WHAT ARE THE WORDS THAT YOU REALLY WANT TO KNOW?

- Do you have trouble remembering the difference between **paragon** and **paradigm,** or **eschatological** and **scatological**?

- Do you suffer from **lethologica** (the inability to remember the right word)?

- Do you long to inject **eclat** and **elan** into your speaking or writing?

THEN *The Quintessential ~~Dictionary~~* IS FOR YO~~U~~

You will find over 31~~~~ ~~~~ ~~~~ ~~~~e-lightful quotations fro~~~~ ~~~~ ~~~~ed columnists, and maga~~~~ ~~~~ ~~~~Buckley, Jr., Thomas Berger, ~~~~ ~~~~ ~~~~es Michener, Irving Wallace, Francine~~~~ ~~~~ ~~~~y, and Roger Kahn.

The impressive range of ~~sources~~ in this dictionary includes such publications as *The New York Times, Newsweek, Time,* and *The New York Review of Books,* on a vast selection of subjects from books, movies, TV shows and stage plays, to art exhibitions, musical performances and architectural commentary.

The Quintessential Dictionary is sure to become your quintessential source book!

THE QUINTESSENTIAL DICTIONARY

I. Moyer Hunsberger

WARNER BOOKS

A Warner Communications Company

This Warner Books Edition is published by arrangement with A&W
Publishers, Inc., 149 Madison Avenue, New York, N.Y. 10016

Warner Books, Inc.
666 Fifth Avenue
New York, N.Y. 10103

 A Warner Communications Company

Printed in the United States of America

First Warner Books Printing: September, 1984

10 9 8 7 6 5 4 3

To that
QUINTESSENTIAL
woman,
my wife Betty

FOREWORD

Most abridged dictionaries designed to increase the reader's vocabulary of interesting words all too often leave the reader wondering: Is that word ever *used*? If so, by whom? Where? In what context? What are some figurative examples of its usage?

The Quintessential Dictionary is like no other dictionary or word book, because it alone emphasizes *actual* examples of *current* word usage, and its scope is limited to "less familiar" words found in newspapers, magazines, and books of recent vintage.

"Less familiar" obviously is a highly subjective category, incapable of lapidary definition even by the author; yet most intelligent people will not, I hope, cavil inordinately with this designation. Readers familiar with some of the words in this dictionary will derive enrichment from the figurative examples of their usage, and all readers will be amused by the witty quotations; edified by the informative, provocative, and lucid commentary on popular culture, current events (including sports), and contemporary ideas and problems; and, above all, challenged by the opportunity afforded to develop a larger, more eclectic, more vivid, and more effective vocabulary.

Indeed, the nearly 1,300 main entries in this dictionary constitute a quintessential vocabulary designed especially for intelligent readers, writers, and students of all ages. Over 3,000 examples of *actual* usage provide a unique and entertaining approach for all who wish (*a*) to increase their capacity for facile, precise, and interesting self-expression; (*b*) to improve the precision of their reading comprehension; and (*c*) to enhance the esthetic pleasure attained from their reading, writing, and speaking.

The excellent popular abridged dictionaries (Webster's New World Dictionary [College Edition], Random House College Dictionary, etc.) devote large amounts of space to two classes of words of little interest to most intelligent people: (*a*) common, everyday words that everyone knows, and (*b*) highly recherché, technical, and specialized words that seldom or never appear in the popular literature most intelligent people read or write. Furthermore, the examples of usage provided in existing dictionaries and word books are often either artificial, very brief, and highly literal or, less frequently, are limited for the most part to quotations from the speeches and writings of well-known persons. The incomparable, but forbidding, Oxford Dictionary alone provides an encyclopedic collection of examples of actual usage for every entry; though invaluable to scholars and word connoisseurs, its weighty tomes can never be up-to-date, even though periodical supplements are issued.

Readers of *The Quintessential Dictionary* will be pleasantly surprised, as I was, to discover the rich variety of useful, intriguing, yet "less familiar" words that appear rather regularly in *Newsweek*, *Time*, syndicated newspaper columns, book reviews, and popular books. The words and examples of usage collected from these sources demonstrate that many contemporary writers delight in vivid and imaginatively figurative use of the English language. The quotations selected are long enough to permit the reader to assimilate the context in which the words are used (and fully appreciate any humor or sarcasm or irony).

Not unexpectedly, three books by William F. Buckley Jr. furnished an incomparably rich source of the vivid use of less familiar words. Indeed, one could probably have compiled an entire dictionary of this kind from Mr. Buckley's writings alone. To read him is a delight even if one disagrees with his point of view, for few contemporary writers use words of any kind with more imagination, flair, precision, and elegance. Among my favorite words are two used by Mr. Buckley with devastating effect, "velleity" (*see p. 409*) and "irenic" (*see p. 206*). Such beautiful words deserve much wider recognition by those interested in elegant and expressive language.

As an inveterate Dodger fan, I was pleased to find in Roger Kahn a loyal follower of the "old" Brooklyn Dodger baseball team as well as a highly knowledgeable and articulate sports writer of genuine literary sensibilities.

Thomas Berger's latest book, a treasure trove of circumlocutory grandiloquence, yielded a plethora of examples of skillful use of less familiar words to create hilarious, logorrheic word pictures.

A recent book and several magazine articles by a prolific and highly talented writer from the other side of the Atlantic, Anthony Burgess, yielded many picturesque examples of the deft use of less familiar words.

Two books by recognized, best-selling authors (James A. Michener and Irving Wallace) provided somewhat less noteworthy examples of the use of the "more familiar" category of less familiar words, but examples of explicit sex in Mr. Wallace's book far outnumbered examples of the use of less familiar words. Mr. Michener appears to have a predilection for the repeated use of certain words; for example, most of the quotations selected to illustrate the use of "acidulous" (*see p. 3*) and "desultory" (*see p. 102*) were taken from *Centennial*.

A wide variety of syndicated columnists, taken together, provided a substantial number of the quotations used in this dictionary, and the ratio of syndicated words read to words selected, though high, was smaller than my initial expectation. More fruitful were reviews and commentary on books, movies, TV shows, stage plays, art exhibitions, musical performances, and architectural matters. Most quotations of this kind came from the *New York Times* (Sections 2 and 7 of the Sunday issues), *Newsweek, Chronicle of Higher Education,* and *Time*. Although less frequently cited, the *New*

York Review of Books constituted a very rich source of quintessential words.

Included among the reviewers and syndicated columnists whose writings were more or less regularly scanned for varying periods of time with uneven rewards were (in alphabetical order): Katrine Ames, Pete Axthelm, Phyllis Batelle, Jim Bishop, Joy Gould Boyum, Patrick J. Buchanan, Newgate Callendar, Vincent Canby, John Chamberlain, Walter Clemons, Allen Cromley, Ray Cromley, John Cunniff, Douglas Davis, The London Economist, Rowland Evans (with Robert Novak), Virginia Fayette, Timothy Foote, Milton Friedman, Francine duPlessix Gray, Paul Gray, Andrew M. Greeley, Meg Greenfield, Doris Grumbach, Jeffrey Hart, Ada Louise Huxtable, Margo Jefferson, T.E. Kalem, Martin Kasindorf, Walter Kerr, James J. Kilpatrick, Hilton Kramer, Jack Kroll, John Leonard, Max Lerner, Melvin Maddocks, Robert Novak (with Rowland Evans), Maureen Orth, Christopher Porterfield, Peter S. Prescott, Desmond Ryan, Hubert Saal, Paul A. Samuelson, Richard Schickel, Harold C. Schonberg, R.Z. Sheppard, John Skow, Henry J. Taylor, Nick Thimmesch, Tom Tiede, Harry F. Waters, George F. Will, Kenneth L. Woodward, Richard L. Worsnop, and Paul D. Zimmerman.

Syndicated news items appear to use a rather limited vocabulary, and were the least productive sources of entries for this dictionary, ranking well below editorials.

In preparing the definitions, the three abridged dictionaries most frequently consulted were: Webster's New World Dictionary (College Edition), Random House College Dictionary (from which phonetic symbols were adopted), and *The New York Times Everyday Reader's Dictionary of Misunderstood, Misused, Mispronounced Words* (Laurence Urdang, editor). In many cases, reference also was made to The Oxford English Dictionary, to the unabridged Webster's and Random House dictionaries, and to Webster's *6,000 Words*. Less frequently, reference was made to Russell Rocke's *Grandiloquent Dictionary* (Prentice-Hall, 1972), *Mrs. Byrne's Dictionary of Unusual, Obscure, and Preposterous Words* (University Books, 1974), and a variety of so-called "word books" and specialized dictionaries.

Interestingly enough, some words currently receiving less than frequent, but more than occasional, usage (for example: *amethystic, dergue, griot*) do not appear in any dictionary or word book of which I am aware.

My wife and all seven of our offspring provided a veritable farrago of advice, a gallimaufry of helpful ideas, and omniscient encouragement as this dictionary was being compiled. On Fathers Day, 1976, my two youngest daughters presented me a copy of a recently published dictionary, memorably inscribed by our youngest daughter Heidi (then 10 years old): "To Daddy, I hope it is your *vade mecum*." A similar hope is extended by the author to all who read *The Quintessential Dictionary*!

I. MOYER HUNSBERGER
Norristown, Pa.
June, 1977

A GUIDE TO THE
USE OF THIS DICTIONARY

Primary and Secondary Words

The Quintessential Dictionary contains nearly 1,300 discrete words, called for convenience *primary words*. *Secondary words* are related to the primary words and follow them in the listing. The total number of primary and secondary entries is well over 3,000 words.

All letters of all primary and secondary words are *capitalized* for emphasis and clarity, regardless of where or how often they appear at other places in the dictionary, with the exception of cases in which a primary word constitutes part of the definition of its own secondary word(s), or vice versa. A capital letter in either a primary or secondary word is underlined.

For all primary (and many secondary) words, the first entry (in parentheses), is the phonetic pronunciation (see *Key to Pronunciation*), followed by an indication of the part of speech (*noun, verb, adj.*, *adv.*, etc.) in italics, and finally by the definition(s). Immediately prior to the definition, the plural form of a noun and, if necessary, its pronunciation are given if the plural is formed in an irregular or unexpected way. Only one form of a verb is entered.

All the foregoing matters are illustrated in the following hypertypical examples and appended notes.

Example 1

ACUMEN (ə-kyōō′ mən, ak′ yə-mən) *noun* superior mental acuteness and discernment; keen insight and perception; shrewdness in understanding and dealing with a situation.

ACUMINOUS *adj.*

ACUMINATE *verb* to make sharp, keen, or pointed.

ACUMINATE *adj.* tapering to a point.

ACUMINATION *noun.*

Note 1. ACUMEN is the *primary word;* the other four capitalized words are *secondary words.*

Note 2. ACUMINOUS is not defined because it is the adjective corresponding to ACUMEN. Similarly, ACUMINATION is the noun corresponding to ACUMINATE, which can be either an adjective or verb.

Note 3. Although all five capitalized words share essentially the same stem, the last three differ significantly in meaning from the first two.

Note 4. There is a substantial difference between the alternate pronunciations of the primary word (see *Key to Pronunciation*). The pronunciation of the secondary words, derivable from the first pronunciation of the primary word, is not indicated separately.

Example 2

JINGO (jiñg′gō) *noun, pl.:* -GOES a person who professes patriotism loudly and excessively, especially one who favors an aggressive foreign policy; CHAUVINIST.

JINGOISM *noun* the spirit, policy, or practice of jingoes; bellicose CHAUVINISM.

JINGOIST *noun, adj.*

JINGOISTIC *adj.*

JINGOISTICALLY *adv.*

Note 1. Both CHAUVINISM and CHAUVINIST are capitalized, this device acting as a cross-reference to their location elsewhere in the dictionary.

Note 2. Since the primary word (JINGOES) is used in defining its own secondary word (JINGOISM), the former is not capitalized in that instance.

Note 3. Either JINGOIST or JINGOISTIC is the adjective corresponding to the nouns JINGOISM and JINGOIST.

Quotations Illustrating Word Usage

Over 3,000 examples of word usage appear in this dictionary. The examples are taken from recent newspapers, popular magazines, and a num-

ber of books (both fiction and non-fiction) of recent
vintage; a summary of these sources appears in the
"Foreword." The illustrative quotations for each
entry, numbered from one to more than twenty,
are entered immediately following the appropriate
primary (and related secondary) words and their
definitions. Where successive quotations come from
the same book, the author's name is followed by
"*Ibid.*" and the page number.

Only the initials and surnames are given for
male authors of quotations, whereas the full names
of female authors are cited as they appear in the
source. In this way, it is hoped to highlight the
extent to which women authored the quotations
used in this book. In those few cases in which the
author's name seemed androgynous (at least, to
the compiler of this dictionary), the full name is
given in the citation, and apologies are offered for
any inadvertent transvestism thereby introduced.

In contrast to the convention outlined above,
the full names of authors, artists, musicians, public
figures, etc. referred to or used in the body of a
quotation usually are given in full, regardless of
sex.

Though syndicated columns often appear in many
different newspapers across the country, only that
newspaper is cited in which the author read the
column in question.

Anonymous authorship is indicated by the usual
abbreviation, "Anon."

If an article has more than two authors, the
name of only the first author is given, followed by
the abbreviation "*et al.*"

Editorials from which examples of usage are

taken are so indicated (in brackets) following the title and preceding the name of the newspaper or magazine.

Local newspapers are identified by the city and state of publication if such information is not apparent from their names.

Key to Pronunciation

The symbol (') indicates that syllable receiving the main stress, and the symbol (-) denotes the end of an unstressed (or less stressed) non-terminal syllable.

All phonetic symbols used in this dictionary are illustrated in the following chart. The pronunciation of most consonants causes no difficulty, but the sounds corresponding to the symbols (ch, sh, th, th̶, and ng̈) should be noted carefully.

Not shown in the chart are four French sounds (indicated in the dictionary by A, N, Œ, R) and one German sound (KH). Since none of these has an English equivalent, the interested reader should seek advice from someone who speaks French or German to obtain the precise pronunciation of those few words involving these sounds.

PRONUNICATION CHART

a	ā	ä	â
bath (ba<u>th</u>)	ale (āl)	arm (ärm)	chair (<u>ch</u>âr)
cat (kat)	bathe (bā<u>th</u>)	char (<u>ch</u>är)	dare (dâr)
hang (haṅg)	gauge (gāj)	farm (färm)	hair (hâr)
mat (mat)	neigh (nā)	jar (jär)	mare (mâr)
tack (tak)	shape (<u>sh</u>āp)	large (lärj)	scare (skâr)
that (<u>th</u>at)	they (<u>th</u>ā)	par (pär)	wear (wâr)

e	ē	i	ī
guess (ges)	geese (gēs)	him (him)	light (līt)
pet (pet)	keel (kēl)	kiss (kis)	rhyme (rīm)
wren (ren)	meat (mēt)	rid (rid)	thigh (<u>th</u>ī)
yet (yet)	these (<u>th</u>ēs)	thin (<u>th</u>in)	time (tīm)

o	ō	ô	oi
cot (kot)	bone (bōn)	fought (fôt)	loin (loin)
lot (lot)	moan (mōn)	saw (sô)	noise (noiz)
not (not)	note (nōt)	short (<u>sh</u>ôrt)	toil (toil)
wasp (wasp)	own (ōn)	walk (wôk)	toy (toi)

u	û	ou	o͝o
come (kum)	fern (fûrn)	cow (cou)	foot (fo͝ot)
judge (juj)	fur (fûr)	growl (groul)	full (fo͝ol)
mud (mud)	learn (lûrn)	mount (mount)	look (lo͝ok)
tough (tuf)	turn (tûrn)	shout (<u>sh</u>out)	nook (no͝ok)

ə	ə	o͞o
allow (ə-lou′)	candle (kan′dəl)	fool (fo͞ol)
Truman (tro͞o′mən)	metal (met′əl)	grew (gro͞o)
boxer (bok′sər)	wire (wīᵊr)	moon (mo͞on)
easily (ē′zə-lē)		mule (myo͞ol)
doctor (dok′tər)		
motion (mō′<u>sh</u>ən)		
measure (me<u>zh</u>′ər)		
murmur (mûr′mər)		

THE QUINTESSENTIAL DICTIONARY

A

AB INITIO (ab i-nish' ē-ō; äb i-nit' ē-ō) from the beginning.

1. Years later, after the War, I found myself having to lecture a large elementary class at Aberdeen, teaching hydrostatics AB INITIO. Right at the beginning came the definitions—a gas having little resistance to change of volume but a liquid having great resistance. (R.V. Jones, "Self-frustration," *A Random Walk in Science*, compiled by R.L. Weber and edited by E. Mendoza, The Institute of Physics and Crane, Russak & Co., 1973, p. 197)

2. Blackford [Oakes] began on the wrong side of Mr. Simon [the Latin teacher at Greyburn, an English school] by suggesting that, as an American, he should . . . be permitted to continue to inflect Latin nouns according to the American sequence—on the grounds that to change now . . . would terribly and prejudicially confuse him . . . . Only the older boy in the back row . . . dared to speak out. "Sir, that's a pretty good point." The boys all laughed, because he was the *other* American, though in fact he had begun Latin, last year, at Greyburn, and had been trained AB INITIO in the English sequence. Mr. Simon replied: ". . . I *suggest* you resolve to learn it the right way, or, I suppose, I had better say . . . the English way." (W.F. Buckley Jr., *Saving the Queen*, Doubleday, 1976, p. 63)

ABJURE (ab-jŏŏr') *verb* to renounce, repudiate, or retract, especially with solemnity, under oath, or publicly; to avoid or shun; to recant.

ABJURATION *noun*.

ABJURER *noun*.

1. Mayor [of Peking] Wu [Teh] made two

significant disclosures [in his speech]. He said the party central committee resolution to make Hua [Kuo-feng] chairman had been passed October 7—the day the "gang of four" [Chiang Ching, Wang Hung-wen, Chang Chun-chiao, and Yao Wen-yuan] are believed to have been arrested . . . . Wu said that on April 30, the ailing chairman [Mao Tse-tung] sent a note to Hua in his own handwriting: "With you in charge, I'm at ease." . . . Mayor Wu said the fear* *(sic)* "forced a so-called final ABJURATION of Chairman Mao, seeking to topple the party central committee headed by Chairman Hua Kuo-feng, and usurp supreme power and state leadership. (*Inquirer* Wire Services, "1 million cheer Hua in Peking," *Philadelphia Inquirer*, 10/25/76, p. 1-A)

2. The story, now current in Washington, that Carter told a group of Democratic Senators at a meeting in Georgia that the Democratic Party must ABJURE force in its foreign policy dealings lest it become know as the perennial war party may be APOCRYPHAL, but the fact that it has been spread indicates something. (J. Chamberlain, "Theories About Jimmy Carter," *Times Herald*, Norristown, Pa., 2/19/77, p. 15)

ABNEGATE (ab' nə-gāt') *verb* to refuse or deny oneself (rights, claims, conveniences, etc.); reject; renounce; to relinquish; give up.

ABNEGATION *noun* self-denial; a giving up of rights, etc.; renunciation.

ABNEGATOR *noun*.

1. The beginnings were HARROWING for the Seven Sisters [Barnard, Bryn Mawr, Mt. Holy-

---

*Should be *four*.

1

oke, Radcliffe, Smith, Vassar, and Wellesley Colleges]. Mt. Holyoke led the way in self-ABNEGATION. Students lived with rawness, penury, puritanical righteousness about lacks in bodily comforts and with heavy domestic work (a) to save money and (b) to show fathers and brothers that though the girls learned science, mathematics and philosophy, their natural roles were not subverted. And all went on in an EXACERBATED state of Christian piety, prayer meetings and religious revivals. (Norma Rosen, Review of *"Peculiar Institutions": An Informal History of the Seven Sister Colleges*, a book by Elaine Kendall, *New York Times*, 4/25/76, Section 7, p. 24)

ABSINTHE or **ABSINTH** (ab' sinth) *noun* wormwood; a green, bitter, aromatic, licorice-flavored liqueur now made with wormwood substitutes and other herbs.

1. [Ellen] Greene is chillingly seductive [in Richard Foreman's production of *The Threepenny Opera*] with her . . . lithe body and AB-SINTHE voice. (J. Kroll, Review, *Newsweek*, 5/17/76, p. 96)

ABSTEMIOUS (ab-stē' mē-əs) *adj.* sparing or moderate in eating and drinking; characterized by abstinence; sparing; not self-indulgent; temperate.

ABSTEMIOUSLY *adv.*

ABSTEMIOUSNESS *noun.*

1. Immigrants not only stuck together after arrival in the United States, but managed to preserve their values in the face of militant "Americanizers"—who equated patriotism with the BOURGEOIS values of rigid work scheduling and ABSTEMIOUSNESS. (R.W. Fox, Review of *Work, Culture and Society in Industrializing America*, by Herbert G. Gutman, *Chronicle of Higher Education*, 5/24/76, p. 21)

2. The publicity stunt intended to show that suburban commuters can get to mid-city Philadelphia faster by train than by automobile might have been a brilliant success except for one thing: The train was late. The contestants in the Great Train-Auto Chase were Thacher Longstreth, president of the Philadelphia Chamber of Commerce, and Jack Kelly, perennial man-about-town and councilman-at-

large. At one point during the train ride, an over-confident Longstreth remarked that Kelly had "probably stopped off somewhere for a couple of quick ones, and we are miles ahead of him." This, of course, is an example of Thacher's well-known humor . . . . Jack Kelly is almost as ABSTEMIOUS as his father, the late John B. Kelly, who thought he was being pretty reckless when he took ginger ale on the rocks. (H.J. Wiegand, "Train was late: It wasn't really so great a race," *Philadelphia Inquirer*, 11/3/76, p. 17-A)

3. The contemporary Chinese are an ABSTEMIOUS, even puritanical people, yet they retain their robust sense of humor and delight in quick-fired exchanges ending in gales of laughter. This is all done on tea . . . . Mao tai, a colorless liquor, is customarily drunk with beer . . . . The glasses are small, but the drink has authority. (D. Middleton, "A Reporter's Notebook: In China Roads Tell of a Changing Society," *New York Times*, 12/5/76, Section 1, p. 32)

ACEDIA (ə-sē'dē-ə) or **ACCIDIE** (ak'sə-dē) or **ACCIDIA** (ak-sid'ē-ə) *noun* spiritual sloth, indifference, boredom, or apathy.

1. Lancelot Lamar [in the book *Lancelot*, by Walker Percy], like the protagonists of all of Percy's novels, is a "somewhat lapsed" man, a victim of ACCIDIE, that SPLENETIC sense of uselessness and alienation, who has come to the end of his rope. (P.S. Prescott, Review, *Newsweek*, 2/28/77, p. 73)

ACERBIC (ə-sûr' bik) or **ACERB** (ə-sûrb') *adj.* sour or ASTRINGENT in taste; sharp, bitter, harsh, or severe in temper, language, expression, etc.

ACERBITY *noun* sourness, with ASTRINGENCY of taste; sharpness, bitterness, harshness, or severity in temper, words, or expression.

ACERBATE (as'ər-bāt) *verb* to make sour or bitter; to exasperate; irritate; vex.

ACERBATE (ə-sûr'bit) *adj.* embittered.

1. Mr. [John] Simon . . . takes note in his preface [to the book *Uneasy Stages*] that he is con-

tinually being called "ACERBIC": "Why," he asks, "can't I sometimes be called the barbed, biting, ACIDULOUS, peppery, sharp, tart, or SARDONIC John Simon?" (R. Brustein, Review, *New York Times*, 1/4/76. Section 2, p. 1)

2. Ninetta [a character in the book, *Women of the Shadows*, by Ann Cornelisen] is ACERBIC and volatile. By day she quarrels with her neighbors; by night she battles her husband. . . . When it all becomes too much, Ninetta substitutes guile for violence. (Margo Jefferson, Review, *Newsweek*, 3/15/76, p. 99)

3. "I am abrasive, ACERBIC, ambitious, angry, arrogant and autocratic," he [President John Silber of Boston University] observed wryly last week, cataloging a handful of charges against him. (J.K. Footlick, "All the President's Woes," *Newsweek*, 5/10/76, p. 75)

4. See (1) under CHOLERIC.

5. . . . Martin Mayer has in recent years conducted informative guided tours of our schools, banks and law offices, identifying error, VENALITY, stupidity and professional HUBRIS wherever he traveled. This small volume [*Today and Tomorrow in America*] contains Mayer's equally ACERBIC but more general judgements upon contemporary America, focused rather more on today and yesterday than on tomorrow. (R. Leckachman, Review, *New York Times*, 3/7/76, Section 7, p. 2)

6. See (3) under VESTIGIAL.

7. See (5) under OBLOQUY.

ACIDULOUS (ə-sij′ə-ləs, ə-sid′ yə-ləs) or **ACIDULENT** *adj.* slightly acid, sour, or tart; sharp; caustic; somewhat sarcastic; having a sour, harsh, or caustic disposition or expression.

ACIDULATE *verb* to make slightly acid or sour.

ACIDULATION *noun*.

1. See (1) under ACERBIC.

2. An ACIDULOUS, correct gentleman [Major George Champlin Sibley, Indian agent at Fort Osage] who dressed in western Missouri as he might have done in Washington, he had been respected when he served at the fort . . . from 1808 through 1813 . . . . But now that he was back, . . . he was actually loved. (J.A. Michener, *Centennial*, Fawcett, 1975, p. 253)

3. The ugly part came at dinner, when Reverend Fenstermacher and his ACIDULOUS wife, Bertha, appeared at the Zendt kitchen for their customary free meal. (J.A. Michener, *Ibid.*, p. 316)

4. "We have to move west," [Captain] Mercy said firmly. "We shall not profane this day [Sunday]," Mrs. Fisher, an unusually ACIDULOUS woman, said. They appealed to Sam Purchas, who listened for less than a minute, then handed down his decision: "After our delay, anybody don't move west as fast as possible got his brains in his ass." (J.A. Michener, *Ibid.*, p. 373)

5. At family prayers Levi [Zendt] was astonished . . . by the minute detail with which Mahlon [Zendt] told God what to do. At each grace the tall, ACIDULOUS man would direct God's attention to evildoers, to men who had stolen money from the bank, to girls who were misbehaving, and Levi began to understand why so much violence had been permitted in Colorado. With God kept so busy in Lancaster [Pa.] prying into petty problems, how could He find time to watch over real crimes like those of the Pasquinel brothers and Colonel Skimmerhorn? (J.A. Michener, *Ibid.*, p. 696)

6. Early next morning he [Sheriff Dumire] rode over to the courthouse in Greeley [Colorado] to consult with Judge Leverton, an ACIDULOUS man who became furious when he learned the purpose of Dumire's visit. "How dare you come to me with shabby details of a case you can't prove? . . . . I ought to throw you in jail." (J.A. Michener, *Ibid.*, p. 791)

ACOLYTE (ak′ə-līt′) *noun* an altar attendant in public worship; altar boy; an attendant or assistant; follower; helper.

1. Hitler's ACOLYTE, he [Albert Speer] was called, a talented young architect who graduated from a unique position of personal friendship with his Fuhrer to become the organizational genius of the failing Third Reich. (F. Spelman, "Albert Speer Talks of Spandau, His Atonement—and Hitler's Strange Affection For Him," *People*, 4/12/76, p. 49)

2. More and more [Ingmar] Bergman's marvelous actors seem like madly dedicated ACOLYTES of his own salvation. Liv Ullmann's performance [in the film, *Face to Face*] is . . . more than acting, it's a ritual . . . of love—the love of an actress and a woman for a great and troubled artist. (J. Kroll, Review, *Newsweek*, 4/12/76, p. 94)

3. He [George Balanchine]'s likely to startle these [ballet] ACOLYTES with a comment like, "Now that you've been through school, you must learn to dance." (Nancy Goldner, "The Inimitable Balanchine," *New York Times*, 5/30/76, Section 6, p. 28)

ACRONYM (ak' rə-nim) *noun* a word formed from the initial letters or groups of letters of words in a set phrase, as *WAC* from *Women's Army Corps*, or *loran* from *long-range navigation*; an acrostic.

ACRONYMIC *adj.*

1. The therapy currently enjoying a phenomenal success in this country is called "EST." The word is an ACRONYM that derives from Erhard Seminars Training, the name given to a self-realization program developed by a former management consultant called Werner Erhard, who has become the acknowledged spiritual leader of thousands of Americans who claim to have been "transformed" by Erhard's program. (Vivian Gornick, Review of *EST: 60 Hours That Transform Your Life*, by Adelaide Bry; and *EST: Playing the Game the New Way*, by Carl Frederick, *New York Times*, 4/4/76, Section 7, p. 5)

2. The [*New York Daily*] *News* would not mention [Branch] Rickey's manager, Burt Shotton, by name. Instead, [Dick] Young lanced the bubble of Shotton as genial PATERFAMILIAS by giving him the ACRONYM "KOBS." The letters, forged in sarcasm, stood for Kindly Old Burt Shotton. The Dodgers lost because of, won despite, KOBS. (R. Kahn, *The Boys of Summer*, Harper and Row, 1971, p. 100)

3. A little Bicentennial show of fortitude by a Pocatello, Idaho, businessman just about killed the Occupational Safety and Health Act, known by the hated ACRONYM of OSHA . . . . Some time ago he [F.G. Barlow] let an OSHA inspector into his front office. But when the OSHA man . . . said, "I'm ready to go back into your shop," Barlow . . . said no. In a lower court appearance Barlow's TEMERITY got him cited for contempt but . . . after six months, a panel of three judges—two from the circuit court, one a chief district judge—handed down a decision that the OSHA section involving inspections was "void and unconstitutionally repugnant to the Fourth Amendment." (J. Chamberlain, "Defending OSHA," *Times Herald*, Norristown, Pa., 1/12/77, p. 19)

4. The President was puzzled at his first Cabinet meeting when members started talking about ERISA, ACRONYM for Employee Retirement Income Security Act, the pension-reform law. When Carter asked what ERISA was all about, Treasury Secretary Blumenthal replied that businessmen call it "Every Ridiculous Idea Since Adam." (Anon., "Washington Whispers," *U.S. News & World Report*, 2/7/77, p. 8)

ACROPHOBIA (ak'rə-fō'bē-ə) *noun* an abnormal fear or dread of being in or looking down from high places.

1. Walter Heller, himself a former CEA [Council of Economic Advisors] chairman, scoffs at the fear of high budget deficits as nothing worse than "fiscal ACROPHOBIA." (M. Ruby and R. Thomas, "The Economy: Almost Booming," *Newsweek*, 1/19/76, p. 62)

2. See (7) under XENOPHOBIA.

3. On a tease from President-elect Jimmy Carter, Billy Carter endured a white-knuckle ride in a hot-air balloon over Americus, Ga. [last week] . . . . For courage and an antidote to ACROPHOBIA, he took along a couple of six-packs of his favorite beer. (Anon., "Newsmakers," *Newsweek*, 1/17/77, p. 40)

4. What is significant about these new behemoths [skyscrapers] is not only their cost . . . . More important, they show a marked change in esthetic attitude . . . . Gone is a taste for the drab, low-cost, functional cigar box . . . . In its place are glistening glass, sensuous marble, gently curved corners, dabs of bright color, eye-popping geometry and ACROPHOBIC illusionism at every turn. On the 26th floor of [Kevin] Roche's 39-story United Nations Plaza

Hotel in New York, the visitor feels suspended in mid-air—caught between an all-glass wall on the left and an all-mirror wall on the right, with a tiny walkway in between. (D. Davis, *et al.*, "Rise of the Come-Hither Look," *Newsweek*, 1/17/77, p. 86)

ACUMEN (ə-kyōō′ mən, ak′ yə-men) *noun* superior mental acuteness and discernment; keen insight and perception; shrewdness in understanding and dealing with a situation.

ACUMINOUS *adj.*

ACUMINATE *verb* to make sharp, keen, or pointed.

ACUMINATE *adj.* tapering to a point.

ACUMINATION *noun.*

1. Banking is not the only profession from which we buy superior ACUMEN [a reference to the fact that banks really sell judgment]. (Leslie Waller, "Banks 'Subsidize' New Immorality," *Norman [Okla.] Transcript,* 1/16/76, p. 6)

2. See (1) under MODUS VIVENDI.

3. From the middle of 1952 through 1958, he [Senator Jacob Javits] wrote, the federal government spent the enormous sum of twenty-eight billion dollars in New York State . . . . What was the liberal Senator . . . trying to tell his constituents, if not that New York, thanks to the ACUMEN of its political representatives . . . is getting an out-size slice of the federal pie? . . . . During the identical period, the federal government received in taxes paid by New York citizens and corporations, $83,600,000,000, or about three times the sum of money that found its way back. (W.F. Buckley Jr., *Up From Liberalism*, Arlington House, 2nd Printing 1968, p. 163)

AD ABSURDUM *see* REDUCTIO AD ABSURDUM.

ADAMANTINE (ad′ə-man′ tĭn, -tēn, -tĭn) *adj.* impenetrably or unyieldingly hard; utterly unyielding or firm in attitude or opinion; adamant; like a diamond in luster.

1. . . . An earth in which the Archbishop of Rome is resigned to the necessity of humiliating his ADAMANTINE Hungarian cardinal [Mindszenty], for the express purpose of avoiding the risk of humiliating his oppressors. (W.F. Buckley Jr., *Execution Eve and Other Contemporary Ballads*, G.P. Putnam's Sons, 1975, p. 495)

2. With my final bite of the one [brownie] I held, I almost broke a tooth on some small ADAMANTINE object . . . . It was a slug of lead. It was very much like a bullet that could have been fired from a .25-caliber Browning automatic. (Thomas Berger, *Who is Teddy Villanova?*, Delacorte Press/Seymour Lawrence, 1977, p. 65)

ADDLE (ad′əl) *verb* to make or become confused or muddled; to make or become spoiled or rotten, as an egg.

ADDLEBRAINED or **ADDLEHEADED** or **ADDLEPATED** (ad′əl-pā′tĭd) *adj.* foolish; silly; having or revealing a muddled or confused mind; stupid.

1. The academic flirtation with Henry Wallace was brief, and . . . by the . . . fall of 1948 . . . , Wallace had lost all but hardened fellow travelers and the advanced ADDLEPATED. (W.F. Buckley Jr., *Execution Eve and Other Contemporary Ballads*, G.P. Putnam's Sons, 1975, p. 473)

2. In any case, I feigned great horror at my ADDLEPATEDNESS . . . (W.F. Buckley Jr., *Ibid.*, p. 421)

3. As was true in Florida, anyone suggesting [George] Wallace will not take North Carolina [in the Presidential primary] risks being considered ADDLEPATED. In 1972, Wallace walloped the state's former Governor, Terry Sanford, by 107,000 ballots, winning more than 50 per cent of the vote to Sanford's 37 per cent. (Smith Hempstone, "Carolina Vote Shapes Up as Rerun," *Daily Oklahoman*, Okla. City, 3/23/76, p.6)

4. And so we still don't know exactly what to do with *Troilus and Cressida*, wise as we are in this 20th century. And so I have another few days to enjoy my perplexity, until *Secret Service* and *Boy Meets Girl* and that Monty Python bunch have driven it out of, or further ADDLED, my head. (W. Kerr, Review, *New York Times*, 4/18/76, Section 2, p. 20)

5. See (2) under FARRAGO.

6. In a place [Washington, D.C.]—and system— where access, acquaintance and a sense of mutual dependence and/or indebtedness are essential to success, it is small wonder that people tend to grow snappish, craven, insecure and slightly ADDLED by a change of government. (Meg Greenfield, "The New Washington Power Game," *Newsweek*, 1/31/77, p. 80)

7. And if doublespeak seems a national second language, it may reflect a calculating mind as easily as an ADDLED one. (C.A. Ridley, Review of *A Civil Tongue*, a book by Edwin Newman, *National Observer*, week ending 2/19/77, p.27)

ADDUCE (ə-dōōs', -dyōōs') *verb*   to give as a reason or proof; to present as evidence; to mention as an example.

ADDUCIBLE or ADDUCEABLE   *adj.*

ADDUCER   *noun.*

1. For democracy—note it well—destroys greatness in every kind, of intellect, of perception, as well as of character. And especially it destroys art . . . . No democracy has ever produced or understood art. The case of Athens is wrongly ADDUCED; for Athens was an aristocracy under the influence of an aristocrat at the time the Parthenon was built. (G. Lowes Dickinson, *A Modern Symposium*, Hart Publishing Co., 1967, p. 140)

AD HOC (ad hok', äd hōk')   *adj.*   for this special or specific purpose, case, or thing, without general application.

1. One of the Treasury boys spotted it [the photograph of Karla in George Smiley's office] during an AD HOC conference about scrapping the operational bank accounts. (J. LeCarré, *The Honourable Schoolboy*, Alfred A. Knopf, 1977, p. 43)

AD HOMINEM (äd hō'mi-nem' , ad hom' ə-nem')   *adj.*   appealing to one's prejudices, emotions, or special interest rather than to intellect or reason, as by attacking one's opponent rather than debating the issue.

1. [Paul J.] Stern's central thesis [in the book, *C.G. Jung: The Haunted Prophet*] is that Jung's life work represents "the creative use of incipient madness.". . . Stern's flippancy and AD HOMINEM style are noisome enough and ill serve the seriousness of the issues at stake. But the stirring of old red herrings is even more pointless—for instance, the anti-Semitism and pro-Nazi INNUENDOS. (J. Hollis, Review, *Chronicle of Higher Education*, 7/26/76, p.9)

2. As soon as the story of "Team B" [asked by President Ford to reevaluate the data on Soviet strategic objectives] was leaked to the press, . . . a campaign got under way to discredit the effort, partly on the ground that the panel consisted of "well-known hard-liners" and/or "right-wingers" who merely found what they had set themselves out to find (that the Soviet Union is out to obtain strategic superiority), and partly that such superiority made no sense in any event. The AD HOMINEM argument can be quickly dismissed . . . . By questioning motives, one seeks to avoid responsibility for dealing with the issues, but one does not thereby dispose of them . . . . Would one deny the existence of civil rights violations on the ground that the panel reporting them found what it wanted to find? (R. Pipes, "Strategic Superiority," *New York Times*, 2/6/77, Section 4, p. 15)

3. "I don't want to hurt your feelings," she [Alice Ellish] said, "but there's a bottle of Scope in the bathroom." Her AD HOMINEM approach was again effective. Though facing the stove and three feet from her, I [Russel Wren] spoke through my hand. (Thomas Berger, *Who is Teddy Villanova?*, Delacorte Press/ Seymour Lawrence, 1977, p. 147)

AD INFINITUM (ad in'fə-nī'təm)   *adv.*   to infinity; endlessly; forever; without limit.

1. The problem, as posed by Fibonacci [13th century Italian mathematician], is this: "Someone placed a pair of rabbits in a certain place enclosed on all sides by a wall to find out how many pairs of rabbits will be born there in the course of one year, it being assumed that every month a pair of rabbits produces another pair, and that rabbits begin to bear young two months after their own birth." . . . . At the end of 12 months the original rabbits and their offspring would number 233 pairs! Fibonacci listed the total pairs of rabbits at the end of each month, and created the following se-

quence of numbers . . . 1, 2, 3, 5, 8, 13, 21, 34, 55, 89, 144, 233 . . . he realized that each number was the sum of the two proceeding* (sic) numbers. In other words, 1 plus 2 equals 3, . . . 3 plus 5 equals 8, 5 plus 8 equals 13, and so on AD INFINITUM . . . . The 100th number in the sequence is a whopping 354,224,848,179, 261,915,075! . . . . If you divide a Fibonacci number by the next highest number, you will discover that it is precisely .618034 times as large as the number that follows. (. . . it works for all numbers after the 14th in the sequence.) And .618034 is a magic number . . . . The front of the Parthenon, including the PEDIMENT when it was intact, would have fitted almost exactly into a golden rectangle [the smaller side is .618034 as long as the larger side]. (W. Hoffer, "A magic ratio recurs throughout art and nature," *Smithsonian*, December 1975, pp. 111–112, 115)

2. See (1) under INCESTUOUS.

3. Thus, in the course of the book [*Friends and Lovers*, by Robert Brain], we learn that our spouses are our friends, our relatives are our friends, the people we do business with are our friends, friends of friends are our friends, and so forth AD INFINITUM. (P. Robinson, Review, *New York Times*, 11/21/76, Section 7, p. 48)

4. See (3) under AD NAUSEAM.

5. Commissions on this and special staff assistants on that and public relations people for such and such and the undersecretary to the assistant administrator and on and on AD INFINITUM—they are all there in government. (C.M. Madigan, "Government Just Grows," *Times Herald*, Norristown, Pa., 2/15/77, p. 11)

ADJURE (ə-jŏŏr′) *verb* to charge, bind, or command solemnly, as under oath or penalty; to entreat, request, or appeal to earnestly; beseech.

ADJURATION *noun* a solemn charge or command; an earnest entreaty.

ADJURER or **ADJUROR** *noun.*

ADJURATORY *adj.*

1. In one of the first policy pronouncements

*Should be *preceding.*

since Mao's death—an editorial that . . . carried the weight of official dogma—Peking said that Mao had "ADJURED" the Chinese people to "act according to the principles laid down." That seemed ambiguous enough to please all of China's ideological factions . . . . (A. Deming, *et. al.*, "Honor Thy Father," *Newsweek*, 9/27/76, p. 45)

AD NAUSEAM (ad nô′zē-əm, -am′, -zhē-, -sē-, -shē-) *adv.* to a sickening or disgusting degree or extreme.

1. [L. Steven] Zwerling says, AD NAUSEAM, that 75 per cent of all students who enter community colleges fail to graduate and less than 12 per cent ever receive the baccalaureate degree. (M.G. Baumann, Review of *Second Best: The Crisis of the Community College*, a book by L. Steven Zwerling, *Chronicle of Higher Education*, 5/17/76, p. 13)

2. Again [Bruce] Dobler has researched his subject AD NAUSEAM and again he has created [in the book, *The Last Rush North*] a veritable horde of stereotyped characters. (S. Frank, Review, *New York Times*, 9/12/76, Section 7, p. 40)

3. For years now our youth have been addicted to tossing in "y'know" after nearly every phrase they utter. You know how it goes . . . : "Well—y'know—I could have dated Marc—y'know—but he's got acne—y'know—and he looks like a creep—y'know . . ." etc., AD INFINITUM, AD NAUSEAM. (E. Midura, "Um's the Word," *Today, The Inquirer Magazine*, 1/30/77, p. 26)

ADONIS (ə-don′is, ə-dō′nis) *noun* (in ancient Greek Mythology) a youth whom Aphrodite loved for his beauty and who was killed by a wild boar; any very handsome young man.

ADONIC *adj.*

1. The image of the cowboy created by movies and television is that of a tall, handsome ADONIS who rides a bullet-proof horse, drinks sasparilla (sic), uses no language stonger than an occasional "heck" or "golly dern," and can fire a six-shooter 15 times before reloading. That image, according to the authors [Charles W. Harris and Buck Rainey] of *The Cowboy: Six-Shooters, Songs and Sex* has little similarity

with the . . . men who rode the range in the Old West. The bit about sasparilla *(sic)* may have been true... ; It was considered an APHRODISIAC. (Anon., Review, *Norman* [Okla.] *Transcript,* 6/27/76, p. 33)

2. Who was it this time [in Ann Smiley's bedroom]? Another beardless ballet dancer . . . ? Her vile cousin Miles, the career politician? Or a one-night ADONIS spirited from the nearby pub? (J. LeCarré, *The Honourable Schoolboy,* Alfred A. Knopf, 1977, p. 111)

ADUMBRATE (ad-um′ brāt, ad′ əm-brāt) *verb* to outline or sketch; to give a faint shadow or resemblance of; to foreshadow; prefigure; to darken or conceal partially; overshadow.

ADUMBRATION *noun.*

ADUMBRATIVE *adj.*

1. See (1) under VOLTE-FACE.

2. But the dog-lovers, greatly aroused, bore down hard and of course the gentleman [who shot a dog "pooping" on a Greenwich Village sidewalk] will be prosecuted, and no one now believes that the final solution to the dog problem was ADUMBRATED by the incident in Greenwich Village. (W.F. Buckley Jr., *Execution Eve and Other Contemporary Ballads,* G.P. Putnam's Sons, 1975, p.423)

3. Sick of the two old parties and looking for a new one? Eugene McCarthy, who in 1968 ADUMBRATED some of the themes that Jerry Brown is now developing, is again running for President, this time as an independent. (W.V. Shannon, "The lasting hurrah," *New York Times,* 3/14/76, Section 6, p. 11)

4. So there is something of everything in this show [*Abroad in America: Visitors to the New Nation,* at the National Portrait Gallery, Washington, D.C.], from the lofty ADUMBRATIONS of poets, politicians and mystics to a first-rate thumbnail evocation of Isadora Duncan on the stage . . . . The National Portrait Gallery exists to give a true picture of what named people were like, and in this case it does it for Cubans, Swedes, Hungarians, Indians and Czechs, with an ideal impartiality. (J. Russell, Review, *New York Times,* 7/11/76, Section 2, p. 27)

5. This book [*The Edwardians: The Remaking of British Society,* by Paul Thompson] is an attempt to describe the . . . middle and working classes in the time of Edward VII, roughly 1900-1914). . . . Conclusions about social patterns and change are merely ADUMBRATED, because . . . it [the book] is "an interim interpretation," full analysis is "still ahead." (Madeline H. Robinton, Review, *The Key Reporter,* Summer 1976, p.5)

6. In this volume [*The Life and Times of Chaucer*] . . . if [author John] Gardner has not come up with the fully realized new Chaucer that we need, the one he ADUMBRATES is quite authentic enough for our present use. (C. Muscatine, Review, *New York Times,* 4/24/77, Section 7, p. 39)

7. See (3) under HIERATIC.

ADVENTITIOUS (ad′vən-tish′əs) *adj.* associated with something incidentally or extrinsically rather than as an integral part; accidentally or casually acquired; added from the outside; not inherent; accidental; occurring in unusual or abnormal places (said of a plant, etc.).

ADVENTITIOUSLY *adv.*

ADVENTITIOUSNESS *noun.*

1. It would be somehow callous, and certainly tedious, to reiterate progressive modifications of McGovern on his domestic score . . . . Or to chronicle his ADVENTITIOUS discoveries: of Jerusalem, for instance. Imagine discovering Jerusalem only under the triangulating guidance of the three kings, Gallup, Harris, and Yankelovich. (W.F. Buckley Jr., *Execution Eve and Other Contemporary Ballads,* G.P. Putnam's Sons, 1975, p.92)

2. Up to then [about 1943] clearly enough, Exxon was about as much a patron of the arts as a man who commissions his portrait. It may scarcely be said to have broadened its scope with the project that served, somewhat ADVENTITIOUSLY, to establish its reputation as an arts sponsor. In 1944, Exxon asked the celebrated documentary film-maker Robert Flaherty to tour the oil fields of Pennsylvania, Oklahoma, and Texas looking for material. The resulting film about oil drilling, *Louisiana Story,* became a great hit, and Virgil Thompson won

a Pulitzer Prize for its musical score. (J. Brooks, "Fueling the Arts, Or, Exxon as a Medici," *New York Times*, 1/25/76, Section 2, p. 30)

AFFLATUS (ə-flā′təs) *noun* inspiration or powerful impulse, as of an artist or poet; divine communication of knowledge.

1. But that kind of resignation hardly becomes those who feel the AFFLATUS to do what they can to steer public opinion, and are prepared to do so even in anticipation of a hard weather helm. (W.F. Buckley Jr., *Execution Eve and Other Contemporary Ballads*, G.P. Putnam's Sons, 1975, p. 392)

2. Evidently, many people now find poetry easier to write than read. The demolitions of old poetic constraints—inaugurated by such elitists as T.S. Eliot and Ezra Pound—have allowed just about any flyspecked page to masquerade as divine AFFLATUS. (P. Gray, "American Poetry: School's Out," *Time*, 4/26/76, p. 95)

AFICIONADO (ə-fish′ yə-nä′dō) *noun* an ardent devotee; a devoted follower of some sport, art, etc.

1. Presenting: Cigars of the Month . . . a years *(sic)* subscription to the worlds *(sic)* finest cigars. As a gift or for yourself. A medley of 12 of the worlds *(sic)* finest handmade cigar brands to delight the AFICIONADO or introduce the novice to the joys of cigar smoking. (Advertisement of Georgetown Tobacco & Pipe Stores, *Smithsonian*, December 1975, p. 139)

2. AFICIONADOS of the mystery GENRE know that "Newgate Callendar" is the PSEUDONYM of the critic who, for the last five years, has written the "Criminals at Large" column in the *New York Times* Book Review. During his tenure the INSCRUTABLE Mr. Callendar has read something like 1,500 mysteries. By now his mind is a collagelike repository of plots, dialogue and style. He has, therefore, devised a mystery story that is at once a MÉLANGE of the whodunit styles that he has encountered, and also a miniature history of the GENRE. (Anon., Introduction to "Endpaper," by Newgate Callendar, *New York Times*, 6/6/76, Section 6, p. 103)

3. See (3) under SCABROUS.

4. AFICIONADOS of wicker and rattan [furniture] will have a world of choices [in 1977]. Some [pieces] look distinctly Oriental. Others have 1930's attic appeal or . . . make a sleek modern statement in combination with chrome. (Grace Madley, "Furniture market is a decorator's delight," *Philadelphia Inquirer*, 10/25/76, p. 1-D)

5. [Will] Weng [*New York Times*' crossword puzzle editor] has also received several puzzles from two prisoners in an Ohio penitentiary, no doubt the source of a rumor among puzzle AFICIONADOS *(sic)* that the puzzles were constructed by inmates. Weng says, however, that the prisoners no longer submit puzzles; probably, he says, they have gained their freedom. (Murray Dubin, "Puzzled? Then Weng has done his job," *Philadelphia Inquirer*, 11/28/76, p. 4-L)

6. (I am aware that content sometimes overwhelms all artistic achievement. Thus, Wagner is not tolerated in Israel, although elsewhere AFICIONADOS are generally considered blameless when they enjoy his operas, even though they themselves might acknowledge that Hitler felt an affinity with Wagner's music based on a genuine appreciation of its contents.) . . . . But if intellectual consent were necessary to esthetic appreciation, life would indeed become impoverished. (Marina Warner, "Mary" [Letter to Editor], *New York Times*, 1/2/77, Section 7, p. 22)

7. See (1) under OENOPHILIST.

AGGLOMERATION (ə-glom′ ə-rā′ shən) *noun* a jumbled cluster or mass; the act or process of agglomerating.

AGGLOMERATE *verb* to collect or gather into a cluster or mass.

AGGLOMERATE *adj.*

AGGLOMERATE *noun* any collection or accumulation of miscellaneous materials.

AGGLOMERATED *adj.*

1. What is sometimes mistaken for conservatism is an ad hoc AGGLOMERATION of forces, brought together temporarily by a PROXIMATE common interest. (W.F. Buckley Jr., *Up From Liberalism*, Arlington House, 2nd Printing 1968, p. 90)

AGITPROP (aj′ it-prop′) *noun* agitation and propaganda, especially for the cause of communism.

AGITPROP *adj.* of or for agitation and propaganda, as used originally in the Communist movement, especially for certain plays, leaflets, etc.

AGITPROPIST *noun.*

1. The Chinese had nothing at all to gain, but unmistakably something to lose, from a concentrated display of AGITPROP as art to a con-scripted audience of Americans who sensed the restraints imposed upon the President [Nixon] by the diplomatic situation; and worried both that he might visibly fret under the strain; and that he wouldn't. (W.F. Buckley Jr., *Execution Eve and Other Contemporary Ballads*, G.P. Putnam's Sons, 1975, p. 31)

2. If the President of the United States [Nixon] is forced to see a ballet on the theme of the decadence, materialism, and SADISM of the non-Communist world, why can't he say: "I thought the thing was lousy—AGITPROP posing as art." (W.F. Buckley Jr., *Ibid.*, p. 55)

3. . . . there is the obstacle of the Olympics, about which everybody knows roughly everything, like how the managers behind the Iron Curtain turn them into AGITPROP, which is the left equivalent of big business. (W.F. Buckley Jr., *Ibid.*, p.221)

4. [Edward] Bond [author of the play, *The Fool*] is the theater's most unsettling multiple personality. Propagandist, poet, rationalist, romantic, pessimist, optimist, he expresses the contradictions that make humanity human. . . . All attempts to pin Bond down as a Marxist, socialist, AGITPROP writer miss the unique complexity of his theatrical effect. *The Fool* vibrates with hate and love; Bond is fair to both sides of the social struggle despite his enmity for the system of competitive capitalism which has created two sides. (J. Kroll, Review, *Newsweek*, 11/1/76, p. 62)

5. Strangely, too, he [film director Rainer Werner Fassbinder] used the film about male homosexuals not so much to say something about homosexuality as to illustrate his leftist conviction that the BOURGEOISIE exploit the PRO-LETARIAT in any milieu. AGITPROP in a feather boa, *Fox*, . . . derives its strength from its discords. Film critics Manny Farber and Patricia Patterson . . . said . . . that his films are a "radical mix of snarl and decoration," and that Fassbinder, himself, is "a mixture of ENFANT TERRIBLE, burgher, and pimp." (R. Tyler, "The Savage World of Rainer Werner Fassbinder," *New York Times*, 3/27/77, Section 2, p. 15)

AGORAPHOBIA (ag′ər-ə-fō′bē-ə) *noun* an abnormal fear or dread of being in open or public places.

1. See (7) under XENOPHOBIA.

2. On the opposite end of the spectrum [from Walter Winchell] was [columnist] O.O. McIntyre, who could write engagingly of Broadway and its bright lights. Secretly, he had AGORA-PHOBIA and seldom left his apartment. (J. Bishop, "Tough Breed," *Times Herald*, Norristown, Pa., 10/27/76, p. 19)

3. The most debilitating, and probably most prevalent of phobias is AGORAPHOBIA—an overwhelming anxiety that results in panic reactions at the thought of leaving the safety of home, of traveling anywhere alone or of being "trapped" in crowded places. As many as one million Americans, most of them women, are known to be AGORAPHOBIC . . . . These phobics gradually hole themselves up at home in fear—refusing even to visit a doctor in search of help. (Phyllis Battelle, "How Do You Feel?" *Times Herald*, Norristown, Pa., 1/28/77, p. 13)

4. See (2) under CREPUSCULAR.

AILUROPHILE (ī-lŏŏr′ə-fīl′, ā-lŏŏr′ə-fīl) or **AELUROPHILE** (ē-lŏŏr′ə-fīl) *noun* a person who likes cats; cat fancier.

AILUROPHILIA (-fīl′ē-ə) or **AELUROPHILIA** *noun* a liking or love of cats.

AILUROPHILIC or **AELUROPHILIC** *adj.*

1. *Cat* (Workman) [is] an album of B. Kliban's drawings sure to delight any AELUROPHILE. (Anon., "Paper Back Talk," *New York Times*, 1/4/76, Section 7, p. 23)

2. *The Cat Catalog*, edited by Judy Fireman (Workman, $6.95). Everything an AILURO-PHILE could want to know about cats. (Anon., Trade Paperbacks, *New York Times*, 1/2/77, Section 7, p. 23)

3. If 1976, with its SPATE of books about cats, was the Year of the AILUROPHILE, this year may well be the Time of the Dog. At any rate, two talented artists have captured the looks and ways of *Canis familiaris*—especially his scruffy lovability—in the two volumes from which the drawings above are reproduced [*Dogs*, by Henry Morgan and George Booth; *Random Dogs*, by Richard Stine]. (Anon., Review, *New York Times*, 4/24/77, Section 7, p. 49)

ALBESCENT (al-bes' ənt) *adj.* becoming white; whitish; moderately white.

ALBESCENCE *noun.*

1. We sensed, all of us, the ALBESCENT tribute to Mr. Nixon's solid good sense . . . (W.F. Buckley Jr., *Execution Eve and Other Contemporary Ballads*, G.P. Putnam's Sons, 1975, p. 22)

ALBINO (al-bīn' ō) *noun; pl.* ALBINOS a person, animal or plant deficient in pigmentation, especially a person with a pale, milky skin, light hair, and pink eyes.

ALBINIC (al-bin'ik) *adj.*

ALBINISM *noun* the state or condition of being an albino.

1. The ceramic flowers blaze crimson and purple about the gray monument [in the graveyard]. An ALBINIC light envelops it all. (Francine du Plessix Gray, "Tribe," *The New Yorker*, 5/31/76, p. 37)

ALEATORIC (ā' lē-ə-tôr' ik) or **ALEATORY** *adj.* of, depending on, or pertaining to chance, luck, or contingency; unpredictable; designating music resulting from purely random successions of tones and noises.

1. The annual event [World Music Days, sponsored by the International Society of Contemporary Music] has also been the setting for annual scandals as composers have used the event as a forum for ever-new explorations of sonic worlds. Atonalism, dodecaphonism, varieties of serialism, minimal music and ALEATORIC examples are among those that have entered the debates in the concerts. (D. Webster, "Boston Hosts World Music Days," *Philadelphia Inquirer*, 10/24/76, p. 15-L)

2. This ENFANT TERRIBLE [Pierre Boulez], who is now past 50, is also a principled anti-Dadaist . . . , has lashed out at the "FETISHISM" of extreme ALEATORY music, and is a proselytizer for a musical system. These contradictions are some of the reasons for the word "enigma" in the subtitle of this biography [*Boulez: Composer, Conductor, Enigma*] by Joan Peyser. (E. Rothstein, Review, *New York Times*, 12/19/76, Section 7, pp. 6-7)

ALEXANDRINE (al' ig-zan' drin, -drēn) *noun* (in Prosody) an iambic line having normally six feet; iambic hexameter.

ALEXANDRINE *adj.* of an alexandrine or alexandrines.

1. So this then was the [black woman] Paola [Belli] had told him [Ronald Beard] [P.R.] Pathan was now shacked up with. Glamour, all right, loads of it, high-breasted, scarlet-swathed, striding from the hip and each stride an ALEXANDRINE jewelled with superbity. The hair too piled high with insolence. (A. Burgess, *Beard's Roman Women*, McGraw-Hill, 1976, pp. 30-40)

ALLITERATION (ə-lit' ə-rā' shən) *noun* the repetition of the same letter or sound at the beginning of two or more words in a phrase, verse of poetry, etc.

ALLITERATIVE *adj.*

ALLITERATE *verb* to show or use alliteration.

1. Twenty-one years ago, the Rev. Robert Schuller gave his first California sermon from the tarpaper roof of a sandwich stand in a ratty drive-in movie theater near Anaheim. Since then, he has become perhaps the country's most successful drive-in preacher, a minister of the evangelical Reformed Church whose sermons are sprinkled with ALLITERATIVE slogans and upbeat advice. (Susan Cheever Cowley, "Park and Pray," *Newsweek*, 5/10/76, p. 103)

2. See (1) under NATTER.

3. This is my 40th year as a follower of the Chicago Cubs . . . . As far as I can recollect, it was the effect of ALLITERATION on the young ear [that was responsible for the choice]. There was something sturdy sounding about "Chicago Cubs". . . the "CC" combination caught

my fancy (more so than the other ALLITERATIVE options offered by the Pittsburgh Pirates and the Boston Bees), captured my devotion . . . . (J.M. Culkin, "Tinkers to Evers to '76," *New York Times*, 6/13/76, Section 5, p. 2)

4. . . . he [Dr. Shock, Channel 17 horror show host] howls his ALLITERATIVE, slightly insulting salutation: "Greetings, my HOKEY hucksters of horror." Or "My nostalgic numskulls of night." Or "My frog-faced fools of fright." At first, he had a one-eyed, scar-faced sidekick named Boris, a hunchbacked CRETIN of dubious sexuality who . . . rinsed his pantyhose out in a urinal. This MESMERIZED the late-night audience. . . . But station management was appalled and banished the show after 13 grisly weeks. Ten thousand hysterical signatures later, Dr. Shock returned . . . . (Maralyn Lois Polak, "Dr. Shock: The Reluctant Ghoul," *Today, The Inquirer Magazine*, 2/13/77, p. 8)

5. A restauranteur with a taste for ALLITERATION and a burn about high coffee prices urges: Drink Tea on Tuesday. And if folks will drink coffee only on days of the week starting with "c," the boycott will really get somewhere. (Anon., Untitled squib on Editorial Page, *Times Herald*, Norristown, Pa., 1/17/77, p. 12)

ALLOCUTION (al′ ə-kyōō′ shən) *noun* a formal speech, especially an incontrovertible or HORTATORY one, or one warning or advising with authority; a pronouncement delivered by the pope to a secret consistory.

1. The day had been crowded, what with the festivities that attended the departure of the Duke, and a number of greetings and ALLOCUTIONS the Queen needed to execute for the Duke to distribute on his rounds through Australia and New Zealand. (W.F. Buckley Jr., *Saving the Queen*, Doubleday, p. 140)

ALTRUISM (al′trōō-iz′əm) *noun* the principle or practice of unselfish or benevolent concern for or devotion to the welfare of others; selflessness.

ALTRUIST *noun.*

ALTRUISTIC *adj.*

1. As I left, [Branch] Rickey remarked, "You know, of course, [Sid] Gordon was born in Brooklyn." His PUTATIVE design was ALTRUISTIC. His real intention was to have me urge the Dodgers to buy Gordon in the pages of the *Herald Tribune*. (R. Kahn, *The Boys of Summer*, Harper and Row, 1971, p. 98)

2. The American people are awakening to the truth that "liberalism" is a costume of ALTRUISM, used to mask an on-going power grab by the "parasitic" professional class to which Neal R. Peirce [*Washington Post* political analyst] and his colleagues belong. (P.J. Buchanan, "New Hampshire's 'Bad Points' Good," *Daily Oklahoman*, Okla. City, 2/3/76, p. 8)

3. [Under "organic growth"] . . . the developed nations would be led to grow somewhat more slowly . . . than their historic curve, with the emphasis on high-technology and conservation-oriented production. Developing countries, stressing labor-intensive industrialization, would grow faster . . . . Nobody spelled out what might bring about such an epidemic of ALTRUISM. (M. Ruby, "The Future: 'Organic Growth,'" *Newsweek*, 4/26/76, p. 84)

4. Geico [Government Employees Insurance Co.], one of the nation's leading automobile insurance companies, faces insolvency unless it receives a massive infusion of capital . . . . Geico's competitors may well come to the rescue . . . . If the competing companies do extend a helping hand, it will not be out of ALTRUISM. They fear that the collapse of Geico . . . might lead to federal regulation of the insurance industry. (R. Worsnop, of ERR, "Casualty insurance risks multiplying," *Norman* [Okla.] *Transcript*, 6/21/76, p. 6)

AMANUENSIS (ə-man′yōō-en′sis) *noun; pl.* -SES (-sēz) a secretary who can write rapidly enough to record dictation; one employed to copy what another has written; secretary: now a somewhat jocular usage.

1. To begin with, these sessions [totaling more than 60 hours] were not interviews [of Chiang Ch'ing by Roxane Witke] in any normal sense, but theatrically wrought performances with Chiang Ch'ing soliloquizing into the early hours of the morning for the benefit of this young foreign scholar, who found herself being transmuted into a retainer, an AMANUENSIS to an empress. (J. Lelyveld, "A Message from

Mao's Widow . . . and how it got here," *New York Times*, 4/3/77, Section 7, p. 7)

2. Whereas that first novel [*Fear of Flying*, by Erica Jong] seemed charged with a bawdy, manic energy, this one [*How to Save Your Own Life*, by Erica Jong] reads flatter than a three-day-old Pepsi. Besides being by turns cutesy and academically stuffy (Isadora [a character in the latter book] refers to herself as an "AMANUENSIS to the ZEITGEIST"), it seems simply mean. (P. Hendrickson, "Erica Jong," *National Observer*, week ending 4/16/77, p. 26)

AMBIENCE (am′ bē-əns) or **AMBIANCE** *noun* that which surrounds or encompasses; environment; the mood, character, atmosphere, etc., of an environment or milieu.

AMBIENT *adj.* completely surrounding; encompassing; on all sides.

1. [Gordon Kahn to Roger Kahn:] "Your mother and I are somewhat concerned about the specific AMBIANCE where you work [referring to Roger Kahn's covering the Brooklyn Dodgers baseball team for the *New York Herald Tribune*]." (R. Kahn, *The Boys of Summer*, Harper and Row, 1971, p. 116)

2. These nights [of reading Joyce's *Ulysses* with his family], begun with a formal opening statement and concluded with coffee, had shown us Stephen Dedalus rising, teaching, walking, Leopold Bloom meditating and lunching, but in an AMBIANCE of humorless intensity. I had not yet grown as fond of *Ulysses* as I was of *Portrait*. (R. Kahn, *Ibid.*, p. 136)

3. He [Carl Furillo] could have qualified marginally [as a pinch-hitter or coach when past his prime], but once he sued, people in baseball's conformist AMBIANCE decided he was a "Bolshevik." (R. Kahn, *Ibid.*, p. 336)

4. Peter Boyle's role [in the movie, *Taxi Driver*] is small . . . as the gently thick Wizard, adjusted to the filth that Travis is coiled up to fight; Boyle gives the film a special New Yorkhack AMBIENCE. (Pauline Kael, Review, *The New Yorker*, 2/9/76, p. 84)

5. . . . the touch of Oxbridge AMBIANCE in the . . . Georgian architecture [of Harvard] . . . . (N.W. Aldrich Jr., "Harvard On the Way

Down," *Harper's*, March 1976, p.41)

6. See (2) under CLOY.

7. Non-specialists will find texts on some capitals [in the book, *World Capitals*, edited by H. Wentworth Eldredge] brisker than others . . . . London belongs to John W. Shepherd of the London School of Economics. Shepherd, like so many of his fellow citizens seems born with a feeling for AMBIENCE and quality-of-life in his bones. (Jane Holtz Kay, Review, *Smithsonian*, December 1975, pp. 129–130)

8. Secondhand clothing stores, whether the AMBIENCE is pawnshop grungy or Hollywood trendy, seem to have an irresistible appeal for certain teenage boys. (Jane Davison, "Mothers buy clothes; boys make costumes," *New York Times*, 3/14/76, Section 6, p. 39)

9. See (2) under ANTEBELLUM.

10. See (4) under ROCOCO.

11. See (3) under SCABROUS.

AMELIORATE (ə-mēl′ yə-rāt′) *verb* to make or become better; improve; MELIORATE.

AMELIORATION *noun.*

AMELIORABLE *adj.*

AMELIORATIVE *adj.*

AMELIORATOR *noun.*

AMELIORANT *noun* a thing that ameliorates.

1. There is an increasingly grim quality about these public queries [as to the content of education], and this is not likely to be AMELIORATED until we come to some larger national understanding as to the kind of nation and the kind of people we think we want. (G.W. Bonham, "Some Vexing Questions About the Liberal Arts" [Editorial], *Change*, May 1976, p. 11)

2. No one [in colonial times] wanted to spend hard-earned money for a transportation system that would only send horsemen tramping all over their land, so roads were allowed to degenerate. King George III could have used taxes to AMELIORATE the situation, but perhaps

he saw the wisdom of keeping his dissatisfied subjects apart. (Michele Derus, *Danbury News-Times*, "Settlers had few pathways," reprinted in the *Norman* [Okla.] *Transcript*, 6/17/76, p. 24)

3. In the exhausting lead role [in Pavel Kohout's play, *Poor Murderer*], Laurence Luckinbill is like a shadow-boxer going fifteen rounds against thin air, and not even the haunted beauty and earthy intelligence of Maria Schell, making her Broadway debut, AMELIORATES what becomes a TRAVESTY of theater itself. (J. Kroll, Review, *Newsweek*, 11/1/76, p. 63)

AMETHYSTIC (am' əthis' tik) *adj.* NOTE: While this word has not yet appeared in any dictionary, it means: having the property of reducing the inebriating effect of alcohol on the bodily functions. This word, of course, is the adjective corresponding to the semi-precious stone, AMETHYST, which is derived from the Greek word AMETHYSTOS, which means: a remedy against drunkenness.

1. Their research [that of Ernest Noble's group at the University of California at Irvine] indicates that a "sober-up pill" may be available soon . . . . The subjects [of this research] . . . tossed off 6 ounces of gin or vodka . . . . They were next given either a moderate dose of one of the three drugs [aminophylline, ephedrine, or L-DOPA]—or a PLACEBO, and their relative degree of inebriation was measured . . . alcoholic impairment of the critical ability to process information was reduced by as much as 50 per cent in those who had taken the drugs, known as AMETHYSTIC* agents. (Anon., "A Sober-Up Pill," *Newsweek*, 11/1/76, p. 63)

AMORPHOUS (ə-môr'fəs) *adj.* without definite form; shapeless; of no definite or particular type, kind, or character; unorganized; vague.

AMORPHISM or AMORPHOUSNESS *noun.*

AMORPHOUSLY *adv.*

1. "First the *société anonyme* [Indocharter

---

*The ancient Greeks believed that amethysts, the semi-precious stones, inhibited the effects of alcohol, and often wore them for that purpose.

Vientiane] was registered in Paris," he [Sam Collins] said. "Second, the *société*, on reliable information, was the property of a discreetly diversified overseas Shanghainese trading company based in Manila, which was itself owned by a Chiu Chow company registered in Bangkok, which in turn paid its dues to a totally AMORPHOUS outfit in Hong Kong called China Airsea . . . which owned everything from junkfleets to cement factories to racehorses to restaurants." (J. LeCarré, *The Honourable Schoolboy*, Alfred A. Knopf, 1977, p. 71)

2. Next . . . is [the book] *Daphnis and Chloe* (Braziller, $55), the Greek pastoral romance newly embellished by Chagall with 58 stunning lithographs in seven colors. The AR-CADIA that he [Chagall] has drawn is stocked with AMORPHOUS domestic animals, . . . skies alive with birds and goddesses, and loving couples who seem most at rest when secure in each other's arms. (P.S. Prescott, Review, *Newsweek*, 12/12/77, p. 105)

AMOUR-PROPRE (ä-moor' prô' pr³) *noun* self-esteem; self-respect.

1. ". . . I shouldn't suppose you suffer . . . from an undue burden of AMOUR-PROPRE, given your seedy calling" [said Donald Washburn]. "Just a moment," I [Russel Wren] cried. "True, my own practice [as a private detective] may at the moment be down-at-heel in a commercial or VENAL sense. But my profession qua vocation is as good as any." (Thomas Berger, *Who is Teddy Villanova?*, Delacorte Press/Seymour Lawrence, 1977, p. 161)

ANACHRONISM (ə-nak'rə-niz'əm) *noun* a person, object, thing, or event that is chronologically out of place, especially one appropriate to an earlier period; an error in chronology in which a person, object, or event is assigned an incorrect date or period.

ANACHRONISTIC or ANACHRONOUS *adj.*

ANACHRONISTICALLY or ANACHRONOUSLY *adv.*

1. Of course, the casting [of the TV show, *Mary Hartman*] is superb. That Louise Lasser is Woody Allen's ex-wife and appeared in sev-

eral of his films is a datum the critical beavers have already gnawed on . . . . They . . . lecture us about the humor of stylized incredulity, ANACHRONISTIC misapprehension, catastrophic pluck, inferiority looking for a complex and so on. (J. Leonard, Review, *New York Times*, 2/1/76, Section 2, p. 1)

2. See (1) under ARTIFACT.

3. See (4) under PEDANT.

4. I have gone over the original edition sentence by sentence [in preparing this edition]. I have corrected the ANACHRONISMS, changed the tenses where appropriate, once or twice entered substantial clarifications. (W.F. Buckley Jr., *Up From Liberalism*, Arlington House, 2nd Printing 1968, p. xxviii)

5. The big question is whether the essential planks of conservatism were ANACHRONIZED by the machine; the big answer is that they were not. (W.F. Buckley Jr., *Ibid.*, p. 222)

6. See (1) under SCAM.

7. The stories [in *The Winthrop Covenant*, by Louis Auchincloss] add little, moreover, to the basic understanding of the workings of the puritan mind that historians like Perry Miller have afforded us. And despite an occasional pass at reproducing 17th and 18th century locutions, these ancient Winthrops sound disconcertingly ANACHRONISTIC. (R. Schickel, Review, *New York Times*, 3/28/76, Section 7, p. 10)

8. See (1) under APARTHEID.

9. Should we, in the ANACHRONISTIC name of "slavery," impose unwanted private associations upon a free if misguided people? Is a "right to contract" an absolute right to buy one's way into any group? It seems to me that when people put up their own money to support their own facility, they have the right to be as exclusive as they please, even if they base their right on reasons we may think to be wrong. (J.J. Kilpatrick, "Private School Issue Troublesome," *Daily Oklahoman*, Okla. City, 5/6/76, p. 10)

10. For it ought to be plain that the liberal arts are as ANACHRONISTIC in the year 1976 as corsets. Indeed, they share similar origins, and have about the same functions—to stifle and conceal. (C. Frankel, "Piercing the Veil of the Commonplace," *Chronicle of Higher Education*, 5/3/76, p. 32)

11. . . . he [author Raymond Chandler] shares with [Philip] Marlowe a code of honor that seems a stubborn ANACHRONISM in both Chandler's fictional world and his real one. (R. Fuller, Review of *The Life of Raymond Chandler*, by Frank MacShane, *Philadelphia Inquirer*, 5/30/76, p. 10-I)

12. . . . a youthful band of hustler-idealists is trying to celebrate the Bicentennial with what might strike some as the ultimate ANACHRONISM—a revolution . . . the Peoples Bicentennial Commission wants a second revolution to overthrow large corporations which, it claims, dominate American life. (Margot Hornblower, *Washington Post*, "New Idea for Bicentennial—a revolution," reprinted in *Norman* [Okla.] *Transcript*, 6/17/76, p. 3A)

13. [Elaine] Kendall's main thesis [in *Peculiar Institutions: An Informal History of the Seven Sister Colleges*] is that the women's colleges are now ANACHRONISTIC, that their continued existence became "highly doubtful" after 1970, that coeducation is "sensible, economical and natural," and that the remaining women's colleges are "vulnerable and unprotected." (C.C. Cole Jr., Review, *Chronicle of Higher Education*, 6/21/76, p. 13)

14. But [Woody] Hayes, who relies on terror rather than science to produce victory, is a relic of football's pre-intellectual era. He is as ANACHRONISTIC as the prose style of Grantland Rice . . . . (G.F. Will, "Is That a Red Dog in the Seam?," *Newsweek*, 9/6/76, p. 102)

15. In a time of ready-to-wear, mass-produced clothes, the kimono of old Japan seems a fabled ANACHRONISM, like phoenix feathers. (R. Hughes, "Furisode and Sō-Hitta," *Time*, 5/24/76, p. 66)

16. See (9) under JINGO.

17. See (10) under IMPECCABLE.

ANAGRAM (an' ə-gram') *noun* the rearrangement of the letters of a word or phrase to form a new word or phrase; the new word or phrase so formed.

ANAGRAMMATIC or **ANAGRAMMATICAL** *adv.*

ANAGRAMMATICALLY *adv.*

ANAGRAMMATIZE (an′ ə-gram′ ə-tīz′) *verb*
to make an anagram of.

1. And if that weren't fun enough, they've embellished it [*Scrambled Exits*, a book by Gyles Brandreth and David Farris] with puzzles of other sorts [than mazes]—riddles, ANAGRAMS, PALINDROMES. (Anon., Review, *New York Times*, 6/19/77, Section 7, p. 47)

ANAMORPHOSIS (an′ə-môr′fə-sis, -môr-fō′sis) *noun* an image distorted so as to appear natural when viewed in a curved mirror or viewed from a certain angle; the method of producing such a drawing or image.

ANAMORPHOSCOPE *noun* an optical device for correcting an image distorted by anamorphosis.

ANAMORPHIC *adj.* having or making unequal magnifications along two perpendicular axes.

1. The word ANAMORPHOSIS comes from the Greek words meaning "shape" and "again," and that is exactly what happens to ANAMORPHIC pictures: When viewed from the correct angle or through specially shaped mirrors, they are re-formed in the viewer's eye . . . . The distorted appearance of ANAMORPHIC images allowed artists to get away with subjects that otherwise would not have passed in polite company. . . . Erhard Scon's *What Do You See?*, a sixteenth century woodcut, combines an ordinary picture of Jonah being spat up by the whale with an ANAMORPHIC picture of a man relieving himself. (B. Marvel, "These Images Aren't What They Seem," *National Observer*, week ending 3/26/77, p. 20)

ANATHEMA (ə-nath′ə-mə) *noun* a person or thing detested, loathed, accursed, or condemned to damnation or destruction; a strong curse or EXECRATION; any imprecation of divine punishment.

ANATHEMATIC (ə-nath′-ə-mat′ik) or ANATHEMATICAL *adj.* loathsome; hateful.

ANATHEMATICALLY *adv.*

ANATHEMATIZE *verb* to pronounce an anathema against.

ANATHEMATIZATION *noun.*

ANATHEMATIZER *noun.*

1. One can only hope, in the heat of so categorical an ANATHEMA, that there is an energy crisis in hell [response to a letter saying "God damn you all" to W.F. Buckley Jr., his friends, and supporters because of Buckley's position on the oil crisis]. (W.F. Buckley Jr., *Execution Eve and Other Contemporary Ballads*, G.P. Putnam's Sons, 1975, p. 283)

2. While considered to be the nation's leading lawyer, [John W.] Davis, Solicitor-General under President Wilson and former ambassador to Great Britain . . . , was ANATHEMA to the progressive Democrats [in 1924] from the West and Midwest because of his representation of Wall Street banks and large utility companies. (M.S. Gwirtzman, "Son of 1924," *New York Times*, 3/14/76, Section 6, p. 91)

3. For at 7 A.M. the next morning, there was smiling Jimmy Carter shaking hundreds of hands at the plant gate of U.S. Steel's huge Homestead plant here [in Pittsburgh], handing out literature promising that if elected he would sign the common-situs picketing bill (vetoed by President Ford) and a repeal of Taft-Hartley's right-to-work section. Both are ANATHEMA to corporate America. (R. Evans, R. Novak, "Carter Displaying Campaign Savvy," *Daily Oklahoman*, Okla. City, 4/26/76, p. 14)

4. Bob [Radnitz] is a practicing HEDONIST . . . . The idea of marriage remains ANATHEMA. (R. Windeler, "Bob Radnitz & Joanna Crawford Collaborate on G-Rated Films and an X-Rated Private Life," *People*, 5/24/76, p. 52)

5. Soviet weapons, possibly accompanied by Soviet advisers and technicians, in neighboring Jordan would be ANATHEMA to Communist-hating Saudi Arabia. (R. Evans, R. Novak, "Pro-Israel U.S. Stance Can Open Foothold in Jordan for Moscow," *Daily Oklahoman*, Okla. City, 6/2/76, p. 6)

6. [Senator Estes] Kefauver won 12 of the 14 primaries he entered that year [1952] . . . . And yet all this availed Kefauver nothing at his party's convention. He was ANATHEMA to the old-line Democratic establishment . . . . Although Kefauver led on the first two ballots, Gov. Adlai E. Stevenson of Illinois swept to victory on the third. (R. Worsnop, "Ford,

Reagan retain strong support: Conventions looming over primaries," *Norman* [Okla.] *Transcript*, 6/8/76, p. 6)

7. A deeper . . . question is whether principles Americans have assumed were part of a free society will be sacrificed by the public's passive acceptance of practices heretofore considered ANATHEMA. Will America tolerate covert arrangements between intelligence agents and academics, authors, journalists and publishers? (J. Nelson, *Los Angeles Times*, "Public might be apathetic about agencies' crimes," reprinted in *Norman* [Okla.] *Transcript*, 6/17/76, p. 11-A)

8. See (2) under ATRABILIOUS.

9. See (4) under LACHRYMOSE.

10. Nevertheless, the [Ford] foundation—which over the years has given away about $5 billion to more than 7,000 organizations and tens of thousands to individuals—has caused periodic headaches for the nation's No. 2 automaker. In the 1950s, for example, the foundation granted $15 million to the Fund for the Republic, whose liberal leanings were ANATHEMA to Ford dealers and customers in the South. (Anon., "Ford's Parting Shot," *Newsweek*, 1/24/77, p. 69)

11. See (1) under ASSIDUOUS.

ANCHORITE (ang' kə-rīt) or **ANCHORET** *noun* a person who lives alone and apart from society for religious meditation; hermit; recluse.

ANCHORITIC (-rit´ ik) or **ANCHORETIC** (-ret´ik) *adj*.

ANCHORESS *noun* a female anchorite.

1. It was in Egypt that monasticism first flowered, nurtured by the formidable example of the great 4th century ANCHORITE, St. Anthony of the Desert. At the height of the movement, before the 7th century Arab invasions, Egypt boasted some 50,000 monks. (Anon., "The Desert Revival," *Time*, 4/19/76, p. 98)

ANDROGYNOUS (an-droj´ə-nəs) *adj*. exhibiting both male and female characteristics, especially sexual ones; hermaphroditic.

ANDROGYNY (an-droj´ə-nē) *noun*.

1. The use of the pronoun "he" to do ANDROGYNOUS duty is out. (W.F. Buckley Jr., *Execution Eve and Other Contemporary Ballads*, G.P. Putnam's Sons, 1975, p. 419)

2. Mao Tse-tung . . . is not considered in China to be a mere man. He is more than a man. More in the divine sense, and more also in the sexual sense. You might say that he is an ANDROGYNOUS god. (W.F. Buckley Jr., *Ibid.*, p. 349)

3. In WJL [*Women: A Journal of Liberation*], feeling has become the paramount judgmental criterion: Revolution is how we feel about our country . . . ; ANDROGYNY is how women feel about their masculine side. The editors accept stereotypical ideas about femininity and then sanctify them. (Suzanne Gordon, Review, *Change*, April 1976, p. 46)

4. . . . there was at the heart of [Coco] Chanel's fashion that ANDROGYNOUSNESS* *(sic)* which conferred to her clothes their notorious timelessness, the staid unchangeability of "men's wear." (Francine Gray, Review of *Chanel*, by Edmonde Charles-Roux, *The New York Review of Books*, 12/11/75, p. 44)

5. Even the most self-deprecating or ANDROGYNOUS male may feel that Miss [Sandra] Hochman's men [in *Happiness Is Too Much Trouble*] are hardly a typical cross-section of their sex. (A. Broyard, Review, *New York Times*, 3/11/76, p.35)

6. He [Lee Clayton (Marlon Brando), in the movie, *The Missouri Breaks*] takes delight in theatre, including ANDROGYNOUS impersonations. (Penelope Gilliatt, Review, *The New Yorker*, 5/31/76, p. 100)

7. In Mattapoisett [in the year 2137, in *Women on the Edge of Time*, by Marge Piercy], humanism controls science and technology. Sex is ANDROGYNOUS; people adopt the ethnic and cultural ancestry of their choice; . . . children have three mothers (male and female). (Margo Jefferson, Review, *Newsweek*, 6/7/76, p. 96)

8. He [director Nicolas Roeg, of *The Man Who Fell to Earth*] seems to have a special insight into the perverse, child-like utopianism of the ANDROGYNOUS rock idol. Bowie is a sweet,

---

*Should be *androgyny*.

sad, touching space-saint with his unisex face and body . . . (J. Kroll, Review, *Newsweek*, 6/14/76, p. 90)

9. See (1) under INNUENDO.

10. . . . I question the existence of the specific solitude of woman-as-intellectual when that woman is a writer, because when it comes to their essential faculty as writers, all writers are ANDROGYNOUS beings. (Nadine Gordimer, "What Makes Us Write?" *The Writer*, October 1976, p. 23)

11. See (8) under MACHISMO.

12. Flaubert called her [George Sand] "this great man," Musset described her as "the most womanly woman I have known." Hers was the creative ANDROGYNOUS mind announced by Coleridge. (Linda Kelly, Review of *The Life of George Sand*, a book by Joseph Barry, *New York Times*, 3/27/77, Section 7, p. 18)

ANGST (ÄNGst) *noun* a gloomy, often neurotic feeling of generalized anxiety and depression; dread; anxiety; anguish.

1. It [William Molcom's *Open House*] is Mahlerian in its clear instrumental colorings, its tunefulness, . . .—a slight, deft piece with Mahler's charm and gaiety and none of his ANGST, now perky, now sentimental, and totally winning . . . (A. Porter, Review, *The New Yorker*, 2/9/76, p. 99)

2. It is less talk about money or socialism that separates Russians and Americans from, say, Englishmen than the existence of a dream and all the ANGST, sacrifice, and spiritual relief (or delusion) attached to it. (G. Feifer, Review of *The Russians*, by Hedrick Smith; and *Russia: The Power and the People*, by Robert G. Kaiser, *Harpers*, March 1976, p. 116)

3. Laverne DeFazio [of ABC's *Laverne and Shirley*], three years out of Millard Fillmore High, is a flip but homely type with a bad case of virginal ANGST. She frets a lot about never having "done the dirty deed," but *seems* resigned to settling for her first facial. (H.F. Waters, "Blue-Collar Boffo," *Newsweek*, 3/29/76, p. 85)

4. *Mary Hartman* [the TV show] certainly is different. Its heroine, played with hilariously understated desperation by Louise Lasser, is a befuddled, ANGST-ridden housewife residing in the mythical blue-collar town of Fernwood, Ohio. (H.F. Waters, M. Kasindorf, "The Mary Hartman Craze," *Newsweek*, 5/3/76, p. 54)

5. In J.D. O'Hara's . . . *A History of Poetry*, there appears a familiar photograph of . . . John Berryman . . . . On the same page are pictures of Robert Lowell, Sylvia Plath and Anne Sexton . . . the caption [reads] . . . "John Berryman along with Sylvia Plath . . . and Anne Sexton . . . all harboring unresolved personal torments, wrote poems filled with ANGST and death wishes that were ultimately fulfilled by suicide." (D. Davie, Review of *The Freedom of the Poet*, a book by John Berryman, *New York Times*, 4/25/76, Section 7, p. 3)

6. This week, 45-year-old Barbara Jill Walters . . . bows in as co-host of the *ABC Evening News with Harry Reasoner and Barbara Walters*. Not since Jack Paar's Second Coming in 1973 has a TV megastar's shift in locus aroused so much speculation, recrimination, promotional ballyhoo and executive-suite ANGST. (H.F. Waters, *et. al.*, "The New Look of TV News," *Newsweek*, 10/11/76, p. 68)

7. . . . the attention of most of us has been riveted recently upon the wit and wisdom of Earl Butz, the unfulfilled lusts of presidential candidates, the ANGST of Air Force generals and the membership policies of a Baptist church in an obscure Georgia village. Meanwhile, . . . OPEC, the most successful and rapacious cartel in the history of price-gouging, has hiked oil prices nearly 400 percent since 1973 . . . . The feeling of those who follow such things closely is that the Doha *sheikhdown* [the meeting of OPEC at Doha, Qatar on Dec. 15] will be somewhere between a 10 and a 25-percent increase in oil prices, effective Jan. 1. (Smith Hempstone, "Over a barrel: Again, the oil price squeeze," *Philadelphia Inquirer*, 11/11/76, p. 11-A)

8. See (4) under FARRAGO.

ANIMADVERSION (an′ ə-mad-vûr′ zhən) *noun* a censorious, critical, unfavorable, or adverse remark or comment (on or upon something); aspersion; derogation; censure; the act or fact of criticizing adversely.

ANIMADVERSIONAL *adj.*

ANIMADVERT   *verb*   to comment critically or with disapproval.

ANIMADVERTER   *noun.*

1. To be blunt about it, Senator McGovern's ANIMADVERSIONS on his fellow human beings are indecent. (W.F. Buckley Jr., *Execution Eve and Other Contemporary Ballads*, G.P. Putnam's Sons, 1975, p. 82)

2. And the next morning an editor who introduced a panel discussion made a minor ANIMADVERSION on the service in the hotel in which we were quartered and got from his fellow editors that spontaneous, raucous, hysterical approval which recalls the startling reception given at San Francisco to General Eisenhower in 1964 when he dropped a crack about the media's bias against Barry Goldwater. (W.F. Buckley Jr., *Ibid.*, p. 172)

3. The gentle ANIMADVERSIONS of the law are not useless. They do become, however, a greater menace than any benefaction they propose to perform when they are taken too literally, and I understand this to be what the critics of the pot laws are fighting against, and I am on their side, not 1000 per cent, . . . but a conservative 100 per cent. (W.F. Buckley Jr., *Ibid.*, p. 393)

4. The book [*The R Document*, by Irving Wallace] contains . . . the better part of an introductory course in the U.S. Constitution, plus extended ANIMADVERSIONS on such topics as the history of the FBI under Hoover, the internment of Japanese Americans during World War II, the history of the company town in America, the Organized Crime Control Act of 1969 and the content and meaning of the Bill of Rights. (Gene Lyons, Review, *New York Times*, 3/14/76, Section 7, p. 5)

5. There was something in this remarkable document [of Paul Hughes] that fed on, and then quickly nourished, every liberal political neurosis of early 1954. Here was evidence of a secret and dark alliance between Eisenhower and [Joseph] McCarthy; . . . of McCarthy's personal views (revealed through a transcription of miscellaneous ANIMADVERSIONS on such disparate persons and things as Attorney General Herbert Brownell, Air Force bases, Drew Pearson, ethics, Leonard Hall . . . . (W.F.

Buckley Jr., *Up From Liberalism*, Arlington House, 2nd Printing 1968, p. 104)

6. He [Time Correspondent Erik Amfitheatrof, in a recent interview] found the celebrated [Gore] Vidal tongue as sharp as ever. A sampling of Vidal's current opinions and ANIMADVERSIONS: Truman Capote—"He's made lying an art form—a minor art form." Norman Mailer—"I think his whole life was destroyed by his name. He should have been called Male-est." (Anon., "Gore Vidal: Laughing Cassandra," *Time*, 3/1/76, p. 64)

7. The House of Commons had since passed a law forbidding the sovereign, and the next in line for the throne, from traveling together in the same plane. [This] was more in the nature of a routine precaution against multiple tragedy than a bill of attainder ANIMADVERTING on the performance of the incumbent monarch. (W.F. Buckley Jr., *Saving the Queen*, Doubleday, 1976, p. 97)

8. "It is he [Teddy Villanova]!" I [Russel Wren] gasped. And Boris, after flinching from my immediate side with a grimace, which I suppose meant Alice [Ellish]'s ANIMADVERSION on my breath had had cause, confirmed in like wonder: "He bestrides the narrow world like a colossus." (Thomas Berger, *Who Is Teddy Villanova?*, Delacorte Press/Seymour Lawrence, 1977, p. 215)

ANIMUS (an' ə-məs)   *noun*   hostile feeling or attitude; animosity; antagonism; strong ill will or hatred; animating spirit or force; intention.

ANIMOSITY   *noun*   a feeling of strong dislike or ill will that tends to display itself in action; hostility; hatred.

1. The bill [to break up major American oil companies] cannot be dismissed as election-year rhetoric by liberal politicians hoping to capitalize on a consumer ANIMUS against the petroleum industry. It must be respected and fought for what it really is: a serious attempt . . . at total nationalization by breaking up the major oil companies into separate smaller units that could not possibly meet the country's energy needs. Then, of course, the government would have to take over. (Anon., "Wrecking Crew at Work" [Editorial], *Satur-*

day Oklahoman & Times, Okla. City, 4/3/76, p. 8)

2. That New York's neutrality [with respect to candidates for nomination for President in 1924] should be questioned at all was indicative of the suspicions and ANIMUS that permeated the [Democratic] party. (R.K. Murray, "The Democrats vs. Frustration City: it was no mix," *Smithsonian*, April 1976, p. 49)

3. Despite good Washington connections, Evans/Novak usually give a one-legged performance, lacking in balance. They early developed an ANIMUS toward Jimmy Carter and reported so many hidden obstacles in his way that if Carter had had to overcome them all, his nomination would have been more impressive than it was. (T. Griffith, "Newswatch," *Time*, 8/16/76, p. 74)

4. The conservative ANIMUS against Big Business has its justification. As Henry Ford II has himself suggested, capitalist foundations are too often inclined to subsidize carriers of what the late Ludwig von Mises called the "anti-capitalist mentality." . . . Big Business spends little advertising money on struggling publications such as Human Events and National Review, . . . while Madison Avenue's copy and cash have gone to media beloved of the liberal Left. (J. Chamberlain, "Conservatives' Turn," *Times Herald*, Norristown, Pa., 2/21/77, p. 15)

5. Thus . . . the Ford Foundation has been helpful to my own journal, The Public Interest, and has made some modest grants to the American Enterprise Institute, with which I am associated. Nevertheless, it is fair and accurate to say that most of the time the Ford Foundation seems more interested in supporting people and activities that display a habitual ANIMUS to the business community. (I. Kristol, "On Corporate Philanthropy," *Wall Street Journal*, 3/21/77, p. 18)

ANKH (ăngk) *noun* a tau-shaped cross with a loop at the top, an ancient Egyptian symbol of life.

1. When the ANKH became the established symbol of *The Love Machine*, she [author Jacqueline Susann] gave away what seemed to be thousands to people who could help . . .

the budget for ANKHS alone amounted to three times the money spent on the average book campaign. (Abby Hirsch, Review of *Dolores*, a book by Jacqueline Susann, *New York Times*, 7/11/76, Section 7, p. 6)

2. In 1972 and 1973 there was a beneficent mood . . . the well-meant but overlooked exhortation "Have a nice day" . . . even appeared on bumper stickers. The ancient Egyptian symbol of life, the ANKH, became popular as a pendant and on rings. The graphic symbol that swept nearly all others off the student bookstore shelves was the Happy Face . . . . (Margaret Lantis, "As times change, so do signs, signals adopted by youth," *Smithsonian*, September 1976, p. 79)

ANODYNE (an′ ə-dīn′) *noun* a medicine that relieves or allays pain; anything that relieves distress.

ANODYNE or **ANODYNIC** (-din′ ik) *adj.* relieving pain; soothing to the mind or feelings.

1. . . . this time the show [*Mrs. Warren's Profession*, performed at the Berliner Ensemble] matches the house décor in ANODYNE prettiness . . . . He [a literary advisor to the Ensemble] explains the collapse . . . of the long-MOOTED plan to take the Ensemble on its first trip to America. (K. Tynan, "Brecht Would Not Applaud His Theater Today," *New York Times*, 1/11/76, Section 2, p. 7)

ANOMALY (ə-nom′ ə-lē) *noun* a deviation from the common rule, type, or form; someone or something anomalous; an incongruity, irregularity, or inconsistency; abnormality.

ANOMALOUS *adj.*

ANOMALOUSLY *adv.*

1. See (4) under GENRE.

2. The moviemakers were particularly on guard against showing the "Woodstein team," as they came to be known in Washington, as anything other than what they were—hungry reporters desperately eager for a break. But the film [*All the President's Men*] will augment what they have since become: very rich reporters in the ANOMALOUS and, for most newsmen, disquieting position of being more famous than

many of their sources. (Anon., "Watergate on Film," *Time*, 3/29/76, p. 54)

ANOMIE (an'ə-mē') *noun* a state or condition of individuals or society characterized by a breakdown or absence of accepted social norms and values, as in the case of uprooted people; lack of purpose, identity, or ethical values in a person or in a society; disorganization; rootlessness.

ANOMIC (ə-nom'ik) *adj.*

1. Travis [in the film, *Taxi Driver*] wants to conform, but he can't find a group pattern to conform to. So he sits and drives in the stupefied LANGUOR of ANOMIE.... He's used his emptiness [later in the film]—he's reached down into his own ANOMIE. Only Brando has done this kind of plunging, and [Robert] DeNiro's performance [as Travis] has something of the undisputed intensity that Brando's had in *Last Tango*. (Pauline Kael, Review, *The New Yorker*, 2/9/76, p. 82)

2. A few scenes [in the film, *Midway*] have been infiltrated by a curiously contemporary ANOMIE, as when Henry Fonda's Admiral Nimitz shrugs off the American victory [at Midway] by wondering, "Were we better . . . or just luckier?" (Janet Maslin, Review, *Newsweek*, 6/28/76, p. 78)

3. Harry Truman had just announced that he would not seek re-election in 1952. Democrats anxiously converged on Illinois Governor Adlai Stevenson and pressured him to make the race. His head buried in his hands, almost on the verge of tears, Adlai blurted: "This will probably shock you, but at the moment, I don't give a damn what happens to the country." By the standards of 1976, when a clutch of candidates are lusting for the presidency, that ANOMIE seems as remote as the Age of Jefferson. But it was typically Stevensonian. (E. Warner, Review of *Adlai Stevenson of Illinois*, a book by John Bartlow Martin, *Time*, 3/22/76, p. 81)

4. If there's something European about [Alan] Rudolph's L.A. [in the movie, *Welcome to L.A.*], reeking of ANOMIE and Antonioni, Robert Benton's Los Angeles in [the movie] *The Late Show* is All-American in its tacky PANACHE, its rueful homage to Raymond Chandler and Howard Hawks. (J. Kroll, Review, *Newsweek*, 2/21/77, p. 88)

ANOREXIA (an' ə-rek' sē-ə) *noun* chronic lack of appetite for food.

ANORETIC (an'ə-ret'ik) *adj.*

1. But the indignation [of V.S. Naipaul] just under the surface takes you back to so many great 19th-century "novelists of society" that I was not surprised to hear him say that reading Balzac was as delicious as eating chocolates. By contrast, the "hippies" he has seen TRAVESTYING Indian religious practices are suffering "intellectual ANOREXIA." (A. Kazin, "V.S. Naipaul, Novelist as Thinker," *New York Times*, 5/1/77, Section 7, p. 7)

2. At 17, Susan looked alarmingly emaciated ....Though she was 5 ft. 5 in. tall, she weighed only 70 lbs. and scorned all but the tiniest morsels of food . . . . Susan was a victim of ANOREXIA nervosa, "the starvation disease" or "Twiggy syndrome" . . . . Of those affected, 80% are female, mostly in their early teens . . . . Some therapists believe that young girls become ANORETICS out of fear of sexuality . . . . Other therapists see the disease as a symbolic "oral rebellion" against overcontrolling and troubled parents. (Anon., "The Self-Starvers," *Times*, July 28, 1975, p. 50-51)

3. See (2) under AUTISM.

ANTEBELLUM (an'tē-bel'əm) *adj.* before the war; (in the U.S.) before or existing before the American Civil War.

1. On July 7, 1924, as the Democratic National Convention prepared to cast its 78th ballot for the Presidential nomination, delegates on the floor of Madison Square Garden stumbled about as if in a terrible and unending dream... "Alabama," the roll call began. William F. Brandon, the Governor of that state, an ANTEBELLUM vision with his string tie and flowing white mustache, rose and for the 78th time boomed out, "Alabama casts 24 votes for Oscar W. Underwood!" (M.S. Gwirtzman, "Son of 1924," *New York Times*, 3/14/76, Section 6, p. 17)

2. There they stand, monumental riddles in the middle of the West African rain forest: old mansions with dignified columns gracing breezy piazzas . . . . These homes belong to the ANTEBELLUM American South, a bygone age

mellowed by AMBIENT nostalgia in the United States, but an era in Liberia still clinging to life by a thread. Soon . . . the mansions and their aging owners will vanish for good. (P. Boorstin, "Liberia's fading echoes of the Old American South," *Smithsonian*, March 1976, p. 82)

ANTEDILUVIAN (an′ tə-di-loo′ vē-ən) *adj.* belonging to the period before the Biblical flood; antiquated or primitive; ancient; very old.

ANTEDILUVIAN *noun* a person who lived before the Biblical flood; a very old or old-fashioned person.

1. And there are Teacher's frequent statements [in the play, *American Buffalo*, by David Mamet] that he and Donny are not apes, that this is not the Middle Ages, when all the while he is acting in a decidedly ANTEDILUVIAN manner. (E. Wilson, Review, *Wall Street Journal*, 2/23/77, p. 24)

2. It's argued that the oil companies have a particular technological expertise that makes it both efficient and expeditious to allow them to dominate competing energy industries. They probably can help by bringing a different and better kind of operational management to the coal industry. But that's not expertise; that's replacing ANTEDILUVIAN ANTHROPOIDS in coal management with men who understand their own employees aren't the enemy. Beyond bringing 20th century labor relations to a 19th century industry, oil has no special expertise outside the oil industry. (N. von Hoffman, "What role will the oil companies play in the energy crisis?" *Philadelphia Inquirer*, 5/14/77, p. 6-A)

ANTHROPOID (an′thrə-poid′) or **ANTHROPOIDAL** *adj.* resembling man; manlike; designating or of any of the most highly developed apes including the chimpanzee, gorilla, orangutan, and gibbon; apelike.

ANTHROPOID *noun* any anthropoid ape.

1. In recent years a site in northeastern Hungary has yielded a small treasure of ANTHROPOID material . . . including three distinct forms. And one of these, called *Rudapithecus hungaricus*, seems to Mr. [Miklós] Kretzoi to be a lot closer to the direct line of human evolution than *Ramapithecus* of India or *Kenyapithecus* of Africa. It is not however a case of parochial CHAUVINISM, nor paleontological olympics . . . . What Mr. Kretzoi points out . . . is that the process of hominization . . . was an evolutionary trend that took place among a whole range of apelike creatures throughout the Afro-Eurasian landscape. (J.K. Page Jr., "Our ancestors—all over," *Smithsonian*, January 1976, p. 12)

2. *American Buffalo* [a play by David Mamet] . . . has three LUMPEN-crooks (played with ANTHROPOID power by Robert Duvall, Kenneth McMillan and John Savage) in a junk shop plotting to rip off a coin collection. (J. Kroll, Review, *Newsweek*, 2/28/77, p. 79)

3. Whether or not the remake [of the movie, *King Kong*] itself is a patch on the powerful [of primitive RKO original, it is slicker and trendier. The Fay Wray character (played by starlet Jessica Lange) at one point chastens her ANTHROPOID amour as "you god-damn CHAUVINIST pig ape." Some EXEGETES even see the picture as a parable condemning the West's exploitation of the Third World. But DeLaurentiis [the producer] hardly seems the man to wage gorilla war on capitalism. (Anon., "Producer DeLaurentiis Sees and Monkey Does—$200 Million, He Hopes," *People*, 12/27/76-1/3/77, p. 74)

4. But. . .the 1976 super-"Kong," for all its super-advanced techniques and technologies, is both elephantine in scale and diminished in thrills. Yes, . . . the new ANTHROPOID is 40 feet tall whereas the 1933 one was a mere 18 inches high. (J. Kroll, "The Movies Go Ape—Again," *Newsweek*, 12/20/76, p. 102)

5. See (2) under ANTEDILUVIAN.

ANTHROPOMORPHIC (an′ thrə-pə-môr′ fik, -pō-) or **ANTHROPOMORPHOUS** *adj.* ascribing human form or attributes to a being or thing not human, especially to a deity; resembling or made to resemble a human form.

ANTHROPOMORPHICALLY or **ANTHROPOMORPHOUSLY** *adv.*

ANTHROPOMORPHISM *noun* the attributing of human shape or characteristics to a god, animal, or inanimate thing; an anthropomorphic conception or representation, as of a deity.

ANTHROPOMORPHIST *noun.*

ANTHROPOMORPHIZE *verb.*

ANTHROPOMORPHOSIS *noun* a transformation into human form.

1. *The Beaver Who Wouldn't Die* . . . , [a book] by 22-year old Monica DeBruyn is precisely the kind of ANTHROPOMORPHIC tale Giblin is talking about. (P.D. Zimmerman, "A Child's Garden of Books," *Newsweek*, 12/15/75, p. 89)

2. The tendency to ANTHROPOMORPHIZE our ideals is an American habit that can get us, indeed has just now gotten us, into deep trouble [this is a reference to equating the good traits of Spiro Agnew with the person Agnew]. (W.F. Buckley Jr., *Execution Eve and Other Contemporary Ballads*, G.P. Putnam's Sons, 1975, p. 331)

3. Thus, . . . the Hildebrandts' [illustrations of] ANTHROPOMORPHIC animals fill the pages [of *The Big City Book*, by Annie Ingle]. So we see a giraffe and an alligator buck the morning rush hour while a blue-suited elephant, briefcase in hand, hurries to the office. (Sidney Long, Review, *New York Times*, 2/8/76, Section 7, p. 16)

4. Ginseng means "man-root" in Chinese. Because the root splits into two "thighs" as it grows underground, mature ginseng struck early observers as human in form. Like the similarly ANTHROPOMORPHIC root known to John Donne ("Get with child a mandrake root"), the bifurcated ginseng fast became associated with sex . . . . Mandrake was thought to promote femaleness—*i.e.* fertility—while ginseng was thought to embody the male principle, potency. (R.A. Sokolov, "Root for all evil," *New York Times*, 4/25/76, Section 6, p. 35)

5. Galleries: Bernard Langlais. Wooden sculptures of animals, mostly with ANTHROPOMORPHIC faces whose features are built up in layers and then painted . . . . (Anon., "Goings On About Town," *The New Yorker*, 5/31/76, p. 8)

6. Chris Conover has her animals [in the book, *Six Little Ducks*] doing things human beings do, but remaining animals not ANTHROPOMORPHIZED Disneyesque mutations. (Barbara Kar-

lin, Review, *New York Times*, 5/30/76, Section 7, p. 10)

7. He [Alec Nisbett, author of the book, *Konrad Lorenz*] follows Lorenz's regrettable tendency to describe animal behavior in human terms—"married love" in monogamous geese, for example. This cannot be dismissed as harmless ANTHROPOMORPHISM in the service of popularization, for it promotes the very misuse of analogy that lies at the heart of Lorenz's problems . . . . Thus, a drake that tried to copulate with Lorenz's boot is a FETISHIST by "exact analogy" . . . . (S.J. Gould, Review, *New York Times*, 2/27/77, Section 7, p. 2)

8. Kong II designers Carlo Rambaldi and Glen Robinson are guilty of the ANTHROPOMORPHIC fallacy. Although their basic ape is well-conceived, with the tartar of centuries on his teeth and a roar like the flushing of a thousand industrial toilets, in moments of deep feeling his features skew themselves into a remarkable resemblance of Jack Nicholson's Satanic tenderness. (J. Kroll, "The Movies Go Ape—Again," *Newsweek*, 12/20/76, p. 103)

9. . . . [Ludwig] Mies [van der Rohe] designed furniture by continuously refining "curvature studies," rather than by the popular mumbo jumbo of ANTHROPOMORPHIC analysis, in which body measurements are fitted to a designed form . . . . Almost everything he produced is superbly comfortable . . . . (Ada Louise Huxtable, "Enduring splendor of Mies van der Rohe," *New York Times*, 2/27/77, Section 6, p. 80)

10. . . . Proteus IV, the oversexed computer of [the movie] *Demon Seed*, has nothing more pressing on his ANTHROPOMORPHIC mind than forcing Julie Christie to bear his child. (Janet Maslin, Review, *Newsweek*, 4/18/77, p. 64, 67)

ANTHROPOPHAGY (an'thrə-pof'ə-jē) *noun* the eating of human flesh; cannibalism.

ANTHROPOPHAGOUS or ANTHROPOPHAGIC or ANTHROPOPHAGICAL *adj.*

ANTHROPOPHAGOUSLY *adv.*

ANTHROPOPHAGITE (-jīt') *noun* cannibal.

ANTHROPOPHAGI (-jī´) *noun, pl.* cannibals.

1. Yet the nudity, free love, longevity and absence of both property and laws which he [Amerigo Vespucci] stressed [in his letters about the New World] were all features of the Golden Age, while ANTHROPOPHAGY, on which he dwelt in gruesome detail, was known from both Mandeville and classical literature. (H. Honour, "America as seen in the fanciful vision of Europe," *Smithsonian*, February 1976, pp. 55–56)

ANTINOMIAN (an´ ti-nō´ mē-ən) *noun* a person who believes that Christians can achieve salvation by virtue of faith alone, obedience to the moral law being therefore unnecessary.

ANTINOMIAN *adj.* of this belief or doctrine.

ANTINOMIANISM *noun.*

ANTINOMY (an-tin´ ə-mē) *noun* the opposition of one law, regulation, etc., to another; a contradiction or inconsistency between two apparently reasonable principles or laws.

1. Perhaps it is easy for me to understand its happening [Howard Hunt's being persuaded to engineer the Watergate burglary] because if someone had on the same occasions bothered to record my own mutterings, they would not have been significantly different, except that my commentary goes out quite safely in newspaper columns and on television, and is prettily laced with brooding historical references to a lowering American ANTINOMIANISM. (W.F. Buckley Jr., *Execution Eve and Other Contemporary Ballads*, G.P. Putnam's Sons, 1975, p. 119)

2. . . . he [Lyndon B. Johnson] was defending due process and constitutional order against the ANTINOMIANISM of the radicals, against the street people who were burning up buildings and the Kunstlers who were debauching the law. (W.F. Buckley Jr., *Ibid.*, p. 262)

3. If the achievement of a [college] degree is a Darwinian process of selection, the nontraditional programs are ANTINOMIAN. If one shares the faith, the degree is a concomitant. Under these circumstances traditional standards will be compromised; no other alternative is possible. (H.I. London, "The Case for Nontraditional Learning," *Change*, June 1976, p. 29)

ANTIPATHY (an-tip´ə-thē) *noun* a basic or habitual repugnance; aversion; an object of repugnance.

ANTIPATHETIC or **ANTIPATHETICAL** *adj.*

ANTIPATHETICALLY *adv.*

1. The very intensity of [Lord] Mountbatten's ANTIPATHY for [Mohammed Ali] Jinnah and opposition to his cause is among the very few new insights that emerge from this long book [*Freedom at Midnight*, by Larry Collins and Dominque Lapierre]. (N. Maxwell, Review, *New York Review of Books*, 12/11/75, p. 15)

2. I did have fun doing an experiment in organic chemistry . . . ; I was also challenged and stimulated . . . I learned at least a snippet about a subject I had approached with ANTIPATHY . . . . [Professor Stanley] Smith and others working with PLATO [a computerized approach to teaching] have consciously built fun into the process. (E. Jenkins, "The Potential of PLATO," *Change*, March 1976, p. 7)

3. For mysterious reasons, he [Carl Furillo] felt ANTIPATHETIC toward Bill Roeder. "That Roeder thinks he's smart, " Furillo said. "Well, he is pretty smart," I said . . . . "Let's ask Roeder [how many feet in an acre] . . . . He'll get it wrong [said Furillo], and that'll show you. He ain't as fucking smart as he thinks." (R. Kahn, *The Boys of Summer*, Harper and Row, 1971, p. 145)

4. The public ANTIPATHY to mass transportation becomes less surprising when one realizes that the classic suburb hardly exists anymore . . . . Today only one-quarter of all suburban workers are employed in central cities. (C.R. Hatch, Review of *The Power Broker: Robert Moses and the Fall of New York*, *Harper's*, January 1975, p. 90)

5. Bands of schoolboys [in Vancouver, British Columbia] have attacked Pakistanis; Sikh temples have been desecrated. Even without violent ANTIPATHY, the mood is reflected by a crop of sick jokes. "I'm starting a collection for a Pakistani family whose house is on fire," says a supposed humorist. "So far I've collected six

gallons of gasoline to keep it going." (G. Clark, "Waking Up from the Canadian Dream," *New York Times*, 6/6/76, Section 6, p. 40)

ANTIPHONAL (an-tif′ə-nəl) or **ANTIPHONIC** *adj.* of, pertaining to, or like an antiphon or antiphony; responsive.

ANTIPHONALLY or **ANTIPHONICALLY** *adv.*

ANTIPHON (an′ tə-fon′) *noun* a hymn, psalm, etc. chanted or sung in responsive, alternating parts; anything composed for responsive chanting or singing.

ANTIPHONY *noun* alternate or responsive singing by a choir in two divisions; a psalm or verse so sung; antiphon; a responsive musical utterance; any response or echo.

ANTIPHONARY *noun* a book of antiphons, especially a book of responsive prayers.

1. Brando and Nicholson [in the movie, *The Missouri Breaks*] are great fun to watch and hear. Their rhythms are beautiful—they are ANTIPHONAL antagonists who confront each other with irony and respect. (J. Kroll, Review, *Newsweek*, 5/24/76, p. 103)

2. . . . Singer [Callaway] cackled on about tea and coffee and Ceylon and Brazil, in an animated monotone which, while it engaged the interest, did not require ANTIPHONAL response, from either Rufus or Blackford [Oakes]. (W.F. Buckley Jr., *Saving the Queen*, Doubleday, 1976, p. 150)

ANTIPODAL (an-tip′ə-dəl) or **ANTIPODEAN** *adj.* diametrically opposite; on the opposite side of the globe (earth).

ANTIPODE (an′ti-pōd′) *noun* anything diametrically opposite; exact opposite.

ANTIPODES (an-tip′ə-dēz) *noun, pl. of antipode* any two places opposite each other on the earth; two opposite or contrary things.

1. Here, then, [in the book, *True Americanism: Green Berets and War Resisters*, by David Mark Mantell] we have two groups serving as ANTIPODAL metaphors of the disastrous sixties—the elite special forces invented by the Kennedy administration as an answer to small explosives in faraway jungles, and the tough young pacifists inadvertently unleashed a few

years later by Lyndon Johnson. (R.J. Margolis, Review, *Change*, Winter 1974-75, p. 62)

2. The true ANTIPODE of peace is violence. And those who want peace in the world should remove not only war . . . but also violence. If there is no open war but there still is violence, that is not peace. (A. Solzhenitsyn, "Will Russia's 'dragon belly' consume the whole world?" *Philadelphia Inquirer*, 3/6/77, p. 3-D)

ANTIQUARIAN (an′tə-kwâr′ē-ən) or **ANTIQUARY** *noun* an expert on or student of antiquities; a collector of antiquities.

ANTIQUARIAN *adj.* pertaining to antiquaries or the study of antiquities; dealing in or pertaining to old or rare books.

1. About 12,000 years ago a huge sheet of ice covered most of North America, but the climate was beginning to warm up and the ice was receding northward . . . . Apparently . . . the warming trend caused a thin layer of ice to move southward, whereupon it rapidly melted, sending water cascading across America into the sea, presumably flooding out whatever coastal cultures were in its path. What is remarkable from the standpoint of the ANTIQUARIAN, the date of this catastrophe—9600 B.C. [determined by radiocarbon dating of fossil shells]—is almost exactly the date which Plato reported for the deluge that destroyed Atlantis. (J.K. Page Jr., "Phenomena, comment and notes," *Smithsonian*, December 1975, p. 10)

2. The remainder of the basement, . . . FESTOONED with loosened insulation . . . , showed nothing of sufficient bulk to hide a man and . . . I shall not here catalogue Sam [Polidor]'s cellar, an inventory of which would interest only the ANTIQUARIAN of that which never had recommendation: disemboweled Morris chairs, ocherous newspaper pages advertising Nehru jackets, etc. (Thomas Berger, *Who Is Teddy Villanova?*, Delacorte Press/Seymour Lawrence, 1977, p. 228)

ANTITHESIS (an-tith′ i-sis) *noun* opposition; contrast; the direct opposite (usually followed by *of* or *to*); a contrast or opposition of thoughts, usually in two phrases, clauses, or sentences.

ANTITHETIC or ANTITHETICAL   *adj.*

ANTITHETICALLY   *adv.*

1. See (2) under HOMOEROTICISM.

2. See (1) under PRELAPSARIAN.

3. I have been maintaining for years that American higher education has mostly developed into an engine for the imposition of the prevailing orthodoxy. It [this statement] is offensive to members of the academic community . . . on several counts . . . . The third relates to the PEJORATIVE connotations that cling to the word "indoctrinator"—the result, primarily, of the false ANTITHESIS between education and indoctrination cultivated by the liberals themselves. (W.F. Buckley Jr., *Up From Liberalism*, Arlington House, 2nd Printing 1968, p. 82)

4. Between 1905 and 1912 [Elie] Nadelman . . . carved dozens of idealized marble heads that are seemingly "Greek," with sharply chiseled profiles and schematically patterned hair . . . . Other heads attain a degree of abstraction (an egg wearing a chignon, for instance) that is the ANTITHESIS of Greek art. (D. Bourdon, "The sleek, witty and elegant art of Elie Nadelman," *Smithsonian*, January 1976, p. 86)

5. In conversations with student groups, housewives, and professionals the name of [California's Governor] Jerry Brown kept cropping up as ANTITHESIS to the plastic politicians running for the presidency. Again and again I listened to resounding praise of his integrity and humanism, his courage in standing for and living by his convictions. (Viola Drath, "A European opinion: U.S. elections too much like a circus," *Chicago Tribune*, 5/6/76, Section 2, p. 4)

6. At the AP [Associated Press] you learned formula and developed speed. The first is ANTITHETIC to creative writing and the second is largely irrelevant, but both are critical to the confidence of every newspaperman. (R. Kahn, *The Boys of Summer*, Harper and Row, 1971, p. 75)

7. Dressen called on Branca, who threw a low fast ball, then a hand-high fast ball, which [Bobby] Thompson, enacting an ANTITHETIC "Casey at the Bat," lined into the left field stands . . . . For the second consecutive year the Dodgers had lost the pennant in the last inning of the last game of the season. (R. Kahn, *Ibid.*, p. 90)

8. The burr haircut and primrose-colored jumpsuit of wine collector Jim Albright, a fifty-year-old Austin [Texas] psychiatrist, suggest a certain eccentricity, and sure enough, his 1,000 bottles are lodged at his home in a separately air-conditioned basement room which, with its deep red walls and silver candelabra, looks like nothing so much as a set from *Rosemary's Baby*. The ANTITHESIS of this is the prefab "wine-vault" that 32-year-old Howard Rachofsky has installed in a bedroom of his ultramodern Dallas duplex. Looking like a sauna bath, though at 58° it feels a lot chillier, the $2850 vault stores about 850 bottles. (Sharon Churcher, "Grape Nuts," *Texas Monthly*, January 1977, p. 66)

APARTHEID (ə-pärt′hāt, -hīt) *noun* (in the Republic of South Africa) the policy of strict segregation and discrimination against native Negroes and other colored people.

1. Glanzi today is little more than a shop, a bar, a church and some rough-and-ready buildings, on the edge of the [Kalahari] desert not far from Botswana's border with South West Africa. In the black-powered Africa of 1976, Glanzi is also something of an ANACHRONISM. For here, in an independent black state, is a white, Afrikaans-speaking community . . . . They suffer from no reverse APARTHEID, for the government believes in nonracial democracy. (J. Reader, "A cattle trek across the wild, wide Kalahari," *Smithsonian*, April 1976, p. 90)

2. In 1952 APARTHEID flowered in what Stanley Woodward [sports editor of the *New York Herald Tribune*] called the American hookworm belt. Blacks attended separate schools, patronized separate restaurants, drank at separate water fountains, relieved themselves at separate urinals, watched baseball from separate sections of the grandstand, bought cokes at separate soft-drink concessions and, at the end of the wearying way, were EULOGIZED in black churches and interred in separate cemeteries for colored only. (R. Kahn, *The Boys of Summer*, Harper and Row, 1971, pp. 103–104)

APERÇU (a-per-sy′, ap′ər-sŏō′) *noun, pl.* -**ÇUS** (-sy′) a hasty glance or quick impression; glimpse; an insight; an outline, digest, survey, or summary.

1. We're asked [in the book, *The Realms of Gold*, by Margaret Drabble] simultaneously to enter into Frances's inner talkativeness . . . and to be barred from her good idea, her professional APERÇU. (C. Ricks, Review, *New York Review of Books*, 11/27/75, p. 43)

2. . . . [Howard] Moss's lines [in the book, *Buried City*], in their lucidity, give us conversation as it would be in Utopia, all light and feeling. [Seamus] Heaney's best poems [in the book, *North*] go back to riddles, charms and ritual; . . . Both poets have, of course, the defects of their virtues: Heaney is least interesting when most explicit, Moss most predictable when he moralizes his APERÇUS. (Helen Vendler, Review, *New York Times*, 4/18/76, Section 7, p. 6)

3. *In the People's Republic* [a book by Orville Schell] has some acute APERÇUS and shrewd comparisons. (R. Terrill, Review, *New York Times*, 5/8/77, Section 7, p. 32)

APHORISM (af′ ə-riz′ əm) *noun* a terse, pithy expression embodying a wise or clever observation or a general truth; maxim; adage.

APHORIST *noun* a person who makes or uses aphorisms.

APHORISTIC *adj.* of, like, or containing aphorisms; given to quoting or making aphorisms.

APHORISTICALLY *adv.*

APHORIZE *verb* to write or speak in aphorisms.

1. See (1) under AVUNCULAR.

2. See (1) under ERRONEOUS.

3. See (3) under MELIORIST.

4. [In 1924] Al Smith, a native New Yorker . . . was second-term governor of the Empire State. A Catholic, wet, and a vigorous opponent of the KKK, Smith rapidly converted his brown derby, cigar and Bowery APHORISMS into tangible signs of the rising influence of the urban masses in political life. (R.K. Murray, "The

Democrats vs. Frustration City: it was no mix," *Smithsonian*, April 1976, p. 49)

5. Her [Lillian Hellman's] reasoning begins back in a less corrupt world where we might find an APHORISTIC line of de Tocqueville: "It is always a great crime to deprive a people of its liberty on the pretext that it is using it wrongly." (Maureen Howard, Review of *Scoundrel Time*, by Lillian Hellman, *New York Times*, 4/25/76, Section 7, p. 2)

6. And Sam Weller dismissed the possibility of their application for any practical purposes on the grounds that, in his experience, tears never yet wound up a clock or worked a steam engine. From which judgment it is apparent Sam spent more time polishing his APHORISMS than in coping with weeping women . . . . (P. Ryan, "No tears about tears from a dry-eyed chauvinist," *Smithsonian*, May 1976, p. 132)

7. These [*The Facts of Life*, by R.D. Laing; and *Heresies*, by Thomas Szasz] are the writings of two most heretical psychoanalysts . . . both are essentially collections of APHORISMS, loosely joined by the IDIOSYNCRASIES of their authors; . . . "An APHORISM stands in the same relation to a description, as a caricature stands to a portrait," Szasz writes. This sentence makes the task of the reviewer extremely difficult, because, in regard to the APHORISMS that form the book, it is then not possible to know whether what Dr. Szasz means to present us with is a true portrait or a caricature. (B. Bettelheim, Review, *New York Times*, 5/30/76, Section 7, pp. 5, 12)

8. See (5) under PARODY.

9. Every Canadian school child for the last 70 years has been brought up to believe the most celebrated of national APHORISMS: "The 19th century was the century of the United States. The 20th century belongs to Canada." (G. Clark, "Waking up from the Canadian Dream," *New York Times*, 6/6/76, Section 6, p. 40)

10. What is wrong here [in the movie, *Alpha Beta*]—very wrong—is the dreary familiarity of the theme, the reworking, still again, of English working-class desperation, the sour brutality of the language, which often sounds too toplofty and APHORISTIC for the people speaking it ("I'm an apostolic alcoholic" . . .).

(Jay Cocks, Review, *Time*, 8/16/76, p. 59)

APHRODISIAC (af′rə-diz′ē-ak′) *noun* an agent, as a drug, arousing or increasing sexual desire.

APHRODISIAC *adj.*

APHRODITE (af′rə-dī′tē) *noun* the ancient Greek goddess of love and beauty, identified by the Romans with Venus.

1. See (2) under PANACEA.

2. Scientists at the U.S. Department of Agriculture . . . say they have discovered the world's first "love potion," which drives female looper moths crazy and stops their male lovers cold . . . the insect APHRODISIAC is believed to be the first authenticated case of a sexually exciting chemical compound. While the flowery-scented odor renders female looper moths helpless to the advances of male looper moths, it also stems the flow of the sexually-attracting odor emitted by the female that is used by the male to locate willing mates. The scientists said that by spreading the APHRODISIAC in areas affected by the moth, males would be unable to locate females and reproduction would be stemmed . . . the APHRODISIAC, 2-phenylethanol, . . . does not do for humans what it does to moths. (Associated Press, "Love Potion breaks up looper moth love life," *Philadelphia Inquirer*, 5/30/76, p. 6-C)

3. I [Adam Malone] remember running through the whole gamut of APHRODISIACS —from stuffing myself with oysters and bananas to trying the Chinese powder that comes from the horn of the rhinoceros, and from taking Spanish fly (made of dried and pulverized beetles) to using yohimbine (made of African tree bark) and none of the NOSTRUMS worked. I was about to try one of the new drugs, PCPA or L-dopa, both of which are said to create hypersexuality in some cases, when suddenly everything came together naturally. (I. Wallace, *The Fan Club*, Bantam Edition, 1975, pp. 370–371)

4. See (1) under ADONIS.

5. And [Prof.] Wallack's young assistant . . . had no idea that the inquisitive and alluring graduate student [a female Russian agent] who had enticed and then yielded to his advances

had been moved by anything more than . . . his irresistible charms, or that she had got from him anything more than a good dinner and a splendid tumble in his quiet little apartment with the computer print-outs on the desk, and the large technical drawing on the wall of a nuclear device, spilling out its APHRODISIAC charms. (W.F. Buckley Jr., *Saving the Queen*, Doubleday, 1976, p. 239)

6. To many of the women he works with, [Robert] DeNiro is most appealing as a workaholic. Kathi McGinnis defines it as an almost APHRODISIACAL quality to his concentration. "It's sexy to work with him; he's so intense. But it's not directed toward women. It's his art." (Susan Braudy, "Robert DeNiro—The Return of the Silent Screen Star," *New York Times*, 3/6/77, Section 2, p. 31)

APLOMB (ə-plom′, ə-plum′) *noun* imperturbable self-possession, poise, or assurance.

1. [Susanne] Farrell (now with hair classically knotted) is high-ROCOCO expression in every limb and joint . . . . Farrell's steps [in Balanchine's ballet, *Chaconne*] are full of surprising new twists; her APLOMB is sublime. (Arlene Croce, Review, *The New Yorker*, 2/9/76, pp. 95–96)

APOCALYPTIC (ə-pok′ə-lip′tik) or **APOCALYPTICAL** *adj.* of or like an apocalypse; prophesying total destruction or great disasters; affording a revelation or prophecy; (if capitalized) pertaining to the Apocalypse or Biblical book of Revelation.

APOCALYPTICALLY *adv.*

APOCALYPSE *noun* revelation; discovery; disclosure; (if capitalized) the last book of the New Testament; book of Revelation.

1. I remember the undergraduate president of the American Veterans Committee [at Yale] announcing at a press conference . . . that it was by no means to be taken for granted that the A.V.C. would countenance the University's announced rise in the tuition rate . . . . And all this nonsense would be duly chronicled in APOCALYPTIC headlines in the undergraduate paper. (W.F. Buckley Jr., *Up From Liberalism*, Arlington House, 2nd Printing 1968, pp. 133–134)

2. At a time when many critics of the arts are expressing feelings of dejection, even a sense of APOCALYPSE about their subjects, Miss [Pauline] Kael continues to write [in the book, *Reeling*] about movies with the breathless delirium of one smitten with young love. (R. Brustein, Review, *New York Times*, 4/4/76, Section 7, p. 1)

3. . . . people who believe that these are APOCALYPTIC times will find such urbane poetry [as that of Leonard Nathan in *Return Your Call* and that of Robert Pinsky in *Sadness and Happiness*] irrelevant, while people who think that poetry must follow the course set out by William Carlos Williams and Charles Olson will find it FINICKY, arch, and too personal. But there is at least some argument for the view that these are not APOCALYPTIC times . . . . Urbane poetry . . . has its place. (Hayden Carruth, Review, *New York Times*, 4/4/76, Section 7, p. 20)

4. From its first APOCALYPTIC public statement, the Club of Rome has been a doomsaying maverick in the optimistic world of Western businessmen . . . . The Club's 1972 study, *The Limits of Growth*, created a furor with its forecasts of exhausted resources and global famine unless growth trends could be reversed. But last week the club seemed to step back into the mainstream of future-think . . . . Under a comparatively optimistic rubric, *New Horizons for Mankind*, the eight-year-old international group of businessmen and intellectuals preached a new gospel called "organic growth" . . . . (M. Ruby, "The Future: 'Organic Growth,' " *Newsweek*, 4/26/76, p. 84)

5. . . . the least we can do is reread him [Robert M. Hutchins]. We might discover what Arthur A. Cohen did about Hutchins: "A visionary without being APOCALYPTIC, hopeful without being optimistic . . . open without being undiscriminating, principled without being fanatic, free without being disorderly." (F.L. Keegan, "It's Time to Reread Robert M. Hutchins," *Chronicle of Higher Education*, 4/26/76, p. 40)

6. The showdown between Brando and Nicholson [in the movie, *The Missouri Breaks*] is an intimate APOCALYPSE, a last spasm of almost quiet violence between two men who know how to behave like myths. (J. Kroll, Review, *Newsweek*, 5/24/76, p. 103)

7. There's no more awesome failure of human intelligence than . . . a bad Broadway musical. So many things have to go wrong to create this kind of debacle that the result has a crazy APOCALYPTIC beauty. There were two such APOCALYPSES on Broadway last week—a highbrow fiasco and a lowbrow disaster. The highbrow was *Rex*, a musical about Henry VIII; the lowbrow was *So Long, 174th Street*, a musical about a SCHLEMIEL who wanted to become an actor. (J. Kroll, Review, *Newsweek*, 5/10/76, p. 76)

8. Briefly, *The Canfield Decision* [a book by Spiro Agnew] is the APOCALYPTIC account of Canfield's callous and opportunistic maneuvering toward his party's 1983 presidential nomination. (D. Shaw, *L.A. Times*, "Agnew 'murders' media and other 'nattering nabobs,' " reprinted in *Norman* [Okla.] *Transcript*, 5/23/76, p. 17)

9. His [Sun Moon's] speeches . . . are full of hell-fire and Korean brimstone punctuated with kicks, karate chops, laughter and tears. (One reporter calls the performance a "kungfu tantrum.") Through his translator [Moon speaks Korean] . . . , Moon tells his audiences of the approaching APOCALYPSE, and offers them one last chance for salvation. (Berkeley Rice, "The pull of Sun Moon," *New York Times*, 5/30/76, Section 6, p. 21)

10. This director [Claude Chabrol], who increasingly reminds me of Simenon in his examination of the APOCALYPSES of the ordinary, has made an absorbing and powerful film [*Une Partie de Plaisir*] about modern men and women. (J. Kroll, Review, *Newsweek*, 6/14/76, p. 90F)

11. See (1) under SUFI.

12. Gazing through the window of a helicopter, Colorado's Governor Richard Lamm, 41, stared in silence at the APOCALYPTIC scene along the banks of the Big Thompson River—splayed bridges, kindling from hundreds of vanished homes, hulks of cars turned upside down like giant beetles. (Anon., "Now There's Nothing There," *Time*, 8/16/76, p. 22)

13. See (3) under NYMPHET.

14. See (3) under CHILIASM.

15. See (3) under QUOTIDIAN.

APOCRYPHAL (ə-pok′ rə-fəl) *adj.* of doubtful sanction, authorship, or authority; uncanonical; false; SPURIOUS; counterfeit; (if capitalized) of or pertaining to the Apocrypha (a group of 14 books, not considered canonical, included in the Septuagint—the oldest Greek version of the Old Testament) and the Vulgate (the Latin version of the Bible prepared chiefly by St. Jerome at the end of the 4th century and used as the authorized version in the Roman Catholic Church) as part of the Old Testament; various religious writings of uncertain origin regarded by some as inspired, but rejected by most authorities.

1. In one of the many stories he liked to tell, where the APOCRYPHAL was not always distinguishable from fact, he [Maxie Rosenblum] said he got into acting after Carole Lombard asked her to teach her to box to help her in fights with her husband Clark Gable. (R.E. Tomasson, "Maxie Rosenblum Dead: Boxer and Actor Was 71," *New York Times*, 3/8/76, p. 28)

2. The scenery and costumes [in the film, *The Magic Flute*] represent a variety of periods that does not include the Egyptian, the only one traditional to the opera. Thus, Pamina is dressed like a Habsburg princess, Monostatos sports a von Stroheim tunic and haircut, and Papagena wears a modern fur-collar coat and matching hat—in the snow, this APOCRYPHAL substance apparently being intended to suggest still another Ordeal to add to those of Water and Fire. (R. Craft, Review, *New York Review of Books*, 11/27/75, pp. 16, 18)

3. . . . the annals of filmmaking are filled with tales of extravagant temper tantrums and the stories one hears about [Orson] Welles, even the unmistakably APOCRYPHAL ones, cannot explain six and a half years of delay [in completing the film he has been making]. (C. Higham, "The Film That Orson Welles Has Been Finishing For Six Years," *New York Times*, 4/18/76, Section 2, p. 15)

4. Legend has it that around the turn of the century a Georgia defense lawyer quoted the famous speech from *The Merchant of Venice*—"The quality of mercy is not strained"—and correctly attributed it to Shakespeare. "Wrong!" shouted the prosecutor. "That quotation is from McGuffey's Readers!" The anecdote may be APOCRYPHAL, but it illustrates the influence of William Holmes McGuffey's primers. (Anon., "Prime Timer: Vintage McGuffey," *Newsweek*, 6/7/76, p. 84)

5. See (1) under FARTHINGALE.

6. The prevailing sense of horror [in Uganda] is perhaps best described by the APOCRYPHAL tale of a freezer in [President Idi] Amin's house that contains the heads of his most distinguished victims . . . ; from time to time, the story goes, Amin walks over to the freezer to lecture his frozen audience about the evils of their ways. (Anon., "Amin: The Wild Man of Africa," *Time*, 3/7/77, p. 24)

7. See (2) under ABJURE.

8. See (3) under FELLAH.

APOGEE (ap′ ə-jē′) *noun* the point in the orbit of a heavenly body, especially of the moon or of a man-made satellite, at which it is farthest from the earth (as opposed to PERIGEE); the highest or farthest point; climax, as of a career.

APOGEAL or **APOGEAN** or **APOGEIC** *adj.*

1. He [Malachi Martin, author of the book, *Hostage to the Devil: The Possession and Exorcism of Five Living Americans*] expresses earnest compassion for the lion-hearted priests who suffer from the physical and psychic toll of the exorcism rite. He provides some cliffhangers when narrating the tumultuous APOGEE of the rite—that moment when the possessing demon identifies himself by name. (Francine Du Plessix Gray, Review, *New York Times*, 3/14/76, Section 7, p. 8)

2. Clive Bell observed that the grandeur and nobility of the Allied cause (during the first World War) "swelled in even vaster proportions every time it was restated"—reaching its APOGEE in our explicitly formulated determination to make the world safe for democracy. The inadequacy of so gross and naive an oversimplification of the national objective is more widely acknowledged today than a generation, or even a decade ago. (W.F. Buckley Jr., *Up From Liberalism*, Ar-

lington House, 2nd Printing 1968, p. 148)

3. See (2) under POLYANDRY.

4. When Scott Fitzgerald and Budd Schulberg arrived in Hanover [N.H.] in 1918 to do the script for a Hollywood movie based upon [Dartmouth College's Winter] Carnival, the pre-World War II version had reached its APOGEE. The atmosphere was one of romance and elegance.... (J. Hart, "Carnival Time," *Times Herald*, Northwestern, Pa., 2/24/77, p. 19)

APOPLECTIC (ap'ə-plek'tik) *adj.* inclined to apoplexy (a sudden, usually marked loss of bodily functions caused by hemorrhage into the tissue of any organ, especially the brain, from rupture or occlusion of a blood vessel).

APOPLECTIC *noun* a person having, or predisposed to, apoplexy.

1. As one would expect, the sainted junior Senator from New York [James L. Buckley] does not reply to APOPLECTIC communications. (W.F. Buckley Jr., *Execution Eve and Other Contemporary Ballads*, G.P. Putnam's Sons, 1975, p. 285)

2. The best, perhaps the only way the Republicans can close the gap with Jimmy Carter is to go with a ticket containing the two men . . . most capable of articulating a populist-conservative alternative and exposing the closet liberalism of Jimmy Carter. That pair is . . . Ronald Reagan and John Connally. The Rockefeller wing of the party would be outraged, the liberal press APOPLECTIC. (P.J. Buchanan, "Carter Very Beatable Candidate," *Daily Oklahoman*, Okla. City, 7/16/76, p. 10)

APOSIOPESIS (ap'ə-sī'ə-pē'sis) *noun, pl.:* -SES a sudden breaking off of a thought in the midst of a sentence, as if from inability or unwillingness to continue.

APOSIOPETIC (ap' ə-sī'ə-pet'ik) *adj.*

1. You ask him [the Italian porter] how much for toting eight bags in his cart from one train to another leaving an hour and a half later. "Seven dollars is the tariff . . ." he will tell you, the final word pitched high, the

Italians having learned the art of APOSIOPESIS from the Greeks 2000 years ago. (W.F. Buckley Jr. *Execution Eve and Other Contemporary Ballads*, G.P. Putnam's Sons, 1975, p. 184)

APOTHEGM (ap' ə-them') or **APOPHTHEGM** *noun* a short, pithy, pointed, instructive saying; a terse remark; APHORISM, maxim.

APOTHEGMATIC or APOTHEGMATICAL *adj.*

APOTHEGMATICALLY *adv.*

1. The lingering sense of Brooklyn as a land of boundless mirth with baseball obbligato was the creation of certain screen writers and comedians . . . it is a Brooklynite who carries the back lot at Paramount Pictures. His speech begins with the APOTHEGM, "Hey, Mac. Ever see steam comin' out a sewer in Flatbush?" (R. Kahn, *The Boys of Summer*, Harper and Row, 1971, p. xiv)

2. Gordon Kahn always answered with APOTHEGMS: "Spring training proves nothing. The Yankees have learned the trick of winning when it counts." (R. Kahn, *Ibid.*, p. 114)

3. See (1) under SENTENTIA.

4. See (3) under DISQUISITION.

APOTHEOSIS (ə-poth' ē-ō' sis, ap'ə-thē' ə-sis) *noun, pl.:* -SES (-sēz, -sēz') the exaltation of a person to the status of a god; deification; the glorification of a person, act, principle, etc. as an ideal; a deified or glorified ideal.

APOTHEOSIZE *verb.*

1. Her [Ellen Greene's] "personalizations" of the songs amount to their stylistic fragmentation, as in her insufferably affected account of *Over the Rainbow*. But then again, one man's "insufferably affected" may be another's emotional APOTHEOSIS. (J. Rockwell, Review, *New York Times*, 2/20/76, p. 23)

2. The APOTHEOSIS of democracy grew out of the EUPHORIA of the nineteenth century. (W.F. Buckley Jr., *Up From Liberalism*, Arlington House, 2nd Printing 1968, p. 148)

3. Despite the deliberately cool, low-key re-

portorial way in which Carl Bernstein and Bob Woodward wrote their book [*All the President's Men*], some critics thought it gave journalists . . . too much credit for something that really belongs to an army of judges, prosecutors, investigators and juries. These critics are really going to gnash their teeth as Woodward and Bernstein are APOTHEOSIZED into Robert Redford and Dustin Hoffman. But those who believe as I do . . . will like the film even more than the book. (J. Kroll, Review, *Newsweek*, 4/5/76, p. 85)

4. See (2) under SOMNAMBULATE.

5. See (5) under EPONYM.

6. His [Ivan Illich's] intended audience . . . is the American public, for the technology, institutional forms, values and processes he describes [in the book, *Medical Nemesis*] have, for better or for worse, reached their APOTHEOSIS in the United States. (H.J. Geiger, Review, *New York Times*, 5/2/76, Section 7, p. 1)

7. The APOTHEOSIS who had entered the White House in January of 1961 was a new Quixote, splendidly armored in an era which had become convinced that all armor was tin. (W. Manchester, Commencement Address, University of Massachusetts, 6/13/65, Mimeographed, p. 3)

8. The leader of a squad of WRENS (women's naval service), Farrell ambles sexily, as though she had a chip on her hip or, just perhaps, an invisible set of bagpipes. If such a thing as an APOTHEOSIS of the sidle can be imagined, Farrell has done it. (W. Bender, Review of *Union Jack*, a ballet choreographed by George Balanchine, *Time*, 5/24/76, p. 70)

9. At 13 an acting veteran (she was the child street walker in *Taxi Driver*), she [Jodie Foster] is well on the road to becoming a new Carole Lombard. Her already brilliant professionalism does a great deal to make [the film] *Bugsy Malone* a perversely appealing APOTHEOSIS of cuteness. (J. Kroll, Review, *Newsweek*, 9/27/76, pp. 89–90)

10. See (1) under ECLOGUE.

APPELATION (ap'ə-lā' shən) *noun* a name, title, or designation of a person or thing; the act of naming or calling by a name.

APPELLATIVE (ə-pel'ə-tiv) *noun* a descriptive name, designation, or title.

APPELLATIVE *adj.*

APPELLATIVELY *adv.*

1. At a later date I want your explanation of this choice of APPELLATION for an imaginary character, and . . . beyond that, I still have no idea of why I am involved in this complex caprice" [said Russel Wren to Natalie Novotny]. (Thomas Berger, *Who Is Teddy Villanova?*, Delacorte Press/Seymour Lawrence, 1977, p. 189)

APPOGGIATURA (ə-poj'ə-tŏor'ə) *noun* a short or long musical note of embellishment preceding another note and taking a portion of its time.

1. He [Boris Bolgin] knew not to expect any explanation of how the mission had been accomplished—these romantic APPOGGIATURAS on the mechanics of the spy business were peculiarly the anxiety of the Americans and the British. (W.F. Buckley Jr., *Saving the Queen*, Doubleday, 1976, p.237)

APPOSITE (ap'ə-zit) *adj.* suitable to the purpose; pertinent; apt; appropriate; relevant.

APPOSITELY *adv.*

APPOSITENESS *noun.*

1. Many of [Tibor] Scitovsky's observations [in his book, *The Joyless Economy*] are APPOSITE. Read and enjoy. (E. Zupnick, Review, *Key Reporter*, Winter 1976-77, p. 5)

2. I [Russel Wren] stared at the cracked ceiling over my desk and quoted one remembered cliché from the letter that was certainly APPOSITE to the whole bag of worms: "Something is rotten in the state of Denmark." (Thomas Berger, *Who Is Teddy Villanova?*, Delacorte Press/Seymour Lawrence, 1977, p. 53)

3. Although both sides [of the negotiations between South African Prime Minister Vorster and Vice President Mondale] were scrupulously courteous and listened attentively to sharply contrasting views and although they spoke English, they might as well have been using two different languages. The sounds were familiar; the words were used with equal

precision; but the ideas they were intended to represent were more often opposite then AP-POSITE. (C.L. Sulzberger, "Opposite Concepts," *New York Times*, 5/22/77, Section 5, p. 19)

A PRIORI (ā′prī-ôr′ī,-ôr′ī, ā′prē-ôr′ē, -ôr′ē, ä′ prē-ôr′ē, -ôr′ē) *adj.* from cause to effect; from a general law to a particular instance; deductive; valid independently of observation; existing in the mind prior to and independent of experience, as a faculty or character trait; not based on prior study or examination; based on theory instead of experience or experiment; before examination or analysis.

1. If one dismisses A PRIORI the possibility that there are rational grounds for resisting the liberal view of things, one necessarily looks elsewhere than to reason for explanation of such discomfiting phenomena as, *e.g.*, the great popularity of the late Robert Taft. (W.F. Buckley Jr., *Up From Liberalism*, Arlington House, 2nd Printing 1968, pp. 90-91)

2. Unless we are so blinded by arrogance as simply to preclude A PRIORI the possibility of ever forfeiting the ability effectively to defend ourselves, the very striving of the Soviet Union for strategic superiority, of which General Brown speaks, should give us cause for concern. (R. Pipes, "Strategic Superiority," *New York Times*, 2/6/77, Section 4, p. 15)

ARABESQUE (ar′ə-besk′) *noun* any ornament or ornamental object in which plant forms, vases, and figures are represented in a fancifully interlaced pattern; (in Fine Arts) a complex and elaborate design of intertwined flowers, foliage, geometric patterns, etc., painted or carved in low relief; a SINUOUS, spiraling, undulating, or serpentine line or linear motif; a pose in ballet in which the dancer stands on one leg with one arm extended in front and the other arm and leg extended behind; a short, fanciful musical piece, typically for piano, with many delicately ornamental passages.

ARABESQUE *adj.* decorated with or characterized by arabesques; fantastic or elaborate.

1. Some of the details of [Marlon] Brando's

performance [in the movie, *The Missouri Breaks*] are certainly improvised ARABESQUES on [Thomas] McGuane's screenplay. (J. Kroll, Review, *Newsweek*, 5/24/76, p. 103)

2. [During the development of SUFISM] Poetry, urban organization, state formation, class structure, architecture, and trading institutions all took form—the styles, alleys, veils, and ARABESQUES we now associate with Islamicate culture—under the aegis of a new cosmopolitanism . . . (C. Geertz, Review of *The Venture of Islam: Conscience and History in a World Civilization. Vol. 1: The Classical Age of Islam; Vol. 2: The Expansion of Islam in the Middle Periods; Vol. 3: The Gunpowder Empire and Modern Times*, by Marshall G.S. Hodgson, *New York Review of Books*, 12/11/75, p. 20)

ARBITRAGE (är′bi-träzḥ) *noun* the simultaneous purchase and sale of the same securities, commodities, or foreign exchange in different markets to profit from unequal prices.

ARBITRAGEUR *noun.*

1. . . . especially since the banks are now revealed to have invested disastrously in flaky real estate speculations, dubious commodity price manipulation, amateurish ARBITRAGE of currency exchange . . . . (Leslie Waller, "Banks 'Subsidize' New Immorality," *Norman* [Okla.] *Transcript*, 1/16/76, p. 6)

ARCADIAN (är-kā′dē-ən) *adj.* of Arcadia; pastoral; rustic; peaceful and simple; innocent.

ARCADIAN *noun* a native or inhabitant of Arcadia; a person of simple habits and tastes.

ARCADIA *noun* a mountainous region of ancient Greece, traditionally known for the pastoral innocence of its people; any place of rural peace and simplicity.

1. In 1972, Sanche de Gramont . . . traveled down the entire 2600 miles of the Niger [River] with his wife.... They saw its ARCADIAN source in the Fouta Djallon highlands of Guinea . . . . (E. Newby, Review of *The Strong God Brown: The Story of the Niger River*, by Sanche de Gramont, *New York Times*, 4/4/76, p. 26)

2. It is too soon, perhaps, for a cool, rational, detached book about what has happened to New York. Those of us who choose to live here are too choked with rage . . . . Rage at the SCABROUS condition of our streets . . . . Rage at the businessmen fleeing to their suburban ARCADIAS. (P. Hamill, Review of *The Year The Big Apple Went Bust*, by Fred Ferretti, *New York Times*, 6/20/76, Section 7, p. 2)

3. Do the ideals of 200 years ago fit the realities of today? Is there really still safety in the vision of free men delegating the most limited powers to those who govern in their name? Or is that an ARCADIAN fantasy unsuited to life in a disorderly country, on a bristling planet? (A. Lewis, "We have really seen the future and IT WORKS!" *New York Times*, 7/4/76, Section 6, p. 85)

4. See (2) under AMORPHOUS.

ARCANE (är-kān') *adj.* mysterious; hidden; secret; obscure; understood by only a few; ESOTERIC.

ARCANUM (är-kā' nəm) *noun,* *pl.*: -NA (-nə) secret or hidden knowledge; a secret; mystery; a supposed great secret of nature that the alchemists sought to discover; a secret and powerful remedy, especially a universal cure for all disease; elixir.

1. . . . it is a refreshing corrective to those who announced the arrival of Jerzy Grotowski as a kind of theatrical Second Coming, bringing a stage scripture composed no longer of language but of ARCANE gesture. (R. Brustein, Review of *Uneasy Stages* and *Singularities*, books by John Simon, *New York Times*, 1/4/76, Section 7, p. 2)

2. Peter Singer [author of *Animal Liberation*] is . . . a young Australian philosophy teacher with the highest philosophical pedigrees who willfully avoids the more ARCANE and technical issues that concern most of his colleagues in the English-speaking world. (C.G. Luckhardt, Review, *New York Times*, 1/4/76, Section 7, p. 5)

3. At thirteen I have a steady date. Elisabeth [the family maid] bathes. I watch. In my mind I prepare an ARCANUM of advances, but I cannot act. (R. Kahn, *The Boys of Summer*, Harper and Row, 1971, p. 31)

4. As the department was organized, reporters specialized in distinct sports . . . . As a result, all that was left for a stringer was ARCANA. One month I found myself . . . "covering" a motorboat race around Manhattan island. (R. Kahn, *Ibid.*, p. 77)

5. But this [the esthetic concept that less is more] is an ARCANE and specialized esthetic . . . . Business clients rarely understand or want it. (Ada Louise Huxtable, "A Skyscraper Fit for a King (Kong)?" *New York Times*, 2/1/76, Section 2, p. 31)

6. But Western ignorance of Peking's ARCANE power struggle is so enormous that humility and caution are advisable. (Anon., "Peking Struggle" [Editorial], *New York Times*, 2/22/76, Section 4, p. 12)

7. Its [the show's, *The Architecture of the Ecole des Beaux-Arts*, at the Museum of Modern Art] calculated objective is to provoke a far-reaching critique of all contemporary architecture. There has already been much criticism and debate about this subject of course, but most of it tends to be either smugly academic or chicly exotic and ARCANE in its cultural and historical references. (Ada Louise Huxtable, Review, *New York Review of Books*, 11/27/75, p. 8)

8. It has been almost a quarter of a century since I dodged, dozed, and doodled my way through high school chemistry . . . . Can such a person, at the ripe age of 40, conduct even a simple experiment in so ARCANE a subject as organic chemistry? (E. Jenkins, "The Potential of PLATO," *Change*, March 1976, p. 6)

9. But the fear of knowing too much is gone from the rank and file of our poets, as is the impulse to remain ARCANE and secure behind a shield of erudition. It is no longer a blot upon poetic credentials to teach, just as it is no longer detrimental to achieving tenure to have published poetry. (D. Lenson, "Can the furtherance of poetry become a more common cause? The Yahoos vs. The Houyhnhnms," *Chronicle of Higher Education*, 4/5/76, p. 20)

10. See (1) under HIERARCHY.

11. Both here [Flint, Mich.] and at . . . Kalamazoo, ardent Reaganites were interested in issues, some of them ARCANE. (R. Evans, R.

Novak, "Reagan Support Not From Party," *Daily Oklahoman*, Okla. City, 5/19/76, p. 6)

12. See (4) under CLERISY.

13. See (1) under ZIGGURAT.

ARCHAISM (är'kē-iz'əm, -kä-) *noun* something archaic, as a word, expression, or mannerism; the use or imitation of something archaic.

ARCHAIC *adj.* marked by the characteristics of an earlier period; antiquated; (of a linguistic form) current in an earlier time but rare in present usage.

ARCHAICALLY *adv.*

ARCHAIZE *verb* to give an archaic appearance or quality to; to use archaisms.

1. But for centuries Christians have recognized that verbal ARCHAISM restricts God's words to an elite. There are readers for whom Shakespearean ARCHAISM raises an impenetrable wall . . . (D. Hall, "To Be or Not to Be, That's What Matters," *New York Times*, 3/14/76, Section 7, p. 39)

ARCHETYPE (är'ki-tīp') *noun* the original pattern or model after which all other things of the same type are made; a model or first form; prototype; a perfect example of a type or group.

ARCHETYPAL or ARCHETYPICAL *adj.*

ARCHETYPALLY or ARCHETYPICALLY *adv.*

1. *The Poison Tree* [a play by Ronald Ribman]'s chief prisoners . . . remind us that the behavioral ARCHETYPES brought to the stage in recent years by black performers are just as important as the previous ARCHETYPES—Irish, English, Jewish—that have enriched our theater. And yet some critics refuse to grant black characters that same universal validity accorded these other ARCHETYPES. (J. Kroll, Review, *Newsweek*, 1/19/76, p. 81)

2. See (4) under PARADIGM.

3. McKeag was especially disturbed over the fact that . . . such children [of one white and one Indian parent] were called *breeds* and were treated with contempt—half-breeds who had a rightful home in neither race. He suspected that the time must come when this PEJO-

RATIVE term would be thrown at young Jacques [son of Pasquinel and Clay Basket]. Then there would be trouble, for the boy gave promise of becoming almost the ARCHETYPE of that word: a real two-breed individual. (J.A. Michener, *Centennial*, Fawcett, 1975, p. 250)

4. Now Lost Eagle rose to stand beside [Captain] Mercy and face the three Cheyenne chiefs. In the next decade his grave, impassive face . . . would be painted by four white artists . . . so that the deep lines down his cheeks would become familiar across the country, and he would represent the ARCHETYPAL Indian chief, the man of unshakable integrity. (James A. Michener, *Ibid.*, p. 437)

5. One matter especially perplexed me [about the book, *Schooling in Capitalist America*, by Samuel Bowles and Herbert Gintis]. How did the ARCHETYPICALLY capitalist Ford Foundation wind up providing three years of research support for a study that concludes: "Capitalism is an irrational system, standing in the way of further social progress. It must be replaced." (Jay S. Goodman, Review, *The Boston Globe*, 3/7/76, p. 15-A)

6. See (2) under SIBYL.

7. . . . there was one special program always associated with the [Jooss ballet] company—his ARCHETYPAL repertory program, . . . and indeed the very program that introduced the Ballets Jooss, the choreographer's own company, to New York more than 40 years ago. (Clive Barnes, "The Joffrey Rejoices in the Genius of Jooss," *New York Times*, 3/28/76, Section 2, p. 8)

8. See (3) under PARODY.

9. See (1) under WELTSCHMERZ.

10. In a character called "Rosy," [James] Watson [in *The Double Helix*] described the ARCHETYPE of the unattractive, aggressive woman scientist, whose anger and frustration, and perhaps lack of ability, served to impede the natural course of scientific discovery. Ms. [Anne] Sayre's book [*Rosalind Franklin and DNA*] is a result of the evident disparity between "Rosy" and the real Rosalind Franklin as Ms. Sayre knew her. (Evelyn Fox Keller, Review, *Change*, Winter 1965-76, p. 59)

11. See (26) under QUINTESSENCE.

ARGOT (är'gō, är'gət) *noun* the vocabulary and idioms, especially the slang, peculiar to a particular class or group of people, especially an underworld group, as thieves, devised for private communication and identification.

ARGOTIC (är-got'-ik) *adj.*

1. And the book [I.K. Martin's *Regan*] is a lexicon of British underworld and police ARGOT: Blag. Slag. Skite. Snout. Agro. Toe-rag. Gell. Shufti. (N. Callendar, Review, *New York Times*, 1/4/76, Section 7, p. 22)

2. See (1) under TAUTOLOGY.

3. [Branch] Rickey's best pitching prospects rapidly destroyed their arms. In trainers' ARGOT, they stripped their gears. (R. Kahn, *The Boys of Summer*, Harper and Row, 1971, p. 96)

ARMAGEDDON (är'mə-ged'ən) *noun* the place where the final battle will be fought between the forces of good and evil before the Day of Judgment, probably so called in reference to the battlefield at Megiddo (*Revelations* 16: 16); any great and decisive battle.

1. See (3) under VACUITY.

2. [Director Gilbert] Moses wanted to take the show *1600 Pennsylvania Avenue* to Los Angeles [after Philadelphia] . . . . But with expenses totaling $100,000 a week, the producers decided to face ARMAGEDDON in New York. (Anon., Review, *Time*, 5/31/76, p. 70)

3. In the fertile fields of California such horror stories [about the dangers of nuclear power plants] are easily rooted. Hereabouts, the world ends in every public park, apostles of AR-MAGEDDON outnumber the purveyors of porn . . . . The case in favor of nuclear power . . . is not as sensational as the case against it. The thought of ARMAGEDDON gives us the nice goose bumps. But the thought of simply turning on the living room lights is not a thought that merits time on the evening news. (J.J. Kilpatrick, "Vote Reaffirms Faith in People," *The Daily Oklahoman*, Okla. City, 6/16/76, p. 6)

4. The native ground [Brooklyn] might be enunciated [in the Brooklyn accent] "Bvooklyn" and "thirty" was a phoneticist's ARMAGED-DON. It would be "tirdy," "toidy," "dirty,"

"doity," "tirty," "toity," "dirdy," or "doidy." (R. Kahn, *The Boys of Summer*, Harper and Row, 1971, p. xiv)

5. By the late 1950's [James] Burnham's . . . amorphous POLEMICS at long last took on a distinctive shape. Unfortunately, . . . it jelled in the form of a cold warriorism so brutally hard that it actually looked forward to ARMAGED-DON. (P. Rosenberg, Review of *Up From Communism*, by John P. Diggins, *New York Times*, 2/23/75, Section 7, p. 23)

6. Even if Carter ekes out a plurality in the statewide popular vote, as seemed likely last week, Jackson stands an excellent chance of gaining first place in the quite separate vote for delegates. Reason: the delegates are elected in 50 local races, each of which is crowded and confused; but Jackson's labor and machine allies can steer voters to the "right" choices. Thus the [Pennsylvania] primary that had been billed as a dramatic ARMAGEDDON was becoming more of a diffuse guerilla war that could yield split results. (Anon., "Pennsylvania's Guerrilla War," *Time*, 4/26/76, p. 14)

ARRANT (ar' ənt) *adj.* out-and-out, thoroughly, confirmed, extreme; notoriously or EGREGIOUSLY bad; shameless.

1. Anthony raised a finger. "I detect Saint Samuel à-Beckett and his fancy French nonsense. ARRANT romantic pessimism." (John Fowles, *Daniel Martin*, Little, Brown, 1977, p. 181)

ARRIVISTE (ar'ē-vēst') *noun* a person who has recently acquired status, power, wealth, or success, often by dubious means, and who is regarded as an upstart; PARVENU.

1. Pursuing her man [the Duke of Westminster] throughout Europe . . . with the ÉLAN of the perpetual ARRIVISTE, [Coco] Chanel desperately tried to have a child by him at the age of forty-six, dragging herself through gynecologists' offices and a series of "humiliating acrobatics" recommended by midwives to achieve pregnancy. . . . But . . . [Westminster] left her for a peer's daughter. (Francine Gray, Review of *Chanel*, a book by Edmonde Charles-Roux, *New York Review of Books*, 12/11/75, p. 45)

2. There is also speculation that [baseball commissioner Bowie] Kuhn acted [to void the sale of three Oakland players to the Yankees] under the powerful influence of Walter O'Malley of Los Angeles and other old-guard owners whose affection for the cantankerous [Charles O.] Finley [of Oakland] is exceeded only slightly by their love for the ARRIVISTE [George] Steinbrenner [of the Yankees]. (P. Axthelm, "Baseball's Money Madness," *Newsweek*, 6/28/76, p. 63)

ARTIFACT (är' tə-fakt') *noun* any object made or modified by man, especially a simple or primitive tool, weapon, vessel, etc.

ARTIFACTITIOUS *adj.*

1. These people [the old activists still on campus] are oddly ANACHRONISTIC on campus today, ARTIFACTS of a time and place that seem light years away. (J.N. Bell, "Silence on Campus," *Harper's*, March 1976, p. 24)

2. See (3) under DETRITUS.

3. See (1) under EFFLUVIUM.

4. The still dominant—politically and economically—Americo-Liberian elite is allowing the ARTIFACTS of its own past to decay unnoticed: architecture, custom and oral history. (P. Boorstin, "Liberia's fading echoes of the Old American South," *Smithsonian*, March 1976, p. 86)

5. See (1) under PHALLIC.

6. See (3) under CHIMERA.

7. In the space of a week [Rupert] Murdoch, an Australian millionaire who collects newspapers the way some people collect Snoopy ARTIFACTS, assumed ownership of the *New York Post* and grabbed control of two liberal, trendy weeklies, the *Village Voice* and *New York* magazine. As an added bonus, Murdoch also got ...the fledgling Los Angeles-based bimonthly *New West*. (Beth Gillin Pombeiro, "In New York the news is Murdoch," *Philadelphia Inquirer*, 1/9/76, p. 1-A)

8. See (3) under NATTER.

9. See (2) under SUBVENTION.

ASCETIC (ə-set'ik) or **ASCETICAL** *adj.* pertaining to asceticism; rigorously abstinent;

austere; exceedingly strict or severe in religious exercises or self mortification; self-denying.

ASCETIC *noun* a person who practices asceticism; any person who abstains from the normal pleasures of life or denies himself material satisfaction; a monk; hermit; ANCHORITE; recluse.

ASCETICISM *noun* austerity of taste, living, etc. that suggests the practices or principles of an ascetic.

ASCETICALLY *adv.*

1. See (1) under CATHARSIS.

2. As [Sanford J.] Ungar describes it [in the book, *FBI*], J. Edgar Hoover was both the making and breaking of the FBI. In 1924, this strange, ASCETIC, lonely man began the transformation of a weak and discredited organization into a modern, remarkably incorruptible crime-fighting force. (P.D. Zimmerman, Review, *Newsweek*, 3/29/76, p. 92)

3. [Unification] Church officials bristle at criticism of [Sun] Moon's luxuries. "Why must a religious leader be an ASCETIC?" asks one. "Look at the Pope," says another....Suppose I described a church that has amassed great wealth and property in this country through charitable donations and profitable investments; a church whose leader lives in splendor while young novitiates live in ASCETIC communes, cut off from family and friends, leading lives of absolute devotion to the church and absolute obedience to its authority. Would this description not fit the Catholic Church as well as that of Sun Moon? (Berkeley Rice, "The pull of Sun Moon," *New York Times*, 5/30/76, Section 6, p. 21)

4. For all their seeming similarities of dynamism, patriotism and ASCETICISM, [Jimmy] Carter and [Admiral Hyman G.] Rickover [who selected Carter to work with him on the Navy's nuclear submarine program] may differ widely. Rickover is as direct, it seems, as Carter's critics say Carter is OBFUSCATORY. (I. Berkow, "Navy's Rickover hero to Carter," *Norman* [Okla.] *Transcript*, 7/15/76, p. 5-A)

ASPERGE (ə-spurj') *verb* to sprinkle, besprinkle.

ASPERGE *noun* a sprinkling of holy water.

ASPERGES (ə-spûr′ jēz, -jez) *noun* the sprinkling of altar, clergy, and people with holy water before High Mass in the Catholic Church.

1. "And, please, [Ronald Beard] said [to Paula Belli], ASPERGING aftershave, "it's been such a long time [since having sexual intercourse]. Don't laugh at me, don't." (A. Burgess, *Beard's Roman Women*, McGraw-Hill, 1976, p. 25)

ASPERITY (ə-sper′i-tē) *noun* roughness or sharpness of tone, temper, or manner; severity; hardship; difficulty; roughness or unevenness of surface; something rough or harsh.

1. Even the sound of [Coco] Chanel's gruff parakeet voice, the ASPERITY of her VITRIOLIC wit, crackle more audibly from the photos than from [author Edmonde] Charles-Roux's tone-deaf prose [in her book, *Chanel*]. (Francine Gray, Review, *New York Review of Books*, 12/11/75, p. 45)

2. He [the wino] was a psychologist of keen penetration, and I [Russel Wren] told him as much. "But praise is as useless to me as punishment!" he replied with ASPERITY. (Thomas Berger, *Who Is Teddy Villanova?*, Delacorte Press/Seymour Lawrence, 1977, p. 132)

3. With ASPERITY I [Russel Wren] yelled: "Though some of you have attained to a level of civilization undreamt of by the low-brow copper of yore, you have acquired a concomitant FECKLESSNESS . . . . " (Thomas Berger, *Ibid.*, p. 218)

ASSEVERATE (ə-sev′ə-rāt′) *verb* to declare or affirm earnestly or solemnly; aver; to state seriously or positively; assert.

ASSEVERATION *noun.*

1. When asked to write a preface to a new edition of *Up From Liberalism* I had a case of jitters at having to read back through ASSEVERATIONS almost ten years old. (W.F. Buckley Jr., *Up From Liberalism*, Arlington House, 2nd Printing 1968, p. xix)

2. Perhaps the single most celebrated ASSEVERATION [relative to Senator Joseph McCarthy's era] was Robert Maynard Hutchins', to the effect that Orthodoxy had closed down

American freedom to the point where it had become hazardous to contribute money to Harvard University. (W.F. Buckley Jr., *Ibid.*, p. 51)

3. Before conservatives arrive at the point where it is appropriate to deal in grandiose ASSEVERATIONS, they must face up to homely analytical chores. (W.F. Buckley Jr., *Ibid.*, p. 196)

4. See (5) under OXYMORON.

5. "I don't have to take that type language," she [Peggy Tumulty] ASSEVERATED in her fire-siren voice, her plump breasts bouncing. (Thomas Berger, *Who Is Teddy Villanova?*, Delacorte Press/Seymour Lawrence, 1977, p. 26)

ASSIDUOUS (ə-sij′ ōō-əs) *adj.* performed with constant and careful attention or application; persistent; unremitting; diligent; persevering; industrious; SEDULOUS.

ASSIDUITY (as′i-dōō′i-tē, -dyōō′-) or ASSIDUOUSNESS *noun.*

ASSIDUOUSLY *adv.*

1. The Carter administration continues to regard [Philadelphia Mayor Frank L.] Rizzo as a political ANATHEMA and ASSIDUOUSLY avoids contact with him. One of the highest-ranking Carter officials on a recent visit to Philadelphia asked a group . . . off the record: "How in the hell do you people let this man get away with what he does?" (C. Stone, "Rizzo's Gone, but Black Stupidity Lingers On," *Philadelphia Daily News*, 11/11/77, p. 2)

2. In foreign policy, [Leonid I.] Brezhnev has ASSIDUOUSLY cultivated the Africans, Latin Americans and other Third World countries—but with more interest in influence than in outright world conquest. With the defeat of Indira Gandhi in India, however, the Soviet Union lost its most important ally in Asia. (R. Carroll, with F. Coleman, *et. al.*, "The Soviets at 60," *Newsweek*, 11/14/77, p. 59)

3. From the outset, the film [*Close Encounters of the Third Kind*] has been shrouded in secrecy to ensure that its suspense not be blown prior to release. Cast and crew have been forbidden to discuss the movie's contents in interviews. Security guards have watched over its sets round the clock, at one point ASSIDUOUSLY

ejecting even [director Steven] Spielberg when he showed up without his ID badge. (F. Rich, Review, *Time*, 11/7/77, p. 102)

4. Conventioneers, traveling salesmen and congressmen, who are the most ASSIDUOUS seekers of feminine companionship on the road, are also the most likely to shy away from a woman who reads Plato. (Alice-Leone Moats, "Plato Travels Well," *Philadelphia Inquirer*, 11/15/77, p. 11-A)

ASTRINGENT (ə-strin′jənt) *adj.* contracting the body tissue and blood vessels, checking the flow of blood or mucus; constrictive; styptic; stern or severe; austere; sharp; harsh; rigorous.

ASTRINGENT *noun.*

ASTRINGENCY *noun.*

ASTRINGENTLY *adv.*

ASTRINGE *verb* to constrict; compress.

1. And the world's diplomats and dignitaries will miss Chou [En-lai]'s unique blend of humor, ASTRINGENCY, and sophistication. (P.G. Kramer and Fay Willey, "Death of a Survivor," *Newsweek*, 1/19/76, p. 47)

2. At 42, the woman [Shirley MacLaine] the British dubbed "the lanky Yankee" is lean, leggy, and fit, with a Buster Brown haircut and the face of a Campbell's Soup Kid. There's nothing childish about her manner, which is ASTRINGENTLY adult. In conversation, she is crisp, even crusty. (Julia Cameron, "Shirley MacLaine—Back in Her Dancing Shoes," *New York Times*, 4/18/76, Section 2, p. 5)

3. My internist, Dr. Jeremiah Barondess, who was in charge of me [in the hospital], was ASTRINGENT about the whole thing [the inability to diagnose the illness]. "Shall I tell you," he asked, "about the Barondess Unified Field Theory of Internal Medicine?" . . . "It's quite simple," he said. "What to do is measurably clearer than what's the matter." (M. Lerner, "Jaundiced view of a jaundiced view: Columnist defends U.S. doctors," *Norman* [Okla.] *Transcript*, 6/16/76, p. 6)

4. Their [his recent poems'] wit and irony . . . both relieve and enforce [Eugenio] Montale's now less involved but no less ASTRINGENT view

of human life as a predicament that is rarely understood, let alone mastered. (J. Galassi, Review of *New Poems*, by Eugenio Montale, translated by G. Singh; and of *Provincial Conclusions*, by Eugenio Montale, translated by Edith Farnsworth, *New York Times*, 5/30/76, Section 7, p. 7)

ASYMPTOTE (as′im-tōt′) *noun* (in Mathematics) a straight line approached by a given curve as one of the variables in the equation of the curve approaches infinity; the tangent to a curve at infinity.

ASYMPTOTIC or **ASYMPTOTICAL** *adj.*

ASYMPTOTICALLY *adv.*

1. Professor Willmoore Kendall of Yale strikingly EPITOMIZED the prevailing theory of higher education. It is based, he said, on "the ASYMPTOTIC approach to truth." An ASYMPTOTE is a line toward which the curve on all these familiar graphs bends, but which the curve, while getting closer and closer to it, never quite touches. ASYMPTOTES, by definition, cannot meet their COMPLEMENTARY curves; as, by definition, higher academic inquiry cannot comprehend truth . . . . (W. F. Buckley Jr., *Up From Liberalism*, Arlington House, 2nd Printing 1968, p. 181)

ATAVISTIC (at′ ə-vis′ tik) *adj.* reverting to or suggesting the characteristics of a remote ancestor or a primitive or earlier type.

ATAVISM (at′ə-viz′əm) *noun* the reappearance in a plant or animal of characteristics of some remote ancestor that have been absent in intervening generations; such a reappearing characteristic; a plant or animal embodying such a reversion; a reversion to an earlier type.

ATAVISTICALLY *adv.*

1. Vince Lombardi was very recently admired for saying that winning was everything, but nowadays his name comes up on the ATAVISTIC side of the ledger. (W.F. Buckley Jr., *Execution Eve and Other Contemporary Ballads*, G. . P. Putnam's Sons, 1975, p. 225)

2. If the Soviet Union persecutes its intellectuals (never mind that it is for writing the truth), the students [at Yale] assembled [to protest Kruschev's treatment of Boris Paster-

nak] concluded, it is no different from a congressional committee's persecuting an intellectual (never mind that it is for writing error). Truth? Error? These are strange words, ATAVISTIC words. (W.F. Buckley Jr., *Up From Liberalism*, Arlington House, 2nd Printing 1968, p. 139)

3. If the majority wills what is socially ATAVISTIC, then to thwart the majority may be the indicated, although concededly the undemocratic, course. (W.F.Buckley Jr., *Ibid.*, p. 158)

4. [Jonah] Raskin [in *Out of the Whale: Growing Up in the American Left*] . . . vividly describes many of the important moments in the new left . . . . When they were writing manifestoes, so was he; . . . and when the left turned to ATAVISTIC violence, Raskin threw a rock and got beaten up by the police. (H.D. Shapiro, Review, *Change*, Winter 1975-76, p. 55)

5. An elegant lampoon of the public school pecking order and other ATAVISMS [the reference is to *The Vampire of Mons*, by Desmond Stewart]. (M. Levin, Review, *New York Times*, 5/30/76, Section 7, p. 14)

6. Later they fly to Mount McKinley National Park, where they learn that 100 hardy souls are threatening this season to assault the 20,320-ft. McKinley. The travelers are not so inclimbed, preferring instead to discover their ATAVISTIC selves by hiking for a day into the bush . . . . (Anon., "Travel '76," *Time*, 6/28/76, p. 62)

7. Circus Vargas' big tent . . . is a cheerful ATAVISM, a reminder of a time when Americans huddled happily on benches under canvas, eating cotton candy and staring at the marvels occurring in the three rings before them. (Anon., "The Circus: Escaping into the Past," *Time*, 5/24/76, p. 18)

8. Today, individuals in France hold an estimated 6,000 tons of gold—15 percent of the world's gold stockpile—worth about $25 billion. Secrecy in money matters is also an honored tradition. . . . "Avarice is the predominant French characteristic," argues cultural history professor Jean-Paul Aron, "because of [our] long peasant history. In all Europe, only the French peasant had to pay off king, bishop and local seigneur . . . . Even when he becomes

an urban, salaried BOURGEOIS, he conserves this ATAVISTIC need to conceal his belongings and wealth, to hide it away in his wool stocking." (A. Deming and Elizabeth Peer, "France's Hidden Wealth," *Newsweek*, 11/22/76, p. 62)

9. See (3) under FERAL.

ATELIER (at' əl-yā') *noun* a workshop or studio, especially of an artist, artisan, craftsman, or couturier.

1. Here and there [in Singapore's Chinatown], in small open-fronted workshops, some of the traditional crafts and services are carried on. In sandalwood-scented ATELIERS on Club Street men are carving and gilding images for Buddhist and Taoist temples, and in a cluttered shop where once opium pipes were made, the artisan makes instead small Chinese signature chops. (Shelley and C. Mydans, "Progress dooms charm and bustle of the Chinatown in Singapore," *Smithsonian*, January 1976, p. 40)

2. She [Rosalind Russell]'d been cultivated by presidents and kings, she'd had lunch on Aristotle Onassis's yacht, dined at the Paris ATELIER of Coco Chanel, and whether she was living in New York or California, she drank her tea out of Royal Copenhagen china cups. (Chris Chase, "She Dined With Kings, But Never Put On Airs," *New York Times*, 12/5/76, Section 2, p. 10)

ATRABILIOUS (a' trə-bil' yəs) or **ATRABILIAR** *adj.* sad; melancholy; morose; gloomy; irritable; cross; bad-tempered.

ATRABILIOUSNESS *noun.*

1. I read the entire manuscript to him [Charles Hamilton, the authority on celebrity letters], including the part where [Frank] Sinatra offers to bet me $100,000 that I can't pull off my hairpiece, and says if I lose he will punch my mouth, and how I'm a pimp, and all that good stuff. "Mmmm," said Mr. Hamilton, "that's an extraordinary letter. An ATRABILIOUS letter, in fact. I'll pay $75 for it." Aha, I knew it. Ol' Blue Eyes is no bargain-basement wise guy. He's ATRABILIOUS (look it up yourself). So the letter is for sale—and my price is $100 or the highest bid, which will be turned over to the Salvation Army. (M. Royko, "A charitable letter after all," *Chicago Daily News*, 5/6/76, p. 3)

2. Further [plays to be performed in Britain's National Theater] . . . include . . . a new John Osborne play, *Watch It Come Down*, which combines an ATRABILIOUS war between the sexes . . . with a heartfelt ANATHEMA on England. (Anon., "A New Treasure on the Thames," *Time*, 3/15/76, p. 81)

3. Picasso's *Vollard Suite*. . . remains the greatest of his etching cycles, just as Georges Rouault would never produce images of a more terse and ATRABILIOUS power than . . . his *Miserere* series, 1916-27. (R. Hughes, "Genius Disguised As a Sloth," *Time*, 6/20/77, p. 69)

ATREUS (ā′ trē-əs, a′ trōōs) *noun* in Classical Mythology) a king of Mycenae and father of Plisthenes, Agamemnon, and Menelaus, upon whose house Thyestes, his brother, pronounced a curse; to avenge the treachery of his brother, Thyestes, Atreus had killed Thyestes' sons and served their flesh to him at a banquet.

1. Their history of the family [in *The Rockefellers*, by Peter Collier and David Horowitz] is not unsympathetic but it is pessimistic; by comparison to the Rockefellers the house of ATREUS was a contented lot. (P.S. Prescott, Review, *Newsweek*, 4/5/76, p. 81A)

2. [Greg] Mullavey is very proud of his show [*Mary Hartman, Mary Hartman*]. "It's part of an English course at Yale," he said. "A professor made it required viewing. He calls it a modern House of ATREUS." In Greek tragedy, the House of ATREUS was smitten by almost ceaseless disaster. (Knight News Service, "'Mary Hartman' Character Draws From Own Past," *Norman* [Okla.] *Transcript*, 7/1/76, p. 22)

3. Yale English professor David Thorburn, who uses the [*Mary Hartman, Mary Hartman* TV] show in one of his courses, has called the Hartman Family "an American house of ATREUS," although there have been no slaughters so far. (Anon., Review, *Time*, 2/23/76, p. 51)

4. Laura's daughter Clara [in *The Widow's Children*, by Paula Fox], who describes herself as a boarder in the house of ATREUS, succumbs to a chronic ache of self-disgust. (P.S. Prescott, Review, *Newsweek*, 9/27/76, pp. 100, 102)

ATTENUATE (ə-ten′yōō-āt′) *verb* to make thin, slender or fine; to weaken, reduce or lessen in force, intensity, severity, effect, quantity or value; to become thin, weak, fine, etc.

ATTENUATE (ə-ten′yōō-it, -āt′) *adj*.

ATTENUABLE *adj*.

ATTENUATION *noun*.

ATTENUATOR *noun*.

1. Liza Minelli, Barry Nelson and a diamond-faceted on-stage and backstage company winged through it [*The Act*], for the most glittering opening-night Broadway audience in years, in two-and-a-half hours, which is not unreasonable for a large-scale musical. But when it did slow down—and that was whenever they were obliged to pay passing attention to the ancient, creaking plot—it seemed forever, especially during the painfully ATTENUATED, drippingly sentimental prelude to what eventually becomes a smash finale. (N. Nadel, "Liza's 'Act' is together," *Times Herald*, Norristown, Pa., 11/12/77, p. 20)

AUBERGINE (ō′bər-zhēn′, -jēn′) *noun* the eggplant or its fruit; the deep purple fruit of the eggplant; the color of eggplant, a dark purple.

AUBERGINE *noun* purple or bishop's purple—purplish black or blackish purple.

1. This week, the international night club queen Régine [Zylberberg] plants her Parisian flag on American soil . . . . Her new nightclub in Delmonico's Hotel is stylishly fitted out in art-deco motifs . . . . There are mirrors everywhere . . . , and the AUBERGINE-colored walls are stenciled in gold. (Linda Bird Francke, "The Reign of Régine," *Newsweek*, 5/17/76, p. 68)

AUGUR (ô′gər) *noun* any soothsayer; prophet.

AUGUR *verb* to divine or predict, as from omens; to foretell the future; prognosticate; foreshadow; betoken; to conjecture; PRESAGE.

AUGURY (ô′ gyə-rē) *noun* divination; an omen, token, or indication.

AUGURAL *adj*.

1. See (1) under PHILIPPIC.

2. Compared to the MAWKISH retreads regularly turned out on John Osborne's assembly line, or the elaborately wrought stylistic repetitions of Harold Pinter, the works of [Trevor] Griffiths, [David] Hare, [Stephen] Poliakoff, [Howard] Brenton, [Howard] Barker, *et. al.*, are AUGURIES of a second coming in English drama. (C. Marowitz, "New Playwrights Stir the British Stage," *New York Times*, 6/20/76, Section 2, p. 12)

3. New World Records, an organization funded by the Rockefeller Foundation, has set out to present . . . a total overview of American music on 100 disks, and there will be a smattering from every area of our remarkably diverse musical history—classical, folk, ethnic, jazz and popular. The first ten releases are now at hand . . . . If these ten . . . are a fair idea of what to expect, New World Records AUGURS to be one of the more important, informative and sheerly enjoyable ventures to emerge from the entire Bicentennial BROUHAHA. (P.G. Davis, "A Deluge of Musical Americana," *New York Times*, 7/4/76, Section 2, p. 1)

AULIC (ô′ lik) *adj.* pertaining to a royal court; courtly.

1. [Eugenio] Montale believes it has been "the dream of every modern poet from Browning on" to make poetry "by juxtaposing the AULIC (formal) and the prosaic," and his mature style has moved increasingly close to the conversational. (J. Galassi, Review of *New Poems*, by Eugenio Montale, translated by G. Singh; and of *Provincial Conclusions*, by Eugenio Montale, translated by Edith Farnsworth, *New York Times*, 5/30/76, Section 7, p. 7)

AUREOLE (ôr′ē-ōl′) or **AUREOLA** *noun* a halo; the sun's corona, as seen during a total eclipse; any encircling ring of light or color.

1. It [the brassiere] was a skimpy garment, made of lace netting, and at the point of each cup was a large aperture that would permit the nipple and AUREOLE to project nakedly. (Thomas Berger, *Who Is Teddy Villanova?*, Delacorte Press/Seymour Lawrence, 1977, p. 107)

AUSCULTATION (ô′ skəl-tā′ shən) *noun* the act of listening, either directly or through a stethoscope or other instrument, to sounds within the body, as a method of diagnosis of illness of internal organs; the act of listening.

AUSCULTATE *verb* to examine by auscultation.

AUSCULTATORY or **AUSCULTATIVE** *adj.*

1. At 20, while engaged in a summer workshop with the poet Charles Olson in which we were asked to keep voluminous journals, I once began a daily entry with the sentence: "I must analyze myself with an INCESTUOUS precision." I think back to that phrase—SO REDOLENT of late adolescent NARCISSISM—as I reread [Paul] Zweig's middle chapter [of *Three Journeys*] on his Paris years, filled with obsessional self-AUSCULTATION of his own twenties. (Francine DuPlessix Gray, Review, *New York Times*, 5/2/76, Section 7, p. 5)

AUTARKY (ô′ tär-kē) *noun* national economic self-sufficiency; a national policy of economic independence, especially of getting along without imports.

AUTARKIC or **AUTARKICAL** *adj.*

AUTARKICALLY *adv.*

AUTARKIST *noun.*

1. And he [John Kenneth Galbraith] has not a word to say [in his book, *The Age of Uncertainty*] about the most influential of all Continental European economists, Friedrich List, whose theories of economic AUTARKY dominated Europe for 100 years and have not lost their appeal to smaller powers even today. (M. Howard, Review, *New York Times*, 4/3/77, Section 7, p. 13)

AUTISM (ô′ tiz-əm) *noun* a state of mind characterized by self-absorption, daydreaming, hallucinations, disregard of external reality, and withdrawal into fantasy.

AUTISTIC *adj.*

1. Some children remain partly arrested at this stage of emotional and intellectual development, and there are others who return to it in part. These are children suffering from infantile AUTISM . . . . Although some AUTISTIC children are as SOLIPSISTIC as infants in their contact with reality, and communicate as little,

they are much farther developed in body. (B. Bettelheim, *The Empty Fortress*, The Free Press, 1967, p. 4)

2. Although some AUTISTIC children . . are ANOREXIC *(sic)*, and others . . emaciated, there are others who are well nourished, even fat . . . . The AUTISTIC child—because inner and outer reality are not separated but are experienced as more or less the same—takes his inner experience for a true representation of the world. (B. Bettelheim, *Ibid.*, p. 65)

AUTOCHTHONOUS (ô-tŏk′thə-nəs) or AUTOCHTHONAL *adj.* pertaining to autochthons; aboriginal; INDIGENOUS (as opposed to heterochthonous); native to a place or thing.

AUTOCHTHONOUSLY *adv.*

AUTOCHTHON (ô-tŏk′thən) *noun* one of the earliest or aboriginal inhabitants of a region; one of the animals or plants of a region.

1. It is hard to believe that Peter Rabbit is only 75 years old, for like the AUTOCHTHONOUS creatures of fables, fairy tales and nursery rhymes, his PROVENANCE is everywhere and his name is legion: Pierre Lapin, Peterchen Hase, Il Coniglio Pierino, Pwtan y Wnigen, Petro Cuniculo. (J. Cott, "Peter Rabbit and Friends," *New York Times*, 5/1/77, Section 7, p. 25)

AUTO-DA-FÉ (ô′ tō-də-fā′) *noun*, *pl.*: AUTOS-DA-FÉ the public declaration of the judgment passed by the courts of the Spanish Inquisition, and the execution of it by secular authorities, especially the public burning of condemned heretics at the stake; literally, act of faith.

1. . . . . I suspect, that the British AUTO-DA-FÉ on [Dylan] Thomas has started up all over again. One has been only too familiar with the view that blames Thomas's poetry because, unlike the bulk of contemporary British poetry, it is vivid and BRAVURA stuff, not civil seepage from stiff lips. He is not like the others, but they are INCESTUOUSLY like one another. (P. West, "Letter to the Editor," *New York Times*, 2/15/76, Section 7, p. 21)

2. "Technology has succeeded in extracting just about the last bit of taste from a loaf of bread," columnist Murray Kempton once told me spiritedly . . . . I assume by now Mrs. Kempton has . . . learned how to bake homemade bread. And Lo! the bread . . . tastes as good as before, and the machine age did not need to be roasted at an AUTO-DA-FÉ to make it all possible . . . . Can one make homemade freedom under the eyes of an OMNIPOTENT state that has no notion of, or tolerance for the flavor of freedom? (W.F. Buckley Jr., *Up From Liberalism*, Arlington House, 2nd Printing 1968, p. 224)

AUTODIDACT (ôt′ō-dī′dakt) *noun* a person who is self-taught.

AUTODIDACTIC *adj.*

1. I think that his [Evelyn Waugh's] Corporal-Major Ludovic, the AUTODIDACT author of *Pensées* and *The Death Wish*, is one of his richest and most brilliant strokes, and that there are many other good things in this his last major work of fiction. (L.E. Sissman, Review of *Evelyn Waugh: A Biography*, by Christopher Sykes, *The New Yorker*, 2/9/76, p. 108)

2. See (1) under GRIFTER.

AUTOEROTISM (ô′tō-er′ə-tiz′əm) or AUTOEROTICISM (ô′tō-i-rot′i-siz′əm) *noun* the arousal and satisfaction of sexual emotion within or by oneself, usually by masturbation; pleasant sensations or tensions arising in the erogenous body zones without external stimulation.

AUTOEROTIC *adj.*

AUTOEROTICALLY *adv.*

1. Central to the whole project [of the book, *Hope and Fear in Washington (The Early Seventies): The Story of the Washington Press Corps*, by Barney Collier] is the FRISSON of the gossip. Can he find out secrets? Will he dare publish them? Yes, Yes, Yes I will, Yes, he screeches to his readers in a kind of terminal AUTOEROTIC frenzy. (A. Cockburn, Review, *New York Review of Books*, 12/11/75, p. 28)

AVANT-GARDE (ə-vänt′ gärd′) *noun* the advance group, the leaders, or the radicals in any field, especially in the visual, literary, or musical arts, whose works are characterized by unorthodox and experimental methods; vanguard.

AVANT-GARDE *adj.* of or pertaining to the experimental treatment of artistic, musical, or literary material; belonging to the AVANT-GARDE.

AVANT-GARDISM *noun.*

AVANT-GARDIST *noun.*

1. See (1) under AVATAR.

2. It is not the least significant thing about [sculptor Mark] diSuvero's career that he belongs to a generation of artists who . . . suffered no delay in winning the acclaim of an influential group of admirers. This. . .separates the experience of this generation. . .from the fate traditionally meted out to members of the AVANT-GARDE. (H. Kramer, "A Playful Storm of Sculpture," *New York Times*, 1/25/76, Section 6, p. 10)

3. See (1) under HALCYON.

4. No other branch of the visual arts has lately been as radically redefined as this one [drawing], which even in the heyday of earlier AVANT-GARDE innovations managed to retain a certain fixed identity. (H. Kramer, "What is Drawing? Where Can We Draw the Line?" *New York Times*, 2/1/76, Section 2, p. 31)

5. See (3) under TITILLATE.

6. His theater has never been AVANT-GARDE, Mr. [Ted] Mann [artistic director of Circle in the Square] said without a hint of embarrassment. (T. Buckley, "Circle in Square, at 25, to Stage a Gala," *New York Times*, 3/8/76, p. 33)

7. He [Arthur Rubinstein] was befriended by Saint-Saëns, rubbed elbows and minds with Hemingway and Picasso . . . and championed the music of such friends as Stravinsky, Albéniz, Granados, Falla, Szymanowski, Ravel, Poulenc and Milhaud when these names were considered part of the accursed AVANT-GARDE. He even . . . knew Sol Hurok before Hurok was an impresario. (D. Henahan; "The ageless hero, Rubinstein," *New York Times*, 3/14/76, Section 6, p. 30)

8. Now AVANT-GARDE economists have long since made known their distrust of the marketplace—which, we are told, lacks the kind of

TRANSCENDENT vision that advances civilization. (W.F. Buckley Jr., *Up From Liberalism*, Arlington House, 2nd Printing 1968, p. 166)

9. See (1) under EMBOUCHURE.

10. See (5) under KITSCH.

11. See (3) under FIN DE SIÈCLE.

AVATAR (av' ə-tär') *noun* (in Hindu Mythology) the descent of a diety to earth in an incarnate form; the incarnation of a god; any embodiment or concrete manifestation of an abstract quality, attitude, concept, or principle in a person.

1. At the beginning of the narrative [*Children of the Sun*, by Martin Green], [Harold] Acton and [Brian] Howard are the darlings of the Sitwells and the AVATARS of the English AVANT-GARDE . . . . (H. Kramer, Review, *New York Times*, 1/25/76, Section 7, p. 3)

2. Berman's first and only piano teacher in Moscow . . . was Alexander Goldenweiser, reportedly an AVATAR of the romantic giants of the 19th century. (M. Mayer, "Berman—A Legend Arrives from Russia," *New York Times*, 2/1/76, Section 2, p. 17)

3. But at its most authentic and popular, the [comic book] form has belonged always to the AVATARS of Superman, beginning most notably with Captain Marvel, Batman and Wonder Woman and toward the end including the Fantastic Four of Stan Lee's Marvel Comics. (Leslie A. Fiedler, "Up, up and away—the rise and fall of comic books," *New York Times*, 9/5/76, Section 7, p. 1)

4. Barry Manilow, once the voice of Big Mac and Kentucky Fried Chicken and more recently *After Dark* magazine's Entertainer of the Year and the AVATAR of Romantic Pop, is pacing the living room of his luxury apartment in the East 20's, his lanky, Ichabod Crane-like figure almost shaking with nervous energy. (R. Palmer, "Barry Manilow—The Master of Romantic Pop," *New York Times*, 9/12/76, Section 2, p. 24)

5. . . .it seems that he [Paul Tillich] was, in the middle part of his life, a high-minded philanderer, making advances to half the women he met, and refusing fidelity from the first moments of his marriage. . . . He begins to

seem the AVATAR of that hero of suburban sex-comedy, the oversexed minister, whom we meet in the novels of Peter DeVries and John Updike, etc. (M. Green, Review of *Paul Tillich: His Life & Thought.* Vol. I: *Life*, by Wilhelm and Marion Pauck, *New York Times*, 12/19/76, Section 7, p. 4)

6. There's Glenna, a girl of the '60's, whom [Lily] Tomlin [in her show] takes through every change, fad and foible of the decade, from scanning the Beatles' albums for secret signs that Paul is dead, to drugs, campus revolution . . . to her final AVATAR as a radical chic lady calling to her maid . . . . (J. Kroll, "Lily Tomlin: Funny Lady," *Newsweek*, 3/28/77, p. 64)

AVERNUS (ə-vûr′ nəs) *noun* a lake in an extinct volcano near Naples, Italy, believed (in Roman mythology) to be at the entrance to Hades; hell; Hades.

1. Eventually, after quite a hike, I [Russel Wren] reached Union Square. I had still not seen a taxi. I was about to descend into the AVERNUS of subways under that complex crossroads . . . . (Thomas Berger, *Who Is Teddy Villanova?*, Delacorte Press/Seymour Lawrence, 1977, p. 133)

AVUNCULAR (ə-vuŋ′ kyə-lər) *adj.* of, pertaining to, or characteristic of an uncle; kind; cheerful.

1. He [Mao Tse-Tung] loved the role of the peasant philosopher, the winking, nose-tapping, canny rube, the AVUNCULAR old cutie with moon face glistening and grimacing, knocking out APHORISMS, parables, and barnyard political wisdom like fungoes! (A. Suehsdorf, "Remembering Chou En-lai in Yenan," *New York Times*, 1/11/76, p. 19)

2. He [Sol Roogow] was a joyless man, who suffered from backaches, but whenever Bob Cooke was around, Roogow became AVUNCULAR: "I'm teaching the kid [Roger Kahn] a lot," he announced inside Cooke's glass office. (R. Kahn, *The Boys of Summer*, Harper and Row, 1971, p. 86)

3. This book [*Growing Up at Grossinger's*, by Tania Grossinger] contains some relatively

harmless CHITCHST;* (sic) about celebrations: Eddie Fisher and Debbie Reynolds; Eddie Fisher and Elizabeth Taylor; Eddie Cantor; Rocky Marciano and other prizefighters; an AVUNCULAR Jackie Robinson, who when Tania told him she had a black boyfriend, counseled her that her family wasn't ready for that. (G. Millstein, Review, *New York Times*, 2/22/76, Section 7, p. 32)

4. America's political cartoonists created, out of their collective genius, Uncle Sam, the symbol of the American nation, the single indisputable contribution of political cartoonists to the political culture. Not quite in the best of taste . . . . Nor yet a gentleman . . . A merchant rather. AVUNCULAR rather than dignified. The name . . . comes from "Uncle" Sam Wilson, a Troy merchant who sold and shipped supplies to the U.S. government during the War of 1812. He so labeled his casks, and "U.S." became "Uncle Sam."** (D.P. Moynihan, "Cartoons still make Uncle Sam nation's witness," *Smithsonian*, December 1975, p. 57)

5. . . . those who enjoy the raised eyebrow, the civilized snicker, and the mild pleasures of a puzzle are not likely to need [Jacques] Barzun's textbook definition of a compound sentence [in the book, *Simple & Direct: A Rhetoric for Writers*] or his gentle, AVUNCULAR scolding about sentence fragments. (M. Hungiville, Review, *Change*, April 1976, p. 55)

6. He [Pandarus, in the Yale Repertory Theater's production of Shakespeare's *Troilus and Cressida*]'s a busy-body, all right . . . . But there is a dotingly AVUNCULAR quality about him. (W. Kerr, Review, *New York Times*, 4/18/76, Section 2, p. 5)

7. "Sunny Jim" Callaghan's first moves belied both his nickname and his AVUNCULAR reputa-

---

*Presumably an alternate spelling of KITSCH.

**Among the eyebrow-raising facts [Joseph Nathan] Kane has ferreted out are these: . . . Samuel Wilson, a provisions [food] inspector during the War of 1812, went by the nickname "Uncle Sam" and he habitually stamped inspected packages with the initials "U.S." This prompted the application of the nickname to the federal government. (A. Rosenthal, AP, "Man gets facts," *Norman* [Okla.] *Transcript*, 7/21/76, p. 23)

tion . . . the new Prime Minister sternly warned factions on both Labor's left and right wings that he intended to maintain party unity at all costs. Said he: "I want no cliques. None of you holds the Ark of the Covenant." (Anon., "Enter Un-Sunny Jim," *Time*, 4/19/76, p. 61)

8. His [Mao Tse-tung's] smooth, moon-like face with its high, sloping forehead and peasant-shrewd eyes gazed out AVUNCULARLY from public portraits all over China. He was praised in song and poetry . . . . Virtually deified by his own countrymen and held in awe even by capitalist societies of the West, he was the source and inspiration of one of history's most extraordinary personality cults. (Anon., "The Last Titan," *Newsweek*, 9/20/76, p. 37)

B

BABEL or **BABEL** (bā′bəl, bab′əl) *noun* (if capitalized) a Biblical city in Shinar in which Noah's descendants tried to build a very high tower intended to reach Heaven, and were prevented from doing so by a confusion of tongues; an impracticable scheme; (often lower case) a confusion of voices, languages, or sounds; tumult; a place of such confusion.

BABELIZE or **BABELIZE** *verb* to make confused or unintelligible.

1. See (1) under EPIGONE.

2. Language scholars . . . tell me that, exclusive of dialects, there are 142 recognized languages spoken by more than a million people . . . . The Oxford scholars here say that the world's 142 language BABEL remains a puzzle without end. (H. J. Taylor, "Fascination of Languages," *Times Herald*, Norristown, Pa., 10/28/76, p. 23)

3. . . . shortly before he left office, Kissinger said: "I do not believe that the Soviet Union is achieving military supremacy over the United States." Seven days later . . . [Secretary of Defense Donald H.] Rumsfeld had the last word: The Kremlin, he said, is "engaged in a serious, steady, and sustained effort which . . . could make it the dominant military power in the world." This BABEL of confusing statements from the outgoing administration did little to help clarify things for the layman . . . . (D.

Southerland, Christian Science Monitor News Service, "Arms Debate Baffles Average Person," *Times Herald*, Norristown, Pa., 3/5/77, p. 1)

4. See (1) under TRADUCE.

BACCHANAL (bā′kə-nàl, bak′ə-nal′, bak′ə-nəl) *noun* a follower of Bacchus, the ancient god of wine and revelry; bacchant or bacchante; a drunken carouser; a dance or song in honor of Bacchus; a drunken party; orgy.

BACCHANAL. *adj.* of Bacchus or his worship; carousing.

BACCHANALIAN *adj.* same as bacchanal.

BACCHANALIA *noun. pl.* an ancient Roman festival in honor of Bacchus; (if lower case) a drunken party; orgy.

BACCHANT *noun* a priest or worshiper of Bacchus; a drunken carouser.

BACCHANTE (bə-kan′te, -kän′-) *noun* a priestess or woman votary of Bacchus; a woman who carouses.

1. Entering a marriage calmly and rationally is like dancing a BACCHANAL calmly and rationally; it is a contradiction in terms. It takes into account everything except what is important: the spirit. (Sydney J. Harris, "Love is adventure, not an investment," *Philadelphia*

Inquirer, 10/6/76, p. 7-A)

BADINAGE (bad′ ənazh′ , bad′ ənij) *noun* light, playful repartee or banter or raillery; teasing.

BADINAGE *verb* to banter or tease (someone) playfully.

1. . . . Bogdanovich [in the film, *At Long Last Love*] challenged fate by attempting to make a spritely musical comedy with a leading lady who can neither sing nor dance and who apparently thinks BADINAGE is something you put on a small cut. (V. Canby, "Movies That Ask To Be Rapped in the Mouth," *New York Times*, 1/4/76, Section 2, p. 11)

2. . . . the Kent School in Kent, Conn., this month gave a daylong retrospective of films starring M-G-M's old master of drawing-room BADINAGE, Robert Montgomery. (C. Michener, M. Kasindorf, "Old Movies Come Alive," *Newsweek*, 5/31/76, p. 48)

3. What the two [characters in the first playlet of *California Suite*, by Neil Simon] are talking about, by means of BADINAGE that is also a secret code, is failed love, fortyish sex, hysterectomies and prostate conditions, the good of a child, the price paid for careers, everything and anything that might link two guardedly loving antagonists, flesh and brain. (W. Kerr, Review, *New York Times*, 6/20/76, Section 2, p. 7)

4. Harry [White, protagonist of Hubert Selby Jr.'s book, *The Demon*] suffers from an excess of heterosexuality. He can't stop taking women to bed . . . . And not just any woman but only married women . . . . Selby has a brilliant ear for the BADINAGE that Harry uses to hustle his quarry and a strong instinct for the intimate relation between the drives of sex and success. (P. D. Zimmerman, Review, *Newsweek*, 11/1/76, p. 84L)

5. Also, in the exchanges between these people and Simon [in *Otherwise Engaged*, a play by Simon Gray] we get the sharpest BADINAGE now on stage in New York; Mr. Gray's characters are masters of the civilized RIPOSTE with the result that a great part of the play is exceedingly funny. (E. Wilson, Review, *Wall Street Journal*, 2/8/77, p. 20)

6. Blackford [Oakes] was in good form for that kind of thing and could have spent a pleasant evening in BADINAGE. . . . (W.F. Buckley Jr., *Saving the Queen*, Doubleday, 1976, p. 118)

BAGATELLE (bag′ə-tel′) *noun* something of little value; an unimportant trifle; a game played with nine balls on a board having at one end nine holes spaced in a diamond shape into which the balls are to be struck with a cue; pinball; a short, light piece of music.

1. . . . if the answer to a puzzle clue is "cancer," [Will] Weng [*New York Times* crossword puzzle editor] makes certain that the clue is not "disease," but rather "constellation" or "Tropic of." But editing decisions like that are mere BAGATELLES (trifles . . .) when the enormity of Weng's work is considered. (M. Dubin, "Puzzled? Then Weng has done his job," *Philadelphia Inquirer*, 11/28/76, p. 4-L)

BAGNIO (ban′yō) *noun* a brothel; house of prostitution.

1. If he had spent those five years [in which he was in prison] alternately drunk and stoned in the most lavish of BAGNIOS, Falconetti would still be as foul-tempered as a dyspeptic bill collector. Some people are just no damned good, and Falconetti is one of them. (Lee Winfrey, "Falconetti to get new eye," *Philadelphia Inquirer*, 10/5/76, p. 4-C)

BALEFUL (bāl′fəl) *adj.* harmful; menacing; threatening harm, evil, or malignity; ominous; deadly; sinister.

BALEFULLY *adv.*

BALEFULNESS *noun.*

1. . . . Craw's large head had turned to Luke, and his moist eyes fixed on him a BALEFUL stare that seemed to go on forever. Luke began to wonder which of Craw's many laws he might have sinned against. (J. LeCarré, *The Honourable Schoolboy*, Alfred A. Knopf, 1977, p. 10)

2. Bakewell flung the door open and entered with a BALEFUL glance for me, then one of discovery for his enormous brogans, which lay where I had dropped them. (T. Berger, *Who Is Teddy Villanova?*, Delacorte Press/Seymour

Lawrence, 1977, p. 176)

BANAL (bə-nal′ , -näl′ , ban′ əl, bān′ əl) *adj.* devoid of freshness or originality; hackneyed; trite; commonplace.

BANALLY *adv.*

BANALITY *noun.*

1. For if the Nazis [on trial at Nuremberg] were normal, then concepts such as Hannah Arendt's "BANALITY of evil," according to which Adolf Eichmann and his ilk could be ordinary men blindly following the command of a murderous system, would be supported. (J. Kovel, Review of *The Nuremberg Mind*, by Florence R. Miale and Michael Selzer, *New York Times*, 2/8/76, Section 7, p. 6)

2. In the Senate version, the [antitrust] bill begins with elaborate findings of fact. Unhappily some of these facts have never been found, and some of the findings are BANAL pronouncements. From this tenuous springboard, the bill dives into a series of grotesque remedies. (J. J. Kilpatrick, "Good Idea Botched in Antitrust Bill," *Daily Oklahoman*, Okla. City, 3/23/76, p. 6)

3. *The Exorcist* was a skillful entertainment that spoke quite subtly about the BANALITY of evil as rationalized by modern science. The same message seems to be intended by Mr. [Malachi] Martin [in *Hostage to the Devil: The Possession and Exorcism of Five Living Americans*], but his book remains as dangerously obscurantist as it is sensationalistic. (Francine DuPlessix Gray, Review, *New York Times*, 3/14/76, Section 7, p. 8)

4. Most students . . . are uninterested in the political world . . . And too often those students who are politically minded behave as though they had taken perpetual vows of BANALITY. (W.F. Buckley Jr., *Up From Liberalism*, Arlington House, 2nd Printing 1968, p. 132)

5. See (1) under EMBOUCHURE.

6. See (1) under CAMP.

7. Harding . . . was the exact opposite of Wilson. His virtues in the eyes of the Senatorial junta that engineered his nomination were precisely the traits that would destroy his administration—BANALITY, laziness, congeniality, lack of convictions. (J.P. Lash, Review of *The President Makers: From Mark Hanna to Joseph P. Kennedy*, by Francis Russell, *New York Times*, 3/28/76, Section 7, p.4)

8. Its theme [*Amoral America*, by George C. S. Benson and Thomas S. Engeman] is familiar, even BANAL: America has lost its moral mooring. Its style is PEDANTIC—one 15-word declarative sentence plodding after another—but the book includes some interesting social-science evidence about the extent of social rot. (T.R. Stizer, Review, *Chronicle of Higher Education*, 4/5/76. p. 20)

9. It sickened her to utter another BANALITY. "Sometimes dreams come true," she [Sharon Fields] said huskily, rather proud of . . . the hackneyed line. (I. Wallace, *The Fan Club*, Bantam Edition, 1975, p. 397)

10. See (3) under FINAGLE.

11. Ford's conservatism, like [Britain's former Prime Minister Harold] Macmillan's, is criticized as BANAL, which it is. Of course, BANAL politics is not the worst kind. Ford can reply, as Macmillan did: "If people want a sense of purpose they can get it from their archbishops." That puts politics in its place, which should not be at the center of the human drama. (G.F. Will, "It Ain't Necessarily So," *Newsweek*, 8/30/76, p. 27)

12. These literary vandals have labored a dozen years [on a revision of the Episcopalian *Book of Common Prayer*] and brought forth a monstrous mishmash that succeeds only in turning the beautiful into the BANAL, the majestic into the mundane, the poetic into the preposterous. (Smith Hempstone, "Taking the poetry out of the prayers," *Philadelphia Inquirer*, 10/6/76, p. 7-A)

13. See (1) under DOWSE.

14. See (6) under SENTENTIOUS.

BANSHEE (ban′shē) or **BANSHIE** *noun* (in Irish and Scottish folklore) a female spirit believed to wail outside a house as a warning that a death will occur soon in the family.

1. I like, too, the chronicles [in the book, *An Encyclopedia of Fairies*, by Katherine Briggs] from the twelfth to the seventeenth centuries in which human involvement in fairy matters is reported as remarkable but not incredible. An English couple in Ireland, for instance, are troubled by a BANSHEE and conclude that BANSHEES flourish in Ireland because the natives are superstitious and lack a proper faith to protect them. (P. S. Prescott, Review, *Newsweek*, 2/21/77, p. 86)

2. "I just found out about these [child-porn] magazines and films this summer, and I've become a raving BANSHEE over it," says Dr. Judianne Densen-Gerber, a Manhattan psychiatrist who has been barnstorming around the country in a crusade against this abuse of minors. (Anon., "Child's Garden of Perversity," *Time*, 4/4/77, p. 55)

BAROQUE (bə-rōk′) *adj.* of or pertaining to a style of art and architecture prevailing in Europe during the 17th and first half of the 18th century that was characterized by elaborate and grotesque forms and ornamentation; of or pertaining to the musical period following the Renaissance, extending roughly from 1600 to 1750 and characterized by highly embellished melodies; fantastically overdecorated; gaudily ornate; ROCOCO; irregular in shape.

BAROQUE *noun* the baroque style or period; anything extravagantly ornamented, especially something so ornate as to be in bad taste; an irregularly shaped pearl.

1. See (1) under MIASMA.

2. Although self-contained [as an appendix in Sacvan Bercovitch's book, *The Puritan Origins of the American Self*], this text [of Cotton Mather's biography of John Winthrop] is a part of what well may be the most revealing unread book in American literature—Mather's fantastic, BAROQUE compendium [1702] of Puritan history, biography, lore, superstition and delusion. (L. Marx, Review, *New York Times*, 2/1/76, Section 7, p. 21)

3. In politics, meanwhile, recent elections have demonstrated that although the old machines have indeed disintegrated (the Chicago of Mayor Richard J. Daley being

always the BAROQUE exception), American-Irish politicians are showing a notable capacity to adapt their style to changed circumstances. They [Edmund G. (Jerry) Brown, Jr. and Hugh Carey] govern the two most populous states, California and New York. (W.V. Shannon, "The lasting hurrah," *New York Times*, 3/14/76, Section 6, p. 11)

BARRATRY (bar′ ə-trē) *noun* originally, the buying or selling of ecclesiastical or civil positions; the criminal offense of habitually stirring up or bringing about quarrels or lawsuits; fraud or gross negligence by a ship's officers or crew that results in loss to the owners.

BARRATROUS *adj.*

BARRATROUSLY *adv.*

BARRATOR or BARRATER *noun* a person guilty of barratry.

1. Fed up with the rising number of medical malpractice suits . . . , doctors in Illinois have begun to launch legal counterattacks . . . . Another Illinois doctor . . . has charged a patient's lawyer with BARRATRY (frivolously stirring up litigation). If convicted, the lawyer could face disbarment proceedings. Indeed, the Illinois State Medical Society feels that overeager attorneys are often the instigators of malpractice suits. (Anon., "Doctors' Counterattack," *Time*, 4/19/76, p. 89)

BARRIO (bar′ ē-ō , bäR′ Ryō) *noun, pl.*: BARRIOS (-ē-ōz , -Ryōs) (in Spanish-speaking countries) a district or suburb of a city; (in U.S. slang) a slum inhabited predominantly by Puerto Ricans or Mexicans.

1. . . . when James Carter is presented with a sombrero in a New York BARRIO it is a journalistic article of faith that it must appear in the evening prints. Never mind that the real news would be if a candidate were not to receive a sombrero . . . . (T. Tiede, "Who's to Blame For Mediocrity?" *Times Herald*, Norristown, Pa., 10/2/76, p. 9)

2. Under the Constitution, a resident alien can live wherever he pleases; okay, but can't we modify the amounts of welfare available to him in such a way as to discourage him from

remaining holed up in some ethnic BARRIO in the South Bronx, and instead encourage him to move to the vast tracts of unused land in other parts of the country? If not, let's amend the Constitution to permit this. (W. A. Rusher, "Bring welfare costs under control," *Philadelphia Inquirer*, 2/7/77, p. 9-A)

BASTINADO (bas' tə-nā' dō, -näd' ō) *noun,* *pl.:* -DOES a blow or a beating with a stick, cudgel, etc., often on the soles of the feet; a stick or cudgel.

BASTINADO *verb* to beat with a stick, cane, or cudgel, often on the soles of the feet.

1. He [the policeman Knox] took a blackjack from a rear pocket and brandished it. "I might just submit you to the BASTINADO" [he said to Russel Wren]. (Thomas Berger, *Who Is Teddy Villanova?* Delacorte Press/Seymour Lawrence, 1977, p. 93)

BATHOS (bā' thŏs) *noun* a ludicrous descent from the exalted or lofty to the commonplace in writing or speech; anticlimax; triteness or triviality in style; false or insincere pathos; obvious sentimentality; MAWKISHNESS; hackneyed quality.

BATHETIC *adj.*

BATHETICALLY *adv.*

1. See (2) under PEDAGOGY.

2. [Gilbert] Murray's verse translations (of Euripides and Aeschylus) [in the early 1900's] . . . were in fact extremely successful on stage; they were also accepted by the public at large and some of the critics as English poetry in their own right. This is a judgment time has rescinded. Murray would occasionally rise in the choral passages to giddy Swinburnian heights (he could also sink to nameless BATHETIC depths), but for the dramatic dialogue he adopted a form which only Donne could handle successfully—rhymed couplets which are, for the most part, not closed. (B. M. W. Knox, Review of *Aeschylus: Suppliants,* translated by Janet Lembke; *Aeschylus: Seven Against Thebes,* translated by Helen Bacon and Anthony Hecht; and *Aeschylus: Prometheus Bound,* translated by James Scully and C. John Herington, *New York Review of*

Books, 11/27/75, p. 27)

3. But even these first volumes [of poetry by Anne Sexton] lapse frequently into BATHOS, betraying an apparent incapacity for self-criticism either moral or esthetic, and such lapses multiply as the career continues. (Patricia Meyer Spacks, Review of *45 Mercy Street,* by Anne Sexton, edited by Linda Gray Sexton, *New York Times,* 5/30/76, Section 7, p. 6)

4. It is frail, BATHETIC stuff, yet touching for the loneliness Balanchine suggests. (W. Bender, Review of *Union Jack,* a ballet choreographed by George Balanchine, *Time,* 5/24/76, p. 70)

5. See (2) under CONTRAPUNTAL.

6. [Fay] Wray's sexual terror [in the original *King Kong* movie], expressed by her incessant opera screams is replaced [in the new *King Kong*] by [Jessica] Lange's ruefully hip repartee. "C'mon, Kong," she sighs, "this thing is never gonna work, can't you see?" When the monster washes her off in a waterfall, he dries her by blowing on her, and this horny halitosis let Lange moaning in arousal. This BATHETIC clunk from the sublime to the ridiculous is characteristic at almost every point of comparison between Kongs I and II. (J. Kroll, "The Movies Go Ape—Again," *Newsweek,* 12/20/76, p. 103)

BATTLEDORE (bat'əl-dôr) *noun* a child's primer, usually made of two or three pages of stiff cardboard on which were printed or impressed the alphabet, numerals, and other rudimentary material and used especially in the 17th and 18th centuries; a child's hornbook (a parchment leaf or page containing the alphabet, a table of numbers, a prayer, etc., covered with a sheet of transparent horn and fixed in a frame with a handle, formerly used in teaching children to read); a primer or book of rudiments.

1. Every conceivable kind of children's book is included [in *Early Children's Books and Their Illustrations,* by Gerald Gottlieb]—bestiaries, hornbooks and BATTLEDORES, courtesy, religious and emblem books, as well as famous books that have been adapted for children such as *Gulliver's Travels* . . . . (W. Claire, Review,

Smithsonian, February 1976, p. 128)

BAUDELAIRE (bōd' ə-lâr', bōd ə-ler') *noun* an important French poet and critic (1821-1867), whose esthetic theories led to the Symbolist movement and who identified strongly with Poe. His only volume of poetry (1857), which long served as a prime example of depravity, morbidity, obscenity and eroticism, led to his conviction for obscenity and blasphemy, a decision only POSTHUMOUSLY reversed. Intending to be Satanic, he created well-known visions of ugliness, sin, and evil.

BAUDELAIREAN *adj* characteristic of Baudelaire or his writings.

1. The astonishing décor [of the Paris Opera's production of *Faust*] transformed itself even into Marguerite's backyard and, with great effect, into a lofty church, a dark prison and the raffish setting for a BAUDELAIREAN orgy on WALPURGIS NIGHT. (H. Saal, Review, *Newsweek*, 9/27/76, p. 105)

2. See (3) under FIN DE SIÈCLE.

BEL CANTO (bel' kan'tō) a smooth, easy-flowing style of singing characterized by brilliant vocal display and purity of tone.

1. She [Paola Belli] spoke English well with British sounds but Mediterranean BEL CANTO. (A. Burgess, *Beard's Roman Women*, McGraw-Hill, 1976, p. 21)

BENISON (ben' i-zən, -sən) *noun* benediction; blessing.

1. . . . we may soon receive the BENISONS of what, in Britain, they call Ambisound, an improvement on conventional stereo and quadraphonic hi-fi systems . . . . British acousticians have dreamed up a system of recording which uses up to 12 "capsules" of four tetrahedrally arranged microphones and requires four, and preferably five, speakers (J.K. Page, Jr., "Sound all around," *Smithsonian*, April 1976, pp. 14, 16)

BÊTE NOIRE (bet nwar', bät' nwär') *noun*, *pl.:* BÊTES NOIRES (bet nwär', bät'nwärz') something or someone that a person particularly dislikes, fears, avoids, dreads, or, loathes; a bugbear.

1. If Reagan is the current darling of the pro-life forces [in the abortion controversy], Birch Bayh is their BÊTE NOIRE. (R. Steele, J. Doyle, "1976's Sleeper Issue," *Newsweek*, 2/9/76, p. 23)

2. The journalists. . . —especially those who are murdered [in *The Canfield Decision*, a book by Spiro Agnew]—are . . . devious SURROGATES for the specific BÊTES NOIRES of Agnew's political career. (D. Shaw, of *Los Angeles Times*, "Agnew 'murders' media and other 'nattering nabobs,' " reprinted in *Norman* [Okla.] *Transcript*, 5/23/76, p. 17)

3. In Atlanta the BÊTE NOIRE among highways was Interstate 485. (C. E. Little, "Atlanta renewal gives power to the communities," *Smithsonian*, July 1976, p. 102)

4. One such passenger, on April 28, 1972, was Ralph Nader, BÊTE NOIR (sic) of the American business establishment, who showed up at the Washington National Airport just five minutes before Allegheny Airlines flight 864 was to take off for Hartford. Nader was on a tight schedule to appear at two consumer rallies in Connecticut. He had no seat. (Anon., "A Big Bump for Bumping," *Time*, 6/21/76, p. 48)

BIBELOT (bib' lō, bēbəlō') *noun* a small decorative object whose value lies in its beauty, unusually small size, or rarity; trinket; a book of unusually small size.

1. [Geoffrey] Wolff turns him [Harry Crosby] around like a BIBELOT, examining him [in the book, *Black Sun: The Brief Transit and Violent Eclipse of Harry Crosby*] as Harry might have examined each part of one of the Egyptian geegaws he treasured during his sun-worshiping phase. (R. Sokolov, Review, *Newsweek*, 9/6/76, p. 63A)

2. Our solid brass [jigsaw] puzzle might take the place of pencil doodling. A handsome desk BIBELOT, the 9-piece puzzle is 5½ " square when assembled. A N-M import from England. $70.00 (Anon., *Neiman-Marcus Christmas Book*, 1976, p. 69)

BIBLIOPHILE (bib' lē-ə-fīl', -fil) or **BIBLIOPHILIST** (bib' lē-of'ə-list) *noun* a person who loves or collects books, especially as examples of fine or unusual printing, binding, or the like.

BIBLIOPHILISM or **BIBLIOPHILY** *noun*.

BIBLIOPHILISTIC or **BIBLIOPHILIC** *adj*.

1. "My idea [David R. Godine says] is to do the best books in the genteel tradition . . . . We're in the . . . toughest corner of the [publishing] ring." BIBLIOPHILES can only hope that, on the way out of that corner, Godine doesn't entirely join the twentieth century. (J. N. Baker, "Holdout for Quality," *Newsweek*, 5/24/76, p. 95)

BIBLIOPOLE (bib' lē-ə-pōl') or **BIBLIOPOLIST** (bib' lē op' ə-list) *noun* a bookseller, especially one dealing in rare or secondhand books.

BIBLIOPOLIC (bib'lē-ə-pol'ik) *adj*.

BIBLIOPOLY (bib'lē-op'ə-lē) or **BIBLIOPOLISM** (bib'lē-op'ə-liz'əm) *noun*.

1. Rare-book dealers and collectors had mixed feelings about the record costs [of first editions by well-known authors]. "The Snopeses are in the market," grumbled one BIBLIOPOLE, as agents for wealthy clients pushed prices to new highs. But as the bidding raised the value of items already in his stock, the same dealer was heard whispering to himself, "Go, go." (Anon., "The New Literary Appreciation," *Time*, 4/25/77, p. 85)

BIBULOUS (bib'yə-ləs) *adj*. addicted to or fond of the drinking of alcoholic beverages; highly absorbent; spongy.

BIBULOUSLY *adv*.

BIBULOUSNESS *noun*.

1. On Christmas Day, 1776, with dazzling audacity, he [General Washington] marched ill-armed, ill-clad troops to the banks of the Delaware . . . . In tubby boats . . . they [John Glover's seafaring men of Marblehead, Mass.] ferried 2,400 Americans across the ice-clogged river to the Jersey shore in the dead of night. For Col. Johann Rall's Hessians, it was a night of WASSAIL . . . . While the Hessians celebrated BIBULOUSLY, the Rebels advanced silently . . . . After a bloody charge, . . . 900 mercenaries surrendered; several hundred more fled in disorder. The half-frozen Americans captured

vast stores of weapons and supplies. (H. LaFay, "The Man Behind the Myths: Geo. Washington," *National Geographic*, July 1976, p. 102)

BIGHT (bīt) *noun* the middle, loop, or slack part of a rope, as distinguished from the ends; a curve in a river, coastline, etc.; a bay formed by such a curve.

BIGHT *verb* to fasten with a bight of rope.

1. For 800 years Ireland, a Catholic country, has been trying to get the Anglican British out of their land, and the six counties of Ulster constitute the last and northernmost BIGHT of the Irish mainland to remain under British rule. (Lucinda Franks, " 'We want peace. Just peace.' " *New York Times*, 12/19/76, Section 6, p. 29)

BIJOU (bē' zhōō, bē-zhōō') *noun, pl.:* **BIJOUX** (bē' zhōōz, bē-zhōōz') a jewel; something delicate and exquisitely wrought; a trinket.

BIJOUTERIE (bi-zhōōt' ər-ē) *noun* jewelry or trinkets generally or collectively.

1. Above all—or perhaps I should say beneath all—lies an IMPLACABLE enmity toward the concept of excellence which John Kennedy exalted. We are confronted by a gray tide of mediocrity. The myth is current that we are all children of the same GRAVID earth bitch, that every homo sap is like every other homo sap, that any suggestion otherwise is PRETENTIOUS, and that every authority is a bugbear . . . . If you receive a Phi Beta Kappa key, or a letter sweater, or a Legion of Honor riband, or any of the BIJOUX in which people once took pride, you are expected to stow it away in a murky backstair corner. (W. Manchester, Commencement Address, University of Massachusetts, 6/13/75, mimeographed, p. 8)

BILDÜNGSROMAN (bil' dōönks rō-män') *noun, pl.:* -MANE (-mä' nə) a novel that details the psychological development of the principal character.

1. It [*The Last Rush North*]'s another half-baked book, neither solid enough to make a compelling documentary [of the building of the Alaska pipeline], nor subtle enough to

qualify as a BILDÜNGSROMAN. He [author Bruce Dobler] is a hard-working novelist with very little to say. (S. Frank, Review, *New York Times*, 9/12/76, Section 7, p. 40)

BILLINGSGATE (bil' ĭngz-gāt', -gĭt) *noun* coarsely or vulgarly abusive language [originally the kind of foul speech often heard at *Billingsgate*, a London fishmarket at the *gate* named after a certain *Billing*].

1. Washington's position on the Addis Ababa summit [of the Organization of African Unity] was simple, if a bit DISINGENUOUS: it wanted the OAU to condemn all foreign intervention . . . and call for a cease-fire and a coalition government [in Angola] . . . . One pro-government [of Nigeria] newspaper ran the headline SHUT UP, while another printed the words TO HELL WITH AMERICA across a photograph of the President [Ford]. Compared with that kind of BILLINGSGATE, the Pravda editorial that confronted Ford early last week looked downright hopeful. (R. Watson, *et al.*, "Angola: Détente Under Fire," *Newsweek*, 1/19/76, pp. 22–23)

2. . . . in the present work [*The Olive of Minerva*] Dahlberg . . . [explains] why the hero . . . left the Big Apple: "He had gone out from that steel and glass GEHENNA, New York. BILLINGSGATE was RIFE in the mouths of the street-gamin . . . and the rabble intelligentsia of the academic dumps of America . . . . Courtesy was regarded as a MALAISE of a MEACOCK GROUTHEAD." Is this complex irony—BILLINGSGATE scolded in BILLINGSGATE; . . . discourtesy discourteously derided? Or is this merely bad writing, over-ripe triteness? (J.D. O'Hara, Review, *New York Times*, 4/18/76, Section 7, p. 20)

3. "You . . . treacherous baggage . . . . A pox on you!" [said Russel Wren to Natalie Novotny]. "You're in real trouble, Russel. I don't think eighteenth-century BILLINGSGATE will answer your needs." (Thomas Berger, *Who is Teddy Villanova?*, Delacorte Press/Seymour Lawrence, 1977, p. 175)

BIMBO (bim' bō) *noun* (in Slang) a woman, especially a sexually promiscuous one.

1. Paul Williams ad-libbed a lascivious remark about wanting to get closer to my letter sweater, and I [Maureen Orth] suddenly thought, "He thinks I'm a BIMBO." (Maureen Orth, "Going, Going . . . Gong!" *Newsweek*, 2/28/77, p. 45)

BLATHERSKITE (blath' ər-skīt') *noun* a person given to voluble, blustery, empty talk; a talkative, foolish person.

BLATHER *noun* foolish talk, loquacious nonsense; babble.

BLATHER *verb* to talk on and on foolishly.

1. Educators accuse politicians of being BLATHERSKITES, compromisers, and opportunists. In turn, politicians see educators as stuffy, SANCTIMONIOUS prigs who are out of touch with reality. (W. McNamara, "The Institute for Educational Leadership," *Change*, February 1975, p. 44)

BLOVIATE (blō' vē-āt) *verb* to orate verbosely and windily.

1. [E. B.] White [former editor of *The New Yorker* magazine] himself was asked to help write a pamphlet on the four freedoms, and at least he saw the joke of that and of committee writing in general. But he did do some BLOVIATING for the Human Spirit, before returning to what he does best: the hammering out of fine sentences about small matters. (W. Sheed, Review of *Letters of E. B. White*, edited by Dorothy Lobrano Guth, *New York Times*, 11/21/76, Section 7, p. 26)

BLOWZY (blou'zē) or **BLOWSY** *adj.* having a coarse, ruddy complexion; fat, ruddy, and coarse looking; disheveled; unkempt; slovenly; frowzy; sluttish.

1. Full-figured in a skirt and sweater, dragging on cigarettes, swilling vodka, Dewhurst was the BLOWZY history professor's wife [in Edward Albee's play, *Who's Afraid of Virginia Woolf?*], a loud and vulgar woman, crackling with passion, intellect, cynicism, sorrow and understanding, the woman whom the audience knows is about to endure a WALPURGISNACHT after 23 years of marriage. (Otile McManus, Review, *Boston Globe*, 3/7/76, pp. 9-A, 14-A)

BOCAGE (bō-käzh') *noun* (in the arts) a decorative pattern consisting of foliage, trees, branches, etc.; countryside or landscape (as of Western France) marked by intermingling patches of woodland and heath, small fields, tall hedgerows, and orchards.

1. . . . the Philadelphia novelist Struthers Burt, who loved Wyoming told [in *Powder River: Let 'er Buck*] of the heroic exploits of the Wyoming volunteers in France in World War I. They cavorted across the BOCAGE as if it were the plains of Wyoming, and their famous battle cry was adopted by other American units and even by the Australians and New Zealanders. (J. A. Michener, *Centennial*, Fawcett, 1975, p. 422)

BOISERIE (bwä-zə-rē) *noun* carved wood paneling.

1. The [private] dinner [of Queen Caroline with Blackford Oakes], discreetly served in the Queen's Drawing Room, in the candlelight with the crystal BOISERIE-effect and, always, the family paintings. . . . (W.F. Buckley Jr., *Saving the Queen*, Doubleday, 1976, p. 189)

BOÎTE (bwAt) *noun*, *pl.*: **BOÎTES** (bwAt) or **BOÎTE DE NUIT** (bwAt də nwē') a small night club; cabaret.

1. Other cities . . . are now trying to lure her [Regine Zylberberg] into their afterhours life. The next BOÎTE will open in Beverly Hills in March of next year . . . . (Linda Bird Francke, "The Reign of Régine," *Newsweek*, 5/17/76, p. 68)

2. Prosperity brought him [Jimmy Carter] a taste of social success among the young crowd in Americus [Georgia], he and Rosalynn fell in with the Bill Popes and the Billy Hornes . . . . They . . . dashed to the Gulf Coast for beach weekends. They tried the twist at a dim and vaguely daring BOÎTE called the Continental Room across the county line in Albany. (Carter preferred waltzing.) (P. Goldman, "Sizing Up Carter," *Newsweek*, 9/13/76, p. 33)

BOLUS (bō' ləs) *noun*, *pl.*: **BOLUSES** a soft, round lump or mass, as of chewed food; (in Medicine) a large (usually spherical) pill.

1. In treating Marianne Moore's work as a BOLUS of IDIOSYNCRASIES, to be dipped into for handy examples of whatever the critic wants at the moment, it [the book, *Marianne Moore*, by Pamela White Hadas] ignores the most marked feature of her development: the fact that in the 1940's she began writing quite differently: publicly, not HERMETICALLY, and by her previous standards, somewhat slackly. (H. Kenner, Review, *New York Times*, 7/17/77, Section 7, p. 14)

BOMBINATE (bäm' bə-nāt') *verb* to buzz, as a fly; hum.

BOMBINATION *noun*.

1. John D. MacDonald, author of the Travis McGee thrillers, does not include his detective hero in the large, motley cast [of his book, *Condominium*] . . . . His MESOMORPHIC Floridian would have collared the dredgers and developers, and punched the crooked county commissioners in the chops. That satisfying fancy is sadly absent from *Condominium*, and so is the author's customary wryness. In its place is a self-righteousness that BOMBINATES at needless length on environmental matters, foolishness and greed. (Anon., Review, *Time*, 7/4/77, p. 53)

BONHOMIE (bon'ə-mē', bô-nô-mē') *noun* friendliness; geniality; good nature; pleasant, affable manner; amiability; kindliness; joviality.

BONHOMOUS (bon'ə-məs) *adj.*

BONHOMOUSLY *adv.*

1. It is the supreme obligation of someone going off duty [on shipboard] to awaken those who are going on duty; and the only civilized way to do it is with a dry, matter-of-fact, faintly compassionate resignation, lint-free, God help us, of BONHOMIE. (W.F. Buckley Jr., *Execution Eve and Other Contemporary Ballads*, G.P. Putnam's Sons, 1975, pp. 249–250)

2. But as the nation's Democrats convened this week for the first Presidential nominating convention to be held there in half a century, the big, aloof Apple [New York City] suddenly blossomed with small-town BONHOMIE.

WELCOME VISITORS signs beckoned, with unlikely cordiality, from windows, kiosks—and massage parlors. The flags of the 50 states fluttered ECUMENICALLY along a 30-block midtown stretch of Fifth Avenue. (D. Gelman, *et al.*, "Polishing The Apple," *Newsweek*, 7/19/76, p. 33)

BON MOT (bôn' mō') *noun, pl.:* BONS MOTS (bôn' mōz') an apt or clever word or remark; witticism.

1. I [Russel Wren] went through the rest of the [directory] board: . . . Corngold & Co., 4A, who I believe dealt in costume-jewelry findings, giving [Sam] Polidor the pretext for a rare BON MOT, "for costumed Jews," he having the habitual New Yorkish derisive regard for his own folk. (Thomas Berger, *Who Is Teddy Villanova?* Delacorte Press/Seymour Lawrence, 1977, pp. 68–69)

2. . . . I [Russel Wren] stepped up my pace, penetrating the sidewalk congestion oblivious to the individuals who made it up, each the hero of his own tragedy or farce, most no doubt involved in both at once, as I believe it was Schopenhauer who stated in a Teutonic BON MOT. (Thomas Berger, *Ibid.*, pp. 68–69)

BON VIVANT (bôn vē-vän', băn vi-vänt') *noun, pl.:* BONS VIVANTS (bôn vē-vän', băn vi-vänts') a person who lives luxuriously and enjoys good food and drink; an epicure; a jovial companion.

1. . . . he [Richard Crossman, a former British Cabinet minister] has produced [in *The Diaries of a Cabinet Minister*] a thoroughly unorthodox political memoir . . . . Other people . . . have tried . . . much the same before—in recent years diplomat Harold Nicolson, BON VIVANT "Chips" Channon and . . . columnist Robert Bruce Lockhart. (A. Howard, Review, *New York Times*, 9/12/76, Section 7, p. 1)

2. Playwright, songsmith, actor, director, wit and BON VIVANT, [Noel] Coward set the tone of sophistication for one age and lived long enough to be discovered by another. He arrived on the London stage a PRODIGY, assumed the mantle of "The Master" as a matter of course, accepted knighthood with IMPECCABLE grace in his twilight years and died on March

26, 1973. . . . (W.B. Collins, "Noel Coward—something there for posterity?" *Philadelphia Inquirer*, 1/30/77, p. 1–D)

BOOBOISIE (bōō bwä-zē') *noun* a class of the general public composed of uneducated, uncultured persons.

1. The Stanford intellectuals' knowledge of the mind and heart of the BOOBOISIE notwithstanding, the television address had the astonishing effect of increasing, rather than diminishing, the number of Americans who believed that Nixon was not telling the truth. (W. F. Buckley, Jr., *Execution Eve and Other Contemporary Ballads*, G. P. Putnam's Sons, 1975, p. 121)

BORBORYGM (bôr' bə-rim) *noun* the noise produced by wind in the bowels; intestinal flatus; a fart.

1. He [Ronald Beard] . . . read what he had written of his new television play and . . . did not much like what he had written. "I've lived with you for ten years, and Christ alone knows how I've done it. Each time you make that double grunting noise prefatory to some weighty BORBORYGM I want to scream and scream and scream and—" (A. Burgess, *Beard's Roman Women*, McGraw-Hill, 1976, p. 17)

BOSKY (bôs' kē) *adj.* covered with trees, bushes, or shrubs; wooded; sylvan; shady.

BOSKET or BOSK or BOSCAGE or BOSKAGE *noun* a small grove or thicket.

1. For the past half dozen years [Frank] Frazetta [the "king" of fantastic art] has been living in East Stroudsburg, in Pennsylvania's Pocono Mountains. There he finds every possible excuse to postpone painting—driving about his 67 BOSKY acres on a tractor, shooting at bats—until the last minute before deadline, when he sits down with his easel and works around the clock in an inspired frenzy. (R. Walters, "Paperback Talk," *New York Times*, 5/1/77, Section 7, p. 68)

2. This play [*A Midsummer Night's Dream*, by William Shakespeare] is moon-struck, magical and mythic . . . . If no real bird song

lilts in a BOSKY dell, the playwright's words linger in the air like INEFFABLE music. (T.E. Kalem, Review of Stratford Festival performance, *Time*, 6/20/77, p. 62)

BOUFFE see OPÉRA BOUFFE.

BOURGEOIS (bŏŏr-zhwä́, bŏŏr'zhwä) *adj.* belonging to, characteristic of, or consisting of the middle class; lacking in refinement or culture; commonplace; conventional; lacking in taste; dominated or characterized by materialistic pursuits or private property concerns.

BOURGEOIS *noun, pl.* -GEOIS a member of the middle class (bourgeoisie); a self-employed person such as a shopkeeper, merchant, or businessman; a person whose values, beliefs, and practices supposedly are petty, materialistic, and conventionally middle-class.

BOURGEOISIE (bŏŏr'zhwä-zē') *noun* the bourgeois (middle) class between the very wealthy aristocracy and the working class (proletariat); (in Marxist theory) the capitalist class opposed to the proletariat (working class).

1. As private individuals, they [members of the middle class] are enticed by their culture to find self-fulfillment through an unbounded and often irrational HEDONISM . . . . When the Protestant ethic finally disappeared from BOURGEOIS society, he [Daniel Bell] concludes [in *The Cultural Contradictions of Capitalism*], "only the HEDONISM remained, and the capitalist system lost its TRANSCENDENTAL ethic." (K.L. Woodward, Review, *Newsweek*, 2/9/76, p. 69)

2. See (1) under FETISHISM.

3. See (2) under SHIBBOLETH.

4. And when the history of its [psychology's] expertise is written it will have to include among its themes the DIALECTIC according to which the technology of behavior analysis arose as a reaction within the BOURGEOIS democracies to the unspeakable degeneration evinced by fascism [under Hitler] . . . . (J. Kovel, Review of *The Nuremberg Mind*, by Florence R. Miale and Michael Selzer, *New York Times*, 2/8/76, Section 7, p. 6)

5. The economic doctrines of Adam Smith were, in part, a reflection of this ZEITGEIST [the Industrial Revolution]. But Smith also was a creative thinker . . . , and it was his formulations of economic theory that helped to shape the new BOURGEOIS order. (P. A. Samuelson, "Adam Smith," *Newsweek*, 3/15/76, p. 86)

6. In [the movie] *Vincent, Francois, Paul and the Others*, Yves Montand wears a mask of ironic bravado over the failed aspirations of a fiftyish BOURGEOIS businessman . . . . Director Claude Sautet, like Hollywood's Paul Mazursky, likes to dissect the sagging BOURGEOISIE . . . . (Maureen Orth, Review, *Newsweek*, 3/29/76, pp. 94–95)

7. See (1) under HORTATORY.

8. See (1) under ABSTEMIOUS.

9. See (1) under PUERILE.

10. See (3) under EXPURGATE.

11. In one of his rare public announcements, [Saul] Bellow has ranked himself among the "large-public writers"—those who voice social concerns and write for a general readership—as distinguished from such "small-public" writers as Eliot, Pound, Joyce and Proust who wrote within the late nineteenth-century romantic tradition of opposing and defying the BOURGEOISIE. (W. Clemons and Chris J. Harper, "Bellow the Word King," *Newsweek*, 11/1/76, p. 89)

12. See (8) under ATAVISTIC.

13. See (2) under POETASTER.

14. See (5) under AGITPROP.

15. See (3) under FIN DE SIÈCLE.

16. See (8) under MORES.

BOWDLERIZE (bōd' lə-rīz') *verb* to EXPURGATE (a play, novel, etc.) prudishly by omitting passages considered indecent, immodest, or offensive [after *Thomas Bowdler (1754-1825)*, English editor of an EXPURGATED edition of Shakespeare].

BOWDLERISM (also BOWDLERIZATION) *noun.*

1. . . . it was much better in the original than in the BOWDLERIZED form. (W.F. Buckley Jr.,

Execution Eve and Other Contemporary Ballads, G.P. Putnam's Sons, 1975, p. 348)

2. [In Heaven] I want every book that was ever written and every magazine that was ever issued stacked out on Cloud Nine for my exclusive use . . . . No EXPURGATED books, no BOWDLERIZED literature. (H.A. Smith, "My requirements of Heaven,"* *New York Times*, 3/14/76, Section 6, p. 111)

3. Shelley translated a play by Euripides . . . . *Cyclops* (BOWDLERIZED at that), and Browning produced a sentimental TRAVESTY of the *Alcestis* and a typically eccentric version of the *Agamemnon*. But these two poet-translators are the exception: for the whole of the eighteenth and nineteenth centuries the Greekless reader saw Attic tragedy through the distorting spectacles of verse written by scholars whose acute perception of the nuances of ancient Greek was exactly matched by their crass insensitivity to the sound and sense patterns of English. (B.M.W. Knox, Review of *Aeschylus: Suppliants*, translated by Janet Lambke; *Aeschylus: Seven Against Thebes*, translated by Helen Bacon and Anthony Hecht; and *Aeschylus: Prometheus Bound*, translated by J. Scully and C.J. Herington, *New York Review of Books*, 11/27/75, p. 27)

4. The last chapter of [Terry] Southern's *The Magic Christian* was cut and BOWDLERIZED by Random House . . . here is what Mr. [J.] Klinkowitz makes of that story [in *Literary Disruptions*]: "That Terry Southern never developed into a major fictionist, and that the black humor movement itself never rose above its own sick jokes, may be ascribed to this castration of the movement's major text." (G. Levine, Review, *Chronicle of Higher Education*, 4/26/76, p. 20)

5. Speaking of the Bicentennial, we are disturbed to learn of a BOWDLERIZED version of the lyrics to "Yankee Doodle," in a children's book published by Parents' Magazine Press. The altered lyric goes "with the *folks* be handy," instead of "with the *girls* be handy" . . . . The Parents' Magazine Press editors decreed that the original version was "sexist." (Anon., "Oddments," *New York Times*, 4/18/76, Section 7, p. 33)

_____
*Smith died a few days after completing this article.

6. Beginning with the University of Chicago series of [classical Greek] tragedy translations . . . there has been widespread effort to produce accessible, exciting versions of those works which have been available to the Greekless English reader only in stilted or even BOWDLERIZED Victorian language. (D. Lenson, "Can the furtherance of poetry become a more common cause?" *Chronicle of Higher Education*, 4/5/76, p. 20)

7. . . . when one reads an Agnew sex scene [in his book, *The Canfield Decision*] ("His hands were busy, as though reading her body Braille. . . she was carried in crashing waves over the falls and deposited in the tranquil pool of slaked desire"), one might almost wish Agnew had been successful in his vigorous campaign to have all literature BOWDLERIZED. (D. Shaw, Of *Los Angeles Times*, Review, reprinted in *Norman* [Okla.] *Transcript*, 5/23/76, p. 17)

8. . . . the imperial censors of Czarist Russia have their Soviet counterparts. And Soviet editors . . . have BOWDLERIZED Chekhov's correspondence. An incorrect political opinion or a sexual reference— prudery and repression going hand in hand—is expunged from the test or given the usual three-dot treatment. (H. Moss, Review of *A New Life of Anton Chekhov*, by Ronald Hingley, *New York Times*, 6/20/76, Section 7, p. 28)

9. When leaks embarrass, the first official cry is that national security has been compromised. On the record of the past few years, this charge simply will not wash. Too much has been stamped confidential in order to conceal hanky-panky and ineptitude, not secrets. Even the celebrated 47 volumes of the Pentagon papers contained, as a Pentagon official admitted, "only 27 pages that gave us real trouble"— and these came to not much. In Daniel Schorr's case, *Village Voice* readers must have nodded over the congressional committee's TENDENTIOUS MAUNDERINGS that Schorr published and its few carefully BOWDLERIZED CIA documents. (T. Griffith, "Plumbing the Real World of Leaks," *Time*, 3/29/76, p. 65)

10. See (3) under GEMÜTLICH.

11. . . . Mr. [Michael] Collins [author of the book, *Flying to the Moon*], like many adults, is

not sure how much of the truth to tell children. When he is in doubt . . . he BOWDLERIZES and edits heavily. (J. Levy, Review, *New York Times*, 2/27/77, Section 7, p. 12)

BRATTLE (brat′əl) *noun* a clattering or rattling noise.

BRATTLE *verb* to clatter or rattle; to scamper noisily.

1. By reputation, [Fresco] Thompson was a wit and he proceeded to fill the morning with a BRATTLE of baseball stories. His voice grated, not unpleasantly, as an anvil moving over firebrick. (R. Kahn, *The Boys of Summer*, Harper and Row, 1971, p. 8)

BRAVURA (brə-vyōōr′ə) *noun* a display of daring; brilliant performance; dash; (in music) a florid passage or piece requiring great skill and spirit in the performer.

BRAVURA *adj.* characterized by bravura.

1. See (1) under AUTO-DA-FÉ.

2. *The Buenos Aires Affair* [by Manuel Puig, translated by Suzanne Jill Levine], his [Puig's] third novel, is . . . a sustained BRAVURA performance by a writer keenly conscious of how . . . the novel as a literary form . . . [has] been caught up in the clichés of popular culture, especially in its Hollywood versions. (R. Alter, Review, *New York Times*, 9/5/76, Section 7, p. 4)

3. The book [*The Education of Patrick Silver*, by Jerome Charyn] . . . has a lilt to it, but the lilt ends up cavorting solo. This effect must be accountable in part to the smallness of the story the book has to tell; the linguistic BRAVURA exists as if to buck a weak plot . . . . (R.P. Brickner, Review, *New York Times*, 9/5/76, Section 7, p. 17)

4. See (3) under NYMPHET.

BRIO (brē′ō) *noun* animation; vivacity; zest.

CON BRIO (kon brē′ō, kōn brē′ō) with vigor or spirit; spiritedly; vivaciously (used as a musical direction).

1. Only Barbra Streisand . . . can GALVANIZE

an audience by showing off the sort of BRIO that made the talented excesses of an Eleanor Powell or James Cagney so infectious. (C. Michener, M. Kasindorf, "Old Movies Come Alive," *Newsweek*, 5/31/76, p. 54)

2. It's an original novel called *The Titans*, latest in John Jake's saga of the progress of one family—the Kents—through 200 years of United States History . . . . With *The Titans* Jakes gets the family halfway through the Civil War. . . . At heart, a history teacher with BRIO, he's now holed up in the basement of his Dayton, Ohio, home doing the extensive research . . . necessary for *The Warriors*, which will carry the tale through Appomattox. (Anon., "Paper Back Talk," *New York Times*, 6/20/76, Section 7, p. 35)

3. Once one accepts the limitations of the director's concept, there is nothing to fault in the BRIO of the cast [of the Royal Shakespeare Company's production of *Henry V*], the racehorse pace or the sense of battle-weary valor conveyed. (T. E. Kalem, Review, *Time*, 5/3/76, p. 75)

4. See (1) under KEEN.

BROBDINGNAGIAN (brob′ ding-nag′ ē-ən) *adj.* of huge size; gigantic [after *Brobdingnag*, a land of giants about 60 feet tall in Jonathan Swift's satire, *Gulliver's Travels* (1726).

1. Though they [1977 Cadillac] are also 3.5 in. narrower, their headlights are positioned farther apart to make them look as wide as ever. Standard engines are no bigger than 425 cu. in., in lieu of the BROBDINGNAGIAN 500 cu. in. of 1976. (Anon., "For '77, An Amazing Shrinking Act, *Time*, 9/13/76, p. 46)

2. The long facade [of the National Gallery's East Wing] on the north, or Pennsylvania Avenue side—a typical Washington BROBDINGNAGIAN expanse of 360 feet—is set back at ground level in a gesture toward human scale that breaks the capital's customary totalitarian-scaled wall. (Ada Louise Huxtable, "A Spectacular Museum Goes Up in Washington," *New York Times*, 5/22/77, Section 2, p. 29)

BROUHAHA (brōō-hä′ hä, brōō′ hä-hä′)

noun excited public interest, discussion, or the like, as the clamor attending some sensational event; a minor episode involving excitement, confusion, etc.; a noisy stir or wrangle; hubbub; uproar; commotion.

1. For some time books have arrived, heralded by extra-literary BROUHAHA, so the story about the book is fastened in the public's memory long after the book itself has disappeared. (Doris Grumbach, "Spring Prospects: A Blend of Self-Help and Self-Righteousness [Review of forthcoming books], *Change*, April 1976, p. 48)

2. . . . the candidates' wives, children, and in-laws spiritedly doing their thing on behalf of numerous . . . smiling . . . issue- skimming hopefuls [running for political office] are likely to be dismissed with the rest of the BROUHAHA by serious-minded European commentators as vulgar and wasteful. (Viola Drath, "A European opinion: U.S. elections too much like a circus," *Chicago Tribune*, 5/6/76, Section 2, p. 4)

3. . . . this [J. D. O'Hara's *A History of Poetry*] conveys the clear impression that Berryman was a confused character who lost his head . . . because of the example of a stronger poet, Lowell, and the critical BROUHAHA that Lowell's developing career provoked . . . this . . . is not at all the figure that emerges from the volume of Berryman's erstwhile un-collected essays and reviews and stories [*The Freedom of the Poet*]. (D. Davie, Review, *New York Times*, 4/25/76, Section 7, p. 3)

4. Is the Soviet military ogre growing to be 10 feet tall . . . ? Or is it possible that he is not growing at all, and that the recent BROUHAHA over increased Russian defense spending is nothing more than gross misrepresentation by American militarists . . . ? (Anon., *The London Economist*, "Aspin, CIA clash over estimates: Soviet defense costs exceed estimate," reprinted in *Norman* [Okla.] *Transcript*, 5/18/76, p. 6)

5. See (3) under AUGUR.

6. Daniel Schorr's book on his CBS-CIA BROUHAHA will be entitled *Final Assignment*. (Which it turned out to be.) (J. X. Dever, "In Focus," *Evening Bulletin*, Philadelphia, Pa., 2/16/77, p. 44)

BRUMMAGEM (brum'ə-jəm) *adj.* gaudy, cheap, and inferior.

BRUMMAGEM *noun* a showy but inferior and worthless thing, especially imitation costume jewelry.

1. But advanced Western civilization is vulnerable. A brief power failure can create chaos. A political miscalculation can be catastrophic. An external attack, ordered, it may be, by some BRUMMAGEM mind from the steppes or from Central Asia, could bring the entire thing to an end, turn it into a twisted mass of horror. (J. Hart, "Jet Plane As Symbol," *Times Herald*, Norristown, Pa., 5/13/77, p. 17)

BUCCAL (buk'əl) *adj.* of or relating to the cheek, the sides of the mouth, or the mouth cavity itself; oral.

BUCCALLY *adv.*

1. "You are a good person," he [Dr. Needles] said, greeting me in his old cardigan. "And these," he said, smiling delightedly into the BUCCAL cavity, "are good teeth." (R. Baker, "Imperial Dentistry," *New York Times*, 5/22/77, Section 6, p. 10)

BUCOLIC (byoo-kol'ik) or **BUCOLICAL** *adj.* of or pertaining to shepherds; pastoral; of pertaining to, or suggesting an idyllic rural life; rustic; rural.

BUCOLICALLY *adv.*

1. At the door of the new house [of Buford Coker] stood Fat Laura, a Virginia woman in her late twenties and obviously a graduate of Ida Hamilton's academy. In her teens she must have been pretty in the buxom, BUCOLIC way that cowboys appreciated, but ten years of hard life and constant movement from one brothel to the next could not be disguised, and the accumulation of forty pounds . . . had made her a slattern. (J. A. Michener, *Centennial*, Fawcett, 1975, p. 702)

2. Only David Smith and Alexander Calder are allowed to show something of their true strength and variety, but then the David Smith area of the exhibition [*200 Years of American Sculpture*, at the Whitney Museum of American Art] is stupidly disfigured by . . . a

huge, curved, blurry color-photo-mural of a landscape employed as a backdrop . . . . I suppose, to remind us . . . that Smith lived and worked much of the time in a BUCOLIC setting in upstate New York. (H. Kramer, Review, *New York Times*, 3/28/76, Section 2, p. 34)

3. Few American generations have ever celebrated life with the enthusiasm of New Yorkers in the 1840s and 1850s. Theirs was an age that captured the fancy of an entire nation by introducing Fifth Avenue mansions, expensive Paris ball gowns, reckless Wall Street speculations, French cuisine and many more extravagances to a still mostly BUCOLIC country. (C. Lockwood, "As near to paradise as one can reach in Brooklyn, N.Y.," *Smithsonian*, April 1976, p. 56)

4. Our community in western Massachusetts would seem to be ideal—800 or so, a village green . . . . We are near a five-college area that provides as much cultural life as we can stand . . . . What could ruin such a BUCOLIC existence? The local utilities company, which has purchased 1,900 acres of land to build a nuclear reactor just outside my backyard. (Beverly Adler, Letter to WRAPAROUND editor, *Harper's*, January 1975, p. 95)

BULIMIA (byōō-lim′ ē-ə) *noun* an abnormally voracious appetite; a continuous, abnormal hunger; a disease in which the patient has an insatiable appetite for food.

BULIMIC *adj.*

1. The record for a BULIMIA victim (a pathological eater), you'll learn [from the *Guinness Book of World Records*], is 384 pounds 2 ounces of food in six days; the champion was 12-year-old Matthew Daking, who ate his way to fame in 1743. (D. Carlinsky, "Something to be thankful for . . . urp, ah, relief," *Times-Union*, Albany, N.Y., 11/25/75, Section 5, p. 9)

BUMPTIOUS (bump′ shəs) *adj.* offensively self-assertive; disagreeably or excessively conceited, arrogant, or forward.

BUMPTIOUSLY *adv.*

BUMPTIOUSNESS *noun.*

1. See (1) under SUPERCILIOUS

2. See (1) under LILLIPUTIAN.

3. The outburst [by Willy Brandt, upon the publication of *The Other German: Willy Brandt's Life & Times*, by David Binder] tells something of the problem of leading the S.P.D. [Socialist Democratic Party], with its FRACTIOUS OLIGARCHS and BUMPTIOUS young Left. But it also tells something about the problem of being Willy Brandt, (D. Schoenbaum, Review, *New York Times* 3/7/76, Section 7, p. 20)

BURGEON (bûr′ jən) *verb* to grow or develop suddenly; to expand quickly; flourish; proliferate.

1. They [the Washburns] made their Manhattan home in a duplex in Sutton Place. The likely amount of Washburn's money continued to BURGEON in my [Russel Wren's] fancy. (Thomas Berger, *Who Is Teddy Villanova?*, Delacorte Press/Seymour Lawrence, 1977, p. 157)

BYZANTINE (biz′ ən-tēn, -tĭn) *adj.* of or pertaining to Byzantium or the Byzantine Empire; noting or pertaining to the architecture of that empire and to architecture influenced by it: characterized by masonry construction, round arches, and low domes over square areas, elaborate mosaics, etc.; (in Fine Arts) designating the style of the above empire, characterized by a highly formal structure, the use of rich colors, especially gold, and emphasis on religious symbolism.

1. Secretary of Defense Donald Rumsfeld and longtime Ford crony Melvin R. Laird are vigorously anti-[John] Connally. So is Connally's fellow Texan, Sen. John Tower, who has been the most steadfast of Ford supporters among conservative Republicans. Beyond such personal dislikes and BYZANTINE rivalries, the President is given concrete arguments against a Ford-Connally ticket. (R. Evans, R. Novak, "Connally Deaf to Ford Wooing," *Daily Oklahoman*, Okla. City, 4/15/76, p. 12)

2. Robert Maheu, the ex-aide who fell out bitterly with [Howard] Hughes, has charged that Hughes instructed him in the early 1960s to set up a link between HAC [Hughes Aircraft Co.] and the CIA so that Hughes could blackmail

the government if it chose to scrutinize his tax and antitrust problems too closely. But the truth seems to be that the connection is far older and less BYZANTINE. (T. Mathews, et al., "The Secret World of Howard Hughes," Newsweek, 4/19/76, p. 34)

3. See (1) under MAGDALENE.

C

CABAL (kə-bal′) noun a small group of plotters, especially against a government; junta; the plottings or intrigues of such a group; a clique; conspiracy; plot.

CABAL verb to form a cabal; to conspire or plot; to join in a cabal.

1. See (1) under FORFEND.

2. See (1) under CABALA.

3. . . . Juan Carlos in the next few months must make some modest gains toward liberalization [in Spain]—hard to achieve with an ultra-right government, but necessary if he is to become a plausible leader of the Spanish people and not merely a front for the repressive CABAL that Franco gathered around himself in order to hang on to absolute power until the last moment. (Barbara Probst Solomon, "Spain on the Brink," New York Review of Books, 11/27/75, p. 22)

4. See (3) under EXPURGATE.

CABALA (kab′ə-lə, kə-bäl′ə) or **KABALA** or **KABBALA** or **CABBALA** noun any occult or secret doctrine or science; an occult religious philosophy developed by certain Jewish rabbis, especially in the Middle Ages, based on a mystical interpretation of the Scriptures; any esoteric doctrine; occultism.

CABALISM noun occult doctrine based on the cabala; any occult doctrine.

CABALIST noun.

CABALISTIC or **CABALISTICAL** adj.

CABALISTICALLY adv.

1. . . . recent [poetic] criticism has altitudinously aggrandized itself with lofty claims that are preposterous (a word which means "before-behind") and snug in its new haven it is all too at home not only with KABBALAH [reference to a book, Kabbalah and Criticism, by Harold Bloom] but also with CABAL. (C. Ricks, Review of Revisionism from Blake to Stevens, by Harold Bloom, New York Times, 3/14/76, Section 7, p. 6)

2. See (1) under SENTIENCE.

CABRIOLE (kab′ rē-ōl) noun a leap in ballet in which one leg is extended horizontally and the feet are struck quickly together; a leg of a table, chair, etc. that curves outward and then tapers inward down to a clawlike foot grasping a ball.

1. He [Mikhail Baryshnikov, in Eliot Feld's ballet, Variations on "America"] . . . rocketed through the air in flashing CABRIOLES that made the audience gasp. (Joan Downs, Review, Time, 3/21/77, p. 88)

CACHET (ka-shā′, kash′ā) noun an official seal or stamp, as on a letter or document; a distinguishing mark or feature; a sign or expression of approval or distinction, especially from someone of great prestige or authority; a mark or sign showing something is genuine, authentic, or of superior quality; prestige; high standing; a slogan, design, etc. stamped or printed on an envelope or folded letter, often as a part of the cancellation.

1. The producers of the joyously lilting, light-footed lark [Very Good Eddie] have had the

good sense . . . not to try to update the book and its jokes. We don't want PASTICHE, we want to know what the original was like . . . . Most of the time the 1915 humors, simple as they are apt to be, have their own CACHET. (W. Kerr, Review, *New York Times*, 1/4/76, Section 2, p. 5)

2. . . . this month [April, 1976] marks the 50th year of existence of the Book-of-the-Month Club . . . . BOMC was the brain-child of . . . Harry Scherman . . . . Mr. Scherman's innovation . . . was to promote new books . . . by hiring a panel of distinguished judges to give a CACHET of literary quality to the selections. (Anon., "Book Ends: BOMC," *New York Times*, 4/25/76, Section 7, p. 53)

3. [Robert] Redford—who plays newsman Bob Woodward in the film *All the President's Men*—has helped give journalists the CACHET of screen idols. (D. Gelman, "Jugular Journalism?" *Newsweek*, 5/10/76, p. 79)

4. Real CACHET is to procure an unreleased film [for home screening]. Often, the stellar social event of the week is a producer's first screening of his new movie . . . . (D. Gelman, Janet Huck, "Picture Parlors," *Newsweek*, 9/13/76, p. 88)

5. Recently, she [photographer Deborah Turbeville] has done ads for designer Calvin Klein, Andrew Geller shoes and Saga Mink, and has given an instant CACHET to New York's huge Barney's department store by photographing its catalog . . . . She chafed against the restrictions imposed by Barney's . . . . (Maureen Orth, *et al.*, "Fashion's Kinky Look," *Newsweek*, 10/4/76, p. 99)

6. He [K. P. Murdoch] had already taken over the afternoon New York Post . . . from the aging hands of 73-year-old Dorothy Schiff. Felker's group [of magazines—New York, New West, Village Voice] . . . would round out the enterprise and underline Murdoch's commitment. "It will give us a little CACHET," he said . . . . (D. Gelman, *et al.*, "Press Lord Captures Gotham," *Newsweek*, 1/17/77, pp. 48–49)

7. See (4) under MÉNAGE.

8. Many hamburgers are made from portions of the cow that the cow had no reason to boast about. So sellers invent distracting names to give hamburgers CACHET. Hence "Whoppers"

and "Heroburgers." (G. F. Will, "Forget the 'Nutty Buddy,' vanilla will do," *Philadelphia Inquirer*, 5/10/77, p. 13-A)

CACHINNATE (kak' ə-nāt') *verb*   to laugh loudly, immoderately, or excessively.

CACHINNATION *noun.*

1. These early [silent] movies are the funniest part of the huge festival of *American Film Comedy* that will turn New York's Museum of Modern Art into a cathedral of CACHINNATION from now until next January. From the first PRIMEVAL Edison shorts, which isolated a sneeze as an epic EPIPHANY of laughter, to the deranged PASTICHES of Woody Allen and Mel Brooks, the museum's show will provide more than 400 examples of madness, PARODY, satire, wit and humor . . . . (J. Kroll, Review, *Newsweek*, 5/31/76, p. 52)

CACOPHONY (kə-kof' ə-nē) *noun*   harsh, jarring, discordant sound; DISSONANCE, a discordant and meaningless mixture of different sounds.

CACOPHONOUS or CACOPHONIC *adj.*

CACOPHONOUSLY or CACOPHONICALLY *adv.*

1. Disenchantment [with Walter O'Malley] struck after my story about the [Junior] Gilliam affair. The phrase I had heard, "How would you like a nigger to take your job?" was, O'Malley insisted, the same as "another Jewish judge," CACOPHONY piped by unchosen lawyers in courthouse smoke rooms. "It's rude, but doesn't mean much," O'Malley said . . . . (R. Kahn, *The Boys of Summer*, Harper and Row, 1971, pp. 423–424)

2. We are now witnessing the quiet, steady intellectual reevaluation of black American communities, generated in part by the heady, CACOPHONOUS days of the late 1960's. (K. Jackson Jr., Review of *Black Consciousness, Identity and Achievement: A Study of Students in Historically Black Colleges*, by Patricia Gurin and Edgar G. Epps, *Change*, February 1976, p. 63)

3. Miss Moorman plays Paik's unique "TV Cello," an electronic instrument capable of CACOPHONIC sound . . . . (B. Forgey, "Art transition is still in transition," *Smithsonian*, March 1976, p. 89)

4. The Ahwanee [Hotel] is really a 50-year old slagpile of stained cement (to simulate timbers) . . . and paper-thin walls. The plumbing at 8 o'clock in the morning is CACOPHONOUS. (M. Olderman, "Yosemite's slagpile with a view," *Norman* [Okla.] *Transcript*, 4/14/76, p. 6)

5. The lights in the Federal courtroom dimmed and a small movie screen near the judge's bench flickered to life. On film, a nude trio—two women and a man—writhed on a motel-room bed amid a CACOPHONY of dubbed moans. (Merrill Sheils, A. Marro, "The Memphis Smut Raker," *Newsweek*, 4/5/76, p. 62)

6. [Caption under a cartoon:] Convention CACOPHONY [of Democratic Party in 1924] was kidded in Berryman cartoon. (R. K. Murray, "The Democrats vs. Frustration City: it was no mix," *Smithsonian*, April 1976, p. 52)

7. [Basil] Cottle . . . draws on his extensive knowledge of the language and of current usage throughout England to argue [in *The Plight of English*] that ambiguity, CACOPHONY, and violations of style and taste are undermining the effectiveness of the language. (J. J. Pappas, Review, *Chronicle of Higher Education*, 5/17/76, p. 13)

8. A CACOPHONY of excited barking announced the arrival of the MFH [Master Fox Huntsman] and his canine entourage. (Barbara Michaels, *Prince of Darkness*, Meredith Press, 1969, pp. 89–90)

9. See (1) under CACOSCOPIC.

10. See (7) under KEEN.

11. I [Russel Wren] was summoned to enter by a score of small forearms . . . , while the ear was smote with the shrieking CACOPHONY in which bluejays couch their peeves. (Thomas Berger, *Who Is Teddy Villanova?*, Delacorte Press/Seymour Lawrence, 1977, p. 192)

12. On the obverse was printed the name of a business (characteristic of CACOPHONOUS New York: Nedick's, Gristede's, Bohack) . . . . (Thomas Berger, *Ibid.*, p. 103)

CACOSCOPIC (kaḱ ə-skôṕ ĭk) *adj.* possibly a neologism whose meaning obviously is: harsh on the eyes; unpleasant to look at.

1. The above paragraph may seem to you to be a very CACOPHONOUS piece of writing (CACO-

SCOPIC really) if you read it only with your eye. Read it aloud and you will find that it sounds like human speech and is not unmelodious. (A. Burgess, "A Shrivel of Critics," *Harper's* February 1977, p. 87)

CADAVEROUS (kə-dav́ ər-əs) *adj.* of or like a corpse or cadaver; pale, wan or ghastly; haggard and thin.

CADAVEROUSLY *adv.*

CADAVEROUSNESS *noun.*

1. Shively glared down at her [Sharon Fields], and his CADAVEROUS face was forbidding. (I. Wallace, *The Fan Club*, Bantam Books, 1975, p. 241)

2. See (2) under PEDAGOGY.

CADGE (kaj) *verb* to obtain by imposing on another's generosity or friendship; to borrow without intent to repay; to beg, sponge, or get by begging or sponging; to fleece; to ask, expect, or encourage another to pay for or provide one's drinks, meals, etc.; to hawk or peddle.

CADGER (kaj́ ər) *noun* an itinerant huckster or truck peddler; one who makes his living by trickery; a beggar; a sponger.

1. [Larry] MacPhail was gutty and brilliant and he rebuilt the [Brooklyn baseball] team with remarkable trades and with monies CADGED from the Brooklyn Trust Company. (R. Kahn, *The Boys of Summer*, Harper and Row, 1971, p. 37)

2. Pasquinel therefore moved from one French license holder [for conducting the fur trade in St. Louis] to the next, trying to CADGE money to outfit his next [trapping] expedition. (J. A. Michener, *Centennial*, Fawcett, 1975, p. 223)

3. They formed a pitiful brigade, plodding along in the dust raised by the thousands who were riding west. They CADGED food where they could, cut timber for other travelers . . . and helped wagons across the Big Blue [River] . . . . (J. A. Michener, *Ibid.*, p. 460)

4. . . . not long ago a Congressman from Michigan found himself without a cent in an airport and had to CADGE money from one of his astonished constituents in order to call home . . . (J. K. Page, Jr., "Phenomena, comments and notes," *Smithsonian*, April 1976, p. 10)

5. The "super bowl" primaries in California, Ohio and New Jersey resulted pretty much in a draw between Jerry Ford and Ronald Reagan. From now on it will be a matter of skillful CADGING in the few remaining states whose delegates to the Republican convention will be decided by district convention and caucus. (J. Chamberlain, "Ford, Reagan Hunt Crucial," *Daily Oklahoman*, Okla. City, 6/16/76, p. 6)

6. See (5) under RIPOSTE.

CALIBAN (kal′ ə-ban′) *noun* an ugly, beastlike person (after *Caliban*, a deformed savage creature, the slave of Prospero, in Shakespeare's *The Tempest*); a man showing brutal and bestial characteristics.

1. Those men . . . [comics of the silent screen] were walking, whirling paradoxes—elegant grotesques, delicate brutes, CALIBANS and Ariels in one overcrowded flesh. The QUINTESSENCE of such hybrids was Fatty Arbuckle, a somewhat disquieting alloy of bully and hero, a pachyderm who moved with a floating grace . . . . (J. Kroll, Review of *American Film Comedy*, at the Museum of Modern Art, *Newsweek*, 5/31/76, p. 52)

CALLIGRAPHY (kə-lig′rə-fē) *noun* beautiful handwriting; fine penmanship; handwriting or penmanship, especially highly decorative handwriting, as with a great many flourishes; the art of writing beautifully.

CALLIGRAPHER or CALLIGRAPHIST *noun.*

CALLIGRAPHIC *adj.*

CALLIGRAPHICALLY *adv.*

1. In the White House workrooms, the staff labored overtime, performing tasks for both the outgoing Fords and the incoming Carters. CALLIGRAPHER John Scarfone turned out photographs inscribed with Ford's signature and reception invitations with Carter's name. (Bonnie Angelo, "It's Just Citizen Ford Now," *Time*, 1/31/77, p. 20)

2. Eleventh-century Kyoto [Japan] doted on festivals and form. The CALLIGRAPHY of a poem was as important as the content, not to mention the quality and scent of the paper used. (F. B. Gibney, Review of the book, *The Tale of Genji*, by Murasaki Shikibu, translated by Ed-

ward G. Seidensticker, *New York Times*, 12/19/76, Section 7, p. 8)

CALLIPYGIAN (kal′ ə-pij′ ē-ən) *adj.* having shapely buttocks.

1. Something doesn't work about *Loose Change* [a book by Sara Davidson] . . . . Ms. Davidson's writing has no core . . . . There is no perspective . . . what is lacking . . . is self-humor . . . . Instead we know how tall Sara is, how long Tasha's white-blond hair is, and the CALLIPYGIAN qualities of Susie. (Lisa Schwarzbaum, Review, *National Observer*, 7/11/77, p. 19)

CALLOW (kal′ ō) *adj.* young; immature; inexperienced.

CALLOWNESS *noun.*

1. Most of us were told at an early age that money isn't really interesting—and most of us, with CALLOW common sense, instantly rejected the HOMILY as so much PHARISAICAL cant. (P. S. Prescott, Review of *The Rockefellers*, by Peter Collier and David Horowitz; and of *The Rockefeller Syndrome*, by Ferdinand Lundberg, *Newsweek*, 4/5/76, p. 81A)

CALUMET (kal′yə-met) *noun* a long-stemmed, ornamented tobacco pipe used by North American Indians on ceremonial occasions, especially as a token of peace; peace pipe.

1. On New Year's Day 1797, Pasquinel reappeared at the Pawnee village to settle affairs with Chief Rude Water: . . . A CALUMET was smoked, and he told Rude Water, "Last year we fight . . . . This year we friends." Again the CALUMET was smoked, and Pasquinel concluded the deal: "I come back, I give you one [beaver] pelt in five." (J. A. Michener, *Centennial*, Fawcett, 1975, p. 224)

CALUMNY (kal′ əm-nē) *noun* a false and malicious statement designed to injure the reputation of someone or something; slander; defamation.

CALUMNIATE (kə-lum′ nē-āt′) *verb* to make false and malicious statements about; slander.

CALUMNIATOR *noun.*

CALUMNIATION *noun* the act of calumniating; slander; calumny.

CALUMNIOUS *adj.*

CALUMNIOUSLY *adv.*

1. The single most useful section of the book [*Who the Hell Is William Loeb?*] by Kevin Cash] is a six-page glossary of Loeb's attacks on political figures. This LITANY of CALUMNY is required because, in his day-in, day-out prose, Loeb sates the imagination and dulls the senses, including outrage. (M. F. Nolan, Review, *New York Times*, 2/20/76, Section 7, p. 6)

2. The CALUMNY Mr. Harriman attempted to pin on Mr. Rockefeller was that he would permit the Transit Authority to . . . raise the fares. But raising subway fares is politically explosive business, which is why Mr. Rockefeller went to infinite pains to express himself as horrified at the very thought of such a thing. (W. F. Buckley Jr., *Up From Liberalism*, Arlington House, 2nd Printing 1968, p. 162)

3. *The Sower*, 1850, was greeted by one conservative [contemporary critic] as an insult to the dignity of work: "I regret that M. [Jean François] Millet so CALUMNIATES the sower," he wrote, disturbed by the faceless and inexplicably menacing colossus striding down the dark hill. (R. Hughes, Review of Millet's centenary exhibition at London's Hayward Gallery, *Time*, 2/23/76, p. 60)

4. Certainly [Secretary of Agriculture Earl] Butz's CALUMNY against blacks [in the ethnic "joke" which caused him to resign] . . . was outrageous, if taken seriously. In fact, not a single individual I have met does take [it] seriously—except when writing rather pompous editorials about the incident. (J. Hart, "Butz's 'Goof,'" *Times Herald*, Norristown, Pa., 10/12/76, p. 11)

5. Train driver Chen Fu-han claimed that the radicals [the four arrested for plotting to depose Chairman Hua Kuo-feng] had hurled CALUMNIES at late Premier Chou En-lai, a political moderate, and that they had forged charges against other leaders. (Inquirer Wire Services, "1 million cheer Hua in Peking," *Philadelphia Inquirer*, 10/25/76, p. 4-A)

CAMP (kamp) *noun* a BANALITY, mediocrity, artifice, ostentation, gesture, style, or form so extreme, PRETENTIOUS, or exaggerated as to amuse or have a perversely sophisticated appeal; a person or his works displaying such characteristics.

CAMP *verb* to act in an amusing PRETENTIOUS way; to perform or imbue (something) with such PRETENTIOUSNESS; to make an ostentatious or FLAMBOYANT display, often in self-PARODY.

CAMPY *adj.* characterized by camp; homosexual.

1. This approach [that used at the Whitney Museum's exhibit of *200 Years of American Sculpture*] may serve a taste for CAMP, a taste for academic BANALITY, or a taste for the lost ideals of civic rectitude—all of them, in the end, a taste for nostalgia—but it certainly does not serve a taste for sculptural excellence. (H. Kramer, Review, *New York Times*, 3/28/76, Section 2, p. 34)

2. See (2) under SCHLOCK.

3. Success-religion was morally productive in its resistance to drift and its nourishment of faith in destination: God died but intentionality survived—a purposefulness stern enough . . . to bear burdens of social responsibility without absurdist CAMP or mugging. Whether equal burdens can be borne by life-experimenters as connoisseurs, as motherhusbands, as wifefathers, as PICARESQUE adventurers is unclear. (B. De Mott, "Beyond the Dream of Success," *Change*, August 1976, p. 37)

4. See (1) under PROGENITOR.

5. See (3) under HALCYON.

6. See (2) under INORDINATE.

CANARD (kə-närd') *noun* a false report, story, or rumor, usually derogatory; hoax.

1. Word is brought to his [Charles Lamont's] bedside [in the TV show, *The Edge of Night*] by his best friend Bruce Sterling that Lamont's wife is being accused by a rapist named Logan of seducing him . . . . Lamont's eyes squinch and his expression seems to say, "Foul CANARD." (K. Kelly, "A drama critic works up lather over TV soaps," *Boston Globe*, 3/7/76, p. 12-A)

2. Actually, American will is remarkably constant. Vietnam utterly disproved the notion that the American people would not hang in

there for a long, . . . costly, confusing war . . . . American troops remain in Europe . . . . No amount of Mideast perversity seems to shake our determination to help our friends . . . . It should put to rest the CANARD that the American people are being conned into dropping their guard. . . . There is a very broad foreign policy consensus. (S. S. Rosenfeld, "U.S. foreign policy direction unclear: Soviets reach status of equality, *Norman* [Okla.] *Transcript,* 4/21/76, p. 6)

3. With Rubinstein, Horowitz and Richter still around, this is not exactly a poor age for the piano. But no need to fear the historians' old CANARD about each epoch of artistic plenty being followed by drought. The best of today's pianists are already being pressed by some younger challengers. (Anon., "Poet of the Piano," *Time,* 5/3/76, p. 60)

4. "Which," I [Russel Wren] added, "might have been no more than the typical vile CANARD a great man's lackeys circulate about his principal rival." (Thomas Berger, *Who Is Teddy Villanova?,* Delacorte Press/Seymour Lawrence, 1977, p. 187)

5. Now, the idea that homosexuals are bent on recruiting children is a CANARD. (F. G. Will, "How Far Out of the Closet?" *Newsweek,* 5/30/77, p. 92)

CANESCENT (kə-nes′ ənt) *adj.* becoming dull white or grayish.

CANESCENCE *noun* dull whiteness.

1. "I got one answer," said Sam [Polidor], grimacing and rubbing the bald spot on his crown, across which he futilely directed strands of the CANESCING hair, barbered long for perhaps that purpose, from his temples. (Thomas Berger, *Who Is Teddy Villanova?,* Delacorte Press/Seymour Lawrence, 1977, p. 23)

CAPTIOUS (kap′ shəs) *adj.* exaggerating trivial faults or defects; made only for the sake of argument or fault-finding; SOPHISTICAL; carping.

CAPTIOUSLY *adv.*

CAPTIOUSNESS *noun.*

1. Still, I don't want to end on a CAPTIOUS note. In this season of Bicentennial cant such a serious effort [as in Sacvan Bercovitch's book, *The Puritan Origins of the American Self*] to define the distinctiveness of our national self-image is a tonic for the mind and spirit. (L. Mark, Review, *New York Times,* 2/1/76, Section 7, p. 22)

2. Why does the author-editor [John Baskin] often sound CAPTIOUS and intrusive, and why the OBFUSCATING ambiguity of the introduction and prologue [of the book, *New Burlington*], instead of hard facts, since this is "history"? (L. Woiwode, Review, *New York Times,* 6/20/76, Section 7, p. 3)

CARAPACE (kar′ə-pās′) *noun* the horny protective covering over all or part of the back of certain animals, as the upper shell of the turtle, armadillo, crab, etc.

1. Both [William and Neaera, two characters in the book, *Turtle Diary,* by Russell Hoban] visit the London Zoo and independently reach the same conclusion: the sea turtles in the aquarium must be liberated and allowed to swim back to their breeding grounds in the Atlantic. Were this CARAPACE the whole story, *Turtle Diary* could pass as standard Disney scenario: unattached, eccentric adults involved in a QUIXOTIC caper because of their love for animals. William realizes that the turtle heist is "the sort of situation that would be ever so charming in a film . . . ." But he has a significant CAVIL: "That sort of film is only charming because they leave out so many details, and real life is all the details they leave out." (P. Gray, Review, *Time,* 2/16/76, p. 72)

2. . . . he [Ronald Beard] had first embraced her [Miriam] when she had been clad as a sergeant of the British auxiliary army. He had then recently become a civilian, and there was a mild PIQUANCY in the contrast of the new . . . softness of his clothes with the rough serge of hers. But, when her clothes were off, the excitement her body aroused was the greater for the lack of the allure of the stiff discarded CARAPACE. (A. Burgess, *Beard's Roman Women,* McGraw-Hill, 1976, p. 42)

3. "Operation Down Under," said Blackford [Oakes to Mrs. Wilson] in a semi-whisper, "is the mechanism that sinks the whole of central Washington underground, under an atomic-proof CARAPACE." (W.F. Buckley Jr., *Saving the Queen,* Doubleday, 1976, p. 43)

CARAVANSARY (kar′ ə-van′ sə-rē′) or **CARAVANSERAI** (kar′ ə-van′ sə-rī′, -sə-rā′)

noun (in the Orient) an inn, usually with a large courtyard, for the overnight accommodation of weary travelers.

CARAVANSERIAL (kar'ə-van-sēr'ē-əl) *adj.*

1. He [Panama's head of government, General Omar Torrijos] paused at one of [Fidel] Castro's CARAVANSERAIS . . . and a photographer . . . maneuvered him for a photograph . . . Torrijos . . . saw that he had been framed against a huge painted red sickle, his own brawny profile supplying the hammer. He was very wroth, . . . demanding, and then destroying the film (W. F. Buckley Jr., "The Panama Canal and Gen. Torrijos," *Evening Bulletin,* Philadelphia, Pa., 10/6/76, p. 19-A)

CARTE BLANCHE (kärt' blanSH', -blänSH') *noun, pl.:* **CARTES BLANCHES** (kärts' blanSH', -blänSH') unconditional authority; full discretionary power to do what one thinks best; a blank sheet of paper that is signed and given by the signer to another person to write in what he pleases.

1. She [Lee Radziwill] hopes . . . to take on varied [decorating] assignments, and her dream of a perfect client is someone who would give her CARTE BLANCHE. (Lisa Hammel, "Lee Radziwill as Decorator: A New Step, Confidently Taken," *New York Times,* 2/20/76, p. 29)

2. One [police] problem [in the book, *Everything Has Its Price,* by Hans Hellmut Kirst] becomes so big that Keller is given CARTE BLANCHE to handle it on his own, as the various heads of the police department hastily avert their eyes. (N. Callendar, Review, *New York Times,* 5/2/76, Section 7, p. 63)

CASSANDRA (kə-san' drə) *noun* (in Classical Mythology) a daughter of Priam and Hecuba, a prophetess cursed by Apollo so that her prophecies, though true, were fated never to be believed; a person who prophesies doom or disaster; a person whose warnings of misfortune are disregarded.

1. . . . one wonders if a zoologist present in Cretaceous times . . . would have known that it was the timid little protomammals . . . that had the future in their genes. Had he seen this, he might then have spent some of his time explaining to the dinosaurs that their particular game was in its ninth inning and he would have been branded a crazed CASSANDRA by the reptilian chamber of commerce. (Anon., "A special issue of *Smithsonian* as America's third century begins" [Editor's Introduction], *Smithsonian,* July 1976, p. 26)

2. Intimates who know him off-tube insist that [Gore] Vidal's public image as a CASSANDRA in drag is a mask protecting a sensitive, even self-sacrificial ally. . . . Says [actress Claire] Bloom, "He is capable of it [love], but he doesn't want others to know, I don't know why." (Anon., "Gore Vidal: Laughing Cassandra," *Time,* 3/1/76, p. 63)

3. [Maj. Gen. George J.] Keegan's case is that the Soviet Union is making massive preparations for a global nuclear war . . . . Such warnings have earned Keegan a reputation as a cold-war CASSANDRA. . . . Keegan believes the U.S. is now standing at the edge of disaster. (M. R. Benjamin and L. H. Norman, "Cassandra of the Cold War," *Newsweek,* 1/10/77, p. 24)

CASTELLATED (kas'tə-lā'tid) *adj.* having turrets and battlements like a castle; having many castles.

1. On July 29 [1844] the column approached that quiet and restful spot where the Laramie joins the Platte [River], and there in the distance . . . they saw the fort, . . . Fort John, a trading post with three towers, CASTELLATED ramparts and adobe walls. (J. A. Michener, *Centennial,* Fawcett, 1975, p. 392)

CASTIGATE (kas'tə-gāt') *verb* to punish in order to correct; to chastise, punish, criticize, rebuke, or reprove severely, especially in a harsh, public manner.

CASTIGATION *noun.*

CASTIGATOR *noun.*

CASTIGATORY (kas'tə-gə-tôr'ē) *adj.*

1. See (2) under VILIFY.

2. See (1) under WASSAIL.

3. Never has a soap stirred up so much lather . . . . an editorial in the Daytime Serial Newsletter, the soapers' Bible, CASTIGATED the show as "a continuing insult to the viewer." . . . Boston *Herald American* critic Anthony LeCamera . . . devoted four consecutive col-

umns to establishing that "there is something sick, sick and twisted, twisted about *Mary Hartman, Mary Hartman*." (H. F. Waters and M. Kasindorf, "The Mary Hartman Craze," *Newsweek,* 5/3/76, p. 54)

4. He [Gore Vidal] has CASTIGATED America as "the land of the dull and the home of the literal:" . . . Like many a gadfly before him, from Twain to Mencken, Vidal has won fame and wealth by biting the hand that feeds him. (Anon., "Gore Vidal: Laughing Cassandra," *Time,* 3/1/76, p. 61)

5. Shortly after CASTIGATING Americans for supporting the IRA, Prime Minister Wilson resigns, bitterly lamenting his failure to solve the Irish problem. (J. C. McGee, "Ireland is Britain's Vietnam," *Philadelphia Inquirer,* 9/15/76, p. 11-A)

6. See (3) under NADIR.

CASTRATO (käs-trät′ ō) *noun, pl.:* -TI (-ē) formerly, especially in the 18th century, a singer castrated as a boy to preserve the soprano or contralto range of his voice.

1. [The opera] *Griselda* was written [by Alessandro Scarlatti] for Rome at a time when women were not allowed to appear there on stage. So in 1721 it had an all-male cast—five CASTRATO principals . . . . In my experience, alto CASTRATO roles have been filled in our day by dashing female mezzos—Janet Baker, Marilyn Horne, Yvonne Milton. (A. Porter, Review of the opera *Griselda,* -as staged at Berkeley, California, *The New Yorker,* 5/31/76, p. 108)

CASUISTRY (kazh′ ōō-i-strē) *noun* application of general ethical principles to particular cases of conscience or conduct; subtle but fallacious, dishonest, or SPECIOUS application of such principles; SOPHISTRY.

CASUISTIC or CASUISTICAL *adj.* of or having to do with casuists; quibbling; SOPHISTICAL; SPECIOUS; intellectually dishonest.

CASUISTICALLY *adv.*

CASUIST *noun* a person expert in, or inclined to resort to, casuistry; an oversubtle or DISINGENUOUS reasoner.

1. 1. Plessy v. Ferguson, despite the CASUISTRY of its reasoning, was the law of the land [at

that time], and both Thurgood Marshall and judges felt compelled to try cases within the "separate but equal" doctrine. (R. Conot, Review of *Simple Justice,* a book by Richard Kluger, *New York Times,* 1/18/76, Section 7, p. 3)

CATACLYSM (kat′ ə-kliz′ əm) *noun* any violent upheaval or disaster causing sudden, sweeping, or violent changes, especially those of a social or political nature; a flood; deluge; a sudden and violent physical action, as an earthquake, producing changes in the earth's surface.

CATACLYSMIC or CATACLYSMAL *adj.*

CATACLYSMICALLY *adv.*

1. . . . CATACLYSMIC events are in store for the [Mary] Hartman folk. The show's architects are considering having sister Cathy embark on an affair with a local priest and her mother Martha could, according to one writer, "become involved with an older black gentleman." (H.F. Waters and M. Kasindorf, "The Mary Hartman Craze," *Newsweek,* 5/3/76, p. 62)

2. What CATACLYSMIC processes of mental evolution mutated the traditionalist wing of conservatism so that it suddenly began to hail the "Middle American" as the repository of all our culture's values, where only a few short years before it had denounced this same Middle American as the "mass man" who symbolized the erosion of the same values? (P. Rosenberg, Review of *The Conservative Intellectual Movement in America,* by George H. Nash, *New York Times,* 6/20/76, Section 7, p. 23)

3. Barring some totally unexpected event of a CATACLYSMIC nature, the next President of the United States will be Jimmy Carter, Gerald Ford or Ronald Reagan. That much seems assured five months before the election. (Anon., "Presidency Important, But . . ." [Editorial], *Daily Oklahoman,* Okla. City, 7/6/76, p. 12)

4. See (1) under MORES.

5. See (2) under SATURNALIA.

CATAFALQUE (kat′ ə-falk′, -fôk′, -fôlk′) *noun* a raised structure on which the coffin of a deceased person lies in state.

1. It was also the case with his [Jasper Johns′

rendition of] ale cans, paint brushes in an empty coffee tin, and the flashlight in its improvised CATAFALQUE. (J. Russell, Review of Jasper Johns' exhibit at Leo Castelli Gallery, *New York Times*, 2/1/76, Section 2, p. 31)

CATAMITE (kat'ə-mīt) *noun* a boy used in homosexual or PEDERASTIC activities.

1. Since September, though, many older, more respectable fellows have been strolling into Playland [the amusement arcade on Times Square between 42nd and 43rd St. in N.Y.C.]. Not skulking, the way such people do when they are sidling into the peep show or the porn movies that stand on either side of it, or when they make eye contact with the lurking CATAMITES . . . . They walk right in, as though they didn't have a single wicked thought in their heads . . . . They're going into Playland to play pinball for a while . . . . (T. Buckley, "Pinball goes electronic," *New York Times*, 1/23/77, Section 6, p. 30)

2. Mr. Simon [the Latin teacher] . . . had many years ago proposed to a lady in Latin and, on finding her response ungrammatical, resolved upon celibacy. Latin was his wife, and mistress, and CATAMITE. (W.F. Buckley Jr., *Saving the Queen*, Doubleday, 1976, p. 63)

3. He [Sir Edmund Backhouse] claimed to have known everyone and done everything. He knew Beardslee and Churchill, corresponded with Tolstoy . . . and was the contented CATAMITE of both Verlaine and Lord Rosebery. (P. Theroux, Review of *Hermit of Peking*, a book by Hugh Trevor-Roper, *New York Times*, 4/24/77, Section 7, p. 36)

4. I [Russel Wren] am immune to the lure of CATAMITES. In fact, I abhor children of either sex. (Thomas Berger, *Who Is Teddy Villanova?* Delacorte Press/Seymour Lawrence, 1977, p. 63)

CATATONIA (kat'ə-tō'nē-ə) *noun* a pathological condition, especially in cases of schizophrenia, characterized by muscular rigidity and mental stupor, sometimes alternating with great excitement and confusion.

CATATONIC *adj.*

1. See (2) under RECIDIVISM.

2. Contrary to my aunt placing her in *One Life to Live*, it's here [in *The Edge of Night*] that poor CATATONIC Geraldine Whitney so numbingly suffers. (K. Kelly, "A drama critic works up lather over TV soaps," *Boston Globe*, 3/7/76, p. 12-A)

3. See (4) under LUGUBRIOUS.

4. See (1) under INANE.

5. See (1) under MESOMORPH.

6. . . . I too [like Byron] awoke to find myself famous. I don't feel Byronic— Bionic maybe, occasionally CATATONIC, but certainly famous . . . . I'd like . . . to tell you what it's like being an event. (Henry **W**inkler, "The Importance of Being Fonzie," *Newsweek*, 9/20/76, p. 11)

7. Sally, Mark and Sandy [characters in Michael Roemer's film *Dying*] came to accept death; Harriet is angry and guilty; and Bill is almost CATATONICALLY depressed. (Honor Moore, Review, *Ms.*, May 1976, p. 18)

CATECHISM (kat'ə-kiz'əm) *noun* an elementary book containing a summary of the principles of a Christian religion, in the form of questions and answers; any series of formal questions and answers used for teaching the fundamentals of a subject; catechetical instruction.

CATECHISMAL or **CATECHISTIC** or **CATECHISTICAL** *adj.*

CATECHETICAL or **CATECHETIC** *adj.* of, like, or conforming to a catechism; consisting of, or teaching by the method of questions and answers.

CATECHIZE *verb* to teach (especially religion) by the method of questions and answers.

CATECHUMEN *noun* a person receiving instruction in the fundamentals of Christianity or of any subject.

CATECHIST or **CATECHIZER** *noun* one who instructs catechumens.

1. In China as elsewhere, the same rule holds: art subjected to the imperatives of politics, and overseen by political functionaries, inevitably becomes repetitive political ICONOGRAPHY, limited to a specific CATECHISM. (R. Chelminski, "In China, a breath of fresh air brightens up the official palette," *Smithsonian*, March 1976, p. 32)

CATHARSIS (kə-thär′sis) *noun* purgation; the purging of an audience's emotions or relieving of its emotional tensions through a work of art; psychotherapy that encourages or permits the discharge of pent-up emotions caused by fears, problems and complexes.

CATHARTIC or **CATHARTICAL** *adj.*

CATHARTIC *noun* a purgative; laxative; physic.

CATHARTICALLY *adv.*

1. Violence is Travis's only means of expressing himself . . . . And, given his ASCETIC loneliness, it's the only real orgasm he can have. The violence in this movie [*Taxi Driver*] is so threatening precisely because it's CATHARTIC for Travis. (Pauline Kael, Review, *The New Yorker*, 2/9/76, p. 85)

2. Psychology does not satisfactorily explain the CATHARSIS—or the *sense* of grace?—achieved by prisoners of Hitler and Stalin who could have become savage, vengeful, animal. The "animal" types crumbled before the others did. A desperately brave belief in human solidarity, despite everything, released the moral energy to go on. (A. Kazin, Review of *The Survivor: An Anatomy of Life in the Death Camps*, by Terrence DesPres, *New York Times*, 3/14/76, Section 7, p. 2)

3. What [Janis] Ian wanted to do was write, and in six hours one night in 1972, she composed *Stars*, a CATHARTIC album about the pitfalls of pop popularity; this was her re-entry into public life. (Mary Alice Kellogg, P.S. Greenberg, "Janis Grows Up," *Newsweek*, 4/5/76, p. 63)

4. [Joe] McGinniss reaches no conclusions about himself [in *Heroes*], no CATHARSIS of any kind . . . . (E. Hoagland, Review, *New York Times*, 4/18/76, Section 7, p. 8)

5. Perhaps the time has come to have liberal arts students from campuses across the country form their own "invisible colleges." They have much to say to each other—part in CATHARSIS and partly in the fruitful sharing of insights and disappointments. (G. W. Bonham, "Some Vexing Questions About the Liberal Arts" [Editorial], *Change*, May 1976, p. 12)

6. The confession [by Sharon Fields] appeared to serve as a CATHARSIS, for now she looked up at [Adam] Malone with mingled pity and contempt. (I. Wallace, *The Fan Club*, Bantam Edition, 1975, p. 238)

7. See (5) under PRATFALL.

CAUSE CÉLÈBRE (kôz′ sə-leb′ rə, -leb′) *noun, pl.:* **CAUSES CÉLÈBRES** (kôz′sə- leb′ rez, -lebz′, kô′ziz-sə-leb′rə, -leb′) any controversy or event that attracts great public attention; a celebrated law case, trial or controversy.

1. Solar energy has gone from being the rather obscure hobby of a handful of backyard inventors to a CAUSE CÉLÈBRE. (S. Love, "Houses designed with nature: their future is at hand," *Smithsonian*, December 1975, p. 46)

2. Testimony in the Andy Messersmith-New York Yankees' dispute will come today from— of all people—Andy Messersmith. The star pitcher will be the star witness in the CAUSE CÉLÈBRE over whether his agent did or didn't commit him to the Yankees. The hearing was to be held in the offices of [baseball] Commissioner Bowie Kuhn . . . . (Associated Press, "Pitcher To Testify," *Norman* [Okla.] *Transcript*, 4/2/76, p. 15)

3. After a period as a CAUSE CÉLÈBRE [following being fired from a tenured position at Stanford], [H. Bruce] Franklin has been spending some lean years scraping up teaching jobs. (He joined Rutgers' Newark faculty this fall.) (H.D. Shapiro, Review of the book, *Back Where You Came From: One life in the death of the empire*, by H. Bruce Franklin, *Change*, Winter 1975-76, p. 55)

CAVIL (kav′əl) *noun* a trivial, annoying, and pointless objection; quibble; the raising of trivial objections.

CAVIL *verb* to raise irritating and trivial objections; to object when there is little reason to do so; to find fault unnecessarily (usually followed by *at* or *about*); to oppose by inconsequential, frivolous, or sham objections; carp; quibble.

CAVILER or **CAVILLER** *noun.*

CAVILINGLY or **CAVILLINGLY** *adv.*

1. The INSOUCIANCE of [Susan] Brownmiller's generalizations [in her book, *Against Our Will:*

Men, Women and Rape] invites CAVIL and risks discrediting her book and with it her subject. (Diane Johnson, Review, *New York Review of Books*, 12/11/75, p. 36)

2. My only CAVIL [with *The Threepenny Opera*] is that [Richard] Foreman's stylization forces the actors . . . to sing with a strain that can be read in their neck muscles. (J. Kroll, Review, *Newsweek*, 5/17/76, p. 96)

3. See (1) under CARAPACE.

CENTRIPETAL (sen-trip′ i-təl) *adj.* moving or directed inward toward a center or axis (opposed to centrifugal).

CENTRIPETALLY *adv.*

1. [Irving] Howe deftly weaves together [in *World of Our Fathers*] an intricate PASTICHE of material ranging from the Rabbinical defense of orthodoxy to the INTERNECINE warfare of the unions and the Left; from the UBIQUITOUS problem of the amorous boarder to the agonies of generational conflict in a social setting that lacked customary CENTRIPETAL forces. (T.L. Haskell, Review, *Chronicle of Higher Education*, 3/29/76, p. 11)

2. "Only two people in our administration quit, and they did so just before they were going to be fired [by President Nixon]. There are things keeping you on [said John Ehrlichman], even when you know things are going wrong. It's almost a physical force, CENTRIPETAL I think the word is. It holds you to the center." (I. Berkow, "Ehrlichman candid in his new book, 'The Company,'" *Norman* [Okla.] *Transcript*, 7/7/76, p. 21)

CEREBRATE (ser′ə-brāt′) *verb* to use the mind or brain; think or think about.

CEREBRATION *noun.*

CEREBRAL (ser′əbrəl, sə-rē′brəl) *adj.* of or pertaining to the cerebrum or the brain; of, appealing to, or characterized by the use of intellect rather than intuition or instinct; intellectual.

CEREBRALLY *adv.*

1. He [Silvio Conte] begins [his letter] by saying that he takes "exception" to my "shrill ode to TRIASSIC CELEBRATIONS." I don't know what that means, but cannot assume that it matters. (W. F. Buckley Jr., *Execution Eve and Other Contemporary Ballads*, G. P. Putnam's Sons, 1975, p. 291)

2. See (2) under HYPOCHONDRIA.

3. See (3) under HERMETIC.

CERULEAN (sə-rōō′lē-ən) *adj.* deep blue; sky-blue; azure.

1. "Be that as it may, would you like to tell me about Mr. Bakewell? Now departed, but, frankly, not lamented by me" [asked Russel Wren]. [Donald] Washburn gave me a generous quota of CERULEAN EYE. "I never heard of him" [he said]. (Thomas Berger, *Who Is Teddy Villanova?* Delacorte Press/Seymour Lawrence, 1977, p. 51)

CHARIVARI (shə-riv′ə-rē′, shiv′ə-rē, shä′ rə-vä′ rē) *noun, pl.:* **CHARIVARIS** a confusion of noises; din; shivaree; a mock serenade or noisy celebration, especially with pans, kettles, horns, etc. to a newly married couple on their wedding night.

CHARIVARI *verb.*

1. At the annual CHARIVARI of the American Booksellers Association in San Francisco three weeks ago, there was one book [*The Public Burning*, by Robert Coover] not listed on any official program . . . . There was a blowup of the book's front cover on display, but generally the book was being described and ordered on faith. (H. Mitgang, "Book Ends: Metafiction," *New York Times*, 6/19/77, Section 7, p. 51)

CHARLATAN (shär′lə-tən) *noun* a person who fraudulently pretends to have expert knowledge, powers, or skill that he does not have; quack; impostor; mountebank; fraud; fake.

CHARLATANISTIC *adj.*

CHARLATANISM or **CHARLATANRY** *noun*

1. See (3) under NOSTRUM.

2. Too easy-riding a personality to show the lacerating self-consciousness of Brando, he [Paul Newman, in *Buffalo Bill and the Indians, or Sitting Bull's History Lesson*] captures a sharp CHARLATANISM that touches pathos when Bill looks at a painting of himself and

says: "Ain't he riding that horse right? Well, if he ain't, how come you all took him for a king?" (J. Kroll, Review, *Newsweek*, 6/28/76, p. 77)

3. And in denouncing the editors of . . . a liberal paper . . . , he [Chekhov] made a prediction: ". . . Russia will one day be ruled by such toads and crocodiles as were unknown even in Spain under the Inquisition . . . every CHARLATAN and wolf in sheep's clothing will have a stage on which to parade his lies . . ." (H. Moss, Review of *A New Life of Anton Chekhov*, by Ronald Hingley, *New York Times*, 6/20/76, Section 7, p. 28)

4. If he [author Denis Mack Smith] has not wholly explained [in the book, *Mussolini's Roman Empire*] how such an absurd system [as Italian fascism] . . . led by such a ridiculous CHARLATAN was ever taken seriously by anyone, he has shown clearly how the vain dreams of Roman imperial glory played their part both in Mussolini's success and in his downfall. (J. Joll, Review, *New York Times*, 6/20/76, Section 7, p. 5)

5. Billy [Martin] seems to have crossed paths with a series of front-office meddlers, neophytes and CHARLATANS—before finally settling into his present semi-idyllic relationship with strong-willed George Steinbrenner of the Yankees. (P. Axthelm, "Billy Martin Country," *Newsweek*, 7/12/76, p. 65)

6. [Paul J.] Stern, a psychotherapist in Cambridge, Mass., has written a psychobiography of Jung [*C.C. Jung: The Haunted Prophet*]. From the lurid mauve cover to the last sour RIPOSTE, Stern convinces the reader that he is not too keen on Jung; . . . He concludes that Jung was a gifted CHARLATAN, vain, sometimes cruel, demagogic, and a constant hustler for the mantle of culture-prophet. (J. Hollis, Review, *Chronicle of Higher Education*, 7/26/76, p. 9)

7. See (3) under HOMILY.

CHARYBDIS (kə-rib' dis) *noun* (in Classical Mythology) the daughter of Gaea and Poseidon, a sea monster mentioned in Homer and later identified with the whirlpool CHARYBDIS, located in the Strait of Messina off the northeast coast of Sicily; *see* SCYLLA.

Between SCYLLA and CHARYBDIS an expression meaning between two equally perilous or evil alternatives, neither of which can be avoided without encountering and probably falling victim to the other.

1. Disturbing rumor from the docks: the ship of marriage, when last seen, was beating its brave way between the SCYLLA of women's liberation and the CHARYBDIS of omnivorous sex. (P.S. Presscott, Review of *A Fine Romance*, by Cynthia Propper Seton; and of *I Hear America Swinging*, by Peter De Vries, *Newsweek*, 5/17/76, p. 108)

2. See (1) under SCYLLA.

3. See (3) under SCYLLA.

4. . . . the submitted puzzles often have people's names in them, either as clues or answers, and [Will] Weng [New York Times' crossword puzzle editor] often finds himself between SCYLLA and CHARYBDIS (hard-pressed . . .). Are the people famous enough? Will they endure? . . . ."I'd use him [TV character, Fonz] in the daily puzzle, but Sunday. . . ." (M. Dubin, "Puzzled? Then Weng has done his job," *Philadelphia Inquirer*, 11/28/76, p. 4-L)

CHASSÉ (sha-sāʹ; or, especially in square dancing, sa-shā) *noun* a gliding step forward or sideways in which one foot is kept in advance of the other.

CHASSÉ *verb* to perform a chassé.

1. [Ronald] Beard gave him [Greg Gregson] a hand [with the big box] . . . . They went up [the stairway] CHASSÉ-wise, a mime of a slowly mobile coat of arms. (A. Burgess, *Beard's Roman Women*, McGraw-Hill, 1976, p. 80)

CHATELAINE (shatʹ ə-lān) *noun* the mistress of a castle or of an elegant or fashionable household; a girdle or clasp for holding keys, a purse, a watch, etc.

1. Fort Osage would have been a lively place even without its CHATELAINE . . . . The boys [Jacques and Marcel Pasquinel] were delighted with the varied activity . . . . Even Marcel, only five at the time, watched OMNIVOROUSLY as mule trains and river boats unloaded. (J. A. Michener, *Centennial*, Fawcett, 1975, p. 255)

CHAUVINISM (shōʹ və-nizʹ əm) *noun*

zealous, belligerent, boastful, militant, unreasoning, excessive, or blind patriotism; JINGOISM; [after N. Chauvin, a soldier in Napoleon's army noted for loud-mouthed patriotism; unreasoning devotion to one's race, sex, etc. with contempt for the other races, the opposite sex, etc.

CHAUVINIST *noun*.

CHAUVINISTIC *adj*.

CHAUVINISTICALLY *adv*.

1. "He [Peewee Reese] came from Kentucky a boy," Red Barber liked to say, his voice warmed by sparks of Southern CHAUVINISM. "And he-ah, right he-ah in Brooklyn, we saw him grow into a man, and more than that, a captain among men." (R. Kahn, *The Boys of Summer*, Harper and Row, 1971, p.312)

2. See (2) under PREDACEOUS.

3. [Coco Chanel's] Great Love numero cinq was a CHAUVINIST right-wing cartoonist and journalist called Iribe. (Francine Gray, Review of *Chanel*, by Edmonde Charles-Roux, *New York Review of Books*, 12/11/75, p. 45)

4. Not too long ago, CHAUVINISM meant excessive patriotism. (Elinor Langer, "The gettingours branch of the movement," *New York Times*, 4/4/76, Section 7, p. 4)

5. See (2) under COGNOSCENTI.

6. See (1) under ANTHROPOID.

7. To sum up, *Aphra* promotes the notion that one's sex organs create a specific and unalterable type of consciousness . . . and that to be an accepted member of one's sex, one must oppress, either verbally or politically, members of the opposite sex. In short, it is a journal of sexual CHAUVINISM. (Suzanne Gordon, Review of *Aphra: The Feminist Literary Magazine*, *Change*, April 1976, pp. 46–47)

8. Over the past decade, [Bud Greenspan's] hauntingly evocative sports specials have won praise around the world. Yet . . . Greenspan's work has been politely spurned by U.S. commercial TV. The three networks . . . do not maintain high-budgeted sports departments to outsiders . . . show up their efforts. Fortunately such CHAUVINISTIC considerations do not burden public television. This month, the 265-station public TV net-

work began presenting Greenspan's most ambitious project—a ten-part series tracing the Olympics from 1896 to the present. (H. F. Waters, "TV's Olympiad," *Newsweek*, 5/24/76, p. 98)

9. At the urging of our friend the New York CHAUVINIST, . . . we went to the Marlborough Gallery . . . to see *Ruckus Manhattan*, an exhibition of sculptures by Red Grooms and the Ruckus Construction Co. . . . *Ruckus* is a funny, MORDANT, garish, loving depiction of the city and its citizens in metal and wood, vinyl and cloth, paint and plaster; it combines the populism of a W.P.A. mural with the irreverence of subway graffiti. (Anon., "Talk of the Town: Teeming," *The New Yorker*, 5/31/76, p. 29)

10. See (1) under INTERNECINE.

11. The husband in this film [Claude Chabrol's *Une Partie de Plaisir*], marvelously played by Paul Gégauff, is perhaps the most authentic and fascinating male CHAUVINIST ever to make a woman cry on the screen. (J. Kroll, Review, *Newsweek*, 6/14/76, p. 90F)

12. For me, obviously a male CHAUVINIST fogey, come soon that bright new future when . . . their ladyships take over the treadmill and all a man has to do is lie around the house . . . . (P. Ryan, "No tears about tears from a dry-eyed chauvinist," *Smithsonian*, May 1976, p. 132)

13. Textbook writers in every nation bring a certain CHAUVINISM to their work. In the French text [covering the American Revolution], . . . the support of France, especially the contributions of the Marquis de Lafayette and General Rochambeau, is hailed as the real key to Colonial victory. A West German textbook teaches that General Washington relied heavily on Friedrich von Steuben, a former officer of Frederick the Great, to train his troops. . . . Canada's history is most interested in . . . why Canadian colonies did not join their neighbors in rebellion. (Merrill Sheils, "As Others See Us," *Newsweek*, 8/9/76, p. 43)

14. Blue-eyed Peanut Princess Karen Bell . . . was aboard [the *Peanut Special*, a leased train from Plains, Ga. to Washington for the Presidential inauguration] giving out peanut leis and chatting away about peanut ham-

burgers and peanut hot dogs. In all, the 382 celebrators ate 275 lbs. of roasted peanuts . . . . Culinary CHAUVINISM, however, was not limited to peanuts. As the train clickety-clacked through the Carolinas, the travelers dined on peanut soup, Georgia ham and Georgia peach ice cream. (G. Taber, "Bound For Fun—And Glory," *Time*, 1/31/77, p. 18)

15. See (3) under ANTHROPOID.

CHIAROSCURO (kē-är′ ə-skyŏŏr′ ō) *noun*, *pl.*: -ROS the treatment of light and shade in a painting, drawing, etc., to produce the illusion of depth, a dramatic effect, etc.; a style of painting, drawing, etc. emphasizing such treatment; a painting, drawing, etc., in which chiaroscuro is used; interplay, variety, or contrast of dissimilar qualities (as of mood, style, character, or spirit) thought of as lightness and darkness.

CHIAROSCURIST *noun*.

1. . . . his [Raymond Chandler's] voice has a kind of loud, domineering quality, strangely monotonal, and perhaps similar to what Chandler heard in the voice of Erle Stanley Gardner. ". . . Years of yapping into a dictaphone have destroyed the quality of his voice, which now has all the delicate CHIAROSCURO of a French taxi horn." (L. Michaels, Review of *The Life of Raymond Chandler*, by Frank MacShane, *New York Times*, 5/16/76, Section 7, p. 26)

2. Even with color, the settings of [the movie] Kong II are no match for the rich black-and-white CHIAROSCURO of Kong I, with its echoes of artists like Gustav Doré and Max Ernst and its sensitivity to the emotional values of tone and texture. (J. Kroll, "The Movies Go Ape—Again," *Newsweek*, 12/20/76, p. 103)

CHICANERY (s̲h̲i-kā′ nə-rē) or **CHICANE** (shi-kān′) *noun* trickery or deception by the use of cunning or clever devices; SOPHISTRY or quibbling or subterfuge used to trick, deceive, or evade; fraud; knavery; deceit.

CHICANE *verb* to trick or get by chicanery; to quibble over; CAVIL at.

1. Since it's our money the banks work with, lending funds for both corporate corruption and private CHICANERY, the banker's reaction

is important . . . . (Leslie Waller, "Banks 'Subsidize' New Immorality," *Norman* [Okla.] *Transcript*, 1/16/76, p. 6)

2. What [Lincoln] Merrill and other PROD members have seen add up to one of the most damning indictments of union corruption in the modern history of the labor movement. It is contained in a book-length PROD report, recently released, which charges the Teamsters with specific instances of fraud, financial CHICANERY and criminal influence. One accusation: a Teamsters' local in New York City is dominated by a Mafia family which "profits handsomely from its two pension funds." (T. Tiede, "NEA Union hierarchy irritates organized crime," *Norman* [Okla.] *Transcript*, 7/9/76, p. 6)

3. [Donald] Washburn's smile turned definitely chilly. "Suddenly," said he, "I see something very CHICANE in your manner. Blackmail, is that it?" (Thomas Berger, *Who Is Teddy Villanova?* Delacorte Press/Seymour Lawrence, 1977, p. 151)

CHI-CHI or **CHICHI** (shē-shē) *adj.* showily or pretentiously elegant, sophisticated, or stylish (usually used in a somewhat derogatory manner); extremely chic; very smart.

1. There's a world glut of anti-American oratory, especially in CHI-CHI Socialist and class-mongering Communist circles in Europe. They TITILLATE themselves with tea-time tales of PROLETARIAN oppression in America . . . . They rarely permit facts to get in the way of their DIALECTICS. (V. Riesel, "Union Capitalists Set an Example," *The Saturday Oklahoman & Times*, Okla. City, 5/15/76, p. 12)

2. A few weeks ago the restored Quincy Market complex opened in Boston . . . the complex will indicate how much Americans want to go back . . . to small merchants providing individual attention in small stores. Although some of the stores are of the downtown CHI-CHI variety, a lot of others are fishmongers, butchers, and the sort of thing you might find on Passyunk [Ave., in Philadelphia]. (T. Hine, "The rarity of the small merchant may save him," *Philadelphia Inquirer*, 9/26/76, p. 9-H)

3. Among the CHI-CHI set, WWD [Women's Wear Daily] has its favorites, and some say the

coverage reflects Mr. [John B.] Fairchild [the publisher]'s personal likes and dislikes. Lee Radziwill . . . and others in Mr. Fairchild's set are relatively immune from criticism. But former reporter [Rosemary] Kent recalls covering a publicity party for Bulgari jewelry that produced an article calling the well-known socialites present "OTBs", or "Old Tired Bags." (Deborah Sue Yaeger, "Middle-Aged Slump: Women's Wear Daily Loses Some of its Clout in the Fashion World," *Wall Street Journal*, 5/12/77, p. 25)

CHILIASM (kil'ē-az'əm) *noun* the doctrine of Christ's expected return to reign on earth for 1000 years; millennialism.

CHILIAST *noun.*

CHILIASTIC *adj.*

CHILIAD *noun* a group of 1000; a period of 1000 years.

CHILIADAL or **CHILIADIC** *adj.*

CHILIARCH *noun* the commander of 1000 men (in ancient Greece or Rome).

1. CHILIASM is in the air, and He is George McGovern, whose incarnation will be effected by the voters in November. (W.F. Buckley Jr., *Execution Eve and Other Contemporary Ballads*, G.P. Putnam's Sons, 1975, p. 76)

2. By the time Al-Ma'mun was caliph in Baghdad—that is, after 813—the ECLECTICISM of Islamicate civilization and the diversity of Islamic faith were indelible characteristics. Greek science and Mazdean occultism, Arabic grammar and Persian poetry, Syrian mercantilism and Iranian absolutism, Medinan traditionalism and Iraqi CHILIASM were all entangled together with a *Thousand and One Nights* folk tradition of jinn and marvels. (C. Geertz, Review of *The Venture of Islam: Conscience and History in a World Civilization. Vol. 1: The Classical Age of Islam; Vol. 2: The Expansion of Islam in the Middle Periods; Vol. 3: The Gunpowder Empire and Modern Times,* by Marshall G.S. Hodgson, *New York Review of Books*, 12/11/75, p. 20)

3. As to why an American author [Kurt Vonnegut] whose Dostoyevskyan preoccupations with the messianic, the APOCALYPTIC and the CHILIASTIC should be popular in the U.S.S.R. today, it is worth noting

that there has been a renewed interest in Dostoyevsky in that country as the centenary of the author's death approaches . . . . (D. M. Fine, "Vonnegut—Big in Russia," *New York Times*, 4/3/77, Section 7, p. 47)

CHIMERA (ki-mēr'ə, kī-) *noun* a horrible or unreal creature of the imagination; a vain, impossible, or idle fancy; (if capitalized) a mythological fire-breathing monster, commonly represented with a lion's head, a goat's body, and a serpent's tail; any similarly grotesque monster having disparate parts, especially as depicted in decorative art.

CHIMERICAL or **CHIMERIC** *adj.* unreal, imaginary, or wildly fanciful.

CHIMERICALLY *adv.*

1. See (1) under TRANSMOGRIFY.

2. Seventy years ago most Europeans would have sooner imagined an army of rabbits than one of Arabs; oil did not dominate politics then and the notion of Arab unity was even more a CHIMERA than it is today. (R. Hughes, Review of *A Prince of Our Disorder*, by John E. Mack, *Time*, 4/12/76, p. 95)

3. Truman's popularity, the author [Joseph C. Goulden] reminds us [in *The Best Years: 1945-50*], was nothing like his POSTHUMOUS acclaim, but a flickering elusive CHIMERA during those years. Harry Truman's success was . . . an ARTIFACT that, like so many, seems more beguiling in retrospect than in contemporary reality. (M.F. Nolan, Review, *New York Times*, 6/20/76, Section 7, p. 4)

4. Authenticity is not a cure-all, and is in fact a CHIMERA. In a completely authentic performance of a Mozart symphony the players would not only wear white wigs but be doomed to lose all their teeth by age 40. (D. Henahan, "How Did They Play Mozart 200 Years Ago?" *New York Times*, 7/11/76, Section 2, p. 13)

5. It's one thing for the agency [MAC— Municipal Assistance Corp. of New York City] to contest a lawsuit aimed at the validity of its crucial expedient, the moratorium on repayment of city notes. It's quite another thing for Judge Simon H. Rifkind, chief legal counsel, to publicly deny that any default had occurred, an incredible stand which the Court of Appeals . . . brushed aside as "merely a

CHIMERA." (R.M. Bleiberg, "Drunk for Bartender?" [Editorial], *Barron's*, 2/21/77, p. 7)

6. But no one has achieved more reform than the activist mothers of Action for Children's Television, based in Newtonville, Mass. ACT is largely credited with persuading the networks to reduce time for commercials on children's weekend shows . . . . ACT's ultimate—perhaps CHIMERIC—goal is to rid kidvid of all advertising. (H. F. Waters, "What TV Does To Kids," *Newsweek*, 2/21/77, p. 70)

CHINOISERIE (shēn-woz'ə-re´, shin' waz-re´) *noun* an 18th century European style of decoration for furniture, ceramics, textiles, etc., in which supposedly Chinese motifs were extensively used; an object or design in this style.

1. See (1) under ORMOLU.

2. As for [Ezra] Pound's interest in China, Mr. [Donald] Davie holds that this was, until late in Pound's life, just 18th century CHINOISERIE, a dallying with Chinese culture rather than an immersion in it. (R. Ellmann, Review of *Ezra Pound: The Last Rower: A Political Profile*, by C. David Heymann; and of *The Cantos of Ezra Pound: The Lyric Mode*, by Eugene Paul Nassar, *New York Times*, 4/4/76, Section 7, p. 25)

3. See (1) under GROSGRAIN.

CHIROGRAPHY (kī-rog´ rə-fē) *noun* handwriting; penmanship.

CHIROGRAPHER *noun*.

CHIROGRAPHIC or CHIROGRAPHICAL *adj*.

1. He [Felix Zigman] recognized [in the ransom note] the distinctly slanted CHIROGRAPHY, the minute dots over the i's, the unclosed tails of the y's, at once. (I. Wallace, *The Fan Club*, Bantam Books, 1975, p. 479)

CHIVVY (chiv'ē) or CHIVY or CHEVY (chev'ē) *verb* to chase; to race or scamper; run after or pursue; to harass, nag, annoy, tease, or torment, especially with persistence and by petty vexations and often for a specific purpose; to acquire, direct, or manipulate by persistent petty maneuvering.

CHEVY *noun* a hunting cry; a hunt, chase,

or pursuit; the game of prisoner's base.

1. Each item [at the Presbyterian mission to the Sac and Fox] was priced in bits—Spanish silver dollars sawed into eight parts so that twenty-five cents was equal to two bits—and they [the Sac and Fox] would not allow the travelers to CHIVVY them down. (J.A. Michener, *Centennial*, Fawcett, 1975, p. 370)

CHOLERIC (kol' ər-ik, kə-ler' ik) *adj*. IRASCIBLE; characterized by anger or quick temper.

CHOLER *noun* anger or ill humor; IRASCIBILITY; irritability.

CHOLERICALLY *adv*.

1. [Wayne] Hays has only himself to blame for his reputation as the CURMUDGEON of Capitol Hill. A former Ohio forensics teacher and proprietor of one of the nimblest minds and most ACERBIC tongues in Congress, he has devoted the better part of fourteen terms in office to cultivating the image of the tough guy with CHOLERIC mien. (D. Chu, H.W. Hubbard "Hays: Bully of the Block," *Newsweek*, 6/7/76, p. 27)

CHORDEE (kor-dē´) *noun* a painful downward curvature of the penis in gonorrhea.

1. Then he [Ronald Beard] noticed his erection swinging in the street-glow. Vast, CHORDEE-like, the fruit of alcohol. (A. Burgess, *Beard's Roman Women*, McGraw-Hill, 1976 p. 68)

CHRESTOMATHY (kres-tom´ ə-thē) *noun* a collection of literary passages, often by one author and in a foreign language.

CHRESTOMATHIC (kres'tə-math'ik) *adj*.

1. The aftereffect of the first blow now . . . began to reassert itself . . . . Sam [Polidor]'s image registered on my retinas as if I were staring through lenses of lemon-lime Jell-O in which banana rounds were embedded. My neck seemed to support a beer barrel, and my thorax was a construction of pipe cleaners. Only mixed metaphors will serve here; I was a CHRESTOMATHY of them at this juncture. (Thomas

Berger, *Who Is Teddy Villanova?*, Delacorte Press/Seymour Lawrence, 1977, p. 14)

CHTHONIC (thŏn′ ik) or **CHTHONIAN** (thō′ nē-ən) *adj.* (in Classical Mythology) of or pertaining to the underworld and its deities and spirits; dark, primitive, and mysterious; infernal; ghostly.

1. The Hispanos [of New Mexico are] Catholic, devout, in a CHTHONIC way . . . [and constitute] a tenacious, tranquil GERARCHY, loosening perhaps under our time's familiar MORDENTS. (E.W. Count, Review of *The Old Ones of New Mexico*, a book by Robert Coles, *The Key Reporter*, Summer 1976, p. 6)

CHUTZPAH or **CHUTZPA** (KHŏŏt′spə, hŏŏts′ pə) *noun* unmitigated effrontery or impudence; shameless audacity; brass; insolence.

1. His [Walter's] son, Thomas [Hoving], his equal in CHUTZPAH, is director of the Metropolitan Museum of Art. (Anon., "For Tiffany's Walter Hoving Silence May Be Golden, But Sounding Off Is Irresistible," *People*, 4/12/76, p. 16)

2. It takes monumental gall—a kind of awesome CHUTZPAH—for any member of Congress to complain about military amenities. In the whole of our government, no group is more petted, pampered, coddled, cuddled and richly subsidized. (J.J. Kilpatrick, "Senators, Congressmen Require Gall to Criticize Amenities for Military," *Daily Oklahoman*, Okla. City, 4/28/76, p. 10)

3. See (1) under MÉLANGE.

4. The book [*The Last Kennedy: Edward M. Kennedy of Massachusetts*] is, [author Robert] Sherrill announces with more than a touch of CHUTZPAH, "anything but the definitive study of Edward M. Kennedy's career. For that you should be grateful. A definitive study of Kennedy would be pretty boring." (G. Hodgson, Review, *New York Times*, 4/18/76, Section 7, p. 3)

5. Last month, his [Dale Reeves'] team [from the Los Angeles County Department of Health Services] accused Al Penni's, a popular, top-rated Culver City restaurant, of the ultimate CHUTZPA: selling "kosher" pastrami that wasn't kosher. The restaurant denies it. (A. J. Mayer, M. Kasindorf, "The Menu Sleuth," *Newsweek*, 10/18/76, p. 101)

6. [Larry] Flynt is an exhibitionist provocateur. His grandstanding and CHUTZPA have offended his enemies far beyond what has appeared in the magazine [Hustler, which he publishes]. . . . No one with any sense would have mailed, as Flynt did, photographs of maimed Vietnam veterans throughout Cincinnati where his trial was to be held. Flynt's stated point was that "violence, not sex, is the real obscenity." The photos, also published in the December Hustler, were enough to make strong men sick. (A. Kretchmer, "Justice for Hustler," *Newsweek*, 2/28/77, p. 13)

CINCTURE (siṅg′ chər) *noun* a belt or girdle; something that surrounds or encompasses, as a belt or girdle; the act of girdling or encompassing.

CINCTURE *verb* to gird, as with a cincture; encircle.

1. America continued to be represented [in Europe in the 18th century] by the exotic feather-CINCTURED Indian . . . . Artists seem to have been drawn INELUCTABLY toward the one remaining exotic element in the North American scene—the Indian. (H. Honour, "America as seen in the fanciful vision of Europe," *Smithsonian*, February 1976, pp. 57–58)

2. See (1) under ORMOLU.

CIRCUMLOCUTION (sûr′ kəm-lō-kyŏŏ′ shən) *noun* a roundabout, indirect, evasive, or lengthy way of speaking; the use of superfluous words; PERIPHRASIS; a roundabout expression.

CIRCUMLOCUTORY (sûr′kəm-lok′yə-tôr′ē) *adj.*

1. It is this concern for sensibilities that gave birth to the EUPHEMISM; for it set into motion the search for the softer word, the blunted explanation, the CIRCUMLOCUTION aimed at mitigating the harshness of a conclusion, or an evaluation. Thus we . . . speak of . . . "underdeveloped" when we mean primitive; . . . and of "unaware" when we mean ignorant. W.F. Buckley Jr., *Up From Liberalism*, Arlington House, 2nd Printing 1968, p. 118)

2. See (2) under QUOTIDIAN.

CLAIRVOYANCE (klâr voi′əns) *noun* the alleged power of seeing objects or actions removed from natural viewing; quick, intuitive knowledge of things and people; keen perception or insight.

CLAIRVOYANT *adj.*

CLAIRVOYANT *noun* a clairvoyant person.

CLAIRVOYANTLY *adv.*

1. And so the exhibition [*The Architecture of the Ecole des Beaux-Arts*] is . . . a revisionist reconsideration of history. But [Arthur] Drexler [director of the Museum of Modern Art's Department of Architecture and Design] brusquely rejects any idea of it as an incentive to revivalism. He does not, however, reject the idea of ECLECTICISM as a next step in architecture, although he claims no CLAIRVOYANCE about the forms it will take. (Ada Louise Huxtable, Review, *New York Review of Books*, 11/27/75, p. 6)

CLANDESTINE (klan des′tin) *adj.* done in secrecy or concealment, especially for purposes of subversion or deception; private or SURREPTITIOUS; furtive; hidden.

CLANDESTINELY *adv.*

1. See (2) under MACHINATION.

2. . . . while men who try to write about these women tend to see the smile behind the shawl as a smile of some CLANDESTINE power, . . . Ann Cornelisen [author of the book, *Women of the Shadows*] knows that the smile . . . is a crafty Trojan horse of a smile, calculated to appease or outwit or confound the enemy. (Jane Kramer, Review, *New York Times*, 4/4/76, Section 7, p. 3)

3. Successive English kings tried to tax Scots whiskey but failed dismally, for there were too many CLANDESTINE distillers in the homes of the Highlands. Scots poet Robert Burns wrote "Whisky and freedom gang (go) together." (P. Dietsch, Agence France-Presse, "Scots nationalists battling over 'bit o' brew,' " *Norman* [Okla.] *Transcript*, 6/16/76, p. 24)

4. The book [*Peculiar Institutions: An Informal History of the Seven Sister Colleges*, by Elaine Kendall] contains good descriptions of . . . Elizabeth Cary Agassiz's efforts to get pro-

fessors for her CLANDESTINE annex in the shadow of Harvard Yard . . . . (C. C. Cole Jr., Review, *Chronicle of Higher Education*, 6/21/76, p. 13)

5. If Transportation Secretary William Coleman, in his ruling last week, had declared auto airbags mandatory, much of America would have taken to cursing and seething. Garages would soon be offering a new, if CLANDESTINE service—the disconnection of airbags. (M. Kilian, Chicago Tribune Service, "Airbags just need the old soft sell," *Philadelphia Inquirer*, 12/16/76, p. 15-A)

CLAUDICANT (klô′ də-kənt) *adj.* lame; having a limp.

CLAUDICATION *noun* a limp; lameness.

1. The [film] project had had its beginnings at a Hollywood party at which Paul Newman or someone similar had said he'd like to play Lord Byron, great handsome limping lecher or layer, also poet, and had then gone into a CLAUDICANT EXOPHTHALMIC routine which Joanne Woodward said was worthier of Frankenstein, meaning the monster. The laughter aroused by what seemed to all present, except one, the total improbability of this COLLOCATION was . . . quenched by this one, a morose rewrite man, who told them all seriously that Byron had probably given serious rewrite advice to the authoress of *Frankenstein*, and then recounted . . . the whole story of that creative summer [spent by Byron and the Shelleys] by the waters of [Lake] Leman. (A. Burgess, *Beard's Roman Women*, McGraw-Hill, 1976, p. 20)

CLAUSTROPHOBIA (klô′ strə-fō′ bē-ə) *noun* an abnormal fear of enclosed, confined, or narrow places.

CLAUSTROPHOBIC *adj.*

CLAUSTROPHOBICALLY *adv.*

CLAUSTROPHOBE *noun.*

1. *The Killer Elite* [is] Sam Peckinpah's most compelling film in several years—a poetic, corkscrew vision of the modern world, CLAUSTROPHOBICALLY exciting. (Anon., Review, *The New Yorker*, 2/9/76, p. 18)

2. But almost the only special technique of the film medium that [Ingmar] Bergman employs [in the film, *The Magic Flute*] is the close-up

. . . and during Pamina's great aria . . . the lens focuses CLAUSTROPHOBICALLY on her mouth and— that currently overpublicized anatomical feature—jaws. (R. Craft, Review, *New York Review of Books*, 11/27/75, p. 16)

3. To change to a spaceship where we must live inside narrow walls, count every resource, cycle everything so tightly that we are constantly aware that our food and water are derived from wastes, would be to give us an unbearable feeling of constriction and CLAUSTROPHOBIA. (I. Asimov., "The Future Mariners," *American Way*, April 1976, p. 10)

4. See (7) under XENOPHOBIA.

5. Like a boxer or a running back who takes time off to make a punk movie, George Higgins had digressed from what he knew how to write well—comedies about the CLAUSTROPHOBIC lives of small-time Boston crooks—to what he didn't: a Washington novel, a Watergate report. If his new story [*The Judgment of Deke Hunter*] isn't as swift as . . . *The Friends of Eddie Coyle*, or as trim as . . . *Coogan's Trade*, . . . it's classy still—good style, sharp moves. (P.S. Prescott, Review, *Newsweek*, 9/6/76, p. 64)

CLERISY (kler′is-sē) *noun* learned persons as a class; literati; intelligentsia; educated people as a class.

1. I am prepared to proceed through life unembittered if, let us say, the jury [hearing W. F. B.'s law suit against Gore Vidal] grants me ten dollars' damage, I having run up a lawyer's fee in six figures. I will not forget it however if the CLERISY indulge themselves in the excess that they cannot bother with it since after all we are dealing with two controversialists. (W. F. Buckley Jr., *Execution Eve and Other Contemporary Ballads*, G. P. Putnam's Sons, 1975, p. 326)

2. Raman [a character in *The Painter of Signs*, by R. K. Narayan], a college-educated painter of signboards, is part of that huge Indian sub-CLERISY, educated but not qualified to rise to the top; he reads himself to sleep with Gibbon's *The History of the Decline and Fall of the Roman Empire* . . . . (A. Thwaite, Review, *New York Times*, 6/20/76, Section 7, p. 6)

3. They [America's leading intellectuals] are dissenters, but by no means revolutionaries. . . . One can thus argue with much plausibility that the intellectual elite is a CLERISY rather than an adversary culture; in fact, the truth is somewhere in between; the intellectuals form an opposition—a very loyal opposition. (P. Steinfels, Review of *The American Intellectual Elite*, by Charles Kadushin, *Harper's*, January 1975, p. 81)

4. . . . football's CLERISY speaks the ARCANE language of "visuals" and "confidence factors" and "seams" and zones that rotate. (G.F. Will, "Is That a Red Dog in the Seam?" *Newsweek*, 9/6/76, p. 72)

CLIMACTERIC (klī-mak′tər-ik) *noun* the period of decreasing reproductive capacity men and women, culminating, in women, in menopause, and, in men, in decreased sexual activity; any critical or crucial period or event; a year in which important changes in health, fortune, etc. are held by some theories to occur, as one's sixty-third year (grand climacteric).

CLIMACTERIC or **CLIMACTERICAL** (klī′mak-ter′i-kəl) *adj.* pertaining to a critical period; crucial.

CLIMACTERICALLY *adv.*

1. Three marriages (the last at 71), uncounted mistresses and illegitimate children and a devastating middle-aged CLIMACTERIC were the results of his [Frank Harris's] amatory career; never, in Miss [Philippa] Pullar [author of *Frank Harris: A Biography*]'s estimation, anything approaching genuine love. (R. Freedman, Review, *New York Times*, 3/28/76, Section 7, p. 8)

CLOCHE (klōsh, klôsh) *noun* a bell-shaped, close-fitting brimless hat for women; a bell-shaped glass jar used to cover delicate plants as protection against frost.

1. *Me and Bessie* [a play]—Perhaps the main weakness of Linda Hopkins' attempt to re-create Bessie Smith by clamping CLOCHE hats on her head and singing Bessie's songs is that she is a jittery and uncertain actress. (Anon., Review, *The New Yorker*, 2/9/76, p. 2)

2. . . . Natalie [Novotny]'s was not the feeble spirit a bigot might expect to find beneath a

stewardess' cap (or, with her airline, a CLOCHE). (Thomas Berger, *Who Is Teddy Villanova?* Delacorte Press/Seymour Lawrence, 1977, p. 144)

CLONE (klōn) or **CLON** *noun* a group of organisms derived from a single individual by various types of asexual reproduction, as by cuttings, bulbs, etc., or by fission, parthenogenesis, etc.

CLONAL *adj.*

CLONALLY *adv.*

1. See (1) under MEGALOMANIA.

2. ABC's top shows are only too familiar comedies such as *Happy Days* and its offspring *Laverne and Shirley*, sci-fi fantasies like the Six Million Dollar Man, from whose stainless-steel rib was CLONED the *Bionic Woman*, and a lineup of crime that includes *Starsky and Hutch* and *S.W.A.T.* (Anon., "The Hot Network," *Time*, 3/15/76, p. 82)

3. Each year local television stations CLONE platoons of handsomely competent news readers, some of whom are expensively promoted to the big time but do not make it. They do all right as long as they just read, but when forced to describe an event at length themselves, they prove uninteresting; in interviews, they lack the knowledge or the dexterity to cross-examine. (T. Griffith, "You Have to Be Neutral to Ask the Questions," *Time*, 9/13/76, p. 72)

4. Eventually it should be technically feasible . . . to make limitless copies, or CLONES, of people considered to be desirable by transplanting their DNA into human eggs. Science-fiction writers already fantasize about armies CLONED from a hybrid Goliath, or a world filled with CLONES of famous and powerful people. . . . "Biologists strongly disavow any interest in human CLONING. Nor would our society today tolerate the attempt" [writes Rick Gore in the September *National Geographic*]. D.J. Frederick, of *National Geographic News*, "New Biology Unlocks The Secrets of Life," *Times Herald*, Norristown, Pa., 10/5/76, p. 8)

5. See (1) under JOCULAR.

CLOY (kloi) *verb* to weary by an excess of something, as of food, sweetness, richness, or pleasure; surfeit; satiate; to become uninterest-

ing or distasteful through overabundance.

CLOYINGLY *adv.*

CLOYINGNESS *noun.*

1. The good religious film has eluded the American industry. To be sure, there has been no shortage of spectaculars (*The Ten Commandments*, . . .), to say nothing of Biblical sexploitations (*David and Bathsheba* . . .), tear jerkers (*Miracle of the Bells*). CLOYING chronicles of clerical culture (*Going My Way* . . .), ventures into the occult (. . . *The Exorcist*), and films with religious background for exotic effect (*Nashville* . . .). (A. M. Greeley, "Why Hollywood Never Asks the Good Question," *New York Times*, 1/18/76, Section 2, p. 1)

2. As the grandson and namesake of Grover Cleveland's Vice-President, Adlai [Stevenson] grew up in a privileged Midwestern AMBIENCE . . . —a weak father and a strong-willed mother whose love for her son was deep, CLOYING, and possessive. (W. Clemons, Review of *Adlai Stevenson of Illinois*, by John Bartlow Martin, *Newsweek*, 3/29/76, p. 8)

3. See (1) under PALLIATE.

4. William Safire, the New York Times columnist and former Nixon speechwriter, charged the authors [of *The Final Days*] with having ridiculed the ex-President—particularly in a scene in which he knelt, prayed and wept with Henry Kissinger. "How square," wrote Safire. "How CLOYINGLY pious. How insufferably un-Georgetown." Anon., "The Furor Over the Book," *Newsweek*, 4/12/76, p. 33)

5. The mass audience first became aware of her [Louise Lasser's] wacky comedic strain when she portrayed a CLOYINGLY sympathetic wife in a Nyquil commercial ("You're a good wife, Mildred." "I know, I know.") (H. F. Waters and M. Kasindorf, "The Mary Hartman Craze," *Newsweek*, 5/3/76, p. 61)

6. Rich prose can CLOY; it is to [Laurie] Lee's credit that this does not often happen [in *I Can't Stay Long*]. (Doris Grumbach, Review, *Smithsonian*, May 1976, p. 114)

7. The 32-year-old entertainer [Diana Ross] shared the Palace stage with two tiers of musicians, mimes and backup singers. The evening . . . had a few good theatrical moments but mostly it ranged from CLOYING to cute, as

much a fashion show as a performance. (Maureen Orth, "Boss Lady," *Newsweek*, 6/28/76, p. 61)

8. Last year brought Claudio Arrau's overly CLOYING version [of Chopin's *Preludes*] on Philips, and now within a month's span here are three more. (Anon., Review of the record: *Twenty-Four* [Chopin] *Preludes*, Op. 28 (Murray Perahia, pianist, Columbia; Maurizio Pollini, pianist, Deutsche Grammophon; Alicia de Larrocha, pianist, London), *Time*, 4/12/76, p. 91)

9. The one illness which never afflicted him [President Kennedy] was the CLOYING NARCISSISM which clots the modern idiom. *He* never felt victimized. *He* never felt alienated. That was left to his assassin. (W. Manchester, Commencement Address, University of Massachusetts, mimeographed, 6/13/65, p. 11)

10. Even in the hands of a great master, of a Cicero or an Austen, classically balanced prose can come to CLOY. It seems, after a while, too smooth and tended, the concord of its cadences too inevitable. (R.A. Sokolov, Review of *Others, Including Morstive Sternbump*, a book by Marvin Cohen, *New York Times*, 2/27/77, Section 7, p. 29)

CLYSTER (klis'tər) *noun* an enema.

1. At Paris' Church of Saint-Gervais, MISERICORDS showing an apothecary administering a CLYSTER to a woman and a couple sharing a bath were hacked almost beyond recognition. A more selective effacement was used at another church with a group of tumblers who were shown exposing their genitals. Often nothing but total obliteration would satisfy the ICONOCLASTS. (Dorothy and H. Kraus, "Naughty notions in holy places," *Smithsonian*, April 1976, p. 98)

COCOTTE (kō-kot', kə-) *noun* a prostitute; a woman who is sexually promiscuous.

1. She [Edmonde Charles-Roux] traces [in her book, *Chanel*] the essence of [Coco] Chanel's style, that taste for unadorned essentials which revolutionized the century's fashions, to two hitherto well-hidden secrets of the designer's youth: her life as a convent girl and her life as a COCOTTE. Coco did not want to be a COCOTTE. (Francine Gray, Review, *New York Review of Books*, 12/11/75, p. 44)

CODA (kō'da) *noun Music* a more or less independent passage concluding a composition or section.

1. [Michael Olmert wrote to the Washington Post:] Their philosophical struggles [those of Norman Mailer and William F. Buckley Jr.] were covered thoroughly by the media, while we watched weekly (it seems) for the familiar LITANY of ideological LEITMOTIFS and CODAS. (W.F. Buckley Jr., *Execution Eve and Other Contemporary Ballads*, G. P. Putnam's Sons, 1975, p. 319)

2. See (2) under WINSOME.

COELACANTH (sē'lə-kanth') *noun* a fish known only in fossil form and thought to have been extinct since the Cretaceous period, but found in 1938 off the coast of southern Africa.

1. Politicans accustomed to swimming in the relatively predictable shallows of the American voter's mood must now be thinking of it as a kind of Loch Ness. This year something is down there. Something unexamined, a different psychological species. An ancient COELACANTH of conservatism? Or some entirely new brand? (Anon., "Running Against Washington," *Time*, 5/24/76, p. 13)

COGNATE (kog-nāt') *adj.* related by family or birth; of the same parentage, descent, etc.; having the same or similar nature or quality.

COGNATE *noun* a person related to another through common ancestry; a cognate word, language, or thing.

COGNATION *noun.*

1. He [Ronald Beard] went into [his studio] where Byron and the Shelleys were waiting, people of his own blood, practitioners of a trade not wholly INCOGNATE with his own.... (A. Burgess, *Beard's Roman Women*, McGraw-Hill, 1976, p. 44)

COGNOMEN kog-nō'mən) *noun* a surname; last name; family name; any name, especially a distinguishing name or nickname.

COGNOMINAL *adj.*

COGNOMINALLY *adv.*

1. . . . whatever he was, there was but one

COGNOMEN that characterized him perfectly. The Milquetoast. (I. Wallace, *The Fan Club*, Bantam Books, 1975, p. 263)

2. What's in a name? For a politician— votes, that's what. The name Kennedy wins elections in Massachusetts; Taft does it in Ohio. In Illinois, Stevenson—coupled with Adlai, of course—is a good bet; and Brown breeds governors in California. But in Texas, the game of political names calls for a Yarborough, a COGNOMEN that has meant liberal votes in the Lone Star State for a generation. (Anon., "The Name's The Thing," *Time*, 8/30/76, p. 62)

3. He [Will Weng] is 69, and sometime next year he will give up the COGNOMEN (title . . .) of being the editor of the toughest and most prestigious crossword puzzle in the nation [the Sunday puzzle of the New York Times]. (M. Dubin, "Puzzled? Then Weng has done his job," *Philadelphia Inquirer*, 11/28/76, p. 4-L)

COGNOSCENTI (kon' yə-shen' tē, kog'nə-) *noun, pl.: sing.* -TE those who are well informed or have superior knowledge and understanding of a certain field, especially fine arts, literature, or the world of fashion; experts.

1. The baseball game—it's softball, actually—has become a hardy London perennial with deeply planted roots . . . . Visiting Americans, Japanese and other COGNOSCENTI, perched along the basepaths, look on amused. Crowds of Londoners . . . congregate to study with hushed respect the habits of Americans at play and to unravel the mysteries perpetrated before them. (N. Gelb, "Riding The Ump Ain't Cricket," *New York Times*, 4/11/76, Section 10, p. 1)

2. To Manhattan's CHAUVINISTIC COGNOSCENTI, the playwright [N. Simon]'s defection [to California] was as unsettling as Fellini leaving the Via Veneto . . . . (H.F. Waters and M. Kasindorf, "Sunshine Boy," *Newsweek*, 4/26/76, p. 75)

3. Whereas so much of the put-down brand of humor that passes for sophistication today seems designed either to separate the dummies from the COGNOSCENTI (*The Fortune*) or to flatten everybody to the level of sitcom awareness, the sophistication of high KITSCH [in old movies] like *Dinner at Eight* was inclusive, not exclusive, UNPRETENTIOUSLY oblique, not assaultive. (C. Michener and M. Kasindorf, Review of the TV movie, *That's Entertainment, Part 2*, *Newsweek*, 5/31/76, p. 51)

4. This sort of inconsistency [in the design of a house] is likely to be of interest primarily to architectural COGNOSCENTI, and it does not deny the real beauty of the main side of the house. (P. Goldberger, "Design," *New York Times*, 6/6/76, Section 6, p. 69)

5. Eventually he [a bull terrier being trained for dog-fighting] is pitted against other contenders in practice matches called "rolls" by the COGNOSCENTI of dogfighting. Here two dogs fight to show their endurance and tenacity, but the fight is halted before one is seriously wounded. (E. Meadows, "An American Pastime," *Harper's*, March 1976, p. 6)

6. On that first day of campaigning [for the Presidency], he [Jimmy Carter] went to the stock car races . . . . Back at the White House President Ford countered Carter by putting on a vest and golf shoes (not at the same time, of course). Political COGNOSCENTE (sic) translated this as "acting presidential." (G. F. Will, "A campaign lacking in substance," *Philadelphia Inquirer*, 9/13/76, p. 7-A)

7. Outside the wine trade, Texas COGNOSCENTI [of wines] tend to be very private people—and more than a little ICONOCLASTIC. The 35-year-old River Oaks lawyer . . . whose collection [of wines] is one of the finest in the country— possibly the world—declines to have his name used, his cellar is so valuable. (Sharon Churcher, "Grape Nuts," *Texas Monthly*, January 1977, p. 66)

COLLEGIALITY (kə-lē' jē-al' ə-tē) *noun* the sharing of authority or power among colleagues.

COLLEGIAL *adj.*

1. She [Nina Totenberg, of National Public Radio] asserted that Chief Justice Warren E. Burger . . . had held back a final decision on the [Watergate] appeal [of Mitchell, Haldeman, and Ehrlichman] so that he could lobby some of his brethren to change their votes . . . . Some Justices are said to have engaged in a shouting match at the first private conference after the news leak . . . . "There is less COLLEGIALITY than one would suspect, or than one might hope" [says one source close to the court]. Another insider agrees: "It is nine people with little in common who don't respect

each other all that much either politically or intellectually." (J. K. Footlick, Lucy Howard, "Supreme Embarrassment," *Newsweek*, 5/9/77, p. 66)

COLLOCATE (kol'ə-kāt) *verb* to arrange or place together, especially side by side; to arrange in proper order.

COLLOCATION *noun* proper arrangement, especially of words in a sentence; the act of collocating; state or manner of being collocated.

1. The [film] project had had its beginnings at a Hollywood party at which Paul Newman or someone similar had said he'd like to play Lord Byron, great handsome limping lecher or layer, also poet, and had then gone into a CLAUDICANT EXOPHTHALMIC routine which Joanne Woodward said was worthier of Frankenstein, meaning the monster. The laughter aroused by what seemed to all present, except one, the total improbability of this COLLOCATION was . . . quenched by this one, a morose rewrite man, who told them all seriously that Byron had probably given serious rewrite advice to the authoress of *Frankenstein*, and then recounted . . . the whole story of that creative summer [spent by Byron and the Shelleys] by the waters of [Lake] Leman. (A. Burgess, *Beard's Roman Women*, McGraw-Hill, 1976, p. 20)

COLLOQUY (kol'ə-kwē) *noun* a conversational exchange, often a formal one; a conference; a literary work written as a dialogue or conversation.

COLLOQUIST *noun.*

COLLOQUIUM *noun* an organized conference or seminar on some subject, involving a number of scholars or experts.

1. In any COLLOQUY in question [when a politician appears briefly on TV] we have a politician saying the obvious things, but those things that he was saying stir the resentments . . . of everyone who deplores (a) paying more for gas or fuel, or (b) finding it hard to get gas or fuel. (W. F. Buckley Jr., *Execution Eve and Other Contemporary Ballads*, G. P. Putnam's Sons, 1975, p. 289)

2. And remembering how the astonishingly sustained six-line stanzas of *The Dream Songs* (1969) [of John Berryman] make up a minstrel show COLLOQUY between "Henry" and "Mr. Bones," how can we fail to make the connection with [Cervantes'] Quixote and his interlocutor Sancho Panza? (D. Davie, Review of *The Freedom of the Poet*, by John Berryman, *New York Times*, 4/25/76, Section 7, p. 4)

3. He [Zwingli] drew Knox aside for an undertoned COLLOQUY. (Thomas Berger, *Who Is Teddy Villanova?*, Delacorte Press/Seymour Lawrence, 1977, p. 93)

COLUMBARIUM (kol'əm-bâr'ē-em) *noun, pl.:* -BARIA a sepulchral vault or other structure with recesses or niches in the walls to receive urns containing the ashes of cremated bodies; such a recess or niche; columbary (a shelter for pigeons or doves; dovecote).

1. Once I drove to a COLUMBARIUM in Reno, Nev., looking for a pigeon-hole with Robinson Jeffers' name on it. I don't think I found it. Anyway, the ashes were largely scattered on the Pacific—apparently against California law at the time. The family had first shipped the body out of state, and then done what they wished to with the remains. (J. Williams, "Paying Respects," *New York Times*, 12/19/76, Section 7, p. 27)

COMATOSE (kō'mə-tōs', kom'ə-) *adj.* affected with or characterized by coma or stupor; lacking alertness or energy; lethargic; TORPID; drowsy.

COMATOSELY *adv.*

1. That President Ford's swing through New Hampshire last weekend, lethargic and unexciting though it was, breathed a little life into his previously COMATOSE campaign here is evidence of his danger in this state's Feb. 24 primary. (R. Evans, R. Novak, "Ford's Campaign Trip 'Humdrum,'" *Daily Oklahoman*, Okla. City, 2/13/76, p. 16)

2. Marianne [in the book, *Hostage to the Devil*, by Malachi Martin] . . . is approached in Washington Square Park by a Man from the Kingdom of Satan who convinces her to enter into "a marriage with nothingness." She launches into a vast and disappointing succession of sexual relationships . . . . Marianne also falls into increasingly frequent paroxysms of violence when confronted with any symbol of her Catholic childhood . . . and grows COMATOSE in her stench-filled room. (Francine DuPlessix

Gray, Review, *New York Times*, 3/14/76, Section 7, p. 8)

3. Karen Ann Quinlan's father won the right in New Jersey Supreme Court on Wednesday to allow his COMATOSE daughter to die, climaxing a legal battle he began almost a year ago. (Associated Press, "Quinlan Wins Right to Let Karen Die," *Daily Oklahoman*, Okla. City, 4/1/76, p. 1)

4. See (3) under PRECOCIOUS.

5. See (1) under HOURI.

6. By the time the featured [after-dinner] speaker staggers out of his chair and approaches the rostrum, the diners are FLATULENT and COMATOSE, the head table is nodding, . . . and the room temperature has begun to approximate that of a sauna inside a tobacco plant. (Sydney J. Harris, "The last speaker talks less," *Philadelphia Inquirer*, 6/8/77, p. 12-A)

COMESTIBLE (kə-mes′ tə-bəl) *noun (usually used in the plural,* COMESTIBLES) food.

COMESTIBLE *adj.* eatable; edible.

1. The thief had made replacements [of the missing items in the refrigerator]: beluga caviar in glass and a tunnel-tinned loaf of Strasbourg pâté de foie gras. . . . The fridge might be mine, but the COMESTIBLES were not. I [Russel Wren] might have dipped into them had they instead been pressed ham, egg salad, and a bottle of Bud. (Thomas Berger, *Who Is Teddy Villanova?*, Delacorte Press/Seymour Lawrence, 1977, pp. 72–73)

COMITY (kom′ i-tē) *noun* mutual courtesy; politeness; civility.

COMITY of nations—the courtesy and respect of peaceful nations for each other's laws and institutions; loosely, the nations showing such courtesy and respect.

1. See (1) under MONOGLOT.

2. . . . what an old-fashioned word [is "treachery"], Black [ford Oakes] thought, in the cosmopolitan world of summit conferences, where the American President, the British Prime Minister, and the Soviet despot [Stalin] make dispositions involving hundreds of thousands of people—millions of people, actually—committing them, for the sake of temporary geopolitical COMITY, to any convenient fate—these men go back to receive the great acclaim, to be gartered by the Queen . . . . (W. F. Buckley Jr., *Saving the Queen*, Doubleday 1976, pp. 197–198)

COMMINATE (kom′ ə-nāt) *verb* to threaten with divine vengeance.

COMMINATION *noun* a denunciation or threat of punishment, especially of sinners.

COMMINATORY (käm′ i-nə-tôr′ ē, kə-min′ ə-) *adj.*

1. What she said now she said mostly in Italian. He [Ronald Beard] bowed his head as if it were COMMINATORY Church Latin. The rain began to hiss outside, like the chorus in Bach's *St. John Passion* demanding crucifixion. (A. Burgess, *Beard's Roman Women*, McGraw-Hill, 1976, p. 134)

COMPLEMENTARY (kom′ plə-men′ tə-rē, -trē) or **COMPLEMENTAL** *adj.* forming or acting as a complement; completing; mutually making up what is lacking.

COMPLEMENT *noun* something that completes or makes perfect; the quantity or amount that completes anything; either of two parts or things constituting a whole.

1. See (1) under PRELAPSARIAN.

2. See (1) under ASYMPTOTE.

3. Balanchine's concept of dance as a COMPLEMENTARY expression of music and, like music, a language onto itself is . . . now . . . a truism of contemporary dance. (Nancy Goldner, "The inimitable Balanchine," *New York Times*, 5/30/76, Section 6, p. 28)

4. See (2) under RECHERCHÉ.

5. It [*Ashmedai*, at the New York City Opera] was also skillfully COMPLEMENTED by [composer Josef] Tal's ECLECTIC score, which used every available musical idiom from electronics to jazz, and it was beautifully served by [director Harold] Prince's production and cast, led by the sprightly Eileen Schauler as the nutty queen and the brooding Paul Ukena as the tragic king. (H. Saal, Review, *Newsweek*, 4/12/76, p. 76)

6. . . . his [Henry Kissinger's] personality ap-

pears remarkably COMPLEMENTARY to that of his patron, Nixon . . . on the one hand [Kissinger was] a highly serious, intellectual projection of the statesman's role as part scholar, part philosopher, part man of action; on the other hand, a skillful bureaucratic technician, scornful of the oral principles of others, secretive, opportunistic, equivocal and ruthless. (O. Johnson, "After eight years the Kissinger enigma remains," *Philadelphia Inquirer*, 1/9/77, p. 4-E)

CON BRIO—See BRIO.

CONCATENATE (kon-kat′ ə-nāt′) *verb* to link or join together; unite in a series or chain.

CONCATENATE *adj.* linked together, as a chain; connected.

CONCATENATION *noun* a linking together or being linked together in a series; a series of things or events regarded as causally or dependently connected.

1. He [David H. Henry] blandly observes [in the book, *Challenges Past, Challenges Present*], "It is possible now to reflect upon McCarthyism as a result of the CONCATENATION of circumstances that exploded in the fifties, not as a creation of one man or an aberration of mid-century politics." Henry acquits the amiable [Joseph] McCarthy of inventing repression and intolerance all by himself. (R. Lekachman, Review, *Change*, April 1976, p. 56)

2. He [Blackford Oakes] was, on the telephone with Peregrine Kirk, required to give as much attention to what he was saying, and to what he must answer in return, as he would give, during a dive in a fighter plane, to replying to the CONCATENATED demands of the instruments on the dashboard. (W.F. Buckley Jr., *Saving the Queen*, Doubleday, 1976, p. 198)

CONCUPISCENCE (kon-kyŌŌ′pi-səns) *noun* ardent, usually sensuous longing; strong or abnormal desire or appetite, especially sexual desire; lust.

CONCUPISCENT *adj.* lustful or sensual; eagerly desirous.

1. In [George C.] Scott's big scene [in the 1958

production of the play, *Children of Darkness*], set in the living quarters of a loathsome jailer and his CONCUPISCENT daughter, ... he [Scott] fixed a cold, rapacious eye upon the jailer's daughter and delivered the line "I propose to enjoy your favors, wench," . . . and the audience shivered with delight. (Barbara Gelb, "Great Scott!," *New York Times*, 1/23/77, Section 6, pp. 11–12)

2. . . . the General Prologue and the first fragment of *The Canterbury Tales* are forced willy-nilly [by John Gardner, author of the book, *The Poetry of Chaucer*] into allegorical treatment with "the old Platonic and Aristotelian scheme of the tripartite soul— rational, IRASCIBLE, CONCUPISCENT." But if Gardner is at home with the EXEGETES, he is not their captive. He is equally at home with the "old humanists". . . who read Chaucer mainly as poetry and always with the amiable suspicion that the poet had his human, non-Christian failings. (C. Muscatine, Review, *New York Times*, 4/24/77, Section 7, p. 39)

3. See (2) under HECTOR.

CONDIGN (kən-dīn′) *adj.* well deserved; fitting; appropriate; suitable: said especially of punishment for wrongdoing.

CONDIGNLY *adv.*

1. . . . Blackford [Oakes] knew that someday he would need to expunge it [the memory of his beating by the headmaster at Greyburn] from his emotional system, though he could not . . . let his mind run over hypothetical means of taking CONDIGN, if asymmetrical, revenge. (W.F. Buckley Jr., *Saving the Queen*, Doubleday, 1976, p. 177)

CONFUTATION (kon′ fyŌŌ-tā-shən) *noun* the act of confuting; something (argument, evidence, etc.) that confutes.

CONFUTE *verb* to prove to be false or invalid; disprove; to prove (a person) to be wrong by argument or proof.

CONFUTATIVE *adj.*

1. Guernica [a Spanish town that was bombed in April 1937 during the Spanish Civil War] is easier to remember because it was the bad guys who did it. The good guys also have done the

same thing a number of times since. We don't need the CONFUTATION of unlikely claims (or allegations against the press, either) to tell us that civilians get hurt if they happen to be in the vicinity. (P. G. Fredericks, Review of *Guernica*, a book by Gordon Thomas and Max Morgan Wills, *New York Times*, 2/15/76, Section 7, p. 16)

CONGERIES (kon' jə-rēz') *noun* (construed as *sing.* or *pl.*) an aggregation of objects or ideas; assemblage; heap; pile.

1. There was a time when the Establishment referred to a New York-based CONGERIES of businessmen, politicians, and academicians who had a pretty tight hold on the policies of America, and were quite satisfied to run things their way. (W.F. Buckley Jr., *Execution Eve and Other Contemporary Ballads*, G. P. Putnam's Sons, 1975, p. 261)

2. The reader of these books [*A Man Called Intrepid: The Secret War*, by William Stevenson; *Bodyguard of Lies*, by Anthony Cave Brown; and *The Spymasters*, by Charles Whiting] comes to realize that British intelligence was a CONGERIES of fiefdoms, each believing in its own supremacy. (W. Clemons, Review, *Newsweek*, 3/22/76, p. 80)

3. . . . I [Russel Wren] could identify . . . a CONGERIES of human beings, among whom I recognized the most and the least: giant Bakewell and the tiny Hindu. . . . (Thomas Berger, *Who is Teddy Villanova?*, Delacorte Press/Seymour Lawrence, 1977, p. 221)

CONSANGUINITY (kon' saṅg-gwin' i-tē) *noun* a relationship by blood; close relationship or connection; affinity.

CONSANGUINEOUS or CONSANGUINE *adj.*

CONSANGUINEOUSLY *adv.*

1. We [Governor Ronald Reagan, James Buckley, and William F. Buckley Jr.] were together [in Reagan's living room] not only because of ideological CONSANGUINITY, or because we are friends, or because we thought . . . to man the same fortress at a moment when Richard Nixon would say something we were alerted to believe would be more than his routine denunciation of wage-and-price controls

. . . There had been no comment in the room, save one or two of those wolfish whistles one hears when someone on one's side in politics says something daringly RISQUÉ. (W.F. Buckley Jr., *Execution Eve and Other Contemporary Ballads*, G. P. Putnam's Sons, 1975, p. 21)

CONSONANCE (kon' sə-nəns) *noun* harmony, accord, or agreement; correspondence of sounds; harmony of sounds.

CONSONANT *adj.* in agreement; agreeable; consistent; in accord; harmonious in tone.

CONSONANTLY *adv.*

1. But one hears this tone [of change] above all in the peculiar CONSONANCE of professorial worldliness—their loyalty to the profession over the institution, their eagerness to sell their advice, to fly to exotic meeting grounds—and the spread of student instrumentalism, that dull and often cynical fascination for the "credential," which is about all that imagination or the spirit of the times seems able to offer them as a reason for going to college, or making sense of it once there. (N.W. Aldrich Jr., "Harvard On The Way Down," *Harper's*, March, 1976, p. 48)

CONSUMMATE (kən-sum' it, kon' sə-mit) *adj.* complete or perfect in every way; superb; supreme; very skillful; highly expert.

CONSUMMATE (kon' sə-māt') *verb* to bring to completion, fulfillment, or perfection; finish; accomplish; to complete (a marriage) by sexual intercourse.

CONSUMMATELY (kon-sum'it-lē) *adv.*

CONSUMMATION (kon'sə-mā'shən) *noun.*

CONSUMMATIVE (kon' sə-mā'tiv) or CONSUMMATORY (kon'sum'ə-tôr'ē) *adj.*

CONSUMMATOR *noun.*

1. Alan Dawson [author of the book, *55 Days: The Fall of South Vietnam*] restricts his canvas to the 55 days that saw the collapse of the splendidly equipped South Vietnamese army and the American withdrawal and frantic evacuation. Dawson was in the eye of the hurricane as the Saigon bureau chief, and here his objective is journalism, plain and simple, and it is achieved admirably with CONSUMMATE professionalism. (L. Swindell, Review, *Phila-*

delphia Inquirer, 11/27/77, p. 16-F)

2. Marie Antoinette and Louis XVI had been married seven years when their marriage was finally CONSUMMATED. It wasn't that they hadn't tried earlier. At night, the queen was too intent on going out late to party, and the king was too tired. (E. Schumacher, Review of *Twilight of the Old Order*, a book by Claude Manceron, *Philadelphia Inquirer*, 11/27/77, p. 17-F)

3. The game [of football], which should support "Semi-Tough," is pushed to the periphery of the movie by [Michael] Ritchie, a CONSUMMATE director of films about winning and losing, in favor of a weakly conceived struggle for the hand of Jill Clayburgh between [Burt] Reynolds and Kris Kristofferson. (Anon., Review, *Philadelphia Inquirer*, 11/27/77, p. 3-F)

CONTENTIOUS (kən-ten'shəs) *adj.* tending to argument or strife; quarrelsome; causing, involving, or characterized by argument, dispute, or controversy; controversial.

CONTENTIOUSLY *adv.*

CONTENTIOUSNESS *noun.*

1. California Rep. Phillip Burton, chairman of the Democratic caucus . . . , bridled briefly. "I have no sense of what our colleagues want," he told [House Majority Leader Thomas P.] O'Neill in a CONTENTIOUS meeting [about the Wayne Hays-Elizabeth Ray affair] on the Hill last week. "How can you say that?" shot the nettled Irishman. ". . . a man is innocent until proven guilty, but in politics, it's like Caesar's wife: you live in a glass bowl—and you step aside until you clear your name." (T. Mathews, *et al.*, "Capitol Capers," *Newsweek*, 6/14/76, pp. 18–19)

2. So the Irish continue to be a stubborn, difficult and CONTENTIOUS people. They were once the scholars who kept learning alive during the Dark Ages, but now everyone knows them to be anti-intellectual. (A.M. Greeley, Review of *The Irish Diaspora in America*, by Lawrence J. McCaffrey; and *The Roman Catholic Church And the Creation of the Modern Irish State, 1878-1886*, by Emmet Larkin, *New York Times*, 6/27/76, Section 7, p. 8)

CONTRAPUNTAL (kon' trə-pun' t'l) *adj.* of or pertaining to counterpoint; composed of

two or more relatively independent melodies sounded together.

CONTRAPUNTALLY *adv.*

CONTRAPUNTIST *noun* a person skilled in the principles and art of counterpoint.

1. Never, in my memory, has the nonsense of academic parties, faculty-student conferences, faculty meetings, faculty hostilities been so amusingly delineated as here [in the book, *The History Man*, by Malcolm Bradbury]. Bradbury's eye is kindly yet sharp, his tongue witty and accurate . . . [examples of typical conversation from the book are given] . . . And on and on in this mode, this fine CONTRAPUNTAL nonsense-cum-plot-revelation, all done in masterly fashion. (Doris Grumbach, Review, *Chronicle of Higher Education*, 3/1/76, p. 14)

2. Foreign Shakespeare critics—and especially French ones—are puzzled and even sometimes quite resentful at the inclusion of low farce into some of the tenser moments of the tragedies. The Porter scene in *Macbeth* is the most famous . . . One elaborate explanation relies on the deliberate use of CONTRAPUNTAL emotion and BATHOS to heighten tension and add an element of macabre unease. Perhaps these scenes have that effect on super-humorless French academic audiences . . . but an English audience usually roars with laughter. (A. Waugh, Review of *English Humor*, a book by J.B. Priestley, *New York Times*, 11/21/76, Section 7, p. 2)

CONTRARIETY (kon' trə-rī'i-tē) *noun* the quality or state of being contrary; something contrary or of opposite character; a contrary fact or statement; inconsistency or discrepancy.

1. He [Oliver Seccombe] had enjoyed thirteen years of happiness with her [his wife Charlotte] . . . she still laughed at the CONTRARIETIES of life and had never once complained that existence in Colorado was less than she had hoped. She loved the range and was an exemplary ranch wife. (J.A. Michener, *Centennial*, Fawcett, 1975, p. 716)

2. . . . it is precisely the fluidity, the ambiguity, the CONTRARIETY, the unfettered independence and consequent spontaneity Shakespeare has given his people that permits them to pass

from year to year, decade to decade, now century to century, without harm. (W. Kerr, "Around the Globe, Shakespeare Remains a Mirror for Mankind," *New York Times*, 9/12/76, Section 2, p. 13)

CONTRETEMPS (kon' trə-täN') *noun, pl.*: **CONTRETEMPS** an inopportune or unfortunate occurrence; an embarrassing mischance; awkward mishap.

1. The [newspaper] reporter did not share with his readers the one CONTRETEMPS of the evening. Some guests . . . wanted young Philip Wendell to join his parents in the duets, but he refused. They asked him to play the violin, but again he proved surly, whereupon Marvin Wendell said sharply, "Play for the people," and the fair-haired young man . . . glared at his father and stomped from the room. (J.A. Michener, *Centennial*, Fawcett, 1975, p. 843)

2. Arraigned last week on the narcotics charge [possession of cocaine] . . . [Louise] Lasser has made no comment on her CONTRETEMPS in a Beverly Hills boutique and a local police station. [When the boutique would not accept her credit card, she refused to leave; police were called, and cocaine was found in her pocketbook.] Anon., "Newsmakers," *Newsweek*, 5/17/76, p. 67)

3. . . . some Americans will welcome the [Wayne] Hays CONTRETEMPS the way columnist Murray Kempton welcomed . . . Sonny Liston, a strikingly unrehabilitated ex-convict, to the heavyweight championship: ". . . he . . . can . . . be a heavyweight champion who will be the discredit his profession has needed all these years." (G.F. Will, "The Hays investigation: Morality won't enter into it," *Philadelphia Inquirer*, 5/31/76, p. 9-A)

4. Of itself, the Hays-Ray episode might have been dismissed as was the Wilbur Mills-Fannie Foxx CONTRETEMPS. Subsequently, however, have come reports that perhaps half a dozen other congressmen have similar arrangements, that Miss Ray shared her favors with a dozen congressmen and two senators, that another young lady was passed around among seven members of a committee with which she was associated. (P.J. Buchanan, "Morality Real Central Issue in Hays Scandal," *Saturday Oklahoman & Times*, Okla. City, 6/12/76, p. 16)

5. Behind the Sunday School manner and the peanut-patch smile, Carter is a warrior as well—a driven man whose loving kindness coexists with a hunger to prove himself in combat . . . . He expects victory and suffers miserably in defeat, in anything from politics to the pickup softball games he pitched during his summer furlough in Plains. He wrangled with umpires, dressed down his own teammates—"Any of you gonna start *helping* me?"—and proposed limiting the other side to press and Secret Service, the better to work up a book on their strengths and weaknesses. "He is an arrogant little son of a bitch," press secretary Jody Powell kidded at one such CONTRETEMPS . . . . Carter overheard, and displayed his non-amusement with a laser stare. (P. Goldman, "Sizing Up Carter," *Newsweek*, 9/13/76, p. 23)

6. It's never pleasant to say "I told you so." But the natural gas industry, if it were disposed to risk a CONTRETEMPS in its public relations with Congress, would be thoroughly justified in calling attention to the fact that it had warned the nation way back in the 1950s that the price policies followed by government regulators would result in a gas famine in the '70s. (J. Chamberlain, "U.S. rules brought gas famine," *Times Union*, Albany, N.Y., 2/2/77, p. 9)

CONTUMACIOUS (kon' tŏō-mā' shəs, -tyŏō-) *adj.* stubbornly perverse or rebellious; obstinately disobedient; insubordinate; contrary; refractory; intractable.

CONTUMACIOUSLY *adv.*

CONTUMACIOUSNESS or **CONTUMACY** (kon' tŏō-mə-sē, -tyŏō-) *noun.*

1. See (1) under SUPERORDINATION.

2. He [U.S. District Court Judge Prentice H. Marshall] denounced the city's refusal to implement the 1974 agreement [involving racial and sexual quotas for hiring in the Chicago police department] as "arrogant" and "CONTUMACIOUS" and enjoined the Treasury Department from sending $95 million in revenue-sharing funds to the city until the police department obeyed his rulings. (R.L. Worsnop, "Chicago becomes major battleground: Reverse discrimination demands ruling," *Norman* [Okla.] *Transcript*, 5/2/76, p. 4)

CONTUMELY (kon' tŏō-mə-lē, -tyŏō, kən-tŏō' mə-lē, -tyŏō‑' , kon' təm-lē) *noun* an insulting display of contempt; haughty and contemptuous rudeness; a humiliating and scornful insult; insulting and humiliating treatment or language; an instance of this.

CONTUMELIOUS *adj.*

CONTUMELIOUSLY *adv.*

1. Colonel Frank Skimmerhorn, who in recent months has suffered CONTUMELY at the hands of the lily-livered segment of our population, was completely vindicated yesterday afternoon when he single-handedly shot the last of the Pasquinels as the half-breed was brazenly trying to commit further depredations in this town. (J.A. Michener, *Centennial*, Fawcett, 1975, p. 510)

2. See (1) under SNIDE.

3. The [House] committee [on "Standards of Official Conduct"] must act [on the charges against Wayne Hays], or it must bear the CONTUMELY it surely will deserve. Never mind Wayne Hays' reputation. The House now must look at its own. (J.J. Kilpatrick, "Hays Affair Requires Quick Action," *Daily Oklahoman*, Okla. City, 6/2/76, p. 6)

4. "No picture ever had such bad talk about it," understates Barbra Streisand as she watches the tide of money roll in from the third reworking of *A Star Is Born*. She was referring to the CONTUMELY heaped upon the film before it was even released . . . (D. Ryan, "Critic's Notebook," *Philadelphia Inquirer*, 1/30/77, p. 1-D)

CONUNDRUM (kənun' drəm) *noun* a riddle whose answer involves a pun; any puzzling question or problem.

1. "Don't be bamboozled by their size: these individuals [young girls] are wily degenerates [said Boris to Russel Wren]. Their games are not the SPILLIKINS and CONUNDRUMS that Jane Austen played with young relatives; they are rather the decadent Roman entertainments that followed Trimalchio's feast." (Thomas Berger, *Who Is Teddy Villanova?*, Delacorte Press/Seymour Lawrence, 1977, p. 202)

CONURBATION (kon' ûr-bā' shən) *noun* an extensive urban area resulting from the expansion of several cities or towns so that they

coalesce but retain their separate identities, usually a complex of suburbs and smaller towns together with a large city at their center.

1. The Paris CONURBATION is being broken up into five coherent communities with local employment opportunities and amenities. In all of these new communities and between all of them, improved public transport is designed to lessen dependence on the private car and, in Le Vaudreuil, an experimental city is being developed to achieve energy conservation, recycling of effluents and reuse of all waste . . . The vast CONURBATIONS, made more intolerable by even deeper poverty and starker social segregation, are a fact. But the whole point of the new directions in urban planning is that half the cities needed for the inevitable population increase of the next 30 years have yet to be built. (Barbara Ward, "Megacities increasingly unfeasible: Half the Cities of 1999 now unbuilt," *Norman* [Okla.] *Transcript*, 6/14/76, p. 6)

2. For to rescue Venice truly—that is, to make of the historic center a practicable modern city, a dormitory town perhaps for the mainland CONURBATIONS, or even a manufacturing city of its own based upon the Arsenale shipyards, would need money beyond the imagination of the Save Venice fund raisers, and moreover would so alter the character of the place that its innocent well-wishers . . . would be appalled at the result. (Jan Morris, Review of *The Death of Venice*, a book by Stephen Fay and Phillip Knightley, *New York Times*, 11/21/76, Section 7, p. 49)

COPROLALIA (kop rə-lā'lē-ə) *noun* excessive or uncontrollable swearing; obsessive use of obscene or SCATOLOGICAL language as sexual gratification; use of words relating to dirt or excrement.

COPROLALIAC *adj.*

1. Tourette's syndrome, which comes and goes, involves tic-like movements, and victims often utter inarticulate words like grunts, hisses and barks. About half of the victims also develop COPROLALIA, which is the uncontrollable urge to utter obscene language. Doctors now have developed several drugs that seem to control this terrible disease. (G. Volgenau, Knight

News Service, "Gutter talk is growing," *Philadelphia Inquirer*, 10/13/76, p. 6-C)

CORNUCOPIA (kôr′nə-kō′pē-ə) *noun* (*in Mythology*) a horn containing food, drink, etc., in endless supply; horn of plenty; a representation of this horn, overflowing with fruits, flowers, and grain, used as a symbol of abundance; an abundant, overflowing supply; any horn-shaped or conical receptacle, container, or ornament.

CORNUCOPIAN *adj.*

1. And if the American job CORNUCOPIA has been depleted, in relative terms, the implications for education are absolutely immense. (G.W. Bonham, "The American Future" [Editorial], *Change*, May, 1975, p. 11)

2. See (1) under DIOGENES.

3. Leaks and even formally published reports on [CIA] activities long since corrected have provided enemies of America with a CORNUCOPIA of details with which to assail our country and its friends for years to come. (W.E. Colby, "What's ahead for the CIA?," *Boston Globe*, 3/7/76, p. 1-A)

4. But these few remembrances of things past are minor compared to the CORNUCOPIA of new marvels in Act 2 [of *The Magic Flute*, which contains] . . . a contrast of ensembles and arias, of tempi, moods, and extremes of vocal range that is unequaled. (R. Craft, Review, *New York Review of Books*, 11/27/75, p. 21)

5. Let us confess that if ever a man in America crossed the liberal ideology, . . . [Senator Joseph] McCarthy did, which is why the McCarthy years are a CORNUCOPIA for the sociologist doing research . . . on American Liberalism . . . (W.F. Buckley Jr., *Up From Liberalism*, Arlington House, 2nd Printing 1968, pp. 39–40)

6. Even in these depressing times, there's a lot of money around in the form of college scholarships . . . . [S. Robert Freede's] Scholarship Search can't do more than acquaint you with opportunities; actually getting the cash is your job from then on. But it does seem to have found a way to tilt the CORNUCOPIA in your direction. (Anon., "Paying For College," *Harper's*, January, 1975, p. 97)

7. And the Senate's Democrats placed delivery

ahead of ideology when they chose [Robert] Byrd over Hubert Humphrey [as Senate Majority Leader], a ravaged but spirited old warrior who might have entered his own CORNUCOPIAN ideas in competition with Carter's. (P. Goldman, *et. al.*, "The New Kings of the Hill," *Newsweek*, 1/17/77, p. 17)

CORPOSANT (kôr′pə-zant′) *noun* same as St. Elmo's Fire (q.v.).

1. Meanwhile, St. Elmo's Fire—a CORPOSANT (*sic*) ball of fiery light you sometimes see on a ship's masts during storms— dances eerily on your [the mountaineer's] ice axe. And the thin air is as hard to breathe as cotton wool. In mountaineering, 99 percent of the way up is called a failure. (H.J. Taylor, "Deadly Eiger Wall," *Times Herald*, Norristown, Pa., 6/8/77, p. 19)

CORUSCATE (kor′ə-skāt′) *verb* to emit vivid flashes of light; glitter; sparkle; scintillate; gleam.

CORUSCATION *noun* the act of coruscating; a sudden gleam or flash of light; a striking display of brilliance or wit.

1. Listen to the way he [Josef Hofmann] plays the Larghetto of Chopin's F minor Concerto— the purity of the line, the CORUSCATING functional embellishments in the right hand . . . . (H. C. Schonberg, "The Greatest Pianist of His Time," *New York Times*, 4/18/76, Section 2, p. 19)

2. As a revival it [*The Heiress*, a play by Ruth and Augustus Goetz] must compete, too, with the memory of earlier incarnations, the 1947 play with Basil Rathbone and an oft-replayed movie starring Ralph Richardson as the CORUSCATING father. (T. E. Kalem, Review, *Time*, 5/3/76, p. 76)

3. And those [TV documentary] specials that do make it on the air seem bland, especially when stacked against the CORUSCATINGLY tough approach of Edward R. Murrow's landmark *See It Now* series. (H. F. Waters, *et al.*, "The New Look of TV News," *Newsweek*, 10/11/76, pp. 78, 81)

COSSET (kos′ it) *verb* to treat as a pet; pamper; coddle; fondle.

COSSET *noun* a lamb brought up without its dam; pet lamb; any pet.

1. Essentially they [the editors who function as co-publishers or independent contractors in a larger publishing company] provide editorial services—signing up, editing and COSSETING writers—while the host publishing company, with which they are tied in a contractual relationship, takes care of sales, administrative and accounting details. (Anon., "Book Ends: Independents," *New York Times*, 2/15/76, Section 7, p. 25)

2. Some impressive figures from Pet Supplies Marketing (a trade publication) show that today's cats are well-treated, even COSSETED, and given a much better deal than many of their ancestors. Barbara Treleven, spokesman for the publication, says retail dollar figures for "cats and cat-related items" increased 17.6 percent between 1973 and 1974. (Mary Daniels, *Chicago Tribune*, "Morris did it: Cats gaining as pets, thanks to TV," reprinted in *Philadelphia Inquirer*, 10/24/76, p. 2-I)

3. I am personally convinced that the American people don't want to be COSSETED, protected and supervised at twice the cost of what they were paying for services four years ago. When it takes 130.5 million work-hours a year to complete government forms, there is a sad waste of time and energy . . . . (J. Chamberlain, "Costly Agencies," *Times Herald*, Norristown, Pa., 11/16/76, p. 11)

COUP DE GRÂCE (kōōd°-gRäs), *pl*.: **COUPS DE GRÂCE** (kōōz-də-gRäs) a death blow, especially one delivered mercifully to end suffering by a mortally wounded person; any finishing or decisive stroke.

1. . . . after noting that Archibald Cox helped write Harvard University's brief supporting preferential admissions, the author [Robert M. O'Neil] informs us [in *Discrimination Against Discrimination: Preferential Admissions and the DeFunis Case*] that Solicitor General Robert Bork, whose demand for federal neutrality in the DeFunis case angered the minorities . . . , was the man who "administered the COUP DE GRÂCE to Messrs. Cox and Richardson" during the infamous Saturday Night Massacre. The implication here is clear, although the accusation, while technically correct, is outrageously misleading. (D. M. Oshinsky, Review, *Change*, May 1976, p. 58)

2. As A.B. Giamatti pointed out in a recent issue of *Yale Alumni Magazine*, the language

and the resultant literature of the new messiahs of this instant cult [the "free speech" and later student protests] gave the COUP DE GRÂCE to the real learning of language, including English. (S. D. Ripley, "While the Three R's are declining in classrooms, we may have to teach them — objectively — in museums," *Smithsonian*, May 1976, p. 2-I)

3. The Dreamer [Adam Malone] had recovered, she [Sharon Fields] could see, had witnessed the COUP DE GRÂCE [her shooting Shively after Malone had stabbed him], . . . and he was now staring at her with an odd expression on his youthful face. (I. Wallace, *The Fan Club*, Bantam Books, 1975, p. 619)

COUP D'ÉTAT (kōō' dä-tä') *noun, pl*.: **COUPS D'ÉTAT** (kōōz dä-tä') a sudden and decisive political action, especially one effecting a change of government illegally or by force, often by a CABAL.

1. *Shogun*, [a book] by James Clavell . . . Englishman embroiled in intrigue and COUP D'ÉTAT in 16th-century Japan. (Anon., Review, *New York Times*, 6/27/76, Section 7, p. 31)

2. It is probable that nuclear weapons technology will come into the hands of lunatic governments before long. Of the 140 or so governments in the world, about two-thirds are run by people who are afraid they might be executed after a violent COUP D'ÉTAT tomorrow. (N. Macrae, "United States can keep growing—and lead—if it wishes," *Smithsonian*, July 1976, p. 37)

3. No doubt Bangladesh . . . is exaggerating both issues [in its dispute with India] . . . Perhaps part of the government's aim is to use this as a means of uniting Bangladesh, no small attraction in a country which has gone through three COUPS D'ÉTAT in 12 months and is facing a new round of instability as next February's election approaches. (NEA/London Economist News Service (LENS), "Bangladesh, India on collision course?" *Times Herald*, Norristown, Pa., 9/7/76, p. 3)

4. . . . the version [of the documentary film, *Idi Amin Dada*, directed by Barbet Schroeder] being shown here is cut in three places [because Dada threatened to kill all Frenchmen in the Ugandan capital if the cuts were not made]: The opening scene, showing a public execution with a commentary noting that the Amin regime had ordered the deaths of thou-

sands since it came to power in a 1971 COUP D'ÉTAT . . . . (Judy Klemesrud, "The Man Who 'Directed' a Dictator," *New York Times*, 9/12/76, Section 2, p. 15)

CRAVEN (krā′vən) *adj.* very cowardly; contemptibly timid or afraid.

CRAVEN *noun* a cowardly person.

CRAVENLY *adv.*

CRAVENNESS *noun.*

1. Unleashed in Spiro Agnew's off-year-election effort of 1970, he [William Safire] gave us "NATTERING NABOBS of negativism" and the JEREMIADS against "permissiveness" and "elitism." Right after Nixon's landslide reelection, Safire became the only right-wing columnist on the *New York Times* op-ed page—a move generally interpreted as a CRAVEN surrender of that proud newspaper to White House pressure. (G. Wills, "William Safire At the Top of the Heap," *New York*, 11/28/77, p. 33)

CREPUSCULAR (kri-pus′kyə-lər) *adj.* of, pertaining to, or resembling twilight; dim; indistinct; active at twilight.

CREPUSCULE or CREPUSCLE *noun* twilight; dusk.

1. For at least 250 million years, beetles have been evolving adaptive strategies to escape from their enemies. During the last two-and-a-half centuries, however, their environment has been invaded by an awesome PREDATOR against which their well-tried defenses afford only minimal protection. None of their earlier pursuers were equipped with vision that had such fine resolving power and perception of color and depth. Nor had beetles been so crudely exposed during their CREPUSCULAR and nocturnal activities by the generation of synthetic light. (M. Emsley, "Nature's most successful design may be beetles," *Smithsonian*, December 1975, p. 105)

2. Though utterly innocent, I [Russel Wren] was a wanted criminal . . . . Claimed by AGORAPHOBIA, I slowed my pace and peered longingly into CREPUSCULAR cellarways and the cozy crannies amidst bales of rubbish . . . . (Thomas Berger, *Who Is Teddy Villanova?*,

Delacorte Press/Seymour Lawrence, 1977, p. 125)

3. I [Russel Wren] opened the hatch and more slid than stepped down the fixed iron ladder so revealed, precipitating myself into a CREPUSCULAR corner of the fifth-floor rear . . . . (Thomas Berger, *Ibid.*, p. 224)

CRETIN (krēt′ən, krē′tin) *noun* a person afflicted with cretinism (a congenital and extreme deficiency of thyroid secretion with resulting deformity and idiocy); a stupid, obtuse, or mentally defective person.

CRETINOID or CRETINOUS *adj.*

1. It [the McGovern Spirit] is the sense of absolute, total self-righteousness. It is manifestly intolerant of different opinions, and disposed, toward those who hold them, to dismiss them as CRETINS. (W.F. Buckley Jr., *Execution Eve and Other Contemporary Ballads*, G. P. Putnam's Sons, 1975, p. 72)

2. The modern liturgists, incidentally are doing a remarkably good job, attendance at Catholic Mass on Sunday having dropped sharply in the ten years since a few well-meaning CRETINS got hold of the power to vernacularize the Mass, and the money to scour . . . the earth in search of the most unmusical men and women to preside over the translation. (W.F. Buckley Jr., *Ibid.*, p. 458)

3. "You're not still sore, are you?" [Adam Malone asked Sharon Fields]. She regarded this nut, this CRETIN, with disbelief. "When was the last time you were gang-banged?" she said bitterly. (I. Wallace, *The Fan Club*, Bantam edition, 1975, p. 337)

4. "For M. Millet, art is slavish copying of nature. He lights his lantern and goes looking for CRETINS . . . imagine a monster with no skull, the eyes extinguished by an idiot's squint, straddling in the middle of a field like a scarecrow. No spark of intelligence humanizes this resting brute. Has he been working or murdering?" So ran one Paris critic's response to Jean François Millet's *Man with a Hoe* at the salon of 1863. (R. Hughes, Review of Millet's centenary exhibition at London's Hayward Gallery, *Time*, 2/23/76, p. 60)

5. See (4) under FLACCID.

6. See (4) under ALLITERATION.

7. The guards in these camps [in Russia for dissidents] . . . are literally CRETINS, and a prisoner who gives a guard even one 3-D postcard will be spared from hard labor for six months. (D. Rottenberg, "To Russia With Levis," *Today*, *The Inquirer Magazine*, 1/9/77, p. 12)

8. See (4) under SUPERANNUATED.

9. "Wait till the summer," she [Mama Stefano] had warned her customers in a snarl . . . . "In the summer he'll find out what [kind of house] he's bought, the CRETIN." In the summer, [owner] slick Franco's mice would storm the bedroom, Franco's fleas would devour him alive, and Franco's . . . hornets would chase him round the garden . . . . (J. LeCarré, *The Honourable Schoolboy*, Alfred A. Knopf, 1977, p. 29)

10. They [the horses in the race] began the long turn before the final straight. "*Come* on, Open Space, stretch for it man, *ride!* Use your whip, you CRETIN!" [Clive] Porton screamed, for by now it was clear . . . that the sky-blue and sea-gray colours of Lucky Nelson were heading for the front . . . . (J. LeCarré, *Ibid.*, p. 157)

CROESUS (krē′səs) *noun* died 546 B.C., king of Lydia 560-546: noted for his great wealth; any very rich man.

1. After the war, her money problems dissolved with the tremendous success of *Pursuit of Love* (1945), *Love in a Cold Climate* (1949) and . . . *The Blessing* (1951). By then, she [Nancy Mitford] had the CROESUS touch, and when she turned to what are now regrettably but ineradicably identified as coffee-table books . . . it was soon apparent that her industry, wit and natural goodness had been rewarded as few writers are in their lifetime . . . (Auberon Waugh, Review of *Nancy Mitford*, by Harold Acton, *New York Times*, 3/28/76, Section 7, p. 7)

2. See (1) under NEBBISH.

3. But for those who stay on top, or near it, life in Hollywood brings riches that would make CROESUS blush. (M. Ruby, M. Kasindorf,

et al., "Inside Hollywood," *Newsweek*, 2/13/78, p. 72)

4. "For what it's worth," Lacon proceeded . . . , "he [Drake Ko] probably does as much to enrich the Colony [Hong Kong] as any other wealthy and respected Chinese businessman. Or as little . . . . In fact, to all outward purposes, he is something of a Hong Kong PROTOTYPE: Steward of the Jockey Club, supports the charities, pillar of the integrated society, successful, benevolent, has the wealth of CROESUS and the commercial morality of the whorehouse." (J. LeCarré, *The Honourable Schoolboy*, Afred A. Knopf, 1977, p. 169)

CUCKOLD (kuk′əld) *noun* the husband of an unfaithful wife.

CUCKOLD *verb* to make a cuckold of.

CUCKOLDRY *noun* the act of making someone a cuckold; the state or quality of being a cuckold.

1. [Bruce] Dobler [in *The Last Rush North*] traces . . . the odyssey of Larry Ransom . . . who travels to Alaska to write a series of articles on the building of the pipeline. The gravel road is laid, Ransom is CUCKOLDED, modular housing is welded together, . . . a couple of earthquakes occur. (S. Frank, Review, *New York Times*, 9/12/76, Section 7, p. 40)

2. . . . François (Michel Picoli) [in the French film, *Vincent, François, Paul and the Others*] is a friend of . . . a highly successful doctor who dislikes everything about his life but the money. The money has its price: his wife, calling him a bloodless cashier, regularly CUCKOLDS him and finally departs. (D. Ryan, Review, *Philadelphia Inquirer*, 9/26/76, p. 6-H)

3. . . . [Saul] Bellow supposed that this novel [*Herzog*] about a middle-aged CUCKOLD who composes unmailed letters to everyone from Willie Sutton to Spinoza might enjoy a narrow critical success and sell 8,000 copies. Instead, it topped the best-seller list for months . . . . (W. Clemons, Chris J. Harper, "Bellow the Word King," *Newsweek*, 11/1/76, p. 89)

4. . . . surely it was none too pleasant for a fellow of his [Donald Washburn's] physique and with his apparent financial resources to

admit to possible CUCKOLDRY . . . . (Thomas Berger, *Who Is Teddy Villanova?*, Delacorte Press/Seymour Lawrence, 1977, p. 56)

5. As the Sganarelle who imagines adultery [in Molière's play, *Sganarelle*, at Yale Repertory Theatre], Michael Gross has the tall, collapsible skeleton of a Ray Bolger; he mimes the comic terror of CUCKOLDRY with admirable ferocity, at one point literally pole-vaulting into the audience in his frenzy. (J. Kroll, Review, *Newsweek*, 2/13/78, p. 34)

CUMSHAW (kum' shô) *noun* a present, gratuity, or tip.

CUMSHAW *verb* to give a present to; to tip.

1. In many respects, [Charles] Durden's book [*No Bugles, No Drums*] seems like a ripoff of [Joseph] Heller's [*Catch-22*]. Hawkins can be read as Yossarian. Pvt. Angelo (Crazy Dago) Cocuzza comes across like Milo Minderbinder's younger brother. . . . Instead of dealing in CUMSHAW, he organizes a scheme to ship 240 pounds of Thai marijuana back to the States in a dead friend's coffin . . . . These incidents seem totally improbable—until you stop to think that just a couple of years ago mortuary workers in Saigon were caught stuffing GI coffins with heroin. (Kim Willenson, Review, *Newsweek*, 8/9/76, pp. 72-73)

CUNNILINGUS (kun'əling'gəs) *noun* oral stimulation (licking) of the female genitalia.

1. Paola gave the telephone a long and rapid and filthy monologue, in which PEDICATION, CUNNILINGUS, FELLATION . . . were presented in a HAGIOGRAPHIC context. (A. Burgess, *Beard's Roman Women*, McGraw-Hill, 1976, p. 113)

CURMUDGEON (kər-muj' ən) *noun* an IRASCIBLE, churlish person; a surly, illmannered, bad-tempered fellow; cantankerous person.

CURMUDGEONLY *adv.*

1. . . . double the fine (or the prison sentence) and you halve the offense. Curiously it is not the CURMUDGEONS alone who are tempted by the argument. (W.F. Buckley Jr., *Execution Eve and Other Contemporary Ballads*, G.P. Putnam's Sons, 1975, p. 399)

2. All this peculiar information [about Welshmen in early America] emerged last week when, in the company of our good pal the old CURMUDGEON, we called on Wynford Vaughan-Thomas, the Welsh Bicentennial Ambassador to the United States. (Anon., "The Talk of the Town: Founding Fathers," *The New Yorker*, 2/9/76, pp. 24-25)

3. He [Howard Hughes] had been a genius and CURMUDGEON, Red-baiter and environmentalist, WASTREL and philanthropist. (T. Mathews, *et al.*, "The Secret World of Howard Hughes," *Newsweek*, 4/19/76, p. 25)

4. See (1) under CHOLERIC.

5. Around the labor federation's . . . headquarters across Lafayette Park from the White House, the possibility of the old CURMUDGEON [82-year-old George Meany, president of the AFL-CIO] leaving office voluntarily was discussed [until recently] only in whispers—if at all. But after a summer marked by a nagging respiratory problem that hospitalized him twice, there seems little doubt that labor's grand eminence will step down. (T. Nicholson, T. Joyce, "Après Meany," *Newsweek*, 12/6/76, p. 81)

CYNOSURE (sī'nə-shŏŏr', sin'ə-) *noun* any person or thing that strongly attracts attention by its brilliance, interest, etc.; a center of attention; something serving for guidance or direction; (if capitalized) an old name for the constellation Ursa Minor, or the North Star in that constellation.

CYNOSURAL (sī'nə-shŏŏr'əl) *adj.*

1. Were you the literary CYNOSURE of the SDS [said John Kenneth Galbraith in a letter to William F. Buckley Jr.] my advice would not be different except as I might suppose your instinct for self-preservation to be less developed. (W. F. Buckley Jr., *Execution Eve and Other Contemporary Ballads*, G. P. Putnam's Sons, 1975, p. 325)

2. But [Jackie] Robinson was the CYNOSURE of all eyes [in Ebbets Field]. (R. Kahn, *The Boys of Summer*, Harper and Row, 1971, p. xviii)

3. Even lounging in a turtleneck, Earl Blackwell is the very figure and CYNOSURE of fashion, and never more so than when he is presiding in

his Manhattan penthouse. (M. Goodman, "Earl Blackwell Chronicles and Entertains Celebrities—For Their Pleasure and His Profit," *People*, 5/24/76, p. 66)

4. [Bob] Marley is Jamaica's superstar. He rivals the government as a political force. The mythical hero of his last album, *Natty Dread*, has already become a national symbol. Marley is a CYNOSURE both in Jamaican society and in the trenchtown ghetto where he grew up. He seldom appears in either milieu, but when he

does, it is with a retinue that includes a SHAMAN, a cook, one "herbsman" laden with marijuana and several athletes. (Anon., "Singing Them A Message," *Time*, 3/22/76, p. 84)

5. Clad in her spotless white blue-bordered sari, Mother Theresa, who ministers to the starving people of Calcutta . . . was the CYNOSURE of the [recent eucharistic] congress. (Anon., "The Catholic Olympics," *Time*, 8/16/76, p. 45)

6. See (1) under EMBAY.

D

DASHIKI (dä-shē′ kē) *noun* a usually bright-colored, loose-fitting one-piece pullover garment worn especially by men.

1. After the decision [to grant him a new trial] was announced, a DASHIKI-clad [Rubin (Hurricane)] Carter appeared at a prison press conference arm in arm with civil rights leader Ralph Abernathy to say that he was looking forward to a "fair trial free of perjured testimony." (Anon., "Justice: Hurricane," *Newsweek*, 3/29/76, p. 30)

2. See (1) under QUIFF.

DEBOUCH (di-boosh′, di-bouch′) *verb* to come forth; emerge; (of a river) to emerge from a narrow valley upon an open plain; (of a body of troops) to march out from a narrow or confined place into open country.

DEBOUCHMENT or DEBOUCHURE (da′ boo-shoor′, di-boo′-) *noun* the act of debouching; a mouth or outlet, as of a river or pass.

1. As I [Russel Wren] DEBOUCHED precipitately from the hallway [into the living room], I saw that [Donald] Washburn stood before the modular sofa . . . . (Thomas Berger, *Who Is Teddy Villanova?*, Delacorte Press/Seymour Lawrence, 1977, p. 160)

2. I [Russel Wren] went to the ground floor and squirted through the lobby . . . , DEBOUCHING onto the sidewalk . . . . (Thomas Berger, *Ibid.*, p. 227)

DEBRIDEMENT (di-brēd′mənt) *noun* the surgical removal of dead or contaminated tissue from a wound to prevent infection.

1. All of Walker Percy's fiction has been written in the service of the same theme that animates *Lancelot*, the search for whatever it is that can banish despair. Percy has spent his entire career DEBRIDING the same wound. His work is narrow but it cuts deep. (R. Todd, Review, *Atlantic*, March 1977, p. 115)

DECIDUOUS (di-sij′ oo-əs) *adj.* shedding the leaves annually, as trees and shrubs; falling off or shed at a particular season, stage of growth, etc., as leaves, horns, or teeth; not permanent; transitory; short-lived.

DECIDUOUSLY *adv.*

DECIDUOUSNESS *noun.*

1. He [Will Weng, *New York Times* crossword puzzle editor] is leery . . . of using [the names of] soap opera stars and cabinet members, their fame often being DECIDUOUS (fleet-

ing . . .). Frequent Presidential candidate Harold Stassen is acceptable, but Maurice Stans, a former secretary of commerce and Nixon fund-raiser, is not. Actor James Arness is a known, durable quantity, but "Hutch," of the television show *Starsky and Hutch*, is not. (M. Dubin, "Puzzled? Then Weng has done his job," *Philadelphia Inquirer*, 11/28/76, p. 4-L)

DÉCLASSÉ (dā′klə-sā′) *adj.* reduced to or having low status.

1. Michael Caine, as a regal safecracker [in *Harry and Walter go to New York*] who enlists Harry and Walter as jailbird valets after the two have failed even at petty larceny, assumes an aristocratic manner so DÉCLASSÉ that it only heightens the picture's comic possibilities. (Janet Maslin, Review, *Newsweek*, 6/28/76, p. 78)

2. In [John] Cheever's suburbias, trying to live up to [patriarch] Leander [Wapshot]'s morality usually results in grotesquely DÉCLASSÉ behavior. (R.Z. Sheppard, Review of *Falconer*, a book by John Cheever, *Time*, 2/28/77, p. 79)

DÉCOLLETAGE (dā′kol-täzh′, -kol-ə-, dek′ə-lə-) *noun* the neckline of a dress cut low in the front or back and often across the shoulders; a décolleté garment.

DÉCOLLETÉ (dā′ kol-tā′, -kol-ə-, dek′ə-lə-) *adj.* (of a garment) low-necked; wearing a low-necked garment.

1. Jackie Onassis wears her [Elsa Peretti's] silver horseshoe belt. Her silver cane and cuffs grace Liza Minnelli's wardrobe. Lauren Bacall's DÉCOLLETAGE glistens with her 36-inch diamond chain. (M. Sneed, "Elsa Peretti— teardrops for Tiffany's," *Chicago Tribune*, 2/20/76, Section 1, p. 1)

2. "You should have put something on top of that DÉCOLLETÉ for lunch," her father grumbled. "Monsieur le Curé almost had a stroke when he gave you Communion this morning." (Francine duPlessix Gray, "Tribe," *The New Yorker*, 5/31/76, p. 37)

3. He [Ronald Beard] liked the Rugantino [restaurant] . . . . Tablecloths were clean, waiters quick, oil and garlic subdued, Anita Ekberg had once danced on a table in profound DÉCOLLETAGE, Jean-Paul Sartre and

Simone de Beauvoir had shared something bland and left their autographs. (A. Burgess, *Beard's Roman Women*, McGraw-Hill, 1976, p. 36)

4. There were no songs [in the film], but atmospheric Trenchmore [who wrote the film's music] was always ready to growl or thump or wax insincerely lyrical over DÉCOLLETAGED passion or the Alps, sometimes both together. (A. Burgess, *Ibid.*, p. 138)

DE FACTO (dē fak′tō) in fact; in reality; actually existing, especially when without lawful authority (distinguished from DE JURE).

1. See (1) under TRANSMOGRIFY.

2. See (1) under PARIAH.

3. See (2) under DE JURE.

4. . . . the [French] government is making no attempt to control wages along with prices. Nor does it plan any measures that would directly aid the faltering franc, which has suffered a DE FACTO devaluation of 9 percent recently. (A. J. Mayer, *et al.*, "Le Plan Barre," *Newsweek*, 10/4/76, p. 85)

5. Administration officials insisted that Ford had only meant [by his "there is no Soviet domination of Eastern Europe" remark] that the U.S. does not recognize Eastern Europe as a Soviet sphere of influence—a position that does not in fact square with DE FACTO American policy. (Susan Fraker and F. Maier, "Jerry Ford Drops a Brick," *Newsweek*, 10/18/76, p. 24)

6. At the same time, the House of which [Tip] O'Neill is now DE FACTO leader rejected the eminently sensible proposal that lame duck congressmen should not take junkets at public expense. (G. Wills, "It's not a home . . . but the House needs a cleaning," *Philadelphia Inquirer*, 12/16/76, p. 15-A)

7. Israel claims that conquest of Sinai gave it DE FACTO oil rights in adjoining Red Sea waters. The U.S. position . . . has been to support Egypt's view that the 1907 Hague convention governing occupied territory forbids developing new resources in such territory. (J. K. Cooley, *Christian Science Monitor* News Service, "Israel Irked Over Oil Rap," *Times Herald*, Norristown, Pa., 2/23/77, p. 17)

DEFALCATION (dĕ´ fal-kā´ shən, -fôl-) *noun* misappropriation or embezzlement of money held by an official, trustee, or other fiduciary; the sum misappropriated or embezzled.

DEFALCATE *verb* to be guilty of defalcation or embezzlement.

DEFALCATOR *noun.*

1. His [Finlay Perkin's] thrust for the jugular was insatiable. He knew that grave misapplications [of funds] had occurred, but he could not easily penetrate to the specific DEFALCATION, and until he could do so, he had no case, and he knew it. (J. A. Michener, *Centennial*, Fawcett, 1975, p. 721)

DEFENESTRATION (dē-fen´ i-strā´ shən) *noun* the act of throwing a person or thing out of a window; a tossing out through a window.

1. In February, the school [Curtis Institute of Music] began a process of DEFENESTRATION that saw dean Peter Schoenbach, artistic administrator Anthony Checchia and opera-department director Dino Yannopoulos pushed out. (D. Webster, "Curtis is ready to move backward," *Philadelphia Inquirer*, 3/6/77, p. 1-I)

2. One of the most precise words in the language never gets the use it deserves. "DEFENESTRATE" means to throw someone or something out a window. It was an old Bohemian custom to DEFENESTRATE nasty people. When a group of Protestant Bohemians so rid themselves of two of their emperor's envoys, that event—called the DEFENESTRATION of Prague—started the Thirty Years War . . . . Who has ever read an account of South Bronx residents DEFENESTRATING their garbage? (B. Wiemer, *Newsday* Service, "The rubric of words," *Philadelphia Inquirer*, 3/27/77, p. 3-L)

3. What Teddy [Villanova] thought of this grappling match could not be known. Perhaps . . . he assessed it as . . . our attempt to DEFENESTRATE an exhausted tart, quite a standard disposal in his degenerate world. (Thomas Berger, *Who Is Teddy Villanova?*, Delacorte Press/Seymour Lawrence, 1977, p. 216)

4. . . .for at the same moment Boris DEFENESTRATED me [Russel Wren] with one great

shove, and willy-nilly . . . I embarked on my career as Flying Wren, death-defying aerialist. (Thomas Berger, *Ibid.*, p. 219)

DEFLORATION (def´ lə-rā´ shən, dē´ flə-) *noun* the act of deflowering; the act of depriving a woman of virginity; the act of ravishing or spoiling; the act of removing flowers from a plant.

1. . . . the book [*The French Consul*, by Lucien Bodard, translated from the French by Barbara Bray] becomes discursive again and again on footbinding, ritual decapitation, leprosy, DEFLORATION and quite incomprehensible wranglings. (P. Theroux, Review, *New York Times*, 3/27/77, Section 7, p. 41)

DÉJÀ VU (dā-zhA-vü) already seen; unoriginal; trite; the illusion of having previously experienced something actually being encountered for the first time.

1. Shively, hands clenched, moved toward Brunner threateningly . . . . Watching the scene with fascination, Adam Malone had a feeling of DÉJÀ VU—like he had lived through a similar scene before, . . . so it seemed less disturbing because it was familiar. (I. Wallace, *The Fan Club*, Bantam Books, 1975, p. 170)

2. . . . in 1972 . . . Nixon signed an agreement conceding to the Soviets a 40 percent numerical advantage in missile launchers . . . . The next agreement may fit this pattern by severely limiting U.S. cruise missiles and insignificantly limiting Soviet Backfire bombers . . . . Feeling a twinge of DÉJÀ VU? (G. F. Will, "Reckless Concessions," *Newsweek*, 9/6/76, p. 84)

3. Watching the current hassle among the networks, the candidates, and the League of Women Voters over tomorrow's Ford-Carter debate in Philadelphia, Bill [Wilson] has a strange feeling of DÉJÀ VU. Sixteen years ago, as Kennedy's representative, HE was arguing with the networks about arrangments. He says they argued then about exactly the same things they're arguing over now . . . . (Marcia Rose, "Showtime: Jimmy, Gerry," *Philadelphia Inquirer*, 9/22/76, p. 1-C)

4. . . . Daniel Menaker's stories [in *Friends and Relations*], trying very hard to be 1970's-

up-to-date, have a wearying sense of DÉJÀ VU about them. It is as if the children of Salinger's characters—or Cheever's or Updike's— . . . are thinking and feeling in all the familiar ways. (Robie Macauley, Review, *New York Times*, 11/21/76, Section 7, p. 50)

DE JURE (dē jŏŏr'ē) by right; according to law, or established by law (distinguished from DE FACTO)

1. See (1) under TRANSMOGRIFY.

2. [President] Ford's bill would authorize busing only to correct DE JURE segregation, racial separation deliberately caused by local decisions, as in drawing school zones or locating school construction. That is distinguished from DE FACTO "segregation," the result of living patterns. (G. F. Will, "Freedom and the Busing Quagmire," *Newsweek*, 7/12/76, p. 76)

3. See (2) under SCINTILLA.

DELIQUESCENCE (del' ə-kwes' əns) *noun* the act or process of deliquescing; the liquid produced when a substance deliquesces.

DELIQUESCE *verb* to melt away; to become liquid by absorbing moisture from the air.

DELIQUESCENT *adj.*

1. Cassavetes [the director of the film, *The Killing of a Chinese Bookie*] breaks things up because he wants you to feel, not read. So he shoots the crazy shows at the cheap Sunset Strip club owned by his hero, Cosmo Vitelli, in bits and pieces—a living collage of delectable breasts, thighs, faces, old pop tunes retreaded on tape and sung by Mr. Sophistication, the EPICENE emcee. You feel the boozy, dozing PRURIENCE of the audience, the giggly sweetness of the girls, the stylized DELIQUESCENCE of the old queen. (J. Kroll, Review, *Newsweek*, 3/15/76, p. 89)

DELTIOLOGY (del' tē-ol' ə-jē) *noun* the hobby of collecting picture postcards.

DELTIOLOGIST *noun* one who collects picture postcards as a hobby.

1. DELTIOLOGISTS (postcard collectors) are to be found everywhere, poking around in old attics and in junk shops, flea markets and antique stores. (The word DELTIOLOGIST was coined by Randall Rhodes of Ashland, Ohio in 1930; from the Greek words *deltion*, a little picture, and *logos*, a branch of knowledge.) (Norah Smaridge, "Would You Pay $150 for a Postcard?" *New York Times*, 5/16/76, Section 2, p. 35)

DEMESNE (di-mān', di-mēn') *noun* a part of an estate occupied, controlled, and worked solely by the owner; a region, district, or domain; the land around a mansion.

1. "This wench is my ward," I [Russel Wren] told him [Boris]. "Toy with her fine foot if you like, but eschew her quivering thigh and the DEMESNES that there adjacent lie." (Thomas Berger, *Who Is Teddy Villanova?*, Delacorte Press/Seymour Lawrence, 1977, pp. 216-217)

DEMIMONDE (dem'ē-mond') *noun* a class of women who have lost social standing because of indiscreet behavior or sexual promiscuity; a demimondaine; prostitutes as a group; any group whose activities are ethically questionable.

DEMIMONDAINE (dem'ē-mon-dān') *noun* a woman of the demimonde.

1. [George] Plimpton describes her [the surrealist artist Vali Myers] as "the symbol of the restless DEMI-MONDE that populated the Left Bank . . . . I'm amazed that she has survived; although she seemed torn and loose, like a cat she always managed to land on four feet." (Rose Hartman, "Vali: Beauty and the Beasts," *Ms.*, May 1976, p. 15)

2. Ernst Lubitsch was deeply influenced by this story [in Charlie Chaplin's film, *A Woman of Paris*] of a provincial girl who becomes a Parisian DEMIMONDAINE. It was, boasted Chaplin in his autobiography, "the first [film] to articulate irony and psychology." (J. Kroll, "Voluptuous Silence," *Newsweek*, 1/10/77, p. 65)

3. As a Sunday school alumna, [New York *Daily News* gossip columnist Mary Elizabeth] Smith has scruples about reporting the seamier doings of the celebrity DEMI-MONDE. She prefers not to write about sex scandals or messy divorces. But she laces her niceness with just enough bitchiness to keep the franchise. (D. Gelman, "Gossip's 'Good Ole Gal,' " *News-

week, 2/28/77, p. 77)

DEMOTIC (di-mot'ik) *adj.* of or pertaining to the common people; popular; vernacular; common; designating or of a simplified system of ancient Egyptian writing: distinguished from HIERATIC.

DEMOTIC *noun* the common dialect of modern Greece.

1. In form it [the book, *Farthing's Fortunes*, by Richard B. Wright] is PICARESQUE, in style DEMOTIC, a cross, if it doesn't sound like too much to say so, between Huck Finn and Thomas Berger's *Little Big Man*. (G. Lyons, Review, *New York Times*, 1/2/77, Section 7, p. 12)

2. Ironically, however, it was not the savants who were responsible for the most outstanding discovery [in Egyptology], but a detachment of [Napoleon Bonaparte's] soldiers working under an officer named Pierre Bouchard on the construction of some coastal fortifications near the western mouth of the Nile at Rosetta. By mere chance they unearthed a slab of basalt [the Rosetta Stone] which bore three inscriptions, one in hieroglyphics, another in a late derivative of the same script known as DEMOTIC and the third in Greek. It was soon guessed that the three inscriptions preserved the same text, written once in Greek and twice in the language of the ancient Egyptians, which no one had been able to read for 1,500 years. (I.E.S. Edwards, "Cracking the Hieroglyphic Code Was Only the Beginning of Egyptology," *New York Times*, 1/2/77, Section 2, p. 1)

3. See (1) under BIBLIOPHYLAX.

4. . . . he [Ronald Beard] wondered why . . . "belly" had become comic or offensive in DEMOTIC speech. (A. Burgess, *Beard's Roman Women*, McGraw-Hill, 1976, p. 24)

5. "And you're somebody who writes things for the great crappy DEMOTIC media [said P.R. Pathan to Ronald Beard]." (A. Burgess, *Ibid.*, p. 61)

6. Parmigian [in the play, *Cold Storage*, by Ronald Ribman] is a character worthy of Saul Bellow in his paradoxical wit, DEMOTIC eloquence and benevolent malice. (J. Kroll, Review, *Newsweek*, 4/25/77, p. 90)

DENIGRATE (den'ə-grāt') *verb* to speak derogatorily or damagingly of; to sully, defame, or disparage the character of; to make black; blacken.

DENIGRATION *noun.*

DENIGRATOR *noun.*

1. It is easy to DENIGRATE any cause by the technique of putting it alongside other, nobler causes. (W.F. Buckley Jr., *Execution Eve and Other Contemporary Ballads*, G.P. Putnam's Sons, 1975, p. 391)

2. See (1) under MAWKISH.

3. Risking inclusion in the DENIGRATED company of "bleeding heart liberals," I see no purpose of society currently being served by keeping [E. Howard] Hunt or [G. Gordon] Liddy locked up in any federal penitentiary. (P. J. Buchanan, "Final Two Watergate Prisoners Punished Enough, Rate Freedom," *Daily Oklahoman*, Okla. City, 4/26/76, p. 14)

4. See (3) under EPHEMERAL.

5. But the women's movement . . . remains stuck with the image of a career elite and, further, haunted by echoes of those early years when many of the more militant feminists were openly DENIGRATING housewives as oppressed and mindless, leading useless lives. (Martha Weinman Lear, " 'You'll probably think I'm stupid,' " *New York Times*, 4/11/76, Section 6, p. 113)

6. The fleeting triumph [of Lillian Hellman's appearance on stage reading the narrative for Blitzstein's opera version of *The Little Foxes*] leads directly to her rejection by old friends, to Dashiell Hammett's illness, the financial necessity of taking on a rotten scriptwriting job in Rome where she becomes the object of a C.I.A. hoax and finally to a self-DENIGRATING affair with a man she has never respected. (Maureen Howard, Review of *Scoundrel Time*, by Lillian Hellman, *New York Times*, 4/25/76, Section 7, p. 2)

7. The story she [Violet Weingarten] . . . tells [in *Half A Marriage*] . . . is that of a deeply passive and self-DENIGRATING woman developing a battery of strategies to retain a manipulative boor [her husband]. (Kathy Pollit, Review, *New York Times*, 4/25/76, Section 7, p. 48)

8. Customarily, we [copyboys at the *New York Herald Tribune*] were summoned with the cry of "Copy," which meant a story had to be moved . . . [Everett] Kallgren ["The Count"] eschewed "Copy" for the DENIGRATION of "Boy!" (R. Kahn, *The Boys of Summer*, Harper and Row, 1971, p. 60)

9. . . . there has now come to light a speech delivered by . . . Leonid Brezhnev in 1973 in which he declared détente a ruse and defined the Soviet goal as decisive superiority [in armed forces and war materials] . . . When the British [intelligence] information [about this speech] reached the Nixon White House, however, top officials DENIGRATED the importance of the speech and no official reference to it occurred until the 1976 National Intelligence Estimate. (J. Hart, "Watch Brezhnev," *Times Herald*, Norristown, Pa., 3/3/77, p. 17)

DÉNOUEMENT (dā´nōō-mäN´) *noun* the final resolution or unraveling of a plot, as of a drama or novel; the point at which this occurs; any final revelation or outcome.

1. The DÉNOUEMENT approached comedy. During a time-out at a varsity football game [at Morgan State College], Joe [Black], ball carrier and linebacker, pulled off his helmet and rubbed the back of one hand upward against his brow. It was a habit he had acquired playing with whites at Plainfield. "Hey," said a Morgan State lineman, "what's that you're doing?" "Brushing the hair out of my eyes." "What hair? Colored people's hair doesn't grow that way." "I mean I'm wiping sweat," Joe said. (R. Kahn, *The Boys of Summer*, Harper and Row, 1971, p. 278)

2. *Candles for the Dead* [a book by Harry Carmichael] is another episode in the saga of Quinn, the crime reporter for *The Morning Post*. This case involves smuggling, a double-cross and even a triple cross and a routine DÉNOUEMENT . . . . Carmichael's writing style can best be described as determined. But, alas, his ear is as flat as the high C of an aging soprano. (N. Callendar, Review, *New York Times*, 3/28/76, Section 7, p. 32)

3. See (2) under SCHMALTZ.

DEPILATE (dep´ə-lāt) *verb* to remove hair from

DEPILATORY (di-pil´ ə-tôr´ ē, -tôr´ē) *adj.* capable of removing hair.

DEPILATION *noun.*

1. The time had then come seriously [to Ronald Beard] to think about being laid, laying rather . . . it was the sense that she [Paola Belli] was real, solid, probably UNDEPILATED, probably also garlic-smelling if one got close enough, . . . that was beginning to indicate to him that the frivolity had to be taken out of this laying business. (A. Burgess, *Beard's Roman Women*, McGraw-Hill, 1976, p. 23)

2. Since having begun regularly to DEPILATE her legs, Peggy [Tumulty] had probably not been north (above-ground) of West Twenty-eighth Street . . . . (Thomas Berger, *Who Is Teddy Villanova?*, Delacorte Press/Seymour Lawrence, 1977, p. 47)

3. The storyteller [in the book, *True Confessions*, by John Gregory Dunne], Thomas Spellacy, is a 72-year-old retired Los Angeles cop who has either witnessed or heard them all. There are the ones about a rapist who preyed on the elderly, the hood who stuffed a rival into a laundry dryer, a sort of Jack the Shaver who DEPILATED his victims with a razor . . . . (R.Z. Sheppard, Review, *Time*, 11/7/77, p. 122)

DERACINATE (di-ras´ə-nāt´) *verb* to pull up the roots; uproot; eradicate; EXTIRPATE; to isolate or alienate (a person or persons) from a native or customary environment.

DERACINATION *noun.*

1. When . . . I first met her, it was instantly clear that unlike the DERACINATED men so typical of this uprooted century, Lillian [Elmlark] was a glad product of a tradition. There was about her a sense of history fulfilled . . . , the maturity of the fully developed human being, the distinctively Jewish blend of pathos and exultation about which the psalmists sing . . . . (W.F. Buckley Jr., *Execution Eve and Other Contemporary Ballads*, G.P. Putnam's Sons, 1975, p. 465)

2. Now no one can deny that Randall Jarrell

[in his book, *Pictures From an Institution*, in which he describes life and manners at "Benton College"] was having himself a whale of a time . . . . He was describing a morally and intellectually DERACINATED environment in which students are encouraged to cut their ties to the world of standards and norms, to march forward as soldiers of a TOTEMIC tolerance; . . . FACTITIOUSLY obsessed with another civilization (any other civilization) and another age (any other age); smooth and urbane—and empty . . . (W.F. Buckley Jr., *Up From Liberalism*, Arlington House, 2nd Printing 1968, p. 124)

3. The only autonomy liberalism appears to encourage is moral and intellectual autonomy; SOLIPSISM. And that is the autonomy of DE-RACINATION; the philosophy that has peopled the earth with . . . presumptuous social careerists diseased with HUBRIS. (W.F. Buckley Jr., *Ibid.*, p. 177)

4. The ties between Paine and the artisan class, even as widely defined here [in the book, *Tom Paine and Revolutionary America*, by Eric Foner], are EXIGUOUS . . . in Foner's argument. It is true that Paine came from the artisan class himself—but so did other DERACIN-ATED pamphleteers of the time, from the best of them (Rousseau) to the shabbier (Cobbett). (G. Wills, Review, *New York Times*, 3/7/76, Section 7, p. 22)

5. See (1) under ESTAMINET.

6. Instead of pride and satisfaction [from his fame], though, [Jed] Tewksbury [in the book, *A Place To Come To*, by Robert Penn Warren] feels only a sense of DERACINATION and shame, as if by leaving his aged mother . . . he has committed some breach of the spirit and is condemned to travel the world alone in search of himself . . . . (G. Lyons, Review, *New York Times*, 3/13/77, Section 7, p. 4)

DERGUE (derg) *noun* a ruling group of military men.

1. The military junta, or DERGUE, running Ethiopia is still basically the same group of men who ousted Emperor Haile Selassie in 1974—with the exception of those killed off in struggles within the group since then. (G.

Godsell, *Christian Science Monitor* News Service, "Ethiopia Upheaval," *Times Union*, Norristown, Pa., 2/15/77, p. 11)

DE RIGUEUR (də Rē-gOER', də-ri-gûr') strictly required, as by etiquette, usage, or fashion; fashionable or faddish.

1. This book [*Scoundrel Time*, by Lillian Hellman] is bound to be widely read. The slim red volume will be DE RIGUEUR on the beaches this summer. (Maureen Howard, Review, *New York Times*, 4/25/76, Section 7, p. 2)

2. But in these triumphant times of women's liberation . . . . Dry eyes and dainty stiff upper lips [as opposed to tears] soon will become DE RIGUEUR [for women]. (P. Ryan, "No tears about tears from a dry-eyed chauvinist," *Smithsonian*, May 1976, p. 132)

3. At some [private home] screenings, catcalls and caustic one-liners flow as freely as liquid refreshments. . . . At Joyce Haber's movie soirées, smart-alec cracks were DE RIGUEUR (*sic*). The bad-mouthing has soured some hosts on screenings. (D. Gelman and Janet Huck, "Picture Parlors," *Newsweek*, 9/13/76, p. 88)

4. In 1972 the movie *Deep Throat* started a SPATE of porn chic. It became DE RIGUEUR to call up your friends and form a giggle party to go watch Linda Lovelace do her thing. It was all soothingly PRURIENT fun, and regrettably it lasted too short a time. (Dorothy Storck, "'Deep Throat,' deep trouble," *Philadelphia Inquirer*, 10/22/76, p. 1-B)

5. Born in 1791, [Giacomo] Meyerbeer made his operatic mark in his native Germany by the time he was 21. He then [moved] to Italy and [mastered] the more melodic style of Italian opera . . . in Paris . . . he came to be regarded as the father of French grand opera, those lavish spectacles in which armies clashed by night and spectacular finales were DE RIGUEUR. (H. Saal, "Small Beer," *Newsweek*, 1/31/77, p. 71)

DERRING-DO (der'ĭng-dōō') *noun* daring action; heroic daring; reckless courage.

1. The need for secret feats of DERRING-DO and manipulation arose in the cold war, and quickly became the vehicle for the agency's spec-

tacular growth. By the late 1950's, security requirements were so pressing that the C.I.A. was spinning off thousands of front companies at home and abroad. (Taylor Branch, "The trial of the C.I.A.," *New York Times*, 9/12/76, Section 6, p. 123)

2. I am proposing a redefinition of hazard that separates daring from DERRING-DO, the kind of jeopardy we experience from the kind we buy. (J. Lipton, "Here Be Dragons," *Newsweek*, 12/6/76, p. 17)

3. Initially, as President Nixon's national security adviser and DERRING-DO negotiator, Kissinger had kept hands off the Middle East. Part of the reason was his preoccupation with the Soviet Union, China, and closing down the war in Vietnam. Another, presumably, was his Jewish background, which Kissinger may have felt would be viewed as a bias in favor of Israel. (Associated Press, "Kissinger influence to linger," *Philadelphia Inquirer*, 12/26/76, p. 11-A)

DESUETUDE (des′ wi-tōōd′, -tyōōd′) *noun*
the state of being no longer used or practiced; disuse.

1. The law's DESUETUDE [re use of marijuana]: the untidy recommendation, in effect, of those who would leave the laws alone, in order to ignore them. (W.F. Buckley Jr., *Execution Eve and Other Contemporary Ballads*, G.P. Putnam's Sons, 1975, p. 400)

2. I do remember wondering, at least once during the period when I heeled for the [Yale Daily] News—which term, I understand, is far-gone in DESUETUDE, rejected alike for its singularity and ignominy—whether there was any justification for an effort so very time-consuming. (W.F. Buckley Jr., *Ibid.*, p. 367)

3. NATO's look is not of dynamism but of division, DESUETUDE and decay. (H.J. Taylor, "Soviets Plan Fast War," *Times Herald*, Norristown, Pa., 5/12/77, p. 23)

DESULTORY (des′ əl-tôr′ ē, -tōr′ ē) *adj.*
lacking in consistency, constancy, or visible order; disconnected; fitful; digressing; not methodical; lacking direct relevancy; incidental; casual; random; passing from one thing to another in an aimless way.

DESULTORILY *adv.*

DESULTORINESS *noun.*

1. The antimarijuana hawks take a position ...hang on to the marijuana laws, ignore them as much as you can, put up with the occasional moral inconvenience of the law applied at the expense of the DESULTORY victim—and relax in the knowledge that the catechism is unchanged. (W.F. Buckley Jr., *Execution Eve and Other Contemporary Ballads*, G.P. Putnam's Sons, 1975, p. 400)

2. It [the beaver] had developed in North America but would spread in DESULTORY fashion through much of Europe; its residence in the streams of Colorado would prove especially fortuitous, bringing great wealth to those Indians and Frenchmen who mastered the trick of getting its pelt. (J. A. Michener, *Centennial*, Fawcett, 1975, p. 116)

3. She [a beaver] climbed ashore and started gnawing DESULTORILY at a cottonwood, but her attention was not focused on the food, and this was good, because as she perched there . . . she heard a movement behind a larger tree and looked up in time to spot a bear moving swiftly toward her. (J. A. Michener, *Ibid.*, p. 118)

4. His [Lame Beaver's] father offered to arrange a marriage, if necessary, but said that Lame Beaver could also look around for himself. In a DESULTORY way he had been doing that, but up to now he had overlooked Blue Leaf. On the trail in an elk-skin dress she was a handsome girl. (J.A. Michener, *Ibid.*, p. 157)

5. They [the Arapaho trio about to steal horses from a Comanche camp] reached the south bank [of the Arkansas], and with deepening anxiety, waited for the night to pass. Comanche guards moved about the camp in DESULTORY fashion, not really attending their work. (J.A. Michener, *Ibid.*, p. 163)

6. In that winter of 1800 the team [Pasquinel and McKeag] acquired six bales of superior [beaver] peltries and were about to head south when a band of Shosone attacked. The Indians were driven off, but returned to lay siege. A DESULTORY gunfight occurred . . . . (J.A. Michener, *Ibid.*, p. 231)

7. Rebecca [Stolzfus] was obviously bored with the dinner [with Levi Zendt], and after a

little DESULTORY conversation, said, "I must get back to help Poppa." Patting him on the arm in a way that sent shivers through his whole body, she pirouetted away. (J.A. Michener, *Ibid.*, p. 312)

8. On July 12 [1844] the three wagons were heading westward in DESULTORY fashion when two Pawnee braves rode up along the north bank of the Platte, and as soon as they came in range Sam Purchas grabbed his Hawken [rifle], took aim, and put a bullet through the head of one of the young men . . . . Purchas grabbed for a second gun and would have shot down the other brave except that Captain Mercy knocked the barrel away, allowing the Pawnee to gallop off. (J.A. Michener, *Ibid.*, p. 376)

9. She [Charlotte, widow of Oliver Seccombe] spent her time in Bristol [England] society . . . she became an attractive target for bachelors . . . who were seeking rich wives . . . in rapid-fire succession, two deaths made her DESULTORY courtships seem unimportant . . . . It fell to Charlotte to supervise both funerals . . . . (J.A. Michener, *Ibid.*, p. 745)

10. For half a year this DESULTORY exchange [between Henry Garrett and Soledad Marquez] continued; only once had the two touched hands. . . . The effect had been electrifying . . . . (J.A. Michener, *Ibid.*, p. 978)

11. Flor [Marquez] arrived first [at the restaurant] and made a DESULTORY effort at helping her father serve the dinner crowd, and after a while [Paul] Garrett drifted in . . . to play the juke box. (J.A. Michener, *Ibid.*, p. 1022)

12. See (1) under PANACEA.

13. See (1) under PELLUCID.

DETRITUS (di-tri′ təs) *noun* debris; any accumulation of disintegrated material; rock fragments or other material broken away from a mass, as by the action of water or glacial ice.

DETRITAL *adj.*

DETRITION *noun* the wearing away by rubbing, abrasion, or friction.

1. Freedom is the indispensable catalyst of a certain kind of greatness, and this is as in-

disputable as that any magnet turned to search out literary genius in Soviet Russia would instantly hone in on Solzhenitsyn, without a quiver's distraction in the direction of the time-serving Lenin Prizees who coo and chuckle over the DETRITUS of Nikolai Lenin as schoolboy. (W.F. Buckley Jr., *Execution Eve and Other Contemporary Ballads*, G.P. Putnam's Sons, 1975, p. 241)

2. As the mountain glaciers [in the Rockies] melted they produced unprecedented amounts of water, which created floods of gigantic proportion. They cascaded down with fierce velocity and submerged traditional rivers . . . . Much DETRITUS was borne down from the mountains, most of it with sharp cutting edges, and it was this mixture of copious water and cutting rock which planed down the lands to the east. (J.A. Michener, *Centennial*, Fawcett, 1975, p. 57)

3. One day, in what we may only hope is the distant future, an archeologist sifting through the DETRITUS of Western civilization may come upon certain puzzling ARTIFACTS. A pair of tennis sneakers, perhaps, with 4-inch platform soles. A goose-quill pen with a felt tip . . . . Or, if Western civilization is lucky, some piano recordings made by Arthur Rubinstein when he was on the brink of 90 and still playing with astonishing vigor, virtuosity and PANACHE. (D. Henahan, "This ageless hero, Rubinstein," *New York Times*, 3/14/76, Section 6, p. 18)

4. Under the head "Capote Strikes Again," the editors of *Esquire* have published the third—and most lurid—installment of Truman Capote's novel-in-progress, *Answered Prayers* . . . . Using the adjective in both senses he is a wicked writer. The narrative flows like a swift stream after a hurricane and flood, and you are swept along with it and with all the DETRITUS of life—the cruel, the funny, the mock tragic, the merely decadent. (M. Lerner, "The true life force not present: Decadence pervades new novel," *Norman* [Okla.] *Transcript*, 5/4/76, p. 6)

5. The two scientists [Alan D. Poole and Robert H. Williams] propose solar plantations and farms in which a plant crop would be turned, by the process of biogasification, into methanol (a liquid fuel ideal for automobiles) and methane (for making electricity), and the

by-products of which would be heat (for industrial steam) and high-grade fertilizers . . . . Indeed, . . . agricultural DETRITUS, such as cornstalks, could also be used as feedstock for the process. (J.K. Page Jr., "Phenomena on Frontiers of Science," *Smithsonian*, July 1976, p. 10)

6. In several of his earlier books [Donald] Barthelme commanded a great range of voices and allusions; he seemed to blend history, personal life, the comedy of manners and verbal DETRITUS into a comic 60's wasteland. It's disheartening to see him here [in the book, *Amateurs*] often coasting on his style . . . . (R. Locke, Review, *New York Times*, 12/19/76, Section 7, p. 18)

7. All four writers [John Cheever, Walker Percy, Joan Didion, and Thomas Berger] . . . are alike in their horror at the weird DETRITUS—ideological, sexual, social—of the sixties. (R. Locke, "Novelists as Preachers," *New York Times*, 4/17/77, Section 7, p. 53)

DEUS EX MACHINA (de'ōōs eks mä'ki-nä, dē'əs eks mak'ə-nə, dä-) *noun* (in Greek drama) a god who resolves the entanglements of the play by his supernatural intervention via stage machinery; an artificial, forced, or improbable device used to resolve the difficulties of a plot; anyone who unexpectedly intervenes to change the course of events.

1. The film [*The Magic Flute*] also uses the eighteenth-century thunder-maker, creaky DEUS EX MACHINA, and other props. (R. Craft, Review, *New York Review of Books*, 11/27/75, p. 16)

2. . . . it behooves Charles LeBaron to tell us what is unique or special about these two [characters in his book, *The Diamond Sky*] that makes them worth pursuing. Unfortunately he leaves the issue in doubt right up to a final DEUX (*sic*) EX MACHINA on a slippery highway. (M. Levin, Review, *New York Times*, 4/11/76, Section 7, p. 37)

3. There is no DEUS EX MACHINA for OPEC [Organization of Petroleum Exporting Countries] in this hazardous world economic situation. OPEC should recognize that oil prices, already too high, are severely jeopardizing international financial stability and ought to be reduced, and not raised, for the sake of their own eco-

nomic future as much as for that of the rest of the world. (Anon., "OPEC Hesitates," [*New York Times* Editorial], reprinted in *Times Herald*, Norristown, Pa., 11/29/76, p. 12)

4. In my now vague recollections of my plane geometry days—when Isaac Asimov was a fellow student at Boys High in Brooklyn, but gave no discernible hints of whom or what he was to mature into—pi appeared out of nowhere, as a DEUS EX MACHINA without real rhyme or reason. The teacher said it was equal to about 3.14, and . . . who could care less? (H. Schwartz, Review of *Asimov on Numbers*, a book by Isaac Asimov, *New York Times*, 4/24/77, Section 7, p. 12)

5. The early 19th century was, in fact, the great age of student rebellions, the tumultuous (*sic*) events of the 1960's notwithstanding . . . . Circumstances had reduced the capacity of the older generation to provide leadership . . . In following these trends to their sources, [Joseph F.] Kett [author of *Rites of Passage: Adolescence in America, 1790 to the Present*] resists the temptation to invoke "industrialization" or that still more encompassing DEUS EX MACHINA, "modernization." (J. Demos, Review, *New York Times*, 4/24/77, Section 7, p. 41)

DIABOLISM (dī-ab'ə-liz'əm) *noun* action aided or caused by the devil; sorcery or witchcraft; the character or condition of a devil; a belief in the worship of devils; action befitting the devil; deviltry.

DIABOLIST *noun*.

DIABOLIC or DIABOLICAL *adj.* of the devil or devils; very wicked or cruel; fiendish.

DIABOLICALLY *adv.*

DIABOLIZE *verb* to make, represent, or portray as diabolical; to subject to diabolical influence.

1. Challenging this DIABOLISM [in the book, *The Boys from Brazil*, by Ira Levin] is Jakov Liebermann, a death-camp survivor who has devoted his post-war life to detecting and exposing unpunished Nazi war criminals. (R.Z. Sheppard, Review, *Time*, 2/23/76, p. 64)

2. The so-called Christmas Bombing of North Vietnam has been fashioned by the Left into a kind of Guernica-like symbol of American evil

and Nixonian DIABOLISM . . . . The definitive treatment of the "Christmas Bombing" appeared in the magazine, Aviation Week and Space Technology, April 23, 1973 issue . . . . The editorial summary says: ". . . most of the official U.S. claims . . . were indeed correct and . . . the claims made by Hanoi and its American dupes were largely false." (J. Hart, "Yule Bombing Seen As Fraud," *Times Herald*, Norristown, Pa., 2/7/77, p. 13)

DIALECTIC (dī'ə-lek'tik) or **DIALECTICAL** *adj.* of, pertaining to, or of the nature of logical argumentation.

DIALECTIC *noun* the art or practice of logical discussion, as of the truth of a theory or opinion; logical argumentation, often by the question and answer method; dialectics, *i.e.*, logic or any of its branches.

DIALECTICALLY *adv.*

DIALECTICS (*often construed as singular*) *noun* the arguments or bases of dialectical materialism, including the elevation of matter over mind and a constantly changing reality with a material basis.

1. Now it is up to him [Peter J. Ognibene, author of *The Life and Politics of Henry M. Jackson*] to compensate by presenting the other side. Such a DIALECTICAL approach to truth has interesting EPISTEMOLOGICAL implications, but it certainly excuses the writer from feeling any guilt . . . . (A. M. Greeley, Review, *New York Times*, 1/11/76, Section 7, p. 3)

2. See (1) under ELEGIAC.

3. These concerns [about the modern self] were articulated [by Lionel Trilling] with characteristic balance, coherence and DIALECTICAL subtlety . . . . (S. Marcus, "Lionel Trilling, 1905-1975, *New York Times*, 2/8/76, Section 7, p. 1)

4. See (4) under BOURGEOIS.

5. The high moral concern, DIALECTICAL cast of mind and rhetorical pugnacity of that epoch [the 1930s] became aspects of his [Ad Reinhardt's] personal style, just as the quest for an "ultimate" art would become a central drive of his life. (P. Schjeldahl, Review of *Art as Art, The Selected Writings of Ad Reinhardt*, edited by Barbara Rose; and *The Art Comics and*

Satires of Ad Reinhardt, by Thomas B. Hess, *New York Times*, 2/15/76, Section 7, p. 7)

6. It was taxation and efficiency [of British administration] that summoned all the toughness and suspicion of the American consciousness and all the DIALECTICAL resources of the American Enlightenment; if taxation and efficiency had come sooner, [Page] Smith argues [in A New Age Now Begins], so too would the Revolution. (G. Dangerfield, Review, *New York Times*, 2/22/76, Section 7, p. 7)

7. See (3) under PIQUANT.

8. See (7) under PUTATIVE.

9. Mr. [Alan] Schneider's staging [of *Zalmen or The Madness of God* at the Lyceum Theater] . . . becomes two-dimensional as a crossword puzzle now that it is locked inside a proscenium, and Mr. Elie Wiesel's DIALECTICS seem far more SENTENTIOUS than before [at the Arena Theater in Washington]. (W. Kerr, Review, *New York Times*, 3/28/76, Section 2, p. 5)

10. See (1) under PICARESQUE.

11. See (1) under PILPUL.

12. See (1) under CHI-CHI.

13. See (4) under TORPID.

DIAPHANOUS (dī-af'ə-nəs) *adj.* very sheer and light; so fine and gauzy in texture as to be almost transparent or translucent; delicately hazy; vague or indistinct; airy.

DIAPHANOUSLY *adv.*

DIAPHANOUSNESS or **DIAPHANEITY** (dī-af'ə-nē'i-tē, dī'ə-fə-) *noun* the property of being transparent.

1. See (2) under PERSPICACIOUS.

2. The scoring of [the Philadelphia Orchestra's Carnegie Hall rendition of Florent Schmitt's *Psalm 47*] has the light DIAPHANOUS quality of French instrumentation at its best, and this despite the large size of the orchestra. (H.C. Schonberg, "Ormandy Conducts a Rather Unusual Program," *New York Times*, 10/14/76, p. 46)

DIARCHY (dī'är-kē) *noun* a government in which power is vested in two rulers.

1. In the past it used . . . to be said that the success of the British rule in India was to establish a "DIARCHY"—whereby the Viceroy's Council functioned alongside the reign of Princes, Nawabs and Maharajahs. (A. Howard, Review of *The Diaries Of a Cabinet Minister*, by Richard Crossman, *New York Times*, 9/12/76, Section 7, p. 370)

DIASPORA (dī-as′pər-ə) *noun* (if capitalized) the scattering of the Jews to countries outside Palestine after the Babylonian captivity; the body of Jews living in such countries; such countries collectively; (if lower case) any scattering of people with a common origin, background, beliefs, etc.

1. *The Irish* DIASPORA *in America* [by Lawrence J. McCaffrey] is the best short history of the Irish in America currently available. (A.M. Greeley, Review, *New York Times*, 6/27/76, Section 7, p. 8)

2. Lebanon has fallen apart. Aside from the passports held by citizens of its fast-growing DIASPORA, Lebanon does not have a single figure, symbol or national institution with any pretense of meaning. (J.M. Markham, "Lebanon, A Country Destroying Itself," *New York Times*, 7/4/76, Section 4, p. 1)

3. . . . sensitive American Jews have returned from visits to Israel in tears. The young Sabras—those born in Israel—are scornful of Jews who live in the DIASPORA. "Why don't you live here," they call, "where you belong?" (J. Bishop, "Troubled Place in the Sand," *Times Herald*, Norristown, Pa., 12/10/76, p. 17)

DIATONIC (dī′ə-ton′ik) *adj.* of, designating, or using any standard major or minor scale of eight tones without the chromatic intervals; of or pertaining to the tones, intervals, or harmonies of such a scale.

1. In this work [the opera, *Jonny Spielt Auf*] of his youth [Ernst Křenek is now 75], DIATONIC and voraciously ECLECTIC, his strength was already apparent. (A. Rich, Review, *New York Times*, 5/31/76, p. 72)

DIATRIBE (dī′ə-trīb′) *noun* a bitter, abusive criticism or denunciation.

1. See (6) under PRESCIENCE.

2. One of the books I read [while in the hospital recently]—a grisly choice on the face of it—was Ivan Illich's DIATRIBE against modern doctors, medicine and hospitals, *Medical* NEMESIS. (M. Lerner, "Jaundiced view of a jaundiced view: Columnist defends U.S. doctors," *Norman* [Okla.] *Transcript*, 6/16/76, p. 6)

3. Her [Mrs. Yost's] range of subject matter, he [Howard Yost] told himself, was awesome . . . . A history of inconsequential phone calls. A DIATRIBE on the prices of food . . . . (I. Wallace, *The Fan Club*, Bantam Edition, 1975, p. 45)

4. . . . he [Adam Malone] was annoyed with Shively's DIATRIBE against the journal [kept by Malone] and no longer in the mood to work on it. (I. Wallace, *Ibid.*, p. 226)

5. See (5) under PRATFALL.

DICHOTOMY (dī-kot′ə-mē) *noun* a division into two parts, kinds, etc.; a sharp difference of opinion; a schism or split.

DICHOTOMOUS *adj.*

DICHOTOMOUSLY *adv.*

DICHOTOMIZE *verb.*

DICHOTOMIST *noun.*

DICHOTOMIZATION *noun.*

1. One day we treated Indians as sovereign nations. Did you know that . . . [Arapaho Chief] Lost Eagle and Lincoln were photographed together as two heads of state? The next day we treated him as an uncivilized brute to be exterminated. And this dreadful DICHOTOMY continues. (J.A. Michener, *Centennial*, Fawcett, 1975, p. 1075)

2. The contrasting of action and contemplation had always been part of his [Michelangelo's] symbolism. But on the Julius tomb . . . —in the two sisters Michelangelo adjoined to the figure of Moses—the old conventional personifications became acutely personal . . . they express a melancholy DICHOTOMY between labor and vision—mournful fertility beggared by the exaltation of divine knowledge. (L. Steinberg, "Michelangelo's last painting: his gift to this century, *Smithsonian*, December 1975, p. 82)

3. Had [Lord] Leighton two lives, a public

and a private . . . ? Perhaps this emotional DICHOTOMY should be pursued when we consider Leighton as an artist. (R. Watson, Review of the book, *Lord Leighton*, by Leonée and R. Ormond, *Smithsonian*, March 1976, p. 103)

DIDACTIC (di-dak' tik) or **DIDACTICAL** *adj.* used or intended for instruction; instructive; inclined to give unwanted teaching or instruction; inclined to teach or lecture others too much; preaching or moralizing; boringly PEDANTIC or moralistic.

DIDACTICS *noun* (construed as singular) the art or science of teaching.

DIDACTICALLY *adv.*

DIDACTICISM *noun.*

1. [John] Adams DIDACTICALLY reminded [the Comte de] Vergennes that under the Articles of Confederation only Congress could make the peace, and that ended further flirtation with a compromise formula. (R.B. Morris, "Was John Adams Really That Important?," *New York Times*, 1/11/76, Section 2, p. 1)

2. . . . [Derek] Lambert [author of the book, *Touch the Lion's Paw*] gets a bit bogged down in detail—detail about the heist and so on. DIDACTICISM aside, the book has a lot to offer, if only for the planning of the caper. (N. Callendar, Review, *New York Times*, 1/11/76, Section 7, p. 25)

3. From Plutarch's day until the present century, biography was presumed to be DIDACTIC, offering lessons in moral history rather than insight into human eccentricity . . . . (P.S. Prescott, Review of *Frank Harris*, by Philippa Pullar, *Newsweek*, 3/15/76, p. 95)

4. It is simplest to say what these two books [*The Boys From Brazil*, by Ira Levin, and *The R Document*, by Irving Wallace] are not: they are not . . . novels . . . they are prose narratives that will take their readers several hours to complete. But in form they are fables: DIDACTIC melodramas constructed to yield meaning as directly and almost as simply as one of Aesop's. Each has A Moral. (Gene Lyons, Review, *New York Times*, 3/14/76, Section 7, p. 4)

5. He [Elie Nadelman] spoke Polish, Russian,

German, French and English and sounded DIDACTIC in most of them. (D. Bourdon, "The sleek, witty and elegant art of Elie Nadelman," *Smithsonian*, January 1976, p. 84)

6. [Jacques] Barzun's gentle wit never provokes more than faint smiles . . . . The problem . . . is that Barzun wants to instruct as well as amuse, and the pleasures of [his book] *Simple & Direct* are often diluted by DIDACTICISM. (M. Hungiville, Review, *Change*, April 1976, p. 55)

7. Not a DIDACTIC writer, like Solzhenitsyn or Doris Lessing, [Nadine] Gordimer stays at home and writes about what she sees and hears and feels. (Penelope Mortimer, Review of *Selected Stories*, by Nadine Gordimer, *New York Times*, 4/18/76, Section 7, p. 7)

8. See (4) under SCATOLOGY.

9. Written in a mock-DIDACTIC style, the book [*The Phrase Droppers' Handbook*, by John T. Beaudouin and Everett Mattlin] is filled with phrases Beaudouin culled from such places as *The New York Review of Books* and from conversations overheard on elevators. Beaudouin is a lover of words who "admires those who are imaginative in their use of language." (Beth Gillin Pombeiro, "Be a phrasedropper," *Philadelphia Inquirer*, 11/9/76, p. 3-C)

DIFFIDENCE (dif'i-dəns) *noun* distrust of one's own ability, worth, or fitness; timidity; shyness; self-effacement.

DIFFIDENT *adj.* lacking self-confidence; marked by a hesitancy to assert oneself; timid; shy; self-conscious; self-effacing; unassuming.

DIFFIDENTLY *adv.*

1. "Lovingly given," he [Charles Luckey] closed the statement, DIFFIDENTLY, "to my congregation and to my good friends if it seems in good taste." (W.F. Buckley Jr., *Execution Eve and Other Contemporary Ballads*, G.P. Putnam's Sons, 1975, p. 499)

2. See (1) under GREGARIOUS.

3. [That the Communists would win China eventually] was . . . said confidently [by Chou En-lai], but with DIFFIDENCE. (A. Suehsdorf, "Remembering Chou En-lai in Yenan," *New*

York Times, 1/11/76, Section 4, p. 19)

4. . . . she [Lillian Elmlark] listened to what you said, and she listened to you. She did so with that combination of DIFFIDENCE and discrimination which over the years were the alchemy that made her husband Harry endurable. . . . (W.F. Buckley Jr., *Execution Eve and Other Contemporary Ballads*, G.P. Putnam's Sons, 1975, p. 465)

5. She [Plum] liked his [Adam Malone's] DIFFIDENT manner and the fact that he was brainy. (I. Wallace, *The Fan Club*, Bantam Edition, 1975, p. 63)

6. The [art] show [*Rooms*, at Project Studios One] . . . is directed by Alanna Heiss . . . . In no way crippled by DIFFIDENCE, she will tell any visitor who crosses her path that in exactly 35 days P.S. 1 got the best artists from all over to do their best work. (J. Russell, "An Unwanted School in Queens Becomes an Ideal Art Center," *New York Times*, 6/20/76, Section 2, p. 41)

DILATORY (dil′ə-tōr′ē) *adj.* inclined to delay or procrastinate; slow; tardy; intended to gain time or defer action.

DILATORILY *adv.*

DILATORINESS *noun.*

1. It was not until 1906 that the art holdings [of the Smithsonian] were brought together as the then National Gallery of Art. Even so, the Smithsonian nevertheless continued to be DILATORY in giving American—or indeed contemporary—art its full due. (S.D. Ripley, "The view from the castle," *Smithsonian*, April 1976, p. 6)

2. The second . . . half of the book [*Life/Situations: Essays Written and Spoken*, by Jean-Paul Sartre, translated by Paul Auster and Lydia Davis] contains three interviews with Sartre: one concerned . . . with his DILATORINESS in coming out in favor of women's liberation, conducted by his liberated but constant companion, Simone de Beauvoir . . . (J. Sturrock, Review, *New York Times*, 4/3/77, Section 7, pp. 11, 22)

DIOGENES (dī-oj′ə-nēz) *noun* the ARCHETYPE of the ancient Greek Cynic philosophers (died about 320 B.C.) who, tradition says, searched for an honest man in broad daylight with a lighted lantern. Seeking to expose the falsity of most conventional standards and beliefs, he and his followers were self-appointed watchdogs of morality. His life exemplified self-sufficiency, outspokenness, and striving for moral excellence through ASCETICISM.

1. The view from our own, admittedly more narrow galaxy—bounded by a typewriter, a telephone, and a CORNUCOPIAN "In" box—suggests that the report of print's demise . . . has been greatly exaggerated . . . we are still getting our share of fritter-texts. The truth is that the process of making a book is usually one part DIOGENES and nine parts NARCISSUS. As Byron observed,

    'Tis pleasant, sure, to see one's name
        in print;
    A book's a book, although there's
        nothing in't.

(R.J. Margolis, "Let's Hear It for Moveable Type" [Editorial], *Change*, April 1975, p. 5)

2. "You have, in other words, opted out of the social contract," said I [Russel Wren]. "Shamelessness is the answer," said this contemporary DIOGENES [the wino]. "All the ills of the world can be traced to the foolish desire to look well in the eyes of others." (Thomas Berger, *Who Is Teddy Villanova?*, Delacorte Press/Seymour Lawrence, 1977, p. 132)

DIONYSIAC (dī′ə-nis′ē-ak′) or **DIONYSIAN** (di ə-nish′ən, -nis′ē-ən) *adj.* pertaining to the Dionysia or to Dionysus; Bacchic; recklessly uninhibited; wild, frenzied, and sensuous; orgiastic.

DIONYSIA *noun* (pl.) the orgiastic and dramatic festivals held periodically in honor of Dionysus, from which ancient Greek comedy and tragedy developed.

DIONYSUS or **DIONYSOS** *noun* the Greek god (in Classical Mythology) of fertility, wine, drama, and revelry; associated with the Roman god Bacchus.

1. The argument . . . which is indeed central to the book [*The Cultural Contradictions of Capitalism*, by Daniel Bell] rests on an alleged contradiction between the prudential, cost-conscious rationality of bureaucratic capitalism and the self-gratifying, self-seeking mode

of the actual lives of its citizens, ranging (in Bell's phrases . . .) from "pop HEDONISM," to "the DIONYSIAC Pack" . . . . (R. Williams, Review, *New York Times*, 2/1/76, Section 7, p. 3)

2. Something of the flavor of Mr. [Martin] Greene's narrative [in *Children of the Sun*] is conveyed in the following passage about Guy Burgess's wartime life: "He lived for a time at the [Lord] Rothschild house . . . , which, together with Guy's other quarters, temporarily became a center of DIONYSIANISM for highly placed people in wartime London . . ." (H. Kramer, Review, *New York Times*, 1/25/76, Section 7, p. 3)

DIPSOMANIAC (dip'sə-mā'nē-ak') *noun* a person with an abnormal, irresistible, and insatiable craving for alcoholic beverages.

DIPSOMANIACAL (dip'sə-mə-nī'ə-kəl) *adj.*

DIPSOMANIA *noun* an irresistible, typically periodic, craving for intoxicating beverages.

1. [David] Hare's [new play] *Teeth 'N Smiles* can be said to have brought nostalgia right up to date. Set in 1969, it is Hare's MORDANT memorial to whatever it was that died in the 60's, here symbolized by the breakup of a touring rock band whose DYPSOMANIAC (sic) lead singer is based (rather too closely for comfort) on Janis Joplin. (C. Marowitz, "New Playwrights Stir the British Stage," *New York Times*, 6/20/76, Section 2, p. 7)

DIPTYCH (dip'tik) *noun* a hinged, two-leaved tablet used in ancient times for writing on with a stylus; a pair of pictures or carvings on two panels, usually hinged together; anything consisting of two parallel or contrasting parts.

1. Sometimes, as in the grey painting called *The Dutch Wives*—which is in effect a DIPTYCH—he [Jasper Johns] confounds expectation by mating like with unlike and leading from an identical formal beginning to two different formal ends. (J. Russell, Review of Jasper Johns exhibit at Leo Castelli Gallery, *New York Times*, 2/1/76, Section 2, p. 31)

DISESTABLISHMENTARIAN (dis'ə-stab'lish-mən-târ'ē-ən) *noun* a person who favors

the separation of church and state, especially the withdrawal of special rights, status, and support granted an established church by the state.

DISESTABLISHMENTARIAN *adj.*

DISESTABLISHMENTARIANISM *noun.*

1. A general assertiveness by Congress is overdue. But to assert control in such a way as to DISESTABLISHMENTARIANIZE the government of the U.S. is to invite chaos. (W. F. Buckley Jr., *Execution Eve and Other Contemporary Ballads*, G. P. Putnam's Sons, 1975, p. 263)

2. It was a measure of the DISESTABLISHMENTARIAN mood abroad in the land that the only surviving stop-Carter candidate striking visible sparks was California's Gov. Edmund G. (Jerry) Brown, Jr., 38, whose first claim to attention . . . is that he is not now and has never been a member of the Federal government. (P. Goldman, *et al.*, "A President 'in Jeopardy,' " *Newsweek*, 5/17/76, p. 22)

DISHABILLE (dis' ə-bēl , dis' ə-bē') or DESHABILLE *noun* the state of being carelessly or partly dressed, or dressed in night clothes; a state of disarray or disorder or disorganization; a disorderly or disorganized state of mind or way of thinking; (*Archaic*) a loose morning dress.

EN DÉSHABILLÉ (än dē-zä bē-yá) partly undressed; dressed in a robe, negligee, etc.

1. Robert Brustein—dean of the Yale Drama School, ex-New Republic theater critic, intellectual roustabout, the ghost at many a symposium on whither the arts—has stitched together [in his book, *The Culture Watch*] 32 sermonettes on the DISHABILLE of culture in these anxious, impacted times. (J. Leonard, Review, *New York Times*, 2/15/76, Section 7, p. 4)

2. One such chat transpires when he [R. D. Laing] removes his shoes and socks on a flight from New Orleans to Buffalo; it hinges on the odd coincidence that an airline regulation prohibits such DISHABILLE and that the stewardess had never gone barefoot . . . . (A. Lacy, Review of *The Facts of Life*, by R.D. Laing; and *R.D. Laing: The Man and His Ideas*, by Richard I. Evans, *Chronicle of Higher Education*, 5/24/76, p. 20)

3. For more than a decade, the best way to catch up with the news in France was to catch L'Express . . . . But last summer, L'Express suddenly switched tracks . . . . L'Express's cameras seemed to zoom mainly toward sex and sensation. "The Story of 'O' " was given two successive covers . . . . "Love After 60" examined sex lives of the elderly, and "Why Get Married?" lured the readers with a head-and-shoulders cover picture of a young couple EN DÉSHABILLÉ. (D. Gelman, Jane Friedman, "One Man's Magazine," *Newsweek*, 4/26/76, p. 72)

DISINGENUOUS (dis' in-jen' yōō əs) *adj.* lacking in frankness, candor, or sincerity; insincere; not straightforward.

DISINGENUOUSLY *adv.*

DISINGENUOUSNESS *noun.*

1. Senator McGovern now advances the contradiction quite formally by proposing a total American commitment to Israeli independence alongside an all but uniform disparagement of U.S. commitments to other countries, most particularly South Vietnam . . . . McGovern likes to point to Israeli democracy as his justification, but this of course is DISINGENUOUS. (W.F. Buckley Jr., *Execution Eve and Other Contemporary Ballads*, G.P. Putnam's Sons, 1975, p. 198)

2. There is even hypocrasy in his own muddled philosophy, as when in the nightclub sequence, he [Lenny Bruce] uses "nigger" and "wop" and "kike" affecting to defuse the words when, in fact, he is DISINGENUOUSLY exploiting them. (W.F. Buckley Jr., *Ibid.*, p. 405)

3. Now that is pure Yankee-charming, jumping-frog DISINGENUOUSNESS. (W.F. Buckley Jr., *Ibid.*, p. 244)

4. See (1) under BILLINGSGATE.

5. [Samuel] Bowles and [Herbert] Gintis evidently believe that all workers who say they would choose another occupation if they were "starting over" are dissatisfied with their present jobs. This may be true. But it seems DISINGENUOUS not to acknowledge [in their book, *Schooling in Capitalist America*] that most of these workers say they are satis-

fied, not dissatisfied, when asked directly. (C. Jencks, Review, *New York Times*, 2/15/76, Section 7, p. 18)

6. As a hero in flowing white robes, Lawrence of Arabia has been somewhat devalued in recent years by investigators probing the personal history of the tormented, often DISINGENUOUS man behind the legend. (W. Clemons, Review of the book, *A Prince of Our Disorder: The Life of T.E. Lawrence*, by John E. Mack, *Newsweek*, 4/12/76, p. 98)

7. [Bob] Woodward and [Carl] Bernstein rely on hearsay evidence [in their book, *The Final Days*] unacceptable in any court. They insist they have two sources for everything but that is DISINGENUOUS: if a Presidential aide tells two people he said such-and-such to the President, and those people independently pass his message to the authors, then it becomes a historical fact that the aide did say it, though of course he may only have concocted a self-serving story. (P.S. Prescott, Review, *Newsweek*, 5/2/76, pp. 89-89D)

8. Given the fiat of the Second Commandment against false idols, she [Cynthia Ozick, author of the book, *Bloodshed and Three Novellas*] questions a bit DISINGENUOUSLY whether a Jew should write stories at all. (P. Gray, Review, *Time*, 4/12/76, p. 95)

9. Chekhov claimed Stanislavsky's interpretations had made "cry-babies" out of his plays, but to call *The Cherry Orchard* a comedy [as Chekhov] did is to be DISINGENUOUS. (H. Moss, Review of the book, *A New Life of Anton Chekhov*, by Ronald Hingley, *New York Times*, 6/20/76, Section 7, p. 27)

10. See (8) under SOLIPSISM.

11. Her [Queen Caroline's] detailed interest in the [hydrogen] bomb was unfeigned but also, Blackford [Oakes] thought, lacking in any aspect of DISINGENUOUSNESS . . . . (W.F. Buckley Jr., *Saving the Queen*, Doubleday, 1976, p. 175)

DISQUISITION (dis' kwi-zizh' ən) *noun* a formal discourse or treatise in which a subject is examined and discussed; dissertation.

1. Footnotes frequently interrupt the tale [*Eaters of the Dead*, by Michael Crichton]

. . . with peculiarly arbitrary DISQUISITIONS on such things as Arab semantics and the "translucent membranes" that cover Norse windows. (J. Sullivan, Review, *New York Times*, 4/25/76, Section 7, p. 22)

2. [B. F.] Skinner starts [the book, *Particulars Of My Life*] with a DISQUISITION on the course of the Susquehanna River . . . as the natural place to begin an autobiography, because the river determined where he was born, of farming, railroading forebears. (E. Hoagland, Review, *New York Times*, 4/11/76, Section 7, p. 6)

3. From the very opening pages when he [Zeno of Bruges, hero of *The Abyss*, by Marguerite Yourcenar, translated from the French by Grace Frick in collaboration with M.Y.] encounters his cousin on the road to the Alps, everything is APOTHEGM, DISQUISITION, EPIGRAM, a new occasion for explicating his own PARLOUS role bestride cultures, innovations and heterodoxies, attuned to every rustle of novelty and danger in the late Middle Ages. (A.A. Cohen, Review, *New York Times*, 7/11/76, Section 7, p. 7)

DISSIDENCE (dis′ i-dəns) *noun* disagreement; dissent; difference of opinion.

DISSIDENT *adj.* or *noun.*

DISSIDENTLY *adv.*

1. Recently in Paris the Ukrainian mathematician, Leonid Plyushch, allowed out of the Soviet Union last month, gave a HARROWING account of his two and a half years as a sane man in the Soviet mental asylum where he had been sent for political DISSIDENCE. (Anon., *The London Economist*, "From Leninists to Libertarians: French Communists Change Style," reprinted in *Norman* [Okla.] *Transcript*, 3/25/76, p. 6)

2. The Russians, with a foothold in both Angola and Mozambique, will surely offer some very attractive bids and plenty of arms to DISSIDENT Rhodesian tribal leaders. (J. Chamberlain, *Times Herald*, Norristown, Pa., 10/5/76, p. 9)

3. See (3) under PUTATIVE.

DISSONANT (dis′ ə-nənt) *adj.* disagreeing

or harsh in sound; discordant; out of harmony; incongruous; at variance; incompatible; opposed in opinion, temperament, etc.

1. . . . his specialty [Bernard Herrmann's, who wrote the score for the film, *Taxi Driver*] was expressing psychological disorder through DISSONANT, wrought-up music. (Pauline Kael, Review, *The New Yorker*, 2/9/76, p. 84)

DITHYRAMB (dith′ ə-ram′, -ramb′) *noun* a Greek choral song or chant of vehement or wildly emotional character and usually irregular form; any wildly emotional speech or writing.

DITHYRAMBIC *adj.*

DITHYRAMBICALLY *adv.*

1. Walk with Burt [Reynolds, in the movie, *Hustle*] through the grubby cubicles of the L.A. Police Department as he hears the Foot Fetish man do his DITHYRAMB about smelly ladies' feet. (J. Kroll, Review, *Newsweek*, 1/12/76, p. 69)

2. I could offer an intellectually seductive explanation of the change [in style between modern skyscrapers and, *e.g.*, the Empire State Building], with DITHYRAMBS about the anti-hero and the anti-symbol and how our vision of men and monuments has altered . . . . (Ada Louise Huxtable, "A Skyscraper Fit for a King (Kong)?," *New York Times*, 2/1/76, Section 2, p. 31)

3. "When someone sees this large piece of wood [the cello], beautifully sculptured, being caressed . . . the player . . . can feel the vibrations through his entire body" [said Lynn Harrell]. It is evident from Harrell's DITHYRAMBIC description that the cello for him is a sensuous instrument as well as an intellectual one. (D. Henahan, "For this Gentle Giant, the Cello Is a Way of Life," *New York Times*, 3/6/77, Section 2, p. 15)

DIURNAL (dī-ûr′nəl) *adj.* daily; happening daily; of or belonging to the daytime (opposed to *nocturnal*).

DIURNALLY *adv.*

1. . . . he [Donald Washburn II] was . . .

completely outfitted—in the same ensemble in which he had appeared [yesterday] at my office. I [Russel Wren] wondered whether it would be politic to ask if he had been home at all; he seemed the sort who would necessarily practice a DIURNAL change of attire. (Thomas Berger, *Who Is Teddy Villanova?*, Delacorte Press/Seymour Lawrence, 1977, p. 156)

DIVOT (div′ ət) *noun* a piece of turf gouged out with a golf club in making a stroke; (in Scotland) a thin slice of turf used as for roofing.

1. On the one hand, the insecure and anxious youth asks your approval of whatever he says with every "y'know." On the other hand, the OMNISCIENT stripling's "y'knows" are simply declaring what he says to be the only possible truth. Indeed, to disagree would be an admission that you had an IQ no higher than an unreplaced DIVOT. (Edmund Midura, "Um's the Word," *Today, The Inquirer Magazine*, 1/30/77, p. 26)

DONNYBROOK (don′ ē-brŏŏk′) *noun* a wild, rowdy, noisy fight; brawl; free-for-all [after Donnybrook Fair, held annually until 1855 in County Dublin, Ireland and famous for riots].

1. In a deadpan manner he [William Marshall] works up some unusually funny situations [in *Yellowthread Street*]. Even the bloody DONNYBROOK at the end, in which a stupid . . . Mongolian monster fights it out with a bunch of hoods and the police department, has its funny aspects. (N. Callendar, Review, *New York Times*, 3/14/76, Section 7, p. 30)

2. [Giant pitcher Jim] Barr hit [Bill] Madlock [of the Chicago Cubs] with a pitch after the warning [about a beanball], an act which would require automatic ejection if the umpire ruled it was done intentionally. When the Cub third baseman advanced on the [pitcher's] mound after being hit, the DONNYBROOK began . . . . (R. Dozer, "Madlock is fined $500, Cardenal $200 by NL," *Chicago Tribune*, 5/6/76, Section 4, p. 1)

3. Edward Albee's play [*Who's Afraid of Virginia Woolf?*] is as fresh and biting as ever. With Colleen Dewhurst and Ben Gazzara as the well-matched married adversaries in a night-long drunken DONNYBROOK. (Anon., Review, *The New Yorker*, 5/31/76, p. 4)

4. He [Stanley Woodward] liked verbs of action and exact adjectives. He disliked "ding-dong battles, horsehides, DONNYBROOKS, myriads of colored lights, fetlock-deep mud, net tilts, grid battles, pile-driving rights . . . ." (R. Kahn, *The Boys of Summer*, Harper and Row, 1971, p. 72)

5. In an instant, Sharon [Fields]'s vision was filled with . . . four of them . . . .The Dreamer [Adam Malone] staggered to his feet. . . .The Salesman [Howard Yost] was holding the Evil One [Shively], restraining him. . . .The Milquetoast [Leo Brunner] was holding off The Dreamer, imploring him not to go on with the DONNYBROOK. (I. Wallace, *The Fan Club*, Bantam Edition, 1975, p. 325)

6. G.O.P. DONNYBROOK . . . by waging INTERNECINE warfare, Ford and Reagan run the risk that when the prize of the nomination is finally won, it will not be worth much. (Anon., "G.O.P. Donnybrook, *Time*, 6/21/76, p. 13)

DOUBLE ENTENDRE (dub′ əl än-tän′ drə, -tänd′) a word or expression with two meanings, one of which is usually RISQUÉ or indecorous; a double meaning; ambiguity.

1. She [Doris Kearns, author of *Lyndon Johnson and the American Dream*] also gave the back of her hand in advance to any speculation about her relationship with Lyndon Johnson (this was before Wayne Hays made "relationship" a DOUBLE ENTENDRE), . . . (Anon., "Book Ends," *New York Times*, 6/20/76, Section 7, p. 37)

2. Restoration drama takes us into a LICENTIOUS world of high style, low morals and ice-cold wit. Interestingly enough, its aim is never bedroom comedy but drawing-room raillery. It is as if sex had been invented as a topic of conversation—either the veiled allusion or the saucy DOUBLE ENTENDRE. (T.E. Kalem, Review of *The Way of the World*, a

play by William Congreve, *Time*, 6/21/76, p. 42)

3. See (3) under HARROWING.

DOWSE (douz) *verb* to search for underground supplies of water, metal, etc., by the use of a divining rod; to seek something with meticulous care, especially with the aid of a mechanical device; to find (as water) by dowsing.

DOWSER *noun* a rod or wand used in dowsing; divining rod; a person skilled in its use.

1. Whifflesnaffer's Law, first enunciated in 1832 by the famed Filipino DOWSER, Eduardo Whifflesnaffer, holds that, when confronted with the choice between news stories, reporters, editors and readers will gravitate, like iron filings to a magnet, to the more trivial, BANAL and superficial. (S. Hempstone, "Over a barrel: Again, the oil price squeeze," *Philadelphia Inquirer*, 11/11/76, p. 11-A)

2. Early settlers in this country gave the witch-hazel its name because the leaves resembled those of the hazel . . . . The witch part of the name comes from its use in DOWSING, as the supple and easily stripped branches are particularly suitable for this ancient art of finding water. (J. Shaw, "A What-Is-It?—The Season's First Flower," *New York Times*, 2/6/77, Section 2, p. 37)

DOXY (dok'sē) *noun, pl.*: DOXIES a slang term for a mistress or paramour; prostitute.

1. "I guarantee that Teddy [Villanova] wouldn't lay a hand on a woman" [said Russel Wren to Peggy Tumulty]. Except a gangland DOXY; but I didn't add that. (Thomas Berger, *Who Is Teddy Villanova?*, Delacorte Press/Seymour Lawrence, 1977, p. 45)

2. "Do you suppose that vanity plays so large a role in my mystique?" [Natalie Novotny asked Russel Wren]. "Certainly pride does not [replied Wren]. I found [Donald] Washburn naked in your bed. I refuse to believe that serving as his DOXY is required by your department [the Treasury]." (Thomas Berger, *Ibid.*, p. 180)

DOYEN (doi-en′, doi′ ən) *noun* the senior member, as in age or rank, of a group, class, profession, etc.; dean.

DOYENNE (doi-en′) *noun* a female doyen.

1. . . . he [Louis Schneider, in his book, *The Sociological Way of Looking at the World*] follows Talcott Parsons, the DOYEN of most modern American sociology, in breaking . . . society into many different systems and subsystems that are functionally related and that move in equilibrium. (Sharon Zukin, Review, *Chronicle of Higher Education*, 3/22/76, p. 13)

2. That event [the conviction of Inez Garcia of second-degree murder of Miguel Jimenez] mobilized feminist forces. At a dozen rallies in the United States and Europe, the DOYENNES of the movement—Kate Millett, Gloria Steinem, Simone de Beauvoir—spoke out on her behalf. The rape victim who had fought back—first Inez Garcia, and later, more successfully, Joan Little—became the new heroine. (D.L. Kirp, Review of *Against Our Will: Men, Women and Rape*, by Susan Brownmiller; and *Rape: The Bait and the Trap*, by Jean McKellar, with the collaboration of Dr. Menachem Amir, *Change*, April 1976, p. 40)

3. . . . Part 3 [of the book, *The Genius of Thomas Hardy*, edited by Margaret Drabble] . . . contains three [essays] by those DOYENS of English letters, A. L. Rowse, Lord David Cecil and Sir John Betjeman. (M. Green, Review, *New York Times*, 4/18/76, Section 7, p. 6)

4. . . . the artistic discipline that makes the first three-fourths of the book first-rate disintegrates as he . . . approaches Harvard graduate school. Whether he [B.F. Skinner, author of the book, *Particulars Of My Life*] tired of the rigor of writing a fine book or grew flighty from overconfidence or, approaching the setting of his successes at Harvard, assumed the perfunctory manner of a DOYEN, isn't clear. (E. Hoagland, Review, *New York Times*, 4/11/76, Section 7, p. 6)

DRACONIAN or **DRACONIAN** (drā-kō′ nē-ən) *adj.* (sometimes lower case) rigorous; severe; cruel; inhuman; (if capitalized) of, pertaining to, or characteristic of Draco or his code of laws.

DRACO *noun* a 7th century B.C. Athenian statesman noted for the severity of his code of laws.

1. President Ford's proposed $394.2 billion budget for the coming fiscal year has widely been termed "austere"—*Newsweek* even referred to it as "DRACONIAN." (M. Friedman, "Ford's Budget," *Newsweek*, 2/9/76, p. 64)

2. His [Colonel Skimmerhorn's] opening strategy was DRACONIAN. Distributing teams along a three-hundred-mile stretch of the Platte [River], he waited for dry and windy days, then set fire to the prairie, producing a conflagration so extensive that it burned all edible fodder from the Platte nearly to the Arkansas [River]. (J. A. Michener, *Centennial*, Fawcett, 1975, p. 509)

3. . . . the vengeance set . . . tend to argue for the imposition [on criminals] of penalties and confinements which (1) defy all ethical and humane logic, (2) like DRACONIAN sentences already on the books, are too severe to be invoked . . . , (3) cost far more money than their proponents have any intention of putting up anyway. (Meg Greenfield, "Death by Friendly Fire," *Newsweek*, 4/12/76, p. 112)

4. The unions have complained volubly about the DRACONIAN cruelty of [New York City's] EFCB [Emergency Financial Control Board] . . . , yet . . . this body . . . recently approved a contract with the teachers' union allowing an average increase of wages and benefits of more than 7% a year. Overall, the board's approval of "cost of living adjustments" has increased personnel costs by 6%. (Anon., "After the Junta" [Editorial], *Wall Street Journal*, 2/22/77, p. 24)

DRECK or **DREK** (drek) *noun* (in Slang) any manufactured item of inferior material, design, workmanship and overall quality; any obviously inferior product; any cheap, gaudy piece of merchandise; a small, cheap, useless item.

1. "[Donald] Barthelme is often guilty of opportunism of subject (the war, street riots, launching pads, etc.) and to be opportune is to succumb to DRECK . . . cleverness is also DRECK. The cheap joke is DRECK. The topical, too, is DRECK." [said William H. Gass] . . . If the modern urban world is DRECK, garbage, sound and fury signifying nothing, how moving, instructive, important can pop art be? (R. Locke, Review of *Amateurs*, a book by Donald

Barthelme, *New York Times*, 12/19/76, Section, pp. 17, 18)

DUN (dun) *verb* to make repeated and insistent demands upon, especially for the payment of a debt; to annoy constantly.

DUN *noun* a person who duns another; an insistent demand for payment.

1. [Last week] The IRS revoked the [Teamsters' $1.4 billion Central States Pension] fund's tax-exempt status retroactive to 1965, charging that the fund was mismanaged and had made "questionable loans." . . . If the ruling stands, the fund will be DUNNED for back taxes and roughly 400,000 active and retired Teamsters will get lower benefits. (Anon., "Squeezing the Teamsters," *Newsweek*, 7/12/76, p. 62)

2. His [Jimmy Carter's] coming of age was utterly ordinary—"the dumbest boyhood of anybody I've ever seen," Miz Lillian [his mother] told him, in despair at being DUNNED for wee-Jimmy anecdotes. (P. Goldman, "Sizing Up Carter," *Newsweek*, 9/13/76, p. 25)

3. People who come to the company's attention as being faithful Jack Daniel's drinkers receive a deed to a square foot of land in the hollow [near the distillery], a certificate of membership [in the Tennessee Squires Association] suitable for framing and a personal letter from the company's president. From time to time, they then get gag letters DUNNING them for taxes or asking permission to hunt on their property. (F. C. Klein, "Jack Daniel's Bets That You Can't Tell Black From Green," *Wall Street Journal*, 2/8/77, p. 19)

DYBBUK (dib'ək) or **DIBBUK** *noun* (in Jewish folklore) a demon or the soul of a dead person that enters the body of a living person and controls him.

1. Throughout the waning day, her [Sharon Fields'] hatred was inflamed by the evil DYBBUK that possessed her. (I. Wallace, *The Fan Club*, Bantam Books, 1975, p. 379)

2. Eventually, the guilt-ridden Jacobo [in *The Fragmented Life of Don Jacobo Lerner*, a book by Isaac Goldemberg] comes to feel that he is possessed by a DYBBUK—the wandering soul of

a dead childhood friend who was obsessed with visions of pogroms, war and holocaust. When the DYBBUK is finally exorcised, Jacobo has nothing left to believe in but "the fact of his own imminent death." (Margo Jefferson, Review, *Newsweek*, 5/9/77, p. 103)

DYKE (dīk) *noun* (in Slang) a LESBIAN, especially one with pronounced masculine characteristics.

DYKEY *adj.*

1. "The threat of female deviance pervades the culture; it is personified in the popular symbols of the witch, the bitch, the de-sexed female, the castrating woman. History casts her up in . . . the spinster symbol Susan B. Anthony; crazy Carrie Nation with her hatchet; . . . and the 20th-century equivalent of the deviant stereotype, the DYKE. It was the threat of such deviance that kept women in line ideologically and emotionally and fettered them psychologically" [Quote from *The Female Experience*, a book by Gerda Lerner]. (Adrienne Rich, Review, *New York Times*, 3/20/77, Section 7, p. 12)

DYSCALCULIA (dis′ kâl-kyŏŏ′ lē-ə) *noun* severe disturbance of the ability to calculate, resulting from CEREBRAL injury.

1. You can wow them at the PTA meeting, too, [using what you learn from *The Phrase Dropper's Handbook*, by John T. Beaudouin and Everett Mattlin] even if your kid is flunking out of second grade. He isn't stupid, merely suffering a "developmental lag," possibly accompanied by a degree of DYSCALCUGLIA (*sic*), which means he can't add two and two. (Beth Gillin Pombeiro, "Be a phrase-dropper," *Philadelphia Inquirer*, 11/9/76, p. 3-C)

DYSLEXIA (dis-lek′sē-ə) *noun* impairment of the ability to read, often as the result of a genetic defect or of brain damage.

DYSLEXIC *adj.*

1. This [disease] is humanus indocilis, the crippler of second-semester-senior college students everywhere. Its early stages are characterized by extremes of temperament (e.g., sudden outbursts of uncontrollable laughter, followed by an impulsive desire to self-destruct). The student may also experience phases of DYSLEXIA, a disturbance of the ability to read . . . . Emotions are also out of tune . . . . Unknowing friends sometimes describe such a student as "weird." (Adriana Signoretta, "College Daze," *Today, The Inquirer Magazine*, 5/15/77, p. 36)

DYSTOPIA (dis-tŏ′pē-ə) *noun* an imagined place or period in which things are as depressingly wretched as they are wonderful in utopia.

DYSTOPIAN *adj.*

1. He [Thomas Disch, author of the book, *Getting Into Death*] has been fabulist, DYSTOPIAN, satirist, hack and poet. (Edna Stumpf, Review, *The Philadelphia Inquirer*, 2/15/76, p. 12-H)

E

ECDYSIAST (ek-diz′ ē-ast′) *noun* stripper; one who rhythmically disrobes; a woman who performs a striptease [coined by H.L. Mencken].

ECDYSIS (ek′ di-sis) *noun* the shedding or casting off of an outer coat by snakes, etc.

ECDYSIASM apparently coined by William F.

Buckley Jr. to mean the profession practised by an ecdysiast.

1. . . . she [Jane Fonda] turned rather earlier than most people to her career, leaving Vassar College prematurely and turning enthusiastically to ECDYSIASM, and on into formal acting. (W. F. Buckley Jr., *Execution Eve and Other Contemporary Ballads*, G.P. Putnam's Sons, 1975, p. 377)

2. The passenger in seat R-25-1 would appear to be a belly dancer practicing her routine . . . Almost since takeoff from Cologne on Lufthansa's flight 408 to New York, she has been rotating her midsection, rolling her eyes, shimmying her shoulders and flexing her thighs. And she is not the only one; just about everyone aboard is doing this "sit-down rumba." Is this a traveling company of *A Chorus Line?* In-flight ECDYSIAST transcendentalists? Not quite. "You are now seated aboard the first airline in which you can get a little exercise while you fly," says a recorded voice. (Anon., "Fitness in Flight," *Time*, 8/1/77, p. 53)

ÉCLAT (ā-klä´) *noun* brilliant or conspicuous success, reputation, etc.; showy or elaborate display; striking effect; a fanfare; acclamation; acclaim; fame; renown.

1. . . . when he [John Law] was 43, he settled in Paris with considerable ÉCLAT. It was the eve of Louis XIV's death, and France was near bankruptcy. "I shall," Law proclaimed to anyone who would listen, "make gold out of paper". . . . Orleans [the old king's nephew], desperate to improve finances, had arranged for Law to charter the first French bank . . . it had the power to issue paper bulls . . . signed by John Law. This was the first paper money to have general circulation on the continent. (R.W. Minton, "John Law's bubble: bigger . . . bigger and then BUST," *Smithsonian*, January 1976, pp. 94, 96)

2. The meal may be just two simple courses, but it is always beautifully prepared, flavorful and served with ÉCLAT. I consider Chuck [Williams] one of the most realistically creative cooks I know. (J. Beard, "New 'toy' will delight pasta fans,"*Philadelphia Inquirer*, 9/26/76, p. 14-I)

ECLECTIC (i-klek´ tik) *adj.* selecting; choosing from or composed of materials from various sources, systems, or doctrines; not following any one system, but selecting and using what are considered the best elements of all, or many, systems; noting or pertaining to works of art, architecture, decoration, etc., produced by a certain person or during a certain period, that derive from a wide range of historic styles.

ECLECTIC or ECLECTICIST *noun* one who follows an eclectic method.

ECLECTICALLY *adv.*

ECLECTICISM *noun* the use or advocacy of an eclectic method; an eclectic system.

1. Her talent is so ECLECTIC that it has established the 53-year-old redhead as something of a Hollywood legend. "Nancy [Walker] can play anything," marvels Valerie Harper. (H.F. Waters, M. Kasindorf, "Funny Lady," *Newsweek*, 12/29/75, p. 57)

2. One would happily applaud this production anywhere else in Germany; here [Berlin], it reinforces one's fear that a company with a hard-won style of its own has surrendered to ECLECTICISM. (K. Tynan, "Brecht Would Not Applaud His Theatre Today," *New York Times*, 1/11/76, Section 2 , p. 7)

3. Critics have found the group [Queen] "pedestrian" while labeling its musical ECLECTICISM "PRETENTIOUS." These brickbats have not discouraged the musicians. . . . "Our audience [says lead singer Freddie Mercury] is sophisticated enough to appreciate our drastic musical variety." (H. Edwards, "Pop Notes: 'Audiences Have Made Our Song Their Anthem,' " *New York Times*, 1/18/76, Section 2, p. 17)

4. But basically, she [Olga Kahn] said, there would be no ["Information Please"] program without Gordon [Kahn]. It was Gordon who polished every question. It was Gordon's ECLECTICISM that established the tone. (R. Kahn, *The Boys of Summer*, Harper and Row, 1971, p. 41)

5. When I sat in on a recent decision-making session to determine recipients of Exxon grants in the arts involving [Harold C.] Roser [Jr.], [Robert E.] Kingsley and three other Exxon people, including a woman and a black man, the criteria brought into play seemed to me as

ECLECTIC and even arbitrary as those of any other person or group with favors to dispense. (J. Brooks, "Fueling the Arts, Or, Exxon as a Medici," *New York Times*, 1/25/76, Section 2, p. 30)

6. One did not go to Ebbets Field for sociology . . . It is not simply that they [the Brooklyn Dodgers] won frequently, brawled with umpires, got into bean-ball fights and endlessly thrashed in the headwaters of a pennant race. The team possessed an astonishing variety of ECLECTIC skills. (R. Kahn, *The Boys of Summer*, Harper and Row, 1971, p. xvii)

7. Having asked questions, feminists must now listen to answers. Perhaps Truman would not have uttered, at a feminist meeting, his famous injunction (or maybe he *would* have): "If you can't stand the heat, get out of the kitchen." Meanwhile, an ECLECTIC perception is necessary if only because thoughtless non-cooperation between the sexes is finally absurd. (L. Tiger, "Fearful Symmetry," *New York Times*, 2/8/76, Section 7, p. 39)

8. Sex as farce, she [Lulu Cartwright, in *Happiness is Too Much Trouble*, by Sandra Hochman] feels, is better than no sex at all. Not every feminist would agree with her, but then Lulu is a sexual ECLECTIC . . . (Anatole Broyard, Review, *New York Times*, 3/11/76, p. 35)

9. In [Adam] Smith, by virtue of the very ECLECTICISM that bores shallow minds, are the roots of the modern theories of general equilibrium. He abandoned a simple and dogmatic labor theory of value to decompose price into its separate wage, interest and profit and landrent components because the brute facts required him to do so. (P.A. Samuelson, "Adam Smith," *Newsweek*, 3/15/76, p. 86)

10. Where liberals used to say, "Make no small plans," [Edmund G.] Brown says, "Think small." ECLECTICISM prevails as he draws upon the thinking of the environmental movement, the discipline of yoga and an ex-Jesuit novice's conviction that, after all, our kingdom is not of this world. (W.V. Shannon, "The lasting hurrah," *New York Times*, 3/14/76, Section 6, p. 11)

11. See (2) under CHILIASM.

12. The John Denver phenomenon is a remarkable example of what is known as "crossover"—a performer whose ECLECTIC style crosses conventional boundaries and therefore appeals to diverse audiences. (Grace Lichtenstein, "John Denver—Pop Music's Wholesome Guru," *New York Times*, 3/28/76, Section 2, pp. 1, 18)

13. See (5) under COMPLEMENTARY.

14. . . . the book [*The New Urban History*, edited by Leo F. Schnore] . . . is a collection of articles . . . on urban history and quantitative methodology. Such compilations are frequently disappointing fare, their ECLECTICISM requiring tent-like umbrella titles to enclose contributions usually uneven in quality and overly particular in focus. (M. Frisch, Review, *Chronicle of Higher Education*, 4/26/76, p. 19)

15. *Feminist Studies* is [a journal] directed at an audience of graduate students and professors. . . .FS has the most to offer women who are interested in investigating feminist issues. The article topics are ECLECTIC, and some issues even contain women's poems. (Suzanne Gordon, Review, *Change*, April 1976, p. 47)

16. [David R.] Godine's list of [published] titles is decidedly ECLECTIC . . . its successes include: *The Wild Gourmet. . . The Anatomical Works of George Stubbs* . . . and *Art of the Printed Book, 1455-1955* . . . (J.N. Baker, "Holdout for Quality," *Newsweek*, 5/24/76, p. 94)

17. See (1) under DIATONIC.

18. See (2) under NEMESIS.

19. While teaching in Stanford's Paris program he [H. Bruce Franklin] became involved with European Marxists and representatives of North Vietnam. By the fall of 1967 his growing opposition to the war found a framework in an ECLECTIC Marxism-Leninism, which he began to teach to his literature students. (H.D. Shapiro, Review of *Back Where You Came From: One life in the death of the empire*, by H. Bruce Franklin, *Change*, Winter 1975-76, p. 55)

20. See (1) under CLAIRVOYANCE.

21. The [New York] *Herald Tribune* was

housed in a twenty-story building...on the block between Seventh and Eighth Avenues, from Fortieth to Forty-first Street...the region was ECLECTIC; in the old *Tribune* neighborhood garment buildings, garages and orange-drink stands mixed into Manhattan dr∗ness. (R. Kahn, *The Boys of Summer*, Harper and Row, 1971, p. 61)

22. See (4) under PEREGRINATION.

23. See (4) under SCABROUS.

ECLOGUE (ek′ lôg, -log) *noun* a pastoral or idyllic poem, often in dialogue form.

1. The private-eye novel, which started out raw and tough and over the years became as formalized as an ECLOGUE, reaches its Bergerian APOTHEOSIS [in *Who Is Teddy Villanova?* by Thomas Berger]: "My name is Zwingli, and I'm a detective. I'll show you my identification, if you'll me yours, as Henry James might say." Cop and suspect . . . swap Modern Library literary references in the book's funniest scene. (W. Clemons, Review, *Newsweek*, 4/4/77, p. 85)

ECTOMORPH (ek′tə-morf′) *noun* a person of the ectomorphic type.

ECTOMORPHIC *adj.* having a slender body build characterized by the relative prominence of structures developed from the embryonic ectoderm (contrasted with endomorphic, MESOMORPHIC), as skin, nerves, brain, and sense organs.

ECTOMORPHICALLY *adv.*
ECTOMORPHY *noun.*

1. ...ERB—[Clint] Eastwood, [Burt] Reynolds and [Charles] Bronson—are dispiriting signs of the confusion in contemporary masculinity. Erb-man is cool. In matters of love and sex his passivity is positively CATATONIC. . . . Erb-man is tough and he knows it. Whether ECTOMORPH (Eastwood) or MESOMORPH (Reynolds and Bronson), he likes his morph and moves like NARCISSUS ambling to the reflecting pond. (J. Kroll, Review of three movies: *Gator; The Outlaw Josey Wales;* and *St. Ives, Newsweek,* 9/13/76, p. 89)

ECUMENICAL (ek′ yŏŏ-men′ i-kəl) or **ECUMENIC** *adj.* general; world-wide; universal; pertaining to the whole Christian church; promoting or fostering Christian unity throughout the world.

ECUMENICALLY *adv.*

ECUMENICALISM or **ECUMENISM** or **ECUMENICISM** *noun.*

ECUMENICIST *noun.*

1. Once a week [when I was a boy] The Sporting News would arrive with an abundance of statistics and an ECUMENICAL editorial policy that gave the same amount of space to each [baseball] team. (J. M. Culkin, "Tinkers to Evers to '76," *New York Times*, 6/13/76, Section 5, p. 2)

2. Whereas FACT [First Annual Conference on Theater, held two years ago at Princeton] was ECUMENICAL in spirit, an attempt to weld an alliance between the commercial stage and the resident theater movement for mutual advantage, the TCG [Theater Communications Group] conference [last month at Yale] was more exclusive in conception, open only to non-profit theaters, and looking for union not with Broadway but with other subsidized arts institutions, such as symphony orchestras, opera and ballet, and museums. (R. Brustein, "Art Versus Arts Advocacy In the Non-Commercial Theater," *New York Times*, 7/4/76, Section 2, p. 5)

3. See (2) under BONHOMIE.

4. See (4) under HOMILY.

5. In keeping with the original vision of a classless, integrated, ECUMENICAL community, the four apartment buildings now standing range from federally assisted low-income housing . . . to co-ops that are comparably priced with East Side Manhattan apartments. (Anon., "The Little Apple," *Time*, 5/24/76, p. 42)

EDEMA (i-dē′ mə) *noun,* pl. **EDEMAS** or **EDEMATA** (i-dē′ mə-tə) an abnormal accumulation of fluid in cells, tissues, or cavities of the body, resulting in swelling.

EDEMATOUS or **EDEMATOSE** *adj.*

1. . . . one of the features of the score [of *The Magic Flute*] as a whole is a delicacy that reflects Mozart's acute aural sensitivity in the last months of his life, when even the singing o

his pet canary caused him physical pain. This symptom, together with EDEMA, stomach trouble, VERTIGO, and spasms of weeping, first suggested a diagnosis of mercury poisoning. If it is true that a stigma increases perception, and that disease, especially one that the sufferer may fear to be fatal, serves to heighten experience, then a purely human explanation can be hypothesized for the ETHEREALITY of *The Magic Flute*—though in Mozart's case we are always inclined to suspect a Divine one. (R. Craft, Review, *New York Review of Books*, 11/27/75, pp. 21–22)

EFFETE (i-fēt′) *adj.* exhausted of vigor or energy; worn out; depleted; decadent; lax; soft, overrefined, etc.; lacking in wholesome vigor, force of character, moral stamina, etc.; unable to produce; spent and sterile; barren.

EFFETELY *adv.*

EFFETENESS *noun.*

1. . . . etiquette is the first value only of the society that has no values, the EFFETE society. (W. F. Buckley Jr., *Up From Liberalism*, Arlington House, 2nd Printing 1968, p. 129)

2. See (3) under SMARMY.

3. We [city boys] used to measure how far a ball traveled by the number of manhole covers it cleared . . . . Some guys could hit a ball three sewers and some four. A four-sewer man was not what you would call EFFETE. (R. Cohen, of Washington Post, "Guinea pig new lawn mower," *Norman Transcript*, 7/16/76, p. 7)

4. The once mandatory identification of poetry with the EFFETE and the sentimental is no longer quite current. This change has come about quickly and without major compromise of the traditional IDIOSYNCRASIES of the profession. (D. Lenson, "Unmasking the Contemporary Poet," *Chronicle of Higher Education*, 8/2/76, p. 9)

5. See (1) under NAMBY-PAMBY.

EFFLORESCENCE (ef′ lə-res′ əns) *noun* the state or a period of flowering; blooming; an example or result of growth and development; the peak or fulfillment, as a career.

EFFLORESCENT *adj.*

EFFLORESCENTLY *adv.*

EFFLORESCE *verb* to blossom out; flower; bloom.

1. See (1) under RECRUDESCENCE.

2. This [the art exhibition, *The Golden Age of Spanish Painting*, at London's Royal Academy] is not a "masterpiece" show, but it does accord with Spanish reality in the 17th century and is required seeing for anyone interested in that singular EFFLORESCENCE. (R. Hughes, Review, *Time*, 2/16/76, p. 66)

3. "[Teddy] Villanova's operations [said Boris] are world-wide. It would be no exaggeration to lay at his door most of the criminal phenomena of the past two decades: the EFFLORESCENCE of the youth cult, obviously; the corruption of most modern languages; the pseudo revolution . . . in sex; the journalistic enshrining of mediocrity . . ." (Thomas Berger, *Who Is Teddy Villanova?*, Delacorte Press/Seymour Lawrence, 1977, p. 204)

EFFLUVIUM (i-flōō′vē-əm) *noun, pl.* -VIA a slight or invisible exhalation or vapor, especially one that is disagreeable or noxious; aura.

EFFLUVIAL *adj.*

1. Indeed, Mr. [Leo] Rosten gradually begins to emanate a whiff of elitism, a preference for the ARTIFACTS of standard high culture . . . . In the book [*The 3:10 to Anywhere*]'s final scene, he strolls the sands of Coney Island, depressed at . . . the vulgar EFFLUVIA of pop culture washed up around him. (R.R. Lingerman, Review, *New York Times*, 3/14/76, Section 7, p. 14)

EFFULGENT (i-ful′-jənt) *adj.* shining forth brilliantly; radiantly.

EFFULGENTLY *adv.*

EFFULGENCE *noun.*

EFFULGE *verb* to shine brightly; flash out.

1. He [President Nixon] returned only to pick up his small glass of liqueur, armed with which he strode to the adjoining table, crowded with Chinese officials, and paused, EFFULGENTLY, to

toast each one of them individually, his cheeks
flushed (with grand purpose—Nixon is to all
intents and purposes a teetotaler), and on to
yet another table of Chinese dignitaries, to do
the same. (W.F. Buckley Jr., *Execution Eve
and Other Contemporary Ballads*, G. P. Putnam's Sons, 1975, p. 30)

EGOCENTRIC (ē′ gō-sen′ trik, eg′ ō-)
adj having or regarding the self as the center
of all worldly things; having little or no regard
for interests, beliefs, or attitudes other than
one's own; self-centered.

EGOCENTRIC *noun* an egocentric person.

EGOCENTRISM or EGOCENTRICITY *noun*.

1. Historians differ on his contributions to
Founding Fatherhood; some see him [Charles
Carroll, the second signer of the Declaration of
Independence, who outlived all other signers]
as a quiet mover and shaker, others as an
EGOCENTRIC money-grubber bent mainly on
enhancing his purse. (Mary H. Cadwalader,
"Charles Carroll of Carrollton: a signer's
story," *Smithsonian*, December 1975, p. 65)

2. . . . the letters and memoirs [of Gordon
Craig] published here [in *'Young Isadora': The
Love Story of Isadora Duncan and Gordon
Craig*, edited by Francis Steegmuller] can only
be described as impatient, self-absorbed—
Steegmuller calls him [Craig] a "tornado of
EGOCENTRICITY"—even incoherent. Why
Steegmuller feels obliged to speak of his
"literary gifts" in connection with them is
beyond me. (J. Atlas, Review, *New York
Times*, 9/5/76, Section 7, p. 3)

3. [Larry] Rivers [a former art student of Hans
Hofmann] once said that "when [Hofmann]
came around to look at the work, he was relaxed enough to beef up the timid hearts and
pompous, blustering and EGOCENTRIC enough
to make every fiber of the delusions of
grandeur puff and puff and puff up until you
saw clearly your name in the long line from
Michelangelo." (D. Davis, "Tale of Hofmann," *Newsweek*, 11/1/76, p. 78)

EGREGIOUS (i-grē′jəs, -jē-əs) *adj*. remarkably, extraordinarily, or outstandingly bad;
glaring; flagrant; outstanding for undesirable
qualities.

EGREGIOUSLY *adv*.

EGREGIOUSNESS *noun*.

1. And he [Silvio Conte] concludes [his letter],
". . . In light of the EGREGIOUSLY excessive profits reported this week by Exxon and all the
other corporate fiefdoms, tell me, how did the
Buckley oil barons fare in 1973?" (W. F.
Buckley Jr., *Execution of Eve and Other Contemporary Ballads*, G. P. Putnam's Sons, 1975,
p. 292)

2. Our host tonight undertook, quite alone
last summer, to right, single-handedly, an inadvertent negligence that might have resulted
in an EGREGIOUS injustice. (W. F. Buckley Jr.,
Ibid., p. 369)

3. We were at a splendid restaurant, and
Harry was at his best, putting on the act for
which he is so famous, affecting an EGREGIOUS
concern for the price of the lettuce, for the
indignities of the service, and for the deficiencies of the Republic. (W. F. Buckley Jr.,
Ibid., p. 466)

4. Just how destructive governmental overkill
at the federal and state levels has become has
emerged clearly from a national survey the
editors of *Change* have just concluded of some
of the more EGREGIOUS examples of governmental intervention. (G.W. Bonham, "Will Government Patronage Kill the Universities?" [Ed-
itorial], *Change*, Winter 1975–76, p. 10)

5. Calling the [energy] bill that finally passed
a "compromise" [President Ford's words] is an
EGREGIOUS case of misleading labeling. (M.
Friedman, "Rising Above Principle," *Newsweek*, 1/19/76, p. 68)

6. The inflating of [John] Adam's public role
seems most EGREGIOUS in the third episode [of
the TV production of *The Adams Chronicles*],
which deals with his diplomacy abroad. (R. B.
Morris, "Was John Adams Really That Important?" *New York Times*, 1/11/76, Section 2,
p. 1)

7. Nothing was left him [Harvard's President
Nathan Pusey, when the 1969 student rebellion
occurred] but power, the power that had come
to him . . . in the course of fifteen years of the
most EGREGIOUS institutional growth. (N. W.
Aldrich, Jr., "Harvard On The Way Down,"
Harper's, March 1976, p. 40)

8. See (2) under PUERILE.

9. See (1) under SPINDRIFT.

10. Next to murder, torture is the most EGREGIOUS violation of personal rights one human being can inflict on another. (Anon., "Torture as Policy: The Network of Evil," *Time*, 8/16/76, p. 31)

EIDOLON (ī-dō´ len) *noun, pl.* -LONS or - LA an image without real existence; phantom; apparition; an ideal person or thing.

EIDOLIC (ī-dō´lik) *adj.*

1. Ideas of love and death glimmer from every page of this book [*The Woman Said Yes: Encounters With Life and Death*, by Jessamyn West], but ideas only in a Platonic sense —EIDOLA: images of beings yet to come. (Nancy Hale, Review, *New York Times*, 5/2/76, Section 7, p. 4)

ÉLAN (ā-län´, ā-lan´) *noun* dash; impetuous ardor; spirited self-assurance; verve; PANACHE.

1. See (1) under ENERVATE.

2. From these strikes [of the shirtwaist-makers in 1909] the Jews had once again fought their way out of captivity and darkness; their ÉLAN . . . was rapidly channeled into the I.L.G.W.U. and the Amalgamated Clothing Workers. (T. Solotaroff, Review of *World of our Fathers*, a book by Irving Howe, *New York Times*, 2/1/76, Section 7, pp. 2, 28)

3. He [Viscount Montgomery] was colorful when soldiering was drab and dangerous business. He was often anything but bold in his troop maneuvers, but the image of British dash, verve, and ÉLAN which he communicated to the world was one of the war's great morale factors among the troops under his command. (Anon., "Montgomery of Alamein" [Editorial], *Daily Oklahoman*, Okla. City, 3/25/76, p. 10)

4. But [Arthur] Rubinstein's reservoir of good humor seems bottomless and his ÉLAN does not desert him even at this dark turn of events [he has only dim peripheral vision]. (D. Henahan, "This ageless hero, Rubinstein," *New York Times*, 3/14/76, Section 6, p. 36)

5. See (1) under ARRIVISTE.

6. The Phillies out-hit, outpitched and out-fielded Cincinnati and reliever Ron Reed seemed to personify all their ÉLAN. (Associated Press, "Phils outplay Cincy," *Norman* [Okla.] *Transcript*, 6/21/76, p. 7)

7. The burglars [who spent the weekend robbing the safe-deposit vault of the Société Générale] evidently decided to call a halt to operations when a flash storm hit Nice, raising waters in the escape sewer to a dangerously high level. Even so, they departed with ÉLAN and prudence. Before exiting through the [underground] tunnel, they wrote their farewell message of peace on the wall ["Without weapons, without hate and without violence"], and welded shut the massive metal door connecting the vault with the bank itself. (Fay Willey and Elizabeth Peer, "Le Grand Fric-Frac," *Newsweek*, 8/2/76, p. 37)

ELDRITCH (el´ drich) or **ELDRICH** *adj.* eerie; weird; spooky; uncanny.

1. Is all this [searching for graves] morbid? I hardly think so . . . . Do not merely seek out "The Great." It meant something to me—and perhaps to them—to find Adelaide Crapsey in Rochester, and H.P. Lovecraft in ELDRITCH and HYPERBOREAN Providence. (J. Williams, "Paying Respects," *New York Times*, 12/19/76, Section 7, p. 27)

ELEEMOSYNARY (el´ə-mos´ə-ner´ē, -moz´-, el´ē-ə) *adj.* of, pertaining to, provided by, or supported by gifts, charity, or charitable donations; charitable; free.

1. Last year, IRS income from this [4% excise] foundation tax exceeded auditing costs by something like $35 million, and that was $35 million less available to the nation's hard-pressed ELEEMOSYNARY institutions . . . . The evidence must be abundantly clear by now that ELEEMOSYNARY institutions need maximum public support . . . . (G. W. Bonham, "The Crisis in Philanthrophy" [Editorial], *Change*, November 1974, pp. 9, 10)

2. . . . the [Supreme] court [of New Jersey] ruled that nonprofit, nonsectarian hospitals may not prohibit the use of their facilities for abortion . . . . Judge Sidney M. Schreiber

[said] on behalf of the 6-1 majority: "Moral concepts cannot be the basis of a non-sectarian, nonprofit, ELEEMOSYNARY regulations where that hospital is holding out the use of its facilities to the general public." (J. Hart, "Issues of our Times," *Times Herald,* Norristown, Pa., 1/13/77, p. 19)

3. Oil, munitions and big business are powerfully entrenched in the chief Congressional committees .... Most powerful among these is the Senate Finance Committee, long notorious as an ELEEMOSYNARY shelter for fat cats and virtually impregnable to White House assault. (R. Baker, "The Old Gang," *New York Times,* 1/23/77, Section 6, p. 4)

ELEGIAC (i-lē′jē-ak′,el′ə-jī′ək) or **ELEGIACAL** *adj.* expressing sorrow or lamentation; sad; mournful; plaintive; used in, or suitable for, or resembling an elegy.

ELEGIST *noun* the author of an elegy.

ELEGIZE (el′i-jīz′) *verb* to commemorate or lament in or as if in an elegy; to compose an elegy.

ELEGY (el′i-jē) *noun* a mournful, melancholy, or plaintive poem, song, etc., especially a lament for the dead.

1. This tone [of the book, *World of our Fathers*], now brisk, now ELEGIAC, also arises from [author Irving] Howe's feeling for the tragic DIALECTIC of his story—that the "normal life" that these self-educated [Jewish] workers ... strove to create proved to be but a staging area for their children's escape from the family, community, and culture. (T. Solotaroff, Review, *New York Times,* 2/1/76, Section 7, p. 30)

2. Uniting [*The Tale of the*] *Heike*'s hundreds of characters and events are certain central themes, mainly inspired by Buddhism, which give a deep meaning to the work and inspire its pervasively ELEGIAC tone. (I. Morris, Review of *The Tale of the Heike,* translated by Hiroshi Kitagawa and Bruce Tsuchida, *New York Times,* 2/8/76, Section 7, p. 24)

3. His [Oliver Seccombe's] deepest regret [at the thought of losing his position at the ranch] would be the loss of [his membership in] the Cheyenne Club, ... that Athens of the west,

where the food was good, the wine better and the talk best of all .... Charlotte Seccombe had no such ELEGIAC thoughts. (J. A. Michener, *Centennial,* Fawcett, 1975, pp. 727-728)

4. See (1) under EULOGY.

ELEPHANTIASIS (el′ə-fan-tī′ə-sis) *noun* a chronic disease of the skin resulting from lymphatic obstruction, characterized by enormous enlargement of the parts affected (especially the legs and genitals) and by hardening and ulceration of the surrounding skin.

ELEPHANTIASIC (el′ ə-fan′ tē-as′ ik, -fan-tī′ə-sik) *adj.*

1. The illegal abduction of ever-larger objects has become an international ambition among the fraternity of thieves. Across the Atlantic, PREDACEOUS ELEPHANTIASIS afflicts the latter-day descendants of Bill Sikes. (P. Ryan, "In decade of the big steal, larceny waxes grander," *Smithsonian,* March 1976, p. 120)

2. Europe, in the late 18th century, suffered from a bureaucratic ELEPHANTIASIS comparable to the one we have been saddled with in the U.S. It took the frightful upheavals of the Napoleonic wars to blast the ... 18th century regulatory construction to bits. That is a price for "reorganization" that Jimmy Carter will surely decline to pay. (J. Chamberlain, "Costly Agencies," *Times Herald,* Norristown, Pa., 11/16/76, p. 11)

ELISION (i-lizh′ən) *noun* the omission of a vowel, consonant, or syllable in pronunciation; (in verse) the omission of a vowel at the end of a word when the next word begins with a vowel; any act or instance of leaving out or omitting a part or parts.

ELIDE (i-līd′) *verb* to pass over; omit; suppress; ignore; to omit (a vowel, consonant, or syllable) in pronunciation.

1. It [Clive Hirschhorn's interview with Stephen Sondheim] was full of journalistic ELISIONS (such as omitting [S.S.'s] plea for subsidized theater ...), distortions ... and fabrications ... (S. Sondheim, Letter to Editor, *New York Times,* 1/11/76, Section 2, p. 19)

ELLIPSIS (i-lip′ sis) *noun, pl.* -SES the omission from a sentence of a word or words that would complete the construction but that are understood in the context; a mark or marks as ---, ..., or *** to indicate an intentional omission or suppression of letters or words, a lapse of time, an incomplete statement, etc.; the use of such marks.

1. [George V.] Higgins lets his characters [in the book, *The Judgment of Deke Hunter*] tell their own stories with the uncannily accurate dialogue that has become his trademark. Every nuance and rhythm of speech, every ELLIPSIS and NON SEQUITUR of conversation rings true. (S. Li, Review, *Philadelphia Inquirer*, 9/5/76, p. 10-E)

EMBAY (em-bā′) *verb* to put or force (a boat, etc.) into a bay for protection or shelter; to shut in; enclose or surround; envelop; to make into a bay.

EMBAYMENT *noun* a forming into a bay; a bay or a formation resembling a bay.

1. He [Sterling Hayden, author of the book, *Voyage*] has a PENCHANT for words like "CYNOSURE" and "braised," which makes one think of cookbooks. He also likes "EMBAYED," which occurs three times in 250 pages, making one feel slightly surrounded by it . . . The plight of the proles [during the presidential contest between McKinley and William Jennings Bryan] is laid on [in the book] with a rather heavy hand, EMBAYING us with Sterling Hayden, the actor's, simplistic theories of the leisure and working classes. (R. Javers, Review, *Philadelphia Inquirer*, 1/30/77, p. 10-D)

EMBOUCHURE (äm′bŏŏ-shŏŏr′) *noun* the mouth of a river; the opening out of a valley into a plain; in *Music*—the mouthpiece of a wind instrument, especially when of metal; the adjustment of a player's lips and tongue to such a mouthpiece.

1. [Harvey] Sollberger [the flutist] acknowledged that "AVANT-GARDE" techniques can be used in a BANAL way—but that, of course, is not what he has in mind when he teaches his students . . . how to make several notes sound simultaneously (it has to do with fingerings and

EMBOUCHURE), . . . and how to change the timbre of a pitch by "alerting the balance of air pressure and EMBOUCHURE." (Joan Peyser, "New Sounds From An Old Instrument," *New York Times*, 3/28/76, Section 2, p. 17)

EMEND (i-mend′) *verb* to edit (a text) by removing errors, flaws, etc.; to free from faults or errors; correct.

EMENDABLE *adj.*

EMENDATION *noun* a correction; the act of emending.

EMENDATORY *adj.*

1. See (1) under MACULATION.

2. Until now [the recent publication of the book, *John Jay. Unpublished Papers 1745-1780*, edited by Richard B. Morris and others], students of Jay's activities have had to rely on old, incomplete and EMENDED two- and four-volume collections of his writings, on an inadequate 40-year-old biography and on various compendia of constitutional and diplomatic documents. (J.M. Banner Jr., Review, *New York Times*, 2/22/76, Section 7, p. 8)

ÉMINENCE GRISE (ā-mē-näNs-gRēz′) *noun pl.* ÉMINENCES GRISES gray eminence; a person who wields unofficial but great power, especially through another person and often surreptitiously and selfishly.

1. In Venice last fall I picked up a book called *Berlinguer e il Professore* . . . Written by an anonymous journalist, . . . it was a political novel about Enrico Berlinguer, the Italian Communist leader, and Amintore Fanfani (the "Professor"), the ÉMINENCE GRISE of the Christian Democrats. The author wrote it in the first person "as a secretary to Fanfani, who in the year 2000 decided to tell all." (M. Lerner, "Political problems characterize times: Communist shadow over Italy," *Norman* [Okla.] *Transcript*, 5/2/76, p. 4)

2. Indeed, raising public consciousness [of non-profit professional American theaters] was the subject of the keynote address [at a Yale conference]. The speaker was W. McNeil

Lowry, former vice president of the Ford Foundation and ÉMINENCE GRISE of the resident theater movement by virtue of being the first to give it substantial financial and moral support. (R. Brustein, "Art Versus Arts Advocacy in the Non-Commercial Theater," *New York Times*, 7/4/76, Section 2, p. 5)

EMOLLIENT (i-mol′yənt) *adj.* having the power of softening or relaxing living tissue, as a medicinal substance; soothing, especially to the skin.

EMOLLIENT *noun* an emollient medicine or agent.

EMOLLIENCE *noun.*

1. The Republican contest in Kansas City provided all the drama of conflict, suspense and heartbreak that had proved so elusive under Jimmy Carter's EMOLLIENT grin last month. (D. Gelman, Lucy Howard, "Hard Work, Hard News," *Newsweek*, 8/30/76, p. 78)

2. The carriage-house factory [of Martha Harper, in Rochester] was greatly expanded [in about 1915] to supply the growing demands of the thriving chain of [beauty] salons. A shipping department was added to send the big bars of castile soap, jars of EMOLLIENT scalp ointment and jugs of the famous tonic to outlets across the nation. (Karen Thure, "Martha Harper pioneered in the hair business," *Smithsonian*, September 1976, p. 98)

EMPIRICISM (em-pir′ i-siz′ əm) *noun* empirical method or practice; search for knowledge by observation and experiment; undue reliance upon experience, as formerly in medicine; quackery; an empirical conclusion.

EMPIRICIST *noun.*

EMPIRICAL *adj.* derived from or guided by experience or experiment; depending upon experience or observation alone, without using science or theory, as formerly in medicine; verifiable or discoverable by experience or experiment.

EMPIRICALLY *adv.*

1. Increasingly, curators, collectors, critics, and the public have come to identify this highly charged EMPIRICISM as the controlling passion of American art. (D. Davis, Mary Rourke, "American Art 200 Years On," *Newsweek*, 2/9/76, p. 67)

2. See (2) under WELTANSCHAUUNG.

EMPYREAN (em-pir′ ē-ən, em′ pə-rē′ ən) *noun* the highest heaven in the cosmology of the ancients, supposed to contain the pure element of fire; the visible heavens; the firmament; the most exalted of heavenly states.

EMPYREAL or **EMPYREAN** *adj.* of the empyrean; heavenly; sublime.

1. . . . [Jonathan] Schell can turn his bleak drama [*The Time of Illusion*] into a marvelous Miltonic PARODY of heaven and hell . . . . The uppermost realm was the EMPYREAN of the [Presidential] summit, where radiant figures, bathed in publicity, seemed to personify the aspirations of a humanity anxious to escape its own extinction. (R. Sherrill, Review, *New York Times*, 1/18/76, Section 7, p. 2)

ENCOMIUM (en-kō′ mē-əm) *noun, pl.* -MIUMS or -MIA a formal expression of high praise; EULOGY; PANEGYRIC; ceremonious praise.

ENCOMIAST *noun* a person who speaks or write encomiums; EULOGIST.

ENCOMIASTIC or **ENCOMIASTICAL** *adj.* of an encomiast; of or like an encomium; EULOGISTIC.

ENCOMIASTICALLY *adv.*

1. He [Senator Barry Goldwater] says that the high court [U.S. Supreme Court] has begun to issue rulings that comport with common sense . . . . The court continues, however, to reject certain cases that would require it to clarify some basic constitutional questions. It has quite a way to go before it fully earns the ENCOMIUM "The Court of Common Sense." (Anon., "The Court of Common Sense" [Editorial], *Daily Oklahoman*, Okla. City, 5/21/76, p. 8)

2. See (1) under TRULL.

ENDEMIC (en-dem′ik) *adj.* peculiar to or restricted to a particular people, country, region, or locality; INDIGENOUS; native.

ENDEMIC *noun* an endemic plant or disease.

ENDEMICALLY *adv.*

ENDEMICITY or **ENDEMISM** *noun.*

1. In the 17th century smallpox, a disease that is now on the verge of eradication, was ENDEMIC everywhere in Europe and probably throughout the world . . . it was in many respects even more loathsome and fearful than that other great killer, plague. (W. L. Langer, "Immunization against Smallpox before Jenner," *Scientific American*, January 1976, p. 112)

2. . . . some beneficently conceived systems pose temptations so glaringly irresistible as to bring on an ENDEMIC demoralization. The ease with which abortions are secured in Sweden appears to have done less in the way of reducing bastardy (the benevolently conceived objective . . .) than in encouraging promiscuity. (W.F. Buckley Jr., *Up From Liberalism*, Arlington House, 2nd Printing 1968, p. 203)

3. Mr. Lim remembers . . . the Twenties and Thirties when [Singapore's] Chinatown was a dangerous place even for foreigners, and crime of all sorts was ENDEMIC. (Shelly and C. Mydans, "Progress dooms charm and bustle of the Chinatown in Singapore," *Smithsonian*, January 1976, p. 45)

4. Hashish is still ENDEMIC in Egypt despite the severe penalties: 25 years of hard labor for dealers and a minimum of five years in prison for smokers. (*The London Economist*, "Promises to be tough nightmare: Egypt passes tough, puritanical law," reprinted in *Norman* [Okla.] *Transcript*, 6/16/76, p. 6)

5. . . . we came to learn styles of rebellion and to sense that the [New York] *Herald Tribune* attracted people who longed to fight ENDEMIC wrongs . . . . (R. Kahn, *The Boys of Summer*, Harper and Row, 1971, pp. 68-69)

6. Though far from an epidemic, the sudden occurrence of the disease [bubonic plague—the "black death"] has disturbed health officials who say that the plague, which is ENDEMIC among wild rodents in the Southwest, is transmitted to humans by flies. (Anon., "Plague in the West," *Newsweek*, 7/4/76, p. 85)

7. Conspiracy [in Italy] has been ENDEMIC since Romulus and Remus began horsetrading from Tiber Island . . . . And the Italians are good conspirators because they love the game and make the rules to suit themselves. (H. J. Taylor, "Unity Lacking in Italy," *Times Herald*, Norristown, Pa., 2/25/77, p. 15)

8. The last reported case of it ["killer" smallpox—variola major] was found Oct. 16, 1975, in Bangladesh. That was also the last reported case of any kind of smallpox on the Indian subcontinent, a place where the disease had been so ENDEMIC that people worship a goddess of smallpox. (J. N. Shurkin, "Smallpox in Somalia delays world campaign again," *Philadelphia Inquirer*, 1/9/77, p. 5-E)

ENDOGAMY (en-dog' ə-mē) *noun* the custom of marrying only within a specific tribe or similar social unit; inbreeding; as opposed to *exogamy*; cross-pollination among flowers of the same plant.

ENDOGAMOUS or **ENDOGAMIC** (en' dō-gam' ik) *adj.*

1. It is in these ethnic parallel institutions—parochial schools, Catholic charities, ENDOGAMOUS marriages, diocesan weeklies—that most ethnic Catholics double-park for a time alongside the core culture. (J. M. Cuddihy, Review of *The American Catholic*, a book by Andrew M. Greeley, *New York Times*, 3/6/77, Section 7, p. 3)

ENERVATE (en'ər-vāt) *verb* to deprive of nerve, force, vigor, or strength; to weaken physically, mentally or morally; enfeeble; devitalize; debilitate.

ENERVATION *noun.*

ENERVATIVE *adj.*

ENERVATOR *noun.*

1. These [openness, enthusiasm, good humor] were not inherent virtues of Communism, of course, but a measure of Yenan's assurance and ÉLAN, as opposed to the ENERVATION of Chungking. (A. Suehsdorf, "Remembering Chou En-lai in Yenan, *New York Times*, 1/11/76, Section 4, p. 19)

2. [Arthur] Rubinstein's voice has lost its rich

timbre by this time and dropped to an ENER-VATED whisper. (D. Henahan, "This ageless hero, Rubinstein," *New York Times*, 3/14/76, Section 6, p. 20)

3. See (3) under RATIOCINATION.

4. . . . [Iris] Murdoch, who once lectured in philosophy, throws Cato [in her book, *Henry and Cato*] up against a superior priest in a sequence of intelligent theological debates. Only these arguments resist Murdoch's shaping and ENERVATING touch; only in them does her story find a genuine human dilemma, a sense of anguish. (P. S. Prescott, Review, *Newsweek*, 1/10/77, p. 69A)

EN FACE (äN-fâs') *adj.* opposite (in the sense of on the opposite pages of a book); having the face forward, as in a portrait.

1. At last Shakespeare has been translated into English. Simon & Schuster has just issued *Macbeth*, *Hamlet*, *King Lear* and *Julius Caesar* in four separate volumes, with the Shakespearean text on the left-hand page and a modern English paraphrase EN FACE. (D. Hall, "To Be or Not to Be, That's What Matters," *New York Times*, 3/14/76, Section 7, p. 39)

ENFANT TERRIBLE (äN-fäN' te-Rê' blə) *noun, pl.* **ENFANTS TERRIBLES** (äN- fäN'te-Rê'blə) an incorrigible child; a person who says and does indiscreet or irresponsible things.

1. Henri Matisse was their leader and senior statesman [that of the "fauves" or "wild beasts"]; Andre Derain and Maurice de Vlaminck were the ENFANTS TERRIBLE (*sic*); among their apostles were men who later came to artistic maturity in different ways—Raoul Dufy, Georges Braque, Kees van Dongen. (D. Davis, Review of an art show, " 'The Wild Beasts': Fauvism and its Affinities," *Newsweek*, 3/29/76, p. 56)

2. [Santiago] Carillo [leader of the Spanish Communist Party] likes to play the "ENFANT TERRIBLE" of the Communist world, discounting such heroes as Marx, Lenin and Mao; but when he does so he is also expressing a longstanding Spanish resentment of the U.S.S.R. (Barbara Probst Solomon, "Spain on the Brink," *The New York Review of Books*, 11/27/75, p. 25)

3. After all, this [the Julliard Quartet] was the ENFANT TERRIBLE of string quartets, an erstwhile collection of young American hellions who attacked their scores with a whiplash urgency, a sharp-edged precision, dramatically wide range of dynamics and—most prominently—a PENCHANT for fast tempos that has become a point of reference . . . in evaluating every other string quartet in sight. (Shirley Fleming, "Woodshedding With the Julliard," *New York Times*, 3/28/76, Section 2, p. 17)

4. Instead of his old 9-foot-high self-portrait . . . as ENFANT TERRIBLE, with an enormous stomach bulging through the open shirt . . . , the new [Al] Leslie is disarmingly humble. (D. Davis, Review of paintings by Al Leslie at Boston Museum of Fine Arts, *Newsweek*, 6/7/76, p. 62)

5. See (2) under ALEATORIC.

6. See (5) under AGITPROP.

ENGAGÉ (äN-GA-zhä') *adj.* involved in or committed to something (as a social or political cause), as opposed to remaining aloof or indifferent.

1. For six years [Paul] Zweig shares a bed with a painter and Communist party militant called Michele, who lives on the heights of Montagne Sainte Genevieve with a band of equally ENGAGÉ brothers but indulges in a number of non-Communist activities, such as laughing. (Francine DuPlessix Gray, Review of the book, *Three Journeys*, by Paul Zweig, *New York Times*, 5/2/76, Section 7, p. 5)

2. In the years since [he was the Trotskyist student leader at C.C.N.Y.], he [Irving Howe] has gone on to become a famous literary critic and professor of literature at the City University. But he has remained politically ENGAGÉ, though slowly moving "right" from Trotskyism to democratic socialism (as represented in his journal, *Dissent*). (I. Kristol, "Memoirs of a Trotskyist," *New York Times*, 1/23/77, Section 6, p. 55)

ENNUI (än-wē', än'wē) *noun* a feeling of weariness and discontent resulting from satiety or lack of interest or inactivity; boredom; indifference.

1. We've just seen *Angel Street* [a play by Bob

Barry], a 35-year-old thriller, . . . only to discover that its intricate MACHINATIONS, with a husband elaborately driving his wife insane, aren't intricate at all but obvious now . . . as worked over by principal players Dina Merrill and Michael Allinson, the gooseflesh of 1941 becomes the ENNUI of today. (W. Kerr, Review, *New York Times*, 1/11/76, Section 2, pp. 7, 19)

2. To those who call me an ungrateful wretch for leaving Nirvana (California) with a less than heavy heart, I must reply that I prefer chaos [in New York] to ENNUI. . . . The ideal in California is to be free from neurosis . . . , to pretend that all those things you would have killed puppies and small children for in the East don't matter any more. (Mary Alice Kellogg, "A Farewell to Nirvana," *Newsweek*, 3/15/76, p. 15)

3. At its worst, this book [*Billy Liar on the Moon*, by Keith Waterhouse] might have been written for a script including canned laughter. At its best it is a very funny testimony to the massive ENNUI of the English middle classes and the welfare state. On the whole, I was impressed with it as an example of the latter. (P. Canby, Review, *Boston Globe*, 3/7/76, p. 15-A)

4. As a character, publishers will tell you, the college professor is only a figure of fun (and television has exhausted that) or ENNUI-producing. . . , a figure in fiction in whom only the author can possibly have any interest. (Doris Grumbach, Review of *The History Man*, by Malcolm Bradbury, *Chronicle of Higher Education*, 3/1/76, p. 14)

5. We think of GENEALOGY as being a musty study with which "first families" fight off ENNUI by tracing their family trees back to William the Conqueror. (E. Park, "Around the Mall and Beyond," *Smithsonian*, April 1976, p. 28)

6. Shively and Yost . . . had . . . shown little interest in what [food] had been served . . . . Somehow, Malone had perceived a muggy air of ENNUI had settled upon the others. (I. Wallace, *The Fan Club*, Bantam Books, 1975, p. 451)

7. The. . .50 reporters, photographers, network-TV cameramen and technicians who accompanied Carter to Plains were at first pleased with the change of pace from Manhattan and the long primary trail. Now, however, they are suffering from advanced ENNUI and frustration—enhanced by South Georgia's sauna-like summer climate and the bountiful swarms of gnats, chiggers and fire ants. (S. Cloud, "Keeping 'Em Down on the Farm," *Time*, 8/16/76, p. 73)

8. See (4) under QUOTIDIAN.

ENTOIL (en-toil´) *verb* to trap in toils or snares; ensnare [Archaic and Poetic].

1. He [Malcolm Muggeridge] does . . . pan authors, if not books, offhand—Eliot, Joyce, Beckett—there is scarcely a great modern for whom he does not have his habitual dismissive phrase. They seem ENTOILED in his impatience with their century. These days he and [his wife] Kitty read Dickens and Jane Austen aloud, finding their way back to what seem better times. (H. Kenner, "At home with St. Mug," *New York Times*, 9/12/76, Section 6, p. 136)

ENTRECHAT (äN-trə-shA´) *noun* a jump in which a ballet dancer crosses his legs or strikes his heels together a number of times while in the air.

1. It is asserted by some . . . that all art and speculative thought after Auschwitz is an affectation, a pornographic exploitation of human suffering when only shocked . . . or prayerful silence is appropriate. Others argue that the ENTRECHATS of art implicitly impose purpose on the purposeless and nobility on the base. But there is a compelling reason for the writer to seek words for the INEFFABLE . . . . [Lawrence L.] Langer's book [*The Holocaust and the Literary Imagination*] . . celebrates . . . the tentative hope [John Donne] expressed in 1612: "This new world may be safer being told/ The dangers and diseases of the old." (J. Hollis, Review, *Chronicle of Higher Education*, 4/5/76, p. 21)

ENTREPÔT (än´trə-pō´) *noun* a center or warehouse for the storage, distribution, or transshipment of goods.

1. As long as men remember, Singapore has

been a center of ENTREPÔT, or transshipment, trade. (Shelley and C. Mydans, "Progress dooms charm and bustle of the Chinatown in Singapore," *Smithsonian*, January 1976, p. 43)

2. As the developing world moves towards . . . technological developments, their cities have already been built as adjuncts to Atlantic trade, vast ENTREPÔT centers—Rio de Janeiro, Buenos Aires, Shanghai, Calcutta—sending out the raw materials, bringing in the manufactured goods. In the 20th century, they have become magnets of a torrential migration long before they . . . have the industrial base . . . to support a fully developed urban system. (Barbara Ward, "Population soars in poorest nations: Jobless flood Third World?" *Norman* [Okla.] *Transcript*, 6/11/76, p. 6)

ENTROPY (en' trə-pē) *noun* a thermodynamic measure of the amount of energy unavailable for useful work in a system undergoing change; the measure of the frequency with which an event occurs within a system; a measure of probability of distribution in a closed or isolated system; a measure of the degree of disorder or randomness; entropy always increases and available energy diminishes in a closed system, as the universe; in information theory and computer science, a measure of the information content of a message evaluated as to its uncertainty; similarity; lack of differentiation.

1. This turned out to be the episode of *The Brady Bunch* in which Miss Henderson (and her three daughters and a cat) married Robert Reed (and his three sons and a dog and Alice, the housekeeper)—in short, the Big Bang that created the Bunch. After which, ENTROPY, I was pleased. I collect such moments. (J. Leonard, "Old Sitcoms and Young Minds," *New York Times*, 3/28/76, Section 2, p. 27)

2. The historian Henry Adams seems particularly TRENCHANT writing, in 1910, about energy and ENTROPY in human affairs in the 20th century. (Anon., "A special issue of Smithsonian as America's third century begins" [Editor's Introduction], *Smithsonian*, July 1976, p. 26)

3. Still, he [T. S. Eliot] had a terrific eye and his own squeamishness sensitized him to the mute, monotonous misery of those furnished

rooms that hardened the heart and congealed the spirit, so that TRANSCENDENCE was no longer possible, not even change—other than the processes of ENTROPY, which we saw everywhere, within and without. What would he make of contemporary New York, where the sense of things running down and falling apart is UBIQUITOUS—a national scandal? (T. Solotaroff, "Alive and together in the park," *New York Times*, 6/13/76, Section 6, p. 37)

4. Here [in *The Judgment of Deke Hunter*, by George V. Higgins] the plot is simply an armature for the talk that reveals . . . Deke Hunter's slouch toward ENTROPY . . . . Any former enlisted man will recognize him: his desperation brought on by a dead-end job, his FULMINATIONS against a perceived incompetence of his superiors . . . . (P. S. Prescott, Review, *Newsweek*, 9/6/76, p. 64D)

5. British science fiction in recent years has had a decidedly un-Imperial tone. In the best work of people like J. G. Ballard and Ian Watson, one can almost hear the dying fall of ENTROPY—the wearing down of all order and structure . . . . Despite his ENTROPIC theme [in *The Jonah Kit*], Watson's prose boils with energy; . . . the exhilarating rush of words and ideas seems to belie the profoundly depressing message. (G. Jonas, Review, *New York Times*, 9/12/76, p. 46)

EPHEMERAL (i-fem' ər-əl) *adj.* lasting a very short time; transitory; lasting but one day.

EPHEMERAL *noun* anything short-lived, as certain insects, or transitory.

EPHEMERA *noun, pl.* -ERAS or ERAE same as above.

EPHEMERALLY *adv.*

EPHEMERALITY or **EPHEMERALNESS** *noun.*

1. Arttransition was a word invented by Otto Piene, himself an artist and . . . director since 1974 of MIT's Center for Advanced Visual Studies (CAVS) . . . . This Center, established in 1967, was one of the less EPHEMERAL acts taken under the A&T (Art and Technology) movement, though one can't be entirely sure even yet whether art was adopted or conquered at MIT. (B. Forgey, "Arttransition is

still in transition," *Smithsonian*, March 1976, p. 88)

2. See (1) under ST. ELMO'S FIRE.

3. . . . that state of institutional wretchedness . . . in which the writer is condemned to produce inferior and EPHEMERAL work to earn a precarious livelihood has not vanished altogether . . . . Despite my sarcasm I intend no DENIGRATION of the scholarly enterprise itself . . . there is much to be said for a purveyor of ideas being involved in the production of them . . . . And the enthusiasm and excitement of original research communicates itself quite readily to students. (I. Grushow, "The Ivory Tower Is Now A High Rise Slum," *Chronicle of Higher Education*, 4/19/76, p. 40)

4. As for equality, we continue to move toward it—although the human condition today sometimes seems to make the goal as distant as in 1776. It is certainly the most EPHEMERAL of Man's ambitions. (S. D. Ripley, "The view from the castle," *Smithsonian*, January 1976, p. 6)

5. . . . individual singers play a more than EPHEMERAL role in musical history. In all ages, they have helped to determine what kind of music was written. (A. Porter, Review of the opera, *Griselda*, by Alessandro Scarlatti, as staged at Berkeley, Calif., *The New Yorker*, 5/31/76, p. 108)

6. See (3) under SHARD.

7. See (14) under HUBRIS.

8. See (1) under JAPONAISERIE.

9. To the extent that American foreign policy in the future, as in most of the past, is destined to be shaped as much by forces outside the control of any administration as by decisions taken in Washington, his [Henry Kissinger's] legacy will have been temporary, if not EPHEMERAL. (O. Johnson, "After eight years, the Kissinger enigma remains," *Philadelphia Inquirer*, 1/9/77, p. 4-E)

10. For some time now the most EPHEMERAL commodity in Hollywood has been the new actress who dazzles the world in her first or second film, is immediately classified "hot"— and promptly sinks back into the crowded ranks of "promising" female faces . . . .

Katharine Ross, Barbara Seagull . . . , Jennifer O'Neill, Stockard Channing, Susan Anspach . . . . (C. Michener, M. Kasindorf, "Year of the Actress," *Newsweek*, 2/14/77, p. 56)

EPICENE (ep'i-sēn') *adj.* belonging to, or partaking of the characteristics of, both sexes; FLACCID; feeble; weak; effeminate; non-masculine; unmanly; designating a noun, as in Latin or Greek, having only one grammatical form to denote an individual of either sex.

EPICENE *noun* an epicene person or thing.

EPICENISM *noun.*

1. Cassavetes [the director of the film, *The Killing of a Chinese Bookie*] breaks things up because he wants you to feel, not read. So he shoots the crazy shows at the cheap Sunset Strip club owned by his hero, Cosmo Vitelli, in bits and pieces—a living collage of delectable breasts, things, faces, old pop tunes retreaded on tape and sung by Mr. Sophistication, the EPICENE emcee. You feel the boozy, dozing PRURIENCE of the audience, the giggly sweetness of the girls, the stylized DELIQUESCENCE of the old queen. (J. Kroll, Review, *Newsweek*, 3/15/76, p. 89)

2. He [the comic book hero] was a man of steel in one guise, but in the other a short-sighted reporter, a crippled newsboy, an EPICENE playboy flirting with a teen-age male companion. PHALLIC but impotent, supermale but a eunuch, incapable of consummating love or begetting a successor; and, therefore, he was a *last hero*, doomed to lonely immortality and banned by an . . . inexplicable taboo from revealing the secret that would make it possible . . . to join the two halves of his sundered self and thus end his comic plight of being forever his own rival for the affection of his best beloved. Ultimately . . . Superman turns out to be not a hero who seems a SHLEMIEL, but a hero who is a SHLEMIEL. If this is not essentially funny . . . , it is because the joke was on all of us and there was no one left to laugh . . . . (Leslie A. Fiedler, "Up, up and away—the rise and fall of comic books, *New York Times*, 9/5/76, Section 7, p. 9)

3. *Survive!* is a quickie rip-off of a quickie rip-off. Exploiting the 1972 plane crash in the Andes in which 16 of the 45 Uruguayans

aboard survived by eating the flesh of those who had died, a Mexican company brought out an instant tamale version of the saga. Allan Carr, 39, an EPICENE Hollywood talent manager and promoter, snapped up the film for $500,000. (Anon., "The Gatsby of Benedict Canyon," *Time*, 8/30/76, p. 52)

4. He [Ronald Beard] had achieved nothing except an award, a Japanese EPICENE figurine called Terry, for the best foreign, to Japan that was, dramatic script of the year. (A. Burgess, *Beard's Roman Women*, McGraw-Hill, 1976, p. 68)

EPICUREANISM or **EPICUREANISM** (ep'ə-kyŏŏ-rē'ə-niz'əm) *noun* (if capitalized) the philosophical system of Epicurus [a Greek, 342?-270 B.C.] which held that pleasure is the highest good; (if lower case) indulgence of luxurious and sensuous pleasures, especially eating and drinking.

EPICURE (ep'ə-kyŏŏr') *noun* a person who enjoys and has a fastidious taste for fine food and drinks, art, music, etc.; connoisseur; a sensualist [Archaic].

EPICUREAN or **EPICUREAN** *adj.* (if capitalized) of, pertaining to, or characteristic of Epicurus or Epicureanism; (if lower case) fond of luxury and sensuous pleasure; fit for an epicure.

EPICUREAN or **EPICUREAN** *noun* (if capitalized) a disciple of Epicurus; (if lower case) a person devoted to the pursuit of pleasure; epicure.

1. My [Russel Wren's] simulation of EPICUREANISM, served to dupe the liberal-lawyer's wife, who was raised in the commercial class of Great Neck, but, owing to my habitual lack of access to true luxury, would scarcely pass muster with a Frederika Washburn. (Thomas Berger, *Who Is Teddy Villanova?*, Delacorte Press/Seymour Lawrence, 1977, p. 59)

EPIGONE (ep'ə-gōn') *noun* an undistinguished imitator of an important writer, painter, etc.; a descendant less gifted than his ancestors; any inferior follower or imitator.

1. "Poetry," [Ezra] Pound insisted, "must be as well written as prose," but he did not reckon on the grunts, snorts and limping NON SE-QUITURS that his EPIGONES would later commit to paper under the banner of the new . . . . contemporary poetry has become a BABEL of IDIOSYNCRASIES. (P. Gray, "American Poetry: School's Out," *Time*, 4/26/76, p. 95)

2. His [Pierre Boulez's] struggle against authority, influence and history is the struggle of the modernist artist . . . who seeks to devour tradition and spring full-grown from the waste. The Oedipal struggle for artistic originality against "EPIGONISM" was Boulez's struggle, and music called for it after Webern's death. (E. Rothstein, Review of *Boulez: Composer, Conductor, Enigma*, a book by Joan Peyser, *New York Times*, 12/19/76, Section 7, p. 7)

3. He [Clement Greenberg] maintains that photography is inherently a realistic medium and that photographers should therefore confine themselves to the dog's work of representation and recording and leave the higher ground of art to painters . . . clearly no red-blooded artist-photographer is going to take [this attitude] lying down . . . . If he is a young modernist like [Carl] Toth and [Michael] Bishop, he will have to prove that he can flatten out picture space as well as any EPIGONE of Cézanne. (Gene Thornton, "Turning The Camera Into a Paint Brush," *New York Times*, 3/27/77, Section 2, p. 23)

4. An empty chamber yawned before me [Russel Wren] . . . No Teddy Villanova, and no hairy, guitar-clutching EPIGONES of that craze of my later youth . . . . (Thomas Berger, *Who Is Teddy Villanova?*, Delacorte Press/Seymour Lawrence, pp. 224-225)

EPIGRAM (ep'ə-gram') *noun* any witty, ingenious, or pointed saying, tersely expressed; epigrammatic expression; a short poem with a witty or satirical point.

EPIGRAMMATIC *adj.*

EPIGRAMMATICALLY *adv.*

EPIGRAMMATIST *noun* a maker of epigrams.

EPIGRAMMATISM *noun* the use of epigrams, epigrammatic character, or style.

EPIGRAMMATIZE *verb* to express in epigrams; to make epigrams.

1. But the true stature of Lincoln is not measured in folksy EPIGRAMS nor symbolized by a willingness to settle for whatever is "feasible." In [the TV show] *Milligan* [*The Case Against Milligan*], Lincoln was again compassionate and EPIGRAMMATIC—but also shrewd and tenacious. (M. Duberman, Review, *New York Times*, 1/11/76, Section 2, p. 27)

2. Even in the lightest of her verse [in *Collected Poems of Stevie Smith*], the briefest EPIGRAM, there is a resonance, the reverberation of a triangle if not a gong. (P. S. Prescott, Review, *Newsweek*, 3/29/76, pp. 88-89)

3. The two performances [in *My Fair Lady*] that hold up are by Robert Coote as . . . Colonel Pickering . . . and by George Rose, whose first-rate characterization of Alfred P. Doolittle. . .exempts him from comparison with the great Stanley Holloway. Rose is a soot-smeared, working-class PUCK, with lascivious eyes, a scampering scuttle and a trumpet-tough voice that blares out amorality in Cockney EPIGRAMS. (J. Kroll, Review, *Newsweek*, 4/5/76, p. 78)

4. . . . everything is here [in *The Complete Works of Saki*, by H. H. Munro]: two novels, a political PARODY, three plays and all of the short stories, with their unexpected EPIGRAMS and quick images . . . . (J. Lukacs, Review, *New York Times*, 3/28/76, Section 7, p. 6)

5. . . . [in] the present work [*The Olive of Minerva*] . . . a cardboard figure named Abel is sent to Majorca to join several others while [author Edward] Dahlberg writes pop-song EPIGRAMMATIC wisdom at us. "Everyman who is Abel, is also Cain," he observes . . . . (J. D. O'Hara, Review, *New York Times*, 4/18/76, Section 7, p. 20)

6. See (3) under DISQUISITION.

EPIGRAPH (ep′ ə-graf′) *noun* an inscription, especially on a building, statue, or the like; an APPOSITE motto or quotation at the beginning of a book, chapter, etc.

EPIGRAPHIC or **EPIGRAPHICAL** *adj.*
EPIGRAPHICALLY *adv.*

EPIGRAPHY (i-pig re-fe) *noun* the study or science of epigraphs or inscriptions, especially of ancient ones; inscriptions collectively; graffiti.

EPIGRAPHIST or **EPIGRAPHER** *noun* a specialist in epigraphy.

1. I [writes M. Patrick Glenville to William F. Buckley Jr.] am stranded here [in Sun Valley, Idaho] without my reference library for a couple of weeks, and have come across a sentence from Terence used as an EPIGRAPH of sorts, which I am unable to translate. (W. F. Buckley Jr., *Execution Eve and Other Contemporary Ballads*, G. P. Putnam's Sons, 1975, p. 354)

2. In publishing this greatly gifted poet [Geoffrey Hill], Houghton Mifflin deserves congratulations upon everything except the omission of the important EPIGRAPHS to each of the three volumes [of *Somewhere in Such a Kingdom*] C. Ricks, Review, *New York Times*, 1/11/76, Section 7, p. 6)

3. For his book, *Three Centuries of Harpsichord Making*, itself so characteristic a [Frank] Hubbard combination of the scholarly and the entertaining, the urbane and the committed, he chose an EPIGRAPH from T.S. Eliot: "I am Lazarus, come from the dead, Come back to tell you all, I shall tell you all." (M. Steinberg, "Frank Hubbard 1920-1976," *Boston Globe*, 3/7/76, p. 10-A)

4. See (1) under SUFI.

5. His [Gavin Lambert's] EPIGRAPH [in the book, *The Dangerous Edge*] from Browning—"Our interest's on the dangerous edge of things . . . ."—provides too vague a metaphor for the cliff-hangings of criminality and detection; and melodrama . . . surely needs no scholarly vindication. (P. Theroux, Review, *New York Times*, 4/25/76, Section 7, p. 8)

6. See (8) under PRETENTIOUS.

EPIPHANY (i-pif′ə-nē) *noun* (if capitalized) the Christian festival (also called Twelfth Day), observed on January 6, commemorating the appearance of Christ to the Gentiles in the person of the Magi; an appearance or manifestation, especially of a deity; (in literature) the sudden realization of the essential meaning of something, or the symbolic representation of such a realization.

EPIPHANIC (ep′ə-fan′ik) *adj.*

1. "...you can't consider this program [of bringing people from business, government, journalism, and the professions to academic campuses as Senior Fellows] on a cost-effectiveness basis. What you are talking about are EPIPHANIES," says Judith L. Pinch of the Woodrow Wilson Foundation. "The results you can measure . . . are things you don't really want to know." (R.K. Rein, "Woodrow Wilson Fellows—Who Are They Now?" *Change*, March 1975, p. 17)

2. See (1) under MIASMA.

3. One thinks back to that moment in 1880 when [W.A.] Bentley [who spent 50 years photographing snowflakes] at 15 first crouched over his new microscope. What was it that had such an impact on him? Was it a single crystal whose unexpected beauty exploded in an EPIPHANY and then melted, barely before he could look twice? (F. Hapgood, "When ice crystals fall from the sky art meets science," *Smithsonian*, January 1976, p. 72)

4. See (1) under CACHINNATE.

5. In the old days [of the Academy Awards] . . . the stars used to come out, as they should, at night. Their exits from the black limos would be lit by EPIPHANIC blasts of flash powder, while searchlights wagged their fingers across the suave Los Angeles sky. (R. Hughes, "The Day for Night Stars," *Time*, 4/12/76, p. 61)

6. See (2) under EUPEPTIC.

EPIPHENOMENON (ep' ē-fə-nom' ə-non' , -nən) *noun pl.* **-MENA** any secondary phenomenon; a secondary complication arising during an illness; a phenomenon that occurs with and seems to result from another but which has no effect or subsequent influence on the process.

EPIPHENOMENAL *adj.*

EPIPHENOMENALLY *adv.*

1. Those of us who, like Herb Kohl [author of *Half the House*], began years ago to criticize the schools have gone on to more inclusive issues, not through despair but because we have usually come to see the process and apparatus of public education as EPIPHENOMENA of deeper forces of social oppression which it

is the school's function to support. (E.Z. Friedenberg, Review, *New York Review of Books*, 11/27/75, p. 30)

EPISTEMOLOGY (i-pis' tə-mol' ə-jē) *noun* the study or theory of the origin, nature, methods, and limits of human knowledge; a branch of philosophy that investigates such matters.

EPISTEMOLOGICAL *adj.*

EPISTEMOLOGICALLY *adv.*

EPISTEMOLOGIST *noun.*

1. See (1) under DIALECTIC.

2. In an age of relativism, one tends to look for flexible devices for measuring this morning's truths. Such a device is democracy; and indeed, democracy becomes EPISTEMOLOGY: democracy will render reliable political truths . . . . Democracy must be justified by its works, not by doctrinaire affirmations of an intrinsic goodness that no mere method can legitimately lay claim to. (W. F. Buckley Jr., *Up From Liberalism*, Arlington House, 2nd Printing 1968, p. 149)

3. Other truths than scientific [e.g., a cancer cure] and methodological ones have no objective existence, the liberals in effect contend, and therefore cannot, under the liberal EPISTEMOLOGY, be apprehended. (W.F. Buckley Jr., *Ibid.*, pp. 181–182)

4. Yet, as [John P.] Diggins observes [in *Up From Communism*], [James] Burnham's divorce from Marxism was never completed. He continued to shift "back and forth between Machiavelli and Marx, between the idea of power and the power of an idea, changing his EPISTOMOLOGY (*sic*) each time he wanted to explain reality." (P. Rosenberg, Review, *New York Times*, 6/20/76, Section 7, p. 23)

5. Completely apart from their educational benefits, [Matthew] Lipman's *Harry* and *Lisa* [two books of elementary philosophy for use in public schools] make delightful reading. The technical terms of philosophy never appear . . . , but logic, EPISTEMOLOGY and even esthetics are elucidated throughout. (M. Sheils, F.V. Boyd, "Philosophy for Kids," *Newsweek*, 9/20/76, p. 86)

EPISTOLARY (i-pis' tə-ler' ē) or **EPISTOLIC** (ep' i-stol' ik) or **EPISTOLICAL** *adj.* contained in or conducted by letters; of, pertaining to, suitable to, or consisting of letters; composed as a series of letters, as certain novels of the 18th century.

1. "Dear Educational Testing Service" in the April 26 [1976] *Chronicle* reads like an attempt by Thomas Pynchon to write an EPISTOLARY novel. It presents, almost humorously, the problem of the use of ambiguity as a substitute for discrimination. (J. Farago, [Letter to the Editor] "Test-makers need 'a touch of humility' and 'an understanding of their own shortcomings,'" *Chronicle of Higher Education*, 6/28/76, p. 17)

2. Nor do I believe the Carter letter [to Dr. Sakharov] will compromise other matters under negotiation between our two countries .... The Soviet Union ... will not forgo the obvious national advantage in, say, reducing the dangers of nuclear war because it regards the American President as an EPISTOLARY busybody. (A. Schlesinger Jr., "Human Rights: How Far, How Fast?" *Wall Street Journal*, 3/4/77, p. 12)

3. Neither of the secret lonely-heart pen-pal lovers happens to have given the other a clue to the fact that they are fellow clerks in the same Budapest *parfumerie*. Ecstatic about each other in print, they are rather allergic to each other in person. When will the EPISTOLARY lovers discover the secret behind their secret? (T. E. Kalem, Review of the musical, "She Loves Me," *Time*, 4/11/77, p. 88)

EPITAPH (ep' i-taf') *noun* a commemorative inscription on a tomb or gravestone; a brief writing in praise of a deceased person.

EPITAPHIC *adj.*

EPITAPHIST *noun.*

1. One evening in Nigeria, the pains of a bruising rugby game had just dissolved when the clubhouse was overtaken by thousands of velvety-gray beetles which had been attracted to the lights. Within minutes, feet, arms, necks and backs were breaking out in burning blisters, each an EPITAPH to a squashed beetle .... We learned that night that it is not for nothing that the textbooks list *Meloidae* as

"blister beetles." (M. Emsley, "Nature's most successful design may be beetles," *Smithsonian*, December 1975, p. 108)

EPITHET (ep' ə-thet') *noun* any word or phrase replacing or added to the name of a person or thing to describe a characteristic attribute; a descriptive name or title; a word, phrase, etc. used invectively as a term of abuse or contempt, to express hostility, or the like.

EPITHETIC or **EPITHETICAL** *adj.*

1. [Coco] Chanel's abrasive, autocratic presence survives mostly through the forty-eight marvelous photographs in this book [*Chanel*, by Edmonde Charles-Roux]. They show the sassy air, the roguish hands-in-pocket stance, the MORDANT, boyish charm which Chanel retained into her eighties and to which the French give the untranslatable EPITHET of "chien." (Francine Gray, Review, *New York Review of Books*, 12/11/75, p. 45)

2. "You"—my speech still came between gasps—"contemptible ... jackal! [said Russel Wren to Donald Washburn II]. Indifferent to the EPITHET, he [D. W. II] summoned Bakewell .... Both left the apartment forthwith. (Thomas Berger, *Who Is Teddy Villanova?*, Delacorte Press/Seymour Lawrence, 1976, p. 176)

3. I [Russel Wren] proceeded to put to him [Boris] a question that would have earned me a beating from the late Pete & Tony, no doubt, with their quick ear for possible vile EPITHETS. (Thomas Berger, *Ibid.*, p. 195)

EPITOMIZE (i-pit'ə-mīz') *verb* to represent ideally; typify; to make an epitome of.

EPITOME *noun* a person or thing that is typical of or possesses to a high degree the features of a whole class; a summary or condensed account; abstract.

1. See (4) under PRESCIENCE.

2. The girls [in the movie, *The Killing of a Chinese Bookie*] are true and touching, beautiful losers, slave-queens of the wild side—EPITOMIZED by the PNEUMATIC Alice Friedland and the awesome Azizi Johari. (J. Kroll, Review, *Newsweek*, 3/15/76, p. 90)

3. See (1) under ASYMPTOTE.

4. See (3) under HAUTEUR.

5. In the case of industrialism, which EPITO-
MIZES the most serious contemporary prob-
lems, he [Louis] Schneider, author of *The
Sociological Way of Looking at the World*
trivializes both its cause and its consequences
. . . (Sharon Zukin, Review, *Chronicle of
Higher Education*, 3/22/76, p. 13)

6. See (5) under PEDANT.

7. If ever there was a case that EPITOMIZED the
old southern whites' need to keep blacks in
their place, it is the [Emmet] Till case. (D. L.
Kirp, Review of *Against Our Will: Men,
Women and Rape*, by Susan Brownmiller; and
Rape: The Bait and the Trap, by Jean
McKellar with the collaboration of Dr.
Menachem Amir, *Change*, April 1976, p. 41)

8. [Guitarist Ralph] Towner's best efforts have
come on two recent recordings, one a duet
album . . . , the other leading a quartet of German and Scandinavian jazzmen. The quartet
recording, *Solstice*, was made in Oslo and is
the EPITOME of ice-cold, diamond-hard European jazz . . . . (S. Davis, "Thrummers Who
Survive in an Electric Era," *New York Times*,
4/18/76, Section 2, p. 18)

9. This story [about a prisoner who ingeniously committed suicide to escape execution] . . .
represented the EPITOME of human determination and ingenuity. (I. Wallace, *The Fan
Club*, Bantam Edition, 1975, p. 377)

10. See (1) under MAGDALENE.

11. Stanley Marsh [a Texas millionaire] is outrageous and silly on purpose . . . Since art is
supposed to be surprising, Marsh holds, it's
best where it's least expected. Here [in Amaril-
lo] alongside Route 66, for instance, where he
got his kicks a few years ago by underwriting a
California design group, called the Ant Eaters,
that wanted to build a memorial to the cult of
the automobile. The Ant Eaters decided that
the automobile was EPITOMIZED by the tailfins
on the postwar Cadillac. So they started the
practice of planting cars—a neat row of 10
Cadillacs plunging into the loam of the prairie
at the angle at which the Titanic plunged into
the icy seas. Cadillac Ranch, it was called. It's
an eye-catcher, all right, sticking out there in
the vastness and emptiness of the Panhandle.

(J. Lelyveld, "Panhandle Pop," *New York
Times*, 5/8/77, Section 6, p. 94)

EPONYM (ep'ǝ-nim) *noun* a real or fictitious person from whom something (a tribe,
institution, nation, place, theory, movement,
historical period, etc.) derives, or is said to
derive, its name.

EPONYMOUS (e-pon'ǝ-mǝs) *adj.*

EPONYMY (e-pon'ǝ-mē) *noun* the derivation of names from EPONYMS.

1. "Look at this," Bavasi said, showing me the
beginning of the book [*The French Lieuten-
ant's Woman*] 'An easterly is the most disagreeable wind in Lyme Bay . . and a person
of curiosity could at once have detected several
strong possibilities about the pair who began to
walk down the quay at Lyme Regis, the small
but ancient EPONYM of the inbite, one incisively sharp and blustery morning in the late
March of 1867.' "Is that a good first sentence?"
(R. Kahn, *The Boys of Summer*, Harper and
Row, 1971, p. 430)

2. The EPONYMOUS poem [in *Open House*, by
W. Olcom] . . . starts: . . . "My heart keeps
open house." (A. Porter, Review, *The New
Yorker*, 2/9/76, p. 99)

3. With the escalating PRETENSIONS to ill-
gotten magnitude that currently beset leading
practitioners in larceny, the day may soon be
here when the sting-merchants take their victims to view the EPONYMOUS edifice of Alexan-
dre Gustave Eiffel, only to be confronted by an
empty skyline—because some earlier-bird col-
leagues-in-crime pinched it overnight. (P.
Ryan, "In decade of the big steal, larceny
waxes grander," *Smithsonian*, March 1976,
p. 120)

4. The EPONYMOUS heroine [of *Aunt Anne*, by
Lucy Clifford] is a sixtyish spinster who is both
sentimental and calculating, weak and determined. (Alison Lurie, Review, *The New York
Review of Books*, 12/11/75, p. 26)

5. *Jonny Spielt Auf* [an opera by Ernst
Křenek] does end with a big [Paul] Whiteman-
esque number, an APOTHEOSIS in which the
EPONYMOUS Jonny, the scoundrelly black jazz-
man, conquers the world with his stolen violin.
(A. Rich, Review, *New York*, 5/31/76, p. 72)

THE QUINTESSENTIAL DICTIONARY

6. Another name now has to be considered, and that is the center's EPONYM, George Pompidou himself . . . . Charles de Gaulle has the Paris international airport and Pompidou the Paris international art center [Centre National d'Art et de Culture Georges Pompidou]. . . . Neither bears the stamp of its EPONYM; those days are over when a great man's personality could, after his death, survive in his monument. (A. Burgess, " 'A $200 million Erector set,' " *New York Times*, 1/23/77, Section 7, pp. 17, 22)

EQUANIMITY (ē' kwə- nim' i-tē, ek' wə-) *noun* calmness or composure, especially under tension; equilibrium; evenness of mind or temper.

EQUANIMOUS (i-kwan' ə-məs) *adj.* having or showing equanimity; even-tempered.

EQUANIMOUSLY *adv.*

1. I am not particularly comfortable with the idea of the university as a mechanism locked into the marketplace, but it would be FATUOUS to pretend it isn't. And I view with EQUANIMITY the fact that technology carries more weight in the marketplace than poetry. If forced to choose between broad-spectrum antibiotics and *Moby Dick*, I would choose the antibiotics every time. (R. Zoellner, "Are Teaching Professors Automatically Losers?" *Chronicle of Higher Education*, 6/28/76, p. 40)

2. [Alejo] Carpentier [author of *Reasons of State*, translated by Frances Partridge] at that time [the late 1950's] was living commodiously under the not entirely liberal regime of Pérez Jiménez in Caracas, and, as an occasional visitor to his native Cuba, seemed to view with some EQUANIMITY the existence of the dictatorship of Fulgencio Batista. (A. Coleman, Review, *New York Times*, 5/2/76, p. 51)

EQUIPOISE (ē' kwə-poiz' , ek' wə-)*noun* an equal distribution of weight; even balance; a counterpoise; counterbalance.

EQUIPOISE *verb* to equal or offset in weight; balance.

1. [Author] David Schoenbrun's skills as journalist and historian attain fruitful EQUIPOISE (*sic*) in the book [*Triumph in Paris: The Ex-*

ploits of Benjamin Franklin]. The result is a witty, urbane, exceptionally astute and lively tale of *mon cher Papa* [Franklin]'s years in Paris, bringing France over to the American cause with a treaty of alliance and military aid. (M. Fineman, Review, *Philadelphia Inquirer*, 11/14/76, p. 14-C)

EQUIPOLLENT (ē' kwə-pol'ənt) *adj.* equal force, power, weight, validity, effect, etc.; equivalent; of two statements, propositions, etc.) logically equivalent in any of the various specified ways.

EQUIPOLLENT *noun* an equivalent.

EQUIPOLLENCE or **EQUIPOLLENCY** *noun.*

EQUIPOLLENTLY *adv.*

1. And [Ronald] Hingley [author of *A New Life of Anton Chekhov*] is not a superb writer; in fact, he is often a dull one, given to odd grammatical quirks, an occasionally highfalutin vocabulary ("SUBVENTION," "SWIVED," "EQUIPOLLENT"), and a style sometimes too sprightly, as if to counteract the drugs of academe. (H. Moss, Review, *New York Times*, 6/20/76, Section 7, p. 29)

EQUIVOCATE (i-kwiv'ə-kāt) *verb* to use ambiguous or unclear expressions, usually to avoid a direct answer or to deceive or mislead; hedge.

EQUIVOCATINGLY *adv.*

EQUIVOCATOR *noun.*

EQUIVOCAL *adj.* of uncertain significance; not determined; of doubtful nature or character; questionable; dubious.

EQUIVOCATION *noun* the use of equivocal or ambiguous expressions, especially in order to mislead or hedge; an equivocal or ambiguous expression; equivoque (ek' wə-vōk, ē' kwə-)

1. The boys in question [in *The Boys From Brazil*, a book by Ira Levin] are Nazi SS men in hiding, and not your equivocating ex-Nazis either, but honest to Adolf, sneering, Jew-hating diabolical villains . . . dedicated to create the Fourth Reich by whatever means necessary. (Gene Lyons, Review, *New York Times*, 3/14/76, Section 7, p. 4)

2. see (2) under FINICKY.

EREMITE (er'ə-mīt') *noun* a hermit or recluse, especially one under a religious vow.

EREMITIC or **EREMITICAL** *adj.*

1. See (1) under RETARDATAIRE.

2. Several years ago, the word "SHUNPIKER" was coined to describe the motorist with lots of time who wanted to escape the traffic on the turnpikes and see more of the countryside . . . . But the most ardent and successful SHUNPIKER was never a hermit. The true EREMITE actually tries to escape reality and the pressures of living with mankind by hiding out on a more or less permanent basis. (Anon., "Shunpikers and Hermits" [Editorial], *Daily Oklahoman*, Okla. City, 4/14/76, p. 8)

ERETHISM (er'ə-thiz'əm) *noun* an unusual or excessive degree of irritability, sensitivity, stimulation, or excitability in an organ or tissue.

ERETHISMIC or **ERETHISTIC** or **ERETHIC** or **ERETHIC** (ə-rəth'ik) *adj.*

1. A man's capacity for orgasm is limited, while a woman's is not . . . . [Dr. Augustus Kinsley] Gardner was ready to hint at this possibility in his popular [19th century] book *Conjugal Sins*. He did so by quoting a French expert, Claude-François Lallemand: "To the man there is the limitation of a physical capability which no stimulants from within or without can goad to further excess. The ERETHISM of women has no boundary," . . . . (Helen Singer Kaplan and David C. Anderson, "Sexual Revolution—The Time of Woman," *New York Times*, 7/4/76, Section 6, p. 95)

ERGOTISM (ûr'gə-tiz'əm) *noun* a diseased condition caused by eating rye and other grains that are infested with ergot fungus or by taking an overdose of medicinal ergot and characterized by cramps, spasms, and a form of gangrene.

1. Convulsive ERGOTISM from eating rye contaminated with an LSD-like ergot, may have induced "trips" in Puritan youngsters whose erratic behavior prompted the Salem witch trials . . . . Ergot grows on a variety of cereal grains, especially rye, and contains a large number of . . . ergot alkaloids including lysergic acid amide, with 10 percent the activity of LSD. Convulsive ERGOTISM symptoms . . . include crawling sensations in the skin, tingling in the fingers, VERTIGO, headaches, hallucinations, epileptiform convulsions and vomiting—all symptoms alluded to in the Salem witchcraft trials. (Anon., "LSD Substance Tied to Trials," *Daily Oklahoman*, Okla. City, 4/5/76, p. 13)

ERISTIC (e-ris'-tik) or **ERISTICAL** *adj.* of, pertaining to, or providing controversy or disputation; controversial; disputatious; CONTENTIOUS; given to SOPHISTICAL argument and SPECIOUS reasoning [after Eris, the ancient Greek goddess of strife and discord].

ERISTIC *noun* a person who engages in disputation; controversialist; eristic discourse; SOPHISTICAL argument.

ERISTICALLY *adv.*

1. And all the lawyers in Christendom, practicing industriously the ERISTIC arts, aren't going to persuade a lot of people that the United States did not in fact acquire the Panama [Canal] Zone in 1903. (W.F. Buckley Jr., "Panama nitpicking canal pact," *Sunday Call-Chronicle*, Allentown, Pa., 10/3/76, p. B-18)

EROGENOUS (i-roj'ə-nəs) or **EROGENIC** or **EROTOGENIC** *adj.* sexually gratifying or sensitive; arousing or tending to arouse sexual desire; designating or of those areas of the body, as the genital, oral, and anal zones, that are particularly sensitive to sexual stimulation.

1. "My career has gone so fast my brain hasn't absorbed it all," says [Henry] Winkler, 30, referring to his possibly most EROGENOUS zone. (Lois Armstrong, "AYYYY—The Fonz Is a Smash, But Henry Winkler Finds Some Nightmares In His Happy Daze," *People*, 5/31/76, p. 41)

2. Chloe models [at Monday's ready-to-wear fashion show in Paris] had midsections so trim they appeared to be minus rib cages. And if Chloe designer Karl Lagerfeld doesn't succeed in making that part of a woman's anatomy the new EROGENOUS zone it won't be for lack of trying. (Elaine Tait, "New from Paris: Pleats and

pretty," *Philadelphia Inquirer*, 10/27/76, p.1-B)

ERRONEOUS (ə-rō′ nē-əs, e-rō′ -) *adj.* containing error; false; mistaken; wrong; incorrect; inaccurate.

ERRONEOUSLY *adv.*

ERRONEOUSNESS *noun.*

1. [Walter] Hoving has plunged into another squabble which is being called the "tiff at Tiffany's." . . . Hoving placed a newspaper ad ERRONEOUSLY attributing 10 right-wing APHORISMS to Abraham Lincoln. Apprised of his mistake by Lincoln buffs, Hoving apologized. But Tiffany charge account holder Dona Fowler Kaminsky, . . . who does not share Hoving's conservatism, was not appeased. "I'll think twice," she wrote Hoving, "before I enter Tiffany's again." "I think you are right," Hoving shot back. "So I'm going to do you a favor. I have closed your account." (Anon., "For Tiffany's Walter Hoving Silence May Be Golden, But Sounding Off Is Irresistible," *People*, 4/12/76, p.16)

2. I [Russel Wren] realized that the unknown Newhouse was registered as of the same office number as my own, 3A, and ERRONEOUSLY so . . . . (Thomas Berger, *Who Is Teddy Villanova?*, Delacorte Press/Seymour Lawrence, p. 18)

3. "I'm not gay!" [said Russel Wren]. She [Alice Ellish] shrugged . . . . "The day is gone in which it was considered a psychological disorder." "I am aware of that [said Wren]. I simply didn't want you to get an ERRONEOUS idea. I have too frequently been the victim of misidentifications lately." (Thomas Berger, *Ibid.*, p. 147)

ERUCT (i-rukt′) or **ERUCTATE** (i-ruk′ tāt) *verb* to belch forth, as wind from the stomach; to emit or issue violently, as matter from a volcano.

ERUCTATION *noun.*

ERUCTATIVE *adj.*

1. . . . .he [Boris Bolgin] knew . . . that the center of their earth [Joseph Stalin] was heaving and fuming and causing great ERUCTATIONS of human misery in its

writhing frustration over the failure of Soviet scientists to develop the hydrogen bomb at the same rate as . . . the Americans . . . (W.F. Buckley Jr., *Saving the Queen*, Doubleday, 1976, p. 104)

ESCHATOLOGY (es′kə-tol′ə-jē) *noun* any system of doctrines concerning last, or final, matters, as death, the afterlife, judgment, immortality, etc.

ESCHATOLOGICAL *adj.*

ESCHATOLOGICALLY *adv.*

ESCHATOLOGIST *noun.*

1. The final commitments of the human species are always ESCHATOLOGICAL, commitments to end purposes in life. To love of family, to redemption, to TRANSCENDENCE. (W. F. Buckley Jr., *Execution Eve and Other Contemporary Ballads*, G. P. Putnam's Sons, 1975, p. 271)

2. Surely . . . an obliging community should be willing to devote itself to matters that do not rise to the status of ESCHATOLOGY. For instance the crazy pot laws. (W.F. Buckley Jr., *Ibid.*, p. 391)

3. Democracy . . . has no ESCHATOLOGY; no vision, no fulfillment, no point of arrival. Neither does academic freedom. Both are merely instruments, the one supposed to induce a harmonious society, the second supposed to advance knowledge. (W.F. Buckley Jr., *Up From Liberalism*, Arlington House, 2nd Printing 1968, p. 140)

4. . . . Communist dogma is ESCHATOLOGICALLY conceived. Communism promises the elimination of poverty, war, inequality, insecurity. Communism offers a view of human history, holds out a millennial vision, indicates the means . . . of effecting this millennium. (W. F. Buckley Jr., *Ibid.*, p. 145)

ESCRITOIRE (es′kri-twär′) *noun* a writing desk or table.

1. Her [Elizabeth Ames'] moral rigidity seems to me to have been exaggerated. Early in her career [as hostess to artists and writers at the Trask mansion in Saratoga Springs, N.Y.] she left admonitory notes on a huge ESCRITOIRE in

the morning room, but when a distinguished man or woman took a lover she didn't seem to much care. (J. Cheever, "The Hostess of Yaddo," *New York Times*, 5/8/77, Section 7, pp. 34–35)

2. She [Ann Smiley] sat alone at her ESCRITOIRE, and she might have composed the scene for him deliberately: the beautiful and conscientious wife, ending her day, attends to matters of administration. (J. LeCarré, *The Honourable Schoolboy*, Alfred A. Knopf, 1977, pp. 109–110)

ESCULENT (es'kyə-lənt *adj.* suitable for use as food; edible; eatable.

ESCULENT *noun* something fit for food, especially a vegetable.

1. Uninformed Parisians believe that Les Halles, the great old market that was Zola's "stomach of Paris," was pulled down to accommodate the new temple of NONESCULENT art [the new Beaubourg Art Center], and they unreasonably resent this. It seems to them like an official subversion of values. (A. Burgess, "A $200 million Erector Set," *New York Times*, 1/23/77, Section 6, p. 17)

ESOTERIC (es'ə-ter'ik) *adj.* understood by or meant for only the select few who have special knowledge or interest; RECONDITE; private; secret; confidential; beyond the understanding or knowledge of most people.

ESOTERICALLY *adv.*

ESOTERICA *noun, pl.* esoteric matters, facts, or things.

ESOTERICISM *noun* esoteric practices, principles, or beliefs.

1. Strikingly, assistance [in a reform of the humanities] may come from what might be thought of as an exceedingly ESOTERIC source— the general theory of culture . . . . Enamored of ESOTERICISM, they [the humanities] must now loose their influence, their power to change anyone or anything. (N. Birnbaum, "The Future of the Humanities" [Editorial], *Change*, Summer 1975, p. 13)

2. See (1) under SENESCENT.

3. James Schlesinger, the former defense secretary, told Congress in October that Russia could be outspending the United States on weapons by up to 50 per cent, and widening the gap. But the official American estimates are the responsibility of the CIA, and its analyses are so ESOTERIC that the differences of view did not come sharply into focus until last month. (*The London Economist*, "Intelligence Officials Astonished: Soviet Defense Budget Zooms," reprinted in *The Norman* [Okla.] *Transcript*, 3/23/76, p. 6)

4. But wherever you go you want to ask, "Who are tramps, really?" thinking that there is something ESOTERIC about their motivation. The mind holds on to stereotypes and you do not want to admit that, under the dirt, tramps are much like the rest of us. (R. Warner, "Riding freights is no picnic for tramps today," *Smithsonian*, December 1975, p. 96)

5. In the early 1950's cell culture was entering a critical period. New culture media and techniques would cause cell culture to go in ten years from an ESOTERIC scientific semi-plaything to an extremely significant, widely employed investigative tool. (L. E. Karp, "The immortality of a cancer victim dead since 1951," *Smithsonian*, March 1976, p. 52)

6. In each [of the two books, *Revelations of New England Architecture*, by Jill Grossman; and *American Classic*, by Laurence Lafore] the emphasis is on people and their buildings, on the way buildings reflect the lives and history of the people who build them—architecture as an expression of life, rather than architecture as an ESOTERIC discipline practiced by professionals. (C. Page, Review, *Smithsonian*, March 1976, p. 105)

7. See (4) under ICONOGRAPHY.

8. See (4) under NECROPHILIA.

9. See (2) under WELTANSCHAUUNG.

10. See (1) under PANTHEON.

ESPRIT DE CORPS (e-sprē'də kôr') group spirit; a sense of union, pride, honor, and of common interests and responsibilities, as developed among a group of persons associated together.

ESPRIT *noun* spirit; sprightliness of wit; lively intelligence.

1. Though numerous HIRSUTE plaintiffs have gone to the U.S. Supreme Court, the Justices had steadfastly refused to get enmeshed in long-hair disputes.... Suffolk county police on Long Island had objected to regulations that banned beards, flared sideburns and hair that went over the collar . . . . William Rehnquist, writing for a six-justice majority, said drily that where the state's standard is not "so irrational that it may be branded arbitrary," the individual's rights must bend "to the overall need for discipline, ESPRIT DE CORPS and uniformity." The nation's policemen could reasonably have expected a more tolerant view from Rehnquist: his own sideburns and locks would not pass the Suffolk County standards. (Anon., "Briefs," *Time*, 4/19/76, p. 90)

ESTAMINET (e-stA-mē-nā', -ne') *noun* a bistro or small cafe.

1. Of the tawdry lines [by T. S. Eliot] in *Gerontion* that describe "the Jew" squatting "on the window sill, the owner/Spawned in some ESTAMINET of Antwerp/ Blistered in Brussels, patched and peeled in London," the editor of *The Norton Anthology of English Verse* EUPHEMISTICALLY notes, "Used unpleasantly by Eliot as a symbol of DERACINATED man." (L. Cole, Review of *Selected Prose by T.S. Eliot*, edited and with an introduction by Frank Kermode, *Change*, August 1976, p. 63)

ETHEREAL (i-thēr'ē-əl) *adj.* light, airy or tenuous; extremely delicate or refined; heavenly or celestial; of the ether or upper regions of space.

ETHEREALLY *adv.*

ETHEREALITY *noun.*

ETHEREALIZE *verb* to make, or treat as being, ethereal.

ETHEREALIZATION *noun.*

1. . . . one of the features of the score [of *The Magic Flute*] as a whole is a delicacy that reflects Mozart's acute aural/sensitivity in the last months of his life, when even the singing of his pet canary caused him physical pain. This symptom, together with EDEMA, stomach trouble, VERTIGO, and spasms of weeping, first sug-

gested a diagnosis of mercury poisoning. If it is true that a stigma increases perception, and that disease, especially one that the sufferer may fear to be fatal, serves to heighten experience, then a purely human explanation can be hypothesized for the ETHEREALITY of *The Magic Flute*—though in Mozart's case we are always inclined to suspect a Divine one. (R. Craft, Review, *New York Review of Books*, 11/27/75, pp. 21-22)

ETHNOCENTRISM (eth' nō-sen' triz-əm) or **ETHNOCENTRICITY** *noun* the belief in the inherent superiority of one's own ethnic group, nation, or culture; a tendency to view alien groups or cultures in terms of one's own.

ETHNOCENTRIC *adj.*

ETHNOCENTRICALLY *adv.*

1. . . . he [John Simon, author of the books, *Uneasy Stages* and *Singularities*] is provocative . . . even when you disagree with him—as I do frequently over his insensitivity to the performance process, his over-lofty view of criticism, and his unexamined conviction that a pluralistic, ETHNOCENTRIC, racially divided, sexually split society like the U.S. could or should have a National Theatre (how can you have a "National Theatre" until you have a nation?). (R. Brustein, Review, *New York Times*, 1/4/76, Section 7, p. 2)

ETIOLATE (ē'tē-ə-lāt') *verb* to cause (a plant) to whiten by excluding light; to cause to be pale and unhealthy; bleach; to deprive of strength; weaken.

ETIOLATION *noun.*

1. . . . three years hence when the trial takes place, the word "Nazi" may have become totally ETIOLATED, causing the jury to wonder that anyone should particularly care about having been so designated. If that is the case I shall be left with nothing more than an expensive footnote in my autobiography, pointing to the irony that it was a conservative who struggled to regulate the use of a word so as to IMMURE within it some sense of the hideousness of Hitler. (W. F. Buckley Jr., *Execution Eve and Other Contemporary Ballads*, G. P. Putnam's Sons, 1975, p. 326)

2. "That is not to say that, as a percentage,

there are brighter boys among the poor than among the rich" [said Mr. Alex-Hiller, headmaster of Eton College]. "No, . . . but I warrant it's true [said Queen Caroline). Probably something gets into us that makes our blood sort of ETIOLATED—do you know that word, Perry? Very useful word . . . . Do you [Sir Alfred Schuler], anywhere in your large book [a biography of George V], . . . use the word in connection with my grandfather [George V]'s speeches?" (W. F. Buckley Jr., *Saving the Queen*, Doubleday, 1976, p. 168)

ETIOLOGY or AETIOLOGY (ē' tē-ol' ə-jē) *noun* the study of the causes of diseases; the cause or origin of a disease; any study of causation, causes, or causality.

ETIOLOGICAL or AETIOLOGICAL *adj.*

ETIOLOGICALLY or AETIOLOGICALLY *adv.*

ETIOLOGIST or AETIOLOGIST *noun.*

1. When right-minded columnists or TV documentaries chastise 210 million Americans for wasting the world's resources, for eating as much annually as would suffice to feed 1.5 billion Third Worlders, the reverberations of the challenge to the "bitch-Goddess" (William James's sexist label for the success deity) resound at their loudest and clearest. For present purposes, however, it is the existence, not the ETIOLOGY, of the challenge to success-religion that matters . . . . (B. DeMott, "Beyond the Dream of Success," *Change*, August 1976, p. 33)

EUDAEMONIA or EUDEMONIA (yōō' di-mō' nē-ə) *noun* happiness.

EUDAEMONIC or EUDEMONIC or EUDAEMONICAL or EUDEMONICAL *adj.* pertaining to or conducive to happiness.

EUDAEMONICS or EUDEMONICS *noun* the theory or art of happiness.

1. The Great Society did not lead us into EUDAEMONIA. It led us into frustration—and the lowest recorded confidence vote in the basic institutions of this country since the birth of George Gallup. (W.F. Buckley Jr., *Execution Eve and Other Contemporary Ballads*, G.P. Putnam's Sons, 1975, p. 477)

EUOLOGY (yōō lə-jē) *noun* a speech or writing in praise of a person, event, or thing, especially a set oration in honor of a deceased person; high praise or commendation.

EULOGIZE (yōō' lə-jīz') *verb* to praise highly; to speak or write a eulogy about; extol; laud; PANEGYRIZE.

EULOGIST *noun.*

EULOGISTIC or EULOGISTICAL *adj.*

EULOGISTICALLY *adv.*

1. . . . she [Lucille Clifton] has now produced [in *Generations: A Memoir*] a short but eloquent EULOGY to her parents. As with most ELEGISTS, her purpose is perpetuation and celebration, not judgment. (Reynolds Price Review, *New York Times*, 3/14/76, Section 7, p. 7)

2. See (2) under APARTHEID.

3. See (1) under TRULL.

EUPEPTIC (yōō-pep'tik) *adj.* of or having good digestion; healthy and happy; cheerful.

EUPEPSIA (yōō-pep shə, -sē-ə) or **EUPEPSY** (yōō pep-se) *noun* good digestion (as opposed to *dyspepsia*).

1. Prodded by the EUPEPTIC booming of the outside master of ceremonies [at the Academy Awards], they [the teenagers] stayed to squeal at [the arrival of] Walter Matthau and . . . at the evening's representative of the muse of irony, Gore Vidal. (R. Hughes, "The Day for Night Stars," *Time*, 4/12/76, p. 61)

2. I recently experienced an unsettling attack of EUPEPSIA (and that's not easy on Sheridan Square [in Greenwich Village]), achieved a flash of EPIPHANY (and that's not easy in New York), and came away with my ears ringing and a sunburned nose. (G. Millstein, "Eine Kleine Strassen-musik," *New York Times*, 4/10/77, Section 4, p. 17)

3. In their bungalow, overlooking a white sand beach [on Contadora island off the Panamanian coast] where they occasionally swim and sun themselves, they [U.S. and Panamanian negotiators] are quickly getting down to basics. Secretary of State Cyrus Vance has been described as "EUPEPTIC" over the

possibility of finally signing a treaty [regarding the Panama Canal] by this summer . . . . (Anon., "Eupeptic over Progress in Panama," *Time*, 2/28/77, p. 14)

EUPHEMISM (yōō´ fə-miz´ əm) *noun* the substitution of a mild, indirect, or vague expression for one considered offensive, distasteful, harsh, ugly, hurtful, or blunt; the expression so substituted.

EUPHEMIST *noun*.

EUPHEMISTIC *adj*.

EUPHEMISTICALLY *adv*.

EUPHEMIZE *verb*.

1. See (1) under CIRCUMLOCUTION.

2. "Majority rule" for Rhodesia today is a EUPHEMISM for a black-minority government, which would almost surely mean both the eviction or exodus of most of the whites and also a drastically lower level of living and of opportunities for the masses of black Rhodesians. (M. Friedman, "Rhodesia," *Time*, 5/3/76, p. 77)

3. . . . [Harold] Yost was about to launch into an explanation of how Mr. Livingston should have the policy on himself owned by his wife— so that if he were taken out of the picture (insurance agents' trusty EUPHEMISM for dying), the insurance benefits would not be subject to inheritance tax. (I. Wallace, *The Fan Club*, Bantam edition, 1975, p. 37)

4. She [Sharon Fields] wondered: . . . But what kind of cooperation did these weirdos [her kidnappers] expect? Did they want only her friendliness . . .? Or was the cooperation they spoke of really a EUPHEMISM for sexual relationship . . .? (I. Wallace, *Ibid.*, pp. 263–264)

5. She [Sharon Fields] began to dig it. Her agent wasn't a talent promoter . . . . Agent was a EUPHEMISM for high-class pimp. (I. Wallace, *Ibid.*, p. 317)

6. . . . it had been suggested to her [Sharon Fields] . . . that the time was nearing when they [her kidnappers] would be finished with her. Release her or—what was the Vietnamese EUPHEMISM?—yes, waste her. (I. Wallace, *Ibid.*, p. 465)

7. See (8) under KITSCH.

8. If Clara Bow could really act—and authors Joe Morella and Edward Z. Epstein claim [in *The 'It' Girl*] that she could —she was scarcely able to show it. All moviegoers wanted was "it," a EUPHEMISM for sex appeal; Miss Bow, like Marilyn Monroe after her, was trapped by her own image. (M. Gussow, Review, *New York Times*, 6/20/76, Section 7, p. 18)

9. See (2) under QUOTIDIAN.

10. See (1) under ESTAMINET.

11. See (2) under FARRAGO.

12. . . . George Cosmatos bridles at the suggestion that *The Cassandra Crossing* is a disaster movie. The film, which . . . centers on passengers aboard a Swiss train who are threatened by or infected by plague, has too much character development to qualify for what the fashion for cinematic EUPHEMISM now calls "group-jeopardy films," he argues. (D. Ryan, "Critic's notebook," *Philadelphia Inquirer*, 1/30/77, p. 1-D)

13. A young woman I know, EUPHEMISTICALLY seeking to report a burial, tells my religious congregation that the lady in question has recently been laid. (Hardly, one thinks, a cause for bereavement). C. A. Ridley, Review of *A Civil Tongue*, by Edwin Newman, *National Observer*, week ending 2/19/77, p. 27)

EUPHORIA (yōō-fōr´ ē-ə, -fôr´ -) *noun* a feeling of vigor, well-being, or high spirits especially an exaggerated or abnormal one having no basis in truth or reality.

EUPHORIC *adj*.

EUPHORICALLY *adv*.

EUPHORIANT *noun* a drug or other agent that produces euphoria.

1. See (2) under APOTHEOSIS.

2. Three years ago, . . . Adm. Elmo R. Zumwalt advised . . . that our NATO plan of reinforcing U.S. forces in Europe and supporting them logistically in the event that Warsaw Pact forces moved west was no longer valid . . . In the aftermath of the Vietnamese war, the bitter residue of Watergate and the EUPHORIA of detente, this ominous warning went un-

noted and unheeded by our Congress. (I. C. Eaker, "U.S. Must Shun Naval 'Parity,'" *Daily Oklahoman*, 4/26/76, p. 14)

3. See (4) under ROCOCO.

4. The Mechanic [Shively] was EUPHORICALLY reflective . . . . [He] began to make public his dreams that now, with the windfall [ransom money], could become reality. (I. Wallace, *The Fan Club*, Bantam Books, 1975, p. 489)

5. . . . there was poor, devastated Adam Malone, anchored to the sofa by too much cannabis and in a mildly EUPHORIC state. (I. Wallace, *Ibid.*, p. 286)

6. He [Adam Malone] went inside . . . his cozy quarters . . . —grateful to leave behind the painful, sick and violent world of reality and return once more to the EUPHORIC and peaceful world of make-believe . . . . (I. Wallace, *Ibid.*, p. 626)

7. See (2) under NARCOSIS.

8. See (7) under ICONOGRAPHY.

EUPHUISTIC (yōō'fyōō-is'tik) or **EUPHUISTICAL** *adj.* of, having the nature of, or characterized by EUPHEMISM; high-flown, affected, PERIPHRASTIC, etc.

EUPHUIST *noun.*

EUPHUISTICALLY *adv.*

EUPHUISM (yōō'fyōō-iz'əm) *noun* any ornate, high-flown, artificial, PERIPHRASTIC style of language or writing, or an instance of this; originally an affected style in imitation of that of John Lyly, fashionable in England at the end of the 16th century, characterized by long series of ANTITHESES, far-fetched figures of speech, ALLITERATION, etc.

1. Thomas Berger's *Who Is Teddy Villanova?* is a black comic PARODY of tough-guy detective fiction out of Hammett and Chandler. Despite its seedy urban setting and HYPERTROPHIED plot, it is written in Berger's arch, allusive and rhetorically exhibitionistic style: loquacious, PERIPHRASTIC, EUPHUISTIC—as if spoken by a demented William F. Buckley. (R. Locke, "Novelists as Preachers," *New York Times*, 4/17/77, Section 7, p. 53)

EVANESCENT (ev'ə-nes'ənt) *adj.* vanishing; passing away; EPHEMERAL; fleeting; tending to become imperceptible; scarcely perceptible.

EVANESCENTLY *adv.*

EVANESCE *verb* to disappear gradually· vanish; fade away slowly.

EVANESCENCE *noun.*

1. It [*The Tale of the Heike*, translated by Hiroshi Kitagawa and Bruce Tsuchida] is a vast work (some 350,000 words . . .), yet the period covered is a mere 25 years, from the sudden rise of the Taira family (Heike), the first military rulers of feudal Japan, through their brief period of glory and HUBRIS, to their dramatic collapse after a series of defeats by the Minamotos, their fierce rivals from the eastern provinces . . . . Among these [central themes of the book] are the EVANESCENCE of worldly glory and the consequent danger of the sort. of HUBRIS exemplified by Kiyomori's brother-in-law when he proudly declared, "Unless a man be a Taira, he is no human being" . . . . (I. Morris, Review, *New York Times*, 2/8/76, Section 7, pp. 23–24)

2. What sustained him [W. A. Bentley, in his long study of snowflakes] were EVANESCENT glimpses of a delicate beauty that was utterly pure and more perishable than a sunset; his photographs [of snowflakes] were . . . a simple diary of his sense of wonder. (F. Hapgood, "When ice crystals fall from the sky art meets science," *Smithsonian*, January 1976, p. 67)

3. . . . the characters [in *The Wanderer*, a book by Knut Hamsun, translated by Oliver and Gunnvor Stallybrass] seem as EVANESCENT as the weather and the days and the hero's whimsical moods. (J. Updike, Review, *The New Yorker*, 5/31/76, p. 116)

4. Physicists are still reconciling Einsteinian relativity with quantum mechanics and dealing with particles so small and EVANESCENT that they themselves seem unsure whether they have revolutionized understanding or merely found another apple in the same old barrel. (J. K. Page Jr., "Frontiers," *Smithsonian*, July 1976, p. 16)

5. [Alain] Resnais's theme [in the movie, *Providence*] is always uncertainty, EVANESCENCE, the mysterious nature of the information sup-

plied by human consciousness. This is a great theme, but Resnais does not voyage daringly into this mystery—he wallows in it. (J. Kroll, Review, *Newsweek*, 2/28/77, p. 73)

EVISCERATE (i-vis'ə-rāt') *verb* to disembowel; to deprive of vital or essential parts; to take away the force, significance, etc., of.

EVISCERATION *noun.*

EVISCERATOR *noun.*

1. The danger comes when a distrust of doctrinaire social systems eases over into a dissolute disregard for principle. A disregard for enduring principle delivers a society, EVISCERATED, over to the ideologists. (W. F. Buckley Jr., *Up From Liberalism*, Arlington House, 2nd Printing 1968, p. xv)

2. It [the liberal Establishment] kept the supposedly best journalistic brains . . . from keeping an eye on the main enemy who sits in the Kremlin . . . . Meanwhile the Communists, without half trying, let us EVISCERATE ourselves. (J. Chamberlain, "Vietnam General Analyzes War," *Daily Oklahoman*, Okla. City, 5/7/76, p. 10)

3. Thailand is spawning a new wave of versatile film makers concerned with such local problems as teenage prostitution and guerrilla terror . . . . A splashy sidelight of the industry is movie-poster art. In Bangkok, block-long billboards picturing grotesque snake-entwined monsters hovering over EVISCERATED women may cost $40,000 and take 36 artists to paint. These gargantuan murals, which used to be thrown away, are suddenly being bought up by European museums. (Anon., "Asia's Bouncing World of Movies," *Time*, 6/28/76, p. 43)

4. "I'm not lukewarm on Europe [said Prime Minister James Callaghan]. But I'm lukewarm about some of the schemes . . . proposed more for the sake of uniformity than unity, like whether only EVISCERATED chickens must be sold within all countries." (Anon., "Callaghan: Winning the Battle," *Time*, 5/24/76, p. 29)

5. See (3) under EXCULPATE.

EXACERBATE (ig-zas'ər-bāt , ik-sas'-) *verb* to increase the bitterness, violence, or viru-

lence of (disease, ill feeling, etc.); aggravate; irritate; exasperate; annoy; to make more intense or sharp.

EXACERBATINGLY *adv.*

EXACERBATION *noun.*

1. *The Impending Crisis* [by David M. Potter] is a book without heroes or villains. But, in striking contrast to the trend of recent writing, Potter reserves his harshest criticism for the abolitionists, whom he depicts as zealots who EXACERBATED sectional tensions by injecting the language of sin into politics. (E. Foner, Review, *New York Times*, 2/22/76, Section 7, p. 7)

2. The EXACERBATION of his [Travis's] desire for vengeance shows in his numbness, yet part of the horror implicit in this movie [*Taxi Driver*] is how easily he passes. The anonymity of the city soaks up one more invisible man. (Pauline Kael, Review, *The New Yorker*, 2/9/76, p. 84)

3. See (1) under ABNEGATE.

4. See (1) under LAGNIAPPE.

5. As nearby sources of wood disappear, [Nepalese] villagers have to travel hours to find firewood, or they burn cow dung. Since the dung is needed to restore fertility, burning it only EXACERBATES the dilemma of the people. (W. Clark, "Big and/or little? Search is on for right technology," *Smithsonian*, July 1976, p. 46)

6. Britain and Italy have become economic basket cases. France, Denmark, Eire, Finland, Belgium, Australia and New Zealand are faced with economic difficulties that will be EXACERBATED by even a modest increase in the price of oil. (Smith Hempstone, "Over a barrel: Again, the oil price squeeze," *Philadelphia Inquirer*, 11/11/76, p. 11-A)

EXCORIATE (ik-skōr'ē-āt', -skôr'-) *verb* to strip off or remove the skin from; to denounce or berate harshly or severely; flay verbally.

EXCORIATION *noun.*

1. . . . what most isn't needed nowadays is a stupendous redundant EXCORIATION of the rich,

but rather a defense of the rich—and the sooner the better, before they are made to disappear, which would be very bad news indeed. (W. F. Buckley Jr., *Execution Eve and Other Contemporary Ballads*, G. P. Putnam's Sons, 1975, p. 479)

2. Of the public figures, only three dared speak out against this inhuman proposal [to totally exterminate the Indians in Colorado] . . . . General Asher pointed out that it was not the habit of the United States Army to sanction mass murder, and he was EXCORIATED as a coward who refused to face up to facts. (J. A. Michener, *Centennial*, Fawcett, 1975, p. 481)

3. Some of his [the historian Francis Parkman's] phrases fester in my [Paul Garrett's] mind. He called Chief Pontiac, one of America's best-balanced Indians, a "thorough savage to whom treachery seemed fair and honorable, the Satan of his forest paradise." . . . he [Parkman] EXCORIATED the farmers passing through as little more than animals, concluding, "Most of them were from Missouri" . . . . he divided the human race . . . into three divisions, "arranged in the order of their merit: white men, Indians and Mexicans" . . . . (J.A. Michener, *Ibid.*, p. 1079)

4. She [Sandy Vogelgesang, in her book, *The Long Dark Night of the Soul: The American Intellectual Left and the Vietnam War*] joins with Chomsky in EXCORIATING intellectuals like Schlesinger who were close to power; she joins with Schlesinger in EXCORIATING intellectuals like Chomsky who were systematically distrustful of power. (P. Steinfels, Review, *Harper's*, January 1975, p. 82)

5. Denenberg is not merely a reporter; he sometimes adds action to EXCORIATION. When he noticed that the antidote on the labels of all wood-alcohol products was medically unsound and possibly fatal, he filed a successful petition with the Consumer Products Safety Commission for new labeling regulations. Two weeks ago Denenberg petitioned the commission to order all U.S. poison labels—some 50,000—rewritten. (Anon., "The Horrible Herb Show," *Time*, 9/13/76, p. 70)

6. A reminder that artist-illustrators, with their printed pictures, were the dominant image-makers throughout most of the nation's history is available this weekend [in the show, *200 Years of American Illustration*] at the New York Historical Society . . . . Among the reminders: Thomas Nast, represented in the show by some of his cartoon EXCORIATIONS of Boss Tweed, also created Santa Claus as we know him, full-bearded, fat, jolly and booted, and Uncle Sam, tall, thin, goat-bearded and pantalooned. (M. Sterne, "Illustrating the American Ideal," *New York Times*, 11/26/76, p. C-13)

7. After the turn of the century, . . . James Ensor painted nothing of consequence for 50 years. His self-pity was increasingly soothed, and this is perhaps why his art did not develop—and why he so eagerly grabbed the honors pressed on him by the grateful nation [Belgium] he had once EXCORIATED. (R. Hughes, "Ensor: Much Possessed by Death," *Time*, 3/7/77, p. 51)

EXCULPATE (ek'skul-pāt', ik-skul'pāt) *verb* to clear from a charge of guilt or fault; free from blame; vindicate; declare or prove guiltless.

EXCULPABLE *adj.*

EXCULPATION *noun.*

EXCULPATORY *adj.* tending to clear from a charge of fault or guilt.

1. See (3) under EXPURGATE.

2. [Anthony] Scaduto [author of the book, *Scapegoat*] also charges that the police suppressed EXCULPATORY evidence and manufactured much of the critical evidence that seemed to connect [Bruno Richard] Hauptmann with the ransom notes and the ransom money [in the 1932 kidnapping of the Lindbergh baby]. (J.K. Footlick and Susan Agrest, "Did Hauptmann Do It?" *Newsweek*, 12/6/76, p. 64)

3. In his son's view, [Alger] Hiss-with-no-tears emerges [in the book, *Laughing Last*, by Tony Hiss] as "Al," a NAIF with terrible flaws, a "sucker" saved—not ruined—by 44 months in a Federal penitentiary. The revision is striking—although one wonders whether in the end it EXCULPATES Hiss or EVISCERATES him . . . . Tony Hiss . . . offers a good deal more

than one needs to know about his father's sex life and a good deal less about his relations with Whittaker Chambers—the confessed Communist whose testimony did Hiss in. (T. Mathews, Review, *Newsweek*, 2/28/77, p. 75)

EXCURSUS (ek-skûr′səs) *noun, pl.:* -SUSES or -SUS a detailed discussion of some point in a book, especially one added as an appendix; a digression, as in a literary work.

EXCURSIVE *adj.* rambling; DESULTORY; digressive.

1. In my favorite poem [in the book, *Comings Back*, by Albert Goldbarth], *Letters to Tony*, the poet [Goldbarth] attempts to cheer up a friend whose wife has left him by discoursing mightily, for 300 or so lines, on human excrement, with EXCURSES on such things as the colonizing of Australia (suggested by "colon") and the mystical importance of the dung beetle to ancient Egypt. (P. Schjeldahl, Review, *New York Times*, 11/21/76, Section 7, p. 64)

2. Giving up the effort to "master reality," the experimental writer retreats into a superficial self-analysis which blots out . . . the external world . . . . "His incursions into the self are as hollow as his EXCURSUS into the world." (C. Lasch, Review of the book, *Gates of Eden: American Culture in the Sixties*, by Morris Dickstein, *New York Times*, 3/13/77, Section 7, p. 30)

3. . . . the general method of the book [*The Life and Times of Chaucer*, by John Gardner] is to amplify and adorn this framework [of chronological facts about Chaucer's life] . . . with discussions of the poems and of Chaucer's development as an artist; with a generous series of EXCURSES or mini-lectures on the culture of the times and on the lives of the principal persons . . . . (C. Muscatine, Review, *New York Times*, 4/24/77, Section 7, p. 13)

EXECRABLE (ek′ sə-krə-bəl) *adj.* utterly detestable; abominable; horrible; accursed; abhorrent; very bad or inferior; of poorest quality.

EXECRABLY *adv.*

EXECRATE *verb* to detest utterly; abhor; abominate; to curse; to call down evil upon;

damn; denounce; to speak abusively or contemptuously of; to loathe; detest.

EXECRATOR *noun.*

EXECRATION *noun.*

EXECRATIVE or **EXECRATORY** *adj.*

1. *A Man Called Intrepid*, EXECRABLY written by a near-namesake [William Stevenson] of its hero, contains brief appearances by minor spies, of whom Greta Garbo is the most surprising and Noel Coward the most amusing . . . . (W. Clemons, Review, *Newsweek*, 3/22/76, p. 80)

2. [Branch] Rickey paid [his ballplayers] EXECRABLE salaries—$7,500 a year was high pay . . . . He had a Puritan dislike for money in someone else's hands. (R. Kahn, *The Boys of Summer*, Harper and Row, 1971, p. 94)

3. The food [on airplanes] is uniformly EXECRABLE. My dog Charlie Chan would prefer to starve. The plastic dishes, the knives and forks are what the wardens give to lifers with a suicide impulse. Anyone who flies a lot can't be overweight. (J. Bishop, "Reporter," *Times Herald*, Norristown, Pa., 2/10/77, p. 19)

4. These movies [that lack heroes] not only lack heroes; more seriously they lack villains. They have all kinds of EXECRABLE characters in them, but they are not real. They are caricatures; badly drawn in the case of a *King Kong* or a *Two-Minute Warning*, well drawn in *Network*. (R. Eder, "Hollywood's Affair With the Anti-Hero," *New York Times*, 1/2/77, Section 2, p. 11)

EXEGESIS (ek′ si-jē′ sis) *noun, pl.* -SES critical explanation or interpretation, especially of scripture.

EXEGETIC (ek′si-jet′ik) or **EXEGETICAL** *adj.*

EXEGETICALLY *adv.*

EXEGETE *noun* a person skilled in exegesis.

1. . . . if he [John Simon, author of the books, *Uneasy Stages* and *Singularities*] ever stopped playing the role of spitting critic, he might relax happily into a learned EXEGETE of Germanic texts, and one possessed of surprising generosity. (R. Brustein, Review, *New York Times*, 1/4/76, Section 7, p. 2)

2. Painter, teacher, POLEMICIST and poet-in-spite-of-himself . . . , he [Ad Reinhardt] had already been a major subterranean influence in the generation of Minimal and post-Minimal art—partly through the work of critical EXEGETES like Rose and Lucy Lippard—and seems ready for wide recognition as one of the most significant cultural figures of the past quarter-century. (P. Schjeldahl, Review of *Art as Art, The Selected Writings of Ad Reinhardt*, edited by Barbara Rose; and of *The Art Comics and Satires of Ad Reinhardt*, by Thomas B. Hess, *New York Times*, 2/15/76, Section 2, p. 7)

3. "My hope," [Bruno] Bettelheim writes, "is that a proper understanding of the unique merits of fairy tales will induce parents and teachers to assign them once again to that central role in the life of the child they held for centuries." . . . Bettelheim's Freudian EXEGESIS of the tales [as contained in his book, *The Uses of Enchantment: The Meaning and Importance of Fairy Tales*] is sure to exasperate many readers. . . .The oral tradition of tale-telling has lapsed, and he believes it should be revived. (W. Clemons, Review, *Newsweek*, 5/24/76, pp. 88, 91)

4. Probably best known as biographer and EXEGETE of Hemingway, Carlos Baker, now in his late 60's, is the author also of a study of Shelley and of an academic (campus) novel, published in 1958, called *A Friend in Power*, which remains a pleasant read . . . . None of this prepares one for the present volume of 12 collected stories [*The Talismans and Other Stories*]. (I. Gold, Review, *New York Times*, 4/11/76, Section 7, p. 34)

5. [Dougald] McMillan [author of *transition, 1927-38*] has been far too solemn about [Eugene] Jolas's theories, at the expense of the rich anecdotal history surrounding the magazine [*transition*]. Most of his book is taken up with relentless EXEGESIS and some of the writers to whom he devotes individual chapters—in particular Dylan Thomas, Beckett and Hart Crane—had only a tenuous relationship with *transition* [edited by E.J.]. (J. Atlas, Review, *New York Times*, 7/11/76, Section 7, p. 16)

6. The Playboy flap alone cost him [Jimmy Carter] a week's EXEGESES and apologies, short-circuiting what momentum he had, curdling his relations with the traveling press—and whetting his appetite for a fight. (P. Goldman and Eleanor Clift, "Mr. Outside in Stride," *Newsweek*, 11/1/76, p. 30)

7. See (3) under ANTHROPOID.

8. As a hard-nosed anti-EXEGETE myself, I find a lot of [author John] Gardner's analysis and analogies [in his book, *The Poetry of Chaucer*] over intricate, far fetched and, finally, cold. EXEGETICAL analysis of Chaucer almost always has an excessive braininess about it that misses the meaning of the poetry as poetry. (C. Muscatine, Review, *New York Times*, 4/24/77, Section 7, p. 39)

9. See (2) under CONCUPISCENCE.

EXIGENT (ek'si-jənt) *adj.* requiring immediate action, attention, or aid; critical; pressing; requiring a great deal, or more than is reasonable; demanding; exacting.

EXIGENTLY *adv.*

EXIGENCY *noun* urgency; a case or situation which demands prompt action or remedy; emergency; the need, demand, or requirement intrinsic to a particular circumstance, condition, etc.

1. In putting forward an ideal and a set of values that even in his own eyes seemed bleak, EXIGENT and yet minimal, [Lionel] Trilling was behaving with characteristic courage . . . . To my mind Trilling's spiritual heroism was in large part bound up with his EXIGENCY and his minimalism—his ability to affirm, without illusion, qualities and virtues that his own group, his own culture, his own audience had largely given up on as being at once excessive in their demands upon us and insufficient in the gratifications they return. (S. Marcus, "Lionel Trilling, 1905-1975," *New York Times*, 2/8/76, Section 7, p. 32)

2. Most peoples' lives are more EXIGENT than those of [Gail] Sheehy's rather privileged subjects [in her book, *Passages*]. (Sara Sanborn, Review, *New York Times*, 5/30/76, Section 7, p. 4)

EXIGUOUS (ig-zig'yōō-əs) *adj.* scanty; little; meager; small.

EXIGUITY (ek'sə-gyōō'i-tē) or

EXIGUOUSNESS *noun.*

EXIGUOUSLY *adv.*

1. That is only for the statistically EXIGUOUS few, that life after death. (W.F. Buckley Jr., *Execution Eve and Other Contemporary Ballads*, G.P. Putnam's Sons, 1975, p. 220)

2. . . . the extra cost of fuel in a jumbo jet as a result of passenger overweight [in luggage] is simply EXIGUOUS. (W.F. Buckley Jr., *Ibid.*, p. 187)

3. . . . give him [the individual] the right of free speech or the right to go to the polling booth, and at best he contributes to a collective determination, contributes as a general rule an EXIGUOUS voice. (W.F. Buckley Jr., *Up From Liberalism*, Arlington House, 2nd Printing 1968, p. 208)

4. The EXIGUOUS setting [of the play, *The Runner Stumbles*, by Milan Stitt] is by Patricia Woodbridge . . . . (Edith Oliver, Review, *The New Yorker*, 5/31/76, p. 51)

5. See (4) under DERACINATE.

EXOPHTHALMOS (ek'sof-thal'məs, -mos) *or* **EXOPHTHALMUS** *or* **EXOPHTHALMIA** *noun* abnormal protrusion of the eyeball, caused by disease or injury.

EXOPHTHALMIC *adj.*

1. Marty Feldman *directing* a movie? The Marty Feldman whose scarecrow physique, Milquetoast manner and EXOPHTHALMIC stare suggest that he needs medical attention? The spirit behind one of the maddest movie projects in the works today is pure FELDMANIA. (Katrine Ames and M. MacPherson, "Feldmania," *Newsweek*, 10/25/76, p. 116)

2. See (1) under CLAUDICANT.

EXORDIUM (ig-zôr'dē-əm, ik-sôr'-) *noun, pl.:* **EXORDIUMS** *or* **EXORDIA** the beginning of anything; the introductory part of an oration or discourse.

EXORDIAL *adj.*

1. There are [in the book, *O America*, by Luigi Barzini] . . . those fights . . . which apparently were deemed necessary for confirming male identity . . . . They were fed with

bootleg liquor, and the EXORDIUM was usually something like "I can lick anybody in this joint." (A. Burgess, Review, *New York Times*, 4/3/77, Section 7, p. 9)

EXPURGATE (ek'spər-gāt') *verb* to amend by removing offensive, obscene, or objectionable matter from (a book, etc.).

EXPURGATION *noun.*

EXPURGATOR *noun.*

EXPURGATORY *or* EXPURGATORIAL *adj.*

1. See (2) under BOWDLERIZE.

2. See (3) under SCATOLOGY.

3. Embattled BOURGEOIS parents of the 1950's, convinced by their shrinks that even the UNEXPURGATED Grimm's fairy tales . . . bred antisocial violence in the young, were appalled to find their children reading in . . . comic books accounts of ball games played with the severed head of a victim whose entrails had been used to make the baselines. . . parents were ready to believe almost any conspiracy theory that EXCULPATED their kids at the expense of someone else: a conspiracy of the masters of media to profit by deliberately corrupting the young (as argued by Frederick Wertham in *Seduction of the Innocent*) or a CABAL of homosexuals (a favorite theory of Gershon Legman's *Love and Death*) against the straight world. . . . (Leslie A. Fiedler, "Up, up and away—the rise and fall of comic books," *New York Times*, 9/5/76, Section 7, p. 10)

4. See (1) under PANJANDRUM.

EXTIRPATE (ek'stər-pāt') *verb* to remove utterly; destroy totally; exterminate; to pull up by or as by the roots; root up.

EXTIRPATION *noun.*

EXTIRPATOR *noun.*

EXTIRPATIVE *adj.*

1. *The Snow Walker* [by Farley Mowat] is a book of tales about the Eskimo, stories ranging from the ancient to the overwhelmingly modern . . . . Mowat draws us into the beauty and anguish of an EXTIRPATED culture; perhaps more than a culture, a microcosmic civilization. (J. Harrison, Review, *New York Times*,

2/22/76, Section 7, p. 4)

2. The illusion of nonconformity [in educational circles] was greatly helped along during the [Senator Joe] McCarthy years, when prominent academic spokesmen ventured hysterical opinions about the death of freedom in the outside world, and its imminent EXTIRPATION in the academic community . . . . Such heady talk persuades the student that the way to nonconformity is—conformity with the precepts of his own intellectual group; which is dominated by liberalism. (W.F. Buckley Jr., *Up From Liberalism*, Arlington House, 2nd Printing 1968, p. 98)

3. See (1) under EXTRAVASATE.

4. It is certainly no part of democratic theory that the Communist Party has a right to free and uninhibited operation. In France and Italy, the Communists as a practical matter are now too powerful to EXTIRPATE. In the U.S. they operate on sufferance. Under a given set of circumstances, the U.S. Communists would certainly be suppressed, just as the German-American Bund was suppressed in 1941. (J. Hart, "Red Pressure in Spain," *Times Herald*, Norristown, Pa., 9/7/76, p. 13)

EXTRAPOLATE (ik-strap'ə-lāt') *verb* (in Statistics) to estimate or infer the value of a variable beyond the known or measured range by assuming the same relationships apply in both the known and unknown ranges; to infer an unknown conclusion or result from something that is known; to speculate or conjecture as to consequences on the basis of known facts.

EXTRAPOLATION *noun*.

EXTRAPOLATIVE *adj*.

EXTRAPOLATOR *noun*.

1. The power of [the movie] "Close Encounters" comes not so much from its careful EXTRAPOLATION of the most respectable UFO data, but rather from the human reality that underlies the whole saucer phenomenon. Astronomer J. Allen Hynek, who worked with [Steven] Spielberg on "Close Encounters," is one of the many scientists who've been forced by the data to suspend their innate skepticism about UFO's . . . . (J. Kroll, "The UFO's Are Coming," *Newsweek*, 11/21/77, pp. 88–89)

2. It is a simple matter of arithmetic to calculate EXTRAPOLATED values for gross national product (GNP) per capita from now until the year 2000 on the assumption that relative growth rates of population and GNP will remain roughly the same . . . . The values shown . . . will almost certainly *not* actually be realized. They are not predictions . . . . It must be recognized, however, that in rejecting EXTRAPOLATED values, one is also rejecting the assumption that there will be *no change* in the system. (Donella H. Meadows, Dennis L. Meadows, Jørgen Randers, William W. Behrens III, *The Limits of Growth*, Potomac Associates and New American Library (Signet), 1972, pp. 49-50)

3. Those Wellesley graduates who stay permanently in the job market . . . work up after 25 years to ceilings that are about equal to the earnings floors of their no more competent cousins and brothers at Dartmouth and Cornell . . . alas, the recent statistics do not show the narrowing of inequality that I had hopefully EXTRAPOLATED a decade ago. (P.A. Samuelson, "Shameful Sex Economics," *Newsweek*, 12/12/77, p. 96)

EXTRAVASATE (ik-strav'ə-sāt') *verb* to force out from the proper vessels, as blood, especially so as to diffuse through the surrounding tissue; to pour forth, as molten lava, from a subterranean source.

EXTRAVASATION *noun*.

1. The question: how can conservatism accommodate revolution? Can the revolutionary essence be EXTRAVASATED and be made to diffuse harmlessly in the network of capillaries that rushes forward to accommodate its explosive force? Will the revolt of the masses moderate when the lower class is risen, when science has EXTIRPATED misery, and the machine has abolished poverty? (W.F. Buckley Jr., *Up From Liberalism*, Arlington House, 2nd Printing 1968, p. 221)

F

FACTITIOUS (fak-tish´ əs) *adj.* artificial, affected, or contrived; not spontaneous, genuine, or natural; forced; feigned.

FACTITIOUSLY *adv.*

FACTITIOUSNESS *noun.*

1. Many of [Geoffrey] Hill's poems [in *Somewhere in Such a Kingdom*] are deep and bitter doubtings as to whether the imaginative life can't too easily become an indulgence in FACTITIOUS high concern . . . . (C. Ricks, Review, *New York Times*, 1/11/76, Section 7, p. 6)

2. [Lionel] Trilling never faltered in his steady commitment to the ideal of autonomy, but what he now thought he saw taking shape was a FACTITIOUS or pseudo-autonomy, the adoption of the adversary program on a relatively massified scale . . . . (S. Marcus, "Lionel Trilling, 1905-1975," *New York Times*, 2/8/76, Section 7, p. 2)

3. See (2) under DERACINATE.

4. By 1968, [Lionel] Trilling had convinced himself that the political issues which paralyzed Columbia University in the spring of that year "were largely FACTITIOUS." [Morris] Dickstein [author of the book, *Gates of Eden: American Culture in the Sixties*], on the other hand, caught in the Columbia uprising a glimpse of what education can become when linked to practice . . . . (C. Lasch, Review, *New York Times*, 3/13/77, Section 7, p. 1)

FAIT ACCOMPLI (fe-tA-kôN-plē´), *pl.*: **FAITS ACCOMPLI** (fe-zA-kôN-plē´) an accomplished fact; a thing already done, so that opposition or argument is useless.

1. And though more [students] than ever piled into buses for a ride to desegregated schools, busing this year was accompanied by a minimum of violence and a growing—if grudging—acceptance of busing as a FAIT ACCOMPLI. (Anon., "Desegregation: Smooth Ride," *Newsweek*, 9/20/76, p. 28)

2. To satisfy the Reagan supporters' stipulation that treaty negotiations [on the Panama Canal] should not be undertaken under duress would require [Panamanian dictator Gen. Omar Torrijos to] say that he has every intention of restraining his students before there is any FAIT ACCOMPLI of violence. (J. Chamberlain, "Panama Negotiations," *Times Herald*, Norristown, Pa., 2/16/77, p. 19)

FANZINE (fan-zēn´) *noun* a periodical written and edited by science-fiction and fantasy enthusiasts and that is frequently prepared by mimeographing.

1. This novel [*Dolores*, by Jacqueline Susann] is a FANZINE version of clippings and rumors about the former First Lady [Jacqueline Onassis] and the people who surround her. The writing is sluggish and the plot limp. (Abby Hirsch, Review, *New York Times*, 7/11/76, Section 7, p. 6)

2. . . . they [children] yearned for a new mythology [in comic books] neither explicitly erotic, overly terrifying nor frankly supernatural, yet essentially PHALLIC, horrific and magical. Such a mythology was waiting to be released in pulp science fiction, a GENRE recreated in the United States in 1926 by Hugo Gernsback . . . . He did not invent the name, however, until 1929, just one year before a pair of 16-year-olds, Jerry Siegel and Joe Shuster, reviewed Philip Wylie's *Gladiator* in one of the

earliest s.f. FANZINES—journals dedicated to amateur criticism of fiction ignored by the critical establishment. (Leslie A. Fiedler, "Up, up and away—the rise and fall of comic books," *New York Times*, 9/5/76, Section 7, p. 1)

3. Initially, the Book Review received a number of letters and calls . . . wondering what the word [FANZINE], used in a Best Seller blurb*, meant . . . we decided to remove FANZINE from the blurb. Readers . . . wrote that FANZINE is in . . . "Webster's Third International" [dictionary] . . . FANZINE's debut in print occurred in 1949 . . . . Now maybe we should all get together and publish a mimeographed newsletter—sort of a "FANZINE" FANZINE. (Anon., "Book Ends," *New York Times*, 12/19/76, Section 7, p. 25)

FARINACEOUS (far′ ə-nā′ shəs) *adj.* consisting or made of flour or meal, as food; containing or yielding starch, as seeds; starchy; mealy in appearance or nature.

FARINOSE *adj.* yielding farina; resembling farina; farinaceous; full of meal; mealy; covered with a mealy powder.

FARINA (fə-rē′nə) *noun* flour or meal made from cereal grains and cooked as cereal, used in puddings, soups, etc; starch, especially potato starch.

1. The committee [of the British Ministry of Agriculture on food standards] was anxious to dispel the argument of some makers [of meat pies] that the meat pie was no more than a "FARINACEOUS article" to which meat was added merely as a flavoring—as little as five percent in some Scottish Forfar Birdies. (Anon., "There'll Always Be An England," *The New Yorker* [reprinted from the *London Sunday Times*], 2/9/76, p. 93)

FARRAGO (fe-rä′gō, rä′-) *noun, pl.: -GOES* a confused mixture; hodgepodge; medley; jumble; confusion.

FARRAGINOUS (fə-raj′ ə-nəs) *adj.* heterogeneous; mixed.

1. At another point [in the book, *Good Evening, Everybody*] he [author Lowell Thomas]

writes of going to Cape Cormorin, on the southern tip of the Indian subcontinent. "I stood alone . . . on the water's edge looking off into the empty distance . . . . I faced about and tried . . . to catch the immensity of the FARRAGO of humanity and hope that stretched away to the north. I could not." (D.R. Boldt, Review, *Philadelphia Inquirer*, 9/26/76, p. 10-H)

2. In [the play, *Dirty Linen & Newfoundland*, by Tom Stoppard], which opened last week in Washington . . . , he [Stoppard] turns the hypocritical hipper-dipper of lecherous legislators into a FARRAGO of verbal PRATFALLS, inadvertent puns, quadruple entendres, EUPHEMISMS and self-exploding lies. Only Stoppard could choreograph such an elegant ballet for foot in mouth. This Select Committee to investigate promiscuity in . . . "both trousers of Parliament," is the most ADDLED colloquium since the Mad Tea Party. (J. Kroll, Review, *Newsweek*, 10/18/76, p. 103)

3. The [IRS tax] code remains our basic tax document, a legal FARRAGO that, as one IRS spokesman has said, "defies human understanding." Prior to last year's Reform Act, it was barely compactible into a single bulky volume. The amending legislation is itself nearly 1,000 pages long. (P. Meyer, "A Short History of Form 1040," *Harper's*, April 1977, p. 24)

4. The moviemakers have tended to play up Papa [Hemingway]'s blatant streaks in MAWKISH romances (*A Farewell to Arms*), pseudoprofound he-man heroics (*For Whom the Bell Tolls*) and FARRAGOES of exotic drinks, sports and ANGST (*The Sun Also Rises*). (C. Porterfield, Review of the movie *Islands In The Stream*, *Time*, 3/21/77, p. 89)

FARTHINGALE (fär′ t͡hing-gāl′) *noun* a hoop or framework worn about the hips to expand a woman's skirt, worn especially in the 16th and 17th centuries; a skirt or petticoat worn over this.

1. According to the APOCRYPHA of the South, the region was once run by cavalier gentlemen and ladies in FARTHINGALES, chased from England by Cromwell and his dour Roundheads. They naturally tended to lord it over the pioneer settlers below them—in the interests of good government. (T. Mathews, *et*

*See (1) above.

al., "The Southern Mystique," *Newsweek*, 7/19/76, p. 30)

FATUOUS (fach' ŏŏ-əs) *adj.* complacently foolish, stupid, or INANE; dim-witted; silly; unreal; illusory; dense.

FATUOUSLY *adv.*

FATUOUSNESS *noun.*

FATUITY *noun* smug foolishness; complacent stupidity; something foolish, as a remark, act, etc.

1. See (1) under IRIDESCENT.

2. From the start it [Jim Lloyd's love for Clemma Zendt] had been a ridiculous thing, scarcely involved with love at all. To speak accurately, it had been nothing but a FATUOUS obsession, but each year it deepened. (J.A. Michener, *Centennial*, Fawcett, 1975, p. 653)

3. One point I think he [Edmund S. Morgan, author of *American Slavery, American Freedom*] misses . . . Bacon's Rebellion excepted, brief and FATUOUS as that was, the bonded servant in Virginia behaved with a docility which his English counterpart never displayed . . . Surely the reason for the passivity of the Virginia bonded servants in the seventeenth century was their youth. The median age in Norfolk County between 1662-1680 . . . was between fifteen and sixteen. (J. H. Plumb, Review, *New York Review of Books*, 11/27/75, p. 4)

4. To think that we instinctively recognize the best is FATUOUS arrogance. . . . The person who hears Bach and finds it "boring" needs to learn that the boredom is in him, not in Bach . . . . Popular music changes every few weeks because it is not satisfying. . . . (Sydney J. Harris, "People aren't born with good taste," *Philadelphia Inquirer*, 10/1/76, p. 9-A)

5. See (1) under EQUANIMITY.

FAUX PAS (fō-pä') , *pl.*: FAUX PAS (fō-päz') a social blunder in manners or conduct; tactless act or remark; indiscretion.

1. So, according to the book [*Tell Them They Are Handsome*, by Janine Alaux], you will never make a FAUX PAS by telling a man that he is handsome, that he looks divine, whether he is a member of the French Academy, a learned scientist, diplomat, political giant, world renowned athlete or young stripling. (Rosette Hargrove, NEA, "Book gives code for women," *Norman* [Okla.] *Transcript*, 6/28/76, p. 4)

2. Two months ago, he [West German Chancellor Helmut Schmidt] set French tempers on edge by comparing Gaullist politicians to Spain's late Fascist dictator, Generalissimo Francisco Franco. He then touched off a furor in Italy by resurrecting the tired joke that Italian tanks have "one forward gear, and three in reverse." . . . neither of those FAUX PAS quite compared with Schmidt's latest misstep . . . Schmidt told reporters that the U.S., West Germany, France and Britain had agreed to deny all future financial aid to Italy if the Communists are given seats in the new Italian cabinet. (M. R. Benjamin, "Schmidt's Lip," *Newsweek*, 8/2/76, p. 35)

3. Carter . . . was occasionally guilty of inaccurate charges and low blows [in the second TV debate with President Ford]—although none of his missteps had the same political or diplomatic reverberations as Ford's FAUX PAS ["there is no Soviet domination of Eastern Europe"]. (R. Steele, *et al.*, "Round Two To Carter," *Newsweek*, 10/18/76, p. 23)

FEBRILE (fē' brəl, feb' rəl) *adj.* pertaining to, caused by, or marked by fever; feverish.

FEBRILITY *noun.*

1. Planning a family vacation is a matter of infinite negotiations as the head of the household attempts to accommodate everyone's tastes and whims. Naturally he whims some, loses some, in an effort to schedule the Cooperstown baseball shrine, an art gallery, an antique market and a genuine prehistoric dinosaur park and rock garden all in one FRACTIOUS, FEBRILE day. (Anon., "Travel '76," *Time*, 6/28/76, p. 62)

2. [Hugh] Trevor-Roper [author of the book, *Hermit of Peking*] writes that [Sir Edmund] Backhouse as a young man "took refuge in the fashionable nonconformity of his time and class: the 'aestheticism,' the FEBRILE eroticism, the aggressive, insolent deviation of the 1890's." (P. Theroux, Review, *New York*

Times, 4/24/77, Section 7, p. 36)

FECKLESS (fek´ lis) *adj.* without worth, spirit, or value; weak; ineffective; inefficient; incompetent; irresponsible; lazy; indifferent; careless.

FECKLESSLY *adv.*

FECKLESSNESS *noun.*

1. In both [books, *H.G. Wells and Rebecca West*, by G.N. Ray; and *H.G. Wells*, by Norman and Jeanne MacKenzie] there was an easygoing, charming, irresponsible, and largely absentee father, and in both there was a dutiful, much put-upon, and visibly wronged mother who devoted herself to the task of raising her children in the face of the difficulties created by the father's FECKLESSNESS. (A. West, Review, *Harper's*, January 1975, p. 84)

2. *Futility* [by Wilhelm Gerhardie] describes the involvement of a young British officer with a FECKLESS Russian family hoping for the restoration of its mining fortunes . . . . (W. Clemons, Review, *Newsweek*, 12/29/75, p. 54)

3. A FECKLESS Western Europe (caused by a weakened NATO) would then stand with a patsy Uncle Sam and allow the Soviets to intimidate this once strong and free Western civilization. (N. Thimmesch of *L.A. Times*, "Democracy, Even in Italy, Worth the Price," *Daily Oklahoman*, Okla. City, 1/15/76, p. 14)

4. "I [Earl Grebe] want to move west," he said. "I want to work where I can own my own place." It was the timeless cry of the man who dreamed of moving on . . . . It . . . had motivated the most diverse types of men: the renegade trapper, the devoted Mormon, the FECKLESS son, the daring entrepreneur . . . . It was the authentic vision of the pioneer American, the dream of freedom and more spacious horizons. (J.A. Michener, *Centennial*, Fawcett, 1975, p. 885)

5. Still, with less serious and talented authors, she [Gail Godwin] shares an essentially reductive image of women, seeing them as almost universally passive and FECKLESS. (Jane Larkin Crane, Review of *Dream Children*, by Gail Godwin, *New York Times*, 2/22/76, Section 7, p. 5)

6. See (1) under RIFE.

7. See (1) under IRASCIBLE.

8. Being a religious people, the Irish see the hand of God in human affairs . . . . The really important things in life . . . cannot be planned for or bargained for. So why not leave them to God's decision? In different circumstances, this folk wisdom can be taken for FECKLESSNESS, fatalism or simple courage. (W. V. Shannon, "The lasting hurrah," *New York Times*, 3/14/76, Section 6, p. 75)

9. The KAMIKAZE attack on the home of [Yoshio] Kadama, the right-wing militarist who stands accused of bribing Japanese politicians on Lockheed's behalf, was launched by a 29-year old part-time pilot and porn-film bit player named Mitsuyasu Maeno. He had no known political connections, and police could find no motive for the act; a somewhat FECKLESS character, Maeno had been most conspicuous in the current erotic film, *Tokyo Emmanuelle*, in which he made love to porn star Kumi Taguchi while piloting his plane. (D. Pauly, *et al.*, "Fastened Seat Belts," *Newsweek*, 4/5/76, p. 65)

10. [Wayne] Hays also threatened Republicans voting against a $10,000 a year raise in congressmen's expenses with cutting the already small minority representation on committees. Naturally, FECKLESS Republicans complied. (N. Thimmesch, "Scandal Probe Lacks Fervor," *Daily Oklahoman*, Okla. City, 6/18/76, p. 10)

11. See (5) under NEMESIS.

12. . . . last week in Ohio the President added to his repertory of FECKLESS rhetorical mannerisms by constantly referring to himself in the third person—"I'm confident that President Jerry Ford can be elected." (Anon., "GOP DONNYBROOK," *Time*, 6/21/76, p. 15)

13. See (3) under ASPERITY.

FECUND (fē´ kund, -kənd, fek´ und, -ənd) *adj.* prolific; fruitful; producing or capable of producing offspring, or fruit, vegetation, etc.; very productive or creative in an intellectual sense.

FECUNDITY (fi-kun'di-tē) *noun.*

FECUNDATE *verb* to make prolific or fruitful; to impregnate; fertilize; pollinate.

FECUNDATION *noun.*

FECUNDATOR *noun.*

FECUNDATORY *adv.*

1. It was obvious to me [Russel Wren] now that Teddy Villanova likely had some connection with the Wyandotte Club. My FECUND response to Peggy [Tumulty]'s despair that there was no money for me (and thus none for her) in the Bakewell killing, my "maybes" now can be interpreted as referring to an INCHOATE, a dim inclination, hardly yet a true plan, to penetrate a roomful of gangsters and, isolating him who was probably Mr. Big, shake him down for a generous fee in return for which I'd stay mum about the corpse. (Thomas Berger, *Who Is Teddy Villanova?*, Delacorte Press/Seymour Lawrence, pp. 43–44)

FEISTY (fī'stē) *adj.* quick-tempered, quarrelsome, aggressive, or belligerent; full of spirit; lively, energetic, or exuberant.

FEISTINESS *noun.*

1. . . . Mahlon [Zendt] told his brothers, "We must all watch Levi. He's getting FEISTY." The three other Zendts agreed. In their earlier days each of them had gone FEISTY at some time or other, had wanted to smoke tobacco, or taste beer at taverns along Hell Street [in Lancaster, Pa.], or ogle the girls, but each had suppressed these urges and had stuck to butchering. (J. A. Michener, *Centennial*, Fawcett, 1975, p. 304)

2. I would rather not have heard about Steve and Patty making free of her grandfather's fantasy-land estate, getting caught in a thunderstorm and tumbling "back in a hot tub, this time a bubble-bath, with two large slices of watermelon." Nor do [Steven] Weed's efforts to convey [in *My Search for Patty Hearst*] how cute Patty was, her FEISTY, little-girl charm, survive transcription. (Sara Sanborn, Review, *New York Times*, 2/15/76, Section 7, p. 5)

3. Most sensible people are going to agree with much of what Mr. [Robert] Brustein says [in *The Culture Watch*] . . . . Popular culture leaves lots to be desired . . . . The FEISTINESS that was supposed to liberate us in the 1960's

had a component of jackboots and goose steps we hadn't suspected. (J. Leonard, Review, *New York Times*, 2/15/76, Section 7, p. 10)

4. See (1) under NE PLUS ULTRA.

5. Occasionally [as children in Oakland's Chinatown], when we all got FEISTY during the Chinese New Year celebrations, we'd have firecracker wars, tossing missiles across hastily barricaded streets. (W. Wong, "Celebrating the Chinese New Year," *Wall Street Journal*, 3/4/77, p. 12)

FELLAH (fel' ə) *noun, pl.:* FELLAHS or FELLAHIN (fel'ə-hēn) a native peasant or laborer in Egypt, Syria, and other Arabic-speaking countries.

1. Egyptians have been making and drinking wine and beer since Pharaonic times and it is a myth . . . that the otherwise very devout Moslem FELLAHIN do not drink. If the government decides to enforce the law [against drinking], Egyptians are likely to come up with their own ingenious brand of speakeasies and bathtub gin. (*The London Economist*, "Promises to be tough nightmare: Egypt passes tough, puritanical law," reprinted in *Norman* [Okla.] *Transcript*, 6/16/76, p. 6)

2. He [the Egyptian man in the street] calls Sadat "Al-Misri"—the Egyptian—and describes him—correctly—as "a man who wants to live and let live." Sadat—a FELLAH, a man of the soil, . . . was born in Meit Abu el-Kom, a secluded village about halfway between Cairo and Alexandria . . . . Sadat still keeps a house at Meit Abu el-Kom. (H. J. Taylor, "Sadat The Statesman," *Times Herald*, Norristown, Pa., 12/1/76, p. 21)

3. The poor Egyptian FELLAH visited a soothsayer for advice. "I am poor and hungry and I can't sleep any more for worrying about feeding my family. What can I do?" he asked. The soothsayer studied the peasant's palm intently, then said: "Your worries are over." The FELLAH brightened. "You mean I'm going to be rich?" The soothsayer shook his head. "No. I mean you will get used to being poor." This is an APOCRYPHAL tale which sometimes is told not only about Egypt, but also about other poor countries in the Middle East. (R. Vicker, "Poverty and Debt Create Tightrope for

Egypt's Sadat," *Wall Street Journal*, 3/4/77, p. 12)

FELLATION (fə-lā'shən) or **FELLATIO** (fə-lā'shē-ō) *noun* buccal coitus; a form of sexual activity in which gratification is accomplished by buccal intromission of the penis; oral stimulation of the penis, especially to orgasm.

1. See (1) under PEDICATION.

2. Other periodicals, with names such as *Naughty Horny Imps*, *Children-Love* and *Child Discipline*, portray moppets in sex acts with adults or other kids. The films are even raunchier. An 8-mm. movie shows a ten-year-old girl and her eight-year-old brother in FELLATIO and intercourse. (Anon., "Child's Garden of Perversity," *Time*, 4/4/77, p. 55)

3. "My brother-in-lore a cocksucker sold me a Valiant once that was a lemon" [said Sam Polidor]. He glared while I [Russel Wren] tried to puzzle out whether his relative and the FELLATOR were one and the same, then went on before I succeeded. (Thomas Berger, *Who Is Teddy Villanova?*, Delacorte Press/Seymour Lawrence, p. 230)

FENESTRATION (fen' i-strā' shən) *noun* (in Architecture) the arrangement of windows and doors of a building; (in Medicine and Surgery) a perforation in a structure or an operation to effect such an opening.

FENESTRATED or **FENESTRATE** *adj.* having windows, openings, or perforations; characterized by windows.

FENESTRA (fi-nes' trə) *noun*, *pl.*: **FENESTRAE** (-trē) a small opening or perforation, as in a bone or membrane; a transparent spot in an otherwise opaque surface, as in the wings of certain butterflies and moths; any small opening in a membrane.

FENESTRAL *adj.*

1. Many FENESTRATIONS, open spaces like windows, perforated the vertebrae of her [diplodocus's] neck and tail, thus reducing their weight. These intricate bones . . . were so exquisitely engineered that they can be compared only to the arches and windows of a GOTHIC cathedral. (J.A. Michener, *Centennial*, Fawcett, 1975, p. 78)

FERAL (fer'əl, fer'əl) *adj.* existing in a natural state, as animals or plants; not domesticated or cultivated; wild; savage; having reverted to the wild state, as from domestication; of or characteristic of wild animals; ferocious; brutal; uncivilized.

1. In 1543 he [the horse] would accompany Coronado on his quest for the golden cities of Quivira, and from later groups of horses brought by other Spaniards some would be stolen by Indians and a few would escape to become FERAL, once domesticated but now reverted to wildness. (J.A. Michener, *Centennial*, Fawcett, 1975, p. 97)

2. Mr. [Al] Demsey is not telling [in *Dog Kill*] a canine horror story . . . . His FERAL pack is composed of a mixture of breeds and personalities most of whom have their special doggy virtues. But their leader, an escaped Doberman . . . , has been inbred and brutalized by man. (M. Levin, Review, *New York Times*, 5/30/76, Section 7, p. 14)

3. How strange (and somehow restful) to find yourself back in the world of American naturalism [when reading *Waiting For the Earthquake*, a book by Lawrence Swain] after all these years!—back in the ATAVISTIC, sweat-stained grimy arena of natural selection and FERAL instincts. . . .(J.R. Frakes, Review, *New York Times*, 2/27/77, Section 7, p. 27)

FESTOON (fə-stoōn') *noun* a wreath or garland of flowers, foliage, ribbon, paper, etc. hanging in a loop or curve; any carved or molded decoration resembling this.

FESTOON *verb* to adorn or hang with festoons; to form into a festoon or festoons.

FESTOONERY *noun* an arrangement of festoons.

1. He [Ronald Beard] embraced her [Paola Belli] an instant, he naked, she dressed like a soldier . . . . She tried a forkful of spaghetti, nodding hot-mouthed that they were done, then FESTOONED his rod with a few white strands, like a maypole. (A. Burgess, *Beard's Roman Women*, McGraw-Hill, 1976, p. 44)

2. Speaking of which takes me [Russel Wren] back to my childhood, when our bathroom was controlled by my sisters; and when they

were physically absent, the place was FES-TOONED with their wet underwear. (Thomas Berger, *Who Is Teddy Villanova?*, Delacorte Press/Seymour Lawrence, 1977, p. 70)

3. See (2) under ANTIQUARIAN.

FETISHISM (fet′i-shiz′əm, fē′ti-) or **FET-ICHISM** *noun* belief in, worship of, or use of fetishes; the compulsive use of some object or non-genital part of the body as a stimulus in attaining sexual gratification, as a shoe, foot, glove, lock of hair, etc.; blind devotion.

FETISHIST *noun.*

FETISHISTIC *adj.*

FETISH or **FETICH** *noun* an object regarded as having magical power; any object, idea, etc. eliciting unquestioning reverence, respect, or devotion; any object or non-genital part of the body that causes a habitual erotic response or fixation.

1. The movie [*Fox*] is a comedy about the pains of upward assimilation: Fox, hopelessly infatuated, submits to his lover Egon's ruthless schooling in the BOURGEOIS FETISHES of gourmet food, boutique clothes, and ghastly antique furniture . . . . Fassbinder's stinging coldness . . . forces us to concentrate on political meanings: the working class will only be corrupted by trying to join the BOURGEOISIE . . . the oppression of the straight world isn't nearly as vicious as the way homosexuals exploit one another. (D. Denby, Review, *New York Times*, 2/1/76, Section 2, p. 13)

2. But the Arttransition conference found [Gyorg] Kepes [first director of MIT's Center for Advanced Visual Studies] . . . in a RUMINATIVE mood, warning against the "dangerous boomerang of a cult of newness" and cautiously suggesting the follies of "technological FETISHISM. (B. Forgery, "Arttransition is still in transition," *Smithsonian*, March 1976, p. 91)

3. The commitment by the liberals to democracy has proved obsessive, even FETISHISTIC. It is part of their larger absorption in Method, and Method is the fleshpot of those who live in metaphysical deserts . . . . Democracy must be justified by its works, not by doctrinaire affirmations of an intrinsic goodness that no mere

method can legitimately lay claim to. (W.F. Buckley Jr., *Up From Liberalism*, Arlington House, 2nd Printing 1968, pp. 148–149)

4. See (7) under ANTHROPOMORPHIC.

5. See (2) under ALEATORIC.

FETOR (fē′tər) or **FOETOR** *noun* any strong, disagreeable smell; stench.

1. . . . it is appropriate that [Jim] Harrison [author of the book, *Farmer*], a man who can choose a learned word like "FETOR" over its synonym "stench," should also enrich his rustic hero's thoughts with some basic details of rural life: oiling an old harness, butchering hogs. (R. Sokolov, Review, *Newsweek*, 8/30/76, p. 70)

2. . . . the tremendous beast [Great Dane dog], assuming the middle-distance stare of canine preoccupation, hunched itself and defecated abundantly. The wind changed, and I was swept into the lobby on a stream of FETOR. (Thomas Berger, *Who Is Teddy Villanova?*, Delacorte Press/Seymour Lawrence, 1977, p. 69)

FEY (fā) *adj.* supernatural; unreal; enchanted; whimsical; strange; otherwordly.

1. See (1) under MOREL.

2. Cat books are appearing on best-seller lists. B. Kliban's softcover *Cat* . . . , about the whimsical, delightfully FEY personality of cats, sold 165,000 copies; another 20,000 are in print. And Kliban is planning a calendar for Christmas and poster for Mother's Day. (Mary Daniels, *Chicago Tribune*, "Morris did it: Cats gaining as pets, thanks to TV," reprinted in *Philadelphia Inquirer*, 10/24/76, p. 2-I)

FINAGLE (fi-nā′gəl) *verb* to get, arrange, or maneuver by cleverness, persuasion, etc., or especially by craftiness, trickery, etc.; to practice deception or fraud; to trick or cheat (a person) (often followed by *out of*); to get or achieve (something) by guile or trickery; to wangle; to use craftiness or trickery.

FINAGLER *noun.*

1. Where we seek answers we are offered [in the *Final Report*, by the Watergate Special Prosecution Force] evasions; where we look for

a recounting of facts and a historical record we are given prosecutorial pussyfooting. Take this example, typical of many, addressed to the dozens of charges made about Bebe Rebozo's financial FINAGLING on Nixon's behalf: ". . . it was concluded by the prosecutors that the evidence would not support an indictment." (Kirkpatrick Sale, Review, *New York Review of Books*, 12/11/75, p. 5)

2. See (1) under RUBATO.

3. The concept for. . .[the book] *1876* must have emerged for [its author, Gore] Vidal in 1972 or 1973, when the country was enduring the shocks of Watergate and reeling under the revelations of BANAL corruption. Why not, then, give the public in the aftermath of Watergate a novel about real, all-American corruption, with classic scoundrels like Boss Tweed . . . ? Give them a real impeachment with William Belknap, President Grant's Secretary of War, and even a stolen election (Samuel J. Tilden outpolled Rutherford B. Hayes, but Hayes FINAGLED a victory in the electoral college). (J. Reston Jr., Review, *Chronicle of Higher Education*, 7/19/76, p. 10)

4. Finally, by ill-conceived and incessant legal FINAGLING—its own legitimacy, indeed, is under challenge in the courts—MAC [Municipal Assistance Corp. of N.Y.C.] has forfeited all claim to the moral imperatives prerequisite to any official watchdog. Drunks, to change the metaphor, just don't make good bartenders. (R.M. Bleiberg, "Drunk for Bartender?" [Editorial], *Barron's*, 2/21/77, p. 7)

FIN DE SIÈCLE (faN d sye′kl⁹) end of the century, especially of or pertaining to the end of the 19th century; formerly used to refer to progressive ideas and customs, but now generally used to indicate decadence.

1. See (1) under MAGDALENE.

2. In *The Obsolete Necessity*, Kenneth [M.] Roemer analyzes the 160 known utopian works published between 1888 and 1900—by far the largest number published in any comparable span in American history . . . . Other historians have found the outlook of FIN DE SIÈCLE America a gloomy one, but Roemer is the first to find its counterpart in utopian writing of the

period. (H.P. Segal, Review, *Chronicle of Higher Education*, 9/27/76, p. 17)

3. But [John] Ensor soon tired of BOURGEOIS respectability. He joined Les Vingt, an AVANT-GARDE group in Belgium with a FIN DE SIÈCLE taste for symbolism, BAUDELAIRE and the occult. Exhibitors turned down much of his work and . . . an overpowering resentment and disgust began to dominate his art. (M. Stevens, "The Energy of Rot," *Newsweek*, 1/31/77, p. 57)

4. See (2) under ODALISQUE.

FINICKY (fin′ə-kē) or **FINICAL** *adj.* excessively particular, exacting, or fastidious; difficult to please; overly dainty; fussy.

FINICALLY *adv.*

FINICALITY or FINICKINESS *noun.*

1. See (3) under APOCALYPSE.

2. Where Ford's press was presidential, Carter's turned FINICAL—a daily catastrophe report on his EQUIVOCATIONS, his trips of the tongue, even such. . .mishaps as a baggage truck bumping into a campaign plane. (P. Goldman and Eleanor Clift, "Mr. Outside In Stride," *Newsweek*, 11/1/76, p. 30)

FLACCID (flak′sid) *adj.* soft and limp; not firm; flabby; hanging in loose folds or wrinkles; lacking force; weak; feeble.

FLACCIDLY *adv.*

FLACCIDITY or FLACCIDNESS *noun.*

1. *The Romantic Englishwoman*—Michael Caine is the pulp-writer husband, and Glenda Jackson is the discontented wife, and this [film] is another FLACCID essay on infidelity, with prissy-mouthed Helmut Berger as the gigolo-intruder. (Anon., Review, *The New Yorker*, 2/9/76, p. 20)

2. See (1) under SMORGASBORD.

3. She [Sharon Fields] looked down. His [Adam Malone's] sorry penis was still FLACCID. (I. Wallace, *The Fan Club*, Bantam edition, 1975, p. 335)

4. The dictatorial father of Freud's time is extinct. Once he roamed the land in vast herds, snorting virile snorts and refreshing himself in

austere men's clubs . . . before thundering home to preside over his cave. In the 1960's he survives as a FLACCID PARODY of his grandfather, a comic figure on televised situation comedies whose CRETIN blunders are deftly corrected by his amused family. He is cheap household help. (W. Manchester, Commencement Address, University of Massachusetts, 6/13/65, mimeographed, p. 8)

5. See (1) under GLISSADE.

6. Many private school officials suspect that the main reason for the prep-school comeback is growing parental dissatisfaction with the FLACCID standards of public schools . . . . Many parents also cite the prep schools' traditional emphasis on student codes of conduct—and their freedom from disruptive teacher strikes and school-budget crises. (Merrill Sheils and F.V. Boyd, "Hello, Mr. Chips," Newsweek, 11/1/76, p. 81)

FLAGELLATE (flaj'ə-lāt') verb to whip; scourge; flog; lash.

FLAGELLATE or **FLAGELLATED** adj. having flagella (whiplike appendages, for locomotion in bacteria, or threadlike shoots or runners, as in strawberries).

FLAGELLANT noun a person who flagellates or scourges himself for religious discipline.

FLAGELLANT adj. flagellating; severely criticizing.

FLAGELLATION noun.

FLAGELLATOR noun.

1. See (1) under INGRATE.

2. But it is time we stopped FLAGELLATING ourselves because of practices that had become commonplace in Washington long before Richard Nixon bugged himself. (J. Chamberlain, "What Value Do Revelations Have?," Daily Oklahoman, Okla. City, 4/14/76, p. 8)

3. The liberal wing of the [Democratic] party is moralistic, hostile to economic growth, guilty about America's role as a major power, and endlessly self-FLAGELLATING about non-white minorities at home and majorities abroad. (J. Hart, "Carter," Times Herald, Norristown, Pa., 11/9/76, p. 11)

FLAMBEAU (flam' bō) noun, pl.: -BEAUX (-bōz) or -BEAUS a flaming torch; a large, ornamental candlestick, as of bronze.

FLAMBOYANT adj. flamelike or brilliant in form or color; strikingly bold or brilliant; too showy; too ornate; conspicuously dashing and colorful; florid; elaborately styled, as speeches; noting or pertaining to French GOTHIC architecture, especially of the late 15th century, characterized by the use of elaborate, flamelike tracery of windows and florid decoration.

FLAMBOYANTLY adv.

FLAMBOYANCE or **FLAMBOYANCY** noun.

1. The distinction between baseball and life was as the transience of the FLAMBEAU to the permanence of night. (R. Kahn, The Boys of Summer, Harper and Row, 1971, p. 43)

2. See (2) under INTERNECINE.

3. He [Arthur Rubinstein] arises at 8 . . . , hungry for breakfast, but first does 20 minutes of setting-up exercises. However, he gets his most strenuous exercise by playing the piano—which is perhaps exercise enough if you play as FLAMBOYANTLY as Arthur Rubinstein. (D. Henahan, "This ageless hero, Rubinstein," New York Times, 3/14/76, Section 6, p. 18)

4. After becoming army chief of staff . . . he [Portugal's first freely elected President, Antonio Ramalho Eanes] cracked down on an army that was infamous for its FLAMBOYANT appearance—long hair, colored T shirts and gaudy silk scarves; its lack of discipline and its propensity for posturing on the political scene. (Fay Willey, Loren Jenkins, "Portugal: Back to Basics," Newsweek, 7/12/76, p. 36)

5. See (4) under TROMPE L'OEIL.

FLAN (flan, flän) noun an open tart filled with custard, fruit, cream, cheese, etc.; (in Spanish cookery) a sweetened egg custard.

1. And a mark of acceptance of the hysterical gooey FLAN into the PANTHEON of human competitive endeavor has been accorded by its current inclusion in the Guinness Book of Records. It is now duly registered that the annual World Custard Pie Championship . . . is held at . . . Coxheath, . . . England. Competitors are ESOTERICALLY required to hurl a pie

of no more than 10¾ inches in diameter at a
target face set at a distance of 8 ft. 3-7/8
inches, and are awarded six points for a bull's-
eye. (P. Ryan, "Pie in the eye is fun—for somebody else," *Smithsonian*, October, 1976,
p. 168)

FLATULENT (flach′ ə-lənt) *adj.* genera-
ting gas in the stomach or intestines, as certain
foods; attended with, caused by, or suffering
from, such an accumulation of gas; having
unsupported PRETENSIONS; pompous; PRETEN-
TIOUS; TURGID; windy or empty in speech.

FLATULENCE *noun.*

1. We are slipping now, and it is clearly not on
account of a universal national FLATULENCE.
(W.F. Buckley Jr., *Execution Eve and Other
Contemporary Ballads*, G.P. Putnam's Sons,
1975, p. 241)

2. The identical letter [stating that new
standards of integrity, responsiveness, and
accountability would be expected of Presidential candidates] went to other avowed candidates for the presidency. Their FLATULENT
responses soon came pouring in . . . Sargent
Shriver sent two pages of FULSOME allegiance.
Mo Udall sent three. (J.J. Kilpatrick, "[Eu-
gene] McCarthy Keeps Rein on Privacy," *The
Daily Oklahoman*, Okla. City, 2/4/76, p. 8)

3. Yet it [*Chanel*, by Edmonde Charles-Roux]
is an excessively long and humorless work.
FLATULENT Gallic bombast stifles any vivid
portraiture. (Francine Gray, Review, *New
York Review of Books*, 12/11/75, p. 45)

4. . . . the entertainer [in New York's Central
Park] offers the audience, particularly those
who are poor and ungrateful, a few ideas for
making money. One of them is a deodorant—
sandalwood, jasmine, musk, etc.—for the
FLATULENT—this being the one orifice and
odor that the cosmetics industry has failed to
exploit. (T. Solotaroff, "Alive and together in
the park," *New York Times*, 6/13/76, Section
6, p. 42)

5. The chance that Hitler was part Jewish is
minimal, but it weighed heavily upon his
mind. He was constantly ill: uncontrollably
FLATULENT, he feared cancer, thought at the
time he came to power that he had only a few

years to live. He developed heart disease . . . .
(P. S. Prescott, Review of *Adolf Hitler*, by John
Toland, *Newsweek*, 9/20/76, p. 87)

6. Explosive FLATULENCE of bus. (Thomas
Berger, *Who Is Teddy Villanova?*, Delacorte
Press/Seymour Lawrence, 1977, p. 237)

7. See (6) under COMATOSE.

FLEWS (flōōz) *noun, pl.*: the large, PENDU-
LOUS sides of the upper lip of certain dogs, as
bloodhounds.

1. So the dog will not get itself hung up on
barbed wire or thorn bushes while working a
trail, a bloodhound's head must be equipped
with a great deal of loose skin. Yankee had
enough skin for Siamese twins . . . . His
FLEWS—the PENDULOUS corners of his upper
lip—were long and deep and doleful . . . . (R.
Caras, "A Boy's Best Dog," *New York Times*,
3/4/76, Section 6, p. 80)

FLUMMERY (flum′ ə-rē) *noun* oatmeal or
flour boiled with water until thick; a soft custard or blancmange; meaningless flattery or
silly talk; foolish humbug; empty compliment;
nonsense.

1. . . . Frederick Warne & Co. has decided
this year to celebrate the 75th anniversary of its
first trade publication of the book [*The Tale of
Peter Rabbit*, by Beatrix Potter] that has sold
approximately 20 million copies around the
world. Its two commemorative offerings are
The History of the Tale of Peter Rabbit—an
informative, 63-page monograph . . . —and
Peter Rabbit's Natural Foods Cookbook—a
lavishly printed piece of FLUMMERY consisting
of . . . a series of soporific recipes that include
. . . "Timmy Willy's Sunny Sunday Scrambled
Eggs." (J. Cott, "Peter Rabbit and Friends,"
New York Times, 5/1/77, Section 7, p. 25)

FORFEND (fôr-fend′) *verb* to forbid; to
ward off; prevent; to fend off; avert; to defend, secure or protect.

1. "I am not an anti-Washington candidate,"
[Jimmy] Carter said. His hosts [in Washington]
seemed equally eager to assure him that they
did not represent—heaven FORFEND—some
kind of anti-Carter CABAL. (Meg Greenfield,
"Mr. Carter Goes to Washington," *Newsweek*,

3/29/76, p. 100)

FRACTIOUS (frak'shəs) *adj.* peevish, irritable, or quarrelsome; hard to manage; refractory or unruly; rebellious; cross.

FRACTIOUSLY *adv.*

FRACTIOUSNESS *noun.*

1. The two lead ones were Levi's own . . . the two nearest the wagon were Mahlon's, and they might do, but the two bought horses in the middle . . . did not feel comfortable working behind the lead pair and showed their uneasiness at every turn in the road . . . . Patiently Levi corrected their FRACTIOUSNESS, and at last he had the satisfaction of feeling them working together. (J.A. Michener, *Centennial*, Fawcett, 1975, pp. 330–331)

2. Levi entered the [Big Blue] river, leading the oxen, which did not want to follow. For one dangerous moment they were FRACTIOUS, but he quieted them, and the big beasts found their footing and proceeded to the spot at which they had to swim. (J.A. Michener, *Ibid.*, p. 372)

3. At a signal from their leader they [the outnumbered Pawnee] retreated eastward to the gibes of the Cheyenne, . . . and all would have passed easily except that one Pawnee lagged, his pinto proving FRACTIOUS, and the farther behind he fell, the more abuse he took, until he turned on his horse and shouted something at the Cheyenne, whereupon Jake Pasquinel and two Cheyenne braves . . . killed him. (J. A. Michener, *Ibid.*, p. 415)

4. A farm which had been worth twenty thousand dollars had been left desolated, and he [Frank Skimmerhorn] had moved homeless from one Minnesota town to the next, hearing the terrible stories of damage done by the Sioux—a hundred ranches burned, two hundred people scalped, a whole section of the nation in disarray, and all because of a few FRACTIOUS Indians. (J.A. Michener, *Ibid.*, p. 479)

5. Their job would be simple: take some twenty-eight hundred FRACTIOUS longhorns safely across thirteen hundred miles of the west's most bruising country. (J.A. Michener, *Ibid.*, p. 535)

6. Mr. [Derek Curtis] Bok's war [as President of Harvard] in 1971 involved a FRACTIOUS faculty and a substantial body of leftist students who in 1969 had been fully prepared to destroy Harvard in order to save the world . . . . (N.W. Aldrich Jr., "Harvard On The Way Down," *Harper's* March 1976, p. 40)

7. . . . what was once a healthy American pragmatism has deteriorated into a wayward relativism. It is one thing to make the allowances to reality that reality imposes. . . . But it is something else to run before political or historical impulses merely because FRACTIOUS winds begin to blow, and to dismiss resistance [to liberalism] as foolish, or perverse idealism. And it is supremely wrong, intellectually and morally, to abandon the norms by which it becomes possible, viewing a trend, to pass judgment upon it. . . . (W.F. Buckley Jr., *Up From Liberalism*, Arlington House, 2nd Printing, 1968, p. 221)

8. See (3) under BUMPTIOUS.

9. See (1) under FEBRILE.

FRANGIBLE (fran'jə-bəl) *adj.* breakable; fragile.

FRANGIBILITY *noun.*

1. CBS-TV had signed him [Evel Knievel] up for a 90-minute *Jaws* show: he was to vault his Harley [motorcycle] over a 64-ft.-wide tub full of "killer sharks." On a trial run before the show, Knievel made it over the sharks but skidded into a retaining wall . . . and for the 13th time in his FRANGIBLE career broke some bones: the right forearm and the left collarbone (his 55th and 56th breaks). (Anon., "People," *Time*, 2/14/77, p. 66)

FRENETIC (frə-net'ik) *adj.* frantic; frenzied.

FRENETICALLY *adv.*

1. Can the Kennedy legacy be transferred to his FRENETIC brother-in-law (Sargent Shriver)? (P.J. Buchanan, "Can Shriver Stand Legacy?", *Saturday Oklahoman & Times*, Okla. City, 2/7/76, p. 8)

2. . . . he [Kubrick] functions best away from the FRENETIC pressures of American life and moviemaking . . . . (Judith Crist, Review of

the film, *Barry Lyndon*, *American Way*, February 1976, p. 29)

3. *Dog Day Afternoon* . . . The pure show-biz energy of the [film] tale—based on a real New York episode—takes it sometimes into the realm of Broadway-comedy glibness, but the mask of FRENETIC cliché doesn't spoil moments of pure reporting on people in extremity . . . . (Anon., Review, *The New Yorker*, 2/9/76, p. 17)

4. "I [Joseph Bean] act as agent for Hermann Bockweiss . . . Silversmith from Germany. Makes wonderful trinkets for the Indian trade." Pasquinel shrugged his shoulders, and Bean continued FRENETICALLY: "Heard you were the best trader on the river. Says he will advance the money for your trip." (J.A. Michener, *Centennial*, Fawcett, 1975, p. 235)

5. Going to his wagon, he [Nacho Gomez] produced three calves, and the Mexicans groaned with delight . . . . Mr. Poteet watched as Nacho entered into FRENETIC bargaining. (J.A. Michener, *Ibid.*, p. 574)

6. Perhaps the most lasting local effect of Professor Wright's FRENETIC invasion [to excavate a skeleton of eohippus, the ancestor of the horse] came in something he casually said to Jim Lloyd as he was packing up after his dig at Rattlesnake Buttes . . . "In their day they [eohippuses] must have been as common as rabbits." (J.A. Michener, *Ibid.*, p. 652)

7. See (1) under SHTICK.

8. Like many encyclopedias, EMD [*Encyclopedia of Mystery and Detection*, by Chris Steinbrunner and Otto Penzler] is a good browsing book, made even more so by its compilers' FRENETIC enthusiasms. The reader will be delighted by all kinds of oddball entries. (N. Callendar, Review, *New York Times*, 4/25/76, Section 7, p. 10)

9. In one FRENETIC decade the Republic survived the rage of the blacks, the revolt of its students, the burning of its cities, rising crime and drug abuse, Watergate and Vietnam. (Yorick Blumenfeld of Editorial Research Reports, "Independence really mystifies Europe," *Norman*, [Okla.] *Transcript*, 7/7/76, p. 6)

FRISSON (frē-sōN′) *noun, pl.*: -SSONS

(-sōN′) a shudder or shiver, as of excitement, fear, or pleasure.

1. It is in the latter works [drawings by Claes Oldenburg, David Hockney, Jim Dine and Andy Warhol], of course, that the exhibition [*Drawing Now: 1955-1975*, at the Museum of Modern Art] provides its intended FRISSON, designed to challenge expectation and reorient esthetic taste . . . (H. Kramer, Review, *New York Times*, 2/1/76, Section 2, p. 31)

2. See (1) under AUTOEROTICISM.

3. . . . I found the four pages on tales of alien beings or states [in the book, *Adventure, Mystery and Romance*, by John G. Cavelti], for which Cavelti has relatively little feeling, the weakest in the book. The characteristic FRISSON in these comes not from an experience of TRANSCENDENCE, but from confrontations with the uncanny apparitions of repressed sex. (G. Stade, Review, *Chronicle of Higher Education*, 9/13/76, p. 16)

4. These are funny scenes [in *Who Is Teddy Villanova?*, a book by Thomas Berger] not simply because they lack justification [for the violence described], but because they are also brilliantly written. They should remind us of the great delight we take in gratuitous, ugly SADISTIC FRISSONS which have become conventional in recent movies, not only in detective thrillers. (L. Michaels, Review, *New York Times*, 3/20/77, Section 7, p. 26)

FROUFROU (frōō′frōō′) *noun* a rustling or swishing, as of a silk skirt when the wearer moves; excessive ornateness or affected elegance; elaborate decoration, especially on women's clothing.

FROUFROU *verb* to move about with a rustle of draperies.

1. The setting [of the play, *A Flea In Her Ear*, by Georges Feydeau] by Robert U. Taylor . . . works most adroitly, while John Helgerson's costumes are frivolously FROUFROU. (C. Barnes, Review, *New York Times*, 12/19/76, Section 1, p. 61)

2. Sometimes, returning as late as three or four in the morning but still not sleepy, he [Jerry Westbury] would hammer on her [his

stepmother's] door to wake her, though often she was awake already; and when she had put on her make-up, he set her on his bed in her FROU-FROU dressing-gown with a king-sized *creme de menthe frappee* in her little claw . . . . (J. LeCarré, *The Honourable Schoolboy*, Alfred A. Knopf, 1977, pp. 92–93)

FULMINATE (ful'mə-nāt') *verb* [Archaic] to thunder and lighten; to explode with sudden violence or a loud noise; detonate; to shout out denunciations, decrees, or the like (usually followed by *against*); to issue or pronounce with vehement denunciation, condemnation, or the like.

FULMINATE *noun* one of a group of unstable, explosive compounds derived from fulminic acid, especially its mercury salt.

FULMINATION *noun* a violent denunciation or censure; violent explosion.

FULMINIC *adj.* highly explosive; unstable.

FULMINOUS *adj.* of, pertaining to, or resembling thunder and lightning.

FULMINANT *adj.* occurring suddenly with great intensity or severity; fulminating.

1. I decided to stick to the point until he would commit himself on the behavior of Mr. [Congressman Wayne] Hays [who had called Congressman B. Carroll Reece a double-crosser]. The best I succeeded in getting out of liberal publicist George Hamilton Coombs—whose FULMINATIONS over the Zwicker incident [a reference to Senator Joseph McCarthy's insinuation that General Zwicker was a pro-Communist unfit to wear his uniform] shattered steel and concrete—was: "Perhaps Mr. Hays' conduct was a little undisciplined." (W. F. Buckley Jr., *Up From Liberalism*, Arlington House, 2nd Printing, 1968, p. 46)

2. . . . the Met season will open on October 11 . . . . There will be the usual FULMINATIONS about the conducting staff . . . . Somehow the Metropolitan Opera will survive. (H.C. Schonberg, "Next Season at the Met—The Accent Will Be French," *New York Times*, 3/28/76, Section 2, p. 17)

3. See (1) under USURIOUS.

4. The manner and tone of James R. Schles-

inger, former secretary of defense, haven't changed since he signed on with the Johns Hopkins School of Advanced International Studies. He remains blunt, LACONIC and wry . . . . He is passionate about what he believes in but he doesn't FULMINATE. (N. Thimmesch, "Lack of American Commitment Major Concern for Schlesinger," *Saturday Oklahoman & Times*, Okla. City, 4/24/76, p. 10)

5. In his simple, impressive descriptions of dedicated lives and eternal causes [in *Inner Companions*], the hysteria and FULMINATIONS of the daily press die away . . . he [Colman McCarthy] is celebrating their victories and encouraging us to make an attempt at ours. (Doris Grumbach, Review, *Smithsonian*, January 1976, p. 102)

6. See (4) under ENTROPY.

FULSOME (fŏōl'səm, ful'-) *adj.* offensive to good taste, especially as being excessive or insincere; gross; disgusting; sickening; repulsive.

FULSOMELY *adv.*

FULSOMENESS *noun.*

1. See (2) under FLATULENT.

2. . . . the insistence on rhyme [in translating Greek tragedy] over hundreds of lines of dramatic dialogue exacts a heavy price in warped syntax, violent inversions, and, above all, FULSOME padding. This was the target of one of Eliot's lethal shots: he pointed out that Medea's prosaic six (Greek) words—"I am a dead woman, have lost all joy in life"—were transformed by [Gilbert] Murray into the ROCOCO jewel, "I dazzle where I stand/ The cup of all life shattered in my hand." (B. M. W. Knox, Review of Aeschylus: *Suppliants*, translated by Janet Lembke; Aeschylus: *Seven Against Thebes*, translated by Helen Bacon and Anthony Hecht; and Aeschylus: *Prometheus Bound*, translated by James Scully and C. John Herington, *New York Review of Books*, 11/27/75, p. 27)

FUMAROLE (fyŏō'mə-rōl') *noun* a vent or hole in a volcanic area, from which smoke and gases rise.

FUMAROLIC (fyōō mə-rol'ik) *adj.*

1. At the bottom of the *Herald Tribune*, as in a valley of FUMAROLES, one was conscious of pressure from underneath. (R. Kahn, *The Boys of Summer*, Harper and Row, 1971, p. 60)

FUNDAMENT (fun' də-mənt) *noun* the buttocks; the anus; the characteristics of a region, as climate, land forms, soils, etc.; a basal principle or foundation.

1. He [Ronald Beard] washed himself thoroughly nevertheless and, on an unbidden image of Saul Bellow the Canadian Jewish novelist for some reason frowning at him, paid special attention to his FUNDAMENT. While on this he heard the telephone and slithered and fell towards it all soapy-arsed. (A. Burgess, *Beard's Roman Women*, McGraw-Hill, 1976, p. 51)

2. Before I [Russel Wren] could make that clear to the stocky detective, he fetched me a kick in the FUNDAMENT that brought me in contact with the floor along my entire length. (Thomas Berger, *Who Is Teddy Villanova?*, Delacorte Press/Seymour Lawrence, 1977, p. 90)

FUNGIBLE (fun' jə-bəl) *adj.* designating movable goods, such as grain or money, any unit or part of which can replace another, as in discharging a debt; interchangeable.

FUNGIBLE *noun* a fungible thing, as money or grain.

FUNGIBILITY *noun.*

1. He [Avery Brundage] had little to do with . . . Russia's successful challenge of Canadian HEGEMONY in hockey, though his agents tried to abort the contest on the grounds that pitting the Russian amateurs against Canadian professionals caused a FUNGIBLE situation: now the amateurs would be thought professionals, and likewise their colleagues in other athletic disciplines. (W.F. Buckley Jr., *Execution Eve and Other Contemporary Ballads*, G.P. Putnam's Sons, 1975, p. 237)

FUSTIAN (fus' chən) *noun* originally a stout coarse fabric of cotton and flax, but now a thick cotton cloth with a short nap, as corduroy, velveteen, etc.; inflated, PRETENTIOUS, or TURGID language in writing or speaking; bombast; rant; claptrap.

FUSTIAN *adj.* made of fustian; pompous or bombastic.

1. Tarden, the hyper-secret agent [in the book, *Cockpit*, by Jerzy Kosinski] . . . can in no way be . . . placed anywhere other than in Tarden's own brutally SADISTIC SOLIPSISTIC world of Faustian FUSTIAN. (C. Ricks, Review, *New York Review of Books*, 11/27/75, p. 44)

G

GAFFE (gaf) *noun* a blunder; FAUX PAS; tactless remark or action.

1. This is, of course, the idea of the Jew as a historic scapegoat for social hatreds—a well-worn idea. . . . "I don't know whether it's true or not" Jimmy Carter said. Can it be that he is not as much at home with ideas as with people? Or — after the "ethnic purity" GAFFE —

is it a case of once-burned-twice-careful? (M. Lerner, of *Los Angeles Times*, "Carter: a calculated artlessness," reprinted in *Norman* [Okla.] *Transcript*, 6/28/76, p. 6)

2. [Jimmy] Carter . . . cast a long, cool shadow at a time when Ford and Reagan were sweating miserably through the last, grueling rounds of their Great Delegate Chase. He was

also husbanding his $21.8 million campaign kitty . . . —and avoiding the dangers of overexposure and GAFFES, in the media and on the stump. (T. Mathews and J. Doyle, "Front-Porch Politics," *Newsweek*, 8/9/76, p. 23)

3. Across the nation, voters of Eastern European origin responded with shock and anger to President Ford's assertion [in the second TV debate with Carter] that "there is no Soviet domination in Eastern Europe." Republicans sought to downplay the GAFFE as simply an unfortunate verbal stumble, while the President himself attempted to clarify his position. (Susan Fraker and F. Maier, "Jerry Ford Drops a Brick," *Newsweek*, 10/18/76, p. 24)

4. The very day the first of the [Joe] Garagiola shows [with President Ford] went on the air, Ford, in a stump-speech, referred to S.I. Hayakawa, California Republican senatorial candidate as "Hiawatha." TV, at least, presented a controlled atmosphere in which GAFFES like that could be edited out of the sound track. (Lee Winfrey, "Ford failed his own commercials," *Philadelphia Inquirer*, 11/10/76, p. 11-C)

5. The President can hardly be delighted with [his brother] Billy's noisy admiration of George Wallace, and a shudder passed through the White House after Billy's one major GAFFE—a "nigger in the woodpile" joke at an Oakland cocktail party last spring. (P. Axthelm, "Brother Billy," *Newsweek*, 11/14/77, p. 33)

GALABEEAH (gə-lä'bə-yə) or **GALABEAH** or **GALABIYA** or **GALABEEYEH** or **GALABIEH** *noun* a smock-like garment worn by Egyptian natives.

1. The average Egyptian earns under $200 a year and is apt to be skin and bones under his flowing GALABIEH. Meanwhile, his government is destitute . . . . (R. Vicker, "Poverty and Debt Create Tightrope for Egypt's Sadat," *Wall Street Journal*, 3/4/77, p. 12)

2. Narrow streets [in Bulaq, a slum district of Cairo] weave through the district. Men in long, flowing GELABEYAS, or robes, sit in cafes puffing on hoses connected to water pipes. Women dressed in black and wearing thick black mascara about their eyes walk to markets, children sidesaddle on their shoulders, a pot or basket on their heads. (T. M. Phelps, "Egypt's Burden of Poverty Seen Shifting to City," *New York Times*, 6/12/77, Section 1, p. 9)

GALLIMAUFRY (gal' ə-mô' frē) *noun* a hodge-podge; jumble; FARRAGO; confused medley; a ragout or hash made from meat scraps.

1. The old guard [in the universities] has liberalized its curriculum so significantly that the once easily defined liberal arts courses are a GALLIMAUFRY of everything from Greek philosophy to modern dance. (H.I. London, "The Case for Nontraditional Learning," *Change*, June 1976, p. 28)

2. [Bartolomé Estaban] Murillo was dedicated to drawing on every level—as sketch, as plan-for-painting, as finished work in itself. Each of these stages is present at [the] Princeton [Art Museum] in a GALLIMAUFRY of mediums (brush, pen, ink, wash, chalk). (D. Davis, "Sentimental Journey," *Newsweek*, 1/10/77, p. 73)

3. If the word "gimmick" did not already exist . . . , one would need to invent it to describe the GALLIMAUFRY with which the BBC producers thought it necessary to liven up John Kenneth Galbraith's already lively text [for the TV show, *The Age of Uncertainty*]. (M. Howard, Review of *The Age of Uncertainty*, a "telebook" by John Kenneth Galbraith, *New York Times*, 4/3/77, Section 7, p. 3)

GALLINACEOUS (gal' ə-nā' shəs) *adj.* pertaining to or resembling the domestic fowls; belonging or pertaining to the order *Galliformes* comprising grouse, pheasants, turkeys, partridges, domestic fowls, etc., which nest on the ground.

GALLINACEAN *noun* a gallinaceous bird.

1. Nicknamed because of his GALLINACEOUS similarity to Big Bird of *Sesame Street*, [Mark] Fidrych [Detroit Tiger pitcher] came to town with an impressive 11-3 won-lost record, and a certifiably manic style of pitching. (Anon., "People," *Time*, 8/16/76, p. 41)

GALVANIC (gal-van' ik) *adj.* of, pertaining to, produced by, or caused by an electric current; producing, stimulating, or stimulated as if by an electric shock; startling; shocking; convulsive.

GALVANICALLY adv.

GALVANISM noun electricity produced by chemical action.

GALVANIZE verb to apply an electric current to; to stimulate as if by an electric shock; startle; excite; to plate (metal) with zinc, originally by galvanic action.

GALVANIZATION noun.

1. Starting from the parent [Union Pacific] line at Julesburg, the rails were thrust westward [toward Centennial] at a GALVANIC rate: ten-, eighteen-, twenty-two miles a day. (J.A. Michener, *Centennial*, Fawcett, 1975, p. 683)

2. In the census records for Alamance County, N.C., for 1870, he [Alex Haley, author of the book, *Roots*] came across the names of his great-grandfather Tom Murray, blacksmith, and his children. "Man, that was GALVANIZING!" he says. "There are something about seeing all those names that grabbed me. I ain't been loose since." (P.D. Zimmerman, Review, *Newsweek*, 9/27/76, p. 96)

3. See (4) under POLEMIC.

4. See (1) under BRIO.

GANGLION (gaṅg′glē-ən) *noun, pl.* GANGLIA (gaṅg′glē-ə) or GANGLIONS a mass of nerve cells serving as a center from which nerve impulses are transmitted; a center of intellectual or industrial force, energy, activity, etc.

1. When the GANGLIA of the New York literary world begin to twitch in this manner [a reference to the abundant publicity *Kinflicks*, a book by Lisa Alther has received], it is a sure sign that something more than literary merit is at work. First books by unknowns do not become events simply because they are good. Frequently, as Mae West once observed in another context, goodness has nothing to do with it. (P. Gray, Review, *Time*, 3/22/76, p. 80)

2. HD [Huntington's Disease] involves the death of cells in two areas of the brain: in the cerebral cortex, causing mental symptoms, and in the basal GANGLIA, producing movement disorders. The onset is insidious, often marked by irritability, restlessness, forgetfulness and subtle changes in speech or balance. (M. Clark and Mariana Gosnell, "The Cruelest Killer," *Newsweek*, 9/27/76, p. 68)

GASTRILOQUIST (gas-tril′ō-kwist) *noun* ventriloquist.

1. It seemed to be a store but it was more like a theater. Its front was plastered with signs announcing Mr. L. Reed, GASTRILOQUIST Extraordinary; Master Haskell, Wizzard of the Ages, THAUMATURGIST and Metamorphisist;... and Last Time to See the Gigantic Elephant Discovered in These Regions by Dr. Albert C. Koch, now of London. (J. A. Michener, *Centennial*, Fawcett, 1975, p. 356)

GAUCHERIE (gō′shə-rē) *noun* lack of social grace; awkwardness; tactlessness; an act, movement, expression, etc., that is GAUCHE.

GAUCHE (gōsh) *adj.* lacking social grace; awkward; tactless.

GAUCHELY adv.

GAUCHENESS noun.

1. I held my tongue, but not in resistance to GAUCHERIE.... R. Kahn, *The Boys of Summer*, Harper and Row, 1971, p. 60)

2. After eight years of living together he [Paul Gegauff, in the French film, *Une Partie de Plaisir*] encourages [his mistress] to take young lovers.... The GAUCHERIE and intellectual PRETENSIONS of her amourous choices enrage him ... he cannot bear what he originally encouraged with urbanity. (D. Ryan, Review, *Philadelphia Inquirer*, 9/26/76, p. 6-H)

GEHENNA (gi-hen′ə) *noun* the valley of Hinnom, near Jerusalem, where propitiatory sacrifices were made to Moloch [II Kings 23:10]; any place of extreme torment or suffering; hell (in the New Testament); a prison or torture chamber.

1. See (2) under BILLINGSGATE.

2. Writing [about the trial of Al Goldstein on

pornography charges in Wichita, Kansas] in a recent issue of Penthouse magazine . . . , Mr. [Alan] Dershowitz [a Harvard professor of Law] said: ". . . the Southern District of New York would have been the natural locus of the . . . trial. But . . . the Feds took out a map of middle America and sought out a Bible belt jurisdiction where Goldstein was likely to be viewed as the devil incarnate and Screw magazine as his GEHENNA Gazette." (S. Grover, "Pornography and Community Standards," *Wall Street Journal*, 2/23/77, p. 24)

GEMÜTLICH (gə-mYt'liKH) or **GEMUETLICH** *adj.* agreeable, cheerful, cozy, etc.: indicating a general sense of well- being.

GEMÜTLICHKEIT or **GEMUETLICHKEIT** *noun.*

1. Ingrid Haebler is regarded by many people, including many Viennese, as the QUINTESSENTIAL Viennese pianist. She exudes GEMÜTLICHKEIT, that peculiar blend of geniality and warm sentiment that is as much a part of legendary Vienna as unsentimental toughness is part of legendary Brooklyn. (D. Henahan, Review of Ingrid Haebler's piano concert at Hunter College, *New York Times*, 3/8/76, p. 32)

2. Unlike other Mozart operas, *The Magic Flute* depicts neither a class struggle, nor, as in *Figaro*, a class hatred. But the opera does contain two truly revolutionary innovations . . . . The first is that Papageno's deficiencies are presented as GEMÜTLICH . . . . The second is that because of its spoken dialogue the opera must be performed in the vernacular. (R. Craft, Review, *New York Review of Books*, 11/27/75, p. 19)

3. If pulled punches, blank cartridges and simulated agony [on TV] pall, we can shift, for the mere price of a ticket, to the less GEMÜTLICH but more vivid precinct of arena or stadium, where the blood is real, the bone sometimes actually snaps (*audibly* to the better seats!), the flesh is truly assailed. And if all else fails, there is Evel Knievel, reciting BOWDLERIZED Kipling before he puts his life on the line. For real. For money. For us! (J. Lipton, "Here Be Dragons," *Newsweek*, 12/6/76, p. 17)

GENEALOGY (jē'nē-ol'ə-jē, -al'-) *noun* a record or account of the ancestry and descent of a person, family, group, etc.; the science or study of family ancestries and histories; lineage; ancestry; pedigree.

GENEALOGICAL *adj.*

GENEALOGICALLY *adv.*

GENEALOGIST *noun.*

1. See (5) under ENNUI.

2. In some areas, the disease [Huntington's Disease] has been traced back GENEALOGICALLY for centuries. Many . . . of the U.S. cases are thought to stem from three men, probably related, who moved from a village in England to Winthrop, Mass., in 1630. (M. Clark, Mariana Gosnell, "The Cruelest Killer," *Newsweek*, 9/27/76, p. 68)

GENOCIDE (jen'ə-sīd') *noun* the deliberate and systematic extermination of a national, a religious, or an ethnic group (first applied to the attempted extermination of the Jews by Nazi Germany).

GENOCIDAL *adj.*

1. Where Indians were concerned, the Colorado press felt few restraints, and one finds in the files numerous invocations to GENOCIDE. Editorial policy called for the extermination of the Indians, and that . . . meant killing every Indian within the state borders. (J. A. Michener, *Centennial*, Fawcett, 1975, p. 666)

2. By remaining mute—or worse—in the face of military takeovers (Latin America), repression (South Korea), torture (Chile, Brazil), and GENOCIDE (Burundi, Bangladesh), the U.S. pays a price internationally and does needless violence to its own constitutional values. (R. J. Lieber and D. Rothchild, "Costs of Amorality," *Harper's*, January 1975, p. 78)

GENRE (zhän'rə) *noun* genus; kind; sort; style; a class or category of artistic or literary endeavor having a particular form, content, technique or the like.

1. See (4) under PSEUDONYM.

2. See (4) under ROMAN À CLEF.

3. See (1) under SCHMALTZ.

4. In a profession that parcels out prestige primarily to the authors of books, Herbert Gutman is something of an ANOMALY. Here is a historian who until now has published only articles—with the sole exception of his recent, book-length demolition of Robert Fogel's and Stanley Engerman's *Time on the Cross*. But Gutman's articles are a GENRE to themselves. (R. W. Fox, Review of *Work, Culture and Society in Industrializing America*, by Herbert Gutman, *Chronicle of Higher Education*, 5/24/76, p. 21)

5. See (2) under SCHLOCK.

6. See (2) under AFICIONADO.

7. The historical novel is a brutal GENRE precisely because it must compel credible life to be pressed through the mesh of OMNISCIENCE. The novelist must know it all—the clangors and alarms of his chosen age, its books, music, art, architecture, its language and intellection; but knowing all these, the novelist must still exhibit them with throb and urgency. The historical novelist must palm his OMNISCIENCE. It's a trick, and perhaps for that reason so few serious novelists try the medium. (A.A. Cohen, Review of *The Abyss*, by Marguerite Yourcenar, translated by Grace Frick in collaboration with Marguerite Yourcenar, *New York Times*, 7/11/76, Section 7, p. 7)

8. See (3) under HOMILY.

9. See (2) under FANZINE.

10. See (7) under SOLIPSISM.

GENUFLECT (jen'yŏŏ-flekt') *verb* to bend the knee or knees in reverence or worship; to express a servile attitude; to act in a submissive or servile way.

GENUFLECTION (jen'yŏŏ-flex'shən) *noun.*

1. It is . . . plain that newspapers constantly find use for confidential communications they feel they cannot transmit. They sit on them, glorying in the possession of knowledge but deterred by reasons of libel or taste or GENUFLECTIONS to national security from letting the readers in on the secret. (A. Cockburn, "The Psychopathology of Journalism," *New York Review of Books*, 12/11/75, p. 29)

2. . . . Jimmy Carter is forced to be a kind of prince, protected by federal centurions, insulated from everyday life, venerated beyond reason and financed in his lofty existence by $21 million from the GENUFLECTING citizenry. (T. Tiede, "Splendid Isolation and Jimmy Carter," *Times Herald*, Norristown, Pa., 10/28/76, p. 23)

GERARCHY (jer' är-kē) *noun* obsolete form of HIERARCHY.

1. The Hispanos [of New Mexico are] Catholic, devout, in a CHTHONIC way . . . [and constitute] a tenacious, tranquil GERARCHY, loosening perhaps under our time's familiar MORDENTS. (E. W. Count, Review of *The Old Ones of New Mexico*, a book by Robert Coles, *The Key Reporter*, Summer 1976, p. 6)

GERONTOCRACY (jer' ən-tok' rə-sē) *noun* government by a council of elders; a governing body consisting of old men.

GERONTOCRATIC *adj.*

1. No better news has come to the Republican camp this Spring than the unconfirmed report that a lifeboat full of aging New Frontiersmen, captained by W. Averell Harriman of the Georgetown GERONTOCRACY, has been whistled aboard the presidential vessel of Jimmy Carter. (P. J. Buchanan, "Reagan Could Be Best Thing for GOP," *Saturday Oklahoman & Times*, Okla. City, 5/15/76, p. 12)

GERRYMANDER (jer'i-man'der, ger'-) *verb* to divide a state, county, etc. into election districts so as to give advantage to one political party [after Elbridge *Gerry* (governor of Massachusetts, whose party redistricted the state in 1812) + (sala)*mander*, whose shape the map of Essex County, Mass., resembled after the redistricting]; to manipulate unfairly so as to gain advantage; to engage in gerrymandering.

GERRYMANDER *noun* a rearrangement of voting districts to the advantage of one political party by concentrating the voting strength of the other party in as few districts as possible.

1. Each time Muhammad [Ali] escaped [Antonio Inoki's head butts to the groin] by scram-

bling to the ropes—a gesture that required the referee to halt the action under the GERRYMANDERED rules. (P. Axthelm, "Rope-a-Dopes," *Newsweek*, 7/4/76, p. 93)

2. A number of racial cases will come to the [Supreme] Court . . . . In New York, under Justice Department orders, the state set up ten legislative districts with populations at least 65 per cent non-white. A group of Hasidic Jews in Brooklyn, whose voting bloc was diluted by the GERRYMANDER, contend that they have been discriminated against because of race. (J. K. Footlick, Lucy Howard, "New Term, New Court," *Newsweek*, 10/11/76, p. 86)

3. Though he [Thomas E. Watson] was a competent congressman—for example he worked with Jimmy Carter's grandfather, a postmaster, to legislate the first Rural Free Delivery—he was too much of a threat to the established order . . . . First they [his opponents] GERRYMANDERED Watson's congressional district so as to prevent his reelection in 1892. Then . . . they stole the 1894 election in one of the most shameful frauds in U.S. history; there were 11,240 registered district voters that year, but Watson's opponent received a majority of 13,780 ballots . . . . Distraught and bitter, Watson became a virulent racist, once describing Booker T. Washington as a "gorilla." (T. Tiede, "Tom Watson's War With Bourbons," *Times Herald*, Norristown, Pa., 12/10/76, p. 17)

4. In 1974, the New York Legislature rearranged state Assembly and Senate districts in Brooklyn to give blacks and Puerto Ricans more voting strength. It was a GERRYMANDER, pure and simple: four districts were redrawn to produce a 65 per cent non-white majority . . . . Last week, the U.S. Supreme Court ruled, 7 to 1, that using race as the primary criterion in drawing legislative boundaries was not unconstitutional. The GERRYMANDER had been challenged by a community of 30,000 Hasidic Jews, who live in an area of Brooklyn called Williamsburg . . . . the new boundaries had split the districts, thus diluting the Hasidic Jews' political influence. They argued that this amounted to racial discrimination against whites . . . . (J. K. Footlick, "Court Docket," *Newsweek*, 3/14/77, pp. 97–98)

GLABROUS (glā′ brəs) or **GLABRATE** (glā′ brāt, -brit) *adj.* smooth; bald; without hair, down, or fuzz.

GLABROUSNESS *noun.*

1. Another few strokes of a comb and he [the detective] would be totally GLABROUS of crown. (Thomas Berger, *Who Is Teddy Villanova?*, Delacorte Press/Seymour Lawrence, 1977, p. 122)

GLISSADE (gli-säd′, -sād′) *noun* a skillful glide over snow or ice in descending a mountain, as on skis or a toboggan; (in dancing) a sliding or gliding step.

GLISSADE *verb* to perform a glissade; to slide or glide.

GLISSADER *noun.*

1. . . . he [Jack Fincher, author of the book, *Human Intelligence*] is . . . asserting that the left hemisphere [of the brain] gives us "the theory of relativity and drafts of the Magna Carta," while the right hemisphere "paints the Sistine chapel and composes *The Flight of the Bumblebee*." This is . . . a huge jump, which any properly cautious scientist would have to deprecate. Having achieved this GLISSADE, . . . Mr. Fincher is able to make any further leap his argument requires, his general thesis being that Western civilization has cultivated the rational left hemisphere to the detriment of the intuitive right hemisphere. All of this, of course, has a familiar ring: the book is, in part, a rather FLACCID reworking of Charles Reich and Theodore Roszak, with ample doses of McLuhan thrown in along the line. (R. Zoellner, Review, *Chronicle of Higher Education*, 9/27/76, p. 18)

GLOSSOLALIA (gläs′ə-lā′lē-ə, glôs′-) *noun* an ecstatic or apparently ecstatic utterance of unintelligible speechlike sounds, viewed by some as a manifestation of a deep religious experience; gift of tongues; speaking in tongues (a prayer characterized by incomprehensible speech originating in primitive Christianity and now practiced by Pentecostal groups in ecstatic forms of worship); nonsensical talk; gibberish.

GLOSSOLALIST (glo-sol′ə-list′) *noun.*

1. While Baptist theology remains conservative, and the "inerrancy" of the Bible remains a common article of faith, the Baptists frown on the emotional phenomena known as the charismatic movement. In the past year, six churches in Texas, Ohio and Louisiana were "disfellowshipped" by their local associations for supporting faith healing and GLOSSOLALIA (speaking in tongues). (Anon., "Let the Church Stand Up," *Time*, 6/21/76, p. 53)

GLOTTOCHRONOLOGY (glot' ō-krə-nol' ə-jē, glot'ə-) *noun* the lexicostatistic study of the relations between the members of a family of languages having a common origin in order to estimate the time of their divergence.

1. As to the fact that the Ute and Aztec spoke languages derived from the same root language, you might want to introduce your readers to GLOTTOCHRONOLOGY, the science of dating origins by language attrition. (J.A. Michener, *Centennial*, Fawcett, 1975, p. 210)

GNOMON (nō'mon) *noun* an early astronomical instrument consisting of a vertical shaft, column, or the like, for determining the altitude of the sun or the latitude of a position by measuring the length of its shadow cast at noon; the raised part of a sundial that casts the shadow.

1. Now [in the high Renaissance world] we have . . . the sun compass with its GNOMON, the shadow of which will tell us the correction. . . . (M. Obregon, "Magic of discovery lures astronauts as it did Argonauts," *Smithsonian*, April 1976, p. 83)

GNOSTICISM (nos'tə-siz'əm) *noun* a system of belief combining ideas derived from Greek philosophy, Oriental mysticism, and ultimately, Christianity, and stressing salvation through gnosis.

GNOSIS (nō' sis) *noun* positive, intuitive knowledge in spiritual matters.

GNOSTIC *noun* a member of any of certain heretical early Christian mystical sects that claimed that matter was evil and denied that Christ had a natural corporeal existence.

GNOSTIC *adj.* of, pertaining to, or having

knowledge, especially of spiritual or mystical things; (if capitalized) pertaining to or characteristic of the GNOSTICS.

1. It [Mecca] was the crossroads of two of the most important trade routes of the seventh century . . . . Wedged in thus between the Sasanian empire . . . Hellenism, ICONOLATRY, and the ecclesiastical spirit—it was exposed as well to Judaism, GNOSTICISM, and the oratorical "moralism" of Bedouin nomads. Muhammad drew on all of these in articulating his prophecy. (C. Geertz, Review of *The Venture of Islam: Conscience and History in a World Civilization. Vol. 1: The Classical Age of Islam; Vol. 2: The Expansion of Islam in the Middle Periods; Vol. 3: The Gunpowder Empire and Modern Times*, by Marshall G. S. Hodgson, *New York Review of Books*, 12/11/75, p. 20)

GOLIARD (gōl'yərd) *noun* any of a class of wandering scholar-poets of the late Middle Ages who wrote satirical Latin verse, often served as minstrels and jesters, and were noted for their rioting and intemperance.

GOLIARDIC *adj.*

1. During a quarter century of poetic folly, I have become more and more GOLIARDIC, PERIPATETIC and simply bizarre. (J. Williams, "Paying Respects," *New York Times*, 12/19/76, Section 7, p. 27)

GOSSAMER (gos'ə-mər) or **GOSSAMERY** or **GOSSAMERED** *adj.* light, thin, and filmy.

GOSSAMER *noun* a filmy cobweb floating in the air or spread on bushes or grass; a very thin, soft, filmy cloth; anything like gossamer in lightness, flimsiness, etc.

1. It [Carter's campaign for the Presidency] traded in personality rather than program; its hallmark was the Carter smile, its genius the Carter gift for surrounding an issue—or submerging it in the GOSSAMER promise of a government "as decent . . . as compassionate . . . as filled with love as our people are." (P. Goldman, "Sizing Up Carter," *Newsweek*, 9/13/76, p. 59)

2. The conducting [by Sarah Caldwell, of

Mikhail Glinka's opera, *Russlan and Ludmilla*, at the Opera Company of Boston] was strong when it had to be, GOSSAMER light when that was necessary. (William Bender, Review, *Time*, 3/21/77, p. 66)

GOTHIC or **GOTHIC** (goth´ik) *adj.* noting or pertaining to a style of literature characterized by a gloomy setting, grotesque or violent events, and an atmosphere of degeneration and decay; pertaining to the Middle Ages; barbarous; uncivilized; rude.

GOTHICALLY or GOTHICALLY *adv.*

GOTHICNESS or GOTHICNESS *noun.*

1. Among other things, [James L.] Browning [chief prosecutor] deflated [F. Lee] Bailey's airy argument that Patty [Hearst] had been brainwashed; he won most of the trial's pivotal battles over evidence; he forced Patty to take the Fifth Amendment 42 times, undermining her GOTHIC story of kidnapping, rape, indoctrination, and terror-stricken flight. (T. Mathews, *et al.*, "Patty: Guilty," *Newsweek*, 3/29/76, p. 23)

2. *Clara Reeve*, by Leonie Hargrave . . . . The sedate manners, the secret obsessions of Victorian England lovingly distilled into a PHANTASMAGORIC dream, the QUINTESSENTIAL GOTHIC novel. (Anon., Review, *New York Times*, 6/27/76, Section 7, p. 31)

3. See (1) under MINATORY.

4. See (4) under PSEUDONYM.

5. See (1) under FENESTRATION.

6. See (3) under NYMPHET.

GÖTTERDÄMMERUNG (goet´ əR-dem´ ə-Rōong´) *noun* (In German mythology) the destruction of the gods and of all things in a final battle with evil powers [literal meaning: twilight of the gods].

1. See (3) under ONTOLOGY.

2. The May 1976 issue of Vision . . . gives a sampling of LACHRYMOSE statistics . . . . Concerning ownership of the capital of leading firms in sixteen European countries, "the state crops up in 40% of them." . . . The Dutch, German and Spanish governments respectively now take in 46, 39, and 22 percent of their GNP's, spending about half for welfare purposes (pensions, health, etc.) . . . . I do not interpret these . . . facts as omens of GÖTTERDÄMMERUNG . . . . Please omit flowers and black cloth as premature [for capitalism]. (P.A. Samuelson, "Capitalism in Twilight?," *Newsweek*, 6/7/76, p. 76)

3. In a bloody, one-man blitzkrieg, he [muscle-builder Frederick Cowan] killed five men—three blacks, an Indian and a white policeman—and wounded five others [in New Rochelle, N.Y.]. Then he put a .45 to his temple and joined his old idol—Adolf Hitler—in suicide. Cowan's GÖTTERDÄMMERUNG fell on Valentine's Day. (T. Mathews and Susan Agrest, "The Nazi of New Rochelle," *Newsweek*, 2/28/77, p. 30)

GRACILE (gras´il) *adj.* gracefully slender; slender; thin.

GRACILITY (gra-sil´i-tē, grə-) *noun.*

1. Their argument [that of Sir Edmund Backhouse and J. O. P. Bland, in their two studies on China published in 1910 and 1914] is so cogent, the insider's view so persuasive, their style so GRACILE, that they are frequently quoted, and even a relatively recent book . . . contains passages . . . from . . . Backhouse and Bland. (P. Theroux, Review of *Hermit of Peking*, a book by Hugh Trevor-Roper, *New York Times*, 4/24/77, Section 7, p. 1)

GRAMA (grä´mə, gram´ə) or **GRAMA GRASS** *noun* any range grass of the genus Bouteloua, of the western and southwestern U.S.

1. On July 5 [1844] the farmers [migrating westward] saw their first buffalo grass, and the next day their first GRAMA. They studied each, pulling the short stems apart and judging that nothing much could come of such stuff. (J.A. Michener, *Centennial*, Fawcett, 1975, p. 374)

2. "True as I'm standin', friends [said the old-time cowboy], that's how stockmen discovered that the useless, brown, scrawny buffalo grass and the blue GRAMA was solid feed, mebbe the best there is . . . ." (J.A. Michener, *Ibid.*, p. 519)

GRANDILOQUENT (gran-dil´ə-kwənt) *adj.*

speaking or expressed in a lofty, high-flown, pompous, or bombastic style.

GRANDILOQUENCE *noun* speech that is lofty or pompous in tone.

GRANDILOQUENTLY *adv.*

1. They aspired to "the honor and freedom of a Harvard permanent appointment," as [McGeorge] Bundy has GRANDILOQUENTLY described it, because they were enthusiastic about studying and talking and writing about certain things, or simply because they were good at it . . . . (N. W. Aldrich Jr., "Harvard On The Way Down," *Harper's*, March 1976, p. 48)

2. See (2) under PROLIX.

3. See (1) under SONOROUS.

4. *The Wind Will Not Subside* [subtitled *Years in Revolutionary China*, a book by David and Nancy Dall Milton] contains occasional patches of GRANDILOQUENT prose echoing the stilted POLEMICS of Peking. (R. Bernstein, Review, *Time*, 4/19/76, p. K9)

5. . . . Longfellow has described Cincinnati as "the Queen City of the West," Churchill has called it "the most beautiful inland city in America," and others have referred to it as "the London of the West," "the Paris of the West," and "the Berlin of the West." The locals, however, eschew such GRANDILOQUENT descriptions. Instead, they refer to themselves as "the machine tool capital of the world." (Skip Myslenski, "Reds reflect the city that nurtures them," *Philadelphia Inquirer*, 10/3/76, p. 5-E)

6. But it was in Shostakovich's massive Symphony No. 5 that [conductor Riccardo] Muti and the [Philadelphia] orchestra really soared . . . . Their GRANDILOQUENT approach produced a big sound, setting the framework for the following movements. (J. V. R. Bull, "Muti, orchestra: Exciting," *Philadelphia Inquirer*, 10/30/76, p. 4-B)

7. See (3) under SHAMUS.

GRAVAMEN (grə-vā'men) *noun, pl.:* **GRAVAMENS** or **GRAVAMINA** (grə-vam'ə-nə) (in legal usage) the essential part of an accusation, namely, that which weighs most heavily or importantly against the accused; a grievance.

1. I very much appreciate your candor in the matter of the alleged lapse in taste in the current NR [National Review]. There are several objections, but the GRAVAMEN appears to be directed against . . . the use of the one word [pussy] conjoined with the verb "stroke." (W. F. Buckley Jr., *Execution Eve and Other Contemporary Ballads*, G. P. Putnam's Sons, 1975, p. 346)

2. Patrick Owens, a colleague, sometimes uses the truly elegant word "GRAVAMEN." It refers to the significant portion of a grievance or complaint. It's the kind of word that comes clothed in black judicial robes and moves into a sentence to the grand march from *Aida*. It's a word that could transform a hangnail from a complaint into a cause. (B. Wiener, *Newsday* Service, "The rubric of words," *Philadelphia Inquirer*, 3/27/77, p. 3-L)

GRAVID (grav'id) *adj.* pregnant.

GRAVIDITY or **GRAVIDNESS** *noun.*

GRAVIDLY *adv.*

1. Above all—or perhaps I should say beneath all—lies an IMPLACABLE enmity toward the concept of excellence which John Kennedy exalted. We are confronted by a gray tide of mediocrity. The myth is current that we are all children of the same GRAVID earth bitch, that every homo sap is like every other homo sap, that any suggestion otherwise is PRETENTIOUS, and that every authority is a bugbear . . . . If you receive a Phi Beta Kappa key, or a letter sweater, or a Legion of Honor riband, or any of the BIJOUX in which people once took pride, you are expected to stow it away in a murky backstair corner. (W. Manchester, Commencement Address, University of Massachusetts, 6/13/75, mimeographed, p. 8)

GREGARIOUS (gri-gâr' ē-əs) *adj.* fond of the company of others; sociable; living in flocks or herds, as animals; having to do with a herd, flock, or crowd.

GREGARIOUSLY *adv.*

GREGARIOUSNESS *noun.*

1. . . . the GREGARIOUS, 42-year-old [Hedrick]

Smith, a Pulitzer Prize winner, takes a broader-gauged approach [in his book, *The Russians*] than his apparently more DIFFIDENT 32-year-old colleague [Robert G. Kaiser, in his book, *Russia*]. (P.D. Zimmerman, Review, *Newsweek*, 1/9/76, p. 71)

2. The last 10 days of Ford's campaign were highlighted by a series of regional half-hour TV shows in which he appeared with TV sportscaster Joe Garagiola. . . . So here came with a smile, and at a bargain fee of only $360 a show, GREGARIOUS Joe Garagiola. (Lee Winfrey, "Ford failed his own commercials," *Philadelphia Inquirer*, 11/10/76, p. 11-C)

3. . . . Helen [Hanks] had long since become accustomed to Blackford [Oakes]'s desire to meet everyone, which she attributed to natural GREGARIOUSNESS, a galloping Anglophilia, and an unconcealed desire to advance his engineering projects . . . . (W. F. Buckley Jr., *Saving the Queen*, Doubleday, 1976, p. 128)

GRIFTER (grif'tər) *noun* (in Slang) a petty swindler, dishonest gambler, or the like; a person who operates a dishonest gambling device at a circus, fair, carnival, etc.; confidence man.

GRIFT *noun* the obtaining of money by swindles, frauds, etc.; money thus obtained.

GRIFT *verb* to obtain money (or other profit) by grift.

1. He [Studs Terkel, author of the book, *Talking to Myself*] grew up in the city that produced the fictional Studs Lonigan and Augie March and the real Al Capone. His mother . . . leased a hotel near the Loop. Its lobby was . . . filled with . . . drifters, GRIFTERS, AUTODIDACTS, a few nuts and bolts from the political machine. (P. Gray, Review, *Time*, 4/18/77, p. 85)

GRIOT (grē'ō) *noun* an African tribal historian.

1. There [in Gambia in 1966] he [Alex Haley, author of the book, *Roots*] discovered villages named after the distinguished Kinte clan and several tribal historians, known as GRIOTS, who knew the history of each village going back hundreds of years. In [the] . . . village of Juf-

fure, Haley met with an old GRIOT . . . who described the family of [Haley's ancestor] Kunta Kinte and told him how, at 17, Kunta had left the village to chop wood and was never seen again. (P. D. Zimmerman, Review, *Newsweek*, 9/27/76, p. 96)

GROSGRAIN (grō' grān) *noun* a heavy, corded, closely woven ribbon or cloth of silk or rayon used for trimming.

1. I associate her [Coco Chanel] with blackness . . . the enormous number of black dresses . . . the flat GROSGRAIN bows . . . the black lacquered CHINOISERIES. (Francine Gray, Review of *Chanel*, a book by Edmonde Charles-Roux, *New York Review of Books*, 12/11/75, p. 44)

GROUTHEAD (grout'həd) *noun* a blockhead; thickhead; dunce.

GROUTHEADED *adj.*

1. . . . in the present work [*The Olive of Minerva*] Dahlberg . . . [explains] why the hero . . . left the Big Apple: "He had gone out from that steel and glass GEHENNA, New York. BILLINGSGATE was RIFE in the mouths of the street-gamin . . . and the rabble intelligentsia of the academic dumps of America. . . . Courtesy was regarded as a MALAISE of a MEACOCK GROUTHEAD." Is this complex irony—BILLINGSGATE scolded in BILLINGSGATE; . . . discourtesy discourteously derided? Or is this merely bad writing, over-ripe triteness? (J.D. O'Hara, Review, *New York Times*, 4/18/76, Section 7, p. 20)

GUIGNOL (gēn-yul') *noun* a dramatic entertainment in which short pieces of a sensational or horrific kind are played successively.

GRAND GUIGNOL or **GRAND GUIGNOL** any dramatic production designed to shock and horrify its audience with its gruesome or macabre content.

1. [Brian] DePalma's approach to his GUIGNOL material [in the film, *Carrie*] is so boldly and—I think—wrongheadedly lyrical that the spectacle of Carrie destroying her tormentors has all the dramatic punch of a small child swatting buttercups. (V. Canby, Review, *New York Times*, 12/5/76, Section 2, p. 13)

2. There is an unwavering, humorless contempt behind so much of the brilliant writing [in Joan Didion's *A Book of Common Prayer*]. Yet even more disturbing is the GRAND GUIGNOL, the melodramatic violence, that sometimes seems to overwhelm the writer and cause the hard-boiled style . . . to become sentimental, self-indulgent. (R. Locke, "Novelists as Preachers," *New York Times*, 4/17/77, Section 7, p. 53)

3. . . . I [Russel Wren] . . . had but lately witnessed a double murder of the most extravagant kind, in fact a legendary mobster-slaying that might well take its place in the annals of gangster GRAND GUIGNOL with the St. Valentine's Day Massacre and the rubbing out of Crazy Joe Gallo in Umberto's Clam House . . . . (Thomas Berger, *Who Is Teddy Villanova?*, Delacorte Press/Seymour Lawrence, 1977, p. 140)

GUSSIE (gus´ē) or GUSSY *verb* to dress up or decorate in a fine or showy way [Slang].

1. Clearly a woman of spirit and grit, with a story worth hearing, if she could tell it straight. But *How It Was* [a book by Mary Welsh Hemingway] is so GUSSIED-up with fancy writing, whimsy and homemaker's hints that one seems to be floundering through a gigantic issue of House & Garden. (W. Clemons, Review, *Newsweek*, 9/27/76, p. 99)

2. Now, in Boston, both sexes seem to want to get all dressed up with someplace to go (in contrast to some little girls in Little Rock, who are more reluctant than boys to get GUSSIED up). The Waltz Evenings [in Boston] are going strong, with dancers ranging in age from 18 to . . . 96. (Jane Davison, "Pick yourself up, dust yourself off," *New York Times*, 12/19/76, Section 6, p. 98)

GYRE (jī˘r) *verb* to whirl; to turn around; to gyrate.

GYRE *noun* a ring or circle; a circular course or spiral motion; whirl; revolution; vortex.

1. That [chivalric] picture [of war] survived in only two arenas [in World War I]. One was the sky, where the Royal Flying Corps, the "knights of the air" in their GYRING Sopwiths, preserved the image of man-to-man conflict. The other was Arabia. (R. Hughes, Review of the book, *A Prince of Our Disorder*, by John E. Mack, *Time*, 4/12/76, p. 93)

H

HAGIOGRAPHY (hag´ē-og´rə-fē, hā´jē-) *noun* the writing and critical study of the lives of the saints; a book or books containing such lives.

HAGIOGRAPHIC or HAGIOGRAPHICAL *adj.* of or pertaining to hagiography; idealizing its subject: said of a biography.

HAGIOGRAPHER *noun* any sacred or holy writer; an author of lives of the saints.

1. The authors [Larry Collins and Dominique Lapierre] treat Gandhi [in the book, *Freedom at Midnight*] in the conventional mode of HAGIOGRAPHY and, as usual, the approach leads to distortion of the historical record . . . . They do not explore those elements of Gandhi's style that led the usually mild and charitable Lord Wavell . . . to describe him as a "malevolent old politician . . . shrewd, obstinate, domineering, double-tongued . . . with little true saintliness in him." (N. Maxwell, Review, *New York Review of Books*, 12/11/75, p. 15)

2. The family members [in the book, *The Rockefellers*, by Peter Collier and David Horowitz] are treated as neither saints nor devils—a fact that may displease . . . both Rockefeller HAGIOGRAPHERS and demonologists. (S. R. Weisman, Review, *New York Times*, 3/28/76, Section 7, p. 1)

3. By Soviet HAGIOGRAPHIC standards, the resultant portrait [of Lenin, by Alexander Solzhenitsyn, in his book, *Lenin in Zurich: Chapters*] is a scandal and a sacrilege, but most of the basic materials for it are all there in documents widely available in the Soviet Union and included in the academic edition of Lenin's collected writings. (S. Karlinsky, Review, *New York Times*, 4/25/76, Section 7, p. 7)

4. Indeed, as Vad Mehta [author of the book, *Mahatma Gandhi and His Apostles*] shows, there is now a sizeable Gandhi industry in the sub-continent, complete with innumerable foundations, museums, colleges and other HAGIOGRAPHICAL institutions, including one that employs 50 researchers and 30 clerks to produce his sayings and writings in 80 volumes. (P. Johnson, Review, *New York Times*, 2/6/77, Section 7, p. 3)

5. See (1) under PEDICATION.

HAGIOLATRY (hag′ē-ol′ ə-trē, hā′ jē-) *noun* reverence for or worship of saints.

HAGIOLATER *noun*.

HAGIOLATROUS *adj.*

1. But the HAGIOLATERS will not be forever denied, as witness the unobtrusive rise, by the Kremlin wall, of the likeness of Stalin, which like the beanstalk is likely now to grow week by week back to full trinitarian status with Marx and Lenin. (W. F. Buckley Jr., *Execution Eve and Other Contemporary Ballads*, G. P. Putnam's Sons, 1975, p. 338)

2. [Laurens] Van Der Post's book [*Jung and the Story of Our Time*] is an extensive summary of Jung's major concepts and present implications . . . . The text occasionally rambles . . . and errs in the direction of HAGIOLATRY, but Van der Post successfully provides the flavor of the man, the warmth, the sustained cheerfulness, and the playfulness

behind his imposing MANDARIN facade. (J. Hollis, Review, *Chronicle of Higher Education*, 7/26/76, p. 9)

HALCYON (hal′ sē-ən) *adj.* calm; peaceful; tranquil; happy; idyllic; wealthy; prosperous; joyful; carefree.

1. Both in the HALCYON days of the Soviet AVANT-GARDE (1917–22) and in the great esthetic flowering of the Bauhaus in Germany (in the 1920's), Constructivism allied itself with vast theoretical programs of social reconstruction. (H. Kramer, "A Playful Storm of Sculpture," *New York Times*, 1/25/76, Section 6, p. 42)

2. The older white residents [of Rosedale, N.Y.] recall the HALCYON days of "melting pot" living (i.e. a "beautiful, white ethnic community"), when doors were left open, windows didn't have to be barred, the streets were safe at night. (J.J. O'Connor, "Taking a Balanced Look at Bias," *New York Times*, 2/1/76, Section 2, p. 27)

3. Truth to tell, [the film] *Deep Throat* was too tacky a vehicle to sustain high porn CAMP, but it managed to gross (you should excuse the expression) more than $25 million and got itself closed down for obscenity in a respectable number of places. That was all back in the HALCYON days before the big movie studios got a heavy lock on bestiality, NECROPHILIA, and Satanism. Downright innocent we were back then. (Dorothy Storck, " '*Deep Throat*,' deep trouble," *Philadelphia Inquirer*, 10/22/76, p. 1-B)

HARBINGER (här′ bin-jər) *noun* a person who goes before and makes known the approach of another; herald; anything that foreshadows a future event; omen; sign.

HARBINGER *verb* to act as harbinger to; herald the coming of.

1. They [the Appalachians] are no longer high; they do not command great plains; and they are impoverished where minerals like gold and silver are concerned. But they are the majestic HARBINGERS of our land; they served their major purpose long before man existed, then lingered on as noble relics to provide man with

an agreeable home when he did arrive. (J.A. Michener, *Centennial*, Fawcett, 1975, p. 53)

2. I wonder how many readers have seen a bluebird in the past 10 years? . . . Yet bluebirds were once the common, accepted HARBINGERS of spring . . . . (Irston R. Barnes, *Washington Post*, "Save Bluebird Crusade Task of 1 Individual," reprinted in *Norman* [Okla.] *Transcript*, 2/26/76, p. 9A)

3. And in California . . . a designer named Mark Goldes has placed a surreylike covering consisting of solar cells on a tiller-steered contraption that looks more like a wheelchair than a car. The machine will cruise for 20 miles non-stop, hardly the answer to the freeway, but Goldes considers his solar-driven one-seater something like the Wright Brothers' Flyer—a HARBINGER of things to come. (J.K. Page Jr., "Solar fiddling," *Smithsonian*, December 1975, p. 12)

4. . . . early poetry and fiction are generally free of memorials of artistic quality to father and mother. Why? . . . The guesses could be endless. But if we search earlier literature, we note only such rare HARBINGERS as Augustine's tribute to his mother and Cowper's poem on his mother's picture, and arrive quickly at Proust, Lawrence, Joyce and their famous long attentions to the matter. (Reynolds Price, Review of *Generations: A Memoir*, by Lucille Clifton, *New York Times*, 3/14/76, Section 7, p. 7)

5. [Woodrow] Wilson used [George] Harvey to achieve the Presidency but did not hesitate to thrust him aside when he no longer fitted his plans. The estrangement with Harvey was itself a HARBINGER of the strength and purpose that Wilson would bring to the Presidency. (J. P. Lash, Review of *The President Makers: From Mark Hanna to Joseph P. Kennedy*, by Francis Russell, *New York Times*, 3/28/76, Section 7, p. 4)

6. Boxed in by [Freddie] Field's package, the talented [director Lamont] Johnson has made [in *Lipstick*] a HARBINGER of the serious erotic film that is inevitably going to be made someday soon by a major American filmmaker. (J. Kroll, Review, *Newsweek*, 4/12/76, p. 94)

7. Elizabeth Cadell's novels are as dependable HARBINGERS of spring as tulips. More dependable, because sometimes the tulips are late. (M. Levin, Review of *Game in Diamonds*, by Elizabeth Cadell, *New York Times*, 5/2/76, Section 7, p. 61)

8. See (1) under NORMATIVE.

HARDSCRABBLE (härd'skra̅'-bəl) *adj.* barely allowing the eking out of an existence or living.

1. The high and mighty Seven [Sister Colleges*] have come far from their unlikely founders and HARDSCRABBLE origins: Vassar and Wellesley were started by fundamentalists; poverty forced Smith's first classes to use potato halves as candleholders. (Ann Marie Cunningham, Review of *Peculiar Institutions*, a book by Elaine Kendall, *Ms.*, May 1976, p. 38)

2. . . .[Wayne] Hays is running as a Presidential favorite son in six southern Ohio districts—and also faces a rather toothless Congressional challenge in his home district near Steubenville, a HARDSCRABBLE corner of Ohio that has also given the country Clark Gable and Dean Martin. (T. Mathews, *et al.*, "Capitol Capers," *Newsweek*, 6/14/76, p. 19)

3. Stumping the HARDSCRABBLE ethnic precincts and the fashionable ballrooms of Pennsylvania, the three most active Democratic candidates last week at times seemed peckish and anxious. All have drastically had to chop their spending and personally phone likely contributors for more aid. Congress had put them in the bind by unconsciously taking off for an Easter recess before a law reviving federal campaign subsidies could be passed. (Anon., "Pennsylvania's Guerrilla War," *Time*, 4/26/76, p. 14)

4. Why is The Lip [West Germany's Chancellor Helmut Schmidt] so waspish? Partly because of a thyroid condition that makes him irritable. Partly because of his HARDSCRABBLE background. . . in a tough Hamburg neighborhood. Partly because of an almost smart-alecky desire to show off. (M. Stevens and A. Collings, "The Lip vs. The Cabbage," *Newsweek*, 9/27/76, p. 51)

*Vassar, Wellesley, Smith, Mt. Holyoke, Bryn Mawr, Radcliffe, and Barnard.

HARRIDAN (har′ĭ-dən) *noun* a scolding, vicious old woman; hag; a disreputable, shrewish old woman.

1. Discarded by a frivolous public, reviled by a wife whom poverty and seven children have turned into a HARRIDAN, [John] Clare [protagonist of Edward Bond's play, *The Fool*]'s mind topples. The last scene takes place in the asylum where Clare spent his last 26 years. (J. Kroll, Review, *Newsweek*, 11/1/76, p. 62)

2. "If her [Chiang Ch'ing's] image and reputation as a HARRIDAN or tyrant or whatever is reinforced [by the book, *Comrade Chiang Ch'ing*] then let it be reinforced," she [author Roxane Witke] said. (J. Lelyveld, "A Message From Mao's Widow . . . and how it got here," *New York Times*, 4/3/77, Section 7, p. 30)

3. Women's radicalism has been condemned as puritanism; the Women's Christian Temperance Union (the largest mass movement of women in the 19th century) went down in history as a joyless, prudish band of HARRIDANS. In fact, it was a women's crusade against the violence inflicted on women by alcoholic husbands, against the liquor industries' financing the anti-suffrage campaigns and against the saloon as a male enclave draining the income of working-class families. (Adrienne Rich, Review of *The Female Experience*, a book by Gerda Lerner, *New York Times*, 3/20/77, Section 7, p. 10)

HARROW (har′ō) *verb* to disturb keenly or painfully; distress the mind, feelings, etc., of; torment; vex.

HARROWING *adj.*

HARROWINGLY *adv.*

1. See (1) under ABNEGATE.

2. See (1) under DISSIDENCE.

3. The contrast [between British and American TV programming] demonstrated that British TV has greater leeway on some matters . . . ; nudity, bedroom scenes and DOUBLE ENTENDRE were in abundance . . . . But to our mind the most daring show . . . was a soap-opera style drama called *Joe Lampton, Man at the Top*. It dealt with the mundane traumas of a middle-aged executive, including a HARROWING bout of unemployment, and it featured an approach almost unknown on American television. The executive was played sympathetically. (Anon., "Daring Television" [Editorial], *Wall Street Journal*, 9/23/76, p. 18)

4. . . . his [Woody Allen's] persona and style are perfect for driving home [in the movie, *The Front*] the HARROWING absurdity of the situation [the 1950's blacklisting of presumed Communists in the entertainment world]. (J. Kroll, Review, *Newsweek*, 10/4/76, p. 89)

HAUTEUR (hō-tûr′) *noun* a lofty or haughty manner, bearing, or spirit; haughtiness; disdainful pride; snobbery.

1. See (1) under MAÎTRE D'HÔTEL.

2. I sat in the spring of 1958 before the television screen and beheld Mr. Truman . . . cavorting from vulgarity to vulgarity, oversimplifying issues, distorting history, questioning motives, provoking base appetites . . . . I espied Dean Acheson and Adlai Stevenson [on the screen] . . . . The HAUTEUR and contempt which they knew so well how to display were not aroused even by so raw a provocation. (W. F. Buckley Jr., *Up From Liberalism*, Arlington House, 2nd Printing 1968, p. 49)

3. Another survival [of the original production of *My Fair Lady*] is Cecil Beaton's costumes, especially the black-and-white extravaganza of the Ascot scene where the toffs are grouped in frozen HAUTEUR across the stage. In its luxury and wit this stage picture EPITOMIZES a great musical whose like may not come this way again. (J. Kroll, Review, *Newsweek*, 4/5/76, p. 78)

4. She [Laura Antonelli] is a vivacious and spirited actress and enjoys some good moments [in the film, *How Funny Can Sex Be?*] with [Giancarlo] Giannini, whose quivering and expressive face can convey everything from unrequited lust to icy HAUTEUR. (D. Ryan, Review, *Philadelphia Inquirer*, 10/22/76, p. 6-C)

HECATOMB (hek′ə-tōm′, -tōōm′) *noun* (in ancient Greece and Rome) a public sacrifice of 100 oxen to the gods; any large-scale slaughter or sacrifice.

1. [John] Ehrlichman's novel [*The Company*] is sure to be grasped by his still frustrated countrymen in hopes of gathering a few SHARDS of

information about the political HECATOMB that was the Nixon White House. (T. Foote, Review, *Time*, 5/31/76, p. 66)

HECTOR (hek'tər) *verb* to treat with insolence; bully; to browbeat; to act in a blustering, domineering way; be a bully; persecute; badger; harass.

HECTOR *noun* a swaggering fellow; bully; a blustering, domineering fellow.

1. . . . [Ronald] Reagan . . . has questioned detente, HECTORED Kissinger and turned the primaries into referendums on the future of the Panama Canal. (P. Goldman, *et al.*, "A President 'in Jeopardy,' " *Newsweek*, 5/17/76, p. 22)

2. A high-tenor voice had apparently been speaking for some moments before I [Russel Wren] regained full consciousness. Its tone must be called morally HECTORING. ". . . leading to wiolence, madness, and strife, and CONCUPISCENCE with vimmin, you see?" (Thomas Berger, *Who Is Teddy Villanova?*, Delacorte Press/Seymour Lawrence, 1977, p. 113)

HEDONISM (hēd'ᵊ niz'əm) *noun* the doctrine that pleasure or happiness is the highest good and the proper aim of action; the self-indulgent pursuit of pleasure as a way of life.

HEDONIST *noun*.

HEDONISTIC or **HEDONIC** *adj*.

HEDONISTICALLY or **HEDONICALLY** *adv*.

1. See (1) under LICENTIOUS.

2. See (1) under BOURGEOIS.

3. See (1) under DIONYSIAC.

4. In a long brilliant sequence [in *The Killing of a Chinese Bookie*] we see Cosmo [Vitelli] pay off a gambling debt to the mob by killing its Chinese rival big shot. This episode is a mini-*Chinatown* all by itself, moving through the freeways to the isolated Xanadu where the ancient Oriental godfather dies amid the trappings of his overripe HEDONISM. (J. Kroll, Review, *Newsweek*, 3/15/76, p. 90)

5. So many of the expressive and stylistic possibilities of art have been rejected by the moder-

nist practitioner either as superfluous HEDONISM or as a dangerous kind of playfulness that is not essential to survival, a rationale and rejection that are the routine, predictable, joyless accompaniment of all revolutionary doctrine. (Ada Louise Huxtable, "Modern Architecture in Question," *New York Review of Books*, 11/27/75, pp. 8, 10)

6. All that's missing [in Washington] is a professional baseball team, but the HEDONISTS here are too fast for baseball anyway. (N. Thimmesch, "Washington Becoming 'Fun City,' " *Daily Oklahoman*, Okla. City, 4/20/76, p. 6)

7. Fidelity to this idea [sacrificing number of followers for ideological purity] allowed the restless, despairing Lenin to reject the offer of money, arms, access to Russia and leadership of the Revolution extended by the remarkable Russian millionaire, Parvus. A HEDONIST and leader of the 1905 uprising, Parvus was Lenin's equal in brilliance and daring, but not his match in stamina or self-discipline. (P.D. Zimmerman, Review of *Lenin in Zurich*, by Alexander Solzhenitsyn, *Newsweek*, 4/12/76, pp. 98, 100)

8. There is a streak of unhidden HEDONISM in Ernest Fleischmann [executive director of the Los Angeles Philharmonic] . . . and he would like to depart this earth with a glass of vintage port in his hand, a Mozart string ensemble playing softly nearby, and in wicked conversation about the PECCADILLOES of his peers . . . . He speaks and reads English, French, Italian, Dutch, and German, and can curse and cry and cajole in each. (T. Thompson, "The importance of being Fleischmann," *New York Times*, 4/11/76, Section 6, p. 36)

9. Brando has become a symbol of lost innocence; Nicholson radiates a new kind of beleaguered innocence, grinning HEDONISTICALLY amid the moral confusion of our time . . . . (J. Kroll, Review of the film *The Missouri Breaks*, *Newsweek*, 5/24/76, p. 103)

10. The Fonz's slogan may be "Live fast, die young and leave a good-looking corpse," but [Henry] Winkler's own life is hardly HEDONISTIC. (Lois Armstrong, "AYYYY, The Fonz Is A Smash, But Henry Winkler Finds Some Nightmares In His Happy Daze,"

People, 5/24/76, p. 44)

11. See (4) under ANATHEMA.

12. He [Leo Brunner] resented the unfairness of the way some Maker, some Cosmic Force, had given . . . a minority like himself the limited means and limited right to be workhorses permitted only the barest minimum of HEDONISTIC indulgence. (I. Wallace, *The Fan Club*, Bantam Edition, 1975, p. 51)

13. See (1) under PUERILE.

14. See (1) under NOSH.

HEGEMONY (hi-jem′ə-nē, hej′ə-mō′nē) *noun, pl.:* -NIES (-nēz) political or economic leadership or predominant influence, especially when exercised by one state or nation over others.

HEGEMONIC *adj.*

1. See (1) under FUNGIBLE.

2. If academic credentialism does not hold its former HEGEMONY, it is not due to the utopian efforts of educational reformers, but to the simple marketplace mechanism which determines that if everybody else carries the same credentials, their ready availability must surely have diminished their market value. (G.W. Bonham, "The Coming Shake-out in Higher Education" [Editorial], *Change*, Summer 1974, p. 12)

3. In a recent convocation address at the University of Massachusetts at Boston, . . . David Riesman observed that "if the U. of Mass. were in Indiana or Georgia, people would recognize it as one of the great state universities; it is only locally, where private higher education has had HEGEMONY for so long, that students who go to the University feel that they really would like to be at Dartmouth or Holy Cross or Smith, Middlebury, Brown or Harvard." (G.W. Bonham, *Ibid.*, p. 12)

4. See (1) under SANGUINARY.

5. Indeed, earlier that year [1973] it seemed that the long HEGEMONY of the local Irish over the uniformed service unions [in New York]—police, fire, sanitation—was also on its way out, for . . . Richard Vizzini defeated Michael Maye to become the first Italian-American head of the firemen's union. (A. Logan,

"Around City Hall: Irishry," *The New Yorker*, 2/9/76, p. 89)

6. Henry Kissinger directed Ford to snub Aleksandr Solzhenitsyn, and then towed Ford to Helsinki. There Ford ratified Soviet HEGEMONY in Eastern Europe. In exchange for that, Brezhnev promised, cross his heart and hope to die, that he would respect human rights. (G. F. Will, "Shazam: The New Ford," *Newsweek*, 3/22/76, p. 88)

7. Senator [Joseph] McCarthy, who was understood by his responsible supporters to be opposing Executive HEGEMONY in matters of internal security, and challenging the open society which presupposes that a Communist has as many rights as a democrat, . . . is spoken of as having outlawed Thomas Jefferson—and is attacked as a homosexual. (W.F. Buckley Jr., *Up From Liberalism*, Arlington House, 2nd Printing 1968, p. 80)

8. The principal reason [the discussion process in America appears to have broken down] is the emphatic indisposition by those whose views prevail in certain quarters to accept any challenge to their intellectual HEGEMONY, to recognize dissent from their conformity as serious. (W.F. Buckley Jr., *Ibid.*, p. 117)

9. This obsession [with method] is most clearly discernible in liberal education theories. At last there is widespread public and even intellectual concern over the HEGEMONY of the instrumentalists over primary and secondary education; . . . In New York State opponents of progressive education . . . have boldly urged that . . . teachers' colleges demand of prospective teachers of physics that they devote as many hours to the study of physics as to the techniques of teaching! (W.F. Buckley Jr., *Ibid.*, p. 179)

10. I worked . . . with Arab women in North Africa, and later with peasant women in Italy, Southern France, and Portugal, and never knew one who was not bitterly amused by our notions of her secret HEGEMONY [over her family], who did not feel betrayed by her sexual circumstance, who did not have the most painful fantasies of freedom . . . her [Ann Cornelisen's] women [in *Women of the Shadows*] vividly corroborate what the women I knew said. (Jane Kramer, Review, *New York Times*,

4/4/76, Section 7, p. 2)

11. Rather than just staking a new claim in the field, they [scholars] have tended . . . to assert disciplinary centrality—if not HEGEMONY—to claim that their new work alters the scholarly landscape in some fundamental way. (M. Frisch, Review of *The New Urban History: Qualitative Explorations by American Historians,* edited by Leo F. Schnore, *Chronicle of Higher Education,* 4/26/76, p. 19)

12. In an effort to challenge the American HEGEMONY in the global computer market, the Japanese government has lavished about $3 billion in subsidies upon local computers makers over the past dozen years and has persuaded the six major companies to team up for research and development. (Anon., "Pacific Overtures," *Time,* 5/24/76, p. 64)

13. These days the machine that secretaries envy is the IBM Selectric, a "single-element" typewriter that replaces the familiar semicircular bank of type keys with a removable bouncing ball of type . . . . This year IBM will hold an estimated 65% of the $600 million office electric typewriter market. The company's HEGEMONY has drawn the attention of the Federal Trade Commission's antitrust division. (Anon., "Chasing the Bouncing Ball," *Time,* 6/21/76, p. 66)

HEGIRA or **HEGIRA** (hi-ji′rə, hej′ər-ə) or **HEJIRA** or **HEJIRA** *noun* (if capitalized) the flight of Muhammad from Mecca to Medina to escape persecution, A.D. 622: regarded as the beginning of the Muslim era; (if lower case) any flight or journey made for the sake of safety or escape; flight.

1. It was a strange HEGIRA on which the horses of Centennial were engaged. It would take them across thousands of miles and onto land that had been under water only a few centuries earlier. For this was the age of ice. (J.A. Michener, *Centennial,* Fawcett, 1975, p. 93)

2. Barbara Howar's first book, *Laughing All the Way,* was a delightful, direct, witty memoir of one woman's HEGIRA through Washington during the L.B.J. administration. . . . *Making Ends Meet,* a novel about a Washington woman torn between dependence and independence, is equally well-written but

somehow less immediate and convincing. (Erica Jong, Review, *New York Times,* 4/25/76, Section 7, p. 1)

3. The book [*Exodusters,* by Nell Irvin Painter]'s dramatic center, though, is Painter's account of the 1879 Exodus—or "the African HEGIRA," as one astonished observer called it. Between February and May of that year, the roads to the Mississippi River were filled with blacks trying to book passage to St. Louis, and from there to "their Mecca," Kansas. (Margo Jefferson, Review, *Newsweek,* 1/17/77, p. 83)

HELIOCENTRIC (hē′ lē-ō-sen′ trik) *adj.* having, regarding, or representing the sun as central; seen or measured as from the center of the sun.

1. His [Charles Colson's] weakness, as generally identified, has been his HELIOCENTRIC concern for one person—Richard Nixon. (W.F. Buckley Jr., *Execution Eve and Other Contemporary Ballads,* G.P. Putnam's Sons, 1975, p. 444)

HELIOTROPE (hē′lē-ə-trōp, hēl′yə-) *noun, adj.* a light tint of purple; reddish-lavender; reddish-purple.

1. I [Russel Wren] used the stairs to inject myself headlong into the fourth floor, of which the rearmore door bore the rubric B and beneath it, from a runny HELIOTROPE stencil: FUN THINGS INC., so often mischievously represented on the lobby directory board . . . as "Fucing," and pronounced by Sam Polidor according to its altered ORTHOGRAPHY. (Thomas Berger, *Who Is Teddy Villanova?,* Delacorte Press/Seymour Lawrence, 1977, p. 225)

HERCYNIAN or **HERCYNIAN** (hər-sin′ ē-ən) *adj.* of or relating to an extensive mountain range covered with forests in ancient Germany; of or relating to the folding and mountain building that took place in the eastern hemisphere in late Paleozoic times.

HERCYNA (hər-sī′ nə) *noun* (in Classical Mythology) a fountain nymph who was the playmate of Persephone.

1. . . . . conceivably there are endless snubs ahead from those who think they are better than we are because their manners are worse,

their pasts shadier, their brainpans smaller . . . .
But there is a pendulum, and it swings. . . .
And when it has reached the end of a cycle, . . .
its own weight reverses it. Then . . . all the incantations of all the druids in all the HERCYN-
IAN groves of NEOSOPHISTRY cannot arrest it. . . .
The change does not announce itself. But certain individuals can hold the mirror up to the
future, and in 1961 such a PRESCIENT statesman
assumed the Presidency of the United States.
(W. Manchester, Commencement Address,
University of Massachusetts, 6/13/65, Mimeographed, p. 9)

HERETICAL (hə-ret′ i-kəl) or **HERETIC**
adj. pertaining to or characteristic of heretics
or heresy.

HERETICALLY *adv.*

HERETIC *noun* a professed believer who
maintains religious opinions contrary to those
of his church; anyone who does not conform
with an established attitude, doctrine, or principle.

HERESY *noun* religious opinion or doctrine
at variance with the orthodox or accepted doctrine; the maintaining of such an opinion or
doctrine; any belief strongly at variance with
established beliefs, MORES, etc.

1. The "Protestant Ethic," which tends to
function as the hero in [Daniel] Bell's book
[*The Cultural Contradictions of Capitalism*],
has historically supported not only a public
conscience but also public repression, and this
has especially been the case when its enemies
are identified as the HERETICAL and LICENTIOUS.
(R. Williams, Review, *New York Times*,
2/1/76, Section 7, p. 3)

HERMENEUTICS (hûr′ mə-nōō′ tiks, -nyōō′ -)
noun (construed as *singular*) the science of
interpretation, especially the study of the principles of Biblical EXEGESIS.

HERMENEUTIC or HERMENEUTICAL *adj.* of
or pertaining to hermeneutics; interpretive; ex-
planatory.

HERMENEUTICALLY *adv.*

1. [Sacvan] Bercovitch's reading [in his book,
The Puritan Origins of the American Self] of
this exemplary "life" [Cotton Mather's bi-

ography of John Winthrop] is a virtuoso performance in contemporary HERMENEUTICS—to
use one of his favorite words. It also is, for
somewhat MERETRICIOUS reasons I suspect, an
extremely modish word in literary circles right
now . . . he [Bercovitch] provides a HERMENEU-
TICAL demonstration of the way Mather, and
the Puritans generally, transformed a traditional (European) HERMENEUTICS in order to
express a distinctive (American) sense of
destiny . . . . But answers to these questions
[about the Puritans], which lie beyond the
boundaries of HERMENEUTICS, are left to the
reader. (L. Marx, Review, *New York Times*,
2/1/76, Section 7, pp. 21-22)

2. [E.D.] Hirsch cogently defends AD HOC
value criteria and the possibility of knowledge
in interpretation; he attacks [in the book, *The
Aims of Interpretation*] relativist and skeptical
HERMENEUTIC theories. (G.A. Cardwell, Review, *The Key Reporter*, Summer 1976, p. 7)

3. We may therefore pass from practical expo-
sition to critical interpretation, to a more speculative, HERMENEUTIC, and crabby view [of the
architecture in Paris's Centre Pompidou]. (N.
Silver, "Le Tour Babel," *Harper's*, April 1977,
p. 90)

HERMETIC (hûr-met′ik) or **HERMETICAL**
adj. made airtight by fusion or sealing; of,
pertaining to, or characteristic of occult
science, especially alchemy; magical; alchem-
ical; hard to understand; obscure.

HERMETICALLY *adv.*

1. Fortunately, even at his loftiest and most
HERMETIC, [Ad] Reinhardt is an intoxicating
writer, a word juggler whose cadences evoke
Beckett and Joyce. (P. Schjeldahl, Review of
*Art as Art, The Selected Writings of Ad Rein-
hardt*, edited by Barbara Rose; and *The Art
Comics and Satires of Ad Reinhardt*, by
Thomas B. Hess, *New York Times*, 2/15/76,
Section 7, p. 8)

2. No use asking me to explain it [the book, 'A'
22 & 23, by Louis Zukovsky]. I've no idea how
an explanation would start: unless by taking
note of the awesome, HERMETIC self-discipline
that has now finished, in 1975, a long poem in
24 parts planned and begun in 1927 . . . . Part
of the poem is its own publication history,

including the fact that *A-24*, the finale, was published three years ago . . . . Mallarmé . . . learned English in order to read the great Poe. Zukovsky learned it to survive in New York, and also to read its riches. One result was *A*, the most HERMETIC poem in English, which they still will be elucidating in the 22nd century. (H. Kenner, Review, *New York Times*, 3/14/76, Section 7, p. 6)

3. But conceptualization [of the artist], no matter how interesting or refined the process of RATIOCINATION on which it is based, is not something we actually experience at first hand in these "drawings." . . . the actual "drawing" that results from . . . CEREBRATION affords, at best, a second-hand experience . . . . The mind is given a system of HERMETIC signs to be decoded, but the eye is given little or nothing to gratify its appetite . . . . Conceptual drawing . . . can fairly be described as the most significant part [of the exhibition, *Drawing Now: 1955-1975*, at the Museum of Modern Art], for it provides the show with its basic RAISON D'ÊTRE. (H. Kramer, Review, *New York Times*, 2/1/76, Section 2, p. 31)

4. His [Morris Dickstein's] book [*Gates of Eden: American Culture in the Sixties*], with its combination of fresh cultural commentary and personal testimony, justifies Dickstein's hope that "criticism, which is often tempted to be HERMETIC, can tell us something about the real world." (W. Clemons, Review, *Newsweek*, 3/28/77, pp. 78–79)

5. See (1) under BOLUS.

HETAERA (hi-tēr'ə, hi-tir'ə) or **HETAIRA** (hi-tī'rə) *noun, pl.*, respectively; **-TAERAE** (- těr'ē) or **-RAI** (-tī'rī) a female paramour, courtesan, or concubine, especially one who was an educated slave in ancient Greece; any woman who uses her charm to gain wealth or social position.

HETAERIC or **HETAIRIC** *adj.*

HETAERISM or **HETAIRISM** *noun* concubinage; a social system in which women are regarded as communal property, supposed to have been practiced among some early peoples.

1. . . . until the current episode of the bedraggled, pathetic relations between Wayne Hays and Elizabeth Ray, much of the national resentment against Washington was against the bureaucracy . . . . Now sex has been added, and for the moment the hustlers and HETAERAE push the bureaucrats aside and take the center of the stage. (M. Lerner, "Washington's sins are not metropolitan: Sex scandal brings resentment," *Norman* [Okla.] *Transcript*, 6/14/76, p. 6)

HIATUS (hī-ā'təs) *noun* a break or interruption in the continuity of a written work, series, or action, etc.; a missing part; LACUNA.

1. Miss [Shirley] Stoler read for the part [of Balthazar, in *The Young Disciple*, in 1956], got it, and has been acting ever since—except for a two-year HIATUS in the late fifties when she married a MACHO Moroccan who expected her to stay in their Manhattan home. (Judy Klemesrud, Review of Lina Wertmuller's film, *Seven Beauties*, *New York Times*, 2/1/76, Section 2, p. 13, 32)

2. After a 22-year HIATUS, Miss [Shirley] MacLaine is clearly pleased to be back on stage [at Las Vegas]. (Julia Cameron, "Shirley MacLaine—Back in Her Dancing Shoes," *New York Times*, 4/18/76, Section 2, p. 1)

3. China and the Soviet Union, which have come close to war over their disputed border, have resumed talks on the issue after a HIATUS of 18 months . . . an early settlement of the two nations' differences is considered unlikely; each has huge military forces near the frontier. (Anon., "China, Soviet Talking Again," *New York Times*, 12/5/76, Section 4, p. 1)

4. . . . John deLancie had been named director [of the Curtis Institute of Music] after a search that had gone on for nearly two years after the resignation of Rudolf Serkin. The long HIATUS in leadership was the result of the active debate among the nine board members about the role Curtis should play in the community. (D. Webster, "Curtis is ready to move backward," *Philadelphia Inquirer*, 3/6/77, p. 1-I)

HIDALGO (hi-dal'gō) *noun, pl.*: **-GOS** (gōz) a man of the lower nobility in Spain; a man of landed property or special prestige in Spanish America.

1. [Patrick] O'Brian's portrait of the artist [Picasso]—especially the ambitious youth and the aging celebrity—is sharply etched [in *Picasso, A Biography*]: the HIDALGO pride that made Picasso a difficult personality at the best of times; the contradiction of his force and daring in art, and his indecisiveness, lack of initiative, his suspiciousness, and summary cruelty in his personal affairs; the bursts of extravagant generosity succeeded by seasons of parsimony . . . ; the seemingly inevitable callousness of his well-publicized love affairs. (J. R. Mellow, Review, *New York Times*, 7/4/76, Section 7, p. 4)

HIERARCHY (hī′ə-rär′kē, hī′rär-kē) *noun* any system of persons or things ranked one above another; government by ecclesiastical rulers; the power or dominion of a hierarch; government by an elite group; an organized body of ecclesiastical officials in successive ranks or orders.

HIERARCHICAL or **HIERARCHIC** *adj.*

HIERARCHICALLY *adv.*

HIERARCH *noun* a person having high position or considerable authority; a person who rules or has authority in sacred things; high priest.

HIERARCHICAL *adj.*

1. Speculation about Peking's political convulutions is ARCANE. But the potential importance of HIERARCHICAL shifts [in the Chinese leadership] to Peking's foreign policy is of enormous concern abroad. (C. L. Sulzberger, "Behind The Great Wall of China," *New York Times*, 5/2/76, Section 4, p. 15)

2. [L. Steven] Zwerling's conclusion [in *Second Best: The Crisis of the Community College*]? To become truly egalitarian we must . . . eliminate the community college and the whole class-serving system of HIERARCHICAL education. Only by granting the baccalaureate, a complete degree, to the lower classes will equality be achieved. (M. G. Baumann, Review, *Chronicle of Higher Education*, 5/17/76, p. 13)

3. He [Lincoln Merrill] calls [Teamsters' chief Frank] Fitzsimmons names. He believes union HIERARCHY is an extension of organized crime. Worse, he has joined a union subculture called

PROD, which wants the U.S. government to force fundamental Teamsters reform. (T. Tiede, of NEA, "Union hierarchy imitates organized crime," *Norman* [Okla.] *Transcript*, 7/9/76, p. 6)

4. See (1) under OSSIFY.

5. See (2) under OSSIFY.

HIERATIC (hī′ə-rat′ik, hī-rat′ik) or **HIERATICAL** *adj* of, pertaining to, or used by priests or the priesthood; priestly; SACERDOTAL.

HIERATICALLY *adv.*

1. What is Islam? . . . Any tradition which reaches from Senegal and Tanzania through Egypt and Turkey to Iran, India, and Indonesia, which extends from the seventh century to the twentieth, which has drawn on Judaism, Byzantine Christianity, Greek philosophy, Hinduism, Arabian paganism, Spanish intellectualism, and the mystery cults of ancient Persia, which has animated at least a half-dozen empires from Abbasid to Ottoman, and which has been legalistic, mystical, rationalist, and HIERATIC by turns, is clearly not readily characterized, though it all too often has been. (C. Geertz, Review of *The Venture of Islam: Conscience and History in a World Civilization. Vol. 1: The Classical Age of Islam; Vol. 2: The Expansion of Islam in the Middle Periods; Vol. 3: The Gunpowder Empire and Modern Times*, by Marshall G.S. Hodgson, *New York Review of Books*, 12/11/75, p. 18)

2. . . . [Paul] Poiret may be credited with having invented the fashion show; he coached and rehearsed his MANNEQUINS as though he were putting on a theatrical spectacle. Paris had never seen anything like it. One critic wrote of the models' "HIERATIC poses" and Cocteau said that Poiret had taught them "a praying-mantis walk." (Waverley Root, *Paul Poiret: Couturier extraordinaire*," *New York Times*, 8/13/76, Section 6, p. 59)

3. Obviously, this failure [of the Turks] to keep up with European military technology was part of a wider economic stagnation. [Lord] Kinross suggests [in his book, *The Ottoman Centuries*] that the tightly organized guilds of artisans of the Ottoman state may have been responsible. The trade guilds or corporations (ADUMBRATIONS of the modern con-

servative trade union) had, of course, helped to wreck the economy of the late Roman empire; they were inherited by Byzantium, which in turn passed the fatal bacillus on to its Ottoman conquerors. Kinross hints, too, at the immense inertial forces of other tightly organized corporations . . . : the elite corps of the army; the MANDARINS of the Ottoman civil service; and, not least, the HIERATIC pressure-groups of the Islamic establishment. (P. Johnson, Review, *New York Times*, 4/10/77, Section 7, p. 12)

HIEROPHANT (hī'ər-ə-fant', hī'rə- , hī-ər'-ə-) *noun* (in ancient Greece) a high priest who presided at sacred mysteries; any interpreter of sacred mysteries or ESOTERIC principles.

HIEROPHANTIC *adj.*

HIEROPHANTICALLY *adv.*

1. An esthete with instincts of a street fighter and a philosopher who was never more serious than when he was clowning, Ad Reinhardt was preeminently his generation's HIEROPHANT of the religion of high art—a difficult and . . . unpopular role that may be assumed by others in the future but surely never with his incredible buoyancy. (P. Schjeldahl, Review of *Art as Art, The Selected Writings of Ad Reinhardt*, edited by Barbara Rose; and *The Art Comics and Satires of Ad Reinhardt*, by Thomas B. Hess, *New York Times*, 2/15/76, Section 7, p. 8)

2. Poor William, quite transfixed by the horror of it all, stood like a statue with a platter of beef poised on his hands, looking just like a HIEROPHANT making an offering. (Barbara Michaels, *Sons of the Wolf*, Meredith Press, 1967, p. 96)

3. It [*Terra Nostra*, a book by Carlos Fuentes] is written in a prose that streams through pages in rushing, cascading, tumbling sentences that squeal, screech, explode, haunt or confide in you until you decide what you are going to do with this teeming language. It is all as if you are overhearing the unceasing incantations of a poet-HIEROPHANT who both terrifies and seduces you. (A.J. Sabatini, Review, *Philadelphia Inquirer*, 11/14/76, p. 14-G)

HIPPIC (hip'ik) *adj.* pertaining to horses, especially horse-racing.

HIPPOID *adj.* horselike; having the characteristics of a horse.

HIPPOPHILE *noun* one who is especially fond of horses.

1. For she [Paola Belli] had been in London taking HIPPIC pictures of Princess Anne . . . . (A. Burgess, *Beard's Roman Women*, McGraw-Hill, 1976, p. 38)

HIRSUTE (hûr'sōōt, hûr-sōōt') *adj.* hairy; shaggy; of, pertaining to, or characteristic of hair; bristly.

HIRSUTENESS *noun.*

1. If 50 businessmen raise $2,000 each for their favorite [presidential] candidate, they go to jail. But if some HIRSUTE rock star holds a one-night concert and turns over the $100,000 in proceeds to his favorite radical, that is perfectly all right with the reformers. (P. J. Buchanan, "Campaign Law Reform Foolish," *Daily Oklahoman*, Okla. City, 2/17/76, p. 8)

2. I [Adam Malone] now have an unruly moustache and beard sprouting. They don't look too good yet, and the store manager made a sarcastic crack about my HIRSUTE adornments. (I. Wallace, *The Fan Club*, Bantam Books, 1975, p. 145)

3. See (1) under ESPRIT DE CORPS.

4. Louise [in the book, *King & Joker*, by Peter Dickinson] is the 13-year old daughter of King Victor II and his Spanish wife, Isabella. They live in a . . . palace where . . . silly practical jokes have begun to disrupt their royal peace of mind. On one occasion, the pet frog of Prince Albert, Louise's older, HIRSUTE brother, pops out of the plate intended for King Victor's breakfast ham . . . . Grand pianos, in herds, arrive unordered and unannounced. (P. D. Zimmerman, Review, *Newsweek*, 8/9/76, p. 72)

HISTORIOGRAPHER (hi-stōr'ē-ōg' rə-fər, -stôr'-) *noun* a historian; an official historian, as of a court, institution, society, etc.

HISTORIOGRAPHY *noun* the body of literature dealing with historical matters; histories collectively; the body of techniques, theories, and principles of historical research and presentation; methods of historical scholarship; the narrative presentation of history based on a critical examination, evaluation, and selection of material from primary and secondary sources and subject to scholarly criteria; an official history.

HISTORIOGRAPHIC or **HISTORIOGRAPHICAL** *adj.*

HISTORIOGRAPHICALLY *adv.*

1. I think it a pity to play along with TENDENTIOUS HISTORIOGRAPHERS, who find it a workaday challenge to their ingenuity to relate linearly the liberalism of Alexander Hamilton and that of Harold Laski; and so I have not—because truthfully I cannot—treated contemporary liberalism except as a contemporary phenomenon. (W. F. Buckley Jr., *Up From Liberalism*, Arlington House, 2nd Printing 1968, p. 178)

2. This falling off of narrative and lapse into hasty HISTORIOGRAPHY will disappoint many readers [of *Roots*, by Alex Haley] . . . . Instead of writing a scholarly monograph of little social impact, Haley has written a blockbuster in the best sense—a book . . . that will reach millions of people and alter the way we see ourselves. (P. D. Zimmerman, Review, *Newsweek*, 9/27/76, p. 95)

HISTRIONICS (his′ trē-on′ iks) *noun* (either singular or plural) a dramatic representation; theatricals; acting; artificial, affected, or exaggerated behavior or speech exhibited insincerely for effect; theatricality.

HISTRIONIC *adj.* of or pertaining to actors or acting; overacting; theatrical; melodramatic; artificial or affected in behavior or speech.

HISTRIONICALLY *adv.*

1. In January , 1974 . . . it seemed that hardly a day went by without some public pronouncement . . . on the new sense of peace and quiet following the shift from a mayor [John Lindsay] famous for HISTRIONICS, to two mild-mannered, UNPRETENTIOUS, strictly-business leaders [Malcolm Wilson and Abraham Beame] with no distracting ambitions for higher office. (A. Logan, "Around City Hall: Irishry," *The New Yorker*, 2/9/76, p. 86)

2. He [John E. Mack, author of *A Prince Of Our Disorder: The Life of T. E. Lawrence*] posits Lawrence as a transitional figure in the history of war. His bright blue eyes and HISTRIONIC accomplishment wowed his contemporaries as they emerged from the slogging slaughter of World War I. But his self-questioning, Mack adds, helped make romantic heroism obsolete. (W. Clemons, Review, *Newsweek*, 4/12/76, p. 98)

3. See (3) under ICON.

4. Devoid of all else, her [Sharon Fields'] flesh and her HISTRIONIC skills were her only weapons [against her kidnappers]. (I. Wallace, *The Fan Club*, Bantam edition, 1975, p. 350)

5. Unlike other early movie magnates, [Adolph] Zukor avoided both Hollywood and HISTRIONICS, preferring to manage his burgeoning entertainment empire from New York, where he ran Paramount until he retired as chairman at 93. (Anon., "Milestones," *Time*, 6/21/76, p. 55)

HOI-POLLOI (hoi′pə-loi′) the common people; the masses: usually patronizing or contemptuous (usually preceded by *the*).

1. Southern ladies, counted upon to be too well-bred to bring up anything embarrassing to their hostess [Cornelia Wallace], had filled the [Alabama governor's] mansion before many of the HOI-POLLOI could get inside [for the reception for Rosalynn Carter]. It remained for the public and the reporters to stand outside . . . . (Maxine Cheshire, Washington Post Service, "The Wallaces: Is Cornelia trying to upstage George?" *Philadelphia Inquirer*, 9/15/76, p. 4–C)

HOKEY (hō kē) *adj.* (in U.S. slang) faked; false; contrived; marked by hokum.

HOKE *verb* (in U.S. slang) to give a false quality or value to; fake.

HOKUM *noun* (in U.S. slang) crudely comic or MAWKISHLY sentimental elements in a story, play, etc., used to gain an immediate emotional response; nonsense; humbug; claptrap; bunk.

HOKEYPOKEY *noun* (in U.S. slang) trickery; deception; hocus-pocus.

1. . . . we are seeing a rapid multiplication of efforts to break out of traditional patterns of undergraduate teaching. They can be characterized as ranging from HOAKY (*sic*) to fundamentally important, and it is often difficult to tell which is which. (G.W. Bonham, "Revitalizing undergraduate learning" [Editorial], *Change*, Winter 1974–75, p. 11)

2. The characters in his [F. Scott Fitzgerald's] earlier novels had been rich either through inheritance or some HOKEY, unexamined, bootlegging magic, and they had certainly never been artists. But the pivot of *The Last Tycoon* is a classical American struggle . . . between the man of imagination and the man of action, between the artist and the tycoon. (S. Koch, Review of the film, *The Last Tycoon*, *Harper's*, March 1977, p. 102)

3. See (4) under ALLITERATION.

HOLISM (hō′liz-əm) *noun* the philosophical theory that whole entities, as fundamental and determining components of reality, have a reality independent of and greater than the sum of their parts.

HOLIST *noun*

HOLISTIC *adj.*

HOLISTICALLY *adv.*

1. The new knowledge [universities came to market], oriented toward the sciences, more specialized, more "objective" in character, was increasingly removed from such HOLISTIC concerns as the nature of social and personal life. It was a knowledge . . . perfectly suited to a ruling—and exploiting—class whose goals had little to do with moral considerations. (D. Siff, Review of *English in America: A Radical View of the Profession*, by Richard Ohmann, *Change*, Winter 1975-76, p. 56)

2. "All the characters [in P. R. Pathan's latest novel] talk alike," said the reviewer, "and it is curious to find a taxi-driver using the same modes of speech as the lecturer in anthropology whom he carries. Men, in point of dialogue alone, are indistinguishable from women, and one wonders what precisely Mr. Pathan is playing at. There may, of course, be some dark HOLISTIC intention of demonstrating that all people are fundamentally the same one person

. . . ." (A. Burgess, *Beard's Roman Women*, McGraw-Hill, 1976, p. 124)

3. We have just produced *Wellness*, a guide to the literature on HOLISTIC healing. (Cris Popenoe, Untitled, *Yes! Bookshop Newsletter*, 5/24/77, p. 1)

HOLOGRAPHIC (hol′ə-graf′ik) or **HOLOGRAPHICAL** or **HOLOGRAPH** *adj.* wholly written by the person in whose name it appears.

HOLOGRAPHIC a will entirely handwritten by the testator.

HOLOGRAPH *noun* a holographic document, letter, etc.

1. Las Vegas, Nev. (AP)—A crudely handwritten document described as the will of the late billionaire Howard R. Hughes was filed with a Nevada court Thursday after it mysteriously arrived at the headquarters of the Mormon Church in Utah . . . . The HOLOGRAPHIC will—so called because it purports to be written in the decedent's own hand—contains no signatures of witnesses. However, a federal judge in Clark County [Nevada] said a HOLOGRAPHIC will does not require witnesses, merely verification from handwriting experts. (Associated Press, "Crude Will Signed by Hughes Found," *Daily Oklahoman*, Okla. City, 4/30/76, pp. 1-2)

HOMILY (hom′ə-lē) *noun* a religious discourse addressed to a congregation; sermon; an admonitory or moralizing discourse, especially a long, dull one.

HOMILETIC or HOMILETICAL *adj.* of or pertaining to preaching or to homilies; of or pertaining to homiletics.

HOMILETICALLY *adv.*

HOMILETICS (hom′ ə-let′iks) *noun* (construed as singular) the art of writing and preaching sermons.

HOMILIST *noun* a person who writes or delivers homilies.

1. See (1) under PHARISAIC.

2. See (1) under MIASMA.

3. [Robert] Altman's film [*Buffalo Bill and the*

Indians] is . . . outside the GENRE [of Westerns] but his perception of Buffalo Bill Cody, deftly played by Paul Newman, is of a CHARLATAN drunkard and exploiter . . . . Bill's phoniness is the springboard for a somewhat HOMILETIC, though enjoyable film about American illusions and their consequences. (D. Ryan, "The Western: A poignant film ushers it out," *Philadelphia Inquirer*, 9/5/76, pp. 1-E, 8-E)

4. Unrepentant, [Archbishop] LeFebre decided to go ahead [last week] with the Mass [in Latin] in Lille, even though Pope Paul had forbidden it. In his emotional, sometimes tearful . . . HOMILY, he explained his position . . . . He attacked the vernacular liturgy, Communists and Freemasons. He denounced Rome's ECUMENICAL dialogues with Protestants: "You cannot marry truth and error . . . " (M. Sheils, Jane Friedman, "The Defiant Bishop," *Newsweek*, 9/13/76, p. 90)

5. Still, Carter was on to something in the American mood after Vietnam and Watergate—a strain identified in [Hamilton] Jordan's memo as an unmet hunger for "strong moral leadership"—and he created a political style to suit it. The campaign blended the perpetual dawn-to-midnight motion of his four-year run for governor with the HOMILETIC I-love-everybody air of caring . . . . (P. Goldman, "Sizing Up Carter," *Newsweek*, 9/13/76, p. 60)

HOMOEROTICISM (hō´ mō-i-rot´ i-siz´ əm) *noun* a tendency to be sexually aroused by a member of the same sex; homosexuality.

HOMOEROTIC *adj.*

1. That's right: the script of the [TV] play [*Song of Myself*] deals with [Walt] Whitman's homosexuality. Indeed, centers on it. Apparently, the more the creators of this dramatization researched Whitman's life, the more they became convinced that HOMOEROTICISM was at its core. (M. Duberman, Review, *New York Times*, 1/11/76, Section 2, p. 27)

2. The PARADIGM of moral "decency" . . . recurs as an important element in Mr. [Martin] Green's new book [*Children of the Sun*], only now it is . . . portrayed . . . as the countervailing ANTITHESIS to the "decadent" thesis of English culture in this century . . . . It is . . . a harlequin, HOMOEROTIC world in which . . . all the conventional standards of British respectability are mocked and repudiated . . . . (H. Kramer, Review, *New York Times*, 1/25/76, Section 7, p. 2)

HORTATORY (hôr´ tə-tōr´ e, -tôr-ē), also **HORTATIVE** (hôr´ tə-tiv) *adj.* urging to some course of conduct or action, especially to do good deeds; exhorting; encouraging; giving advice.

1. The Chinese Communist Party never made any bones about using art as a tool, fitted to propaganda purposes . . . . Official Chinese art became HORTATORY posters, filled with symbolic figures representing the soldier, the factory worker, the peasant, the oppressed foreign minorities, the BOURGEOISIE, the capitalist and so on. (R.Chelminski, "In China, a breath of fresh air brightens up the official palette," *Smithsonian*, March 1976, p. 32)

2. Undoubtedly the story [*The Little Engine That Could*] came out of the glory days of railroading, when there were steam engines that really did go chuff chuff chuff, providing the LEITMOTIF "I think I can—I think I can." . . . . Yet it is too glib to interpret the Little Blue Engine's HORTATORY message as a sort of capitalistic locomotive cheer—the inner-directed man's Jesus prayer—to call the story, as did a Time writer, "an Establishment epic." Actually, *The Little Engine That Could* is more attuned to the folklore of children than the folklore of capitalism. (R. R. Lingeman, Review, *New York Times*, 5/2/76, Section 7, p. 49)

3. But in a discussion of *Lady Sings the Blues* [in *The Devil Finds Work*, by James Baldwin], Baldwin finds that old HORTATORY, rhythmic voice; . . . He notes that the movie "is related to the black American experience in about the same way . . . that Princess Grace Kelly is related to the Irish potato famine . . ." (Orde Coombs, Review, *New York Times*, 5/2/76, Section 7, p. 7)

HOURI (hŏŏr´ ē, hour´ e) *noun, pl.: -*RIS one of the beautiful virgins provided in Paradise for all faithful Muslims; a seductively beautiful woman.

1. Marvin (Jack Weston [in Neil Simon's play, *California Suite*]) has come West to celebrate the bar mitzvah of his nephew and been given the surprise present of a blonde hooker (Leslie Easterbrook). After a night of amnesiac pleasure, Marvin wakes to find this HOURI, a vodka overachiever, COMATOSE in his bed. (T. E. Kalem, Review, *Time*, 6/21/76, p. 43)

2. See (1) under KHOL.

HOYDEN (hoid´ᵊn) or HOIDEN *noun* a boisterous, bold, rude girl or woman; a tomboy.

HOYDEN or HOYDENISH *adj.* boisterous and bold; rude; tomboyish.

HOYDENISHNESS or HOYDENISM *noun*.

1. . . . she [Tammy Grimes] knew what it was to agonize through an awards ceremony, having won a Tony early in her career for her work as the HOYDENISH heroine of the 1960 musical hit, *The Unsinkable Molly Brown*, and again for *Private Lives*. (R. Berkvist, "Tammy Talks About Neil," *New York Times*, 6/20/76, Section 2, p. 7)

2. He [Oliver Barrett IV, in *Love Story*, by Erich Segal] defied his father . . . to marry the lovely Radcliffe HOYDEN Jenny Cavilleri, daughter of a humble Cranston, R.I. pastry baker. (B. Cook, "Segal Tries Harder, and That's the Trouble," *National Observer*, week ending 3/26/77, p. 21)

HUBRIS (hyōō´bris, hōō-) *noun* excessive, insolent, or wanton pride (or self-assurance or arrogance).

HUBRISTIC (hyōō-bris´tik) *adj.*

HUBRISTICALLY *adv.*

1. Landslides [in presidential elections] breed the kind of HUBRIS that produced Vietnam and Watergate; hard campaigns . . . build character even as they test it. (P. Goldman and J.J. Lindsay, "The Torture Trail," *Newsweek*, 1/12/76, p. 28)

2. . . . I agree with such acute monitors of the controversy as James Burnham and Jeffrey Hart who insist that science is not only HUBRISTIC but childish to the extent that it finds itself saying that the case for the harmlessness of pot

is substantially established. (W.F. Buckley Jr., *Execution Eve and Other Contemporary Ballads*, G. P. Putnam's Sons, 1975, p. 392)

3. . . . he [Shockley] is a live carrier of scientific HUBRIS. (W.F. Buckley Jr., *Ibid.*, p. 472)

4. According to the traditional academic HUBRIS, political leaders who pose such questions [as Gov. Edmund G. Brown Jr.'s "Why is it better to have a smaller number of students in each class?"] ask essentially political questions, and thus deserve less than full disclosure as to what the evidence does or does not in fact show. But . . . such questions . . . deserve to be answered with candor. (G.W. Bonham, "Back to First Principles" [Editorial], *Change*, October 1975, p. 12)

5. See (1) under EVANESCENT.

6. Thucydides was really a most fitting author for [ex-President of Harvard, Nathan M. Pusey's] study; the historian's study, after all, is Athens, the HUBRIS and decline of an imperial democracy . . . (N.W. Aldrich Jr., "Harvard On The Way Down," *Harper's*, March 1976, p. 40)

7. . . . Herodotus . . . did his historical bit in compliment of the Persian letter-carriers of 5 B.C., and if only we hadn't HUBRISTICALLY inscribed his paean of praise on the facade of the New York Post Office, innumerable postmasters would have been spared listening to customers inquiring if it was snow, rain, heat or gloom of night that stayed their local courier from his appointed round? (P. Ryan, "Postmen can blame it on Old Horsley," *Smithsonian*, December 1975, p. 144)

8. . . . it seems to me time for some of the high-and-mighty ones [doctors who believe laetrile is effective against cancer], the know-it-all ones, to put HUBRIS aside and to acknowledge the vastness of their ignorance of the human being. (J.J. Kilpatrick, "Brawl Brewing Over Laetrile," *Saturday Oklahoman & Times*, 4/3/76, p. 8)

9. In another ten years . . . Mr. [Arthur] Schlesinger may make considerable progress, taking his lead from Mr. Patrick Moynihan and Mr. Richard Goodwin, both of them ardent and self-proclaimed liberals . . . , who now speak about . . . the HUBRIS of centralized

power, about the failures of canonical liberalism to help the race question or do much about poverty. (W.F. Buckley Jr., *Up From Liberalism*, Arlington House, 2nd Printing 1968, p. xxv (New Preface))

10. See (3) under DERACINATE.

11. And then, as if Elly Zendt had been guilty of the sin of HUBRIS, on the night of August 10 [1844], when the road lay clear and easy to Oregon, her husband Levi . . . knew that he was destined to turn back. (J.A. Michener, *Centennial*, Fawcett, 1975, p. 401)

12. See (4) under NEMESIS.

13. See (5) under ACERBIC.

14. The battle plan . . . called for him [Jimmy Carter] to finesse the March 2 Massachusetts primary with only a token effort . . . . But a post-New Hampshire attack of HUBRIS tempted him into Massachusetts, on the strength of a . . . scouting trip by [Charles] Kirbo and an EPHEMERAL surge in the polls . . . Carter limped in fourth . . . . (P. Goldman, "Sizing Up Carter," *Newsweek*, 9/13/76, p. 60)

15. See (2) under LIBIDINOUS.

HUMMOCK (hum'ǝk) *noun* an elevated well-drained tract of land rising above the general level of a marshy region; a knoll or hillock; a low, rounded hill; a tract of fertile, heavily wooded land, higher than a surrounding marshy area.

HUMMOCKY *adj.*

1. Just to sign up for a paltry hour [on the Central Park tennis courts] you must make a special, early-morning trip to the courts . . . and confront a formidable line which eventually leads you [to] a formidable lady . . . who seems to take perverse pleasure in informing you that . . . the only thing . . . available is one of the HUMMOCKY clay courts, and that only between 6 and 7 p.m. (R. Schickel, "Playing Tennis Here is Fun if You Survive the Obstacles," *New York Times*, 1/11/76, Section 5, p. 2)

HYPERBOLE (hī-pûr'bǝ-lē) *noun* obvious and intentional exaggeration for effect; an extravagant or deliberately inflated statement or figure of speech not intended to be taken literally.

HYPERBOLIC *adj.*

HYPERBOLICALLY *adv.*

HYPERBOLISM *noun* the use of hyperbole.

HYPERBOLIZE *verb* to use hyperbole; exaggerate; to represent or express with hyperbole or exaggeration.

1. Sometimes . . . [in André Malraux, author Jean] Lacouture takes off on clouds of that French HYPERBOLE the English language does not accommodate without irony. (Mavis Gallant, Review, *New York Times*, 1/11/76, Section 7, pp. 1-2)

2. . . . the fact is that Nixon's HYPERBOLIC patriotism and garrulous bellicosity and itchy piety are pretty standard for our Presidents. (R. Sherrill, Review of *The Time of Illusion*, by Jonathan Schell, *New York Times*, 1/18/76, Section 7, p. 2)

3. He [the ringmaster of the Cartwright Circus] delivered an introduction that rose in HYPERBOLE, and at the end he was shouting at the top of his powerful voice, "Daring Dan and his tribe of Wild Apache . . . ." (J.A. Michener, *Centennial*, Fawcett, 1975, p. 763)

4. The strange thing about this pamphlet [describing the attractions of the town of Centennial] was that it contained no HYPERBOLE. The palatial homes shown had been built by men who arrived . . . with no money. The crops of the farmers were exactly as pictured . . . . (J.A. Michener, *Ibid.*, p. 842)

5. But what of . . . the patient, who did not live to witness her contribution to medical science and who went to her grave ignorant that her tumor was very much alive [because of cell culture techniques] in George Gay's laboratory? . . . . "Helen Lane [the dead patient] has achieved immortality, both figuratively and literally," intoned my medical school professor. At the time, I thought the comment a little HYPERBOLIC, but over the years . . . I came to realize that Helen Lane had become an item of true medical folklore. (L.E. Karp, "The immortality of a cancer victim dead since 1951," *Smithsonian*, March 1976, p. 55)

6. If the Introduction—by Eugene Ionesco—

to *Volcano*, by Maurice and Katia Krafft] is a masterpiece of HYPERBOLE, it is exactly right, for the volcano is HYPERBOLIC in action. (M. Kernan, Review, *Smithsonian*, March 1976, p. 104)

7. . . . the fragility of Miss [Pauline] Kael's HYPERBOLIC claims [in the book, *Reeling*] is nowhere better illustrated than in her notorious review of *Last Tango in Paris* . . . . "Bertolucci and Brando have altered the face of an art form . . . . This is a movie people will be arguing about . . . for as long as there are movies." (R. Brustein, Review, *New York Times*, 4/4/76, Section 7, p. 2)

8. A not-so-new electronic gadget—the Citizens Band radio—is suddenly sweeping the country. And when I say "sweeping," I'm not being HYPERBOLIC. The Federal Communications Commission . . . received no fewer than 73,000 [license applications and renewals] . . . in January 1975; in January 1976, more than half a million arrived . . . (M. Harwood, "America with its ears on," *New York Times*, 4/25/76, Section 6, p. 28)

9. In his book, *Witness*, [Whitaker] Chambers, with his usual HYPERBOLE, says,"Alger Hiss and his wife I had come to regard as friends as close as a man ever makes in his life," but . . . Chambers was full of wrong information about his "close friend." (R. Sherrill, Review of *Alger Hiss: The True Story*, by John Chabot Smith, *New York Times*, 4/25/76, Section 7, p. 42)

10. In [Philip] Marlowe's case, the blend [of his narration] is smoother than Jack Daniels'—a mix of wisecracks, HYPERBOLE, dialogue that you hear coming off the pages, and a richness of simile that will give you a literary high. (R. Fuller, Review of *The Life of Raymond Chandler*, by Frank MacShane, *Philadelphia Inquirer*, 5/30/76, p. 10-I)

11. His [President Ford's] current slogan— "Peace, Prosperity and Trust"—is HYPERBOLE, but as slogans go it isn't too bad. (M. Lerner, "Conventions promise to be exciting," *Norman* [Okla.] *Transcript*, 6/4/76, p. 6)

12. For once, circus HYPERBOLE comes close to fact. At one end of the Gyro-Wheel's arms [in the Ringling Brothers and Barnum & Bailey Circus] is a heavy counterweight; at the other

is a circular wire-mesh cage 8 ft. in diameter. Bale and his wife Jeanette give the cage a mighty push. As it begins to turn, Bale hops inside, then makes like a hamster in an exercise wheel. As the cage rises, he runs up the inside to help maintain speed. When it reaches the top, Bale backpedals frantically to slow the shooshing descent, reversing again at the bottom to propel himself around the loop once more . . . . Cardiac-arrest time . . . comes when Bale climbs outside the cage and does the whole heart-stopping routine standing on top, with nothing between him and a nasty tumble but an exquisite sense of balance. (Anon., *Time*, 4/26/76, pp. 85-86)

13. See (1) under QUIFF.

14. Says Carl Sanders, the liberal whom Carter defeated for the Georgia governorship: "Hell, Carter is a lot more liberal than I ever was." Adds Carter with some HYPERBOLE: "My socioeconomic positions are not really different from Mo Udall's." (Anon., "Stampede to Carter," *Time*, 6/21/76, p. 12)

15. See (1) under PROCRUSTEAN.

HYPERBOREAN or **H̲YPERBOREAN** (hī′pər-bôr′ē-en, -bôr′, -bə-rē′-) *adj.* (if lower case) pertaining to or of the extreme north; frigid; arctic; very cold; (if capitalized) of the Hyperboreans.

HYPERBOREAN or **H̲YPERBOREAN** *noun* (if capitalized) an inhabitant, according to Greek Mythology, of a northern region of sunshine and everlasting spring beyond the mountains of the north wind; (if lower case) a person of a far northern region.

1. Is all this [searching for graves] morbid? I hardly think so . . . . Do not merely seek out "The Great." It meant something to me—and perhaps to them—to find Adelaide Crapsey in Rochester, and H. P. Lovecraft in ELDRITCH and HYPERBOREAN Providence. (J. Williams, "Paying Respects," *New York Times*, 12/19/76, Section 7, p. 27)

HYPERTROPHY (hī-pûr′ trə-fē) *noun* abnormal growth or enlargement of a part or organ; excessive growth; excessive accumulation of any kind.

HYPERTROPHY *verb* to affect with or undergo hypertrophy.

HYPERTROPHIC *adj.*

1. Or sometimes we augment our own knowledge so that we know too much to teach. Several distinguished scholars who are immersed in large and important subjects suffer from this HYPERTROPHY. If a well-informed person asks them penetrating questions about their field, they will reply freely; but if they have to talk about it to laymen or beginning students, they have scarcely any idea where to begin . . . . They know it all; but they do not know what other people do not know about it. (G. Highet, "The Need to 'Make It New,'" *Chronicle of Higher Education*, 6/21/76, p. 40)

2. See (1) under PERIPHRASTIC.

3. See (2) under PROXIMATE.

HYPERTYPICAL (hi'pər-tip'i-kəl) *adj.* surpassing the type; showing abnormal development of characteristics.

1. As the book [*A New Age Now Begins*, by Page Smith] goes deeper and deeper into its military phase, Smith's HYPERTYPICAL revolutionary emerges as a man without whom even Washington's magic might have been in vain—and that is the common soldier of the Continental line. (G. Dangerfield, Review, *New York Times*, 2/22/76, Section 7, p. 7)

HYPOCHONDRIA (hī'pə-kon'drē-ə) or **HYPOCHONDRIASIS** *noun* an abnormal condition characterized by a depressed emotional state and imaginary ill health; excessive worry or talk about one's health.

HYPOCHONDRIAC *noun* a person suffering from or subject to hypochondria; a person who worries or talks excessively about his health.

HYPOCHONDRIAC or **HYPOCHONDRIACAL** *adj.* pertaining to, suffering from, or produced by hypochondria.

HYPOCHONDRIACALLY (hī'po-kon-drī'ak-ə-lē) *adv.*

1. The R. D. Laing who emerges in . . . [Richard I.] Evans' book [*R.D. Laing: The Man and His Ideas*] is extraordinarily self-centered, and one sympathizes with the explosion of Amitai Etzioni over Laing's HYPOCHONDRIACAL NARCISSISM. (A. Lacy, Review, *Chronicle of Higher Education*, 5/24/76, p. 20)

2. "You know," Casey Stengel said about a quiet Arkansan named John Sain, "he don't say much, but that don't matter much, because when you're out there on the mound, you got nobody to talk to." Pitchers are individualists, brave, stubborn, CEREBRAL, HYPOCHONDRIACAL and lonely. (R. Kahn, *The Boys of Summer*, Harper and Row, 1971, p. 96)

3. "I agree with him [Ivan Illich] in part [said Dr. Lewis Thomas]. In recent years we've become obsessed with health to such an extent that we are almost a HYPOCHONDRIACAL society. We're now spending $120 billion a year on health compared to $10 billion in 1950 . . . . I do agree there is a tendency these days to 'medicalize' a great many social problems which are really beyond the scope of medicine . . . . On the other hand, I do have to disagree with Illich on doctor-made disease—what he calls IATROGENESIS." (Lee Edson, "The Dark Secret of Doctors: Most Things Get Better By Themselves," *New York Times*, 7/4/76, Section 6, p. 115)

4. See (2) under NEBBISH.

HYPOTHERMIA (hī'pə-thûr'mē-ə) *noun* a subnormal body temperature; (in Medicine) the artificial reduction of body temperature to slow metabolic processes, usually for facilitating heart surgery.

HYPOTHERMAL *adj.* lukewarm; tepid; of or characterized by hypothermia.

1. . . . photographers [in cold weather] caught up in the ecstasy of making great pictures can needlessly end up with frostbite or even HYPOTHERMIA. (B.W. Most, "On Taking Pictures in Cold Weather," *New York Times*, 2/6/77, Section 2, p. 38)

I

IATROGENIC (ī-ă′ trə-jen′ ik, ē-ă′ -) *adj.* (of a neurosis or physical disorder) caused by the diagnosis, manner, or treatment of a physician or surgeon; caused by medical treatment: said especially of imagined symptoms, disorders, or ailments induced by a physician's words or actions.

IATROGENICITY *noun.*

1. . . . Louis Schneider [in the book, *The Sociological Way of Looking at the World*] . . . has found a metadigm for social action in irony, or, for those who prefer the medical term, the IATROGENIC principle . . . . Schneider means by "irony" what sociologists used to call "unanticipated" or "unintended" consequences. (Sharon Zukin, Review, *Chronicle of Higher Education*, 3/22/76, p. 13)

2. [Ivan] Illich thinks that . . . modern medicine has turned the citizens of advanced industrial nations into lifelong patients who are presumed sick until proven healthy. The paradoxical result, Illich argues in his brilliant new book *Medical Nemesis*, is an epidemic of multiple "IATROGENESIS"—the ancient Greek term for physician-induced illness. (K.L. Woodward, Review, *Newsweek*, 6/7/76, p. 87)

3. See (3) under HYPOCHONDRIA.

ICON (ī′ kon) *noun* a picture, image, figure, or other representation; (in the Orthodox Eastern Church) a representation in painting, enamel, etc. of some sacred personage, as Christ or a saint or angel, itself venerated as sacred.

ICONIC or **ICONICAL** *adj.*

1. . . . Levine [Metropolitan Opera Music Director] explained, "we feel you don't create grandeur with lots of papier-mache ICONS. You put on stage a grandeur made up of space and height." (R.M. Braun, "The Met's New Team Rediscovers 'Aida,'" *New York Times*, 2/1/76, Section 2, p. 17)

2. By the end of the war [World War I] the machine gun was . . . assured a permanent niche in the pantheon of armaments. In fact, 50 years after its invention, it had become something of a contemporary ICON. (W.V. Thomas, Review of *The Social History of the Machine Gun*, by John Ellis, *Chronicle of Higher Education*, 3/1/76, p. 14)

3. In *Missouri Breaks* they [Marlon Brando and Jack Nicholson] face off against one another, not only as characters but as magic ICONS of our lives. Brando is Robert E. Lee Clayton, a HISTRIONIC, half-mad bounty hunter, Nicholson is his quarry, Tom Logan, the easygoing leader of a gang of rustlers. (J. Kroll, Review, *Newsweek*, 5/24/76, p. 103)

4. See (1) under SIMIAN.

5. The peasants [in paintings by Jean Francois Millet] are large. The fill the foreground. They make it uncomfortable to be the traditional audience of salon painting, the middle-class observer. They are also deliberately ICONIC. (R. Hughes, Review of Millet's centenary exhibition at London's Hayward Gallery, *Time*, 2/23/76, p. 60)

6. If there is a hero of *The Best Years* [a book by Joseph C. Goulden] it has to be the doughty clubhouse politician from Kansas City [Harry Truman] who defied the experts, who transformed the election of 1948 into a ceremonial smashing of the ICONS of technology. (M.F.

Nolan, Review, *New York Times*, 6/20/76, Section 7, p. 4)

ICONOCLAST (ī-kon′ə-klast′) *noun* a person who attacks or ridicules cherished beliefs, traditional institutions, etc., as being based on error or superstition; a breaker or destroyer of images, especially those set up for religious veneration.

ICONOCLASM *noun* the action, doctrines, beliefs, or spirit of an iconoclast.

ICONOCLASTIC *adj.*

ICONOCLASTICALLY *adv.*

1. . . . we are reminded . . . of Jimmy Cannon's deflating words—that they [baseball heroes] are just little boys playing baseball. As much might be said, in the same ICONOCLASTIC mode, about Toscanini, or Flagstad. (W.F. Buckley Jr., *Execution Eve and Other Contemporary Ballads*, G.P. Putnam's Sons, 1975, p. 218)

2. The traces of skepticism [John Kenneth] Galbraith shows are temperamental, not ICONOCLASTIC. They are hardly intended to induce an organic or principled rejection in the reader [of *China Passage*] of modern Chinese society, the most advanced totalitarian society in the world. (W.F. Buckley Jr., *Ibid.*, p. 279)

3. The public exercises, in particular over a politician, a genuine tyranny, the conservative justification for which is: It is right that public figures should not express themselves, concerning an issue of grave social moment, ICONOCLASTICALLY. (W.F. Buckley Jr., *Ibid.*, p. 394)

4. . . . Lenny Bruce . . . required a nation riding on a frenzy of ICONOCLASM, where grown-ups, sitting around a bar, felt a sense of liberation on hearing taboo words spoken out loud, smuttily, leeringly, by a "comedian." (W.F. Buckley Jr., *Ibid.*, p. 403)

5. Somebody has got to rescue us from the women's liberation movement, and if Miss [Germaine] Greer gets over her fundamentalist ICONOCLASM, she might be just the person to do it. (W.F. Buckley Jr., *Ibid.*, p. 418)

6. In . . . 1956 *Collier's* published the article [about Duke Snider preferring farming to professional baseball if the latter didn't pay so

well], Snider and myself [Roger Kahn] sharing the by-line. The piece stands as accurate, reasonably balanced and mild compared to the commercial sports ICONOCLASM of the 1970's. (R. Kahn, *The Boys of Summer*, Harper and Row, 1971, p. 378)

7. It is ironic . . . that [Evelyn] Waugh began as an ICONOCLAST . . . and ended as a stern, constricted moralist. . . . It is his grandest oddity. (L.E. Sissman, Review of *Evelyn Waugh: A Biography*, by Christopher Sykes, *The New Yorker*, 2/9/76, p. 108)

8. "It's [the desire for vests is] a temporary pomposity of the young," replied John Weitz, the designer and a well-known ICONOCLAST. (L. Sloane, "Suits Take On a Vested Interest," *New York Times*, 3/28/76, Section 3, p. 9)

9. His [T.E. Lawrence's] newest biographer [John E. Mack, author of *A Prince of Our Disorder: The Life of T.E. Lawrence*] is a professor of psychiatry at Harvard Medical School. But . . . Mack's interest in T.E. Lawrence is neither ICONOCLASTIC nor clinical . . . [Says Mack:] "I unabashedly regard him as a great man and an important historical figure." (W. Clemons, Review, *Newsweek*, 4/12/76, p. 98)

10. Apostles of the new quantification [of history], Eric Lampard observes in the witty introduction to this collection [entitled *The New Urban History*, edited by Leo F. Schnore], come on with the zeal of new converts, converts whose "ICONOLCASTIC boorishness has often brought out the fretfulness, clownishness, and downright ugliness" latent in the priests of a defensive orthodoxy. (M. Frisch, Review, *Chronicle of Higher Education*, 4/26/76, p. 19)

11. See (1) under PISCICIDE.

12. For years, [Steven J.] Ross [head of Warner Communications, Inc.] has been vainly trying to convince *Mad* publisher William Gaines to carry advertising in his ICONOCLASTIC magazine, which already nets better than $2 million a year on revenues of about $6 million. (A.J. Mayer, M. Kasindorf, "Entertainment: The Undertaker," *Newsweek*, 6/7/76, p. 73)

13. But with creativity [at a newspaper office] comes unorthodoxy, ICONOCLASM and passionate, if sometimes misdirected, integrity. (R.

Kahn, *op. cit.*, p. 72)

14. See (1) under CLYSTER.

15. See (2) under LUDDITE.

16. See (2) under MANDALA.

17. See (7) under COGNOSCENTI.

ICONOGRAPHY (ī kə-nog′ rə-fē) *noun* a symbolic representation or pictorial illustration of conventional meanings by means of images or figures; the study or analysis of subject matter and its meaning in the visual arts; iconology.

ICONOGRAPHER or **ICONOLOGIST** noun.

ICONOGRAPHIC or **ICONOGRAPHICAL** or **ICONOLOGICAL** *adj.*

1. Of the several André Malraux incarnations available, current ICONOGRAPHY usually offers two: the artist-as-antifascist . . . and the watchful old man . . . . (Mavis Gallant, Review of *André Malraux*, a book by Jean Lacouture, *New York Times*, 1/11/76, Section 7, p. 1)

2. See (1) under SARCOPHAGUS.

3. See (1) under CATECHISM.

4. The question that has lately been at issue with these [early abstract] paintings is whether they are really abstract, or, as many specialists now believe, actual representations of an ESOTERIC religious ICONOGRAPHY. (H. Kramer, Review of Angelica Rudenstine's catalog of the Guggenheim Museum's exhibition, *Paintings: 1880-1945*, *New York Times*, 4/18/76, Section 2, p. 33)

5. In two recent ones, *Not To Disturb* and *The Hot House by the East River*, the [Muriel] Spark techniques—obliqueness, blatant contrivance, deliberate mystification; her ICONOGRAPHIC characters, as in medieval morality plays; and her love of the grotesque—succeed only in being irritating. (Gail Kessler Kinetz, Review of *The Abbess of Crewe: A Modern Morality Tale*, by Muriel Spark, *Ms.*, May 1976, pp. 26-27)

6. See (1) under JAPONAISERIE.

7. A new city under the EUPHORIA of the coming of FDR was literally springing up around [Merian C.] Cooper and [Ernest B.] Schoed-

sack [creators of the original *King Kong* movie]: their plan to end with Kong scaling the city's highest building had to be changed three times, climaxing in the incredible ICONOGRAPHIC luck of the just-completed Empire State Building. (J. Kroll, "The Movies Go Ape—Again, *Newsweek*, 12/20/76, p. 103)

ICONOLATRY (ī′ kə-nol′ ə-trē) *noun* the worship or adoration of ICONS or images.

ICONOLATER *noun*.

ICONOLATROUS *adj.*

1. It [Mecca] was the crossroads of two of the most important trade routes of the seventh century . . . . Wedged in thus between the Sasanian empire . . . Hellenism, ICONOLATRY, and the ecclesiastical spirit—it was exposed as well to Judaism, GNOSTICISM, and the oratorical "moralism" of Bedouin nomads. Muhammad drew on all of these in articulating his prophecy. (C. Geertz, Review of *The Venture of Islam: Conscience and History in a World Civilization. Vol. 1: The Classical Age of Islam; Vol. 2: The Expansion of Islam in the Middle Periods; Vol. 3: The Gunpowder Empire and Modern Times*, by Marshall G.S. Hodgson, *New York Review of Books*, 12/11/75, p. 20)

ID (id) *noun* (in Psychoanalysis) the part of the psyche that is the source of primal, instinctive urges, it is dominated by the pleasure principle and irrational wishing, and its impulses are modified by the ego and the superego.

1. For the past hundred years a single, powerful concept has infused almost every doctrine in the social sciences. That is the idea that under the rational surface appearance of the world is an underlying structure of irrationality . . . . For Freud, under the veneer of civilization (the social super-ego) was the turbulent, aggressive ID. (D. Bell, Review of *Structural Anthropology, Vol. II*, by Claude Lévi-Strauss, translated by Monique Layton, *New York Times*, 3/14/76, Section 7, p. 23)

2. His [Donald Barthelme's] true American ancestor is S.J. Perelman, his predecessor at the *New Yorker*....Perelman's antic haymakers spring from the irrepressible ID, the old Adam (Groucho Marx) who screams

"hands off!" to mass culture. Barthelme . . . has no such angry all-American optimism. (R. Locke, Review of *Amateurs*, a book by Donald Barthelme, *New York Times*, 12/19/76, Section 7, p. 17)

3. "War abhors the individual, and this is war [said Natalie Novotny]. I for example have had to eradicate the last VESTIGES of my own self. I have neither the ID nor ego." "That explains much" [said Russel Wren]. By which I suppose I meant her LASSITUDE in bed. (Thomas Berger, *Who Is Teddy Villanova?*, Delacorte Press/ Seymour Lawrence, 1977, p. 181)

IDIOPATHIC (id′ ē-ə-path′ ik) *adj.* of unknown or uncertain cause, as a disease.

IDIOPATHY (id′ ē-op′-ə-thē) *noun* a disease not preceded or occasioned by any other.

1. . . . Miss [Lisa] Alther and Mrs. [Doris] Lessing share an energetic intelligence, an absence of self-pity, an appetite for experience . . . . They are pioneers of the IDIOPATHIC, not bookkeepers of the emotions. (J. Leonard, Review of *Kinflicks*, a book by Lisa Alther, *New York Times*, 3/14/76, Section 7, p. 4)

IDIOSYNCRASY (id′ ē-ə-sing′ krə-sē, -sin′-) *noun* a characteristic, habit, mannerism, or the like, that is peculiar to an individual.

IDIOSYNCRATIC *adj.*

IDIOSYNCRATICALLY *adv.*

1. See (1) under LONGUEUR.

2. One asks: are there characteristic IDIOSYN-CRASIES of the liberal mind at work? I think there are. (W.F. Buckley Jr., *Up From Liberalism*, Arlington House, 2nd Printing 1968, p. 37)

3. See (3) under PARVENU.

4. See (7) under APHORISM.

5. I look to the folks [Caterine Milinaire and Carol Troy] who wrote *Cheap Chic* like I look to myself: stylish yet refreshingly IDIOSYN-CRATIC; classic yet breezily irreverent; elegant, witty, original, devil-may-care. (Jane Shapiro, Review, *Ms.*, May 1976, p. 34)

6. But one of it [the book, *The Woman Said Yes: Encounters With Life and Death*, by Jessamyn West]'s guesses, of which our awareness grows without being forced, is that . . . each of us dies in a personal, IDIOSYNCRATIC way. (Nancy Hale, Review, *New York Times*, 5/2/76, Section 7, p. 4)

IMMACULATE (i-mak′ yə-lit) *adj.* free from spot or stain; spotlessly clean; free from moral blemish or impurity; pure; undefiled; innocent; without sin; free from fault or flaw; free from errors, as a text.

IMMACULATELY *adv.*

IMMACULATENESS or IMMACULACY *noun.*

1. Her [Sharon Fields'] attire was IMMACULATE. (I. Wallace, *The Fan Club*, Bantam Books, 1975, p. 343)

2. "She [Charlotte Douglas] was IMMACULATE of history, innocent of politics. . . " [Quote from the book, *A Book of Common Prayer*, by Joan Didion]. (Joyce Carol Oates, Review, *New York Times*, 4/3/77, Section 7, p. 34

IMMOLATE (im′ə-lāt′) *verb* to sacrifice; to kill, as a sacrificial victim, especially by fire; offer in sacrifice.

IMMOLATOR *noun.*

IMMOLATION *noun.*

1. Mr. [Robert] Littell's technique [in his book, *The October Circle*] is oblique and impressionistic; its effect is haunting. When a bitter character named Lev IMMOLATES himself as an act of political protest, he does not cease to be an unperson. The press simply reports his suicide as being prompted by an incurable disease. (M. Levin, Review, *New York Times*, 2/15/76, Section 7, p. 20)

2. Based on a real front-page case in the 1930's, [*In the Realm of the Senses*, a Japanese film] follows an affair between a novice in a geisha house and the MACHO husband of the madam . . . there is beauty and terror in the explicit sex scenes in which human flesh IMMO-LATES itself in an excess of ecstacy. (J. Kroll, Review, *Newsweek*, 10/18/76, p. 115)

IMMURE (i-myŏŏr′) *verb* to enclose within walls; to shut in; confine; seclude; imprison; to build or entomb in a wall.

IMMUREMENT *noun.*

1. . . . three years hence when the trial takes place, the word "Nazi" may have become totally ETIOLATED, causing the jury to wonder that anyone should particularly care about having been so designated. If that is the case I shall be left with nothing more than an expensive footnote in my autobiography, pointing to the irony that it was a conservative who struggled to regulate the use of a word so as to IMMURE within it some sense of the hideousness of Hitler. (W.F. Buckley Jr., *Execution Eve and Other Contemporary Ballads*, G.P. Putnam's Sons, 1975, p. 326)

IMPECCABLE (im-pek' ə-bəl) *adj.* faultless; flawless; irreproachable; without defect or effort; not liable to sin; exempt from the possibility of doing wrong.

IMPECCABLY *adv.*

IMPECCABILITY *noun.*

IMPECCANT *adj.* not sinning; sinless; blameless.

IMPECCANCE or **IMPECCANCY** *noun.*

1. This IMPECCABLY edited volume [*John Jay. Unpublished Papers 1745-1780*, edited by Richard B. Morris and others] . . . will, at last, make possible, along with its successors, a full life and just appreciation of this statesman of the early Republic. (J.M. Banner Jr., Review, *New York Times*, 2/22/76, Section 7, p. 8)

2. James Aldridge's IMPECCABLE regional novel [*The Untouchable Juli*] whisks you on a trip into the 1930's, as lived in an Australian bush town called St. Helen. What Mr. Aldridge summons up is not nostalgia but a mix of small-town bigotry, cultural poverty and a kind of innocence that can lead to complications. (M. Levin, Review, *New York Times*, 3/14/76, Section 7, p. 32)

3. To all these issues and events [in the career of Frances Perkins] George Martin [author of the book, *Madame Secretary: Frances Perkins*] brings the fruits of early access to the Perkins papers, ample admiration for his subject, almost IMPECCABLE scholarship, a sure grasp of the milieus in which Perkins operated and a clear if somewhat plain style. (J. MacGregor Burns, Review, *New York Times*, 4/25/76, Section 7, p. 6)

4. "He [Henry Winkler] was unassuming and polite, with IMPECCABLE manners . . . ," reports executive producer [of *Happy Days*] Tom Miller. (Lois Armstrong, "AYYY—The Fonz A Smash, But Henry Winkler Finds Some Nightmares In His Happy Days," *People*, 5/24/76, p. 42)

5. That evening, Earl Blackwell is IMPECCABLE as always as he greets the guests on opening night of Manhattan's new private club, Doubles. (M. Goodman, "Earl Blackwell Chronicles And Entertains Celebrities—For Their Pleasure and His Profit," *People*, 5/24/76, p. 67)

6. It [the book, *A Big Wind for Summer*, by Gavin Black]'s all very British, in the best sense of the word. Black is a fine writer, and his plotting is IMPECCABLE. Put this high on your list. (N. Callendar, Review, *New York Times*, 5/2/76, Section 7, p. 63)

7. See (2) under SARTORIAL.

8. Le Cirque [a French restaurant in N.Y.] was where he noted also such exquisitely IMPECCABLE tastebuds as those of Margaret Truman, Rex Harrison . . . . (J. O'Brian, "Broadway," *Times Herald*, Norristown, Pa., 3/3/77, p. 28)

9. See (2) under BON VIVANT.

10. A gentleman [as reported in the May issue of *Atlantic*] requested a ham and cheese sandwich that the Burger King calls a Yumbo . . . . He walked out rather than call a ham and cheese a Yumbo. His principles are ANACHRONISMS but his prejudices are IMPECCABLE, and he is on my short list of civilization's friends. (G.F. Will, "Forget the 'Nutty Buddy,' vanilla will do," *Philadelphia Inquirer*, 5/10/77, p. 13-A)

11. She [Natalie Novotny] had the most IMPECCABLE rear I had ever seen among human kind . . . . It gave me [Russel Wren] no pleasure to make this identification now. (Thomas Berger, *Who Is Teddy Villanova?*, Delacorte Press/ Seymour Lawrence, 1977, pp. 154-155)

IMPLACABLE (im-plak'ə-bəl, -plā'kə-) *adj.* not placable; not to be appeased or pacified; relentless; inexorable; unappeasable; irreconcilable.

IMPLACABLY *adv.*

IMPLACABILITY *noun.*

1. See (1) under SPECIOUS.

2. The conservative must, therefore, guard against the self-discrediting generalization that our society is no longer "free," while insisting, as IMPLACABLY as the liberal does every time a Communist is harassed by a disciplinary law, that not an appropriation is passed by the legislature, but that our freedom is diminished. (W.F. Buckley Jr., *Up From Liberalism,* Arlingington House, 2nd Printing 1968, pp. 211-212)

3. Shively remained IMPLACABLE . . . . "We're not letting you out of here, least not till you and us get better acquainted." (I. Wallace, *The Fan Club,* Bantam Books, 1975, p. 263)

4. IMPLACABLY, cold-bloodedly, in short years, shattering egos, even careers, breaking up marriages, she [Sharon Fields] had used men in her climb to the pinnacle. (I. Wallace, *Ibid.,* p. 318)

5. See (5) under PARODY.

6. See (1) under GRAVID.

IMPORTUNATE (im-pôr′ chə-nit) or IMPOR-
TUNE (im′ pôr-tōōn′, -tyōōn′, im-pôr′ chən)
adj. urgent or persistent in solicitation; PER-
TINACIOUS, as in solicitations or demands;
troublesome; annoyingly urgent; refusing to be
denied.

IMPORTUNATELY or IMPORTUNELY *adv.*

IMPORTUNITY *noun.*

IMPORTUNE *verb* to beset with solicitations; demand with urgency or persistence; to make improper advances toward (a person); to beg for (something) urgently or persistently.

IMPORTUNER *noun.*

1. There is very little suffering going on these days as a result of IMPORTUNATE grand juries going after newspapermen. (W.F. Buckley Jr., *Execution Eve and Other Contemporary Ballads,* G.P. Putnam's Sons, 1975, p. 431)

2. "Yesterday I was IMPORTUNATE," Wainwright apologized. "Today I want you to meet

our minister," and he led Levi and Elly [Zendt] to the porch . . . . "Reverend Oster," Wainwright said, "I wish you'd inform these strangers that I'm a man of reasonably decent character." (J.A. Michener, *Centennial,* Fawcett, 1975, p. 355)

3. "You're wanted for heroin-pushing and the gypsy is prepared to charge you IMPORTUNED a schoolboy for immoral purposes if need be" [said Natalie Novotny to Russel Wren.]. (Thomas Berger, *Who Is Teddy Villanova?,* Delacorte Press/Seymour Lawrence, 1977, p. 188)

4. The schoolgirls, who wore ribboned lavender pancake hats and striped blazers with silver crests over their nonexistent left breasts . . . , now tried to seize me [Russel Wren] like IMPORTUNATE harlots. (Thomas Berger, *Ibid.,* p. 193)

IMPUNITY (im-pyōō′ ni-tē) *noun* exemption from penalty, harm, or punishment; immunity from detrimental effects, as of action.

1. During Prohibition, indiscriminate tipplers discovered that whisky could be downed with IMPUNITY in public places if it were concealed in a glass of milk. A few learned to like it that way and kept the habit after repeal, continuing to order an occasional brandy alexander (cream, brandy, and crème de cacao) or a sombrero (milk and Kahlua). But now drinkers are turning in larger numbers to the milky way. Liquor-store shelves are displaying a growing variety of dairy-based, premixed cocktails combining booze and moos . . . . Among leaders of the herd are Malcolm Hereford's Cows . . . . Heublein's ads show Cow bottles grazing in a green pasture and describe how Malcolm Hereford, a fictitious bull breeder, invented the drink. Concludes Hereford "A Cow-on-the-rocks is not a bum steer." (Anon., "Cows with a Kick," *Time,* 4/19/76, p. 69)

2. . . . I want to destroy for all time the myth that grandchildren are dear little creatures who can be adored and spoiled with IMPUNITY by their doting grandparents and then returned to their parents for the application of a proper upbringing. (T. Longstreth, "Notes on a dreary vacation," *Philadelphia Inquirer,* 10/5/76, p. 11-A)

3. Knowing I [Russel Wren] could do so with

IMPUNITY, I made a joke: "I might have been on my way to a golden shower." "I don't care what brand of soap you take baths with, sir!" she [Peggy Tumulty] said indignantly, making . . . a commercial interpretation of a term alien to her. (Thomas Berger, *Who is Teddy Villanova?*, Delacorte Press/Seymour Lawrence, 1977, p. 101)

INANE (i-nān′) *adj.* lacking sense or ideas; silly; foolish; empty; void; pointless.

INANELY *adv.*

INANITY (i-nan′ i-tē) *noun* lack of sense or ideas; silliness; emptiness; lack of depth or meaning; something inane.

INANITION *noun* exhaustion or depletion from lack of nourishment; starvation; lack of mental or moral vigor or spirit; emptiness.

1. At [Louise] Lasser's urging, the [*Mary Hartman* TV] show's writers have added more dimensions to the central character. Mary Hartman still utters INANE NON SEQUITURS. She is apt to inform phone callers: "I can't talk now . . . I'm on the telephone." But of late Mary is fitfully emerging from her CATATONIC trance to confront her doll's-house condition. (H.F. Waters and M. Kasindorf, "The Mary Hartman Craze," *Newsweek*, 5/3/76, p. 56)

2. Utterly outrageous, utterly self-possessed, an imp who can tease and startle and charm with a single remark, he [Malcolm Muggeridge] was the only M.C. who could have drawn [TV] viewers to a dreary summer filler called *Stop to Think*, where he nearly overcame the INANITY of the scripted questions. (H. Kenner, "At home with St. Mug," *New York Times*, 5/12/76, Section 6, p. 39)

3. DeLaurentiis . . . spent $24 million to produce *Kong* . . . . DeLaurentiis deserves the big payoff just for the INANE brilliance of his idea to re-Kong the king thriller of all time—an idea so INANELY brilliant that the universal minds at Universal had it too. (J. Kroll, "The Movies Go Ape—Again," *Newsweek*, 12/20/76, p. 102)

INCARNADINE (in-kär′ nə-dīn′ , -din, -dēn′) *verb* to make incarnadine.

INCARNADINE *noun* the color of either flesh or blood.

INCARNADINE *adj.* flesh-colored; pale pink; blood-red; crimson.

1. Bands of blue jays winging by at 100 or 200 feet in businesslike silence against a sky matching their azure are as much a part of autumn's rites in the East as the INCARNADINING of the multitudinous woods beneath them. (C. Ogburn, "In fall's clear skies birds part the air and raise the spirit," *Smithsonian*, September 1976, p. 65)

INCESTUOUS (in-ses′ chōō-əs) *adj.* of, involving, or having the nature of incest; guilty of incest.

INCEST *noun* sexual intercourse, cohabitation, or marriage between persons so closely related that marriage is legally or ritually forbidden.

INCESTUOUSLY *adv.*

INCESTUOUSNESS *noun.*

1. Unlike their colleagues in mathematics and the natural sciences, who train their students to become practicing biochemists, physicists, computer analysts, or laboratory technicians, humanists train humanists to train humanists to train humanists, AD INFINITUM. It is a narrow path leading inevitably to INCESTUOUS elitism and intellectual NARCISSISM. (Elinor Lenz, "The Humanities Go Public," *Change*, February 1976, p. 53)

2. See (1) under AUTO-DA-FÉ.

3. See (1) under AUSCULTATION.

4. Nothing could be more INCESTUOUS than a claque of Dodger fans rehearsing the merits of Pete Coscarart or Dolph Camilli. (J.M. Culkin, "Tinkers to Evers to '76," *New York Times*, 5/13/76, Section 5, p. 2)

5. See (3) under PEDOPHILIA.

INCHOATE (in-kō′ it) *adj.* just begun; in the early stages; incipient; rudimentary; imperfect; incomplete; not yet clearly or completely formed or organized.

INCHOATELY *adv.*

INCHOATENESS or INCHOATION *noun* beginning; origin; early stage.

1. The Constitution, to be sure, speaks of the impeachment procedure as available against a President found guilty of "high crimes and misdemeanors," but the phrase in question was probably accepted either because it was legal boiler plate (a misdemeanor, after all, is defined...as including a trivial misuse of the mailing frank, let alone the misuse of Air Force One for political purposes—it is inconceivable that a President goes a week without committing a legal misdemeanor), or as a sop to those, fearing the INCHOATE despot, Alexander Hamilton sought to reassure. (W.F. Buckley Jr., *Execution Eve and Other Contemporary Ballads*, G.P. Putnam's Sons, 1975, pp. 116–117)

2. In a world of INCHOATE change, an unpredictable electorate and an unmanageable Congress, the problems of the presidency . . . are less philosophic and more pedestrian . . . (S. Pett, Associated Press, "The Presidency: 'A Decline in Authority?'" *Sunday Oklahoman*, Okla. City, 1/29/76, p. 8-B)

3. [The] Wounded [female] diplodocus and the four young dinosaurs that had witnessed this massacre [of the male diplodocus by allosaurus] now swam back to the lagoon. In the days that followed, she began to experience the last INCHOATE urge she would ever know . . . . She was drawn by some inexplicable force back to the swamp . . . for some pressing reason she had never felt before. (J.A. Michener, CENTENNIAL, Fawcett, 1975, p. 82)

4. You can be sure that one day, perhaps just as Mary [Hartman] is enmeshed in an IN-CHOATE "Cuckoo's Nest" trauma, she will once again . . . pronounce . . . "Everything is going to be all right . . . . And afterward, we're all going to go to the House of Pancakes." (H.F. Waters, M. Kasindorf, "The Mary Hartman Craze," *Newsweek*, 5/3/76, p. 63)

5. A President is the articulator of collective aspirations, or he is not much . . . he should be able to elicit and . . . shape public sentiments that otherwise would be INCHOATE. (G.F. Will, "Ford's Real Weakness," *Newsweek*, 5/17/76, p. 114)

6. Debbie [in the book, *Find Debbie!* by Roy Brown] is a psychotic 14-year old, given to uncontrolled fits of rage . . . . Tied to Debbie's IN-CHOATE and disorderly life by bonds of love and hate, her family is by turns angry, remorseful, hopeful and guilt-stricken. (Gloria Levitas, Review, *New York Times*, 5/2/76, Section 7, p. 36)

7. The interrogator's need to be respected by his victims is one notable feature of a vague, INCHOATE subculture that exists in every country where torture is an established practice. (Anon., "Macabre World of Words and Ritual," *Time*, 8/16/76, p. 32)

8. See (1) under FECUND.

INCUBUS (in' kyǝ-bǝs, iṅg'-) *noun, pl.: -BI* (-bī) or -**BUSES** a demon supposed to descend upon sleeping persons, especially one in male form fabled to have sexual intercourse with women in their sleep; anything that oppresses one like a nightmare; a burden; a nightmare.

1. The controversies in which Senator [Joseph] McCarthy was engaged have no relevance whatever to what follows, whose meaning is the same for those who hated, and those who loved McCarthy . . . . I beg the reader who is anti-McCarthy to bear this in mind in the next few pages, during which he will be face to face with the INCUBUS; and I caution the reader who is pro-McCarthy . . . not to lose sight of the ball . . . . (W.F. Buckley Jr., *Up From Liberalism*, Arlington House, 2nd Printing 1968, p. 40)

2. He [Ronald Beard] hurried shuddering on to the Viale, which was an INCUBUS of traffic, the drivers operatic on their horns . . . . (A. Burgess, *Beard's Roman Women*, McGraw-Hill, 1976, p. 35)

3. "To those who see the past as an INCUBUS from which we must set ourselves free, I would reply, with Freud, that obsessions are purged only by understanding, not by repudiation. We cannot profitably look forward without also looking back" [Quote from a 1969 lecture by Hugh Trevor-Roper at London School of Economics]. (Caroline Seebohm, "Hugh Trevor-Roper: History Is Relevant," *New York Times*, 4/24/77, Section 7, p. 37)

INCULPATE (in-kul'pāt, in'kul-pāt') *verb* to charge with fault; blame; accuse; to involve in a charge; incriminate.

INCULPATION noun.

INCULPATORY adj.

1. During his imprisonment in the detention center near Pisa and the Washington hospital, [Ezra] Pound clung to his [Fascist] views. His release . . . was psychologically a letdown. He . . . assessed his past with the same severity that he had once applied to others. The ensuing silence was interrupted by occasional expressions of remorse. He had botched his life, he now felt . . . . Happily, he did not quit work on The Cantos, though he included them in the general INCULPATION. . . . (R. Ellmann, Review of Ezra Pound: The Last Rower; A Political Profile, by C. David Heymann; and The Cantos of Ezra Pound: The Lyric Mode, by Eugene Paul Nassur, New York Times, 4/4/76, Section 7, p. 25)

INCUNABULA (in′ kyŏŏ-nab′ yə-lə) noun (plural), sing.: **INCUNABULUM** early printed books, especially extant copies of books printed before 1500; the earliest stages of anything; infancy; beginnings.

INCUNABULAR adj.

1. There [at the 13th Annual International Antiquarian Book Fair, at New York's Plaza Hotel] celebrities like Zero Mostel and Jackie Onassis . . . and youth . . . browsed through more than $2 million worth of books, manuscripts and INCUNABULA. Among the items for sale was a two-volume set of Adolf Hitler's MEIN KAMPF, (inscribed by the author. The price . . . : $4,600. (Anon., "The New Literary Appreciation," Time, 4/25/77, p. 85)

INDIGENOUS (in-dij′ ə-nəs) adj. characterizing, or originating, existing, or growing in a particular region or country; native (usually followed by to); innate; inherent; inborn; natural (usually followed by to); AUTOCHTHONOUS; aboriginal.

INDIGENOUSLY adv.

INDIGENOUSNESS or **INDIGENITY** noun.

1. Iran is also committed to the development of an INDIGENOUS nuclear technology which will give it the capacity to construct nuclear weapons. (D. Oakley, "For Arabians . . . Oil Money Buys Guns," Norman [Okla.] Transcript, 2/5/76, p. 6)

2. The Arapaho and Cheyenne arrived very late on the scene [in Colorado]. They occupied land which wiser Indians like the Pawnee and more INDIGENOUS ones like the Ute had inspected for several centuries and found unproductive . . . their previous wanderings from east of the Mississippi and north to the Missouri to the arid plains had deprived them of most of their cultural heritage . . . . (J.A. Michener, Centennial, Fawcett, 1975, p. 206)

3. See (1) under OLIGARCHY.

4. National Review's prophecy coincides exactly with my own: "The Zimbabwe regime that would succeed the present Rhodesian government is going to be one more of those despotic, arbitrary, usually personalized, often tribal, frequently bloody political arrangements that are Africa's INDIGENOUS political products." (J.J. Kilpatrick, "New Morality, Old Hypocrisy," Daily Oklahoman, Okla. City, 4/14/76, p. 8)

5. When the dam [Tunxis Reservoir] was completed, Bloomfield [Conn.] signed a 50-year lease . . . to allow use of the floodwater storage basin behind the dam as a park. The state restricted the use of the land to things that would enhance or be INDIGENOUS to the surrounding environment. (V. Anderson, "Neighbors Grow Their Best Vegetables By a Dam Site," New York Times, 3/28/76, Section 2, p. 35)

6. When the Smithsonian Institute was founded 130 years ago, there was little recognized INDIGENOUS art in the United States except for the largely unappreciated arts of the Indians. (S.D. Ripley, "The view from the castle," Smithsonian, April 1976, p. 6)

7. The seeds of cassava and the sweet potato brought by early Portuguese explorers . . . have since become part of the basic diet for millions of Africans, who happen to live on a continent strangely unendowed with INDIGENOUS foods. (J. Grimond, "Europe's African Legacy: Mostly Bad, Some Good," New York Times, 5/2/76, Section 4, p. 2)

8. See (2) under SEDULOUS.

9. There are some very special streets in American cities, long recognized as anchors of place

and identity, that have suffered serious vicissitudes. Magazine Street in New Orleans is one . . . . Long blocks are now a "mirage like" mix of restoration and neglect . . . . Take your choice of Uncle Bill's Pool Hall or Tucci's elegant restaurant; enjoy the balconied and arcaded, INDIGENOUS and irreplaceable architecture in casual, INSOUCIANT decay. But, make no mistake, Magazine Street is reviving. (Ada Louise Huxtable, "The fall and rise of Main Street, *New York Times*, 5/30/76, Section 6, pp. 13-14)

10. See (4) under ROCOCO.

11. A recent study of industries and employment in developing countries by the International Labour Office (ILO) in Geneva concluded that new research and development is needed to bring about a "shift to INDIGENOUS raw materials, small hand-operated machinery and the use of various waste materials for the generation of energy in individual industrial plants." (W. Clark, "Big and/or little? Search is on for right technology," *Smithsonian*, July 1976, p. 44)

12. See (2) under PERSPICACITY.

INEFFABLE (in-ef´ ə-bəl) *adj.* too overwhelming to be expressed or described in words; inexpressible; too awesome or sacred to be spoken; unspeakable; unutterable.

INEFFABLY *adv.*

INEFFABILITY or **INEFFABLENESS** *noun*

1. See (1) under ENTRECHAT.

2. There were INEFFABLE glimpses [at the Republican convention] of Betty Ford dancing with Tony Orlando, Nelson Rockefeller displaying a telephone ripped out by an angry Reagan supporter, and a sea of kooky delegates' hats. (D. Gelman, Lucy Howard, "Hard Work, Hard News," *Newsweek*, 8/30/76, p. 78)

3. . . . a low-keyed, middle-size Australian, he is prosaic, pin-striped and so soft-spoken that his commands barely carry across a between-editions pressroom. But at 45, [Keith Rupert] Murdoch has stamped his INEFFABLE brand on newspapers of three continents—and last week after the peaceable take-over of the afternoon daily *New York Post* and an electrifying board-

room battle for control of Clay Felker's New York Magazine Co., he had established a solid beachhead at the center of the publishing world. (D. Gelman, *et al.*, "Press Lord Captures Gotham!" *Newsweek*, 1/17/77, p. 48)

4. See (1) under PANJANDRUM.

5. See (2) under BOSKY.

INELUCTABLE (in'i-luk'tə-bəl) *adj.* incapable of being avoided or evaded; inescapable; certain; inevitable.

INELUCTABILITY *noun*.

INELUCTABLY *adv.*

1. So it will be, not necessarily for McGovern himself: but for McGovern's dreams, surely; INELUCTABLY. It is necessarily so for anyone who seeks to do what only God can do. (W.F. Buckley Jr., *Execution Eve and Other Contemporary Ballads*, G.P. Putnam's Sons, 1975, p. 77)

2. When looking again into the camera, the President [Nixon] said, "Two wrongs do not make . . . ," a muted but fatalistic plea escaped me, as if to the headsman whose stroke is already committed, "No! Don't!" But it was INELUCTABLE, and we were informed that two wrongs do not make a right . . . . (W.F. Buckley Jr., *Ibid.*, p. 113)

3. See (1) under CINCTURE.

4. In the mid-16th century Bramante's memorial chapel would have leaped to the mind of any Roman whenever he thought of the locale of St. Peter's death. And this INELUCTABLE association turns the strange wheeling motion of the executioners [in Michelangelo's *Crucifixion of St. Peter*] into a topographical clue. (L. Steinberg, "Michelangelo's last painting: his gift to this century," *Smithsonian*, December 1975, p. 81)

5. A 23 ends with . . . [the] final syllables "are but us," namely the arbutus. All of which would be a frigid PEDANTIC game but for [author Louis] Zukovsky's INELUCTABLE passion to order a half-century's public and domestic experience. (H. Kenner, Review, *New York Times*, 3/14/76, Section 7, p. 6)

6. What has befallen us, that liberalism should be, INELUCTABLY, the only approach to

democratic government, mid-twentieth century? (W.F. Buckley Jr., *Up From Liberalism*, Arlington House, 2nd Printing 1968, p. 177)

7. And yet the myth holds, . . . that France and especially Paris, is the home of enlightenment, of the most exquisite refinement of sensuous pleasure, and of a pursuit of the good life, which is conducted . . . in full philosophical awareness of the horror of history and the INELUCTABILITY of death. (A. Burgess, "'A $200 million Erector Set,'" *New York Times*, 1/23/77, Section 6, p. 14)

8. I [Russel Wren] ducked into the inner office and found that reality INELUCTABLY opposed my capricious decision to forget about [Teddy] Villanova, *et al.* Bakewell's tremendous body covered my studio couch. (Thomas Berger, *Who Is Teddy Villanova?*, Delacorte Press/ Seymour Lawrence, 1977, p. 32)

INGANNATION (in' gan-ā' shən) *noun* cheat; fraud; deception [Obsolete].

1. At President Truman's press conferences, reporters often got more than they bargained for: *Q:* Mr. President, the Republican national campaign director today accuses you of INGANNATION . . . . *A:* INGANNATION? I don't use $40 words like that in my language. That's a Republican word. It isn't democratic. (Anon., "Here's Harry! Candid Quips and Quotes from the Remarkable Mr. Truman," Hallmark Treasures (designed by Rainer K. Koenig), Unpaged, 1975)

INGÉNUE (àn'zhə-nōō',-nyōō') or **INGENUE** *noun,* *pl.:* -NUES (-nōōz', -nyōōz') the role of an INGENUOUS girl, especially as represented on the stage; an actress who plays such a role or specializes in playing such roles; an innocent, inexperienced, unwordly young woman.

1. But I don't mean that we are simply being taken back to 1927, when an INGENUE came down a curving staircase like a swallow returning to Capistrano and the bad boy of the celebrated clan simply bolted over the balustrade to get at his fencing partner. (W. Kerr, Review of *The Royal Family*, by George S. Kaufman and Edna Ferber, *New York Times*, 1/11/76, Section 2, p. 7)

2. The face [of Claire Bloom] has weathered

the decades well, too. It is no longer that of the 21-year old INGENUE who achieved international stardom in Chaplin's film, *Limelight*, but it is still very pretty. (A. Haas, "Claire Bloom still takes her acting seriously," *Philadelphia Inquirer*, 10/3/76, p. 1-H)

3. See (1) under TERMAGANT.

INGENUOUS (in-jen'yōō-əs) *adj.* free from reserve, restraint, or dissimulation; simple; artless; innocent; NAIVE; frank; open; candid; without guile.

INGENUOUSLY *adv.*

INGENUOUSNESS *noun.*

1. European democrats have marveled at the apparent Italian Communist conversion to democracy; but they would also be INGENUOUS to trust completely a party which still subscribes in significant measure to an antidemocratic creed and which is still untried in government. (*The London Economist*, "Italians examine Communism," Reprinted, *Norman* [Okla.] *Transcript*, 4/19/76, p. 6)

2. The question raised by this group of books [*Enterprising Women*, by Caroline Bird; *Women, Money & Power*, by Phyllis Chesler and Emily Jane Goodman; *Women in the Pulpit*, by Priscilla and William Proctor; *Lawyering*, by Helene E. Schwartz; and *Notes of a Feminist Therapist*, by Elizabeth Friar Williams] is whether, if the equality sought by American feminists were achieved, it would have the slightest transforming effect on either our social institutions or our characters . . . . It was debated as INGENUOUSLY in the 19th century as by the 20th century women's movement . . . . Not facing it leads to a narrowminded feminism—it might be called the "getting ours" branch of the movement—that is as embarrassing for its moral as for its economic NAÏVETÉ. (Elinor Langer, Review, *New York Times*, 4/4/76, Section 7, p. 4)

INGRATE (in' grāt) *noun* an ungrateful person.

1. But the sporting press hurried to FLAGELLATE us for unorthodoxy [in publishing an article saying Duke Snider preferred farming to professional baseball if the latter had not

paid so well]. At least fifty newspaper articles described Snider as an INGRATE. (R. KAHN, *The Boys of Summer*, Harper and Row, 1971, p. 378)

INNUENDO (in'yōō-en'dō) *noun, pl.:* -DOS or -DOES an indirect intimation (remark, gesture, or reference) about a person or thing, especially of a derogatory nature; insinuation.

1. [Edmonde] Charles-Roux intimates obliquely that [Coco] Chanel's thirty-year friendship with Misia Sert was a lesbian one, but she does so in obscene Victorian INNUENDOES. . . . Thus, one of the most relevant aspects of Chanel's character—that bisexuality which might seem to have given her work its ANDROGYNOUS timelessness—is never directly considered in these 380 pages [of the book, *Chanel*]. (Francine Gray, Review, *New York Review of Books*, 12/11/75, p. 45)

2. Love is enacted [in *A Dance to the Music of Time*, by Anthony Powell] in speculation and INNUENDO about the sex lives of other people: is Gwinnett a NECROPHILIAC? Scorpio Murtlock . . . homosexual? (C. Michener, Review, *Newsweek*, 4/5/76, p. 80)

3. There being no decent reason for this petty demand [that President Ford made on Ronald Reagan to release his 1975 tax returns], it was left to stand as an INNUENDO. (G.F. Will, "Ford's Real Weakness," *Newsweek*, 5/17/76, p. 114)

4. See (1) under AD HOMINEM.

INORDINATE (in-or'dᵊnit) *adj.* not within proper limits; immoderate; excessive; unrestrained in conduct, feelings, etc.; intemperate; not regulated; irregular; extreme; exorbitant; disordered; too great or too many.

INORDINATELY *adv.*
INORDINATENESS *noun.*

1. The real point [of Daniel P.] Moynihan's thinking is the bearing of the Third World attacks on the theme of the INORDINATE sense of guilt among American liberal intellectuals. The Moynihan group rejects the guilt, both on a global and an internal national level. (M. Lerner, "New political mood pervades U.S.," *Norman* [Okla.] *Transcript*, 5/14/76, p. 6)

2. Miss [Natalie] Wood, wearing an INORDINATE amount of makeup for the sweltering Deep South [in NBC's production of *Cat On a Hot Tin Roof*], confuses ferocious tenacity with something resembling childish pique. At times, wielding a cigarette, she seems to be offering a CAMPY imitation of Bette Davis. Robert Wagner . . . is so low-keyed that it is an effort to remember he is there at all. (J.J. O'Connor, "This Tribute Smacks of Exploitation," *New York Times*, 12/5/76, Section 2, p. 29)

3. Natalie Novotny was not given to INORDINATE displays of emotion . . . . It may be ungallant of me [Russel Wren] to reveal that when making love she often seems asleep. (Thomas Berger, *Who Is Teddy Villanova?*, Delacorte Press/Seymour Lawrence, 1977, p. 129)

4. "Wren, are you a deviate of some sort? I [Donald Washburn II] catch a whiff of underwear addiction—then I remember too your recent INORDINATE demonstration on my recovering my own supporter from under the bed." (Thomas Berger, *Ibid.*, p. 159)

INSCRUTABLE (in-skrōō'tə-bəl) *adj.* not easily understood; mysterious; completely obscure; unfathomable; enigmatic; incomprehensible; undiscoverable; inexplicable; incapable of being searched into or scrutinized; impenetrable to investigation.

INSCRUTABLY *adv.*

INSCRUTABILITY *noun.*

1. See (1) under SURREPTITIOUS.

2. The most intriguing crew-member of the Star Trek spaceship Enterprise is an INSCRUTABLE, pointy-eared man from Vulcan named Mr. Spock. (Anon., "Paper Back Talk," *New York Times*, 1/4/76, Section 7, p. 23)

3. So *that's* how they do it, in the INSCRUTABLE, revolutionary People's Republic of China! (W.F. Buckley Jr., *Execution Eve and Other Contemporary Ballads*, G.P. Putnam's Sons, 1975, p. 28)

4. See (5) under PARODY.

5. See (2) under AFICIONADO.

6. See (3) under QUONDAM.

INSOBRIETY (in′sə-brī′i-tē) *noun* lack of sobriety; intemperance or immoderation; drunkenness.

1. [British artist John Calcott] Horsley's design [of the first Christmas card in 1843] was centered around a convivial family gathering in which everyone from tots to grandpa was benevolently engaged in drinking the health of absent loved ones. He was later CASTIGATED by temperance organizations for giving Yuletide encouragement to the spread of INSOBRIETY, alcoholism and wild WASSAIL. (P. Ryan, "Postmen can blame it on Old Horsley," *Smithsonian*, December 1975, p. 144)

INSOUCIANCE (in-sōō′ sē-ans) *noun* the quality of being insouciant; lack of care or concern; indifference.

INSOUCIANT *adj.* free from concern; without anxiety; carefree; calm and unbothered; indifference.

INSOUCIANTLY *adv.*

1. Meanwhile . . . Israeli strategists observe Congress INSOUCIANTLY prepared to deliver South Vietnam to the North Vietnamese. (W.F. Buckley Jr., *Execution Eve and Other Contemporary Ballads*, G.P. Putnam's Sons, 1975, p. 57)

2. He [the hero of *Saving the Queen*, by William F. Buckley Jr.] is extraordinarily self-assured, with an indefinable cultural INSOUCIANCE, and his rhythms are never disharmonious. (W. Goodman, Review, *New York Times*, 1/11/76, Section 7, p. 8)

3. . . . these INSOUCIANTLY matter-of-fact entertainers . . . . (W. Kerr, Review of *Tuscaloosa's Calling Me . . . but I'm Not Going*, *New York Times*, 1/25/76, Section 2, p. 5)

4. . . . the recent publication of two [brightly colored, oversized picture books about city life] shows that it is still possible to take an INSOUCIANT view of the subject—an accomplishment expecially remarkable for Annie Ingle's *The Big City Book* since the city it purports to introduce to children bears an unmistakable resemblance to New York. (Sidney Long, Review, *New York Times*, 2/8/76, Section 7, p. 16)

5. [Adlai] Stevenson's losing [presidential] campaign in 1952 is rightly famous. "There was a gaiety, a spontaneity, a freshness, an INSOUCIANCE about it," [John Bartlow] Martin writes [in his book, *Adlai Stevenson of Illinois*], "that was extraordinarily appealing to countless people weary of pompous politicians." (W. Clemons, Review, *Newsweek*, 3/29/76, pp. 87-88)

6. See (1) under CAVIL.

7. "Shrieks" and "teases" were favorite pursuits of this pretty aristocrat [Nancy Mitford] who liked pretending to be the sort of woman the eighteenth century called a "rattle"—INSOUCIANT, frivolous, heedlessly high-spirited. (W. Clemons, Review of *Nancy Mitford: A Memoir*, by Harold Acton, *Newsweek*, 5/3/76, p. 91)

8. We see Clayton [in the film, *The Missouri Breaks*] caught at an instant of deadly danger in a foam bath. A pistol is pointed at him by Logan. Clayton . . turns his back to the pistol-pointer, and goes on talking idly . . . . The heavy shoulders and the INSOUCIANCE bring off the voluptuous risk. (Penelope Gilliatt, Review, *The New Yorker*, 5/31/76, p. 100)

9. Ronald Reagan recently found himself in Detroit in front of a spiffy audience, the Economic Club. With the INSOUCIANCE that makes politicians do daring deeds with careless smiles, he praised the automobile. (G.F. Will, "Taking A Ride With Ronnie," *Newsweek*, 5/31/76, p. 76)

10. See (9) under INDIGENOUS.

11. Whatever happens in politics over the next four nights [at the Democratic convention], a television star could be born. Someone's pluck, wit, INSOUCIANCE or rhetorical style . . . may catch the national fancy, as the crisp Huntley-Brinkley byplay did in 1956, or as the quip, "This is John Chancellor, from somewhere in custody," did when the now-anchorman but then-reporter was arrested on camera during the chaos of 1968 in Chicago. (L. Brown, "The Games the Networks Play At Convention Time," *New York Times*, 7/11/76, Section 2, p. 21)

12. The most famous of these [glamorous

Edwardian society women]—Lily Langtry and Lady Warwick—had been the mistresses of the King [Edward VII], a fact of which everyone was aware, including the Queen [Alexandra], who handled that situation with the same INSOUCIANT charm that she handled everything. (J.H. Plumb, Review of *The 1900's Lady*, by Kate Caffrey, *New York Times*, 9/5/76, Section 7, p. 3)

13. "Fuck this [gun]," said the mustachioed patrolman. "It don't matter. Let's haul the garbage [the corpse]." . . . Surely the police had not, despite the INSOUCIANT obscenity, brushed away the matter of the gun. (Thomas Berger, *Who Is Teddy Villanova?*, Delacorte Press/Seymour Lawrence, 1977, pp. 35-36)

INSULAR (in′sə-lər, ins′yə-lər) *adj.* of or pertaining to an island or islands; dwelling or situated on an island; detached; standing alone; isolated; narrowly exclusive; illiberal; provincial.

INSULAR *noun* an inhabitant of an island.

INSULARITY or INSULARISM *noun.*

INSULARLY *adv.*

1. The tools of controversy are tough . . . . But I wonder when else, in the history of controversy, there has been such consistent intemperance, INSULARITY and IRASCIBILITY as the custodians of the liberal orthodoxy have shown toward conservatives who question some of the orthodoxy's premises. (W.F. Buckley Jr., *Up From Liberalism*, Arlington House, 2nd Printing, 1968, p. 55)

2. See (2) under QUONDAM.

3. See (1) under MONOGLOT.

INTEGUMENT (in-teg′yə-mənt) *noun* an outer covering, as a skin, hide, shell, husk, rind, etc.; any covering, coating, or enclosure.

INTEGUMENTARY *adj.*

1. . . . . this took Black [ford Oakes] a little by surprise, even as Anthony [Trust]'s language did when it shucked off the aw-shucks INTEGUMENT he usually wrapped it in . . . . (W.F. Buckley Jr., *Saving the Queen*, Doubleday, 1976, p. 38)

INTERDICT (in′ tər-dikt′) *noun* (in Civil Law) any official prohibitory act or restraint; (in the Roman Catholic Church) a punishment by which the faithful are prohibited from participation in certain sacred acts.

INTERDICT *verb* to forbid with authority; prohibit; to impede by steady bombardment; to cut off authoritatively from certain ecclesiastical functions and privileges.

INTERDICTION *noun* the act or an instance of interdicting; the state of being interdicted; an interdict.

INTERDICTOR *noun.*

INTERDICTORY or INTERDICTIVE *adj.*

1. But [Moshe] Dayan added a chilling corollary: Arab mayors [in the West Bank] should be warned that if their towns exploded again, they would be placed under a blanket INTERDICTION. It would be designed to deal a crippling blow to Arab livelihoods by preventing delivery of food supplies to market in a designated town, . . . or barring sheep from leaving for pasture. (Anon., "Fighting A Cancer," *Time*, 5/31/76, p. 28)

2. In A.D. 1120—. . . the year that the Chinese are said to have invented playing cards—the Bishop of Lyons INTERDICTED the region's caterpillars and field mice. And in 1485, . . . the High Vicar of Valence hauled all the local caterpillars before his court, assigned a lawyer to speak for them, and commanded them to leave the area. (M. Olmert, Review of *The Constant Pest: A Short History of Pests and their Control*, by George Ordish, *Smithsonian*, June 1976, p. 110)

INTERNECINE (in′tər-nē′sēn, -sīn, -nes′ēn, -nes′īn) *adj.* mutually destructive, harmful or deadly; of or pertaining to conflict, feuding, or struggle within a group; original meaning: characterized by great slaughter.

1. He [Harry Truman], it is said, is more responsible than any man in America for the Cold War, for the INTERNECINE alliances, for United States militarism and CHAUVINISM, for a delay in discharging our obligations to racial equality. (W.F. Buckley Jr., *Execution Eve and Other Contemporary Ballads*, G.P. Putnam's Sons, 1975, p. 475)

2. [President] Ford intensely dislikes INTERNE-CINE squabbling and has told his aides that he wants the bickering stopped. And Kissinger has been known to criticize Moynihan's FLAM-BOYANT ways. (A. Deming, "Moynihan's Complaint," *Newsweek*, 2/9/76, p. 32)

3. *The Clewiston Test* [by Kate Wilhelm] is a scary book. Outwardly, at least, it tells of the INTERNECINE warfare at a pharmaceutical company. (J. Charyn, Review, *New York Times*, 2/22/76, Section 7, p. 37)

4. See (1) under CENTRIPETAL.

5. The young couple, Nick (Richard Kelton) and Honey (Maureen Anderman), who join them for a savage 2 a.m. - to 5 a.m. session of show-and-tell are simply deployed by George and Martha [in Albee's play, *Who's Afraid of Virginia Woolf*] as fodder for their IN-TERNECINE warfare. (T.E. Kalem, Review, *Time*, 4/12/76, p. 83)

6. See (6) under DONNYBROOK.

INTRANSIGENT (in-tran'si-jənt) *adj.* uncompromising or inflexible; irreconcilable.

INTRANSIGENT *noun* an intransigent person, especially in politics.

INTRANSIGENTLY *adv.*

INTRANSIGENCE or **INTRANSIGENCY** *noun.*

1. Unless President Kenneth Kaunda of Zambia, who has been trying to promote "detente" between South Africa, Rhodesia and the IN-TRANSIGENT all-black African nations, can get some sort of loan from the West, . . . the Russians will be in a position to present the political bill for those tanks [given to Zambia by Russia]. (J. Chamberlain, "Soviets Read Maps With Purpose," *Daily Oklahoman*, Okla. City, 3/24/76, p. 10)

2. After the 93rd ballot [of the 1924 Democratic National Convention], he [William G. McAdoo] and [Alfred E.] Smith met privately . . . . Saying it was obvious neither could be nominated, Smith offered to withdraw if McAdoo did. The latter refused. His INTRANSIGENCE caused Smith to denounce him so vehemently that after the meeting McAdoo told friends Smith had been drunk. (M.S. Gwirtzman, "Son of 1924," *New York Times*, 3/14/76, Section 6, p. 94)

3. In the students' fiery INTRANSIGENCE [during the Great Proletarian Cultural Revolution] Mao [Tse-Tung] must have seen embers of his own youth. (R. Bernstein, Review of *The Wind Will Not Subside: Years in Revolutionary China, 1964-69*, *Time*, 4/19/76, p. K9)

4. Uganda's INTRANSIGENCE seemed to have seeds in President Carter's press conference last Wednesday. It blossomed early Friday, when President Idi Amin ordered the Americans to stay in his East African nation until he met with them Monday. It faded over the weekend when Amin postponed the meeting. (Associated Press, "Uganda Situation: The Crisis-That-Wasn't," *Times Herald*, Norristown, Pa., 3/3/77, p. 36)

INTREPID (in-trep'id) *adj.* fearless or dauntless; very brave; courageous; bold.

INTREPIDITY *noun.*

INTREPIDLY *adv.*

1. Nine months after telling her so [how much he loved her], he [G.B. Shaw] married Charlotte Payne-Townshend, a union that apparently left Ellen imperturbed. "What IN-TREPIDITY," she wrote him. (Helen Bevington, Review of *The Life and Times of Ellen Terry*, by Tom Prideaux, *New York Times*, 1/4/76, Section 7, p. 3)

2. Thus far I [Russel Wren] had been less than a hero . . . , and yet I had accepted a punishment that could be termed Herculean. But suddenly I was in an INTREPID mood. I had not been touched by the ALBINO's shotgun lightning that sent two other souls to Hades. (Thomas Berger, *Who Is Teddy Villanova?*, Delacorte Press/Seymour Lawrence, 1977, p. 190)

INTUIT (in-tōō'it, -tyōō'- , in'tōō-it, -tyōō-) *verb* to know or understand by intuition.

INTUITABLE *adj.*

INTUITION *noun* the direct knowing or learning of something without the conscious use of reasoning; immediate apprehension or understanding; a keen and quick insight.

INTUITIVE *adj.*

INTUITIVELY *adv.*

1. Claude Lévi-Strauss [author of *Structural Anthropology, Vol. II*, translated by Monique Layton] and Noam Chomsky have argued, independently and in different ways, that behind the disorder and flux of the world, beneath the large variety of cultures and the extraordinary number of languages, is a substructure of rationality and order. For Chomsky . . . mind has the power to generalize rules, while language itself . . . has a set of logical properties embedded in deep structures that can be INTUITED by mind. (D. Bell, Review, *New York Times*, 3/14/76, Section 7, p. 23)

INVETERATE (in-vet′ər-it) *adj.* confirmed in a habit, practice, feeling, or the like; firmly established by long continuance, as a disease; chronic; deep-rooted; habitual.

INVETERATELY *adv.*

INVETERACY *noun.*

1. Venice and Rome call forth some historical set-pieces written [by Leo Rosten, in *The 3:10 to Anywhere*] with the infectious enthusiasm of an INVETERATE teacher. Some anecdotes from the Soviet Union suggest that Mr. Rosten is at his best as a RACONTEUR with a superb ear for linguistic eccentricities. (R.R. Lingeman, Review, *New York Times*, 3/14/76, Section 7, p. 14)

INVIDIOUS (in-vid′ē-əs) *adj.* causing or tending to cause animosity, resentment, ODIUM, or envious dislike; offensively or unfairly discriminating; harmful; injurious; hateful.

INVIDIOUSLY *adv.*

INVIDIOUSNESS *noun.*

1. . . . his [Shockley's] palaver encourages an Archie Bunkerite racial INVIDIOUSNESS. (W.F. Buckley Jr., *Execution Eve and Other Contemporary Ballads*, G.P. Putnam's Sons, 1975, p. 472)

2. Shopping is the chief activity in the Soviet Union for some members of the [tour] group. Purchases are much-debated and compared, sometimes INVIDIOUSLY. (R.W. Stock, *Group Tour of Russia: A Collective Triumph, New York Times*, 1/11/76, Section 10, p. 18)

3. . . . it was never thought strange or INVIDIOUS that Evelyn's publisher-father, Arthur [Waugh], frequently reviewed books he had himself edited and published . . . . (L.E. Sissman, Review of *Evelyn Waugh: A Biography*, by Christopher Sykes, *The New Yorker*, 2/9/76, p. 106)

IPSO FACTO (ip′sō fak′tō) by the fact itself; by the very nature of the deed; literally, by that very fact.

1. Unintentionally, therefore, [Secretary of Agriculture Earl] Butz had violated an important convention. He thought he was speaking in private [when he told the ethnic joke that lead to his resignation], but, fatally, he was in the presence of John Dean, the human tape recorder. IPSO FACTO, it was all public, not private. For Dean, who had been instrumental in the destruction of a president, a mere Cabinet officer was hardly more than an appetizer. (J. Hart., "Butz's Goof," *Times Herald*, Norristown, Pa., 10/12/76, p. 11)

IRASCIBLE (i-ras′ə-bəl) *adj.* easily angered; quick-tempered; characterized or produced by anger; testy; touchy; irritable; CHOLERIC.

IRASCIBLY *adv.*

IRASCIBILITY *noun.*

1. There are some sharp portraits [in *Kings and Queens: The Plantagenets of England*, by Janice Young Brooks]: the FECKLESS Edward II; the capable but IRASCIBLE Henry II; the determined, slightly mad Margaret of Anjou. (T. Lask, Review, *New York Times*, 2/22/76, Section 7, p. 16)

2. See (1) under INSULAR.

3. Radio-TV interviewer Mike Wallace, in his column . . . for the *New York Post*, introduces Randolph Churchill as "an IRASCIBLE snob." Now, for all I know, that is just what Mr. Churchill is; but this is not the way to introduce one's guests, not even obstreperous conservative guests, to one's readers . . . (W.F. Buckley, Jr., *Up From Liberalism*, Arlington House, 2nd Printing 1968, p. 61)

4. There's the original office [at the Jack Daniel's distillery] where Jack worked, and in

it the balky safe that the IRASCIBLE old
gentleman kicked so hard one morning in 1905
that it eventually cost him his leg and his life.
(F.C. Klein, "Jack Daniel's Bets That You
Can't Tell Black From Green," *Wall Street
Journal*, 2/8/77, p. 1)

5. See (2) under CONCUPISCENCE.

IRENIC (ī-ren′ ik, ī-rē′ nik) or **IRENICAL**
adj. tending to promote peace; peaceful;
pacific.

IRENICALLY *adv.*

IRENICS *noun* (construed as *singular*) the
doctrine or practice of promoting conciliation
among Christian churches; irenic theology.

1. He [Blackford Oakes] lay back in bed,
opening the curtains and looking out in the
moonlight past the garden over those IRENIC
fields that had bred, according to the famous
adage, the flower of British youth. (W.F.
Buckley Jr., *Saving the Queen*, Doubleday,
1976, p. 176)

2. "Are you aware . . . of the dollar drain we
poor English are sustaining as a result of your
vulgar commercial success?" [Queen Caroline
asked Blackford Oakes] . . . . "I am aware [he
replied] that the Industrial Revolution that
began here [in England] germinated quite
nicely on American soil." Queen Caroline
smiled. "Yes, indeed, indeed. Thanks in large
part, would you not agree, Mr. Oakes, to the
IRENIC circumstances your industrial gardens
enjoyed due to the protection of the British
fleet?" (W.F. Buckley Jr., *Ibid.*, p. 223)

IRIDESCENCE (ir′i-des′əns) *noun* exhibiting a play of lustrous changing colors like those
of the rainbow, as when seen from different
angles.

IRIDESCENT *adj.*

IRIDESCENTLY *adv.*

1. This is what we call IRIDESCENCE without
illumination. It was not misuse of the horse
that dragged the Indian back to defeat; it was
the arrival of the white man on a superior iron
horse. But there I go, doing it myself, and it is
just as FATUOUSLY IRIDESCENT when I do it as
when another guy does. (J.A. Michener, *Cen-*

tennial, Fawcett, 1975, p. 512)

2. By tea time, his [Malcolm Muggeridge's]
IRIDESCENT talk has hovered round perhaps a
dozen subjects and still yielded nothing shocking, unless you are shocked by the notion that
Sir Harold Wilson's career was shaped not by
Socialist orthodoxy but by his secret fantasy of
emulating Sir Winston Churchill. (H. Kenner,
"At Home with St. Mug," *New York Times*,
9/12/76, Section 6, p. 127)

3. Before his nomination he [George McGov-
ern] was a wonderful hayseed, a simple man
in a green IRIDESCENT suit who had a vision for
America. Then the campaign got him. In the
end he would up a twisted zealot, wearing
tailored attire. . . . (T. Tiede, "Splendid Isolation and Jimmy Carter," *Times Herald*, Norristown, Pa., 10/28/76, p. 23)

IRREDENTIST (ir′i-den′ tist) *noun* (usually capitalized) a member of an Italian association that became prominent in 1878, advocating the redemption, or the incorporation
into Italy, of certain neighboring regions
(Italia irredenta) under foreign control but
having a primarily Italian population; any person in any country advocating the acquisition
of some neighboring region formerly a part of
his country and tied to it historically, ethnically, and culturally.

IRREDENTIST *adj.*

IRREDENTISM *noun.*

IRREDENTA *noun* a region linked
historically, ethnically, and culturally with
one nation but governed by another.

1. The trouble with the cliché [that only people with a small vocabulary use dirty words] is
(a) it isn't true; (b) it doesn't take into account
the need to use the resources of the language;
and (c) the kind of people who use it are almost
always engaged in IRREDENTIST ventures
calculated to make "dirty" words and ex-
.pressons that no longer are, and even some that
never were . . . . I had reason to reach, some
time back, for a word to comment upon a line
of argument I considered insufferably SANC-
TIMONIOUS. "Crap," I wrote: And the IRREDEN-
TIST hordes descended upon me in all their
fury. (W.F. Buckley Jr., *Execution Eve and*

Other Contemporary Ballads, G.P. Putnam's Sons, 1975, p. 408)

2. Syria, which has never forgotten its IRREDENTIST designs, has issued a stern warning to the Christian right-wingers that it will intervene in force if they seriously try to partition Lebanon—even if that meant war with Israel. (J.W. Markham, "Lebanon, An Artificial Nation, May Not Endure," *New York Times,* 1/18/76, Section 4, p. 1)

3. For the past six years the British military have been predicting the enemy [IRA]'s defeat, yet Irish IRREDENTISTS continue . . . to strike where and whenever they choose. (J.C. McGee, "Ireland is Britain's Vietnam," *Philadelphia Inquirer,* 9/15/76, p. 11-A)

4. "One is not an American anymore, he's a Black Muslim, or a Red Indian, or an Irish Catholic. . . . We are more POLYGLOT than Czechoslovakia. Why do you think the United States should be exempt from IRREDENTISM, the disease of our time?" [says Roger, in *The Company of Friends,* a book by John Crosby]. (G.

Lyons, Review, *New York Times,* 5/15/77, Section 7, p. 14)

IRRUPTION (i-rup′shən) *noun* a breaking or bursting in; a violent incursion or invasion; a sudden increase in an animal population.

IRRUPT *verb* to burst suddenly or violently into; to manifest violent activity or emotion; (of animals) to increase suddenly in numbers through a lessening in the number of deaths.

IRRUPTIVE *adj.*

IRRUPTIVELY *adv.*

1. As I recall, the poem comes with a perception—a breakthrough into nature . . . . And married to the IRRUPTION of nature must be something live that surfaces out of language; the language . . . brings a formal element without which nothing happens, nothing is *made* [said John Updike to Helen Vendler in an interview]. (Anon., "John Updike on Poetry," *New York Times,* 4/10/77, Section 7, p. 3)

J

JAPE (jāp) *noun* a joke; jest; quip; a trick or practical joke; a wisecrack.

JAPE *verb* to joke; jest; play tricks.

JAPER *noun.*

JAPINGLY *adv.*

1. Neither James Burnham, nor Priscilla, nor I was familiar with the JAPE. (W.F. Buckley Jr., *Execution Eve and Other Contemporary Ballads,* G.P. Putnam's Sons, 1975, p. 348)

2. Modern witches, Dr. [Lynn A.] McMillan [of Oklahoma Christian College] asserts, are nearly unanimous in their claim that they are good witches . . . it is a tenet of witchery that good is returned to the doer threefold and evil

likewise. What witch is going to invite triple whammy, even if it's only for a small JAPE like inhabiting a cat or yowling? (J.L. Jones, "Wonders of Science Providing Field Day for Devil," *Sunday Oklahoman,* Okla. City, 6/6/76, p. 17-A)

3. On TV, singer John Davidson in his relentless search for Don Rickles' career is just a 14-year-old PRURIENT, his JAPES embarrassing and his effects juvenile comic delinquency. (J. O'Brian, "Broadway," *Times Herald,* Norristown, Pa., 10/4/76, p. 17)

4. TV's McLean Stevenson will co-host Thanksgiving parade video coverage, for kids, mostly. We trust he'll quit his annoying SCATO-

LOGICAL JAPES which make his *Tonight* odoriferous. (J. O'Brian, *Ibid.*, 10/25/76, p. 17)

5. See (2) under SAPPHISM.

6. He [Donald Washburn II] put his lips together and frowned his immunity to this JAPE. (Thomas Berger, *Who Is Teddy Villanova?*, Delacorte Press/Seymour Lawrence, 1977, p. 50)

7. See (4) under QUOTIDIAN.

JAPONAISERIE (jap'ə-nez'ər-ē) or **JAPANE-SERY** *noun* Japanese ornaments, knick-knacks, etc.

1. The art nouveau line—whip-like, airy, eddying back on itself—was common to high art as well. A good example is Gauguin's portrait of the painter Roy, 1889, with its serpentine forms of background and hair. Such serpentine curves had been discovered by the French in Japanese art: the first shops for JAPONAISERIE had been set up in Paris in the 1870s. Moreover, the designers of the *Belle Epoque* seized on the reverence for EPHEMERAL nature in Japanese art, importing a fresh ICONOGRAPHY of fugitive things: mist, shivering grasses, winding shoots, morning glories and insects. (R. Hughes, "The Snobbish Style," *Time*, 9/13/76, p. 67)

JEJUNE (ji-jōōn') *adj.* (of food) not nourishing; barren; without interest; dull; insipid; empty; lacking wisdom; juvenile; immature; childish.

JEJUNELY *adv.*

JEJUNENESS or JEJUNITY *noun.*

1. To those trained in the long perspectives of literary history, the . . . presumption [of the "beat" writers] of finally capturing the very essence of mind and actuality can easily seem JEJUNE. (P. Parisi, Review of *Naked Angels: The Lives and Literature of the Beat Generation, Chronicle of Higher Education,* 5/10/76, p. 19)

2. See (2) under PUERILE.

3. The last of the biographies [*Thomas Merton*, by Cornelia & Irving Süssman] is JEJUNE and embarrassingly juvenile. It is about the 20th-century mystic—some say saint—

Thomas Merton. (Jane Yolen, Review, *New York Times*, 5/2/76, Section 7, p. 34)

4. Most people have a general idea that the pill works as a contraceptive because it interferes with the natural balance of hormones in a woman's body so that the normal process of ovulation . . . does not take place . . . . For reproductive biologists, though, such an explanation would be JEJUNE. They point out that the pill could be producing its contraceptive effect in a variety of ways. (P. Vaughan, "The pill turns twenty," *New York Times*, 6/13/76, Section 6, p. 9)

5. We know what was wrong with [Edvard] Munch's childhood and youth, and just why he responded so intensely to his environment. But when the time comes to tackle the art, Mr. Watkins [in his film, *Edvard Munch*] doesn't do quite so well. There is too much of Munch scratching around on canvas, and there is too much JEJUNE analysis of the pictorial process. (J. Russell, 'Edvard Munch'—A Film Truer to Life than to Art," *New York Times*, 9/12/76, Section 2, p. 33)

6. . . . while certain masterpieces enlist the love of both children and adults, on the merits of lesser works we are bound to differ. After all, to adore everything a small child adores, an adult would have to be pretty JEJUNE, if not sometimes dirty-minded and downright barbaric. (X. J. Kennedy, "The Flat, Fat Blatt," *New York Times*, 5/1/77, Section 7, p. 31)

JEREMIAH (jer'ə-mī'ə) or **JEREMIAH** *noun* (if capitalized) a Major Prophet of the 6th and 7th centuries, B.C., known for his pessimism; a book of the Bible bearing his name; (if lower case) a person pessimistic about the future; a person who complains about the evil, decay, and disaster that he sees about him and who foresees and predicts a calamitous future (after the Hebrew prophet Jeremiah).

JEREMIANIC or JEREMIANIC or JEREMIAN or JEREMIAN *adj.*

JEREMIAD (jer'ə-mī'ad) *noun* a lamentation or tale of woe, in allusion to the Lamentations of Jeremiah; mournful and denunciatory complaint; a dolorous tirade.

1. The meeting [of the "Club of Rome"] . . . had its share of JEREMIAHS. Brazilian political

scientist Helio Jaguaribe de Maltos, for one, predicted that unless corrective steps were taken "a technocratic version of Oriental despotism . . ." would brutally reduce population to match resources . . . (M. Ruby, "The Future: 'Organic Growth,'" *Newsweek*, 4/26/76, p. 84)

2. See (2) under RISIBLE.

3. But Lancelot's confession [in the book, *Lancelot*, by Walker Percy] is anything but repentant. It is both a funny and a scarifying JEREMIAD on the modern age. (P. Gray, Review, *Time*, 3/7/77, p. 86)

4. In [Paddy] Chayefsky's riotous vision [in his screenplay for the film, *Network*], . . . we have half a film of exalted satire followed by a half of JEREMIAD full of mythic symbols. (D. Ryan, Review, *Philadelphia Inquirer*, 12/17/76, p. 9-I)

5. See (1) under CRAVEN.

JINGO (jǐng′gō) *noun, pl.* -GOES A person who professes patriotism loudly and excessively, especially one who favors an aggressive foreign policy; CHAUVINIST.

JINGOISM *noun* the spirit, policy, or practice of jingoes; bellicose CHAUVINISM.

JINGOIST *noun, adj.*

JINGOISTIC *adj.*

JINGOISTICALLY *adv.*

1. The Olympics and war are both born from the same JINGOISTIC temperament, according to Edwards [a sociologist], "the same training, the same drives work for both. The same rituals prevail—anthems, martial music, prayers for victors, medals for heroes." (R.T. Runfola, "Violence in Sports," *New York Times*, 1/11/76, Section 5, p. 2)

2. Appalled by World War I's horrors, he [Bertrand Russell] threw himself totally into the peace movement, lecturing up and down England on the senselessness and waste of the conflict . . . . So successful was he in challenging the country's devout JINGOISM that by 1916 . . . he had become one of the most hated men in Britain. (M. Rosenthal, Review of *The Life of Bertrand Russell*, by R.W. Clark; *My Father Bertrand Russell*, by Katherine Tait;

and *The Tamarisk Tree*, by Dora Russell, *New York Times*, 2/15/76, p. 2)

3. How homegrown, how American can opera be? The Minnesota Opera Company . . . has replied with some of the most original ventures in musical theater, such as *Horspfal*, a satire on JINGOISM and the rape of the American Indian . . . . (H. Saal, Review of the opera, *The Voyage of Edgar Allan Poe*, by Dominick Argento, as performed by the Minnesota Opera Co., *Newsweek*, 5/10/76, p. 121)

4. All last week, [Ronald] Reagar struck responsive Republican chords with his neo-JINGOIST stand on the Panama Canal—"It's ours. We paid for it. . .and we darn well intend to keep it". . . .(D.M. Alpern, *et al.*, "Ford's New Start," *Newsweek*, 5/17/76, p. 25)

5. The most depressing part of a remarkably foolish and JINGOISTIC piece on westerns by Grace Lichtenstein in the *Times* of May 16 was the news of a coming six-day conference in Sun Valley on "Western Movies; Myths and Images," whose participants will include: one western star, one western director, one western writer, one film historian, one Yale historian, one American Heritage magazine staffer, and two *Time* film reviewers. (J. Simon, Review of the movie, *The Missouri Breaks*, *New York*, 5/31/76, p. 73)

6. Ford may not have wished to tip off Panama to the eventual U.S. negotiating position, and he clearly did not want to confront the issue in an election year. If Ford lacked some political candor, his attitude nevertheless was much more sensible than Reagan's JINGOISTIC refusal even to consider that outright, unyielding ownership of the canal may no longer serve any vital U.S. interest. (Anon., "Panama Theatrics," *Time*, 4/26/76, p. 16)

7. JINGOISM, black or white, is not going to solve the real problems—the deterrence of terrorism, the longer-term partnership between black and white in and out of Africa, and the attempt to make sure that Africa's political problems can be solved without any outside intervention at all. (The London Economist, "Stone throwing no real solution," *Norman* [Okla.] *Transcript*, 8/3/76, p. 6)

8. But the fear in Dacca [capital of

Bangladesh] is that, if Mrs. Gandhi stumbles on the road to her New Democracy in India, she might exploit the quarrel with Bangladesh to create a wave of JINGOIST popularity to keep her in power. (NEA/London Economist News Service (LENS), "Bangladesh, India on collision course? *Times Herald*, Norristown, Pa., 9/7/76, p. 3)

9. That [1966] decision [of a Federal District Court, co-authored by then-Judge Griffin Bell, upholding the refusal of the Georgia legislature to seat Julian Bond because of his criticism of the Vietnam war] was quickly and unanimously reversed by the Supreme Court. Read today, . . . it seems like something from the dark ages of judicial JINGOISM during World War I. No one would bother to read such an ANACHRONISTIC, discredited opinion now— except that it so recently was the considered judgment of the man named to be the next Attorney General of the United States. (A. Lewis, "Griffin Bell's Record, *New York Times*, 12/30/76, p. 23)

JOCULAR (jok′yə-lər) or **JOCOSE** (jō-kōs′) *adj.* given to or characterized by joking or jesting; humorous.

JOCULARLY or JOCOSELY *adv.*

JOCULARITY or JOCOSENESS or JOCOSITY (jō-kos′i-tē) *noun* the state or quality of being jocular or jocose; joking or jesting; a joke or jest.

1. But it now appears possible, in principle, to produce a dozen or a thousand identical twins of a valued racehorse or a prize athlete or a noted genius or a vain dictator. Since word got out about this possibility a few years ago, there has been JOCULAR speculation of mass-producing Albert Einsteins, Arthur Rubinsteins, Mao Tse-Tungs, Margot Fonteyns, or Mickey Mantles. The process for duplicating or mass-producing copies of an individual is best known today as CLONING. (Vance Packard, *The People Shapers*, Little, Brown and Co., as excerpted in *Allentown (Pa.) Morning Call*, 12/1/77, p. 46)

K

KAFKAESQUE (kaf′kə-əsk) *adj.* of, relating to, or suggestive of Franz Kafka (1883-1924) or his obscure writings. Kafka's protagonists encounter monstrous dilemmas in a world they cannot understand.

1. See (1) under OPPROBRIUM.

2. It [*Comrades*, by Alan Siegler] is an easy, enjoyable book to read, chock full of calculated incongruities, humorous, WINSOME, slight. There are KAFKAESQUE episodes, paranoiac as dreams, of encircling plots, maddeningly coy informants, mysterious women. (J. Yohalem, Review, *New York Times*, 3/7/76, Section 7, p. 24)

KAMIKAZE (kä′mə-kä′zē) *noun* (in World War II) a member of a corps in the Japanese air force, charged with the suicidal mission of crashing his aircraft, laden with explosives, into an enemy target, especially a ship; the airplane or pilot used in such a mission.

1. See (1) under THROMBOTIC.

2. See (9) under FECKLESS.

3. The pilot put on a World War II flying suit, with the patch of the Rising Sun on the right sleeve. . . . Then, as he circled his Piper Cherokee over a residential district outside Tokyo, he placed the white band of a KAMIKAZE pilot around his head. He . . . dived headlong into the second-floor veranda of a sprawling suburban home. The pilot died in the crash. But the target of the attack, Japanese power

broker Yoshio Kodama, escaped with no more than a scare. D. Pauly, *et. al.*, "Fastened Seat Belts," *Newsweek*, 4/5/76, p. 65)

4. Writing *The Best Man* had inspired him [Gore Vidal] to become the Democratic candidate for Congress in New York State's bedrock Republican 29th District. It was a KAMIKAZE assignment. Vidal advocated such positions as federal aid to education and diplomatic recognition of Communist China . . . . He lost by 25,000 votes (out of a total of 183,000 cast . . . . He also ran ahead of Presidential Candidate John F. Kennedy. (Anon., "Gore Vidal: Laughing Cassandra," *Time*, 3/1/76, p. 63)

KEEN (kēn) *noun* a wailing lament or dirge for the dead.

KEEN *verb* to wail in lamentation for the dead.

1. Depending on one's immediate mood, a lot can be found wrong in the writing of Farley Mowat: all sorts of laughable excesses, from sloppy style, OVERWEENING sentimentality, a kind of CON BRIO enthusiasm for windmill tilting, to the sort of verbal KEENING one associates with a traditional Irish wake, with the whiskey flowing so freely one forgets just who is dead and why. (J. Harrison, Review of *The Snow Walker*, by Farley Mowat, *New York Times*, 2/22/76, Section 7, p. 4)

2. Read these portraits [in *Women of the Shadows*, by Ann Cornelisen]; they are like KEENS. These harsh, vulnerable women shine because they have a courage that the condition of their lives makes very nearly meaningless. (Jane Kramer, Review, *New York Times*, 4/4/76, Section 7, p. 3)

3. Few of us are anxious to paint bridges; real risk exists and our sense of self-preservation asserts itself in distaste for high winds that KEEN through suspension cables. (R. Kahn, *The Boys of Summer*, Harper and Row, 1971, p. 345)

4. There is a strong smell of revenge in his [Harry Crews'] writing and, behind his comic grotesquerie [in *A Feast of Snakes*] KEENS the angry cry of a man enraged that life can be so cruel and people so victimized by the LUMPEN conditions of their lives. (P.D. Zimmerman,

Review, *Newsweek*, 8/2/76, p. 75)

5. Concentrated, dense, hectic, descriptive, the music [of Alban Berg's opera, *Lulu*, as played by the Metropolitan Opera's orchestra] is deeply involved in the drama onstage, and the wild trumpet and saxophone KEENINGS are as expressive as the human voice. (H. Saal, Review, *Newsweek*, 4/11/77, p. 106)

6. Having failed . . . to murder me with a butt . . . , the van now lurched to a brake-KEENING halt . . . , reversed its gears . . . , and came viciously back . . . . (Thomas Berger, *Who Is Teddy Villanova?*, Delacorte Press/Seymour Lawrence, 1977, p. 193)

7. He went into a howl of exquisite agony . . . and entered the elevator. And even above the hoarse moan of the motor, the CACOPHONY of cable, I could hear the thrill of his KEEN as he sang earthwards. (Thomas Berger, *Ibid.*, p. 237)

KIERKEGAARDIAN or KIERKEGAARD-IAN (kēr'kə-gär'dē-ən) *adj.* of or relating to the Danish philosopher and theologian Kierkegaard or his existentialist philosophy.

KIERKEGAARDIAN or KIERKEGAARDIAN *noun* a follower or adherent of Kierkegaardian philosophy.

1. By the end of the book [*Triton*, by Samuel R. Delany] Bron's despair has reached almost KIERKEGAARDIAN proportions. (G. Jonas, Review, *New York Times*, 3/28/76, Section 7, p. 31)

KITSCH (kich) *noun* art, literature, etc., of a PRETENTIOUS, but shallow kind, calculated to have an immediate popular appeal.

KITSCHY *adj.*

1. The real, though unacknowledged, subject of [Bevis Hiller's] surpassingly ugly collection of illustrations [in *Austerity/Binge: Decorative Arts of the Forties and Fifties*] is nostalgic KITSCH. (Dale Harris, Review, *New York Times*, 1/4/76, Section 7, p. 24)

2. Lewis and Elizabeth [in the film, *The Romantic Englishwoman*] are so hypnotized— or tranquilized—by images from KITSCH romance that they are incapable of taking any responsibility for their actions. (S. Farber,

Review, *New York Times*, 1/18/76, Section 2, p. 13)

3. *The Red Shoes* (1948) . . . . Written, produced, and directed by Michael Powell and Emeric Pressburger—master purveyors of high KITSCH. . . . (Anon., Review, *The New Yorker*, 2/9/76, p. 20)

4. See (1) under ST. ELMO'S FIRE.

5. Writer David Royfiel and director Lamont Johnson are making [in the film, *Lipstick*] murky connections between sex, religion, repression and the emotional sterility of AVANT-GARDE art. The result is both SPECIOUS and seductive, a KITSCHY ode to the pervasive eroticism of contemporary culture. (J. Kroll, Review, *Newsweek*, 4/12/76, p. 94)

6. See (3) under COGNOSCENTI.

7. And all the rest of them [were present], the celebrity mix, . . . Sy Yeager, the hot new filmmaker, EUPHEMISM for director, who . . . had the arrogance to make a cult of the KITSCH peddlers of the past like Busby Berkeley, Preston Sturges, Raoul Walsh. (I. Wallace, *The Fan Club*, Bantam Edition, 1975, p. 181)

8. See (3) under AVUNCULAR.

KLAXON (klak′sən) *noun* a kind of electric horn (for automobiles, trucks, etc.) with a loud, shrill sound.

1. His [Russel Wren's] secretary, Peggy Tumulty, is the book [*Who Is Teddy Villanova?* by Thomas Berger]'s best creation—a plump, KLAXON-voiced Catholic . . . , whose sexual attitudes, Wren observes, "dated from a by-gone age . . . she still looked first at a man's third finger and not at the swell of his groin." (W. Clemons, Review, *Newsweek*, 4/4/77, p. 85)

KLEPHT (kleft) *noun* a Greek brigand, exalted in the war of independence as a patriotic robber; guerrilla; brigand.

KLEPHTIC *adj.*

1. From the autumn of 1820 through the summer of 1821, [author Harry Mark] Petrakis takes the reader [of the book, *The Hour of the Bell*] first to the . . . gathering of the [Greek] guerrilla forces in their mountain camps under the leadership of Vorogrivas, who is heir-apparent of the KLEPHT, Capt. Boukouvalas. Vorogrivas holds a deep, loving respect for the

old warhorse, spoon-feeding him warm milk and consenting to allow Boukouvalas to ride—strapped to his horse—against the Turks, so that the old captain may die in the saddle. (Charlotte Green, Review, *Philadelphia Inquirer*, 11/14/76, p. 15-G)

KLEPTOMANIA (klep′tə-mā′nē-ə, -man′yə) *noun* an abnormal, persistent impulse or tendency to steal, not prompted by need.

KLEPTOMANIAC *noun.*

1. Messily directed by John Berry, [the film] *Thieves* also features . . . . Mercedes McCambridge as a KLEPTOMANIAC with a PENCHANT for hats. (Janet Maslin, Review, *Newsweek*, 2/21/77, p. 92)

KNOUT (nout) *noun* a whip with leather thongs formerly used in Russia to flog criminals.

KNOUT *verb* to flog with a knout.

1. Mr. [V.S.] Pritchett [author of the book *The Gentle Barbarian*] starts . . . with . . . . [Turgenev's] SADISTIC mother, absolute ruler of 5,000 serfs, a woman who understood that a test of power lies in the caprice with which it can be wielded. Ivan's childhood was "a training for the innocence of the rich . . . ," but also a training in the flash of the KNOUT, the shame of the bended knee. Deep into adult life Turgenev struggled against the memory of this tyranny. (I. Howe, Review, *New York Times*, 5/22/77, Section 7, p. 1)

KOAN (kō′än) *noun* in Zen, a nonsense question asked of a student to force him, through contemplation of it, to a greater awareness of reality.

1. . . . trying to understand a 4-year old's notion of a really top-notch joke or riddle is a bit like trying to understand a Zen KOAN like "What is the sound of one hand clapping?"—it simply cannot be done with our limited, linear, Western, adult minds. (D. Greenburg, "Knock, Knock. Who's There," *New York Times*, 5/1/77, Section 7, p. 35)

KOHL (kōl) *noun* a fine powder of antimony sulfide, used especially in certain Eastern countries as a cosmetic to darken the eyelids, eyebrows, etc.

1. . . . her [Peggy Tumulty's] normally swart

hair . . . had turned to red-gold ringlets; . . . her lips were gore-red as the wound of clichéd metaphor and her eyes KOHLED like a HOURI's. (Thomas Berger, *Who Is Teddy Villanova?*, Delacorte Press/Seymour Lawrence, 1977, p. 208)

KRIEGSPIEL (krēg' spēl) *noun* literally, war game; a game using small figures and counters that represent troops, ships, etc., played on a map or miniature battlefield, developed for teaching military tactics to officers; a form of chess in which each player sees only his own pieces, his opponent's moves being told to him by a referee.

1. In 1969, . . . Jack Trout wrote in . . . the magazine *Industrial Marketing*, "Positioning is the game people play in today's me-too marketplace." Positioning became the magic word, the winning move in the KRIEGSPIEL. What was positioning? . . . . You look at the marketplace. You see what vacancy there is. You build your campaign to position your product in that vacancy. (T. Morgan, "New! Improved! Advertising!" *New York Times*, 1/25/76, Section 6, p. 56)

KUDOS (kōō'dōz, -dōs, kyōō⁴) *noun* (*construed as singular*)*—credit or praise for an achievement; glory; fame.

1. In his autobiography, *Living It Up: Or, They Still Love Me in Altoona!* he [George Burns] displays reason for veneration in the touching description of his feelings following the death of his wife and partner, Gracie

*Kudos is not the plural of the imagined word kudo!

Allen. He gains further KUDOS upon viewing the body of his best friend, Jack Benny . . . . "He [Benny] looked as though he were taking one of his long pauses." (H. Teichmann, Review, *New York Times*, 11/21/76, Section 7, p. 51)

2. We like the idea of the AMA's also sending KUDOS to a list of least violent [TV] advertisers, asking them to keep up the good work. (Anon., "TV Violence 'Blasted,'" [Editorial from *Christian Science Monitor*], *Times Herald*, Norristown, Pa., 2/24/77, p. 18)

3. "That means the ruse worked. She [Natalie Novotny] will follow the red herring to Teterboro Airport, and meanwhile I shall single-handedly capture [Teddy] Villanova, garnering all KUDOS and plaudits" [said Boris]. (Thomas Berger, *Who Is Teddy Villanova?*, Delacorte Press/Seymour Lawrence, 1977, p. 203)

KVETCH (kᵊ-vech′) *verb* to complain; to whine.

KVETCH *noun* someone who complains or whines, especially in a nagging manner.

1. On set, she [Louise Lasser] would patronizingly advise her co-workers on how to read their lines . . . . "We're getting on to her game," sighs Greg Mullavey, who plays husband Tom. "The crises she precipitates really mean 'Help Me!' Underneath that little-girl Mary Hartman costume is another human being who is scared to death. It's all ritual. Louise is a KVETCH." (H.F. Waters, M. Kasindorf, "The Mary Hartman Craze," *Newsweek*, 5/3/76, p. 62-63)

L

LACHRYMOSE (lak'rə-mōs′) *adj.* inclined to shed many tears; tearful; causing tears; sad.
LACHRYMOSELY *adv.*

LACHRYMATION or **LACHRIMATION** or **LACRIMATION** *noun* normal or excessive shedding of tears.

LACHRYMAL or **LACRIMAL** *adj.* of, pertaining to, or characterized by tears; producing tears; indicative of weeping.

LACHRYMATORY *adj.* of, causing, or producing tears.

LACHRYMATOR *noun* a substance that irritates the eyes and produces tears; tear gas.

1. . . . a British high court judge, hearing a [recent] case alleging breach of contract over onion-peeling machines, transported the full PANOPLY of his court to a Welsh onion-pickling factory. There they solemnly watched weeping Welsh women peeling 120 odoriferous bulbs a minute. . . . The weeping women of Wales may take some comfort from the opinion of Charles Dickens that their LACHRYMOSE labors may, after all, be SALUBRIOUSLY beneficial to females . . . . "It [weeping] opens the lungs, washes the countenance, exercises the eyes, and softens the temper," he [Mr. Bumble, in *Oliver Twist*] said. (P.Ryan, "No tears about tears from a dry-eyed chauvinist," *Smithsonian*, May 1976, p. 132)

2. And when you eventually depart from this vale of tears, . . . your loved ones, you hope, will launch you into the hereafter on a family floodtide of heartbroken LACRIMATION activated, if need be, by . . . onions concealed in handkerchiefs. (P. Ryan, *Ibid.*, p. 132)

3. See (2) under GÖTTERDÄMMERUNG.

4. . . . he [Don Siegel] knows full well that pity is ANATHEMA to a self-made, self-sufficient figure like [J.B.] Books [chief character in the film, *The Shootist*]. Rather than milking this potentially LACHRYMOSE situation, Siegel directs most of the film with an eloquent restraint, culminating in a heartbreaking final exchange between [John] Wayne and [Lauren] Bacall. (Janet Maslin, Review, *Newsweek*, 8/16/76, p. 68)

LACONIC (lə-kon' ik) *adj.* using few words; expressing much in few words; concise; brief; pithy; terse; succinct.

LACONICALLY *adv.*

LACONISM or **LACONICISM** *noun* laconic brevity; a laconic speech or expression.

1. An Apache matriarch stares long and

LACONICALLY [in the 1950 film, *Broken Arrow*] at James Stewart and his new bride, Debra Paget. Finally, she addresses Paget, twice saying something close to "Keewahnah." (W. Markfield, "Hollywood's Greatest Absurd Moments," *New York Times*, 1/25/76, Section 2, p. 15)

2. See (4) under FULMINATE.

3. He [Captain Culpepper of the L.A. Police Department] was speaking [on the telephone] in a LACONIC undertone to someone, and his two dozen subordinates pretended not to listen. (I. Wallace, *The Fan Club*, Bantam Edition, 1975, p. 530)

4. Throughout the wedding [the groom, James H.] Randall seemed shy, spaced out and LACONIC—and effusively manhandled by women. But when he and his bride [Marisa Berenson] would cross paths, they would embrace laughingly and dance warmly as they nuzzled. (Dewey Gram and Jeanne Gordon, "Marriage, Marisa Style," *Newsweek*, 12/6/76, p. 103)

LACUNA (lə-kyōō′ nə) *noun, pl.* -NAE or -NAS a gap or missing part; a space where something has been omitted or has come out; HIATUS.

LACUNAL or **LACUNAR** or **LACUNARY** *adj.*

1. Until now the outstanding LACUNA [in Japanese literature accessible in English] had been *The Tale of the Heike* . . . , and we can be grateful indeed that Mr. [Hiroshi] Kitagawa has completed [with Bruce Tsuchida] the gargantuan task of providing a full annotated text in English. (I. Morris, Review, *New York Times*, 2/8/76, Section 7, p. 24)

2. "The appearance of an English translation of Kṛṣṇadāsa Kavirāja Gosvāmī's *Śrī Caitanya-caritāmṛta* by A.C. Bhaktivedanta . . . is a cause for celebration among both scholars in Indian Studies and lay-people seeking to enrich their knowledge of Indian spirituality . . . . It will fill a most serious LACUNA in our libraries and in our courses on the religious traditions of India." (J. Bruce Long [Quoted in Kṛṣṇa Consciousness Pamphlet], Undated, 7th last page)

3. But he [Supreme Court Justice Rehnquist] cannot resist the out-of-town word. Thus he

speaks of "a LACUNA in the statute." In ordinary parlance, a LACUNA is a gap, a hole, a blank space. Why not say so? (J.J. Kilpatrick, "Court Opinions Not Made to Read," *Daily Oklahoman*, Okla. City, 7/6/76, p. 12)

4. "I will arrange for you [Boris Bolgin] to see Comrade Sakharov in the morning. He will familiarize you with the technical information we need [to build a hydrogen bomb], to give you an idea of the LACUNAE in our own work." (W.F. Buckley Jr., *Saving the Queen*, Doubleday, 1976, p. 109)

LAGNIAPPE (lan-yap´) *noun* something given with a purchase to a good customer for good measure; a gratuity or tip; something given or obtained gratuitously.

1. Miscalculations associated with the Russian grain sale of summer 1972 and the dollar devaluaton of February 1973 further EXACERBATED the situation; the effectiveness of the oil producers' cartel was an added LAGNIAPPE. (M. Mayer, "How Banks Destroy the Economy," *Harper's*, January 1975, p. 58)

2. Some rituals [of today's witches in the U.S.] are held in the buff, the theory being that clothing interferes with the vibes of Nature. This may also provide itchy witches with the added LANGNIAPPE (*sic*) of VOYEURISM. (J.L. Jones, "Wonders of Science Providing Field Day for Devil," *Sunday Oklahoman*, 6/6/76, Section A, p. 17)

3. For LAGNIAPPE, [Hugh] Trevor-Roper [in the book, *Hermit of Peking: The Hidden Life of Sir Edmund Backhouse*] tosses out a disturbing suggestion: How many other pathological liars [like Backhouse] have left scholars—and readers—with fraudulent documents long since accepted as fact? (S. Schoffman, Review, *Time*, 5/9/77, p. 86)

LAISSEZ FAIRE or **LAISSEZ-FAIRE** (les´ā fâr, lez´-) the concept that government should intervene as little as possible in the direction of economic affairs; the practice or doctrine of noninterference in the affairs or conduct of others.

1. [President] Ford himself is a fiscal conservative, who spent most of his years in the Congress trying to hold down Government spending on social programs in keeping with the most orthodox LAISSEZ-FAIRE doctrine. (J. Kraft, "Right for Ford," *New York Times*, 4/25/76, Section 6, p. 106)

2. In the long middle section [of the book, *Tom Paine and Revolutionary America*] he [author Eric Foner] concentrates on three main points: (1) the independence movement leading up to the Pennsylvania Constitution of 1776; (2) Paine's LAISSEZ-FAIRE stance by the end of the economic crisis of 1779; and (3) Paine's support of the Bank of North America in the 1780's. (G. Wills, Review, *New York Times*, 3/7/76, Section 7, p. 21)

3. Milton Friedman, who was awarded the Nobel Prize in economics yesterday, is an unorthodox LAISSEZ-FAIRE theorist whose activities as an adviser to conservative politicians almost cost him the prize . . . . His philosophy is generally associated with a . . . hands off policy in regard to business and trade. . . . Friedman believes that interest rates within countries and the value of world currencies internationally should be free to seek their own levels. (Anon., Inquirer Wire Service, "A hands-off point of view," *Philadelphia Inquirer*, 10/15/76, p. 4-B)

4. Rep. Henry Reuss of Wisconsin, respected liberal chairman of the House Banking Committee, never has championed LAISSEZ FAIRE capitalism but believes that even asking for standby wage-price controls now would be severely damaging. Without question, a secret ballot on standby authority would lose badly today in both House and Senate. (R. Evans, R. Novak, "Carter reassures businessmen," *Philadelphia Inquirer*, 11/30/76, p. 19-A)

LAMBENT (lam´bənt) *adj.* running, moving, or playing lightly or gracefully over a surface or subject; flickering; brilliantly playful; dealing gently and brilliantly with a topic; softly bright, radiant, or glowing.

LAMBENTLY *adv.*

LAMBENCY *noun.*

1. As the weeks passed, . . . Tranquilino discovered anew what a jewel he had in Sarafino Gómez. She had a disposition like the clotted milk he ate . . . , gentle, LAMBENT,

always the same. (J.A. Michener, *Centennial*, Fawcett, 1975, p. 836)

2. See (2) under SCHLOCK.

LANGUOR (laNG'gər) *noun* physical weakness or faintness; lack of energy, spirit, vigor, or vitality; lack of interest; indifference; sluggishness; stillness; tenderness of mood or feeling.

LANGUOROUS adj.

LANGUOROUSLY *adv.*

1. See (1) under ANOMIE.

2. Millions who have never read him [Gore Vidal] recognize his electronic presence: elegance bordering on NARCISSISM, feline LANGOUR, throaty self-assurance. (Anon., "Gore Vidal: Laughing Cassandra," *Time*, 3/1/76, p. 61)

3. See (3) under SUPINE.

4. See (1) under ODALISQUE.

LAPIDARY (lap' i-der' ē) or **LAPIDARIAN** *adj.* of or pertaining to the cutting of precious stones; characterized or distinguished by an exactitude and refinement suggestive of gem cutting; short, precise, and elegant; of, pertaining to, or suggestive of inscriptions on stone monuments.

LAPIDARY *noun* a workman who cuts, polishes, and engraves precious stones; the art of such a workman; an expert in precious stones; a collector of or dealer in gems.

1. Political exchanges are not LAPIDARY models of the SYLLOGISTIC art. (W.F. Buckley Jr., *Execution Eve and Other Contemporary Ballads*, G.P. Putnam's Sons, 1975, p. 61)

2. If Mr. Nixon knew ahead of time about Watergate, he is a rogue and (such was the LAPIDARY insinuation) should be impeached. (W.F. Buckley Jr., *Ibid.*, p. 120)

3. But there is the LAPIDARY distinction: the purpose [of impeachment] cannot be to punish the President, only to effect his removal. (W.F. Buckley Jr., *Ibid.*, p. 120)

4. If the power-conscious Mr. Kissinger can endorse a SALT treaty which with LAPIDARY relish relegates the U.S. to inferior status as a

strategic nuclear power, then it should not so much surprise us that a Hungarian, a Pole, and a Cuban together outwitted and outnumbered—enjoying advantages both cultivated and ONTOLOGICAL—an Italian and a Puerto Rican at a critical moment in an athletic contest between Us and Them. (W.F. Buckley Jr., *Ibid.*, p. 242)

5. [Marvin] Cohen [author of the book *Others, Including Morstive Sternbump*] can be made out, but his LAPIDARY phrasing stands in the way of a quick read . . . . Cohen wants us to stop and puzzle over his halting yet jazzy personal idiom. He has gone to great trouble to make English sound foreign to native ears. (R.A. Sokolov, Review, *New York Times*, 2/27/77, Section 7, p. 29)

6. In their intermingling of myth and reality and their playful creation of imaginary worlds, these stories [in *Kingdoms of Elfin*, by Sylvia Townsend Warner] call to mind the moral tales of Jules Laforgue . . . . Their hothouse atmosphere, their LAPIDARY sheen and their supreme artifice may be too much for those accustomed only to the confessional alphabet-adventure soup of the moment. (W.J. Smith, Review, *New York Times*, 3/27/77, Section 7, pp. 6–7)

LAPIN (lap'in) *noun* rabbit fur, generally dyed in imitation of more valuable furs; a rabbit; its fur.

1. This potent little book [*The Tale of Peter Rabbit*, by Beatrix Potter] has made its influence felt in every burrow of our national life—the Playboy dress code, the Hare Krishna movement, my own LAPINE (sic) novels, etc. (J. Updike, Box quotation in the following article: J.Cott, "Peter Rabbit and Friends," *New York Times*, 5/1/77, Section 7, p. 25)

LASSITUDE (las'ə-tōōd', -tyōōd') *noun* weariness of body or mind from strain, oppressive climate, etc.; LANGOUR; a condition of indolent indifference; a state of being tired and listless.

1. The "wily Vietnamese" themselves, heirs to a MANDARIN tradition of LASSITUDE and graft, were not always eager to carry the battle to the enemy—and Douglas MacArthur's injunction

("Treat them as you did your cadets," he told [General] Westmoreland in late 1963) was apparently ineffective. (W. Just, Review of the book, *A Soldier Reports*, by General William C. Westmoreland, *New York Times*, 2/1/76, Section 7, p. 5)

2. Although centrist [Jim] Wright's selection [as House majority leader] represents some mellowing by House Democrats, he is well to the right of their consensus. His election was more the product of intense, semi-hysterical personal emotions aroused by Rep. Philip Burton of California, petty ambitions, a strange LASSITUDE by liberal lobbyists and just plain luck. (R. Evans and R. Novak, "Wright may surprise people. . . , " *Philadelphia Inquirer*, 12/16/76, p. 15-A)

3. See (3) under ID.

LATITUDINARIAN (lat′ i-tōōd′ ³nâr′ ē-ən, -tyōōd²) *noun* a person who is latitudinarian in opinion or conduct; a person who has very liberal views and, in religion, cares very little about particular creeds and forms.

LATITUDINARIAN *adj.* allowing or characterized by latitude or wide difference in opinion or conduct, especially in religious matters; liberal in one's views; very tolerant of different opinions.

LATITUDINARIANISM *noun.*

1. Part of the problem [with the book, *Friends and Lovers*, by Robert Brain] is that Brain is a LATITUDINARIAN. He absolutely refuses to make a distinction . . . precisely because he won't attempt a definition, friendship becomes a meaningless, inclusive category: all human relationships are embraced within it. (P. Robinson, Review, *New York Times*, 11/21/76, section 7, p. 48)

LEITMOTIF (līt′mō-tēf′) *noun* a motif or theme, *i.e.*, a musical phrase, associated throughout a musical drama with a particular person, situation, or emotion; a dominant theme or underlying pattern.

1. See (1) under CODA.

2. If the LEITMOTIF of Henriette [Brull]'s life [as described in *Letter To My Mother*, by

Georges Simenon] was her obsession with providing for her old age, her son's, in this deathbed vigil is, "Can I hold it against you?" For . . . a crime has been committed, and the "crime" is Henriette's failure to love her son [Georges Simenon] . . . . After his mother has died, he concludes what has stood between them was her "ferocious need to be good." In a novel, . . . Simenon would never have tolerated such a defiance of VERISIMILITUDE. (Erica Abeel, Review, *New York Times*, 1/25/76, Section 7, p. 6)

3. But the real LEITMOTIF of this book [*From the Last Row*, by Jean Dalrymple] (unfortunately marred by factual errors) is the conflict between two opposing philosophies of performing arts centers. (Anna Kisselgoff, Review, *New York Times*, 2/20/76, p. 39)

4. See (2) under HORTATORY.

5. If Vietnam or something equally traumatic hadn't happened, American history would have had to invent it. That ultimate collision of traditional optimism against the new pessimism began . . . a resolution of the immense sense of loss that has been the LEITMOTIF of this American century. (R. MacLeish, "National Spirit: pendulum begins to swing," *Smithsonian*, July 1976, p. 32)

LESE MAJESTY (lēz′maj′is-tē′) or LÈSE MAJESTY or LÈSE MAJESTÉ *noun* a crime or offense against the sovereign power in a state, especially an offense against a ruler's dignity as head of state; treason; any insolent or slighting behavior toward a person to whom deference is due; an attack or outrage upon any traditional custom, venerated belief, etc.

1. *Saving the Queen*, [a book] by William F. Buckley Jr. . . . Heroic C.I.A. man involved in a bit of friendly LÈSE MAJESTÉ. (Anon., Review, *New York Times*, 3/7/76, Section 7, p. 33)

2. It was hard to see how such melodrama [Vice President Rockefeller giving the uplifted finger to hecklers] could help the campaign . . . . President Ford reacted to his Vice President's doigt du seigneur with "reserved amusement." And in a final gesture of LESE MAJESTY—at his own expense—the Rock cheerfully agreed to give friends autographed photos of himself—finger aloft. (T. Mathews, *et al.*,

"The Most Happy Fella," *Newsweek*, 9/27/76, p. 35)

3. Yet what is becoming quite common is for reporters . . . to think it their right and duty to follow public figures wherever they go, on official business or otherwise, to ask in interviews the most personal questions and to expect them to be answered. I have yet to hear President, Cabinet officer or Congressman reply it was none of a reporter's business. To do so would be branded evasion, and LESE-MAJESTE in the kingdom of the media. (Vermont Royster, "The Prying Eye," *Wall Street Journal*, 2/2/77, p. 16)

LETHOLOGICA (leth'ō-loj'i-kə) *noun* inability to remember the right word; temporary inability to remember a word or name, or an intended action.

1. For years I suffered terribly from LETHOLOGICA, until a nice doctor friend prescribed Mrs. Byrne's Dictionary of Unusual, Obscure, and Preposterous Words. Yes, for years I couldn't remember the right words . . . . I was leaving blanks in my love letters and suicide notes. I found how bleak the future was when I tried a little cephalonamancy (fortune telling by boiling an ass head), and tyromancy (fortune telling by watching cheese coagulate). I went from doctor to doctor for help, finally becoming a confirmed iatrapistiac (one having little faith in doctors), especially when one suggested I needed a hepaticocholangiocholecystenterostomy (look it up). Then I found Mrs. Byrne's Dictionary . . . . Now . . . I browse instead of groak (watching people silently while they eat, hoping they'll ask you to join them). I don't care anymore that we have a kakistocracy (government of rule by the worst). Leslie Hanscom in *Newsday*: " . . . Only a clinchpoop could scan these pages without a feeling of awe at the undiscovered boundaries of the English tongue." (Advertisement of *Mrs. Byrne's Dictionary* by University Books, Inc., *American Scientist*, March–April 1976, p. 215)

LIBIDINOUS (li-bid'ə -nəs) *adj.* of, pertaining to, or characteristic of the libido; full of or characterized by lust; lustful; lewd; lascivious.

LIBIDINOUSNESS *noun*.

LIBIDO (li-bē'dō, li-bī'dō) *noun* all of the instinctual energies and desires that are derived from the ID; the sexual instinct or urge.

LIBIDINAL *adj.*

LIBIDINALLY *adv.*

1. Question: "Didn't Hitler feel a certain homosexual attraction toward you?" Answer [by Albert Speer]: "Probably yes. A historian once wrote that I was Hitler's unrequited love. There probably was something in him toward me which had some deep LIBIDINOUS tinge." (F. Spelman, "Albert Speer Talks of Spandau, His Atonement—and Hitler's Strange Affection For Him, *People*, 4/12/76, p. 51)

2. Casanova's long johns look like the wrappings of a LIBIDINOUS mummy. And [Federico] Fellini has treated Donald Sutherland [who plays Casanova in the film, *Fellini's Casanova*] like a Frankenstein monster, shaving his hairline, ski-lifting his nose, extending his jaw to turn his head into a grotesque caricature of PHALLIC HUBRIS. (J. Kroll, Review, *Newsweek*, 1/24/77, p. 61)

LICENTIOUS (lī-sen' shəs) *adj.* sexually unrestrained; lewd; unrestrained by law or morality; lawless; immoral; lascivious; libertine; lustful; going beyond customary or proper bounds or limits; abandoned; profligate.

LICENTIOUSLY *adv.*

LICENTIOUSNESS *noun*.

1. A special church document on sex also: . . . . Accused the mass media and entertainment sectors of spreading LICENTIOUS HEDONISM." (Associated Press, "Vatican Hits Sex Outside of Marriage," *Daily Oklahoman*, Okla. City, 1/15/76, p. 20)

2. The "Protestant Ethic," which tends to function as the hero in [Daniel] Bell's book [*The Cultural Contradictions of Capitalism*], has historically supported not only a public conscience but also public repression, and this has especially been the case when its enemies are identified as the HERETICAL and LICENTIOUS, (R. Williams, Review, *New York Times*, 2/1/76, Section 7, p. 3)

3. See (2) under DOUBLE ENTENDRE.

4. Casanova, on his way [in the film, *Fellini's Casanova*] to an assignation with a LICENTIOUS nun, rows his boat across the Adriatic made up of plastic waves whipped to an oily froth with off-screen wind machines. (J. Kroll, Review, *Newsweek*, 1/24/77, p. 60)

LILLIPUTIAN (lil' i-pyōō′ shən) *noun* a very small person [after the tiny inhabitants of Lilliput, an imaginary country described in Swift's satire, *Gulliver's Travels* (1726)]; any person who is narrow, petty, or has little influence.

LILLIPUTIAN *adj.* extremely small; diminutive; tiny; narrow-minded; petty.

1. . . . Mr. Murray Kempton was not satisfied to make the point that I poke at straw men (he is too rigorous a sport to refuse to acknowledge that the most BUMPTIOUS liberal POLEMICISTS are here repulsed); nor even to make the point . . . that I should take on not the contemporary LILLIPUTIANS, but their SEMINAL antecedents; John Dewey and O.W. Holmes, J.S. Millard, Charles Darwin, Auguste Comte and Rousseau . . . . (W.F. Buckley Jr., *Up From Liberalism*, Arlington House, 2nd Printing 1968, p. xxvii)

2. A rare collection of bonsai plants, a Bicentennial . . . gift from Japan to the United States, will be presented at dedication ceremonies at the National Arboretum in Washington on Friday . . . . The 53 tiny trees, ranging in age from 30 to 350 years, and valued at $4 million will be appropriately displayed in a specially designed Japanese garden . . . . Each plant . . . seems to have something unique to admire. One container holds a miniature beech grove, with each LILLIPUTIAN tree growing as naturally as in a woodland. (Lee Lorick Prina, "A Bicentennial Gift of Bonsai to the People of America from the Japanese," *New York Times*, Section 2, p. 29)

3. See (1) under SHILL.

LIMN (lim) *verb* [Archaic] to paint or draw; to portray in words; describe.

LIMNER (lim′ nər, lim′ ər) *noun* a painter, especially a portrait painter.

1. Such constrictions [as those in some of the stories in *Obituaries*, by Bernard Kaplan] are not entirely chronic. The author manages to break out of them in "One Small Death in Saratoga," because he LIMNS his conceptual play with the specific gravity of a "real" setting; the month of August in Saratoga Springs. (J. Charyn, Review, *New York Times*, 2/22/76, Section 7, p. 37)

2. In the *Last Judgment* fresco, . . . Michelangelo has LIMNED his self-portrait within the flayed human skin held up to the gaze of Christ by St. Bartholomew; as if his wretched self were on trial. (L. Steinberg, "Michelangelo's last painting: his gift to this century," *Smithsonian*, December 1975, p. 83)

3. Written with considerably more PANACHE, as befits its subject, is Noel [B.] Gerson's *The Sad Swashbuckler: The Life of William Walker* . . . this is . . . the story of a remarkable general-of-fortune-who-would-be-King of Nicaragua . . . the book LIMNS its peculiar hero with sure strokes. (Jane Yolen, Review, *New York Times*, 5/2/76, Section 7, p. 34)

4. The un-solemn, deftly patient text [of *Learning To Say Good-By*, by Eda LeShan] finds an exact match in Paul Giovanopoulos's cross-hatched, literal drawings, in which the headstones' not-quite-gibberish inscriptions LIMN the weirdness of death itself. (P. West, Review, *New York Times*, 5/1/77, Section 7, p. 45)

LITANY (lit′ə nē) *noun* a ceremonial or liturgical form of prayer consisting of a series of invocations or supplications with responses that are the same for a number in succession; a recitation or recital that resembles a litany; any prolonged or drearily monotonous and repetitive account.

1. See (1) under CALUMNY.

2. It is interesting that nowhere in these books [*The Boundless Resource: A Prospectus for an Education-Work Policy*, by Willard Wirtz; and *Bridging the Gap: A Study of Education-to-Work Linkages*, by Richard I. Ferrin and Solomon Arbeiter] is the argument made that further education can make workers more satisfied—an argument that until recently has been a regular part of the LITANY. (G. Weathersby, Review, *Chronicle of Higher Education*, 6/28/76, p. 16)

3. Now it appears that at least 10 per cent of the programs' [Medicare's and Medicaid's] budgets may be pilfered annually as a result of abuses and outright fraud by all segments of the medical profession. At hearings last week by a Senate subcommittee on health . . . witnesses recited a LITANY of medical ripoffs ranging from nursing-home purchases of boats and trips to Hawaii to laboratory kickbacks for new accounts. (Sandra Salmans, Henry McGee, "Physician, Heal Thyself," *Newsweek*, 8/9/76, p. 24)

4. See (1) under CODA.

LITIGIOUS (li-tij'-əs) *adj.* of or pertaining to lawsuits or litigation; excessively inclined to litigate; inclined to dispute or disagree; argumentative; disputatious; quarrelsome.

LITIGIOUSLY *adv.*

LITIGIOUSNESS *noun.*

LITIGATION *noun* the act or process of litigating; a lawsuit.

LITIGATE *verb* to contest at law.

LITIGABLE *adj.* subject to litigation.

LITIGATOR *noun.*

1. No scrap of luridly LITIGIOUS prose [about William Loeb] escapes [Kevin] Cash's vacuum cleaner [in the book, *Who the Hell is William Loeb?*], including . . . an alienation-of-affection suit against Loeb, his own mother's law-suit against her son and—after she disinherited him—Loeb's suit against his mother's estate. (M.F. Nolan, Review, *New York Times*, 2/1/76, Section 7, p. 6)

LITTÉRATEUR (lit'ər-ə-tûr', lē-tä-Ra-tŒR) or **LITTERATEUR** *noun* a writer of literary works; person of letters.

1. Of Farley Mowat's 19 or so books I've read 12, and . . . it seems to me *The Snow Walker* is the best. The precious sniping of the LITTÉRATEUR is simply not relevant here. *The Snow Walker* is a book of tales about the Eskimo, stories ranging from the ancient to the overwhelmingly modern. (J. Harrison, Review, *New York Times*, 2/22/76, Section 7, p. 4)

2. Howard Prince [played by Woody Allen, in the movie, *The Front*] has never heard of the blacklist [in the entertainment world of the 1950's] and becomes a front just to do a buddy a favor. He has never read anything but the Racing Form, but in his new role as LITTÉRATEUR he heads for the nearest bookstore saying, "Gimme two Hemingways and two Faulkners." (J. Kroll, Review, *Newsweek*, 10/4/76, p. 89)

LITTORAL (lit' ər-əl) *adj.* of, pertaining to, on, or along the shore of a lake, sea, or ocean.

LITTORAL *noun* a region along the shore.

1. It [the Niger] was a river difficult to get to from the north because of the Sahara and its fanatical inhabitants; and it was equally inaccessible from the fever-ridden Atlantic LITTORAL to the south and west, for which the title "White Man's Grave" was expressly invented. (E. Newby, Review of *The Strong God Brown: The Story of the Niger River*, by Sanche de Gramont, *New York Times*, 4/4/76, Section 7, p. 26)

2. Returning [to Anzio] after many years, I was agreeably surprised to find it less squalid than it might have been, blessedly free of the cement-cube slums blighting most of the Italian LITTORAL, pleasantly laced with green belts of pine and sprinkled with mimosas in feather yellow bloom. (Claire Sterling, "The View from Anzio: They Do Not Love Us," *New York Times*, 7/4/76, Section 6, p. 107)

LOBOTOMY (lō-bot'ə-mē, lə-) *noun* the cutting into or across a lobe of the brain, usually of the cerebrum, to alter brain function and to change the behavior of a person, a surgical procedure used especially in the treatment of mental disorders.

1. I wonder . . . if we have not already offered so much "help" that we have done more to LOBOTOMIZE students than more obvious forms of repression. Perhaps we foster the Peter Principle—people reaching their level of incompetence, instead of stopping at their highest level of success. (M.G. Baumann, Review of *Second Best: The Crisis of the Community College*, by L. Steven Zwerling, *Chronicle of Higher Education*, 5/17/76, p. 13)

2. One of their [John S. and Ardelia Willis's] grandchildren is a tenured professor at Princeton. Another, who suffered from what the Peruvian poet called "anger that breaks a man into children," was picked up just as he entered his teens and emotionally LOBOTOMIZED by the reformatories and mental institutions specifically designed to serve him. (Toni Morrison, "A Slow Walk of Trees (as Grandmother Would Say). Hopeless (as Grandfather Would Say)," *New York Times*, 7/4/76, Section 6, p. 104)

LOGOPHILIA (lŏ' gə-fĭl' ē-ə) *noun* fondness for or love of words.

1. I enjoyed [in the book, *François Rabelais: A Study*, by Donald M. Frame] the analysis of Rabelais' "exuberant style,..., his LOGOPHILIA, his verbal game-playing,..." (Doris Grumbach, Review, *New York Times*, 7/17/77, Section 7, p. 18)

2. The OED [Oxford English Dictionary], available in a two-volume microtext edition since 1971, is indisputably the most complete English-language dictionary ever made. But even those LOGOPHILES who like to page through it hunting for rare words . . . may not have guessed that its principal editor was more than a SEDULOUS savant . . . . But James Murray was a stupefying dynamo and even a bit of a sport. He and his wife Ada rode a runaway tandem tricycle into a ditch when Murray was 48. His eleventh child was born when he was 51. (R. Sokolov, Review of *Caught in the Web of Words: James A.H. Murray and the 'Oxford English Dictionary,'* a book by K.M. Elisabeth Murray, *Newsweek*, 11/7/77, p. 97-D)

LOGORRHEA (lŏ'gə-rē'ə, log'ə-) *noun* excessive talkativeness, especially when incoherent and uncontrollable; a medical condition in which speech is incoherent and repetitious.

LOGORRHEIC *adj.*

1. Take David Mamet . . . and his first play to risk Broadway, *American Buffalo*. Mr. Mamet is unquestionably talented . . . . Something of what he hears is funny, something of it is wickedly human. But it's surely a mistake to urge him to make whole evenings out of LOGOR-

RHEA, out of the compulsive, circular, run-on and irrelevant flow of words that tend to spill from folk when they're otherwise impotent and can't even get anyone interested in a game of gin rummy. (W. Kerr, "Language Alone Isn't Drama," *New York Times*, 3/6/77, Section 2, p. 3)

LONGUEUR (lôn-gĕr', long-gûr') *noun* a long, boring, tedious stretch, as of time or of a passage in a musical or literary work.

1. Ultimately, the very IDIOSYNCRASY and detachment of [Gail] Godwin's characters and the world they inhabit [in the book, *Dream Children*] lend to her writing a tedium and consequence that paralyze even her deftest effects. As one reads through the LONGUEURS that take up so much room in these stories, one becomes increasingly impatient for some breakthrough to the real world. . . . (Jane Larkin Crain, Review, *New York Times*, 2/22/76, Section 7, p. 22)

LOUCHE (lōōsh) *adj.* of questionable character; disreputable; devious, oblique.

1. With success firmly in his grasp, however, Mr. [Lorenz] Hart continued to make the midnight rounds, disappearing for days on end and counting among his true friends a LOUCHE character named Milton "Doc" Bender . . . he maintained his destructive course . . . . Shortly after it [*A Connecticut Yankee*]'s triumphant return to Broadway in 1943, Hart died at the age of 48. (Bobbie Short, Review of *Thou Swell, Thou Witty*, Edited and with a Memoir by Dorothy Hart; and *Rogers & Hart*, by Samuel Marx and Jan Clayton, *New York Times*, 11/21/76, Section 7, p. 53)

LUBRICIOUS (lōō-brĭsh' əs) or **LUBRICOUS** (lōō' brə-kəs) *adj.* of a surface, coating, etc.; having an oily smoothness; slippery; unstable; uncertain; shifty; unsteady; wavering; undependable; sexually wanton; lewd; lustful; lecherous; lascivious; obscene.

LUBRICIOUSLY *adv.*

LUBRICITY (lōō-brĭs'ĭ-tē) *noun* oily smoothness as of a surface; slipperiness; ability or capacity to lubricate; instability; shiftiness; trickiness; lewdness; wantonness; salaciousness.

1. See (1) under SCABROUS.

2. I hope that somewhere along the line hard investigation will reveal that the reports of J. Edgar Hoover's LUBRICIOUS renditions to Lyndon Johnson of the moral habits of some of his important critics will prove to have been exaggerated. (W.F. Buckley Jr., *Execution Eve and Other Contemporary Ballads*, G.P. Putnam's Sons, 1975, p. 411)

3. This winded frontier comedy [the movie, *The Duchess and the Dirtwater Fox*] concerns one of those fun couples who, sadly, amuse only each other. The Duchess (Goldie Hawn) is a Barbary Coast hooker trying to get off her back and onto her feet by turning a dishonest dollar. The Dirtwater Fox (George Segal) is a sharpie whose smart schemes always collapse in chaos. These two hook up to defraud a LUBRICIOUS Mormon—a bit of bunko that helps keep the Dirtwater Fox a few steps ahead of some bad guys who are giving him heated chase. (J. Cocks, Review, *Time*, 4/26/76, p. 48)

LUCUBRATE (loo´kyoo-brāt´) *verb* to work, write, or study laboriously, especially at night; to write in a learned or scholarly manner.

LUCUBRATION (loo kyoo-brā´ shən) *noun* laborious work, study, writing, etc., especially at night; something produced by such study, especially a learned or carefully elaborated work.

LUCUBRATOR *noun.*

LUCUBRATORY (loo´kyoo-brā´tō-rē) *adj.*

1. Under the Eisenhower Program one could, simultaneously, declare for a free market economy and veto . . . the gas bill which aimed at a free market on gas; . . . LUCUBRATE over constitutional rights and freedoms and forever abandon captured American soldiers; and over the whole package . . . there was suffused a general benignity of a kind that bewitched the multitude of the voters. (W.F. Buckley Jr., *Up From Liberalism*, Arlington House, 2nd Printing 1968, p. 12)

2. Settle that point once and for all, and we will know, when we hear the LUCUBRATIONS of Mr. Sevareid, that when he walks out it's

because he chooses to walk out: that it has nothing to do with any contractual obligation [to a labor union] to walk out. (W.F. Buckley Jr., *Execution Eve and Other Contemporary Ballads*, G.P. Putnam's Sons, 1975, p. 259)

3. Well, lift up your head and shout "Hallelujah!" Erase those lines of LUCUBRATION that fret your brow! Come out into the sunshine and get yourself a copy of the 1976 Neiman-Marcus "Christmas Preview" catalog! (D. West, "The Lighter Side," *Times Herald*, Norristown, Pa., 10/5/76, p. 9)

LUDDITE (lud´īt) *noun* any of a group of workers in England (1811-16) who smashed new labor-saving textile machinery in protest against reduced wages and unemployment [believed to be after Ned Ludd, who smashed two frames of a Leicestershire employer (*ca.* 1779)].

1. *Medical Nemesis,* [a book] by Ivan Illich . . . . Another Illich neo-LUDDITE barrage, this time directed at medical care. (Anon., Review, *New York Times*, 5/30/76, Section 7, p. 17)

2. [Ivan] Illich—priest, historian, theologian, philosopher, POLEMICIST, ICONOCLAST, and, in some ways, the leading LUDDITE of the 20th century—is thus back with another major critique [the book, *Medical Nemesis*] of the restless industrialization of our society . . . . No POLEMICIST writing today has his passion, his range, his glittering and pyrotechnic arsenal. (H.J. Geiger, Review, *New York Times*, 5/2/76, Section 7, p. 1-2)

3. And Lord Russell mocked what he described as "the superior virtue of the oppressed." They were treated as LUDDITES. Every intellectual had VICARIOUSLY shared the sufferings of the misfit, the noncomformist, the anti-authoritarian, the PICARESQUE rebel at war with society. Alienation . . . had become a cultural vogue. (W. Manchester, Commencement Address, University of Massachusetts, 6/13/65, Mimeographed, p. 3)

4. . . . there does appear to exist, especially on and around the campus, a collection of individuals both ignorant of and opposed to all forms of advanced technology. These are middle- and upper-class LUDDITES, as the 19th

century English workmen were called who tried to smash up labor-saving machinery. Thus, recently, I debated the New Left anarchist Karl Hess—a thorough-going LUDDITE—at Dartmouth. The Hess partisans in the audience were a peculiar looking crew . . . their questions tended to be incoherently passionate. (J. Hart, "N-Plants Safe," *Times Herald*, Norristown, Pa., 5/27/77, p. 13)

LUGUBRIOUS (lŏŏ-gŏō′brē-əs, -gyŏō′-) *adj.* mournful or gloomy in manner or tone, especially exaggeratedly or ridiculously so; mournful; melancholy; doleful.

LUGUBRIOUSLY *adv.*

LUGUBRIOUSNESS *noun.*

1. Asked to sing a merry Irish song at a St. Patrick's Day party last year, he [Gov. Carey of New York] said there was no such thing, quoted some LUGUBRIOUS lines from *Mother Machree*, and added "You try to tell a woman today that you love her 'brow that's all furrowed and wrinkled with care.' You'll never get away with it." (A. Logan, "Around City Hall Irishry," *The New Yorker*, 2/9/76, p. 90)

2. "Mom told us that God sent the roadrunner to show us the way through difficult places," he [Lasater] said, and this started a LUGUBRIOUS discussion of mothers and other noble women the cowboys had known. Tale after tale of frontier heroism unfolded, invariably with some gallant woman at the core of the action. (J.A. Michener, *Centennial*, Fawcett, 1975, p. 572)

3. So Jim [Lloyd] caught the night train to Chicago, and . . . hurried to Kilbride's Kerry Roost, where the white-haired, LUGUBRIOUS owner remembered Clemma Ferguson: "Fine-looking girl. Good waitress." (J.A. Michener, *Ibid.*, p. 740)

4. [The narrator in a volume of the trilogy preceding *Travesty*, by John Hawkes] recalls a friend telling him that he lives his "entire life in a coma" and his numbed LUGUBRIOUS itemization of past incidents, present encounters . . . suggests a state of feeling degree zero, an estranged consciousness somehow communicating from the other side of CATATONIA. (T. Tanner, Review, *New York Times*, 3/28/76, Section 7, p. 23)

5. . . . [George H.] Nash [author of *The Conservative Intellectual Movement in America*] is not entirely to blame for his shallowness, inasmuch as he wasn't given very much to work with. American conservative thought in the postwar period is a LUGUBRIOUS affair, shrill and repetitive, filled with a good measure of self-pity and an inordinate pride in its lack of intellectual subtlety. (P. Rosenberg, Review, *New York Times*, 6/20/76, Section 7, p. 23)

6. Other metals that are likely to be mined out before long are mercury, gold, silver and lead, followed by zinc and chromium . . . . He [Brian J. Skinner] is LUGUBRIOUS about the prospects of finding substantial metal ores in the Earth's crust below the oceans. . . . (J.K. Page Jr., "We may run out of metals," *Smithsonian*, July 1976, p. 14)

7. Can a former president find happiness once he leaves the White House? . . . The answer to that is as LUGUBRIOUS as any soap opera: Don't bet on it. Over the years, most of them . . . spent their remaining years bitterly missing the pomp and the power. (Virginia Fayette, "Getting Richer," *Times Herald*, Norristown, Pa., 1/26/77, p. 17)

8. See (5) under WELTSCHMERZ.

9. See (2) under TRULL.

LUMPEN (lum′pən) *adj.* of, pertaining to, or designating disenfranchised and uprooted individuals or groups, especially those who have sunk to a low or contemptible status in their class because of their unproductiveness, shiftlessness, alienation, degeneration, etc.

LUMPEN *noun* a person or group that is lumpen.

1. He [Cosmo Vitelli, in the film *The Killing of a Chinese Bookie*] is an upside-down Gatsby, a social ZIRCON with a diamond morality. [Director] Cassavetes records his downfall with a fine sense of the casualness of doom in the LUMPEN world. (J. Kroll, Review, *Newsweek*, 3/15/76, pp. 89-90)

2. Mack Sennett, the catalytic force who generated almost all the great comic personalities [of silent films], loved this atmosphere of LUMPEN rebellion, and boasted that his movies . . . "whaled the daylights out of Authority and

PRETENSION." (J. Kroll, Review of *American Film Comedy*, at Museum of Modern Art, *Newsweek*, 5/31/76, p. 53)

3. See (4) under KEEN.

4. See (2) under ANTHROPOID.

LUPINE (lōō′ pīn) *adj.* pertaining to, resembling, or related to the wolf; fierce or savage; ravenous; predatory.

1. Old ball players [referring to George Shuba] pursue the pleasures of eating with LUPINE directness. (R. Kahn, *The Boys of Summer*, Harper and Row, 1971, p. 228)

LUSTRATE (lus′ trāt) *verb* to purify by performing certain rituals or ceremonies to make amends for a wrong, as by offering a propitiatory sacrifice or performing a ceremonial washing.

LUSTRATION *noun.*

LUSTRATIVE (lus′trə-tiv) *adj.*

1. The following morning [Ronald] Beard LUSTRATED against a lonely day by sitting in two cold inches [of water] and sopping with a logged sponge. (A. Burgess, *Beard's Roman Women*, McGraw-Hill, 1976, p. 51)

M

MACHICOLATION (mə-chik′ə-lā′shən) *noun* an opening in the floor of a projecting gallery or parapet through which missiles, molten lead, etc. could be dropped on an enemy by the defenders of a fortress; a projecting gallery or parapet with such openings.

MACHICOLATE *verb* to provide with machicolations.

1. "After the next war, when we shall all have exchanged hydrogen bombs, I [Queen Caroline] should think these [Windsor Castle] archives would be tremendously useful, since whoever is left over will be reduced to defending himself by the use of things like moats and MACHICOLATIONS and bows and arrows . . ." (W.F. Buckley, *Saving the Queen*, Doubleday, 1976, p. 172)

MACHINATION (mak′ə-nā′shən) *noun* the act, an instance, or the process of machinating or plotting; (usually used as the plural) crafty schemes, secret plots; intrigues, especially those with evil intent.

MACHINATE *verb* to contrive, devise, or plot, especially artfully or with evil purpose.

MACHINATOR *noun.*

1. See (1) under ENNUI.

2. The treatment of power [in *The Rockefellers*, a book by Peter Collier and David Horowitz] begins with John D. Rockefeller, Sr., the man whom Robert La Follette called "the greatest criminal of the age." Describing the intricate web of rebates, CLANDESTINE agreements and ruthless MACHINATIONS that John D. Rockefeller employed to build the Standard Trust, the authors write: "Under the Trust arrangement, it was never clear who owned what or who was responsible for which actions. . . . As Ida Tarbell later wrote: 'You could argue its existence from its effects, but you could never prove it.' " (S.R. Weisman, Review, *New York Times*, 3/28/76, Section 7, p. 1)

3. The bulk of the book [*The Invisible Primary*, by Arthur T. Hadley] is a chronicle of candidates' MACHINATIONS in the past three years, and these are usually interesting,

whether they determine the final outcome or merely contribute to it. (B. Shafer, Review, *New York Times*, 3/28/76, Section 7, p. 22)

4. See (3) under PEDERASTY.

MACHISMO (mä-chiz′ mō) *noun* (in Hispanic cultures) maleness, virility, or aggressiveness; strong or assertive masculinity; male domination.

MACHO (mä′chō) *noun* a strong, virile man.

MACHO *adj.* masculine, virile, courageous, etc.

1. See (1) under HIATUS.

2. Everyone who has worked with [Alan] Greenspan seems struck by his lack of ego, his unconcern with MACHISMO, his disposition to emphasize his subject more than himself. (J. Kraft, "Right, for Ford," *New York Times*, 4/25/76, Section 6, p. 109)

3. [Jerome] Robbins unveiled his new PAS DE DEUX for Natalia Makarova and Mikhail Baryshnikov . . . at Lincoln Center. . . . In their first solos they spin off flickering images of remembered youth, of athletic bravado in the boy's case and of uncomplicated innocence in the girl's. But in their second variations, the man's MACHISMO becomes softened by poetry, the girl's innocence tempered by understanding. (H. Saal, "Gala Trio of Ballets," *Newsweek*, 5/24/76, p. 87)

4. He [Julius Erving, the Doctor J of the New York Nets] has mixed playground MACHISMO and team-oriented unselfishness in a perfect blend; his steel-spring legs and huge hands are matched by a keen, inquiring mind. (P. Axthelm, "Sky King" *Newsweek*, 5/24/76, p. 55)

5. See (1) under SUPERNAL.

6. Their efforts [those of female Spanish bullfighters] have provoked varying degrees of amusement, astonishment and hostility in a profession that is perhaps the peak of MACHISMO. (J. Hoagland, of *Washington Post*, "Crowd Reaction varies as women take up bullfighting," *Norman* [Okla.] *Transcript*, 6/27/76, p. 27)

7. See (2) under IMMOLATE.

8. An unhappy aspect of the women's move-ment has been the oddly ANDROGYNOUS MACHISMO some of its leaders have developed. This has expressed itself in fashion, in sex, in distinctly masculine lifestyles. Meantime, the other kind of MACHISMO seems to be settling in. I was agreeably surprised by the number of women who watched *Gone With the Wind* and remarked, glowingly, on the "virility" of Clark Gable. (Harriet Van Horne, "Feminity succeeds," *Philadelphia Inquirer*, 11/16/76, p. 11–A)

9. See (5) under TRANSVESTITE.

MACULATION (mak′yə-lā′shən) *noun* the act of spotting; a spotted condition; a marking of spots, as on an animal; a disfiguring spot or stain; defilement; blemish.

MACULATE *verb* to mark with a spot or spots; stain; to sully or pollute; defile.

MACULATE (mak′yə-lit) *adj.* spotted; stained; blotched; impure; defiled.

MACULA (mak′yŏŏ-lə) or MACULE *noun* a spot, stain, blotch, etc., especially a discolored spot on the skin or a dark spot on the sun.

1. . . .the new conservatives, many of whom go by the name of Modern Republicans, have not been very helpful. Their sin consists in permitting so many accretions, modifications, EMENDATIONS, MACULATIONS, and qualifications that the original thing quite recedes from view. The conservative movement in America has got to put its theoretical house in order. (W.F. Buckley Jr., *Up From Liberalism*, Arlington House, 2nd Printing 1968, p. 189)

MAGDALENE (mag′də-lēn′) or MAGDALEN mag′ də-lən) *noun* a reformed and repentant prostitute; (in Britain) a reformatory for prostitutes.

1. But Alphonse Mucha was a sculptor too, and nothing in this show EPITOMIZES the art nouveau vision (or fantasy) of woman better than a bust he designed around 1899 for a Parisian jeweler. This astonishing object, whose form shifts like water in the twining reflections of silver flesh and gold hair, is perversely liturgical—a PARODY (done, one should recall, for a public whose cultural background was still Catholic) of medieval head RELIQUARIES. The im-

age, however, is not a saint or a MAGDALEN but that SIBYLLINE bitch of the FIN-DE-SIÈCLE imagination, the Fatal Woman, *La Belle Dame sans Merci*—enigmatic as a sphinx, cruelly indifferent as a BYZANTINE empress, wearing the features of the Divine Sarah and the aggressive glitter of a vintage Cadillac fender. (R. Hughes, "The Snobbish Style," *Time*, 9/13/76, p. 67)

MAIEUTIC (mā-yōo´-tik) *adj*. noting the method used by Socrates in bringing forth knowledge by interrogation and insistence on close and logical reasoning; designating or pertaining to the Socratic method—so-called because Socrates held that teaching is providing help for the eliciting of latent ideas; intellectual midwifery [Socrates played the part of a midwife in helping students "give birth" to universal ideas hidden in their mind because of prejudice or bigotry].

MAIEUTICS *noun* obstetrics; the Socratic method

1. He [Mike Wallace] proposes to do a television program on the subject [of the ethics of junketing], and I am grateful to him for his MAIEUTIC inquiry about *my* own views, which had not crystallized. (W.F. Buckley Jr., *Execution Eve and Other Contemporary Ballads*, G.P. Putnam's Sons, 1975, p. 434)

2. The Braddock-Louis fight, like the Schmeling-Louis fight, was more than just sport, but sport was the MAIEUTIC agent in that stride toward racial parity. (W.F. Buckley Jr., *Ibid.*, p. 224)

MAÎTRE D'HÔTEL (mā´ tər dō-tel´, mā´ trə) *noun, pl.*: **MAÎTRES D'HÔTEL** (mā´ tərz dō-tel´, mā´ trəz) a headwaiter, butler, or steward; major-domo; the owner or manager of a hotel.

MAÎTRE D' (mā´ tər dē´, mā´ trə), *pl.*: **MAÎTRE D'S** an informal expression for maître d'hôtel.

1. Instead of a friendly greeting [at *Top of the Park* restaurant], HAUTEUR from a MAÎTRE D'HÔTEL who implies that you're lucky to get into the place (and from the way the tables are filled, perhaps you are). (J. Canaday, "Hauteur, but a View, at Top of the Park," *New York Times*, 2/20/76, p. 27)

2. This is not to say the Palace Court [restaurant in Las Vegas] is unmitigated highway robbery. Service there is good and the MAÎTRE D' is practically enchanting, though his French accent reminds me less of France than of Sid Caesar speaking "French." (R. Vare, "Where Dining Is a Big Gamble," *National Observer*, week ending 4/2/77, p. 11B)

MALAISE (ma-lāz´, ma-lez´) *noun* a condition of general bodily weakness or discomfort; an unfocused, vague feeling of mental uneasiness or physical discomfort; a vague awareness of moral or social decline.

1. Beyond statistics lies the MALAISE of the spirit. For the British, there are no more parades. Gone in a whirl of platitudes is that empire upon which the sun never set. The genius that nurtured Milton and Shakespeare and seeded the minds of our Founding Fathers now sleeps in bitter TORPOR, unbidden to greatness. (Smith Hempstone, "Wilson Evasion Fine Art Form," *Daily Oklahoman*, Okla. City, 3/24/76, p. 10)

2. See (2) under BILLINGSGATE.

3. The mid-70's guess-who novel is ingeniously designed to feed our particular MALAISE even while symbolizing it . . . we are all too ready to reduce not only the novel but history to its lowest common denominator: gossip. (M. Maddocks, "Now for the Age of Psst!," *Time*, 6/28/76, p. 69)

MALAPROPISM (mal´ ə-prop-iz´ əm) *noun* an instance or the habit of ludicrous misuse of words, especially by the confusion of words that are similar in sound; an instance of this [named after Mrs. Malaprop, a character in Sheridan's humorous play, *The Rivals* (1775), noted for her misapplication of words].

MALAPROPOS (mal´ap-rə-pō´) *adj*. inappropriate; untimely; inopportune; at an awkward or improper time or place.

MALAPROPOS *adv*. inappropriately; inopportunely.

1. . . . I've become concerned about the sad state of humor in the White House. We've been a long time in the desert between intelligent oases of laughter, as distinguished from mirages of MALAPROPISMS and PRATFALLS. May-

be memories of Lincoln, FDR and Kennedy never die, but they do fade somewhat. (A. Epstein, "The wit of Jimmy Carter—it's a short story," *Philadelphia Inquirer*, 9/24/76, p. 11-A)

2. Though we have been hearing a great deal about political apathy, . . . 80 per cent of the students [at Dartmouth College] said they intended to vote . . . . What these figures demonstrate is that "normalcy," to use President Warren Harding's famous MALAPROPISM, has returned to the college campus. (J. Hart, "Student Normalcy," *Times Herald*, Norristown, Pa., 10/28/76, p. 23)

3. If the message was appealing, Ford's delivery was seldom incandescent; his speeches were sprinkled with astonishing semi-sequiturs and MALAPROPS . . . . He spoke glowingly of his visits to Lawton, Texas and Joliet, Ind.—they are in Oklahoma and Illinois, respectively—and announced in Lincoln, Ill., that it was "great to be in Pontiac." (T. Mathews and T.M. DeFrank, "Out Of The Rose Garden," *Newsweek*, 11/1/76, pp. 23-24)

4. The narrator and most of the other guys [in the book, *The Secret of Fire 5*, by Jack Olsen] talk in a heavy locker-room jargon studded with MALAPROPISMS: "nothing seems to phrase him"; "a regular Jackal and Hyde"; the men are "orgling James Mansfield in the TV"; "I feel like Alice in Wanderland." (D. Wakefield, Review, *New York Times*, 5/1/77, Section 7, p. 10)

5. Similarly, David Mamet's play [*American Buffalo*] is a sort of junk shop of language . . . . The speech of Mamet's three main characters . . . is an incrustation of street slang, NON SEQUITURS, MALAPROPISMS and compulsive obscenity. The playwright revels a bit too much in this SCATOLOGY and blasphemy. (C. Porterfield, Review, *Time*, 2/28/77, p. 54)

MALEFACTION (mal′ə-fak′shən) *noun* an evil deed; crime; wrongdoing.

MALEFACTOR *noun* a person who violates the law; criminal; evil-doer.

MALEFACTRESS *noun* a female malefactor.

1. Watching the emergence of the tall building in New York in 1913, the critic Mont-

gomery Schuyler could still write ". . . . It is a public MALEFACTION to protrude a shapeless bulk above the purple crowd of humbler roofs." (Ada Louise Huxtable, "A Skyscraper Fit for a King (Kong)?" *New York Times*, 2/1/76, Section 2, p. 31)

MALENTENDU (mAl-äN-täN-dY) *noun* a misunderstanding.

1. When she [my mother-in-law Aranka] next came . . . . Bob [my husband] was out of town. "So where is he?" In Phoenix, I [Jessica Mitford] explained, on a case for the union. Aranka looked at me accusingly. "Always for the union he is doing things. Isn't it about time he did something for himself?" (A typical Aranka MALENTENDU; the union in question happened to be one of the law firm's most lucrative accounts.) (Jessica Mitford, "Memoirs of a Not-So-Dutiful Daughter," *New York Times*, 4/17/77, Section 6, p. 37)

MALINGER (mə-liñg′gər) *verb* to pretend or feign illness or other incapacity in order to avoid or escape duty, work, etc.; shirk.

MALINGERER *noun*.

1. The Labor Department's administration of the [federal government's compensation] program [for employees suffering on-the-job injuries] has sparked allegations of frequent MALINGERING by federal employees, shoddy administration by the government and unnecessary expenses paid by taxpayers . . . . "We know that MALINGERERS get away with their dishonesty," said Larry P. Hackler, safety director at the Norfolk, Va., Naval Shipyard in an appearance before the House Education and Labor Committee. (Associated Press, "Paid Hookey," *Allentown (Pa.) Morning Call*, 12/2/77, p. 13)

MALLEABLE (mal′ē-ə-bəl) *adj.* capable of being extended or shaped without breaking by hammering or by pressure from rollers; adaptable or tractable; capable of being changed, molded, trained, etc.

MALLEABILITY or **MALLEABLENESS** *noun*.

1. In this MORDANT comedy of manners, Sweet William [the title character] hasn't any. A

playwright by profession, he pumps around on a borrowed bicycle, reading good-night stories to his children, taking supper at the table of his second wife, bursting into the bedroom of Ann Walton, the novel's MALLEABLE heroine, then gallivanting off with Ann's cousin whom he has seduced in the course of supervising her abortion. (P. D. Zimmerman, Review of the book, *Sweet William*, by Beryl Bainbridge, *Newsweek*, 3/22/76, p. 82)

MANA (mä′nä) *noun* a generalized, impersonal supernatural force or power, which may be concentrated in objects or persons and to which certain primitive peoples attribute good fortune, magical powers, etc.

1. In many tribes, women who are having their periods are confined in special menstrual huts, located some distance from the village, to protect the rest of the community from their threatening supernatural power, or MANA. (Jean Seligman, Review of the book, *The Curse: A Cultural History of Menstruation*, by Janice Delaney, Mary Jane Lupton and Emily Toth, *Newsweek*, 9/13/76, p. 82)

MANDALA (mun′ dᵊlᵊ) *noun* (in Oriental Art) a schematized representation of the total cosmos, chiefly characterized by a concentric organization of geometric shapes, each of which contains an image or attribute of a deity.

1. Throughout conversations with those who build and study solar devices and related technologies, one theme keeps recurring— solar collectors create a different consciousness. They are a MANDALA, a universal, mystical symbol that is said to reveal the wisdom of the way the world works. (S. Love, "Houses designed with nature: Their future is at hand." *Smithsonian*, December 1975, p. 50)

2. In 1969 graphics appeared all over. The peace symbol and the upraised fist were now common . . . . Finally MANDALAS (Hindu or Buddhist symbols of the universe), advertised as "sacred meditation symbols," appeared. Perhaps the most subtly revealing was the old photo of W.C. Fields, hatted and gloved, peering in a secretive and calculating way over a hand of cards. The old, roguish ICONOCLAST

made defiance of the MORES appear amusing. (Margaret Lantis, "As times change, so do signs, signals adopted by youth." *Smithsonian*, September 1976, pp. 77-78)

3. *Dispatches* reprints the reports that [Michael] Herr sent home from the [Vietnam] war, eyewitness accounts of combat . . . . "But disgust was only one color in the whole MANDALA, a gentleness and pity were other colors, there wasn't a color left out . . . . I remembered the way a Phantom pilot had talked about how beautiful the surface-to-air missiles looked as they drifted up toward his plane to kill him." (P. Gray, Review, *Time*, 11/7/77, p. 119)

MANDARIN (man′dᵊ-rin) *noun* a high official of the old Chinese Empire; a member of any elite group; a leading intellectual, political figure, etc., sometimes one who is pompous, arbitrary, etc.

MANDARIN *adj.* designating or of a Chinese style of dress, especially a narrow, close-fitting, stand-up collar parted in the front; designating or of an elegant, over-refined literary style.

1. [Laurens] Van der Post's book [*Jung and the Story of Our Time*] is an extensive summary of Jung's major concepts and present implications . . . . The text occasionally rambles . . . and errs in the direction of HAGIOLATRY, but Van der Post successfully provides the flavor of the man, the warmth, the sustained cheerfulness, and the playfulness behind his imposing MANDARIN facade. (J. Hollis, Review, *Chronicle of Higher Education*, 7/26/76, p. 9)

2. See (1) under ORMOLU.

3. See (1) under LASSITUDE.

4. See (2) under PALADIN.

5. See (3) under HIERATIC.

MANICHEISM (man′ə-kē′ iz-əm) or **MANICHAEISM** or **MANICHAEANISM** or **MANICHEEISM** *noun* a religious philosophy taught from the 3d to 7th century by the Persian Mani, or Manichaeus, and his followers, combining Zoroastrian, Gnostic Christian, and pagan elements, and based on the doctrine of the two contending principles of good (light,

God, the soul) and evil (darkness, Satan, the body).

MANICHEAN or MANICHAEAN or MANICHEE *noun* an adherent of Manicheism.

MANICHEAN or MANICHAEAN *adj.*

1. He [Malachi Martin] enounces [in his book, *Hostage to the Devil: The Possession and Exorcism of Five Living Americans*] a primitivistic and antiquated MANICHEEISM in which the world is viewed as a battleground between God and a highly exteriorized Kingdom of Satan. (Francine DuPlessix Gray, Review, *New York Times*, 3/14/76, Section 7, p. 8)

2. Fairy stories—and *The Magic Flute* is one—are based on MANICHAEAN oppositions; the right side triumphs in the end and the moral is made. But in this opera, while the audience is frequently advised of Sarastro's virtues, he actually shows himself as vindictive, and both he and the Speaker of the brotherhood are revealed as rabid MISOGYNISTS . . . . No sharply contrasting character traits are distributed to either side, in fact, and the real contest reduces to one between the sexes, a war actually fought in the opera's PENULTIMATE scene—and predictably won by the men in five seconds flat. (R. Craft, Review, *New York Review of Books*, 11/27/75, pp. 18-19)

3. Terry Nation [author of *Survivors*] chooses an "On the Beach" prospectus and shows how a few English survivors cope with the aftermath of something like the Black Death. Not many folks are left alive, and those who are reveal their best and their worst . . . a MANICHEAN conflict pervades the book. (M. Levin, Review, *New York Times*, 11/21/76, Section 7, p. 69)

MANNEQUIN (man'ə-kin) or **MANIKIN** or **MANNIKIN** *noun* a model of the human figure used for displaying clothing, and by tailors, dress designers, etc. for fitting or making clothes; a girl or woman employed to model clothes for potential buyers.

1. As romantic comedy . . . [the French film] *Salut l'Artiste* is not very "evolved" either. But because its characters seem made of flesh and blood, because they don't fit the current American pattern of being either psychotic or MANNEQUINS of old movie stars, it's enjoyable . . . . (Maureen Orth, Review, *Newsweek*, 3/29/76, p. 94)

2. The note that appeared here about the difficulty of finding a Herbert Hoover-type collar for the Orville Wright MANNEQUIN in the Air and Space Museum has resulted in a letter from Mari deCuir, a costume designer of New Orleans. (E. Park, "Around the mall and beyond," *Smithsonian*, December 1975, p. 36)

3. See (2) under HIERATIC.

4. See (2) under SINUOUS.

5. See (4) under PROSCRIBE.

6. See (5) under MISOGYNY.

7. See (1) under ONANISM.

MANQUÉ (män-kā́) or **MANQUÉE** (feminine) *adj.* having failed, missed, or fallen short, especially because of circumstances or a defect of character; unfulfilled; unsuccessful or defective; potential but unrealized; would-be (placed after the noun it modifies).

1. Although [Ronald W.] Clark [author of the book, *The Life of Bertrand Russell*] effectively demolishes the simplistic notion of Russell as a logic chopper without needs, the "romantic MANQUÉ" he finds lying beneath the surface is altogether too bland and pleasant. The complex human failings, as both Katherine Tait [in *My Father Bertrand Russell*] and Dora Russell [in *The Tamarind Tree*] make clear, are as important a part of Russell as the very real nobility. (M. Rosenthal, Review, *New York Times*, 2/15/76, Section 7, p. 3)

2. In Michael Winner's [film] *Won Ton Ton, The Dog Who Saved Hollywood*, a would-be actress (Madeline Kahn), a would-be director (Bruce Dern) and a studio mogul MANQUÉ (Art Carney) make good by riding in on the tail of a talented German shepherd as he becomes a star of the silent screen. (Katrine Ames, Review, *Newsweek*, 6/14/76, p. 90)

3. [*The Buenos Aires Affair*, a book by Manuel Puig; translated by Suzanne Jill Levine] starts . . . as a tale of a kidnapped woman, a threat of sexual violation, an impending murder, but turns out to be a probing study of two souls

disabled by indifferent or perverse parenting: Gladys Hebe D'Onofrio, a sculptress MANQUÉE in her thirties, frightfully isolated, racked with sexual fantasies . . .; and Leopoldo Druscovich, a gifted art critic and editor . . . , in the grips of a terrible guilt that manifests itself in the bizarre pattern of his repeated sexual failures. (R. Alter, Review, *New York Times*, 9/5/76, Section 7, p. 4)

4. Auden and Chaucer are involved on the fly-leaf [of *Pleasure Seeker's Guide*, by Judith Leet], but I find rather a frustrated fabulist or a novelist MANQUÉ. . . it is not intelligence alone that makes a poet. A gift for language, a talent for things singingly . . . said is also required—and this Judith Leet lacks. (Erica Jong, Review, *New York Times*, 9/12/76, Section 7, p. 14)

5. Virginia Marbalestier [protagonist of the book, *Raw Silk*, by Janet Burroway]—fabric designer, painter MANQUÉ and California-born wife of a British textile firm's manager—watches the company's silk looms at work and sees a metaphor for her life. (Margo Jefferson, Review, *Newsweek*, 4/4/77, p. 88)

MANTRA (man' tra, mun' tra) *noun* (in Hinduism) a word or formula to be recited or sung; a hymn or portion of text, especially from the Veda, to be chanted or intoned as an incantation or prayer.

1. Unlike California's MANTRA-minded Gov. Jerry Brown, another spokesman for government retrenchment at a time of reduced resources, [Gov.] Carey [of New York] gets along with working politicians—when he isn't twisting their arms for support. (D.M. Alpern, "A Puzzle Named Carey," *Newsweek*, 1/19/76, p. 33)

2. The recommended means for achieving the mature stage of love of God in this age of Kali, or quarrel, is to chant the holy names of the Lord. The easiest method for most people is to chant the Hare Kṛṣṇa MANTRA:

Hare Kṛṣṇa, Hare Kṛṣṇa, Kṛṣṇa, Kṛṣṇa, Hare Hare.
Hare Rama, Hare Rama, Rama, Rama, Hare, Hare.

(Anon.,Kṛṣṇa Consciousness Pamphlet (received in O'Hare Airport), Undated, Unpaged, 2nd last page)

3. See (1) under RUMPELSTILTSKIN.

4. Each student [undergoing initiation to TM] brought fruit and flowers to be placed on the altar by Teacher Janet Aaron, who then recited a Sanskrit *puja* (hymn of worship) and whispered each student's MANTRA, the secret word that must be repeated to aid meditation. (Anon, "Tempest over TM," *Time*, 3/1/76, p. 34)

5. See (2) under STASIS.

6. See (2) under SAPIENTIAL.

MANUMIT (man' yə-mit) *verb* to release from slavery or servitude.

MANUMITTER *noun*.

MANUMISSION *noun* liberation; emancipation; a freeing or being freed from slavery.

1. . . . he [Charles Carroll] preferred life at Doughoregan Manor where he was now growing wheat instead of tobacco, liming and manuring his fields to prevent depletion of the soil. He housed 300 slaves as well or better than his white tenants, and MANUMITTED some of them. (Mary H. Cadwalader, "Charles Carroll of Carrollton: a signer's story," *Smithsonian*, December 1975, p. 69)

2. The liberals can proclaim a reign of terror, promulgated by Senator [Joseph] McCarthy and Roy Cohn, and be taken seriously the world over. Then, after a while, it is generally agreed that the reign of terror has terminated. We look about, eager to enjoy our MANUMISSION—only to find that life is about as it was before; whereupon one's instinct is to call into question whether that reign of terror ever existed. (W.F. Buckley Jr., *Up From Liberalism*, Arlington House, 2nd Printing 1968, p. 188)

MAQUETTE (ma-ket') *noun* a small preliminary model or three-dimensional study for a sculpture or an architectural work.

1. In tracing the evolution of the Statue [of Liberty] from its first MAQUETTE in 1870 to its unveiling, [Marvin] Trachtenberg [author of the book, *The Statue of Liberty*] has been obliged to investigate the political currents of 19th-century France, the biography and tem-

perament of [Frédéric Auguste] Bartholdi [its creator], the history of colossi in the ancient and modern world, the effects of new technology on mechanical and engineering methods, the story of how the money was raised in the United States to pay for the base of the monument, the transportation of the statue to New York, and what it has come to mean in our day. (H. Rosenberg, Review, *New York Times*, 3/28/76, Section 7, p. 3)

MARCEL (mär-sel´) or **MARCEL WAVE** *noun* a series of even waves put in the hair with a curling iron (after *Marcel* Grateau, 1852-1936, the French hairdresser who originated the process).

MARCEL *verb* to put such waves in (hair).

1. Of course, we're watching a period piece [*The Royal Family*, by George S. Kaufman and Edna Ferber]: we'd know that from the Ina Claire coiffure that Rosemary Harris flows so serenely beneath, a sort of seawave MARCEL, if seawaves were ever blonde. (W. Kerr, Review, *New York Times*, 1/11/76, Section 2, p. 7)

MARTINET (mär´tə-net´) *noun* a strict disciplinarian, especially a military one [named after General Jean Martinet (died 1672), French inventor of a system of drill]; any stickler for rigid regulations.

1. But [Hedrick] Smith [author of the book, *The Russians*], who sent his kids to rigid Russian schools for a time, also takes the reader to the Moscow equivalent of a PTA meeting at which a MARTINET of a school mistress publicly chews out parents for the failures of their progeny. (P.D. Zimmerman, Review, *Newsweek*, 1/19/76, p. 71)

2. *Night Cover* [a book by Michael Z. Lewin] . . . introduces Police Lieut. Leroy Powder. Powder is a veteran, an irritable, tough, honest cop who is something of a MARTINET and also a stickler for the rules. (N. Callendar, Review, *New York Times*, 3/14/76, Section 7, p. 28)

3. See (1) under VIGNETTE.

4. See (3) under MAWKISH.

5. Only one shadow mars this idyllic land: that of Uganda's PORCINE President-for-Life,

Field Marshal Idi Amin Dada, 49, a man of mercurial personality, who in a short six years has caught the world's attention with unpredictable and often deadly antics. He is killer and clown, big-hearted buffoon and strutting MARTINET. He can be as playful as a kitten and as lethal as a lion. (Anon., "Amin: The Wild Man of Africa," *Time*, 3/7/77, p. 19)

MARZIPAN (mär´zə-pan´) or **MARCHPANE** (märch´pān) *noun* a confection of ground almonds, sugar, and egg white made into a paste and variously shaped and colored.

1. William Kotzwinkle's new novel [*Fata Morgana*] is a lurid confection; like MARZIPAN, it is tempting but not very digestible. The coloring, the flavors, the ingredients themselves are all artificial, and though Kotzwinkle mixes them ingeniously, he disappoints the appetite that he arouses. (S. Goodwin, Review, *Philadelphia Inquirer*, 4/24/77, p. 13-H)

MASOCHISM (mas´ə-kiz´əm, maz´-) *noun* the condition in which sexual gratification depends on suffering, physical pain, and humiliation, especially inflicted on oneself; gratification gained from pain, deprivation, etc, inflicted or imposed on oneself [named after Leopold Sacher-Masoch (1835-95), an Austrian writer who described it].

MASOCHIST *noun*.

MASOCHISTIC *adj*.

MASOCHISTICALLY *adv*.

1. *Swept Away*—Lina Wertmuller's Marxist story [on film] of a wealthy industry-upheld bitch on a yacht who finds herself marooned in a state of heavily erotic political MASOCHISM. (Anon, Review, New Yorker, 2/9/76, p. 21)

2. Infatuation is explained [in *The Young Person's Guide to Love*, by Morton Hunt] through the story of Wilbur Mills and his South American stripper; unrequited love through Elaine of Astolat who languished lengthily after Lancelot . . . , and vengeful and MASOCHISTIC love through the tale of the New York lawyer who, when she rejected him, had his beloved burned with lye, went to jail, yet nevertheless emerged from it having convinced her to marry him. (Linda Wolfe, Review, *New York*

Times, 2/15/76, Section 7, p. 12)

3. Called everything from a liar to a Vietnam-operation murderer, [William] Colby demonstrated [in his paper to the conference whose collected papers constitute the book, *The CIA File*, edited by Robert L. Borosage and John Marks] a cool equaled only by the MASOCHISM that brought him to the scene to begin with. (J. Flannery, Review, *Boston Globe*, 3/7/76, p. 16-A)

4. [John E.] Mack [in the book, *A Prince of our Disorder: The Life and Times of T.E. Lawrence*] also places in humane perspective the recent discovery that this heroic figure [T.E.L.] was a MASOCHIST who discovered his pleasure under torture at Dara in 1917 and recruited a fellow enlisted man to whip him at intervals between 1923 and 1935. (W. Clemons, Review, *Newsweek*, 4/12/76, p. 98)

5. [Swiss] voters have blocked new government spending programs, which must be approved in tax referenda. "Someone proposes to the Fribourgers that they pay more taxes. They refuse. They are not MASOCHISTS" [commented Le Tribune de Genève] . . . . "Think small" could serve as the Swiss national motto. (J. Plummer, "Weapons production flouts neutrality: Model Swiss democracy in transition," *Norman* [Okla.] *Transcript*, 4/27/76, p. 6)

6. He [Adam Malone] was so out of touch with reality . . . that he had actually managed to inspire his fellow hoodlums to act on one fantasy—that in the end their victim [Sharon Fields] would not mind having been kidnapped or held prisoner, that she would be MASOCHISTIC enough to like it, . . . [and] invite their aggression and attention. (I. Wallace, *The Fan Club*, Bantam Edition, 1975, pp. 261-262)

7. MASOCHISTICALLY, she [Sharon Fields] pursued [with Adam Malone] the aftermath of her terrible blunder . . . . "He [Shively] wants to kill me, doesn't he?" (I. Wallace, *Ibid.*, p. 515)

8. See (5) under TRIAGE.

9. See (6) under NECROPHILIA.

MAUNDER (môn′ dər) *verb* to talk in a rambling, foolish, or incoherent way; drivel; to move, go, or act in an aimless, dreamy, vague manner.

MAUNDERER *noun*.

1. . . . seeking a quotation from a man universally appealing, admired and beloved, [Branch] Rickey began with five MAUNDERING lines from Herbert Hoover. (R. Kahn, *The Boys of Summer*, Harper and Row, 1971, p. 100)

2. It was necessary that the Bicentennial be televised in order to assure us that it has, indeed, taken place. No fooling. . . . Next to *Yankee Doodle Cricket*, I liked the movie version of *1776* . . . . Running third were various PBS programs, especially *Goodbye America*. As for the rest, John Chancellor bravely admitted patriotism. Howard K. Smith sermonized on democracy and bureaucracy. Walter Cronkite MAUNDERED. Disney overproduced the fireworks. (J. Leonard, "Overdosing on the Bicentennial," *New York Times*, 7/11/76, Section 2, p. 21)

3. One of the most shocking aspects of the Watergate affair . . . was the revelation that our President and his advisers regularly used the most vulgar language in the Oval Room . . . these fellows did not curse and blaspheme with flair, . . . as Andrew Jackson might have, and Lincoln too; no, they dropped them unthinkingly as they MAUNDERED along their dark path, like ill-disciplined horses in a Fourth of July parade. (J. Smith, *L.A. Times*, "Obscenity sometimes becomes a routine," *Norman* [Okla.] *Transcript*, 8/8/76, p. 6)

4. See (9) under BOWDLERIZE.

MAVIN (mā′ vən) or MAVEN *noun* an expert, especially in everyday matters.

1. [Will] Weng [editor of N.Y. Times' crossword puzzles] is certain that his puzzles are the "least VAPID," and he promises to continue to do them when he retires next year . . . . Will Weng (puzzle MAVEN, 2 words). (M. Dubin, "Puzzled? Then Weng has done his job," *Philadelphia Inquirer*, 11/28/76, p. 4-L)

2. (Maralyn Lois Polak, "Maxine Schnall: Sexuality MAVEN," *Today, The Inquirer Magazine*, 5/22/77, p. 11)

MAWKISH (mô′kish) *adj.* having a sweet, weak, sickening taste or flavor; insipid; nauseating; sickly sentimental; feebly emotional.

MAWKISHLY *adv.*

MAWKISHNESS *noun.*

1. An American back from a sojourn abroad minces no words in describing his impression of American television. "There is scarcely an adjective of DENIGRATION that cannot be mustered to assault it," says Robert MacNeil [anchorman for the Public Broadcasting Service program, the *MacNeil Report*]. "It is trivial, mindless, blatant, MAWKISH, vulgar, strident." (Don Oakley, "Alternatives? Television Denigrated," *Norman* [Okla.] *Transcript*, 3/25/76, p. 6)

2. See (2) under AUGUR.

3. Mr. [Edward] Crankshaw [author of the book, *The Shadow of the Winter Palace: Russia's Drift to Revolution 1825-1917*] is a superbly literate historian . . . . His greatest forte is a sympathetic yet never MAWKISH insight into the psyche of the men on whom rested the burden of ruling the vast empire [Czarist Russia] . . . . His portrait of [Czar] Nicholas I is a masterpiece. I know of no better picture of this unattractive MARTINET, whose icy exterior seems to have concealed a desperately insecure, almost hysterical, personality. (R. Pipes, Review, *New York Times*, 9/5/76, Section 7, p. 3)

4. . . . the haunting "Londonderry Air" is a fairy tune, learned by mortal pipers, to which only MAWKISH human words have ever been fitted . . . . (P. S. Prescott—Review of *An Encyclopedia of Fairies*, a book by Katharine Briggs, *Newsweek*, 2/21/77, p. 85)

5. See (4) under FARRAGO.

MEACOCK (mē´käk) *noun* a cowardly or effeminate man.

1. . . . in the present work [*The Olive of Minerva*] Dahlberg . . . [explains] why the hero . . . left the Big Apple: "He had gone out from that stink and glass GEHENNA, New York. BILLINGSGATE was RIFE in the mouths of the street-gamin. . . and the rabble intelligentsia of the academic dumps of America . . . . Courtesy was regarded as a MALAISE of a MEACOCK GROUTHEAD." Is this complex irony—BILLINGSGATE scolded in BILLINGSGATE;

. . . discourtesy discourteously derided? Or is this merely bad writing, over-ripe triteness? (J.D. O'Hara, Review, *New York Times*, 4/18/76, Section 7, p. 20)

MEDINA (mə-dē´nə) *noun* the old native quarter of a North African city.

1. Here [in the book, *A Street in Marrakech*], in a modest, almost humble . . . manner, she [Mrs. Elizabeth Warnock Fernea] records how she and her husband and their three children took up a year's residence in the MEDINA of Marrakech . . . and how, eventually, they won acceptance [by their neighbors]. (Anon, Review, *The New Yorker*, 2/9/76, p. 111)

MEGALOMANIA (meg´ə-lō-mā´nē-ə) *noun* a mental disorder marked by delusions of greatness, wealth, power, etc.; an obsession or passion for doing extravagant and grand things; a tendency to exaggerate.

MEGALOMANIAC *noun.*

MEGALOMANIAC or MEGALOMANIACAL or MEGALOMANIC *adj.*

1. The 94 otherwise undistinguished victims [in the book, *The Boys from Brazil*, by Ira Levin] are . . . the adoptive fathers of 94 CLONES (exact genetic duplicates) made from the preserved tissues of Hitler himself. By killing the fathers as the sons turn 14 [Doktor Josef] Mengele hopes to duplicate the precise psychological circumstances of Hitler's youth, thereby producing a bumper crop of inspired MEGALOMANIACS with whom to plague the world. (G. Lyons, Review, *New York Times*, 3/14/76, Section 7, p. 4)

2. See (1) under SADISM.

3. [Director] Hall unveiled [at last week's opening of the Olivier Theatre in London] a [version of *Tamburlaine The Great*] that was only slightly abridged and staged with a bold eye for spectacle and a sharp ear for Marlowe's roaring verse. To signal the MEGALOMANIA of the Scythian shepherd who conquered half of Asia and Africa, Hall had him riding in a carriage pulled by two captive kings with bits in their mouths. (M. MacPherson, Review, *Newsweek*, 10/18/76, p. 103)

4. From the beginning, a sizable element among the German General Staff considered Hitler's MEGALOMANIA to be disastrous. (J. Skow, Review of *Bodyguard of Lies*, by Anthony Cave Brown, *Time*, 2/16/76, p. 74)

5. The reader [of the book, *The Assassins*, by Joyce Carol Oates] is compelled to ask if the MEGALOMANIACAL Petrie was (1) a mere crackpot, (2) a latter-day Henry Adams, or (3) a pernicious William F. Buckley minus the charm. (Anon., Review, *Time*, 2/23/76, p. 65)

MEIOSIS (mī-ō'sĭs) *noun* expressive understatement; litotes, *i.e.*, an understatement; especially one in which an affirmative is expressed by the negative of its contrary; e.g., "not a small man" for a very tall man.

MEIOTIC *adj.*

MEIOTICALLY *adv.*

1. A MEIOTIC cynicism is a part of his [John Kenneth Galbraith's] literary and analytical style, and he takes it with him wherever he goes. (W.F. Buckley Jr., *Execution Eve and Other Contemporary Ballads*, G.P. Putnam's Sons, 1975, p. 280)

2. . . . even allowing for the MEIOTIC tradition of the English . . . . (W.F. Buckley Jr., *Ibid.*, p. 460)

3. He [Arnold Lunn] took an unrestrained, unaffected pleasure in his work, which was amiably sarcastic, in the MEIOTIC British tradition, wonderfully well-tuned, unrelenting but good-natured. (W.F. Buckley Jr., *Ibid.*, pp. 482-483)

MÉLANGE (mā-länzh) *noun* a mixture; medley; hodgepodge.

1. Only Norman Lear has the power—and the CHUTZPAH—to bring such a mind-blowing MÉLANGE [as in the *Mary Hartman* show] to television. (H.F. Waters and M. Kasindorf, "The Mary Hartman Craze," *Newsweek*, 5/3/76, p. 56)

2. See (2) under AFICIONADO.

3. When I came to, another face was close to mine: its skin was polished brown . . . . It wore a white turban. Its breath smelled of a

MÉLANGE of spices which I was in no state to identify severally and name, though no doubt cumin, coriander, and tumeric would have been among them. (Thomas Berger, *Who Is Teddy Villanova?*, Delacorte Press/Seymour Lawrence, 1977, p. 113)

4. [Donald] Washburn touched his temples. "Please, Wren, please! Never have I encountered such a MÉLANGE of truths, whole, half, quarter, and misapprehensions in the same variety and profusion." (Thomas Berger, *Ibid.*, p. 165)

MELIORISM (mēl'yə-riz'əm, mē'lē-ə-) *noun* the doctrine that the world naturally tends to become better, and especially that it may be made better by human effort; the betterment of society by improving people's health, living conditions, etc.

MELIORIST *noun or adj.*

MELIORISTIC *adj.*

MELIORITY *noun* superiority.

MELIORATE *verb* to ameliorate (to make or become better; improve).

MELIORABLE or **MELIORATIVE** *adj.*

MELIORATION *noun.*

MELIORATOR *noun.*

1. See (1) under SENTENTIA.

2. See (1) under NIHILIST.

3. One's answer to such questions [as "What is *your* answer to the race problem?"], if one is a conservative, is either evasively APHORISTIC . . . or else it is MELIORISTIC, or even milleniarist. There is of course no "answer" to the "racial problem," and anything one would "do" sounds downright unconcerned, if not MISANTHROPIC. (W.F. Buckley Jr., *Up From Liberalism*, Arlington House, 2nd Printing 1968, pp. xx-xxi)

4. The events of the past 100 years, however, more than suffice to undercut the assumptions of the MELIORISTS that the mere accumulation of knowledge and good will would ease the world's woe. The Holocaust, in particular, grimly denies the Socratic assertion that right knowledge predictably leads to virtuous conduct. (J. Hollis, Review of *The Holocaust and*

the Literary Imagination. by Lawrence L. Langer, *Chronicle of Higher Education.* 4/5/76, p. 21)

MELLIFLUOUS (mə-lif′loo-əs) or **MELLIFLUENT** *adj.* sweetly or smoothly flowing; smooth- and sweet-sounding; flowing with honey; sweetened with or as with honey; honeyed.

MELLIFLUOUSLY or **MELLIFLUENTLY** *adv.*

MELLIFLUOUSNESS or **MELLIFLUENCE** *noun.*

1. Those of us who, by accident of birth and by choice of profession, toil in the language of the Anglos and the Saxons are acutely aware that the absence of gender endings on our nouns and verbs and so forth gives us a considerable problem. We must now employ the word "chairperson" and a host of other functional but un-MELLIFLUOUS terms. (J.K. Page Jr., "On People," *Smithsonian,* December 1975, p. 14)

2. When Alan Curtis conducted Cavalli's *Erismena* at the Holland Festival two years ago, he assembled four countertenors of markedly different type: the MELLIFLUOUS Paul Esswood as his hero. . . . (A. Porter, Review of the opera, *Griselda,* by Alessandro Scarlatti, as staged at Berkeley, California, *The New Yorker,* 5/31/76, p. 108)

3. See (3) under PSEUDONYM.

4. His [Senator Howard Baker's] on-camera presence and MELLIFLUOUS flow of sophisticated country wisdom enchanted audiences during the Watergate hearings—although his tendency to sermonize diluted his effectiveness as an interrogator. (Anon., "People on the Podium," *Time,* 8/16/76, p. 17)

MÉNAGE (mā-näzh′) or **MENAGE** *noun* a domestic establishment; household; the management of a household's housekeeping.

MÉNAGE À TROIS (mā-näzh A trwä′) *noun* a household consisting of a married couple and the lover of one of them.

1. *The Family Arsenal* [a book by Paul Theroux] deals with four apprentice terrorists loosely connected to the IRA . . . . He [Valentine Hood] lives [in London] . . . with Mayo,

"a barbarian with taste," who works for the IRA . . . and with two scruffy teenagers, a boy who makes bombs and a girl who delivers them to railroad luggage lockers. Their MENAGE is a PARODY of marriage, of a family. (P.S. Prescott, Review, *Newsweek,* 7/19/76, p. 70)

2. Modern writers . . . seem to have lost sight of the homely fact that what is really exciting . . . is the way we behave toward those closest to us, and the way they behave toward us . . . only the [current] mystery novels seem to have grasped this essential truth. When the vicar is foully stabbed in the rose garden, it is never a stranger who did it, but always a member of the MENAGE. (Sydney J. Harris, "For the real drama, knock on any door," *Philadelphia Inquirer,* 10/7/76, p. 11-A)

3. [Helmut] Newton's [photographic] series, entitled *The Story of Oh-h-h,* featured a male model openly fondling a woman and a seductive MÉNAGE À TROIS on vacation, while [Deborah] Turbeville photographed the season's bathing suits in a cold public bathhouse . . . ambiguous sexual settings and desperate loneliness have filtered down to commercial ads, catalogs and window displays. (Maureen Orth, *et. al.,* "Fashion's Kinky Look," *Newsweek,* 10/4/76, p. 99)

4. New York's Continental Baths used to enjoy a steamy CACHET as a chic refuge for the gaily incontinent . . . . It resurfaces here [in Philadelphia] for a one-week stand with *Saturday Night at the Baths,* a film . . . shot through with the solemn fervor common to homosexual advocacy and acted out in a poorly managed MENAGE À TROIS. (D. Ryan, Review, *Philadelphia Inquirer,* 12/18/76, p. 8-A)

MENDACIOUS (men-dā′ shəs) *adj.* false or untrue; lying; untruthful; dishonest.

MENDACIOUSLY *adv.*

MENDACIOUSNESS or **MENDACITY** (men-daś i-tē) *noun.*

1. For the colleges and universities, the more MENDACIOUS aspects of complying with socially beneficial programs are particularly vexing, since most educators are ideologically in favor of their legislative intent. (G.W. Bonham, "Will Government Patronage Kill the Univer-

sities?" [Editorial], *Change*, Winter 1975-76, p. 61)

2. Rarely in military history has there been a battle communique more MENDACIOUS and self-aggrandizing than the one issued by Colonel Skimmerhorn at Zendt's Farm on the day after his attack upon an undefended Indian village whose occupants were unarmed and eager to surrender. (J.A. Michener, *Centennial*, Fawcett, 1975, p. 506)

3. New journalism has always been fair game for abuse, and . . . most members of the profession readily concede the fact. Indeed the more seasoned of these members will invariably commend Evelyn Waugh's novel *Scoop* to novices, explaining that this chronicle of MENDACITY, idleness, VENALITY, and ignorance is a splendidly accurate distillation of their calling. (A. Cockburn, "The Psychopathology of Journalism," *New York Review of Books*, 12/11/75, p. 28)

4. On the whole it [*The First Casualty: From the Crimea to Vietnam—The War Correspondent as Hero, Propagandist, and Myth Maker*, by Phillip Knightley] is an interesting, if slightly dogged account of how newspaper reports of almost every conflict since the Crimean war turn out, upon examination, to be unrelievedly MENDACIOUS. (A. Cockburn, Review, *ibid.*, p. 29)

5. For all of Ma Bell's politeness, the telephone is a fundamentally rude instrument. Of course, one can hire a secretary to say, "He's not in the office," but if the he in question doesn't actually step out of the office every time the phone rings, this practice institutionalizes MENDACITY. (J.K. Page Jr., "The unwanted phone call," *Smithsonian*, January 1976, p. 16)

6. At present the mechanism for picking purveyors of detergents (free market competition plus MENDACIOUS advertising plus independent assessments by consumers' associations) is plainly working better than the mechanism (known as the great democratic process) for picking presidents and mayors. (N. Macrae, "United States can keep growing—and lead—if it wishes," *Smithsonian*, July 1976, p. 39)

7. [King] Victor [in *King & Joker*, by Peter Dickinson] is constipated and carefully MENDA-

CIOUS; the neurotic [Queen] Isabella is convinced unreasonably that she carries hemophilia . . . . (P.D. Zimmerman, Review, *Newsweek*, 8/9/76, p. 72)

8. No American in his right mind is going to criticize the British for using the black arts to make up for their lack of military preparedness in 1940. But it is a different story when little countries such as South Vietnam and South Korea turn to MENDACITY in perhaps misguided attempts to preserve their menaced identity. (J. Chamberlain, "Handle Korea With Caution," *Times Herald*, Norristown, Pa., 12/3/76, p. 13)

MENDICANT (men'də-kənt) *adj.* begging; living on alms; pertaining to or characteristic of a beggar.

MENDICANT *noun* a person who lives by begging; beggar; a mendicant friar.

MENDICANCY or **MENDICITY** *noun* the practice of begging; the state or condition of being a beggar.

1. It [New York] has become a MENDICANT city, begging its way from the edge of default on a promise of good budgetary behavior. Only three weeks ago, Treasury Secretary William E. Simon approved a Federal loan to help New York meet yet another deadline for debt and payroll obligations—a boon the city earned by persuading its municipal labor unions to accept a continued wage freeze. The choice of New York as the convention site came as a Democratic gesture of charity in the city's season of penances. (D. Gelman, *et al.*, "Polishing The Apple," *Newsweek*, 7/19/76, pp. 33–34)

MERETRICIOUS (mer' i-trish' əs) *adj.* alluring by a show of false, flashy, or vulgar charms or attractions; tawdry; based on pretense, deception, or insincerity; superficially plausible; SPECIOUS; showy, gaudy; SPURIOUS; sham; false; *originally*, of, like, or characteristic of a prostitute.

MERETRICIOUSLY *adv.*

MERETRICIOUSNESS *noun*.

1. See (1) under HERMENEUTICS.

2. Walk and gates still encircle Harvard Yard,

ut Cambridge has become a "college town" in the full MERETRICIOUS sense that was unimaginable in a community riven by town and gown. Harvard Square is an expensive shopping center where the quantity of bookstores . . . seems less significant than the UBIQUITY of expensive boutiques. (N.W. Aldrich, Jr., "Harvard On The Way Down," Harper's, March 1976, p. 39)

3. Not least among the pleasures of *Reeling* [a book by Pauline Kael] is to come upon her capsule put-downs of MERETRICIOUS movies like *Day of the Dolphin* ("the most expensive Rin Tin Tin movie ever made") or of vaguely NARCISSISTIC actors like Robert Redford ("has turned almost alarmingly blond—he's gone past platinum, he must be into plutonium; his hair s coordinated with his teeth"). (R. Brustein, Review, *New York Times*, 4/4/76, Section 7, p. 1)

4. When the English edition [of *Ragtime*, by E. L. Doctorow] was published over there in January, the critics pounced on it with derisory war whoops in a sort of Boston Tea Party in reverse. . . . Peter Ackroyd in *The Spectator* was . . . unfriendly: "sentimental and MERETRICIOUS," he said. (Anon., "Reverse English," *New York Times*, 3/7/76, Section 7, p. 33)

5. It [the billfold] had been Peggy [Tumulmulty]'s gift to me [Russel Wren] at lunchtime on the previous Xmas Eve (in response to the collapsible plastic rain hood I had given her that morning, taking her aback some distance, owing to my only lately having denounced the holiday as MERETRICIOUS . . .). (Thomas Berger, *Who Is Teddy Villanova?*, Delacorte Press/Seymour Lawrence, 1977, pp. 77-78)

6. I'm sure it was Calvin whom I [Russel Wren] saw on Union Square, in a Cadillac, both MERETRICIOUSLY adorned, the car in mother-of-pearl, he in white sombrero and scarlet jacket . . ." (Thomas Berger, *Who Is Teddy Villanova?*, pp. 163-164)

MERINO (mə-rē'nō) *noun* a knitted fabric of merino wool, often mixed with cotton; (if capitalized) one of a hardy breed of sheep, raised originally in Spain, valued for its fine, soft wool; wool from such a sheep.

MERINO *adj.* designating or of this sheep or wool.

1. His [multimillionaire Stephen Whitney's] funeral at Trinity Church [in New York City] was equally impressive. Six clergymen met the procession at the front door. The eight pallbearers were men of wealth and position . . . .The body lay in a MERINO and satin shroud and rested in a coffin of rosewood with silver hardware. (C. Lockwood, "As near to paradise as one can reach in Brooklyn, N.Y.," *Smithsonian*, April 1976, p. 56)

MESHUGA (mə-shŏŏg´ə) or MESHUGGA or MESHUGAH *adj.* a slang expression for crazy; mad; insane.

1. Only at the end of the book [*The Girl on the Coca-Cola Tray*, by Nancy Winters] does Jenny discover what a MESHUGGENER her husband really is, and that only because she has found his secret journal of sexual adventures. (M. Levin, Review, *New York Times*, 11/21/76, Section 7, p. 69)

2. *Honey* [a book by Honey Bruce] is a love story: wacky, sick, totally MESHUGGE and frightening . . . . (Rosalyn Drexler, Review, *New York Times*, 3/6/77, Section 7, p. 12)

MESMERIZE (mez´mə-rīz´, mes´-) *verb* to hypnotize; to spellbind; fascinate; to compel by fascination.

MESMERIZER *noun*.

MESMERIZATION *noun*.

MESMERISM *noun* hypnosis as induced by the Austrian physician, F.A. Mesmer (1733-1815), through animal magnetism; hypnotism; a compelling or irresistable attraction; fascination.

MESMERIC *adj.*

MESMERICALLY *adv.*

MESMERIST *noun*.

1. Most conventions are tiresomely wordy. Arttransition . . . was no exception. In fact, there was not all that much art to *see* at MIT, unless one chose . . . to MESMERIZE oneself in videotape recordings and film viewings for five or six hours just to top off the day in cheery fashion. (B. Forgey, "Arttransition is still in transition," *Smithsonian*, March 1976, p. 94)

2. See (9) under TITILLATE.

3. . . . at the outset [of *Scottish and Canadian Guard Regiments*, a part of George Balanchine's ballet, *Union Jack*] everybody does the same steps. But the women . . . do them very differently from the men . . . they're like a feminine melody set against a masculine drone bass. The distinction, absolutely MESMERIZING, is something you'll see on no parade ground in the world. (Arlene Croce, Review, *The New Yorker*, 5/3/76, p. 113)

4. It should be noted that Canucks (and all Jennies) [both are names of early airplanes] spoke a language that MESMERIZED pilots. (J. Keasler, "Tracking the 'lost' barn-storming pal of 'Slim' Lindbergh." *Smithsonian*, May 1976, p. 62)

5. MESMERIZED by her [Sharon Fields'] proximity . . . . [Adam] Malone was momentarily rendered speechless. (I. Wallace, *The Fan Club*, Bantam Edition, 1975, p. 68)

6. Her [Sharon Fields'] heart stood still. She stared up MESMERIZED. . . . It was—Oh God—The Evil One [Shively], the worst of the lot. (I. Wallace, *Ibid.*, p. 266)

7. See (4) under ALLITERATION.

MESOMORPH (mez'ə-môrf', mes'- , mē'zə- , mē'sə-) *noun* a person of the mesomorphic physical type.

MESOMORPHIC *adj.* having or pertaining to a muscular or sturdy athletic body build characterized by the relative prominence of structures developed from the embryonic mesoderm (muscle, bone, and connective tissue), as contrasted with ECTOMORPHIC and endomorphic; related to or being in an intermediate state.

MESOMORPHISM or **MESOMORPHY** *noun.*

1. . . . ERB—[Clint] Eastwood, [Burt] Reynolds and [Charles] Bronson—are dispiriting signs of the confusion in contemporary masculinity. Erb-man is cool. In matters of love and sex his passivity is positively CATATONIC . . . . Erb-man is tough and he knows it. Whether ECTOMORPH (Eastwood) or MESOMORPH (Reynolds and Bronson), he likes his morph and moves like NARCISSUS ambling to the reflecting pool. (J. Kroll, Review of three movies: *Gator; The Outlaw Josey Wales;* and *St. Ives, Newsweek,* 9/13/76, p. 89)

2. John D. MacDonald, author of the Travis McGee thrillers, does not include his detective hero in the large, motley cast [of his book, *Condominium*]. . . . His MESOMORPHIC Floridian would have collared the dredgers and developers, and punched the crooked county commissioners in the chops. That satisfying fancy is sadly absent from *Condominium*, and so is the author's customary wryness. In its place is a self-righteousness that BOMBINATES at needless length on environmental matters, foolishness and greed. (Anon., Review, *Time*, 7/4/77, p. 53)

METASTASIS (me-tas'tə-sis) *noun, pl.:* -SES the transference of disease-producing organisms or of malignant or cancerous cells to other parts of the body by way of the blood vessels, lymphatics, or membranous surfaces; transformation; change of form or manner.

METASTATIC *adj.*

METASTATICALLY *adv.*

METASTASIZE (mə-tas'tə-sīz) *verb.*

1. But as government generally has become less efficient and more routinized, even the most liberalizing legislation has been METASTASIZED into a series of mindless enforcement and regulatory procedures that could have come out of *Alice in Wonderland*. (G.W. Bonham. "Will Government Patronage Kill the Universities?" [Editorial], *Change*, Winter 1975-76. p. 10)

2. On the SALT talks he [Kissinger] has yet to show his basic stance toward the Soviet METASTASIS on weaponry. (M. Lerner, "At Home in a Jekyll-Hyde World: Kissinger: Flamboyant, Enigmatic," *Norman* [Okla.] *Transcript*, 3/22/76, p. 6)

3. That bizarre incident [the KAMIKAZE attack on the home of Yoshio Kodama] seemed to be the highlight of the METASTASIZING Lockheed scandal [in Japan] last week. (D. Pauly, *et. al.*, "Fastened Seat Belts," *Newsweek*, 4/5/76, p. 65)

4. The problem . . . is that at a certain level of acquisition money METASTASIZES: it not only assumes a life of its own, it takes control of its owners, making it difficult . . . for them to per-

form as human beings. (P.S. Prescott, Review of *The Rockefellers*, by Peter Collier and David Horowitz; and of *The Rockefeller Syndrome*, by Ferdinand Lundberg, *Newsweek*, 4/5/76, p. 81A)

5. *Ratner's Star* [a book by Don DeLillo] is twice too long; as its terminal signs (failing inspiration, METASTASIS of exhausted ideas and dialogue) progress in the second half it becomes virtually unbearable. (P.S. Prescott, Review, *Newsweek*, 6/7/76, p. 90)

MEZUZAH (mə-zŏŏz′-ə) or **MEZUZA** *noun* (in Judaism) a small piece of parchment inscribed with the Shema (verses 4-9 of *Deut.* 6 and 13-21 of *Deut.* 11), rolled and put into a case, and traditionally attached to the doorpost of the home.

1. . . . by the middle of May [1953] he [Gil Hodges] was batting .187 and Charlie Dressen sent him to the bench. The fans of Brooklyn had warmed to the first baseman as he suffered his slump . . . . Packages [from fans] arrived with rosary beads, rabbits' feet, MEZUZAHS, scapulars. (R. Kahn, *The Boys of Summer*, Harper and Row, 1971, pp. 345-346)

2. Among bracelet charms and neck pendants, the big sellers during the Christmas season [of 1974] were crosses and zodiac signs . . . . Next in popularity came St. Christopher medals . . . and the Italian horn . . . There was some demand for the fisherman's . . . cross; the Star of David, the Hand of Fatima, Southwest Indian jewelry, even a few star and crescent pendants, and small gold MEZUZAHS but without the scroll that a real MEZUZAH should contain. (Margaret Lantis, "As times change, so do signs, signals adopted by youth," *Smithsonian*, September 1976, p. 80)

MIASMA (mī-az′m^ə, mē-) *noun* foul-smelling gases emitted by marshes, decomposing organic matter, etc.; poisonous EFFLUVIA or germs infecting the atmosphere; a dangerous, foreboding, deathlike, unwholesome, or befogging influence or atmosphere.

MIASMIC (also **MIASMAL, MIASMATIC**) *adj.*

1. All of this moves along [in the book, *A Very Human President*] in the [J.] Valenti style, for the most part a kind of Texas BAROQUE compounded of cliches and HOMILIES, phrases that can soar high and flop hard . . . . Amid the "EPIPHANIES" of legend and personal slights that "swelled into gargoyle masses" comes the language, "it was a helluva lunch" . . . . LBJ "slotted in his mind" what he proposed to do, murder hung like a "MIASMIC mist," people played on the White House "varsity," . . . .(E.F. Goldman, Review, *New York Times*, 2/1/76, Section 7, p. 4)

2. "This is an impartial inquiry into the general events that occurred at Rattlesnake Buttes last November," he [General Harvey Wade] announced . . . . At the Denver Hotel, under his skillful questioning, he began to penetrate the MIASMA engulfing this sorry affair [massacre of the Indians]. (J.A. Michener, *Centennial*, Fawcett, 1975, p. 500)

3. Dan Golenpaul, the man who came to him [Gordon Kahn] for help [with the "Information Please" radio program], owns it all. And as Golenpaul grows rich, his arrogance rises like a MIASMA and he finds this short, bald, mustached man from Brooklyn, who remembers poetry, Jeffersonian sentences and the sequence in which roads intersect Saw Mill River Parkway, a thorn to conscience but a necessity to the program. No one can prepare and edit so many questions on so many topics as Gordon J. Kahn. (R. Kahn, *The Boys of Summer*, Harper and Row, 1971, p. 32)

4. Joseph Henry hated vanity and self-promotion as much as all other modes of deception, humbugging and quackery. What a wrench it must have been for such a man to leave the ivied halls of Princeton . . . and descend into the MIASMA of Washington. (S.D. Ripley, "Comments on The Papers of Joseph Henry," *Vol. II*, edited by N. Reingold, *Smithsonian*, December 1975, p. 6)

5. A decade ago . . . . James Baldwin . . . seemed . . . so certain in his vision of this country . . . . Because he existed we [black students] felt that the racial MIASMA that swirled around us would not consume us . . . . (Orde Coombs, Review of *The Devil Finds Work*, by James Baldwin, *New York Times*, 5/2/76, Section 7, p. 6)

6. . . . during the war I lived for 9 months in a tent with five other marines in such a stultify-

ing MIASMA of variations on the all-purpose four-letter word that I had to read a little Will Durant every night . . . to remind myself that there were alternate adjectives, verbs and adverbs in the English language. (J. Smith, of *Los Angeles Times*, "Obscenity sometimes becomes a routine," *Norman* [Okla.] *Transcript*, 8/8/76, p. 6)

7. Sources admit the [U.S.] government would rather encourage than stop the Chinese nuclear tests, for this is more a worry to Russian than to U.S. interests. Therefore, left to their own devices, without a peep of contrary opinion, the Chinese will likely continue to spread on the winds of the MIASMA of their weaponry. (T. Tiede, "Negative Effect of Selective Outrage," *Times Herald*, Norristown, Pa., 11/30/76, p. 11)

MICAWBERISH (mi-kô bər-ish) *adj.*

MICAWBER   a carelessly improvident character in Dickens' *David Copperfield* who is a SANGUINE idler trusting that something good will turn up.

1. . . . it is impossible to be too critical of the MICAWBERISH attitude that if we can just keep the GNP growing, something will turn up. (M. Mayer, "How Banks Destroy the Economy," *Harper's*, January 1975, p. 59)

MIDDEN (mid'ᵊn) *noun* (in British dialect) a dunghill or refuse heap.

KITCHEN MIDDEN   a mound consisting of shells of edible mollusks, animal bones, and other refuse, such as often marks the site of a prehistoric human habitation.

1. See (3) under SPOOR.

2. Beer-can MIDDEN behind a Montana tavern marks a sad misuse of private land, one legacy of America's throw-away society. (N. Devore III, Caption on picture, National Geographic, July 1976, pp. 74-75)

3. In this respect the press resembles a gigantic MIDDEN heap from which, over varying periods of time, the innumerable but miscellaneous fragments of truth can be fitted together into the shape of invention or a new idea. (L.H. Lapham, "Confusion Worse Confounded," *Harper's*, April 1977, p. 14)

4. . . . it could be supposed that a cushion of rubbish lay at the bottom of the [dumbwaiter] shaft, a veritable MIDDEN the lowest level of which might well date from the turn of the century.... (Thomas Berger, *Who Is Teddy Villanova?*, Delacorte Press/Seymour Lawrence, 1977, p. 36)

MILLIARD (mil'yərd, -yärd) *noun* (in Britain) one thousand millions; one billion.

1. When we landed here, Laghouat [in the Algerian Sahara] was as quiet . . . as if a plague had struck. And it had; a locust plague. Nothing compares to this devouring MILLIARD except perhaps the waves on waves of little yellow mice that attack the wheat on the plains of Hungary and Yugoslavia and then suddenly disappear . . . . There are only a handful of automobiles here, but their wheels skid on the carcasses of the MILLIARD that blacked the sky. (H.J. Taylor, "Lonesome Sahara," *Times Herald*, Norristown, Pa., 10/14/76, p. 21)

MIMESIS (mi-mē'sis, mī-) *noun* imitation or reproduction of the supposed words or behavior of another; imitation; mimicry.

MIMETIC *adj.* of or characterized by imitation; imitative; of or characterized by mimicry.

MIMETICALLY *adv.*

1. A race cannot hate itself, mock its ideals and institutions, and—survive . . . . He [Duncan Williams, author of *Trousered Apes*] quotes Toynbee: "A failure of creative power in the minority, an answering withdrawal of MIMESIS on the part of the majority, [bring on] consequent loss." (W.F. Buckley Jr., *Execution Eve and Other Contemporary Ballads*, G.P. Putnam's Sons, 1975, p. 406)

2. Here is a small sample of glaring errors [in the book, *Butterflies: Their World, Their Life Cycle, Their Behavior*, by Thomas C. Emmel]: "One example of mimicry familiar to Americans is the monarch [butterfly], . . . whose caterpillars feed on poisonous milkweeds and thus become poisonous themselves, and the viceroy, a harmless [butterfly] whose caterpillars feed on nonpoisonous willows but resemble monarch larvae." (The MIMETIC resemblance is actually between adults). (J.M.

Burns, Review, *Smithsonian*, December 1975, pp. 131-132)

3. See (2) under VELLEITY.

MINATORY (min´ə-tôr´ ĕ, -tôr´ -ē) or **MINATORIAL** *adj.* menacing; threatening.

MINATORILY *adv.*

1. The prizes awarded [at the Boston Printmakers 28th Annual Exhibition] by Richard Teitz [the juror] went to Robert A. Nelson's lithograph *Cat and Mice*, a GOTHIC fantasy where a MINATORY feline, who is also part Sphinx glowers over a toppling file of armorclad Breughel-esque mice . . . . (R. Tayor, Review, *Boston Globe*, 3/7/76, p. 11-A)

MINOTAUR (min´ə-tôr) *noun* (in Classical Mythology) a monster with the body of a man and the head of a bull, confined in a Cretan labyrinth and annually fed seven youths and seven maidens from Athens, until killed by Theseus.

1. . . . did [Howard] Hughes, like the Cretan MINOTAUR, get caught in the windings and twistings of the very labyrinth he had created and sit there lonely in its bowels because he could no longer find a way out. (M. Lerner, "No Woman with him when he died: He cared for money and power," *Norman* [Okla.] *Transcript*, 4/22/76, p. 6)

MISANTHROPE (mis´ ən-thrŏp´ , miz´-) or **MISANTHROPIST** (mis-an´ thrə-pist, miz-) *noun* one who hates or distrusts mankind (or many people) or who shuns company.

MISANTHROPIC or MISANTHROPICAL *adj.*

MISANTHROPICALLY *adv.*

MISANTHROPY (mis-an´thrə-pē, miz-) *noun* hatred, dislike, distrust, or avoidance of mankind.

1. Such complainers [about postal service] tend to be more forgiving at Christmas . . . unless one is equipped with the MISANTHROPIC hide of the unreformed Ebenezer Scrooge. Whose mention points up a diverting coincidence-in-time: for Charles Dickens published the first edition of *A Christmas Carol* in December 1843, just as Sir Henry Cole was making his inaugural offering of 1,000 Christmas cards. (P. Ryan, "Postmen can blame it on Old Horsley," *Smithsonian*, December 1975, p. 144)

2. See (3) under MELIORISM.

3. Senator Paul Douglas, a professionally trained economist and sometime professor of the subject, can harangue the voters of Illinois, as he did in 1954 . . . , with dire talk of impending mass poverty ensuing upon the MISANTHROPIC stewardship of a Republican administration. But when years go by and that poverty fails to materialize, he is not brought to account, nor are his credentials as an economist publicly reviewed. (W.F. Buckley Jr., *Up From Liberalism*, Arlington House, 2nd Printing 1968, p. 188)

4. . . . Bob Merrill's screenplay is not without its insights into the great MISANTHROPE's character. Director Arthur Hiller has captured with some color. and texture Field's crazy household and the Hollywood of the 30's and 40's. And most of all Rod Steiger gives probably his best performance as Fields in [W.C. Fields and Me]. (J. Kroll, Review, *Newsweek*, 4/12/76, p. 94)

5. These ideals [of Southern brotherhood] are summed up [in the second play of *A Texas Trilogy*, by Preston Jones] by Red Grover, a MISANTHROPIC saloon keeper (Patrick Hines) who describes the difference between White Magnolianism and the Ku Klux Klan: "Anybody who's got to put on a white bed sheet to kick a coon's ass has got to be a fool." (J. Kroll, Review, *Ibid.*, 5/17/76, p. 9)

6. See (3) under PONTIFICAL.

7. Georges Clemenceau . . . said that the voice of the people is the voice of God and the leader's job is to follow that voice *shrewdly*. Clemenceau packed into the word "shrewdly" a lifetime of hearty MISANTHROPY and cynicism that he didn't bother to conceal. But if you take Carter at his word, there is not a skeptical, let alone a cynical, atom in his body . . . . (G.F. Will, "Carter and 'The People,' " *Newsweek*, 10/18/76, p. 118)

MISCEGENATION (mis´ i-jə-nā´ shən, misej´-ə-) *noun* marriage or cohabitation between a man and a woman of different races, especially in the U.S. between a white and a black; interbreeding between members of different races.

MISCEGENETIC *adj.*

1. Real or imaginary, the tragedies of MISCEGENATION have never been simple—ever since Othello did what he had to do to Desdemona. (K. Miller, Review of *Guerrillas*, by V.S. Naipaul, *New York Review of Books*, 12/11/75, p. 4)

2. His [J. Edgar Hoover's] searing contempt for Dr. Martin Luther King was based on MISCEGENATION and Dr. King's public criticism of the FBI. (J. Bishop, "Tribute to Hoover," *Times Herald*, Norristown, Pa., 9/4/76, p. 11)

3. . . . this engrossing and gravely beautiful Soviet film [Andrei Tarkovsky's *Solaris*] is like a strange MISCEGENATION of Chekhov and H.G. Wells. The Russian scientists in their . . . space station are like Chekhovian characters in their country house—trapped between . . . action and paralysis. (J. Kroll, Review, *Newsweek*, 10/25/76, pp. 104, 107)

MISERICORD (miz'ər-ə-kôrd', mi-zer'ə-kôrd') or **MISERICORDE** *noun* a small projection on the underside of a hinged seat of a church stall that gives support, when the seat is raised, to a person standing in the stall; a medieval dagger, used for the COUP DE GRÂCE to a wounded foe.

1. Late in the 11th century . . . appeared . . . a hidden ledge that came into use when the seat [for the priest] was raised [the priest being required to stand while chanting the Divine Office]. On this jutting console the cleric could rest while ostensibly standing. Its adoption was rapid throughout Western Europe, the object taking the name . . : MISERICORD [from the *misericordia*—mercy—indulgence] . . . . Our five-year canvass of thousands of MISERICORDS revealed the use of scriptural themes in only three percent of the carvings . . . . Since the use of the underseat ledge brought the sitter's buttocks in contact with the carving beneath, it would have been irreverent to put the form of Jesus, Mary, Peter or Paul there. (Dorothy and H. Kraus, "Naughty notions in holy places." *Smithsonian*, April 1976, p. 96)

2. See (1) under CLYSTER.

MISHMASH (mish' mash) or **MISHMOSH** *noun* a hodgepodge; jumble.

1. Imagery [in the *Cruel Garden*, performed by Britain's Ballet Rambert] taken from García Lorca himself, the Moon and Death, the defeated bullfighter, the glimpses of a rejected America, are mixed up with a MISHMASH of symbols deriving from Mr. [Lindsay] Kemp himself [who conceived the ballet]. (C. Barnes, "Ballet: A la Recherche du Rambert," *New York Times*, 7/17/77, Section 1, p. 41)

MISOGAMY (mi-sog' ə-mē, mī-) *noun* hatred of marriage.

MISOGAMIST *noun.*

MISOGAMIC (misə-gam'ik, mī -sə-) *adj.*

1. And most of it [Edward Dahlberg's often incomprehensible wisdom, as expressed in the book, *The Olive of Minerva*] dwells on sex: "Void of MISOGAMY, he cowered when he considered the paps; the uterine tribe is spiteful." (J.D. O'Hara, Review, *New York Times*, 4/18/76, Section 7, p. 20)

MISOGYNY (mi-soj' ə-nē, mī-) *noun* hatred of women, especially by a man.

MISOGYNIC or **MISOGYNOUS** or **MISOGYNISTIC** *adj.*

MISOGYNIST *noun* a person, especially a man, who hates women.

1. See (2) under MANICHEEISM.

2. [In the film, *Murder By Death*] Peter Falk plays incisively upon Sam Spade's mythic MISOGYNY, forever brushing off Eileen Brennan, a clinging moll. ("I'm scared, Sam—hold me!" "Hold yourself, I'm busy.") (Janet Maslin, Review, *Newsweek*, 7/4/76, p. 101)

3. "She [Italian filmmaker Lina Wertmuller] is a female MISOGYNIST masquerading as a political crusader," complains London critic Alexander Walker, unfurling a battle flag that attracts many allies in America. (Anon., "The Irresistible Force and The Immutable Object," *Time*, 2/16/76, p. 58)

4. All men are MISOGYNISTS, deficient in humanity and undeveloped in affection; fearful and resentful of women, they turn to a

"supernaturalizing of the penis" [according to Adrienne Rich, in her book, *Of Woman Born: Motherhood As Experience and Institution*] . . . .(P.S. Presscott, Review, *Newsweek*, 10/18/76, p. 107–D)

5. Lovely Linda, Harry's wife [in the book, *The Demon*, by Hubert Selby Jr.], remains the angelic MANNEQUIN one would expect from a writer of Selby's apparently MISOGYNISTIC frame of mind. Their marriage . . . seems more abstracted than observed. (P.D. Zimmerman, Review, *Newsweek*, 11/1/76, p. 87)

6. In her role as church symbol Mary expresses the basic theme of MISOGYNY that runs through the Church's history. While we are told to emulate her and become mothers, we cannot do so without suffering to lose our virginity, which the Church also exhorts us to hold . . . . The author [Marina Warner, of the book, *Alone Of All Her Sex*] says the [Virgin Mary] legend's lyricism will and should survive, but the cult of Mary as a form of moral exhortation and expression of MISOGYNY "has been exhausted." (Mary Ann Maggiore, Review, *Philadelphia Inquirer*, 11/7/76, p. 13-K)

7. In dozens of interviews he [Federico Fellini]'s expressed his hatred of Casanova—" . . . . [He is] the kind of man who . . . is well-dressed, who can make love several times a night . . . , [who is] basically MISOGYNISTIC, with the NARCISSISTIC impulses that are behind the Italian male's professed adoration of the female sex." (J. Kroll, "A Sterile Casanova," *Newsweek*, 1/24/77, p. 60)

8. He [Ishmael Reed, author of the book, *Flight To Canada*] is also afflicted with a MISOGYNY that blunts his tone and timing: women are sneered at rather than satirized, and accorded a suspiciously unequal share of follies and stupidities. (Margo Jefferson, Review, *Newsweek*, 12/20/76, p. 96)

9. See (2) under SANS-CULOTTE.

MISPRISION (mis-prizh′ ən) *noun* misconduct or neglect of official duty, especially by one in public office; failure by one not an accessory to prevent or notify of treason or felony; a contempt against the government, monarch, or courts, as sedition or contempt of court; contempt; disdain.

MISPRISON OF FELONY concealing knowledge of a felony (or treason) by one who has not participated or assisted in it.

1. Finally the report [of the Watergate Special Prosecution Force] ignores the amazing performance of former Attorney General Richard Kleindienst, in charge of the investigation, who seems, at least, to be guilty of obstruction of justice and MISPRISION of felony in failing to come forth with information he had from the very beginning about the involvement of top White House and re-election people in the Waterbugging. (K. Sale, Review, *New York Review of Books*, 12/11/75, p. 8)

MITOSIS (mī-tō′sis, mi-) *noun* the usual method of cell division, characterized typically by the resolving of the chromatin in the nucleus into a threadlike form that separates into segments or chromosomes, each of which separates longitudinally into two parts, one part of each chromosome being retained in each of two new cells resulting from the original cell.

MITOTIC (mī-tot′ik) *adj.*

MITOTICALLY *adv.*

1. In its MITOSIS from cold print to cathode tube, however, *Helter Skelter* has taken on the odor of lurid, sensationalist exploitation . . . . The ritualistic butcherings of actress Sharon Tate, her four household visitors and the LaBianca couple are shown in flashback frames that go by so lickety-split that the shock effects are almost SUBLIMINAL. (H.F. Waters, Review, *Newsweek*, 4/5/76, p. 61)

MNEMONIC (nē-mon′ik, ni-) *adj.* assisting or intended to assist the memory; of or pertaining to mnemonics or memory.

MNEMONICALLY *adv.*

MNEMONICS *noun* (construed as *singular*) the process or technique of improving or developing the memory by the use of certain formulas; such formulas.

MNEMOSYNE *noun* the ancient Greek goddess of memory, and mother of the Muses.

1. As a star for the New York Knickerbockers, Jerry Lucas was famous for his long, one-handed jump shots, his pinpoint passes—and his phenomenal feats of MNEMONIC magic. He

once memorized 500 columns of the Manhattan telephone book and co-authored the best seller *The Memory Book*. (Susan C. Cowley, Sylvester Monroe, "The Gospel of Lucas," *Newsweek*, 1/19/76, p. 56)

2. " . . . there's a very sharp signaling device the disease uses, you know, rather like the light flashing a warning about no juice left in the tank [Dr. Bloomfield told Ronald Beard]. The left eye starts to twitch, always the left apparently. If it's the right it means nothing. Useful language, English, full of MNEMONICS. Right: all right. Left: not much [time] left [to live]." (A. Burgess, *Beard's Roman Women*, McGraw-Hill, 1976, p. 142)

3. There were . . . long stories on its technical complexities, with paeans to the crew at the New York Metropolitan Opera House and to the Wilson-Glass troupe for its physical endurance and MNEMONIC ability in staging the five-hour production [of the opera, *Einstein on the Beach*, by Robert Wilson and Philip Glass]. (F.J. Spieler, Review, *Harper's*, March 1977, p. 107)

MODUS OPERANDI (mō'dŏŏs ŏ' pə-Rän'dē, mō'dəs op'ə-ran'dī) *noun, pl.:* **MODI OPERANDI** mode or system of operating or working; procedure; way of doing or making.

1. The title of the book [*Ogilvie, Tallant & Moon*, by Chelsea Quinn Yarbro] is the name of a law firm in San Francisco, and Moon is a full-blooded Indian . . . when Moon solves a mystery by calling upon something in his racial subconscious, we all nod our heads undoubtedly. All, probably, except a few doubters—atheists or Communists, most likely—who consider this kind of MODUS OPERANDI a lousy copout. (N. Callendar, Review, *New York Times*, 2/15/76, Section 7, p. 20)

2. . . . last week the Old Lady of Threadneedle Street [Bank of England] stood accused of losing her virtue. The bank and the Treasury announced that they were investigating the possibility that bank officials had broken the nation's exchange-control laws, and presumably made a bundle for themselves and certain unscrupulous British speculators . . . . Such skullduggery would be easy to hide; the bank's gentlemanly MODUS OPERANDI does not stress careful record keeping, and one press account

suggested that some of what records there were had been "mistakenly" shredded. (Anon., "Is Nothing Sacred?" *Newsweek*, 5/10/76, p. 89)

3. And because he is so repelled by [Robert] Moses' personality, his class and racial biases, and his blatantly extra-legal MODUS OPERANDI, [Robert A.] Caro [author of *The Power Broker: Robert Moses and the Fall of New York*] cannot fairly evaluate why or what Big Bob built. (C.R. Hatch, Review, *Harper's*, January 1975, p. 88)

4. For my money, Carter is no more angelic than, say, the average Democratic committee chairman on the Hill. And his MODUS OPERANDI is weirdly akin to Nixon's. (N. Thimmesch, of *Los Angeles Times*, "Carter's Methods Akin to Nixon's," *Daily Oklahoman*, Okla. City, 7/9/76, p. 8)

MODUS VIVENDI (mō'dŏŏs wē-wen'dē, mō'dəs vi-ven'dī), *noun, pl.:* **MODI VIVENDI** (mō'dē wē-wen'dē, mō dī vi-ven'dī) manner of living or getting along; a temporary arrangement between persons or parties pending a settlement of matters in debate.

1. Leopold's business ACUMEN had not been transmitted to his son [Wolfgang Mozart], and it would be difficult to conceive of anyone less prepared for such a MODUS VIVENDI. (R. Craft, "A Prodigy of Nature," *New York Review of Books*, 12/11/75, p. 12)

2. But Carter's more immediate concern was reaching a productive MODUS VIVENDI with his own lopsided party majorities of 62-38 in the Senate and 292-143 in the House . . . he comes to Washington trailed by a florid record of combat with the Georgia legislature. (P. Goldman, *et. al.*, "The New Kings of the Hill," *Newsweek*, 1/17/77, p. 18)

MOIRÉ (mwä-rā', mōr'ā, môr'ā) *adj.* (of silk, other fabrics, and metal surfaces) presenting a watery or wavelike appearance suggestive of rippling water.

MOIRÉ or **MOIRE** (mwär, mōr, môr) *noun* a design pressed on silk, rayon, etc., by engraved rollers; any fabric with a watery or wavelike appearance.

1. Blinded by strobe light explosions and VERTIGO-inducing MOIRES, directors [of museums]

cautiously navigated through the superproductions known as "light shows." . . . they stoically endured assaults on their PRISTINE white spaces. They saw their walls splattered with molten lead and flinched while their new TRAVERTINE floors groaned under the weight of timber and steel plate. (M. Friedman, "Museums and Artists Learn To Live With the 70's," *New York Times*, 9/12/76, Section 2, p. 33)

MOLET (mol'it) or **MULLET** (mul'it) *noun* a figure of a usually five-pointed star; American star; Scottish star.

1. It was the MOLET, this so-called "Star of American Liberty," that in time became the PARADIGM of all modern stars used on flags. (W. Kalyn, "Rally Round the Stars and Stripes, Pinetrees and Rattlesnakes," *New York Times*, 3/28/76, Section 2, p. 37)

MOLLIFY (mol'ə-fī') *verb* to soften in feeling or temper, as a person; pacify; appease; to mitigate or reduce.

MOLLIFICATION *noun*.

MOLLIFIER *noun*.

1. See (1) under PREDACEOUS.

2. To try to fend off the good House keepers who assembled to dump him last week, [Wayne] Hays stood down temporarily from his job as the chief dispenser of Democratic campaign funds. UNMOLLIFIED, House Majority Leader Thomas P. O'Neill pressed Hays for an unconditional resignation from all his chairmanships . . . . (T. Mathews, *et. al.*, "Capitol Capers," *Newsweek*, 6/14/76, p. 18)

MONOCOQUE (män'ə-kōk'-käk') *adj.* designating or of a kind of construction (of airplanes, boats, cars, etc., in which the fuselage, outer casing or skin bears all or most of the structural load; designating or of a kind of construction, as of an automobile, in which the body and chassis are one unit.

1. You cruise even the roughest roads with confidence, the result of the [Mercedes-Benz] 450 SEL's* SYNERGISTIC combination of independent suspension, 116.7-inch wheelbase

*Price is more than $22,000.

and welded—not bolted—MONOCOQUE construction. Ad for Mercedes-Benz, *Newsweek*, 10/18/76, p. 54)

MONOGLOT (män'ə-glot) *adj.* speaking or writing only one language.

MONOGLOT *noun* a monoglot person.

1. "I would like to write in Italian [Ronald Beard wrote to Paola Belli], but I remain at the end a MONOGLOT Englishman, unworthy to enter the COMITY of nations, tied to one tongue as to one cuisine and one INSULAR complex of myths." (A. Burgess, *Beard's Roman Women*, McGraw-Hill, 1976, p. 149)

MONOMACHY (mō-nom'ə-kē) *noun* a duel; a single combat.

MONOMACHIST *noun* one who fights in single combat; duelist.

1. No wonder [Anthony] Powell is reminded of another of Robert Burton's torrential passages: "I hear new news every day, and those ordinary rumours of war, plagues, fires, inundations, thefts, murders, massacres, meteors, comets, spectrums, PRODIGIES, apparitions, MONOMACHIES, shipwrecks . . . ." (G. Hicks, Review of *Hearing Secret Harmonies*, by Anthony Powell, *American Way*, May 1976, p. 39)

MONOPHTHONG (mon'əf-thông) *noun* a simple vowel sound during the utterance of which the vocal organs remain in a relatively unchanging position, as (o) in *go*.

MONOPHTHONGAL *adj.*

1. "Both of them weeds." How clear and MONOPHTHONGAL that high front vowel, positively Mediterranean. (A. Burgess, *Beard's Roman Women*, McGraw-Hill, 1976, p. 139)

MOOT (mōōt) *adj.* subject to or open for argument or discussion; debatable; on which opinions differ; doubtful; as a moot point; of little or no practical value or meaning; purely academic; not actual; theoretical; hypothetical.

MOOT *verb* to discuss or debate; to present or introduce for discussion; to reduce or remove the practical significance of (a question);

to argue (a case), especially in a mock court.

MOOT *noun* an argument or discussion, especially of a hypothetical legal case, as in a law school.

1. See (1) under ANODYNE.

2. Both of the works under review here [*The Conservative Intellectual Movement in America*, by George H. Nash; and *Up From Communism*, by John P. Diggins] are outlandishly expensive. Even inflation cannot justify charging $20 for a moderately-sized book. In Nash's case this complaint is MOOT, for his book would be expensive at any price. Diggins, however, has been done a gross disservice by his publisher. (P. Rosenberg, Review, *New York Times*, 6/20/76, Section 7, p. 25)

3. The word "Yid," for instance, is now printable [in Russia]. But whether this is a relaxation of censorship or a footnote to unofficial anti-Semitism remains MOOT. According to [Ronald] Hingley [author of *A New Life of Anton Chekhov*], the word was less PEJORATIVE in Chekhov's time than it is now. (H. Moss, Review, *New York Times*, 6/20/76, Section 7, p. 28)

MORDANT (môr′ dənt′) *adj.* biting, cutting, caustic, or sarcastic, as of speech, wit, expression, etc.

1. Clement Attlee led a delegation of Englishmen there [to Red China] eighteen years ago, one of whom wrote a MORDANT little book called *No Flies in China*, urbanely mocking the only absolutely verifiable revolutionary achievement in the city of Shanghai—in fact, the reporter hadn't seen a single fly. (W.F. Buckley Jr., *Execution Eve and Other Contemporary Ballads*, G.P. Putnam's Sons, 1975, p. 27)

2. Downstairs in ICP [International Center for Photography]'s bookstore, a more MORDANT view of America is presented . . . . In every picture [in his exhibit], [Robert] D'Alessandro . . . [is] suggesting that it [the flag] stands not for noble and praiseworthy ideals, but for impulses and interests that are cheap and vulgar if not VENAL and vicious. (Gene Thornton, Review, *New York Times*, 1/11/76, Section 2, p. 31)

3. See (1) under MALLEABLE.

4. See (1) under EPITHET.

5. [Caption below a reproduction of a Peggy Bacon sketch] : A crayon study of the MORDANT Dorothy Parker, about to deliver, probably, a deservedly mortal verbal blow. (F. Getlein, "A serious, yet funny artist," *Smithsonian*, January 1976, p. 61)

6. Once he [Alexander Woollcott] cabled a friend whose wife had just died, "You lucky bastard to have had all those years with that exquisite person." To those who remember Woollcott at his MORDANT best, the same sentiment applies. (P.D. Zimmerman, Review of *Smart Aleck*, by Howard Teichmann, *Newsweek*, 5/17/76, p. 110)

7. See (9) under CHAUVINISM.

8. Moods change swiftly in *Three Journeys* [by Paul Zweig], which is part of its seduction and power, and this Paris chapter can be as MORDANTLY witty as the preceding chapter is nebulously contemplative. (Francine DuPlessix Gray, Review, *New York Times*, 5/2/76, Section 7, p. 5)

9. See (1) under DIPSOMANIAC.

10. . . . *Slap Shot*'s [film] script does manage to break through its own conventions and cliches to offer some wry and MORDANT observations on our culture's skewed value system, in which immaturity can be mistaken for masculinity and nudity is thought to be more obscene than violence. (Joy Gould Boyum, Review, *Wall Street Journal*, 3/7/77, p. 15)

MORDENT (môr′dənt) *noun* (not to be confused with MORDANT, *see above*) a melodic musical embellishment made by a quick alteration of a principal tone with an auxiliary tone, usually a half-step lower.

1. See (1) under CHTHONIC.

2. To the slurs he [Bing Crosby] added (although he could probably not have identified or defined) the MORDENT, which became an early hallmark of his singing. A MORDENT is simply the introduction of an unscheduled short note adjacent to the note of destination. The additional note may be the note above or the note below. Crosby's MORDENTS were light

and fast, and they produced the effect of a slight catch, or choke, or sob which was to remain one of the most attractive of his vocal devices. Initially he used only the upper MORDENT. In later years he added the lower, articulating it more slowly and very effectively. (H. Pleasants, "A Bel Canto Baritone Named Bing Crosby," *New York Times*, 12/5/76, Section 2, p. 18)

MOREL (mə-rel') *noun* any edible mushroom of the genus *Morchella*, especially *M. esculenta*, resembling a sponge on a stalk.

1. It (the MOREL) is the golden prince of mushrooms and it has the same relationship to other edible fungi that golden Iranian caviar has to the catfish . . . . Millions of American mushroom eaters have never seen or tasted a MOREL. It is as FEY as a UNICORN. (J.R. Phelan, "May is morel time," *New York Times*, 5/9/76, Section 6, p. 80)

2. See (2) under SERENDIPITY.

MORES (mōr' āz, -ēz, môr' -) *noun*, *pl.* folkways of central importance accepted without question and embodying the fundamental beliefs of a group and which often become part of the formal legal code.

1. "I'm striving to learn what is truly important [said John Ehrlichman]. What happened in the [Nixon] White House, that CATACLYSM, may have been the best thing to ever happen to me. It blew away all my MORES . . . for the first time I have a compendium of unanswered questions." (I. Berkow, "Ehrlichman candid in his new book, 'The Company,' " *Norman* [Okla.] *Transcript*, 7/7/76, p. 21)

2. Lyndon Johnson's probity consequently joined the political power of Catholic bishops, abortion, Clarence Kelley's valances, the Burger court, redistribution of income through tax reform, and sexual MORES as extraneous issues obscuring Democratic discontent with the economy and Republican administration. While Democratic politicians still believe those issues are strong enough to defeat Mr. Ford, Carter's performance has introduced an element of doubt. (R. Evans, R. Novak, "Bad trip for Carter: A train ride to nowhere," *Philadelphia Inquirer*, 9/24/76, p. 11-A)

3. See (2) under MANDALA.

4. See (9) under POLEMIC.

5. The sketches [in the film, *How Funny Can Sex Be?*] deal with Italian sexual MORES . . . . The conception is funny and the execution sharp as the couple argue over PUTATIVE lovers and then pick their way across the sleeping forms of their progeny to copulate . . . . (D. Ryan, Review, *Philadelphia Inquirer*, 10/22/76, p. 6-C)

6. The gorilla act [transformation of a woman into a gorilla] is the latest gimmick . . . to attract new customers and dollars to San Francisco's North Beach area . . . . What is happening here is as indicative of the country's changing sexual MORES as the advent of topless here a dozen years ago. (D. Johnston, *Los Angeles Times* Service, "Now, X-rated bars try gorillas," *Philadelphia Inquirer*, 1/17/77, p. 10-A)

7. Why did this man [George Washington] shy away from power and self-aggrandizement? . . . . Washington himself would have answered that he did not desire to rule over others (though, paradoxically, as a product of his time and MORES, he was absolute master over others who happened to be black) . . . . He possessed the kind of humility only truly great men possess. (Anon., "George Washington Made It Work" [Editorial], *Times Herald*, Norristown, Pa., 2/21/77, p. 14)

8. Actually, I [Russel Wren] am a complete maverick in the BOURGEOIS world and in no way conform to its MORES and norms. (Thomas Berger, *Who Is Teddy Villanova?*, Delacorte Press/Seymour Lawrence, 1977, p. 31)

MORIBUND (mor'ə-bund) *adj.* in a dying state; near death; on the verge of extinction or termination; not progressing; stagnant; having little or no vital force left.

MORIBUNDITY *noun.*

MORIBUNDLY *adv.*

1. See (2) under RECIDIVISM.

2. [In the first play of *A Texas Trilogy*, by Preston Jones] We see LuAnn [Hampton, played by Diane Ladd] getting wiser and harder, her cheerleader's skirt becoming a

beautician's uniform and then the hostess dress of the Howdy Wagon in which she welcomes new citizens of a MORIBUND town. (J. Kroll, Review, *Newsweek*, 5/17/76, p. 9)

3. See (2) under NEURASTHENIA.

4. . . . [Myles] Arber's big story [in the Crested Butte (Colo.) Chronicle, suggesting that Pres. Ford's campaign manager, Howard (Bo) Callaway, was guilty of conflict of interest] had backfired badly . . . . He estimates that he has lost nearly $20,000 in advertising revenue . . . , and his paper has shrunk from a healthy 24 pages to a MORIBUND eight . . . the Justice Department cleared Callaway of all conflict-of-interest charges, and four officials of Callaway's Crested Butte Development Corp. have sued Arber for libel and slander. (Anon., "The Price of Success," *Newsweek*, 1/31/77, pp. 5-8)

5. Shortly after Elizabeth II began her reign, John Osborne, king of the Angry Young Men, took time between hit plays to pronounce the British monarchy MORIBUND—"A gold filling in a mouth full of decay." (M. Maddocks Review of *Majesty: Elizabeth II and The House of Windsor*, by Robert Lacey, *Time*, 3/7/77, p. 87)

6. See (1) under PSYCHOPOMP.

MORPHOLOGY (môr-fol' ə-jē) *noun* the form or structure of anything; the study of the form or structure of anything, especially the scientific study.

MORPHOLOGIC or MORPHOLOGICAL *adj*.

MORPHOLOGICALLY *adv*.

MORPHOLOGIST *noun*.

1. See (1) under SURREPTITIOUS.

2. I . . . challenge the idea . . . that you cannot know about life in Harlem, or about the MORPHOLOGY of Presidential campaigns, or about the life of a fire fighter, without yourself being involved or, failing that, applying yourself as a Boswell, on the scene. (W.F. Buckley Jr., *Execution Eve and Other Contemporary Ballads*, G.P. Putnam's Sons, 1975, p. 467)

MOUE (mo͞o) *noun* a pouting grimace; wry face.

1. His [Marlon Brando's] cutesy MOUES in the notorious bathroom scene [in the film, *The Missouri Breaks*] are matched only by the abject ineptitude of Kathleen Lloyd as Jane Braxton. (J. Simon, Review, *The New Yorker*, 5/31/76, p. 75)

2. "Merde!" cried Boris, in answer . . . to the raised fist displayed by a taxi driver whose vehicle he had but narrowly missed defending. Then, MOUING into the rear-vision mirror [to his young passengers]: "Je fais mes excuses, mes petites!" (Thomas Berger, *Who Is Teddy Villanova?*, Delacorte Press/Seymour Lawrence, 1977, p. 196)

3. "Just a moment, who really is Natalie Novotny?" [asked Russel Wren]. [Sam] Polidor MOUED lavishly. "Uh nairline stew with a great sensa yooma." (Thomas Berger, *Ibid.*, p. 235)

MUCKRAKE (muk'rāk) *verb* to search for and publicize in newspapers, etc. real or alleged corruption, scandal, or the like, especially in politics; *obsolete*: a rake for use on muck or dung [inspired by the allusion by T. Roosevelt in a speech (1906) to the man with the *muck rake* in Bunyan's *Pilgrim's Progress*].

MUCKRAKER *noun*.

1. Last year in a seminar at the Troy State University School of Journalism in Alabama, I assigned two books as samples of the beginning and end of MUCKRAKING. One was Lincoln Steffen's *Autobiography*, the other was *All the President's Men*, by Washington Post reporters Carl Bernstein and Bob Woodward. (J. Chamberlain, "What Value Do Revelations Have?" *Daily Oklahoman*, Okla. City, 4/14/76, p. 8)

2. Of course, the rise of social ethics, from the MUCKRAKERS to the civil-rights enthusiasts, was a reaction to the selfish and corrupting inconsistency of individuals living by the strains of Protestant gentility. (T.R. Sizer, Review of *Amoral America*, by George C.S. Benson and Thomas S. Engeman, *Chronicle of Higher Education*, 4/5/76, p. 20)

3. MUCKRAKER Jack Anderson is now dishing out his political tidbits on ABC-TV's *Good Morning, America*, along with Rona Barrett, who covers Hollywood. (Linda Bird Francke, *et. al.*, "Gossip Mania," *Newsweek*, 5/24/76, p. 60)

4. The 1880's were another period of concern, when the Indian Rights Association and other humanitarian reform organizations made repeated demands that tribal relations and the Indian reservations be destroyed, so that the Indians, newly . . . educated, and Christianized, could be absorbed as citizens into the body politic. Then came the MUCKRAKING campaign against the Bureau of Indian affairs in the 1920's, with cries for the reversal of the very plans of Americanization that had been in high favor in 1890. (F.P. Prucha, "An Awesome Proliferation of Writing About Indians," *Chronicle of Higher Education*, 5/24/76, p. 19)

5. See (1) under SERIATIM.

6. It used to be called MUCKRAKING. More recently the term investigative journalism has taken hold. Whatever it's called, it is undergoing a major reflowering . . . . Americans like to hear the worst . . . . (D.T. Bazelon, Review of *Power, Inc.*, a book by Morton Mintz and Jerry Cohen; and *The Average Man Fights Back*, a book by David Hapgood, in collaboration with Richard Hall, *New York Times*, 3/27/77, Section 7, p. 32)

MULCT (mulkt) *verb* to punish (a person) by fine or forfeiture; to obtain (money or the like) by fraud, deceit, etc.; to deprive (someone) of something, as by fraud.

MULCT *noun* a fine or similar penalty.

1. An infamous old prison has long since been demolished, leaving only the legends of its two most illustrious occupants: "Boss" Tweed, who served time in 1874 after MULCTING the city of $200 million; and Mae West, who was gilded-caged for overacting in a 1927 play called—what else?—*Sex*. (Anon., "The Little Apple," *Time*, 5/24/76, p. 42)

MULLIGAN (mul′ ə-gən) *noun* (in U.S. slang) a kind of stew containing odd bits of meat, vegetables, etc., especially as prepared by hobos.

1. On the road he [a hobo] could depend on finding jungles or encampments adjacent to the railroad yards. The jungles were run by democratic rules: Any man was welcome. Anyone could get something to eat, though if he had food he should add it to the MULLIGAN, or stew. Mirrors, pots, and pans were to be returned to their nails on the trees, and everything spotlessly cleaned for the next fellow. (R. Warner, "Riding freights is no picnic for tramps today," *Smithsonian*, December 1975, p. 97)

MURRAIN (mûr′in) *noun* any of various diseases of cattle, as anthrax, foot-and-mouth disease, or tick fever; a plague or pestilence.

1. None of the authors . . . that I have known ever felt this way [grateful to colleagues, indexers, and their family] during the throes of preparing a book. A much more candid . . . preface would run this way: "A MURRAIN on all my stupid PETTIFOGGING colleagues who keep interrupting my work with their ridiculously inept suggestions." (Sydney J. Harris, "A book's preface doesn't tell it all," *Philadelphia Inquirer*, 9/27/76, p. 9-A)

MYTHOMANIA (mith′ə-mā′nē-ə) *noun* an abnormal tendency to lie or exaggerate.

MYTHOMANIAC *adj.*

MYTHOMANIAC *noun.*

1. His [the French artist-designer Erté's] first big chance in the theater . . . was the costume he designed for an exotic young dancer named Mata Hari in her hit show, *The Minaret*, in 1913 . . . . "She pretended to be a Hindu, although she was completely Dutch," he said. "She was one of those people who invented themselves, a MYTHOMANE. There was nothing in that espionage business. If she'd been willing to defend herself and speak openly, the case would have been dismissed." Mata Hari was executed during World War I as a German spy . . . . (Flora Lewis, "Erté Recalls the Glamour of His Art," *New York Times*, 12/19/76, Section 1, p. 62)

2. It is of course unlikely that one man would have experienced even a third of Mr. Crabb's claims. Half? Incredible! All? A MYTHOMANIAC! . . . . I can certify that whenever Mr. Crabb has given precise dates, places, and names, I have gone to the available references and found him frighteningly accurate—when he can be checked at all. (T. Berger, *Little Big Man*, Fawcett, 1964, p. 447)

N

NABOB (nā′bob) or **NAWAB** (nə-wôb′) *noun* a person, especially a European, who has made a large fortune in India or another country of the East; any very wealthy or powerful person.

NABOBISH *adj.*

1. Knowledgeable sources say the Prince [Bernhard, of the Netherlands] would sometimes mix his old "drinking pals" with the NABOBS of European business—a blend that sometimes worked and sometimes didn't. (M. Ruby, *et. al.*, "A Slap for the Prince," *Newsweek*, 4/5/76, p. 68)

2. See (1) under NATTER.

NACRE (nā′kər) *noun* mother-of-pearl.

NACRED *adj.* lined with or resembling nacre.

NACREOUS *adj.* of, pertaining to, or resembling nacre; lustrous; pearly; IRIDESCENT.

1. He [Ronald Reagan] is using the [Panama] canal issue as Andrew Jackson used the national-bank issue, as a piece of sand around which he hopes NACRE will form, producing in time a pearl beyond price, a broad new consensus about national purpose. (G.F. Will, "Ford's Real Weakness," *Newsweek*, 5/17/76, p. 114)

NADIR (nā′dər, nā′dir) *noun* that point of the celestial sphere directly opposite to the zenith and directly below the observer; the lowest point; time of greatest depression or dejection.

1. Tom Dardis has written the best book so far [*Some Time in the Sun*] on the Hollywood careers of five famous writers . . . . His subjects are Scott Fitzgerald, William Faulkner, Aldous Huxley, Nathanael West and James Agee . . . . Though Fitzgerald went to Hollywood at the NADIR of his career, Dardis argues, he was not a broken-down victim of the studio system as he has usually been portrayed. Like Huxley, he was able to command top pay; he regained his creative powers while doing movie piecework and acquired confidence to embark on his unfinished novel, *The Last Tycoon*. (W. Clemons, Review, *Newsweek*, 7/19/76, p. 70)

2. JFK, Estes Kefauver and Adlai Stevenson were but a few of the Democrats who took some distance [from Harry Truman]; and the press Truman got, reread today, makes the coverage of Richard Nixon at his Watergate NADIR look like the nomination for the Nobel peace prize. (Meg Greenfield, "The Man They Loved to Hate," *Newsweek*, 9/13/76, p. 92)

3. There's been no word yet about whither [the TV show] *Spencer's Pilots*, despite critics' CASTIGATION and a near-NADIR Nielsen. Rumor has its Friday-night niche going to an information and interview show . . . . (H. Harris, "New deals follow the departure of CBS' penny-pinching president," *Philadelphia Inquirer*, 10/25/76, p. 4-D)

NAÏVETÉ (nä-ēv-tā′) or **NAIVETÉ** or **NAIVENESS** *noun* the quality or state of being naive; artless simplicity; a naive action, remark, etc.

NAÏVE or **NAIVE** or **NAÏF** or **NAIF** (nä-ēf′) *adj.* having or showing natural simplicity; unaffectedly, sometimes foolishly, simple; unsophisticated; childlike; artless; INGENUOUS; not suspicious; credulous.

NAÏVELY or **NAIVELY** *adv.*

1. See (2) under INGENUOUS.

2. . . . the President [Ford] in fact struck one of his worried advisers as calm to the point of NAÏVETÉ about his prospects [for being nominated]. (P. Goldman, *et. al.*, "A President in Jeopardy," *Newsweek*, 5/17/76, p. 22)

3. Jodie [Foster, who played the teen-age prostitute in the film, *Taxi Driver*] is neither a button-nosed NAÏF like the young Hayley Mills, nor hard-edged PRECOCIOUS, like Tatum O'Neal . . . . She does not date or attend Hollywood functions. (Anon., "Hooker Hooked," *Time*, 2/23/76, p. 49)

4. Some of the humor here [in the film, *General Idi Amin Dada*] is surely unintentional, but Amin is so frequently made to look foolish, by sequences he both staged and approved, that the viewer is forced to weigh the dictator's NAÏVETÉ against his guile. (Janet Maslin, Review, *Newsweek*, 9/6/76, p. 65)

5. See (3) under EXCULPATE.

NAMBY-PAMBY (nam' bē pam' bē) *noun*, *pl.*: **NAMBY-PAMBIES** namby-pamby writing or talk; a namby-pamby person; namby-pamby sentiment.

NAMBY-PAMBY *adj.* weakly sentimental; insipid; without vigor; wishy-washy; weak or indecisive; lacking in moral or emotional strength.

1. Nick Nolte is no EFFETE NAMBY-PAMBY. After graduating from Westside High in Omaha, he won a series of football scholarships and insists that one Arizona college kicked him out after he was caught in the girls' dorm. (Lenore Hershey, "Nick Nolte Surfaces," *Ladies Home Journal*, July 1977, p. 57)

2. When I read about declining SAT scores, the "functional illiteracy" of our students, the NAMBY-PAMBY courses, the army of child psychologists, reading aides, educational liaisons, starry-eyed administrators and bungling fools who people our school systems, my heart sinks. (Suzanne Britt Jordan, " 'I Want to Go to the Prose,' " *Newsweek*, 11/14/77, p. 23)

NARCISSISM (när' si-siz' əm) or **NARCISM** *noun* self-love; EGOCENTRICITY; excessive admiration of one's self; excessive interest in one's own appearance, comfort, importance, abilities, etc.; (in PSYCHOANALYSIS) erotic gratification derived from admiration of one's own physical or mental attributes.

NARCISSIST or **NARCIST** *noun*.

NARCISSISTIC or **NARCISTIC** *adj*.

NARCISSUS (in classical mythology) a beautiful youth who fell in love with his own image reflected in a pool and wasted away from unsatisfied desire, whereupon he was transformed into the flower now called narcissus.

1. See (1) under TITILLATE.

2. See (1) under PEDERASTY.

3. Partly in response to the 1969 Tax Reform Act, foundations have grown more cautious as well as more sensitive to their public images, and a kind of corporate NARCISSISM has spread in the foundation field that one would have thought inappropriate. (G.W. Bonham, "Hard Choice For Foundations" [Editorial], *Change*, September 1975, p. 11)

4. As is characteristic of a certain kind of benevolent American NARCISSISM, the best notions about American education have always been thought exportable to much of the rest of the world, preferably unhampered by local custom and circumstance . . . . (G.W.B., "The American Disease" [Editorial], *Ibid.*, June 1975, p. 11)

5. See (1) under DIOGENES.

6. See (1) under INCESTUOUS.

7. New York Times columnist Russell Baker . . . wrote . . . last year, ... To be part of Washington [D.C.] is to live in a fever of NARCISSISM. (R.L. Worsnop, "Metropolitan Areas Lose Prestige," *Norman* [Okla.] *Transcript*, 2/23/76, p. 6)

8. And although he [Malcolm Braly] spent eighteen of his first 40 years in places like San Quentin and Folsom, he recounts [in the book, *False Starts*] these experiences [as a convict] with none of the NARCISSISM or self-pity in so much confessional writing. (P.D. Zimmerman, Review, *Newsweek*, 3/15/76, p. 91)

9. . . . the mirror of hindsight combines revelation and NARCISSISM to a seductive

degree. (Ada Louise Huxtable, "Modern Architecture in Question," *New York Review of Books*, 11/27/75, p. 8)

10. It is not the thinkers of the past who are blind but twentieth-century social science, which long ago committed itself to the view that things get better and better . . . . It dignifies chaos as "pluralism," moral collapse as an expansion of "personal choice," NARCISSISM as autonomy. (C. Lasch, Review of *The Wish to be Free: Society, Psyche, and Value Change*, by Fred Weinstein and Gerald M. Platt, *New York Review of Books*, 11/27/75, p. 42)

11. . . . the period . . . between the mid-tenth and mid-thirteenth centuries . . . was the definitive one for both the religious and cultural dimensions of Islam . . . a distinctive social structure, . . . a complex organization of craft and training guilds, and the shining triumph of male NARCISSISM, the harem system, appeared through the whole Islamic world. (C. Geertz, Review of *The Venture of Islam: Conscience and History in a World Civilization. Vol. 1: The Classical Age of Islam; Vol. 2: The Expansion of Islam in the Middle Periods; Vol. 3: The Gunpowder Empire and Modern Times*, by Marshall G.S. Hodgson, *New York Review of Books*, 12/11/75, p. 20)

12. It's too early for a complete theory of the psychopathology of journalists but I would commend...Heinz Kohut's essay on NARCISSISM and NARCISSISTIC rage . . . . Kohut talks about the desire among those suffering NARCISSISTIC rage to "turn a passive experience into an active one." (A. Cockburn, "The Psychopathology of Journalism," *New York Review of Books*, 12/11/75, p. 31)

13. See (3) under MERETRICIOUS.

14. See (1) under HYPOCHONDRIA.

15. [Madeline] Kahn, [Bruce] Dern, [Art] Carney and Ron Leibman (who plays a wonderfully NARCISSISTIC matinee idol [in *Won Ton Ton, The Dog Who Saved Hollywood*] would probably have fared better without a director. (Katrine Ames, Review, *Newsweek*, 6/14/76, p. 90)

16. And his [Roman Polanski's] fascination with the morbid extremes of NARCISSISM has never been more painfully obvious: here [in

The Tenant, in which he is the protagonist], when he contemplates leaping out the window in drag, he imagines an attentive audience cheering his performance from below. Moviegoers are likely to urge him on. (Janet Maslin, Review, *Newsweek*, 6/28/76, p. 78)

17. In *Live or Die* (1966), which won the Pulitzer Prize [for Anne Sexton], the speaker describes herself in one poem as daughter, sweet meat, priest, mouth, and bird of the sun: images of altogether uncritical self-adoration. A poem on the death of Sylvia Plath quickly becomes yet another means for talking about the self, that self endlessly jealous of attention. The shrill NARCISSISM of such lyrics appears to have attracted more readers than it repelled. (Patricia Meyer Spacks, Review of *45 Mercy Street*, by Anne Sexton, edited by Linda Gray Sexton, *New York Times*, 5/30/76, Section 7, p. 6)

18. See (1) under AUSCULTATION.

19. See (2) under LANGUOR.

20. See (9) under CLOY.

21. [Barbra] Streisand's constant upstaging of [Kris] Kristofferson [in the movie, *A Star Is Born*] often goes beyond the bounds of run-of-the-mill NARCISSISM; the camera spends a great deal of time watching her watch him talk, and when he nearly breaks his neck running a motorcycle off a concert stage, we get a better look at her reaction than we do at the accident. (Janet Maslin, Review, *Newsweek*, 1/10/77, p. 64)

22. See (7) under MISOGYNY.

23. See (2) under SANS-CULOTTE.

24. See (1) under MESOMORPH.

NARCOHYPNIA (när′ kə-hip′ nē-ə) *noun* numbness following sleep.

1. Having been imprisoned under the Nixon Administration, served most of my prison sentence during Ford's Presidency, to emerge ultimately on parole under Jimmy Carter, I feel a NARCOHYPNIA equal to Rip Van Winkle's. (E.H. Hunt, "How America Looks to Me Now," *Newsweek*, 4/4/77, p. 15)

NARCOLEPSY (när′kə-lep′sē) *noun* a condition of frequent and overwhelming desire for sleep.

NARCOLEPTIC *noun.*

1. "I [said Lily Tomlin] had [as a premed student at Wayne State University], what do you call it, NARCOLEPSY—I'd go home at 3 to study, fall asleep and wake up at 9 the next morning." (J. Kroll, "Lily Tomlin: Funny Lady," *Newsweek*, 3/28/77, p. 65)

NARCOSIS (när-kō′ sis) *noun* a state of sleep or drowsiness; a state of deep stupor, unconsciousness, or drowsiness produced by a drug, or by heat, cold, or electricity.

NARCOSE *adj.* characterized by stupor; stuporous.

NARCOTIC (när-kot′ ik) *adj.* having the power to produce narcosis, as a drug; pertaining to or of the nature of narcosis; pertaining to narcotics or their use.

NARCOTIC *noun* any of a class of addictive substances, as opium, morphine, heroin, codeine, etc., that blunt or distort the senses and in large quantities produce EUPHORIA, stupor, coma, or death: used in medicine to relieve pain, cause sedation, and induce sleep; anything that exercises a soothing or numbing effect or influence.

NARCOTISM *noun* addiction to narcotics; the action or influence of narcotics; narcosis; an abnormal inclination to sleep.

NARCOTIZE *verb* to subject to a narcotic; stupefy; to make dull; deaden the awareness of; to act as a narcotic.

NARCOTIZATION *noun.*

1. For an instant I allowed myself to think what lay locked within the skull [of the dead Jackie Robinson Jr.], Gibran and Herbie Mann and the colored taxi at Vero Beach and night patrols near Pleiku and the NARCOSIS of heroin and the shock of withdrawal and a father's tender voice. (R. Kahn, *The Boys of Summer*, Harper and Row, 1971, p. 409)

2. In deeper dives, the risks multiply. Nitrogen NARCOSIS, or "rapture of the deep," can occur in depths as shallow as 100 feet . . . . At the increased pressure, nitrogen becomes toxic to some divers, giving them a sense of EUPHORIA that can often be fatal. (Linda Bird Francke, *et. al.*, "Life Under Water," *Newsweek*, 7/12/76, p. 47)

NATATORIUM (nāt′ə-tōr′ ĕ-əm) *noun, pl.: -RIUMS or -RIA* - a swimming pool, especially one indoors.

NATATORIAL or **NATATORY** *adj.* of, pertaining to, or characterized by or adapted for swimming.

NATATION (nā-tā′ shən, na-) *noun* the act or art of swimming.

NATATIONAL *adj.*

NATANT *adj.* swimming or floating, especially floating on the surface of water.

1. In the future, heated pools may have to be called NATATORIUMS, while their owners brandish doctors' certificates attesting that they are polio victims. (Anon., "Modern Living," *Time*, 2/23/76, p. 62)

NATES (nā′ tēz) *noun, pl.* the buttocks; rump.

1. [Donald] Washburn sneered. "Its [the Sforza figurine's] value, of course, would be rather in the millions, if at all calculable. The very materials from which it is molded, gold, with sapphire eyes for the boy and ruby for the bearded ancient, NATES of chalcedony, diamond member—" I [Russel Wren] said: "How vulgar." (Thomas Berger, *Who Is Teddy Villanova?*, Delacorte Press/Seymour Lawrence, 1977, p. 171)

NATTER (nat′ ər) *verb* (*Chiefly British*) to complain; grumble; nag; scold; find fault peevishly. (*Australian*) to chatter idly.

NATTER *noun* (*Chiefly British*) a chat or talk. (*Canadian*) gossip.

1. . . . why read *The Canfield Decision* [by Spiro Agnew]? For the small pleasure of discovering some new Agnew ALLITERATION, perhaps? No, there is not even the literary equivalent of his "NATTERING NABOBS of negativism." (D. Shaw, of *Los Angeles Times*, "Agnew 'murders' media and other 'nattering nabobs'," *Norman* [Okla.] *Transcript*, 5/23/76, p. 17)

2. [In *Ratner's Star*, by Don De Lillo] The time is 1979 . . . . Billy [Terwilliger, 14, a Nobel Laureate in Mathematics] must decipher a message the center thinks has come from a planet circling a distant star . . . . Billy and his friends retreat to a gigantic cavern . . . , there to continue NATTERING, to solve the cipher and to work at composing an intergalactic language. (P.S. Prescott, Review, *Newsweek*, 6/7/76, p. 90)

3. Many [of Donald Barthelme's stories] have little nervous bursts of violent action . . . that interrupt the deadpan descriptions and lists of ARTIFACTS and urban TOTEMS, the samples of technical jargon and intellectual NATTERING. (R. Locke, Review of *Amateurs*, by Donald Barthelme, *New York Times*, 12/19/76, Section 7, p. 17)

4. Alas, some NATTERING by her [Shirley MacLaine, in her TV special, *Where Do We Go From Here*] about saving cities, enjoying New York and gentle jokes about Fun City—including maybe declaring the burg Disneyland East—are high on relevance, low on humor. (Jay Sharbutt, AP, "TV-Radio Comments," *Times Herald*, Norristown, Pa., 3/12/77, p. 22)

NEBBISH (neb′ ish) *noun* a person who is pitifully inept, ineffective, shy, dull, etc.

1. He [Howard Yost] had come here [where the ransom money was to be left] . . . a poor, middle-class NEBBISH. He would leave here, glory be, a CROESUS. (I. Wallace, *The Fun Club*, Bantam Books, 1975, p. 553)

2. [Linda] Blandford [author of *Super-Wealth: The Secret Lives of the Oil Sheikhs*] uncovers reams of fascinating material . . . but, alas, she tells her story in a style which at times reads like vintage Rona Barrett. "Arabs are HYPOCHONDRIACS of the first order," she tells us, and "Most Saudi women fall into two categories: NEBBISH and mezzo NEBBISH." (D.G. Snell, Review, *Barron's*, 3/7/77, p. 20)

NECROLOGY (nə-krol′ ə-jē, ne-) *noun* a notice of death; obituary; a list of persons who have died within a certain period of time.

NECROLOGICAL or **NECROLOGIC** *adj.*

NECROLOGICALLY *adv.*

NECROLOGIST *noun.*

1. Neither of the above instances [references to the death of Gracie Allen and Jack Benny] should be taken as an indication that Mr. [George] Burns's book [*Living It Up*] is a NECROLOGY. Far from it. It is, rather, a celebration of life—his reminiscences of everyone in show business . . . , a clutch of recollections of hilarious anecdotes . . . . (H. Teichmann, Review, *New York Times*, 11/21/76, Section 7, p. 51)

NECROPHILIA (nek′ rə-fil′ ē-ə) or **NECROPHILISM** *noun* a morbid, abnormal fascination with death and the dead, especially an erotic attraction to corpses.

NECROPHILE *noun.*

NECROPHILIAC or **NECROPHILIC** or **NECROPHILOUS** *adj.*

1. The movie [*Gable and Lombard*] doesn't pick up Lombard's famous line about her movie-stud husband being a "lousy lay." Director Sidney J. Furie apparently wants to become Hollywood's leading NECROPHILIAC (he violated Billie Holliday in *Lady Sings the Blues*). As a NECROPHILIAC, Furie is a lousy lay. (J. Kroll, Review, *Newsweek*, 3/15/76, p. 90)

2. See (2) under INNUENDO.

3. He [Shively] was . . . positioning himself over her once more, and she [Sharon Fields] could see that his violence had stimulated him to the hilt. She waited for the act of NECROPHILIA to begin. He lifted her legs, parted them roughly . . . . (I. Wallace, *The Fan Club*, Bantam Books, 1975, p. 323)

4. Readers of commercial fiction enjoy ESOTERIC information, and tasteful NECROPHILIA should be worth 30,000 copies just for starters. Paul Konig, the protagonist of this long, involved story [*City of the Dead*, by Herbert Lieberman], is a forensic pathologist, the chief medical examiner of New York City . . . . In plot and characterization it's about as distinguished as *Cannon* would be if Cannon wore a white coat and stethoscope. (P.S. Prescott, Review, *Newsweek*, 7/19/76, p. 76)

5. See (3) under HALCYON.

6. A Spanish king, Felipe II, is the novel

[*Terra Nostra*, by Carlos Fuentes]'s dominating presence. This Felipe . . . builds the Escorial, a bleak mausoleum in which his royal ancestors will be reinterred and Felipe will be free to wallow in NECROPHILIC mysticism. A MASOCHIST in search of salvation, Felipe . . . commits crimes to insure that this life is a hellish contrast to the heaven he expects; he refuses to consummate his marriage on the ground that one cannot possess the thing one loves . . . . (P.S. Prescott, Review, *Newsweek*, 11/1/76, p. 84)

7. Even so, the book [*The Don: The Life and Death of Sam Giancana*, by William Brashler] stands as a useful corrective to fashionably relaxed attitudes toward violence in entertainment, and at the same time strews enough corpses around to satisfy the most demanding NECROPHILE. (D. Goddard, Review, *New York Times*, 2/27/77, Section 7, p. 18)

8. And [Lawrence] Schiller angrily denies that he practices what some reporters call "NECROPHILIC journalism." In the [Gary] Gilmore case, he was no more than the ringmaster in what became a media circus, with sophisticated newsmen behaving like throwbacks to "The Front Page" days. (At one point, when warden Samuel Smith announced that the execution of Gilmore would take place at dawn, a TV producer shouted: "Can't you be a little more precise? We have a live show to do here.") (D. Gelman, *et. al.*, "Ringmaster at the Circus," *Newsweek*, 1/31/77, p. 78)

9. Swille [a character in the book, *Flight to Canada*, by Ishmael Reed] collects whips and engages in NECROPHILIA with his sister's corpse. (Margo Jefferson, Review, *Newsweek*, 12/20/76, p. 96)

NECROPOLIS (nə-krop′ ə-lis) *noun, pl.*: -LISES a cemetery, especially a large one or one belonging to an ancient city.

NECROPOLITAN *adj.*

1. . . . I could see monuments, high crosses, small angels, a prosperous imposing Catholic NECROPOLIS in this poor town [Woonsocket, R.I., where Clem Labine—former Dodger pitcher—lives]. (R. Kahn, *The Boys of Summer*, Harper and Row, 1971, p. 221)

2. "My heart is a cemetery," she [George Sand] remarked in a despairing moment to Saint-Beuve. "A NECROPOLIS," was the comment of a discarded lover. (Linda Kelly, Review of "Infamous Woman: The Life of George Sand," by Joseph Barry, *New York Times*, 3/27/77, Section 7, p. 20)

NEMESIS (nem′ i-sis) *noun, pl.* -SES (sēz) (if capitalized), the mythological Greek goddess of retributive justice or vengeance; an agent or act of retribution or just punishment; anyone (or anything) which a person seemingly cannot conquer (or achieve), etc.; an opponent or rival whom a person cannot overcome or best.

1. See (2) under IATROGENIC.

2. An ECLECTIC repertory it isn't. And that—depending on one's taste—is the [New York City Ballet] company's glory or NEMESIS. (Nancy Goldner, "The inimitable Balanchine," *New York Times*, 5/30/76, Section 6, p. 28)

3. See (2) under DIATRIBE.

4. I was fascinated to see how it [my stay in the hospital] would turn out . . . . Would I be a factor in the punishment to be meted out to the medical establishment for their HUBRIS and a factor also in the medical NEMESIS that will overtake them [a reference to Ivan Illich's book, *Medical Nemesis*]? . . . . But, most of all I liked the toughminded honesty . . . . I came out, recovered from a disease whose coming and subsiding was still unexplained. Whatever this was, it was not the HUBRIS—the arrogance in the face of the gods—which Illich attributed to medicine. (M. Lerner, "Columnist defends U.S. Doctors," *Norman* [Okla.] *Transcript*, 6/16/76, p. 24)

5. [Viola Herms] Drath . . . begins [her book, *Willy Brandt*] with Brandt in the trough in Bonn in 1974, caught in an undignified position by an East German spy, the FECKLESSNESS of his security apparatus and the NEMESIS of his own complicated character. (D. Schoenbaum, Review, *New York Times*, 3/7/76, Section 7, pp. 19-20)

6. . . . last week, [Viktor] Korchnoi walked into police headquarters in Amsterdam and asked for political asylum . . . . As the second-ranking chess player in the world, he remains qualified to play in next year's world cham-

pionship match series. That competition could bring him face to face with Soviet players— and perhaps pit him against his old NEMESIS, Anatoly Karpov. (R. Carroll, Friso Endt., "Korchnoi's Complaint," *Newsweek*, 8/9/76, p. 38)

NEOLOGISM (ne-ol′ə-jiz′əm) *noun* a new word, usage, idiom, or phrase; the introduction or use of new words or of new meanings of established words; a new doctrine, especially a new interpretation of sacred writings.

NEOLOGISTIC *adj.*

NEOLOGIZE *verb.*

1. For a writer so sensitive to faulty translations and grammatical abominations (he shudders at "the horrid NEOLOGISM 'anymore' in the title of Tennessee Williams's latest play"), [John] Simon seems oddly unconscious of the excesses of his own prose, which is riddled with puns, word quibbles, Latinisms, and PEDANTRIES. (R. Brustein, Review of *Uneasy Stages* and *Singularities*, by John Simon, *New York Times*, 1/4/76, Section 7, p. 2)

2. Ezra Pound, who . . . set forth the technical rules for what he called "Imagisme" in 1912, charged that Amy Lowell appropriated his NEOLOGISM for purposes he considered irrelevant. Still, her three-volume anthology, *Some Imagist Poets* (1915, 1916, 1917), includes poems that embody at least some of these principles. (Grace Schulman, Review of *Amy Lowell*, by Jean Gould, *New York Times*, 1/25/76, Section 7, p. 22)

3. The first duty of a man trying to plot a course for clear thinking is to produce words that really apply to the situations he is trying to describe. I don't mean a fresh set of NEOLOGISMS devised, like thieves' cant or double talk, to hold the uninitiated at arm's length. We have seen enough of that in the jargon of the academic sociologists . . . . (W.F. Buckley Jr., *Up From Liberalism* [Foreword, by John Dos Passos], Arlington House, 2nd Printing 1968, p. ix)

4. The living pieces in this mosaic [the movie, *Buffalo Bill and the Indians, or Sitting Bull's History Lesson*] have never been better— especially—Joel Grey, whose nutty NEOLOGISMS ("tremendable, futurable") make Nate

Salsbury [Buffalo Bill's partner] the Sam Goldwyn of the Gilded Age. (J. Kroll, Review, *Newsweek*, 6/28/76, p. 77)

5. "The difference between the right word and the almost right word," Mark Twain once observed, "is the difference between lightning and the lightning bug." Since Twain's day, in the view of many newspaper editors, a plague of fireflies has filled the sky: NEOLOGISMS proliferate and the rules of grammar have raveled badly. (Anon., "Sacred and Profane," *Time*, 2/26/76, p. 77)

6. The book [*Childhood and History in America*, by Glenn Davis] presents a veritable lexicon of ugly NEOLOGISMS. (J. Demos, Review, *New York Times*, 4/24/77, Section 7, p. 42)

NE PLUS ULTRA (ne plŏŏs ŏŏl′tRä, nē plus ul′trə) the highest point or culmination; acme; the utmost limit; the highest point of perfection.

1. What do Richard Nixon, Robert Redford, Truman Capote and Julia Child have in common? . . . they have all allowed their homes to be photographed for Architectural Digest, the slick, clubby, NE PLUS ULTRA monthly magazine that appears on the best coffee tables from Monaco to Manhattan to Malibu . . . . Under the FEISTY leadership of 42-year-old Paige Rense, AD has increased its circulation from 25,000 in 1970 to 200,000 today—at a stiff $2.95 per copy. (Mary Alice Kellogg, Martin Kasindorf, "Status Digest," *Newsweek*, 9/20/76, p. 84)

2. See (2) under SCHLOCK.

NESCIENCE (nesh′ əns, nesh′ ē-ans) *noun* ignorance; lack of knowledge; agnosticism.

NESCIENT *adj.*

1. "And if I [Reuben Mendoza] am to tell you my inmost thought, I must confess on what a flood of NESCIENCE we, who seem to direct the affairs of nations, are borne along together with those whom we appear to control." (G. Lowes Dickinson, *A Modern Symposium*, Hart Publishing Co., 1967, p. 51)

NEURASTHENIA (nŏŏr əs-thē nē-ə, nyŏŏr′-)

noun nervous disability and exhaustion, as from overwork or prolonged mental strain; nervous prostration; nervous breakdown; a type of neurosis, usually the result of emotional conflicts, characterized by irritability, fatigue, weakness, anxiety and, often, localized pains (headaches, etc.) or distress without apparent physical causes: formerly thought to result from weakness or exhaustion of the nervous system.

NEURASTHENIC *adj.*

NEURASTHENICALLY *adv.*

1. Thus, there is about conservative writing an air of impenetrable smugness, a sense of being pleased with itself that makes the NEURASTHENIC frigidity of liberal POLEMICS seem almost refreshing by contrast. (P. Rosenberg, Review of *The Conservative Intellectual Movement in America*, by George H. Nash; and of *Up From Communism*, by John P. Diggins, *New York Times*, 6/20/76, Section 7, p. 23)

2. Consistent with [Paris couturier Paul] Poiret's sense for the dramatic was his fondness for strong colors . . . . Poiret explained in his autobiography," . . . . Into the sheepfold of MORIBUND mauves and NEURASTHENIC pastels, I hurled hell-bent wolves—reds, greens, purples, royal blues, orange, lemon." (Waverly Root, "Paul Poiret: Couturier extraordinaire," *New York Times*, 6/13/76, Section 6, p. 59)

3. Feminist historians have recognized that periods of history regarded as progressive for men have often been regressive for women. . . . The affluence gained by upwardly mobile, "self-made" American men removed their wives from essential, life-supporting activity and created the passive, economically dependent, NEURASTHENIC "lady of leisure." (Adrienne Rich, Review of *The Female Experience*, a book by Gerda Lerner, *New York Times*, 3/20/77, Section 7, p. 5)

NEXUS (nek′ səs) *noun, pl.:* NEXUSES or NEXUS a means of connection; tie; link; a connection, tie, or link between individuals of a group, members of a series, etc.; the group or series so connected.

1. But there is no significant lobby . . . to defend the rights of the libertarian when concern is with property rights, because of the elemen-

tary failure to establish the NEXUS betwen individual freedom and property rights. (W.F. Buckley Jr., *Up From Liberalism*, Arlington House, 2nd Printing 1968, p. 210)

2. The speeches of congratulations and thanks wore on [at the Academy Awards]. The patriotic NEXUS was established: "A great nation," Walter Mirisch intoned, "like a great film, can stand the test of time and the glare of critical examination." . . . When Elizabeth Taylor unaccountably asked the crowd to sing it [*America the Beautiful*] along with her, no one knew the words. (R. Hughes, "The Day for Night Stars," *Time*, 4/12/76, p. 61)

NICTITATE (nik′ ti-tāt′) or NICTATE *verb* to wink; to blink rapidly, as birds and animals with a nictitating membrane.

NICTITATING membrane—a thin membrane, or inner or third eye-lid, present in many animals, capable of being drawn across the eyeball, as for protection.

NICTITATION or NICTATION *noun.*

1. Holding his hands at eye level, [Red] Smith used the paper to wipe sweat from his palms. "This," he announced, "is a brute of a ball game" [3rd game of the 1953 World Series, in which Carl Erskine set a Series strikeout record against the N.Y. Yankees]. Rud Rennie gazed toward center field, eyes filmed as by a NICTITATING membrane. (R. Kahn, *The Boys of Summer*, Harper and Row, 1971, p. 183)

NIHILISM (nī′ ə-liz′ əm, nē′ , ni′ hi-) *noun* total rejection of established laws and institutions; extreme skepticism, especially with regard to customary values or moral judgments; the denial of the existence of any basis for knowledge or truth; total and absolute destructiveness toward the world at large and oneself; the doctrine of a 19th century Russian revolutionary group that existing social, political, and economic institutions must be completely destroyed to make way for new institutions.

NIHILIST *noun.*

NIHILISM *noun.*

NIHILISTIC *adj.*

NIHILITY (nī-hil′i-tē, nē-) *noun* the state of

being nothing; nothingness.

1. Notwithstanding such occasional flashes of affirmation and MELIORATION, [Gail] Godwin [author of *Dream Children*] is essentially a chronicler of life on the edge, where isolation and alienation move toward the extremes of NIHILISM and madness. (Jane Larkin Crain, Review, *New York Times*, 2/22/76, Section 7, p. 5)

2. Bishop Sheen once called Heywood Broun, whom he had never met but whose NIHILISTIC columns he read every day, and told him he wanted to see him. "What about?" asked Broun gruffly. "About your soul," said Bishop Sheen. (W.F. Buckley Jr., *Up From Liberalism*, Arlington House, 2nd Printing 1968, p. 129)

3. In seeking out the bland, the modulated approach, in blurring distinctions, and in acclimatizing men to life without definition, we erode the Western position; . . . . The NIHILIST tidal wave continues to build up power . . . . Effective resistance to it will call for supreme individual and collective exertion. (W.F. Buckley Jr., *Ibid.*, p. 128)

4. There is nothing so ironic as the NIHILIST or relativist (or the believer in the kind of academic freedom that postulates the equality of ideas) who complains of the anti-intellectualism of American conservatives. Such is *our* respect for the human mind that . . . we credit it with having arrived at certain great conclusions. (W.F. Buckley Jr., *Ibid.*, p. 182)

5. It [*Travesty*, a book by John Hawkes] moves very quickly, for something of the same reason *Macbeth* moves very quickly—we are moving towards and through horror with a madman, locked up within the sealed-off acceleration of his mania, incapable of interrupting the suave NIHILISM of his resolve. (T. Tanner, Review, *New York Times*, 3/28/76, Section 7, p. 23)

6. But mentally he [the narrator in *Travesty*, by John Hawkes] is psychopathic, in the impenetrable SPECIOUSNESS of his NIHILISM that to him, apparently, seems totally and beautifully rational. (T. Tanner, *Ibid.*, p. 23)

7. The Bertold Brecht of 1928 was a divided genius, split between his early NIHILISM and his

later Marxism. That genius exploded on August 31, 1928, when *The Threepenny Opera* opened in Berlin. (J. Kroll, Review of Richard Foreman's production of *The Threepenny Opera*, as performed at Lincoln Center, *Newsweek*, 5/17/76, p. 96)

8. In the extralegal world of baseball, a dissatisfied player may protest to the Commissioner . . . . Turning to the courts [as Carl Furillo did] is considered NIHILISTIC. No one in baseball, or in the law, knows just when a judge will decide that the official player's contract is itself invalid. (R. Kahn, *The Boys of Summer*, Harper and Row, 1971, p. 335)

9. . . . yes, the anger had gone out of him, and now . . . what had replaced it . . . Depression, of course, but there was more. He [Adam Malone] was pervaded by a feeling of utter hopelessness. He was suffused with a feeling of NIHILISM. He felt as one with Sartre . . . . (I. Wallace, *The Fan Club*, Bantam Edition, 1975, p. 296)

10. See (4) under TORPID.

11. NIHILISM is the moral equivalent of weightlessness . . . . The NIHILISM—and the deadening effect—of many recent films lies in the fact that everything is colored the same color as the main characters. If they are hopeless, so is the world. (R. Eder, "Hollywood Is Having An Affair With the Anti-Hero," *New York Times*, 1/2/77, Section 2, p. 11)

NOBLESSE OBLIGE (nō-bles′ ō-blēzh) the moral obligation of the rich or highborn to display honorable or charitable conduct.

1. My friend Mort Tenner, principal of Franklin High School has sent me . . . a copy of a booklet published by the Los Angeles High School District on the subject of sex discrimination in education . . . . A bus boy, the booklet says, is to be called a waiter's assistant. On this point I do not speak from some lofty pinnacle of NOBLESSE OBLIGE. I was a bus boy, and, if I ever write my memoirs, I hope I don't try to upgrade my station, or disguise my sex, by calling myself a waiter's assistant. (J. Smith, "Any Other Name: A Rose is a Rose is . . . ," *Norman* [Okla.] *Transcript*, 4/4/76, p. 16A)

2. . . . [he] has raised $130,000 for his favorite charity: the Walter Hoving home for drug ad-

dicted young women. NOBLESSE OBLIGE is part of Hoving's Social Register life-style. (Anon., "For Tiffany's Walter Hoving Silence May Be Golden, But Sounding Off Is Irresistible," *People.* 4/12/76, p. 16)

3. [Sir Edmund] Hillary's personal aid program [to the Sherpas in Nepal] is a combination of Victorian NOBLESSE OBLIGE . . . and a deep concern for the mountain people. (B. Smith, "Triumph, Death and Love: It is the story of the Himalayas and Edmund Hillary," *People,* 5/24/76, p. 16, 18)

4. Carter Sr. [Jimmy's father] . . . believed in hard work, sharp trading, church on Sunday and the separation of blacks from whites except in the fields. He developed . . . a sense of NOBLESSE OBLIGE; he taught Sunday School, stood for the school board and the state legislature, and indulged in a good many secret philanthropies . . . he was good to his black labor . . . . (P. Goldman, "Sizing Up Carter," *Newsweek,* 9/13/76, p. 25)

NOM DE GUERRE (nom' də-gâr') *noun, pl.:* NOMS DE GUERRE an assumed name; pseudonym.

1. We [The Fan Club] met twice in the week . . . . (I [Adam Malone] will be discreet in referring to each persona. I will employ a NOM DE GUERRE in referring to each participant in our joint effort [to kidnap Sharon Fields]). (I. Wallace, *The Fan Club,* Bantam Books, 1975, p. 139)

2. "I must pay, I must pay," he kept mumbling. Costas Georgiou, a Cypriot-born British subject who goes by the NOM DE GUERRE Tony Callan, sat in his prison cell in the Angolan capital of Luanda—a soldier of fortune turned condemned criminal. (M. Stevens, J. Pringle, "Angola: Death for 'Dogs of War,' " *Newsweek,* 7/12/76, p. 32)

3. When the Russians and the Germans signed their nonaggression pact of 1939, [André] Malraux began to abandon his leftist views. During the war, under the NOM DE GUERRE Berger, he led a branch of the French Resistance. (P.D. Zimmerman, "Malraux: L'Homme Engagé," *Newsweek,* 12/6/76, p. 88)

4. "I have reason to believe," he [Donald Washburn II] went on "that I contracted this [social] disease . . . from my wife . . . . I don't suppose you know some obscure sawbones to whom I could go anonymously or . . . under a NOM DE GUERRE?" (Thomas Berger, *Who Is Teddy Villanova?,* Delacorte Press/Seymour Lawrence, 1977, p. 156)

NOM DE PLUME (nom' də-plōōm') *noun, pl.:* NOMS DE PLUME pen name; PSEUDONYM.

1. Perhaps the author [Malachi Martin] of this lucrative horror show [the book, *Hostage to the Devil: The Possession and Exorcism of Five Living Americans*] would also have done better to take on another NOM DE PLUME. (Francine DuPlessix Gray, Review, *New York Times,* 3/14/76, Section 7, p. 8)

2. In 1966, the Russian critic and novelist Andrei Sinyavsky (NOM DE PLUME: Abram Tertz) was sentenced to seven years' servitude for circulating manuscripts of his work in the West. During his incarceration . . . he kept a journal that has now been translated into beautifully flexible English by Kyril FitzLyon and Max Hayward [*A Voice From The Chorus*]. (P.D. Zimmerman, Review, *Newsweek,* 7/12/76 p. 71E)

NONPAREIL (non' pə-rel') *adj.* having no equal; unequaled; unrivaled; peerless.

NONPAREIL. *noun* a person or thing having no equal; a small pellet of colored sugar for decorating candy, cake, and cookies; a flat, round bite-sized chocolate covered with this sugar; a 6-point type (in Printing).

1. But seldom has a book with such an exciting idea [as *Raise the Titanic!* by Clive Cussler] been so poorly written. Cussler is the cliché expert NONPAREIL . . . . When not using clichés, Cussler tries for Elegant Writing, with even more appalling results. (N. Callendar, Review, *New York Times,* 12/19/76, Section 7, p. 24)

2. If he has not attained the stature or public recognition of Nabokov or Pynchon or John Barth . . . . [Donald] Barthelme at 45 enjoys a secure reputation as a genuine original, a technicial NONPAREIL. (R. Locke, Review of the book, *Amateurs,* by Donald Barthelme, *New York Times,* 12/19/76, Section 7, p. 17)

NON SEQUITUR (non sek' wi-tər) an inference or conclusion that does not follow logically from the premises; a remark having no bearing on what has just been said.

1. Intentionally substituting fitful caricature for coherent characterization, and a steady stream of NON SEQUITUR and fantastic monologue for dialogue, the production [of Rick Bailey's play, *Mean Woman*] does succeed in suggesting its own bizarre, vaguely futuristic dimension. (J. Brandenburg, Review, *Daily Oklahoman*, Okla. City, 3/23/76, p. S1)

2. My reluctance is to concede that the cogency of one's criticisms [of liberalism] depends upon the subsequent cogency of one's affirmation [of the benefits of conservatism] (a logical and psychological NON SEQUITUR). To indict the law-breaker shouldn't require that the prosecutor define the good life. (W.F. Buckley Jr., *Up From Liberalism*, Arlington House, 2nd Printing, 1968, p. xx)

3. See (1) under INANE.

4. Sometimes she [Lily Tomlin] is relaxed and charming; on other occasions, she seems intentionally to have set herself adrift in a sea of NON SEQUITURS; or her honest reaction to a question may make her seem rude or abrupt. (Ellen Cohn, "Lily Tomlin: Not just a funny girl," *New York Times*, 6/6/76, Section 6, p. 94)

5. See (1) under EPIGONE.

6. See (1) under ELLIPSIS.

7. See (5) under MALAPROPISM.

NORMATIVE (nor' mə-tiv) *adj.* of, pertaining to, or establishing an accepted standard or norm of correctness in behavior, speech, writing, dress, etc.; reflecting the assumption or favoring the establishment of such a standard or norm.

NORMATIVELY *adv.*

1. There is no longer a single NORMATIVE Judaism today—a development of which Spinoza himself was one of the HARBINGERS . . . . We have Orthodox and secular Jews, Conservative and Reform Jews, Zionist and anti-Zionist Jews, and nuances and sub-categories within all of these. (Yirmiahu Yovel, "Why Spinoza was Excommunicated," *Commentary*, November 1977, p. 52)

NOSH (nosh) *verb* to eat between meals, especially to nibble at tidbits; to eat (a snack).

NOSH *noun* a snack.

NOSHER *noun.*

1. David Zelag Goodman's screenplay [in the film, *Logan's Run*] . . . takes place in the 23rd century, when the post-catastrophe earthling live in a doomed city near Washington, D.C. It's a world of pure HEDONISM where everyone just NOSHES and necks until the age of 30, when they're rubbed out . . . . (J. Kroll, Review *Newsweek*, 7/4/76, p. 102)

NOSTRUM (nos'trəm) *noun* a pet scheme, theory, device, etc., especially one to remedy social or political ills; PANACEA; a patent medicine of a kind sold with exaggerated claims; a quack medicine; a medicine prepared by the person selling it.

1. Experiencing Professor John Kenneth Galbraith is always a pleasant pleasure, though one must be on one's guard, and the Republic is wise to steel itself to resist his seductive NOSTRUMS. (W.F. Buckley Jr., *Execution Eve and Other Contemporary Ballads*, G.P. Putnam's Sons, 1975, pp. 286-287)

2. See (14) under POLEMIC.

3. Perhaps the very smallness of the scientific community [in Joseph Henry's time] made vulnerable to such CHARLATANS and hucksters of commercial science as the medicine men who laid the foundations of vast fortunes with their NOSTRUMS and remedies for aches and pains (often laced with forbidden alcohol) (S.D. Ripley, Comments on *The Papers of Joseph Henry, Vol. II*, edited by Nathan Reingold. *Smithsonian*, December 1975, p. 6)

4. See (3) under APHRODISIAC.

5. By traditional measure the 6,800,000 Americans who were unemployed last month should have been a big, painful political lump demanding the ministrations of Henry ("Scoop") Jackson or Hubert Horatio Humphrey. These two were ready, bags filled with NOSTRUMS

(H. Sidey, "The Presidency," *Time*, 6/21/76, p. 18)

NOVA (no' və) *noun*, *pl.*: **NOVAE** or **NOVAS** a star that suddenly becomes thousands to millions of times brighter than it was originally and then gradually fades over a period of months to years.

1. In a lovely, subtle sequence [in the film, *The Killing of a Chinese Bookie*], Cosmo [Vitelli], dressed in tuxedo and bearing orchids, goes in a limousine to pick up three of his girls at their homes for a night on the town. Through oblique but perfectly detailed glimpses we catch the true identity of these friendly young women whose marvelous bodies hide their humanity in a NOVA of sexuality. (J. Kroll, Review, *Newsweek*, 3/15/76, p. 89)

NUGATORY (nōō' gə-tôr' ē, -tôr' ē, nyōō'-) *adj.* trifling; of no real value; of no force or effect; futile; worthless; ineffective; insignificant.

1. On the one hand, to review TV programs is . . . to experience the self as NUGATORY. You might as well be a weatherman, reporting a day-late: a low-pressure WELTSCHMERZ moved last night across the Waltons, unbunching at least one Brady and leaving thousands of Efrem Zimbalists without an excuse; meanwhile, drought continues in the mid-Kojak. (J. Leonard, "Reflections on My Seven Years of Being at Swords' Points," *New York Times*, 4/17/77, Section 2, p. 27)

2. The rewards for running in this unique race [the Boston Marathon] are NUGATORY. The winner receives a laurel wreath; other top finishers get medals worth little more than the cost of the bus ride they have just avoided; all finishers are granted a bowl of generally inedible beef stew. (P. Stoler, Review of *The Boston Marathon*, a book by Joe Falls, *Time*, 4/18/77, p. 89)

3. In quest of it [the letter] I [Russel Wren] went into my back pocket. It was gone. I prowled the rest of my person unsuccessfully, then dashed into the front office and looked there, with results quite as NUGATORY. (Thomas Berger, *Who Is Teddy Villanova?*, Delacorte Press/Seymour Lawrence, 1977, p. 53)

4. The foregoing deliberations were rendered NUGATORY by Washburn's coming up from his naked squat with a fistful of gun, not money. (Thomas Berger, *Ibid.*, p. 152)

NUMINOUS (nōō'mə-nəs, nyōō'-) *adj.* of, pertaining to, or like a numen; divine; spiritual or supernatural; surpassing comprehension; mysterious; arousing elevated or deeply spiritual emotions.

NUMEN (nōō' min, nyōō'-) *noun*, *pl.*: **NUMINA** a deity, especially one presiding locally or believed to inhabit a particular object; a presiding spirit; guardian deity; an indwelling guiding force or spirit.

1. Norman Mailer, deploying those NUMINOUS phrases for which he is justly loved, talked in his piece on Miami about walking through the Democratic convention and suddenly realizing why it was an exhilarating experience: because he sensed only love among the delegates . . . . (W.F. Buckley Jr., *Execution Eve and Other Contemporary Ballads*, G.P. Putnam's Sons, 1975, p. 95)

2. And what about the "tongue speaking" that is often associated with healing? Psychologically it appears similar to chanting or primal screaming. Could its reappearance suggest that the overly moralized and cerebral forms of spirituality in the West are giving way to a direct encounter with the NUMINOUS as the core of faith? (H.G. Cox, Review of *All Things Are Possible*, by David Edwin Harrell Jr., *New York Times*, 2/22/76, Section 7, p. 6)

3. His daughter's portrait [of Samuel Sayles Sr., in the book, *Generations: A Memoir*, by Lucille Clifton] is of a man who worked in a steel mill for 30 years, who took pride in an orally transmitted history of strong female ancestors, who spent his life . . . leaning hard on two wives, several mistresses and daughters, and who is remembered by one of them at least not as callous and self-serving but as NUMINOUS with grace, generosity and power . . . . (R. Price, Review, *New York Times*, 3/14/76, Section 7, p. 7)

NUMISMATIC (nōō'miz-mat'ĭk, -mis-, nyōō'-)

adj. of, pertaining to, or consisting of coins, medals, or the like; pertaining to numismatics; of or having to do with currency.

NUMISMATICALLY *adv.*

NUMISMATICS or NUMISMATOLOGY *(the former is construed as singular)* the study or collecting of coins, medals, paper money, and the like.

NUMISMATIST or NUMISMATOLOGIST *noun* a specialist in numismatics; a person who collects numismatic items, especially coins.

1. Two robbers posing as police officers forced their way into the home of Abe Forman . . . where he operates a NUMISMATIC mail order business. They stole coins valued at $75,000 . . . (Anon., "From the police blotter," *New York Times,* 2/20/76, p. 35)

NYMPHET (nim′ fət, nim-fet′) *noun* a sexually attractive young girl; a pubescent girl, especially one who is sexually PRECOCIOUS; a young or little nymph.

NYMPHETIC *adj.*

1. Perhaps the most ambitious TV-as-art course is given by social scientist Arthur Asa Berger at San Francisco State . . . . Cher . . . poses no threat [to male egos]. "She is more of a NYMPHETTE* figure," Berger explains, "—a tease who raids the fridge and then goes to bed alone." (Anon., "Modern-Day Classics," *Newsweek,* 5/24/76, p. 100)

2. Who, for instance, had the inspiration to name the PROTOTYPICAL NYMPHET-woman "Gidget?" The name blends midget with gadget—the plaything never dangerous, fun, and unthreatening. This tootsie still fills the heads of men in their foolish fifties. (G. Wills, "Visions of playthings dance in our heads," *Philadelphia Inquirer,* 2/7/77, p. 9-A)

3. Whatever doubts critics may have had about the merits of a wryly elegant piece of GOTHIC trash called *Carrie,* they had none

*This spelling is not used in any dictionary of which I am aware.

about Sissy Spacek's BRAVURA performance in the title role—that of a naive NYMPHET who wreaks APOCALYPTIC revenge on the senior prom on the high-school classmates who have persecuted her. (C. Michener, M. Kasindorf, "Year of the Actress," *Newsweek,* 2/14/77, p. 63)

4. . . . I still think it was more fun covering [old] movies like *The African Queen, High Noon,* and *Gigi.* Back when a star was a star, not a nekkid NYMPHET on the half shell. (Virginia Fayette, "The Good Old Days," *Times Herald,* Norristown, Pa., 2/22/77, p. 9)

5. The grandfather [in the play, *The Transfiguration of Benno Blimpie,* by Albert Innaurato] will have Benno nowhere near him; he is far too busy seducing, or being seduced by, a NYMPHET bold and skilled enough to give Lolita cold chills; . . . however, the young slut puts a knife in the man before she has done with him. (W. Kerr, "When Did Sex Become The Villain?" *New York Times,* 3/27/77, Section 2, p. 3)

NYMPHOMANIA (nim′ fə-mā′ nē-ə) *noun* an abnormally strong and uncontrollable desire in women for sexual intercourse.*

NYMPHOMANIAC or NYMPHOMANIACAL *adj.*

NYMPHOMANIAC *noun.*

1. This picture [*The Royal Harlot*] is a true-life story of the Empress Valeria Messalina, third wife of the Emperor Claudius of ancient Rome and the most notorious adulteress and NYMPHOMANIAC in history. (I. Wallace, *The Fan Club,* Bantam Books, 1975, p. 17)

2. To appreciate both her historic accomplishments and her personality, it is imperative to disabuse oneself at once of the notion that Catherine [II, of Russia] was nothing but a royal NYMPHOMANIAC who indulged her insatiable sexual appetites to the total neglect of her oppressed subjects. (R. Pipes, Review of *Catherine the Great,* a book by Joan Haslip, *New York Times,* 3/27/77, Section 7, p. 4)

*In men, this condition is called SATYRIASIS (sat′ə-rī′ə-sis).

O

OBFUSCATE (ob′-fə-skāt′, ob-fus′ kāt) *verb* to confuse, muddle, perplex, bewilder, or stupefy; to cloud over, make obscure, or darken.

OBFUSCATION (ob′fus-kā′-shun) *noun*.

1. Someone [of the tourists to Russia] asks about Jewish emigration. "It is an issue that has been exaggerated in the American press," an [Russian] academician responds, and then proceeds to OBFUSCATE . . . . (R.W. Stock, *Group Tour of Russia: A Collective Triumph*, New York Times, 1/11/76, Section 10, p. 1)

2. "Do you know what 'Regor' is?" Gary [Lapolla] said. "It's Roger in a little-known tongue, the OBFUSCATED dialect of Serutan." (R. Kahn, *The Boys of Summer*, Harper and Row, 1971, p. 40)

3. Suppose, [the editor of the Wall Street Journal] mused, all the lawyers just stayed home . . . . "The wheels of commerce would turn more swiftly as people without training in OBFUSCATION and logic-chopping made clear and understandable agreements." (C. Black, "For the legal profession, a time of soul searching." *Philadelphia Inquirer*, 2/15/76, p. 7-I)

4. But most of the book [*The Bugles Blowing*, by N. Freeling] is an attempt to create a strange character; and a lot of it is, or at least seems to be, deliberately OBFUSCATORY . . . . Some will call this both philosophic and subtle. Others . . . will consider it a waste of time. (N. Callendar, Review, New York Times, 2/22/76, Section 7, p. 38)

5. His objective, he [Robert Sherrill, author of *The Last Kennedy: Edward M. Kennedy of Massachusetts, Before and after Chappaquiddick*] says, is not . . . "to convict Kennedy of anything in particular, but rather to present a case study of how a famous politician—by delays, by OBFUSCATION, by propaganda, by all sorts of tricks and wiles—can kill somebody under mysterious circumstances and still regularly receive more than 40 percent of the support in Presidential preference polls." (G. Hogdson, Review, *New York Times*, 4/18/76, Section 7, p. 3)

6. See (2) under CAPTIOUS.

7. See (4) under ASCETIC.

8. There was never a moment during his first news conference when Mr. Carter was not completely in control . . . . He indulged in a little sly humor but the point of an answer was never lost in rhetoric or deliberate OBFUSCATION. (R. Roth, "National media can do better," Sunday Bulletin, Philadelphia, Pa., 2/13/77, p. 7)

9. For if, as Voltaire said, men used speech to conceal their thoughts, they often used jargon and OBFUSCATION to conceal their lack of thought, or their purposes . . . . Yet if government is to be close to the people, . . . it has to speak to them in a civil tongue, in language they understand. (Anon., "Challenge of Plain English" [Editorial], *Philadelphia Inquirer*, 2/7/77, p. 8–A)

OBITER DICTUM (ob′ i-tər dik′təm) *noun, pl.:* **OBITER DICTA** an incidental or passing remark, opinion, etc.; an incidental or supplementary opinion by a judge, not essential to a decision and therefore not binding.

1. There are various bibliographies, many specialized works (especially in the Sherlock Holmes area), such OBITER DICTA as Jacques

Barzun's *A Catalogue of Crime*, and handbooks like *The Mystery Writer's Art*, edited by Francis M. Nevins, Jr. But it has remained for the [Chris] Steinbrunner-[Otto] Penzler team to give us a real encyclopedia [*Encyclopedia of Mystery and Detection*] . . . . (N. Callendar, Review, *New York Times*, 4/25/76, Section 7, p. 8)

2. The rambling nature of [James A.] Michener's essay—chapter headings [of *Sports in America*] range from *The Media* to *Government Control*—allows him plenty of room for OBITER DICTA. They are all too predictable. Solemnly he warns against "the jungle of juvenile sports competition." (M. Maddocks, Review, *Time*, 6/28/76, p. 63)

OBLOQUY (ob'lə-kwē) *noun, pl.:* -QUIES (-kwēz) ill repute, disgrace, or infamy resulting from public censure; verbal abuse or condemnation by the general public; censure; VITUPERATION; revilement; reproach; blame; CALUMNY; aspersion.

1. If the public is persuaded that the Committee for the Reelection of the President was in fact an adjunct of the White House, then any crime or abomination committed by the Reelection Committee contributes to the OBLOQUY in which . . . the investigating staff desires to suspend the Nixon administration. (W.F. Buckley Jr., *Execution Eve and Other Contemporary Ballads*, G.P. Putnam's Sons, 1975, pp. 126-127)

2. . . . he [Bertrand Russell] advocated such subversive notions as birth control and trial marriages. For their candor and enlightenment, these ideas brought down on Russell a generous amount of OBLOQUY from the aggrieved guardians of church and state. (M. Rosenthal, Review of *The Life of Bertrand Russell*, by Ronald W. Clark; *My Father Bertrand Russell*, by Katherine Tait; and *The Tamarind Tree*, by Dora Russell, *New York Times*, 2/15/76, Section 7, p. 3)

3. I have urged a full pardon for Mrs. d'Aquino [so-called "Tokyo Rose"], who has suffered almost 30 years of OBLOQUY and shame for crimes she did not commit. (S.I. Hayakawa, "Woman Labeled 'Tokyo Rose' Deserves Pardon," *Saturday Oklahoman & Times*, 4/3/76, p. 8)

4. See (3) under PRETENTIOUS.

5. In picking Bob Dole, 53, Ford signed on the most accomplished gunslinger in the party, a man who makes his points not with OBLOQUY or the cement fist or leaden tongue of a Spiro Agnew, but with an ACERBIC wit that often leaves everyone but the victim laughing. (Anon., "Has Gun Will Travel," *Time*, 8/30/76, p. 24)

OBMUTESCENCE (ŏb-myōō-tes'əns) *noun* loss of speech; keeping of silence.

OBMUTESCENT *adj.* becoming or remaining silent.

1. Meanwhile, Mr. Nixon's critics, always willing to believe the worst about him, took the curdling SANCTIMONY of his speech as a personal challenge to uproot any SCINTILLA of evidence linking the President to Watergate . . . . The OBMUTESCENCE of the President in the past fortnight suggests that he knows now the grave mistake he made on the evening of April 30. (W.F. Buckley Jr., *Execution Eve and Other Contemporary Ballads*, G.P. Putnam's Sons, 1975, p. 127)

OBSEQUY (ob'sə-kwē) *noun, pl.:* OBSEQUIES (usually used in the plural) a funeral rite or ceremony.

1. According to the *New York Times*, the funeral of Albert Anastasia (1903-57) was sparsely attended. Even his priest brother failed to witness the burial, although he did say prayers over the empty grave prior to the final OBSEQUIES. Today Albert's small, flat stone, crowded into an unclassy corner of Green-Wood Cemetery in Brooklyn, is overgrown with grass. (P. Nobile, "The Tombs of the Dons," *New York*, 11/28/77, p. 53)

OCHLOCRACY (ok-lok'rə-sē) *noun* government by the mob; mob rule.

OCHLOCRAT *noun.*

OCHLOCRATIC *adj.*

1. She [Queen Caroline] found it increasingly easy to achieve informality—to the dismay of—her impossibly PUNCTILIOUS husband who desired OCHLOCRACY abroad but, at home, to be paid homage by the baboons of the zoo.

(W.F. Buckley Jr., *Saving the Queen*, Doubleday, 1976, p. 130)

ODALISQUE (ōd'əlisk) or **ODALISK** *noun* a female slave or concubine in a harem, especially in that of the Sultan of Turkey; a painting of a reclining odalisque in the style of Matisse and others.

1. His [E.J. Bellocq's] PANACHE was enhanced by the bravado of the girls themselves [who posed for his camera] and the culture [of the Storyville section of New Orleans] that nourished them. They are consummate actresses, skilled at conveying precisely the secrets of their varied appeal, whether it is the cool stolidity of the demi-slipped lady in black stockings, the loose-limbed good humor of the striped-stocking lass with a glass, or the seductive LANGUOR of a naked ODALISQUE—"low art" mimicking the high art of Goya and Manet. (D. Davis, "Bellocq's Girls," *Newsweek*, 3/14/77, p. 89)

2. Even Rudolph's occasional FIN DE SIÈCLE over-ripeness [in the film, *Welcome to L.A.*] (a nude [Geraldine] Chapman (sic) presents herself to [Keith] Carradine in front of a Matisse ODALISQUE) are (sic) the excesses of a young talent making an extraordinary debut. (J. Kroll, Review, *Newsweek*, 2/21/77, p. 88)

ODIOUS (ō'dē-əs) *adj.* deserving or causing hatred; hateful; repugnant; detestable; highly offensive; disgusting; abominable; objectionable; despicable; EXECRABLE; loathsome; repellent; repulsive.

ODIOUSLY *adv.*

ODIOUSNESS *noun.*

ODIUM *noun* hatred, especially of a person or thing regarded as loathsome or contemptible; the state or fact of being hated; the disgrace brought on—by hateful action; OPPROBRIUM; abhorrence.

1. *Cockpit* [a book by Jerzy Kosinski] is a reel of such willed nastiness as to constitute perhaps the most coldly ODIOUS reading I have ever been subjected to. (C. Ricks, Review, *New York Review of Books*, 11/27/75, p. 44)

2. After all, in the Arlington Heights [a Chicago suburb] case the court of appeals tried to impose on a *town* the sort of "affirmative action" that is ODIOUS when imposed on employers whose payrolls do not have a government-approved racial or sexual composition. That is, the court said, in effect, that Arlington Heights' traditional zoning standards must be changed because they help produce a community with the "wrong" racial statistics. [This decision later was overturned by the U.S. Supreme Court]. (G.F. Will, "Common Sense on Race," *Newsweek*, 1/24/77, p. 80)

3. However ODIOUS and universally hated she was, Chiang Ching [Mao Tse-tung's wife] enjoyed immunity as long as Mao was alive precisely because it would have been impossible to denounce her without attacking her husband . . . . Chinese citizens . . . must be wondering how Mao could ever have chosen such a companion. (S. Leys, *Newsweek* International Service, "Secretly the Chinese people always liked Teng," *Philadelphia Inquirer*, 1/23/77, p. 4-F)

OENOLOGY or **ENOLOGY** (ē-nol' ə-jē) *noun* the science or study of wines, winemaking, and viniculture (cultivation of wine grapes).

OENOLOGIST or ENOLOGIST *noun.*

OENOLOGICAL or ENOLOGICAL *adj.*

1. [Barbara] Walters says her most frequent escorts are White House economics adviser Alan Greenspan, management consultant John Diebold and ENOLOGIST Alexis Lichine. (H.F.Waters, "How Barbara Tuned Up," *Newsweek*, 10/11/76, p. 70)

2. Yes, [Chateau] Pétrus has its own staff OENOLOGIST; but [Chateau] La Conseillante's vinification is supervised by Prof. Emile Peynaud, the most famous and successful OENOLOGIST in all Bordeaux. (R. Daley, "Great Bargains of Bordeaux," *New York Times*, 3/27/77, Section 6, p. 114)

OENOPHILIST (ē-nof'ə-list) or **OENOPHILE** (ē'nə-fīl) *noun* a lover of wines.

1. Not all Texas OENOPHILES have separate cellars; some simply keep their cherished bottles around the house. These AFICIONADOS split into two camps—those who pamper their

wines by turning up the air conditioning and those who don't. Bill English, a robust Austin restauranteur . . . sleeps under blankets year-round because "I share the bedroom with part of my personal wine collection." (Sharon Churcher, "Grape Nuts," *Texas Monthly*, January 1977, p. 66)

2. The choice of wines (there are only four) includes a potable Blanc de Blanc ($6) which went pretty well with the fish. This [The Mosholu restaurant in Penn's Landing] is no place for an OENOPHILE. (B. Collins, "Mood is great, food ordinary on ship converted to restaurant," *Philadelphia Inquirer*, 12/24/76, p. 4-B)

3. Blackford [Oakes] wondered where the OENOPHILES' journals were [in Ellison's apartment] and thought Ellison must be a real sport to pass himself off as a winetaster, working in the sunkissed vineyards of Washington, D.C. (W.F. Buckley Jr., *Saving the Queen*, Doubleday, 1976, p. 29)

OLEAGINOUS (ō'lē-aj'ə-nəs) *noun* having the nature or quality of oil; containing or producing oil; greasy; oily; oily in manner; UNCTUOUS.

OLEAGINOUSLY *adv.*

OLEAGINOUSNESS *noun*.

1. Is Senator Everett Dirksen unclean? Does he fight unethically? I am not aware that he does, or even that his opponent Mr. Stengel ever charged him with doing so. It is not relevant that *Time* magazine once called Dirksen OLEAGINOUS. The question is, is he unclean? By implication the Appeal [sponsored by Elmer Davis and Archibald MacLeish] says that he is. Where is the proof? (W.F. Buckley Jr., *Up From Liberalism*, Arlington House, 2nd Printing 1968, p. 78)

2. [Ronald] Beard saw a sunset-glow blow-up of Leonardo da Vinci's "Last Supper" and heard an OLEAGINOUS recorded commentary. (A. Burgess, *Beard's Roman Women*, McGraw-Hill, 1976, p. 19)

3. Nevertheless, his [Bakewell's] fist, having reached the limit of its upward travel, came forward. The movement, however, was as yet OLEAGINOUSLY slow . . . (Thomas Berger, *Who Is Teddy Villanova?*, Delacorte Press/Seymour

Lawrence, 1977, p. 8)

OLIGARCHY (ol'ə-gär'kē) *noun* a form of government in which the power is vested in a few persons; a state or organization so ruled; the persons or class so ruling.

OLIGARCHIC or OLIGARCHICAL or OLIGARCHAL *adj.*

OLIGARCHICALLY *adv.*

OLIGARCH *noun* one of the rulers in an oligarchy.

1. Yet, ironically, like the American on which they patterned their new nation, Liberia's own system was also flawed by inequality. For the minority whose ancestors were immigrants from America (about 50,000 today) made up a powerful (and often corrupt) OLIGARCHY, while the INDIGENOUS majority who make up more than 97 percent of the population, tribal peoples like the Kpelle, Gola, Kru and Mandingo (about 1.6 million), remained voiceless and exploited. (P. Boorstin, "Liberia's fading echoes of the Old American South," *Smithsonian*, March 1976, p. 83)

2. To the TV industry, the four-month-old soap spoof [*Mary Hartman, Mary Hartman*] represents a radical departure in form—and a potential threat to the networks' OLIGARCHIC dominance of entertainment programming. After the show was spurned by all three networks, the indomitable [Norman] Lear personally peddled it to local stations on a syndication basis. (H.F. Waters, M. Kasindorf, "The Mary Hartman Craze," *Newsweek*, 5/3/76, p. 54)

3. See (3) under BUMPTIOUS.

4. "All government is rule by the few over the many [according to Robert Strausz-Hupé]. That, in an OLIGARCHY, the ruling class is more exclusive than it really is, this is aristocratic PRETENTIOUSNESS. That, in a democracy, the ruling class is more open than it really is, this is egalitarian cant. Both conceits are necessary for the welfare of the respective establishments." (G.F. Will, "Carter and 'The People'," *Newsweek*, 10/18/76, p. 118)

OMNIPOTENT (om-nip' ə-tent) *adj.* almighty, or infinite in power, as God or a deity; having very great or unlimited authority or power; all-powerful.

OMNIPOTENTLY *adv.*

OMNIPOTENCE *noun.*

1. See (1) under OMNISCIENT.

2. See (1) under SAPIENTIAL.

3. . . . he [Spiro Agnew] shares at least one dangerous oddity with many of those on the left he most despises: a belief in the OMNIPOTENCE of this country and the aimless suggestibility and emptiness of everyone else. (Meg Greenfield, "Agnew's Revenge," *Newsweek*, 5/24/76, p. 104)

4. See (2) under AUTO-DA-FÉ.

5. In a nation where 70 per cent of the economy depends on agriculture—. . . where hydroelectric power for industry also depends on rainfall—the monsoon is the mysterious, confounding, OMNIPOTENT phenomenon that preoccupies India. (Sharon Rosenhause, of *Los Angeles Times*, " 'May rains come in season; the earth springs to life,' " *Norman* [Okla.] *Transcript*, 7/7/76, p. 19)

OMNIPRESENT (om' ne-prəz' ənt) *adj.* present everywhere at the same time.

OMNIPRESENCE *noun.*

1. See (1) under SHTETL.

2. You know *Troilus* and *Cressida* . . . . Disillusioned to the outer edges of despair, bitter about war and positively livid on the subject of an OMNIPRESENT lechery, rudely dismissive of romance, cynical to the seething core. (W. Kerr, Review of Yale Repertory Theater's production of Shakespeare's *Troilus and Cressida*, *New York Times*, 4/18/76, Section 2, p. 5)

OMNISCIENT (om-nish' ənt) *adj.* having complete or infinite knowledge, awareness, or understanding; knowing or perceiving all things; having extensive knowledge.

OMNISCIENCE *noun.*

OMNISCIENTLY *adv.*

1. The United States, as events in Vietnam and Cuba and Angola have painfully reminded us, is not OMNIPOTENT, much less OMNISCIENT. (Anon., "Issues for '76" [Editorial], *New York Times*, 3/28/76, Section 4, p. 14)

2. Leopold's teaching and guidance were a SINE QUA NON, for without the father's long and OMNISCIENT supervision, the son [Wolfgang Mozart] would doubtless have become a different composer from the one the world adulates. (R. Craft, "A Prodigy of Nature," *New York Review of Books*, 12/11/75, p. 9)

3. The most common journalistic complaint, aside from the question of taste, was the style of the book [*The Final Days*, by Bob Woodward and Carl Bernstein]. Its form is OMNISCIENT narrative; it is written largely without attributions, and is studded with direct quotations from private conversations and with characterizations of the thoughts and emotions of the participants. (Anon., "The Furor Over The Book," *Newsweek*, 4/12/76, p. 33-34)

4. See (4) under PRETERNATURAL.

5. See (7) under GENRE.

6. See (1) under DIVOT.

OMNIVOROUS (om-niv'ər-əs) *adj.* eating all kinds of foods indiscriminately; eating both animal and plant foods; taking in everything indiscriminately, as with the mind.

OMNIVOROUSLY *adv.*

OMNIVOROUSNESS *noun.*

OMNIVORE *noun* a person or animal that is omnivorous.

1. Fort Osage would have been a lively place even without its CHATELAINE . . . . The boys [Jacques and Marcel Pasquinel] were delighted with the varied activity . . . . Even Marcel, only five at the time, watched OMNIVOROUSLY as mule trains and river boats unloaded. (J. A. Michener, *Centennial*, Fawcett, 1975, p. 255)

2. See (1) under CHARYBDIS.

ONANISM (ō'nə-niz'əm) *noun* withdrawal of the penis in sexual intercourse so that ejaculation takes place outside the vagina; masturbation [after *Onan*, son of Judah (Genesis 38:9)]

ONANIST *noun.*

ONANISTIC *adj.*

1. This [Federico Fellini's film, *Casanova*] is an inbred, studio-made work of a fevered imagination in which Casanova's conquests are perceived as ONANISTIC symbols to a point where he finally ends up in bed with a MANNEQUIN. (D. Ryan, "There's no joy in Fellini's view of 'Casanova,' " *Philadelphia Inquirer*, 3/9/77, p. 13-B)

2. The rest of the incident [in *Falconer*, a book by John Cheever] is largely prison incident—the killing of cats, the bickering and petty blackmails, the ONANISM, the homosexual attachments and jealousies, the drafting of appeals and the picking of guitars . . . . (Joan Didion, Review, *New York Times*, 3/6/76, Section 7, p. 24)

ONOMASTICS (onə'·mas'tiks) *noun, plural* (construed as *singular*) or **ONOMATOLOGY** the study of the origin, form, meaning, and use of names, especially proper names.

ONOMASTIC or ONOMATOLOGIC or ONOMATOLOGICAL *adj.* of or having to do with a name or names.

ONOMATOLOGIST *noun.*

1. "You're a student? Who are these? [asked Ronald Beard of the girls who had invaded his apartment] . . . . "I'm not sure that we need ONOMASTICS either, but I'm Arlene and that's Donatella . . . and that's Maria and that's Paola." (A. Burgess, *Beard's Roman Women*, McGraw-Hill, 1976, p. 108)

ONOMATOPOEIA (on'ə-mat'ə-pē-ə, -mät'-) *noun* the formation of a word by imitating the natural sound associated with the object or action involved; echoism (example: *buzz*); the use of such words for poetic or rhetorical effect.

ONOMATOPOEIC or ONOMATOPOETIC *adj.*

ONOMATOPOEICALLY or ONOMATOPOETICALLY *adv.*

1. "ONOMATOPOEIA" is a great word in itself. It sounds like the opening rhythms of a spirited Croatian folk dance . . . . But it also describes a class of words . . . that imitate the sounds of the things they describe. How about "SUSURROUS" to describe the whispering of the wind in the trees? Or how about "TINTINNABULATION,"

an old word given broad currency by Edgar Allen Poe when he used it to describe the sound of bells? (B. Wiemer, Newsday Service, "The Rubric of Words," *Philadelphia Inquirer*, 3/27/77, p. 3-L)

2. A great, rushing, rhythmic, ONOMATOPOEIC piece of machinery, the roller coaster distills our emotions and describes our physical boundaries. The achingly slow climb to the top, the high-speed plunge to the bottom . . . . (B.J. Phillips, "Those Roller Rides in the Sky," *Time*, 7/4/77, p. 36)

ONTOLOGY (on-tol'ə-jē) *noun* the branch of metaphysics that studies the nature of existence, reality, or ultimate substance; (loosely) metaphysics.

ONTOLOGICAL *adj.*

ONTOLOGICALLY *adv.*

ONTOLOGIST *noun.*

1. Sculpture is, after all, the art of making an object, and it was the very ONTOLOGY of the object that [Alberto] Giacometti had come to question. He felt obliged to begin again from the beginning . . . . (H. Kramer—Review of Alberto Giacometti's memorial exhibit at Sidney Janis Gallery, *New York Times*, 1/18/76, Section 2, p. 29)

2. The persistent misuse of the word democracy reflects either an ignorance of its ONTOLOGICAL emptiness; or . . . the pathetic attempt to endow it with substantive meaning. (W.F. Buckley Jr., *Up From Liberalism*, Arlington House, 2nd Printing 1968, p. 146)

3. His [Richard Foreman's] name for his own productions, the ONTOLOGICAL—Hysteric Theatre, is perfect for the divided Brecht of *Threepenny Opera* . . . . Stanley Silverman's musical direction [of *The Threepenny Opera*, at Lincoln Center] makes you feel the ONTOLOGICAL hysteria that drove the Berliners of the '20's to dance the Charleston while their society was sliding toward the GÖTTERDÄMMERUNG of Hitler. (J. Kroll, Review, *Newsweek*, 5/17/76, p. 96)

4. [Peter] Singer [author of *Animal Liberation*] rejects an ONTOLOGY of rights which would have us "get" them from some source and, having gotten them, "possess"

them, as we do a book or car. (C.G. Luck-hardt, Review, New York Times, 1/4/76, Section 7, p. 5)

5. See (4) under LAPIDARY.

6. In the seventies the new conformists . . . have chosen relativism as the best game in town . . . . They are the real flower children of the seventies; their ONTOLOGY is clear and crisp: "Yoko and me, that's reality." . . . . They've chosen cynical relativism as the shrewdest strategy for operating within our premised economy . . . . What they will lack is the dimension of outrage, the capacity to thunder "No" when some injustice has been wrought on something other than their own self-interests. (M. Kaplan, "The Ideologies of Tough Times,' " Change, August 1976, pp. 29-30)

OPÉRA BOUFFE (op' ər-ə boof) or **BOUFFE** *noun, pl.:* OPÉRA BOUFFES or OPERAS BOUFFE a comic, usually farcical, opera.

1. . . . said Blackford [Oakes] with a feigned air of OPÉRA BOUFFE secretiveness, as if he were privy to the plays to be used in the fall's offensive by the Yale football team . . . . (W. F. Buckley Jr., Saving the Queen, Doubleday, 1976, p. 171)

2. See (2) under SANS-CULOTTE.

OPHIDIAN (ō-fid′ē-ən) *adj.* pertaining to or like a snake.

OPHIDIAN *noun* a snake or serpent.

OPHIOLOGY *noun* the study of snakes.

1. Underneath, the gray sea took on a pale OPHIDIAN flecking without shine. (W.F. Buckley Jr., Execution Eve and Other Contemporary Ballads, G.P. Putnam's Sons, 1975, p. 251)

OPPROBRIUM (ə-prō′ brē-əm) *noun* the disgrace, infamy, or reproach incurred by conduct considered outrageously or grossly shameful; infamy; dishonor; reproachful contempt for something regarded as inferior.

OPPROBRIOUS *adj.*

OPPROBRIOUSLY *adv.*

1. Mr. Ford has contrived, moreover, the

strategic myth that the real problem is "the irresponsible and dangerous exposure of our nation's intelligence secrets." Its purpose is to divert OPPROBRIUM from the culprits to their accusers, and the culmination of the strategy is in the KAFKAESQUE "reforms" [proposed by Ford] that would largely prevent further disclosures while doing little about what was actually exposed—not vital secrets but the blunders, abuses and crimes of the C.I.A. (T. Wicker, "Protecting the Culprits, Punishing the Accusers," New York Times, 2/22/76, Section 4, p. 13)

2. Yes, there are circumstances when the minority can lay claim to preeminent political authority, without bringing down upon its head the moral OPPROBRIUM of just men. (W.F. Buckley Jr., Up From Liberalism, Arlington House, 2nd Printing 1968, p. 157)

3. A compulsive planner—and a congenital optimist—Carter is already well along in his plans to take over the White House, risking the OPPROBRIUM of being considered too cocky in order to be sure he is ready. (Anon., "Campaign Kickoff," Time, 9/13/76, p. 18)

ORDONNANCE (ôr′ dᵊ-nəns) *noun* the proper or orderly arrangement or disposition of parts, as of a building, a picture, or a literary composition; an ordinance, law, or decree.

1. But [Lamar] Herrin [in his book, The Rio Loja Ringmaster] seems to wish to insist, sometimes TAUTOLOGICALLY and sometimes inventively, that fiction like baseball is a game, and arbitrary, with artificial references and topographies and ORDONNANCES and chronologies. (G. Wolff, Review, New York Times, 2/27/77, Section 7, pp. 26-27)

ORGIASTIC (ôr′jē-as′tik) *adj.* of, pertaining to, resembling, or having the nature of an orgy; tending to arouse or excite unrestrained emotion.

ORGY (ôr′jē) *noun* wild, drunken, riotous, or LICENTIOUS festivity or revelry; debauchery; a party characterized by public promiscuous sexual intercourse; any proceedings marked by unbridled indulgence of passions; unrestrained indulgence in any activity.

1. "The battle of books has broken out again,"

rejoiced Marshall McLuhan 30 years ago in a typically ORGIASTIC essay on philosophies of higher learning. "The SPLENETIC interchanges of educators and scholars . . . are shrieking across the no man's land of the curriculum." (R.J. Margolis, "Let's Hear It for Moveable Type" [Editorial], *Change*, April 1975, p. 5)

2. See (2) under SADOMASOCHISTIC.

3. See (3) under SATURNALIA.

ORMOLU (ôr′mə-lōō′) *noun* an imitation gold made of an alloy of copper and tin, used in making ornaments, moldings, cheap jewelry, etc.; gilded metal, especially brass or bronze; imitation gold leaf.

1. While feather headdresses and CINCTURES indicated the alien and exotic characteristics of the Indian, . . . the nakedness of the rest of their bodies permitted their assimilation into the classically based European [art] tradition . . . feathered Indians quickly took their places alongside CHINOISERIE MANDARINS, delicately modeled or painted on porcelain, cast in OR-MOLU or chased in silver, peeping out of ROCOCO scrolls on gilt and enameled snuff boxes. (H. Honour, "America as seen in the fanciful vision of Europe," *Smithsonian*, February 1976, p. 56)

OROGENY (ō-roj′ənē, ô-roj′-) or **OROG-ENESIS** *noun* the process of mountain formation, especially by folding and faulting of the earth's crust.

OROGENIC or OROGENETIC *adj.*

OROGRAPHY *noun* the branch of physical geography dealing with mountains.

OROGRAPHIC or OROGRAPHICAL *adj.*

OROGRAPHICALLY *adv.*

1. As to my dating of classical geological periods, I have followed the most conservative . . . dates . . . . There are discrepancies. Ogden Tweto, the foremost expert on the Laramide OROGENY, believes the New Rockies began to emerge 72,000,000 years ago, with the process terminating about 43,000,000 years ago. Others have preferred beginning dates like 80,000,000 to 65,000,000 and terminal dates as late as 39,000,000. (J.A. Michener, *Centennial*, Fawcett, 1975, p. 67)

OROTUND (ôr′ə-tund′, ôr′-) *adj.* (of the voice or speech) strong, full, resonant, deep, and clear; (of a speaking or writing style) pompous or bombastic.

OROTUNDITY *noun.*

1. His [the hero's, in *Saving the Queen*, a book by William F. Buckley Jr.] mentors in the Company [CIA], who bear names like Anthony Trust, Singer Callaway, King Harman and Jonathan Hanks, also list toward the ORO-TUND in their conversation. (W. Goodman, Review, *New York Times*, 1/11/76, Section 7, p. 8)

2. Churchill was not, as [Hanson W.] Baldwin suggests [in his book, *The Crucial Years 1939-1941*], a Victorian. That imperialist braggadocio, that brandy-swilling, cigar-smoking insolence, that OROTUND wit dated from the days, not of the great Queen, but of good King Edward. (M. Howard, Review, *New York Times*, 2/8/76, Section 7, p. 7)

3. Whatever her subject . . . [Adrienne] Monnier wrote in a vivacious, intimate voice, at once OROTUND (in other words, typically French) and conversational . . . . (J. Atlas, Review of *The Very Rich Hours of Adrienne Monnier*, translated, with an Introduction and Commentaries, by Richard McDougall, *New York Times*, 7/11/76, Section 7, p. 14)

4. It is strange that there is little pithy about this book [*O America*, by Luigi Barzini] which, though it drips down the throat gracefully like white wine dispensed from an invalid-feeder, glories in a middle-aged OROTUNDITY that is at variance with the sharp cinematic memories of bar fights, necking and viewing gangster corpses in the line of duty. (A. Burgess, Review, *New York Times*, 4/3/77, Section 7, p. 9)

5. Johnny [Liebman] got OROTUND when he was tight, and Blackford [Oakes] smiled at the familiar chiding . . . . (W.F. Buckley Jr., *Saving the Queen*, Doubleday, 1976, p. 7)

ORTHOGRAPHY (ôr-thŏg′ rə-fē) *noun* spelling in accord with accepted usage; spelling as a subject of study.

ORTHOGRAPHER *noun* a person skilled or expert in spelling.

ORTHOGRAPHIC or **ORTHOGRAPHICAL** *noun.*

ORTHOGRAPHICALLY *adv.*

1. I [Russel Wren] used the stairs to inject myself headlong into the fourth floor, of which the rearmore door bore the rubric B and beneath it, from a runny HELIOTROPE stencil: FUN THINGS INC, so often mischievously represented on the lobby directory board . . . as "Fucing," and pronounced by Sam Polidor according to its altered ORTHOGRAPHY. (Thomas Berger, *Who Is Teddy Villanova?*, Delacorte Press/Seymour Lawrence, 1977, p. 225)

OSCULATION (os'kyə-la' shən) *noun* the act of kissing; a kiss; the contact between two osculating curves or the like.

OSCULATE *verb* to kiss or embrace; to touch closely; to make close contact with; to have characteristics in common; (of a curve) to touch another curve or another part of the same curve so as to have the same tangent and curvature at the point of contact.

OSCULATORY *adj.*

OSCULAR *adj.* of or pertaining to the mouth or kissing.

OSCULANT *adj.* sharing certain characteristics in common; adhering closely; embracing.

1. [Mel] Torme, known in his heyday as "The Velvet Fog," managed the whole OSCULATION [with Chita Rivera] without a tremor of the hand or spilling a drop [of his drink]. (Anon., "Star Tracks: The Velvet Fog Kisses," *People*, 5/24/76, p. 33)

2. What is more timely for St. Valentine's Day than *The Art of Kissing*, a Doubleday reprint of a 1936 how-to treatise? Contains 45 illustrations. Price: $1.95. Evidently Doubleday doesn't think too much of postgraduate OSCULATORY instruction. (B.A. Bergman, "Cover to Cover," *Sunday Bulletin*, Philadelphia, Pa., 2/13/77, p. 16)

3. Peggy [Tumulty] had put pencil to paper as ordered. Now she raised the former, put the eraser to her lips and withdrew it with an OSCULATORY sound . . . . "If a Teddy Villanova ever played for Brooklyn, I never heard of him" [said she]. (Thomas Berger, *Who Is Ted-*

dy Villanova?, Delacorte Press/Seymour Lawrence, 1977, p. 28)

OSSIFY (os'ə-fī') *verb* to convert into or to harden or become like bone; to become rigid or inflexible in practice, outlook, habits, attitudes, etc.

OSSIFICATION *noun.*

1. New forms of business organization will have to be found, probably changing big corporations into confederations of entrepreneurs. The firms and countries that will go bust in these circumstances are those that try to replace HIERARCHICAL corporations by even more OSSIFIED forms of HIERARCHY—say, by deciding that you mustn't have a boss trying to arrange what free men do with their imaginations, but can have a trade union committee doing so instead. (N. MacRae, "United States can keep growing—and lead—if it wishes," *Smithsonian*, July 1976, p. 39)

2. Many elements contributed to the American saga of economic progress. Our vast continent teemed with unexpected natural resources; our immigrants (apart from our shame of slavery) came as volunteers driven by venturesomeness and ambition; our social environment was not OSSIFIED by feudal HIERARCHIES or medieval traditions. We were a wonderful laboratory for an experiment with [Adam] Smith's free-market system. (A.M. Okun, "Equal Rights but Unequal Incomes," *New York Times*, 7/4/76, Section 6, p. 102)

3. Catherine's doctor father [in *The Heiress*, a play by Ruth and Augustus Goetz] . . . is a SARDONIC man who resents his daughter bitterly. To him, Catherine is an aching reminder that his wife died in giving birth to her. He violently opposes the match [with Townsend]. Having diagnosed Townsend's intentions, the doctor is quite unconcerned about the condition of Catherine's OSSIFYING heart. (T.E. Kalem, Review, *Time*, 5/3/76, p. 76)

OSTRACISM (os'trə-siz'əm) *noun* the act of ostracizing; the fact or state of being ostracized; (in ancient Greece) temporary banishment of a citizen, decided by popular vote; exile.

OSTRACIZE *verb* to exclude or bar, by

general consent, from a group, society, privileges, etc.; to banish (a person) from his native country; expatriate; exile.

OSTRACIZABLE   adj.

OSTRACIZER   noun.

1. See (2) under WASTREL.

2. . . . the mid-19th century . . . scientists were seeking to legitimize their profession and to establish institutions politically structured to bring about the OSTRACISM of dabblers and quacks. (R.C. Post, Review of *The Formation of the American Scientific Community: The American Association for the Advancement of Science, 1848-1860*, by Sally Gregory Kohlstedt, *Smithsonian*, May 1976, p. 108)

3. Coventry is a town in England where, long ago, defeated soldiers were sent for penitence; since then "go to Coventry" has throughout the English-speaking world meant OSTRACISM. The phrase is now quaint and obsolete. (T. Tiede, of NEA, "Union hierarchy imitates organized crime," *Norman* [Okla.] *Transcript*, 7/9/76, p.6)

4. They . . . encouraged her [the Princess of Jaipur] to abandon PURDAH, that social and sexual OSTRACISM endured by even the most upper class of Indian women. (Caroline Seebohm, Review of *A Princess Remembers*, by Gayatri Devi of Jaipur and Santha Rama Rau, *New York Times*, 3/13/77, Section 7, p. 5)

OTIOSE (ō'shē-ōs , ō'tē-ōs) adj.   leisured; idle; indolent; slothful; ineffective; futile; sterile; pointless; unnecessary; superfluous; useless.

OTIOSELY   adv.

OTIOSITY or OTIOSENESS   noun.

1. About your un-negotiable Style Book UKASE: Fowler says the comma before the "and" [in a series of terms] is considered OTIOSE (his word). Too many sections. (W.F. Buckley Jr., *Execution Eve and Other Contemporary Ballads*, G.P. Putnam's Sons, 1975, p. 352)

OUBLIETTE (ōō'blē-ət') noun   a concealed dungeon, as in certain old castles, having a trap door in the ceiling as its only opening.

1. The leftists also gleefully watched as Giscard's customary supporters attacked the new tax idea for precisely the opposite reason: that it was too radical. Proclaimed Gaullist Deputy Hector Rolland: "This bill should be thrown into the OUBLIETTE, from which it should never have escaped. (Anon., "The Revolt Over Reform," *Time*, 6/21/76, p. 32)

OUROBOROS* (ŏr'ə-bôr'əs) noun   an ancient mythical serpent, symbol of the GNOSTICS and the alchemists, represented as continuously devouring its own tail and being reborn from itself, thereby symbolizing the unity and indestructibility of both material and spiritual things: things never disappear but only change form in a perpetual cycle of destruction and recreation.

1. In his early thirties, [Dennis R.] Holloway [University of Minnesota architecture professor] is a conventionally dressed dynamo of energy and imagination. His scheme [which embodies a solar-heated house] is called Project OUROBOROS, after a mythical serpent that lived by devouring its own waste and feces. (S. Love, "House designed with nature: Their future is at hand," *Smithsonian*, December 1975, p. 47)

OUTRÉ (ōō-tRā') adj.   passing the bounds of what is usual or considered acceptable, decent, or proper; exaggerated; eccentric; bizarre.

1. On a first reading, *Dream Children* [a book by Gail Godwin] arrests and engrosses. But on closer inspection, the reader recognizes that the deepest and most consistent response the writer elicits is no more than a sauna-like self-pity, and that the specific effects are rather frequently too OUTRÉ for genuine resonance. (Jane Larkin Crain, Review, *New York Times*, 2/22/76, Section 7, p. 22)

OVERWEENING (ō'vər-wē'nĭng) adj.   (of a person) conceited, overconfident, presumptuous; (of opinions, PRETENSIONS, characteris-

---

*As a matter of ESOTERIC interest, OUROBOROS also is the name of a highly informal society of academic chemists in New England, of which the author of this book is a member.

tics, etc.) exaggerated, excessive, arrogant.

OVERWEENINGLY *adv.*

1. See (1) under KEEN.

2. . . . the people may have some reason for encouragement in the war against foolish and needless regulation . . . . In arriving at the Great Bat Agreement the CPSC [Consumer Products Safety Commission] swung the whole might . . . of the United States government against a danger to Western civilization . . . [caused] when the striking component of an aluminum baseball bat accidentally separates itself during a swinging motion . . . Owners of the faulty bats may now obtain new . . . kits [for attachment to the bats]. [Rep. Del] Clawson and [Sen. Paul] Laxalt are not concerned with aluminum bats, as such, but with the broad picture of excessive or OVERWEENING regulation of our lives. (J.J. Kilpatrick, "Red Tape War Gains Reported," *Daily Oklahoman*, Okla. City, 4/1/76, p. 10)

3. In season and out, I have fought the doctors' battle against OVERWEENING government. (J.J. Kilpatrick, "Brawl Brewing over Laetrile," *Saturday Oklahoman & Times*, Okla. City, 4/3/76, p. 8)

4. . . . there are those who already have warned that distinctions will need to be made if the absolute law is passed, and that those distinctions might then be OVERWEENING. For example, who exactly is and who isn't a newspaperman, or a reporter, or a free-lance television or radio consultant? (W.F. Buckley Jr., *Execution Eve and Other Contemporary Ballads*, G.P. Putnam's Sons, 1975, pp. 430-431)

5. Charles Willey [Republican candidate for Congress from 15th district of New Jersey] is apparently the first aspirant for congressional election to make an issue of OVERWEENING judicial interference with the legislative arm's right to control the taxing power. Never in our historical past have judges presumed to tell legislatures how or in what quantities they must spend the taxpayers' money. (J. Chamberlain, "Separation of Powers Threatened by Recent Judicial Branch Tyranny, *Daily Oklahoman*, Okla. City, 6/18/76, p. 10)

6. [General George A.] Custer's exploits [in the Civil War] won him national fame as well as a reputation for impetuousness and OVER-

WEENING egotism. (R. Worsnop of Editorial Research Reports, "Death was swift for legendary leader," *Norman* [Okla.] *Transcript*, 6/27/76, p. 6)

7. Without him [Mahatma Gandhi], it is very probable that countless more lives would have been lost to the OVERWEENING passions of our bloodthirsty century. (P. Johnson, Review of *Mahatma Gandhi and His Apostles*, a book by Ved Mehta, *New York Times*, 2/6/77, Section 7, p. 3)

OXYMORON (ok'si-mōr'on) *noun, pl.:* OXYMORA a figure of speech by which an effect is produced by combining opposite or contradictory ideas or terms, as in *cruel kindness*, *to make haste slowly*, *thunderous silence*, or *sweet sorrow*, etc.

1. See (1) under SCATOLOGY.

2. To begin with, it was during the years of the Regnerys' martial Quakerism—if Professor Vivas will permit the OXYMORON. (W.F. Buckley Jr., *Execution Eve and Other Contemporary Ballads*, G.P. Putnam's Sons, 1975, p. 490)

3. "The college [Henry Steele Commager said in an address to the Society for College and University Planning] should relegate play and games to the students themselves, which means that it should do away with professional and semi-professional athletics. There is no reason why any college should waste its resources on stadia, on a galaxy of high-priced coaches, on athletic scholarships—an OXYMORON if ever there was one." (J. Magarrell, "Historian Thinks Modern College May Be an Anachronism," *Chronicle of Higher Education*, 8/2/76, p. 3)

4. Bruno Sammartino designates himself a "scientific wrestler," a term that, while verging on the OXYMORONIC, indicates he endeavors to apply "clever, beautiful" regulation holds. Until, that is, the crude countermoves of his opponent (read: kicks, bites, jabs, slashes) fill him with such utter frustration that he turns crowdward as if for permission to transgress. Finally he too lapses into brawling buffoonery. (Maralyn Lois Polak, "Interview: Bruno Sammartino," *Today: The* [Philadelphia] *Inquirer Magazine*, 10/24/76, p. 8)

5. "It is not OXYMORONIC to say that your

[Russel Wren's] role has been massively petty," [Donald] Washburn ASSEVERATED, "yet essential, because the same could be said of a shoelace." (Thomas Berger, *Who Is Teddy Villanova?*, Delacorte Press/Seymour Lawrence, 1977, p. 170)

P

PAELLA (pä-yel′ə) *noun* a Spanish dish consisting of chicken, rice, saffron, tomatoes, seasonings, stock, and often shellfish, all cooked slowly together until the moisture is absorbed.

1. To a fellow soldier he must execute for cowardice, [Sebastian] Rosales [in the book, *Journey of the Wolf*, by Douglas Day] says: "I will behave with respect, and we will do this business as quickly and cleanly as it can be done." This is pure Hemingway when the master was cooking up his favorite pot of PAELLA. (R. Freedman, Review, *New York Times*, 3/27/77, Section 7, p. 8)

PAILLASSE (pal-yas′, pal′yas) or **PALLIASSE** *noun* a mattress of straw or sawdust; pallet.

1. . . . he [McKeag] pleaded with Pasquinel to amputate the arm [which had been wounded by a Shoshone tomahawk], and again the Frenchman refused. Instead, he took his ax, chopped a mass of fine wood and built a fire. When it crackled he plunged the ax in, allowing it to become red-hot. Without warning, he slammed the incandescent metal against the corrupt shoulder, pinning McKeag to the PAILLASSE as he did so. . . . This drastic treatment halted the corruption. . . . (J.A. Michener, *Centennial*, Fawcett, 1975, p. 231)

PALADIN (pal′ə-din) *noun* any of the twelve legendary peers or knightly champions attendant on Charlemagne; a knight or a chivalrous champion; any champion of a noble cause.

1. If anything, we've been busy lately glamorizing journalists as the PALADINS of the Republic, private eyes with the public for a client, justices of the supreme court of Our Right to Know Everything That's Going On. (J. Leonard, "In Praise of Nasty Surprises," *New York Times*, 5/16/76, Section 2, p. 39)

2. The donators of great works to the [French] Museum of Modern Art were not happy about the transfer of 35 Braques, 100 Laurens, 26 Marquets, 800 Roualts, 47 Picassos, 200 Dufys, etc., etc. to what some newspapers still call the *folie Beaubourg* [the newly constructed Centre National d'Art et de Culture Georges Pompidou]. The ghost of the honorary president of the Association des Donateurs still walked—Malraux the MANDARIN . . . . Between the MANDARINS and the pop PALADINS there seemed to be a great gulf fixed. Now, I am assured, everything will be all right on opening night. (A. Burgess, " 'A $200 million Erector Set,' " *New York Times*, 1/23/77, Section 6, p. 17)

PALETTE (pal′it) *noun* a thin and usually oval or oblong board or tablet with a thumb hole at one end, used by painters for holding and mixing colors; the set of colors on such a board; the range of colors used by a particular artist; the elements of any art considered as to quality or range.

1. In China, a breath of fresh air brightens up the official PALETTE [title of article]. (R. Chelminski, *Smithsonian*, March 1976, p. 31)

PALIMPSEST (pal′imp-sest) *noun* a parchment tablet or the like that has been written upon or inscribed two or three times, the previous text or texts having been imperfectly erased and remaining, therefore, partly visible.

1. The old buildings [in Beirut, Lebanon] are completely gone . . . . In a PALIMPSEST of Beirut's layered history, columns of the old Roman law school stuck out of shell holes near the crusader church which had been converted into a mosque in the Middle Ages . . . . A few merchants made their way past the [peacekeeping] Syrian troops to see if anything was left of their shops. (W. Blakemore, The Christian Science Monitor News Service, "Change in Beirut," Times Herald, Norristown, Pa., 11/19/76, p. 17)

PALINDROME (pal′ in-drōm′) noun a word, line, phrase, sentence, or verse that reads the same backward or forward.

1. And if that weren't fun enough, they've embellished it [Scrambled Exits, a book by Gyles Brandreth and David Farris] with puzzles of other sorts [than mazes]—riddles, ANAGRAMS, PALINDROMES. (Anon., Review, New York Times, 6/19/77, Section 7, p. 47)

PALLADIAN (pə-lā′dē-ən) adj. of or in the classical Roman style of Andrea Palladio.

PALLADIAN window a window in the form of an archway with two narrow, flatheaded side compartments.

1. In the first section [of the American Revolution Bicentennial Administration's official exhibit, The World of Franklin and Jefferson, at the Metropolitan Museum of Art] are photographic montages of life in the 18th century: studies of windows from the simplest to arched PALLADIAN extravaganzas, or of gravestones, or eating implements. (Amei Wallach, of Newsday, "Americans view famed artifacts," Norman [Okla.] Transcript, 4/18/76, p. 33)

PALLIATE (pal′ ē-āt) verb to attempt to mitigate or conceal the gravity of (an offense) by excuses, apologies, etc.; extenuate; to relieve without curing, as a disease; mitigate; alleviate; ease.

PALLIATION noun.

PALLIATOR noun.

PALLIATIVE (pal′ē-āt′iv, -ə-tiv) adj. serving or tending to palliate; alleviating; extenuating.

PALLIATIVE noun a thing that palliates.

PALLIATIVELY adv.

1. With laughs he [Joyce] PALLIATES the sense of doom that is the heritage of the Irish Catholic. True humor needs this background of urgency: Rabelais is funny, but his stuff CLOYS. His stuff lacks tragedy. (W. Saroyan, Review of Stories and Plays, by Flann O'Brien, New York Times, 3/28/76, Section 7, p. 8)

2. See (2) under PRELAPSARIAN.

PANACEA (pan′ ə-sē′ ə) noun a supposed remedy for all disease or ills; cure-all; an answer for all problems or solution to all difficulties; (if capitalized) an ancient Greek goddess of healing.

PANACEAN adj.

1. There are 5,000 debt collectors in the United States. Last year $3 billion in debts were turned over to them for collection, of which they collected more than $850 million. Yet only 38 states and the District of Columbia have laws regulating collectors. Most of these laws are enforced in a DESULTORY fashion . . . . So the federal law, however well written, will be no PANACEA. (R. Cromley, "The end no longer justifies the means: Debt collectors retain tyrannical power," Norman [Okla.] Transcript, 4/27/76, p. 6)

2. Known throughout the Orient for centuries as a PANACEA able to ward off all manner of ills from the common cold to diabetes . . . , ginseng's reputation as an APHRODISIAC goes back to the days when it was the exclusive prerogative of lustful Chinese emperors. (R.A. Sokolov, Root for all evil, New York Times, 4/25/76, Section 6, p. 35)

3. None of the distinguished doctors who contributed to this volume [of essays, Universities in the Western World, edited by Paul Seabury] offers an easy PANACEA [for the discouraging features of the contemporary campus] or an optimistic prognosis, but they do, at least, share an implicit faith: If the infantilization of

the university can be diagnosed, understood, and explained, then it might in some manner be resisted. (M. Hungiville, Review, *Change*, May 1976, p. 60)

PANACHE (pə-nash´, -näsh´) *noun* an ornamental plume or tassel, especially of feathers, usually worn on a helmet or cap; a grand, FLAMBOYANT, or dashingly elegant manner; a stylish or swaggering manner; verve; style; FLAMBOYANCE; spirited self-confidence or style.

1. See (3) under DETRITUS.

2. The National Theater of the Deaf was about to present its new production, *Parade* . . ., and any skepticism in the audience regarding deaf actors would soon dissolve in enthusiasm for the entertainment's swirl of color and movement and its PANACHE. (Jean Stratton, "The 'eye-music' of deaf actors fills stage eloquently," *Smithsonian*, March 1976, p. 67)

3. And she [Goldie Hawn]'s partnered [in *The Duchess and the Dirtwater Fox*] by George Segal, who has developed PANACHE along his comic way and for once has bits to suit his easy comedy style. (Judith Crist, Review, *American Way*, April 1976, p. 46)

4. Operators of other New York night haunts say they welcome her [Régine Zylberberg]. "Régine has wonderful PANACHE [says Hugh Allen, manager of El Morocco]. She also has four of what most men only have two of." (Linda Bird Francke, "The Reign of Régine," *Newsweek*, 5/17/76, p. 68)

5. When he [painter Al Leslie] struck his great theme—the death of O'Hara—he re-created the setting with characteristic PANACHE. (D. Davis, Review of paintings by Al Leslie at the Boston Museum of Fine Arts, *Newsweek*, 6/7/76, p. 62)

6. See (3) under LIMN.

7. See (3) under PANOPLY.

8. Bloomingdale's new store: New York PANACHE in suburban Washington? (Lynn Langway, *et. al.*, [Caption under picture in] "Bloomie's South," *Newsweek*, 9/13/76, p. 76)

9. See (4) under ANOMIE.

10. Egalitarian manners have taken their toll,

of course, and the PANACHE of [the] 1938 [Winter Carnival at Dartmouth College] is probably irrecoverable, but the campus seems relaxed, all immediate problems manageable, most people this year appeared to be genuinely like each other, and they are clearly able to have a good time. (J. Hart, "Carnival Time," *Times Herald*, Norristown, Pa., 2/24/77, p. 19)

11. See (1) under ODALISQUE.

12. Ralph Lauren, who has brought a special PANACHE to his women's sports clothes, became the newest member of fashion's Hall of Fame yesterday. (Bernadine Morris, *Ralph Lauren*, 6/10/77, *New York Times*, 6/10/77, p. 18

13. At 26, Stephen Burrows was the brightest star of American Fashion. He did things with clothes that had never been done before and he did them with style and PANACHE. That was in 1970. By the time he was 31, he was a has-been, washed up on the shores of Seventh Avenue. Now, at 33, he's up again. (Jean Butler, "Fashion," *New York Times*, 6/12/77, Section 6, p. 72)

PANDEMIC (pan-dem´ ik) *noun* a pandemic disease.

PANDEMIC *adj.* (of a disease) prevalent throughout an entire country, continent, or the whole world; general; universal.

1. . . . the streets beckoned and ball games ruled streets before the automobile PANDEMIC . . . . Stickball is famous. (R. Kahn, *The Boys of Summer*, Harper and Row, 1971, p. 19)

2. Despite this small incidence of swine flu—in a winter in which 1,300 deaths from other kinds of influenza occurred across the nation—medical experts took note because this strain of flu is thought to be responsible for the 1918 PANDEMIC that killed 20 million people. (Anon., "Flu Shots for Everyone," *Newsweek*, 4/5/76, p. 64)

3. In less than a year, [the 1918-19 flu] PANDEMIC killed more than 500,000 Americans and some 20 million people world-wide—the greatest number ever killed in so short a period by any natural or man-made catastrophe . . . . The Asian flu PANDEMIC of 1957 infected some 45 million Americans and killed 70,000 of them. The Hong Kong PANDEMIC of 1968-69 af-

flicted 50 million Americans, caused 33,000 deaths, and cost perhaps $3.9 billion in medical care, industrial absenteeism and the future earnings of those who died. Thus, it may be worth the effort and expense necessary to avert even a "normal" PANDEMIC [of swine flu]. (P.M. Boffey, "Soft evidence and hard sell," *New York Times*, 9/5/76, Section 6, pp. 8–9)

4. [Admiral] Rickover ran his team [of scientists developing the nuclear submarine] . . . brutally hard. Eighty-hour weeks were commonplace, chewings-out frequent, compliments unheard of, fear and trembling PANDEMIC. Carter bent to the Admiral. . . ready to work and anxious to please. The experience left him as rigorously perfectionist as the OLD MAN himself. (P. Goldman, "Sizing Up Carter," *Newsweek*, 9/13/76, p. 30)

5. The earth's fictional population is being decimated in an epidemic of plague novels, most of which end with the PANDEMIC being arrested. Not in this infectious epic [*Survivors*, by Terry Nation] from Britain. (M. Levin, Review, *New York Times*, 11/21/76, Section 7, p. 69)

PANEGYRIC (pan´i-jir´ik, -ji´rik) *noun* a formal oration, discourse, or writing in praise of a person or event; EUGOLY; a formal or elaborate commendation; high or HYPERBOLIC praise; laudation.

PANEGYRICAL *adj.*

PANEGYRICALLY *adv.*

PANEGYRIST *noun.*

PANEGYRIZE (pan´i-jə-riz) *verb* to speak or write a panegyric about; EULOGIZE; to indulge in panegyric; bestow praises.

1. A few days before the New York Senate's primary election last week, readers of the New York Times were startled by an un-Timeslike effusion on the editorial page [endorsing Daniel P. Moynihan]. Not only was the style toastmasterish, but the editorial "we" . . . was a rather imperious "I." Publisher Arthur Ochs (Punch) Sulzberger himself had written the PANEGYRIC . . . and ordered it printed over the objections of his editorial-page editor (and cousin), John B. Oakes . . . last April . . . .

[Sulzberger] . . . named Sunday editor Max Frankel to replace Oakes as head of the editorial page, effective next January. (D. Gelman, Ann Lallande, "The Editorial 'We,' " *Newsweek*, 9/27/76, p. 87)

2. Chairman Mao has now been gathered up with his ancestors and the news media of the world have been writing PANEGYRICS. How fortunate for Han Suyin that her epic biography of Mao [*Mao Tse-tung and the Chinese Revolution, Vol. 2: Wind In The Tower (1949-1975)*] has just been issued. (E. Lawson, Review, *Philadelphia Inquirer*, 10/3/76, p. 12-H)

3. . . . [Norman] Lear . . . has admitted its recent shortcomings—and he is personally supervising an emergency resuscitation [of the TV show, *Mary Hartman, Mary Hartman*] . . . . Basically the folks who put together "MH2" grew so enraptured with the show's critical PANEGYRICS that they forgot what made it so successful. (H.F. Waters and M. Kasindorf, "Remodeling Mary," *Newsweek*, 12/27/76, p. 51)

PANHANDLE (pan´han´d³l) *verb* to accost passers-by on the street and beg from them; to accost and beg from; to obtain by accosting and begging from someone.

PANHANDLER *noun* a beggar, especially one who begs on the streets.

1. . . . it seems worthwhile to devote considerable space to a report by three researchers at the University of Washington on . . . PANHANDLING. (J.K. Page Jr., "Phenomena, comments and notes," *Smithsonian*, April 1976, p. 10)

2. They were good neighbors, Manhattan-style, neither looking at nor addressing strangers (the chummy, in New York, are invariably perverts, PANHANDLERS, or footpads) . . . . (Thomas Berger, *Who Is Teddy Villanova?*, Delacorte Press/Seymour Lawrence, 1977, p. 43)

PANJANDRUM (pan-jan´ drəm) *noun* a self-important, pompous, or PRETENTIOUS official.

1. William Burrough's earliest novel, *Junky*, has just been published in "the first complete and unEXPURGATED edition." Until now, *Junky*,

has been issued only in an Ace paperback in 1953 . . . and it is doubtful whether many readers ever saw the debut of the man who is now a grand PANJANDRUM of the drug culture and the experimental "prose novel," as Allen Ginsberg calls it in his characteristically INEFFABLE introduction. (A. Broyard, Review, *New York Times*, 4/10/77, Section 7, p. 14)

2. When Joe Baum came on the scene, most of the restaurants in Manhattan were judged according to a single standard. French. The grand PANJANDRUM of the Gotham milieu was, as he had been for more than two decades, Henri Soulé, proprietor of Le Pavillon, then considered almost indisputably the greatest French restaurant in the United States. (C. Claiborne, "Joe's in His Heaven—His Windows on the World," *Holiday*, Summer 1977, p. 35)

PANOPLY (pan´ ə-plē) *noun* a complete suit of armor; any protective covering; a complete covering or array, either material or ideal, and especially splendid.

PANOPLIED *adj.*

1. For at least the immediate future, the major portion of the Persian Gulf's new riches will continue to be spent on the acquisiton of a PANOPLY of the most lethal armaments now for sale, predicts this observer [Professor Marvin Zonis of the University of Chicago]. (D. Oakley, "For Arabians . . . Oil Money Buys Guns, *Norman* [Okla.] *Transcript*, 2/5/76, p. 6)

2. See (1) under LACHRYMOSE.

3. [Alejo] Carpentier's earlier novels and stories were often pretty heavy going, what with their tiresome philosophizing and heavily laid-on historical PANOPLIES. [*Reasons of State*, translated by Frances Partridge] is something different—a jocular view of imaginative idealism, repressive power and burgeoning revolution, all done with breezy PANACHE. (A. Cockburn, Review, *New York Times*, 5/2/76, Section 7, p. 51)

4. It was not so long ago—a matter of 20 years—that art nouveau was considered a minor style, deservedly forgotten. Those tendriled doorknobs and flowing pedestals, that PANOPLY of rare materials . . . , that air of hothouse elegance, glazed and nuanced—what

did such things amount to but decoration? And what was decoration but a sin against the purity of modern art? (R. Hughes, "The Snobbish Style," *Time*, 9/13/76, p. 64)

PANTHEON (pan´ thē-on´ , -ən) *noun* all the gods of a people or of a particular mythology considered collectively; a temple dedicated to all the gods.

1. And a mark of acceptance of the hysterical gooey FLAN into the PANTHEON of human competitive endeavor has been accorded by its current inclusion in the Guinness Book of Records. It is now duly registered that the annual World Custard Pie Championship . . . is held at . . . Coxheath, . . . England. Competitors are ESOTERICALLY required to hurl a pie of no more than 10 3/4 inches in diameter at a target face set at a distance of 8 ft. 3 7/8 inches, and are awarded six points for a bull's-eye. (P. Ryan, "Pie in the eye is fun—for somebody else," *Smithsonian*, October, 1976, p. 168)

2. One hopes that a long-delayed three-disk album of his great songs of the past decade, due out this fall, will establish him [Neil Young] rightfully in the PANTHEON of post-war American popular art. (J. Rockwell, "Neil Young—As Good as Dylan?," *New York Times*, 6/19/77, Section 2, p. 35)

3. Since this new awareness, the woman novelist who also happens to be a feminist and who seeks to depict a religious vision uniquely "female" in character is not likely to have her heroine discover the predominantly male cast of the Judeo-Christian PANTHEON at the end of her spiritual pilgrimage. (Francine duPlessix Gray, "Nature as The Nunnery," *New York Times*, 7/17/77, Section 7, p. 3)

4. By combining his love of jazz, respect for its musicians, a lifelong fascination with recordings and a militant civil-righteousness, [John] Hammond won a singular place in American music. Without him, a PANTHEON of immortals from Billie Holiday and Benny Goodman to Count Basie and Bob Dylan might never have been heard so well—or at all. (H. Saal, Review of *John Hammond On Record*, a book by John Hammond with Irving Townsend, *Newsweek*, 11/7/77, p. 93)

PARABOLIC (par´ ə-bol´ ik) or **PARABOLI-CAL** *adj.* of, pertaining to, in the form of, involving, or expressed by a parable.

PARABOLICALLY *adv.*

PARABOLIZE *verb* to tell in a parable or parables.

PARABLE *noun* a short simple story, usually of an occurrence of a familiar kind, from which a moral or religious lesson may be drawn; a short, allegorical story designed to convey a truth or moral lesson; any statement conveying its meaning indirectly, as by analogy.

PARABOLIZER noun.

1. Her [Joan Samson's] PARABOLIC novel [*The Auctioneer*] was a choice of five book clubs, received good reviews, sold quite well in the bookstores (30,000) but never made the hardcover best-seller list . . . . To date, [the Avon soft-cover edition has sold] 1,118,500 copies. (Anon., "Paper Back Talk," *New York Times*, 2/27/77, Section 7, p. 35)

PARACLETE (par´ə-klēt´) *noun* (if lower case) a person called in to aid; an advocate; intercessor; pleader; (if capitalized) the Holy Spirit, considered as comforter, intercessor, or advocate in Christian theology.

1. Potter Daventry [a character in *In A Shallow Grave*, a book by James Purdy] turns out to be the oddest of PARACLETES, a murderous Christ. "Heaven-crazy," he slashes himself and forces Garnet [another character] to drink his blood out of a tin cup . . . . (J. Charyn, Review, *New York Times*, 2/8/76, Section 7, p. 3)

PARADIGM (par´ə-dim, -dīm) *noun* an example; pattern; model to use as a standard; mold; ideal; standard; PARAGON; (in Grammar) an example of a declension or conjugation giving all the inflected forms of a word.

PARADIGMATIC (par´ə-dig-mat´ik) *adj.*

PARADIGMATICALLY *adv.*

1. See (2) under HOMOEROTICISM.

2. The beauty of *Long Day's Journey* is that it is PARADIGMATIC. [Eugene] O'Neill had struggled in other plays to create symbolic figures representing America, Mankind, Motherhood. These plays are failures . . . . Paradoxically, in *Long Day's Journey* O'Neill succeeded where he had failed before by clinging to the hard facts of the case and the techniques of the strictest realism. (M. Feingold, "Robards Returns to O'Neill's 'Journey,' " *New York Times*, 1/25/76, Section 2, p. 5)

3. Publicity is the PARADIGM of salesmanship. (R. Kahn, *The Boys of Summer*, Harper and Row, 1971, p. 98)

4. In the comedian's story, Carl Erskine has been having difficulty throwing strikes. Someone scratching a single. Two men walk. Now with nobody out and bases loaded, that PARADIGM of constancy, the ARCHETYPAL [Brooklyn] Dodger fan, rises in Ebbets Field. "Come on, Oiskine," he bellows. "These guys stink." (R. Kahn, *Ibid.*, p. 242)

5. Also in [Irving] Howe's descriptions [in *World of Our Fathers*] of the . . . struggle between the left and right, of the slow giving way of radical aspirations to practical ambitions in the rank-and-file, one can find an evolving PARADIGM of the political behavior of Jews in America as well, perhaps, of the ideological tensions that mark one's own politics. (T. Solotaroff, Review, *New York Times*, 2/1/76, Section 7, p. 28)

6. They [liberals] are men and women who tend to believe that the human being is perfectible and social progress predictable, . . . that all peoples and societies should strive to organize themselves upon a rationalist and scientific PARADIGM. (W.F.Buckley Jr., *Up From Liberalism*, Arlington House, 2nd Printing 1968, p. 137)

7. See (1) under MOLET.

8. Past [Carnegie] commission reports, which were responsive to the turmoil of the sixties when liberal arts was still the PARADIGM of the university, are inadequate to explain either the new trends and problems attendant on the now "stable" enrollment picture or the current swing to career goals. (Joan Baum, Review of *The Useful Arts and the Liberal Tradition*, by Earl F. Cheit, *Change*, April 1976, p. 54)

9. Acceptance of the PARADIGM of rape [as proposed by Susan Brownmiller in the book, *Against Our Will*] as the root source of

women's oppression becomes, finally, a matter of faith, not facts. (D.L. Kirp, Review, *Change*, April 1976, p. 41)

10. See (2) under RUBATO.

11. See (1) under SHAMUS.

12. There is nothing so rare as a good evening of exhibition football on television, except possibly an intelligent pregame show. Fans will find both when they tune in the Super Bowl rematch between Pittsburgh and Dallas on August 28. Before the game, ABC will air not the usual image-burnishing salute to the sport but a realistic study of football as a way of making a living. . . . *It's Tough to Make It in This League* neither glosses over the problems players face nor flogs the cliché of football as a PARADIGM of society's ills. (Anon., "Telling It Tough," *Time*, 8/30/76, p. 55)

13. See (2) under TECTONIC.

PARAGON (par′ ə-gon′ , -gən) *noun* a model or pattern of excellence or perfection.

1. . . . when you consider all the weaseling, fudging, flakking, boosting, PETTIFOGGING, and downright lying that passes these days for theater criticism, [John] Simon emerges as a PARAGON of candor, almost a voice in the wilderness. (R. Brustein, Review of *Uneasy Stages* and *Singularities*, by John Simon, *New York Times*, 1/4/76, Section 7, p. 2)

PARAMETER (pə-ram′ i-tər) *noun* something used as a standard against which other things are measured; any constant, with variable values, used as a referent for determining other variables.

PARAMETRIC (par′ə-met′rik) or **PARAMETRICAL** *adj.*

1. I wish we could reach some sort of national consensus on the extent of the consumer's responsibility for his own welfare, or, conversely, the extent of the business-government responsibility. As it is, we are following a painful process . . . , defining the PARAMETERS of responsibility one case at a time . . . . Neither the economy nor the consumer can stand many more tris-type fiascos [a reference to the government requirement that children's clothing be fireproofed and the subsequent government ban of "tris," a fire-retardant, because of the possibility it causes cancer]. (R.L. Lesher, "The Great Pajama Flap," *Times Herald*, Norristown, Pa., 6/27/77, p. 12)

2. . . . they [Kate and Harvey Holroyd] haven't, it develops [in the book, *The Serial: A Year in the Life of Marin County*, by Cyra McFadden], come to terms about their basic lifestyle, having failed to finalize the PARAMETERS of their own interface. (C. Michener, Review, *Newsweek*, 6/20/77, p. 96)

PARANOIA (par′ə-noi′ə) *noun* a mental disorder characterized by systematized delusions, as of grandeur or persecution, and the projection of personal conflicts, that are ascribed to the supposed hostility of others.

PARANOID or **PARANOIDAL** or **PARANOIAC** *adj.* of or like paranoia; characterized by oversuspiciousness, grandiose delusions or delusions of persecution.

PARANOID *noun* a person afflicted with paranoia.

1. There can be no doubt that Hitler was emotionally responsive to music—especially Wagner's . . . . And, of course, Hitler must have known intuitively that the neuroses and PARANOIA in many of Wagner's music-dramas reinforced the German susceptibility to the myth of the "Master Race." (Carleton Smith, "Tracking down original scores missing in the war," *Smithsonian*, December 1975, p. 90)

2. One approaches *FBI* [a book by Sanford J. Ungar] in the hope that it will provide a much-needed perspective on our one and only national police force . . . . It turns out, for instance, that much of the so-called PARANOIA of the left—old and new—should not have been so-called at all. (V.S. Navasky, Review, *New York Times*, 3/14/76, Section 7, p. 3)

3. Talking with John Dean sets up a strong pull of conflicting emotions . . . he can be viewed as a virtual national hero—he blew the whistle on the warped Nixon crew whose power-hungry PARANOIA was subverting our national purpose . . . . On the other hand, he was a knowing and fully participating member of that crew. (MARCIAROSE, "Ambition led Dean's list," *Philadelphia Inquirer*, 10/27/76, p. 1-B)

4. [Saul] Bellow may be the best exponent

since Charles Dickens of monomaniac eccentricity. Among the most memorable examples: the millionaire Einhorn in *The Adventures of Augie March*; the fast-talking Dr. Tamkin who relieves Tommy Wilhelm of his last dollar, and, most recently, the PARANOIAC poet Von Humboldt Fleisher—"a hectic nonstop monologist and improvisator, a champion detractor." (W. Clemons and Chris J. Harper, "Bellow the Word King," *Newsweek*, 11/1/76, p. 89)

PARIAH (pə-rī′ə) *noun* an outcast; any person or animal generally despised or rejected by others; (*cap.*)—a member of one of the lowest castes in southern India.

1. "At a stroke, the [Supreme Court] justices had severed the remaining cords of DE FACTO slavery through the 'Brown' decision. The Negro no longer could be fastened with the status of official PARIAH." Anon., "From the Book Shelf" [Editorial quote from *Simple Justice*, by R. Kluger], *The Norman* [Okla]. *Transcript*, 2/19/76, p. 6)

2. On Friday, when he [Levi Zendt] walked from the farm to Lancaster, no passer-by would offer him a ride. The black sleighs skidded past as if he were a PARIAH. And when he reached the market, none of the merchants would talk to him. (J.A. Michener, *Centennial*, Fawcett, 1975, pp. 319-320)

3. The subject of this fascinating, often gripping book [*A Man Called Intrepid*, by William Stevenson] is Sir William Stephenson, the British intelligence chief who came to New York in 1940 to establish an immense network for the gathering and processing of information. His code name—given by Winston Churchill—was Intrepid . . . . But Stephenson was constantly in touch [during pre-war business trips to Germany] with the political PARIAH Winston Churchill and he was involved in securing (read stealing) the Enigma machine, the German signaling device used throughout the war, the breaking of which undoubtedly had a profound influence on the war's outcome. (Margaret Manning, Review, *The Boston Globe*, 3/7/76, Section A, p. 16)

4. John B. Connally, treated like a king instead of a PARIAH at the White House recently, left Washington without the slightest intention of making the endorsement President Ford desperately seeks in Texas—a fact that points up the political forces and intrigues now swirling within the Ford camp. (R. Evans, R. Novak, "Connally Deaf to Ford Wooing," *Daily Oklahoman*, 4/15/76, p. 12)

5. The victory for those within the Department of State who have long pushed for a policy of "relentless opposition" to the pro-Western and white governments in southern Africa is complete. The secretary wants all Americans out of Rhodesia. He warns against any U.S. citizen visiting the PARIAH republic. He applauds the action of Rhodesia's neighbors in cutting ties to Salisbury. (P.J. Buchanan, "U.S. Wants Part of Rhodesia Spoils," *Daily Oklahoman*, 5/4/76, p. 8)

6. But if [Mark] Felt [a top F.B.I. official] turned public informer, Nixon asked [on one of his tapes]: "Who is going to hire him? . . . He would go to a job at Life [Magazine], and everyone would treat him like a PARIAH." (R. Sherrill, Review of *Alger Hiss: The True Story*, by J.C. Smith, *New York Times*, 4/25/76, Section 7, p. 44)

7. So neither of the two books under review [*The Irish Diaspora in America*, by Lawrence J. McCaffrey; and *The Roman Catholic Church and the Creation of the Modern Irish State, 1878-1886*, by Emmet Larkin] can be expected to create a stampede to the book stores. If everyone knows everything . . . about a PARIAH people, there is no reason to read books about them. (A.M. Greeley, Review, *New York Times*, 6/27/76, Section 7, p. 8)

8. [Milan] Kundera [author of *The Farewell Party*, translated from the Czech by Peter Kussi]—a poet, playwright, critic, musicologist as well as novelist and short-story writer—suffered [after the Soviet invasion of Czechoslovakia in 1968] . . . exclusion from the writers' union; loss of his teaching post . . . ; denial of passport; banning of his plays . . . . An official PARIAH, he . . . went on writing and he has steadily gained a Western European reputation, including the 1973 Prix Médicis Etranger for his novel, "Life Is Elsewhere." (S. Maloff, Review, *New York Times*, 9/5/76, Section 7, p. 4)

PARLOUS (pär'ləs) *adj.* Chiefly Archaic—perilous; dangerous; difficult to escape from or deal with; risky; dangerously clever; cunning; shrewd; mischievous.

PARLOUSLY *adv.*

PARLOUSNESS *noun.*

1. Although all 80,187 tickets [for Super Bowl X] and an undetermined number of counterfeits have been sold for $20 and up, although receipts for the box office, television, radio, and films on this one game will exceed $5 million, although postseason loot will exceed $25,000 for each winning player and $15,000 for each loser, these remain PARLOUS times in the czarist [Pete Rozelle] view. (Red Smith, "Can't Find Czars Like Pete," *New York Times*, 1/18/76, Section 5, p. 3)

2. The absence of dependable statewide polls makes political forecasting a PARLOUS pastime. (S. Hempstone, "Carolina Vote Shapes Up as Rerun," *Daily Oklahoman*, Okla. City, 3/23/76, p. 6)

3. But his [Harold Wilson's] long stay [as Britain's prime minister] ended with a leaving that itself makes this year more PARLOUS than it was already likely to be. It is now marginally more likely . . . that a general election will come sooner than the Labor party or the Conservative party—or the country—can afford one: perhaps even within the year. (*The London Economist*, "Who Will Pick Up The Pieces? Feeble Legacy of Harold Wilson," *Norman* [Okla.] *Transcript*, 4/2/76, p. 6)

4. Explaining the PARLOUS state of his campaign, he [Morris Udall] says his mistakes have been tactical, not ideological. (G.F. Will, "The Loneliness of the Long-Distance Runner," *Newsweek*, 5/3/76, p. 100)

5. See (3) under DISQUISITION.

PARODY (par'ə-dē) *noun* a humorous, satirical, or ridiculous imitation of a serious piece of literature, musical composition, person, event, etc.; a poor or feeble imitation; TRAVESTY; burlesque.

PARODY *verb* to imitate (a composition, author, etc.) for purposes of ridicule or satire; to imitate poorly or feebly; TRAVESTY.

PARODIC (pə-rod'ĭk) or **PARODICAL** *adj.*

PARODIST *noun* a writer of parodies.

PARODISTIC *adj.*

1. See (4) under EPIGRAM.

2. See (2) under TRAVESTY.

3. [Elie] Nadelman produced his most important works—a suite of wood carvings—soon after his arrival in this country. These wooden figures merely PARODY ARCHETYPAL figures in modern society, but are rendered in a quasi-archaic style that suggests the cigar-store Indians and ships' figureheads of American folk art. (D. Bourdon, "The sleek, witty and elegant art of Elie Nadelman," *Smithsonian*, January 1976, p. 88)

4. See (1) under EMPYREAN.

5. Peter Sellers, as a Charlie Chan figure [in the movie, *Murder By Death*], PARODIES both the INSCRUTABLE sage's fondness for silly APHORISMS and the merciless exploitation of his children. When No. 3 Son asks why he is forever getting stuck with the dirty work, Sellers IMPLACABLY replies, "Cause your mother not here to do it." (Janet Maslin, Review, *Newsweek*, 7/4/76, pp. 101-102)

6. Vampires may still have some of their old power over us because their stories so often PARODY class relations in a supposedly classless society, the incessant patterns of dominance and submission. (L. Braudy, "Review of the book, Interview With the Vampire," by Ann Rice, *New York Times*, 5/2/76, Section 7, p. 7)

7. See (1) under MÉNAGE.

8. See (4) under FLACCID.

9. See (1) under MAGDALENE.

10. See (1) under CACHINNATE.

11. The play [Bullshot Crummonds] is a PARODY of the 1920s pulp literature character Bulldog Drummond, an ex-British Army officer who imagines himself an amateur sleuth . . . . The theater [showing this play in San Francisco], right next door to the mostly empty skin houses, draws busloads of children, families and couples. (D. Johnston, *Los Angeles Times* Service, "Now, X-rated bars try gorillas," *Philadelphia Inquirer*, 1/17/77, p. 10-A)

PARTHENOGENESIS (par'thə-nō-jen'i-sis)

noun reproduction by the development of an unfertilized ovum, seed, or spore, as in certain polyzoans, insects, algae, etc., or as artificially induced in many animals.

PARTHENOGENETIC *adj.*

PARTHENOGENETICALLY *adv.*

1. [Quotation from the book, *Edward Kennedy and the Camelot Legend*, by James McGregor Burns:] But he [Kennedy] would, "if the delegates nonetheless nominated him"—in the political equivalent of PARTHENOGENESIS, presumably—" . . . accept the nomination." (G. Hodgson, Review, *New York Times*, 4/18/76, Section 7, p. 3)

PARVENU (pär′və-nōō′, -nyōō′) *noun* a person who has suddenly acquired wealth, power, or importance, who is not fully accepted socially into the class into which he has risen; an upstart.

PARVENU *adj.* being, resembling, or characteristic of a parvenu.

1. One of these [buccaneers of the Gilded Age, in *The House of Mirth*, a play by Edith Wharton] is Rosedale, the PARVENU Jew whose desire for Lily [Bart] has a business-like rapacity more honest than the devious aristocrats who pant after her. (J. Kroll, Review, *Newsweek*, 4/26/76, p. 105)

2. . . . [Preston] Jones completes [in the third play of *A Texas Trilogy*] his Bradleyville [Texas] social spectrum by presenting its PARVENU country-club set . . . . (J. Kroll, Review, *Newsweek*, 5/17/76, p. 90)

3. . . . he [Mao Tse-Tung] . . . launched the century's most IDIOSYNCRATIC social upheaval: the Great Proletarian Cultural Revolution . . . . When the upheaval spreads fear among "rightists," many join ultraleftist factions in frantic overcompensation . . . . Even then, as the authors [David and Nancy Dall Milton, of the book, *The Wind Will Not Subside: Years in Revolutionary China, 1964-69*] indicate, irony is not played out. PARVENU ultraleftists are branded "counterrevolutionary," and the rightists are restored to power. (R. Bernstein, Review, *Time*, 4/19/76, p. K9)

4. See (2) under SISYPHEAN.

5. He [President Valery Giscard d'Estaing, of

France] impresses you as the absolute opposite of a familiar figure in today's world: the PARVENU. (H.J. Taylor, "Giscard Under Pressure," *Times Herald*, Norristown, Pa., 9/21/76, p. 13)

6. [A.R.] Gurney [Jr., author of the play, *Children*] has taken one of John Cheever's stories and made it into a rueful, ironic portrait of a classic Wasp family that's losing its Waspishness . . . . Barbara, the divorced daughter, is having a sneaky affair with a married Catholic PARVENU. Son Randy is a . . . post-adolescent whose soul wears a permanent jock strap; he even dances with his party-dressed wife in a football uniform. (J. Kroll, Review, *Newsweek*, 11/8/76, p. 109)

PAS DE DEUX (pä′də-dŒ′) *noun, pl.*: PAS DE DEUX (pä′də-dŒz′) a dance or figure for two persons.

1. [Jerome] Robbins unveiled his new PAS DE DEUX for Natalia Makarova and Mikhail Baryshnikov . . . at Lincoln Center. . . . In their first solos they spin off flickering images of remembered youth, of athletic bravado in the boy's case and of uncomplicated innocence in the girl's. But in their second variations, the man's MACHISMO becomes softened by poetry, the girl's innocence tempered by understanding. (H. Saal, "Gala Trio of Ballets," *Newsweek*, 5/24/76, p. 87)

PASQUINADE (pas′kwə-nād′) *noun* a satire, sarcastic squib, or lampoon, originally one posted in a public place.

PASQUINADE *verb* to criticize or ridicule with such satire; to lampoon.

1. I revere my Anglican friends, and highly respect their religion, but it is true that it sometimes lends itself to such PASQUINADE as Auberon Waugh's, who wrote . . . : "In England we have a curious institution called the Church of England . . . . Its strength has always lain in the fact that on any moral or political issue it can produce such a wide divergence of opinion that nobody—from the Pope to Mao Tse-Tung—can say with any confidence that he is not an Anglican. Its weaknesses are that nobody pays much attention to it and very few people attend its functions." (W.F. Buckley Jr., *Execution Eve and Other Contmporary*

Ballads, G.P. Putnam's Sons, 1975, p. 459)

PASTICHE (pa-stēsh´, pä-) *noun* a literary, musical, or artistic piece consisting wholly or chiefly of motifs, techniques, or bits borrowed from one or more sources; such a piece intended to imitate or ridicule another artist's style; potpourri; a jumbled or incongruous mixture; hodgepodge.

1. See (1) under CACHET.

2. Jack Gold and Adrian Mitchell should be sued for malpractice. Gold's direction [of the movie, *Man Friday*] is heavy-handed and obvious. Mitchell's screenplay is a PASTICHE of every cliché about class and race prejudice and the corruption of power. (Katrine Ames, Review, *Newsweek*, 3/22/76, p. 84)

3. Of the thousand and one protests against the House Committee on Un-American Activities I have seen, I think the one a few years ago by Mr. John Crosby, the columnist, most worth relating in this PASTICHE of the liberal in controversy. (W.F. Buckley Jr., *Up From Liberalism*, Arlington House, 2nd Printing 1968, p. 72)

4. See (1) under CENTRIPETAL.

5. See (1) under CACHINNATE.

6. Dr. [Roger] Gould [a Los Angeles psychiatrist] says her book [*Passages*, by Gail Sheehy] is a "terrible PASTICHE" of his own ideas. (Anon., "Book Ends," *New York Times*, 5/30/76, Section 7, p. 17)

PATAPHYSICS (pad´ə-fiz´iks) *noun* (construed as *singular*)—intricate and whimsical nonsense intended as a PARODY of science.

PATAPHYSICAL *adj.*

PATAPHYSICIAN *noun.*

1. [Quote from Max Ernst:] "Rebellious, heterogeneous, full of contradiction, [my work] is unacceptable to specialists of art, culture, morality. But it does have the ability to enchant my accomplices: poets, PATAPHYSICIANS* and a few illiterates."
[*Footnote:] "PATAPHYSICS," wrote its founder, Poet Alfred Jarry, in 1898, is "the science of the realm beyond metaphysics." It will study the laws that govern exceptions and "explain the

universe supplementary to this one." (R. Hughes, "Max Ernst: The Compleat Experimenter," *Time*, 4/12/76, p. 57)

PATERFAMILIAS (pä´tər-fə-mil´ē-əs, pä´-, pat´ər-) *noun*, *pl.:* **PATERFAMILIASES** or **PATRESFAMILIAS** (pä´trēz-fə-mil´ē-əs, pä´-, pa´-) the father of a family; male head of a household: an expression used generally of a man when surrounded by his children or in his capacity as a father.

1. Married, and happily, to Laura Herbert in 1937, . . . he [Evelyn Waugh] settled down in a handsome Georgian country house . . . and became a sort of squire and a serious PATERFAMILIAS . . . . (L.E. Sissman, Review of *Evelyn Waugh: A Biography*, by Christopher Sykes, *The New Yorker*, 2/9/76, p. 107)

2. See (2) under ACRONYM.

3. Poor O.J. Simpson. He turns 29 next month, and he is itching to move back to California after seven years as a running back for the Buffalo Bills. "I've paid my dues in Buffalo," he feels. . . . So O.J. is looking for locker space with some team closer to home and his acting career, in which he has appeared most recently as a North African PATERFAMILIAS in the ABC-TV movie *Roots*. (Anon., "People," *Time*, 6/28/76, p. 39)

PATINA (pat´ə na) *noun* a sheen, glow, aura, etc., especially as the result of age, usage, or association; a film or incrustation, usually green, produced by oxidation on the surface of old bronze and thought to add to its ornamental value; any incrustation or film appearing gradually on a surface.

1. One wonders why [Norma] Klein [author of the book, *Blue Trees*] depends on tasteless conversations to give her work the PATINA of authenticity. (Alice Bach, Review, *New York Times*, 2/8/76, Section 7, p. 16)

2. Underneath a PATINA of professionalism, the Dodgers I joined [as a reporter] in 1952 twitched in shock and mortification. No major league baseball club before had been both as gifted and as consecutively disappointing. (R. Kahn, *The Boys of Summer*, Harper and Row, 1971, p. 89)

3. Both [William Jennings] Bryan and [Jim-

my] Carter have a benevolent smile; the glow and PATINA of quiet charm. But they also have an icy eye. It suggests an unmatched talent with a dirk and a temper that can explode phfft like a celluloid collar. And neither seems able to keep his balance on the invisible tightrope that stretches between himself and personal ambition. (H.J. Taylor, "Intriguing Comparisons," *Times Herald*, Norristown, Pa., 9/1/76, p. 19)

4. She [Leonora Beard] glowed with an old-guinea PATINA in the dim light [of the hospital], a few shallow breaths from the end. He waited about three minutes to confirm that he was now Ronald Beard the widower. (A. Burgess, *Beard's Roman Women*, McGraw-Hill, 1976, p. 15)

5. See (1) under PUDENDUM.

6. See (1) under RAPTORIAL.

PATOIS (pat'wä) *noun*, pl.: PATOIS (pat' wäz) a rural or provincial form of speech differing from the accepted standard; local dialect; jargon.

1. With its food, however, the [Caesar's] Palace Court [restaurant] rolls almost nothing but snake eyes. In the PATOIS of [Las] Vegas, it craps out. (Robert Vare, "Where Dining Is a Big Gamble," *National Observer*, Week ending 4/2/77, p. 11-B)

2. "Yet they speak only French?" [asked Russel Wren] . . . "But surely when not at school, when at home —" "Oh [said Boris], they gibber in an American PATOIS, but I assure you they have understood nothing of what we've said since going into formal English." (Thomas Berger, *Who Is Teddy Villanova?*, Delacorte Press/Seymour Lawrence, 1977, p. 201)

PATRICIATE (pə-trish'ē-it, -āt) *noun* the patrician class; patrician rank; aristocracy.

PATRICIAN *noun* any person of noble or high rank; aristocrat.

PATRICIAN *adj.*

1. In his case . . . that "mission" may be defined as a quiet but passionately-held desire to explain the strange ways of the class into which the writer [Louis Auchincloss] was born, the WASP PATRICIATE of the Eastern seaboard in

general, the inhabitants of what might be called Brownstone New York in particular . . . . (R. Schickel, Review of *The Winthrop Covenant*, by Louis Auchincloss, *New York Times*, 3/28/76, Section 7, p. 10)

PATRIMONY (pa' trə-mō' nē) *noun* an estate inherited from one's father or ancestors; any quality, characteristic, etc., that is inherited; inheritance; heritage; the estate or endowment of a church, religious house, etc.

PATRIMONIAL *adj.*

1. Stewart Mott, the clown prince of the General Motors empire, may now squander his PATRIMONY promoting the cause of Fred Harris. But if he and Harris coordinate the spending of the funds, both go to the slammer. (P.J. Buchanan, "Campaign Law Reform Foolish," *Daily Oklahoman*, Okla. City, 2/17/76, p. 8)

2. During the war [World War II] she [Winifred Wagner, the composer's daughter-in-law] transferred them all [Wagner's original manuscripts] to a hospital where they were kept four stories underground. In 1973, she created the Richard Wagner Foundation of Bayreuth to preserve "his universal PATRIMONY for all time." Had [Adolf] Hitler listened to her and followed her wishes the precious [original] manuscripts [in Hitler's possession] would be safe today. (Carleton Smith, "Tracking down original scores missing in the war," *Smithsonian*, December 1975, p. 90)

3. Parisians . . . were privileged to be the first to see the breathtaking and now-famous exhibit of ancient archeological treasures unearthed since the new order came to power [in China] . . . . It was evidence that . . . the excesses of the Cultural Revolution had not eroded China's basic respect and admiration for its artistic PATRIMONY. (R. Chelminski, "In China, a breath of fresh air brightens up the official palette," *Smithsonian*, March 1976, p. 31)

4. Among the appropriate questions one directs to the theorists of academic freedom: . . . . If the community makes positive provisions to encourage an individual scholar to search out truths, is the community not entitled to expect that the scholar's concerns shall be more than subjectively important, that the scholar, if suc-

cessful, will contribute to the intellectual or moral or scientific PATRIMONY? (W.F. Buckley Jr., *Up From Liberalism*, Arlington House, 2nd Printing, 1968, p. 180)

5. He [Howard Hughes] also guessed badly in selling off his PATRIMONY, the Hughes Tool Co. He sold his stock at $30 a share, raked in $150 million—and then looked on helplessly as the Arab oil embargo struck, and a new boom in oil drilling broke and the price of the stock more than doubled. (T. Mathews, *et. al.*, "The Secret World of Howard Hughes," *Newsweek*, 4/19/76, p. 32)

6. See (4) under SENTENTIOUS.

PATRISTIC (pə-tris′ tik) or **PATRISTICAL** *adj.* of or pertaining to the fathers of the Christian church or their writings or doctrines or the study of the latter.

PATRISTICALLY *adv.*

1. Their homeland [Soviet Russia], using the cant phrase, is a peculiar combination of TROPISMS, some of them nationalistic and PATRISTIC, some of them egotistic. (W.F. Buckley Jr., *Execution Eve and Other Contemporary Ballads*, G.P. Putnam's Sons, 1975, p. 242)

PATRONYMIC (pa′ trə-nim′ ik) *noun* a family name; surname; a name showing descent from a given male ancestor, as by the addition of a prefix or suffix: O'Brian (descendant of Brian) or Williamson (son of William).

PATRONYMIC *adj.* of or derived from the name of a father or male ancestor.

PATRONYMICALLY *adv.*

1. He [Boris] provided neither a family name nor, conspicuous failure in one who stems from the steppes, a PATRONYMIC. (Thomas Berger, *Who Is Teddy Villanova?*, Delacorte Press/ Seymour Lawrence, 1977, p. 194)

2. A secretary who worked on a book with me several years ago never accorded anybody a PATRONYMIC. As far as I could figure there were at least three Bobs among the people she mentioned and, in an effort to tell them apart, I asked, "Has any of these Bobs a last name?" "I don't know," was the reply. (Alice-Leone Moats, "Dear Fifi and Harry: Who Are You?," *Philadelphia Inquirer*, 6/8/77, p. 11-A)

PECCADILLO (pek′ə-dil′o) *noun*, *pl.*: -LOES, -LOS a minor or petty sin or offense; slight or trifling fault.

1. Now in discussing these episodes [*re* the moral behavior of persons investigated by J. Edgar Hoover], the commentator for Time magazine referred airily to the transcribed "PECCADILLOES" of the gentlemen in question. Now a PECCADILLO is a slight offense, a petty fault—like, say, slurping your soup, or picking your nose, or neglecting to use the object pronoun after a proposition . . . . But a PECCADILLO that is less than professionally incapacitating is . . . not only none of the FBI's business, it shouldn't have any capacity to shock. Yet it does. I cannot imagine a Congressman running for reelection saying to the voters: "I work every day and every night of the week in the public interest, except Saturday nights which I spend in a brothel." The public, one gathers, doesn't share the urbanity of Time magazine on what constitutes a PECCADILLO. (W.F. Buckley Jr., *Execution Eve and Other Contemporary Ballads*, G.P. Putnam's Sons, 1975, pp. 412-413

2. An account of Nixon's presidency that dwells on "Watergate"—the bizarre combinations of crimes, PECCADILLOES, usurpations, felonies, abuses of power, crackpot capers and violations of constitutional law . . .—necessarily misses one of the main points of recent political history: the emergence of the Presidency as a fourth branch of government in its own right, wielding vast powers, conducting much of its business in secret, justifying illegal actions in the name of "national security" and accountable, in its own eyes, to no one but itself. (C. Lasch—Review of *Nightmare*, by J. Anthony Lukas, *New York Times*, 1/25/76, Section 7, pp. 23-24)

3. A beastly bunch . . . whose PECCADILLOES are designed to provide lip-smacking and head-shaking. [*The Sisters*, a book by Anne Lambton, is] Hot stuff, crisply prepared for the escapist who wants to believe the worst. (M. Levin, Review, *New York Times*, 1/25/76, Section 7, p. 30)

4. The PECCADILLOES of Citizen [William] Loeb receive far more attention from [author Kevin] Cash [in *Who the Hell Is Citizen Loeb?*] than the motivations of his political

philosophy. We are TITILLATED by a second-hand tale of how the pistol-packin' publisher once shot the office cat. (M.F. Nolan, Review, *New York Times*, 2/1/76, Section 7, p. 6)

5. See (8) under HEDONISM.

6. If Elizabeth Ray received $14,000-a-year for a job she didn't do—couldn't do, as she says—then Wayne Hays is guilty of far more than a sexual PECCADILLO . . . . To paraphrase a famous joke, that was no lady we caught him with. That was our tax money. (Elsa Gross, "The Hays-Ray affair: This scandal is the public's business," *Philadelphia Inquirer*, 5/30/76, p. 7-E)

7. America continues . . . to represent a number of ideals to Europeans: that real freedom . . . can exist; that under such freedom man can achieve his highest potential; and that despite all of man's PECCADILLOS, government ought to be moral. (Yorick Blumenfeld, of ERR, "Independence reality mystifies Europe," *Norman* [Okla.] *Transcript*, 7/7/76, p. 6)

8. That big one [in the picture] with the moustache is Ben Davidson . . . . The little one he's holding is Jim Bouton, the ex-New York Yankee pitcher who threw curves at the baseball establishment with *Ball Four*, his 1970 book about drinking, dallying and other big-league PECCADILLOES. (Anon., "People," *Time*, 5/24/76, p. 40)

PECCANT (pek' ənt) *noun* sinful; sinning; erring morally; disregarding or violating a rule or practice; faulty; wrong.

PECCANCY *noun* sinfulness.

PECCANTLY *adv.*

PECCABLE *adj.* liable to or capable of sin or error.

PECCABILITY *noun*.

1. We meet up with an interesting PECCANT Chaucer [in *The Life and Times of Chaucer*, a book by John Gardner], an intimate, "forgiving and fascinated," of Edward III's notorious mistress Alice Perrers; a man who probably did seduce a lower-class girl named Cecily Chaumpaigne, and who could hardly have been expected to resist . . . the unofficial fiscal opportunities of his various offices . . . . (C.

Muscatine, Review, *New York Times*, 4/24/77, Section 7, p. 38)

PECKSNIFF (pek' snif) a character (Seth Pecksniff) in *Martin Chuzzlewit* (an 1843 novel by Charles Dickens) who was an UNCTUOUS hypocrite.

PECKSNIFFIAN (pek-snif' ē-ən) *adj.* hypocritically affecting benevolence or high moral principles; falsely moralistic; insincere.

1. If [ex-President] Nixon can perform that service [go to China and tell the Chinese that our country still has great physical and spiritual resources] in a quiet way, and if the PECKSNIFFS and POPINJAYS back here can keep their heads clear over the man for even 10 minutes, perhaps our slipping relationship with the Chinese will be strengthened. (N. Thimmesch. "Nixon's Visit to China Good Sign, " *Daily Oklahoman*, Okla. City, 2/13/76, p. 16)

PECTORAL (pek' tər-əl) *noun* something worn on the breast, as an ornamental plate; (in Anatomy) a pectoral part or organ, as a muscle or fin.

PECTORAL *adj.* of, in, on, or pertaining to the chest or breast; thoracic; worn on the breast or chest; of or for diseases of the lungs; influenced by or resulting from personal feelings; subjective.

1. Sally Field, the old Flying Nun herself, takes off her habit and everything else in a touching performance as a country girl [in the film, *Stay Hungry*] . . . and Arnold Schwarzenegger, a former Mr. Universe, is surprisingly good as the muscle man with heart—and PECTORALS of gold. (J. Kroll, Review, *Newsweek*, 5/17/76, p. 111)

2. . . . he [the policeman] seized my [Russel Wren's] Ban-Lon bosom and . . . got a handful of PECTORAL as well in fingers stern as tongs. (Thomas Berger, *Who Is Teddy Villanova?*, Delacorte Press/Seymour Lawrence, 1977, pp. 34–35)

3. One had the detective's gun . . . . Another, his knitted shirt straining across the massive PECTORALS, had taken the officer's . . . blackjack. . . . (Thomas Berger, *Ibid.*, p. 124)

PECULATE (pek' yə-lāt) *verb* to steal or

take dishonestly (money or property entrusted to one's care); embezzle.

PECULATION *noun*.

PECULATOR *noun*.

PECULATORY *adj*.

1. His [Louis Auchincloss's] novels are littered with men and women who broke their code—whether through PECULATION or adultery or simply by marrying beneath their stations—and paid the price. (R. Schickel, Review of *The Winthrop Covenant*, by Louis Auchincloss, *New York Times*, 3/28/76, Section 7, p. 10)

PEDAGOGY (ped'ə-gō'jē, -goj'ē) *noun* the profession, function, or work of a teacher; teaching; the art or method of teaching, especially instruction in teaching methods.

PEDAGOGIC (ped'ə-goj'ik, -gō'jik) or PEDAGOGICAL *adj*.

PEDAGOGICALLY *adv*.

PEDAGOGUE (ped'ə-gog', -gôg') *noun*.

1. See (5) under PEDANT.

2. Despite [Irving] Wallace's lumbering PEDAGOGIC dialogue [in the book, *The R Document*], frequent near-comic stylistic lapses (my favorite is: "his CADAVEROUS—but not unhandsome—visage"), and his often BATHETIC use of the rhetorical question as an all-purpose plot intensifier . . . , it is hard not to be cheered by democracy's survival [in the book]. (Gene Lyons, Review, *New York Times*, 3/14/76, Section 7, p. 5)

PEDANT (ped'ənt) *noun* a person who makes an excessive or inappropriate display of learning, or who displays scholarship lacking in judgment, sense of proportion, or common sense; a narrow-minded person or teacher who overemphasizes and gives unnecessary stress to rules or minor or trivial details of learning.

PEDANTIC or PEDANTICAL *adj*.

PEDANTICALLY *adv*.

PEDANTICISM *noun* pedantry.

PEDANTRY *noun* the character, quality, or practices of a pedant, as undue display of learning; slavish attention or adherence to rules, details, etc.; an instance of being pedantic.

1. See (1) under NEOLOGISM.

2. His [Sacvan Bercovitch's] sort of intensive textual analysis is enough, I realize, to limit his audience to specialists, but an unfortunate taste for polysyllabic theological terms [in *The Puritan Origins of the American Self*] creates an almost impenetrable aura of PEDANTRY. (L. Marx, Review, *New York Times*, 2/1/76, Section 7, p. 21)

3. See (5) under INELUCTABLE.

4. The technique of counterpoint that Mozart had learned at the age of fourteen was not only remote from Bach, however, but also was dead, an ecclesiastical ANACHRONISM practiced only by such PEDANTS as Padre Martini, who became Mozart's teacher in Bologna during the summer of 1770. (R. Craft, " 'A Prodigy of Nature,' " *New York Review of Books*, 12/11/75, p. 14)

5. Stanley Smith, a lean 44-year-old Californian who has taught at the University of Illinois since 1960, EPITOMIZES PEDAGOGY without PEDANTRY. . . he reveals a deep love for his subject [organic chemistry] and a quiet zeal for imparting its charms and mysteries to the uninitiated. (E. Jenkins, "The Potential of PLATO," *Change*, March 1976, p. 6)

6. See (3) under VERISIMILITUDE.

7. See (8) under BANAL.

8. Hurriedly dressing, he [Leo Brunner] babbled on and on PEDANTICALLY about the thin line that distinguished seduction and rape, finally satisfying himself . . . that there could be no such thing as rape once there was consummation. (I. Wallace, *The Fan Club*, Bantam Edition, 1975, p. 333)

9. [Maury] Fitzgerald [a professor at the College of San Mateo], who brought us here [to the Jewish cemetery in Colma, California, where Wyatt Earp is buried], has more than a PEDANTIC interest in grave sites, too. He is executive secretary-treasurer of the [Cemetery Workers] union [Local 265]. . . . A hundred yards from Wyatt Earp's urn stands the crypt of William Randolph Hearst, . . . the im-

mensely influential newspaper tycoon who was the model for "Citizen Kane." He lies in adjoining Cypress Lawn Cemetery. (M. Olderman, NEA, "Earp Lies Among The Respectable," *Times Herald*, Norristown, Pa., 11/9/76, p. 10)

10. Churchill . . . was accused of ending sentences with a preposition. "This," he said in response, "is the type of arrant PEDANTRY up with which I will not put." (J. Bishop, "Reward of Wit," *Times Herald*, Norristown, Pa., 1/5/77, p. 17)

PEDERASTY (ped'ə-ras'tē, pē'də-) *noun* sexual relations (sodomy, i.e. anal intercourse) between two males, especially when one is a minor.

PEDERAST *noun* a man who engages in pederasty.

PEDERASTIC *adj.*

PEDERASTICALLY* *adv.*

1. It [the English culture of this century] is a world in which, as Mr. [Martin] Green observes [in *Children of the Sun*], "power idolizes the young man as the supreme form of life"—a world of NARCISSISM, PEDERASTY and artifice . . . . It is a world in revolt against fathers and fatherhood . . . . (H. Kramer, Review, *New York Times*, 1/25/76, Section 7, p. 2)

2. Charles Laughton was a homosexual. Clara Bow was sexually insatiable . . . . Rin Tin Tin was a PEDERAST. So what else is new? Clearly sexual revelations TITILLATE publishers—if not readers. (M. Gussow, Review of *Charles Laughton*, by Charles Higham; *The 'It' Girl*, by Joe Morella and Edward Z. Epstein; and of *Hollywood Is A Four Letter Town*, by James Bacon], *New York Times*, 6/20/76, Section 7, p. 16)

3. It is not only that *The Abyss* [by Marguerite Yourcenar, translated by Grace Frick in collaboration with M.Y.] . . . moves with deliberateness and MACHINATION, coincidence being too coincidental and surprise almost wholly absent . . . . The difficulty is with Zeno [the hero] himself. He is throughout utterly

---

*All of the above also may be spelled PAED.

tentative . . . : PEDERAST, but also lover of women; vegetarian, but lest he be doctrinaire, an occasional stew; . . . sympathetic to the Church, but pliant to the Reformation; hospitable to everything except stupidity. (A.A. Cohen, Review, *New York Times*, 7/11/76, Section 7, p. 32)

4. "Impatient ungrateful little Roman swine. I give them [two boys] a flat and I furnish it for them and that's the bloody thanks—" [said P.R. Pathan]. "You furnish it?" [said Ronald Beard] . . . . "PEDERASTIC set-up, is it, is that what it's all about?" "It is what it is and none of your business," Pathan said. (A. Burgess, *Beard's Roman Women*, McGraw- Hill, 1976, p. 64)

5. . . . the denizens of the rear loft [of the building], who, I [Russel Wren] suspected from the name of their operation, The Ganymede Press, printed pornography of the PEDERAST persuasion. (Thomas Berger, *Who Is Teddy Villanova?*, Delacorte Press/Seymour Lawrence, 1977, p. 4)

6. The most culturally resplendent era in the history of man, the time of Pericles, when more philosophers, poets, and heroic sculptors were extant synchronously than have been accumulated in the twenty-five centuries since, was also the Golden Age of PEDERASTY. (Thomas Berger, *Ibid.*, pp. 62-63)

7. Nor did I [Russel Wren] wish to ask change [to make a telephone call] from . . . a comely, almost beautiful young boy in the beanie and blazer of a private school; because . . . he might have assumed I was but another of the PEDERASTS no doubt familiar to him on his homeward route. (Thomas Berger, *Ibid.*, p. 112)

8. See (5) under PEDOPHILIA.

PEDICATION (ped' i-kā' shən) *noun* anal coitus.

1. Paola gave the telephone a long and rapid and filthy monologue, in which PEDICATION, CUNNILINGUS, FELLATION . . . were presented in a HAGIOGRAPHIC context. (A. Burgess, *Beard's Roman Women*, McGraw-Hill, 1976, p. 113)

PEDIMENT (ped'ə-mənt) *noun* (in ARCHI-

TECTURE) a low gable or gable-like feature, typically triangular and outlined with cornices, in the Grecian style; any similar triangular piece used ornamentally, as over a doorway, fireplace, etc.; (in GEOLOGY) a gently sloping rock surface at the foot of a steep slope.

PEDIMENTAL or **PEDIMENTED** *adj.*

1. There were no soaring peaks [in the ancestral Rockies], like their successors, but they did rise from sea level and would have seemed higher above their PEDIMENT than today's Rockies, which although they lift far into the sky, take their start from plains already high. (J.A. Michener, *Centennial*, Fawcett, 1975, p. 50)

2. See (1) under AD INFINITUM.

PEDOPHILIA (pē'də-fil'ē-ə, -fil' yə) *noun* abnormal sexual desire in an adult for children.

1. As [Frank] Deford notes [in the book, *Big Bill Tilden*], a brilliant sketch of Tilden in decline appears in Vladimir Nabokov's *Lolita*. It glitters with multiple refractions. Humbert Humbert, literature's most famous PEDOPHILE, is talking about one of the most notorious in real life [Tilden] . . . ". . . in California, I got her to take a number of very expensive lessons with a famous coach, a husky, wrinkled oldtimer, with a harem of ball boys . . ." (T. Buckley, Review of *Big Bill Tilden*, by Frank Deford, *New York Times*, 6/20/76, Section 7, p. 8)

2. Not since the child-obsessed Hollywood 1930's have kids occupied so much of the cultural consciousness. Then, a demoralized America needed an innocence fix, and producers were like PEDOPHILIAC Frankensteins, creating a race of mutant moppets who played a costumed TRAVESTY of adult life. (J. Kroll, "The Children's Hour," *Newsweek*, 9/27/76, p. 89)

3. Among recent developments: Underground sex magazines are heavily stressing INCEST and PEDOPHILIA. One current West Coast periodical ran ten pages of photos, cartoons, and articles on sex with children. (Anon., "Child's Garden of Perversity," *Time*, 4/4/77, p. 55)

4. ". . . . Lewis Carroll, by the way, was at least a latent if not a practicing PEDOPHILE . . ."

[said Russel Wren]. (Thomas Berger, *Who Is Teddy Villanova?*, Delacorte Press/Seymour Lawrence, 1977, p. 189)

5. "Yes, I [Russel Wren] think I see it clearly now: Bakewell and Washburn . . . pretend to be PEDERASTS, when actually they are PEDOPHILES. Though the common root of both words is the Greek for 'boy,' and with the notorious Attic bias, also by extension 'child'—female liberationaries should take note . . .—the suffixes 'rast' and 'phile' make all the difference for the English-speaking deviate." (Thomas Berger, *Ibid.*, pp. 199-200)

6. . . . and you had an ensemble the wearer of which deserved the pistol-whipping planned for Teddy Villanova, whose PEDOPHILIA now might seem a harmless caprice. (Thomas Berger, *Ibid.*, p. 208)

PEDOPHOBIA (ped'ə-fō'bē-ə) *noun* an irrational fear of children.

1. [From a letter from Sir Arnold Lunn:] "Yesterday's paper recorded a case of PAEDOPHOBIA [a term Lunn liked to use for *fear of children*] . . . one of the results of what is fraudulently described as the permissive society . . . ." (W. F. Buckley Jr., *Execution Eve and Other Contemporary Ballads*, G.P. Putnam's Sons, 1975, p. 486)

PEJORATIVE (pi-jôr' ə-tiv, -jor' -) *adj.* having a disparaging or derogatory effect or force; deprecatory; making lower in worth or quality.

PEJORATIVE *noun* a pejorative word or form.

PEJORATIVELY *adv.*

PEJORATION (pej'ə-rā'shən) *noun* a worsening; depreciation; a lessening in worth or quality.

1. "They called me carpetbagger when I moved the Dodgers from Brooklyn to Los Angeles," O'Malley said. "One man wrote I left because I believed the colored, Puerto Ricans and Jews were taking over Brooklyn. Lies. PEJORATIVE lies . . ." (R. Kahn, *The Boys of Summer*, Harper and Row, 1971, p. 429)

2. "A *Froebel* boy should know how to evaluate things realistically," O'Malley said [to

Roger Kahn], and "Froebel boy" had never sounded so PEJORATIVE. (R. Kahn, *Ibid.*, p. 424)

3. The word elitism is of recent vintage: it does not appear in the American Heritage Dictionary published in 1969. It is a PEJORATIVE label for social philosophies opposed to the notion that rigorous egalitarianiam (*sic*) is a democratic imperative. And elitist is a label for people (like me) who believe that, frequently, egalitarianism is envy masquerading as philosophy. (G.F. Will, "D is for Dodo," *Newsweek*, 2/9/76, p. 84)

4. The term "egghead," with all of its PEJORATIVE implications, became the identifying mark of Adlai Stevenson. (Elinor Lenz, "The Humanities Go Public," *Change*, February 1976, p. 52)

5. See (3) under ARCHETYPE.

6. See (3) under ANTITHESIS.

7. See (3) under MOOT.

8. Profits are called by many names these days, many of them bad. *Obscene, exorbitant, excessive* are the leading PEJORATIVES. (D.B. Tinnin, "Profits: How Much Is Too Little," *Time*, 8/16/76, p. 54)

9. I knew her [Barbara Walters'] old man. Lou Walters was a producer of cut-rate Ziegfeld shows . . . . His daughter is, in my estimation, a tough tomato. This is not a PEJORATIVE. The job of the interviewer is to be merciless in keeping the interviewee on the track, and Barbara Walters can do that. (J. Bishop, "Viewing Barbara," *Times Herald*, Norristown, Pa. 10/28/76, p. 23)

10. [Senator Joe] McCarthy, using the [Freda] Utley research [on Owen Lattimore], jumped to PEJORATIVE conclusions, which defeated his own purpose. The unadorned Utley parallels [of Lattimore's views with those of Stalinists and Maoists] were enough. (J. Chamberlain, "TV Picks 'The Hatchet,'" *Times Herald*, Norristown, Pa., 2/25/77, p. 15)

PELLUCID (pə-loo´ sid) *adj.* allowing the maximum passage of light; clear or limpid; transparent or translucent; clear in meaning; easy to understand; clear and simple in style.

PELLUCIDLY *adv.*

PELLUCIDITY or PELLUCIDNESS *noun.*

1. The PELLUCID quality of [Robert M.] Hutchins's prose was brought home to me a few weeks ago . . . professors who spend their time cultivating their scholarly gardens of rare herbs and leafless plants and professors who teach DESULTORILY to their captive audiences, may find him difficult and dangerous. (F.L. Keegan, "It's Time to Reread Robert M. Hutchins," *Chronicle of Higher Education*, 4/26/76, p. 40)

2. Marital dry rot in suburbia. A clinging mama and her growing-up boy. An alcoholic advertising salesman in search of himself. These are three of the whitest elephants in the attic of contemporary fiction—and author Richard Yates, 50, has devoted a tight, PELLUCID novel to each one. (P. Gray, Review of *The Easter Parade*, by Richard Yates, *Time*, 8/30/76, p. 71)

3. . . . . [Will] Weng [editor of the N.Y. Times' daily and Sunday crossword puzzles] is a gentle German from Terre Haute, Ind. "I was invited to join the Chinese Society of Columbia University," he says, with PELLUCID (transparent . . .) glee. (Murray Dubin, "Puzzled? Then Weng has done his job." *Philadelphia Inquirer*, 11/28/76, p. 4-L)

PEMMICAN (pem´ ə-kən) or **PEMICAN** *noun* a loaf or small, pressed cake of shredded dried meat mixed with fat and dried fruits or berries, originally prepared by North American Indians; dried beef, suet, dried fruits, etc., prepared as a concentrated, high-energy food, used for emergency rations, as on arctic expeditions.

1. During the first summer [at Zendt's Farm] . . . . Levi returned to his old habits . . . started making large links of PEMMICAN, which he considered as nothing but buffalo sausage. (J. Michener, *Centennial*, Fawcett, 1975, p. 16)

PENCHANT (pen´ chənt) *noun* a strong taste, liking, or fondness for something; an inclination or leaning toward.

1. See (3) under ENFANT TERRIBLE.

2. He [Brunner] said . . . she [Sharon Fields] possesses an impressive degree of experience and an admirable PENCHANT for sexual experimentation. (I. Wallace, *The Fan Club*,

Bantam Books, 1975, p. 445)

3. There are embarrasing passages that might have been edited out of this volume [*The Diary of Anaïs Nin: 1955-1966,* edited by Gunther Stuhlmann]: Miss Nin is inclined to believe that critics are "evil" if they are not supportive, and she has a PENCHANT for reprinting letters from admirers whose claims for her art can only arouse disbelief . . . (Joyce Carol Oates, Review, *New York Times,* 6/27/76, Section 7, p. 5)

4. [In his campaign to unseat Senator James Buckley] Moynihan has kept his PENCHANT for sputtering from the lip under control. After squeaking through a primary as the most conservative candidate in a five-way race that included Rep. Bella Abzug, Moynihan has been busier healing Democratic wounds than taking shots at Buckley . . . (Susan Fraker and H.W. Hubbard, "The Choice Races: Roughhouse," *Newsweek,* 11/1/76, p. 34)

5. See (1) under EMBAY.

6. See (1) under KLEPTOMANIA.

PENDULOUS (pen' jə-ləs, pen' də-, -dyə-) *adj.* hanging down freely or loosely; drooping; swinging freely; oscillating.

PENDULOUSLY *adv.*

PENDULOUSNESS *noun.*

1. So the dog will not get itself hung up on barbed wire or thorn bushes while working a trail, a bloodhound's head must be equipped with a great deal of loose skin. Yankee had enough skin for Siamese twins . . . . His FLEWS—the PENDULOUS corners of his upper lip—were long and deep and doleful . . . . (R. Caras, "A Boy's Best Dog," *New York Times,* 3/14/76, Section 6, p. 80)

2. . . . a small hole had been punctured between his eyes, and a filament of red ran from it along the bridge of his nose, collecting in a PENDULOUS drop at the tip. (Thomas Berger, *Who Is Teddy Villanova?,* Delacorte Press/Seymour Lawrence, 1977, p. 33)

3. Natalie [Novotny] laughed rhetorically, by which I mean not with sufficient energy to agitate her breasts, which anyway were firm cones and not of the PENDULOSITY that is sensi-

tive to reverberations. (Thomas Berger, *Ibid.,* p. 183)

PENTIMENTO (pen' tə men' tō) *noun, pl.:* **PENTIMENTI** (-tē) a reappearance in a painting of a design which has been painted over.

1. Many of us are engaged these days in examining the PENTIMENTO of old movies in order . . . to see what was there for us once, what is there for us now. (C. Michener, M. Kasindorf, "Old Movies Come Alive," *Newsweek,* 5/31/76, p. 48)

PENULTIMATE (pi-nul' tə-mit) *adj.* next to the last; of or pertaining to a penult or penults.

PENULTIMATE *noun* a penult.

PENULTIMATELY *adv.*

PENULT or **PENULTIMA** *noun* the one next to the last; the next to the last syllable in a word.

1. Then Gordon Manning, the PENULTIMATE managing editor of *Collier's* called me [Roger Kahn] for lunch and asked if I had any article ideas. (R. Kahn, *The Boys of Summer,* Harper and Row, 1971, p. 375)

2. If elite negotiations are undeniably influential in deciding who gets nominated [for the Presidency], so are a number of other factors . . . . The author implicitly admits as much in his PENULTIMATE chapter . . . . (B. Shafer, Review of *The Invisible Primary,* by Arthur T. Hadley, *New York Times,* 3/28/76, Section 7, p. 22)

3. If this [character in the book, *The Midas Consequence,* by Michael Ayrton] is supposed to be Picasso, he is a somewhat nicer guy than the people-eater depicted by Françoise Gilot Picasso's PENULTIMATE companion (in *Life With Picasso*). (M. Levin, Review, *New York Times,* 4/18/76, Section 7, p. 28)

4. When Fred Astaire rolls his eyes ever so slightly as he fox-trots with Judy Garland in the PENULTIMATE scene from *Easter Parade,* it's a secret, irresistible invitation to us . . . to share his delight. (C. Michener, M. Kasindorf. Review of the TV movie, *That's Entertainment, Part 2, Newsweek,* 5/31/76, p. 51)

5. See (2) under MANICHEISM.

PENUMBRA (pi-num′ brə) *noun* the partly lighted area surrounding the complete shadow of any body, as the moon, in full eclipse; a vague, indefinite, or borderline area.

PENUMBRAL *adj.*

1. . . . he [Hubert Humphrey] put in his last call, to the AFL-CIO's George Meany, sitting in a PENUMBRA of cigar ash in his office . . . . "Hubert says he hasn't made up his mind," Meany told an aide. "That means he's not going to run." Meany was right . . . . (P. Goldman, *et. al.*, "Carter's Sweep," *Newsweek,* 5/10/76, p. 35)

2. Legend has it that Hemingway, broken in mind and about to die, spoke well of Vance Bourjaily's talent . . . . Fifteen years and three novels later, Bourjaily still hovers in that PENUMBRA where able writers try and fail to write a book of real significance. His new novel [*Now Playing at Canterbury*] is not that book . . . : the big American Novel that would let him bask finally in the glare of a major literary reputation. (P.S. Prescott, Review, *Newsweek,* 9/13/76, p. 81)

3. He [Dr. Chase, headmaster of Greyburn] hung up the telephone and eased his chair forward into the light's territory, no longer a PENUMBRAL figure with a disembodied hand reaching like a tentacle from under the rock into the lit spaces of the world to transact necessary business. (W.F. Buckley, *Saving the Queen,* Doubleday, 1976, p. 74)

PERCIPIENT (pər-sip′ ē-ənt) *adj.* perceiving, especially keenly or readily; having powers of perception or insight; discerning; discriminating.

PERCIPIENT *noun* a person who perceives.

PERCIPIENTLY *adv.*

PERCIPIENCE or PERCIPIENCY *noun.*

1. Lord [C.P.] Snow [in his book, *Trollope: His Life and Art*] picks on what he calls "PERCIPIENCE" as the secret of the [Trollope] magic. PERCIPIENCE, as he defines it, is the faculty of looking into things—people, in this case—and divining the hidden workings of the mechanisms. It includes the power to see each person not simply as he is now but as he was once and as he will be in years to come. This power is, of course, essential to the novelist whose characters must run through several volumes . . . though the word [PERCIPIENCE] is a good one it is only a substitute for our old friends perception, intuition, sympathy, understanding . . . . "When we lose our grip/A word comes in handy" said Goethe, and Lord Snow would seem to have reached for a Word. (N. Dennis, Review, *New York Review of Books,* 12/11/75, pp. 34-35)

PERDURABLE (pər-dŏŏr′ ə-bəl, -dyŏŏr′) *adj.* extremely durable or lasting; permanent; everlasting.

PERDURABLY *adv.*

PERDURABILITY *noun.*

PERDURE (pər-dŏŏr′ , -dyŏŏr′) *verb* to remain in existence; continue; last; to endure permanently.

1. Perhaps the most PERDURABLE Brand Name author today is Janet Taylor Caldwell of Buffalo, N.Y., who at the moment has 35 novels in print from four paperback publishers. (R. Walters, "Paperback Talk: Sagas," *New York Times,* 5/22/77, Section 7, p. 46)

2. *Engaged.* Glenn Ford, 61, PERDURABLE, soft-spoken, intense Hollywood leading man, and Actress Cynthia Hayward, 30, his three-year flame. (Anon., "Milestones," *Time,* 8/1/77, p. 71)

PEREGRINATION (per′ə-grə-nā′shen) *noun* travel from one place to another, especially on foot; a course of travel; journey.

PEREGRINATE (per′ə-grə-nāt′) *verb* to travel or journey, especially on foot; to travel over; traverse.

PEREGRINATOR *noun.*

PEREGRINE (per′ ə-grin, -grēn, -grīn) *adj.* foreign; alien; coming from abroad; traveling or migratory.

PEREGRINITY *noun.*

1. Alas, the book [*Growing Up in America*, by Fred M. and Grace Hechinger] concludes its PEREGRINATION [through American education] with a group of final sentences so inoffensive they might easily be overlooked. (C. Truehart,

Review, *Change*, Winter 1975-76, p. 54)

2. If he [a writer for the *Post*] means that [Whittaker] Chambers was reliably an evangelist for this or that position in the sense that, say, Billy Graham and Robert Ingersoll were, then he knows nothing at all about Chambers' intellectual PEREGRINATIONS, which is too bad. (W.F. Buckley Jr., *Execution Eve and Other Contemporary Ballads*, G.P. Putnam's Sons, 1975, p. 317)

3. *Heat and Dust*, [a book] by Ruth Prawer Jhabvala. A scandal involving her grandmother in the day of the Raj haunts a young Englishwoman's PEREGRINATIONS of soul in a modern, but obscurely lit India. (Anon., "Editor's Choice," *New York Times*, 4/11/76, Section 7, p. 45)

4. . . . although the book [*The Devil Finds Work*, by James Baldwin] purports to be an examination of the way American films distort reality, its ECLECTICISM is so pervasive, that all we are left with are PEREGRINATIONS of the mind and ideas that jump around and contradict each other. (O. Coombs, Review, *New York Times*, 5/2/76, Section 7, p. 6)

PERFERVID (pər-fur' vid) *adj.* extremely fervid, ardent, or intense.

PERFERVIDLY *adv.*

1. From this unfortunate beginning [Reverend] Bluntworthy [whose text was "Feed my Lambs"] launched into a PERFERVID oration [before a congregation of cattlemen] about sheep as the symbol of humankind, Jesus as the shepherd, and the world as a great meadow in which right-thinking men took it . . . as a holy obligation to *Feed my sheep* . . . . The collection was one of the bleakest ever taken at Union Church, and in the closing hymn only the minister's voice could be heard. (J.A. Michener, *Centennial*, Fawcett, 1975, p. 738)

2. Joseph L. Rauh, Jr., his PERFERVID concern over lawbreakers notwithstanding, did *not* report to the Justice Department the illegalities of a man [Paul Hughes] who went about town getting money under false pretenses from credulous liberals, flashing forged credentials as an alleged member of a Senate Committee. (W.F. Buckley Jr., *Up From Liberalism*, Arlington House, 2nd Printing 1968, p. 112)

3. Reporters and editors . . . are [in the book, *The Canfield Decision*, by Spiro Agnew] variously (sometimes simultaneously) drunks, simpletons, troublemakers, dupes, traitors, liars, sheep and—worst of all in Agnew's PERFERVID lexicon—"left-wing liberals who work for left-wing liberals." Agnew creates for these "liberals" a formal alliance . . . dedicated to jointly but SURREPTITIOUSLY promoting (and punishing) the candidates (and causes) of their preference (and disdain). (D. Shaw, *Los Angeles Times*, "Agnew 'murders' media and other 'nattering nabobs,'" *Norman* [Okla.] *Transcript*, 5/23/76, p. 17)

PERGOLA (pûr' gə-lə) *noun* an arbor formed of horizontal trelliswork supported on columns or posts, over which vines or other plants are trained; a colonnade having the form of such an arbor.

1. Pioneer Square's cast-iron PERGOLA was built [in Seattle] in 1910. (Anon., Caption on Picture, Bill Speidel's *Seattle Guide*, February 27, March 6, 1976, p. 21)

PERIGEE (per' i-jē) *noun* the point in the orbit of a heavenly body, especially the moon or an artificial satellite, at which it is nearest the earth; the lowest or nearest point.

PERIGEAN or PERIGEAL *adj.*

1. [Gore] Vidal's PERIGEE as a public debater came during the turbulent 1968 Democratic Convention in Chicago. Appearing on ABC-TV, while demonstrators and police rioted in the streets, Vidal called Fellow Commentator William F. Buckley Jr. a "crypto Nazi." Buckley RIPOSTED: "Now listen, you queer. Stop calling me a crypto Nazi or I'll sock you in your goddam face and you'll stay plastered." Mutual lawsuits finally came to a well-earned nothing. (Anon., "Gore Vidal: Laughing Cassandra," *Time*, 3/1/76, p. 63)

PERIPATETIC (per' ə-pə-tet' ik) *adj.* (if capitalized) of or pertaining to Aristotle, who taught philosophy while walking in the Lyceum in ancient Athens; (if lower case) walking or traveling about; itinerant; moving from place to place.

PERIPATETICALLY *adv.*

1. Going to Florida and back is not a very big

deal, in this PERIPATETIC age. (W.F. Buckley Jr., *Execution Eve and Other Contemporary Ballads*, G. P. Putnam's Sons, 1975, p. 434)

2. See (3) under SCATOLOGY.

3. Revealed by echo sounders, the mid-depths [of the ocean] teem with PERIPATETIC, almost invisible but exotic fish with buoyant swim bladders. (J. McCarthy, "Ups and downs of Deep Scattering Layers in oceans," *Smithsonian*, April 1976, p. 73)

4. . . . Jon Cleary [author of the book, *A Sound of Lightning*] is finely attuned to the outdoors. So is his hero, Jack Random, a PERIPATETIC Englishman who has come from Tasmania to manage the Montana holdings of a multi-national wood-pulp octopus. (M. Levin, Review, *New York Times*, 5/30/76, Section 7, p. 14)

5. See (1) under GOLIARD.

PERIPHRASTIC (per′ ə-fras′ tik) *adj.* CIRCUMLOCUTORY; roundabout.

PERIPHRASIS (pə-rif′ rə-sis) *noun, pl.:* -SES (- sēz) CIRCUMLOCUTION; a roundabout way of speaking, or an instance of it.

PERIPHRASTICALLY *adv.*

1. Thomas Berger's *Who Is Teddy Villanova?* is a black comic PARODY of tough-guy detective fiction out of Hammett and Chandler. Despite its seedy urban setting and HYPERTROPHIED plot, it is written in Berger's arch, allusive and rhetorically exhibitionistic style: loquacious, PERIPHRASTIC, EUPHUISTIC—as if spoken by a demented William F. Buckley. (R. Locke, "Novelists as Preachers," *New York Times*, 4/17/77, Section 7, p. 53)

2. Writing about the magical [Greta] Garbo, Alistair Cooke said that all his highfalutin verbiage was just "professional PERIPHRASIS for a yen." (J. Kroll, Review of *Anna Christie*, a play by Eugene O'Neill, *Newsweek*, 4/25/77, p. 89)

PERORATION (per′ə-rā′ shən) *noun* the concluding part of a speech or discourse, which sums up and emphatically recapitulates the principal points; a high-flown or bombastic speech.

PERORATIONAL *adj.*

PERORATE *verb* to speak at length; make a speech; to bring a speech to a close with a formal summing-up or conclusion.

PERORATOR *noun.*

1. These burdens we inherit from the past teach us to be sure the future will bring more of the same. [In *Family Feeling*, a book by Helen Yglesias] Anne's son speaks the PERORATION which sorrows for them all: "There's no way without torment. Unless you forget the whole thing. Throw it all away. Fatherhood. Sons. Fathers and sons. Family." (B. Allen, Review, *Boston Globe*, 3/7/76, p. 17-A)

2. . . . [In *Generations: A Memoir*, a book by Lucille Clifton] Mrs. Clifton delivers her PERORATION: "Things don't fall apart. Things hold. . . ." I call it a PERORATION because the form of this seemingly random collection of memories becomes apparent only at the end (a funeral oration), in a modification of the style and language of America's great orators, Negro preachers. (R. Price, Review, *New York Times*, 3/14/76, Section 7, pp. 7-8)

3. A crowd estimated at 7.5 million persons . . . turned out for a MacArthur ticker-tape parade in New York City [to welcome him home from Korea]. The general's speech before a joint session of Congress was acclaimed as a classic of oratory . . . . In his PERORATION, MacArthur said, " . . . old soldiers never die, they just fade away." . . . . Today it is "give 'em hell" Harry who is fondly remembered, while MacArthur is thought of as a museum piece. (R. Worsnop, "Truman-MacArthur Feud Retold: Generals, Presidents Clash Often," *Norman* [Okla.] *Transcript*, 1/9/76, p. 16)

4. The PERORATIONS from bunting-draped platforms across the land this coming summer are likely to drift away like summer mist. If another Gettysburg Address should emerge as a surprise, so much the better. (S.D. Ripley, "The View from the castle," *Smithsonian*, January 1976, p. 6)

5. The show's Bruce Jenner was Tory Ray Hatter, 25, vice chairman of the Young Conservatives and new holder of the world record for non-stop political speeches—29 hr., 12

min. 30 sec. of PERORATION on codfishing, women's rights and other matters. (Anon., "The People," *Time*, 9/13/76, p. 45)

6. John Connally, 59, was the most apparent loser. Usually a spellbinder, he hurried through a strangely flat address to an underwhelmed convention. His PERORATION was so gloomy that he sounded like a Texas Spengler: "How long this civilization, this free society of America will exist, I do not know." (Anon., "Some Soared, Some Sank," *Time*, 8/30/76, p. 35)

PERQUISITE (pûr' kwi-zit) *noun* an emolument over and above fixed income or salary, especially something customary or expected; any bonus or fringe benefit granted an employee; something demanded or due as a particular privilege because of a person's status, position, etc.; a tip or gratuity.

1. The Dulanys were Irish Marylanders who had converted to the Church of England and thus enjoyed PERQUISITES [in colonial times] denied the [Catholic] Carrolls, who had no great opinion of them anyway. (Mary H. Cadwalader, "Charles Carroll of Carrollton: A signer's story," *Smithsonian*, December 1975, p. 68)

2. . . . [Wayne] Hays has capitalized [as Chairman of the House Administration Committee] on the implied threat that congressmen who choose to cross him might find some of their cherished PERQUISITES missing. (D. Chu and H.W. Hubbard, "Hays: Bully of the Block," *Newsweek*, 6/7/76, p. 27)

3. "Do you mind telling me," I [Russel Wren] asked Washburn, "who controls the money in your family?" . . . . I was amazed to hear him say: "Freddie [my wife] does . . . . It's been a damned good six years, though, and well worth the trouble for the PERQUISITES alone . . . . Vintage vino and fine fodder." (Thomas Berger, *Who Is Teddy Villanova?*, Delacorte Press/Seymour Lawrence, 1977, p. 58)

PERSIFLAGE (pûr' sə-fläzh') *noun* light, frivolous, or bantering talk; banter; a light, frivolous, or flippant style of writing or speaking.

1. She [Eleanor Herbert, in the book, *Miss Herbert: The Suburban Wife*, by Christina Stead] takes a job as a hotel maid, teases the men who brush against her in the corridors and slides into experimental promiscuity that in no way affects her belief in her virginal respectability. She darts off to Paris, where a would-be lover listens to her hypocritical PERSIFLAGE about decency, fair dealing and self-control. (W. Clemons, Review, *Newsweek*, 7/26/76, p. 75)

PERSONA NON GRATA (peR-sō' nä nōn gRä' tä; par-sō' nə non grä' tə, grä -, grat'ə) *noun*, *pl.*: **PERSONAE NON GRATAE** (peR-sō' nī nōn gRä tī, par-sō' nē non grä tē, grä -, grat'ē) an unwelcome or unacceptable person, especially a diplomatic representative unacceptable to the government to which he is accredited.

1. That PERSONA NON GRATA status [of Wayne Hays] is not likely to improve after the confessions of Elizabeth Ray hit the bookstalls this week. The publishers insisted last week that the book was pure fiction, but the search for telltale profiles was likely to become the hottest parlor game in Washington. (T. Mathews, *et. al.*, "Capitol Capers," *Newsweek*, 6/14/76, p. 20)

PERSPICACITY (pûr' spə-kas' i-tē) *noun* keenness of mental perception; discernment; penetration.

PERSPICACIOUS *adj.*

PERSPICACIOUSLY *adv.*

1. To gain an idea, however hazy, of *Survivor's* [a book by Marc Brandel] excitement and PERSPICACITY, one might imagine an Agatha Christie mystery crossbred with Henry James's *Aspern Papers*. (M. Mewshaw, Review, *New York Times*, 3/28/76, Section 7, p. 18)

2. As he progressed in style from DIAPHANOUS Empire or Hellenic to opulent neo-Oriental, [Paris couturier Paul] Poiret drew from all sources at hand, with unerring PERSPICACITY for the best of everything, old and new. At the close of his . . . career, his fashions were what we immediately recognize as "ethnic," but love of INDIGENOUS artisanship prevailed all through his designing days. (Phyllis Feldkamp, Review of *Paul Poiret, King of Fashion*, a show at the

Fashion Institute of Technology, *New York Times*, 6/13/76, Section 6, p. 59)

3. The truth is that Khalifa Ibn Hamed al-Thani [oil minister of Qatar] and his chums have the U.S. and the rest of the world over a barrel of oil. And that is both an ignoble and a defenseless posture, as the PERSPICACIOUS Whifflesnaffer* would have been the first to note. (S. Hempstone, "Over a barrel: Again, the oil price squeeze," *Philadelphia Inquirer*, 11/11/76, p. 11-A)

4. See (1) under PERSPICUOUS.

PERSPICUOUS (pər-spik'yōō-əs) *adj.* clear in statement or expression; lucid; easily understood.

PERSPICUITY (pûr'spə-kyōō'i-te) or **PERSPICUOUSNESS** *noun.*

PERSPICUOUSLY *adv.*

1. I [Russel Wren] record this utterance [of Peggy Tumulty] as literally as I can remember it, to demonstrate that . . . bizarre syntax is often as PERSPICUOUS as the king's English. Peggy's supposition also was PERSPICACIOUS. Her elaboration of it, however, proved preposterous. (Thomas Berger, *Who Is Teddy Villanova?*, Delacorte Press/Seymour Lawrence, 1977, p. 41)

2. She [Natalie Novotny] found in a drawer a pair of spectacles rimmed in very thin horn and with perfectly round lenses of a diameter so vast that . . . half her forehead and most of her bangs were visible through the PERSPICUOUS discs, surely nonprescription circles cut from a window. (Thomas Berger, *Ibid.*, pp. 186-187)

PERTINACIOUS (pûr' tə-nā' shəs) *adj.* holding tenaciously to some purpose, belief, intention, or action, often stubbornly or obstinately; persevering; extremely or stubbornly persistent; hard to get rid of; unyielding.

PERTINACIOUSLY *adv.*

PERTINACITY *noun.*

1. In some of the writers whom he [Lionel Trilling] most admired—in Hazlitt, Arnold, Tocqueville, Mill, and George Orwell . . .

*See (1) under DOWSE.

—that faculty of rational intellect, rigorously and PERTINACIOUSLY exercised, had led to its own TRANSCENDENCE and to its transformation into literature. In the writings of Lionel Trilling we can observe the same processes at work. (S. Marcus, "Lionel Trilling, 1905-1975," *New York Times*, 2/8/76, Section 7, p. 34)

2. I don't know how many innocent young people will go away from the screen representation of the Woodward-Bernstein Watergate exposé, *All the President's Men*, with a feeling that two PERTINACIOUS news hounds saved the republic by hanging on for a year of investigative reporting . . . . History, however, may return an entirely different verdict. (J. Chamberlain, "Vietnam General Analyzes War," *Daily Oklahoman*, Okla. City, 5/7/76, p. 10)

PETTIFOG (pet' ē-fog' , -fôg') *verb* to bicker or quibble over trifles; to carry on a petty, shifty, or rascally law business; to practice chicanery of any sort.

PETTIFOGGER *noun* a lawyer who handles petty cases, especially one who uses unethical methods in conducting trumped-up cases; a trickster; cheater; a quibbler; CAVILER.

PETTIFOGGERY *noun.*

1. See (1) under PARAGON.

2. If . . . liberalism is reshaping itself . . . , then the entire world stands to benefit, and it would be PETTIFOGGING to remind those who carefully drew up their skirts from contact with the old positions and their old apostles, that they all grew up together in intimate communion. (W.F. Buckley Jr., *Up From Liberalism*, Arlington House, 2nd Printing 1968, p. xxv)

3. If ideology calls for a fifteen billion dollar program of public health, the assumption is that the fifteen billion dollars are there—somewhere. It becomes PETTIFOGGERY and obstructionism to maintain that the money is not "there" in the sense of being readily available and uncommitted. It is reactionary to insist that to produce the money it becomes necessary either to raise the level of economic production, . . . raise existing taxes, or inflate the money into existence. (W.F. Buckley Jr.,

Ibid., pp. 169-170)

4. See (1) under MURRAIN.

PHALANSTERY (fal' ən-ster' ē) *noun* the community itself or the buildings occupied by a community known as a phalanx (the unit of society in the utopian social system called Fourierism); any similar association or the buildings it occupies; any communal association or its buildings.

PHALANSTERIAN *adj.*

PHALANSTERIANISM *noun* Fourierism.

1. P.S. 1 [Project Studios One, a new art center in an old school in Queens] has two models . . . . One is the PHALANSTERY of practicing artists which flourished not long ago at St. Katherine's Dock in London . . . . The other parallel . . . is Documenta, the panorama of modern art which turns up from time to time at Kassel in Germany. (J. Russell, "An Unwanted School in Queens Becomes an Ideal Art Center," *New York Times*, 6/20/76, Section 2, p. 41)

PHALLIC (fal'ik) or **PHALLICAL** *adj.* of, like, or pertaining to the phallus or phallicism; genital.

PHALLICISM or PHALLISM *noun* worship of the phallus as symbolic of the creative power of nature, as in the Dionysiac festivals in ancient Greece.

PHALLICIST or PHALLIST *noun.*

PHALLUS *noun* an image of the penis, symbolizing in certain religions the generative power in nature; the penis or the clitoris.

1. In front of the cabin stood some sort of curious-looking Indian ARTIFACT . . . the place is called Camp Peter Rock . . . . See the Indian relic in front of the shack? . . . . It's a six-foot PHALLIC rock, with an amazing resemblance to a penis. (I. Wallace, *The Fan Club*, Bantam Edition, 1975, p. 207)

2. In studying [Alfred] Kinsey, [Paul] Robinson makes good investigative use [in *The Modernization of Sex*] of the tension that resulted from his struggle . . . between scientific neutrality on the one hand and, on the other, a strong commitment to certain values (pleasure, freedom of sexual experimentation) and some powerful biases (toward the rights of youth and against the myth of PHALLIC superiority). (R. Gilman, Review, *New York Times*, 5/30/76, Section 7, p. 5)

3. The architectural solution, by Gyo Obata of . . . . Hellmuth, Obata and Kassabaum, has been to make the building [the Air and Space Museum of the Smithsonian Institution] as big as possible, with a modular structural system strong enough to hang planes from, and flexible enough to accommodate the rockets that used to stand in surrealist PHALLIC splendor in front of the red brick Smithsonian. (Ada Louise Huxtable, "Supermuseum Comes to the Mall," *New York Times*, 7/4/76, Section 2, p. 22)

4. See (2) under FANZINE.

5. See (2) under EPICENE.

6. In Chicago, [architect] Stanley Tigerman, 46, makes houses with a sense of humor bordering on farce. For the former owner of a Las Vegas strip joint, he has designed "The Daisy House," shaped like a PHALLUS. (D. Davis, Mary Rourke, *Real Dream Houses*, *Newsweek*, 10/4/76, p. 69)

7. Kong fighting off the planes [in the new movie, *King Kong*] while straddling the Art Deco PHALLUS [World Trade Center Towers] of the megalopolis is an image that probably even atomic holocaust will never erase from human consciousness, should it survive. (J. Kroll, "The Movies Go Ape—Again," *Newsweek*, 12/20/76, p. 103)

8. At the outset of their drive for equal treatment, militant homosexuals . . . , led by blatantly effeminate men and masculine women, sometimes featured obscene banners and deliberately provocative displays such as a giant PHALLUS on a float. (J.K. Footlick and Susan Agrest, "Gays and the Law," *Newsweek*, 10/25/76, p. 101)

9. It was one of the more unusual weddings of 1973—or indeed of any year. The bride, a 46-year old American photojournalist named Wyn Sargent, wore a bra and an orchid-fiber skirt; the groom, the chief of a cannibal tribe in Indonesian New Guinea, sported only a necktie of spider-web fibers and a PHALLIC

sheath. According to Sargent, the marriage was never consummated and was merely part of her effort to settle a feud among three warring chiefs of the Dani tribe. (Anon., "The Chief's Token Bride," *Newsweek*, 10/25/76, p. 16)

10. See (2) under LIBIDINOUS.

11. He [Donald Washburn] wore fawn-colored trousers of luxuriant cavalry twill . . . . His fly, however, was open, and a view of a naked, small, seemingly withered PHALLUS was offered. (Thomas Berger, *Who Is Teddy Villanova?*, Delacorte Press/Seymour Lawrence, 1977, p. 49)

PHANTASMAGORIA (fan-taz′ mə-gōr′ ē-ə, -gôr′ -) or **PHANTASMAGORY** *noun* a shifting series of phantasms or deceptive appearances, as in a dream; a changing scene made up of many elements; the optical illusion produced by a magic lantern or the like, in which figures increase or diminish in size, pass into each other, dissolve, etc.; any rapidly changing scene.

PHANTASMAGORICAL or **PHANTASMAGORIC** or **PHANTASMAGORICAL** *adj.*

PHANTASMAGORIALLY or **PHANTASMAGORICALLY** *adv.*

PHANTASM *noun* an apparition or specter; a creation of the imagination or fancy; a perception of something that has no physical reality; figment of the mind.

PHANTASMAL or **PHANTASMIC** *adj.*

1. *A Dreambook For Our Time*, by Tadeusz Konwicki . . . . A man whose loyalties shuttled while a fighter in World War II tries to come to terms with his past and postwar present: a PHANTASMAGORIA that is an outstanding example of the modern Polish novel. (Anon., "Paperbacks: New and Noteworthy," *New York Times*, 3/14/76, Section 7, p. 35)

2. Nathaniel Hawthorne spoke of the "PHANTASMAGORICAL antics" he had played in describing the socialist community which appears in *The Blithedale Romance*: the antics played in the commune conceived by Ahmed [in the book, *Guerrillas*, by V.S. Naipaul] could also be called PHANTASMAGORICAL. (K. Miller, Review, *New York Review of Books*,

12/11/75, p. 3)

3. [Paul] Hughes unfolded to [Joseph L.] Rauh [Jr.] a PHANTASMAGORIA of treacherous doings on the part of [Senator Joseph] McCarthy and his associates—so grotesque and bizarre . . . that they would surely have struck Rauh as incredible had they been imputed to a Communist, rather than to Senator McCarthy. But Rauh was instantly taken in . . . so hot was his lust for anti-McCarthyana. (W.F. Buckley Jr., *Up From Liberalism*, Arlington House, 2nd Printing 1968, pp. 103-104)

4. See (2) under GOTHIC.

PHARISAIC (far′ i-sā′ ik) or **PHARISAICAL** *adj.* practicing or advocating strict observance of external forms and ceremonies of religion or conduct without regard to the spirit; self-righteous; SANCTIMONIOUS; hypocritical; (if capitalized) of or pertaining to the Pharisees.

PHARISAICALLY *adv.*

PHARISEE *noun* a SANCTIMONIOUS, self-righteous or hypocritical person; (if capitalized) a member of an ancient Jewish sect which observed the letter but not the spirit of religious law.

PHARISAISM or **PHARISAISM** *noun.*

1. Most of us were told at an early age that money isn't really interesting—and most of us, with CALLOW common sense, instantly rejected the HOMILY as so much PHARISAICAL cant. (P.S. Prescott, Review of *The Rockefellers*, by Peter Collier and David Horowitz; and of *The Rockefeller Syndrome*, by Ferdinand Lundberg, *Newsweek*, 4/5/76, p. 81A)

PHATIC (fat′ ik) *adj.* of, constituting, or given to formulistic talk, meaningless sounds, etc. used merely to establish social contact rather than to communicate ideas.

PHATICALLY *adv.*

1. Many Western ears will find it hard to tell whether [W.S.] Merwin [in his book of poetry, *The Compass Flower*] is being VATIC or PHATIC. (P. Gray, Review, *Time*, 3/21/77, p. 91)

PHILIPPIC (fi-lip′ ik) *noun* (if lower case) any discourse or speech characterized by bitter denunciation or invective; (if capitalized) any of the orations delivered by Demosthenes against Philip II of Macedon.

1. There is a brilliantly written piece called *The Warrior Intellectuals*, by Frances Fitzgerald, subtitled *A Philippic Against Daniel P. Moynihan and the AUGURS on the Right*. It is a full-dress intellectual attack not only on Moynihan but on the whole school of thought of which he is a leader and the best-known symbol. Despite my basic disagreement with the piece . . . . (M. Lerner, "New political mood pervades U.S.," *Norman* [Okla.] *Transcript*, 5/14/76, p. 6)

2. "Good legs," Gordon [Kahn] said, "but he [Al Gionfriddo] doesn't qualify as an intelligent man." Gordon turned to his daughter and lectured on the basics of positioning oneself in defensive baseball. Her round face lit, as though she were hearing a PHILIPPIC. After a while, I excused myself, pleading homework. The Yankees won the Series [from the Dodgers], four games to three. (R. Kahn, *The Boys of Summer*, Harper and Row, 1971, p. 46)

PHILISTINE or PHILISTINE (fil′ i-stēn′) *noun* a person lacking in or smugly indifferent to culture, esthetic refinement, etc., or contentedly commonplace, narrow, or conventional in ideas and tastes.

PHILISTINE or PHILISTINE *adj.* lacking in, indifferent to, or hostile to culture; smugly conventional.

PHILISTINISM or PHILISTINISM *noun.*

1. None of this [reduced attention to education in magazines and newspapers] . . . represents a conspiracy against the educators. It comes as a result of a number of confluent trends, including in very large measure the growing PHILISTINISM in American higher education. (G.W. Bonham, "Change and the Academic Future" [Editorial], *Change*, June 1974, p. 10)

2. See (2) under SANCTIMONIOUS.

3. Kipling . . . was on the wrong side; as [Kingsley] Amis says [in his book, *Rudyard Kipling And His World*], citing LeGallienne,

the Englishman as brute and PHILISTINE never before had an admired writer on his side, nor progressive thought so literary an enemy . . . he [Kipling] became a show-off and fake. (M. Green, Review, *New York Times*, 4/18/76, Section 7, p. 14)

4. There are a number of other memorable stories in the collection [*Selected Stories*, by Nadine Gordimer] . . . . The isolation of one timid, sensitive woman at a rowdy PHILISTINE party in *The Night the Favourite Came Home*; . . . in all these Gordimer has been inspired by her belief that ". . . the whole value of writing should be its dispassionate view. The injustices will come through." (Penelope Mortimer, Review, *New York Times*, 4/18/76, Section 7, p. 7)

5. She [Olga Kahn] took secret pride in the intellectual level of the TJHS [Thomas Jefferson High School] English Department and never relaxed her vigilance for PHILISTINISM. She entertained elegantly, taught five days a week, relished radical theater and feasted on concerts conducted by Serge Koussevitzky, which still left time to exorcise PHILISTINISM from her home. (R. Kahn, *The Boys of Summer*, Harper and Row, 1971, p. 11)

6. "Is that child [Roger] playing ball in the hall again? He should be reading." Olga [Kahn] was again exorcising PHILISTINISM. She thrust forward *Little Stories of Great Musicians* . . . . (R. Kahn, *Ibid.*, p. 22)

7. The old guard has responded to nontraditional [college] programs as if they were assaults by the PHILISTINES on the liberal arts tradition. They intend to preserve what is left of a badly battered orthodoxy. (H.I. London, "The Case for Nontraditional Learning," *Change*, June 1976, p. 28)

8. Now that she stands tiptoe in sensible shoes on the threshold of becoming Britain's first woman Prime Minister, Margaret Thatcher is out to convince the voters she still is, at heart, only a shopkeeper's daughter . . . . No figure in public life here [Britain] in recent memory has been called as many names . . . . "The Female PHILISTINE from Finchley"—an attack on her education policies with reference to the London suburb she represents. (H.A. Milligan, Associated Press, "Shopkeeper's daughter may be next prime minister," *Norman* [Okla.]

Transcript, 6/20/76, p. 36)

9. Some PHILISTINES say football is more brawn than brain . . . . But football is the last frontier of intellect. It is *very* complicated and getting more so. . . . (G.F. Will, "Is That A Red Dog in the Seam?" *Newsweek*, 9/6/76, p. 72)

10. They ["affirmative action" decrees] abridge the academy's most fundamental freedom, the freedom to select its professorship solely in accordance with standards of scholarly excellence. And in attempting to regulate the racial and ethnic composition of student bodies, PHILISTINES from the government have tried to abridge the freedom of the university to control its curriculum. (G.F. Will, "Common Sense on Race," *Newsweek*, 1/24/77, p. 80)

PICARESQUE (pik'ə-resk') *adj.* pertaining to, characteristic of, or characterized by a form of prose fiction, originally developed in Spain, in which the adventures of an engagingly roguish hero are described in a series of usually humorous or satiric episodes that often depict, in realistic detail, the everyday life of the common people; of, pertaining to, designating, or resembling rogues or sharp-witted, likable vagabonds and their adventures.

1. [Northrop] Frye risks becoming the great homogenizer of literature. *The Golden Ass* of Apuleius, a curious and effective mixture of PICARESQUE incident and Neoplatonic fancy, is glanced at by Frye [in *The Secular Scripture: A Study of the Structure of Romance*] in both of its aspects, but with small sense of the book's DIALECTICAL or even self-contradictory nature. (H. Bloom, Review, *New York Times*, 4/18/76, section 7, p. 21)

2. These big books [*Surface of the Earth*, by Reynolds Price; and *Beyond the Bedroom Wall*, by Larry Woiwode] are not filled with dramatic tension. The characters do not possess weird or PICARESQUE qualities intended to grab the reader in the first eight pages. (J. Weston Jr., "A 'Boomlet' in American Letters: The Return of the Family," *Chronicle of Higher Education*, 5/3/76, p. 12)

3. Next to the United States Government, Mark Russell is one of Washington's most durable institutions, a PICARESQUE, stand-up comic whose lines are as fresh as the afternoon headlines—and twice as interesting. But in eighteen years of entertaining Capital insiders and tourists, Russell has never had much of a national image; his wit has been too specialized for an audience unlikely to know that Wayne Hays' home base is Steubenville, Ohio. (J.J. Lindsay, [Introduction to] "The Insider," *Newsweek*, 7/19/76, p. 58)

4. See (3) under LUDDITE.

5. Pfc. Jamie Hawkins [in *No Bugles, No Drums*, by Charles Durden] is a foul-mouthed Georgia pothead of 20 who finds, soon after he is shipped to South Vietnam, that the Army is at war with his soul . . . . Hawkins' PICARESQUE journey through the war is marked by some of the funniest, ghastliest military scenes put to paper since Joseph Heller's *Catch 22*. (Kim Willenson, Review, *Newsweek*, 8/9/76, p. 72)

6. See (3) under CAMP.

7. See (1) under DEMOTIC.

PICARO (pik'ə-rō, pē'kä-Rо') or **PICAROON** (pik'ə-rōōn') *noun, pl.:* **PICAROS** (-rōz,-Rōs) an adventurous rogue, vagabond, thief, or brigand; a pirate or corsair; a pirate ship (picaroon).

PICAROON *verb* to act or operate as a pirate or brigand.

1. Kelly P. Gast [in the book, *Murphy's Trail*] mingles light-fingered humor with an offbeat cattle drive to San Diego from Baja California. This is where a PICAROON named Mike Murphy jumps ship (a cattle boat) in the year 1911, which is just in time for the Mexican civil war. (M. Levin, Review, *New York Times*, 4/18/76, Section 7, p. 29)

PIED-À-TERRE (pyä-dä-teR') *noun, pl.:* **PIED-À-TERRE** a small dwelling for temporary or part-time use, as an apartment maintained in a foreign city.

1. Her [Lee Radziwill's] New York apartment, which for many years was used as a PIED-À-TERRE when she came back here for visits, is a sea of staunchly elegant French and English period pieces, with acres of fabric. (Lisa Hammel, "Lee Radziwill as Decorator: A New Step, Confidently Taken," *New York Times*,

2/20/76, p. 29)

PIETISM (pī′ə-tiz′əm) *noun* a system that stresses the devotional ideal in religion; exaggeration or affectation of piety.

PIETISTIC *adj.*

PIETISTICALLY *adv.*

1. [Marshall G.S. Hodgson, author of the book, *The Venture of Islam: Conscience and History in a World Civilization*] sees the history of Islam . . . as an extended struggle of a gentle PIETISM to escape from an arid legalism. (C. Geertz, Review, *New York Review of Books*, 12/11/75, p. 24)

2. Corruption moulted the last third of the previous century, in contrast to the PIETISTIC patriotism in fashion at the time . . . . In the 1880s the price of a Senate seat (paid by bribing state legislatures, which then elected senators) was high—and there were plenty of takers. (R. MacLeish, "National spirit: pendulum begins to swing," *Smithsonian*, July 1976, p. 30)

3. It [Carter's inaugural address] was, on balance, a strongly religious speech—too simply PIETISTIC perhaps. But it was also an accurate expression of Carter's faith . . . (Anon., "Waltzing Into Office," *Time*, 1/31/77, p. 10)

PILLION (pil′ yən) *noun* a cushion attached behind a saddle for an extra rider, especially a woman, as in medieval times; an extra saddle behind the driver's on a motorcycle.

1. It was part of Roman culture—two young grinners on a Vespa or Lambretta, coming in suddenly from the rear, the PILLION-boy making the grab, then off, triumphant, waving, grinning, holding trophy [Ronald Beard's leather case] aloft. (A. Burgess, *Beard's Roman Women*, McGraw-Hill, 1976, p. 78)

PILPUL (pil′po͞ol) an ingenious, hair-splitting, penetrating argument, especially in Jewish Talmudic study.

1. "It was a terrifying, sometimes even a SADISTIC, method of teaching," says [Irving] Howe [in *World of Our Fathers*], "and only the kinds of students that came to Cohen [at

City College of New York] could have withstood it—Jewish boys with minds honed to DIALECTIC, bearing half-conscious memories of PILPUL, indifferent to the prescriptions of gentility, intent on a vision of lucidity." (T.L. Haskell, Review, *Chronicle of Higher Education*, 3/29/76, p. 11)

2. Harry Kemelman's series about David Small, the Massachusetts rabbi who solves murder cases with an application of PILPUL, Talmudic reasoning, has been a favorite ever since the first one came out in 1964. Now we [have] *Wednesday The Rabbi Got Wet* . . . when Rabbi Small gets busy with his PILPUL there is a neat solution to the case. (N. Callendar, Review, *New York Times*, 9/12/76, Section 7, p. 47)

PIQUANT (pē′ kant, -känt) *adj.* agreeably pungent or sharp in taste or flavor; biting; tart; interesting, provocative, stimulating, or lively; spicy; intriguing.

PIQUANCY or **PIQUANTNESS** *noun.*

PIQUANTLY *adv.*

1. I did not send a telegram of congratulations to the Right Honorable Edward Heath, but your letter thanking me for doing so reminds me how ill-mannered I was not to have done so, and emphasizes a wonderful PIQUANCY, that the former editor of the *New Statesman* should be thanking the editor of the *National Review* for congratulating the people of Great Britain for emancipating themselves from the influence of the *New Statesman*. (W.F. Buckley Jr., *Execution Eve and Other Contemporary Ballads*, G.P. Putnam's Sons, 1975, p. 362)

2. He [Sir Arnold Lunn] found, as other modern critics, notably Malcolm Muggeridge, have done, a high PIQUANCY in the forms and implications of the great sexual revolution. (W.F. Buckley Jr., *Ibid.*, p. 486)

3. Schedule a really hot debate, and students will come out of the woodwork to hear it. Let them anticipate . . . high forensic or DIALECTICAL skill (e.g., the polished Professor Fred Rodell . . . vs. the formidable James Jackson Kilpatrick on the subject of the Supreme Court . . . or a PIQUANT personal situation (Owen Lattimore vs. Fred Utley . . .) —sometimes the fires that are kindled at such meetings stay lit. But

. . . political life on campus seems to have reduced to a few spectaculars. (W.F. Buckley Jr., *Up From Liberalism*, Arlington House, 2nd Printing 1968, p. 132)

4. See (2) under CARAPACE.

PISCICIDE (pis'ə-sīd', pis'kə-sīd') *noun* a substance used to kill fish.

PISCICIDAL *adj.*

1. [Red] Smith is the third sportswriter ever honored with a Pulitzer [Prize] . . . . Certainly Smith had his faults. For one, he wasted an inexplicable amount of prose on fishing, which can be boring even when rendered in such vintage Smith terms as "PISCICIDE." . . . For the newcomers who claim a patent on hard-hitting and ICONOCLASTIC reporting, Smith recalls the Trib's great editor Stanley (Coach) Woodward . . . . (P. Axthelm, "The Master's Touch," *Newsweek*, 5/17/76, p. 75)

PISCINE (pis' īn, pis' ēn, pis' in, pī' sēn) *adj.* of, pertaining to, or resembling a fish or fishes.

1. . . . I [Russel Wren] said in an undertone, with the knowledge that "Bombay duck" was not fowl but rather a PISCINE dish: "This whole affair is quite fishy." (Thomas Berger, *Who Is Teddy Villanova?*, Delacorte Press/Seymour Lawrence, 1977, p. 150)

PISONIA or **PISONIA** (pī-sō' nə-yə) *noun* (after Dr. Pison, 1611-1678, a Dutch botanist) a genus of trees and shrubs having flowers without petals, and stony fruits.

1. Bird-catcher tree is the common name sometimes applied to PISONIA, because the seed pods have a sweet gum which attracts birds. Another name for PISONIA is heimerliodendron. [Caption above picture]. (Anon., "PISONIA: Focus Look-Alike," *Plants Alive*, May 1976, pp. 12-13)

PLACATORY (plā'kə-tōr' ē, -tôr' ē, plak'ə) or **PLACATIVE** *adj.* serving, tending, or intended to placate.

PLACATE (plā' kāt, plak-āt') *verb* to appease or pacify; MOLLIFY; to stop from being angry.

PLACATER *noun.*

PLACATION *noun.*

PLACABLE *adj.* capable of being placated or appeased; readily pacified; forgiving.

PLACABLY *adv.*

PLACABILITY *noun.*

1. As for the recent Rhodesian statement [by Henry Kissinger], he [Gov. Jerry Brown] approved it, but he was skeptical of merely PRECATORY admonitions. What was that word again? . . . . I thought he had said "PLACATORY," a nice $2.95 word, but I ran after him . . . to check. He had said "PRECATORY," a three-dollar word if there ever was one . . . . I'm skeptical of Brown; but I'm impressed. (J.J. Kilpatrick, "Brown Leaves Jaded Washington Press Corps Wagging Their Heads," *Daily Oklahoman*, 5/21/76, p. 8)

PLACEBO (plə-sē' bō) *noun*, *pl.:* -BOS or -BOES a harmless substance having no pharmacological effect but given to a patient merely to humor him, or given to one group of subjects acting as a control in an experiment in which another group is given a drug that is being tested; something said or done to win the favor of another.

1. Doctors gave [Adam] Smith [author of the book, *Powers of Mind*] little lectures on PLACEBOS, on drugs, on the RUMPELSTILTSKIN effect (naming an ailment makes a patient get better), on split-brain research . . . . He half-practices TM and discloses (shame!) his secret MANTRA. (M. Gardner, Review, *New York Review of Books*, 12/11/75, p. 46)

2. Their research [that of Ernest Noble's group at the University of California at Irvine] indicates that a "sober-up-pill" may be available soon . . . . The subjects [of this research] . . . tossed off 6 ounces of gin or vodka . . . . They were next given either a moderate dose of one of the three drugs [aminophylline, ephedrine, or L-DOPA]—or a PLACEBO, and their relative degree of inebriation was measured . . . alcoholic impairment of the critical ability to process information was reduced by as much as 50 percent in those who had taken the drugs, known as AMETHYSTIC agents. (Anon., "A Sober-Up Pill," *Newsweek*, 11/1/76, p. 63)

PLANGENT (plan' jənt) *adj.* resounding loudly and resonatingly, especially with a vibrating, plaintive, or mournful sound, as a bell; beating with a loud or deep sound, as the breaking of waves.

PLANGENCY *noun.*

PLANGENTLY *adv.*

1. And [Peter] Martins achieves [in *Chaconne*, a Balanchine ballet] a rhythmic PLANGENCY that is independently thrilling. (Arlene Croce, Review, *The New Yorker*, 2/9/76, p. 96)

2. Miss [Alicia] deLarrocha does not observe the repeats and takes tempos that show off her dazzling fingers [on the piano]. This performance is PLANGENT and urgent in its pace. Haydn is given a full dynamic treatment together with modern force and drive. (D. Webster, "Decorative artistry in 10 Haydn sonatas," *Philadelphia Inquirer*," 10/24/76, p. 3-L)

3. A loud female voice at Da Meo Patacca was singing, PLANGENTLY, that song about the funicular railway. (A. Burgess, *Beard's Roman Women*, McGraw-Hill, 1976, pp. 66-67)

PLEBEIAN (plə-bē' ən) *adj.* belonging or pertaining to the common people; common, commonplace, coarse, or vulgar.

PLEBEIAN *noun* one of the common people; a vulgar, coarse person.

PLEBEIANLY *adv.*

1. Waiting time for a new Mercedes-Benz ranges from five months to 14 (for the relatively PLEBEIAN-priced $6,738 diesel 200 model . . . and would-be buyers . . . are getting annoyed. (Anon., "Mercedes' Buy-Back," *Time*, 5/31/76, p. 55)

2. He [James Hanley] has perfected a gritty, PLEBEIAN realism that leaves one emotionally exhausted yet persuaded that here is a writer of high integrity and considerable achievement. Hanley's new novel, *A Dream Journey*, is one of his best . . . . (I. Howe, Review, *New York Times*, 12/19/76, Section 7, p. 1)

PLETHORA (pleth' ər-ə) *noun* overfullness; superabundance; excess; glut.

PLETHORIC *adj.* overfull; TURGID; inflated.

PLETHORICALLY *adv.*

1. Governmental responses . . . have come primarily on the education side of the education-work relationship. The early 1960's saw a PLETHORA of such programs, including the Manpower Development Training Act, The Economic Opportunity Act, the Neighborhood Youth Corps, the Job Corps and many other federal, state and local initiatives. (G. Weathersby, Review of *The Boundless Resource: A Prospectus for an Education-Work Policy*, by Willard Wirtz; and *Bridging the Gap: A Study of Education-to-Work Linkages*, by Richard I. Ferrin and Solomon Arbeiter, *Chronicle of Higher Education*, 6/28/76, p. 16)

2. When he died at the age of 85 in 1961, Carl Gustav Jung left . . . both disciples and detractors; a PLETHORA of papers, letters, and RECONDITE studies that are still being translated and published; and a continuing controversy as to his significance for our century. (J. Hollis, Review of *C.G. Jung: His Myth in Our Time*, by Marie-Louise von Franz, translated by William H. Kennedy; and *C.G. Jung: The Haunted Prophet*, by Paul J. Stern; and *Jung and the Story of Our Time*, by Laurens van der Post, *Chronicle of Higher Education*, 7/26/76, p. 9)

3. In a sense, art nouveau invented female chic in the popular arts. Not since the 16th century mannerists had there been such a PLETHORA of delicately icy women as now appeared on that new form, the advertising poster. (R. Hughes, "The Snobbish Style," *Time*, 9/13/76, p. 67)

4. See (2) under SATURNALIA.

PNEUMATIC (nŏō-mat'ĭk, nyŏō-) *adj.* of or pertaining to air, gases or wind; operated by air or by the pressure or exhaustion of air; filled with or containing compressed air, as a tire; (in Theology) of or pertaining to the spirit or soul; spiritual.

PNEUMATICALLY *adv.*

1. See (2) under EPITOMIZE.

2. John Leonard just wrote a bitter-hilarious essay in the New York Times on the way supposedly adult men seek out PNEUMATIC chil-

dren and shy away from women. (G. Wills, "Visions of playthings dance in our heads," *Philadelphia Inquirer*, 2/7/77, p. 9-A)

3. A mustached woman in a filthy saffron dressing gown, showing a PNEUMATIC cleavage, leaned forward on her camp chair . . . and beckoned to me in what she believed was a lascivious gesture. . . . (Thomas Berger, *Who Is Teddy Villanova?*, Delacorte Press/Seymour Lawrence, 1977, p. 112)

POETASTER (pō'it-as'tər) *noun* an inferior or poet; a writer of indifferent or mediocre verse; rhymester; would-be poet.

1. [Harry] Crosby the man—the master of orgies, the worshiper of books, the self-conscious opium eater and neurotic poseur—far outran Crosby the POETASTER or Crosby the publisher, under his own Black Sun imprint, of Joyce and other vanguard writers of the '20's. His brief career exaggerated the frantic side of the "lost generation" of writers who lived in Paris after World War I. (R. Sokolov, Review of *Black Sun: The Brief Transit and Violent Eclipse of Harry Crosby*, by Geoffrey Wolff, *Newsweek*, 9/6/76, p. 63A)

2. Born into a BOURGEOIS Parisian family in 1901, he [André Malraux] waged a "fight against destiny" that at first took the form of dandyism and POETASTING, clothing him in silk-lined cloaks and setting him toward Indochina where he sought to ransack jungle treasures that would bring him an easy life. Instead he found colonialism and a conscience. (P.D. Zimmerman, "Malraux: L'Homme Engagé," *Newsweek*, 12/6/76, p. 88)

POIGNANT (poin' yənt, poin' ənt) *adj.* keenly distressing to the feelings; keen or strong in mental appeal; affecting or moving the emotions of pity and compassion; pungent to the smell; sharp, biting, penetrating, pointed, etc.

POIGNANCY *noun.*

POIGNANTLY *adv.*

1. I am aware that it is fashionable to speak of the widening [economic] gap between the less developed and the developed nations. And if one looks at the divergences between humanitarian hopes and the sad reality for India, Pak-

istan, Bangladesh, Haiti and numerous former colonies in Africa, Latin America and Asia, one appreciates the POIGNANCY of the shortfall. (P.A. Samuelson, "Capitalism in Twilight?," *Newsweek*, 6/7/76, p. 76)

2. Haunted by fear and despair after twice being attacked and robbed, these aged New Yorkers [Hans and Emma Kabel] slashed their wrists and hanged themselves in the apartment they had shared for 50 years. This POIGNANT human tragedy occurred because of America's failure to ensure safe living conditions for old people in her cities. (Anon., "Blood On Our Hands [Editorial]," *Times Herald*, Norristown, Pa., 10/14/76, p. 20)

3. See (3) under TRANSVESTITE.

4. Highly sensitive matters will be discussed—assuming, of course, that the Vietnamese government agrees to receive a delegation [headed by former senator Mike Mansfield] as the State Department has requested. The POIGNANT question of a full accounting as to the fate of the missing U.S. servicemen is only one of the many to be taken up in a preliminary way. (Anon., "U.S. Emissary To Hanoi [Editorial]," *Times Herald*, Norristown, Pa., 3/3/77, p. 16)

POINTILLISM (pwan' tə liz' əm, -tē-iz' əm, poin'-) *noun* (in Painting) a theory and technique developed by the Neo-Impressionist painters, based on the scientific theory that the juxtaposition of points or spots of pure colors, as blue and yellow, are optically mixed into the resulting hue, as green, by the viewer.

POINTILLIST *noun.*

POINTILLISTIC or **POINTILLIST** *adj.*

1. Five of the works [on Afro-American culture and history published in the last year or so] are of special distinction: Eugene Genovese's . . . . *Roll, Jordan, Roll*; Theodore Rosengarten's recording of the life-chronicle of the black Alabama farmer Nate Shaw in *All God's Dangers*, which verges on being a type of POINTILLISM in language form; Martin Kilson's. . . . *Ethnicity: Theory and Experience*; and Ralph Gleason's . . . . *Celebrating the Duke*. An unexpected entry into these ranks is this thoroughgoing, scholarly presentation [in *Black Consciousness, Identity, and Achievement: A Study of Students in Historically Black Col-*

leges] by [Patricia] Gurin and [Edgar G.] Epps. (K. Jackson Jr., Review, *Change*, February 1976, p. 63)

2. In our POINTILLISTIC attack this month in WRAPAROUND [a feature of Harper's], the villain takes his licks in a variety of ways. For some curious reason, humor—itself a form of socially acceptable wickedness—seems to be a popular weapon [against villains]. (N.W. Aldrich Jr., "Villains: Who's to Blame?," *Harper's*, January 1975, p. 5)

POLEMIC (pə-lem'ik, pō-) *noun* a controversial argument, as one against some opinion, doctrine, etc.; a person who argues in opposition to another; controversialist.

POLEMIC or POLEMICAL *adj.* of, pertaining to, or involving disputation or controversy; controversial; disputatious.

POLEMICALLY *adv.*

POLEMICIST or POLEMIST *noun* a person engaged or skilled in polemics.

POLEMICS *noun* (construed as singular) the art or practice of disputation or controversy.

1. I had scored a POLEMICAL checkmate [by saying I hoped Braddock would win because he was a Catholic after my black butler (also a Catholic) had said he hoped Louis would win the Louis-Braddock fight]. (W.F. Buckley Jr., *Execution Eve and Other Contemporary Ballads*, G.P. Putnam's Sons, 1975, p. 224)

2. Strangely, the subject of Mr. Nixon's perfidies did not wholly occupy Mr. [John Kenneth] Galbraith, a man of personal generosity not always visible through his POLEMICS. (W.F. Buckley Jr., *Ibid.*, p. 287)

3. . . . all he is is a POLEMICIST for the Left: Congress could never have meant to extend to him the immunities intended for objective newspapermen. (W.F. Buckley Jr., *Ibid.*, p. 431)

4. I had an encounter with Ms. Germaine Greer, the antisexist sex bomb who has wrangled with lots of people including Norman Mailer, about whom, incidentally, she wrote the most GALVANIZING POLEMIC in the recent history of the art. (W.F. Buckley Jr., *Ibid.*, p. 418)

5. [F.R.] Leavis was distinctively English, a central figure at Cambridge, founder of a school of criticism, with disciples and enemies, a passionate moralist, a grand POLEMICIST, a true believer in the redemptive powers of literature. (S. Marcus, "Lionel Trilling, 1905-1975," *New York Times*, 2/8/76, Section 7, p. 1)

6. Hence, the POLEMICAL line of discourse that [Lionel] Trilling now took up [in *Beyond Culture*] was essentially aimed at the excesses of irrationalism and self-abandonment that the "success" of the adversary culture had made popular and even chic. (S. Marcus, *Ibid.*, p. 30)

7. See (1) under SISYPHEAN.

8. See (2) under EXEGESIS.

9. . . . whether [Bertrand] Russell is writing about educational theory or sexual MORES, his POLEMICAL intent is to free men from the spectre of both [ignorance and fear]. (M. Rosenthal, Review of *The Life of Bertrand Russell*, by Ronald W. Clark; *My Father Bertrand Russell*, by Katherine Tait; and *The Tamarind Tree*, by Dora Russell, *New York Times*, 2/15/76, Section 7, p. 2)

10. The authors [Samuel Bowles and Herbert Gintis] combine the sophisticated technical skills of modern economics with an uncompromising Marxism. Applying these two perspectives to American education gives an odd hodgepodge of a book. Part [of *Schooling in Capitalist America: Educational Reforms and the Contradictions of Economic Life*] is complicated analysis of school performance. Part is shrill anti-capitalist POLEMIC. (Jay S. Goodman, Review, *Boston Globe*, 3/7/76, p. 15A)

11. This book [*The CIA File*, edited by Robert L. Borosage and John Marks] is a deck overwhelmingly loaded against the CIA's covert operations, a relentless indictment of its record, and a virtual POLEMIC of demand that covert operations be dismantled. (J. Flannery, Review, *Boston Globe*, 3/7/76, p. 16A)

12. It seems important, in attempting to assess the value or seriousness of Susan Brownmiller's POLEMIC on rape [*Against Our Will*], to under-

stand that there are really two audiences for it, one which will know much of what she has to say already, and another which is ill-equipped by training or sympathy to understand it at all. (Diane Johnson, Review, *New York Review of Books*, 12/11/75, p. 36)

13. Inasmuch as the Committee [for Cultural Freedom] was composed of some of the most discriminating intellectuals in America, I shrank from the conclusion that, their attention having been forced to the document [*A Clean Politics Appeal*, by Elmer Davis and Archibald MacLeish], they should have failed to smell out what was so reekingly there, namely, POLEMICAL foulness. I was therefore relieved to come across evidence that the Committee was distressed by the political venture of fellow members MacLeish and Davis. (W.F. Buckley Jr., *Up From Liberalism*, Arlington House, 2nd Printing 1968, p. 79)

14. Students [after the war] went about the campus weighted down by a macrocosmic concern for the human race. As ever, most of the NOSTRUM-peddlers pointed Left: we must nationalize the railroads, inaugurate world government, throw our bombs into the sea . . . It was generally believed that every . . . point scored, every pamphlet distributed, every POLEMIC delivered, contributed to the crystallization of the historical impulse. (W.F. Buckley Jr., *Ibid.*, pp. 137-138)

15. See (1) under LILLIPUTIAN.

16. Give me the right to spend my dollars as I see fit —. . . to travel, to food, to learning, to taking pleasure, to POLEMICIZING, and, if I must make the choice, I will surrender you my political franchise in trade, confident that by the transaction, assuming . . . that no political decision affecting my sovereignty over my dollar can be made, I shall have augmented my dominance over my own affairs. (W.F. Buckley Jr., *Ibid.*, p. 208)

17. Conversations with several Dodgers strengthened [Dick] Young's harsh conclusion that a number of [Dodger] pitchers lacked heart and, after one losing game in 1948, he composed a POLEMICAL lead: "The tree that grows in Brooklyn is an apple tree and the apples are in the throats of the Dodgers." (R. Kahn, *The Boys of Summer*, Harper and Row,

1971, p. 99)

18. See (1) under NEURASTHENIA.

19. See (5) under ARMAGEDDON.

20. See (2) under LUDDITE.

21. See (4) under GRANDILOQUENT.

22. A p.r. man before he became a Nixon speechwriter, Safire has had a hard time abandoning a cute, punning style and glib judgments. He is most interesting when most irritating, being unfair in his opinions as the worst of liberal POLEMICISTS. (T. Griffith, "Newswatch," *Time*, 8/16/76, p. 74)

POLLYANNA (pol' ē-an' ə) *noun* an excessively, blindly, or persistently optimistic person [after the name of the heroine of the novels of Eleanor H. Porter (1868 - 1920), an American writer].

1. The group [*Make The Day Count*, whose members are fatally ill] is neither a gathering of HEDONISTS nor POLLYANNAS. Kelly [the founder] says members aim to make the best use of their time "to do what we can for ourselves and each other." Not a bad philosophy even for those without terminal disease. (T. Tiede, "Life Merits Full Respect," *Norman* [Okla.] *Transcript*, 1/16/76, p. 6)

2. Mozart wrote much of *The Magic Flute's* most glorious music for Pamina, yet she is not a real character but a Never-Never Land POLLYANNA. By contrast, Papageno is so human that he seems to belong in another kind of opera. (R. Craft, Review, *New York Review of Books*, 11/27/75, p. 19)

3. See (1) under SAPIENTIAL.

4. From its first issue in April 1970, this magazine has been wary of doomsayers— partly on the ground that they rarely offer solutions— and POLLYANNAS (they frequently don't even see the problems). (Anon., "A special issue of Smithsonian as America's third century begins" [Editor's Introduction], *Smithsonian*, July 1976, p. 26)

5. Waiting impatiently for publication of *How To Cure Yourself of Positive Thinking*. The author, Donald G. Smith, is a semantics teacher who explains, with wit, how to survive in a world of POLLYANNAS. (Seemann Publish-

ers. $7.95). (B. A. Bergman, "Cover to Cover," *Sunday Bulletin*, 2/13/77, p. 16)

6. What this country needs is a new national song. Not one that ruins your throat, like the *Star-Spangled Banner*. Not one that sounds POLLYANNA, like *America the Beautiful*. And of course not *The Battle Hymn of the Republic*. But a song that captures the spirit of playing while working, that moves along easily, that is not too much of a strain. A song like *Dixie*. (Anon., "How to Whistle Dixie," *Texas Monthly*, January 1977, p. 58)

7. . . . [Ray] Dirks had always been something of a maverick on Wall Street—an individualist who delighted in deflating corporate POLLYANNAS and shaking up the investment Establishment. So, when an employee of Equity Funding Corp. came to him with evidence that executives of the insurance firm were kiting its stock by writing phony policies, Dirks investigated—and then informed his clients and tipped off the press. The fraud involved tens of millions of dollars . . . , and was one of the worst corporate scandals ever to hit the insurance industry. (T. Nicholson, *et al.*, "The High Cost of Whistling," *Newsweek*, 2/14/77, p. 75)

POLTERGEIST (pōl'tər-gīst') *noun*   a noisy ghost or other spirit supposed to show its presence by breaking crockery, banging doors, knockings, table rappings, etc.

1. It [Ireland] has become a place where fact and fiction, myth and reality, bigotry and generosity fly about indiscriminately like so many faeries and POLTERGEISTS. (Lucinda Franks, "'We want peace. Just peace.'" *New York Times*, 12/19/76, Section 6, p. 29)

POLTROON (pol-trōōn) *noun*   a thorough coward; craven.

POLTROON *adj.*

POLTROONERY *noun.*

1. I have only just now seen your spread of August 12, under the heading "Some of the Best People are Afraid of Flying," and featuring a gallery of faces including what I hope is the most POLTROONISH photograph of me ever taken. (W.F. Buckley Jr., *Execution Eve and Other Contemporary Ballads*, G.P. Putnam's Sons, 1975, p. 321)

2. Liberty Tavern (known before 1776 as Stranger's Resort) is a New Jersey inn from which Thomas Fleming [in the book of the same name] looks into the hearts and minds of some patriots and POLTROONS caught up in the Revolution. (M. Levin, Review, *New York Times*, 5/2/76, Section 7, p. 60)

POLYANDRY (pol' ē-an' drē) *noun*   the practice or condition of having more than one husband at one time (distinguished from monandry).

POLYANDROUS or **POLYANDRIC** *adj.*

POLYANDRIST *noun*   a woman who practices or favors polyandry.

1. Eventually, civilization, like that of the ancient Greeks, got rid of polygamy and POLYANDRY and substituted monogamy. (I. Wallace, *The Fan Club*, Bantam Books, 1975, p. 149)

2. In a semi-polygamous (and less formally POLYANDROUS) society [of the ancient Japanese Heian court] the marriage game reached an APOGEE of perfection as the governing Fujiwara family plotted for its daughters to marry Emperors' sons or vice versa. (F.B. Gibney, Review of *The Tale of Genji*, by Murasaki Shikibu, translated by Edward G. Seidensticker, *New York Times*, 12/19/76, Section 7, p. 8)

POLYGLOT (pol' ē-glot') *adj.*   knowing many or several languages; multilingual; containing, composed of, or written in several languages.

POLYGLOT *noun*   a mixture or confusion of languages; a person in command of several languages; a book, especially the Bible, containing the same text in several languages.

1. A seaman aboard a Greek freighter he [Anthanasios Plessias] jumped ship six years ago in Newark, N.J., and simply melted into the POLYGLOT urban crowd. (A.J. Mayer, *et. al.*, "Immigration: The Alien Wave," *Newsweek*, 2/9/76, p. 56)

2. It [the Bicentennial art show] is a characteristically American crusade—big, well-heeled and POLYGLOT, long on zest, short on ideas. (D. Davis and Mary Rourke, "American

Art 200 Years On," *Newsweek*, 2/9/76, p. 66)

4. See (4) under IRREDENTIST.

POLYMATH (pol' ē-math') *noun* a person learned in many fields; a person of great and diversified learning.

POLYMATHIC *adj.*

1. Ernest Becker [author of the book, *Escape from Evil*] began as a cultural anthropologist, but he ended as a formidable POLYMATH. (A. Lacy, Review, *Chronicle of Higher Education*, 2/17/76, p. 15)

2. Vintage [Arnold] Toynbee, then, this book [*Mankind and Mother Earth*], and yet not the place to start if one wants to wrestle with the POLYMATH's vision of the world. (Robin W. Winks, Review, *New York Times*, 9/12/76, section 7, p. 31)

3. [Julian] Jaynes is a fiftyish professor of psychology at Princeton University. He is also, on the evidence of this book [*The Origin of Consciousness in the Breakdown of the Bicameral Mind*], a POLYMATH and monomaniac who takes all knowledge as his province and squeezes it down to a corroboratory footnote to his central argument. (G. Jonas, Review, *New York Times*, 3/13/77, Section 7, p. 6)

POLYMORPHOUS (pol'ē-môr'fəs) or **POLYMORPHIC** *adj.* having, assuming, or passing through many or various forms, stages, or the like.

POLYMORPHOUSLY *adv.*

POLYMORPHISM *noun.*

1. Should a writer of history need reminding of how frequently issues turn out to be double-edged, false-bottomed and POLYMORPHOUSLY perverse? (Norma Rosen, Review of *'Peculiar Institutions': An Informal History of the Seven Sister Colleges*, by Elaine Kendall, *New York Times*, 4/25/76, Section 7, p. 26)

2. In her sexual attitudes Peggy [Tumulty] dated from a bygone age. Despite the public harangues of POLYMORPHOUS perverts and their tracts on venereal liberation, she still looked first at a man's third finger and not at the swell of his groin. (Thomas Berger, *Who Is Teddy*

Villanova?," Delacorte Press/Seymour Lawrence, 1977, p. 27)

3. See (1) under SODOMY.

PONTIFICAL (pon-tif'i-kəl) *adj.* pompous or dogmatic; of, pertaining to, or characteristic of a pontiff or pope; papal; arrogant or haughty.

PONTIFICATE *verb* to speak pompously; to act or speak as if infallible; to discharge the duties of a pontiff.

PONTIFICATOR *noun.*

1. And then came the PONTIFICAL voice she [Sharon Fields] knew so well, that of Sky Hubbard with his exclusive about her on today's Noontime News . . . . (I. Wallace, *The Fan Club*, Bantam Books, 1975, p. 341)

2. "Under the new Homestead Act—" he [Oliver Seccombe] began PONTIFICALLY . . . . "Under this act the trick is to get title only to those parcels of land that control water. Get a hundred and sixty acres of such land, and you control ten thousand acres of range land that has no water. . . . " (J.A. Michener, *Centennial*, Fawcett, 1975, p. 522)

3. . . . I learned that the Jaques of *As You Like It* need not be a surly MISANTHROPE or a PONTIFICAL reciter of set pieces. He could be, as the young and already brilliant George C. Scott made him, an extraordinarily witty, extraordinarily funny gentleman-cynic, key to the entire play. (W. Kerr, "Around the Globe, Shakespeare Remains a Mirror for Mankind," *New York Times*, 9/12/76, Section 2, p. 5)

4. When, a century ago, Victor Hugo PONTIFICATED that "henceforth the nations unanimously recognize Paris as the leading city of the human race,"...so far as the transatlantic art world was concerned, Hugo was only trumpeting an obvious truth. (H. Kramer, "France's new culture palace," *New York Times*, 1/23/77, Section 6, p. 13)

POPINJAY (pop' in-jā') *noun* originally a parrot; a person given to vain displays and empty chatter; coxcomb; a foppish, empty-headed person; a talkative, conceited person.

1. See (1) under PECKSNIFF.

2. *Women of the Shadows*, [a book] by Ann Cornelisen . . . . Five beautifully drawn portraits of the women in a small Sicilian village, their POPINJAY husbands, their SYMBIOSIS with the land they love and hate and the courage of their enduring. (Anon., "Editor's choice," *New York Times*, 4/25/76, Section 7, p. 53)

3. . . . [Pavel] Kouhout's juggling of illusion and reality [in the play, *Poor Murderer*] lacks the precision of the Italian master [Pirandello]'s. Can this PRESTIDIGITATING probe of a devious POPINJAY be Kouhout's idea of an allegory about his own ambiguous imprisonment? (J. Kroll, Review, *Newsweek*, 11/1/76, p. 63)

4. "My dander is easily aroused, I'm afraid. Only yesterday I put my shoe through a TV screen. I could not endure the haircut of the POPINJAY on the six o'clock news" [said Donald Washburn II]. (Thomas Berger, *Who Is Teddy Villanova?*, Delacorte Press/Seymour Lawrence, 1977, p. 154)

PORCINE (pôr′sīn, pôr′sin) *adj.* of or pertaining to swine; hoggish; piggish.

PORCINITY *noun.*

1. In America he [Frank Harris, author of *My Life and Loves*] lectured "on the PORCINITY of the American people, the poverty of letters, the stupidity, the lack of liberal culture" in the Republic. (P.S. Prescott, Review of *Frank Harris*, by Philippa Pullar, *Newsweek*, 3/15/76, p. 95)

2. At the cash-register counter, a bald, stoop-shouldered pot-bellied man . . . was busily wrapping a purchase and gossiping with a rotund, PORCINE-looking woman. (I. Wallace, *The Fan Club*, Bantam Books, 1975, p. 587)

3. It [Sassafras] has to be one of the most beautiful little taverns in town . . . . The dominant eye-catchers . . . are a couple of spectacular paintings by a young South American artist. My favorite is of a pink, PORCINE mermaid recumbent in a dream. (B. Collins, "Two first-class places turn up on Second Street," *Philadelphia Inquirer*, 10/22/76, p. 3-C)

4. See (5) under MARTINET.

5. . . . he [Peregrine Kirk] . . . walked down Brompton Road across to Harrods, . . . asked by name for a salesman with whom he talked about the necessity of a strategic plan for replenishing his supply of French silk shirts which were only now, ever so slowly, making their way back to the English market, after the endless period during which they were available only in America, and other PORCINE countries that had accumulated by military and geopolitical opportunism their squalid surplus of the world's hard currency. (W.F. Buckley Jr., *Saving the Queen*, Doubleday, 1976, p. 156)

6. Also, the swine was trespassing in my [Russel Wren's] sanctum, had perhaps found [the manuscript of] my play and wiped his PORCINE posteriors on it . . . (Thomas Berger, *Who Is Teddy Villanova?*, Delacorte Press/Seymour Lawrence, 1977, p. 206)

PORTE-COCHERE (pôrt′kō-shâr′,-ka-,pôrt²) *noun* a covered carriage entrance leading into a courtyard; a porch roof at the door of a building for sheltering persons entering and leaving carriages.

1. The actual door [of the house] is blunt, its PORTE-COCHERE a modest attempt at automobile-age formality. (P. Goldberger, "Design, *New York Times*, 6/6/76, Section 6, p. 69)

POSTHUMOUS (pos′chə-məs, tyŏŏ-, -chŏŏ-) *adj.* published after the death of the author; born after the father's death; arising, occurring, or continuing after a person's death.

POSTHUMOUSLY *adv.*

1. To me it [the portrait of George Washington given to Ramdoolal Dey] will always be a great portrait with a great history, unique in representing General Washington's romantic VICARIOUS, POSTHUMOUS passage to India and back. (D. Emrich, "A Yankee gift to a Bengali," *Smithsonian*, February 1976, p. 119)

2. . . . *Dolores*, her [Jacqueline Susann's] newly published POSTHUMOUS novel, includes bitchy artist and vicious gossip named Horatio Capon. *Dolores* itself is the ROMAN À CLEF in its most preposterous incarnation. It is about Dolores Ryan, the beautiful widow of an assassinated U.S. President, who marries one of the

world's richest men for his money. Is this truly the story of the fabulous Jackie O.? (M. Maddocks, "Now for the Age of Psst!," *Time*, 6/28/76, p. 68)

3. I don't find the second Republican item of POSTHUMOUS praise [for Truman] much more compelling; the admiration expressed by President Ford . . . for Truman's doughty ability to beat the terrible odds against him in the election of 1948. The odds were that terrible . . . in large part because of the slanderous things Republicans had been putting out about Harry Truman. (Meg Greenfield, "The Man They Loved to Hate," *Newsweek*, 9/13/76, p. 92)

4. See (3) under CHIMERA.

POSTPRANDIAL (pōst-pran' dē-əl) *adj.* after a meal, especially after dinner.

POSTPRANDIALLY *adv.*

1. And, sitting in the little drawing room [the only room not "bugged" by his superiors] that had served as the children's nursery, he [Pyotr Ilyich] explained to his wife why, in the future, they must retreat here for any intimate discussions, and routinely after dinner, when, he knew, the POSTPRANDIAL relaxation loosens the tongue. (W.F. Buckley Jr., *Saving the Queen*, Doubleday, 1976, p. 106)

POT-AU-FEU (pô-tô-fŒ') *noun* a French dish made by boiling meat and vegetables, etc., with the broth customarily strained and served separately.

1. And with the thrift of a French housewife making POT-AU-FEU out of last week's table scraps, [Coco] Chanel copied in fake stones the treasures he [the Duke of Westminster, a lover who rejected her] had left her, thus pioneering the famous costume jewelry she sold. (Francine Gray, Review of *Chanel*, a book by Edmonde Charles-Roux, *New York Review of Books*, 12/11/75, p. 45)

2. Every culture has its boiled-meat dinner, from New England to Vienna, from Mexican and Spanish pucheros to Irish stew, Italian bollito misto and the French POT-AU-FEU. . . . There is the rich and beautiful bouillon from the boiling that you may begin the meal with . . . . Your main course is a platter of tender meat surrounded by as large a variety of vegetables as your heart desires. (Julia Child, "Pot-au-feu: French version of the boiled-meat dinner," *Philadelphia Inquirer*, 1/9/77, p. 14-G)

PRATFALL (prat' fôl) *noun* [Slang] a fall on the buttocks, especially one for comic effect, as in a burlesque.

1. Lattimore and Arrowsmith [editors of the University of Chicago Press's translations of Greek classics] can be depended on to produce English verse that, while it does not always scale the heights of Parnassus, never stumbles into a PRATFALL. (B.M.W. Knox, Review of *Aeschylus: Suppliants*, translated by Janet Lembke; *Aeschylus: Seven Against Thebes*, translated by Helen Bacon and Anthony Hecht; and *Aeschylus: Prometheus Bound*, translated by James Scully and C. John Herington, *New York Review of Books*, 11/27/75, p. 27)

2. Chevy Chase—not the town outside Washington but the TV performer who takes PRATFALLS imitating the President on "NBC's Saturday Night"—bumped into the real Gerald Ford last week. No problem; the two traded laughs as star guests at the Radio & Television Correspondents Association dinner at the Washington Hilton . . . . In New Hampshire, said Chase, "President Ford accidentally kissed a snowball and threw a baby." . . . cracked the President, "Mr. Chevy Chase, you're a very, very funny suburb." (Anon., "Newsmakers," *Newsweek*, 4/5/76, p. 58)

3. His [President Ford's] PRATFALLS on an airplane ramp in Austria and on a ski slope in Colorado . . . inspired a long series of Jerry-the-Bumbler jokes and political cartoons . . . . From all accounts the President felt that the gibes were good-natured rather than malicious. (R. Worsnop, "President maintains sense of humor," *Norman* [Okla.] *Transcript*, 4/19/76, p. 6)

4. What a setup for a PRATFALL. (G. Wolff, Review of *A Hero in His Time*, by Arthur A. Cohen, *New York Times*, 1/25/76, Section 7, p. 4)

5. The human body is one of comedy's supple tools. In agility, it releases tonic exuberance.

As an object of humiliation through banana-peel PRATFALLS or pies in the face, it evokes instant delight. Even distortions or grotesqueries of the body—obesity, dwarfishness, eccentric gaits, tics, stutters, deafness and drunken staggers—have all been known to provoke a startling comic CATHARSIS in playgoers . . . . Britain's Monty Python troupe, which opened live at Manhattan's City Center last week, renews that comic tradition, and its success in television, movies and now, onstage, shows that many audiences are parched for it. In *Monty Python Live!* the operative word is "live," for almost all of the routines have been seen before on American TV. Fortunately, they are unkillably hilarious even in repetition . . . . When John Cleese delivers a DIATRIBE to a shyster petshop owner while flogging the dead parrot that has been sold to him, the funning is lethally potent. (T.E. Kalem, Review, *Time*, 4/26/76, p. 67)

PRECATORY (prek′ ə-tōr′ ē) *adj.* characterized by, relating to, or expressing entreaty or supplication; supplicatory.

1. As for the recent Rhodesian statement [by Henry Kissinger], he [Gov. Jerry Brown] approved it, but he was skeptical of merely PRECATORY admonitions. What was that word again? . . . I thought he had said "PLACATORY," a nice $2.95 word, but I ran after him . . . to check. He had said "PRECATORY," a three-dollar word if there ever was one. . . . I'm skeptical of Brown; but I'm impressed. (J.J. Kilpatrick, "Brown Leaves Jaded Washington Press Corps Wagging Their Heads," *Daily Oklahoman*, 5/21/76, p. 8)

PRECIOSITY (presh′ē-os′i-tē) *noun* an affected refinement or excessive fastidiousness, as in language, style, or taste.

1. Though [Herbert] Gold often substitutes SHTIK for character development in his novels, so do quite a few other authors—J.P. Donleavy comes to mind—without suffering any loss of popularity. A novel like John Hawkes' *Sleep, Death and the Traveler*, depends on SHTIK too, but it is very PRETENTIOUS, international SHTIK, the poor man's Lawrence Durrell, who might, in turn, be described as the patron saint of PRECIOSITY. (A. Broyard, Review of *Waiting for Cordelia*, by Herbert Gold, *New York Times*, 5/22/77, Section 7, p. 14)

PRECOCIOUS (pri-kō′ shəs) *adj.* forward in development, especially mental development; prematurely developed, as the mind, faculties, etc.; of, pertaining to, or showing premature development.

PRECOCIOUSLY *adv.*

PRECOCITY (pri-kos′ i-tē) or **PRECOCIOUSNESS** *noun.*

1. See (3) under SCATOLOGY.

2. Janis Ian has had her fill of dreams. At 14 the PRECOCIOUS songwriter from New York captured the spirit of her generation with her hit record *Society's Child*, a bitter lament about interracial dating. At 20, with three album flops behind her, she vanished from sight. Now 24, Ian is back on top with two hit albums . . . and a Grammy award last month as best female vocalist for her hit single, *At Seventeen* . . . . (Mary Alice Kellogg, P.S. Greenberg, "Janis Grows Up," *Newsweek*, 4/5/76, p. 63)

3. Such facts as Original Sin cannot be made to disappear . . . ; that human beings are not equal, cannot be made equal, and must not be deemed equal other than before the law; such facts as that excellence can be distinguished from mediocrity, and that PRECOCITY is not an affront on democratic society . . . . Our mania for a COMATOSE togetherness keeps these facts remote from view. (W.F. Buckley Jr., *Up From Liberalism*, Arlington House, 2nd Printing 1968, p. 130)

4. . . . he [Hugo Weisgall] began composing when he was 10. As a student, he was thrown out of the Peabody Institute of Music, despite his PRECOCIOUS gifts. (G. Gelles, "A 'Dead' Composer Returns to Life," *New York Times*, 4/18/76, Section 2, p. 19)

5. See (3) under NAÏVETÉ.

6. . . . the skinny kid (jockey Steve Cauthen) with the perfect poise on horseback emerges as a multifaceted hero—a 95-pound blend of the riding mastery of a Bill Shoemaker, the incredible PRECOCITY of a miniature Paul Bunyan and the level-headed acceptance of sudden fame that distinguished . . . 16-year-old Chris Evert . . . (P. Axthelm, "Racing's Boy Wonder," *Newsweek*, 2/14/77, p. 83)

PREDACEOUS or **PREDACIOUS** (pri-dā′shəs) *adj.* predatory; rapacious; preying on other animals.

PREDACEOUSNESS or **PREDACIOUSNESS** or **PREDACITY** (pri-das′i-tē) *noun.*

PREDATOR (pred′ə-tər) *noun* a predatory person, animal, or thing.

PREDATORY *adj.* of, pertaining to, or characterized by plunder, exploitation, etc.; living by plunder, exploitation, etc.

PREDATORILY *adv.*

1. [Charles] Carroll . . . early felt that independence from Britain was an ultimate necessity, writing in 1762 that he saw no alternative. In his letters he is forever on guard against PREDATORY English dictates. When Parliament passed the Stamp Act, Carroll seethed; the Act's Repeal a year later (1766) contained a declaration that still claimed for England broad power over Colonial affairs, and Carroll was not MOLLIFIED. (Mary H. Cadwalader, "Charles Carroll of Carrollton: a signer's story," *Smithsonian*, December 1975, p. 68)

2. Not only do species of firefly have subtly different flash sequences to attract mates of their own kind, but there are PREDATORY species whose females (CHAUVINISTS please note) mimic the signals of up to four other species and lure aroused lovers to their death. (M. Emsley, "Nature's most successful design may be beetles," *Smithsonian*, December 1975, p. 107)

PREDILECTION (pred′əlek′shən, prēd -) *noun* a preconceived liking; partiality or preference (for).

1. He [Governor E.G. Brown, Jr.] came to power a liberal Democrat by bloodline—his father, Pat, had been governor before Ronald Reagan—and, as far as anyone knew, by personal PREDILECTION. (P. Goldman, E.G. Lubenow, *Mr. Small—Is Beautiful, Newsweek*, 12/15/75, p. 47)

2. When composing the Declaration of Independence, the founders listed 26 specific charges against King George III, one of which was that he had "erected a multitude of new Offices and sent hither Swarms of Officers to harass our people, and eat out their Substance." George was not the first American ruler with this PREDILECTION, however, and not the last. (T. Tiede, "Harassment Takes Toll," *Norman* [Okla.] *Transcript*, 1/14/76, p. 6)

3. Owing largely to a PREDILECTION for flying low and close to the shoreline, the [trumpeter] swans were an easy prey for hunters. The white man quickly turned them into an item of commerce. The swans were hunted mercilessly for their feathers, which reputedly made the finest pen quills . . . . From 1820 to 1860 the Hudson's Bay Company marketed 108,000 [breast] skins [for clothing]. (W.D. Jorgensen, "Isolated family lives in symbiosis with trumpeters," *Smithsonian*, January 1976, p. 56)

4. Marxist PREDILECTIONS surface less happily in the hostile judgments meted out to Marx's anarchist rivals, P.J. Proudhon and Michael Bakunin. (W.W. Wagar, Review of *The Age of Capital: 1848-1875*, by E.J. Hobsbawm, *Chronicle of Higher Education*, 5/10/76, p. 21)

5. Acting out of fear, ideological PREDILECTION, a genuine concern for improvement of academic conditions, or simply not knowing what else to do, university administrators bureaucratized student demands into nontraditional educational enterprises. What students sought—and generally received—was a style of education different from the lecture/classroom/exam mode . . . . (H.I. London, "The Case for Nontraditional Learning," *Change*, June 1976, p. 25)

6. Once in the wash, the [old 100% wool] union suits were uncooperative. They had a PREDILECTION for shrinkage and discoloration. Homemakers of the time remember leaving size 44s on the line at night, and collecting two-thirds of that in the morning. (T. Tiede, NEA, "Son of 'Union Suit,' " *Times Herald*, Norristown, Pa., 2/19/77, p. 15)

PREHENSILE (pri-hen′sil, -sīl) *adj.* adapted for seizing or grasping something, as a prehensile limb; fitted for grasping by wrapping around an object, as a prehensile tail.

PREHENSILITY *noun.*

PREHENSION *noun* the act of seizing or

grasping; mental apprehension.

PREHENSIBLE adj. able to be seized or grasped.

1. From the surface of the lake an enormous construction began slowly to appear, an inch at a time, muddy waters falling from it as it rose. Slowly, slowly the thing [diplodocus] in the lagoon came into view, until it disclosed a monstrous prison of dark flesh to which the PREHENSILE neck was attached. (J.A. Michener, *Centennial*, Fawcett, 1975, p. 72)

2. It was allosaurus, king of the carnivores, with jaws that could bite the neck of diplodocus in half. When the great beast entered the water to attack her, she lashed at him with her tail and knocked him slightly off course. Even so, the mostrous six-inch claws on his PREHENSILE front feet raked her right flank, laying it open. (J.A. Michener, *Ibid.*, p. 81)

3. Later that night, in Sally's car, they did it for the last time under the shadow of West Rock. She was silent, but PREHENSILE. He was distracted, but taken by lust, and he had to remind himself to be tender, and was glad when the moon was suddenly blotted out by the huge stone because she . . . wouldn't be able to see . . . that he was thinking about subjects other than Sally, and the Last Copulation at West Rock. (W.F. Buckley Jr., *Saving the Queen*, Doubleday, 1976, pp. 27-28)

4. . . . the pressure on my [Russel Wren's] chest . . . was due to the kneeling of this man thereupon. It was far from easy to dislodge him: . . . his sharp little kneecaps were seemingly PREHENSILE at, or in, my rib cage. (Thomas Berger, *Who Is Teddy Villanova?*, Delacorte Press/Seymour Lawrence, 1977, p. 113)

PRELAPSARIAN (prē-lap' sâr ē-ən) adj. characteristic of or belonging to the time or state before the fall of man.

1. The classical instance is the survival for centuries of ANTITHETICAL primitivisms, labeled "soft" and "hard," and reflecting COMPLEMENTARY attitudes to work. Both kinds are involved in the story of Adam, who lived in a paradise of pleasure but had to cultivate it: a situation Milton found a bit difficult, for having declared the work virtually unnecessary, a mere disinterested tidying up of superfluous growth with PRELAPSARIAN SECATEURS, he gave Eve victorious arguments for the division of labor. (F. Kermode, Review of *Work and Play: Ideas and Experience of Work and Leisure*, by Alasdair Clayre, *New York Review of Books*, 11/27/75, p. 35)

2. [Gov. Willie] Stark [in Robert Penn Warren's book, *All The King's Men*] wants to make [Adam] Stanton [his boyhood friend who now is a surgeon] the director of a new hospital he is building as a monument to his greatness and a PALLIATIVE to his betrayed idealism. But it is no deal. Stanton, a PRE-LAPSARIAN purist . . . , will not serve Stark. (G. Lyons, Review of *A Place To Come To*, a book by Robert Penn Warren, *New York Times*, 3/13/77, Section 7, p. 4)

PREMONITORY (pri-mon' i-tôr' ē, -tôr'ē) adj. giving premonition; serving to warn beforehand.

PREMONITION noun a forewarning; an intuitive anticipation of a future event; presentiment; foreboding.

1. So the Zendts went up the gangplank and for some time they lingered on deck . . . but Levi saw [thinking back] only the elephant, massive and plodding and filling the sky with its PREMONITORY form. (J.A. Michener, *Centennial*, Fawcett, 1975, p. 358)

2. See (5) under PRESCIENCE.

PREPOTENT (pri-pōt' ənt) adj. preeminent in power, authority, or influence; predominant; noting, pertaining to, or having prepotency.

PREPOTENCY noun superiority in power, force, or influence; the greater capacity of one parent to transmit certain characteristics to off-spring: a concept now discredited.

PREPOTENTLY adv.

1. He [the young bull brought from England to Centennial, Colorado] had only two conspicuous qualities—extremely substantial rear quarters . . . and a PREPOTENT power to stamp upon his offspring . . . the physical attributes he possessed. (J.A. Michener, *Centennial*, Fawcett, 1975, p. 747)

2. He [Emperor IX, a bull brought from Eng-

land] was a stunning animal, a PREPOTENT bull with the precious capacity of stamping only his better qualities on his progeny. (J.A. Michener, *Ibid.*, p. 938)

PREPUCE (prē′ pyōōs) *noun* the fold of skin that covers the head of the penis; foreskin; a similar fold over the end of the clitoris.

PREPUTIAL (pri-pyōō′shəl) *adj.*

1. She [Sharon Fields] would call upon her endless experience, her deep knowledge of sensual enchantment, drawn from a Who's Who of PREPUCES in her past. (I. Wallace, *The Fan Club*, Bantam Edition, 1975, p. 351)

PRESAGE (pres′ij, pri-sāj′) *verb* to have a foreboding or presentiment of; to portend; foreshadow; to forecast; predict; to make a prediction.

PRESAGE (pres′ ij) *noun* a presentiment or foreboding; something that portends or foreshadows a future event, as an omen; prophetic significance; AUGURY; foresight; PRESCIENCE.

PRESAGER *noun.*

1. . . . currently the United States Army wants Wounded Knee rewritten as a battle rather than a massacre. Maybe this PRESAGES "The Battle of My Lai." (J. Harrison, Review of the book, *The Snow Walker*, by Farley Mowat, *New York Times*, 2/22/76, Section 7, p. 4)

2. In the years covered [1832-1835] by this volume [*The Papers of Joseph Henry, Vol. II*, edited by Nathan Reingold] he [Henry] was concerned not only with the need to teach, but also with the need to work on his research studies in electromagnetism, which led to the principles of conductivity and eventually PRESAGED the development of wireless telegraphy. (S.D. Ripley, "The view from the castle," *Smithsonian*, December 1975, p. 6)

3. As the [Last Judgment] fresco in its entirety embodies simultaneities of then and now—the crucifixion as a historic moment and as the PRESAGE of its own afterlife and commemoration—so the artist, too, may be portrayed in the full span of his moral history. The turbaned rider [in the fresco] then stands for a younger Michelangelo . . . . (L. Steinberg; "Michelangelo's last painting: his gift to this century,"

Smithsonian, December 1975, p. 84)

PRESCIENCE (prē′shē-əns, -shəns, presh′ē- ; presh′ əns) *noun* apparent knowledge of things before they exist or happen; foreknowledge; foresight.

PRESCIENT *adj.*

PRESCIENTLY *adv.*

1. A powerful monolithic man [Carl] Furillo possessed an astonishing throwing arm and a PRESCIENT sense of how the ball would carom off the [outfield] barrier. (R. Kahn, *The Boys of Summer*, Harper and Row, 1971, p. xviii)

2. One might add that Mr. [Frank] Fischer's PRESCIENT concerns [about the dissatisfactions of college graduates who are underemployed] are not shared or understood by a preponderance of people in higher education . . . the subject of how one might best be able to manage human expectations of material decline remains as appallingly removed from educational agendas as life in an Alaskan igloo. (G.W. Bonham, "The American Future," [Editorial], *Change*, May 1975, p. 11)

3. The [Jack] Valenti worshipfulness [in the book, *A Very Human President*] is not confined to L.B.J. or even to his group . . . . John Connally does things "awesomely," a "PRESCIENT" man, who "unfastens others' fears, dissolves all hesitancies" . . . . (E.F. Goldman, Review, *New York Times*, 2/1/76, Section 7, p. 4)

4. That evening [August 25, 1844] . . . she [Elly Zendt] stayed in the wagon, writing to Laura Lou. This letter stands as an epistle of hope and PRESCIENCE, EPITOMIZING the contributions made by the brave women who crossed the plains in pioneer days. (J.A. Michener, *Centennial*, Fawcett, 1975, p. 405)

5. "I don't want women looking at those bleak empty spaces," [Mervin] Wendell had said with the PRESCIENCE that marked his dealings. "You show a bunch of Iowa women those prairies, and they'll panic." . . . now as Alice Grebe looked at it [the photograph of the land], she had a PREMONITION of the loneliness she could expect . . . . (J.A. Michener, *Ibid.*, p. 884)

6. It [*The CIA File*, edited by Robert L.

Borosage and John Marks] is a collection of papers, presented not last week but over two days in September, 1974. (Accordingly, a reader marveling at the PRESCIENCE of a publisher rushing to print now, when CIA's future is an increasingly national debate, should realize he is reading DIATRIBES a year and a half old; held today, the conference's output would doubtless be printed in VITRIOL.) (J. Flannery, Review, *Boston Globe*, 3/7/76, p. 16-A)

7. It was a shame, she [Mrs. Goddard] added, that Bob Goddard never lived to see the moon rockets whose feasibility he had predicted with such PRESCIENCE—not merely predicted, but demonstrated—at a time when the world's other space pioneers were still working equations on paper. (M. Kernan, "50th anniversary of step toward space," *Smithsonian*, March 1976, p. 80)

8. See (1) under HERCYNIAN.

9. . . . the First Congress passed a statute prescribing 39 lashes for larceny, and one hour in the pillory for perjury. And one PRESCIENT congressman opposed the "cruel and unusual" clause [in the Constitution] because it might someday be construed to ban such "necessary" punishments as ear cropping. (G.F. Will, "In Cold Blood," *Newsweek*, 11/29/76, p. 116)

PRESCIND (pri-sind´) *verb* to detach, abstract, separate, or isolate (a meaning, one's mind, etc.) to remove; to withdraw attention (from).

1. [Question from Helen Vendler to John Updike:] "You've decided, in your new collection of verse, to PRESCIND from taste altogether, in some of the poems about sex . . . . It is possible to avoid the ridiculous in such an enterprise?" [Answer by John Updike:] "Well, why avoid the ridiculous? . . . . I think taste is a social concept, not an artistic one." (Anon., "John Updike on Poetry," *New York Times*, 4/10/77, Section 7, p. 28)

PRESTIDIGITATION (pres´ ti-dij´ i-tā´ shən) *noun* sleight of hand; legerdemain; conjuring; the performance of tricks by quick, skillful use of the hands.

PRESTIDIGITATOR *noun*.

1. [Tennessee] Williams has written so much and with such seeming authority about the rural South that we must always take care to remember that he was a big-city boy from St. Louis and that much of his drawling Southerness, like Truman Capote's, is a feat of literary PRESTIDIGITATION; he was Tom Williams before he was Tennessee. (B. Gill, Review of *27 Wagons Full of Cotton*, a play by Tennessee Williams, *The New Yorker*, 2/9/76, p. 78)

2. Many of his [Stanley Elkin's] heroes [in the book, *The Franchiser*] are businessmen whose urges go beyond a Cash McCall drive for power and money. They see business as part of a cosmic magic show, an exuberant PRESTIDIGITATION of goods and services. (R. Z. Sheppard, Review, *Time*, 5/24/76, p. 88)

3. See (3) under POPINJAY.

PRETENTIOUS (pri-ten´ shəs) *adj.* full of pretense or pretension; characterized by assumption of dignity, importance, or excellence; ostentatious; pompous; showy; affectedly grand, superior, etc.

PRETENTIOUSLY *adv.*

PRETENTIOUSNESS *noun.*

PRETENSION *noun* laying of a claim or title to something; a claim or title to something; a claim made, especially indirectly or by implication, to some quality, merit, title, dignity, importance, or the like; pretentiousness; the act of pretending or alleging; an allegation of doubtful veracity; pretext; ostentation.

1. See (2) under SIBYL.

2. See (3) under COGNOSCENTI.

3. Other paintings of [Jean François Millet] met similar critical OBLOQUIES: *The Gleaners*, 1857, "have enormous PRETENTIONS (*sic*)—they pose like the three fates of pauperdom" [said one contemporary critic]. (R. Hughes, Review of Millet's centenary exhibition at London's Hayward Gallery, *Time*, 2/23/76, p. 60)

4. See (1) under GRAVID.

5. Most probably, both of these books [*The Cleveland Street Scandal*, by H. Montgomery Hyde; and *The 1900's Lady*, by Kate Caffrey] will be forgotten in two or three years' time, alas long before many far more PRETENTIOUS

and less enjoyable books. And it's a pity that this should be so. These books are lively, witty and written with exceptional professional competence by practiced writers. (J.H. Plumb, Review, *New York Times*, 9/5/76, Section 7, p. 2)

6. See (1) under HISTRIONICS.

7. See (4) under OLIGARCHY.

8. There are several EPIGRAPHS in this [*Instructions To The Double*], Tess Gallagher's first book of poems; they include passages from Rilke, Cavafy, Anaïs Nin and Simone de Beauvoir. That sounds PRETENTIOUS, but in this case it's not. The quotes are all choice in themselves and . . . are extremely informative about this poet and her enterprise. (P. Schjeldahl, Review, *New York Times*, 11/21/76, Section 7, p. 64)

9. See (3) under ECLECTIC.

10. See (3) under EPONYM.

11. See (2) under GAUCHERIE.

12. See (2) under LUMPEN.

13. See (1) under PRECIOSITY.

PRETERNATURAL (prē'tər-nach'ər-əl) *adj.* differing from or beyond what is normal or what is normally found in or expected from nature; exceptional, unusual, abnormal, extraordinary, or unnatural; supernatural.

PRETERNATURALLY *adv.*

1. In time [Dick] Young came to know the Dodgers [baseball team] better than any other newspaperman and better, too, than many Dodger officials. He sensed when to flatter, when to cajole, when to threaten . . . . Young possessed a PRETERNATURAL sense of the rhythms and balances of human relations. (R. Kahn, *The Boys of Summer*, Harper and Row, 1971, p. 99)

2. It had been Brumbaugh who had devised the clever system of importing boxcar loads of bat manure from the recently discovered deposits at the bottom of Carlsbad Caverns in New Mexico. This new-type fertilizer was dry and compact and easy to handle. It was also PRETERNATURALLY rich in mineral deposits;

where it was used, crops grew. (J.A. Michener, *Centennial*, Fawcett, 1975, p. 815)

3. In the South, the white community is entitled to put forward a claim to prevail politically because, for the time being anyway, the leaders of American civilization are white—as one would expect given their PRETERNATURAL advantages of tradition, training, and economic status . . . . The white South perceives, for the time being at least, qualitative differences between the level of its culture and the Negroes', and intends to live by its own. (W.F. Buckley Jr., *Up From Liberalism*, Arlington House, 2nd Printing 1968, p. 157)

4. Deified in the Soviet Union and other Communist countries, credited with PRETERNATURAL foresight and OMNISCIENCE, Lenin is frequently regarded in the West as a libertarian whose ideas were corrupted and distorted by Stalin . . . . (Simon Karlinsky, Review of *Lenin in Zurich*, by Alexander Solzhenitsyn (translated by H.T. Willetts), *New York Times*, 4/25/76, Section 7, p. 7)

5. On a sign outside Caesar's Palace here in Las Vegas a larger-than-life Shirley MacLaine is shown tossing off a PRETERNATURALLY high kick . . . this sign means Shirley MacLaine is back on the stage and kicking up her heels. (Julia Cameron, "Shirley MacLaine—Back in Her Dancing Shoes," *New York Times*, 4/18/76, Section 2, p. l)

PRIAPIC (prī-ap'ik) or **PRIAPEAN** (prī ə-pē'ən) *adj.* (sometimes capitalized) of or pertaining to Priapus; PHALLIC; exaggeratedly concerned with masculinity, male sexuality, and virility.

PRIAPUS (prī-ā'pəs) (in Classical Mythology) a god of male procreative power, the son of Dionysus and Aphrodite; (if lower case) PHALLUS.

PRIAPISM (prī'ə-piz'em) *noun* a pathological condition characterized by continuous erection of the penis, especially without sexual excitement; PRURIENT or lascivious behavior, display, or attitude.

PRIAPISMIC *adj.*

1. After the [vasectomy] operation . . . I felt like an apostate . . . . On the other hand, I couldn't miss the opportunity to fully enjoy my

new, safe identity. So I . . . ran off with my wife on a second honeymoon. We drove 400 miles for our PRIAPIC holdiay to the site of our original honeymoon . . . . We couldn't have imagined more joy—until about seven weeks after our return. It was then that Susan began getting sick in a way that we knew meant another little Catholic was in formation . . . . Dr. M. was running twin clinics, one for phony vasectomies and one for real abortions . . . . We're suing him for $300,000. (Anon., name withheld, Letter to WRAPAROUND, *Harper's*, January 1975, pp. 92–93)

2. Whether he's copulating with a marquise or a maid-servant, poor Donald Sutherland [in the film, *Fellini's Casanova*] as the great lover is simply shown doing PRIAPIC push-ups until his breath rattles and his eyes roll back in their sockets. (J. Kroll, Review, *Newsweek*, 1/24/77, p. 60)

3. . . . Fellini's vision and invention are dragged down [in the film, *Fellini's Casanova*] by his rage against the PRIAPIC hero. It is gaudy and in the end a depressing film. (Anon., "Love Machine," *Newsweek*, 1/24/77, p. 3)

PRIMEVAL (prī-mē'vəl) . *adj.* of or pertaining to the earliest times or ages, especially of the world; primal; PRISTINE; primordial.

PRIMEVALLY *adv.*

1. See (1) under CACHINNATE.

2. . . . kelp is one of the key links needed to maintain the precious chain of ecological balance in Pacific coastal waters. The giant kelp, its strands stretching like PRIMEVAL fingers toward the surface, is the home of a vast menagerie of aquatic life. (T.G. Branning, "Giant kelp: its comeback against urchins, sewage," *Smithsonian*, September 1976, p. 103)

PRIMIPARA (prī-mip'ər-ə) *noun, pl.:* **PRIMIPARAE** (-ə-rē') a woman who has borne only one child or who is pregnant for the first time.

PRIMIPARITY (prī'mi-par'i-tē) *noun.*

PRIMIPAROUS (prī-mip'ər-əs) *adj.*

1. In pre-abortion days, Dr. [Howard I.] Diamond [of Beth Israel Medical Center in N.Y.C.] was every PRIMIPARA's dream. He took

no vacations lest one of his patients go unexpectedly into labor. (Norma Rosen, "Between Guilt and Gratification: Abortion Doctors Reveal Their Feelings," *New York Times*, 4/17/77, Section 6, p. 74)

PRISTINE (pris'tēn, -tin, pris-tēn') *adj.* of, pertaining to, or characteristic of the earliest, or an earlier, period or state; having its original purity; uncorrupted; unspoiled.

PRISTINELY *adv.*

1. It takes a little willing suspension of disbelief to appreciate *Piero Ventura's Book of Cities*, which could well be subtitled "Urbanization Without Tears." But once the reader accepts the artist's PRISTINE point of view, there are pages of delicate drawings to enjoy. (Sidney Long, Review, *New York Times*, 2/8/76, Section 7, p. 16)

2. . . . everything properly Islamic proceeds from the PRISTINE period of Mecca and Medina, when faith, law, custom, and political authority are conceived to have been completely fused through the person of the Prophet [Muhammad] and the pronouncements of the Quran. (C. Geertz, Review of *The Venture of Islam: Conscience and History in a World Civilization. Vol. 1: The Classical Age of Islam; Vol. 2: The Expansion of Islam in the Middle Periods; Vol. 3: The Gunpowder Empire and Modern Times*, by Marshall G.S. Hodgson, *New York Review of Books*, 12/11/75, p. 18)

3. The conservationists would turn livid if the very thought of building a 100-room hostelry in this PRISTINE Sierra valley were even broached. (M. Olderman, "Yosemite's slagpile with a view," *Norman* [Okla.] *Transcript*, 4/14/76, p. 6)

4. . . . the serious speculation which constitutes the novel [*Eaters of the Dead*, by Michael Crichton]'s appendix is downright debilitating. Here we find a summary of all the arguments . . . over whether the "eaters of the dead" were PRISTINE Neanderthal men or retarded *Homo sapiens*. (J. Sullivan, Review, *New York Times*, 4/25/76, Section 7, p. 22)

5. In Kong I it's Fay Wray's purity that's the central commodity— . . . for the savages of Skull Island who placate their beast deity with

a yearly virgin. In Kong II the savages . . . must know that [Jessica] Lange is no PRISTINE package, but as with everything else their standards have fallen. (J. Kroll, "The Movies Go Ape—Again," Newsweek, 12/20/76, p. 103)

PROCLIVITY (prō-kliv'i-tē) *noun* a natural or habitual tendency or inclination.

1. Pronatalism, a word that was coined by population control advocates about a decade ago, is the notion that all adults should bear children if they are biologically able to do so, regardless of their own needs or PROCLIVITIES. (L. Lear, "Pronatalism: We don't have to be parents," *Philadelphia Inquirer*, 7/21/77, p. 11-A)

2. I do not believe that there is an "innate feminine PROCLIVITY" for gossip, as [Lucy S.] Dawidowicz playfully asserts [in the book, *The Jewish Presence*] . . . . (E. Rothstein, Review, *New York Times*, 7/24/77, Section 7, p. 13)

PROCRUSTEAN (prō-krus'tē-ən) *adj.* of, like, pertaining to, or suggestive of Procrustes or his actions; designed or acting to secure conformity at any cost; drastic or ruthless.

PROCRUSTES *noun* (in Greek Mythology) a robber who seized travelers, tied them to a bedstead, and either stretched them or cut off their legs to make them fit the bed.

1. First novels are the stepchildren of the book family. Publishers—when they agree to print one at all—seem to run off only enough copies for the author and his immediate family. Which is just as well, since none but the most cavernous bookstores bother much about making shelf space for debuts. The self-fulfilling prophecy is then in full operation: the book fails to sell, and no one is surprised . . . . Exceptions to this PROCRUSTEAN rule are rare enough to be newsworthy. Lisa Alther's *Kinflicks* is enjoying a first printing of 30,000 copies, is a forthcoming alternate selection of the Book-of-the-Month Club and the subject of considerable prepublications HYPERBOLE. (P. Gray, Review, *Time*, 3/22/76, p. 80)

2. Just as evidence about the behavior of political intellectuals is, more often than not, trimmed to fit the Platonic idea, or, rather the PROCRUSTEAN bed, which we have inherited from a long line of conservative thinkers since

Edmund Burke, so the attitude toward intellectuals in forming our discussion of them is commonly that of condescension [as is the case with Sandy Vogelgesang, author of *The Long Dark Night of the Soul: The American Intellectual Left and the Vietnam War*]. (P. Steinfels, Review, *Harper's*, January 1975, p. 82)

3. His [Jimmy Carter's] most imposing monument [as Governor of Georgia] was a wide-ranging record of reforms . . . . He shook up the state's Procrustean prison system. He promoted measures to upgrade education and humanize welfare . . . . He sponsored an anti-secrecy "sunshine law." (P. Goldman, "Sizing Up Carter," *Newsweek*, 9/13/76, p. 52)

4. Each story [selected for the public TV series, *The American Short Story*] could find its natural length, whether 23 minutes or 56 minutes, rather than having to be fitted to the PROCRUSTEAN bed of network television, where things happen only in increments of 30 minutes. (B. Marvel, "Rendering Language Visible: The Short Story as TV Fare," *National Observer*, week ending 4/16/77, p. 24)

PRODIGY (prod'i-jē) *noun* a person having extraordinary talent or ability, especially a child of highly unusual talent or genius; something wonderful or marvelous.

PRODIGIOUS *adj.* extraordinary, as in size or amount; wonderful, marvelous, or amazing; enormous, huge.

PRODIGIOUSLY *adv.*

PRODIGIOUSNESS *noun.*

1. See (1) under MONOMACHY.

2. Leopold Mozart's description of his eight-year-old son might well have added that the boy [Wolfgang] was also a PRODIGY of Leopold himself, whose expert tutelage and unrelenting ambition had cultivated and exploited the child's gifts. (R. Craft, "'A Prodigy of Nature,'" *New York Review of Books*, 12/11/75, p. 9)

3. When her older brother—"a PRODIGY who campaigned in Spanish for Al Smith at the age of 3"—choked to death on a quarter, she [Sissy Farenthold] became, in the words of her father a "two-in-one child." (Patricia Burstein, "Maverick Sissy Farenthold Takes A Sabbatical from Texas Politics to Run a Yankee College,"

People, 4/12/76, p. 19)

4. Tucked away on one program [at the Romantic Music Festival in Indianapolis] is a short piece—the *Polonaise Américaine,* by Josef Hofmann . . . a pianist who, many think, was the greatest of his time; . . . the Indianapolis audience will be hearing in the *Polonaise Américaine* the work of a 10-year- old PRODIGY. (H.C. Schonberg, "The Greatest Pianist of His Time," *New York Times,* 4/18/76, Section 2, p. 19)

5. Henry James marveled at her [Edith Wharton's] energy, and commented on it to friends: "The arrangement of [Edith's] life is to me one of the PRODIGIES of time," he said. (G. Hicks, Review of *Edith Wharton: A Biography,* by R.W.B. Lewis, *American Way,* February 1976, p. 30)

6. The article [the obituary of a black slave, Thomas Fuller, in the Dec. 9, 1790 issue of the Alexandria Gazette] states that Fuller was "a PRODIGY . . ." [He was asked] how many seconds has a man lived who is 70 years, 17 days, and 12 hours. He answered in 1½ minutes, 2,219,500,800. One of the gentlemen, who employed himself with his pen in making these calculations, told him . . . the sum was not so great as he had said—upon which the old man hastily replied, "Stop, Massa, you forget de leap year." (Athelia Knight, The Washington Post, *Virginia Bicentennial exhibit tells black's accomplishment,* Norman [Okla.] Transcript, 7/7/76, p. 24)

7. See (2) under BON VIVANT.

8. See (2) under SATURNINE.

PROGENITOR (prō-jen′i-tər) *noun* a forefather; ancestor in direct line; an original or model for later development; predecessor; precursor.

PROGENITIVE *adj.* capable of having offspring; reproductive.

1. . . . Calloway claims [in the book, *Of Minnie The Moocher and Me,* by Cab Calloway and Bryant Rollins] he is the ultimate practitioner, if not the PROGENITOR, of "jive" talk. He attempts to prove it by including . . . a rather long-winded "dictionary of jive." It's

CAMPY . . . but space-consuming. (M. Torme, Review, *New York Times,* 9/12/76, Section 7, p. 10)

2. . . . if [Lowell] Thomas understands . . . his own career as the PROGENITOR of the documentary and the first-ever network news commentator, he isn't telling [in the book, *Good Evening, Everybody*] . . . (D.R. Boldt, Review, *Philadelphia Inquirer,* 9/26/76, p. 10–H)

PROGNATHOUS (prog′nə-thəs, prog-nā′thəs) or **PROGNATHIC** *adj.* having projecting or protrusive jaws.

PROGNATHISM *noun.*

1. The influence of Darwinian ideas [on cartoons] is to be seen, for example, in Grant Hamilton's 1898 depiction of Spain as a bloody and PROGNATHOUS semibeast. This fate particularly befell the Irish during the 19th century, whose jaws jutted and jutted until the creature was indeed very apelike. (D.P. Moynihan, "Cartoons still make Uncle Sam nation's witness," *Smithsonian,* December 1975, p. 57)

PROLETARIAN (prō′li-târ′ē-ən) *adj.* pertaining or belonging to or of the proletariat.

PROLETARIAN *noun* a member of the proletariat; worker.

PROLETARIAT *noun* the poorest class in a society, especially the industrial working class who do not possess capital and must sell their labor to survive.

PROLETARIANIZE *verb* to convert or transform into a proletarian; to make (language, manners, etc.) proletarian.

PROLETARIANIZATION *noun.*

1. See (1) under CHI-CHI.

2. Rising above technology's PROLETARIAT may prove greatest challenge to tomorrow's scientists. (D.S. Greenberg, "Scientists wanted—pioneers needn't apply: call AD 2000," *Smithsonian,* July 1976, p. 66)

3. Hubert Selby Jr. [author of the book, *The Demon*] owes his literary reputation largely to *Last Exit to Brooklyn,* a fascinating, fevered voyage into the violent urban underworld of

pimps and whores, thieves, toughs, TRANSVES-
TITES and their PROLETARIAN boyfriends. (Paul
D. Zimmerman, Review, *Newsweek*, 11/1/76,
p. 84-L)

4. See (5) under AGITPROP.

PROLIX (prō-liks', prō'liks) *adj.* unnecessarily or tediously long and wordy; (of a person) given to speaking or writing at great
length; verbose; using more words than is
necessary; long-winded.

PROLIXITY *noun.*

PROLIXLY *adv.*

1. Apart from a few PROLIX and repetitive
passages, it [*The Tale of the Heike*, translated
by Hiroshi Kitigawa and Bruce Tsuchida] is an
eminently readable and exciting book, full of
lively anecdotes . . . . (I. Morris, Review, *New
York Times*, 2/8/76, Section 7, p. 23)

2. [Branch] Rickey, bushy-browed, PROLIX,
GRANDILOQUENT, leaned back in his chair and
told the Indiana Erskines about his farm
boyhood in "Oh-hi-yuh." The father and
mother were overwhelmed. (R. Kahn, *The
Boys of Summer*, Harper and Row, 1971,
p. 256)

3. The Trilateral Commission [an international group organized by David Rockefeller to
stimulate dialogue among Western Europe,
Japan and the U.S.] holds meetings every nine
months or so on one continent or another to
discuss international problems. It hires professors to write PROLIX reports with epochal
titles . . . . Most of these reports read like a big
yawn . . . . The new President is a member. So
is Vice-President Walter F. Mondale. (W.
Greider, Washington Post Service, "Trilateralists have taken over the U.S. government,"
Philadelphia Inquirer, 1/23/77, p. 1-F)

PROPINQUANT (prō-piñg'kwənt) *adj.*
near; neighboring; adjacent.

PROPINQUITY *noun* closeness; proximity;
nearness in place, time, or relationship; affinity.

1. Pinnacle is not alone in the westward movement. The "religious department" of Harper &

Row has already moved to San Francisco . . . .
Thus far most of its callers have been West
Coast writers . . . to whom the prospect of a
PROPINQUANT editor is most attractive. (R.
Walters, "Paperback Talk: Westward Ho,"
New York Times, 5/15/77, Section 7, p. 46)

PROROGUE (prō-rōg') *verb* to discontinue
a session of the British Parliament or other
legislative assembly; to postpone; to discontinue for a period.

PROROGATION *noun.*

1. Stopping the narrative [of *The Shadow of
the Winter Palace. Russia's Drift to Revolution
1825-1917*, by Edward Crankshaw] in 1914 is
mystifying. Mr. Crankshaw justifies himself
with the assertion that "from the beginning of
1914 [Nicholas II] ceased to play any effective
part in the government of the country." In
fact, the Emperor's decision in the summer of
1915 to PROROGUE the parliament (Duma) and
to assume personal command of the armed
forces was a reassertion of autocratic power
which had the profoundest effect on the fate of
Russia and its government. (R. Pipes, Review,
New York Times, 9/5/76, Section 7, p. 18)

PROSCRIBE (prō-skrīb') *verb* to forbid the
practice, use, etc., of; to denounce or condemn; to prohibit; outlaw; to banish or exile;
to deprive of the protection of the law; INTERDICT.

PROSCRIBER *noun.*

PROSCRIPTION *noun* the act of proscribing; the state of being proscribed; outlawry;
INTERDICTION; prohibition.

PROSCRIPTIVE *adj.*

PROSCRIPTIVELY *adv.*

1. In overturning a court-ordered racial quota
designed to protect the jobs of black and Puerto Rican school principals, the United States
Court of Appeals for the Second District
recently in effect PROSCRIBED racial discrimination even when it is intended to aid disadvantaged minorities. (Anon., "Seniority Dilemma"
[Editorial], *New York Times*, 2/20/76, p. 32)

2. Clay Basket [Pasquinel's wife] enjoyed being with McKeag and loved anew this quiet,

gentle man, but he was mortally afraid of her, PROSCRIBED as she was by being the wife of his partner. (J.A. Michener, *Centennial*, Fawcett, 1975, p. 257)

3. Princeton (and the same is true of other colleges) would never be caught corporately urging a dedication of the intellectual faculties to the service of a particular world view. Such a thing being, in an age of relativism, unmodish, and in any case PROSCRIBED by the rites of academic freedom. (W.F. Buckley Jr., *Up From Liberalism*, Arlington House, 2nd Printing 1968, p. 136)

4. Well before World War I, when [Paris Couturier Paul] Poiret sent harem-panted MANNEQUINS off to the races at Longchamps, they drew angry hoots and catcalls . . . . Poiret, who upset a good many fashion applecarts, likes to point out that "there has never been a truly new fashion which has not caused, at the outset . . . a general hue and cry, a universal chorus of hatred and PROSCRIPTION" . . . .(Phyllis Feldkamp, Review of *Paul Poiret, King of Fashion*, a show at Fashion Institute of Technology, *New York Times*, 6/13/76, Section 6, p. 59)

5. As recently as six month ago, [King] Juan Carlos made it clear in published interviews . . . that the Communists should continue to be PROSCRIBED [in Spain]. . . . Certainly the Spanish Communists, if PROSCRIBED, would lay claim to being the "repressed opposition" — but if the regime were perceived as moving toward free institutions such a claim could have little more than a short-term rhetorical effect. (J. Hart, *Red Pressure in Spain*, *Times Herald*, Norristown, Pa., 9/7/76, p. 13)

6. The choice seems to be one of complete freedom of expression (with all that implies in the way of nudity, outspoken language and obscene behavior or thought). Or there will have to be some form of censorship that PROSCRIBES those actions and thoughts and photographs that so many find detestable . . . the likelihood is that . . . freedom of expression will prevail (in all its forms). (Stephen Grover, "Pornography and Community Standards," *Wall Street Journal*, 2/23/77, p. 24)

7. But I suspect that we may have reached the end of the line so far as usefully further defining and PROSCRIBING conflict of interest is concerned. At some point you need to assume that most people are not VENAL or corrupt and do not enter government to make a killing. (Meg Greenfield, "Let's Not Overdo It," *Newsweek*, 12/20/76, p. 104)

PROTOTYPE (prō′ tə-tīp′) *noun* the original or model on which something is based or formed; someone or something that serves as an example of its kind; something analogous to another thing of a later period; an ARCHETYPE; pattern; model; a primitive form regarded as the basis for a group; a perfect example of a particular type.

PROTOTYPICAL or **PROTOTYPAL** or **PROTOTYPIC** *adj.*

PROTOTYPICALLY *adv.*

1. Led by the PROTOTYPICAL evil genius Doktor Josef Mengele, the infamous medical experimenter of Auschwitz, eight assassins are sent [in the book, *The Boys from Brazil*, by Ira Levin] . . . to kill—on specified dates—94 sixty-five-year-old civil servants living in Europe and North America. (G. Lyons, Review, *New York Times*, 3/14/76, Section 7, p. 4)

2. Well, the Peltzer case was the PROTOTYPE for the scheme he [Adam Malone] had in mind for [Leo] Brunner. (I. Wallace, *The Fan Club*, Bantam Books, 1975, p. 600)

3. For Secretary of State Mr. Carter nominated Cyrus Vance, almost PROTOTYPICAL of the so-called Eastern Establishment. He . . . served in major defense and diplomatic positions in both the Kennedy and Johnson administrations . . . . He is . . . almost universally respected by those who know his past performance. (Anon., "Kissinger, the Old Cyrus Vance," *New York Times*, 12/5/76, Section 4, p. 1)

4. See (2) under NYMPHET.

PROVENANCE (prov′ ə-nəns) *noun* a place of origin; source; derivation.

1. But the PROVENANCE of a suggestion does not define the merit of it. (W.F. Buckley Jr., *Execution Eve and Other Contemporary Ballads*, G.P. Putnam's Sons, 1975, p. 364)

2. Mr. [Justice] Goldberg . . . made no criticism of the book [Lasky's book on Goldberg], merely of its PROVENANCE. (W.F. Buckley Jr., *Ibid.*, p. 439)

3. Blazoned across the top of the page is: "From His Grace the Duke of Leinster." This is in case the majesty of the PROVENANCE of this form letter should miss you. (W.F. Buckley Jr., *Ibid.*, p. 181)

4. "At the foot of the [Chalk] cliff, in 1875, [Kennedy explained], . . . Professor Wright of Harvard dug out the great dinosaur that can be seen in Berlin." . . . "I knew the dinosaur but not its PROVENANCE." (J.A. Michener, *Centennial*, Fawcett, 1975, p. 35)

5. . . . having first described [in *A New Age Now Begins*] the PROVENANCE of the various colonies, the author [Page Smith] sees them (however disparate their backgrounds) in terms of a special American consciousness. (G. Dangerfield, Review, *New York Times*, 2/22/76, Section 7, p. 7)

6. . . . the language of this play [*Prometheus Bound*] shows so little of the metaphorical exuberance and complexity typical of Aeschylus that . . . many scholars have doubted its Aeschylean PROVENANCE—doubts finally laid to rest . . . by Herington's work . . . . (B.M.W. Knox, Review of *Aeschylus: Suppliants*, translated by Janet Lembke; *Aeschylus: Seven Against Thebes*, translated by Helen Bacon and Anthony Hecht; and *Aeschylus: Prometheus Bound*, translated by James Scully and C. John Herington, *New York Review of Books*, 11/27/75, p. 29)

7. . . . I was impressed with the bail-free release of [Hanafi] terrorist leader Khaalis, ne´ Ernie McGhee, on the liberal grounds that he had a "stable residence" and no prior convictions. Although I met those same criteria at the time of my 1973 guilty plea, Judge Sirica demanded from me a cash bail of $100,000 plus information concerning its PROVENANCE. But then my associates and I hadn't killed a man, wounded others, and terrorized 134 hostages. (E.H. Hunt, "How America Looks to Me Now," *Newsweek*, 4/4/77, p. 15)

8. There was just a trace of an accent there [in Rudolph's speech], and Blackford [Oakes] could not guess its PROVENANCE, and of course

would not have presumed to inquire. (W.F. Buckley Jr., *Saving the Queen*, Doubleday, 1976, p. 33)

9. See (1) under AUTOCHTHONOUS.

PROVENDER (prov´ ən-dər) *noun* dry food (hay, corn, oats, etc.) for livestock; fodder; food; provisions.

1. . . . Sam [Polidor] . . . left . . . though not without giving me his plan for lunch: "I'm going for chinks." Which was to say, chow mein. He added that . . . he would not disclose which of the Oriental establishments he headed for. He was safe: I [Russel Wren] don't care for toy PROVENDER. (Thomas Berger, *Who Is Teddy Villanova?*, Delacorte Press/Seymour Lawrence, 1977, p. 25)

PROXIMATE (prok´ sə-mit) or PROXIMAL *adj.* next or nearest in space, order, time, etc.; close; very near; approximate; fairly accurate; forthcoming; imminent.

PROXIMATELY *adv.*

PROXIMATENESS or PROXIMATION *noun.*

PROXIMITY *noun* the state or quality of being near; nearness in space, time, order, occurrence, etc.

1. What is sometimes mistaken for conservatism is an ad hoc AGGLOMERATION of forces, brought together temporarily by a PROXIMATE common interest. (W.F. Buckley Jr., *Up From Liberalism*, Arlington House, 2nd Printing, 1968, p. 90)

2. Donald Cammell's film [*Demon Seed*] takes place in the PROXIMATE future when a giant computer with a HYPERTROPHIC brain outwits the human beings running it, and turns Julie Christie into a captive in her own house. The computer half rapes and half seduces her, and . . . she bears what appears to be his child. (Ruth Gilbert, Review, *New York*, 11/28/77, p. 15)

PRURIENT (proŏr´ ē-ənt) *adj.* having or tending to have lascivious, lewd, or lustful thoughts, ideas, or desires; causing lasciviousness or lust; full of changing desires, itching curiosity, or abnormal craving.

PRURIENTLY *adv.*

PRURIENCE or PRURIENCY *noun.*

1. See (1) under EPICENE.

2. In his newest venture [*Hostage to the Devil: The Possession and Exorcism of Five Living Americans*] . . . Mr. [Malachi] Martin cashes in simultaneously on our appetite for PRURIENCE and on the vogue for the occult that made *The Exorcist* one of the largest box office draws in film history. (Francine Du Plessix Gray, Review, *New York Times*, 3/14/76, Section 7, p. 8)

3. Because rape is an important topic of a potentially sensational and PRURIENT nature, it is too bad that the book [*Against Our Will*, by Susan Brownmiller] is not a model of surpassing tact and delicacy, unassailable learning and scientific methodology. (Diane Johnson, Review, *New York Review of Books*, 12/11/75, p. 36)

4. Particularly in England a good gossip page is regarded as a SINE QUA NON of such papers as *The Daily Mail* or *The Daily Express* or *The Evening Standard*. More avowedly serious newspapers such as the London *Sunday Times* or *The Observer* acknowledge the need, with gossip columns purged of excessive PRURIENCE or outrageous snobbery . . . . In the United States PRURIENT and snobbish gossip is reserved for the huge mass circulation papers like the *National Inquirer*. . . (A. Cockburn, "The Psychopathology of Journalism," *New York Review of Books*, 12/11/75, p. 28)

5. [Joseph L.] Rauh told the jury that he had been interested only in developing a legal case against [Senator Joseph] McCarthy, not in having a PRURIENT view of McCarthy's personal affairs. In that case, why did he not instruct Hughes to limit his reports to evidence of legal wrongdoing? (W.F. Buckley Jr., *Up From Liberalism*, Arlington House, 2nd Printing, 1968, p. 106)

PSEUDONYM (sōōd' ənim) *noun* a fictitious name, especially one used by an author to conceal his identity; pen name; NOM DE PLUME.

PSEUDONYMITY *noun* pseudonymous character; the use of a pseudonym.

PSEUDONYMOUS *adj.* bearing a false or fictitious name; writing or written under a fictitious name.

PSEUDONYMOUSLY *adv.*

1. In 1773 a clash in the press brought [Charles] Carroll to the forefront of public notice . . . . Daniel Dulany, eloquent lawyer and scornful of the Carrolls . . . , argued the governor's side in a dialogue between "First Citizen" and "Second Citizen," which he published in the *Maryland Gazette*. Charles Carroll then assumed the PSEUDONYM of "First Citizen" in order to attack Dulany's position. Soon the "First Citizen"—Carroll—was reaping praise and acclaim. His letters were given credit for a landslide election that year, when every Maryland county sent antiestablishment delegates to Annapolis. (Mary H. Cadawalader, "Charles Carroll of Carrollton: a signer's story," *Smithsonian*, December 1975, p. 68)

2. Mr. [Malachi] Martin is a former Jesuit priest and the author of several other colorful and controvesial books on religion . . . . Among them [is] *The Pilgrim*, a gossipy account of the Vatican Council that he authored under the PSEUDONYM of Michael Serafian. (Francine DuPlessix Gray, Review of *Hostage to the Devil: The Possession and Exorcism of Five Living Americans*, by Malachi Martin, *New York Times*, 3/14/76, Section 7, p. 8)

3. "Your name," author John Jakes was once told by an editor, "sounds like a piece of clanking machinery. You should use a PSEUDONYM." Under his real, if UNMELLIFLUOUS, name Jakes is doing very well. He is the first writer ever to make the best-seller list with three books in a single year. (Anon., "John Jakes Spins Out Paperback Best-Sellers On the Bicentennial," *People*, 4/12/76, p. 25)

4. Jennifer Wilde, PSEUDONYMOUS author of *Love's Tender Fury*, is a Texan who has written a dozen successful GOTHICS under other names, took this first flight into the burgeoning historical romance GENRE at the suggestion of a Warner editor . . . (Anon., "Paper Back Talk: Daydreams," *New York Times*, 4/25/76, Section 7, p. 51)

5. . . . the more or less immature work [of Chekhov] . . . is subdivided [in the book, *A New Life of Anton Chekhov*, by Ronald Hingley] into four distinct periods, the earliest

being that of the skits, jokes, one-liners, puns and sketches Chekhov turned out for the humor magazines of the day under the PSEUDONYM of Antosha Chekonte to help support himself while studying medicine. (H. Moss, Review, *New York Times*, 6/20/76, Section 7, p. 26)

6. See (2) under AFICIONADO.

7. Charles Lamb is remembered as the transparently PSEUDONYMOUS essayist "Elia," a connoisseur of nostalgia and whimsy, old china, and roast pig. (Rachel Brownstein, Review of *The Letters of Charles and Mary Lamb: Vol. I and Vol. II*, Edited by Edwin W. Marrs, Jr., *New York Times*, 7/11/76, Section 7, p. 18)

PSORIASIS (sə-rī ə-sis) *noun* a chronic skin disease characterized by reddish patches covered with white scales.

PSORIATIC (sōr'ē-at'ĭk) *adj.*

1. The scrawny detective [Zwingli] nodded his PSORIATIC nose. (Thomas Berger, *Who Is Teddy Villanova?*, Delacorte Press/Seymour Lawrence, 1977, p. 97)

PSYCHOPOMP (sī' kō-pomp) *noun* one who conducts souls to the place of the dead, as Hermes in classical mythology.

PSYCHOPOMPAL or PSYCHOPOMPOUS *adj.*

1. THANATOLOGY was a comparatively new discipline. Not many sought the services of a PSYCHOPOMP . . . . Perhaps the look of MORIBUNDITY was mandatory in a PSYCHOPOMP; it begot confidence in the patient, suggesting that here was one who would literally lead the way. (A. Burgess, *Beard's Roman Women*, McGraw-Hill, 1976, pp. 140-141)

PTOMAINE (tō'mān, tō-mān') *noun* any of a class of basic nitrogenous substances produced during putrefaction of animal or plant protein and that cause food poisoning.

1. But [Spiro] Agnew's VILIFICATIONS [in his book, *The Canfield Decision*] are not limited to the press; he writes in the same simple-minded, single-minded fashion about Jews, liberals and intellectuals—all of whom . . . seem interchangeable in his tedious PTOMAINE.

(D. Shaw, *Los Angeles Times*, "Agnew 'murders' media and other 'nattering nabobs,' " *Norman* [Okla.] *Transcript*, 5/23/76, p. 17)

PUCKISH or **PUCKISH** (puk'ish) *adj.* mischievous; impish.

PUCKISHLY or PUCKISHLY *adv.*

PUCKISHNESS or PUCKISHNESS *noun.*

PUCK or PUCK (if lower case) a mischievous sprite or elf; (if capitalized) the mischievous sprite in Shakespeare's *A Midsummer Night's Dream*.

1. With loving attention to detail, at times unexpectedly PUCKISH, [Sviatoslav] Richter traced each phrase [on the piano]. (Anon., Review of a record of music by Brahms: *Sonata No. 2 in A, Op. 100*; by Prokofiev: *Sonata No. 1 in F Minor, Op. 80* (David Oistrakh, violin; Sviatoslav Richter, piano; Angel/Melodiya), *Time*, 4/12/76, p. 89)

2. The ROMAN À CLEF . . . holds an eminent position in literary history. . . . *Robinson Crusoe* was based on the desert-island experiences of one Alexander Selkirk off the coast of Chile, and *Tristram Shandy* caused not-always-comic shocks of recognition among the York neighbors of PUCKISH Laurence Sterne. (M. Maddocks, "Now for the Age of Psst!," *Time*, 6/28/76, p. 68)

PUDENDUM (pyōō-den' dəm) *noun, pl.:* PUDENDA (-də) the external genital organs of the female; vulva; the plural form is used to mean the external genital organs of either sex.

PUDENDAL *adj.*

1. "He had dialed . . . in search of six little girls to take to view the Statue of Liberty . . . American maidens, said he, should be made aware of the source of the national mystique, which happens to be both colossal and feminine. Small wonder, he added, that male homosexuals abound: the thought of that massive copper PUDENDUM beneath that great skirt of green PATINA must be terrifying to a certain type of juvenile constitution—male, that is; a female's must find it exhilarating" [said Boris]. (Thomas Berger, *Who Is Teddy Villanova?*, Delacorte Press/Seymour Lawrence, 1977, pp. 210-211)

PUERILE (pyōō′ər-il, pyōōr′il) *adj.* of, or pertaining to a child; childishly foolish; silly; boyish; youthful; juvenile; trivial.

PUERILELY *adv.*

PUERILITY *noun.*

PUERILISM *noun* childish behavior of an adult.

1. Paradoxically [Daniel] Bell argues [in *The Cultural Contradictions of Capitalism*], the HEDONISM made possible by capitalism's mass-marketing techniques has encouraged PUERILE imitations of the artists' antiBOURGEOIS values. (K.L. Woodward, Review, *Newsweek*, 2/9/76, p. 69)

2. I'd like to see . . . [an] experiment in which callers describe the [TV] show just seen in three adjectives. Within reason of course. ("We have a Mr. Buckley here who finds *Laverne* and *Shirley* EGREGIOUS, PUERILE, and JEJUNE.") (D. Cavett, of NEA, "Television 'Wasteland' Revisited," *Norman* [Okla.] *Transcript*, 6/23/76, p. 6)

PUISSANCE (pyōō′i-sans, pyōō-is′əns) *noun* great power, might, force, or influence.

PUISSANT *adj.*

PUISSANTLY *adv.*

1. [Arthur] Rubinstein's physique has often been mentioned as a reason for his continuing PUISSANCE. He is not tall (5 feet, 8 inches) or heavy (about 165), but he has a powerful chest, blacksmith biceps and disproportionately long legs. (D. Henahan, "This ageless hero, Rubinstein," *New York Times*, 3/14/76, Section 6, p. 18)

PULLULATE (pul′ yə-lāt′) *verb* to send forth sprouts, buds, etc.; to germinate; to breed, produce, or create rapidly; to increase rapidly; multiply; to exist in large numbers; swarm; teem; to be produced as offspring.

PULLULATION *noun.*

1. . . . [at the American Booksellers Assocation Trade Exhibit] there are the cocktail parties which PULLULATE in riotous (no pun) profusion and range from small suite affairs to lavish SATURNALIAS. (Anon., "Book Ends," *New York Times*, 6/27/76, Section 7, p. 33)

2. Four years of war [World War I] had left much of the world ripe for all sorts of epidemics, and many varieties of pneumonia-causing bacteria were PULLULATING. (Anon., "Plagues of the Past," *Time*, 8/16/76, p. 67)

PUNCTILIO (puṅgk-til′ ē-ō) *noun, pl.:* -LIOS a fine point, particular, or detail, as of conduct, ceremony, or procedure; strictness or exactness in the observance of petty formalities or amenities.

PUNCTILIOUS *adj.*

PUNCTILIOUSLY *adv.*

PUNCTILIOUSNESS *noun.*

1. A fortnight later a few of us met in Manhattan and decided, as a matter of PUNCTILIO, to suspend our formal support for . . . President Nixon. (W.F. Buckley Jr., *Execution Eve and Other Contemporary Ballads*, G.P. Putnam's Sons, 1975, p. 22)

2. See (1) under OCHLOCRACY.

PURBLIND (pûr′blīnd) *adj.* nearly or partially blind; dim-sighted; slow or deficient in understanding, imagination, or vision.

1. See (1) under STUPOR MUNDI.

2. It was curious that a state so advanced in all other directions should have been so permanently blind in its understanding of Mexicans. Colorado was where sensible labor relations were first worked out, where old-age pensions would be developed, where education was generously supported. . . . Colorado was a state where good ideas flourished, yet on this great basic question of human rights it remained PURBLIND. It could never admit that for farmers to use labor for personal gain and then to dismiss that labor with no acceptance of responsiblity was immoral. And any Anglo brave enough to raise the question ran the risk of having his teeth kicked in. (J.A. Michener, *Centennial*, Fawcett, 1975, p. 926)

3. But Carter remains vulnerable, open to a political counteroffensive if only the PURBLIND Republicans will use and seize the opportunity. The concessions Carter has been forced to make to win the acceptance of the McGovern

wing of his party have made him susceptible to an attack from the center and right. (P.J. Buchanan, "Carter Very Beatable Candidate," *Daily Oklahoman*, Okla. City, 7/16/76, p. 10)

PURDAH (pûr′də) or **PURDA** or **PARDAH** *noun* (in India, Pakistan, etc.) a screen, curtain, or veil, used for hiding women from the sight of men or strangers; seclusion in this manner or the practice of such seclusion.

1. In the Netherlands, preliminary word was that the evidence against Prince Bernhard would prove convincing, but stop short of signed receipts for the $1.1 million he is accused of receiving from Lockheed—and . . . Dutch officials were hinting at a reprimand and official PURDAH for the Prince. He would probably be forced to resign most of his corporate directorships and told to be more careful in choosing friends . . . . (D. Pauly, *et al.*, "Fastened Seat Belts," *Newsweek*, 4/5/76, p. 67)

2. Political tremors elsewhere in the world have thrust two upcoming books into prominence. The first is *Comrade Ch'ing*, by Roxane Witke, a biography of Mao Tse-tung's widow, who was forced into political PURDAH after Mao's death. (Anon., "Book Ends," *New York Times*, 2/27/77, Section 7, p. 37)

3. The Maharaja of Jaipur's second wife was so rigidly confined by PURDAH that when she was ill "the doctor had to make his diagnosis from the passage outside her room, getting details of her symptoms"—temperature and pulse—from her maids. (Caroline Seebohm, Review of *A Princess Remembers*, by Gayatri Devi of Jaipur and Santha Rama Rau, *New York Times*, 3/13/77, Section 7, p. 5)

4. See (4) under OSTRACISM.

5. The writing throughout [of the book, *A Princess Remembers*, by Gayatri Devi of Jaipur and Santha Rama Rau] betrays very little emotion or even irony; the prose is veiled like the PURDAH women from whom the Maharani had managed to escape. (Caroline Seebohm, Review, *New York Times*, 3/13/77, Section 7, p. 5)

PURLIEU (pûr′ lōō, pûrl′ yōō) *noun* a district or area at the edge of a town, forest,

etc.; a place where one has the right to come and go at will and wander freely; a place one habitually frequents; a haunt; (in the plural:) bounds, limits; environs; neighborhood.

1. The movie [*Mikey and Nicky*] follows them [the two main characters] for one careening night through the seedy PURLIEUS of Philadelphia as the bumbling hit man (Ned Beatty) attempts to catch up with Nicky [on whom the syndicate has put out a contract]. (J. Kroll, Review, *Newsweek*, 12/27/76, p. 56)

2. Social journalists with more class than Jerry [Westerby], shrewdly observing his progress through the PURLIEUS of the Charing Cross Road, would have recognized the type at once: the mackintosh brigade personified, cannon-fodder of the mixed-sauna parlors and the naughty bookshops. (J. LeCarré, *The Honourable Schoolboy*, Alfred A. Knopf, 1977, p. 108)

PUSILLANIMOUS (pyōō′ sə-lan′ə-məs) *adj.* timid, cowardly, or irresolute; fainthearted; proceeding from or showing a lack of courage or resolution.

PUSILLANIMITY *noun.*

PUSILLANIMOUSLY *adv.*

1. "We must take her [a young Arapaho girl who was kidnapped by the Pawnee to use as a human sacrifice] back," he [Lame Beaver] stormed, unwilling to consider any alternative. Trade for her? Never. Surrender more hunting land? Never. Horses, pelts, guns? He would listen to no such PUSILLANIMITY. (J.A. Michener, *Centennial*, Fawcett, 1975, p. 197)

2. Then, in late October, a very brave young captain named Salcedo grew impatient with the PUSILLANIMOUS behavior of the fat generals and devised a daring plan . . . . The plan worked, and by the end of October the revolution at Temchie was doomed. (J.A. Michener, *Ibid.*, p. 825)

PUTATIVE (pyōō′ tə-tiv) *adj.* generally regarded as such; reputed; supposed.

PUTATIVELY *adv.*

1. But this only partially explains his compulsion to retaliate against his PUTATIVE tormentors by pouring personal insult on their heads.

(R. Brustein, Review of *Uneasy Stages* and *Singularities*, by John Simon, *New York Times*, 1/4/76, Section 7, p. 1)

2. Watergate is coming up right soon now. As a judicial matter, before the relevant court, and as an extra-judicial matter, before Congressional committees that are raring to go, their thirst for justice no doubt stimulated by the happy coincidence that the Congressional committees are run by Democrats, and the victims are, at least PUTATIVELY, Republicans. (W.F. Buckley Jr., *Execution Eve and Other Contemporary Ballads*, G.P. Putnam's Sons, 1975, p. 107)

3. Four decades of unrelenting turmoil, domestic and international, have created in the public a willingness to grant almost unlimited powers to the President, now in the hope that he will "get America moving again," now in the hope that he will clamp down on malcontents and DISSIDENTS, the PUTATIVE source of all the troubles that afflict the nation and disturb the peace. (C. Lasch, Review of *Nightmare*, by J. Anthony Lukas, *New York Times*, 1/15/76, Section 7, p. 24)

4. See (1) under ALTRUISM.

5. There was much more excitement over Senator [Joseph] McCarthy's methods—(did he or did he not—observe approved methods of interrogation?)—than over the PUTATIVE revelations that ensued . . . . (W.F. Buckley Jr., *Up From Liberalism*, Arlington House, 2nd Printing, 1968, p. 140)

6. The liberal sees no moral problem . . . in divesting the people of that portion of their property necessary to finance the projects certified by ideology as beneficial to the Whole. Mr. J.K. Galbraith wages total war against any PUTATIVE right of the individual to decide for himself how to allocate his resources. (W.F. Buckley Jr., *Ibid.*, p. 170)

7. Leaving aside the question *whether* the Keynesian formula could bring about the advertised economic result, Lord Keynes' point was DIALECTICALLY self-contained: *if* he could bring about, by his razzle-dazzle economics, the desired economic result, the PUTATIVE injuries to the long term are worth worrying

about only as one worries, in moments of morbid vanity, about whether one's grave will be kept green. (W.F. Buckley Jr., *Ibid.*, p. 187)

8. The liberal ideology is PUTATIVELY based on the maximization of choice at every level. What is important to the liberal, again PUTATIVELY, is that there be choice; whereas to the conservative, what is important is, What choices will man . . . go on making? In actual practice, the choices, under applied liberalism, are limited by the pressures of an over-arching and highly repressive conformity. (W.F. Buckley Jr., *Ibid.*, p. 183)

9. The nature of that war [between the sexes] and the paramount role that rape plays in it form the crux of the argument in *Against Our Will* [by Susan Brownmiller] and the PUTATIVE basis for feminist ideology. (D.L. Kirp, Review, *Change*, April 1976, p. 41)

10. Joe McGinniss was sent out with a lucrative contract to look for "the vanishing American hero." . . . his first book, *The Selling of the President, 1968*, had made him at 26 the youngest author to stand number one on the nonfiction bestseller list . . . . The PUTATIVE heroes for McGinniss are, of course, from somewhere around that same era when he was Number One . . . . (E. Hoagland, Review of *HEROES*, by Joe McGinniss, *New York Times*, 4/18/76, Section 7, p. 8)

11. The Hechingers [Fred M. and Grace], clearly, are writing [Growing Up in America] for the ages . . . and references to events in the quite recent past, accordingly, are written for some PUTATIVE reader a century hence: "The last quarter of the twentieth century began . . ." (C. Truehart, Review, *Change*, Winter 1975-76, p. 54)

12. See (1) under SCHLEPP.

13. [In the film, *Robin and Marian*] Will brings Robin and Little John up to date by singing a popular ballad about the PUTATIVE exploits of the merry men in their pre-Crusades youth. "But Will," Robin protests, pleased, "we never did any of those things." (Jay Cocks, Review, *Time*, 3/22/76, p. 78)

14. See (5) under MORES.

Q

QUARK (kwôrk) *noun* any of three hypothetical elementary particles postulated by some physicists as forming the basis of all matter in the universe [an arbitrary use by M. Gell-Mann of a word coined by James Joyce in *Finnegan's Wake*]

1. While the remedies to [the technical problems in gathering TV news] seem as elusive as the charmed QUARK, network executives view the coming of a one-hour newscast as an eminently helpful first step. But that prospect is far less appealing to the affiliates, who would have to surrender a half hour from their own schedules—along with the lucrative local advertising revenue that comes with it. (H.F. Waters, *et al.*, "The New Look of TV News," *Newsweek*, 10/11/76, p. 78)

QUERENCIA (kā rens'yə) *noun* an area in the arena taken by the bull for a defensive stand in a bullfight.

1. Black [ford Oakes] eased away toward Sally—his QUERENCIA, his love—to lick his wounds. (W.F. Buckley Jr., *Saving the Queen*, Doubleday, 1976, p. 44)

QUERULOUS (kwer'ə-ləs, kwer'yə-ləs) *adj.* full of complaints; inclined to find fault; complaining; characterized by or uttered in complaint; peevish; petulant; testy; carping.

QUERULOUSLY *adv.*

QUERULOUSNESS *noun.*

1. It is not my intention to be QUERULOUS and churlish in such an amicable place as Heaven, but I've always been led to expect rare and noble treatment behind those walls of jasper.

(H.A. Smith, "My requirements of Heaven,"* *New York Times*, 3/14/76, Section 6, p. 111)

2. . . . they [Eugenio Montale's first poems] were imbued with a passionate sense of moral disillusionment and alienation—verging at times on QUERULOUSNESS—which has remained the poet's characteristic attitude. (J. Galassi, Review of *New Poems*, by Eugenio Montale, translated by G. Singh; and of *Provincial Conclusions*, by Eugenio Montale, translated by Edith Farnsworth, *New York Times*, 5/30/76, Section 7, p. 6)

3. [Ronald] Reagan's campaign manager, John Sears, correctly senses another Reagan advantage and a Ford liability in the QUERULOUS mood of the country: "This may be a year when people don't know what they want, but they know they don't want what they've got." (Anon., "G.O.P. Donnybrook," *Time*, 6/21/76, p. 15)

4. See (4) under SANG-FROID.

QUIDDITY (kwid' i-tē) *noun* that which makes a thing what it is: the essential nature or quality of a thing that makes it unique; a trifling nicety or subtle distinction; quibble.

1. But the [magazine] article said something about its being very rare indeed for a husband to want his wife back from the dead . . . . New fresh sex, of course, had a lot to do with it, hot loveless but also guiltless sex, a totally different QUIDDITY from marital love. (A. Burgess, *Beard's Roman Women*, McGraw-Hill, 1976, pp. 103-104)

*This article was completed a few days before the author's death.

QUIDNUNC (kwid'nuñgk') *noun* a person who is eager to know the latest news and gossip; a gossip or busybody; a newsmonger.

1. Harry Sheer's QUIDNUNC? [Boxed questions about sports]—Last call for the names of the pitchers who served up Ernie Banks' 300th, 400th, and 500th home runs . . . . Today's trivia: . . . the 1911 New York Giants under John McGraw stole a record 347 bases in 154 games and won a pennant . . . but could steal only four bases in the World Series and lost to the Philadelphia A's, four games to two! (H. Sheer, *Chicago Tribune*, 5/6/76, Section 4, p. 2)

QUID PRO QUO (kwid'prō-kwō') one thing in return for another; tit for tat; something given or taken in return for something else, as a favor; substitute; something equivalent.

1. In 1951 he [Prince Bernhard] came home from Buenos Aires with a $60 million order from Juan Perón's government for Dutch railroad equipment; at the time, the only QUID PRO QUO was thought to be a Dutch decoration for Perón's wife, Eva. But . . . the Netherlands government disclosed that the deal had also involved a payoff of $12 million in cash for the Peróns, $1 million in jewelry for Evita, and a deluxe private train for them both. (M. Ruby, *et al.*, "A Slap for the Prince," *Newsweek*, 4/5/76, p. 68)

2. There are some who will argue that we should continue to help India's teeming millions faced with starvation. Maybe so, but there ought to be some QUID PRO QUO in our own interest—like telling Mrs. Gandhi to shut up about "American imperialism" over the U.S. Navy's desire to expand a small service and communications facility 1000 miles south of India on the island of Diego Garcia. (Anon., "More Foreign Aid Policy," [Editorial], *Daily Oklahoman*, Okla. City, 4/20/76, p. 6)

3. "Old Blue Eyes" is to receive a doctorate of humane letters from the University of Nevada—Las Vegas, Sunday. . . . The degree . . . has the earmarks of a QUID PRO QUO. In a story about the University's . . . highly successful basketball team, Barry McDermott of Sports Illustrated wrote: ". . . Stars like Frank Sinatra have been known to influence recruits" to enroll at the university and try out for the team. (R.L. Worsnop, "And now it's Dr. Sinatra, *Oklahoma City Times*, 5/19/76, p. 50)

4. Some [women in Washington] are idealists . . . . Some see a Congressional post as just a job, some as a stepping-stone to careers in business or politics. Some are looking for husbands, some are excited by the power and celebrity of the men around them, and some, to be sure, fall into sexual attachments with congressmen—though rarely on the QUID PRO QUO basis that [Elizabeth] Ray alleges [in her relationship with Wayne Hays]. (A. Deming, *et al.*, "Women of Washington," *Newsweek*, 6/14/76, p. 28)

5. [J. Edgar] Hoover wreaked vengeance on reporters who used the FBI for information, but who refused to be used by Hoover in a QUID PRO QUO. (J. Bishop, "Tribute to Hoover," *Times Herald*, Norristown, Pa., 9/4/76, p. 11)

6. [Rep. John] Brademas claims he did nothing to "earn" his $5,000 from [Tong Sun] Park . . . . The money was meant to buy friendship, if not directly, then indirectly. Cordial relations with an influential congressman, even if no specific QUID is given for the QUO, help to legitimate a man like Park as he moves through the legislative labyrinth. (G. Wills, "It's not a home . . . but the House needs a cleaning, *Philadelphia Inquirer*, 12/16/76, p. 15-A)

QUIFF (kwif) *noun Slang:* a sexually promiscuous woman.

1. His novel [*The Education of Patrick Silver*, by Jerome Charyn] is a vigorous performance, . . . its notably fluent language a kind of novelistic blarney, lavish with HYPERBOLIC verbs . . . . "There were QUIFFS at the terminal, QUIFFS and spies, with the imprint of shotguns under their DASHIKIS, police aerials climbing up their backs, newspaper stuffed in a brassiere . . ." (R.P. Brickner, Review, *New York Times*, 9/5/76, Section 7, p. 5)

QUINCUNX (kwiñg'kuñgks, kwin'-) *noun* an arrangement of five objects, as trees, in a square or rectangle, one at each corner and one in the middle.

QUINCUNCIAL (kwin-kun'shəl) or QUINCUNX-

IAL (kwin-kuñg′ sē-əl) *adj.* consisting of, arranged, or formed like a quincunx or quincunxes.

QUINCUNCIALLY *adv.*

1. In Masonic ritual, a Brother placed three dots after his signature, and a Sister five dots, in QUINCUNX, after hers . . . . Fives and threes occur in rhythms, chords, and key signatures throughout the opera [*The Magic Flute*]. (R. Craft, Review, *New York Review of Books*, 11/27/75, p. 21)

QUINTESSENCE (kwin-tes′əns) *noun* the pure and concentrated essence of anything; the most perfect embodiment or manifestation of a quality or thing; (in ancient and medieval philosophy) the 5th element or essence, ether, supposed to be the constituent matter of the heavenly bodies, the others being air, fire, earth, and water.

QUINTESSENTIAL *adj.*

QUINTESSENTIALLY *adv.*

1. For more than 50 years, André Malraux has been the QUINTESSENTIAL man of letters as man of action, hurling himself into the great events of his time as the only antidote to an overriding sense of the absurd. (P.D. Zimmerman, Review of *André Malraux*, by Jean Lacouture, *Newsweek*, 12/29/75, p. 56)

2. Senator Hubert Humphrey emerged as the *best*, *i.e.*, the QUINTESSENTIAL spokesman for the Democratic approach to such questions. (W.F. Buckley Jr., *Execution Eve and Other Contemporary Ballads*, G.P. Putnam's Sons, 1975, p. 264)

3. QUINTESSENTIALLY, the community college is close to home, it is accessible. (R. Dugger, "The Community College Comes of Age," *Change*, February 1976, p. 34)

4. With the visiting professors [who meet with people in small towns through a program sponsored by the National Endowment for the Humanities], the QUINTESSENTIAL outsiders, leading the postprogram discussion, layers of conventional responses were peeled away to reach many never before publicly aired local issues . . . . (Elinor Lenz, "The Humanities Go Public," *Change*, February 1976, p. 55)

5. Sherry Duffy, now with the county crime prevention unit, proved herself in the QUINTESSENTIAL police showdown: she shot and killed a man who had fired at another man and then turned on her. (Sue Chastain, "Wilmington policewomen: A notice to Philadelphia," *Philadelphia Inquirer*, 2/15/76, p. 18-A)

6. He [André Malraux] still seems somewhat larger than life, the QUINTESSENTIAL portrait of the artist as activist. (J.B. Steele, Review of *André Malraux*, by Jean Lacouture, *Philadelphia Inquirer*, 2/15/76, p. 12-H)

7. These quotations [from a wide variety of philosophers, politicians, journalists, etc.] have the . . . virtue of condensing the . . . argument [in *The Peter Plan*, by Norma Klein], providing its QUINTESSENCE while opening paradoxical windows on the surrounding intellectual landscape. (F. Golfing, Review, *New York Times*, 2/8/76, Section 7, p. 18)

8. Men with waist-length hair and dirt under their fingernails no longer represent rebellious charisma to me, education notwithstanding. Happy former rat-race proponents who have left to paint driftwood and have no sense of humor are not attractive. The damnable thing about this new tribe of QUINTESSENTIAL Californians is that they are so *serious* about it all. (Mary Alice Kellogg, "A Farewell to Nirvana," *Newsweek*, 3/15/76, p. 15)

9. Archie Rice [the protagonist in *The Entertainer*, a TV special] is the QUINTESSENTIAL show-biz failure, a tired, shamelessly vulgar comic with a shine on the seat of his conscience . . . . (H.F. Waters, Review, *Newsweek*, 3/15/76, p. 55)

10. Oct. 18, 1974 marked the beginning of a one-man spree of sexual violence that lasted eight months and was unprecedented in Great Britain and Europe. Before it was over, the slim man with the flashlight and knife would attack nine women and turn contemplative Cambridge [England], a QUINTESSENTIAL college community, into a place of mindless fear and suspicion. (G.M. O'Neil, "Only the terror was undisguised," *Boston Globe*, 3/7/76, p. 1-A)

11. Anne, directionless, later bereft, works [in the book, *Family Feeling*, by Helen Yglesias] at her biography of Frederick Law Olmstead, the architect of Central Park . . . : the QUINTES-

SENTIAL striving American, plunged deep into the social and political problems that have obsessed all her generation. (B. Allen, Review, *Boston Globe*, 3/7/76, p. 16-A)

12. See (1) under GEMÜTLICH.

13. It's a QUINTESSENTIALLY journalistic passage; one gossip relating the gossip of a second gossip who himself is admitting to gossiping to a third person who is quite prepared to gossip about himself to yet another gossip who is putting together a book about first sexual experiences. (A. Cockburn, "The Psychopathology of Journalism," *New York Review of Books*, 12/11/75, p. 31)

14. My reason for abstracting social security is [that] . . . it has an almost unique symbolical significance in American social controversy, where it holds down a position as the QUINTESSENCE of modern welfarism. (W.F. Buckley Jr., *Up From Liberalism*, Arlington House, 2nd Printing 1968, p. 201)

15. He [H.H. Munro] was fond of his father and of his Scottish ancestry; still there is something in his writing that is QUINTESSENTIALLY English . . . . (J. Lukacs, Review of *The Complete Works of Saki*, by H.H. Munro, *New York Times*, 3/28/76, Section 7, p. 6)

16. [Werner] Erhard himself received the message [you are the cause of your own experience] in a blinding flash while driving . . . down some California highway. In that QUINTESSENTIAL California instant, some four and a half years ago, "est" [Erhard Seminars Training] was born. (Vivian Gornick, Review of *est: 60 Hours That Transform Your Life*, by Adelaide Bry, *New York Times*, 4/4/76, Section 7, p. 6)

17. See (3) under SYBARITE.

18. A QUINTESSENTIAL New Yorker, the private Louise Lasser seems as disoriented as a beached carp in her rustic rented house atop Los Angeles' Benedict Canyon. (H.F. Waters and M. Kasindorf, "The Mary Hartman Craze," *Newsweek*, 5/3/76, p. 61)

19. The mean that mainstream sociologists have chosen is a search for the QUINTESSENTIAL metaphor of social action—one that their audience will take as true, yet not immediately obvious . . . . (Sharon Zukin, Review of *The Sociological Way of Looking at the World*, by Louis Schneider, *Chronicle of Higher Education*, 3/22/76, p. 13)

20. In Rumer Godden's latest novel [*The Peacock Spring*], Sir Edward Gwithiam, a QUINTESSENTIALLY hard-working, kindly and tepid British diplomat posted in Delhi with the United Nations, finds himself madly in love with Alix Lamont, a beautiful Eurasian who is "not quite right." (Katha Pollitt, Review, *New York Times*, 4/25/76, Section 7, p. 48)

21. The leading man's Best Pal: Frank McHugh . . . . The QUINTESSENTIAL McHugh can be seen stealing or saving *Boy Meets Girl* (1938), *Dodge City* (1939) and *The Roaring Twenties* (1929). (Wallace Markfield, "Somebody Should Have Put Their Names in Lights," *New York Times*, 4/18/76, Section 2, p. 15)

22. See (1) under CALIBAN.

23. In [James] Watson [author of the book, *The Double Helix*] we have the image of the QUINTESSENTIALLY American scientist on the make—young, brash, impulsive . . . . (Evelyn Fox Keller, Review of *Rosalind Franklin and DNA*, by Anne Sayre, *Change*, Winter 1975-76, p. 59)

24. See (2) under GOTHIC.

25. [Giancarlo] Giannini . . . offers [in the film, *How Funny Can Sex Be?*] a ripely funny portrait of the QUINTESSENTIAL Italian husband who discovers on his honeymoon that his sexual powers desert him unless he essays the act under moving conditions, namely a train, an elevator or the back of a truck. (D. Ryan, Review, *Philadelphia Inquirer*, 10/22/76, p. 6-C)

26. Young surpasses not only [David] Crosby, [Stephen] Stills and [Graham] Nash, but indeed the vast majority of contemporary singer-songwriters on several grounds . . . . Neil Young is the QUINTESSENTIAL hippy-cowboy loner, a hopeless romantic struggling to build bridges out from himself to women and through them to cosmic ARCHETYPES of the past and of myth. (J. Rockwell, "Neil Young—As Good as Dylan?" *New York Times*, 6/19/77, Section 2, p. 2)

QUISLING (kwiz'liŋ) *noun* a person who betrays his country by aiding an invading enemy, often serving later in a puppet government; a traitor; a fifth-columnist; collaborationist [after Vidkun *Quisling* (1887-1945), pro-Nazi Norwegian leader who in 1940 aided the German invaders of his native Norway].

1. When last seen as the starched, love-parched maid in *Upstairs, Downstairs*, British actress Jean Marsh was helping the Allies win World War I by serving tea at the Bellamys and moonlighting as a bus conductor. But lately she has been embroiled in World War II, filming *The Eagle Has Landed*, in which she plays a British WAC gone awry aiding Michael Caine, a German colonel, in a plot to kidnap Winston Churchill. How could the prim Rose of *Upstairs* switch from kitchenling to QUISLING? Easy, she says: "I'd do it to anyone for the money." (Anon., "People," *Time*, 6/28/76, p. 38)

2. . . . Saul Bellow contended [recently] that most people don't pay any mind to writers, and his assessment struck me as correct . . . many of my fellow travelers [writers] must be under the illusion that their lives are as interesting to the general public as Mary Hartman's. But before I'm branded a QUISLING for the vulgar herd, I must confess a degree of sympathy for the writer's plight. (J. Flaherty, "Hi-Diddely-Dee—The Writer's Life for Me!" *New York Times*, 3/13/77, Section 7, p. 43)

QUIXOTIC (kwik-sot' ik) or **QUIXOTICAL** *adj.* [after Don Quixote, the hero of a novel by Cervantes] extravagantly chivalrous or romantic; visionary; impractical or impracticable; romantically idealistic; pursuing lofty but impractical ideals.

QUIXOTICALLY *adv.*

QUIXOTISM *noun* a quixotic character, practice, idea, or act.

1. A more dramatic example of the QUIXOTIC nature of this process occurred recently when HEW informed colleges and universities, albeit too late, of the availability of $375 million in grants under Title X of the Public Works and Economic Development Act. (G.W. Bonham, "Will Government Patronage Kill the Universities?" [Editorial], *Change*, Winter 1975-76, p. 12)

2. One of the frustrations of academic realities is the QUIXOTIC nature of academic reform. (G.W. Bonham, "Academic Reform: Still a Pseudoscience" [Editorial], *Change*, November 1975, p. 11)

3. All this is remarkable in light of [Jimmy] Carter's performance in 1972 when he attempted a QUIXOTIC stop-McGovern drive at the national governor's conference in early June. (R. Evans and R. Novak, "Carter Woos McGovernites," *Daily Oklahoman*, Okla. City, 2/3/76, p. 8)

4. The war [revolution in Mexico] strung out from February till October [1900], with the miners organizing their village as a redoubt capable of withstanding almost any assault. The American engineers and their families were . . . now in Chihuahua city. The Germans were gone too, all except one QUIXOTIC young man who elected to stay with Frijoles [the revolutionary leader] and the miners. (J.A. Michener, *Centennial*, Fawcett, 1975, p. 825)

5. It is difficult now to imagine Arvo Gus Hallberg as the scourge of America, a man so notorious he had to alter his name to get work. Yet Gus Hall and his American Communist Party threw fear into millions in days past . . . . Almost forgotten now, except for his quadrennial and QUIXOTIC presidential campaigns, he is a figure of failure. (T. Tiede, "Age Takes Toll: Hall Antique Not Menace," *Norman* [Okla.] *Transcript*, 3/24/76, p. 6)

6. He [Ian Richardson as Professor Higgins, in *My Fair Lady*] also lacks the sexiness, perverse but unmistakable, that lies beneath Higgins's academic epidermis and makes him a QUIXOTIC lover rather than a cold cad. (J. Kroll, Review, *Newsweek*, 4/5/76, p. 78)

7. [John] Berryman's suicide was QUIXOTIC; . . . and we owe it to him to learn what he thought the QUIXOTIC figure signified. (One thing it signified was "humility" . . . ; one way to regard all Berryman's poems of the 1960's is as one long potential exercise in self-humiliation). (D. Davie, Review of *The Freedom of the Poet*, by John Berryman, *New York Times*, 4/25/76, Section 7, p. 4)

8. The Soviet Constitution upon which the pos-

sibly QUIXOTIC American effort [to help Soviet Jews emigrate to Israel] was based can hardly be improved—on paper . . . . No discrimination because of nationality or race is permitted . . . .Yet there is only slightly more concordance today between the word and the deed of Soviet justice than there was in Stalin's day. (H.E. Salisbury, Review of *Courts of Terror: Soviet Criminal Justice and Jewish Immigration*, by Telford Taylor, *New York Times*, 4/18/76, Section 7, p. 5)

9. Since the coup against the late, disgraced Emperor Haile Selassie nearly two years ago, Ethiopa's revolutionary experiment in "scientific socialism" has proved to be as eccentric and QUIXOTIC as anything decreed by the old kingdom. (Anon., "Ethopia: A Land of Anarchy and Bloodshed," *Time*, 5/31/76, p. 29)

10. See (l) under CARAPACE.

11. . . . Humphrey got a phone call from unpredictable Jerry Brown. He wanted to join Humphrey in a ninth inning drive to stop Carter. Humphrey turned him down . . . QUIXOTICALLY, Brown continued to fight. (Anon., "Stampede to Carter," *Time*, 6/21/76, p. 9)

12. When Eugene McCarthy joined forces with Lester Maddox last week in an attempt to gain inclusion in the crucial TV debates between President Ford and Jimmy Carter, his action was not entirely unexpected. McCarthy, 60, has, since his 1968 campaign, made the QUIXOTIC gesture his hallmark. (Anon., "Will McCarthy Matter?," *Time*, 9/13/76, p. 17)

QUONDAM (kwon'dam) *adj.* that formerly was or existed; former; of earlier times.

1. "It was our habit," recalled the QUONDAM dean of this [Harvard] faculty, McGeorge Bundy, "to ask ourselves, about every really first-rate scholar everywhere, why he should not be at Harvard." (N.W. Aldrich Jr., "Harvard On The Way Down," *Harper's*, March 1976, p. 42)

2. It [the Supreme Court's "one man, one vote" decision and LBJ's legislation] also produced a new class of liberal Southern senators, U.S. representatives and governors. They ranged from QUONDAM Presidential contenders

such as North Carolina's former Gov. Terry Sanford to Georgia's Julian Bond, and they all pressed for an end to the South's INSULARITY. (T. Mathews, *et al.*, "The Southern Mystique," *Newsweek*, 7/19/76, p. 31)

3. Well, as so often happens in the affairs of men, fate uses as its instrument such an otherwise unrewarding person as my QUONDAM nurse to further its INSCRUTABLE aims. (T. Berger, *Little Big Man*, Fawcett, 1964, p. 12)

QUOTIDIAN (kwō-tid'ē-ən) *adj.* daily; recurring every day; usual, ordinary, or everyday.

QUOTIDIAN *noun*.

1. There is something democratic and enlivening in their [the "beat" writers'] celebration of "our QUOTIDIAN inspired lives," the beauty of common speech, the intrinsic artfulness of the mind's first thoughts, and, finally, in their indignation at the forces that obscure these potentials. (P. Parisi, Review of *Naked Angels: The Lives and Literature of the Beat Generation*, by John Tytell, *The Chronicle of Higher Education*, 5/10/76, p. 19)

2. Surrealist poetry seems to be the strongest influence on their work [that of poets with comic masks who amuse and entertain], which is frequently a satirical attack on the QUOTIDIAN habits of its audience. Their success depends upon acute perception of the detail of behavior and the EUPHEMISMS and CIRCUMLOCUTIONS used to dignify it. (D. Lenson, "Unmasking the Contemporary Poet," *The Chronicle of Higher Education*, 8/2/76, p. 9)

3. Science fiction regularly shows us humanity in trouble. Mutants, monsters, alien intelligences and creeping plant life all figure the possible end of a human world, but they also suggest something more QUOTIDIAN, less APOCALYPTIC: a change of life, a suspicion that humanity itself has simply been mislaid or thrown away in some recent corridor of history. And in this light science fiction seems less a marginal or extravagant form of fiction than a caricatured version of what is going on all over the place. (M. Wood, Review of *Plus*, a book by Joseph McElroy, *New York Times*, 3/20/77, Section 7, p. 6)

4. Until this moment I [Russel Wren] had no

quite been able to rise above a suspicion that the entire affair . . . was the elaborate JAPERY by which a pampered parasite, and his enormous retainer, sought to allay QUOTIDIAN ENNUI. (Thomas Berger, *Who Is Teddy Villanova?*, Delacorte Press/Seymour Lawrence, 1977, p. 172)

5. She [Peggy Tumulty] displayed even more flesh than I had supposed she carried beneath her QUOTIDIAN attire, yet in a form of more luxuriant definition. . . (Thomas Berger, *Ibid.*, p. 209)

6. She [Peggy Tumulty] wore her office attire and her QUOTIDIAN hair and eyes. (Thomas Berger, *Ibid.*, p. 239)

R

RACONTEUR (rak'on-tûr') *noun* a person skilled in relating anecdotes or telling stories.

1. See (1) under INVETERATE.

2. If they're lucky, visitors to Mr. Chui [Cheong Tai]'s shop [in Hong Kong] also get a bit of entertainment with their purchase, since the tailor is an accomplished RACONTEUR. A favorite story is about what happened to Mr. Chui during the Japanese occupation . . . in World War II. (Veronica Huang, "For This Tailor, Needles and Pins are Fabric of Life," *Wall Street Journal*, 9/23/76, p. 25)

RAISON D'ÊTRE (rā'zōn de'trə) *noun, pl.:* **RAISONS D'ÊTRE** (rā'zōns de'trə) reason or justification for being or existence.

1. In 1971, after 26 consecutive years of support, the [Woodrow Wilson National Fellowship] foundation had to suspend its prestigious RAISON D'ÊTRE because it couldn't scare up a dime in support of graduate school fellowships . . . (R.K. Rein, "Woodrow Wilson Fellows— Who Are They Now?", *Change*, March 1975, p. 17)

2. See (3) under HERMETIC.

3. In comparison [with Pamina], Tamino is without any background, and, for the first part of the action [in Mozart's *The Magic Flute*], his only RAISON D'ÊTRE is the search for a wife who has been selected for him by a stranger. (R. Craft, Review, *New York Review of Books*, 11/17/75, p. 19)

4. She must transform herself from Miss Susan Klatt to Miss Sharon Fields, the legend, the dream, the wish, the sex symbol, the RAISON D'ÊTRE of The Fan Club. (I. Wallace, *The Fan Club*, Bantam Edition, 1975, p. 351)

5. His [Felix Zigman's] RAISON D'ÊTRE, his value to mere mortals, . . . his success itself, each was based on his ability to remain unruffled and to think clearly in any crisis. (I. Wallace, *Ibid.*, p. 481)

6. Another live Wagner recording, a *Die Meistersinger* from the 1943 Bayreuth festival is an equally fascinating historical document . . . . The RAISON D'ÊTRE of this Meistersinger is the conducting of Wilhelm Furtwängler. (P.G. Davis, Review, *New York Times*, 6/20/76, Section 2, p. 27)

RANDY (ran' dē) *adj.* sexually aroused; lustful; lascivious; amorous; lecherous; rude and aggressive; coarse; crude; vulgar.

1. Back in the days when the Society for the Suppression of Vice rode tall in the saddle and the friendly neighborhood candy store pushed pornography instead of pot, whole generations

of RANDY schoolboys would . . . spend their allowances collecting the grimy volumes of Frank Harris's *My Life and Loves.* (R. Freedman, Review of *Frank Harris: A Biography,* by Philippa Pullar, *New York Times,* 3/28/76, Section 7, p. 8)

2. Indeed, I tried ginseng myself over a period of several weeks. . . . Nothing seemed to happen. Finally I took an especially big spoonful of extract one morning in my coffee. And all that day I was RANDY as a teen-age mink. (R.A. Sokolov, "Root for all evil," *New York Times,* 4/25/76, Section 6, p. 35)

3. By mid-decade [of the '60's] . . . . Rock music had scrounged for and found its own RANDY legitimacy. (Anon., "McCartney Comes Back," *Time,* 5/31/76, p. 41)

RAPTORIAL (rap-tôr´ē-əl) *adj.* predatory; preying upon other animals; PREDACEOUS; adapted or equipped for seizing prey, as the strong, notched beak and the sharp talons of certain birds (eagles, hawks, owls, vultures, etc.)

1. When I [Russel Wren] had moved in, . . . , the couch was flanked by matching end tables bearing tall lamps of false copper with a fake PATINA; and a mirror, framed by the RAPTORIAL wingspread of a gilded (and deformed) eagle, had hung on the parallel wall above a chair upholstered in glossy maroon plastic. (Thomas Berger, *Who Is Teddy Villanova?,* Delacorte Press/Seymour Lawrence, 1977, p. 70)

RATIOCINATION (rash´ē-os´ə-nā´shən, rat´ē-ō´sə-nā´shən, -äs´ə-) *noun* the process of logical reasoning.

RATIOCINATIVE *adj.*

RATIOCINATE *verb* to reason, especially by using formal logic.

RATIOCINATOR *noun.*

1. There is no question that Joyce and Nabokov . . . brilliantly explored and expanded the limits of language and structure of novels, yet both were led irresistibly and obsessively to cap their careers with those cold and lifeless masterpieces, *Finnegan's Wake* and *Ada,* more to be deciphered than read by a handful of scholars whose pleasure is strictly RATIOCINATION. (J. Hofsess, "How I Learned to Stop Worrying and Love 'Barry Lyndon,' " *New York Times,* 1/11/76, Section 2, p. 13)

2. See (3) under HERMETIC.

3. [Lawrence L.] Langer [in *The Holocaust and the Literary Imagination*] discusses a number of writers whose works are available in English translations. Each bears witness to such themes as the violation of innocence, the displacement of normality, the ENERVATION of body and spirit, and the disruption of RATIOCINATIVE modes of experiencing the world. Among the perspectives marshalled are:. . .the Boschean grotesqueries of Jerzy Kosinski, the WALPURGISNACHT of Elie Wiesel's faith, . . . (J. Hollis, Review, *Chronicle of Higher Education,* 4/5/76, p. 21)

4. [Robert] Redford is an actor who does not find a character through RATIOCINATION or conversation, but rather by getting as quickly as possible into action and seeing where his instincts lead him. (Anon., "Watergate on Film," *Time,* 3/29/76, p. 57)

5. The prose of novelists, being concerned with action and emotion rather than with RATIOCINATION, tends to be verse-like and essay poetic effects. Dickens . . . often wrote unconsciously in blank verse. (A. Burgess, "A Shrivel of Critics," *Harper's,* February 1977, p. 90)

6. Blackford [Oakes] ran his mind over the cliché—Watson, motionless during the RATIOCINATIVE convulsions of Sherlock Holmes; Archie Goodwin, silent lest he distract the great Nero Wolfe. (W.F. Buckley Jr., *Saving the Queen,* Doubleday, 1976, p. 149)

RECHERCHÉ (rə-shâr´shā, Rə-sher-shā´) *adj* sought out with care; very rare, uncommon, exotic, or choice; of studied refinement or elegance; precious; too refined; too studied.

1. Light years away from Volkswagen's losses or housewives' hamburger menus there remains a RECHERCHÉ world impervious to the ravages of unemployment, inflation, recession, and economic gloom. (Jan M. Rosen, "Far From the Madding Recession—Sales Boom in Luxury Categories," *New York Times,* 1/25/76, Section 3, p. 65)

2. To [Paris couturier Paul] Poiret, a dress was an object of art. He reserved his chefs-d'oeuvre for his ideal woman (his wife). Some of these were one-of-a-kind dresses . . . . Every detail was studied—from the judicious placement of a single spot of color to the perverse but perfect sense of what RECHERCHÉ fabric would COMPLEMENT another. (Phyllis Feldkamp, Review of *Paul Poiret, King of Fashion*, a show at Fashion Institute of Technology, *New York Times*, 6/13/76, Section 6, p. 59)

RECIDIVISM (ri-sid'ə-viz'əm) *noun* repeated, habitual, or chronic relapse, as into crime or antisocial behavior.

RECIDIVIST *noun.*

RECIDIVISTIC or **RECIDIVOUS** *adj.*

1. . . . I know that when I face downhill [on skis] bravely and bob down before each turn, and up, triumphantly, after completing the turn, on those happy occasions when I succeed in completing a turn, she [my ski instructor] is a little embarrassed, looking around at the fancy company that is witness to her student's RECIDIVISM [return to his old and improper techniques]. (W.F. Buckley Jr., *Execution Eve and Other Contemporary Ballads*, G.P. Putnam's Sons, 1975, p. 247)

2. Our tribe [the estimated 25 million people who are terrified in an airplane] continues to increase and our rate of RECIDIVISM to soar . . . . I happen to be one of the silent, sullen ones, a sort of MORIBUND Wallenda . . . . Despite our CATATONIC appearance on boarding [an airplane], we will have committed each of you to photographic memory, considered your potential for heroic action in an emergency and marveled glumly . . . at how very much . . . you resemble a typical casualty list. (Meg Greenfield, "What Not to Say at 37,000 Feet," *Newsweek*, 3/15/76, p. 104)

3. . . . it seems clear that for the moment most proposed reforms [in rape laws] will be merely conciliatory—directed at improving the way a rape victim is treated, but not particularly concerned with methods of prosecution of offenders or even of identifying RECIDIVISTS. (Diane Johnson, "The War Between Men and Women," *New York Review of Books*, 12/11/75, p. 36)

4. We do not know what to do with the men and women we put in jail, or how long to keep them there, or when they are ready for parole . . . . We don't know how to cut back on the RECIDIVISM—the repeats who apparently account for such a high proportion of our crime. (R. Cromley, "Elderly citizens increasingly victimized: Research ignored as crime preventive," *Norman* [Okla.] *Transcript*, 5/2/76, p. 4)

5. "They are a depraved lot of hardened criminals, most of them RECIDIVISTS, on whom compassion would be wasted [said Boris]. In the reformatory they'll make indecent pottery and finger paintings." (Thomas Berger, *Who Is Teddy Villanova?*, Delacorte Press/Seymour Lawrence, 1977, p. 202)

RECONDITE (rek'ən-dīt', ri-kon' dīt) *adj.* dealing with very profound, difficult, or abstruse subject matter; beyond ordinary knowledge or understanding; ESOTERIC; little known; obscure.

RECONDITELY *adv.*

RECONDITENESS *noun.*

1. Such synthesizing ideas—Bohr's model of the atom, or Einstein's theories—are the ultimate scientific achievment; yet . . . since the 1920's, everyone agreed that fewer truly imperial concepts were emerging. Some thought that modern science had become too specialized, RECONDITE, swamped with detail. (F. Hapgood, "Why The Tortoise Is Kind And Other Tales of Sociobiology," *Atlantic*, March 1976, p. 100)

2. So what kind of laws should govern them [people in space colonies] . . . ? Or should treaty-like constitutions be thought through now which will permit spacekind to develop their own laws? It may seem a bit RECONDITE to worry about such matters, but as [George] Robinson points out [in his book, *Living in Outer Space*], we are, after all, in the Space Age right now, whether we like it or not. (J.K. Page Jr., "Phenomena, comments, and notes," *Smithsonian*, December 1975, p. 18)

3. Through this aperture into the occult, the reader views [in *Divine Comedies*, by James Merrill] a tapestry as large and ornate as any to be found in recent poetry. Merrill's allusions are often RECONDITE. But his loving attention to

brilliant surfaces outdazzles difficulties. (P. Gray, Review, *Time*, 4/26/76, p. 95)

4. See (2) under PLETHORA.

RECRUDESCENCE (rē'krōō-des'əns) *noun* a fresh outbreak or spell of renewed activity, as of a disease or an undesirable condition; revival or reappearance in active existence.

RECRUDESCENT *adj*.

RECRUDESCE *verb* to break out again after lying latent or relatively inactive.

1. This new commitment to navigating the passages to tomorrow cannot be directed by some centralized bureaucracy . . . . This new EFFLORESCENCE of human intelligence . . . is well suited to higher learning institutions, particularly as their national influence is now on the wane . . . . It is also possible that this RECRUDESCENCE of the moral conscience in college youths and their institutions will help shape a happier nation, and fulfill as well a central purpose of American institutions of higher learning . . . . (G.W. Bonham, "An American Agenda: I" [Editorial], *Change*, February 1975, p. 9)

REDOLENT (red' əlent) *adj*. having a pleasant, sweet-smelling, fragrant, or aromatic odor; odorous, odoriferous, or smelling; suggestive, reminiscent, or evocative (of).

REDOLENCE *noun*.

1. When the wind was right, it should have been easy to pick up her [Cleopatra's] scent, and that of her equally REDOLENT handmaidens, as the royal barge proceeded up the Nile. (C.J. Oppenheim III, "Perfume is social dynamite in an expensive package," *Smithsonian*, February 1976, p. 76)

2. Pooling their imaginative resources, the six [who founded the enterprise] came up with the Circle in the Square name . . . . They called themselves the Loft Players, a name REDOLENT of what has come to be called the artsy-craftsy. (T. Buckley, "Circle in the Square, at 25, to Stage a Gala," *New York Times*, 3/8/76, p. 33)

3. REDOLENT of the decadence of Germany between the world wars, [Kurt] Joos' two [ballet] masterpieces [*The Green Table* and *The Big City*] are both completely of that time and per-

tinent today. (H. Saal, Review, *Newsweek*, 3/29/76, p. 97)

4. So, desperately, one casts about for some inventive phrase-making [to replace such words as "chairperson"], turning by chance to a recent issue of *People* . . . , a magazine with a title REDOLENT of nonexist opportunity. (J.K. Page Jr., "On People," *Smithsonian*, December 1975, p. 14)

5. Some of Munro's war reportage is missing [from *The Complete Works of Saki*, by H.H. Munro], and so is his earliest work, *The Rise of the Russian Empire*, a rare history book that he wrote at 29, full of marvelous passages, REDOLENT of the essence of all of his later writing. (J. Lukacs, Review, *New York Times*, 3/28/76, Section 7, p. 6)

6. Vibrant, colorful, REDOLENT of China as it used to be, today Tua Pho—[Singapore's] Chinatown—is giving way to modern times. (Shelley and C. Mydans, "Progress dooms charm and bustle of THE Chinatown in Singapore," *Smithsonian*, January 1976, p. 39)

7. See (1) under AUSCULTATION.

8. New Yorkers who take taxis . . . sometimes wonder what they're paying for. It can be a jolting ride in cramped quarters REDOLENT with exhaust fumes. (Harriet Heyman and M. Leebow, "Uncramped Taxis," *New York Times*, 6/20/76, Section 4, p. 6)

9. Roman Catholic. The words are REDOLENT of rich and solemn rituals chanted amid clouds of incense in an ancient tongue. (Anon., "A Church Divided," *Time*, 5/24/76, p. 48)

REDUCTIO AD ABSURDUM (ri-duk'tē-ō' ad ab-sûr'dəm) *adj*. a reduction to an absurdity; the refutation of a proposition by showing its logical consequences to be impossible or absurd.

1. Dr. [Paul R.] Ehrlich [in his book, *The Population Bomb*] goes through what he calls the "absurd" exercise of assuming that the population of the world will double every thirty-seven years for the next nine centuries and concludes that there would then be roughly a hundred people for each square yard of solid ground. He discovers by REDUCTIO AD ABSURDUM that the geometric growth of

population must at some point be interrupted . . . . (John Maddox, *The Doomsday Syndrome*, McGraw-Hill, 1973, p. 41)

REFULGENT (ri-ful′jənt) *adj.* shining; radiant; glowing; resplendent.

REFULGENCE or **REFULGENCY** *noun.*

REFULGENTLY *adv.*

1. She [Clemma Zendt] would make Jim [Lloyd]'s life miserable, but also REFULGENT. (J.A. Michener, *Centennial*, Fawcett, 1975, p. 654)

2. My auxiliary documents of identification were gone. In a way, looking at the REFULGENT side of this murky adventure, I [Russel Wren] was relieved that I had not found them and again read the name Villanova on each. (Thomas Berger, *Who Is Teddy Villanova?*, Delacorte Press/Seymour Lawrence, 1977, p. 79)

REGNANT (reg′nənt) *adj.* reigning; ruling (usually used following the noun it modifies); exercising authority, rule, or influence; prevalent; widespread; of greatest power; predominant.

REGNANCY *noun.*

REGNAL *adj.* pertaining to a sovereign, sovereignty, or reign.

1. [David Edwin] Harrell [author of the book, *All Things Are Possible*] believes that the healing revival . . . began to die out in about 1958 when the more respectable and subdued "charismatic" movement arose and began to spread among the middle classes and within the standard denominations, including the Roman Catholic. Some writers call this the "neopentecostal" movement but whatever one calls it, it presented the REGNANT evangelists with a vexing dilemma. (H.G. Cox, Review, *New York Times*, 2/22/76, Section 7, p. 6)

REIFY (rē′ə-fī) *verb* to convert an abstraction into a concrete thing, or to regard an abstract thing as concrete or real.

REIFICATION *noun.*

1. . . . the [McGovern] legions intend to win. They hope to REIFY George McGovern's dream.

(W.F. Buckley Jr., *Execution Eve and Other Contemporary Ballads*, G.P. Putnam's Sons, 1975, p. 76)

2. The terms of the proposed cease-fire [in Vietnam] continually REIFY, like the photographs in Mr. Land's new camera, which however will give us in fifty seconds what, respecting Vietnam, it will take fifty hours or days—or months?—to perceive distinctly enough to evaluate. (W.F. Buckley Jr., *Ibid.*, p. 272)

3. . . . this book [*Family Feeling*, by Helen Yglesias] is an example of one kind of first-rate fiction: the REIFICATION and artful shaping of the obvious and overlooked. (I. Gold, Review, *New York Times*, 2/1/76, Section 7, p. 6)

4. Notions such as psychopathy pretend to explain something, but they have as much value as the equally REIFIED concept of "moral idiocy" that prevailed at the turn of the century. (J. Kovel—Review of *The Nuremberg Mind*, by Florence R. Miale and Michael Selzer, *New York Times*, 2/8/76, Section 7, p. 34)

5. Until the objection to involuntary participation in social security REIFIES in the public mind as something more than a ritualistic exercise in libertarian crankiness, we are not going to set the nation marching to our rescue. (W.F. Buckley Jr., *Up From Liberalism*, Arlington House, 2nd Printing, 1968, p. 210)

RELIQUARY (rel′ə-kwer′ē) *noun* a small box, casket, or shrine in which relics are kept and shown.

1. But Alphonse Mucha was a sculptor too, and nothing in this show EPITOMIZES the art nouveau vision (or fantasy) of woman better than a bust he designed around 1899 for a Parisian jeweler. This astonishing object, whose form shifts like water in the twining reflections of silver flesh and gold hair, is perversely liturgical—a PARODY (done, one should recall, for a public whose cultural background was still Catholic) of medieval head RELIQUARIES. The image, however, is not a saint or a MAGDALEN but that SIBYLLINE bitch of the FIN-DE-SIÈCLE imagination, the Fatal Woman, *La Belle Dame sans Merci*—enigmatic as a sphinx, cruelly indifferent as a BYZANTINE empress, wearing the features of the Divine Sarah and

the aggressive glitter of a vintage Cadillac fender. (R. Hughes, "The Snobbish Style," *Time*, 9/13/76, p. 67)

RENEGE (ri-nig′, ri-neg′) *verb* to go back on one's word or promise; to back out of an agreement; (in card games) to play a card of another suit, against the rules, when one can follow suit.

RENEGER *noun*.

1. Until the last moment, the President [Carter] had hoped to make as much of the [planned 9-nation] trip as possible . . . . Sensitive anyway about RENEGING on his long-planned trip, the President was under heavy pressure to salvage the leg to Paris, where [French President] Giscard [d'Estaing] has been counting on a boast to his party's election chances next March—and where Carter had planned to deliver a major foreign-policy speech. (R. Booth, with Eleanor Clift, *et. al.*, "Mr. Stay-at-Home," *Newsweek*, 11/14/77, p. 30)

2. The [*New York*] *Times*, in general far more than the *Washington Post*, which seems to have gone bland on this administration, had kept Carter's feet to the fire. Square in the middle, of course, is Bill Safire. The inaugural bunting hadn't been put away (he called the speech "pedestrian") before Safire was peppering away with columns accusing Carter of politicizing the Justice Department, RENEGING on human-rights pledges, ignoring the Korean scandal, betraying Israel, and, eventually, Bert Lance. (N. Thimmesch, "Siege at the White House," *New York*, 11/28/77, p. 37)

3. Although HEW Secretary Joseph A. Califano still strenuously objects, White House aides believe that President Carter will keep his controversial campaign pledge to create a separate Cabinet-level Department of Education . . . . Califano argued that the fields of health, education and welfare are too interrelated to be split . . . . As White House aides see it, Califano was also trying to protect his domain. "The idea that we would RENEGE on a campaign promise just because it was his turf really grated on us," said one Carter aide. (B. Roeder, "School's In," *Newsweek*, 12/12/77, p. 3)

RETARDATAIRE (rə-täR′də-teR′) a French word meaning: late; behind-time; in arrears; backward.

1. But Michelangelo's avowed nostalgia for a life of visionary inaction is RETARDATAIRE, harking back to the EREMITIC religiosity of the Middle Ages; it is as discordant with his own irrepressible creativity as with the spirit of the times. (L. Steinberg, "Michelangelo's last painting: his gift to this century," *Smithsonian*, December 1975, p. 82)

REVANCHISM (ri-vänch′iz-əm, ri-vänsh′-) or **REVANCHE** *noun* the revengeful spirit moving a defeated nation to aggressively seek restoration of its lost territories, etc.

REVANCHIST *noun*.

1. Before attributing the negative reviews [of *Ragtime*, by E.L. Doctorow, in Britain] to a mood of latent REVANCHISM among British intellectuals, it should be pointed out that hostile receptions over there for books that have beguiled stateside readers are not unusual (and vice versa), while American writers without honor in their own country occasionally find a little green corner of English appreciation. (Anon, "Reverse English," *New York Times*, 3/7/76, Section 7, p. 33)

REVENANT (rev′ ə-nənt) *noun* a person who returns, as after a long absence; a person who returns as a spirit after death; ghost.

1. [From *The Wanderer*, a book by Knut Hamsun, translated by Oliver and Gunnvar Stallbrass] "Before leaving the churchyard I found a serviceable thumbnail, which I pocketed . . . . No one cried: 'That is mine!' " That the bit of corpse evidently lay on the ground . . . instead of needing to be dug for, may shed light on the deplorable condition of Norse cemeteries, or it may serve as a symbol for the manner of this indifferent little fiction, in which the author picks up his own name and what incidents he finds strewn on the surface of his mind, and no REVENANTS of buried significance cry out, "That is mine!" (J. Updike, Review, *The New Yorker*, 5/31/76, p. 116)

RIFE (rīf) *adj.* of common or frequent occurrence; prevalent; in widespread existence, activity, or use; current in speech or report; abundant, plentiful, or numerous; plenteous; multitudinous.

RIFENESS *noun.*

1. The illusions were many. The American believed that a whole society accepted the rhetoric of rebellion and was ready to sacrifice and turn out full force to oppose British suppression. The British believed the colonies were RIFE with Loyalists upon whom they could depend. They believed, too, that the FECKLESS Rebels had no heart for a long conflict and surely would accept reconciliation before the year was gone. (G.F. Scheer, Review of *1776: Year of Illusions*, by Thomas Fleming, *New York Times*, 2/22/76, Section 7, p. 10)

2. See (2) under BILLINGSGATE.

RIPOSTE (ri-pōst´) or **RIPOST** *noun* a quick, sharp and often witty response or retort in speech or action; counterstroke.

RIPOSTE *verb* to make a riposte.

1. Years earlier [Walter] Hoving had bested New York's Mayor Fiorello LaGuardia in a battle of one-liners. Angry at Hoving's opposition to rising sales taxes, LaGuardia thundered, "We can't turn the city over to a floorwalker." Hoving's RIPOSTE was swift. "After all, Mr. Mayor," he cooed, impaling LaGuardia upon his celebrated nickname, "every floorwalker has a little flower in his buttonhole." (Anon., "For Tiffany's Walter Hoving Silence May Be Golden, But Sounding Off Is Irresistible," *People*, 4/12/76, p. 16)

2. Lord Keynes was facetious about the long term, but the success of his RIPOSTE [he said, "In the long run we all are dead" in response to criticism of the long range effect of his economic program] was due in large part to the undoubted fact that conservatives have cheapened the vocabulary of caution . . . . If one is on record as reiterating the prediction that the social security law will bring slavery to America in our time, after a while one's warnings will be automatically discounted. (W.F. Buckley Jr., *Up From Liberalism*, Arlington House, 2nd Printing 1968, p. 188)

3. Benjamin Franklin watched the ascent [of the hot-air balloon of the Montgolfier brothers in Paris on November 21, 1783]. When someone demanded "What good is it?" Franklin supposedly RIPOSTED, "Of what use is a newborn babe?" (E. Park, "New Smithsonian Museum records Man's thrilling affair with flight," *Smithsonian*, June 1976, p. 48)

4. See (1) under PERIGEE.

5. The door of his fashionably appointed den proves to be revolving. Through it stream people whose untidy problems and messy personalities make Simon [Michael Gambon, in the play, *Otherwise Engaged*, by Simon Gray,] seem almost a genteel charmer, though his witty RIPOSTES are fashioned from barbed wire. His upstairs lodger, a sociology student, enters to CADGE money and denounce Wagner as a fascist. Simon's older brother, an academic mole, mewls and pules about the disadvantages of not having an Oxford degree. (T.E. Kalem, Review, *Time*, 4/19/76, p. 80)

6. See (6) under CHARLATAN.

7. When the party's over, do you lie in bed, stare at the ceiling and dream up witty RIPOSTES and devastating conversation stoppers, when all you said all night was "How fascinating!" and "No, really?" (Beth Gillin Pombeiro, "Be a phrase-dropper," *Philadelphia Inquirer*, 11/9/76, p. 1-C)

8. See (5) under BADINAGE.

RISIBLE (riz´ə-bəl) *adj.* having the ability, disposition, or readiness to laugh; causing or capable of causing laughter; laughable; comical; funny; amusing; pertaining to or concerned with laughter.

RISIBILITY *noun.*

1. Higher education may well be a "high-rise slum," but I disagree with Prof. Ira Grushow as to the reason . . . . Primarily, the cause is not that professors . . . are frantically churning out unreadable minutiae, but rather that they submit to salary scales that an unskilled day laborer would find RISIBLE. (S. Sandler, "Exploitation, empire-building, and wages 'an unskilled laborer would find risible.'" [Letter to the editor], *Chronicle of Higher Education*, 6/28/76, p. 17)

2. Conventions [of political parties] display an aspect of human behavior too often neglected today: the proclivity for buffoonery . . . . [Man] is not merely a distributor of platitudes and a JEREMIAH. He is also . . . capable of all sorts of RISIBLE posturings and gorgeous PRATFALLS. Such is the magic of a convention that when the pols convene, they become mysteriously enslaved to this clownish impulse. (R.E. Tyrell Jr., "Hurrah for the Conventions!" *Newsweek*, 8/23/76, p. 11)

3. Dick Dixon [protagonist of the book, *The Rio Loja Ringmaster*, by Lamar Herrin], during his first nine-innings game, a RISIBLE performance against a mob of Mexican *beisbolistas* that seems to be heading for a no-hitter . . . , realizes that he has "a bent toward the cosmological." (G. Wolff, Review, *New York Times*, 2/27/77, Section 7, p. 27)

4. "Are you a detective, as well?" [asked Russel Wren, of Donald Washburn II]. His RISIBILITIES were once again provoked. "My dear fellow, I'm an avid filmgoer, and keenly follow the gossip columns." (Thomas Berger, *Who Is Teddy Villanova?*, Delacorte Press/Seymour Lawrence, 1977, p. 163)

RISQUÉ (ri-skā') *adj.* daringly close to indelicacy or impropriety; off-color; suggestive.

1. We [Governor Ronald Reagan, James Buckley, and William F. Buckley Jr.] were together [in Reagan's living room] not only because of ideological CONSANGUINITY, or because we are friends, or because we thought . . . to man the same fortress at a moment when Richard Nixon would say something we were alerted to believe would be more than his routine denunciation of wage-and-price controls . . . . There had been no comment in the room, save one or two of those wolfish whistles one hears when someone on one's side in politics says something daringly RISQUÉ. (W.F. Buckley Jr., *Execution Eve and Other Contemporary Ballads*, G.P. Putnam's Sons, 1975, p. 21)

ROCOCO (rə-kō'kō) *adj.* pertaining to or noting a style of elegant and refined architecture, sculpture, or painting; ornate or florid in speech, literary style, etc.; antiquated; outmoded; too profuse or elaborate in ornamentation.

ROCOCO *noun* the rococo style in the fine arts.

1. I replied with a story impossibly labored, yet splendidly ROCOCO, which I had come across years before in the autobiography of G.K. Chesterton. (W.F. Buckley Jr., *Execution Eve and Other Contemporary Ballads*, G.P. Putnam's Sons, 1975, p. 366)

2. See (1) under ORMOLU.

3. See (2) under FULSOME.

4. In a recent interview in the ROCOCO splendor of his Goodspeed headquarters, [executive director Michael] Price [of the Goodspeed Opera House in East Haddam, Conn.] explained . . . . "It took us a long time to decide who and what we were . . . . The musical is probably America's only INDIGENOUS performing art . . . . We offer . . . 180 minutes of EUPHORIA, and this place provides one hell of an AMBIENCE for the kind of theater we like to do." (P. Gardner, "A Connecticut Playhouse With That Broadway Touch," *New York Times*, 4/18/76, Section 2, p. 5)

5. Aeschylus paraded in the ROCOCO trappings of [a translation by] Potter—"But you, my friends, amid these rites/Raise high your solemn warblings . . . . " (B.M.W. Knox, Review of *Aeschylus: Suppliants*, translated by Janet Lembke; *Aeschylus: Seven Against Thebes*, translated by Helen Bacon and Anthony Hecht; and *Aeschylus: Prometheus Bound*, translated by James Scully and C. John Herington, *New York Review of Books*, 11/27/75, p. 27)

6. See (1) under APLOMB.

RODOMONTADE (rod'ə-mon-tād', -täd', rō'də-,-mən-) *noun* vainglorious of arrogant boasting, bragging; braggadocio; PRETENTIOUS, blustering, ranting talk.

RODOMONTADE *adj.* bragging; arrogantly boastful.

RODOMONTADE *verb* to boast; brag.

1. The telephone rang. It was his [Blackford Oakes'] father—jovial as ever, but this time with a little less of the RODOMONTADE, a great deal more of the furtive purpose and quiet authority of many years ago . . . . (W.F. Buckley

Jr., *Saving the Queen*, Doubleday, 1976, p. 157)

ROMAN À CLEF (rô-mä'na-klä) *noun*, *pl.*: ROMANS À CLEF (-män'za-klä') a novel that presents real events and characters under the guise of fiction.

1. Veteran readers of Miss Susann's ROMANS À CLEF about the show-biz, jet-set world will have no trouble guessing the real-life inspiration for the title character [in *Dolores*]—Mrs. Warren Gamaliel Harding, of course. (Anon., "Book Ends: Jackie," *New York Times*, 1/11/76, Section 7, p. 29)

2. Legend tells us that Midas was given not only the golden touch, but also ass's ears . . . . The late Michael Ayrton has worked both these mutations into a concentration of musings [in the book, *The Midas Consequence*] that the publisher calls a "ROMAN À CLEF about Picasso." (M. Levin, Review, *New York Times*, 4/18/76, Section 7, p. 28)

3. The real-life counterparts of most of the characters [in *The Canfield Decision*, by Spiro Agnew] . . . are . . . so easily identified that the readers are even denied the who's who guessing game they have come to expect of the ROMAN À CLEF. (D. Shaw, of Los Angeles Times, "Agnew 'murders' media and other 'nattering nabobs,'" *Norman* [Okla.] *Transcript*, 5/23/76, p. 17)

4. Gossip is even the latest literary GENRE to be attempted by Truman Capote. With a tongue so tart it must sting, Capote has taken on—and apart—the jaded members of international society in his ROMAN À CLEF *Answered Prayers* . . . . "The Tiny Terror," as Women's Wear Daily calls him, mingles real people with thinly-veiled fictional ones—and stabs them all. (Linda Bird Francke, *et al.*, "Gossip Mania," *Newsweek*, 5/24/76, p. 58)

5. Is *The Canfield Decision* [by Spiro Agnew] a ROMAN À CLEF, then, one of those novels in which the characters are thinly disguised versions of real-life people? . . . . It is a ROMAN À CLEF in which everyone is Agnew . . . they all tend to share his strange outlook on people and events . . . (Meg Greenfield, "Agnew's Revenge," *Newsweek*, 5/24/76, p. 104)

6. Down in Atlanta flogging her D.C. ROMAN

À CLEF, *Making Ends Meet*, Washington socialite Barbara Howar confessed she's flattered to be referred to as a writer: "I'm really just a professional big mouth." (Anon., "Chatter," *People*, 5/24/76, p. 92)

7. A Washington ROMAN À CLEF it [*The Company*, by John Ehrlichman] is; . . . . Readers will have no difficulty in making out the shaggy outlines of Presidents JFK, LBJ, RMN, not to mention Henry Kissinger (Carl Tessler in the book), J. Edgar Hoover (Elmer Morse) and others . . . . (T. Foote, Review, *Time*, 5/31/76, p. 66)

8. What exactly is a ROMAN À CLEF? There is no equivalent in English for this phrase that literally means novel with a key—a story whose characters are modeled on real people . . . thanks to Ehrlichman and *The Company*, Truman Capote and *Answered Prayers*, and Elizabeth Ray and *The Washington Fringe Benefit*, the ROMAN À CLEF may become not only the form the bestselling novel takes in 1976 but the symbol of a rather shoddy year that could just possibly go down in history as the Age of Psst!—Have-You-Heard? (M. Maddocks, "Now for the Age of Psst!," *Time*, 6/28/76, p. 68)

9. See (2) under POSTHUMOUS.

10. See (2) under PUCKISH.

ROUÉ (rōō-ā', rōō'ā) *noun* a debauchee or rake; profligate; a dissipated man.

1. It's hard to believe that the coming together of a withered Puritan and a middle-aged ROUÉ would light up the sky with the glittering display of fireworks that the director [of *Summertime*] . . . provides, but this is one of those . . . romantic movies . . . that many people remember with considerable emotion. (Anon., Review, *The New Yorker*, 5/31/76, p. 23)

2. "Cut," murmured the director . . . —but no one noticed. Trevor Howard, playing [in the film, *The Last Remake of Beau Geste*] a geriatric ROUÉ in British military garb, continued to mount a grand staircase, wheezing as he pulled off his clothes and tossed them over the banister. (Katrine Ames and M. MacPherson, "Feldmania," *Newsweek*, 10/25/76, p. 116)

RUBATO (rōō-bä'tō) *adj.* having certain

musical notes arbitrarily lengthened while others are correspondingly shortened, or vice versa; intentionally deviating from a strict tempo.

RUBATO   noun, pl.: -TOS a rubato phrase or passage.

RUBATO   adv.   in a rubato manner.

1. Nor do the dancers [at Balanchine's New York City Ballet] FINAGLE with RUBATO; the weave of the steps is too tight for that. (Nancy Goldner, "The inimitable Balanchine," *New York Times*, 5/30/76, Section 6, p. 28)

2. Last week in Carnegie Hall he [Arthur Rubinstein] played Beethoven's *Sonata No. 18 in E Flat* with the same lithe rhythms and robust tone that brought him fame in the first place. He played a Chopin group . . . as though he, Rubinstein, had invented RUBATO and the triplet! But most of all, he played Schumann's *Carnaval*, that PARADIGM of whimsy and frolic, as if only old age could understand the joy of being young. (Anon., "Rubenstein at 89," *Time*, 3/29/76, p. 53)

RUBICUND (rōō′bə-kund)   adj.   red or reddish; ruddy.

RUBICUNDITY   noun.

1. RUBICUND shame suffused Knox's beefy face, and he slunk away. (Thomas Berger, *Who Is Teddy Villanova?*, Delacorte Press/Seymour Lawrence, 1977, p. 98)

RUFOUS (rōō′ fəs)   adj.   reddish; tinged with red; brownish-red; rust-colored.

1. It was late winter when a seven-year-old male of this herd [of bison] shook the ice off his beard, hunched his awkward shoulders forward . . . and tossed his head belligerently, throwing his RUFOUS mane first over his eyes and then away to one side. (J.A. Michener, *Centennial*, Fawcett, 1975, p. 98)

RUMINATE (rōō′mə-nāt′)   verb   to chew the cud, as a cow does; to meditate or muse; ponder; to chew again or over and over.

RUMINATION   noun.

RUMINATIVE   adj.

RUMINATIVELY   adv.

RUMINATOR   noun.

RUMINANT   adj.   ruminating; chewing the cud; contemplative; meditative.

RUMINANT   noun   any even-toed mammal comprising cloven-hoofed, cud-chewing quadrupeds (cattle, deer, camels, buffaloes, goats, giraffes, etc.).

1. Drew Middleton of the New York Times, in a scholarly and pessimistic study on NATO v. Warsaw Pact, asks: "Can America Win the Next War?" In Brussels, General Haig begins to RUMINATE aloud about the purpose of the astonishing and inexplicable Russian military buildup opposite West Germany. (P.J. Buchanan, "Foreign Policy Debate Missing," *Daily Oklahoman*, Okla. City, 3/23/76, p. 6)

2. *The Role of the Supreme Court in American Government,* [a book] by Archibald Cox . . . . Graceful, deceptively modest RUMINATIONS on the Supreme Court, which carry a number of corrective as well as original notions. (Anon., Review, *New York Times*, 3/14/76, Section 7, p. 37)

3. See (2) under FETISHISM.

4. His tone is more relaxed and RUMINATIVE . . . . (J. Updike, Review of *The Wanderer*, by Knut Hamsun, translated by Oliver and Gunnvar Stallybrass, *The New Yorker*, 5/31/76, p. 116)

5. Her RUMINATIONS were interrupted by voices on two levels. She [Sharon Fields] was startled. It was the first time she had been able to hear voices from the next room. (I. Wallace, *The Fan Club*, Bantam Books, 1975, p. 339)

6. This is not the first time I [Adam Malone] have RUMINATED upon the subject of sex. In fact, . . . I had planned to undertake an article on the constant preoccupation with sex in our culture. (I. Wallace, *Ibid.*, p. 440)

RUMPELSTILTSKIN (rum′ pəl-stilt′ skin) noun   a dwarf in a German folk tale who spins flax into gold for a maiden to meet the demand of the prince she has married, on the condition that she give him her first child or else guess his name: she guesses his name and he vanishes or destroys himself in a rage.

1. Doctors gave [Adam] Smith [author of the book, *Powers of Mind*] little lectures on

PLACEBOS, on drugs, on the RUMPELSTILTSKIN effect (naming an ailment makes a patient get better), on split-brain research . . . . He half-

practices TM and discloses (shame!) his secret MANTRA. (M. Gardner, Review, *New York Review of Books*, 12/11/75, p. 46)

S

SACERDOTAL (sas'ǝr-dōt'ǝl, sak-') *adj.* of priests; priestly; characterized by a belief in the divine authority of the priesthood.

SACERDOTALLY *adv.*

SACERDOTALISM *noun* the system, spirit, practices, or methods of the priesthood; excessive reliance on a priesthood.

1. . . . Arthur Schlesinger warned, "as long as the President is perceived as a SACERDOTAL figure, Presidents will begin to regard worship as their due, and that is a state of mind which leads easily to excess." (S. Pett, *Associated Press*, "The Presidency: 'A Decline in Authority?,'" *Sunday Oklahoman*, Okla. City 1/29/76, Section B, p. 8)

2. Its origin [the story of Peter's martyrdom] is post-Biblical. St. Jerome refers to it briefly in the first of his *Lives of Illustrious Men*: "[Peter] pushed on to Rome . . . and held the SACERDOTAL chair there for twenty-five years until the last . . . year of Nero. At his hands he received the crown of martyrdom being nailed to the cross with his head downwards . . . , asserting that he was unworthy to be crucified in the same manner as his Lord." (L. Steinberg, "Michelangelo's last painting: his gift to this century," *Smithsonian*, December 1975, p. 75)

SACRALIZE (sak'rǝ-līz) *verb* to make sacred or holy.

SACRALIZATION *noun.*

SACRAL *adj.* of, pertaining to, or for sacred rites or observances.

1. With telling economy he [Sacvan Bercovitch, author of *The Puritan Origins of the American Self*] follows the development of this "symbolic mode" from the 17th-century Puritans to the era of Jonathan Edwards and Benjamin Franklin and . . . to the great flowering of the SACRALIZED image of America in the age of Emerson and Lincoln. (L. Marx, Review, *New York Times*, 2/1/76, Section 7, p. 21)

SADISM (sad'iz-ǝm, sā'diz-ǝm) *noun* sexual gratification gained through dominating, mistreating, humiliating, or causing physical pain to one's partner [after Marquis de Sade, French soldier and novelist (1740–1814), notorious for his perverted sexual activities]; any enjoyment from being cruel to or inflicting physical or psychological pain on another or others.

SADIST *noun.*

SADISTIC *adj.*

SADISTICALLY *adv.*

1. . . . he [Barney Collier] describes Sally Quinn [in *Hope and Fear in Washington (The Early Seventies): The Story of the Washington Press Corps*] as having a "heavyset rump held up by thick, sturdy legs." This is just before a startling burst of SADISTIC MEGALOMANIA in which he announces that "I was angry at myself . . . for seeing her so harshly . . ." (A. Cockburn, Review, *New York Review of Books*, 12/11/75, p. 28)

2. See (1) under PILPUL.

3. That reminded [Vincent] Price, unpleas-

antly, of the time he had to perform "with a 10-foot boa constrictor around my neck. The director—who was as SADISTIC as most directors are—made me stand there for an hour." (Jean McGarry, "Vincent Price just can't escape it—he's scary," *Oklahoma City Times*, 5/19/76, p. 30)

4. See (2) under AGITPROP.

5. See (1) under FUSTIAN.

6. See (4) under FRISSON.

7. See (1) under KNOUT.

SADOMASOCHISM (sad′ ō-mas′ ə-kiz′ əm, -maz-′, sä′ dō-) *noun* SADISM and MASOCHISM regarded as complementary aspects of a fundamental tendency that associates pleasure with the infliction of pain.

SADOMASOCHIST *noun.*

SADOMASOCHISTIC *adj.*

SADOMASOCHISTICALLY *adv.*

1. From inside the book [*Hope and Fear in Washington (The Early Seventies): The Story of the Washington Press Corps*, by Barney Collier] a bad novel about journalism is probably struggling to get out, but Collier cannot manage this, and presents a series of SADOMASOCHISTIC encounters with some of the well-known journalists in Washington. There are no conclusions, no judgments. The point merely lies in the SADOMASOCHISTIC exercise, whereby Collier presents himself visibly to the readers as a shit, but at the same time makes it plain that there will be hell to pay when the book is finally published. (A. Cockburn, Review, *New York Review of Books*, 12/11/75, p. 28)

2. . . . members of the SADOMASOCHISTIC set wouldn't be disappointed [in the TV production, *Helter-Skelter*]. The Manson girls describe their horrors with ORGIASTIC relish. (H.F. Waters, Review, *Newsweek*, 4/5/76, p. 61)

3. Anyone who has endured the purgatory of most New York cab rides knows that this is not transportation; it is SADOMASOCHISM. The average New York taxi is a combination of dilapidation, filth, inefficiency and acute Rube Goldbergian discomforts designed to torture, humiliate and frustrate, for a price. (Ada Louise Huxtable, "Help Is on the Way for Discouraged Taxi Riders," *New York Times*, 6/20/76, Section 2, p. 41)

4. In the 1950's, E.C. Comics under the direction of William M. Gaines set the pattern by moving from priggish Super-heroes at war to tales of war for violence's sake, to crime and finally to SADOMASOCHISTIC fantasy. They found an audience among . . . children of the white middle classes, for whom the crime in the street . . . could be enjoyed only VICARIOUSLY . . . . (Leslie A. Fiedler, "Up, up and away—the rise and fall of comic books," *New York Times*, 9/5/76, Section 7, p. 10)

5. Most vice squads these days concentrate on hard-core pornography involving bestiality, SADO-MASOCHISM and—lately—the abuse of children. (Susan Fraker, *et al.*, "Crackdown on Porn," *Newsweek*, 2/28/77, p. 21)

SAINT ELMO's FIRE (or LIGHT) (el′ mōz) *noun* [after St. Elmo (died 303 A.D.), patron saint of sailors] a visible electric discharge (corona) from charged, especially pointed, objects, as the tips of masts, spires, trees, etc.: seen sometimes during electrical storms.

1. For these reasons—because it is so full of "masterpieces," because it is so full of KITSCH—*Reeling* [a book by Pauline Kael] ultimately grinds you down. It is always an entertaining book, and piece by piece a brilliant one, but taking it in large doses, you may get frazzled by all the feverish energy, flashing like ST. ELMO's FIRE, around so many EPHEMERAL works. (R. Brustein, Review, *New York Times*, 4/4/76, Section 7, p. 2)

2. See (1) under CORPOSANT.

SALUBRIOUS (sə-lōō′ brē-əs) *adj.* favorable to or promoting health or welfare; healthful; wholesome; salutary.

SALUBRIOUSLY *adv.*

SALUBRITY or SALUBRIOUSNESS *noun.*

1. The argument [as to how far America had fallen short of being the best of all possible New Worlds] was taken a stage further in 1768 by Cornelius de Pauw, who declared that in the UNSALUBRIOUS climate of the American continent all mammals degenerated, not ex-

cepting Europeans who settled there. (H. Honour, "America as seen in the fanciful vision of Europe," *Smithsonian*, February 1976, p. 57)

2. [Quote from official statement about Boston Printmakers 28th Annual Exhibition by Richard Stuart Teitz, juror of selection and awards:] "Some artists' names will be familiar to previous exhibition visitors while others will be unknown. Although this was not done deliberately by the juror, I believe it is indicative of a SALUBRIOUS development." (R. Taylor, Review, *Boston Globe*, 3/7/76, p. 11-A)

3. See (1) under LACHRYMOSE.

SALVIFIC (sal-vif′ik) *adj.* offering salvation; tending to save, help, or secure safety.

SALVIFICALLY *adv.*

1. This is a signal advantage, not only because it produces a SALVIFIC insensitivity as one learns to tune out criticism, but because by one's strategic indifference to it one discourages the critic. (W.F. Buckley Jr., *Execution Eve and Other Contemporary Ballads*, G.P. Putnam's Sons, 1975, p. 240)

SANCTIMONIOUS (saṅg̑k′tə-mō′nē-əs) *adj.* making a hypocritical show of piety or righteousness.

SANCTIMONIOUSLY *adv.*

SANCTIMONIOUSNESS or **SANCTIMONY** (saṅg̑k′tə-mō′nē) *noun* affected piety or righteousness; religious hypocrisy.

1. See (1) under BLATHERSKITE.

2. The libretto of *The Magic Flute*, once dismissed as absurd and undeserving of serious scrutiny, is today overmined for buried "meaning" and "significance," and often uncritically praised as a "faultless dramatic structure." Nor will a balance between PHILISTINE ridicule and SANCTIMONIOUS approbation be found in the latest SPATE of books about the opera . . . . (R. Craft, Review, *New York Review of Books*, 11/27/75, p. 16)

3. See (1) under OBMUTESCENCE.

4. See (1) under IRREDENTIST.

SAND (sand) *noun* firm resolution; courage; stamina; a circular footscraping used as a jazz dance step.

1. Margaret Farrar . . . [edited] the daily and Sunday [New York] Times [crossword] puzzle from 1942 until she retired in 1969. She was replaced by [Will] Weng . . . . "She was hard to follow," Weng says. ". . . the VITUPERATIVE mail stacked up . . . . Many people wrote, 'bring back Margaret Farrar.' " But Weng had SAND (perseverance, slang . . .), and he ignored the nasty mail. (M. Dublin, "Puzzled? Then Weng has done his job," *Philadelphia Inquirer*, 11/28/76, p. 4-L)

SANG-FROID (säN-fRWA′) *noun* coolness of mind, calmness in face of danger or annoyance; composure; cool self-possession; poise; EQUANIMITY.

1. A puppet show [at the Smithsonian's new National Air and Space Museum] tells the hilarious story of Jean-Pierre Blanchard and Dr. John Jeffries who made it across the English Channel in a hydrogen balloon in 1785 . . . . Though they jettisoned all their sand ballast, anchors, books, food, clothing and even, unthinkably, their last bottle of brandy, their basket bounced on the waves and when they finally skittered across the shoreline they were clinging, nearly naked, to the shrouds with barely enough SANG-FROID left to accept congratulations. (E. Park, "New Smithsonian Museum records Man's thrilling affair with flight," *Smithsonian*, June 1976, pp. 48-49)

2. Affirmative Action Make Believe that a lot of black people did believe because they also believed that the white people in those nice offices were not like the ones in the general store or in the plumbers union—that they were fundamentally kind, or fair, or something. Anything but the desperate prisoners of economics they turned out to be, holding on to their dominion with a tenacity and SANG-FROID that can only be described as Nixonian. (Toni Morrison, "A Slow Walk of Trees (as Grandmother Would Say). Hopeless (as Grandfather Would Say)," *New York Times*, 7/4/76, Section 6, p. 160)

3. The principle *(sic)* objectives of the [Republican] attack will be to picture Carter as untried and untruthful; to yoke him to the tax-and-spend liberalism of his running mate, Walter F. Mondale, and the Democratic Congress—and if possible to drive him into losing his relentlessly smiling SANGFROID. (P. Gold-

man, T.M. DeFrank, H. Bruno, "The Under-dogs," *Newsweek*, 8/30/76, p. 25)

4. Beneath [Harry] Reasoner's studied SANG-FROID lies a temperament that seems to have grown increasingly testy. On a recent broad-cast, in the midst of a Washington correspon-dent's report on the latest CIA scandal, Reaso-ner QUERULOUSLY inquired: ". . . . Why is it leading off our newscast?" (H.F. Waters, *et al.*, "The New Look of TV News," *Newsweek*, 10/11/76, p. 76)

5. . . . her cold little green eyes were diminish-ing in circumference as she prepared to squeeze the trigger. How grotesque to be shot by a SANG-FROID schoolgirl. (Thomas Berger, *Who is Teddy Villanova?*, Delacorte Press/Seymour Lawrence, 1977, p. 197)

SANGUINARY (sañg gwə-nər′ e) *adj.* full of, characterized by, accompanied by, or de-lighting in much bloodshed, murder, or car-nage; ready or eager to shed blood; blood-thirsty; composed of or marked with blood; bloodstained; bloody.

SANGUINARILY *adv.*

SANGUINARINESS *noun.*

1. The culminating clash [in the battles be-tween the Taira family and the Minamotos] was the SANGUINARY naval battle of Dannoura in 1185, which brought the HEGEMONY of the Tairas to an abrupt end. (I. Morris, Review of *The Tale of the Heike*, translated by Hirôshi Kitagawa and Bruce Tsuchida, *New York Times*, 2/8/76, Section 7, p. 23)

2. See (2) under SPOOR.

3. Given its SANGUINARY shock valve, the story of the Charles Manson atrocities was probably destined to end up on celluloid. But the nag-ging question is whether a film treatment of the Tate-LaBianca murders wouldn't be more appropriate in the movie theaters than on prime-time television . . . . (H.F. Waters, Re-view of the TV movie, *Helter-Skelter*, *News-week*, 4/5/76, p. 61)

4. Outraged citizens were heard to cry [during the Hanafi Muslims' reign of terror in Wash-ington, D.C.]: "Why didn't the FBI know about this in advance?" The answer is . . . that

the bureau . . . is itself cowed and demoral-ized. After all, the Hanafis are United States citizens: how dare our law-enforcement agen-cies penetrate their sect and report its SANGUI-NARY intentions? (E.H. Hunt, "How America Looks to Me Now," *Newsweek*, 4/4/77, p. 15)

SANGUINE (sañg′ gwin) *adj.* cheerful, hopeful, confident, or optimistic; reddish; rud-dy; blood-red; red.

SANGUINELY *adv.*

SANGUINENESS *noun.*

SANGUINEOUS or SANGUINOUS *adj.* of, pertaining to, or containing blood; of or hav-ing the color of blood; red; involving much bloodshed; SANGUINARY; SANGUINE; confident; hopeful.

SANGUINOLENT *adj.* of, pertaining to, containing, or tinged with blood; bloody.

SANGUINOLENCY *noun.*

1. While we work, sleep, drink, or think about Jimmy Carter's teeth, our children, tethered to the TV hitching post, absorb the situation comedies of the 1950's and 1960's . . . . Are we SO SANGUINE about the values and perceptions of these programs—their portrayal, for in-stance, of women and fathers—that we let them mess up uninformed minds? Whatever happened to network programs designed spe-cifically for children? In the 1950's we had "Howdy Doody," Kukla, Fran & Ollie," . . . . (J. Leonard, "Old Sitcoms and Young Minds," *New York Times*, 3/28/76, Section 2, p. 27)

2. That same year [1922] a former Secretary of the Navy, Josephus Daniels, joined in the SAN-GUINE predictions: "Nobody now fears that a Japanese fleet could deal an unexpected blow on our Pacific possessions . . . . Radio makes surprises impossible." (E. Barnouw, "So You Think TV is hot stuff? Just you wait," *Smithso-nian*, July 1976, p. 83)

3. This week a "novel" called *The Washington Fringe Benefit* by Elizabeth L. Ray joins the mass market best seller list . . . in June, 1975 . . . William Grose, Dell's editor-in-chief, bought it from an outline submitted by John Cush-man, a leading New York literary agent. [Yvonne] Donleavy was to collaborate with

Ray, split a $25,000 advance with her. SAN-GUINELY Dell ordered 250,000 copies for release in August. When Hays and Ray suddenly became household words in late May, Dell moved fast . . . . A fortnight later 500,000 copies were churned out . . . . As of now, there are 1,600,000 copies in print of this slapdash memoir . . . . (Anon., "Paper Back Talk," *New York Times,* 7/4/76, Section 7, p. 15)

4. Some wonder whether the CB fad has finally said "10-4." . . . . Analyst Charles Hill . . . is more SANGUINE. "I think it will probably be a decent year for CB once the dust has settled," he says. (Lynn Langway and Elaine Sciolino, "10-4 for CB?," *Newsweek,* 1/24/77, p. 69)

5. If you ask any ice hockey fan what he likes about the game . . . , he'll probably talk about its speed, skill and excitement. Still, so much of what makes for that excitement is SANGUINE and undisguised brutality that some of this fan's pleasure simply has to derive from the spectacle of cruelty. (Joy Gould Boyum, Review of the movie, *Slap Shot, Wall Street Journal,* 3/7/77, p. 15)

6. See (1) under SHIKSA.

SANS-CULOTTE (sänz'-kyŏō-lot) *noun, pl.:* **SANS-CULOTTES** (sänz' kyŏō-lots) (in the French Revolution) a term of contempt applied by aristocrats to the poorly clad revolutionary soldiers of the poorer class who substituted pantaloons for knee breeches; any radical revolutionary or person of extreme republican views.

SANS-CULOTTIC or **SANS-CULOTTISH** *adj.*

SANS-CULOTTISM *noun.*

1. President of the [New York] City Council Paul O'Dwyer introduced a bill proposing that the name of Grand Army Plaza, at Fifty-Ninth Street and Fifth Avenue, be changed to Common Sense Plaza (The historian Henry Steele Commager commented later that Paine, a certifiable SANSCULOTTE, "might have expected Heaven for his lot, but not a site next to the Plaza Hotel"). (A. Logan, "Around City Hall: Irishry," *The New Yorker,* 2/9/76, p. 86)

2. The most lamentable effect of this mind-body split has been literature of sexual explicitness which has degenerated this year into a lucrative new SANS-CULOTTISM. One in which dizzy sexpot heroines, oral sex, NARCISSISTIC self-pity and that most fashionable accessory of porn chic—the lesbian episode—merge into a GRAND BOUFFE of female exhibitionism to date unsurpassed for MISOGYNY. (Francine duPlessix Gray, "What Are Women Doing?," *New York Times,* 4/24/77, Section 7, p. 40)

SAPIENTIAL (sā' pē-en' shəl) *adj.* having, providing, expounding, or characterized by wisdom.

SAPIENT (sā' pē-ənt) *adj.* wise or sage; sagacious; full of knowledge; discerning; of fancied wisdom.

SAPIENCE or **SAPIENCY** *noun.*

SAPIENTLY *adv.*

1. In Robert Theobald's view . . . "We must abandon our POLLYANNA optimism and encourage new styles of leadership which will have the imagination to lead us in new directions." What is needed, he said, is SAPIENTIAL leadership, or that based on competence, wisdom and knowledge, rather than on the ability to coerce or impress. Leadership that admits it isn't OMNIPOTENT, but which is willing to join in a search for answers. (J. Cunniff, "Leadership role takes new directions," *Norman* [Okla.] *Transcript,* 5/9/76, p. 6)

2. We older and wiser heads know that well-placed "uhs" and "ums" in our speech serve good and useful purposes. For instance the "uh" allows your listeners the time to savor the rich SAPIENCE of your discourse while you are composing new gems. The "um" user is actually uttering his Transcendental Meditation MANTRA. (E. Midura, "Um's the Word," *Today, The Inquirer Magazine,* 1/30/77, p. 26)

SAPPHISM (saf'iz-əm) *noun* lesbianism.

SAPPHIST *noun* a lesbian.

SAPPHO *noun* an ancient Greek poetess, born in Lesbos.

1. Of all the VIGNETTES [in the book, *Peculiar Institutions*], however, [author Elaine] Kendall is best on Martha Carey Thomas . . . the legendary, gifted, single-minded spirit of the college [Bryn Mawr] in which she was dean,

president, teacher. Her instincts and choices were SAPPHIST; she had been educated at a number of places, including Johns Hopkins, under "certain conditions" that turned out to be that she was forbidden to attend classes or seminars with men students. (Doris Grumbach, Review, *Change*, May 1976, p. 61)

2. "I [Russel Wren] refer to your [Natalie Novotny's] asserted SAPPHISM. Confirm my sense that you spoke in jest—strange JAPERY, perhaps, but these are unique times . . . . (Thomas Berger, *Who Is Teddy Villanova?*, Delacorte Press/Seymour Lawrence, 1977, p. 185)

SARCOPHAGUS (sär-kof´ ə-gəs) *noun, pl.* -GI (jī) *or* -GUSES a stone coffin, especially one bearing sculpture, inscriptions, etc., often on display, as in a monumental tomb.

1. The [ancient] Egyptians, as Dexter and Levine [of the Metropolitan Opera] conceive them, are a people locked into a rigid, uncompromising society, like the ICONOGRAPHIC figures found in the SARCOPHAGUSES of Luxor. (R.M. Braun, "The Met's New Team Rediscovers *Aida*," *New York Times*, 2/1/76, Section 2, p. 17)

SARDONIC (sär-don´ ik) *adj.* characterized by bitter or scornful derision; disdainfully or bitterly sneering, ironical, or sarcastic; biting; MORDANT; contemptuous.

SARDONICALLY *adv.*

SARDONICISM *noun.*

1. See (1) under ACERBIC.

2. Success in advertising is hard to explain, but in the case of Scali, McCabe, Sloves it has to do with perceiving the 70's as a decade of lost illusions and tight money. To separate the consumer from his dollar, they have emphasized a kind of SARDONIC toughness. (T. Morgan, "New! Improved! Advertising!," *New York Times*, 1/25/76, Section 6, p. 13)

3. Watching Duke Snider turned Bill Roeder [a reporter] SARDONIC . . . "do you notice when he's happiest?" Roeder complained. "When he walks." (R. Kahn, *The Boys of Summer*, Harper and Row, 1971, p. 147)

4. When he reached the Pawnee lands, Rude

Water [the chief] greeted him as a son, then set eight braves to wrecking his canoe, stealing his rifle and running off with the precious bales of [beaver] pelts. Unarmed and without food, Pasquinel was left alone, a hundred and fifty miles from Missouri . . . . He walked by night, relieved in a SARDONIC way that he no longer had to carry his packs. (J.A. Michener, *Centennial*, Fawcett, 1975, p. 220)

5. Her [Helen Yglesias's] style [in *Family Feeling*] is elegant, evocative, simultaneously humane and SARDONIC. (B. Allen, Review, *Boston Globe*, 3/7/76, p. 17-A)

6. Her voice [in *Collected Poems of Stevie Smith*] is bold, individual, occasionally SARDONIC, but her poems are not the least confessional . . . . (P.S. Prescott, Review, *Newsweek*, 3/29/76, p. 88)

7. What can one do to kindle in the liberal bosom a spirit of antagonism toward the Communists equal in intensity to that which moved the liberals to fight against Senator [Joseph] McCarthy? . . . . I wrote: "A few years ago a SARDONIC observer indulged in a little wishful thinking. 'If only,' he said, 'Mao Tse-tung, back in 1946 or 1947, had criticized Margaret Truman's singing! China might have been saved! Perhaps some day . . . Nikita Krushchev . . . will sputter out, 'You know, I like old Joe—McCarthy, that is.' Then will the liberals . . . join the fray, prepared to shed their blood to devastate the newly discovered enemy.'" (W.F. Buckley Jr., *Up From Liberalism*, Arlington House, 2nd Printing, 1968, pp. 115-116)

8. When the traders were safely out of Dakota territory [after a "close call" with the Indians], Pasquinel said [to McKeag], "If you give an Indian a fair chance, you can avoid killing . . . . In years to come those braves will sit around the campfire and tell about the coup they made on the two white men," . . . He smiled SARDONICALLY, then added, "And you will sit in Scotland and tell of the tomahawks and the arrows." (J.A. Michener, *Centennial*, Fawcett, 1975, p. 230)

9. [Robert] Sherrill's book [*The Last Kennedy: Edward M. Kennedy of Massachusetts, Before and After Chappaquiddick*] is slim . . . . Yet it is a small, SARDONIC masterpiece. (G. Hodgson, Review, *New York Times*, 4/18/76, Section 7, p. 12)

10. Traditionalists argue that "language" as learned by chimps differs in serious ways from human language, and the barrier separating ape and human remains unbreached. Their opponents point out, somewhat SARDONICALLY, that the traditionalists keep redefining language to include only those functions not yet mastered by chimpanzees. (J. Church, Review of *Why Chimps Can Read*, by Ann J. Premack, *New York Times*, 4/11/76, Section 7, p. 20)

11. Loss and anger over loss are reflected in contemporary literature from the SARDONIC rages of Kurt Vonnegut Jr. to the exquisitely delicate despair of Joyce Carol Oates. (R. MacLeish, "National Spirit: pendulum begins to swing," *Smithsonian*, July 1976, p. 31)

12. See (3) under OSSIFY.

13. . . . most presidents feel, as did Andrew Jackson, that they must secure both liberty and the "integrity of the Constitution against the Senate, the House, or both." So it is that the feud between the executive and legislative branches has become the longest continuously SARDONIC crap game in town. (T. Tiede, "Subject Carter to Third Degree?," *Times Herald*, Norristown, Pa., 12/11/76, p. 15)

14. Dorothy Parker collided with a woman leaving a fashionable restaurant . . . . The stranger stepped back with a SARDONIC smile. "Age before beauty," she said. Miss Parker stepped through the doorway. "Pearls before swine," she said . . . . (J. Bishop, "Reward of Wit," *Times Herald*, Norristown, Pa., 1/5/77, p. 17)

SARTORIAL (sär-tŏr′ē-əl, -tôr′.) *adj.* of or pertaining to a tailor or to tailoring; of clothing or dress, especially men's.

SARTORIALLY *adv.*

SARTOR *noun* a tailor: literary or humorous term.

1. The recent surge in vest volume was sparked by young men who wanted a new SARTORIAL fashion, and by the stores and manufacturers that supply this "contemporary market." (L. Sloane, "Suits Take On a Vested Interest," *New York Times*, 3/28/76, Section 3, p. 1)

2. . . . some of my happiest memories are of Saturday excursions to the State-Lake Theater in Chicago's Loop to watch him [Cab Calloway], IMPECCABLY dressed in white tails and shiny patent-leather shoes, . . . shout his "hi-de-ho's" . . . . (I sometimes wonder if the SOUBRIQUET "Duke" might not have been more applicable in Calloway's case, at least where SARTORIAL splendor was concerned). (M. Torme, Review of *Of Minnie the Moocher and Me*, by Cab Calloway and Bryant Rollins, *New York Times*, 9/12/76, Section 7, p. 8)

3. I had reached new levels of SARTORIAL eccentricity. (Jane Shapiro, Review of *Cheap Chic*, by Caterine Milinaire and Carol Troy, *Ms.*, May 1976, p. 33)

4. From man's earliest efforts to protect his crops he has relied upon scarecrows . . . . They range from simple stick figures draped with old gunny sacks to elaborate SARTORIAL masterpieces, some of them fit for display in a museum. (Avon Neal, "Scarecrows provide an antic art form," *Smithsonian*, September 1976, p. 115)

SATURNALIA or **SATURNALIA** (sat′ ər-nā′lē-ə, -nāl′yə) *noun, pl.* **-LIA** or **-LIAS** (sometimes construed as *singular*) (if capitalized) the ancient Roman festival of Saturn, observed about December 17 as a time of general feasting and unrestrained merrymaking in celebration of the winter solstice; (if lower case) any period or occasion of unrestrained, often ORGIASTIC, revelry.

SATURNALIAN or **SATURNALIAN** *adj.* (if capitalized) of the Saturnalia; (if lower case) riotously merry or ORGIASTIC.

1. See (1) under PULLULATE.

2. The current movie season offers the customary PLETHORA of remakes, sequels, CATACLYSM and supernatural SATURNALIA. (D. Ryan, "The Skeptic: Rated 'R' (for 'Repulsive')," *Philadelphia Inquirer, Today* Magazine, 10/17/76, p. 6)

3. The film [*Fellini's Casanova*], for all its ORGIES and SATURNALIAS, is really un-erotic . . . here the heavy, jackhammer sex isn't sexy, touching or funny . . . . (J. Kroll, Review, *Newsweek*, 1/24/77, p. 60)

SATURNINE (sat′ ər-nīn′) *adj.* heavy; gray; gloomy; morose; dull; the opposite of *mercurial*; sluggish; sullen; of, pertaining to, or resembling lead; affected by or suffering from lead poisoning.

SATURNINELY *adv.*

SATURNINENESS or **SATURNINITY** *noun.*

1. I can see [Sal] Maglie, SATURNINE in the brightness of May [1955], winding up and throwing. [Jackie] Robinson started to duck and then, with those extraordinary reflexes, hunched his shoulders and froze. The ball sailed wild behind him. (R. Kahn, *The Boys of Summer*, Harper and Row, 1971, p. 395)

2. What SATURNINELY handsome actor is signed up for 170 movies, with 50 of them currently in production? No need to feel abashed at not knowing the answer: Indian actor Shashi Kapoor, 38, is one of the stars in the Asian movie-making world whose output is PRODIGIOUS by Hollywood standards but who is seldom seen in the U.S. . . . For the most part, that is just as well. (Anon., "Asia's Bouncing World of Movies," *Time*, 6/28/76, p. 40)

3. . . . Teddy [Villanova] decompressed his lips and smiled, true, in a fashion that might be seen as SATURNINE . . . . (Thomas Berger, *Who Is Teddy Villanova?*, Delacorte Press/ Seymour Lawrence, 1977, p. 215)

SATYR (sā′ tər, sat′ ər) *noun* (in Greek mythology) a woodland nymph fond of riotous living and lechery; a lustful or lecherous man; a man having satyriasis.

SATYRIC (sə-tir′ik) or **SATYRICAL** *adj.*

SATYRIASIS (sat′ə-rī′ə-sis, sa′tə) or **SATYRO-MANIA** *noun* abnormal and uncontrollable desire by a man for sexual intercourse.

SATYROMANIAC *noun* a lustful man.

1. [Bianca's] Father [in the play, *White Marriage*, by Tadeusz Rozewicz] is a SATYR who sometimes literally turns into a bull as he tramples after wife and servants. Grandfather is a senile SATYR who can't shake off lust even at the

*This condition in women is known as NYMPH-OMANIA.

gates of death. (J. Kroll, Review, *Newsweek*, 5/9/77, p. 115)

2. . . . I [Russell Wren] am a bachelor of thirty (but heterosexual, as some have said, to the threshold of SATYRIASIS). (Thomas Berger, *Who Is Teddy Villanova?*, Delacorte Press/Seymour Lawrence, 1977, p. 2)

3. He was a short and slight-built man—a figure very common among SATYRS, incidentally—but could laugh as robustly as a worthy of twice his bulk. (Thomas Berger, *Ibid.*, p. 2)

4. From the filthy wallpaintings of Ashanti, not to mention the *Kama Sutra*, available in recent years on every paperback rack, we know the Indians as a carnal people. A serpentine body [of a yogi] is no impediment to a SATYR. (Thomas Berger, *Ibid.*, p. 57)

SCABROUS (skab′ rəs, skā′ brəs) *adj.* having a rough surface, as a file, because of minute points or projections; scaly or scabby; blotchy; encrusted; full of difficulties; shocking; improper; scandalous; indecent; obscene.

SCABROUSLY *adv.*

SCABROUSNESS *noun.*

1. Bought under the counter and read under the counterpane, [Frank] Harris's SCABROUS memoirs [*My Life and Loves*] seemed heady stuff [in earlier times] . . . . But now that it is readily available . . . who is prepared to wade through its 983 pages of TURGID LUBRICITY and dubious anecdotes? (R. Freedman, Review of *Frank Harris: A Biography*, by Philippa Pullar, *New York Times*, 3/28/76, Section 7, p. 8)

2. SEE (2) UNDER ARCADIAN.

3. It is the SCABROUS underbelly of Middle American culture, this "sport" of dogfighting. In Texas, Florida and Georgia, Southern California, the Rocky Mountains, and even on the outskirts of New York, dogfighting AFICIO-NADOS gather in barns and back bedrooms to SURREPTITIOUSLY conduct their matches . . . . The AMBIENCE is of naked violence. (E. Meadows, "An American Pastime," *Harper's*, March 1976, p. 6)

4. Born in Ostend, Belgium, in 1860, he [John Ensor] was a reclusive man with an ECLECTIC

brush, who turned a wide range of styles and influences into a SCABROUS, satirical vision of grinning skulls and tormented masks. (M. Stevens, "The Energy of Rot," *Newsweek*, 1/31/77, p. 57)

5. It [the film, *Slap Shot*] is, on the one hand, foul-mouthed and unabashedly vulgar, on the other, vigorous and funny. So, like certain off-color jokes and certain SCABROUS comic classics, it's bound to offend at the same time as it amuses. (Joy Gould Boyum, Review, *Wall Street Journal*, 3/7/77, p. 15)

SCAM (skam) *noun* confidence game [slang].

SCAM *verb* to cheat or swindle, as in a confidence game [slang].

1. Odd things are happening on our movie screens. ANACHRONISTIC outdoor telephone booths show up in *The Godfather* and *Hearts of the West*. In *The Sting*, set in 1936 Chicago, SCAM artist Paul Newman outhustles the canny Robert Shaw while wearing a 1945 snap-brim. (M.E. Mullen Jr., "Dismemberment of Things Past," *New York Times*, 3/28/76, Section 2, p. 15)

2. . . . the book [*The Track*, by Bill Surface] is chocked with fascinating information and delicious SCAMS. For instance, I learned that . . . trainers trying to put a horse over for a betting coup work their horse far out from the inner rail, so that the workout time that appears in the Racing Form is much slower than the actual work. (J. Flaherty, Review, *New York Times*, 6/27/76, Section 7, p. 2)

3. [Zachary] Swann's genius lay in the SCAMS he devised to import his products [drugs] into the U.S. . . . He looked for his carriers [of drugs], he says (and [Robert] Sabbag [author of the book, *Snowblind: A Brief Career in the Cocaine Trade*] doesn't seem to question what Swann says), and designed into each SCAM an escape hatch so that the carrier could walk away from the dope if he was caught. Example: a customs inspector discovers cocaine in a woman's suitcase. She protests: it's the wrong case; the clothes are all the wrong size, and there—her real suitcase, identical in design, is still on the luggage rack with her clothes and identification in it. (P.S. Prescott, Review, *Newsweek*, 1/31/77, p. 75)

SCATOLOGY (skə-tol'ə-jē') *noun* obscenity, especially words or humor referring to excrement; preoccupation or obsession with excrement, excretion, or obscenity; the study of feces or of fossil excrement.

SCATOLOGICAL or **SCATOLOGIC** *adj.*

1. Now I don't much like SCATOLOGICAL humor, and it works only when the OXYMORONIC effect outweighs the vulgarity—as in Bill Rickenbacker's legendary "Conservatives are organizing a paean to the Warren Court." (W.F. Buckley Jr., *Execution Eve and Other Contemporary Ballads*, G.P. Putnam's Sons, 1975, p. 348)

2. Notwithstanding that the word [crap] has these clearly nonSCATOLOGICAL uses [nonsense, drivel], there is an Anglo-Saxon earthiness to it which performs for the writer a function altogether different from such a retort as, say, "Flapdoodle." (W.F. Buckley Jr., *Ibid.*, p. 409)

3. The emotional damage resulting from Mozart's PERIPATETIC early life [traveling with his father] was even further reaching. He had not much of a childhood, already being at the age of five a PRECOCIOUS and serious young man . . . the frequent separations from his mother, and her overshadowing by her husband, must have hurt him and may account for his later failures with women, as well as for the expressions of adolescent SCATOLOGICAL sexuality in his letters—until recently considered unfit to publish except in EXPURGATED form. (R. Craft, "A Prodigy of Nature," *New York Review of Books*, 12/11/75, p. 12)

4. A cookbook of recipes from the Renaissance, a mildly SCATOLOGICAL novel written anonymously during the American Revolution and a DIDACTIC tract on preserving whales—these are a few of the notable oddities about to be published by David R. Godine, Publishers, a small Boston firm dedicated to the vanishing belief that books should not be just printed but printed well. (J.N. Baker, "Holdout for Quality," *Newsweek*, 5/24/76, p.94)

5. The most loathsome thing I have read recently [says Josh Logan] is the first chapter of

Truman Capote's *Answered Prayers*. It's simply terrible how he has bitten the hands that fed him—people who invited him to dinner and to weekends in the country. And then to write so SCATOLOGICALLY about them. (Associated Press, "Director Logan completes book after 3 years," *Norman* [Okla.] *Transcript*, 6/4/76, p. 12)

6. But two of the words in the quoted—and undenied—remark [of Earl L. Butz], and a crude and unfunny and indefensibly anti-black remark it was, are unfit, we believe, for publication here. One was a sexual vulgarism, the other a common SCATOLOGICAL term. (Anon., "Mr. Butz rightly resigns, lacking common decency," [Editorial], *Philadelphia Inquirer*, 10/5/76, p. 10-A)

7. . . . James Joyce's *Ulysses* and Henry Miller's *Tropic of Cancer* probably carried as much if not more of the SCATOLOGICAL message [than *Lady Chatterley's Lover*]. (G. Volgenau, Knight News Service, "Gutter talk is growing," *Philadelphia Inquirer*, 10/13/76, p. 6-C)

8. See (4) under JAPE.

9. Larry Flynt's magazine [*Hustler*] is as shamelessly vulgar as its reputation suggests. It is not merely sexually explicit, it is perverse; the magazine thrives on gross, racist and SCATOLOGICAL humor. (A. Kretchmer, "Justice for *Hustler*," *Newsweek*, 2/28/77, p. 13)

10. See (5) under MALAPROPISM.

SCHADENFREUDE (shäd′ ′n-froi′ də) *noun* glee at another's misfortune.

1. We are so aware of U.S. troubles that we tend to overlook how badly other countries are doing. As an exercise in SCHADENFREUDE (what the dictionary defines as "malicious joy at the misfortune of others"), let's review some current facts. Switzerland, that utopia of right-wingers, has had about the worst stagnation of production since 1970 of any European country. (P.A. Samuelson, "A Year of Opportunity," *Newsweek*, 1/31/77, p. 67)

2. . . . more than once I [Russel Wren] had after a brief perusal hurled the sheaf [of manuscript pages] away in chagrin: I won't say why and so nourish the SCHADENFREUDE of other would-be dramatists whose scenes, after a vig-

orous start, founder in the middle . . . . (Thomas Berger, *Who Is Teddy Villanova?*, Delacorte Press/Seymour Lawrence, 1977, p. 83)

SCHLEMIEL (shlə-mēl′) or SCHLEMIHL or SHLEMIEL *noun Slang:* an awkward, ineffectual, unlucky, or bungling person who habitually fails or is easily victimized [after Peter Schlemihl, title character of an 1814 novel by the German author Adelbert van Chamisso (1781-1838)].

1. While others were touching the acme, you [Yuri Maximovich, in *A Hero in His Time*, by Arthur A. Cohen] became . . . a nonentity . . . . But this SHLEMIEL [Y.M.] is also a communicant, and his church is form, and his faith is poetry, and he is discovered by his author as "great waters of verse were rising within him." (G. Wolf, Review, *New York Times*, 1/25/76, Section 7, p. 4)

2. David Selig, the first-person narrator [of *Dying Inside*, by Robert Silverberg], is that familiar figure in modern fiction—the failed-intellectual-Jewish SCHLEMIEL—with one important difference: He was born with the ability to look inside other people's minds. (G. Jonas, Review, *New York Times*, 4/25/76, Section 7, p. 47)

3. [How many were the] "most one-handed catches of easy throws in one inning [made] by a first baseman," [statistician Allan Roth asked Roger Kahn], "Three," I said. "Eh?" Roth said. "Three. Very Good. Very Good. But who, SHLEMIEL?"(R. Kahn, *The Boys of Summer*, Harper and Row, 1971, p. 127)

4. See (7) under APOCALYPSE.

5. See (2) under EPICENE.

6. American sex fantasies are endearingly infantile—poor King Kong is a subway-smashing SCHLEMIEL who dies for love but never gets the girl . . . . The mythical monster in *The Beast* [a film directed by Walerian Borowczyk] gets the girl . . . and then expires from sheer ecstasy . . . . (J. Kroll, Review, *Newsweek*, 5/9/77, p. 110)

SCHLEPP (shlep) or SCHLEP or SHLEP or SHLEPP *noun* a slang expression for an ineffectual person.

SCHLEPP or **SCHLEP** or **SHLEP** or **SHLEPP** *verb* (in Slang) to go or move with effort; drag oneself; to drag about, especially unnecessarily or burdensomely.

1. In fact, Kolokolov [in the book, *A Hero in His Time*, by Arthur A. Cohen] is no poet at all; he is a showman and careerist, and on the night . . . of a wonderfully comic testimonial dinner in his honor he calls for [Yuri Maximovich] Isakovsky . . . and is annoyed to find that unsung SHLEPPER, his PUTATIVE comrade, unfashionably costumed. (G. Wolf, Review, *New York Times*, 1/25/76, Section 7, p. 4)

SCHLOCK (shläk) *noun* anything cheap or inferior; trash [colloquial].

SCHLOCK or **SCHLOCKY** *adj.* cheap and trashy; inferior [colloquial].

1. See (3) under VACUITY.

2. For followers of vamp CAMP (not to mention the Carlos Castaneda variety of pop SCHLOCK—otherworldly visions and LAMBENT presences dancing a macabre do-si-do on the head of a pin), this magical mystery tour through 200 years of a vampire's life, loves and suffering [in the book, *Interview With a Vampire*, by Anne Rice] is the NE PLUS ULTRA mit schlag of the GENRE. (Alix Nelson, Review, *Ms.*, May 1976, p. 27)

3. [Scott] Fitzgerald, [William] Faulkner and [Aldous] Huxley all wrote for top [Hollywood] studios. Nathanael West entered at the bottom, grinding out for Republic such long-forgotten SCHLOCK as *Jim Hanvey—Detective* (starring Guy Kibbee) and *Ticket to Paradise* (with Roger Pryor and Wendy Barrie). Says [Tom] Dardis [author of *Some Time in the Sun*]: "It was junk all the way. [Yet] no American writer got as much out of Hollywood as did West." The place gave him money he desperately needed and the material for *The Day of the Locust* . . . . (W. Clemons, Review, *Newsweek*, 7/19/76, p. 73)

4. He [Barry Manilow] landed a job as music director for a CBS television show, *Callback*, and developed the ability to write idiomatic, perfectly serviceable arrangements for rock-and-roll tunes, opera, Broadway pop, and sing-along SCHLOCK, 16 arrangements a week. (R. Palmer, "Barry Manilow—The Master of Romantic Pop," *New York Times*, 9/12/76, Section 2, p. 24)

5. See (3) under SHTICK.

SCHMALTZ (shmälts, shmôlts) or **SCHMALZ** *noun* exaggerated or sickly sentimentalism or BANALITY, as in music, soap operas, or literature.

SCHMALTZY *adj.*

1. The title sequence [of *That's Entertainment, Part 2*] . . . lists the stars in a send-up of just about every title sequence ever contrived to fit the GENRE: for SCHMALTZ, Nelson Eddy and Jeanette MacDonald spelled out in blossoms floating on a pond . . . . (C. Michener, M. Kasindorf, Review, *Newsweek*, 5/31/76, p. 51)

2. The DÉNOUEMENT [of *Bread Givers*, a book by Anzia Yezierska] is a SCHMALTZY attempt at realism. (Lilly Rivlin, Review, *Ms.*, May 1976, p. 37)

SCIAPHOBIA (sī′ə-fō′bē-ə) or **SKIAPHOBIA** (skī′ə-) *noun* fear of shadows.

1. But you can take it from us that there will be another 40 days of winter if marmota monax [the groundhog] suffers an attack of SCIAPHOBIA today. If not, you can break out the garden tools. (Anon., "Halfway to Spring" [Editorial], *Norman* [Okla.] *Transcript*, 2/2/76, p. 6)

SCINTILLA (sin-til′ə) *noun* a minute trace; a minute particle; a spark; a shred.

1. See (1) under OBMUTESCENCE.

2. Today there are judges and others who seem convinced that once a SCINTILLA of DE JURE segregation has been found in a school system, the Constitution mandates that no school shall be all white or more than half black. (G.F. Will, "Freedom and the Busing Quagmire," *Newsweek*, 7/12/76, p. 76)

SCIOLISM (sī′ə-liz′əm) *noun* superficial knowledge or learning.

SCIOLIST *noun.*

SCIOLISTIC *adj.*

1. . . . he [the painter James Ensor] was in-

trigued with the masks that were donned—and
the inhibitions that were shed—during the
pre-Lenten carnival in Ostend [Belgium] . . . .
"Bloated vicuna faces . . . obtuse SCIOLISTS
with moldy skulls, hairless vivisectionists, odd
insects, hard shells giving shelter to soft beasts"
[he exclaimed]. (M. Stevens, "The Energy of
Rot," *Newsweek*, 1/31/77, p. 57)

SCLEROTIC (skli-rot'ik) *adj.* hard; sclerosed; of, characterized by, or having sclerosis;
of the sclera.

SCLEROUS (sklir'əs, sklēr'əs) *adj.* hard,
bony; thick; firm.

SCLEROID *adj.* hard or hardened.

SCLEROSED *adj.* hardened or indurated,
as by sclerosis.

SCLEROSIS *noun* a hardening of the cell
wall of a plant; an abnormal hardening of
body tissues or parts, especially of the nervous
system or the walls of arteries; a disease characterized by such hardening.

1. Today the [Christian Democratic] party is
maligned and ridiculed as never before—and
from every corner of Italian society. Urban
youths rail against it as SCLEROTIC and estab-
lishmentarian. (Anon., "Christian Democrats:
On a Shaky Unicycle," *Time*, 5/24/76, p. 24)

SCREED (skrēd) *noun* a long and tedious
letter, essay, discourse, speech, or the like.

1. It is a SCREED, this book [*Winners & Losers:
Battles, Retreats, Gains, Losses and Ruins
from a Long War*, by Gloria Emerson] . . . it is
not carefully written; it is sloppy and disconnected. (J.M. Perry, Review, *National Observer*, week ending 3/26/77, p. 21)

SCRIMSHAW (skrim'shô) *noun* careful decoration and carving of shells, bone, ivory,
etc., done especially by sailors on long voyages;
an article so made or such articles or work collectively; the art or technique of producing
such work.

SCRIMSHAW *verb* to carve or engrave
(shells, bone, ivory, etc.) in making a scrimshaw.

1. Around Dr. [William] Rashbaum [of Beth

Israel Medical Center]'s neck was a delicate
macramé band on which was strung a SCRIM-
SHAW whistle. I admired it. He told me, with
evident satisfaction, that he had made it himself. (Norma Rosen, "Between Guilt and Gratification: Abortion Doctors Reveal Their Feelings," *New York Times*, 4/17/77, Section 6,
p. 78)

SCRIVENER (skriv'nər) *noun* a scribe,
copyist, or clerk; a notary.

1. Now some of these mostly unheralded
SCRIVENERS will achieve recognition of a sort in
the form of the first annual Pushcart Prize
(Anon., "Book Ends: Thinking Small," *New
York Times*, 1/11/76, Section 7, p. 29)

SCURRILOUS (skûr'ə-ləs) *adj.* grossly or
obscenely abusive; coarsely jocular or derisive;
vulgar; foulmouthed; containing coarse vul-
garisms or indecent abuse.

SCURRILOUSLY *adv.*

SCURRILOUSNESS or **SCURRILITY** *noun*.

1. At the moment, however, the reflective
critic [in John Simon] is being eclipsed by the
SCURRILOUS public performer, and the worse
qualities of the man are in the ascendant. (R.
Brustein, Review of *Uneasy Stages* and *Singularities*, by John Simon, *New York Times*,
1/4/76, Section 7, p. 2)

SCYLLA (sil'ə) *noun* a rock in the Strait of
Messina, off the southern coast of Italy; (in
Classical Mythology) a sea nymph who was
transformed into a sea monster, later identified
with the rock SCYLLA; *see* CHARYBDIS.

Between SCYLLA and CHARYBDIS an expression meaning between two equally perilous or
evil alternatives, neither of which can be
avoided without encountering and probably
falling victim to the other.

1. Modern Argentina has been trapped between the SCYLLA of Peronism and the
CHARYBDIS of the army, never able to escape
from the one without disappearing straight into the other. (*London Economist*, "Peronism
due dishonorable discharge? Argentina's army's fighting chance," *Norman* [Okla.] *Transcript*, 4/20/76, p. 6)

2. See (1) under CHARYBDIS.

3. "The chapter tonight is about Hamlet and simply full of puns." She [Olga Kahn] was carrying the red-covered Modern Library *Ulysses* [by James Joyce]. "In Dublin on June 16, 1904, it is two o'clock in the afternoon . . . the scene symbolizes the classic SCYLLA and CHARYBDIS." (R. Kahn, *The Boys of Summer*, Harper and Row, 1971, p. 137)

4. See (4) under CHARYBDIS.

SECATEURS (sek'ə-tərz, -tûrz') *noun* construed as *plural* or *singular* scissors or shears, especially pruning shears.

1. The classical instance is the survival for centuries of ANTITHETICAL primitivisms, labeled "soft" and "hard," and reflecting COMPLEMENTARY attitudes to work. Both kinds are involved in the story of Adam, who lived in a paradise of pleasure but had to cultivate it: a situation Milton found a bit difficult, for having declared the work virtually unnecessary, a mere disinterested tidying up of superfluous growth with PRELAPSARIAN SECATEURS, he gave Eve victorious arguments for the division of labor. (F. Kermode, Review of *Work and Play: Ideas and Experience of Work and Leisure*, by Alasdair Clayre, *New York Review of Books*, 11/27/75, p. 35)

SEDENTARY (sed'ᵊn-ter'ē) *adj.* characterized by or requiring a sitting posture; accustomed to sit or rest a great deal or to take little exercise; (of birds) remaining in one locality; not migratory.

SEDENTARILY *adv.*

SEDENTARINESS *noun.*

1. . . . in his slim volume of theater essays, *Singularities*, . . . in these leisurely pieces, written for more SEDENTARY occasions than review deadlines, [author John] Simon emerges as a drama critic of distinction . . . . (R. Brustein, Review, *New York Times*, 1/4/76, Section 7, p. 2)

2. Why does [Harold] Bloom [in *Poetry and Repression: Revisionism from Blake to Stevens*] feel bound to be muscle-bound? Partly it's the situation that George Bernard Shaw understood—that of a university-trained writer feel-

ing he and his work are not somehow as manly as other men and their work and, so Shaw says, wallowing "in violence and muscularity of expression, as only literary men do when they become thoroughly depraved by solitary work, SEDENTARY cowardice, and starvation of the sympathetic centers." (C. Ricks, Review, *New York Times*, 3/14/76, Section 7, p. 6)

3. . . . no newspaper can match the Sunday *New York Times*, all 4½ lbs., 450 pages and 500,000 words—give or take a few thousands—of it. Indeed, the city's sanitation department once estimated it cost New York $6 million annually just to dispose of the Sunday *Times* poundage. For years the edition has provided a Sabbath's activity for the city's SEDENTARY and a rich lode of guilt for those who know they should read all the news fit to print on any Sunday, but don't quite succeed. (Anon., "Changes at the Times," *Time*, 4/19/76, p. 87)

4. There are hitchhiking adventures [in *Indian Action*, by Stuart Mitchner] that will ring true to any traveler and even amuse the SEDENTARY—such as the time they had to paint a restaurant mural in Kabul in three days for food and board before the last plane to New Delhi. (J. Yohalem, Review, *New York Times*, 9/5/76, Section 7, p. 14)

SEDULOUS (sej'ə-ləs) *adj.* diligent in application or attention; persevering; persistently, unremittently, or carefully maintained; ASSIDUOUS; constant; untiring; tireless.

SEDULOUSLY *adv.*

SEDULOUSNESS or **SEDULITY** (si-dyōō'li-tē, -dōō-) *noun.*

1. . . . [André] Malraux has remained obscured—encrusted by a mythology he SEDULOUSLY cultivated. (P.D. Zimmerman, Review of *André Malraux*, by Jean Lacouture, *Newsweek*, 12/29/75, p. 56)

2. . . . it is prudent . . . to suppose that the young American [John Berryman, in England in 1940] . . . was bamboozled by the cherished and SEDULOUSLY promoted fictions of a foreign culture into thinking . . . that Dylan [Thomas] represented a Celtic, an INDIGENOUSLY Welsh, imaginative tradition challenging the . . .

authenticated English establishment. (D. Davie, Review of *The Freedom of the Poet*, by John Berryman, *New York Times*, 4/25/76, Section 7, p. 4)

3. See (2) under LOGOPHILIA.

SEGUE (seg'wā, sā'gwā) *noun* an immediate transition from one part to another, as in music.

SEGUE *verb* to continue or blend into without interruption (the next part or item), usually of a musical performance.

1. What a strange memoir this [book, *Talking To Myself*, by Studs Terkel] is, written like a movie scenario, employing fade-outs and quick cuts and filled with wondrously ingenious SEGUES between subjects that are programmed sequentially in his [the author's] fertile mind. (M.J. Bandler, Review, *Philadelphia Inquirer*, 4/24/77, p. 13-H)

2. . . . Phil Donahue, we are also told, was offered the host post on "The Today Show" just a couple of days ago. Philip . . . has created such an unbeatable TV niche with his own "Phil Donahue Show," I personally think he'd be silly to SEGUE from his own spotlight to become one of a group, no matter how prestigious that group is. (Shirley Eder, "Day For Night for Brokaw," *Philadelphia Daily News*, 11/9/77, p. 58)

SEMINAL (sem' ə-n'l) *adj.* pertaining to, containing, or consisting of semen or seed; having possibilities of future development or reproduction; highly original, as an idea, style, etc., and influencing future events or developments; germinal; originative.

SEMINALLY *adv.*

SEMINALITY *noun.*

1. For Professor Husen [of the University of Stockholm] and other competent observers, even the SEMINAL definitions of the future purposes of education seem now surprisingly ambiguous and tenuous. (G.W. Bonham, "The American Disease" [Editorial], *Change*, June 1975, p.11)

2. Books are proliferating on Art Moderne and Deco and the Skyscraper Style and such early figures as George Howe, who, with William Lescaze, designed the SEMINAL Philadelphia Savings Fund Society Building. (Ada Louise Huxtable, "Modern Architecture in Question," *New York Review of Books*, 11/27/75, p. 8)

3. See (1) under LILLIPUTIAN.

4. French couturier [Paul] Poiret (1879-1944), the man who shucked the corset, has in recent years been shaping up as the SEMINAL figure of 20th-century fashion . . . . The show [*Paul Poiret, King of Fashion*] at F.I.T. [Fashion Institute of Technology] should establish Poiret in permanence as grandpère of the retinue of great dressmakers who came after him. (Phyllis Feldkamp, Review, *New York Times*, 6/13/76, Section 6, p. 59)

SEMIOTIC (sē'mē-ot'ik, sem'ē- , sem'ī-) or **SEMIOTICS** (construed as *singular*) *noun* a general theory of signs and symbols; especially, the analysis of the nature and relationships of signs in language, usually including three branches, syntactics, semantics and pragmatics.

SEMIOTIC or **SEMIOTICAL** *adj.* of or pertaining to signs or semiotics; of or relating to medical symptoms.

SEMIOTICISM *noun.*

SEMIOLOGY *noun* the science of signs in general; the study of signs; sign language.

SEMIOLOGIC or **SEMIOLOGICAL** *adj.*

SEMIOLOGIST *noun.*

1. "Marriage," Ronald Beard observes [in the book, *Beard's Roman Women*, by Anthony Burgess], "is complex SEMIOTICS." In 26 years of it he and Leonora developed a private language and a shared, eventually sexless history. (P.S. Prescott, Review, *Newsweek*, 10/25/76, p. 110)

SENESCENT (sə-nes' ənt) *adj.* growing old; aging.

SENESCENCE *noun.*

1. The second theory [as to why dinosaurs became extinct] is more difficult to assess, because it deals with psychological factors, which . . . are so ESOTERIC that they cannot be quantitatively evaluated. Classes of animals,

like men, empires, and ideas, have a predestined length of life, after which they become SENESCENT and die out. (J.A. Michener, *Centennial*, Fawcett, 1975, p. 84)

2. [Nelson] Rockefeller does symbolize because of the liberal Republicans' decline—SENESCENCE. Like Hugh Scott of Pennsylvania, Clifford Case of New Jersey and Edward Brooke of Massachusetts, he has grown weary of the fray and just doesn't care that much what happens to his party. (D.S. Broder, "Say goodbye to the GOP liberals," *Philadelphia Inquirer*, 8/29/76, p. 7-G)

SENTENTIA (sən-ten' shē-ə) *noun*, *pl.*: -TIAE (-shē-ē) an APHORISM, maxim, or brief comment on living, usually used in the *plural* form.

SENTENTIAL *adj.*

1. The author [Lawrence J. Peter]'s views and his recommendations [in the book, *The Peter Plan*] are quite practicable. Both follow a MELIORIST model derived from behaviorist psychology . . . . His argument is periodically interspersed with APOTHEGMS, maxims, SENTENTIAE by a wide variety of philosophers, politicians, journalists, or simply, wits. (F. Golffing, Review, *New York Times*, 2/8/76, Section 7, p. 18)

SENTENTIOUS (sən-ten' shəs) *adj.* abounding in pithy APHORISMS or maxims; given to excessive moralizing; self-righteous; given to or using pithy sayings, maxims, and proverbs; of the nature of a maxim; APHORISTIC, especially in a way that is ponderously trite and moralizing.

SENTENTIOUSLY *adv.*

SENTENTIOUSNESS *noun.*

1. Yiddish theater began as the one refuge in the years of darkness, serving up lofty SENTENTIOUSNESS, flooded emotionality and low pageantry: Moshe Lieb Halpern called it a cross between a synagogue and a bawdy house. (T. Solotaroff, Review of *World of Our Fathers*, by Irving Howe, *New York Times*, 2/1/76, Section 7, p. 29)

2. See (9) under DIALECTIC.

3. The line between tragic horror and joking make-believe has got smudged; the film [*Robin and Marian*] is so SENTENTIOUS that it's difficult to gauge when to laugh and when to be appalled. (Anon., Review, *The New Yorker*, 5/31/76, p. 22)

4. Zeno [hero of *The Abyss*, by Marguerite Yourcenar, translated from the French by Grace Frick in collaboration with M.Y.] is never quite whole. Lacking a PATRIMONY, bastard son that he is, Zeno is born into a mercantile Flemish family in 1510, raised by a SENTENTIOUS merchant banker uncle, packed off to a seminary and allowed to fester for himself. (A.A. Cohen, Review, *New York Times*, 7/11/76, Section, 7, p. 7)

5. Without any wish to be overly SENTENTIOUS about it, we sadly call attention to the fact that man has begun littering on Mars. Among photographs radioed back . . . from the Viking II lander is one showing the ejected cover of a soil sampler nestled in what may once have been a tiny watercourse among the Martian rocks. (Anon., "Litterbug on Mars" [Editorial], *The Times Herald*, Norristown, Pa., 9/30/76, p. 24)

6. Farragut [the protagonist in *Falconer*, a book by John Cheever] is admittedly a man keenly aware of the BANAL ironies of his life and of his own SENTENTIOUS observations. Yet at times Cheever imposes them on the reader as if the novel itself were a correctional institution. "We prisoners," says Farragut, . . ."have suffered for our sins . . ." Another SENTENTIOUS observation would be equally true: crime's victims are no strangers to grief. (R.Z. Sheppard, Review, *Time*, 2/28/77, p. 79)

SENTIENCE (sen' shəns) or **SENTIENCY** *noun* sentient condition or character; capacity for sensation of feeling; consciousness; mere awareness or sensation that does not involve thought or perception.

SENTIENT (sen' shənt) *adj.* having the power of perception by the senses; characterized by sensation; conscious.

SENTIENT *noun* a sentient person or thing.

SENTIENTLY *adv.*

1. Zeno [of Bruges, hero of *The Abyss*, by

Marguerite Yourcenar, translated from the French by Grace Frick in collaboration with M.Y.], like the KABBALISTIC* image of the primordial man, is body, SENTIENCE, and intelligence; however Marguerite Yourcenar has not made him an Everyman, for hers is no simple-minded allegory. (A.A. Cohen, Review, *New York Times*, 7/11/76, Section 7, p. 7)

SEPTENTRIONAL (sep-ten′ trē-ə-nəl) *adj.* northern; boreal; belonging to the north: as opposed to *meridional* (southern).

1. It's all good clean fun, of course, watching Brother Billy Carter putting on the Yankee reporters. And it's kind of amusing to watch SEPTENTRIONAL types struggle with the redneck idiom. It's not long before they are in a heap of trouble with accents, syntax, BUCOLIC metaphors, or the simple fact that neither grits nor "y'all" is of any use to anybody in the singular. (G.B. Tindall, "A Surfeit of Southern Fried Chic," *Wall Street Journal*, 2/9/77, p. 22)

SERENDIPITY (ser′ ən-dip′ i-tē) *noun* an apparent aptitude for making fortunate or desirable discoveries by accident.

SERENDIPITOUSLY *adv.*

1. [Professor Gerard K.] O'Neill's space-colony concept is a classic case of SERENDIPITY in science. In 1969 he assigned the idea as a hypothetical problem in his introductory physics course. He was startled by the speed with which critical physical problems were apparently solved by his students, and he began to take the concept seriously. (R. Chernow, "Colonies in space may turn out to be nice places to live," *Smithsonian*, February 1976, p. 64)

2. Since that day my father and I found and ate four pounds of MORELS—$272 worth, at today's prices—I have only one comparable instance of SERENDIPITY. Some years ago I wandered into a Las Vegas casino and . . . put $20 on a novice crapshooter rolling the dice for the first time. The shooter shredded the laws of probability, rolled 18 straight passes, and I walked off a $3,200. winner. (J.R. Phelan, "May is morel time," *New York Times*, 5/9/76, Section 6, p. 81)

*See CABALA.

3. As it has always been for him [the Italian poet, Eugenio Montale], the moment of vision, the rare SERENDIPITOUS "flash" of insight, though vouchsafed to few, remains the one validating human experience. (J. Galassi, Review of *New Poems*, by Eugenio Montale, translated by G. Singh; and of *Provincial Conclusions*, by Eugenio Montale, translated by Edith Farnsworth, *New York Times*, 5/30/76, Section 7, p. 7)

4. Mathematical and other logical calculations which would have taken a month for any team to complete 25 years ago can now be done in much less than a second. This would be an odd prelude to a period during which the world's advance in knowledge by deduction, induction or SERENDIPITY abruptly slowed down. If my guess is right, Man's main problem in the next few decades will be . . . that he is likely to be given some very dangerous toys to play with during another period of VERTIGINOUS economic advance . . . . (N. Macrae, "United States can keep growing—and lead—if it wishes," *Smithsonian*, July 1976, p. 34)

5. And it [New York City] is still, despite its congestion and litter, a stunning place to visit. It is not only the multitude of museums, theaters, restaurants. There are the pedestrian attractions—the SERENDIPITOUS architectural and shopping treats of its endlessly various neighborhoods. (D. Gelman, *et al.*, "Polishing the Apple," *Newsweek*, 7/19/76, p. 34)

6. Doctors aren't sure exactly how propranolol lowers high blood pressure . . . . Through SERENDIPITY, doctors are finding other uses for propranolol. Dr. Maxwell Gelfand . . . has found it very effective in treating migraine headaches. And Dr. Norman M. Kaplan . . . says he has achieved effective temporary relief of anxiety and weight loss in some 50 patients with thyroid imbalance. (Gail Bronson, "A Case of Caution: Heart Patients in U.S. Can't Use Vital New Drugs," *Wall Street Journal*, 3/7/77, p. 18)

SERIATIM (sēr′ē-ā′tim, ser′-) *adj., adv.* in a series; singly in succession; one after another in order; point by point; serial (ly).

SERIATE *adj.* arranged or occurring in one or more series.

SERIATELY *adv.*

SERIATION noun.

1. . . . MUCKRAKERS like Fred Cook in his book, *The FBI Nobody Knows,* and Max Lowenthal in *The Federal Bureau of Investigation,* not to mention former agents like William Turner (*Hoover's FBI: The Men and the Myth*) and Norman Ollestad (*Inside the FBI*) had all, in one way or another, blown the whistle and the siren on the FBI. One difference between then and now is that until recent years the Bureau had won the public relations war. In addition to attacking the character and motives of its detractors, the Bureau encouraged Harry and Bonaro Overstreet to write *The FBI in Our Open Society,* an attempt to refute its critics SERIATUM (sic). (S. Navasky, Review of *FBI,* by Sanford J. Ungar; and *Cointelpro,* edited by Cathy Perkus, *New York Times,* 3/14/76, Section 7, p. 3)

SESQUIPEDALIAN (ses'kwi-pi-dā'lē-ən, -dāl'yən) adj. measuring a foot and one-half; very long: said of words; given to or characterized by the use of long words.

SESQUIPEDALIAN noun a long word.

SESQUIPEDALIANISM noun.

1. . . . a modest vocabulary used with skill and precision is better than a voluminous and SESQUIPEDALIAN one sloshed recklessly about with the finesse of a year-old, fingerpainting chimpanzee. (Lesley Conger, "A Writer's Alphabet," *The Writer,* May 1977, p. 8)

2. . . . not even Buckley's wittiest SESQUIPEDALIAN SONORITIES can allay the impression that he is writing [the book, *Saving the Queen*] with his foot in his cheek. (P. Gray, Review, *Time,* 1/5/76, p. 66)

SHAMAN (shā'mən, shä mən, sham'ən) noun a medicine man or witch doctor; a person who works with the supernatural as both priest and doctor.

SHAMANIC adj.

SHAMANISM noun the animistic religion of northern Asia, embracing a belief in powerful good and evil spirits who can be influenced only by shamans; any similar religion, as among the Eskimos and the Indians of the American Northwest.

1. [Anne] Waldman's poems are a kind of high-energy shorthand . . . and, most recently . . . repetitive chant-like "songs," which bring to mind tribal SHAMAN ceremonies. (Aram Saroyan, Review of *Journals & Dreams: Poems,* by Anne Waldman, *New York Times,* 4/25/76, Section 7, p. 18)

2. But perhaps [R.D.] Laing does not mean to be taken seriously . . . . Perhaps . . . he is really a SHAMAN, and SHAMANS need not operate within the frigid limits of rational discourse and canons of evidence. (A. Lacy, Review of *The Facts of Life,* by R.D. Laing; and of *R.D. Laing: The Man and His Ideas,* by Richard I. Evans, *Chronicle of Higher Education,* 5/24/76, p. 20)

3. See (4) under CYNOSURE.

4. The Democrats have won [the Presidency] without him [Senator Edward Kennedy]. The Kennedy spell had been broken by a lackluster but effective SHAMAN from Georgia . . . . And so the last of the Kennedys is being relegated to something less than regal status. (T. Tiede, "The Fading of Teddy," *Times Herald,* Norristown, Pa., 12/6/76, p. 13)

SHAMUS (shā'məs, shä'·) noun a slang expression for a private detective or policeman.

1. Twenty years after his last bow, the PARADIGM of detective-as-Lochinvar is still Raymond Chandler's incorrodable SHAMUS, Philip Marlowe. (S. Kanfer, Review of *The Life of Raymond Chandler,* by Frank McShane, *Time,* 6/21/76, p. 74)

2. Playleft Lillian Hellman preaches her own PRISTINE standards and integrity (read her books and she's the John Wayne of the militant left, rigged Joe McCarthy up to self-destruct, faced down the House Un-American Committee, created the private-SHAMUS novel, considers her almost adult-long liaison with Dashiell Hammett the tidiest life in the free intellectual world, all by her own autobiographical implications) just did the famous magazine-ad commercial for Blackglama mink coats which pays the stars of "What Becomes a Legend Most" with the freebee little animals. (J. O'Brien, "Broadway," *Times Herald,* Norristown, Pa., 2/11/77, p. 25)

3. A former college English teacher, the SHA-

MUS [Russel Wren, in the book, *Who Is Teddy Villanova?* by Thomas Berger] speaks in Victorian GRANDILOQUENT, and the burden of his remarks is composed of snippets from the Great Books and library paste. (P. Gray, Review, *Time*, 4/4/77, p. 86)

SHARD (shärd) *noun* a fragment, especially of broken earthenware; potsherd; a hard covering, as a scale or a shell (of an egg or snail; the hard wing-case of a beetle.

1. His [Peter deVries'] new novel [*I Hear America Swinging*] opens with a newly discovered SHARD from Whitman ("I hear America swinging/The carpenter with his wife or the mason's wife, or even the mason . . ." (P.S. Prescott, Review, *Newsweek*, 5/17/76, p. 109)

2. See (1) under HECATOMB.

3. The winged and SHARDED insects, the chitin-clad EPHEMERA that so greatly outnumbered all other forms of active life we see, are announcing not only a season [summer] but a whole lifetime. (Anon., "Summer" [Editorial], *New York Times*, 6/20/76, Section 4, p. 16)

4. Here was a book about a Nazi soldier who, somehow, had tripped on a SHARD of conscience, which magically restored his perspective. (W.F. Buckley Jr., *Saving the Queen*, Doubleday, 1976, p. 33)

5. . . . the brownie that crumbled in my jaws was quite OK, rather better than those of yore, from which my aunt seldom had been precise enough in eliminating SHARDS of walnut shell. (Thomas Berger, *Who Is Teddy Villanova?*, Delacorte Press/Seymour Lawrence, 1977, p. 62)

SHIBBOLETH (shib' ə-lith) *noun* a peculiarity (of pronunciation, behavior, opinion, mode of dress, custom, etc.) which distinguishes a particular class or group of people; a test word or password or favorite phrase of a party, class, sect, etc.; in the *Bible* (Judges 12: 4-6), the test word used by the Gileadites to distinguish the escaping Ephraimites, who pronounced the initial *sh* as *s*.

1. The modernists held that history was just about to begin, that limits were there to be transcended, constraints so many SHIBBOLETHS to be destroyed. (N. Birnbaum, *The Future of the Humanities* [Editorial], *Change*, Summer 1975, p. 12)

2. Beginning now, the black BOURGEOISIE should strive to break the history of financial dependency on white philanthropy. It should attempt this not out of adherence to some political SHIBBOLETH but out of plain pride of possession and desire of moderate autonomy. (K. Jackson, Jr., Review of *Black Consciousness, Identity, and Achievement: A Study of Students in Historically Black Colleges*, by Patricia Gurin and E.G. Epps, *Change*, February 1976, p. 64)

3. The facile comparison of football and the Vietnam war [*re* violence] was one of the SHIBBOLETHS of the 60's. (S. Kanfer, "Doing Violence to Sport," *Time*, 5/31/76, p. 64)

4. The idea (attributed to Vince Lombardi) that winning isn't everything, that it's the only thing, is the SHIBBOLETH of sports. It makes sports nothing more than a continuing struggle to maintain a pecking order . . . the only satisfaction is of prevailing over someone else, and the only motivation for playing is to be No. 1. (T. Tutko, "Winning Isn't Everything It's Cracked Up To Be," *New York Times*, 7/4/76, Section 5, p. 2)

5. With the ardor of a medieval dance craze men from places "of light, of liberty, and of learning" stampede toward the new SHIBBOLETHS. The highest of all . . . is unconventionality. (W. Manchester, Commencement Address, University of Massachusetts, 6/13/65, Mimeographed, p. 6)

6. His [author Harrison E. Salisbury's] questions [in the book, *Travels Around America*] are quiet, thoughtful, provocative. But he disdains the SHIBBOLETH of objectivity . . . . (W. Manchester, Review, *New York Times*, 3/6/77, Section 7, p. 33)

SHIKSA (shik' sə) *noun* a girl or woman who is not Jewish.

1. I [Jessica Mitford] looked forward to meeting [my mother-in-law] Aranka, to being clasped to the warm and loving bosom of a Jewish family . . . . Bob [my husband] was far from SANGUINE about this prospect . . . a SHIKSA of radical persuasion with a 2-year old child, he suggested, was arguably not the ideal bride

for the apple of Aranka's eye. (Jessica Mitford, "Memoirs of a Not-So-Dutiful Daughter," *New York Times*, 4/17/77, Section 6, p. 35)

SHILL (shil) *noun* a slang expression for a person who poses as a customer in order to decoy others into participating, as at a gambling house, auction, etc.

1. Mason Reese and Rodney Allen Rippy are LILLIPUTIAN super-SHILLS, lisping their TV sales pitches to the consumer millions. (J. Kroll, "The Children's Hour," *Newsweek*, 9/27/76, p. 89)

2. A series of odd jobs ranging from janitor to SHILL at a Las Vegas casino supported him [W. Michael Blumenthal, chairman of the Bendix Corp.] through the University of California at Berkeley, where he graduated Phi Beta Kappa and won a scholarship to Princeton. In five years there, he earned three graduate degrees including a Ph.D. in economics. (A.J. Mayer and Jon Lowell, "Blumenthal's Money Machine," *Newsweek*, 12/20/76, p. 82)

SHTETL (shtet'l) *noun, pl.:* **SHTETLACH** (-läkh) or **SHTETLS** any of the former Jewish village communities of Eastern Europe, especially in Russia.

1. Leonard Kriegel [author of *Notes for the Two Dollar Window: Portraits From an American Neighborhood*]'s neighborhood was a Jewish-Irish-Italian section of the northwest Bronx . . . . Lennie's OMNIPRESENT SHTETL grandmother in silent strength shakes her fist at the heavens . . . (Vivian Gornick, Review, *New York Times*, 4/18/76, Section 7, pp. 8, 10)

2. And it was to Paris that much of the best talent in other countries—the young Picasso in Spain, the young Chagall in his Russian SHTETL, the young Calder in America—was drawn for ideas and inspiration, for fellowship with other artists and a way of life in which the artistic vocation could prosper without the nagging prejudices that surrounded it elsewhere. (H. Kramer, "France's new culture palace," *New York Times*, 1/23/77, Section 6, p. 13)

SHTICK or **SCHTICK** (shtik) *noun* [Slang] a comic scene or piece of business, as in a

vaudeville act; an attention-getting device; a special trait, talent, etc.

1. In *Boy Meets Girl* [actress Marybeth] Hurt escapes from the creaky old carousel of farce with her charming and tender playing of the dumb girl whose illegitimate baby becomes a movie superstar. The other actors are forced to show off in bits of SHTIK (*sic*)—[Charles] Kimbrough's FRENETIC hack screenwriter, [Joe] Grifasi's studio tunesmith who whirls like a mad dervish to his own silly symphonies. (J. Kroll, Review, *Newsweek*, 4/26/76, p. 105)

2. She [Sharon Fields] had done it, the whole bit, the entire SHTICK—. . . desiring and promising orgasmic delight and ecstasy— and then the delivering . . . (I. Wallace, *The Fan Club*, Bantam Edition, 1975, p. 351)

3. It is certainly difficult to explain precisely what makes Steve Martin funny but what emerges is a relentless assault on show-business SCHTIK (*sic*) and pop-culture SCHLOCK. (Maureen Orth, "Silly Putty," *Newsweek*, 1/31/77, p. 59)

4. In a way they [Art Carney and Lily Tomlin] become [in the movie, *The Late Show*] the muses of Los Angeles—the slipperiest burg in America, where you can't tell life from SHTIK (*sic*). (J. Kroll, Review, *Newsweek*, 2/21/77, p. 90)

5. See (1) under PRECIOSITY.

SHUNPIKING (shun'pīk-ing) *noun* the practice of avoiding superhighways, especially for the pleasure of driving on back roads.

SHUNPIKE *verb.*

SHUNPIKER *noun.*

1. Several years ago, the word "SHUNPIKER" was coined to describe the motorist with lots of time who wanted to escape the traffic on the turnpikes and see more of the countryside . . . . But the most ardent and successful SHUNPIKER was never a hermit. The true EREMITE actually tries to escape reality and the pressures of living with mankind by hiding out on a more or less permanent basis. (Anon., "Shunpikers and Hermits," [Editorial], *Daily Oklahoman*, Okla. City, 4/14/76, p. 8)

SIBYL (sib'il) *noun* any of certain women

of antiquity reputed to possess powers of prophecy; a prophetess or witch; sorceress; fortuneteller.

SIBYLLINE (sib′ əlēn′, -lĭn) *adj.* prophetic or oracular

1. Inverting [Ruby V.] Redinger's position [in *George Eliot: The Emerging Self*], we might say George Eliot's achievement lay in her never entirely becoming George Eliot, in her continuing fidelity to her own earlier, unsatisfied, beseeching self, an uncompromising creature who lived on, tamed but not silenced, in the dispiriting Victorian SYBIL.[*] (M. Wood, Review, *New York Review of Books*, 11/27/75, p. 13)

2. Miss [Meredith] Monk, who worries about sounding PRETENTIOUS, explains the title [*Quarry*] as a "digging up of memory of racial unconsciousness. I don't want to say it's a prophecy, but I am very interested in ARCHETYPES. The one I'm coming to more and more is the oracle of the SIBYL. I'm not so PRETENTIOUS to think I am one. But when I sing, I feel the energy taking me over. The voice of the gods or something . . ." (J. Rockwell, "Meredith Monk's Tapestry of Music and Dance," *New York Times*, 3/28/76, Section 2, p. 8)

3. See (1) under MAGDALENE.

4. Willie [played by Janice Rule in the movie, *3 Women*,] is a silent, SIBYLLINE figure who paints every surface . . . with grotesque humanoid figures in which a fierce, PRIAPIC male terrorizes three females. (J. Kroll, Review, *Newsweek*, 4/18/77, p. 64)

SIMIAN (sim′ē-ən) *adj.* of, pertaining to, resembling, or characteristic of apes or monkeys.

SIMIAN *noun* an ape or monkey.

SIMIANITY *noun.*

1. These [World War II] films, as well as magazines and best-selling books, were supplying ICONS of hatred—inhuman Nazis, SIMIAN Japs and strutting Fascisti—images unlikely to lay the ground for a tolerant postwar internationalism. (P.D. Zimmerman, Review of *V Was*

---

*An erroneous spelling.

For Victory: Politics and American Culture During World War II, by John Morton Blum, *Newsweek*, 6/7/76, p. 89)

SIMULACRUM (sim′yə-lā′krəm) *noun, pl.*: -CRA (-krə) a slight, unreal, vague, deceptive, or superficial likeness or semblance; an effigy, image, likeness, or representation; a mere pretense; sham.

1. Most parents regard TV's *Sesame Street* as a benevolent baby sitter, but viewer Edward Hoagland [author of the book, *Red Wolves & Black Bears*], 43, has noticed something more. Animals, he suggests, are now an endangered species in the realm of make-believe. The Muppets are perky humanoids or cuddly monsters; Big Bird is barely the SIMULACRUM of an ostrich. (P. Gray, Review, *Time*, 5/3/76, p. K3)

2. Lacking challenge, we seek "excitement." Finding excitement unsatisfying, we look for "thrills," which provide a SIMULACRUM of hazard without subjecting us to any greater risk than choking on our beer or popcorn. (J. Lipton, "Here Be Dragons," *Newsweek*, 12/6/76, p. 17)

3. From the start, he [Samuel Beckett] was profoundly uninterested in the standard material of literature: heroes and heroines, SIMULACRA of daily reality, incidents, resolution, endings happy or otherwise. (P. Gray, Review of *Ends and Odds and Fizzles*, books by Samuel Beckett, *Time*, 2/7/77, p. 84)

SINECURE (sī′nə-kyŏor′, sĭn′ə-) *noun* an office or position requiring little or no work or responsibility, especially one yielding honor or profitable returns; a church office that pays a salary without involving care (cure) of souls.

1. There are three superb people in *The Last Chronicle* [a book by Anthony Trollope]. One is the Reverend Septimus Harding who, in the remunerative SINECURE of Warden of Hiram's Hospital, years earlier had launched Trollope in Barsetshire in *The Warden*. (J.K. Galbraith, *Political Novels Past and Present*, *New York Times*, 9/12/76, Section 7, p. 18)

2. Never since Australia gained independence in 1901 has there been such a storm surround-

ing an office [the Governor Generalship] that always had been considered a SINECURE for lesser royalty, retired generals and faded politicians [until John Kerr assumed the office in 1974]. (B. Newman, "Angst in Australia," *Wall Street Journal,* 3/23/77, p. 1)

SINE QUA NON (sī′ ne kwä nōn′, sī′ nē kwä nōn′, sin′ā kwä nōn′) something essential; an indispensable condition or requirement; an absolute prerequisite.

1. See (2) under OMNISCIENT.

2. But to the guardians of a high technology society, chrome is the SINE QUA NON that makes modern defense tick. It is the only available component that can be alloyed with other metals to withstand high temperatures under extreme stress. There could be no space program without chrome. Nuclear submarines are dependent on it. So are jet planes. Ditto for missiles. (J. Chamberlain, "Rhodesian Chrome Vital for Nation," *Daily Oklahoman,* Okla. City, 4/15/76, p. 12)

3. And most [adult students] assume that teachers and classrooms are the SINE QUA NON for learning. (H.I. London, "The Case for Non-traditional Learning," *Change,* June 1976, p. 27)

4. Of course, H.G. Wells is the SINE QUA NON of technological crystal-balling, and probably the best way to get technological assessment done these days is still . . . by reading good science fiction. (Anon., "A special issue of Smithsonian as America's third century begins," [Editors' Introduction], *Smithsonian,* July 1976, p. 26)

5. I have finally found an organization I can wholeheartedly support . . . the letter that announced the organization to me had no title on it, but it did have a nonprofit mailing permit— the SINE QUA NON of all worthwhile organizations. This one is against the mowing of lawns. (R. Cohen, of the *Washington Post,* "Guinea pig new lawn mower," *Norman* [Okla.] *Transcript,* 7/16/76, p. 7)

6. Graduate schools too have found that applicants have less proficiency in those subjects [reading, writing, arithmetic] once regarded

as SINE QUA NON of all learning and the responsibility has been placed largely on the shift in colleges from required courses to electives. (Anon., "Too Many Poor Scores" [Editorial reproduced from St. Louis Post-Dispatch], *Times Herald,* Norristown,Pa., 9/17/76, p. 10)

SINISTRAL (sin′i-strəl) *adj.* of, pertaining to, or on the left-hand side; left (as opposed to right); left-handed; having whorls that rise to the apex in clockwise spirals: said of the shells of certain mollusks with the apex toward the viewer.

SINISTRALLY *adv.*

SINISTRALITY *noun.*

SINISTRAD *adv.* to the left; leftward; sinistrally.

1. Ms. [Sue] Alpert . . . runs a mail-order firm called The Left Handed Complement here [in Anaheim, Calif.] that supplies such items as left-handed mustache cups, cameras and boomerangs to the estimated 15-20 per cent of the population that is SINISTRAL, or left-handed . . . . Her company is now selling more than 125 products nationwide, including SINISTRAL coffee pots, scissors (the biggest seller), can openers and potato peelers. (S. Fox (AP), "Left-Handers get right items," *Norman* [Okla.] *Transcript,* 7/11/76, p. 5)

SINUOUS (sin′yōō-əs) or **SINUATE** *adj.* having many curves, bends, or turns; wavy; winding; indirect; not straightforward; crooked; devious; twisting; curved; serpentine; coiled; twining; roundabout.

SINUOUSLY or **SINUATELY** *adv.*

SINUOUSNESS or **SINUOSITY** or **SINUATION** *noun.*

SINUATE *verb* to curve or wind in and out; to be sinuous or wavy.

1. See (1) under SLAVER.

2. The lines are soft and flowing. The MANNEQUINS [in the retrospective show, *Paul Poiret, King of Fashion*] in SINUOUS crepes and sheer cottons do not wear bras . . . . There are headwraps, boots, harem pants. (Phyllis Feldkamp, Review, *New York Times,* 6/13/76, Section 6, p. 59)

SISYPHEAN (sis'ə-fē'ən) *adj.* of, pertaining to, or like Sisyphus; endless, toilsome, and unavailing, as labor or a task.

SISYPHUS (sis'ə-fəs) (in Greek Mythology) a son of Aeolus and greedy ruler of Corinth, noted for his trickery: he was punished in Tartarus (Hades) by being forever compelled to roll a heavy stone to the top of a slope, the stone escaping him near the top and rolling down again.

1. He [Harvard sociologist Nathan Glazer, in the book, *Affirmative Discrimination*] has written a tempered, factually argued, vigorous POLEMIC against the predominant drift of public policy on racial issues over the past decade. He demonstrates that the Government effort to make good on President Johnson's promise "to fulfill these rights [to equality as a fact] . . . has led to an increasingly tangled skein of lawsuits, busing orders and racial quotas. . . ." With regard to the aggressive efforts of the Federal courts . . . to realign school populations in order to achieve an ideal racial balance, Glazer is illuminating on the SISYPHEAN nature of this task. (W. V. Shannon, Review, *New York Times*, 2/8/76, Section 7, p. 4)

2. The same note echoes through all of his [Gore Vidal's] writings. Affairs are in the hands of PARVENUS and thugs; the best and the brightest cannot bail out the sinking ship. Vidal obviously considers himself among this SISYPHEAN elite. His tone is that of the seer scorned. (Anon., "Gore Vidal: Laughing Cassandra," *Time*, 3/1/76, p. 61)

3. In Greek mythology, SISYPHUS is doomed to push a rock uphill. Every time he gets it there, it rolls down again. That's about the way it is with Philadelphia jazz. Although it has its ups and downs, jazz is very much available in the Philadelphia area. (B. Thompson, "A Guide to jazz," *Philadelphia Inquirer*, 10/15/76, p. 1-C)

SLAVER (slav'ər, slā'vər, slä'-) *verb* to let saliva trickle from the mouth; slobber; drool; to cover with saliva or slobber on.

SLAVER *noun* saliva drooling from the mouth.

1. Pandarus [in the Yale Repertory Theater's production of Shakespeare's *Troilus and Cressida*] is not quite the SLAVERING pimp we look for, and make a legend of, not quite the probably impotent VOYEUR who contrives his own satisfaction out of assignations SINUOUSLY arranged. (W. Kerr, Review, *New York Times*, 4/18/76, Section 2, p. 5)

SLUD (slud) or SLUDDER *noun* a slippery mass (as of mud or slush).

1. Tapes of these sessions [monthly meetings of writers and top editors of L.A. Times] . . . would show that my colleagues and I were very sparing in our use of the kind of words Mrs. Lyman objects to [words used in the Washington Post newsroom in the movie, *All the President's Men*], but we used them without apology—just as we might use SPINDRIFT, EGREGIOUS or SLUD—when no other word would do . . Most of us can use an obscene or blasphemous word when the circumstances require one, but we are not wasteful of these precious parts of speech. (J. Smith, *Los Angeles Times*, "Obscenity sometimes becomes a routine," *Norman* [Okla.] *Transcript*, 8/8/76, p. 6)

SLUGABED (slug'ə-bed') *noun* a lazy person who stays in bed after others are up.

1. Most humanities professors [at state universities in Colorado], those unfunded SLUGABEDS, have to be kept alive on "Denver dollars." Science professors make little demand on the limited—and shrinking—pool of state funds. In many cases, only *one* of their "ninths" comes from Denver. The other 10½ ninths [of their salaries]—substantially more than $40,000 on a gross, say, of $50,000— comes from Washington. (R. Zoellner, "Are Teaching Professors Automatically Losers?," *The Chronicle of Higher Education*, 6/28/76, p. 40)

2. Your typical early-bird day person . . . is a physical, outdoorsy, success-driven doer who zips out of bed at dawn and has everything done by lunch time. Your average SLUG-A-BED night owl on the other hand, functions poorly, if at all, during daylight hours and the very thought of a jog through the park at sunrise is enough to drive him to drink into the wee small hours—as will anything else. (A. Hoppe, "Night and day do mix," *Philadelphia Inquirer*, 6/7/77, p. 7-A)

SMARMY (smär´mē) *adj.* British informal: excessively, FULSOMELY, or UNCTUOUSLY flattering, fawning, ingratiating, servile, affectionate, etc.; speaking obsequiously; (of hair) plastered-down.

SMARM or **SMARMINESS** *noun* British informal: trite, CLOYING sentimentality.

1. Devane [in the film, *Family Plot*] is the ultimate Hitchcock villain who cannot quite repress a vicious, toothy grin from breaking through his suave, SMARMY manner. (Katrine Ames, Review, *Newsweek*, 4/5/76, p. 86)

2. About "glamorizing" SMARMY characters: well, yes, it is disturbing, although one of the characteristics of egomaniacs like John Dane [who claimed on "60 minutes" that the Jewish Defense League had offered him $250,000 to assassinate Yasir Arafat] . . . is that they must be flattered if they are to talk at all. (J. Leonard, "In Praise of Nasty Surprises," *New York Times*, 5/16/76, Section 2, p. 29)

3. Utterly lamentable, too, is [Marlon] Brando's performance [in the film, *The Missouri Breaks*] . . . . Starting with a correspondence-school brogue and bits of mannerisms left over from *The Nightcomers*, he adds to them an EFFETENESS and SMARMINESS that would keep even the likes of Braxton from hiring him, he comes across as a mixture of Rod Steiger doing *Hennessy* and Tallulah Bankhead doing Tallulah. (J. Simon, Review, *New York*, 5/31/76, p. 75)

4. SMARMY as this may sound to any fan used to high-voltage tales about the profligate life of rock stars, [Paul] McCartney draws enough sustenance from his rigorously imposed family structure to have it re-created for the current Wings tour. (Anon., "McCartney Comes Back," *Time*, 5/31/76, p. 43)

SMORGASBORD (smôr´ gəs-bōrd´ , -bôrd´) *noun* a buffet meal of a wide variety of hot and cold appetizers (hors d'oeuvres), salads, casserole dishes, fish, meats, cheeses, etc.

1. The official sculpture produced in the United States in the 19th century is, for the most part, an unrelieved tale of genteel pieties and patriotic sentiments in an unholy alliance with FLACCID forms and second-rate ideas. To serve up this SMORGASBORD of provincial monuments and mementos as if it were a feast of artistic delicacies is an absurdity, but that . . . is what *200 Years of American Sculpture* [an exhibition at the Whitney Museum of American Art] succeeds in doing. (H. Kramer, Review, *New York Times*, 3/28/76, Section 2, p. 34)

2. For the opening exhibition [of the Cooper-Hewitt Museum] she [director Lisa Taylor] chose Hans Hollein . . . , who in turn invited nine wide-ranging international talents to design special exhibits and rooms . . . . The result is an amazingly varied SMORGASBORD—too varied, perhaps. (D. Davis, "Grand Designs," *Newsweek*, 10/18/76, p. 104)

SNIDE (snīd) *adj.* derogatory in a nasty, insinuating manner; slyly malicious or derisive.

SNIDELY *adv.*

SNIDENESS *noun.*

1. Not all the newsmen and newswomen in [Spiro] Agnew's novel [*The Canfield Decision*] are terminated with such extreme prejudice [*i.e.*, murdered], however. Most are merely consigned to the ovens of the author's CONTUMELY. Scarcely a page . . . fails to include some SNIDE mention of the press . . . . (D. Shaw, *Los Angeles Times*, "Agnew 'murders' media and other 'nattering nabobs,' " *Norman* [Okla.]*Transcript*, 5/23/76, p. 17)

SOBRIQUET (sō´ brə-kā´ , -ket´) or **SOUBRIQUET** *noun* a nickname; an assumed name.

1. In many parts of the world last week, soldiers of fortune—and those who openly accepted the less elegant SOBRIQUET of "mercenaries"—were laying plans and packing bags [for Angola]. (R. Carroll, *et al.*, "The Mercenary Life," *Newsweek*, 2/9/76, p. 30)

2. These multiple enterprises have . . . earned him [Earl Blackwell] the obvious SOBRIQUET "The Pearl Mesta of show business." (M. Goodman, "Earl Blackwell Chronicles and Entertains Celebrities—For Their Pleasure and His Profit," *People*, 5/24/76, p. 68)

3. Twenty years ago [New York] Giant pitcher

Sal Maglie was given the SOBRIQUET "The Barber" because of the close shaves his fast ball gave the faces of the hitters. (S. Kanfer, "Doing Violence to Sport," *Time*, 5/31/76, p. 64)

4. [William Jennings] Bryan was called "The Great Commoner." His SOUBRETTE (*sic:* should be SOBRIQUET) derives from "The Commoner" weekly political journal he edited in Lincoln, Neb. [Jimmy] Carter constantly features his peanut farmer image as a shirt-sleeve fellow in Plains, Ga. (H.J. Taylor, "Intriguing Comparisons," *Times Herald*, Norristown, Pa., 9/1/76, p. 19)

5. See (2) under SARTORIAL.

6. The university [Stanford] . . . , founded in 1885 by railroad magnate and politician Leland Stanford, began rising to national prominence in the 1950's, earning along the way the SOBRIQUET "Harvard of the West." (W. Wong, "Harvard West?," *Wall Street Journal*, 9/23/76, p. 1)

SOCKDOLAGER (sok-dol′ ə-jər) or **SOCK-DOLOGER** *noun* *Slang:* something unusually large, heavy, outstanding, etc.; a heavy, finishing blow; finisher; something so effective or forceful as to be final or decisive [coinage based on *sock* (a blow) plus *doxology* (in slang sense of *finish*)].

1. I nearly fell out of my chair when I read a statement on the American corporation made by Eugene J. McCarthy, who should be on the ballot in a fair number of states by November . . . The real McCarthy SOCKDOLAGER concerned the oil industry. "Of all major industries," he said, "the oil companies are probably the most competitive. Certainly they are more competitive than the major automobile companies . . . . If the oil companies are to be faulted, it is for having provided the country with too much inexpensive oil and gasoline, in consequence of which wasteful, over-sized automobiles were developed, and wasteful fuel consumption practices followed both in industry and in consumer use." (J. Chamberlain, "Some Common Sense," *Times Herald*, Norristown, Pa., 9/7/76, p. 13)

SODOMY (sod′ ə-mē) *noun* unnatural, especially anal, sexual intercourse with a man, woman, or animal; bestiality.

SODOMITE or **ṢODOMITE** *noun* (if lower case) a person who practices sodomy; (if capitalized) an inhabitant of Sodom.

ṢODOM *noun* an ancient city destroyed, with Gomorrah, because of its wickedness (see Gen. 18-19); any very sinful, corrupt, vice-ridden place.

1. "From all we know," Boris shouted, "he [Teddy Villanova] may well be a POLYMORPHOUS pervert, as ready to SODOMIZE a man as flog a strumpet or molest a child of either sex." (Thomas Berger, *Who Is Teddy Villanova?*, Delacorte Press/Seymour Lawrence, 1977, p. 218)

2. "He possessed what was surely one of the world's most extensive collections of indecent literature and pictorial art, all of the SODOMIST persuasion . . ." [said Donald Washburn]. (Thomas Berger, *Ibid.*, p. 170)

3. . . . I [Russel Wren] slunk to the corner, where one of the new public-phone arrangements stood . . . . Involved in a conversation, you might have your pockets picked—or, in certain areas . . . , be quickly, deftly SODOMIZED while making an apology for dialing a wrong number. (Thomas Berger, *Ibid.*, p. 111)

SOI-DISANT (SWA dē-zäN′) *adj.* calling oneself thus; alleging oneself to be; self-styled; so-called or pretended.

1. . . . in his earliest days it is said that [Lorenz] Hart often provided lyrics for others, extracting little or no payment in return. (There is a fascinating tale . . . in both books [*Thou Swell, Thou Witty*, Edited and with a Memoir by Dorothy Hart; *Rodgers & Hart*, by Samuel Marx and Jan Clayton] about the $100 bills handed him by Billy Rose, then a producer and SOI-DISANT composer. There is no absolute proof as to which Rose songs actually contained the Hart lyrics, but one can guess at those with Hart's intricate rhyming.) (B. Short, Review, *New York Times*, 11/21/76, Section 7, p. 3)

SOIGNÉ (swän-yā′) *adj.* carefully or elegantly done, operated, or designed; neat; tidy; well-groomed; well cared for or attended to.

SOIGNÉE *adj.* the feminine form of soigné.

1. Exotically beautiful women [at the wedding of Marisa Berenson and James. H. Randall] elegantly kissed the air alongside each other's ears, lest they smudge their lip gloss, while SOIGNÉ men worked the room, embracing each other. There were far too many choice celebrities to linger long with just one. (Dewey Gram and Jeanne Gordon, "Marriage, Marisa Style," *Newsweek*, 12/6/76, p. 102)

2. A few months back, we sampled a minceur dinner prepared by M. Guérard himself at Régine's, a SOIGNÉ local B.P. hangout, and found it memborable, innovative and refreshingly free from caloric aftershock. (Anon., "Book Ends," *New York Times*, 2/27/77, Section 7, p. 37)

3. He [publisher John B. Fairchild] took WWD [Women's Wear Daily], a dullish trade journal for the women's and children's clothing and cosmetic industries, and spiced it up with photographs and chatty copy about the Beautiful People ("BPs") such as Jacqueline Kennedy Onassis . . . . WWD staffers staked out BP haunts like La Grenouille, the SOIGNÉE Manhattan restaurant that Mr. Fairchild calls "The Frogpond." (Deborah Sue Yaeger, "Middle-Aged Slump: Women's Wear Daily Loses Some of Its Clout in the Fashion World." *Wall Street Journal*, 5/12/77, p. 1)

SOLECISM (sol'i-siz'əm) *noun* a substandard or ungrammatical usage of words; any mistake, breach of propriety, or inconsistency; a breach of good manners or etiquette.

SOLECIST *noun.*

SOLECISTIC or SOLECISTICAL *adj.*

SOLECISTICALLY *adv.*

1. What Mr. [Lucien] Bodard [author of *The French Consul*, translated by Barbara Bray] makes a glorious naval battle was in fact a much more complex encounter in which the Chinese . . . offered fierce resistance. This is a liberty, a minor defect in the book, but an annoying SOLECISM . . . (P. Theroux, Review, *New York Times*, 3/27/77, Section 7, p. 41)

2. "Does the palace have a listed number?" [Blackford Oakes asked]. The Queen [Caroline] laughed. "Over here [in England], Mr. Oakes, we say: 'Is the palace's number ex-directory?' " Blackford knew that, but knew

also that idiomatic American SOLECISMS carried one further, in certain circumstances, than total acclimatization. He smiled. "I'm glad you're in the book." (W.F. Buckley Jr., *Saving the Queen*, Doubleday, 1976, p. 131)

SOLIPSISM (sol'ip-siz'əm) *noun* the theory that the self can be aware of nothing but its own experiences and states; the theory that only the self exists or can be proved to exist.

SOLIPSISMAL *adj.*

SOLIPSIST *noun* or *adj.*

SOLIPSISTIC *adj.*

1. See (1) under FUSTIAN.

2. I recently refused to accept, as a topic for a graduate term paper, an astrological interpretation of *Ulysses* . . . . "Astrology," I said, "implies that the earth is the center of the universe." To which he [the Ph.D. candidate] replied, "I feel that it is." . . . . For a moment I felt that I was in the presence of madness; then I thought, No, he's not insane, he's just a SOLIPSIST. This is SOLIPSISM, nothing more. . . . For SOLIPSISM so unquestioning makes rational discourse impossible. . . . A conversation between Humpty Dumpty and Mr. Pickwick wouldn't get anywhere. Nevertheless, these two SOLIPSISTS are English majors now, and they are everywhere. (J.M. Morse, "Nothing Is True, Nothing Is False," *Chronicle of Higher Education*, 4/5/76, p. 40)

3. See (3) under DERACINATE.

4. It is hard to know when the solitary ego [of Howard Hughes] yielded to a kind of SOLIPSISM—the belief that it alone existed and no one else counted. (M. Lerner, "No woman with him when he died: He cared for money and power," *Norman* [Okla.] *Transcript*, 4/22/76, p. 6)

5. Philosophers of science say that it is only by . . . wedging of details into theory that scientists can find the subtle SOLIPSISMS between idea and reality that lead to new theories. (J.K. Page Jr., "Frontiers," *Smithsonian*, July 1976, p. 16)

6. See (4) under TORPID.

7. The pure woman-on-woman story can eventually become an exercise in SOLIPSISM . . .

this intensive GENRE is on the way to creating new stereotypes of its own . . . . (Robie Macauley, Review of *In the Looking Glass: Twenty-one Modern Short Stories by Women*, edited by Nancy Dean and Myra Stark, *New York Times*, 3/27/77, Section 7, p. 7)

8. The self-indulgence, SOLIPSISM, crankiness and spite of [Erica] Jong's new opus [*How To Save Your own Life*] can be perversely amusing. But underlying everything is an irritating DISINGENUOUSNESS. Jong is a real performer, but this time she is too unbecomingly petty to be entertaining. (Janet Maslin, Review, *Newsweek*, 3/28/77, p. 83)

9. See (1) under AUTISM.

SOMMELIER (sum' əl-yā, sô-mə-lyā') *noun* a wine waiter or wine steward, as in a club or restaurant.

1. I thought this dish [a salmon mousse] an insult at $5 a serving [at the Palace Court, in Las Vegas, Nevada], but it turned out to be a veritable loss leader compared with my dealings with the SOMMELIER, a man better versed in the ways of P.T. Barnum than of Alex Lichine . . . . The vintages were dull, the prices hideous. (R. Vare, "Where Dining Is a Big Gamble, "National Observer, week ending 4/2/77, p. 11-B)

2. At times as many as five people may be milling around a table [at New York's Palace Restaurant]: tuxedoed waiters explaining the menu . . . the SOMMELIER suggesting a wine, a busboy refilling your water glass and another whisking away a barely used ashtray. (R.B. May, "At New York's Palace Restaurant Time Isn't of Essence, but Money Is," *Wall Street Journal*, 3/23/77, p. 26)

SOMNAMBULATE (som-nam' byə-lāt') *verb* to get up and move about in a trancelike state while asleep.

SOMNAMBULANT *adj.*

SOMNAMBULATION *noun.*

SOMNAMBULATOR *noun.*

SOMNAMBULISM *noun* the act or habit of walking about, and often performing various other acts, while asleep; sleepwalking; the trancelike state of one who somnambulates.

SOMNAMBULIST *noun.*

SOMNAMBULISTIC *adj.*

SOMNAMBULISTICALLY *adv.*

1. But [Michelangelo's] *Crucifixion* fresco . . . projects painful detachment from action . . . : The henchmen about the cross revolve like SOMNAMBULISTS; the soldiers at the lower left come unwillingly; and the horsemen are too marginal in the design to activate a humanity given over to resignation. (L. Steinberg, "Michelangelo's last painting: his gift to this century," *Smithsonian*, December 1975, p. 82)

2. With her bangs and braids, puff-sleeved mini-dresses, great doe eyes and dreamy, SOMNAMBULANT voice, [Louise] Lasser's Mary [in the TV soap opera, *Mary Hartman, Mary Hartman*] is the APOTHEOSIS of a child-woman trying to grow up before she cracks up. (H.F. Waters and M. Kasindorf, "The Mary Hartman Craze," *Newsweek*, 5/3/76, p. 55)

SONOROUS (sə-nôr' əs, -nôr' -, son' ər-es) *adj.* emitting or capable of emitting a sound, especially a deep, resonant sound, as a thing or place; loud, deep, or resonant, as a sound; rich and full in sound, as language, verse, etc.; high-flown; GRANDILOQUENT.

SONOROUSLY *adv.*

SONOROUSNESS *noun.*

SONORITY *noun* the condition or quality of being resonant or sonorous; resonance.

1. This [*Interview With A Vampire*, a book by Anne Rice] is the tape-recorded memoir of a *reluctant* vampire whose SONOROUS GRANDILOQUENCE is absolutely unparalleled in the annals of things that go bump in the night. (Alix Nelson, Review, *Ms.*, May 1976, p. 27)

2. Since 1969, when Milan-born [Claudio] Abbado became music director of LaScala, he has labored to bring the orchestra to a concert pitch rare among opera orchestras, which are used to playing the less-refined SONORITIES of opera. (H. Saal, "Nights at the Opera," *Newsweek*, 9/27/76, p. 107)

3. See (2) under SESQUIPEDALIAN.

SOPHISTRY (sof'ĭ-strē) or **SOPHISM** *noun*

a subtle, tricky, superficially plausible but generally fallacious method of reasoning, especially if used to deceive or defeat someone; a false argument; fallacy.

SOPHIST *noun* (in ancient Greece) any of a class of professional teachers of philosophy, rhetoric, etc., noted for their ingenuity and SPECIOUS argumentation; a learned person; any person practicing clever, SPECIOUS reasoning.

SOPHISTIC or SOPHISTICAL *adj.* of the nature of sophistry, sophism, or sophists; clever and plausible, but unsound and tending to mislead; fallacious.

SOPHISTICALLY *adv.*

1. At the moment the nation is very much attracted by the SOPHISM of Professor [John Kenneth] Galbraith . . . , namely that we are not as consumers really free, inasmuch as we are pawns of the advertising agencies. (W.F. Buckley Jr., *Up From Liberalism*, Arlington House, 2nd Printing 1968, p. 207)

2. A New York University coed talked eloquently [at a recent Harvard conference on the liberal arts] . . . in terms of fundamental choices . . . . "We must all be very clear that we are not discussing delectable SOPHISTRIES, but actions and events that drive to the VISCERA of whether our children's children will be around to work in that nourishing . . . garden of Thomas Huxley's." (G.W. Bonham, "Some Vexing Questions About the Liberal Arts," [Editorial], *Change*, May 1976, p. 12)

3. See (1) under HERCYNIAN.

SOUBRETTE (soo-bret′) *noun* (in the theater) a lady's maid or maidservant, especially a pretty, coquettish one involved in intrigue; any pretty, flirtatious, or frivolous young woman character; an actress who plays such roles; any vivacious, lively, or pert young woman.

1. The dance [Balanchine's *The Steadfast Tin Soldier*] is continuously absorbing, . . . and [Patricia] McBride brings an ageless vitality to the doll's character. She has the sparkle of an experienced SOUBRETTE . . . (Arlene Croce, Review, *The New Yorker*, 2/9/76, p. 94)

2. See (1) under TERMAGANT.

SOUPÇON (soop-sôN′, soop′ sôN) *noun* a slight trace or flavor; hint; suggestion; suspicion; a very small amount; bit.

1. "I hit it big with [the book] *The Eagle Has Landed* [said its author Harry Patterson], which is also now a film, and continued with my formula of stressing character. It involves a SOUPÇON of history, plus documentary fact and fiction, usually centered on World War II." (H. Mitgang, "Behind the Best Sellers: Harry Patterson," *New York Times*, 4/24/77, Section 7, p. 46)

2. There's page after page of information [in *Condominium*, by John D. MacDonald] on building codes, . . . , tide tables, wind currents, mixed drinks. But far from overwhelming us, MacDonald delivers this barrage of factual material in such tidy doses—interspersed with a little sex here, a SOUPÇON of violence there—that our interest never flags. (D.G. Snell, Review, *Barron's*, 6/20/77, p. 26)

3. The . . . [Cole] Porter career is one beloved by backstage biographers. As Brendan Gill's brisk, uncritical [book] *Cole* showed, the life was filled with laughter, tragedy, a SOUPÇON of scandal and above and below all, money. (G. Clarke, Review of *Cole Porter, A Biography*, by Charles Schwarz, *Time*, 7/25/77, p. 64)

SPATE (spāt) *noun* a sudden rush or outpouring of words, emotion, customers, etc.; (in British usage) a flood.

1. See (2) under SANCTIMONIOUS.

2. Walter Spink, professor of Indian Art at the University of Michigan, who has been working more than a decade on the detailed analysis of the caves, believes that all the . . . painting at Ajanta [in India] was done, in one SPATE of furious activity, from about A.D. 460 to 480. (Madhur Jaffrey, "Ancient beauty of Ajanta's painted caves is restored," *Smithsonian*, August 1967, p. 35)

3. See (4) under DE RIGUEUR.

4. See (3) under AILUROPHILE.

SPAVINED (spav′ind) *adj.* suffering from or afflicted with spavin (a disease of the hock joint of horses in which enlargement occurs due to collection of fluids, bony growth, or distention of the veins, and which usually causes lameness); being in a decrepit condition; lame.

1. After the landscape we are shown [in the book, *Hills of Home*, by Bob Minick] the houses, the SPAVINED barns, the weathered front porches with rush-bottomed chairs. (M., Kernan, Review, *Smithsonian*, December 1975, p. 133)

2. This comedy [*The New York Idea*, by Langdon Mitchell] was written by a Harvard-educated lawyer and first presented in 1906. The play is surprisingly UNSPAVINED by age. (T.E. Kalem, Review, *Time*, 4/11/77, p. 88)

3. Boris turned [the van] right and shot through the routine filthy side street of parked cars, SPAVINED dogs, scarred cats, and a living gallery of manifest rogues . . . (Thomas Berger, *Who Is Teddy Villanova?*, Delacorte Press/Seymour Lawrence, 1977, p. 201)

SPECIOUS (spē'shəs) *adj.* seemingly good, sound, correct, logical, etc., but lacking real merit; plausible but not genuine; pleasing to the eye but deceptive; misleading.

SPECIOUSLY *adv.*

SPECIOUSNESS *noun.*

1. Women sense . . . that the institution of rape is mysteriously protected by an armor of folklore, Bible tales, legal precedents, SPECIOUS psychological theories. Most of all it seems protected by a rooted and IMPLACABLE male belief that women want to be raped . . . (Diane Johnson, "The War Between Men and Women," *New York Review of Books*, 12/11/75, p. 36)

2. See (6) under NIHILISM.

3. See (5) under KITSCH.

4. . . . [Steven] Kellogg [illustrator of the children's book, *Yankee Doodle*, by Edward Bangs] was convinced by the editors at Parents' [Magazine Press] that the familiar chorus [of the song, *Yankee Doodle*] was "sexist." So, instead of the traditional "Mind the music and the step/And with the girls be handy," the last line now reads "And with the folks be handy." Kellogg explains . . . that "this Bicentennial edition alters that very chorus to suit the realities of our own [time]." . . . . This is SPECIOUS logic of the highest order. . . . such misguided sensitivity is . . . a triumph for the . . . people who want to integrate "penpersonship" and "personkind" into the English language. (S.

Krensky, Review, *New York Times*, 5/2/76, Section 7, p. 27)

5. Yes, there is most assuredly something SPECIOUS about the history-as-reflected-in-postage-stamps technique of imparting knowledge to the young. But frankly, we stamp collectors welcome and celebrate any and all such books [as *A Stamp Collector's History of the United States*, by Samuel A. Tower; *History Through Stamps*, by David Keep; *The Bible Through Stamps*, by Ord Matek; *Stamps Tell the Story of Space Travel*, by Emery Kelen]. (C. Lehmann-Haupt, Review, *New York Times*, 5/2/76, Section 7, p. 44)

6. See (4) under SPURIOUS.

SPELEOLOGY (spē' lē-ol' ə-jē') *noun* the exploration and scientific study of caves.

SPELEOLOGIST *noun.*

SPELEOLOGICAL *adj.*

SPELAEAN or SPELEAN *adj.* of, relating to, or like a cave; dwelling in caves.

1. If you are a weekend SPELEOLOGIST and you also happen to have got most of the way up Mount Everest on your own two feet, you are just the person to get the most out of Project Studios One, the new art center which is now open to visitors in Long Island City, Queens. Until 1963 P.S. 1 was a school. Roughly the size of the Plaza Hotel . . . , it dominates the landscape for some way around. (J. Russell, "An Unwanted School in Queens Becomes an Ideal Art Center," *New York Times*, 6/20/76, Section 2, p. 41)

SPELUNKER (spi-luńg'kər) *noun* a person who explores caves as a hobby.

SPELUNKING *noun.*

SPELUNK *verb.*

1. She [Paula Fox, author of *The Widow's Children*] makes difficulties for herself in writing fiction, approaches a novel like a SPE-LUNKER; hunching slowly over real rocks, the searchlight on her forehead describing delicate arcs in the darkness; her beam makes pleasing patterns, but there's not much room for an audience. (P.S. Prescott, Review, *Newsweek*, 9/27/76, p. 100)

PIFF (spif) *noun* push money, *i.e.* a commission paid (as by a manufacturer) to a salesperson to push the sale of a particular item or one of merchandise.

, SPIFFING—or paying a retail clerk to push a manufacturer's product—is defended not only as an effective marketing technique but as a practice given legal justification by the Robinson-Patman Act . . . . One justification for SPIFFING is that the product involved, often an electrical appliance, already has been purchased from the manufacturer before the clerk is paid to promote it. (J. Cunniff, "Scandals presage domestic turmoil? Business corruption may come home," *Norman* [Okla.] *Transcript*, 5/19/76, p. 6)

PILLIKIN (spil' ə-kin) *noun* a jackstraw; *plural* form with *singular* verb] the game of jackstraws.

, "Don't be bamboozled by their size: these individuals [young girls] are wily degenerates said Boris to Russel Wren? Their games are not the SPILLIKINS and CONUNDRUMS that Jane Austen played with young relatives; they are rather the decadent Roman entertainments that followed Trimalchio's feast." (Thomas Berger, *Who Is Teddy Villanova?*, Delacorte Press/Seymour Lawrence, 1977, p. 202)

PINDRIFT (spin' drift) or **SPOONDRIFT** *noun* spray swept by a violent wind along the surface of the sea.

, Tapes of these sessions [monthly meetings of writers and top editors of L.A. Times] . . . would show that my colleagues and I were very sparing in our use of the kind of words Mrs. Lyman objects to [words used in the Washington Post newsroom in the movie, *All the President's Men*], but we used them without apology—just as we might use SPINDRIFT, GREGIOUS or SLUD—when no other word would do . . . . Most of us can use an obscene or blasphemous word when the circumstances require one, but we are not wasteful of these precious parts of speech. (J. Smith, *Los Angeles Times*, "Obscenity sometimes becomes a routine," *Norman* [Okla.] *Transcript*, 8/8/76, . 6)

PLENETIC (spli-net' ik) or **SPLENETICAL**

adj. irritable; bad-tempered; peevish; spiteful; IRASCIBLE; testy; petulant; of the spleen.

SPLENETIC *noun* a splenetic person.

SPLENETICALLY *adv.*

1. "The battle of books has broken out again," rejoiced Marshall McLuhan 30 years ago in a typically ORGIASTIC essay on philosophies of higher learning. "The SPLENETIC interchanges of educators and scholars . . . are shrieking across the no man's land of the curriculum." (R.J. Margolis, "Let's Hear It for Moveable Type," [Editorial], *Change*, April 1975, p. 5)

2. Lancelot Lamar [in the book, *Lancelot*, by Walker Percy], like the protagonists of all of Percy's novels, is a "somewhat lapsed" man, a victim of ACCIDIE, that SPLENETIC sense of uselessness and alienation, who has come to the end of his rope. (P.S. Prescott, Review, *Newsweek*, 2/28/77, p. 73)

3. On Third Ave. I [Russel Wren] caught a cab and had to endure the abuse of the driver when I confessed that I hadn't yet thought of where I was going . . . . "I'll tell you this," he assured me SPLENETICALLY, "I'm putting the meter on while you decide." (Thomas Berger, *Who Is Teddy Villanova?*, Delacorte Press/Seymour Lawrence, 1977, p. 109)

SPOONERISM (spoō' nə-riz' əm) *noun* the interchange or transposition of initial or other sounds in two or more words, usually by accident [after W.A. Spooner (1844-1930), English clergyman of New College, Oxford, noted for such slips of the tongue].

1. History remembers the Rev. Dr. William A. Spooner as warden of New College, Oxford, in the early 1900's and as a famous classicist. Language students remember him for his famous slips of the tongue . . . Some of his . . . delicious distortions include: (addressing a rural audience) "Noble tons of soil"; (on observing a fight) "He delivered a blushing crow." Perhaps Spooner's best known blooper is the one he uttered in what was intended as a graceful reference to Queen Victoria. This came out as "the queer old dean" instead of "the dear old Queen." Over the years such errors of speech have become known as SPOONERISMS . . . . William Spooner's finest example (on dismissing an inadequate student): "You have hissed all

my mystery lectures. You have tasted the whole worm, and must leave by the first town drain." (C. Panati, "Tips of the Slongue," *Newsweek*, 7/26/76, p. 80)

SPOOR (spŏŏr, spôr, spŏr) *noun* a track or trail, especially of a wild animal hunted as game or of a person.

SPOOR *verb* to track by or follow a spoor.

1. The beauty of the tales [in *The Snow Walker*, by Farley Mowat] purge, exhaust, draw us out of our skin, but the pain involved is so deep that we feel the free-floating remorse that characterizes modern man on those rare occasions he has the wit and humility to turn around and look at his SPOOR. (J. Harrison, Review, *New York Times*, 2/22/76, Section 7, p. 4)

2. The true nature of the bloodhound is little understood by most people. That scarifying SANGUINARY name has nothing to do with their lusting for blood or even with following blood SPOOR . . . . (R. Caras, "A Boy's Best Dog," *New York Times*, 3/14/76, Section 6, p. 82)

3. [Caption under a picture of trash containing the sign: "Help keep the Baja clean so it dozent look like America!"]: Uncollected trash MIDDENS—SPOOR of the tourist—pile up at Bahía Concepción in Baja California. (T.W. Pew Jr., "The blacktopping—and littering—of Baja California," *Smithsonian*, January 1976, p. 82)

4. The other day . . . a liberal friend of mine came up with a conspiracy theory to end all conspiracy theories. Did I think it possible, he asked darkly, that all the bloodhound sniffing at the SPOOR of illicit sex in Washington could be a plot to pay back the liberals for Watergate? Hadn't I noticed that the congressional culprits whose sex lives had been unmasked were unfailingly liberals? (M. Lerner, of *Los Angeles Times*, "Democrats Paid For Watergate," *Norman* [Okla.] *Transcript*, 7/6/76, p. 6)

5. "We have left many a false SPOOR . . . . Gus [Bakewell] and I [Donald Washburn] have been a team since . . . the Second German War." (Thomas Berger, *Who Is Teddy Villanova?*, Delacorte Press/Seymour Lawrence, 1977, p. 169)

SPURIOUS (spyŏŏr′ē-əs) *adj.* not genuine, authentic, or true; counterfeit; false; sham; of illegitimate birth; bastard.

SPURIOUSLY *adv.*

SPURIOUSNESS *noun.*

1. His [Frank Harris's] interminable and largely SPURIOUS autobiography *My Life and Loves* was one of the century's most notorious books; it is now, in this brass age of UBIQUITOUS pornography, a book no longer in demand. (P.S. Prescott, Review of *Frank Harris*, by Philippa Pullar, *Newsweek*, 3/15/76, p. 95)

2. In 1952, he [Adlai Stevenson] was gravely suspicious of unions and regarded Keynesian economics, to the extent that he understood it, as a transparently SPURIOUS alibi for a sloppy management of public finances. (J.K. Galbraith, Review of *Adlai Stevenson of Illinois* by John Bartlow Martin, *New York Times*, 3/7/76, Section 7, p. 2)

3. "You will at any rate admit [said Russel Wren to Donald Washburn] that the assignment for which you hired me was totally SPURIOUS. There is no Frederika Washburn and she has no illicit lover; in fact, you are unmarried." (Thomas Berger, *Who Is Teddy Villanova?*, Delacorte Press/Seymour Lawrence, 1977, p. 164)

4. ". . . Bakewell and Washburn are making their escape, no doubt having exchanged millions of their . . . superficially SPECIOUS but actually SPURIOUS bills for the genuine, . . . and will deposit the real in a Swiss vault." [said Russel Wren]. (Thomas Berger, *Ibid.*, p. 184)

STAKHANOVITE (stə-kä′nə-vīt′) *noun* worker rewarded under Stakhanovism.

STAKHANOVISM *noun* (in the Soviet Union) a method for increasing production (developed in 1935 and named after A.G. Stakhanov (b. 1905), Russian efficiency expert) by rewarding with bonuses and privileges those workers who are able to increase production by improving efficiency.

1. "By 1933 we were shooting movies in five days . . . hell, we could have *phoned* them in!" said James Cagney—and he [Cagney] was one of its [the movie industry's] STAKHANOVITE

R. Berkvist, Review of the book, *Cagney by Cagney*, by James Cagney, *New York Times*, 8/18/76, Section 7, p. 16)

STASIS (stā′sis, stas′is) *noun* the state of equilibrium, balance, stagnation, or inactivity.

The filth, STASIS, boredom and despair that were the overmastering realities of trench warfare between 1914 and 1918 destroyed the chivalric picture of conflict. (R. Hughes, Review of the book, *A Prince of Our Disorder*, by John E. Mack, *Time*, 4/12/76, p. 93)

Devoid of faith in the human potential for decisive change, relativists leave boats unrocked. In a song called *Revolution*, far from calling even for liberal dissent and inquiry, the Beatles assure us that it's gonna be all right. Not long afterward, they would distill this ethical STASIS into a single crystalline MANTRA: "Let It Be." (M. Kaplan, "The Ideologies of 'Tough Times,' " *Change*, August 1976, p. 28)

The great fan [of the helicopter] overhead made one last lazy swish and came to STASIS. The engine sounded a few gasps and mumbles and expired. (Thomas Berger, *Who Is Teddy Villanova?*, Delacorte Press/Seymour Lawrence, 1977, p. 223)

STENTORIAN (sten-tôr′ē-ən, -tôr′-) *adj.* very loud or powerful in sound.

STENTOR *noun* a Greek herald in the Trojan War, described in the *Iliad* as having the voice of 50 men; (if not capitalized) a person having a very loud voice.

He [Nixon] got up there several times before the television cameras and deplored in STENTORIAN tones the [Watergate] cover-up. (W.F. Buckley Jr., *Execution Eve and Other Contemporary Ballads*, G.P. Putnam's Sons, 1975, p. 159)

. . . when suddenly there was a STENTORIAN knock on the door . . . (W.F. Buckley Jr., *Ibid.*, pp. 421-422)

The central role of Henderson [in *Lily*, an opera by Leon Kirchner] is all-important; bass Ara Berberian has the physical stature and STENTORIAN voice to make Henderson come alive. (H. Saal, Review, *Newsweek*, 4/25/77, p. 103)

4. My assailant was a purple-faced wino . . . . He . . . said [to Russel Wren]: " . . . . Buy me a refill [of the bottle], else I'll abuse you in a STENTORIAN voice, embarrassing you in front of your fellow man, and you'll have no recourse, because I fear nothing . . ." (Thomas Berger, *Who Is Teddy Villanova?*, Delacorte Press/ Seymour Lawrence, 1977, p. 133)

5. . . . and Boris' STENTORIAN mirth roared in competition with the engine. (Thomas Berger, *Ibid.*, p. 197)

STERTOROUS (stûr′ tər-əs) *adj.* characterized by stertor or heavy snoring; breathing in this manner.

STERTOR *noun* loud, raspy, labored breathing or snoring, caused by obstructed respiratory passages; a heavy snore.

STERTOROUSLY *adv.*

STERTOROUSNESS *noun.*

1. Snore therapist? That's how he [Marcus H. Boulware]'s described on the jacket of his book, *Snoring*, and that's what he'd like to be if only more research is done on STERTOROUS breathing or snoring. One of his dreams is to establish a sleeping-laboratory center which would have snorers under the watchful eyes of researchers. But he says people yawn at the idea. (B. Koon, "He's the Snorer's Friend," *National Observer*, week ending 3/26/77, p. 1)

2. He [Sam Polidor] turned, walked rapidly away, returned to breathe STERTOROUSLY at the banister . . . (Thomas Berger, *Who Is Teddy Villanova?*, Delacorte Press/Seymour Lawrence, 1977, p. 232)

STRIDULATE (strij′ə-lāt′) *verb* to produce a shrill, harsh, grating, or chirping sound, as a cricket or grasshopper does, by rubbing together certain hard parts of the body; to shrill; to cry shrilly.

STRIDULATION *noun.*

STRIDULATORY or **STRIDULOUS** or **STRIDULANT** *adj.* producing or having a shrill, harsh, or grating sound.

STRIDULOUSLY *adv.*

STRIDULOUSNESS noun.

1. Summer comes as quietly as sunrise . . . . And from now on the hot afternoons and late dusks will throb with the hum and scratch, the throb and STRIDULATION of bees and beetles and all their strident insect kin. (Anon., "Summer" [Editorial], New York Times, 6/20/76, Section 4, p. 16)

STUPOR MUNDI (stoo'pər mûn'dē)   the object of wonder; marvel of the world.

1. [Quote from Whittaker Chambers' letter to William F. Buckey Jr.:] "Mr. Nixon may do wonders; he may astonish us (and himself), a new STUPOR MUNDI. Then I shall have proved the man who, privileged to see the future close up, was PURBLIND." (W.F. Buckley Jr., Execution Eve and Other Contemporary Ballads, G.P. Putnam's Sons, 1975, p. 337)

SUBLIMINAL (sub-lim' ə-nəl, -li' mə-) adj. noting, pertaining to, or employing stimuli that exist or operate below the threshold of consciousness and that become effective subconsciously by repetition.

SUBLIMINALLY adv.

1. See (1) under MITOSIS.

2. In one scene [in the movie] Rocky, a Kentucky Fried Chicken bucket, albeit turned upside down, can be seen in . . . star Sylvester Stallone's apartment for a few seconds . . . . "That ad . . . for chicken is very effective," [Wilson] Key [author of the book, Subliminal Seduction] says, because . . . it suggests that an immensely popular star eats Kentucky Fried Chicken . . . over the long haul this SUBLIMINAL linkage with a big star can't help but sell more chicken. (J.W. Schwada, "How Secret Ads Get Into Movies," National Observer, 5/30/77, p. 1)

SUBORN (sə-bôrn') verb   to bribe or induce (someone) unlawfully or secretly to perform some misdeed or to commit a crime; (in Law) to induce (a person, especially a witness) to give false testimony, or commit perjury.

SUBORNATION noun.

SUBORNATIVE adj.

SUBORNER noun.

1. Horrified, Riccardo [who has been transformed to a falcon in Imbroglio Valpolicella's opera, Metaxis in Accidie] at first resists, then yields and wings away to Cyprus, where he alights to learn that Umbriago had arrived earlier and had already SUBORNED the Russian Patriarch . . . (H. Goldberg, "What Was This Opera Doing in the Rubble of the Roxy?" New York Times, 1/25/76, Section 2, p. 19)

2. These nineteen [who arrived from California] had one hell-raising time at the rendezvous; a few days after they departed, they were jumped by a band of Mohave Indians who had been SUBORNED by the Mexican governor of California . . . [eight] were murdered. (J.A. Michener, Centennial, Fawcett, 1975, p. 293)

3. . . . the FBI has confessed to robbing the mail boxes of the institute [Institute for Policy Studies], going through its trash, SUBORNING employees, and generally spying on this group of left scholars as part of its violation of the rights of American citizens throughout the country. (G. Wills, "Tyranny: More than Chile's problem," Philadelphia Inquirer, 10/3/76, p. 7-L)

4. See (3) under UMBRAGE.

SUBVENTION (səb-ven' shən) noun a grant of money, as by a government or some other authority, in aid or support of some institution, study, or undertaking, especially in connection with science or the arts; the furnishing of aid or relief; subsidy.

SUBVENTIONARY adj.

SUBVENE verb   to arrive, occur, or serve as a support or relief; to come to one's assistance.

1. See (1) under SWIVE.

2. He [K.G. Pontus Hulten, the Swedish director of Plastic Arts at the newly constructed Centre National d'Art et de Culture George Pompidou] has written a book on Jean Tinguely, the Swiss sculptor who makes sculptural machines that work . . . . In Stockholm, in the vestibule of the Moderna Museet [where he had been director], he had a Tinguely ARTIFACT that worked when you put a coin in the slot. I earned enough to SUBVENE the purchase of other, less kinetic, works. (A. Burgess, " 'A $200 million Erector Set,' " New York Times

1/23/77, Section 6, p. 17)

3. To finance them [the *Lebensborns*, Nazi homes for breeding a Nordic "super-race"], the SS relied on SUBVENTIONS from the state, involuntary charitable contributions from big industry and . . . funds realized from the seized property of Jews. (A. Whitman, Review of *Of Pure Blood*, a book by Marc Hillel and Clarissa Henry, translated from the French by Eric Mossbacher, *New York Times*, 3/13/77, Section 7, p. 26)

SUFI (sōō' fē) *noun* a member of an ASCETIC, retiring, and mystical Muslim sect.

SUFISM *noun*.

SUFISTIC *adj*.

1. Miss [Lisa] Alther, for instance, seems to share with Mrs. [Doris] Lessing a weakness for SUFISM: quotations from Idries Shah are used as EPIGRAPH and epilogue [in her book, *Kinflicks*] . . . . There is even a character in *Kinflicks*, Hawk, who is writing an APOCALYPTIC "historical science fiction," just like Mark Coleridge in *The Four-Gated City*. (J. Leonard, Review of *Kinflicks*, a book by Lisa Alther, *New York Times*, 3/14/76, Section 7, p. 4)

2. See (2) under ARABESQUE.

SUPERANNUATED (sōō' pər-an' yōō-ā' tid) *adj*. retired because of age or infirmity, especially with a pension; too old for use, work, or service; antiquated or obsolete; old-fashioned; outdated.

SUPERANNUATION *noun* a superannuating or being superannuated; a pension received by a superannuated person.

SUPERANNUATE *verb* to set aside as, or because, old-fashioned or obsolete; to retire from service, especially with a pension, because of age or infirmity.

1. The animal [the bison], as it had developed in Asia, was so powerful that it had, as an adult, no enemies. Wolves tried constantly to pick off newborn calves or SUPERANNUATED stragglers, but they avoided mature animals in a group. (J.A. Michener, *Centennial*, Fawcett, 1975, p. 98)

2. There were also the SUPERANNUATED bulls,

pitiful cases, bulls who had once commanded the herd. They had lost their power either to fight or to command and dragged along as stragglers with the herd, animals of no consequence. (J.A. Michener, *Ibid.*, p. 99)

3. The picture of a bunch of SUPERANNUATED old goats down in Washington capering around with their hired sweeties is one of the funniest presented to us in some time. When the Hays business first came to light, I laughed till my sides hurt. I didn't stop until I realized that there is a possibility that Mr. [Wayne] Hays' pleasure was partially paid for by me. (W.J. Slatterly, Untitled article, *New York Times*, 6/13/76, Section 4, p. 19)

4. It is a mistake to believe that every [airline] stewardess is but a SUPERANNUATED cheerleader—for that matter, it may be wrong as well to assume that all cheerleaders are happy CRETINS, or that all CRETINS are blissful . . . (Thomas Berger, *Who Is Teddy Villanova?*, Delacorte Press/Seymour Lawrence, 1977, p. 128)

SUPERCILIOUS (sōō' pər-sil' ē-əs) *adj*. haughtily disdainful or contemptuous, as a person, his expression, bearing, etc.; arrogant; scornful.

SUPERCILIOUSLY *adv*.

SUPERCILIOUSNESS *noun*.

1. Unseating the champion is a universally satisfying thing to do, and if the theatrical circumstances combine a controlled titan and a BUMPTIOUS challenger (Spassky vs. Fischer), or better still a SUPERCILIOUS defender and a poorboy challenger (Canada vs. Russia), the satisfaction sweetens. (W.F. Buckley Jr., *Execution Eve and Other Contemporary Ballads*, G.P. Putnam's Sons, 1975, p. 239)

SUPEREROGATORY (sōō' pər-ə-rog' ə-tōr' ē) *adj*. going beyond the requirements or expectations of duty; greater than that required; superfluous.

SUPEREROGATORILY *adv*.

SUPEREROGATE (sōō' pər-ər'ə-gāt') *verb* to do more than duty requires or expects.

SUPEREROGATION *noun*.

SUPEREROGATOR *noun*.

1. My own view is that the generalizations [of Mr. T.W. Adorno], where they are not groundless, are meaningless; that to the extent they say a conservative is something else than what he is, they are wrong, and to the extent they prove a conservative is a conservative, they are SUPEROGATORY . . . his thesis is marvelously convenient for those who refused to concede that there are rational grounds for conservative dissent from the liberal orthodoxy. (W.F. Buckley Jr., *Up From Liberalism*, Arlington House, 2nd Printing 1968, pp. 92-93)

2. "I don't investigate rackets," said the boss. "Surely the combined resources at your disposal would render my efforts SUPEREROGATORY." (N. Callendar, "The mystery mystery," *New York Times*, 6/6/76, Section 6, p. 103)

SUPERFETATION (sōō′ pər-fē-tā′ shən) *noun* the fertilization of an ovum in a female mammal already pregnant; the piling up of one growth on another; cumulative development.

SUPERFETATE (sōō′pər-fē′tāt) *adj., verb.*

1. "And what about Big Jake the Wop?" [Russel Wren asked]. "No, Jake the Wop or Big Jake [replied Zwingli]. To combine them is SUPERFETATION." (Thomas Berger, *Who Is Teddy Villanova?*, Delacorte Press/Seymour Lawrence, 1977, p. 99)

SUPERNAL (sōō-pûr′ n ³l) *adj.* heavenly, celestial, or divine; lofty; of more than human excellence, powers, etc.; being on high or in the sky or visible heavens.

SUPERNALLY *adv.*

1. His movie [Marco Ferreri's *La Grande Bouffe*] is about a young engineer (Gerard Depardieu) whose wife has left him with their year-old son. He shacks up with a girl (the SUPERNALLY lovely Ornella Muti) who objects to his MACHO ways . . . (J. Kroll, Review, *Newsweek*, 6/14/76, p. 90- F)

SUPERNUMERARY (sōō′ pər-nōō′mə-rer′ē, -nyōō′) *adj.* being in excess of the usual, proper, or prescribed number; extra; that is beyond the number or quantity needed or desired; superfluous.

SUPERNUMERARY *noun* a supernumerary person or thing; (in theater) a person with a small, non-speaking part, as in a mob scene.

1. A woman looked at [Greg] Gregson and then at [Ronald] Beard, and then again at Beard. Beard looked at her and his eyes beat like SUPERNUMERARY hearts. It could not be that Paola [Belli] had crept back to Rome . . . (A. Burgess, *Beard's Roman Women*, McGraw-Hill, 1976, p. 86)

2. The only remaining character to deal with was the main, the grand, the motive for all this play of passion and volition, to which the other performers were but SUPERNUMERARY: Teddy Villanova . . . (Thomas Berger, *Who Is Teddy Villanova?*, Delacorte Press/Seymour Lawrence, 1977, p. 235)

SUPERORDINATE (sōō′ pər-ôr′də-nit′) *adj.* of higher or superior condition, rank, kind, etc.

SUPERORDINATE *noun* a superordinate person or thing.

SUPERORDINATE (sōō′ pər-ôr′ də-nāt′) *verb* to elevate to superordinate position.

1. I have said it until I am blue in the face that in my opinion Mr. Nixon ought not to be impeached even if he is established to have had knowledge of Watergate before March, but it does not follow from that judgment, based on the SUPERORDINATION of the health of the state over the demands of individual justice, that Mr. Nixon's behavior is anything less than CONTUMACIOUS. (W.F. Buckley Jr., *Execution Eve and Other Contemporary Ballads*, G.P. Putnam's Sons, 1975, pp. 123-124)

SUPERVENE (sōō′ pər-vēn′) *verb* to take place or occur as something additional, unexpected, foreign, or extraneous to the normal course of events or the matter at hand; to take place; ensue.

SUPERVENIENCE or **SUPERVENTION** *noun.*

SUPERVENIENT *adj.*

1. . . . some educational institutions are more than the sum of their parts—we are well acquainted, I think, with colleges that somehow achieve a level of academic excellence, a tradi-

tion of intellectual commitment, that cannot be accounted for merely by an enumeration of the talents of their students or the accomplishments of their faculty. Indeed there are institutions in this [Connecticut] valley that exhibit just such an emergent, or SUPERVENIENT, quality. This university [University of Massachusetts] is not one of them. In fact, it manages by some unfortunate sleight of hand, to be less than the sum of its parts. (R.P. Wolff, *Appearance and Reality in Higher Education* [Chancellor's Lecture at University of Massachusetts at Amherst], Mimeographed, 2/2/75)

SUPINE (sōō-pīn') *adj.* lying on the back, face upward; mentally or morally inactive, passive, or inert; sluggish; listless; (of the hand) having the palm upward.

SUPINELY *adv.*

SUPINENESS *noun.*

SUPINATE (sōō pə-nāt') *verb* to turn to a supine position; rotate (the hand or forearm) so that the palm is upward or away from the body; to become supinated.

SUPINATION *noun.*

1. Within two days he [General Harvey Wade] satisfied himself and the board that General Laban Asher had been incompetent and morally SUPINE. (J.A. Michener, *Centennial*, Fawcett, 1975, p. 500)

2. If [the] Venneford [ranch] sat by SUPINELY while sheepmen invaded the range, . . . pretty soon the whole intricate structure would begin to fall apart, the trend would accelerate, and a noble way of life would be lost. (J.A. Michener, *Ibid.*, p. 703)

3. Leo Brunner sat up, looking fixedly at the full-length photograph of the half-clad Sharon Fields in a LANGUOROUS, fetching SUPINE position. (I. Wallace, *The Fan Club*, Bantam Edition, 1975, p. 61)

SUPPURATE (sup'yə-rāt') *verb* to produce or discharge pus, as a wound; fester.

SUPPURATION *noun* the process of suppurating; the matter produced by suppuration; pus.

SUPPURATIVE *adj.*

SUPPURATIVE *noun* a medicine that promotes suppuration.

1. Eventually they arrived in [Queen Caroline's] ornate drawing room, SUPPURATING with velvet and bric-a-brac. (W.F. Buckley Jr., *Saving the Queen*, Doubleday, 1976, p. 166)

SURCEASE (sûr-sēs') *verb* to stop; end; to cease from some action; desist; to come to an end; to cease from; leave off.

SURCEASE *noun* cessation; end.

1. Author of the lovable H*Y*M*A*N K*A*P*L*A*N books, screenwriter, novelist, humorist, sociological student of Hollywood folkways, one-man chautauqua-in-residence at Look magazine, popular lexicographer of Yiddish, he [Leo Rosten, author of *The 3:10 to Anywhere*] has led a busy life SURCEASED by love of travel. (R.R. Lingeman, Review, *New York Times*, 3/14/76, Section 7, p. 14)

2. There is a charming chapter [in *Born Again*, by Charles W. Colson] called *The President's Night Out*, in which Our Man Colson scrambles to help the President, who looks forward to an evening of musical SURCEASE at the Kennedy Center with conductor Eugene Ormandy. But no one seems to know if Ormandy is actually appearing. A resourceful White House operator eventually tracks down Ormandy himself in his Philadelphia lair . . . . Eventually Colson learns that four military bands are playing; the President, restless, settles for them. (Molly Ivins, Review, *New York Times*, 3/28/76, Section 7, p. 5)

SURREPTITIOUS (sûr'əp-tish' əs) *adj.* obtained, done, made, etc., by stealth or in secret; acting in a stealthy way; CLANDESTINE.

SURREPTITIOUSLY *adv.*

SURREPTITIOUSNESS *noun.*

1. The MORPHOLOGY of championship chess is INSCRUTABLE, something that contributes to the game's fascination and edges it SURREPTITIOUSLY away from sport in the direction of art. (W.F. Buckley Jr., *Execution Eve and Other Contemporary Ballads*, G.P. Putnam's Sons, 1975, p. 238)

2. In England it [the book, *Trousered Apes*]

was the nearest thing to a SURREPTITIOUS volume since the days when pornography was effectively banned. (W.F. Buckley Jr., *Ibid.*, p. 406)

3. See (3) under PERFERVID.

4. See (3) under SCABROUS.

SURROGATE (sûr'ə-gāt', -git) *noun* a person appointed to act for another; deputy; substitute.

SURROGATE *verb* to put into the place of another as a successor, substitute, or deputy; substitute for another; to subrogate.

SURROGATION *noun.*

1. Humor is likely to be in short supply in this year's presidential election campaign . . . . Perhaps the two nominees should take one week off in mid-October and let Chevy Chase and David Frye campaign as their SURROGATES. (R. Worsnop, "President maintains sense of humor," *Norman* [Okla.] *Transcript*, 4/19/76, p. 6)

2. Mary [Hartman] does not know how to talk to her boorish husband about his connubial dysfunction so she brings in a sex therapist to act as a "SURROGATE." The plan collapses when Mary belatedly discovers what sex SURROGATES actually do. (H.F. Waters, M. Kasindorf, "The Mary Hartman Craze," *Newsweek*, 5/3/76, p. 55)

3. The theater for Carter's triumph was the Pennsylvania primary, and his victory . . . was devastatingly complete . . . . He whipped Humphrey's unwilling SURROGATE, Henry M. (Scoop) Jackson . . . and drove him from the race before the week was out. (P. Goldman, *et al.*, "Carter's Sweep," *Newsweek*, 5/10/76, p. 26)

4. See (2) under BÊTE NOIRE.

5. Year by year [since the death of J. Edgar Hoover], FBI men themselves began to feel free to tell what they knew of The Boss [JEH], a man they treated as God or at least his 20th-century SURROGATE in Washington. Associated Press, "Stories about Hoover reveal his power," *Norman* [Okla.] *Transcript*, 6/11/76, p. 13)

6. See (2) under VATICINATION.

7. Wavering delegates [at the Republican convention] received last-minute phone calls from the President, others found themselves pressured by a squad of high-ranking Ford SURROGATES and, as the crucial vote approached, the White House command post flooded the floor with its whips to hold the line. (D.M. Alpern, *et al.*, "How Ford Did It," *Newsweek*, 8/30/76, p. 28)

SUSURROUS (sŏŏ-sûr' əs) or **SUSURRANT** (sŏŏ-sûr'ənt) *adj.* full of whispering or rustling sounds; softly murmuring; whispering; gently rustling.

SUSURRATION (sŏŏ'sə-rā'shən) *noun* a soft murmur; whisper.

SUSURRATE *verb* to whisper; murmur; rustle.

SUSURRUS *noun* a soft murmuring or rustling sound; whisper.

1. "ONOMATOPOEIA" is a great word in itself. It sounds like the opening rhythms of a spirited Croatian folk dance . . . . But it also describes a class of words . . . that imitate the sounds of the things they describe. How about "SUSURROUS" to describe the whispering of the wind in the trees? Or how about "TINTINNABULATION", an old word given broad currency by Edgar Allan Poe when he used it to describe the sound of bells? (B. Wiemer, *Newsday* Service, "The Rubric of Words," *Philadelphia Inquirer*, 3/27/77, p. 3-L)

2. The telephone proceeded to ring several times . . . . I [Russel Wren] picked up the instrument . . . . I utter a hopeful "Yes?" But now I was humiliated to hear it emerge, owing to stress, as a SUSURRANT whimper. "Teddy, we're gonna ice you," said a voice . . . (Thomas Berger, *Who Is Teddy Villanova?*, Delacorte Press/Seymour Lawrence, 1977, p. 33)

3. He [Zwingli] rustled some pages in a new volume . . . . Again the SUSURRUS of pages. (Thomas Berger, *Ibid.*, pp. 88-89)

4. Until the poetry of Baudelaire, the "unhappy consciousness of modern man" seemed merely a fatigued SUSURRATION from the grey pages of Hegel. (C. Bernard, Review of *Baudelaire: Prince of Clouds*, a book by Alex de

Jonge, *Philadelphia Inquirer*, 5/15/77, p. 13-I)

5. See (2) under THRENODY.

SUTLER (sut´lər) *noun* a merchant who followed an army and sold provisions, liquor, etc. to the soldiers.

1. . . . at this moment only two [new buildings] were in operation at Fort Laramie—the SUTLER's store . . . and the residential building . . . (J.A. Michener, *Centennial*, Fawcett, 1975, p. 425)

SUZERAIN (soō´zə-rin, -rān´) *noun* a sovereign or a state exercising political control over a semiautonomous dependent state; historically, a feudal overlord.

SUZERAIN *adj.* characteristic of or being a suzerain.

SUZERAINTY *noun* the position or power of a suzerain; the domain or area subject to a suzerain.

1. A strong but kind tortoise [one who showed mercy on a tortoise defeated in battle] could thus surround himself with intimidated underlings; he would become a local SUZERAIN. (F. Hapgood, "Why The Tortoise Is Kind and Other Tales of Sociobiology," *Atlantic*, March 1976, p. 100)

SWIVE (swīv) *verb* to copulate with; to have sexual intercourse with.

1. And [Ronald] Hingley [author of *A New Life of Anton Chekhov*] is not a superb writer; in fact, he is often a dull one, given to odd grammatical quirks, an occasionally highfalutin vocabulary ("SUBVENTION," "SWIVED," "EQUIPOLLENT"), and a style sometimes too sprightly, as if to counteract the drugs of academe. (H. Moss, Review, *New York Times*, 6/20/76, Section 7, p. 29)

SYBARITE (sib´ə-rīt´) *noun* (if capitalized) an inhabitant of Sybaris (an ancient Greek city in southern Italy noted for its wealth and luxury); (if lower case) a person devoted to or fond of luxury, pleasure, or sensuous self-indulgence; sensualist; voluptuary.

SYBARITIC (sib´ə-rit´ik) or **SYBARITICAL** *adj.*
SYBARITICALLY *adv.*
SYBARITISM *noun.*

1. At midday, the vacationing SYBARITES de-

voured countless platters of grilled fish and steak, sumptuous . . . salads and pâtés and . . . mounds of fresh fruit and French pastries. (Linda Bird Francke, Jane Friedman, "Sun Spots," *Newsweek*, 1/5/76, p. 44)

2. For many years, he has enjoyed the best wines and the most expensive cigars . . . and, in his [Rubinstein's] SYBARITIC approach to daily existence, has long been the Winston Churchill of the piano. (D. Henahan, "This ageless hero, Rubinstein," *New York Times*, 3/14/76, Section 6, p. 18)

3. . . . author [Neil] Simon—as QUINTESSENTIALLY New Yawky as a graffiti-stained subway—recently relocated West, to an imitation white frame farmhouse in sunny, SYBARITIC Bel-Air. (H.F. Waters, M. Kasindorf, "Sunshine Boy," *Newsweek*, 4/26/76, p. 75)

4. Unlike stock-car drivers, Grand Prix racers are rich SYBARITES who zip through the industrialized world in futuristic "Formula I" nodules of fiber glass. Theirs is a life of death and daring where excess baggage means two cars and a couple of glacé blondes. (Anon., "On the Road at Long Beach," *Time*, 4/12/76, p. 82)

5. In one of the slickest, sassiest and most SYBARITIC thefts in history, a team of burglars [last week] lifted a cool $10 million from Société Générale's safe-deposit vault [in Nice]. The robbery may well be a world record, and Frenchmen promptly dubbed it "le fric-frac du siècle"—the burglary of the century . . . they [the burglars] were good at their trade—and had fun on the job. They provided themselves with every necessary tool, and they also brought ample stocks of food, wine and candy. (Fay Willey and Elizabeth Peer, "Le Grand Fric-Frac," *Newsweek*, 8/2/76, p. 36)

6. Situated in a commercial district not far from Universal Studios, the Yes is part of the SYBARITIC world of so-called adult motels—mini-pleasure domes whose main purpose clearly isn't to provide a restful night's sleep for weary travelers. What is the purpose? Well, . . . just flick on the large, swiveling color-television set . . . you'll find closed- circuit hard-core pornographic movies that leave nothing to the imagination. (S.J. Sansweet, "Playing to Fantasies: Some Motels Thrive On Adult Patronage," *Wall Street Journal*, 3/2/77, p. 1)

7. He [Edward M. Henley, in the book, *Evidence of Love,* by Shirley Ann Grau] is guiltlessly dedicated to his pleasures, which include exotic women and an occasional boy . . . . Instead of following Edward's SYBARITIC path, Stephen [his son] becomes a Unitarian minister and a classics scholar. (R.Z. Sheppard, Review, *Time,* 2/7/77, p. 92)

8. Again, for an anti-materialist, [Mahatma] Gandhi led what some would consider a remarkably SYBARITIC existence, surrounded by doting female servants and secretaries, who waited on him literally hand and foot . . . . These ladies were also invited to share his bed, naked, as exercises in resisting temptation. (P. Johnson, Review of *Mahatma Gandhi and His Apostles,* a book by Ved Mehta, *New York Times,* 2/6/77, Section 7, pp. 3-4)

9. When he [Clay Felker] overspent his board-authorized start-up budget for [the magazine] New West last year by a reported $2 million or so—partly on SYBARITIC expense allowances for employees—some shareholders began howling for his head. (D. Gelman, *et al.,* "Press Lord Captures Gotham," *Newsweek,* 1/17/77, p. 50)

SYCOPHANT (sik'ə-fənt) *noun* a self-seeking, servile flatterer (of people of wealth or influence); fawning parasite; toady.

SYCOPHANTIC or SYCOPHANTICAL or SYCOPHANTISH *adj.*

SYCOPHANTICALLY or SYCOPHANTISHLY *adv.*

SYCOPHANCY (sik'ə-fən-sē) or SYCOPHANTISM *noun* self-seeking or servile flattery; the character or conduct of a sycophant.

1. Says former Nixon speechwriter Pat Buchanan, now a columnist: "It tells us that Camelot was an utter fraud, a hoax perpetrated . . . by Kennedy SYCOPHANTS and a compliant press . . . " (D. Gelman, S. Leshner, "Closets of Camelot," *Newsweek,* 1/19/76, p. 71)

2. The victory [of Ronald Reagan] in Texas was simply unassimilable by strategists in the Ford campaign . . . Ford came in as a sitting champion, only slightly dented in North Carolina. He poured into Texas everything a President has to vouchsafe: his royal presence, the Air Force Fleet, the large SYCOPHANTIC crowds, the wife, the son, military bases, judgeships. (W.F. Buckley Jr., "Ford has no excuses now—Reagan's the man," *Chicago Daily News,* 5/6/76, p. 12)

3. "Then there are those in her [Sharon Fields'] circle who are afraid of her, who are weak SYCOPHANTS" [Adam Malone said]. (I. Wallace, *The Fan Club,* Bantam Edition, 1975, p. 88)

4. Now freshly combed and suited up for a triumphal appearance they would never make, they still seemed an implausible pair. Ronald Reagan was surrounded by his gleaming staff of Californians, and so the anguish of the moment in which he finally lost the nomination was somewhat obscured. But Richard Schweiker was alone; without friends and SYCOPHANTS, he showed his dismay. (R. Ajemian, "The End of the Ride," *Time,* 8/30/76, p. 32)

5. In a recent interview, he [Australian foreign minister Andrew Peacock] said Australia was finished being a puppet of the United States. "Heaven forbid that we have some SYCOPHANTIC relationship in which we simply accept everything your government wants to do." (B. Newman, "Australia Bids to Bridge Gap Between the West and Developing States," *Wall Street Journal,* 3/4/77, p. 1)

6. A lot of people [in Washington] just plain want jobs . . . . In the presence of any Georgian, of others known to be well-connected with the new Administration and of those who had already gotten the nod for high posts, I saw would-be assistant secretaries behaving with a kind of sickly-grin SYCOPHANCY. . . (Meg Greenfield, "The New Washington Power Game," *Newsweek,* 1/31/77, p. 80)

7. [Singer] Callaway's veneration of Rufus was transparent, but a world removed from SYCOPHANCY. (W.F. Buckley Jr., *Saving the Queen,* Doubleday, 1976, p. 146)

8. "I played that [piece on the piano] more competently than I do now when I was a girl of thirteen, but in those days my audience listened less acutely and applauded less heartily. It is extraordinary how my anointment as Queen has improved the quality of my audiences." There was scattered laughter, as ever,

after the Queen [Caroline] drew attention to the enveloping SYCOPHANCY. (W.F. Buckley Jr., *Ibid.*, p. 172)

SYLLOGISM (sil'ə-jiz'əm) *noun* an argument or form of reasoning in which two statements or premises are made and a logical conclusion drawn from them; reasoning from the general to the particular; deductive logic; an instance of subtle, sophisticated, tricky, or SPECIOUS reasoning.

SYLLOGISTIC or **SYLLOGISTICAL** *adj.*

SYLLOGISTICALLY *adv.*

SYLLOGIZE *verb* to reason or infer by use of syllogisms.

1. See (1) under LAPIDARY.

2. I suggest Mrs. [Eleanor] Roosevelt's philosophy of hand-shaking does not emerge from the data. If we were to set up a SYLLOGISM, here is how it would look; Proposition A: E.R. will not shake hands with those who are guilty of mass killings. Proposition B: E.R. will shake hands with Andrei Vishinsky. Conclusion: Vishinsky is not guilty of mass killings.*

*Mr. Daniel Bell, . . . now a professor of sociology at Columbia, wrote me [W.F. Buckley Jr.] that the SYLLOGISM was incorrect, and offered to buy a year's subscription to *National Review*, against my promise to buy a copy of his book (*The New American Right*), if I could get the SYLLOGISM certified by a professional philosopher. The SYLLOGISM was, of course, duly validated . . . , and Mr. Bell took out his subscription . . . . P.S. I bought and read Mr. Bell's book anyway. (W.F. Buckley Jr., *Up From Liberalism*, Arlington House, 2nd Printing 1968, pp. 41-42)

3. Some federal agencies and federal judges actually seem to view patents as contrary to the public interest, charges T.L. Bowes, executive director of Intellectual Property Owners, Inc., a Washington-based organization devoted to preserving the patent incentive. They apparently subscribe to the faulty SYLLOGISM, he says: Monopolies are bad for the nation, patents are monopolies, therefore patents are bad for the nation. (Anon., "Patent Problems" [Editorial], *Times Herald*, Norristown, Pa. 12/3/76, p. 12)

SYMBIOSIS (sim'bī-ō'sis, -bē-) *noun*, *pl.*: -SES - *Biology:* the living together of two dissimilar organisms, especially when this association is mutually beneficial; a similar relationship of mutual interdependence between persons or groups.

SYMBIOTIC or **SYMBIOTICAL** *adj.*

SYMBIOTICALLY *adv.*

1. Some of the newer work-study arrangements provide young people . . . with useful exposure to the disciplines (and frustrations) of real work, provide opportunities for worker collaboration, and instruct students in the SYMBIOTIC relationship between individual productivity and economic survival. (G.W. Bonham, "Revitalizing Undergraduate Learning" [Editorial], *Change*, Winter 1974-75, p. 12)

2. Their [the women's, in *Women of the Shadows*, by Ann Cornelisen] loyalties are to the children they bear and raise so grudgingly, and to the land they work and hate . . . . They live in a greedy, desperate SYMBIOSIS with the enslaving presences of their everyday world. (Jane Kramer, Review, *New York Times*, 4/4/76, Section 7, p. 3)

3. The old adventurer [an 80-year old lady in *Ahmed and the Old Lady*, a book by Jon Godden] is admittedly "foolish, headstrong and rash" . . . Ahmed is an ambivalent charmer out of Kipling. The two know the best and the worst of one another—and their SYMBIOSIS makes an irresistible fable. (M. Levin, Review, *New York Times*, 4/4/76, Section 7, p. 33)

4. Isolated family lives [in British Columbian wilderness] in SYMBIOSIS with trumpeters [swans]. [Title of article]. (W.D. Jorgensen, *Smithsonian*, January 1976, p. 56)

5. See (2) under POPINJAY.

6. She [Céleste Albaret, author of the book, *Monsieur Proust*] became bound to him [Marcel Proust] . . . , she became the sole servant of his elaborate, invalid's ritualistic nightmare life . . . . Hundreds of egoists, of course—invalid mothers and worn-out daughters—have lived in such a dismal SYMBIOSIS, but few ignorant young girls and dying geniuses. (A. Wilson, Review, *New York Times*, 4/11/76, Section 7, pp. 6-7)

7. The [colonial] Americans saw themselves as a new race of Israelites created in the latter day and endowed with the same SYMBIOTIC relationship that God had conferred upon his first chosen people. (R. MacLeish, "National spirit: pendulum begins to swing," *Smithsonian*, July 1976, p. 28)

8. [Michael] Graves and his peers [among architects] create SYMBIOTICALLY with their clients. But some of them are also determined to elevate the architect's role to that of artist-thinker, above that of collaborator, builder, engineer. (D. Davis, Mary Rourke, "Real Dream Houses," *Newsweek*, 10/4/76, p. 66)

9. [Roswell] Angier's investigation [described in his book, " . . . A Kind of Life": *Conversations in the Combat Zone*] goes well beyond stereotypes. What seems at first an adversary relationship between the [striptease] girls and their customers is often a SYMBIOSIS. (P.D. Zimmerman, Review, *Newsweek*, 11/1/76, pp. 84-H, 84-L)

SYNAPSIS (si-nap'sis) *noun, pl.*: SYNAPSES (-sēz) the conjugation of homologous chromosomes, one from each parent, during early MEIOSIS; synapse.

SYNAPSE *noun* the point of contact between adjacent neurons, across which nerve impulses are transmitted.

SYNAPTIC or SYNAPTICAL *adj.*

SYNAPTICALLY *adv.*

1. [Robert] Hayden [author of the book, *Angle of Ascent*] has always been a symbolist poet struggling with historical fact, his rigorous portraits of people and places providing the SYNAPTIC leap into the interior landscape of the soul, where prayer for illumination and perfection are focused on the oneness of mankind. (M.S. Harper, Review, *New York Times*, 2/22/76, Section 7, p. 34)

2. In sci-fi terms, I have the sensation of being trapped in a time warp. While the rest of the universe was kinetic, I remained static [in prison], and it will take me a while to catch up, to get the SYNAPSES back in phase again. (E.H. Hunt, "How America Looks to Me Now," *Newsweek*, 4/4/77, p. 15)

SYNCRETISM (siṅg'kri-tiz'əm, sin'-) *noun* the union or reconciliation of different or opposing principles, beliefs, practices, or groups in religion, philosophy, etc., or an attempt to do so.

SYNCRETIC or SYNCRETISTIC *adj.*

SYNCRETIZE *verb* to combine, unite, or reconcile or to attempt to do so.

1. Modern Zionism, so determined to negate the unhealthy, exclusivist elements of traditionalism, has allowed some of the most coercive aspects of Orthodoxy to seep in and gain a SYNCRETIC foothold in the [Israeli] State . . . the most fiery issue in the last election campaign, prior to the Yom Kippur War, was the issue of religion in the State, embodied in the question, "Who is a Jew?" The "Who is a Jew" controversy stems from the denial of individual rights: for instance, a man is denied the right to marry the woman he loves because he is not [legally] a Jew. (*Moment*, 6/19/77, p. 22)

SYNDYASMIAN (sin' di-as' mē-ən) *adj.* pertaining to or marked by sexual union without exclusive coition or with temporary cohabitation; of or relating to sexual pairing, as of animals while procreating and rearing their young.

SYNDYASMOS *noun* the Greek word for pairing, coupling, or sexual intercourse.

1. It used to be called "shacking up." Since achieving the status of a sociological phenomenon, it has been labeled everything from cohabiting in "quasi-conjugal diads" to "consorting in SYNDYASMOS." Most folks doing it just say they're living together . . . (According to the U.S. Census Bureau, some 1.3 million American adults share 660,000 two-person households with an unrelated adult of the opposite sex—double the number in 1970.) (D. St. Albin Greene, " 'Living in Sin' Is in Style," *National Observer*, 5/30/77, p. 1)

SYNECDOCHE (si-nek'də-kē') *noun* a figure of speech in which a part is used for the whole or the whole for a part, the special for the general or the general for the special.

SYNECDOCHIC (sin' ik-dok'ik) or SYNECDOCHICAL *adj.*

SYNECDOCHICALLY *adv.*

1. Will no one tell the people at Scott, Foresman about the SYNECDOCHE? [in reference to their editors' requirement that "early humans" be used instead of "early men," etc.]. (W.F. Buckley Jr., *Execution Eve and Other Contemporary Ballads*, G.P. Putnam's Sons, 1975, p. 419)

2. . . . although I have dealt with the federal social security program as a SYNECDOCHE, I am aware that I have come to conclusions based on quantitative evaluation of the costs of social security which would not necessarily be warranted if one were reckoning the cost of the entire apparatus of social welfare in this country. Whereas it is true that federal social security, insofar as it incurs a modest operating deficit, has a negligible economic effect, it is not true that the entire overhead of social welfare has negligible economic effects. (W.F. Buckley Jr., *Up From Liberalism*, Arlington House, 2nd Printing 1968, p. 201)

SYNERGISM (sin' ər-jiz'əm, si-nûr' jiz-əm) or SYNERGY *noun* the simultaneous action of agents, as drugs, that work toward the same end but that, when used together, have a greater total effect than the sum of the individual effects; the combined or correlated action of different organs or parts of the body, as of muscles working together.

SYNERGISTIC or SYNERGIC or SYNERGETIC *adj.* working together; cooperating.

SYNERGISTICALLY *adv.*

SYNERGIST *noun* a synergistic organ, drug, etc.

1. The word these days seems to be "SYNERGISM," a term biologists use to describe the action of two or more organisms to achieve an effect that neither one is capable of individually . . . . MG [Michigan General Corporation] says it intends to develop Pinnacle [its publisher of paperbacks] into a major mass-market house and will shortly "acquire a major hardcover house." It expects the two firms to "SYNERGIZE" each other . . . . Sometimes a publisher finds a SYNERGISTIC partner in show business. (Anon., "Paper Back Talk," *New York Times*, 1/4/76, Section 7, p. 39)

2. For fullest enjoyment I find most red wines are far more dependent than whites on SYNERGETIC combination with food. Dry white wine, on the other hand, is as much of a joy alone . . . as it is with food. (M. Pakenham, "The whites are winning," *Philadelphia Inquirer*, 9/26/76, p. 1-I)

3. See (1) under MONOCOQUE.

T

TABETIC (tə-bet' ik) *adj.* pertaining to tabes.

TABES (tā' bēz) *noun* a gradually progressive emaciation, wasting away, or atrophy due to disease.

TABESCENT *adj.* wasting or withering away; becoming emaciated.

TABESCENCE *noun*.

1. Near the entrance of the cooperative stood a mother with her son. The boy was TABETIC, respectful. Both were in mourning. (Osip Mandelstam, "Hello, Cézanne! Good Old Grandfather!"(translated by Clarence Brown), *New York Times*, 3/20/77, Section 7, p. 35)

TABULA RASA (tab'yə-lə rē'sə, rä'sə) *noun* pl.: TABULAE RASAE (tab'yə-lē'rä'sē', rä'sē)

a blank tablet; clean slate; the mind not yet
affected by experiences, impressions, etc.

1. How do we create a TABULA RASA where
measurement is concerned so that we can begin thinking in the metric system? (Ingeborg
Boudreau, Review of the book, *Metric Can Be
Fun!*, by Munro Leaf, *New York Times*,
5/30/76, Section 7, p. 11)

TALISMAN (tal′is-mən, -iz-) *noun* an object (ring, stone, etc.) bearing engraved figures
or symbols and supposed to possess occult powers and worn as an amulet or charm to bring
good luck and keep away evil; any amulet or
charm.

TALISMANIC or TALISMANICAL *adj.*

TALISMANICALLY *adv.*

1. It is a pity that there has developed the TAL-
ISMANIC view of democracy, as the indispensable and unassailable solvent of the free and virtuous society . . . . The humbler claims for
democracy are not only legitimate but realistic. It is right that the views of the individual
who stands to be affected by a law or ordinance, should be canvassed . . . . And if these
views argue for barbarism or regimentation, it
is proper to circumvent them, even if, in doing
so, democracy is flouted; as it deliberately is
under the Constitution of the United States.
(W.F. Buckley Jr., *Up From Liberalism*,
Arlington House, 2nd Printing, 1968,
pp. 159-160)

2. Dancing about him [FDR] in a circle,
hands clasped, his ecstatic braintrusters sang
together the magical incantation . . .: "*We
Owe It* [the national debt] *To Ourselves!*" In
five TALISMANIC words the planners had disposed of the problem of deficit spending.
(W.F. Buckley Jr., *Ibid.*, p. 168)

3. In it [a short story in the book, *Mauve
Gloves & Madmen, Clutter & Vine*] he [author
Tom Wolfe] tells of a black athlete who has
just attained that ultimate TALISMAN of super-
stardom—a chance to do a commercial—and
the anguish of that athlete over the fact that in
making the commercial he must make fun of
himself. (D.R. Boldt, Review, *Philadelphia Inquirer*, 1/30/77, p. 10-D)

TATTERDEMALION (tat′ ər-di māl′ yən,
-mal′-) *noun* a person in tattered or ragged
clothing; a ragged fellow; ragamuffin.

1. In San Clemente country one hears a good
deal about Richard Nixon and his TATTERDE-
MALION life, the weekly attritions on his professional staff, his personal staff, the overgrown
ivy, the weedy tennis court, the languishing
lawn, the mysterious nonappearance of Mrs.
Nixon's personal belongings, packed late on the
night of August 8, 1974. (W.F. Buckley Jr.,
*Execution Eve and Other Contemporary Bal-
lads*, G.P. Putnam's Sons, 1975, p. 163)

2. The boys returned, three hours later, TAT-
TERDEMALION, . . . (W.F. Buckley Jr., *Ibid.*,
p. 232)

3. He [Major Mercy] whistled as a signal to the
[Indian] outlooks who must be hidden somewhere in the rocks, but none appeared, and he
realized that this TATTERDEMALION group [of
Indians] was without organization or guards.
(J.A. Michener, *Centennial*, Fawcett, 1975,
p. 485)

4. He [Blackford Oakes] was agreeably surprised to notice that he would be paying eight
dollars a day, including breakfast, for a room
[in Paris] positively awesome in its only slightly
TATTERDEMALION Empire splendor. (W.F.
Buckley Jr., *Saving the Queen*, Doubleday,
1976, p. 113)

TAUTOLOGY (tô-tol′ ə-jē) *noun* needless
repetition of an idea in different words; re-
dundancy; neoplasm; the instance of such a
repetition; (in logic) a law that can be shown
on the basis of certain rules to exclude no logical possibilities; an instance of such a law.

TAUTOLOGICAL or TAUTOLOGIC or TAU-
TOLOGOUS *adj.*

TAUTOLOGICALLY or TAUTOLOGOUSLY
adv.

TAUTOLOGIZE *verb* to use tautology; be
repetitious.

TAUTOLOGIST *noun.*

1. New York. Chicago. Indianapolis. Hong
Kong. All have something in common this
month: the police procedural (which is a TAU-
TOLOGY, really; procedural means police story

in the ARGOT). (N. Callendar, "Criminals at Large," *New York Times*, 3/14/76, Section 7, p. 28)

2. Too often he [T.S. Eliot] formulates his arguments in the negative, nor is it uncommon for him to let TAUTOLOGIES take the place of logic, as when he archly informs us that "to define maturity without assuming that the hearer already knows what it means, is almost impossible: let us say then, that if we are properly mature . . . we can define maturity in a civilization and in a literature." (L. Cole, Review of *Selected Prose of T.S. Eliot*, edited and with an introduction by Frank Kermode, *Change*, August 1976, p. 63)

3. "I know now that there is no one thing that is true," says the wounded Hudson [in the film, *Islands in the Stream*]. "It is all true." Hemingway's whole life was an attempt—often noble—to breathe life into that TAUTOLOGY. (J. Kroll, Review, *Newsweek*, 3/14/77, p. 96)

4. See (1) under ORDONNANCE.

5. [What other comedian than Steve Martin] Studied so much philosophy in the hot sun at Long Beach State that he emerged paralyzed by TAUTOLOGY and addicted to a sense of the absurd? (Maureen Orth, "Silly Putty," *Newsweek*, 1/31/77, p. 59)

6. "Listen carefully, you slow-witted idiot, sorry, that's what do you call it TAUTOLOGOUS or whatever the fucking word is, listen [said Leonora's voice over the telephone to Ronald Beard]." (A. Burgess, *Beard's Roman Women*, McGraw-Hill, 1976, p. 102)

TECTONIC (tek-ton'ik) *adj.* of or pertaining to building or construction; constructive; architectural; pertaining to the structure of the earth's crust.

TECTONICS *noun* (construed as *sing.*) the study of the earth's crustal structure and the forces that produce changes in it; structural geology; the art or science of construction, as of buildings, furniture, etc.

1. The meaning of the event [Peter's martyrdom] as a rite of foundation and an affirmation of faith is expressed again [in Michelangelo's *Crucifixion of St. Peter*] in the TECTONIC characters of the design: It has the four-square sol-

emnity composers give to the *Credo* . . . . The component groups—the soldiers at the left, the horsemen, the friendly chorus at upper center, the marchers in echelon descending at the right, and the huddle of women below—all form compact rectangular units. (L. Steinberg, "Michelangelo's last painting; his gift to this century," *Smithsonian*, December 1975, p. 81)

2. Geologists, the last to be presented with a new idea—or PARADIGM, as the jargon has it—are busily weaving all previous and current geological observations into the grand tapestry of plate TECTONICS. (J.K. Page Jr., "Frontiers," *Smithsonian*, July 1976, p. 16)

3. . . . the Palmdale bulge . . . lies along a stretch of the 600-mile San Andreas fault, a deep fracture that runs from below the Mexican border to about 100 miles north of San Francisco, where it meets the Pacific Ocean. The fault is actually the boundary of two TECTONIC plates, huge sections of the earth's outer layer that are sliding in opposite directions. A western sliver of California, on the Pacific plate, is moving northwest. The remainder of the state is being carried by the North American plate toward the southeast. (Anon., "The Palmdale Bulge," *Time*, 4/19/76, p. 85)

TELEOLOGY (tel' ē-ol' ə-jē, tē' lē-) *noun* the doctrine that final causes exist; the study of final causes; the study of the evidences of design or purpose in nature; such design or purpose; the belief that an overall purpose and design are a part of or are apparent in nature; the fact or quality of being directed toward a definite end or of having an ultimate purpose, especially as attributed to natural processes.

TELEOLOGICAL or **TELEOLOGIC** *adj.*

TELEOLOGICALLY *adv.*

TELEOLOGIST *noun.*

1. Of all existentialist plays *The Flies* [by Sartre] is most obviously written in the wake of Nietzsche's "God is Dead." Yet Orestes [the protagonist], though fully testifying to the loneliness and futility of life without God or cosmic TELEOLOGY, concludes with a positive note. "On the far side of despair," he proclaims, "life begins." (Hazel E. Barnes, "Greek

Mythical Figures As Contemporary Images," *The Key Reporter*, Summer 1976, p. 3)

TELOS (tel′ əs) *noun* end; purpose; ultimate object; aim.

1. The one dissenting voice is still that of Hegel, who discerned under the apparent disorder of the world an irresistible current of reason that would drive men . . . to the mastery of nature and themselves. It is this historical TELOS or goal that provided the utopian component of Marxism . . . (D. Bell, Review of *Structural Anthropology, Vol. II*, by Claude Lévi-Strauss, translated by Monique Layton, *New York Times*, 3/14/76, Section 7, p. 23)

TEMERITY (tə-mer′ i-tē) *noun* foolish or reckless boldness; rashness; foolhardiness; recklessness; daring.

TEMERARIOUS *adj.* rash; reckless; impetuous.

TEMERARIOUSLY *adv.*

1. And the present TEMERITY of [philanthropic] foundations must be replaced by a new intellectual and philosophic outreach that encourages more than a replication of what has worked before. (G.W. Bonham, "The Filer Report: Lessons for the Future" [Editorial], *Change*, February 1976, p. 20)

2. Given the intimidation many readers have felt on confronting the new quantification [of history], it is surprising to discover that the work here [in *The New Urban History*, edited by Leo F. Schnore] . . . is . . . more limited by TEMERITY than by arrogance. (M. Frisch, Review, *Chronicle of Higher Education*, 4/26/76, p. 20)

3. In ten years, Chadburn had not even had the TEMERITY to inquire whether Zigman was or ever had been married. (I. Wallace, *The Fan Club*, Bantam Books, 1975, p. 485)

4. How about the ways [Wayne] Hays berated Alexander Butterfield, then Federal Aviation Administration head, because an FAA cop had the TEMERITY to arrest Rep. William Alexander, a Democratic pal of Hays, for being abusive at the National Airport here. Naturally, Alexander got off, and Butterfield caved in so his appropriations wouldn't suffer. (N.

Thimmesch, "Scandal Probe Lacks Fervor," *Daily Oklahoman*, Okla. City, 4/18/76, p. 10)

5. See (3) under ACRONYM.

TENDENTIOUS (ten-den′ shəs) *adj.* having, showing, or characterized by a definite tendency, bias, purpose, or aim; especially, advancing a definite point of view; lacking impartiality; not fair or just.

TENDENTIOUSLY *adv.*

TENDENTIOUSNESS *noun.*

1. [Dennis] Smith's success, in this extraordinary book [*Report from Engine Co. 82*], is a major achievement, comparable to Claude Brown's telling us about Harlem and drugs in *Manchild in the Promised Land*, and Joe McGinniss' telling us (however TENDENTIOUSLY) about Presidential political packaging in *The Selling of the President*. (W.F. Buckley Jr., *Execution Eve and Other Contemporary Ballads*, G.P. Putnam's Sons, 1975, p. 468)

2. More accessible . . . are 23 pages done in 1946-47 for the newspaper *P.M.*, telling "How to Look" at the works and ideas, inventions and posturings, good guys and bad guys of modern art. Though almost crudely TENDENTIOUS, the anti-"humanist" slant of this series long eluded the right-thinking leftist editors of *P.M.*, according to [Thomas B.] Hess [in the book, *The Art Comics and Satires of Ad Reinhardt*]. When they did catch on, Reinhardt was fired. (P. Schjeldahl, Review, *New York Times*, 2/15/76, Section 7, p. 8)

3. A negotiating formula for the West Bank [occupied by Israel] will not be found easily or quickly. But it must be found if a peace settlement is to be achieved . . . . This, not TENDENTIOUS resolutions, should be the focus of United Nations attention, if peace is the objective. (Anon., "Necessary Veto" [Editorial], *New York Times*, 3/28/76, Section 4, p. 14)

4. See (1) under HISTORIOGRAPHER.

5. In an earlier book, *The Freudian Left*, [Paul] Robinson took up the work of three writers—Geza Roheim, Wilhelm Reich and Herbert Marcuse—who dwelt not so much on sexual behavior in itself as on its social and political implications, and who were of a more

philosophical, abstract and TENDENTIOUS nature than the people he examines here [in *The Modernization of Sex:* Havelock Ellis, Alfred Kinsey, William Masters and Virginia Johnson]. (R. Gilman, Review, *New York Times,* 5/30/76, Section 7, p. 4)

8. See (9) under BOWDLERIZE.

9. Meg Greenfield, a normally hard-headed *Newsweek* columnist, apparently also endorses the same goal of Communist legitimacy [in Spain]. In a recent feature column, she uses TENDENTIOUS quotations to do so: . . . . Spaniards "argue that the government's intention...to keep the Communist Party outlawed...would be a moral and tactical calamity, casting doubt on the independence and legitimacy of the other parties." (J. Hart, "Red Pressures in Spain," *Times Herald,* Norristown, Pa., 9/7/765, p. 13)

TENEBROUS (ten′ə-brəs) or **TENEBRIOUS** (tə-neb′rē-əs) *adj.* dark; gloomy; obscure.

TENEBRIFIC *adj.* producing or causing darkness; obscuring.

TENEBROUSNESS or **TENEBRIOUSNESS** *noun.*

1. If we look long and closely at *Diver,* the huge and TENEBROUS drawings by [Jasper] Johns which dominate the *Drawing Now* exhibition at the Museum of Modern Art, we may decide that its true point of comparison is not so much with anything else as with Rembrandt. (J. Russell, Review, *New York Times,* 2/1/76, Section 2, p. 31)

TERATOGEN (ter′ə-tə-jən) *noun* an agent, as a chemical, disease, etc., that causes malformation of a fetus.

TERATOGENIC *adj.*

TERATOID *adj.* resembling a monster; malformed or abnormal.

TERATISM *noun* a malformed fetus; monstrosity.

TERATOLOGY *noun* the scientific study of biological monstrosities and malformations.

TERATOLOGICAL *adj.*

TERATOLOGIST *noun.*

1. The story behind 2,4,5-T offers a disturbing case study of federal neglect in dealing with chemicals which may be TERATOGENIC [presumably due to the impurity dioxin]—that is, which deform babies still in the womb. (D. Zwerdling, "Deformity or death: The threat of 2,4,5-T," *Philadelphia Inquirer,* 2/15/76, p. 4-I)

TERGIVERSATE (tûr′ ji-vər-sāt′) *verb* to change repeatedly one's attitude or opinions with respect to a cause, subject, etc.; to desert a cause, party, etc.; to use evasions or subterfuge; EQUIVOCATE; vacillate; to turn or become a renegade; apostasize.

TERGIVERSATION *noun.*

TERGIVERSATOR or **TERGIVERSANT** *noun.*

TERGIVERSATORY (tûr′ji-vûr′sə-tōr′ē, -tôr′ē) *adj.*

1. [Hubert] Humphrey skewered another of [George] McGovern's TERGIVERSATIONS very neatly when he asked how come McGovern was against subsidies for Lockheed, when he was in favor of subsidies for American Motors. (W.F. Buckley Jr., *Execution Eve and Other Contemporary Ballads,* G.P. Putnam's Sons, 1975, p. 62)

2. There is a very sad witlessness in the TERGIVERSATIONS of George McGovern, whether on income redistribution, or on bases in Thailand, or on Thomas Eagleton, or on defense policies, or on Mayor Daley, or on the Mideast. (W.F. Buckley Jr., *Ibid.,* p. 92)

3. The only defense of the West against it [Communism] is the tenderest solicitude for Western values, the fastidious cultivation of the Western position, so sorely ravaged by the imprecisions and TERGIVERSATIONS of the leaders of the West. (W.F. Buckley Jr., *Up From Liberalism,* Arlington House, 2nd Printing, 1968, p. 195)

4. One [booby prize], surely, goes to lame-duck Democratic Governor [of Utah] Calvin Rampton. Though he says he believes in capital punishment, he nevertheless issued the original stay of execution [to Gary Gilmore] that opened the door to endless legal TERGIVERSATION. (J. Hart, "Crisis of Authority," *Times Herald,* Norristown, Pa., 12/18/76, p. 15)

TERMAGANT (tûr′mə-gənt) *noun* a bois-terous, quarrelsome, turbulent, brawling, scolding woman; shrew; (if capitalized) a mythical deity believed by Christians of the Middle Ages to be worshiped by Muslims and introduced into morality plays as a violent, boisterous overbearing person.

TERMAGANT *adj.* violent; turbulent; brawling; shrewish; quarrelsome; scolding.

1. On stage she [Metropolitan Opera Star Benita Valente] transforms herself into tempt-resses and TERMAGANTS and INGENUES and cour-tesans and SOUBRETTES and murderesses and princesses and an occasional sweetheart. (Mar-alyn Lois Polak, "Interview: Benita Valent," *Today*, The Inquirer Magazine, 1/30/77, p. 8)

2. She [film actress Miriam Hopkins] had tem-perament and she could act. She was also a TERMAGANT who went through a half-dozen husbands, believed in astrology and numerolo-gy, and became progressively bitchier . . . with every movie she made. (J. Barkham, Review of the book, *Ginger, Loretta, and Irene Who?* by George Eells, *Philadelphia Inquirer*, 1/9/77, p. 12-L)

THANATOLOGY (than′ə-tol′ə-jē) *noun* a description or an account of death.

THANATOLOGIST *noun.*

1. Death not only feels good, it is such a "peaceful and beautiful experience" that peo-ple who have been there—or close—do not even want to come back to this life . . . . A re-markable similarity has been noted in survi-vors' independent accounts of visions and feel-ings gathered not only by Dr. [Elisabeth Kubler-] Ross but also by other noted THANA-TOLOGISTS (those who study death). (R. Chan-dler, *Los Angeles Times*, "Life after death: 'Beyond the shadow of a doubt,' " *Norman* [Okla.] *Transcript*, 7/30/76, p. 8)

2. [Ronald] Beard [protagonist of the book, *Beard's Roman Women*, by Anthony Burgess] contracts a fatal disease and seeks the help of a THANATOLOGIST. What must he learn in order to die? (P.S. Prescott, Review, *Newsweek*, 10/25/76, p. 112)

3. See (1) under PSYCHOPOMP.

THAUMATURGE (thô′ mə-turj′) or **THAU-MATURGIST** *noun* a worker of wonders or miracles.

THAUMATURGY (-tûr′jē) *noun* the work-ing of wonders or miracles; magic.

THAUMATURGIC or **THAUMATURGICAL** *adj.* pertaining to a thaumaturge or to thau-maturgy; having the powers of a thaumaturge.

THAUMATOLOGY *noun* the study, descrip-tion, or lore of miracles.

1. It seemed to be a store but it was more like a theater. Its front was plastered with signs an-nouncing Mr. L. Reed, GASTRILOQUIST Extraor-dinary; Master Haskell, Wizzard of the Ages, THAUMATURGIST and Metamorphosist; . . . and Last Time to See the Gigantic Elephant Dis-covered in These Regions by Dr. Albert C. Koch, now of London. (J.A. Michener, *Cen-tennial*, Fawcett, 1975, p. 356)

THEOCRACY (thē-ok′ rə-sē) *noun* a form of government in which God or a deity is re-cognized as the supreme civil ruler; a system of government by priests claiming a divine com-mission; a state under such a form of govern-ment.

THEOCRAT *noun* a person who rules or governs as a representative of God or a deity, or is a member of the ruling group in a theoc-racy, as a divine king or a high priest; a person who favors theocracy.

THEOCRATICALLY *adv.*

THEOCRATIC or **THEOCRATICAL** *adj.*

1. But the kingdom [of Saudi Arabia] was still a deeply conservative THEOCRATIC state whose only law was the *sharia*, which is rather as if the Constitution of the United States were actually the Ten Commandments. The depth of the King [Faisal]'s personal commitment to Islam, and a touch of paranoia in his old age, sometimes gave this unpleasantly XENOPHOBIC aspects. He retained until the end, for exam-ple, personal control of the issue of visas for Jews and journalists, both of whom he seemed to regard rather indiscriminately as potential enemies of the state. (D. Holden, "A Family Affair," *New York Times*, 7/6/75, Section 6, p. 9)

2. The Alteration [by Kingsley Amis] is unquestionably a science-fiction novel, falling into the subdivision of "alternate worlds." The world in this case is one of the present day—but the Reformation has never occurred, the Holy Roman Empire is still with us, and young and innocent male sopranos (not to mention the world at large) are subject to physical and metaphysical castration at the hands of a brutal THEOCRACY. (Edna Stumpf, Review, *Philadelphia Inquirer*, 1/30/77, p. 10-D)

THEODICY (thē-od′i-sē) *noun* a vindication of the goodness of God in respect to the existence of evil.

THEODICEAN *adj.*

. Trained as an empirically oriented physician, . . . [C.G.] Jung claimed to have analyzed over 67,000 dreams of patients . . . . Jung subsequently generated prodigious research into such widely divergent subjects as mythology, alchemy, THEODICY, aesthetics, and flying saucers, as well as the full range of psychic disorders. (J. Hollis, Review of *C.G. Jung: His Myth in Our Time*, by Marie-Louise von Franz, translated by William H. Kennedy; *C.G. Jung: The Haunted Prophet*, by Paul J. Stern; and *Jung and the Story of Our Time*, by Laurens van der Post, *Chronicle of Higher Education*, 7/2/76, p. 9)

THEOSOPHY (thē-os′ə-fē) *noun* any of various philosophies or religious systems that propose to establish direct, mystical contact with divine principle through contemplation, revelation, etc.; the doctrines and beliefs of a modern sect (Theosophical Society) of this nature that incorporates elements of Buddhism and Brahmanism.

THEOSOPHIC or THEOSOPHICAL *adj.*

THEOSOPHICALLY *adv.*

THEOSOPHIST *noun.*

. It was Annie Besant, the social reformer and THEOSOPHIST, who first insisted that society must be reformed "by the slow process of evolution, not by revolution and bloodshed." (M. Holroyd, Review of *The Fabians*, a book by Norman and Jeanne MacKenzie, *New York Times*, 3/27/77, p. 38)

THRENODY (thren′ ə-dē) or **THRENODE** (thrē′nōd) *noun* a poem, speech, or song of lamentation, especially for the dead; dirge; funeral song; lament.

THRENODIAL or THRENODIC *adj.*

THRENODIST *noun.*

1. This [the traditional empathy with the loser] . . . underlies the old adage . . . ("The proud Tairas endure but for a little time"); and it informs the opening THRENODY of *The Tale of the Heike* [translated by Hiroshi Kitagawa and Bruce Tsuchida], surely one of the most affecting statements in literature about the uncertainty of human fortunes and the ultimate futility of worldy endeavor. (I. Morris, Review, *New York Times*, 2/8/76, Section 7, p. 23)

2. In "Tom" [one of the stories in *The Shrine And Other Stories*, by Mary Lavin] the story begins with . . . : "My father's hair was black as the Devil's, and he flew into black, black rages." It continues . . . through the mounting THRENODY of the daughter-narrator to inform us of the fate of this particular family: of courtship, of marriage, a wife's death, a widower's survival, of possibilities not grasped to live differently, SUSSERANT (sic) echoes of old pain as promises cease to shine. (M. Fineman, Review, *Philadelphia Inquirer*, 11/13/77, p. 12-H)

THROMBOSIS (throm-bō′sis) *noun* intravascular coagulation (clotting) of the blood in any part of the circulatory system, as in the heart, arteries, veins, or capillaries.

THROMBOTIC *adj.*

1. His [Norman Lear's] situation comedies, especially *All in the Family* and *Maude*, wear their wisecracks like strings of grenades; every two minutes somebody pulls a pin . . . . Each weekly program, moreover, is . . . a KAMIKAZE attack on the attention, THROMBOTIC. (J. Leonard, Review of the soap opera, "Mary Hartman, Mary Hartman," *New York Times*, 2/1/76, Section 2, p. 27)

TIMOROUS (tim′ ər-əs) *adj.* full of fear; fearful; subject to fear; timid; characterized by or indicating fear.

TIMOROUSLY *adv.*

TIMOROUSNESS *noun.*

1. TIMOROUSLY, he [Leo Brunner] gave these [signed and addressed postcards] up to The Mechanic [Shively] . . . to be forwarded on to the chick in Baltimore, who in turn would see that they were mailed [to Mrs. Brunner] at three intervals between June 23rd and June 30th. (I. Wallace, *The Fan Club*, Bantam Books, 1975, p. 155)

2. The chestnut [horse] alone wanted to investigate this mystery [a frozen mammoth embedded in a glacier], and in succeeding days he returned TIMOROUSLY to the small canyon, still puzzled, still captivated by a situation that could not be understood. In the end he knew nothing, so he kicked his heels at the silent mammoth, returned to the grassy area, and led his herd back toward the main road to Asia. (J.A. Michener, *Centennial*, Fawcett, 1975, p. 95)

3. The four [Pasquinel, Lise and Grete Bockweiss, McKeag] ate together frequently, but between Grete and McKeag little was happening. He was TIMOROUS with ladies and blushed as red as his beard when pretty Grete teased, "I'll bet you have a squaw hidden upstream." (J.A. Michener, *Ibid.*, p. 237)

4. He [author Morris Dickstein] portrays himself [in the book, *Gates of Eden: American Culture in the Sixties*] as a TIMOROUS marcher on the Pentagon in 1967, a "good boy" who found it hard to decide what "good" meant any more. (W. Clemons, Review, *Newsweek*, 3/28/77, p. 78)

TINTINNABULATION (tin′ti-nab′yə-lā-shən) *noun* the ringing or sound of bells.

TINTINNABULAR or TINTINNABULATORY or TINTINNABULOUS *adj.* of or pertaining to bells or bell ringing.

1. These ghostly scenes [in the opera, *The Voyage of Edgar Allan Poe*, by Dominick Argento], laced with lines from Poe's writing and accompanied by the frequent TINTINNABULATION of bells, evoke the hallucinatory quality of his work. (H. Saal, Review, *Newsweek*, 5/10/76, p. 121)

2. See (1) under SUSURROUS.

3. The Medieval city was dominated by the sound of church bells and (indoors) the great

cathedral organs . . . . And so, when the TINTINNABULATIONS of church bells began to give way to the clamor of industry and the thunder of traffic it was a sure sign that a shift of power—from the sacred to the secular—was taking place. (B. Marvel, Review of *The Tuning of the World*, a book by R. Murray Schafer, *National Observer*, 7/11/77, p. 19)

TITILLATE (tit′ə lāt′) *verb* to excite a tingling sensation in, as by touching or stroking lightly; to excite agreeably, especially superficially.

TITILLATINGLY *adv.*

TITILLATIVE *adj.*

TITILLATION *noun.*

1. Whether, if a tape recorder had existed in the nineteenth century, the Presidents then would have gone to the NARCISSISTIC excesses of recording every expletive uttered in the privacy of their quarters for the TITILLATION of future historians, one simply cannot guess. (W.F. Buckley Jr., *Execution Eve and Other Contemporary Ballads*, G.P. Putnam's Sons, 1975, p. 149)

2. See (4) under PECCADILLO.

3. Professor [Daniel] Bell [author of *The Cultural Contradictions of Capitalism*] sees the evolution of AVANT-GARDE art as a movement from a daring venture . . . to a mere mood of mutinousness, which attacks undefended citadels and deludes its purchasers into believing that it is outrage when it is only TITILLATION. (Anon., Review, *The New Yorker*, 2/9/76, p. 111)

4. . . . . Father Peter decides to exorcise her after all medical and psychiatric tests have proved negative . . . . This is the most credible episode in the quintet of contemporary case histories of demoniacal possession that make up Malachi Martin's TITILLATING new book [*Hostage to the Devil: The Possession and Exorcism of Five Living Americans*]. (Francine duPlessix Gray, Review, *New York Times*, 3/14/76, Section 7, p. 8)

5. . . . much of what she [Lucy Clifford] produced was the standard Victorian and Edwardian stew of romance, melodrama, high-

mindedness, and high life, spiced with just enough passion to TITILLATE but not actually shock the reader. (Alison Lurie, Review of Lucy Clifford's Writings, *New York Review of Books*, 12/11/75, p. 26)

6. Here [in *Against Our Will: Men, Women and Rape*, by Susan Brownmiller] . . . is every admonitory rape story you were ever told, horrifying in the way that propaganda is horrifying and also TITILLATING just in the way publishers hope a book will be TITILLATING . . . the exemplary anecdotes . . . must appeal at some level to the instincts they illustrate and deprecate . . . . (Diane Johnson, Review, *New York Review of Books*, 12/11/75, p. 36)

7. Eva [in *Eva's Man*, by Gayl Jones] murdered and sexually mutilated a man she met by chance . . . and spent five days with. Her crime appalls but TITILLATES . . . (Margo Jefferson, Review, *Newsweek*, 4/12/76, p. 104)

8. Composed of bizarre individuals [fish] and characterized by baffling behavior, the Deep Scattering Layers [of oceans] retain enough mystery to TITILLATE almost anyone. (J. McCarthy, "Ups and Downs of Deep Scattering Layers in Oceans," *Smithsonian*, April 1976, p. 78)

9. He [Ronald Reagan] charmed the commonfolk clustered at the Battle Creek airport, MESMERIZED an audience of real estate people in Kalamazoo, and TITILLATED an audience of 2,000 at . . . Detroit's prestigious Economic Club. (A. Cromley, "Reagan Uses Actor's Skill in Michigan," *Saturday Oklahoman & Times*, Okla. City, 5/15/76, p. 16)

10. Not all the media are TITILLATED by the move toward personality reporting . . . . The New Yorker . . . maintains rigid notions of what is fit to print. (Linda Bird Francke, *et al.*, "Gossip Mania," *Newsweek*, 5/24/76, p. 64)

11. No mass-marketed movie has ever been better gauged [than *That's Entertainment, Part 2*] to TITILLATE the superiority complexes of old-movie buffs . . . (C. Michener, M. Kasindorf, Review, *Newsweek*, 5/31/76, p. 51)

12. *Helter Skelter*, CBS's TITILLATING treatment of the Manson murders, was blacked out by stations in Pittsburgh, San Francisco and Portland, Me. (H.F. Waters, Betsy Carter, "Affiliates' Lib," *Newsweek*, 6/7/76, p. 53)

13. See (1) under CHI-CHI.

14. In the old, innocent moviegoing days the term "foreign film" had overtones of something exotic, TITILLATING, shocking, and perhaps outrageous. (J. Kroll, Review of three foreign films, *Newsweek*, 6/14/76, p. 90-E)

15. ". . . she [Sharon Field]'s taking off this Thursday morning for London . . . . The TITILLATING question is—Why this sudden change in schedule? . . . . We have one guess, and his initials are Roger Clay" [radio report]. (I. Wallace, *The Fan Club*, Bantam Edition, 1975, p. 167)

16. See (2) under PEDERASTY.

17. He [Billy Carter] hates reporters, . . . but he talks with them endlessly, giving the most TITILLATING observations ("I recall when on Sunday morning you could go out and take a leak in the main street of Plains [Georgia] and nobody would see you; now you got 2,000 people or more crawling all over the place.") (T. Tiede, "Will Billy Carter Be Humiliation?" *Times Herald*, Norristown, Pa., 12/15/76, p. 17)

TONTINE (ton' tēn, ton-tēn´) *noun* a form of annuity in which the amount left to each subscriber increases as other subscribers die [after Lorenzo Tonti, a Neapolitan banker who introduced the system into France in the 17th century]; the annuity so shared; the group of subscribers.

1. He [David Hackett Fischer] assembles [in the book, *Growing Old in America*] anecdotes of the high . . . social status of the old in pre-17th-century cultures where, few in number, they had both the prestige derived from being clan heads and grandparents, and the concentration of economic power natural to survivors. Property ownership was a kind of TONTINE, in which the last survivor took the kitty. (A. Comfort, Review, *New York Times*, 4/17/77, Section 7, p. 9)

TOPIARY (tō' pē-er´ē) *noun*, *pl.*: **TOPIARIES** a garden containing topiary work; topiary art or work.

TOPIARY *adj.* of, pertaining to, or designating the art of trimming and training shrubs or trees into unnatural ornamental shapes.

1. The Dickens era [in Public Broadcasting Service programming] is well begun with this production of *Hard Times*, which is as spare as [Trollope's] *The Pallisers* is lush . . . the two series are ideal companions. Trollope wrote of power struggles in Parliament and of intrigue under the TOPIARY at the country house of the Duke of Omnium. In *Hard Times* Dickens explained what life was like for those who could only peer through the gates—and how much misery it cost to maintain those ducal shrubs in such well-shaved elegance. (G. Clarke, "And Now, Here's Charles Dickens," *Time*, 5/16/77, p. 57)

TORPID (tôr′pid) *adj.* inactive or sluggish; slow; dull; apathetic; lethargic; dormant.

TORPIDLY *adv.*

TORPIDITY or **TORPIDNESS** *noun.*

TORPOR *noun* a state of suspended physical powers and activities; sluggish inactivity or inertia; dormancy; lethargic dullness or indifference; apathy; stupor.

1. I assume that directed physical exertion can proceed thoughtlessly, without the philosophical benediction of a culture otherwise TORPID, shiftless, and prideless. (W.F. Buckley Jr., *Execution Eve and Other Contemporary Ballads*, G.P. Putnam's Sons, 1975, p. 227)

2. See (1) under MALAISE.

3. There's a scene [in the play, *Zalmen or The Madness of God*, by Elie Wiesel] that apparently won't work no matter how you stage it, and since the scene goes straight to the heart of the play its brief failure is fatal. A company of foreign actors touring Russia asks permission to attend Yom Kippur services in a village synagogue. Zalmen, the local rabbi's hoptoad of a sexton, . . . urges the . . . rabbi to shake off his TORPOR and speak out to the strangers during his sermon. This act is rash to the point of madness because a commissar and guards will be on hand. (W. Kerr, Review, *New York Times*, 3/28/76, Section 2, p. 5)

4. At its bleakest, relativism brings TORPOR, NIHILISM, meaninglessness: humanity as a mass of impotent cockroaches . . . relativism is opportunism and expedience, the core of the decadent hippie ideology . . . . This decadence springs in part from SOLIPSISTIC origins. Lennon's song . . . finally retreats from the burden of critical work and hibernates: He believes, finally, only in himself . . . . Dealing with burned-out hippies—. . . to whom critical commitments are as alien as the Fortune 500 or the Resurrection—trashing these poor sixties souls as if they were exemplary of the best their generation has to offer, or as if their SOLIPSISM were the root moral message of the last decade, has, alas, become fashionable . . . . What happened in America in the sixties, we are told by those unable to distinguish DIALECTIC from decadence, resulted because no one had any values. (M. Kaplan, "The Ideologies of 'Tough Times'," *Change*, August 1976, p. 28)

5. Soon forgotten by his [Russian Army] superiors, he [Private Ivan Chonkin, in the book, *The Life and Extraordinary Adventures of Private Ivan Chonkin*, by Vladimir Voinovich] moves in with the local spinster and is gradually assimilated into the TORPID life of the town. (P.S. Prescott, Review, *Newsweek*, 2/14/77, p. 87)

TOTEM (tō′təm) *noun* a natural object or an animate being, as an animal or bird, assumed as the emblem of a clan, family, or group; an object or natural phenomenon with which a primitive family or sib considers itself closely related.

TOTEMIC *adj.*

TOTEMICALLY *adv.*

TOTEMISM *noun* the practice of having or believing in totems and totemic relationships; the system of tribal division according to totems; social customs based on this division.

TOTEMIST *noun.*

1. Of Communist China's leaders I believe he [Chou En-lai] was least stylized, least TOTEMIC, most comfortably himself, most truly the man he seemed to be . . . (A. Suehsdorf, "Remembering Chou En-lai in Yenan," *New York Times*, 1/11/76, Section 4, p. 19)

2. See (2) under DERACINATE.

3. If Russia is hard to fathom except by reli-

ance on TOTEMISM, China is far worse. The great wall of secrecy makes it almost impossible even for Sinologists to be certain what is taking place. (C.L. Sulzberger, "Behind the Great Wall of China," *New York Times*, 5/2/76, Section 4, p. 15)

4. If you can fit your numbers into a bell curve, or establish congruency with some statistical generalization . . . , you may safely assume that your data reflect the existence and behavior of a real entity. In this way statistical method itself becomes statistical proof, and numbers become TOTEMS. Moreover, the aggregate thrust of *The I.Q. Controversy* [a book edited by N.J. Block and Gerald Dworkin] suggests that I.Q. may be the biggest TOTEM of them all. (R. Zoellner, Review, *Chronicle of Higher Education*, 9/27/76, p. 18)

5. See (3) under NATTER.

TRADUCE (trə-dōōs', -dyōōs') *verb* to speak maliciously and falsely of; slander; defame; malign; vilify; to make a mockery of; betray.

TRADUCEMENT *noun*.

TRADUCER *noun*.

TRADUCINGLY *adv*.

1. [Quote from a letter to the Parisian Director of Public Works from a large number of artists protesting the erection of the Eiffel Tower:] "We writers, painters, sculptors, architects, all passionately concerned with that spirit of beauty which, till now, had been preserved intact in Paris, wish to protest with all possible strength, all possible indignation, in the name of the TRADUCED taste of France, in the name of French art and history, now menaced and threatened, against the erection, in the very heart of our capital, of this useless monster, which an affronted public . . . has already baptized 'The Tower of Babel.' " (A. Burgess, " 'A $200 million Erector Set' " *New York Times*, 1/23/77, Section 6, p. 22)

2. You could call this caper Roots TRADUCED, or maybe The Revenge of the Confederacy. It seems that in two widely separated locales, copies of *Roots* [by Alex Haley] have turned up with the text of *Gone With the Wind* [by Margaret Mitchell] bound inside. That is, the

books had *Roots* jackets and binding, but the words on the pages were all about Scarlett O'Hara and Rhett Butler. (R.R. Lingeman, "Gone With the Roots," *New York Times*, 3/27/77, Section 7, p. 63)

3. "The biggest problem with our contemporary bookchat critics is that they are incapable of describing, or apprehending, or comprehending what they see. Is it the Taj Mahal? Is it a pavilion? A coliseum? . . . . All distinction is resented, and that which has been distinguished is TRADUCED . . ." said Gore Vidal. (Diane Johnson, "Gore Vidal, Scorekeeper," *New York Times*, 4/17/77, Section 7, p. 47)

TRANSCENDENTAL (tran' sen-den' t°l) or **TRANSCENDENT** *adj*. surpassing or superior; being beyond ordinary or common experience, thought, or belief; extraordinary; supernatural; abstract or metaphysical; abstruse.

TRANSCENDENCE *noun*.

TRANSCEND *verb* to rise above or go beyond the limts of; overstep; exceed; to outdo or exceed in excellence, degree, etc.; surpass; excel.

TRANSCENDINGLY *adv*.

1. See (1) under BOURGEOIS.

2. In this way Europe [between 1850 and 1950] disbursed a quarter of its population [by emigration] and was able to double its tilled land and treble its pastureland, thus temporarily resolving its food and population problems. By this grandiose TRANSCENDENCE of his limits, Western Man lost his awareness of the biological constraints of our globe. (G. Borgstrom, "The numbers force us into a world like none in history," *Smithsonian*, July 1976, p. 72)

3. See (3) under ENTROPY.

4. See (8) under AVANT-GARDE.

5. See (3) under FRISSON.

6. See (1) under ESCHATOLOGY.

7. See (1) under PERTINACIOUS.

TRANSMOGRIFY (trans-mog'rə-fi', tranz-) *verb* to change completely in appearance or form, especially grotesquely; transform.

TRANSMOGRIFICATION *noun*.

1. [Nathan] Glazer's handling of some particular issues [in his book, *Affirmative Discrimination: Ethnic Inequality and Public Policy*] is striking, at once closely argued and witty, as . . . in his discussion of the distinction between DE FACTO and DE JURE segregation and the wonderful TRANSMOGRIFICATION of the former into the latter in some arguments for numerical quotas by affirmative-action agencies. Or in his treatment of the CHIMERAS of the "unitary" school district and the stably integrated neighborhood. (C. Cohen, Review, *Chronicle of Higher Education*, 3/1/76, p. 13)

2. If she can steady her grip on her terrifying, TRANSMOGRIFYING wit, there may yet be a great novel in the already vast [Joyce Carol] Oates canon. (Anon., Review of *The Assassins*, by Joyce Carol Oates, *Time*, 2/23/76, p. 65)

3. Racked by the humiliating pains of what seems to be rectal cancer, the tough old guy [Clive Langham, a character in the film, *Providence*] sweats out his ordeal while composing a novel whose characters are TRANSMOGRIFICATIONS of the people in his life. (J. Kroll, Review, *Newsweek*, 2/28/77, p. 73)

4. Throughout much of human history, the old . . . have held positions of privilege, as many of our honorific words imply—senator, veteran, guru, alderman, seigneur, presbyter—all TRANSMOGRIFICATIONS of the words for "old." So why in modern America, are the old regarded so vindictively? (A. Comfort, Review of *Growing Old in America*, a book by David Hackett Fischer, *New York Times*, 4/17/77, Section 7, p. 9)

TRANSPONTINE (trans-pon' tin, -tïn) *adj.* across or beyond a bridge; on the southern side of the Thames River in London.

1. Jesse Abramson, the skilled hard-boiled boxing writer, said my dressing-room story [after the Dodgers' loss to the Yankees in the 7th game of the 1953 World Series] showed excessive emotional involvement. Bob Cooke and Irving Marsh agreed. The TRANSPONTINE madness had me in thrall. "Take a week off," Cooke said. "Get more perspective." (R. Kahn, *The Boys of Summer*, Harper and Row, 1971, p. 185)

2. [Quote from Stanley Woodward, sports

editor of N.Y. Herald Tribune]: "We found it advisable to shift Brooklyn writers frequently. If we hadn't, we would have had on our hands a member of the Brooklyn baseball club, rather than a newspaper reporter. The TRANSPONTINE madness seems to affect all baseball writers, no matter how sensible they outwardly seem. You must watch a Brooklyn writer for symptoms and, before they become virulent, shift him to the Yankees or to tennis or golf." (R. Kahn, *Ibid.*, p. xiii)

TRANSVESTITE (trans-ves' tït, tranz' -) *noun* a person who derives sexual pleasure from dressing in the clothes of the opposite sex.

TRANSVESTISM or **TRANSVESTITISM** *noun* the practice of wearing clothing appropriate to the opposite sex, often as a manifestation of homosexuality.

TRANSVESTIC or **TRANSVESTITE** *adj.*

1. She [Coco Chanel] cultivated a tomboyish *jeune fille* look, dressing in strict tailor-made suits and a boater, inventing costume parties so she could attend them in her lover's clothes. This TRANSVESTITISM became the backbone of her style. Throughout the next forty years she would raid her men's closets and bureau drawers for inspiration. (Francine Gray, Review of *Chanel*, a book by Edmonde Charles-Roux, *New York Review of Books*, 12/11/75, p. 44)

2. Are the sex-change operations just a more sophisticated TRANSVESTISM or do they actually reverse sexuality? . . . . There's no consensus at this point, and chances are there won't be for some time to come. (J.E. Baxter, "Why Shouldn't We Change Sex?," *Newsweek*, 9/27/76, p. 21)

3. [Dino] Risi and Ruggiero Maccari, who wrote the sketches [for the film, *How Funny Can Sex Be?*], include some tasteless failures, most notably . . . one about a bumpkin and a TRANSVESTITE that tries to be POIGNANT and ends up being shabby. (D. Ryan, Review, *Philadelphia Inquirer*, 10/22/76, p. 6-C)

4. See (3) under PROLETARIAN.

5. And there's Rick, the bar stud, [Lily] Tomlin's first major male character. Tomlin pays back Chaplin's TRANSVESTITE VIGNETTES with this masterpiece of MACHO desperation—Rick

hitching up his fly as he talks sports . . . (J. Kroll, "Lily Tomlin: Funny Lady," *Newsweek*, 3/28/77, p. 64)

TRAVERTINE (trav′ ər-tin, -tēn) *noun* a form of light-colored limestone deposited by mineral springs, especially hot springs, used in Italy for building.

1. See (1) under MOIRÉ.

2. The walls of the stage [of Avery Fisher Hall] are made of dark brown oak, and the brown is carried outside to the foyers, where the massive TRAVERTINE pillars are now painted a chocolate brown. The downstairs areas also have a good deal of brown. (H.C. Schonberg, "Fisher Hall, Redone, Faces the Real Test," *New York Times*, 10/14/76, p. 35)

TRAVESTY (trav′i-stē′) *noun* a literary or artistic burlesque of a serious work or subject, characterized by grotesque or ludicrous incongruity of style, treatment, subject matter, etc.; a literary or artistic composition so inferior in quality as to seem merely a grotesque imitation of its model; any grotesque, crude, or debased likeness.

TRAVESTY *verb* to make a travesty on; burlesque; counterfeit; mock.

1. See (3) under BOWDLERIZE.

2. A TRAVESTY is a "burlesque or ludicrous imitation of a serious work," a "grotesque image or likeness," a PARODY. Murder is a TRAVESTY of love, sickness is a TRAVESTY of health, death is a TRAVESTY of life. Psychopathic derangement is a TRAVESTY of human reason, and our amiable narrator [in the book, *Travesty*, by John Hawkes] is a kind of diabolic genius at the perverse art of TRAVESTY. (T. Tanner, Review, *New York Times*, 3/28/76, Section 7, p. 24)

3. One song [in *So Long, 174th Street*] is a TRAVESTY of Leporello's "catalog" aria from *Don Giovanni* . . . (J. Kroll, Review, *Newsweek*, 5/10/76, p. 76)

4. See (2) under PEDOPHILIA.

5. See (3) under AMELIORATE.

6. By current standards, the trial [of Bruno Richard Hauptmann for kidnapping the Lindbergh baby] was a TRAVESTY. Publisher William Randolph Hearst paid Hauptmann's lawyer, Edward J. Reilly, $25,000 in exchange for exclusive rights to the family's story. Four times a day, the jurors trekked through crowds that shouted "Burn Hauptmann." (J.K. Footlick and Susan Agrest, "Did Hauptmann Do It?" *Newsweek*, 12/6/76, p. 64)

7. See (1) under ANOREXIA.

TREACLE (trē′ kəl) *noun* originally, a remedy for poison; a molasses, especially that which is drained from the vats used in sugar refining; a mild mixture of molasses, corn syrup, etc., used in cooking or as a table syrup; contrived or unrestrained sentimentality.

TREACLY (trē′klē) *adj.*

1. His [Paul McCartney's] tunes are elaborately homespun, lined with shifting, driving rhythms and coy harmonies, their lyrics full of flights of gentle, sometimes TREACLY fantasy. (Anon., "McCartney Comes Back," *Time*, 5/31/76, p. 41)

2. Marilyn and Alan Bergman, who may well be the worst cornball lyricists that Hollywood has ever spawned, crank out [for the movie, *Harry and Walter Go To New York*] just the right brand of TREACLE to explain why the [Elliott] Gould—[James] Caan duo will never strike it rich in their ill-chosen field. (Janet Maslin, Review, *Newsweek*, 6/28/76, pp. 77–78)

3. With the Air and Space Museum, Washington and the Smithsonian have finally moved into the 20th century architecturally . . . . It has been a slow, hard trip . . . . There is a certain TREACLE-like logic about the process and the result. (Ada Louise Huxtable, "Supermuseum Comes to the Mall," *New York Times*, 7/4/76, Section 2, p. 22)

4. During the period in which they were competing for the [Olympic Games] contract, both ABC and CBS produced shows about the USSR that were uncritical to the point of embarrassment. CBS even sent Mary Tyler Moore to Moscow for a TREACLY show. (J. Hart, "NBC Defends Moscow Deal," *Times Herald*, Norristown, Pa., 5/12/77, p. 23)

TRENCHANT (tren′chənt) *adj.* incisive or keen, as language or a person; penetrating;

forceful; vigorous; effective; energetic; clearly or sharply defined; clearcut; distinct.

TRENCHANTLY adv.

TRENCHANCY noun.

1. . . . in the present work [The Olive of Minerva: Or The Comedy of a Cuckold] [author Edward] Dahlberg aims many a barb of TRENCHANT wit at this target [culture]. (J.D. O'Hara, Review, New York Times, 4/18/76, Section 7, p. 20)

2. And though the Yale company has given us a plain, followable reading [of Shakespeare's Troilus and Cressida], it hasn't done more than that; the level is academic stock-company with some mumblers and some reasonably TRENCHANT warrior-lovers in the group. (W. Kerr, Review, New York Times, 4/18/76, Section 2, p. 20)

3. Despite his TRENCHANT criticism of the medical establishment, [Ivan] Illich has elicited enthusiastic responses [to his book, Medical Nemesis] from its members at Harvard, Yale, and other medical schools during a tour in May of U.S. campuses. (K.L. Woodward, Review, Newsweek, 6/7/76, p. 87)

4. See (2) under ENTROPY.

5. Until his recent death, W.K. Wimsatt . . . was an extraordinary force in practical criticism and in theory of poetry. His final collection [Day of the Leopards: Essays in Defense of Poems] shows him at his most subtle, TRENCHANT, and logical. (G.A. Cardwell, Review, The Key Reporter, Summer 1976, p. 7)

6. Auberon Waugh . . . has tried his hand at fiction but is a much more TRENCHANT observer and wit in his frequent reviews of fiction for Books & Bookmen and The Evening Standard [of London]. (F. Lipsius, "What happens to books crossing the Atlantic?," Philadelphia Inquirer, 1/30/77, p. 11-D)

TREPIDATION (trep' i-dā' shən) noun tremulous fear, alarm or agitation; apprehension; fearful uncertainty, anxiety, etc.; perturbation; trembling or quivering movement; vibration; tremor; quaking.

1. Reagan's speech to the prestigious Economic Club of Detroit, dominated by Ford supporters, was well received (despite his own TREPIDATIONS that he might flop there). (R. Evans, R. Novak, "Reagan Support Not From Party," Daily Oklahoman, Okla. City, 5/19/76, p. 6)

2. With TREPIDATION, he [Adam Malone] had returned for one last inspection of the master bedroom and the Celestial Bed, and found that Shively's body had been covered by a white linen sheet. (I. Wallace, The Fan Club, Bantam Books, 1975, p. 623)

3. It must have been with a quiver of TREPIDATION that he [Paul Hughes] told his thirsting little group that Senator [Joseph] McCarthy and his staff had amassed an arsenal of pistols, lugers, and submachine guns in the basement of the Senate Office Building. (W.F. Buckley Jr., Up From Liberalism, Arlington House, 2nd Printing 1968, p. 110)

TRIAGE (trē' äzh) noun the provision of aid (in a situation in which the total need exceeds the capacity for providing help) only to those most likely to benefit; a system of assigning priorities of medical treatment to battlefield casualties on the basis of urgency, chance for survival, etc.; refuse of coffee beans.

1. No one really likes TRIAGE—the selection of those nations most likely to survive and the concentration of our available food aid on them. The question can only arise if we should reach the point where the world population outruns food resources. When such a situation arises, some people will die no matter what the disposition of the inadequate food supply . . . . In that event, some hard decisions will have to be made. (Advertisement of The Environmental Fund, Smithsonian, March 1976, p. 29)

2. What the [philanthropic] foundations now face with increasing frequency is economic TRIAGE, where exceedingly worthy programs must be sacrificed in favor of the few that are supportable . . . . For [the] Danforth [Foundation], TRIAGE arrived somewhat earlier than for most . . . . (G.W. Bonham, "Hard Choices for Foundations" [Editorial], Change, September 1975, p. 11)

3. . . . anyone who regards eugenics as of "marginal interest" in a world of Shockley,

psychosurgery and talk of TRIAGE, is not a very acute observer of the contemporary scene. (S.J. Gould, "S.J. Gould replies" [to an author disturbed by Gould's review of his book], *New York Times*, 1/11/76, Section 7, p. 28)

4. Limited resources of manpower and money are in fact forcing us into employing on a planetary scale an environmental form of TRIAGE, the practice evolved by Allied forces in World War I of sorting the wounded into three groups: those likely to die despite medical care, those so lightly wounded as to probably recover without care, and the remainder on whom medical resources were concentrated. Should we be deciding on which species and which ecosystems to use our meager conservation resources? And which . . . shall we decide to write off? (T. Lovejoy, "We must decide which species will go forever," *Smithsonian*, July 1976, p. 56)

5. "I think this city [New York] is falling and burning apart," says a Bronx fire official. "Last July I was working as a dispatcher and there was a call every 50 seconds. My gut feeling is we're under siege. TRIAGE—that's where I think we're at. You've got to be a MASOCHIST, or in a rut, to stay here." (D. Gelman, "Polishing The Apple," *Newsweek*, 7/19/76, pp. 34-35)

6. Dr. [Gerrett] Hardin, an ecologist at the University of California, Santa Barbara, is well known as an advocate of TRIAGE or "the lifeboat ethic," in world food matters. He has argued that as global food shortages become more intense, the United States should not grant food aid but instead should permit famines to reduce the number of people in developing countries. If the United States shares its food, Dr. Hardin argues, it will hurt this country's chance of survival and in other countries merely postpone a worse famine later . . . . Statements from the audience [at a conference in Philadelphia on food and nutrition] that Dr. Hardin was wrong and that his views should have been discarded long ago drew a strong round of applause. (Boyce Rensberger, "Serious World Food Gap Is Seen Over the Long Term by Experts," *New York Times*, 12/5/76, Section 1, p. 67)

TRIASSIC (trī-as'ik) *adj.* noting or pertaining to the first period of the Mesozoic era occurring from 180 million to 220 million years ago; characterized by volcanic activity and the advent of dinosaurs and marine reptiles.

TRIASSIC *noun* the Triassic period or system.

1. He [Silvio Conte] begins [his letter] by saying that he takes "exception" to my "shrill ode to TRIASSIC CEREBRATIONS." I don't know what that means, but cannot assume that it matters. (W.F. Buckley Jr., *Execution Eve and Other Contemporary Ballads*, G.P. Putnam's Sons, 1975, p. 291)

TRIPTYCH (trip'tik) *noun* (in Fine Arts) a set of three panels or compartments side by side, bearing pictures, carvings, or the like, and often hinged together so that the two side panels may be folded over the central one, as in some altar pieces.

1. Yet even here we are reminded of an architectural precedent: Michelangelo's final design for the tomb of Julius II, composed as a monumental TRIPTYCH. On the tomb, the central figure of Moses—like St. Peter a ruler, founder and seer—is flanked by the statues of Leah and Rachel, the Old Testament sisters who, like Martha and Mary of the New Testament, symbolize the active and the contemplative life. (L. Steinberg, "Michelangelo's last painting: his gift to this century," *Smithsonian*, December 1975, p. 81)

TROGLODYTE (trog'lə-dīt') *noun* a cave man or cave dweller; a person, as a hermit, living in seclusion or in a primitive or degraded state; a recluse; one who shuns the society of others; any person of a primitive or degraded way of thinking; an ANTHROPOID ape.

TROGLODYTIC or TROGLODYTICAL *adj.*

1. It is possible today, without being branded as a woebegone TROGLODYTE, to question the "damn the cost, full speed ahead" drive behind the Great Society programs as the fiscal iceberg looms ominously ahead. (G. Hauge, "Everybody's Special Interest," *Newsweek*, 12/15/75, p. 19)

2. If the President [Ford] wins his party's nomination at Kansas City in August, only a

handful of super-TROGLODYTES will want to sit on their hands and sulk. (J.J. Kilpatrick, "Republican Partisans Encouraged to Stay Unified by 'Cooling It,' " *Daily Oklahoman*, Okla. City, 1/14/76, p. 8)

3. After the Somme, a new kind of battleground had been given to England: an open mass grave under a leaking sky, inhabited by shell-shocked TROGLODYTES. (R. Hughes, Review of the book, *A Prince of Our Disorder*, by John E. Mack, *Time*, 4/12/76, p. 93)

4. . . . not even mountain climbers understand the pale, mud-smeared TROGLODYTES whose curious passion it is to worm their way down through the clammy dark into the deepest and narrowest capillaries of caves. (J. Skow, Review of *The Longest Cave*, a book by Roger W. Brucker and Richard A. Watson, *Time*, 8/16/76, p. 70)

5. Malta has been settled since the Stone Age. Descend into the Stone Age caves and you find engineering skill simply astounding. The strategic island, with its ancient TROGLODYTE houses built in the sides of the cliffs, has been ruled successively for 35 centuries by Phoenicians, Greeks, Carthaginians, Romans, Arabs, Normans, the Knights of Malta, France and Britain . . . . (H.J. Taylor, "Vance Unhappy Over Malta," *Times Herald*, Norristown, Pa., 2/23/77, p. 17)

6. He [Blackford Oakes] had taken to exercising in the morning and weekends, and was a trim 170 pounds, and his light suntan belied the TROGLODYTIC life spent plumbing the mysteries of the spooks. (W.F. Buckley Jr., *Saving the Queen*, Doubleday, 1976, p. 41)

TROMPE L'OEIL (trômp′lä′) visual deception, especially in paintings in which such a strong illusion of reality is created that the viewer on first sight is in doubt as to whether the thing depicted is real or a representation; a painting, mural, or panel of wallpaper designed to create such an effect; an illusion or effect of this kind.

1. Logan's professional dishonesty is matched by the unscrupulousness of a mercenary hired by Braxton, a man called Lee Clayton (Marlon Brando), who first appears [in the film, *The Missouri Breaks*] on an apparently unridden

horse. A piece of TROMPE L'OEIL. There is an earnest-looking head of a man hanging upside down below the horse's neck. (Penelope Gilliatt, Review, *The New Yorker*, 5/31/76, p. 100)

2. *The October Circle* [title of a book by Robert Littell] is a coterie of Bulgarian expartisans whose disillusionment is deepening during 1969 *(sic)*, the year of the Soviet invasion of Hungary . . . . Significantly, the centerpiece of the hotel lobby where they met is a TROMPE L'OEIL painting of a mirror. In it, the October Circle can see what appears to be a reflection of the lobby. But they cannot see themselves. (M. Levin, Review, *New York Times*, 2/15/76, Section 7, p. 20)

3. By deciding to celebrate legs or bury them, to glorify bosoms or flatten them, by floating women's bodies in capes and drapes, shawls, cloaks, trains, panels, hoods, furbelows and twiddlybits, the great fashion houses emerge, year after year, as masters of TROMPE L'OEIL. (Anon., "Fashion: Oxygen for an Aging Lady," *Time*, 2/7/77, p. 76)

4. There are no FLAMBOYANT signs indicating that it [New York's U.N. Plaza Hotel]'s a hotel and the glass wall is laced with a repetitive aluminum grid that gives no clue as to where floors and windows fall . . . . Inside, [Architect Kevin] Roche plays tricks with glass . . . . Along with the constant TROMPE L'OEIL effects of the glass-mirror corridors . . ., there is an "infinity chamber" restaurant . . ., topped off with a ceiling surfaced in pentagonal mirrors . . . the eye is confronted with angled reflections that challenge the sense of what is real and what is mirrored. (D. Davis, *et al.*, "Rise of the Come-Hither Look," *Newsweek*, 1/17/77, p. 87)

TROPE (trōp) *noun* any literary or rhetorical device, as metaphor, metonymy, SYNECDOCHE, and irony, that consists in the use of words in other than their literal sense; an instance of this figurative usage; a figure of speech.

1. Often precise and witty, [John] Simon will just as often go into painful contortions in order to set up a TROPE (as in his elaborate description of a "baked-Alaska performance" by "Scott of the Antarctic") . . . (R. Brustein, Re-

view of the books, *Uneasy Stages* and *Singularities*, by John Simon, *New York Times*, 1/4/76, Section 7, p. 2)

TROPISM (trō′piz-əm) *noun* the tendency of a plant, animal, or part to grow or turn in response to an external stimulus, either by attraction or repulsion, as a sun-flower turns toward light; any movement, action, etc., in response to stimuli.

TROPISMATIC or **TROPISTIC** *adj*.

1. Their homeland [Soviet Russia], using the cant phrase, is a peculiar combination of TRO-PISMS, some of them nationalistic and PATRIS-TIC, some of them egotistic. (W.F. Buckley Jr., *Execution Eve and Other Contemporary Ballads*, G.P. Putnam's Sons, 1975, p. 242)

TROVE (trōv) *noun* something valuable or pleasing, especially something that has been kept hidden or is discovered: short for *treasure trove*; any valuable discovery.

1. Recently brought to light by Marion Balderston, this TROVE of correspondence . . . is published here [in *The Lost War: Letters from British Officers During the American Revolution*, edited by Marion Balderston and David Syrett] in full. (G.F. Scheer, Review, *New York Times*, 2/22/76, Section 7, p. 12)

2. . . . he [Harold Yost] leaped forward . . . and there they were . . ., both of them, the two bulging brown suitcases, . . . the heaping treasure TROVE, the booty of Blackbeard. (I. Wallace, *The Fan Club*, Bantam Books, 1975, p. 554)

3. See (3) under WELTANSCHAUUNG.

TRUCKLE (truk′ əl) *verb* to submit or yield obsequiously, abjectly, or tamely (usually followed by *to*); to be servile; to cringe, submit, toady, etc. (usually followed by *to*)

1. No longer . . . can we purchase chrome from Rhodesia . . . . But apparently it's perfectly OK to buy chrome from the Soviet Union where . . . every muzhik can vote—in fact *must*—for the single party of the Kremlin's choice . . . to me there's just a whiff of hypocrisy . . . in TRUCKLING to the U.N.'s sanction. (E.H. Hunt, "How America Looks to Me Now," *Newsweek*, 4/4/77, p. 15)

TRUCULENT (truk′ yə-lent, trōō′ kyə-lent, truk′ yōō-lent) *adj*. fierce; cruel; savagely brutal; brutally harsh; ferocious; rude; mean; VITRIOLIC; scathing; aggessively hostile; belligerent; pugnacious; bellicose; defiant.

TRUCULENCE or **TRUCULENCY** *noun*.

TRUCULENTLY *adv*.

1. Gradually people are introduced [in the book, *Hills of Home*, by Bob Minick] to us, or we to them. They stare out at us, sometimes with suspicion or TRUCULENCE, occasionally with tentative friendliness. (M. Keman, Review, *Smithsonian*, December 1975, p. 133)

2. All of this [the decline of congressional power] and more is set forth in a timely book by House Minority Leader John Rhodes of Arizona entitled *The Futile System*. The normally courteous and urbane Rhodes rips into Congress with surprising candor and TRUCU-LENCE. (Anon., "Presidency Important, But . . ." [Editorial], *Daily Oklahoman*, Okla. City, 7/6/76, p. 12)

TRULL (trul) *noun* a prostitute; strumpet; trollop.

1. Remembering Whitman, I asked a celebrated poet of my generation whether he contemplated a tribute to President Kennedy. He answered that he was thinking of a EULOGY for Oswald. One marvels that no one has written an ENCOMIUM to Jack Ruby and his TRULLS. (W. Manchester, Commencement Address, University of Massachusetts, Mimeographed, 6/13/65, p. 3)

2. A smirk was peculiarly unattractive on Peggy [Tumulty]'s visage, which was rather pretty when totally . . . without expression, and nearly beautiful when truly LUGUBRIOUS, probably in imitation of the Pietà, an ever-available model for Catholic women and greatly preferable to, say, a motion-picture TRULL. (Thomas Berger, *Who Is Teddy Villanova?*, Delacorte Press/Seymour Lawrence, 1977, p. 27)

3. "He [Teddy Villanova] is the personification of evil [said Boris]. I hope only that these little TRULLS are young enough to meet the requirements of his appetite." (Thomas Berger, *Ibid.*, p. 203)

TRUNCATED (truṅg′kā-tid) or **TRUNCATE** *adj.* cut short or appearing as if cut short; shortened by or as by having the apex, vertex, or end cut off by a plane (in geometry).

TRUNCATE *verb* to shorten by cutting off a part; cut short; lop.

TRUNCATION *noun.*

1. . . . the new [Rick] Bailey script [of the play, *Mean Woman*] seems content to pilot its five luckless characters recklessly into the looney bin and leave them there, on their own devices. Which is to say that the inmates of Bailey's TRUNCATED limbo (and by extension the audience) must do everything the hard way, from the inside out. (J. Brandenburg, Review, *Daily Oklahoman*, Okla. City, 3/23/76, p. S-1)

2. [Manuel] Puig [author of *The Buenos Aires Affair*, translated by Suzanne Jill Levine] is, like Faulkner . . . , a master of occluded narrative . . . . Perhaps the most extreme instance of occluded narrative here is . . . the elliptical shorthand account taken down by a police stenographer . . . of a call informing about a supposed murder. In the asyntactical jumble of TRUNCATED statements a plot emerges . . . (R. Alter, Review, *New York Times*, 9/5/76, Section 7, p. 4)

TUMBREL (tum′ brəl) or **TUMBRIL** *noun* one of the carts used during the French Revolution to convey victims to the guillotine; a dump cart, especially one for carrying dung.

1. They [the delegates to the Democratic convention] had fire in their bellies, that hot ideological fire that says: We're going to change America and you, boy, are going to ride in the TUMBREL to Execution Square, and we're going to enjoy your suffering. (W.F. Buckley Jr., *Execution Eve and Other Contemporary Ballads*, G.P. Putnam's Sons, 1975, p. 95)

2. An endless panning shot [in the film] of the jammed Place Louis XVI, . . . with the mobs cheering and jeering . . . , until the camera held on the TUMBRIL, then slowly moved in to reveal the ill-fated King Louis XVI being led up the steps to the guillotine. (I. Wallace, *The Fan Club*, Bantam Books, 1975, p. 574)

3. "We're worried as hell over what Stalin is

up to. He has turned more secretive than ever. A purge, maybe of classic proportions, is under way. The TUMBRILS are full and, as usual, full of his own past intimates" [said Anthony Trust]. (W.F. Buckley Jr., *Saving the Queen*, Doubleday, 1976, p. 122)

TU QUOQUE (tōō-kwō′ kwe, tōō-kwō′ kwē, tyōō-kwō′ kwē) a Latin expression meaning *thou too:* a retort charging an accuser with a similar crime or failing.

1. Mr. John Cogley . . . was . . . the most courageous of the lot [of reviewers of W.F. Buckley's book]. He admitted that ". . . the weaknesses that Mr. Buckley finds in liberalism are genuine flaws . . ."—but then picked himself up from abjection by the TU QUOQUEISM that conservatives are Just As Bad, rejecting . . . the point I make . . . that one judges a movement not merely by the deeds of its qualified spokesmen, but also by their acceptance as spokesmen by the larger community of the faithful. (W.F. Buckley Jr., *Up From Liberalism*, Arlington House, 2nd Printing 1968, pp. xxvi-xxvii)

TURGID (tûr′ jid) *adj.* swollen; bloated; distended; tumid; inflated; overblown; pompous; bombastic; GRANDILOQUENT.

TURGIDITY or **TURGIDNESS** *noun.*

TURGIDLY *adv.*

1. See (1) under SCABROUS.

2. These birds [Supreme Court Justices] are busy writing the supreme law of the land . . . . Yes, they must try to write precisely. But do they have to write precisely TURGIDLY? Can't they write precisely lucidly instead? (J.J. Kilpatrick, "Court Opinions Not Made to Read," *Daily Oklahoman*, Okla. City, 7/6/76, p. 12)

3. He [Admiral Hyman G. Rickover] is known to be indefatigable and single-minded in pursuit of a goal, like (Jimmy) Carter. He is considered a genius electrical engineer; he was a pioneer and prodder of the TURGID Navy in developing the nuclear submarine. (I. Berkow, "Navy's Rickover hero to Carter," *Norman* [Okla.] *Transcript*, 7/15/76, p. 5-A)

4. *The Shootist* is handsomely set and honestly directed by Don Siegel and it leaves one an-

guished that [John] Wayne was not better served by the authors of the script, Scott Hale and Miles Hood Swarthout. Despite their frequent TURGIDITY, Wayne survives with eloquence. (D. Ryan, Review, *Philadelphia Inquirer*, 9/5/76, p. 8-E)

TUTTI (tŏō′ tē) *noun* a musical passage played or sung by all performers; the tonal product or effect of a tutti performance.

TUTTI *adj.* all; (in Music) all the voices or instruments together; intended for all these together.

1. Vern Bickford's first pitch to him [Jackie Robinson] broke wide, and . . . the blacks, who ringed the entire outfield, cheered in triumph. Robinson fouled the next pitch, hopping in an awkward follow-through. A roar went up from the whites. In the end, to a TUTTI of enthusiasm and disappointment, Robinson hit a short fly to left. (R. Kahn, *The Boys of Summer*, Harper and Row, 1971, p. 107)

U

UBEROUS (yōō′ bər-əs) *adj.* (of breasts) supplying milk or nourishment in abundance; rich in fertilizng moisture; richly productive; fertile; abundant; copious; full.

UBERTY *noun* abundance; fruitfulness; fertility.

1. . . . he [John Simon] almost invariably imbalances his reviews with a VITUPERATIVE assault on the morbid failings of some playwright, director or other critic, and particularly on the "flipper-like limbs" or "UBEROUS" left breast of some hapless actress whose personal appearance has violated his esthetic sense. (R. Brustein, Review, of *Uneasy Stages* and *Singularities*, books by John Simon, *New York Times*, 1/4/76, Section, p. 1)

UBIQUITOUS (yōō-bik′ wi-təs) *adj.* being or seeming to be everywhere or many places at the same time; omnipresent.

UBIQUITOUSLY *adv.*

UBIQUITY (yōō-bik′ wi-tē) or **UBIQUITOUSNESS** *noun.*

1. Uniforms are UBIQUITOUS [in Soviet Russia]. (R.W. Stock, "Group Tour of Russia: A Collective Triumph," *New York Times*, 1/11/76, Section 10, p. 1)

2. Even the narrator [in *A Brief Life*, by Juan Carlos Onetti, translated by Hortense Carpentier] . . . never becomes more than a UBIQUITOUS gray shade who seems to be able to slip under doors and through walls . . . (Anon., Review, *The New Yorker*, 2/9/76, pp. 108, 110)

3. But a continuing factor preventing their recovery was the ruthless competition of the aggressive starling and the UBIQUITOUS house sparrow [with the bluebird] for any suitable nesting cavity. (Irston R. Barnes, of the *Washington Post*, "Save Bluebirds Crusade Task of 1 Individual," *Norman* [Okla.] *Transcript*, 2/26/76, p. 9-A)

4. See (1) under SPURIOUS.

5. See (2) under MERETRICIOUS.

6. The confusion [when the Bucklands arrived in Omaha] was compounded by the four UBIQUITOUS American journalists who wanted to talk with everyone . . . (J.A. Michener, *Centennial*, Fawcett, 1975, p. 619)

7. Beetles, like some other insects, have a high tolerance to radioactivity; thus, should Man

exterminate himself in a nuclear war, the UBIQUITOUS beetles will surely inherit the Earth. (M. Emsley, "Nature's most successful design may be beetles," *Smithsonian*, December 1975, p. 108)

8. If the Irish seem UBIQUITOUS in national politics, they are also still highly visible in numerous fields where they long ago made their names, such as labor unions (A.F.L.-C.I.O. president George Meany), . . . law enforcement (F.B.I. director Clarence Kelley), . . . business (Peter Grace of W.R. Grace & Co. . . .) and the church (Cardinal Cooke of New York). (W.V. Shannon, "The lasting hurrah," *New York Times*, 3/14/76, Section 6, p. 72)

9. Georgina Spelvin, star of *The Devil in Miss Jones*, is charged with being part of the "nationwide conspiracy," as is the UBIQUITOUS Harry Reems, who starred in both films [*Deep Throat* and *The Devil*] . . . . Can an actor like Reems, for example, who made only $100 on *Deep Throat* and had nothing to do with its distribution, be held legally responsible for its distribution? (Merrill Sheils, A. Marro, "The Memphis Smut Raker," *Newsweek*, 4/5/76, p. 62)

10. (Anyone nostalgic for that vomitous green, once UBIQUITOUS color of a thousand furnished rooms, of kitchens and bathrooms of boarding houses, . . . will be delighted to hear that it is used to spectacular ill-effect in this exhibition [*200 Years of American Sculpture* at the Whitney Museum of American Art]). Rotten installations are scarcely a rarity on the museum scene, but this one really does take the cake. (H. Kramer, Review, *New York Times*, 3/28/76, Section 2, p. 34)

11. . . . he [Howard Hughes] was left [after his 1946 crash of the experimental Hughes XF-11 plane] with permanent bladder and prostate trouble, a severe constipation problem and a monomaniacal fear of germs. He took to refusing to shake hands with people and covering his hands with the UBIQUITOUS sheets of Kleenex when he had to hold a glass or open a door . . . . He considered air conditioners deadly germ machines and he even suspected clothes as germ collectors; he is said to have taken to sitting naked in darkened sweltering hotel rooms, surrounded by crinkled Kleenex and

covered only with a few sheets over his privates. (T. Mathews, *et al.*, "The Secret World of Howard Hughes," *Newsweek*, 4/19/76, p. 31)

12. . . . Americans own about half of Canada's industry . . . . The American influence in Canadian culture is equally UBIQUITOUS. (P.W. Semas, "U.S. Academics' Influence Rankles Canadian Nationalists," *Chronicle of Higher Education*, 3/1/76, p. 3)

13. It is hard to find [in Singapore's Chinatown] the once-UBIQUITOUS roadside medicine men who would set any broken bones you might have with a quick sleight of hand. (Shelley and Carl Mydans, "Progress dooms charm and bustle of the Chinatown in Singapore," *Smithsonian*, January 1976, p. 41)

14. It is vitally important for [Susan] Brownmiller [in *Against Our Will*] to demonstrate that the victims of rape do not in any sense will their fate, for to admit that possibility calls into question the UBIQUITY of oppression. In the teeth of substantial and contrary psychological evidence, Brownmiller denies that women ever fantasize about rape. . . . It is the UBIQUITOUS metaphoric rape of women to which Simone de Beauvoir, Juliet Mitchell, Shulamith Firestone, and even Betty Friedan speak . . . . If rape cannot be equated with oppression, it can be comprehended as an important missing link in feminist ideology. (D.L. Kirp, Review, *Change*, April 1976, pp. 41-42)

15. While it is true that in Russia personal life is the only form of free enterprise allowed by the UBIQUITOUS state, plunging into sex as much as these characters do [in *Moscow Farewell*, by George Feifer] is precisely the final surrender to the State. (J. Brodsky, Review, *New York Times*, 4/18/76, Section 7, p. 4)

16. See (1) under CENTRIPETAL.

17. A subject becomes liberal when it is taught and studied for the purposes that our medieval forebears saw in the quadrivium and trivium. What does it teach . . . about UBIQUITOUS and recurrent characteristics of the human scene and human destiny? . . . . The liberal arts are liberal if they pierce the veil of the commonplace, if they lift the student from the domination of what is conventional and near at hand.

(C. Frankel, "Piercing the Veil of the Commonplace," *Chronicle of Higher Education*, 5/3/76, p. 32)

18. When [Kurt] Jooss gave up his international [ballet] touring group about 20 years ago . . his reputation slipped. Apart from the inevitable and UBIQUITOUS *Green Table*, no one seemed to want to revive his other works. Clive Barnes, "The Joffrey Rejoices in the Genius of Jooss," *New York Times*, 3/28/76, Section 2, p. 8)

9. The Associated Press found, in a series of interviews conducted across the nation, that the trend among college men is not only toward shorter hair but toward more neatness in general. That does not mean a return to the crewcut, or that the UBIQUITOUS blue jean is fading from the scene. (G.G. LaBelle of the Associated Press, "Campus trend to neater look noted," *Norman* [Okla.] *Transcript*, 6/16/76, p. 10)

0. See (3) under ENTROPY.

1. Morris Udall, whose candidacy may not survive another disappointment, was most severely handicapped by the money crimp. Pennsylvania," he complained, "may turn out to be a busted play for me because of it. Last week he had to give up his chartered plane and his hopes of coming from behind with a TV blitz, but he did not surrender his candor. For the first time he acknowledged that the UBIQUITOUS non-candidate, Hubert Humphrey, "has real chance." (Anon., "Pennsylvania's Guerilla War," *Time*, 4/26/76, p. 14)

2. As many cost-minded managers are acutely aware, the UBIQUITOUS office copier is just as andy for duplicating Aunt Tillie's strudel recipe as for running off copies of business mail. ow Manitou Systems, Inc., of Bensenville, l., is offering a way of preventing office orkers, as President Paul Leopold puts it, om "thinking of the copier in the same way ey think of the water fountain." The company has developed a device . . . that switches ie machines on only when the user inserts a lastic identification card issued by his employer. (Anon., "Copy Cut," *Time*, 4/19/76, 77)

KASE (yōō'kās, yōō-kāz) *noun* (in Czar-

ist Russia) an edict or order of the Czar having the force of law; any order or proclamation by an absolute or arbitrary authority.

1. A UKASE. *Un*-negotiable. The only one I have issued in seventeen years. It goes: "John went to the store and bought some apples, oranges, and bananas." NOT: "John . . . some apples, oranges and bananas." . . . . National Review's Style Book, effective immediately, makes the omission of the second comma a capital offense. (W.F. Buckley Jr., *Execution Eve and Other Contemporary Ballads*, G.P. Putnam's Sons, 1975, p. 351)

2. See (1) under OTIOSE.

3. And in Boston . . . a judge is taking it upon himself to prescribe the most meticulous rules for running the schools even after his busing UKASE has been obeyed. (J. Chamberlain, "Separation of Powers Threatened by Recent Judicial Branch Tyranny," *Daily Oklahoman*, Okla. City, 6/18/76, p. 10)

4. He [Sam Polidor] showed his teeth in an evil smile, very like the expression of a dog suffering an unwanted snout at his hind parts but restrained by his master's UKASE against combat. (Thomas Berger, *Who Is Teddy Villanova?*, Delacorte Press/Seymour Lawrence, 1977, p. 230)

ULTRAMONTANISM (ul'trə-mon'tə-niz'əm) *noun* the policy of the party in the Roman Catholic Church that favors increasing and enhancing the power and authority of the pope.

ULTRAMONTANIST *noun*.

ULTRAMONTANE *adj.* situated beyond the mountains; of or pertaining to the area south of the Alps, especially Italy; of, pertaining to, or advocating ultramontanism.

ULTRAMONTANE *noun* a person living beyond the mountains; a person living south of the Alps; a person who supports ultramontanism.

1. During the sixties, many Jesuits, far from toiling in the vineyards of ULTRAMONTANISM, became self-consciously, not to say obstreperously, independent, the hero of the group in question being of course their fellow Jesuit Father Daniel Berrigan. (W.F. Buckley, *Exe-*

cution Eve and Other Contemporary Ballads, G.P. Putnam's Sons, 1975, p. 152)

ULULATE (yōōl' yə-lāt', ul' -) *verb* to howl, as a dog or a wolf; hoot, as an owl; to utter howling sounds, as in shrill, wordless lamentation; wail; to lament loudly and shrilly.

ULULANT *adj.* howling; ululating.

ULULATION *noun.*

1. . . . in the current issue of Harper's magazine, reviewing the Republican convention in Miami, he [Kurt Vonnegut Jr.] strikes the tuning fork for the ULULATORS, coast to coast. (W.F. Buckley Jr., *Execution Eve and Other Contemporary Ballads*, G.P. Putnam's Sons, 1975, p. 94)

2. His [Evelyn Waugh's] biographer [Christopher Sykes] cites [in the book, *Evelyn Waugh*] scores of incidents [of his reputation as an ogre]: . . . . Waugh, in a small and crowded restaurant, demanding a book from Sykes "in a manner of a two-year old child, gurgling between ear-splitting ULULATIONS 'I-want-the-book-now' . . ." (L.E. Sissman, Review, *The New Yorker*, 2/9/76, p. 108)

3. It was the sound of the coyotes that tormented Alice [Grebe], and one lonely night . . . she heard the ULULATING cries in the darkness, and they sounded to her like the voice of doom. (J.A. Michener, *Centennial*, Fawcett, 1975, p. 898)

4. . . . they [the bloodhound puppies] . . . displayed the same docile, affectionate disposition shown by their parents, both of whom greeted us with lovely rolling ULULATIONS that fairly shook the Maryland countryside. (R. Caras, "A Boy's Best Dog," *New York Times*, 3/14/76, Section 6, p. 13)

5. President Anwar Sadat was welcomed home from Israel Monday night as "the man of peace" by thousands of Egyptians standing shoulder-to-shoulder along the 26-mile route from the airport to his home in the city [Cairo] . . . . The crowds cheered, laughed, chanted, clapped, whistled, beat drums and made clicking ULULATING sounds with their tongues. (Anon., "Sadat Rides in Triumph Across Cairo," *Kansas City Times*, 11/22/77, p. 1)

UMBRAGE (um'brij) *noun.* offense; resentment, annoyance, or displeasure; a sense of slight or injury; foliage that affords shade.

UMBRAGEOUS *adj.* giving shade; shady; easily offended; taking, or inclined to take, umbrage.

UMBRAGEOUSLY *adv.*

1. But I . . . think that television is the greatest teaching tool since the Egyptians invented the pencil, and . . . you can use it to overcome most of the damage done to kids in the name of public education. And so I take UMBRAGE with those studies that ask youngsters if the violence on TV scares them and, when they say it does, proceed to draw profound socio-psychological meaning from it all. (Virginia Fayette, "About TV . . . ," *Times Herald*, Norristown, Pa. 3/24/77, p. 19)

2. In his early poems Mr. [Anthony] Hecht . . took pleasure in recourse to the older dictionaries . . . . When he used the word "UMBRAGE," it was the UMBRAGE given by trees in a garden not the kind taken by people who choose to be offended. (D. Donoghue, Review of *Millions of Strange Shadows*, by Anthony Hecht, *New York Times*, 3/27/77, Section 7, p. 6)

3. . . . Dee Brown does a good job [in the book, *Hear That Lonesome Whistle Blow*] with the drama and with the scalawaggery of the great railroad promoters: he's still angry at . . . the Big Four . . . who organized the Central Pacific, for gypping the 19th-century American taxpayers. I think he would have had an even better book if he'd extended his UMBRAGE into the recent past and told . . . the story of the new generation of railroad desperadoes of the 1950's and 60's who again SUBORNED government officials, this time to destroy the passenger trains the 19th-century bruisers had gouged to create. (T. Hiss, Review, *New York Times*, 5/15/77, Section 7, p. 15)

UNCTUOUS (ungk'chōō-as) *adj.* of the nature of or characteristic of an unguent or ointment; oily; greasy; characterized by excessive piousness or moralistic fervor; excessively smooth, suave, complacent, or smug; having an oily or soapy feel; plastic; moldable.

UNCTUOSITY or **UNCTUOUSNESS** *noun.*

NCTUOUSLY *adv.*

NCTION *noun* an act of anointing, especially as a medical treatment or ritual symbol; something soothing or comforting; a soothing, sympathetic, and persuasive quality in discourse, especially on religious subjects; a professional, conventional, or affected earnestness or fervor in utterance.

She [Mrs. Trimmer] was joined by others in the latter part of the 18th century] who produced, as Ryskamp says [in the Preface to *Early Children's Books and Their Illustrations,* a book by Gerald Gottlieb], "moral tales [for children] of UNCTUOUS edification." (W. Blaire, Review, *Smithsonian,* February 1976, p. 129)

Lopez is a captivatingly UNCTUOUS minor character [in *Double Honeymoon,* by Evan S. Connell] . . . (R.Z. Sheppard, Review, *Time,* 4/21/76, p. 74)

"Can I show you something in a suit, sir?" the investment counselor might say UNCTUOUSLY. "A lawsuit I mean. A really blue-chip group of defendants and prospects for an impressive award for damages." Buying shares in a lawsuit? Why not, asks Manhattan Attorney Carl E. Person, who has reason to believe that he is on his way to creating just such an investment possibility. (Anon., "Suits for Sale," *Time,* 5/3/76, p. 46)

NICORN (yōō'nə-kôrn') *noun* a mythical creature resembling a horse and having a single horn in the center of its forehead: often symbolic of chastity or purity.

It (the MOREL) is the golden prince of mushrooms and it has the same relationship to other edible fungi that golden Iranian caviar has to the catfish. . . . Millions of American mushroom eaters have never seen or tasted a MOREL. It is as FEY as a UNICORN. (J.R. Phelan, "May is morel time," *New York Times,* 5/9/76, Section 2, p. 80)

RSINE (ûr'sīn, ûr'sin) *adj.* of, like, or characteristic of a bear; bearlike.

Somewhere in Such a Kingdom [by Geoffrey Hill] comprises . . . three books, . . . a sequence of extraordinary prose-poems, humorous and URSINE. (C. Ricks, Review, *New York Times,* 1/11/76, Section 7, p. 6)

USUFRUCT (yōō'zŏō-frukt', -sŏō-, yōōz'yŏō-, yŏōs'-) *noun* the right to use or benefit from something which belongs to another, short of destroying or harming it; use, enjoyment, or profitable possession of something.

USUFRUCTUARY *adj.* of, pertaining to, or of the nature of usufruct.

USUFRUCTUARY *noun* a person who has the temporary use and reaps the profits of an estate, office, etc.

1. He [President Nixon] likes the power of the Presidency, the USUFRUCTS of the Presidency, and the romance of the Presidency. (W.F. Buckley Jr., *Execution Eve and Other Contemporary Ballads,* G.P. Putnam's Sons, 1975, p. 141).

2. "Now really what the hell kind of a word is this [USUFRUCTS] to use in a column directed to the average person with the average vocabulary" [from the letter of Robert Moran to William F. Buckley Jr.]. (W.F. Buckley Jr., *Ibid.,* p. 339)

3. What then would you do to the nursery rhyme, Could eternal life afford / That tyranny should thus deduct / From this fair land / . . . A year of the sweet USUFRUCT? [from response of William F. Buckley Jr., to Robert Moran]. (W.F. Buckley Jr., *Ibid.,* p. 340)

USURIOUS (yōō-zhŏōr'ē-əs) *adj.* constituted of, characterized by, or practicing usury; charging illegal or exorbitant interest rates for the use of money.

USURIOUSLY *adv.*

USURIOUSNESS *noun.*

USURER *noun* a person who lends money, especially at an exorbitant or unlawful rate of interest.

USURY *noun* an exorbitant, illegal, or extortionate amount or rate of interest; the lending of money at such a rate.

1. Mr. [Eugene Paul] Nassar has had the excellent idea of assemblying [in *The Cantos of Ezra Pound: The Lyric Mode*] the lyrical fragments

of Pound's *Paradiso*, as they occur sporadically throughout *The Cantos*. These are moments of stillness, serenity, insight, and they are Pound's evocation of a positive universe to counter a USURIOUS one. They come as a relief after the politics, and seem to touch a more fundamental stratum, where fascist FULMINATIONS are irrelevant. (R. Ellmann, Review, *New York Times*, 4/4/76, Section 7, p. 26)

2. It [Blumstein's] is the principal department store on 125th Street, free with credit, persistent with demands for payment, the very cliché of the USURIOUS exploitive, Jewish white. (R. Kahn, *The Boys of Summer*, Harper and Row, 1971, pp. 401-402)

UXORIOUS (uk-sōr' ē-əs, -sôr- , ug-zōr- , -zôr-) *adj.* doting upon, irrationally fond of, or affectionately oversubmissive toward one's wife.

UXORIOUSLY *adv.*

UXORIOUSNESS *noun.*

UXORIAL *adj.* of, befitting, or characteristic of a wife.

UXORIALLY *adv.*

1. Farragut [in the book, *Falconer*, by John Cheever] is a tender parent and UXORIOUS husband . . . (W. Clemons, "Cheever's Triumph," *Newsweek*, 3/14/77, p. 61)

V

VACUITY (va-kyōō'i-tē) *noun* the state of being vacuous or empty; an empty space; a void; a vacuum; emptiness of mind; absence or lack of something specified; absence of thought or intelligence; something, as a statement, revealing such absence; inanity.

VACUOUS (vak' yōō-əs) *adj.* without contents; empty; lacking in or showing a lack of purpose, ideas, intelligence, interest, or thought; purposeless; idle; stupid; inane; senseless.

VACUOUSLY *adv.*

VACUOUSNESS *noun.*

1. The most frightening aspect of this new intellectual VACUITY lies not in the fact that people in higher education are apathetic, which they are not. What has happened is that they increasingly confuse their intense present concern for structuralism and organizational survival . . . with moving forward, which they are not doing. (G.W. Bonham, "Change and the

Academic Future," [Editorial], *Change*, June 1974, p. 9)

2. Winthrop [Rockefeller], exiled in Arkansas, died a drunk; John D 3 . . . saw the family leadership wrested from him by Nelson; Nelson . . . ruined his own chances of becoming President and slid into bitterness and anger; Laurance, who invested in real estate, "lacked a center of balance" and lapsed into cynicism; even David, "the Chairman of the Board of the Establishment," is described [in *The Rockefellers*, by Peter Collier and David Horowitz] as "VACUOUS" and finally a doubtful success as a banker. (P.S. Prescott, Review, *Newsweek*, 4/5/76, p. 82)

3. Actually there's little to choose between the manic SCHLOCK of *174th Street* and the VACUOUS classiness of *Rex*. In both cases the failure of a concept at the center results in a theatrical ARMAGEDDON. (J. Kroll, Review, *Newsweek*, 5/10/76, p. 76)

VADE MECUM (vā' dē mē' kəm, vä-), pl.

VADE MECUMS something carried about by a person for frequent or constant use, especially a reference book, handbook, manual, etc.

1. Random House now has an encyclopedia worthy to set alongside its dictionary, which is my personal VADE MECUM. (J. Barkham, Review of *The Random House Encyclopedia*, Editor-in-Chief: Jess Stein, *Philadelphia Inquirer*, 11/27/77, p. 17-F)

VAPID (vap'id) *adj.* lacking life or flavor; insipid; without liveliness or spirit; dull or tedious; flat; uninteresting; boring.

VAPIDLY *adv.*

VAPIDITY or **VAPIDNESS** *noun.*

1. Throughout the scandal in 1889 and 1890, there were rumors that the Queen's grandson, H.R.H. Prince Albert Victor, had visited the place [a male brothel on Cleveland Street]. (. . . He [also] was accused of being Jack the Ripper in spite of the fact that his movements show him to have been miles and miles from the murders when they were committed.) There is no shred of evidence that he went anywhere near Cleveland Street . . . . But he was a weak and VAPID young man and so gossips were ready to believe anything. (J.H. Plumb, Review of *The Cleveland Street Scandal*, by H. Montgomery Hyde, *New York Times*, 9/5/76, Section 7, p. 2)

2. Her [author Anne Rivers Siddons'] central concern [in her book, *Heartbreak Hotel*] is the metamorphosis of one Maggie Deloach from VAPID Southern belle to thoughtful modern woman. The catalysts are the looming civil rights movement and a young newspaper reporter whose chance remarks make a profound impression on Maggie. (Kathy Carey, Review, *Philadelphia Inquirer*, 10/3/76, p. 12-H)

3. See (1) under MAVIN.

VARIOLATION (vâr'i-ō-lā'shən) *noun* inoculation with the virus of smallpox, a medical procedure antedating vaccination.

VARIOLA *noun* any of a group of virus diseases characterized by pustular eruptions and including smallpox, cowpox, horsepox, etc.

VARIOLAR or **VARIOLOUS** *adj.*

1. Educated people came to call this practice of folk medicine [for the prevention of smallpox] inoculation, after the Latin *inoculare*, to graft. They also called it VARIOLATION; variola, from the Latin *varus*, pimple, was the scholarly name for smallpox. (W.L. Langer, "Immunization against Smallpox before Jenner," *Scientific American*, January 1976, p. 112)

VATICINATION (vat' i-sə-nā'shən) *noun* the act of prophesying; a prophecy.

VATICINATE (və-tis' ə-nāt') *verb* to prophesy; to foretell the future.

VATICINATOR *noun.*

VATICINAL *adj.* of, pertaining to, or characterized by prophecy; prophetic.

VATIC or **VATICAL** *adj.* of, pertaining to, or characteristic of a prophet; prophetic.

1. Vindictiveness is a bore, and I dwell here on some of the preelection VATICINATIONS of Professors Schlesinger and Galbraith not so much because I desire to tease them, though I take the normal man's pleasure in doing that, as because I think there is something to be learned about punditry from meditating on them. (W.F. Buckley Jr., *Execution Eve and Other Contemporary Ballads*, G.P. Putnam's Sons, 1975, p. 100)

2. The time-honored position of the VATIC or oracular poet also endures, despite the decline of guruism . . . . Theirs is the essentially romantic stance of the SURROGATE priest who . . . believes that poetry must assume the defense of the spirit where defunct traditional religions have failed. (D. Lenson, "Unmasking the Contemporary Poet," *Chronicle of Higher Education*, 8/2/76, p. 9)

3. See (1) under PHATIC.

VELLEITY (və-lē'i-tē) *noun* volition in its weakest form; a mere wish or desire, unaccompanied by the slightest effort or action to obtain it.

1. But whereas most people who want the street poop [of dogs] removed are indulging a VELLEITY, those who want their dogs are indulging a passion. (W.F. Buckley Jr., *Execution Eve and Other Contemporary Ballads*,

G.P. Putnam's Sons, 1975, p. 424)

2. The driver . . . confessed that he rather hoped the United States would get into the War [World War II] . . . . Black [ford Oakes] . . . discoursed on the illogic and immorality of the United States getting involved in a European war, recapitulating with considerable skill, analytic and MIMETIC, the phrases and paragraphs he had so often heard his father so seriously intone. The driver retreated, leaving the impression that his desire for war was at most a VELLEITY . . . (W.F. Buckley Jr., *Saving the Queen*, Doubleday, 1976, p. 52)

3. A generation of Soviet bureaucrats responded in one way to barked commands, in an entirely different way to whispered VELLEITIES. (W.F. Buckley Jr., *Ibid*, p. 237)

VENAL (vēn'l) *adj.* open to bribery; able to be purchased, as something not rightfully offered for sale; associated with or characterized by corruption or bribery; willing to use influence or authority improperly for mercenary gain.

VENALITY *noun.*

VENALLY *adv.*

1. See (2) under MORDANT.

2. [Jack] Lemmon lacks the reptilian VENALITY of Sir Laurence Olivier, who played the original Archie [in *The Entertainer*]; at times Lemmon seems about as threatening as a kumquat. (H.F. Waters, Review, *Newsweek*, 3/15/76, p. 55)

3. See (3) under MENDACIOUS.

4. I do not pretend that the recounting . . . of the [Paul] Hughes episode does not afford a wry amusement. For [Joseph L.] Rauh [Jr.] and company had for years moralized about the VENALITY of the secret informer . . . (W.F. Buckley Jr., *Up From Liberalism*, Arlington House, 2nd Printing 1968, p. 114)

5. The VENALITY of Italian politics was underlined dramatically by the news of bribery abroad by American oil and airplane companies. The irony is that the American legislative exposure of this tawdry practice has had little political impact in the American elections but may have a strong one in Italy. (M. Lerner, *Los Angeles Times*, "Communists seek Italian victory," *Norman* [Okla.] *Transcript*, 6/21/76, p. 6)

6. But the get-rich-quick schemes [to defraud Medicaid] could not have worked without the cooperation of VENAL clinic owners, many of them non-physicians. The favorite ploy was to disguise kickbacks as rent. (Anon., "The Medicaid Scandal," *Time*, 2/23/76, p. 37)

7. See (5) under ACERBIC.

8. See (7) under PROSCRIBE.

9. See (1) under AMOUR-PROPRE.

VENDETTA (ven-det' ə) *noun* a private feud, as formerly in Corsica and Italy, in which the family of a murdered person seeks to kill the murderer or members of his family; any prolonged and bitter feud, rivalry, contention, etc.

VENDETTIST *noun.*

1. Trevose, Pa. (AP)—A young bachelor who an official said was apparently carrying out a "personal VENDETTA" has been charged with the execution-style slayings of six persons, including five of his neighbors. (*Associated Press*, "Vendetta Seen in 6 Slayings," *Norman* [Okla.] *Transcript*, 3/23/76, p. 1)

2. The civil rights movement claimed that J. Edgar Hoover was conducting a personal VENDETTA against the movement's spiritual leader, Martin Luther King, and now we learn that in addition to other harassments the Bureau probably attempted through anonymous threats to move the late Dr. King to suicide. (V.S. Navasky, Review of *FBI*, a book by Sanford J. Ungar; and of *Cointelpro*, edited by Cathy Perkus, *New York Times*, 3/14/76, Section 7, p. 3)

VERDANT (vûr' dənt) *adj.* green with vegetation; of the color green; inexperienced; unsophisticated.

VERDANCY *noun.*

VERDANTLY *adv.*

1. The occasion is the debut of *The Adams Chronicles*, a thirteen-part [TV] series that

took six years and $5.2 million to produce, employs 1100 actors and is based on no fewer than 300,000 pages of historical documents about the nation's most intellectually VERDANT family tree. (H.F. Waters, Review, *Newsweek*, 1/19/76, p. 78)

2. Many once-flourishing vacation resorts in the Catskills have gone out of business in recent years, done in by a combination of cheap jet travel that lured tourists elsewhere and heavy property taxes. The former resorts, in their lush, VERDANT settings, have proved popular with church groups and other organizations that do not pay taxes. (Beth Gillin Pombeiro, "Praise the Lord, and grant them tax relief," *Philadelphia Inquirer*, 9/28/76, p. 1-A)

3. . . . from roughly 1965 to 1975 the forces of unbridled liberalism have been moving across the land like latter-day blitzkriegers, stomping upon traditions and customs; insisting that America was (in the territory they held, anyway) turning VERDANT like a well-fertilized fairway, and generally wreaking havoc. But the impetus has clearly gone out of their assaults in recent years . . . (D.R. Boldt, Review of *Mauve Gloves & Madmen, Clutter & Vine*, a book by Tom Wolfe, *Philadelphia Inquirer*, 1/30/77, p. 10-D)

4. In 1969 it [Cambodia] was a small, VERDANT country of about 6 million. It lived in a state of inglorious but relatively peaceful political compromise. (R.L. Strout, *Christian Science Monitor* News Service, *Times Herald*, Norristown, Pa., 2/19/77, p. 15)

VERDIGRIS (vûr' də-grēs , -gris) *noun* a green or bluish PATINA formed, after long exposure to air, on copper, brass, or bronze surfaces, consisting principally of basic copper sulfate.

1. It [the water bucket] stood alone in a patch of weeds, with a pair of hot and itchy sparrows on its rim, yet it did not have the melancholy air of old, discarded household tools—that grin of rust, the solitude of VERDIGRIS. (Marguerite Dorian, "The Water Bucket," *The New Yorker*, 2/9/76, p. 33)

2. My mouth tasted as if I [Russel Wren] had licked the VERDIGRIS off a half-dozen pennies.

(Thomas Berger, *Who Is Teddy Villanova?*, Delacorte Press/Seymour Lawrence, 1977, p. 127)

VERISIMILITUDE (ver' i-si-mil' i-tōōd' , -tyōōd') *noun* the appearance or semblance of truth or fact; likelihood; probability; something, as a statement, having merely the appearance of truth.

VERISIMILAR *adj.* having the appearance of truth; likely; probable; plausible.

VERISIMILARLY *adv.*

1. Great effort [in the TV special, *The Adams Chronicles*] has gone into choosing sites and furnishing them to capture an aura of VERISIMILITUDE. (R.B. Morris, Review, *New York Times*, 1/11/76, Section 2, p. 1)

2. See (2) under LEITMOTIF.

3. After a while, this straining toward VERISIMILITUDE [by use of frequent footnotes in *Eaters of the Dead*, a book by Michael Crichton] becomes a PEDANTIC mannerism . . . (J. Sullivan, Review, *New York Times*, 4/25/76, Section 7, p. 22)

4. One would assume that a former Vice President of the United States could at least invent such a tale [as in *The Canfield Decision*], a book by Spiro Agnew] with some degree of VERISIMILITUDE. . . . But there are no special insights, no startling revelations. (D. Shaw, *Los Angeles Times*, "Agnew 'murders' media and other 'nattering nabobs,' " *Norman* [Okla.] *Transcript*, 5/23/76, p. 17)

5. [Barbra] Streisand has always favored glamour over VERISIMILITUDE, but she never before has gone to such an untenable extreme; this time [in the movie, *A Star Is Born*], the sets are almost compulsively overdecorated and the costumes take precedence over the action at every turn. (Janet Maslin, Review, *Newsweek*, 1/10/77, p. 64)

6. Her [Harriet Beecher Stowe's] scrupulous efforts [in *Uncle Tom's Cabin*] remind me of [Alex] Haley's [in *Roots*]. Both sought to achieve VERISIMILITUDE. And both, inevitably, made errors of fact. And both also bent reality for the sake of their message, painting things sharper and simpler than they really were . . . .

On the large historical truth, both win hands down. . . . Haley's book, like Mrs. Stowe's, is a work of historical imagination and re-creation. (Meg Greenfield, "Uncle Tom's Roots," *Newsweek*, 2/14/77, p. 100)

7. *Freaky Friday* is [a movie] about a mother and daughter who magically exchange bodies for a day . . . . With Barbara Harris as an adorably adolescent woman and Jodie Foster as a 35-year-old child, this Disney production takes on an air of VERISIMILITUDE that ought to make it at least as interesting to adults as it is to children . . . (Janet Maslin, Review, *Newsweek*, 2/28/77, p. 72)

VERISM (věr'iz-əm, ver'iz-əm) *noun* the theory that strict representation of truth and reality is essential to art and literature and, therefore, the ugly and vulgar must be portrayed.

VERIST *noun*.

VERISTIC *adj.*

1. The ending [of the book, *A Killing for Charity*] is curious—highly VERISTIC, even bitter. (N. Callendar, Review, *New York Times*, 2/22/76, Section 7, p. 38)

2. [Police] Procedurals vary. They can be Boy Scout and icky . . . . Or they can be realistic and even VERISTIC, as in Michael Z. Lewin's [book] *Night Cover*. (N. Callendar, *Ibid.*, 3/14/76, Section 7, p. 28)

VERMEIL (vur'mil, vər-mā') *noun* vermilion red; metal, as copper, silver or bronze, that has been gilded.

VERMEIL *adj.* of the color vermilion.

1. A VERMEIL pin in his [Walter Hoving's] lapel says, "Try God." (Anon., "For Tiffany's Walter Hoving Silence May Be Golden, But Sounding Off Is Irresistible," *People*, 4/12/76, p. 16)

VERNAL (vûr'nəl) *adj.* of, pertaining to, or occurring in spring; appropriate to or suggesting spring; springlike; youthful; fresh, warm, and mild; fresh and young.

1. [Madeline] Kahn, a proficient comedienne, caricatures herself at times [as Amalia, in the musical, *She Loves Me*]. She lacks the VERNAL

innocence intrinsic to the role. (T.E. Kalem, Review, *Time*, 4/11/77, p. 88)

VERNISSAGE (vûr' ni-säzh') *noun* the opening day of an art exhibit; the day before this, reserved for painters to varnish or touch up their paintings.

1. It cost $75 a person merely to walk into Cartier for the VERNISSAGE of 150 original Louis Cartier designs (the exhibition can now be seen by ordinary mortals, without cost, until Oct. 29) . . . the whole shebang was a tax-deductible contribution to the American Cancer Society's New York division . . . (Enid Nemy, "Throng of Sparkling Celebrities Outshines a 108-Carat Diamond," *New York Times*, 10/14/76, p. 32)

VERTIGINOUS (vər-tij'ə-nəs) *adj.* whirling or spinning about; rotary, as the action of a top; affected with vertigo; dizzy; liable to, affected by, or threatening to cause vertigo

VERTIGINOUSLY *adv.*

VERTIGINOUSNESS *noun.*

VERTIGO (vûr'tə-gō') *noun, pl.:* VERTIGOES or VERTIGINES a disordered sensation of dizziness in which a person feels that he or his surroundings are whirling about.

1. Americans value technology, and the social sciences owe their VERTIGINOUS postwar rise to the promise that they would generate a new social technology. (N. Birnbaum, *The Future of the Humanities* [Editorial], *Change*, Summer 1975, p. 11)

2. . . . the whole movie [*Taxi Driver*] has a sense of VERTIGO . . . (Pauline Kael, Review, *The New Yorker*, 2/9/76, p. 82)

3. Cassavetes [the director of the film, *The Killing of a Chinese Bookie*] doesn't want to show you a fight [between Cosmo Vitelli's black girlfriend and a new stripper he is interviewing], he wants you to feel the VERTIGO of jealousy. (Jack Kroll, Review, *Newsweek*, 3/15/76, p. 89)

4. See (1) under ETHEREAL.

5. See (4) under SERENDIPITY.

6. Sheila Redden, a Belfast wife and mother in her late 30's, stops in Paris on her way to the

Riviera . . . she falls into an affair with an American eleven years her junior . . . . When her VERTIGINOUS passion dissolves her orderly existence, her physician husband suspects she is undergoing early menopause. (W. Clemons, Review of *The Doctor's Wife*, by Brian Moore, *Newsweek*, 9/20/76, pp. 88D-89)

7. See (1) under MOIRÉ.

VESTIGIAL (ve-stij´ē-əl) *adj.* of, pertaining to, or of the nature of a vestige.

VESTIGIALLY *adv.*

VESTIGE *noun* a mark, trace, or visible evidence of something that has disappeared or no longer exists; a trace; bit.

1. Although anti-war and anti-military sentiment has largely evaporated as a factor with the voters, it seems to survive VESTIGIALLY as a factor against Jackson. This opposition to Jackson will dog him right up to the July convention. (*The London Economist*, "Primary elections serve their purpose: Jimmy Carter new political wonder," *Norman* [Okla.] *Transcript*, 4/27/76, p. 6)

2. One of the striking aspects of the book [*The Brothers Reuther*, by Victor G. Reuther] is Victor's repeated assertion of his and Walter's patriotism, a VESTIGIAL reflex following a lifetime of smears. (P.D. Zimmerman, Review, *Newsweek*, 5/17/76, pp. 108D, 108J)

3. "You have a VESTIGIAL memory of what spontaneity is like," the ACERBIC Gore Vidal told producer Norman Lear at a Los Angeles party. "If you ever open up your operation to the outside world, I would be interested in participating." . . . starting the week after next, he [Vidal] will appear on six episodes of Lear's *Mary Hartman, Mary Hartman*. (Susan Cheever Cowley, "Newsmakers," *Newsweek*, 10/4/76, p. 63)

4. Every woman who has ever had the experience of being a pathfinder in a field previously reserved for men knows the very ambivalent feelings it raises. We want to achieve; yet we are terrified that our achievements will cost us love. We want to succeed; yet another VESTIGIAL part of us seems to be saying it is more "feminine" to fail. (Erica Jong, "Speaking of Love," *Newsweek*, 2/21/77, p. 11)

5. See (3) under ID.

VEXILLOLOGY (vek´sə-lol´ə-jē) *noun* the study of flags.

VEXILLOLOGICAL *adj.*

VEXILLOLOGIST *noun.*

1. The United States is in the middle of a "flag boom," according to Dr. Whitney Smith, one of the country's leading VEXILLOLOGISTS (a person who studies flags) and head of the Flag Research Center in Winchester, Mass., an organization of flag historians devoted to coordinating and promoting the study of flags. (W. Kalyn, "Rally Round the Stars and Stripes, Pinetrees and Rattlesnakes," *New York Times*, 3/28/76, Section 2, p. 35)

VICARIOUS (vī-kar´ē-əs, vi-) *adj.* performed, exercised, held, handled, received, or suffered by one person in place of another; taking the place of another person or thing; substitute; deputy; felt or enjoyed through imagined participation in the words, deeds, or experience of others.

VICARIOUSLY *adv.*

VICARIOUSNESS *noun.*

1. See (1) under POSTHUMOUS.

2. "And in today's society," [Garry] Marshall [executive producer of the TV show, *Happy Days*] continued, "with people getting pushed around—losing their jobs and things like that—Fonzie becomes a kind of folk hero to them because no one takes advantage of him. They get VICARIOUS pleasure in watching him do what they can't." (Jill Gerston, "The 'Fonz' fad: The secret is a super 'cool'," *Philadelphia Inquirer*, 5/30/76, pp. 1-H, 5-H)

3. I [Adam Malone] found the following quotation attributed to the playwright Robert E. Sherwood: "Imagine the plight of a Hollywood heroine . . . who has been boosted suddenly to a dizzy eminence . . . . She awakens in the night with the realization, 'At this moment I am being subjected to VICARIOUS rape by countless hordes of Yugoslavs, Peruvians, Burmese, Abyssinians, Kurds, Latvians and Ku Klux Klansmen!' " (I. Wallace, *The Fan Club*, Bantam Edition, 1975, p. 138)

4. There is nothing new in saying that the Anzeati [people of Anzio, Italy] are not in love with Americans any more . . . . Nor need that necessarily mean much, considering how few they are—26,000 in all, today, two out of three of them too young for any but VICARIOUS knowledge of the last war. (Claire Sterling, "The View From Anzio: They Do Not Love Us," *New York Times*, 7/4/76, Section 6, p. 106)

5. See (3) under LUDDITE.

6. See (4) under SADOMASOCHISM.

7. . . . by his high-school graduation today's typical teen-ager will have logged at least 15,000 hours before the small screen . . . . And at present levels of advertising and mayhem, he will have been exposed to 350,000 commericals and VICARIOUSLY participated in 18,000 murders. (H.F. Waters, "What TV Does To Kids," *Newsweek*, 2/21/77, p. 63)

VIDUITY (vi-dōō′ə-tē) or **VIDUAGE** (vid′yōō-əj) *noun* widowhood or its duration.

VIDUOUS or **VIDUAL** *adj.* widowed; bereaved.

VIDUATION *noun* the state of being widowed or bereaved.

1. Above, too, in a pleasant narrow apartment Olga Kahn survives, brave as Brunnelhilde in VIDUITY. (R.Kahn, *The Boys of Summer*, Harper and Row, 1971, p. 437)

VIGNETTE (vin-yet′) *noun* a decorative design or small illustration used on the title page of a book or at the beginning or end of a chapter; any small, pleasing picture or view; a short graceful literary sketch.

1. . . . rather than helpful, straightforward statements such as "Henry Kissinger was a liar" or "Bob Haldeman was a MARTINET," one is given only an occasional VIGNETTE [in the book, *Born Again*, by Charles W. Colson]. Christian Colson will not dwell on the dark sides of his former associates. (Molly Ivins, Review, *New York Times*, 3/28/76, Section 7, p. 5)

2. See (1) under SAPPHISM.

3. See (5) under TRANSVESTITE.

VILIFY (vil′ə-fī′) *verb* to defame or slander; to speak ill of; disparage; malign; calumniate; revile.

VILIFICATION *noun.*

1. See (1) under PTOMAINE.

2. Charles Sumner is CASTIGATED [in the book, *The Impending Crisis 1848-1861*, by David M. Potter] for his "pompous rectitude and studied VILIFICATION," while the incompetent proSouthern President James Buchanan is merely termed "foolish." (E. Foner, Review, *New York Times*, 2/22/76, Section 7, p. 7)

VISCERAL (vis′ ər-əl) *adj.* of, pertaining to, or affecting the viscera; intuitive, instinctive, emotional, etc., rather than intellectual.

VISCERALLY *adv.*

VISCERA *noun, pl.: singular:* VISCUS the organs in the cavities of the body, especially those in the abdominal cavity; the intestines; bowels.

1. See (2) under SOPHISTRY.

2. . . .Americans are so haunted by it [the loss of the Vietnam War] that they have wiped an eraser across the blackboard of their minds. Occasionally a playwright comes along to chalk up the score all over again. David Rabe did it with VISCERAL force in *Sticks and Bones*, a play in which the hero is at peace only with the skeletons who stalk his mind. (T.E. Kalem, Review of *Medal of Honor Rag*, a play by Tom Cole, *Time*, 4/12/76, p. 82)

3. Its excitement is VISCERAL, but unlike other "road" films, it doesn't insult the intelligence . . . (V. Canby, Review, *New York Times*, 6/20/76, Section 2, p. 25)

VISCID (vis′id) *adj.* having a glutinous or thick, sticky consistency; sticky; adhesive; viscous.

VISCIDLY *adv.*

VISCIDITY *noun.*

1. Spiros Constantinides of the University of Rhode Island has suggested that okra—whose VISCID green pods provide the distinctive ingredient in gumbo dishes—could become an important source of protein if cooks would use its

ripe seeds as well as its tasty pods. (Anon., "Searching for Superplants," *Time*, 5/31/76, p. 48)

VITRIOL (vĭ'trē-əl) *noun* oil of vitriol; sulfuric acid; something highly caustic, sharp, bitter, or severe in effect; venom.

VITRIOLIC *adj.* of, pertaining to, obtained from, or resembling vitriol; extremely biting; severely caustic; extremely hurtful; scathing; sharp and bitter.

1. See (6) under PRESCIENCE.

2. See (1) under ASPERITY.

3. About 40 players among the 600 major leaguers are still looking from a distance—and refusing to sign. Among them are seven [Charles O.] Finley stars. "I put figures on the table," says [Jerry] Kapstein, agent for five of the [Oakland] A's. "And Charlie just issued VITRIOLIC statements." (P. Axthelm, "Baseball's Money Madness," *Newsweek*, 6/28/76, p. 65)

4. Perhaps the foremost example of a cartoonist's political power came from the deft hand of Thomas Nast. Shortly after the Civil War a gang of crooks headed by "Boss" William M. Tweed muscled into control of New York City and began to plunder its treasury. That prompted Nast to launch . . . a continuing drumfire of humorously styled, but devastating editorial cartoons lambasting the Tweed ring. Nast's VITRIOL soon had Tweed in a frenzy . . . . Nast's campaign was given major credit for the eventual jailing of Tweed. However, Tweed escaped and fled to Spain, only to be arrested in the little town of Vigo and shipped back to the United States. In Vigo, it seems, authorities had recognized Tweed from one of Nast's cartoons! (F. Stilley, "Cartoonist's art changes history," *Norman* [Okla.] *Transcript*, 7/15/76, p. 8-A)

5. Lyndon Johnson, who inspired some of the most vicious and VITRIOLIC commentary of any President in our time, is . . . in the process of being absolved and actually *pinned for* by a number of his most scourgelike critics. (Meg Greenfield, "The Man They Loved to Hate," *Newsweek*, 9/13/76, p. 92)

6. Since he began his evening-news spots on Philadelphia's WCAU-TV 16 months ago (af-

ter losing a 1974 bid for the Democratic U.S. Senate nomination), Denenberg has flayed the makers of more than 150 products, from sedatives to sugarless gum. Horrible Herb, as he is known among his victims, spices his VITRIOL with humor. One recent broadcast: "I make sure I get my exercise, get enough rest, and eat healthy food. So I don't need Geritol." (Anon., "The Horrible Herb Show," *Time*, 9/13/76, p. 70)

VITUPERATE (vī-tōō'pə-rāt', -tyōō- , vĭ-) *verb* to find fault with; censure harshly or abusively; berate; revile; CASTIGATE.

VITUPERATOR *noun.*

VITUPERATION *noun.*

VITUPERATIVE *adj.*

VITUPERATIVELY *adv.*

1. See (1) under UBEROUS.

2. *Marilyn the Wild* [by Jerome Charyn] is flawed by its own rampaging vitality. A Charyn character cannot simply put on a coat: Esther Rose's "fist burrowed into her sleeve like the skull of a groundhog." Too many adversaries shrill in the same VITUPERATIVE key. Even lovers snarl their sweet nothings, as if they were pouring poison into each other's ears. Yet the author endows his most grotesque characters with a certain beauty. His kinkiest people . . . are the imaginings of a major talent. (Le Anne Schreiber, Review, *Time*, 4/19/76, p. 96)

3. See (1) under SAND.

VOLTE-FACE (volt'fäs) *noun* the act of turning so as to face in the opposite direction; a complete change of attitude or opinion.

1. If Richard Nixon can go to Peking and ADUMBRATE there the similarities between George Washington's revolution and Mao Tse-Tung's, we have a VOLTE-FACE at least the equivalent of the Soviet defeat of a Canadian hockey team . . . . (W.F.Buckley Jr., *Execution Eve and Other Contemporary Ballads*, G.P. Putnam's Sons, 1975, p. 242)

2. "We are therefore not only protecting Hong Kong from the *Russians* . . . , we are protecting her from the wrath of Peking . . . . However,"

said Lacon, and to emphasize the VOLTE-FACE went so far as to arrest Smiley's arm with his long hand so that he had to put down his glass. "However," he warned . . . "whether our masters will swallow all that is quite another matter altogether." (J. LeCarré, *The Honourable Schoolboy*, Alfred A. Knopf, 1977, p. 89)

VOYEUR (vwä-yûr′, voi-yûr′) *noun* a person who compulsively engages in the practice of obtaining sexual gratification by looking at sexual organs, acts, or objects, especially secretively; peeping Tom.

VOYEURISM *noun.*

VOYEURISTIC *adj.*

1. Most of them [reviewers of the first edition of *Up From Liberalism*, by William F. Buckley Jr.] took the easiest way out—. . . they simply dissociated themselves from such spokesmen for liberalism as I had photographed in this book in embarrassing postures. Indeed I was treated by some reviewers as a VOYEUR, for having read the altogether public pronouncements of some of these [liberal] ladies and gentlemen (an interesting question: do good manners require us not to look when a ritualistic liberal is speaking?) (W.F. Buckley Jr., *Up From Liberalism*, Arlington House, 2nd Printing 1968, p. xxvi)

2. I do truly hope, and I do truly expect, that in another ten years, events will have moved so as to confirm that we have come up from liberalism, and that only historical VOYEURS will want to study the reasons why, as given, some of them, in this little volume. (W.F. Buckley Jr., *Ibid.*, p. xxviii)

3. [Peter] Collier and [David] Horowitz's narrative [The Rockefellers] takes VOYEURISM and gossip to a grand scale and uses them to clarify an era of American industrial growth. (S.R. Weisman, Review, *New York Times*, 3/28/76, Section 7, p. 1)

4. They all [*Travesty*, by John Hawkes, and the two earlier volumes in the trilogy] share a "preoccupation with the myths and actual practices of sexuality," all are in differing ways VOYEURISTIC (photographs play a distinct role in each book), all seem to accept . . . "the obvious multiplicity of love," and discuss with . . . fond anatomical detail their own and their

wives' enlightened extramarital relationships, and . . . they all claim to be beyond jealousy and the petty rages and fears of the conventional egotistical mind. (T. Tanner, Review, *New York Times*, 3/28/76, Section 7, p. 23)

5. See (1) under SLAVER.

6. The result is the first "pornographic film" [*The Empire of the Senses*] that is an occasion for contemplation—not VOYEURISM. (C. Michener, "New Films at Cannes," *Newsweek*, 6/7/76, p. 98)

7. See (2) under LAGNIAPPE.

8. She was fair game . . . . Unless this one, The Salesman [Howard Yost], and the others were . . . more sensitive to her feelings, and would only appear briefly as VOYEURS. (I. Wallace, *The Fan Club*, Bantam Books, 1975, p. 283)

9. [Leo] Brunner seemed entirely transformed into the VOYEUR. "Howard, what was her reaction? . . . . Yost shrugged. "I think it's all familiar to her. I mean, having men go to bed with her." (I. Wallace, *Ibid.*, p. 287)

10. VOYEURS here [in Washington] relish the daily accounts about which Democratic congressman or senator was pleasured in the feathers by which congressional chick who got her job through which Democratic official. (N. Thimmesch, "Scandal Probe Lacks Fervor," *Daily Oklahoman*, Okla. City., 6/18/76, p. 10)

11. . . . this piece [the desk] . . . was not equipped with a so-called modesty panel; perhaps that had been extracted by some previous VOYEUR. . . (Thomas Berger, *Who Is Teddy Villanova?*, Delacorte Press/Seymour Lawrence, 1977, p. 44)

12. After an era of revolution [in sexual behavior], is a counterrevolution under way? Is it even possible that the revolution never really succeeded, that much of America watched the New Morality—VOYEURISTICALLY—without abandoning the Old Morality? Recent years undeniably have brought major changes to America's social patterns, most notably a greater openness about sex and a greater acceptance of premarital sex, homosexuality and abortion. But young people who favor the new standards are still paying a high price in family conflicts, and conservative protesters are increasingly vociferous. (Anon., "The New Morality," *Time*, 11/21/77, p. 111)

W

WALPURGISNACHT (väl-pŏŏr′gis-naK̲H̲t′) or **WALPURGIS NIGHT** the evening preceding May 1st, the feast day of St. Walpurgis, on which, according to a formerly popular German superstition, witches held a demonic orgy on Brocken mountain to renew allegiance to the devil; something (as an event or situation) having an ORGIASTIC or nightmarish character.

1. See (1) under BLOWZY.

2. The play [Who's Afraid of Virginia Woolf? by Edward Albee] was a WALPURGISNACHT of marital ferocity in which George, a history professor, and Martha his wife, using some of the most uninhibited language the American theater had known until that evening, tore each other to bits. (D. Stern, "Albee: 'I Want My Intent Clear,'" New York Times, 3/28/76, Section 2, p. 1)

3. See (3) under RATIOCINATION.

4. See (1) under BAUDELAIREAN.

WASSAIL (wos′əl, wos′āl, was′-, wo-sāl′) noun a salutation to a person, used in England in early times when presenting a cup of drink or when drinking to a person's health; a festivity or revel with drinking of healths, especially at Christmas time; carousal; liquor, especially spiced ale, for drinking healths on festive occasions; a song sung in wassailing.

WASSAIL verb to drink healths; revel with drinking; toast.

WASSAILER noun.

1. [British artist John Calcott] Horsley's design [of the first Christmas card in 1843] was centered around a convivial family gathering in which everyone from tots to grandpa was benevolently engaged in drinking the health of absent loved ones. He was later CASTIGATED by temperance organizations for giving Yuletide encouragement to the spread of INSOBRIETY, alcoholism and wild WASSAIL. (P. Ryan, "Postmen can blame it on Old Horsley," Smithsonian, December 1975, p. 144)

2. See (1) under BIBULOUS.

WASTREL (wā′strəl) noun a wasteful person; spendthrift; a waif; abandoned child; an idler or good-for-nothing.

1. Olga [Roger Kahn's mother] is saying something must be done. Shrill fragments rattle down the hall like shrapnel. "WASTREL . . . Dodgers! Baseball! Sex fiend!" (R. Kahn, The Boys of Summer, Harper and Row, 1971, p. 31)

2. The novella [in The Smell of Hay, by Giorgio Bassani, translated by William Weaver] is called The Gold-rimmed Eye-glasses, and is about a gentle provincial doctor who is OSTRACIZED for having an affair with a young WASTREL. (Anon., Review, The New Yorker, 2/9/76, p. 110)

3. The first series of letters [in the book, Nancy Mitford, by Harold Acton] describes her love for Hamish Erskine, an elegant young WASTREL who never got around to marrying her, or, indeed anyone else. (Auberon Waugh, Review, New York Times, 3/28/76, Section 7, p. 6)

4. See (3) under CURMUDGEON.

5. Of course, the voyage [described in the book, Voyage, by Sterling Hayden] is doomed, the captain obsessed, the mates brutal and the men hapless WASTRELS with hearts of gold and

philosophical turns of mind. (R. Javers, Review, *Philadelphia Inquirer*, 1/30/77, p. 10-D)

WELTANSCHAUUNG (velt' än-shou ŏŏng) *noun* a comprehensive, especially a personal, philosophy, conception, or image of civilization, of the universe, and of man's relation to it.

1. The conscious philosophical relativism of the academy, filtering down past the scholars and the intelligentsia to the masses, becomes less a WELTANSCHAUUNG, more an attitude of mind. (W.F. Buckley, Jr., *Up From Liberalism*, Arlington House, 2nd Printing 1968, p. 125)

2. One of the most provocative aspects of [Marie-Louise] von Franz's book [*C.G. Jung: His Myth in Our Time*] is her discussion of current social phenomena from a Jungian perspective . . . ."the drop-out" and the drug culture are seen as misguided . . . reactions to a world that denies the legitimacy of spiritual needs. Nascent interest in Eastern thought is similarly considered an effort to redress an imbalance in the Western EMPIRICAL WELTANSCHAUUNG. Encounter groups are also efforts to redress imbalances; . . . The strength of von Franz's book is its ability to elucidate Jung's often ESOTERIC thought and to identify its broader implications. (J. Hollis, Review, *Chronicle of Higher Education*, 7/26/76, p. 9)

3. What is so intriguing about this treasure TROVE of pre-1919 Wodehouse that [editor] David A. Jasen has brought together [in the book, *The Uncollected Wodehouse*] is its commonality with post-1919 Wodehouse. Some of the early pieces . . . may be a bit parochial, but the WELTANSCHAUUNG is the same . . . (M. Levin, Review, *New York Times*, 2/6/77, Section 7, p. 13)

WELTSCHMERZ (velt' shmers) *noun* sorrow which one feels and accepts as his necessary portion in life; sentimental pessimism or melancholy over the state of the world.

1. The Hartmans' down-homey neighbors [Loretta and Charlie Haggars] are the perfect foils of the WELTSCHMERZ of Mary and Tom. Ol' Charlie may be an oaf, but Loretta—the

ARCHETYPAL Southern sexpot—adores him because in bed he gives her "four minutes of sky-rockets *plus*." (H.F. Waters, M. Kasindorf, "The Mary Hartman Craze," *Newsweek*, 5/3/76, p. 56)

2. The remaining two-thirds of the book [*Moscow Farewell*, by George Feifer] are devoted to rather monotonous accounts of the protagonist's WELTSCHMERTZ (*sic*) . . . and to interesting speculations about the essence of Soviet life. (J.B. Brodsky, Review, *New York Times*, 4/18/76, Section 7, p. 4)

3. You don't want to wash the dinner dishes? Don't tell the family you feel lazy. Instead, assume a pained expression and complain of a mild attack of WELTSCHMERZ, pronounced VELT-shmairts, which means anguish about the state of the world. Everything sounds so much more important in German. (Beth Gillin Pombeiro, "Be a phrase-dropper," *Philadelphia Inquirer*, 11/9/76, p. 3-C)

4. See (1) under NUGATORY.

5. Pouches of WELTSCHMERZ hung below his [Boris's] eyes; his heavy mouth was LUGUBRIOUS. (Thomas Berger, *Who Is Teddy Villanova?*, Delacorte Press/Seymour Lawrence, 1977, p. 193)

6. A pseudo-sophisticate is someone who confuses cafe WELTSCHMERZ with a tragic sense of life. (A. Broyard, Review of *Goodbye*, a book by W.H. Manville, *New York Times*, 5/15/77, Section 7, p. 12)

WINDROW (wind'rō, win'-) *noun* a row or line of hay, sheaves of wheat, etc., left to dry; a row of dry leaves, dust, etc., swept together by the wind.

WINDROW *verb* to rake, sweep, arrange, etc., in a windrow or windrows.

1. It (the 1917-18 flu epidemic) came in silently, gliding on the wings of the same autumn wind which carried the crisp leaves . . . . No one noticed it at first . . . . Then it hit . . . . There was no vaccine . . . . In San Francisco and San Antonio and Denver and Omaha; in London and Manchester and Bristol; in Bordeaux and Paris and Château-Thierry; in Heidelberg and Berlin and Stettin the people died in WINDROWS. (J. Bishop, "Silent

Scourge," *Times Herald*, Norristown, Pa., 12/3/76, p. 13)

WINSOME (win′ səm) *adj.* attractive in a sweet, engaging way; winning, engaging, or charming.

WINSOMELY *adv.*

WINSOMENESS *noun.*

1. . . . Mary, or Molly, as she was called, was a WINSOME, outgoing girl and in June 1768, Charles Carroll of Carrollton, aged 30, made her his bride. (Mary H. Cadwalader, "Charles Carroll of Carrollton: a signer's story," *Smithsonian*, December 1975, p. 67)

2. I don't know what's worse in this excruciating CODA [the film, *Logan's Run*], director Michael Anserson's ham-handedness or [Peter] Ustinov's cynical WINSOMENESS. (J. Kroll, Review, *Newsweek*, 7/4/76, p. 102)

3. See (2) under KAFKAESQUE.

4. The original [*King Kong*] film created a monster whose fearfulness was real though there was a ghost of charm behind it. The new monster is positively SMARMY in its WINSOMENESS. (R. Eder, "Hollywood Is Having An Affair With the Anti-Hero," *New York Times*, 1/2/77, Section 2, p. 1)

WUNDERKIND (vŏŏn′ dəR-kint′, vŏŏn′ dər-kind′) *noun, pl.:* -KINDER (-kin′ dəR) or -KINDS a wonder child or child PRODIGY.

1. Celebrating its 25th season, the Baltimore Opera Company produced the world premiere of *Inez de Castro*, the twelfth opera by 30-year old WUNDERKIND Thomas Pasatieri. (H. Saal, Review, *Newsweek*, 4/12/76, p. 76)

2. . . . during 1952 . . . four plays he [Jose Ferrer] had either produced, directed or acted in were appearing simultaneously in the vicinity of Times Square . . . . In the same year . . . , Ferrer also made two movies, *Anything Can Happen* and *Moulin Rouge* . . . So far, 1976 has found Ferrer considerably less terrifying. 1952's WUNDERKIND has fallen on some hard artistic times in his 65th year . . . (A. Haas, " 'Medal of Honor' gives Ferrer that old zest," *Philadelphia Inquirer*, 9/26/76, p. 1-H)

3. Mr. [Arthur R.] Taylor came to CBS in July of 1972 with a reputation as a financial WUNDERKIND, having been selected . . . after an extensive search for a worthy successor to Dr. Frank Stanton, who had been the CBS president since the 1940's . . . (L. Brown, "CBS Ousts Taylor as Its President . . . ," *New York Times*, 10/14/76, p. 66)

4. Not until 1958, when he [Hans Hofmann] was nearly 80, did he turn to painting full-time, and for the last eight years of his life he created like a WUNDERKIND: canvas after canvas pulsating with light and color, dynamic patterns and youthful vigor. (D. Davis, "Tale of Hofmann," *Newsweek*, 11/1/76, p. 78)

5. [John] Updike is 44 now, no longer the WUNDERKIND of *Rabbit, Run*, who amazed and annoyed critics with his lush prose and jewel-like short stories of life as a teacher's son in Pennsylvania . . . (Sally Quinn, *Washington Post* Service, "John Updike: On women and living together," *Philadelphia Inquirer*, 1/9/77, p. 3-H)

X

XENOPHOBIA (zen′ ə-fō′ bē-ə) *noun* an unreasonable or excessive dread, fear, or hatred of foreign or strange people or things. XENOPHOBIC *adj.*

1. All hard evidence thus far indicates a take-over plan [of last week's abortive coup in Nigeria] drawn up hastily and haphazardly by a relatively small group of disgruntled officers . . . . If this is correct, it would be far better for the Government to say so, rather than to level dubious accusations and provoke a XENOPHOBIA in Nigeria that would be difficult to control. (Anon., "Nigerian Scapegoat" [Editorial], New York Times, 2/22/76, Section 4, p. 12)

2. Did the conditions under which humans lived in the Stone Age spread a genetic basis for behavior like territoriality, XENOPHOBIA, and male dominance? he [Prof. Edward O. Wilson, of Harvard] asks [in his textbook, Sociobiology]. (F. Hapgood, "Why the Tortoise is Kind and Other Tales of Sociobiology," Atlantic, March 1976, p. 101)

3. The view that emerges [in The Venture of Islam, by M.G.S. Hodgson] . . . challenges the commonly accepted version of Islam as a narrowly exclusivist creed combining fanaticism, fundamentalism, and XENOPHOBIA in equal proportions. (C. Geertz, Review, New York Review of Books, 12/11/75, pp. 18–20)

4. . . . a professor at UCLA wrote that, in [Senator Joseph] McCarthy's XENOPHOBIC America, anyone caught buying a foreign car was likely to be boycotted by members of the American Legion. (W.F. Buckley Jr., Up From Liberalism, Arlington House, 2nd Printing 1968, p. 51)

5. And "how do you get on a blacklist? Well, some actors have got on by having foreign names" [wrote Mr. John Crosby] (tacit premise: blacklisters are reckless, provincial, XENOPHOBIC). (W.F. Buckley Jr., Ibid., p. 73)

6. Like China, Albania is isolated, XENOPHOBIC and deeply secretive. Remarks one Western analyst: "Compared to Albania, China is positively scrutable." (M.R. Benjamin, T. Nater, "Albania: The Inscrutable West," Newsweek, 5/10/76, p. 56)

7. . . . Vincent Price said ". . . The Pit and the Pendulum . . . has every single element of human fear in it: CLAUSTROPHOBIA, AGORAPHO-BIA, XENOPHOBIA, ACROPHOBIA . . ." (Jean McGarry, "Vince Price just can't escape it—he's scary," Oklahoma City Times, 5/19/76, p. 30)

8. It is hard to swallow [J.M.] Blum's assertion [in V Was For Victory: Politics and American Culture During World War II] that a more enlightened American foreign policy could have appreciably eased the cold war, given Stalin's XENOPHOBIA and underhandedness. (P.D. Zimmerman, Review, Newsweek, 6/7/76, p. 89)

9. There are, in her [Diane Keaton's] performance [in the play, The Primary English Class, by Israel Horowitz], a dozen Debbies: a falsely easy-mannered hipster, a stern elementary school disciplinarian, a sexual paranoiac (she is convinced the school janitor is a rapist), a multiprejudiced XENOPHOBE, a cruelly playful child and, finally, a vulnerable woman. (R. Schickel, Review, Time, 3/1/76, p. 51)

10. See (1) under THEOCRATIC.

11. The military government [of Nigeria] recently has shown increasing signs of renewed self-confidence after a period of hesitation, XENOPHOBIA and acute security-consciousness. That is no small accomplishment . . . (J.C. Randall, Washington Post Service, "Military tries to push progress in wealthy but divided Nigeria," Philadelphia Inquirer, 3/6/77, p. 4-C)

12. Loyalist [New York Magazine Co.] staffers scrawled XENOPHOBIC graffiti on their office walls (SEND THIS WALLABY BACK, JACK), then walked off the job—leaving [new owner K.P.] Murdoch and other directors to get out this week's New York [magazine] issue with the help of some Murdoch minions. (D. Gelman, et al., "Press Lord Captures Gotham," Newsweek, 1/17/77, p. 49)

13. There is about the whole enterprise [at Paris's Centre National d'Art et de Culture Georges Pompidou] an air of borrowed prestige [from other countries] that the XENOPHOBIC French are bound to resent . . . (H. Kramer, "France's new culture palace," New York Times, 1/23/77, Section 6, p. 13)

Y

YARMULKE (yär′məl-kə, yä′məl-kə) or **YAR-MELKE** or **YAMALKA** or **YAMULKA** *noun*   a man's skull cap, worn especially during prayer and religious study in Judaism.

1. In 1972, in Florida, . . . he [Henry Jackson] talked not just against busing but about a Constitutional amendment against busing. Perhaps he only seems to wear a YARMULKE more than other candidates . . . Jackson is an overdoer in substance and in style. (Elizabeth Drew, "A Reporter in Washington, D.C.: Winter Notes—II," *The New Yorker*, 5/31/76, p. 88)

2. As it happens, I pass a volleyball game [in Central Park] and stop to watch, attracted by the racial and ethnic differences among the players . . . . The leader of the . . . team is a burly affable white with a pirate's mustache . . . There is also a bandy-legged man in a jogging outfit with a YARMULKE pinned to his hair; . . . and a very serious Arab . . . who is all over the court. (T. Solotaroff, "Alive and together in the park," *New York Times*, 6/13/76, Section 6, p. 42)

3. Carter publicly confronted the religious issue early last week in Elizabeth, N.J. Responding to a question from a predominantly Jewish audience of 2,000, the candidate—a blue velvet YARMULKE perched atop his head—declared extemporaneously: "I worship the same God you do . . . " (Anon., "Carter and the Jews," *Time*, 6/21/76, p. 13)

YENTA or **YENTE** (yen′tə)   *noun*   (in colloquial usage) a woman gossip or busybody; an unpleasant, scandalmongering woman.

1. The kids [in *Some Swell Pup*, a book by Maurice Sendak and Matthew Margolis] are monsters, the dog's not so hot either and the WP [Wise Passerby] is a drag. A line like "I kiss your head, Madam," amuses adults, and inexplicably (not so inexplicably, because the little girl is a YENTA), much of the dialogue like "Now me already!" . . . is vintage Group Theater. (Nora L. Magid, Review, *New York Times*, 9/5/76, Section 7, p. 16)

Z

ZEITGEIST (tsīt′gīst′)   *noun*   the spirit of the time; general trend of thought or feeling of an era.

1. See (5) under BOURGEOIS.
2. As an expert compromiser, Mr. [Derek C.] Bok must have seemed to the serious men who

called him to his post [as President of Harvard] almost perfectly endowed to accomplish what they saw as his most pressing task for the Seventies: the restoration of peace to a torn faculty, and modesty to the student body. With the help of the ZEITGEIST and a shrinking economy, he appears to have done both. (N.W. Aldrich Jr., "Harvard On The Way Down," *Harper's*, March 1976, p. 47)

3. Between 1945 and 1958 he [Robert Moses] built 148,000 low-income housing units, as many as the rest of the country put together . . . . He was the ZEITGEIST personified: the man who hammered together the nation's only organization . . . capable of building with a regional view of transportation, recreation, and population dispersal. (C.R. Hatch, Review of *The Power Broker: Robert Moses and the Fall of New York*, by Robert A. Caro, *Harper's*, January 1975, p. 88)

4. . . . the American art museum was subject to forces in the late 60's . . . with which it has not been able to cope . . . . Artists, affected by the change in the ZEITGEIST, began to direct their concerts not only against the museum as a symbol of established culture but against the idea of ownership itself. (M. Friedman, "Museums and Artists Learn To Live With the 70's," *New York Times*, 9/12/76, Section 2, p. 33)

5. See (2) under AMANUENSIS.

ZIGGURAT (zig′ ŏŏ-rat′) or **ZIKKURAT** or **ZIKURAT** *noun* (among the ancient Babylonians and Assyrians) a temple of Sumerian origin in the form of a pyramidal tower with a shrine at the top and consisting of a number of stories and having about the outside a broad ascent winding round the structure, presenting the appearance of a series of terraces.

1. Arecibo [the Puerto Rican location of the world's largest radio telescope], it occurred to me, was the Stonehenge, the Babylonian ZIGGURAT, perhaps even the Pyramids of the technological age, and men like [Thomas] Matthews and [William] Erickson and [Frank] Drake [director of the National Astronomy and Ionosphere Center at Arecibo] were its priests, their lore just as ARCANE and incomprehensible and awe-inspiring as was the ability of the ancient sages to predict eclipses, the coming of comets, the time of the sunrise. (T. Buckley, "Is anybody out there?," *New York Times*, 9/12/76, Section 6, p. 68)

2. One of [Ivan] Van Sertima's main arguments [in his book, *They Came Before Columbus*] is based on the pyramids of Central America; these he [mistakenly] believes to be derived from the Egyptian pyramids . . . . He also confuses the pyramids of Egypt with the ZIGGURATS of Mesopotamia. They are entirely different things. (Glyn Daniel, Review, *New York Times*, 3/13/77, Section 7, p. 14)

ZIRCON (zûr′kon) *noun* a common mineral, zirconium silicate, used as a refractory when opaque and as a gem when transparent.

1. He [Cosmo Vitelli, in the film *The Killing of a Chinese Bookie*] is an upside-down Gatsby, a social ZIRCON with a diamond morality [Director] Cassavetes records his downfall with a fine sense of the casualness of doom in the LUMPEN-world. (J. Kroll, Review, *Newsweek*, 3/15/76, pp. 89-90)

By the year 2000, 2 out of 3 Americans could be illiterate.

It's true.

Today, 75 million adults… about one American in three, can't read adequately. And by the year 2000, U.S. News & World Report envisions an America with a literacy rate of only 30%.

Before that America comes to be, you can stop it… by joining the fight against illiteracy today.

Call the Coalition for Literacy at toll-free **1-800-228-8813** and volunteer.

Volunteer Against Illiteracy. The only degree you need is a degree of caring.

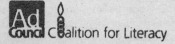
Warner Books is proud to be an active supporter of the Coalition for Literacy.